HANDBOOK OF
ILLINOIS EVIDENCE

cite this book:
Cleary & Graham's Handbook of Illinois Evidence §
(7th ed. 1999).

CLEARY & GRAHAM'S
HANDBOOK OF
ILLINOIS EVIDENCE
Seventh Edition

MICHAEL H. GRAHAM
Member, Illinois Bar

ASPEN LAW & BUSINESS
A Division of Aspen Publishers, Inc.
Gaithersburg   New York

Permissions
Aspen Law & Business
1185 Avenue of the Americas
New York, NY 10036

Printed in the United States of America

Library of Congress Cataloging-in-Publication Data

Graham, Michael H.
    [Handbook of Illinois evidence]
    Cleary & Graham's handbook of Illinois evidence / Michael H. Graham. — 7th ed.
        p.   cm.
    Includes index.
    ISBN 0-7355-0351-6 (hc)
    1. Evidence (Law)—Illinois.   I. Title.   II. Title: Cleary and Graham's handbook of Illinois evidence.
KFI1740.C58   1999
347.773'06—dc21   98-55066
                                                                            CIP

About Aspen Law & Business

Aspen Law & Business—comprising the former Prentice Hall Law & Business and Little, Brown and Company's Professional Division—is a leading publisher of authoritative treatises, practice manuals, services, and journals for attorneys, financial and tax advisors, corporate and bank directors, and other business professionals. Our mission is to provide practical solution-based how-to information keyed to the latest legislative, judicial, and regulatory developments.

We offer publications in the areas of banking and finance; bankruptcy; business and commercial law; corporate law; pensions, benefits, and labor; insurance law; securities; taxation; intellectual property; government and administrative law; matrimonial and family law; environmental and health law; international law; legal practice and litigation; and criminal law.

Other Aspen Law & Business products treating litigation issues include:

Almanac of the Federal Judiciary
Civil False Claims and Qui Tam Actions
DC Federal Courts Handbook
Directory of Federal Court Guidelines
Discovery Practice
DOJ Manual
Drunk Driving Defense
Handbook of Connecticut Evidence
Handbook of Massachusetts Evidence
Handbook of New York Evidence
Inside Litigation
Jury Selection
Modern Evidence
Motion Practice
New York Defender Digest
Tax Court Litigation
The Law of Civil RICO
Voir Dire
Wigmore on Evidence

ASPEN LAW & BUSINESS
A Division of Aspen Publishers, Inc.
A Wolters Kluwer Company

SUBSCRIPTION NOTICE

This Aspen Law & Business Product is updated on a periodic basis with supplements to reflect important changes in the subject matter. If you purchased this product directly from Aspen Law & Business, we have already recorded your subscription for the update service.

If, however, you purchased this product from a bookstore and wish to receive future updates and revised or related volumes billed separately with a 30-day examination review, please contact our Customer Service Department at 1-800-234-1660, or send your name, company name (if applicable), address, and the title of the product to:

ASPEN LAW & BUSINESS
A Division of Aspen Publishers, Inc.
7201 McKinney Circle
Frederick, MD 21701

To my wife,
Marilyn Graham
1942–1998

Summary of Contents

Contents

ARTICLE II   JUDICIAL NOTICE

CONTENTS

CONTENTS

ARTICLE IV   RELEVANCY AND ITS LIMITS

CONTENTS

CONTENTS

CONTENTS

CONTENTS

ARTICLE VI   WITNESS

CONTENTS

CONTENTS

CONTENTS

CONTENTS

ARTICLE VII   OPINION AND EXPERT TESTIMONY

CONTENTS

CONTENTS

CONTENTS

CONTENTS

CONTENTS

ARTICLE IX   AUTHENTICATION AND
              IDENTIFICATION

CONTENTS

ARTICLE X   ORIGINAL WRITING RULE

CONTENTS

Preface

The Handbook of Illinois Evidence has served the bar and judiciary of the State of Illinois through six editions and numerous supplements for nearly 43 years. I had the pleasure of joining with Professor Edward W. Cleary on the third edition of the Handbook published in 1979. Full responsibility for the Handbook fell upon my shoulders with the publication of the fourth edition in 1984. The friendly reception each of the prior editions received has warmed the hearts of its authors. Professor Edward W. Cleary died on January 19, 1990, in Scottsdale, Arizona.

The preface to the first edition, written by Professor Cleary in 1956, is as apt now as it was when it was penned.

> Like time and tide, points of evidence during a trial wait for no man. A ready command of general principles is indispensable.
>
> This book is designed to instill those principles by setting them forth without undue elaboration, but with sufficient illustrative references to decided cases to make their application clear. It will thus be found useful, it is hoped, not only to the practitioner as a means of tightening his grasp on the rules from time to time, but also to the student who is preparing for admission to the Bar of Illinois.
>
> Brevity serves another purpose for which the work is intended—finger-tip accessibility of a concise statement of each rule and the authorities supporting it, to meet the unexpected situations which so frequently develop in the course of a trial.
>
> An evidence book must be organized around general principles and theories, rather than around types of cases, since the same general principles and theories are encountered in many types of cases. This kind of organization creates difficulty in

solving a particular problem when doubt exists as to the principle or theory which is involved. The difficulty is overcome by the inclusion of a very full index in the back of the book, containing catch words and phrases and references to situations, in addition to principles and theories. Consulting it will make the book practical to the highest degree.

Citation and discussion of all the Illinois decisions would make a compact book impossible. The cases cited have been selected for their treatment of the problem, discussion of earlier cases, and likelihood of being cited in other cases on the point.

Liberal use should be made of the tables of cases, statutes, and rules found in the back of the book. A detailed table of contents, the pertinent part of which is repeated at the beginning of each [article], provides a helpful analysis of the subject matter.

The seventh edition generally follows the organization and style of earlier editions. The text reflects the continuing selective adoption by the Illinois Supreme Court of the Federal Rules of Evidence by decision and by court rule. The most important adoption by decision is *Wilson v. Clark,* 84 Ill. 2d 186, 49 Ill. Dec. 808, 417 N.E.2d 1322 (1981), which incorporated into the evidence law of Illinois the concept of reasonable reliance on facts, data, and opinions by an expert witness and eliminated the mandatory use of the hypothetical question, Rules 703 and 705 of the Federal Rules of Evidence. Also important was the abandonment of the voucher rule by adoption of Rule 607 of the Federal Rules of Evidence as Illinois Supreme Court Rule 238(a).

The text includes hypothetical illustrations explaining several of the more difficult evidentiary concepts, such as the collateral-noncollateral distinction, the definition of hearsay, and multiple level hearsay in conjunction with the hearsay exception for business records. It also includes expanded discussions of other crimes, wrongs, or acts, prior conviction impeachment, expert reconstruction testimony, reasonably relied upon by expert, subsequent remedial measures, rereading of testimony, and sexual and physical abuse, among other subjects.

Several of the illustrations also appear in T. Mauet, Fundamentals of Trial Techniques, third edition, 1992 by Thomas A. Mauet. Further material is reprinted from M. Graham, Handbook of Federal Evidence, fourth edition, 1996 by West Publishing Company. Permission to reprint is gratefully acknowledged.

The citations in this edition are current through volume 231 of the Illinois Decisions Reporter.

Michael H. Graham

March 1999

HANDBOOK OF
ILLINOIS EVIDENCE

ARTICLE I

General Provisions

§101   Applicability

§101.1   *Scope of Rules of Evidence: Commentary*

The rules of evidence as set forth in this Handbook are applicable to all proceedings in the supreme court, the appellate court, and the circuit courts of the State of Illinois, with the exception of the following:

(1) Preliminary questions of fact, *see* §104.1.

(2) Proceedings before grand juries.

(3) Proceedings for extradition or rendition; preliminary examinations in criminal cases; sentencing, or granting or revoking probation; issuance of warrants for arrest, criminal summonses, and search warrants; proceedings with respect to release on bail or otherwise; and contempt proceedings in which the court may act summarily.

However, at all stages of all proceedings, the rules as to privilege do apply.

With respect to hearsay evidence at a sentencing hearing, *see People v. Thompkins*, 181 Ill. 2d 1, 228 Ill. Dec. 909, 690

N.E.2d 984 (1998); *People v. Bounds,* 171 Ill. 2d 1, 215 Ill. Dec. 28, 662 N.E.2d 1168 (1995) (hearsay that is reliable is admissible). *See also People v. Tenner,* 157 Ill. 2d 341, 193 Ill. Dec. 105, 626 N.E.2d 138 (1993); *People v. Patterson,* 154 Ill. 2d 414, 182 Ill. Dec. 592, 610 N.E.2d 16 (1992); *People v. Williams,* 149 Ill. 2d 467, 174 Ill. Dec. 829, 599 N.E.2d 913 (1992); *People v. Jett,* 294 Ill. App. 3d 822, 229 Ill. Dec. 209, 691 N.E.2d 145 (1998); *People v. Blanck,* 263 Ill. App. 3d 224, 200 Ill. Dec. 773, 635 N.E.2d 1356 (1994). With respect to double level hearsay, at least some parts of the testimony need to be corroborated. *People v. Williams,* 181 Ill. 2d 297, 229 Ill. Dec. 898, 692 N.E.2d 1109 (1998); *People v. Moore,* 171 Ill. 2d 74, 215 Ill. Dec. 75, 662 N.E.2d 1215 (1996). As to gang related evidence, autopsy evidence, and other crime, wrong, or act evidence at a sentencing hearing, *see People v. Hope,* 168 Ill. 2d 1, 212 Ill. Dec. 909, 658 N.E.2d 391 (1995); *People v. Sims,* 167 Ill. 2d 483, 212 Ill. Dec. 931, 658 N.E.2d 413 (1995); *People v. Williams,* 164 Ill. 2d 1, 206 Ill. Dec. 592, 645 N.E. 2d 844 (1994); *People v. Alksnis,* 291 Ill. App. 3d 347, 225 Ill. Dec. 35, 682 N.E. 2d 1112 (1997). With respect to hearsay evidence, evidence of gang membership, and evidence of other crimes, wrongs, or acts at a capital sentencing hearing, *see People v. Simms,* 168 Ill. 2d 176, 213 Ill. Dec. 576, 659 N.E.2d 922 (1995).

In adjudicatory proceedings under the Juvenile Court Act, the rules of evidence applicable in criminal proceedings apply to delinquent minor determinations, 705 ILCS 405/5-18; rules applicable in civil proceedings are applied in determinations of abused, neglected, or dependent minors, *id.,* 2-18, and minors requiring authoritative intervention, *id.,* 3-20. In hearings to determine whether it is in the best interest of the child to be made a ward of the court, all helpful evidence is admissible. *Id.,* 2-22 and 3-23.

In small claims actions, Supreme Court Rules 281-289, the rules of evidence frequently are not applied. *Demeo v. Manville,* 68 Ill. App. 3d 843, 25 Ill. Dec. 443, 386 N.E.2d 917 (1979).

Attorney disciplinary proceedings are governed by rules of

evidence developed by the supreme court; the legislature is without authority to regulate the admission of evidence in a disciplinary proceeding. *In re Ettinger,* 128 Ill. 2d 351, 131 Ill. Dec. 596, 538 N.E.2d 1152 (1989). The common law rules of evidence, however, need not be strictly applied in attorney disciplinary proceedings. *In re Blank,* 145 Ill. 2d 534, 165 Ill. Dec. 709, 585 N.E.2d 105 (1991); *In re Silvern,* 92 Ill. 2d 188, 65 Ill. Dec. 272, 441 N.E.2d 64 (1982).

Proceedings conducted before the court of claims are not governed by the rules of evidence. 705 ILCS 505/1 through 505/29.

With respect to proceedings conducted under the Illinois Administrative Procedure Act, 5 ILCS 100/1-1 to 100/15-10, rules of evidence are governed by *id.,* 100/10-40(a) and (b), which provides:

> In contested cases:
>
> (a) Irrelevant, immaterial or unduly repetitious evidence shall be excluded. The rules of evidence and privilege as applied in civil cases in the circuit courts of this State shall be followed. Evidence not admissible under those rules of evidence may be admitted, however, (except where precluded by statute) if it is of a type commonly relied upon by reasonably prudent men in the conduct of their affairs. Objections to evidentiary offers may be made and shall be noted in the record. Subject to these requirements, when a hearing will be expedited and the interests of the parties will not be prejudiced, any part of the evidence may be received in written form.
>
> (b) Subject to the evidentiary requirements of subsection (a) of this Section, a party may conduct cross-examination required for a full and fair disclosure of the facts.

The hearsay rule is to be applied in administrative proceedings. *Abrahamson v. Illinois Department of Professional Regulation,* 153 Ill. 2d 76, 180 Ill. Dec. 34, 606 N.E.2d 1111 (1992); *Jackson v. Board of Review,* 105 Ill. 2d 501, 86 Ill. Dec. 500, 475 N.E.2d 879 (1985); *Cochrane's of Champaign v. Liquor Control,* 285 Ill. App. 3d 28, 220 Ill. Dec. 755, 673 N.E.2d 1176 (1996).

Section 10-40(a) creates an additional hearsay exception for trustworthy statements, that is, those commonly relied upon by reasonably prudent people in the conduct of their affairs. *Metro Utility v. Illinois Commerce Commn.*, 193 Ill. App. 3d 178, 140 Ill. Dec. 455, 549 N.E.2d 1327 (1990).

In criminal cases, the rules of evidence apply to both the prosecution and the defense. A criminal defendant does not by virtue of either the compulsory process, confrontation, or due process clauses have the right to ignore "established rules of evidence designed to assure fairness and reliability in the ascertainment of guilt or innocence." The accused does not have "the unfettered right to offer testimony that is incompetent, privileged, or otherwise inadmissible under standard rules of evidence." *People v. Smith*, 152 Ill. 2d 229, 266, 178 Ill. Dec 335, 351, 604 N.E.2d 858, 874 (1992) quoting from *Chambers v. Mississippi*, 410 U.S. 284, 302 (1973) and *Taylor v. Illinois*, 484 U.S. 400, 410 (1988).

§102 Purpose and Construction

§102.1 Commentary

The purpose of rules of evidence — like rules of procedure — is the speedy and final resolution of controversies according to the substantive rights of the parties. *See* Code of Civil Procedure §5/1-106, 735 ILCS 5/1-106. Rules of evidence should be interpreted and applied to secure fairness in administration, to foster the ascertainment of truth, to prevent unfair prejudice, to eliminate unjustifiable expense and delay, and to protect all involved from harassment or undue embarrassment. *Cogan v. Kal Leasing, Inc.*, 190 Ill. App. 3d 145, 137 Ill. Dec. 396, 546 N.E.2d 20 (1989) (quoting Handbook).

§103   Rulings on Evidence

§103.1   An Overview

The function of reviewing courts is to correct errors committed by trial courts. Evidentiary rulings are within the sound discretion of the trial court; rulings on evidence will be reviewed applying the clear abuse of discretion standard. *People v. Hayes*, 139 Ill. 2d 89, 151 Ill. Dec. 348, 564 N.E.2d 803 (1990); *People v. Kidd*, 147 Ill. 2d 510, 169 Ill. Dec. 258, 591 N.E.2d 431 (1992); *People v. Hope*, 168 Ill. 2d 1, 212 Ill. Dec. 909, 658 N.E.2d 391 (1995). *Compare Halleck v. Coastal Building Maintenance Co.*, 269 Ill. App. 3d 887, 207 Ill. Dec. 387, 647 N.E.2d 618 (1995) (whether a statement is hearsay is reviewed applying the *de novo* standard). Clear abuse of discretion will be found only where the court's decision is arbitrary, fanciful, or unreasonable, or where no reasonable person would take the view adopted by the trial court. *People v. Illgen*, 145 Ill. 2d 353, 164 Ill. Dec. 599, 583 N.E.2d 515 (1991).

A trial court is not generally regarded as committing error in the admission or exclusion of evidence unless the error and the specific ground thereof come to the attention of the court, and it nevertheless persists. The policy is designed to afford the opponent an opportunity to confront the objection, to afford the court an intelligent basis of decision, and to enable the opponent to take possible corrective steps. *Bafia v. City International Trucks, Inc.*, 258 Ill. App. 3d 4, 196 Ill. Dec. 121, 629 N.E.2d 666 (1994). Moreover, a mere technical violation of a rule of evidence is not a sufficient basis for reversal unless it appears that the admission or exclusion affected a substantial right of a party. Supreme Court Rule 615; *Wilson v. C. & W.I.R.R.*, 365 Ill. 405, 6 N.E.2d 634 (1937). The burden of showing that substantial rights were affected rests with appellant. The clear abuse of discretion test, discussed supra, is applied in determining whether an evidentiary ruling is in error. Only if discretion was clearly abused is the ruling error subject to the substantial right test. Such error not affecting a substantial right of a party is often characterized as harmless. *Kotteakos v. United States,* 328 U.S. 750 (1946).

There are three categories of error well recognized in statutory law and judicial opinions. "Harmless error" is error raised at trial but found not to affect substantial rights. "Prejudicial" or "reversible" error is error raised at trial that is found to affect substantial rights. "Plain error" is error not raised at trial but nevertheless considered by a reviewing court and found to affect substantial rights. With respect to plain error and harmless error, *see* §103.10 infra.

No formal exception need be taken in order to make any ruling or action of the court reviewable.

Trial counsel should not permit the immediate objective of convincing the trier of fact to obscure the importance of making up a proper record for possible review. *See* §§103.2, 103.3, and 103.7 infra. With regard to the necessity to preserve error for appeal in post-trial motions, *see* §103.8 infra.

In making or responding to objections with respect to the admission or exclusion of evidence, it is of course improper for counsel to make any statements solely for the purpose of inflaming, prejudicing, or merely addressing the jury. The making of such speeches for the benefit of the jury may constitute reversible error. *Ryan v. Monson,* 33 Ill. App. 2d 406, 179 N.E.2d 449 (1961).

Persistent asking of questions after an objection has been sustained in violation of the court's ruling may result in the granting of a new trial. *People v. Thomas,* 261 Ill. App. 3d 366, 199 Ill. Dec. 43, 633 N.E.2d 839 (1994).

In general, a mistrial will be awarded where there has been an error of such gravity that it has infected the fundamental fairness of the trial, such that continuation of the proceeding would defeat the ends of justice, *People v. Redd,* 135 Ill. 2d 252, 323, 142 Ill. Dec. 802, 553 N.E.2d 316 (1990), i.e., the jury was so influenced and prejudiced that it can not be fair and impartial and that the damaging effect can not be cured by admonitions and instructions. *See also Dupree v.*

County of Cook, 287 Ill. App. 3d 135, 222 Ill. Dec. 3d 504, 677 N.E.2d 1303 (1997). The trial court's denial of a defendant's request for mistrial will not be disturbed unless the trial court's decision was a clear abuse of discretion. *People v. Sims,* 167 Ill. 2d 483, 212 Ill. Dec. 931, 658 N.E.2d 413 (1995); *People v. Hall,* 114 Ill. 2d 376, 102 Ill. Dec. 322, 499 N.E.2d 1335 (1986).

With respect to the conduct of such affairs outside the presence of the jury, *see* §§103.9, 104.3, and 506.3 infra.

§103.2 Error in Admitting: Objection, Presentation, and Waiver

The making of a proper objection is essential in order to save for review a contention that evidence was admitted erroneously. *Casson v. Nash,* 74 Ill. 2d 164, 23 Ill. Dec. 571, 384 N.E.2d 365 (1978), court is not required to exclude evidence *sua sponte.*

The admission of evidence cannot be assigned as error if no objection was made, *People v. Carlson,* 79 Ill. 2d 564, 38 Ill. Dec. 809, 404 N.E.2d 233 (1980), or if an objection was made but not ruled upon, *Palatine v. Dahle,* 385 Ill. 621, 53 N.E.2d 608 (1944); *Department of Public Works v. Anastoplo,* 14 Ill. 2d 126, 151 N.E.2d 337 (1958), or if evidence was admitted subject to connection and no motion to strike was later made, *Kloster v. Markiewicz,* 94 Ill. App. 3d 392, 49 Ill. Dec. 966, 418 N.E.2d 986 (1981), or if ruling was reserved but never made, *People v. Waller,* 67 Ill. 2d 381, 10 Ill. Dec. 517, 367 N.E.2d 1283 (1977), or if the objection was not made promptly. *People v. Waller* supra; *People v. Driver,* 62 Ill. App. 3d 847, 20 Ill. Dec. 7, 379 N.E.2d 840 (1978), a delayed objection by defendant at end of defendant's case to prosecution exhibit offered during prosecution's case was not made in ample time. *Compare Decker v. St. Mary's Hospital,* 249 Ill. App. 3d 802, 188 Ill. Dec. 912, 619 N.E.2d 537 (1993) (objection to evidence offered in violation of motion in limine timely when made at first recess; immediate objection would have emphasized objectionable testimony). Nor can the admission of evidence at trial be assigned as error by the party procuring the admission of the evidence in the absence of a timely motion to strike. *People v. Randall,* 84 Ill. App. 3d 888, 40 Ill, Dec. 177, 405 N.E.2d 1269 (1980).

The concept of waiver of the right to assert error on appeal based upon failure to object applies as well to matters such as the absence of an affidavit supporting a motion to dismiss. *Cuerton v. American Hosp. Supply Corp.* 136 Ill. App. 3d 231, 90 Ill. Dec. 480, 482 N.E.2d 187 (1985). A suggestion or acquiescence in a procedure for the court to resolve an objection raised at trial constitutes a waiver of any objection to the procedure. *People v. Miller,* 120 Ill. App. 3d 495, 75 Ill. Dec. 814, 457 N.E.2d 1373 (1983).

To be effective on review, the objection must state the specific ground relied upon for exclusion, unless the ground is so obvious from the context that it must have been apparent. *Massey v. Farmer's Natl. Bank,* 104 Ill. 327 (1882). Where the ground of the objection is of a character that may be remedied, an opportunity to do so is thus provided. *Central Steel & Wire Co. v. Coating Research,* 53 Ill. App. 3d 943, 11 Ill. Dec. 686, 369 N.E.2d 140 (1977). A specific objection is a waiver of all grounds not specified; in other words, one ground cannot be urged below and another on appeal. *People v. Lewis,* 165 Ill. 2d 305, 209 Ill. Dec. 144, 651 N.E.2d 72 (1995), objection as to lack of foundation does not preserve hearsay objection for appeal; *People v. Barrios,* 114 Ill. 2d 265, 102 Ill. Dec. 522, 500 N.E.2d 415 (1986), objection on the ground of unfair prejudice does not preserve hearsay objection for appeal; *People v. O'Neal,* 104 Ill. 2d 399, 84 Ill. Dec. 481, 472 N.E.2d 441 (1984), objection on one ground to jury instruction waives all grounds not specified; *Forest Preserve Dist. v. Lehmann,* 388 Ill. 416, 58 N.E.2d 538 (1945), objection that sale was agricultural precluded assigning as error that it was too remote in time, and circumstances had changed; *People ex. rel. Blackmon v. Brent,* 97 Ill. App. 2d 438, 240 N.E.2d 255 (1968), objection as not original writing is waiver of objection for lack of proper foundation; *Bear v.*

Holiday Inns of America, Inc., 1 Ill. App. 3d 786, 275 N.E.2d 457 (1971), objection as to changed conditions of carpet depicted in photograph would not support review of objection relating to changed lighting conditons; *Bosel v. Marriot Corp.,* 65 Ill. App. 3d 649, 22 Ill. Dec. 267, 382 N.E.2d 587 (1978), objection as to relevancy does not preserve objection on grounds of hearsay, improper opinion, or original writing rule; *Zerbenski v. Tagliarino,* 67 Ill. App. 3d 166, 23 Ill. Dec. 846, 384 N.E.2d 753 (1978), objection to question as argumentative is waiver of objection on grounds of unfair prejudice; *Diorio v. City of Chicago,* 99 Ill. App. 3d 1047, 55 Ill. Dec. 50, 425 N.E.2d 1223 (1981), objection on the ground of the lawyer-client privilege does not preserve objection on the ground of relevancy; *People v. Brown,* 275 Ill. App. 3d 1105, 212 Ill. Dec. 441, 657 N.E.2d 642 (1995), objection as to authentication does not preserve objection as to relevance or unfair prejudice.

However, if a specific objection is erroneously sustained, the action of the trial court in excluding evidence will be upheld on appeal if the ruling excluding the evidence was proper for some other reason and if with respect to the proper reason the objection could not have been obviated. *Levin v. Welsh Brothers Motor Services, Inc.,* 164 Ill. App. 3d 640, 115 Ill. Dec. 680, 518 N.E.2d 205 (1987). *Accord Hamling v. United States,* 418 U.S. 87 (1974).

The words "I object" need not be used; all that is necessary is that a reasonable indication of an objection be given. *People v. Pankey,* 58 Ill. App. 3d 924, 16 Ill. Dec. 339, 374 N.E.2d 1114 (1978). A general objection such as "I object, the evidence is irrelevant, immaterial, incompetent, and inadmissible" raises only the question of relevance. *Johnson v. Bennett,* 395 Ill. 389, 69 N.E.2d 899 (1946); *Calumet & C. Canal & Dock Co. v. Morawetz,* 195 Ill. 398, 63 N.E. 165 (1902); *Buntain v. Bailey,* 27 Ill. 409 (1862). The objection "incompetent" made alone, being equivalent to inadmissible, fails to state any ground of objection. *Forrest v. Industrial Commn.,* 77 Ill. 2d 86, 32 Ill. Dec. 346, 395 N.E.2d 576 (1979). Similarly, objections such as "Your Honor, he can't do that," and "It is unfair," should be held not even to raise the question of relevance. Following a general objection, specific grounds may not be raised for the first time on appeal. *Clifford-Jacobs Forging Co. v. Industrial Commn.* 19 Ill. 2d 236, 166 N.E.2d 582 (1960); *Johnson v. Jackson,* 43 Ill. App. 2d 251, 193 N.E.2d 485 (1964); *Chubb/Home Insurance v. Outboard Marine,* 238 Ill. App. 3d 558, 179 Ill. Dec. 591, 606 N.E.2d 423 (1992).

Where the proper ground for sustaining the objection can only be raised by a specific objection (a ground other than relevance), and a general objection is in fact sustained, the decision will be upheld on appeal only if it would be useless to reverse the case because counsel would be sure to use the correct specific objection if the case was retried to exclude what already was excluded and the specific objection could not obviated. The party offering the evidence may discover the specific ground relied upon by the court by asking the court to state or have opposing counsel state the basis of the ruling. Once the specific ground is discovered, it is possible that the objection may then be obviated.

A party who has objected is not required to repeat the objection each time such evidence is offered when a continuing objection has been interposed or when the attitude of the court is clear and repetition of the objection would aggravate the situation and tend to prejudice the jury. *Chicago Union Traction Co. v. Lauth,* 216 Ill. 176, 74 N.E. 738 (1905); *Schoolfield v. Witkowski,* 54 Ill. App. 2d 111, 203 N.E.2d 460 (1964). Conversely, in the absence of either of the foregoing, a failure to object to similar evidence waives any claim that the evidence actually objected to was admitted erroneously. *Beltz v. Griffin,* 244 Ill. App. 3d 490, 184 Ill. Dec. 178, 612 N.E.2d 1054 (1993).

An objection by a party to the admissibility of evidence does not preserve error on behalf of a nonobjecting opposing party. *Brown v. Timpte,* 137 Ill. App. 3d 1053, 92 Ill. Dec. 677, 485 N.E.2d 488 (1985), objection by one defendant does not inure to plaintiff. An objection by a party aligned in interest also has been held not to preserve error on behalf of a nonobjecting aligned party. *Martino v. Barra,* 10 Ill. App. 3d

97, 293 N.E.2d 745 (1973). *Martino* is incorrect and should not be followed. *See Loose v. Offshore Navigation, Inc.*, 670 F.2d 493 (5th Cir. 1982) (it is both dilatory and fatuous for each aligned party to voice "me-too" objections).

If a portion only of an exhibit is objectionable, the objection must be directed specifically to that part. *Gamble-Robinson Commn. Co. v. Union Pac. Ry.*, 262 Ill. 400, 104 N.E. 666 (1914). Similarly, if evidence is admissible against less than all adverse parties or for a limited purpose, error in excluding the evidence for all purposes is not preserved unless such limited admissibility is specifically presented to the court. *Tokar v. Crestwood Imports, Inc.*, 177 Ill. App. 3d 422, 126 Ill. Dec. 697, 532 N.E.2d 382 (1988).

The requirement that a proper objection be made to preserve error for review on appeal applies as well to improper remarks of counsel. *People v. Skorusa*, 55 Ill. 2d 577, 304 N.E.2d 630 (1973). With respect to preserving error with regard to jury instructions, *see* §611.27 infra.

§103.3 Error in Admitting: Time of Objection, Motion to Strike; Curative Instructions

Objections to evidence should be made as soon as the ground for objection becomes apparent. *People v. Trefonas*, 9 Ill. 2d 92, 136 N.E.2d 817 (1956); *Goldberg v. Capitol Freight Lines*, 382 Ill. 283, 47 N.E.2d 67 (1943), which generally is the time the evidence is being offered. *Hunter v. Chicago & North Western Transportation Co.*, 200 Ill. App. 3d 458, 146 Ill. Dec. 253, 558 N.E.2d 216 (1990). However, sometimes the ground for objection may not be apparent or available until after the evidence has been given, and in that event a motion to strike is appropriate. *People v. Fritz*, 84 Ill. 2d 72, 48 Ill. Dec. 880, 417 N.E.2d 612 (1981). For example, a proper question may evoke an inadmissible answer, *Chicago, P. & St. L. Ry. Co. v. Blume*, 137 Ill. 448, 27 N.E. 601 (1891); or an unresponsive answer, *People v. Fritz*, 84 Ill. 2d 72, 48 Ill. Dec. 880, 417 N.E.2d 612 (1981); *People v. Rose*, 77 Ill. App. 3d 330, 32 Ill. Dec. 700, 395

N.E.2d 1081 (1979). Or evidence may become immaterial through dismissal of the pertinent count of the complaint. *Bell v. Toluca Coal Co.,* 272 Ill. 576, 112 N.E. 311 (1916). Or evidence may not be produced to connect up evidence admitted subject to being connected up. *Gillespie v. Chrysler Motor Corp.,* 135 Ill. 2d 363, 142 Ill. Dec. 777, 553 N.E.2d 291 (1990); *Krengiel v. Lissner Corp., Inc.,* 250 Ill. App. 3d 288, 190 Ill. Dec. 222, 621 N.E.2d 91 (1993). Or the thrust of an expert's testimony may not be readily apparent at the outset. *Department of Transp. v. Bouy,* 69 Ill. App. 3d 29, 25 Ill. Dec. 499, 386 N.E.2d 1163 (1979). Or cross-examination may establish that the direct testimony was based upon hearsay. *Louis L. Weinzelbaum, Inc. v. Abbell,* 49 Ill. App. 2d 442, 200 N.E.2d 43 (1964).

Once the ground of the objection becomes apparent and available, the motion to strike must be timely. *Krengiel v. Lissner Corp., Inc.,* 250 Ill. App. 3d 288, 190 Ill. Dec. 222, 621 N.E.2d 91 (1993). A motion to strike made either at the close of the witness's testimony, at the close of the party's case, or at the close of the opponent's opportunity to present his case in chief, is not made in apt time. *Holden v. Caselton,* 275 Ill. App. 3d 950, 212 Ill. Dec. 479, 657 N.E.2d 680 (1995); *Johnson v. Hoover Water Well Serv.,* 108 Ill. App. 3d 994, 64 Ill. Dec. 476, 439 N.E.2d 1284 (1982); *People v. Driver,* 62 Ill. App. 3d 847, 20 Ill. Dec. 7, 379 N.E.2d 840 (1978).

If evidence is struck, an instruction to the jury to disregard should be given on request. *People v. Jackson,* 84 Ill. 2d 350, 49 Ill. Dec. 719, 418 N.E.2d 739 (1981). The sufficiency of such a corrective measure must be determined under all the circumstances. "The human mind is not a slate, from which can be wiped out, at the will and instruction of another, ideas and thoughts written thereon." *People v. Deal,* 357 Ill. 634, 643, 192 N.E. 649 (1934). Nevertheless, the giving of the instruction is considered sufficient in all but the most aggravated situations, and a mistrial need not be declared. *People v. Ward,* 154 Ill. 2d 272, 181 Ill. Dec. 884, 609 N.E.2d 252 (1992). *Accord People v. Alvine,* 173 Ill. 2d 273, 219 Ill. Dec. 546, 671 N.E.2d 713 (1996); *People v. Hobley,* 159 Ill. 2d 272, 202 Ill. Dec. 256, 637 N.E.2d 992 (1994); *People v. Cisewski,*

118 Ill. 2d 163, 113 Ill. Dec. 58, 514 N.E.2d 970 (1987) (instruction to jury to disregard the answer or remark generally will correct the error). *See, e.g., Williams v. Consumers Co.,* 352 Ill. 51, 185 N.E. 217 (1933), inadvertent disclosure of liability insurance in unresponsive answer was cured; *People v. Wilson,* 51 Ill. 2d 302, 281 N.E.2d 626 (1972), prejudice resulting from inadmissible evidence cured by court instruction to disregard; *People v. Baptist,* 76 Ill. 2d 19, 27 Ill. Dec. 792, 389 N.E.2d 1200 (1979), prejudicial effect of final argument cured by court admonition to jury; *People v. Olinger,* 112 Ill. 2d 324, 97 Ill. Dec. 772, 493 N.E.2d (1986), prejudice, caused by questioning on cross-examination as to a nonexistent prior inconsistent statement, cured by jury instruction; *People v. Travis,* 94 Ill. App. 3d 983, 50 Ill. Dec. 325, 419 N.E.2d 433 (1981), improper reference in question to handgun rendered harmless by motion to strike and instruction to disregard; *People v. Romano,* 139 Ill. App. 3d 999, 94 Ill. Dec. 28, 487 N.E.2d 785 (1985), improper admission of accident reconstruction testimony adequately cured by instruction to disregard; *People v. Johnson,* 199 Ill. App. 3d 577, 145 Ill. Dec. 676, 557 N.E.2d 466 (1990), the striking of a hearsay description of the defendant testified to by a police officer cured any prejudice. *Cf. People v. Gregory,* 22 Ill. 2d 601, 177 N.E.2d 120 (1961), error in admitting evidence of other crimes not cured by instruction to disregard; *People v. Garreau,* 27 Ill. 2d 388, 189 N.E.2d 287 (1963), prejudicial effect of remarks in final argument not cured by sustaining objections to the remarks and admonishing jury to disregard them; *People v. Lewis,* 269 Ill. App. 3d 523, 206 Ill. Dec. 938, 646 N.E.2d 305 (1995), unresponsive reference to polygraph examination denied the defendant the right to a fair trial in spite of instruction to disregard; *People v. Rivera,* 277 Ill. App. 3d 811, 214 Ill. Dec. 575, 661 N.E.2d 429 (1996), prejudicial unresponsive testimony as a prior identification not cured by instruction to disregard in light of prosecution's follow up question and reference in closing argument. *See also* §105.1 infra, discussing similar considerations in connection with limiting instructions.

§103.4 Error in Admitting: Waiver of Right to Object by Other than Failure to Make; Opening the Door

Waiver of the right to object may also occur in ways other than by failure to make an objection. Thus a party introducing evidence of a particular kind cannot complain if the opposing party thereafter offers similar evidence. *Lincoln v. Chicago & A.R. Co.*, 262 Ill. 98, 104 N.E. 282 (1914), introducing testimony that property would not benefit in amount of assessment precluded objection that ultimate issue rule was violated by testimony that it would benefit in said amount; *Grundy County Natl. Bank v. Myre*, 65 Ill. App. 3d 368, 21 Ill. Dec. 660, 381 N.E.2d 1204 (1978), introducing evidence of settlement negotiations precluded objection to other testimony concerning the settlement discussions; *Tokar v. Crestwood Imports, Inc.*, 177 Ill. App. 3d 422, 126 Ill. Dec. 697, 532 N.E.2d 382 (1988), party who called adverse party's expert to testify as an expert is foreclosed from later asserting the witness was not qualified. This aspect of waiver is not applied broadly to rules of evidence but only to particular kinds of evidence, so that a party offering hearsay evidence, for example, would not waive the right thereafter to object to any hearsay whatever but only to that particular kind of hearsay.

The principle of waiver does not require a party to stand on an overruled objection. She may follow the law as laid down by the trial judge and herself offer similar evidence without waiving her objection. *Chicago City Ry. v. Uhter*, 212 Ill. 174, 72 N.E. 195 (1904), overruled objection to hearsay evidence of physical condition not waived by offering similar hearsay thereafter; *People v. Spates*, 77 Ill. 2d 193, 32 Ill. Dec. 333, 395 N.E.2d 563 (1979), after denial of motion to preclude use of prior conviction to impeach, disclosure of prior conviction on direct examination does not waive error. *Cf. People v. Nicholls*, 236 Ill. App. 3d 275, 177 Ill. Dec. 626, 603 N.E.2d 696 (1992), the questioning of a witness on cross-examination concerning evidence admitted over the cross-examiner's objection during direct examination waives any error for appeal; incorrectly decided.

The failure of the opposing party to object is of no consequence if the evidence offered is relevant and otherwise admissible. Whether admitting proof of inadmissible facts without objection opens the door to rebutting them finds no clear answer in the decisions. Some cases take the view that the party offering the original evidence cannot complain if the trial judge accepts the boundaries of the controversy as set by him and permits not only cross-examination and redirect examination but also the admission of rebuttal evidence. *People v. Payne,* 98 Ill. 2d 45, 74 Ill. Dec. 542, 456 N.E.2d 44 (1983), cross-examination by defense attorney of police officer inquiring whether the defendant was searched when arrested implying nothing was found opened the door to admission of illegally seized evidence; *People v. Nastasio,* 30 Ill. 2d 51, 195 N.E.2d 144 (1964), defendants testifying on direct examination that they were never convicted of any crime other than those mentioned opens door to proof of commission of crime not otherwise employable for purpose of impeachment; *People v. Johnson,* 42 Ill. App. 3d 194, 355 N.E.2d 577 (1976), witness testimony on direct examination that he never was arrested made cross-examination as to prior arrests permissible; *People v. Mendez,* 53 Ill. App. 1038, 11 Ill. Dec. 758, 369 N.E.2d 212 (1977), cross-examination by defense attorney of police officer as to why confession not reduced to writing opened door to testimony of defendant's silence following the giving of *Miranda* warnings; *People v. Penland,* 64 Ill. App. 3d 656, 21 Ill. Dec. 513, 381 N.E.2d 840 (1978), testimony of defense witnesses that they had never seen defendant with a shotgun opened door to testimony that defendant was seen with a shotgun in a discotheque; *People v. Rasmussen,* 143 Ill. App. 3d 11, 97 Ill. Dec. 176, 492 N.E.2d 612 (1986), once defendant testifies to his good character for morality and decency, state may cross-examine as to homosexual preference and misconduct with boys; *People v. Ford,* 163 Ill. App. 3d 497, 114 Ill. Dec. 611, 516 N.E.2d 766 (1987), testimony on direct by accused that he had never "cut" anyone before permitted prosecution to prove the contrary by extrinsic proof; *People v. Riggins,* 205 Ill. App. 3d 904, 151 Ill. Dec. 145, 564 N.E.2d 122 (1990), testimony on direct examination, concerning whether the arresting officer advised of the charges, opened the door to cross-examination and extrinsic evidence as to the defendant having been given his constitutional rights; *People v. Le Cour,* 273 Ill. App. 3d. 1003, 210 Ill. Dec. 245, 652 N.E.2d 1221 (1995), cross-examination of police officer as to having sworn out a search warrant that was never executed, opened door to explanation that process of obtaining warrant took too long thereby giving the defendant too much time to dispose of the drugs to expect drugs to be found in the house; *People v. Woodard,* 276 Ill. App. 3d 242, 212 Ill. Dec. 878, 658 N.E.2d 55 (1995), testimony on direct by accused that police did not tell him why he was arrested opened door to cross-examination concerning his arrest for fleeing and evading a police officer. Such door opening is sometimes referred to as "curative admissibility." *People v. Wright,* 261 Ill. App. 3d 772, 198 Ill. Dec. 376, 632 N.E.2d 706 (1994). Other cases sustain the trial court in excluding the rebuttal evidence, pointing out that an adequate remedy was available by way of objection to the original evidence or that the doctrine of "opening the door," designed to prevent unfairness, should not be permitted to be used to inject prejudice. *Saputo v. Fatla,* 25 Ill. App. 3d 775, 324 N.E.2d 34 (1975).

Admissibility ultimately turns on a balancing of the need to rebut the inference raised against the risk of prejudice that would be posed by the introduction of the rebutting evidence, § 403.1 infra. *People v. Manning,* 182 Ill. 2d 193, 230 Ill. Dec. 933, 695 N.E.2d 423 (1998); *People v. Chambers,* 179 Ill. App. 3d 565, 128 Ill. Dec. 372, 534 N.E.2d 554 (1989). Relatively harmless excursions into irrelevancy are subject to the discretion of the trial judge. However, if more than mere irrelevancy is involved, and substantial harm results either from the nature of the evidence introduced or from denial of rebuttal, a ruling of admission or of exclusion is grounds for reversal. *People v. Newman,* 261 Ill. 11, 103 N.E. 589 (1913), error to allow prosecution to prove other offenses by codefendant witness for accused who testified on direct that police were persecuting him; *People v. Simmons,* 274 Ill. 528,

113 N.E. 887 (1916), error to foreclose accused from going into motives for change of testimony by witnesses produced by state only for purpose of showing they had committed perjury to obtain new trial for accused. Generally speaking, when inadmissible facts are admitted without objection, it appears that the opponent will be permitted by the trial court to introduce contrary evidence limited in scope and extent to that needed to eliminate the unfair prejudice that might otherwise ensue from the original evidence. *People v. Boclair,* 129 Ill. 2d 458, 136 Ill. Dec. 29, 544 N.E.2d 715 (1989); *People v. Chambers,* 179 Ill. App. 3d 565, 128 Ill. Dec. 372, 534 N.E.2d 554 (1989); *Wine v. Bauerfreund,* 155 Ill. App. 3d 19, 107 Ill. Dec. 491, 507 N.E.2d 155 (1987). In this connection, consider also the rule against impeaching witnesses on collateral matters, §607.2 infra.

Inadmissible matters brought out on cross-examination cannot be used by the cross-examiner to open the door to otherwise inadmissible rebuttal evidence. *People v. Kirkwood,* 27 Ill. 2d 23, 160 N.E.2d 766 (1959). *See generally People v. Cruz,* 162 Ill. 2d 314, 205 Ill. Dec. 345, 643 N.E.2d 636 (1994) (cross-examiner may not ask a question to elicit a certain response and then assert witness has "opened the door" to otherwise inadmissible evidence on that particular subject). *See also Dalton v. People,* 224 Ill. 333, 79 N.E. 669 (1906), error to allow prosecution to prove other offenses in rebuttal of overly broad assertion of innocence elicited from accused on cross-examination; *People v. Harris,* 224 Ill. App. 3d 649, 167 Ill. Dec. 165, 587 N.E.2d 47 (1992), cross-examination by prosecution of defendant relating to his character does not trigger right on part of prosecution to introduce reputation testimony as to the defendant's character by way of rebuttal. *Cf. People v. Gordon,* 82 Ill. App. 3d 906, 38 Ill. Dec. 339, 403 N.E.2d 570 (1980), approving admission of evidence to rebut without discussing issue. With respect to whether cross-examination directed toward matters on direct examination opens the door to otherwise inadmissible evidence, *see People v. Jenkins,* 209 Ill. App. 3d 249, 154 Ill. Dec. 122, 568 N.E.2d 122 (1991). With respect to whether evidence admitted under the concept of completeness, §§106.1 and 106.2 infra, opens the door to otherwise inadmissible evidence, *see People v. Wright,* 261 Ill. App. 3d 772, 198 Ill. Dec. 376, 632 N.E.2d 706 (1994).

Objections not raised at the first trial of a case may be urged at a later trial and are not waived, even though the later trial is one *de novo* on appeal or on remand. *Belskis v. Dering Coal Co.,* 246 Ill. 62, 92 N.E. 575 (1910); *Baker v. Brown,* 18 Ill. 91 (1856). A contrary result should be reached if the objection is based on the confidential nature of information that was disclosed without objection at the earlier trial, since the confidentiality cannot be restored. *See* 8 Wigmore, Evidence §2328 (McNaughton Rev. 1961).

A party cannot complain of evidence that she herself has introduced or brought out. *People v. Cortes,* 181 Ill. 2d 249, 229 Ill. Dec. 918, 692 N.E.2d 1129 (1998); *People v. Scott,* 148 Ill. 2d 479, 171 Ill. Dec. 365, 594, N.E.2d 217 (1992); *Gillespie v. Chrysler Motors Corp.,* 135 Ill. 2d 363, 142 Ill. Dec. 777, 553 N.E.2d 291 (1990); *Auton v. Logan Landfill, Inc.,* 105 Ill. 2d 537, 86 Ill. Dec. 438, 475 N.E.2d 817 (1985); *People v. Brown,* 275 Ill. App. 3d 1105, 212 Ill. Dec. 441, 657 N.E.2d 642 (1995); *Chubb/Home Insurance v. Outboard Marine,* 238 Ill. App. 3d 558, 179 Ill. Dec. 591, 606 N.E.2d 423 (1992). Neither can a party complain when evidence similar to that objected to is admitted without objection, *Gillespie v. Chrysler Motors Corp.* supra; *Cunningham v. Millers General Insurance Co.,* 227 Ill. App. 3d 201, 169 Ill. Dec. 200, 591 N.E.2d 80 (1992), or admitted by stipulation, *People v. Ross,* 63 Ill. App. 3d 884, 20 Ill. Dec. 688, 380 N.E.2d 897 (1978); *People v. Hawkins,* 27 Ill. 2d 339, 189 N.E.2d 252 (1963), or when evidence is offered on cross-examination to develop all circumstances that explain, qualify, discredit, or destroy the witness's direct testimony although such examination may incidentally raise new matter. *People v. Williams,* 66 Ill. 2d 478, 6 Ill. Dec. 854, 363 N.E.2d 801 (1977); *People v. Suter,* 292 Ill. App. 3d 358, 226 Ill. Dec. 568, 685 N.E. 2d 1023 (1997). *See also* §611.11 infra.

A party who proceeds to trial without objection and permits

the opposing party to introduce proof waives failure of the opponent to have interposed an answer, *Larson v. R.W. Borrowdale Co.,* 53 Ill. App. 2d 104, 203 N.E.2d 77 (1964); to file an answer to an amended complaint, *American Natl. Bank and Trust Co. of Chicago v. City of Chicago,* 4 Ill. App. 3d 127, 280 N.E.2d 567 (1971); or to file a reply to an affirmative defense, *Sottiaux v. Bean,* 405 Ill. 25, 95 N.E.2d 899 (1950); and the absence of the pleading does not constitute an admission, *Mooney v. Underwriters at Lloyd's,* 33 Ill. 2d 566, 213 N.E.2d 283 (1966).

The admissibility of evidence offered to refute admissible evidence does not involve the concept of door opening. For a discussion of the scope of refutation, *see* §611.12 (concerning redirect examination) and §§611.1 and 611.3 (regarding rebuttal). *Cf. People v. Smith,* 105 Ill. App. 3d 84, 60 Ill. Dec. 816, 433 N.E.2d 1054 (1982); *People v. Wydra,* 265 Ill. App. 3d 597, 202 Ill. Dec. 202, 637 N.E.2d 741 (1994); *People v. Pursley,* 284 Ill. App. 3d 597, 220 Ill. Dec. 237, 672 N.E.2d 1249 (1996), incorrectly employing the term "opened the door."

§103.5   Error in Admitting: Depositions

Objections to depositions are governed in detail by Supreme Court Rule 211. The underlying principle is that an objection must be made in ample time to afford opportunity to correct the defect with minimum inconvenience, if it is one subject to correction. An incidental effect is to reduce the likelihood of encountering an unanticipated objection at the trial. Some defects can be obviated by serving a new notice or taking a new deposition, and some can be obviated at the taking; others cannot be corrected at all. The rule is tailored accordingly as to the time of objecting:

Before taking.   Defects in notice, Rule 211(a); disqualification of officer if known or discoverable with reasonable diligence, Rule 211(b); form of written questions, Rule 211(c)(3).

At taking of oral deposition. Grounds of objection to competency of the deponent or admissibility of evidence that could be corrected if presented during taking, such as the form of question or answer, Rule 211(c)(1); errors and irregularities in taking, oath, or misconduct that might be corrected if presented promptly, Rule 211(c)(2). Illustrations are found in earlier cases: insufficiency of proof of loss of original document as foundation for secondary evidence of its contents, *Hutchinson v. Bambas*, 249 Ill. 624, 94 N.E. 987 (1911); insufficient preliminary proof of account books, *Williams v. Press Publishing Co.*, 126 Ill. App. 109 (1906). Lack of adequate support establishing the basis of an expert's opinion has also been added to the list. *Lundell v. Citrano*, 129 Ill. 2d 390, 84 Ill. Dec. 581, 472 N.E.2d 541 (1984).

After taking but before trial. Irregularities as to completion and return, Rule 211(d).

At trial. Objections to the competency of the deponent or admissibility of testimony on grounds that could not have been corrected if presented at the taking, Rule 211(c)(1). Immateriality and irrelevancy fall in this category. *See, e.g., Bird v. Thanhouser*, 160 Ill. App. 653 (1911), testimony of one party to contract as to what he meant by language immaterial under parol evidence rule. Moreover, their existence may not be apparent at the time of taking. The fact that the matter might have been proved by another witness or by another kind of evidence seems not to remove the situation from this category. *Albers Commission Co. v. Sessel*, 193 Ill. 153, 61 N.E. 1075 (1901), incompetency of deponent under Dead Man's Act, §606.1 *infra*, may first be raised at trial. *Contra Balkwill v. Bridgeport Wood Finishing Co.*, 62 Ill. App. 663 (1895), relating to failure to object, prior to trial, to deposition testimony as to whether May 30 was a legal holiday. If the objection could not possibly be known at time of deposition, it may be made at trial. *Prince v. Hutchinson*, 49 Ill. App. 3d 990, 8 Ill. Dec. 311, 365 N.E.2d 549 (1977), sufficiency of evidence in record to support hypothetical question.

Objections prior to taking should be in writing and served

on the opposite party. Illinois Supreme Court Rule 211(a), (b) and (c)(3). Objections during the taking are noted in the deposition by the officer, Rule 206(f). Objections to completion and return are by motion to suppress, Rule 211(d). Otherwise objections are disposed of at the trial unless a party on notice and motion avails himself of his right to obtain a ruling in advance of trial, Rules 211(c)(1) and (4).

§103.6   Error in Admitting: Nonjury and Chancery Cases

In nonjury cases, it is assumed that the trial judge in reaching a decision disregarded improperly admitted evidence, if the record contains sufficient competent evidence to sustain the result. *Knight v. Collings,* 227 Ill. 348, 81 N.E. 346 (1907), action at law; *Oswald v. Nehls,* 233 Ill. 438, 84 N.E. 619 (1908), suit in chancery; *People v. Harris,* 57 Ill. 2d 228, 314 N.E.2d 465 (1974), *People v. Berland,* 74 Ill. 2d 286, 24 Ill. Dec. 508, 385 N.E.2d 649 (1978); *People v. Tye,* 141 Ill. 2d 1, 152 Ill. Dec 249, 565 N.E.2d 931 (1990), bench trial. The principle also applies to arguments and remarks of counsel. *People v. Miller,* 30 Ill. 2d 110, 195 N.E.2d 694 (1964). The effect of the assumption is to prevent a substantial right of the party from being affected, *see* §103.1 supra. *See, e.g., Superior Structures v. City of Sesser,* 277 Ill. App. 3d 653, 214 Ill. Dec. 413, 660 N.E.2d 1362 (1996). The assumption may be rebutted by a showing to the contrary. *People v. Gilbert,* 68 Ill. 2d 252, 12 Ill. Dec. 142, 369 N.E.2d 849 (1977); *McFail v. Braden,* 19 Ill. 2d 108, 166 N.E.2d 46 (1960); *People v. Cassell,* 283 Ill. App. 3d 112, 218 Ill. Dec. 512, 669 N.E.2d 655 (1996); *People v. Koch,* 248 Ill. App. 3d 585, 188 Ill. Dec. 77, 618 N.E.2d 647 (1993). Possible methods of making the requisite showing include statements from the bench, *People v. Rivers,* 410 Ill. 140, 102 N.E.2d 303 (1951); *People v. Alford,* 111 Ill. App. 3d 741, 67 Ill. Dec. 340, 444 N.E.2d 576 (1982), the overruling of an objection made to the introduction of the evidence, *People v. Hampton,* 96 Ill. App. 3d 728, 52 Ill. Dec. 330, 422 N.E.2d 11 (1981); *People v. DeGrott,* 108 Ill. App. 2d 1, 257 N.E.2d 177 (1968), and special findings and propositions of law, McCaskill, Illinois Civil Practice Act Annotated 178 (1936). Special findings and propositions of law, while not required, are beneficial in a complicated case. *Robinhorne Constr. Corp. v. Snyder*, 113 Ill. App. 2d 288, 251 N.E.2d 641 (1969).

In chancery cases the general rule that proper objection must be made in the court below in order to preserve for review any error in admitting evidence prevails as in other cases, *Doty v. Doty*, 159 Ill. 46, 42 N.E. 174 (1895); *Dunlavy v. Lowrie*, 372 Ill. 622, 25 N.E.2d 67 (1940), and earlier cases indicating the contrary must be regarded as overruled. In cases heard before a master, the usual and proper procedure is to include objections to evidence in objections filed to the master's report and to renew the objections before the court as exceptions to the master's report. An alternative method is to obtain a ruling of the court by motion while the case is still pending before the master. *Peck v. Peck*, 16 Ill. 2d 268, 157 N.E.2d 249 (1959).

With respect to court considering evidence not introduced at trial, *see* §605.2 infra.

§103.7   Error in Excluding: Offer of Proof

Just as the objection is the key to saving for review any error in admitting evidence, the offer of proof is the key to saving error in excluding evidence. *People v. Thompkins*, 181 Ill. 2d 1, 228 Ill. Dec. 909, 690 N.E.2d 984 (1998) (citing Handbook); *People v. Andrews*, 146 Ill. 2d 413, 167 Ill. Dec. 996, 588 N.E.2d 1126 (1992) (citing Handbook); *People v. Ramirez*, 244 Ill. App. 3d 136, 184 Ill. Dec. 524, 613 N.E.2d 1116 (1993) (citing Handbook). The purpose of the offer of proof is to disclose the nature of offered evidence to which objection is interposed, for the information of the trial judge and opposing counsel, and to enable the reviewing court to determine whether the exclusion was erroneous and harmful. *People v. Thompkins* supra; *People v. Andrews* supra; *Little v. Tuscola Stone Co.*, 234 Ill. App. 3d 726, 175 Ill. Dec. 812, 600

N.E.2d 1270 (1992) (citing Handbook); *Holden v. Caselton,* 275 Ill. App. 3d 950, 212 Ill. Dec. 479, 657 N.E.2d 680 (1995); *Premier Electrical Construction Co. v. American National Bank of Chicago,* 276 Ill. App. 3d 816, 213 Ill. Dec. 128, 658 N.E.2d 877 (1995). When the circumstances and the question itself sufficiently indicate the purpose and substance of the evidence sought, and when the question is in proper form and clearly admits of a favorable answer, an offer is not required although clearly the safer course. *People v. Lynch,* 104 Ill. 2d 194, 83 Ill. Dec. 598, 470 N.E.2d 1018 (1984); *Creighton v. Elgin,* 387 Ill. 592, 56 N.E.2d 825 (1944); *Moss v. Miller,* 254 Ill. App. 3d 174, 192 Ill. Dec. 889, 625 N.E.2d 1044 (1993); *Wright v. Stokes,* 167 Ill. App. 3d 887, 118 Ill. Dec. 853, 522 N.E.2d 308 (1988). *See also Overcast v. Bodart,* 266 Ill. App. 3d 428, 203 Ill. Dec. 425, 639 N.E.2d 984 (1994), while preferable, failure to state why evidence should be admitted was excused where reason had previously been made known to the court. When it is not clear what the witness would say, what is the basis for her so saying, and what the purpose of the evidence is, a detailed and specific offer of proof is required. *People v. Keen,* 206 Ill. App. 3d 940, 151 Ill. Dec. 652, 564 N.E.2d 1314 (1990); *People v. Jackson,* 180 Ill. App. 3d 78, 129 Ill. Dec. 321, 535 N.E.2d 1086 (1989); *People v. Brown,* 104 Ill. App. 3d 1110, 60 Ill. Dec. 843, 433 N.E.2d 1081 (1982) (merely alluding to what might be divulged does not preserve error for appeal). Unless excused because apparent from the context, failure to make an offer of proof precludes raising the question on appeal. *People v. Andrews,* 146 Ill. 2d 413, 167 Ill. Dec. 996, 588 N.E.2d 1126 (1992); *Tarshes v. Lake Shore Harley Davidson,* 171 Ill. App. 3d 143, 121 Ill. Dec. 88, 524 N.E.2d 1136 (1988). A proper offer of proof by one party preserves the question for review on appeal when raised by a co-party aligned in interest. *Country Cas. Insurance Co. v. Wilson,* 144 Ill. App. 3d 28, 98 Ill. Dec. 225, 494 N.E.2d 152 (1986). *See also Howard v. Gonzales,* 658 F.2d 352, 355 (5th Cir. 1981).

Questions concerning offers of proof usually arise with respect to evidence excluded during direct examination of a friendly witness. Sometimes, however, similar questions arise when evidence is excluded upon cross-examination or direct examination of an adverse witness. Under such circumstances, an offer of proof is frequently unnecessary in that the substance of the evidence being excluded is apparent from the context. This may occur when a particular answer to a leading question permits, and examining counsel obviously expects, an answer favorable to his client. The substance of excluded evidence may also be sufficiently apparent as well when the cross-examiner expects an unfavorable response and obviously intends to pursue a given line of inquiry.

Sometimes, however, on cross-examination or direct examination of an adverse witness not only is the substance of the evidence excluded not apparent, it cannot be anticipated even by examining counsel. Under such circumstances, there is authority creating an additional exception to the requirement of an offer on the theory that the examination being exploratory, counsel is not in a position to know what the witness could or would testify to if permitted to do so. *See Alford v. United States,* 282 U.S. 687 (1931); *People v. Kellas,* 72 Ill. App. 3d 445, 28 Ill. Dec. 9, 389 N.E.2d 1382 (1979). However, since such a difficulty is overcome by the taking of the offer of proof in question and answer form outside the presence of the jury, combining a liberal interpretation of when the substance of the evidence is apparent from the context with a requirement of an offer of proof on cross-examination or direct of an adverse witness when the substance is not apparent seems preferable to recognizing an exception to the requirement of an offer of proof. *See People v. Jones,* 174 Ill. App. 3d 737, 124 Ill. Dec. 255, 528 N.E.2d 1363 (1988).

The classic method of making an offer is actually to place the witness on the stand, ask the question, and, upon the sustaining of an objection, permit the witness to state with particularity what the witness would answer if permitted to do so. Under some early authority, nothing less constitutes an offer, *Mulhern v. Talk of the Town,* 138 Ill. App. 3d 829, 93 Ill. Dec. 282, 486 N.E.2d 383 (1985), and an indication by the trial judge that he would not admit the evidence was not an exclusion in the absence of such an offer. *Chicago City Ry. v. Carroll* supra. This approach was unduly strict, as well as time-consuming.

An offer is sufficient if counsel makes known to the court, outside the hearing of the jury, with particularity, the substance of the witness's anticipated answer even if the witness is not actually produced, provided no question is raised as to her ability to produce the witness who would so testify. *Belfield v. Coop,* 8 Ill. 2d 293, 134 N.E.2d 249 (1956); *State Farm v. Best in the West Foods,* 282 Ill. App. 3d 470, 217 Ill. Dec. 764, 667 N.E. 2d 1340 (1996); *People v. Caselton,* 275 Ill. App. 3d 950, 212 Ill. Dec. 479, 657 N.E.2d 680 (1995); *People v. McMillan,* 239 Ill. App. 3d 467, 180 Ill. Dec. 516, 607 N.E.2d 585 (1993). A statement by counsel that the witness would contradict certain testimony is also sufficient. *People v. Andrews,* 146 Ill. 2d 413, 167 Ill. Dec. 996, 588 N.E.2d 1126 (1992); *Hall v. Northwestern Univ. Med. Clinics,* 152 Ill. App. 3d 716, 105 Ill. Dec. 496, 504 N.E.2d 781 (1987). *Accord Slezak v. Girzadas,* 167 Ill. App. 3d 1045, 118 Ill. Dec. 677, 522 N.E.2d 132 (1988), statement of counsel is adequate when it "show[s] what the offer of proof is or what the expected testimony will be, by whom or how it was made, and what its purpose is"; *People v. Phillips,* 186 Ill. App. 3d 668, 679, 134 Ill. Dec. 468, 475, 542 N.E.2d 814, 821 (1989), "An offer of proof is sufficiently specific, therefore, if it adequately shows the court what the evidence would be, allowing a court of review to assess the prejudice allegedly inuring from the exclusion." Conversely an offer of proof by counsel that merely summarizes the witness's testimony in a conclusionary manner is insufficient. *People v. Andrews* supra; *Molitor v. Jaimeyfield,* 251 Ill. App. 3d 725, 190 Ill. Dec. 933, 622 N.E.2d 1250 (1993); *People v. Files,* 260 Ill. App. 3d 618, 198 Ill. Dec. 476, 632 N.E.2d 1087 (1994); *People v. Caselton,* 275 Ill. App. 3d 950, 212 Ill. Dec. 479, 657 N.E.2d 680 (1995). Obviously an offer of proof by counsel based upon conjecture and speculation as to the nature of the excluded testimony is inadequate. *Abbinante v. O'Connell,* 277 Ill. App. 3d 1046, 214 Ill. Dec. 772, 662 N.E.2d 126 (1996).

On the other hand, the court may, in its discretion, permit or direct counsel to make an offer of proof in question-and-answer form. The making of the offer in question-and-answer form resolves all doubts as to the content of the proposed testimony. In nonjury cases the making of the offer of proof in question-and-answer form provides the appellate court with material for a possible final disposition of the case in the event of reversal of a ruling that excluded evidence. *See People v. Duarte,* 79 Ill. App. 3d 1113, 34 Ill. Dec. 657, 398 N.E.2d 332 (1979); *People v. Petitt,* 245 Ill. App. 3d 132, 184 Ill. Dec. 766, 613 N.E.2d 1358 (1993), suggesting preference for question-and-answer form whenever a witness is readily available.

Cross-examination with respect to the offered evidence may be permitted in the discretion of the court. If the evidence included consists of a document authenticated in the record or by offer of proof, a sufficient offer of proof is made by requesting the reporter to insert the exhibit in the record. *Allen v. Howard Bowl, Inc.,* 61 Ill. App. 2d 314, 210 N.E.2d 342 (1965).

Trial courts are required to permit counsel to make an offer of proof, *In re Estate of Undziakiewicz,* 54 Ill. App. 2d 382, 203 N.E.2d 434 (1964). A refusal to permit counsel to make an offer of proof is error. *People v. Thompkins,* 181 Ill. 2d 1, 228 Ill. Dec. 909, 690 N.E.2d 984 (1998); *In re Marriage of Strauss,* 183 Ill. App. 3d 424, 132 Ill. Dec. 245, 539 N.E.2d 808 (1989). Similarly, an extremely hostile attitude on the part of the trial judge to the offer will excuse the making of an offer. *People v. Lynch,* 104 Ill. 2d 194, 83 Ill. Dec. 598, 470 N.E.2d 1018 (1984); *People v. Pressley,* 160 Ill. App. 3d 867, 112 Ill. Dec. 312, 513 N.E.2d 921 (1987).

The purpose of the offered evidence, if not readily apparent, should be stated by counsel. *People v. Hoffee,* 354 Ill. 123, 188 N.E. 186 (1933); *Reavely v. Harris,* 239 Ill. 526, 88 N.E. 238 (1909). The court in its discretion may add a statement showing the character of the offered evidence, the form in which offered, the objection, and ruling. A reviewing court will consider the propriety of an exclusionary ruling only in the light of the stated purpose. *Hairgrove v. City of Jacksonville,* 366 Ill. 163, 8 N.E.2d 187 (1937); *Light v. Steward,* 128 Ill. App. 3d 587, 83 Ill. Dec. 760, 470 N.E.2d 1180 (1984). Similarly, a reviewing court will consider the propriety of an exclusionary ruling only in light of the particular legal theory presented. *Salcik v. Tassone,* 236 Ill. App. 3d 548, 177 Ill. Dec. 723, 603 N.E.2d 793 (1992) (past recollection recorded argument does not preserve impeachment under prior inconsistent statement theory).

Sustaining an objection to an offer that contains competent as well as incompetent matter is not error. *Hairgrove v. City of Jacksonville* supra; *Donnan v. Donnan,* 256 Ill. 244, 99 N.E. 931 (1912); *People v. Duarte,* 79 Ill. App. 3d 1113, 34 Ill. Dec. 657, 398 N.E.2d 332 (1979). It is the obligation of the party making the offer of proof to adequately distinguish each matter and obtain a separate ruling with respect to each matter. *Rinesmith v. Sterling,* 293 Ill. App. 3d 344, 227 Ill. Dec. 709, 687 N.E.2d 1191 (1997). Excluding for a wrong reason is not error if there is in fact a valid reason that could not be obviated in the trial court. *Morrison v. Hinton,* 5 Ill. 473 (1843). Impropriety in the form of the question, being correctable, does not fall in the latter category. *People v. Allen,* 378 Ill. 164, 37 N.E.2d 854 (1941).

§103.8   Effect of Erroneous Ruling: Preserving Error for Review; Formal Exception

No formal exception is required to save an unfavorable ruling on evidence for review. Attention, however, is directed to the requirement that post-trial motions in civil jury cases must specify with particularity the grounds in support thereof. 735 ILCS 5/2-1102. A general assertion of error in admitting or excluding evidence is not in compliance with this section. *Lawler v. Pepper Const. Co.,* 33 Ill. App. 2d 188, 178 N.E.2d 687 (1961); *Perez v. Baltimore & O.R. Co.,* 24 Ill. App. 2d 204, 164 N.E.2d 209 (1960). Error alleged with respect to the trial court admitting or excluding evidence is waived in a criminal jury trial if not included in a written post-trial motion even though the alleged error had properly been preserved at trial. 725 ILCS 5/116-1; *People v. Williams*, 165 Ill. 2d 51, 208 Ill. Dec. 341, 649 N.E.2d 397 (1995); *People v. Enoch*, 122 Ill. 2d 176, 119 Ill. Dec. 265, 522 N.E.2d 1124 (1988); *People v. Edwards*, 74 Ill. 2d 1, 23 Ill. Dec. 73, 383 N.E.2d 944 (1978); *People v. Pickett*, 54 Ill. 2d 280, 296 N.E.2d 856 (1973). Error alleged with respect to the trial court admitting or excluding evidence, not properly preserved at trial, is not preserved merely by its inclusion in a written post-trial motion. *People v. Enoch*, 122 Ill. 2d 176, 119 Ill. Dec. 265, 522 N.E.2d 1124 (1988); *Gausselin v. Commonwealth Edison Co.*, 260 Ill. App. 3d 1068, 197 Ill. Dec. 787, 631 N.E.2d 1246 (1994). The waiver principle applies to alleged error with respect to jury instructions as well. *People v. Thurman*, 104 Ill. 2d 326, 84 Ill. Dec. 454, 472 N.E.2d 414 (1984); *People v. Huckstead*, 91 Ill. 2d 536, 65 Ill. Dec. 232, 440 N.E.2d 1248 (1982). However, a written post-trial motion is not required with respect to appeals from delinquent minor proceedings under the Juvenile Court Act. *In re W.D.*, 194 Ill. App. 3d 686, 141 Ill. Dec. 364, 551 N.E.2d 357 (1990).

The purposes of the waiver rule are (1) to ensure that the trial court is informed of possible errors so that the court has an opportunity to correct them; (2) to give the reviewing court the benefit of the judgment and observation of the trial court with regard to the issues raised on appeal; (3) to prevent a party from objecting to matters in which he has acquiesced throughout the course of the trial; (4) to eliminate unnecessary reviews and reversals; and (5) to prevent the possibility of unlimited litigation. *People v. Harrawood*, 66 Ill. App. 3d 163, 22 Ill. Dec. 899, 383 N.E.2d 707 (1978).

Where the prosecution fails to object to the post-trial motion as being oral, the defendant is not precluded on appeal from raising errors that appear on the record, although not specified in the oral motion for a new trial. *People v. Whitehead*, 35 Ill. 2d 501, 221 N.E.2d 256 (1966); *People v. Welte*, 77 Ill. App. 3d 663, 33 Ill. Dec. 90, 396 N.E.2d 315 (1979). Similarly, participation by the prosecution in argument of the post-trial motion precludes the prosecution from raising its untimeliness for the first time on appeal. *People v. Eddington*, 129 Ill. App. 3d 745, 84 Ill. Dec. 887, 473 N.E.2d 103 (1984). In a bench trial, a post-trial motion is not necessary to preserve for review questions addressing issues that were first presented to the trial court. *People v. Crowder*, 174 Ill. App. 3d 939, 124 Ill. Dec. 366, 529 N.E.2d 83 (1988).

In the absence of proper preservation, review on appeal is limited to plain error, sufficiency of the evidence, and constitutional issues properly raised at trial that could be raised in a post-conviction hearing petition. *People v. Enoch,* 122 Ill. 2d 176, 119 Ill. Dec. 265, 522 N.E.2d 1124 (1988).

§103.9   *Hearing of Jury; Motion in Limine*

To the extent practicable, proceedings are to be conducted so as to prevent inadmissible evidence from being suggested to the jury by any means. *Crystal Lake Park Dist. v. Consumers Co.,* 313 Ill. 395, 145 N.E. 215 (1924). Thus objectionable questions should not be purposely propounded to the witness in the hearing of the jury, and offers of proof should be made outside the jury's hearing. *See also Holda v. Kane,* 88 Ill. App. 3d 522, 43 Ill. Dec. 522, 410 N.E.2d 552 (1980), request for jury to view premises should be made outside the presence of the jury. The jury may be excused, the court and counsel may retire to chambers, or counsel may approach the bench, as means of preventing the question or offer from coming to the jury's attention. If the jury is to be excused, the offer will frequently be made after the witness's testimony has been concluded.

A motion in advance of the commencement of trial, called a motion in limine, may be made seeking an order (1) precluding the introduction of specified evidence, (2) permitting the introduction of specified evidence, or (3) requiring that counsel refrain at trial from referring in any manner to particular evidence in the presence of the jury prior to obtaining a ruling as to admissibility. *Department of Pub. Works &*

Bldgs. v. Sun Oil Co., 66 Ill. App. 3d 64, 22 Ill. Dec. 826, 383 N.E.2d 634 (1978). A motion in limine is particularly well suited to protect against prejudicial impact on the minds of the jury from having been exposed to inadmissible evidence such as privileged information, use of alcohol, or subsequent remedial measures; *Kutchins v. Berg,* 264 Ill. App. 3d 926, 202 Ill. Dec. 805, 638 N.E.2d 673 (1994); *Lundell v. Citrano,* 129 Ill. App. 3d 390, 84 Ill. Dec. 581, 472 N.E.2d 541 (1984). Because motions in limine are a fertile ground for confusion and misunderstanding at trial, a written motion and a written proposed order should be prepared by the moving party. *Lundell v. Citrano* supra; *Decker v. St. Mary's Hospital,* 249 Ill. App. 3d 802, 188 Ill. Dec. 912, 619 N.E.2d 537 (1993). *Accord Cunningham v. Millers General Insurance Co.,* 227 Ill. App. 3d 201, 169 Ill. Dec 200, 591 N.E.2d 80 (1992) (motion and order should both be in writing).

Until recently it was assumed that a motion in limine preserved error for appeal with regard to evidence ruled admissible or inadmissible; an objection or offer of proof was not required at trial. *Cf. Luce v. United States,* 469 U.S. 38 (1984), requiring the defendant to testify to preserve error with respect to a ruling on a motion in limine permitting the use of a prior conviction to impeach. *Accord People v. Hartfield,* 137 Ill. App. 3d 679, 92 Ill. Dec. 281, 484 N.E.2d 1136 (1985); *People v. Redman,* 141 Ill. App. 3d 691, 95 Ill. Dec. 866, 490 N.E.2d 958 (1986). *See also People v. Henne,* 165 Ill. App. 3d 315, 116 Ill. Dec. 296, 518 N.E.2d 1276 (1988), extending the *Luce* requirement that the witness testify at trial to impeachment by a prior inconsistent statement. An objection at trial to evidence offered at trial following a denied motion in limine to exclude was required to preserve error for appeal in *Romanek-Golub & Co. v. Anvan Hotel Corp.,* 168 Ill. App. 3d 1031, 119 Ill. Dec. 482, 522 N.E.2d 1341 (1988). The trend of authority is in this direction. *Accord Illinois State Toll Highway Authority v. Heritage Standard Bank & Trust Co.,* 163 Ill. 2d 498, 206 Ill. Dec. 644, 645 N.E. 2d 896 (1994); *Wingo by Wingo v. Rockford Memorial Hospital,* 292 Ill. App. 3d 896, 226 Ill. Dec. 939, 686 N.E. 2d 722 (1997); *Chubb/Home Insurance v.*

Outboard Marine, 238 Ill. App. 3d 558, 179 Ill. Dec. 591, 606
N.E.2d 423 (1992) (the Illinois case law is clear that an objection must be raised at trial or the right to raise the issue on appeal is waived). *See also Cunningham v. Millers General Ins. Co.* supra; *Gonzales v. Prestress Engineering Corp.*, 194 Ill. App. 3d 819, 141 Ill. Dec. 606, 551 N.E.2d 793 (1990). *Cf. People v. Easley*, 148 Ill. 2d 281, 170 Ill. Dec. 356, 592 N.E.2d 1036 (1992), where question turns on legal and not factual considerations, requiring that the accused actually testify to preserve issue for appeal might not be appropriate; *Reuter v. Korb*, 248 Ill. App. 3d 142, 186 Ill. Dec. 731, 616 N.E.2d 1363 (1993), offer of proof not required at trial to preserve issue for appeal following denial of admissibility on motion in limine. *See generally People v. Williams*, 161 Ill. 2d 1, 204 Ill. Dec. 72, 641 N.E.2d 296 (1994), where the Illinois Supreme Court appears to have assumed without discussion that it was not necessary to renew an objection to the admissibility of a prior conviction ruled admissible before trial to impeach prior to anticipatory disclosure of such conviction by the criminal defendant or direct examination to preserve error on appeal. The safest course is to renew the objection or make an offer of proof at trial.

A trial court is under no obligation to decide the admissibility of evidence or other matters in advance of trial as actual circumstances at trial may differ from the proffer. *People v. Whitehead*, 116 Ill. 2d 245, 108 Ill. Dec. 376, 508 N.E.2d 687 (1987). Rulings on motions in limine are reviewed on appeal applying the abuse of discretion standard. *Rinesmith v. Sterling*, 293 Ill. App. 3d 344, 227 Ill. Dec. 709, 687 N.E.2d 1191 (1997); *Wingo by Wingo v. Rockford Memorial Hospital*, 292 Ill. App. 3d 896, 226 Ill. Dec. 939, 686 N.E. 2d 722 (1997); *Congregation of the Passion v. Touche Ross*, 224 Ill. App. 3d 559, 166 Ill. Dec. 642, 586 N.E.2d 600 (1991). Violation of a motion in limine may result in a new trial or reversal on appeal. *Kutchins v. Berg*, 264 Ill. App. 3d 926, 202 Ill. Dec. 805, 638 N.E.2d 673 (1994).

Rulings on motions in limine are interlocutory orders subject to reconsideration during trial. *Krengiel v. Lissner Corp.*,

Inc., 250 Ill. App. 3d 288, 190 Ill. Dec. 222, 621 N.E.2d 91 (1993); *Chubb/Home Insurance v. Outboard Marine* supra; *Cunningham v. Millers General Ins. Co.* supra; *Crawford County State Bank v. Grady,* 161 Ill. App. 3d 332, 112 Ill. Dec. 869, 514 N.E.2d 532 (1987). *See also People v. Mosley,* 145 Ill. App. 3d 753, 99 Ill. Dec. 591, 495 N.E.2d 1326 (1986) (motion in limine made *at* trial is interlocutory). Having once ruled, however, the court should be extremely hesitant to reverse its position lest unfair prejudice result. *People v. Cooper,* 66 Ill. App. 3d 205, 23 Ill. Dec. 1, 383 N.E.2d 768 (1978), improper to reverse ruling with respect to admissibility of prior conviction of defendant for purpose of impeachment after defendant had taken stand in reliance on prior ruling.

In order to preserve an objection that certain evidence offered at trial violates an order in limine, an objection must be made at trial. *Beasley v. Huffman Mfg. Co.* supra.

With respect to the admissibility of prior convictions to impeach, a decision prior to trial may be a significant factor in planning trial strategy and in the criminal defendant's decision as to whether to testify. Nevertheless the necessity of evaluating all of the factors to be considered in deciding admissibility of a prior conviction in light of the testimony actually introduced at trial permits the court to withhold decision until after the defendant testifies. *People v. Rose,* 75 Ill. App. 3d 45, 30 Ill. Dec. 662, 393 N.E.2d 698 (1979). The admissibility of convictions for impeachment is treated in §§609.1 to 609.10 infra.

A motion in limine precluding the offering of evidence at trial should be employed with caution as it may unduly restrict the opposing party's presentation of its case, *Reidelberger v. Highland Body Shop, Inc.,* 83 Ill. 2d 545, 48 Ill. Dec. 237, 416 N.E.2d 268 (1981); *People v. Eddington,* 77 Ill. 2d 41, 31 Ill. Dec. 808, 394 N.E.2d 1185 (1979), especially with respect to excluding evidence offered by the criminal defendant. *People v. Brumfield,* 72 Ill. App. 3d 107, 28 Ill. Dec. 422, 390 N.E.2d 589 (1979), reversible error to exclude evidence of involuntary intoxication on motion in limine; *People v. Hood,* 244 Ill. App. 3d 728, 185 Ill. Dec. 201, 614 N.E.2d 335 (1993), improper under circumstances to exclude defense witness on motion in limine as cumulative. Such evidence should, of course, be excluded when clearly collateral or extraneous. *People v. Downey,* 162 Ill. App. 3d 322, 113 Ill. Dec. 553, 515 N.E.2d 362 (1987); *People v. Berquist,* 239 Ill. App. 3d 906, 181 Ill. Dec. 738, 608 N.E.2d 1212 (1993). Because of this danger, it is imperative that the in limine order be clear and that all parties have an accurate understanding of its limitations. *Reidelberger v. Highland Body Shop, Inc.* supra; *Lockett v. Bi-State Transit Auth.,* 94 Ill. 2d 66, 67 Ill. Dec. 830, 445 N.E.2d 310 (1983); *People v. Batchelor,* 202 Ill. App. 3d 316, 147 Ill. Dec. 608, 559 N.E.2d 948 (1990). Under many circumstances, the most appropriate response to such a motion is the issuance of an order requiring that the matter be brought to the attention of the court prior to being disclosed in any fashion to the jury.

It is suggested that the proper approach to motions in limine was presented in *Bradley v. Caterpillar Tractor Co.,* 75 Ill. App. 3d 890, 900, 31 Ill. Dec. 623, 394 N.E.2d 825 (1979), quoting from *Lewis v. Buena Vista Mut. Ins. Assn.,* 183 N.W.2d 198, 200-201 (Iowa 1971):

> The motion in limine is a useful tool, but care must be exercised to avoid indiscriminate application of it lest parties be prevented from even trying to prove their contentions. That a plaintiff may have a thin case or a defendant a tenuous defense is ordinarily insufficient justification for prohibiting such party from trying to establish the contention. Nor should a party ordinarily be required to try a case or defense twice—once outside the jury's presence to satisfy the trial court of its sufficiency and then again before the jury. Moreover, the motion in limine is not ordinarily employed to choke off an entire claim or defense, as it was here. . . . Rather, it is usually used to prohibit mention of some specific matter, such as an inflammatory piece of evidence, until the admissiblity of that matter has been shown out of the hearing of the jury. . . .
>
> . . . The motion is a drastic one, preventing a party as it does from presenting his evidence in the usual way. Its use should be exceptional rather than general. . . . The motion should be used, if used at all, as a rifle and not as a shotgun, pointing out

the objectionable material and showing why the material is inadmissible and prejudicial. Since no one knows exactly how the trial will proceed, trial courts would ordinarily be well advised to require an evidentiary hearing on the motion when its validity or invalidity is not manifest from the face of the motion.

With respect to the hearing of preliminary matters outside the presence of the jury, *see* §104.3 infra; as to the assertion of a privilege, *see* §506.3 infra.

§103.10 Plain Error; Harmless Error

The adversary system, based on party responsibility, is deeply engrained in our jurisprudence, particularly in the field of evidence. *People v. Williams,* 28 Ill. 2d 114, 190 N.E.2d 809 (1963), court is normally not required to exclude evidence *sua sponte* when a party fails to object. Occasionally, however, the error committed so affects substantial rights as to induce the reviewing court to consider the issue even where, since no proper objection was made, strict adherence to the adversary system would require affirmance. *People v. Young,* 128 Ill. 2d 1, 131 Ill. Dec. 86, 538 N.E.2d 461 (1989); *People v. Carlson,* 79 Ill. 2d 564, 38 Ill. Dec. 809, 404 N.E.2d 233 (1980). This so-called doctrine of plain error, designed as a means of ameliorating the harshness of strict application of the general waiver rule, *People v. Pickett,* 54 Ill. 2d 280, 296 N.E.2d 856 (1973), finds greater application in criminal cases. *People v. Gard,* 158 Ill. 2d 191, 198 Ill. Dec. 415, 632 N.E.2d 1026 (1994), plain error to admit the results of a polygraph test taken by a witness; *People v. Winchester,* 352 Ill. 237, 185 N.E. 580 (1933), error in murder case to admit damaging hearsay statement, though no objection made; *People v. Green,* 53 Ill. App. 3d 820, 11 Ill. Dec. 521, 368 N.E.2d 1129 (1977), use of defendant's silence after receiving *Miranda* warnings to impeach is plain error; *People v. Godsey,* 74 Ill. 2d 64, 23 Ill. Dec. 117, 383 N.E.2d 988 (1978), use of silence before grand jury in reliance upon privilege against self-incrimination to impeach defense witness constitutes plain error; *People v. Szabo,* 94 Ill. 2d 327, 68 Ill. Dec. 935, 447 N.E.2d 193 (1983), doctrine of plain error applicable to sentencing hearing applying the death penalty. *See also* Illinois Supreme Court Rule 615(a), providing for plain error or defects affecting substantial rights to be noticed on appeal of criminal cases. The doctrine of plain error, however, may not be invoked when a defendant collaterally attacks a conviction or sentence under the Post-Conviction Hearing Act, 725 ILCS 5/122-1 *et seq. People v. Owens,* 129 Ill. 2d 303, 135 Ill. Dec. 780, 544 N.E.2d 276 (1989). On occasion the circumstances of a civil case may fall within it. *Muscarello v. Peterson,* 20 Ill. 2d 548, 170 N.E.2d 564 (1960), conduct of insurer in suppressing portion of statement used by opponent for impeachment, though no effort was made to question witness further after discovery of deletion. With respect to plain error where misconduct on the part of the trial judge is alleged, *see People v. Sprinkle,* 27 Ill. 2d 398, 189 N.E.2d 295 (1963); *People v. Berry,* 244 Ill. App. 3d 14, 184 Ill. Dec. 534, 613 N.E.2d 1126 (1991).

The infrequency with which the doctrine is applied precludes deliberate reliance upon it during the trial of a case. *People v. Precup,* 72 Ill. 2d 7, 21 Ill. Dec. 863, 382 N.E.2d 227 (1978), before plain error will be considered, it must be plainly apparent from the record that an error affecting substantial rights was committed; *People v. Pastorino,* 91 Ill. 2d 178, 62 Ill. Dec. 172, 435 N.E.2d 1144 (1982), plain error is a narrow limited exception to the general waiver rule; *People v. Beasely,* 108 Ill. App. 3d 301, 63 Ill. Dec. 942, 438 N.E.2d 1305 (1982), not plain error to fail to give limiting instruction with respect to prior inconsistent statement in light of the competent evidence offered. In the nature of things the application of the plain error rule will be more likely with respect to the admission of evidence than to exclusion, since failure to comply with normal requirements of offers of proof is likely to produce a record that simply does not disclose the error.

The relationship between the doctrines of reversible error, brought to the attention of the trial court as one affecting a "substantial right," and plain error, providing for the consideration on appeal of errors affecting a "substantial right" when not brought to the attention of the trial court, is less than totally clear. If the term *substantial right* is given the same meaning with respect to each doctrine, failure to object at trial would be inconsequential. Not surprisingly, plain error is defined as obvious error of a somewhat more fundamental or serious nature than mere reversible error. Some such error is called "grave error." *People v. Pisani,* 180 Ill. App. 3d 812, 129 Ill. Dec. 563, 536 N.E.2d 247 (1989). In short, while all plain errors are reversible errors, not all reversible errors are also plain errors. *People v. Keene,* 169 Ill. 2d 1, 214 Ill. Dec. 194, 660 N.E.2d 901 (1995) (citing Handbook).

As a practical matter, however, it is not clear how much more serious an error must be in order to permit plain error treatment, or how to determine whether a given error is more serious than reversible error. Decisions finding plain error reflect little more than the conclusions reached by the court, and the attempted definitions are probably best viewed only as general indicators of the nature of the inquiry. *See, e.g.,* 3A Wright, Federal Practice and Procedure §856 (1982) ("indeed the cases give the distinct impression that 'plain error' is a concept appellate courts find impossible to define, save that they know it when they see it"); 8B Moore's Federal Practice ¶52.02[2] (2d ed. 1984) ("Many appellate decisions *speak* as if premised on this distinction [in degree between reversible errors raised below and reversible errors not raised below] but one cannot find any real difference in the way the different verbal formulae are actually applied to the facts of particular cases" (emphasis in original)). However, it can safely be said that the probability of treatment as plain error is greater when a constitutional right is violated. McCormick, Evidence §52 (4th ed. 1992). Overall it is fair to conclude that a substantial right has been affected and thus plain error treatment will be given when the asserted error results in fundamental unfairness because of a breakdown in the adversary system as distinguished from typical trial mistakes, i.e., the asserted error is something fundamental to the integrity and reputation of the judicial process. *People v. McNeal,* 175 Ill. 2d 335, 222 Ill. Dec. 307, 677 N.E.2d 841 (1997); *People v. Keene,* 169 Ill. 2d 1, 214 Ill. Dec. 194, 660 N.E.2d 901 (1995).

In connection with the foregoing discussion of plain error in criminal cases, consider the position taken with respect to Supreme Court Rule 615(a) supra in *People v. Howell,* 60 Ill. 2d 117, 120-121, 324 N.E.2d 403 (1975):

> [G]enerally, failure to raise an issue in the trial court constitutes a waiver and that this general waiver rule also applies to constitutional issues. We [have] held that Rule 615(a) does not mandate that a reviewing court consider all errors involving substantial rights whether or not they had been raised in the trial court. Rather the rule is intended as a means of meliorating the harshness of the strict application of the waiver rule. It permits the court on review to take notice of errors appearing upon the record which deprive the accused of substantial means of enjoying a fair and impartial trial and in criminal cases in which the evidence is closely balanced to consider errors that have not been properly preserved.

The importance of the "closely balanced" criterion in determining plain error was emphasized in *People v. Carlson,* 79 Ill. 2d 564, 576, 38 Ill. Dec. 809, 404 N.E.2d 233 (1980):

> A significant purpose of the plain error exception to the waiver doctrine is to correct any serious injustices which have been done to the defendant. It therefore becomes relevant to examine the strength or weakness of the evidence against him; if the evidence is close, there is a possiblity that an innocent person may have been convicted due to some error which is obvious from the record, but not properly preserved. Thus, this court has held that where the evidence is closely balanced, a court of review may consider errors that have not been properly preserved for review.

In summary, in addition to the "closely balanced" criterion, the plain error doctrine is also to be applied whether a substantial right has been affected, i.e., in those exceptional circumstances where application of the rule is necessary to preserve the integrity and reputation of the judicial process because the fairness of the trial has been undermined. The doctrine of plain error is thus disjunctive. Failure to properly preserve error below may be excused either because the error affected a substantial right or, independent of the right affected, simply because the evidence in this case was closely balanced. *People v. McNeal,* 175 Ill. 2d 335, 222 Ill. Dec. 307, 677 N.E.2d 841 (1997); *People v. Keene,* 169 Ill. 2d 1, 214 Ill. Dec. 194, 660 N.E.2d 901 (1995). Accord *People v. Bounds,* 171 Ill. 2d 1, 215 Ill. Dec. 28, 662 N.E.2d 1168 (1995) (closely balanced or error so fundamental that it denied the defendant a fair proceeding); *People v. Ward,* 154 Ill. 2d 272, 181 Ill. Dec. 884, 609 N.E.2d 252 (1992), the doctrine of plain error may be invoked in criminal cases where the evidence is closely balanced or where the error is of such magnitude that the accused was denied a fair and impartial trial.

Multiple errors considered together can amount to plain error. *People v. McMurtry,* 279 Ill. App. 3d 865, 216 Ill. Dec. 390, 665 N.E.2d 450 (1996). The doctrine of plain error as applied to jury instructions, Supreme Court Rule 451(c), is restricted to correction of "grave errors" or to situations where the case is close factually and fundamental fairness requires that the jury be properly instructed. *People v. Fierer,* 124 Ill. 2d 176, 124 Ill. Dec. 855, 529 N.E.2d 972 (1988); *People v. Huckstead,* 91 Ill. 2d 536, 65 Ill. Dec. 232, 440 N.E.2d 1248 (1982). The doctrine of plain error will be applied where an unauthorized sentence has been imposed as a substantial right has been affected. *People v. Hicks,* 181 Ill. 2d 541, 230 Ill. Dec. 244, 693 N.E. 2d 373 (1998).

In civil cases the waiver doctrine is applied strictly unless the prejudicial error involves flagrant misconduct or behavior so inflammatory that the jury verdict is a product of biased passion, rather than an impartial consideration of the evidence. *Gillespie v. Chrysler Motors Corp.,* 135 Ill. 2d 363, 142 Ill. Dec. 777, 553 N.E.2d 291 (1990).

Finally, an exception to the waiver rule is found when an

issue of public importance, decided by the appellate court but not by the trial court, is presented. Under these circumstances, the Illinois Supreme Court may consider the issue. *In re Marriage of Minear,* 181 Ill. 2d 552, 230 Ill. Dec. 250, 693, N.E.2d 379 (1998).

Harmless error is a technical violation of a rule of evidence, properly brought to the attention of the trial court, not considered a sufficient basis for reversal because the admission or exclusion did not affect a substantial right of a party. *See* Supreme Court Rule 615(a); *Kotteakos v. United States,* 328 U.S. 750 (1946); *Wilson v. C. & W.I.R.R.,* 365 Ill. 405, 6 N.E.2d 634 (1937).

With respect to applying the harmless error standard, the supreme court in *People v. Lindgren,* 79 Ill. 2d 129, 141, 37 Ill. Dec. 348, 402 N.E.2d 238 (1980), stated:

> [A] conviction will be upheld only if the properly admitted evidence is so over-whelming that no fair-minded jury could have voted for acquittal (*see People v. Tranowski* (1960), 20 Ill. 2d 11, 17, 169 N.E.2d 347, *cert. denied,* (1960), 364 U.S. 923, 81 S. Ct. 290, 5 L. Ed. 2d 262, or, to put it another way, only if the record affirmatively shows that the error was not prejudical (*People v. Romero* (1977), 66 Ill. 2d 325, 5 Ill. Dec. 817, 362 N.E.2d 288; *People v. Stadtman* (1974), 59 Ill. 2d 229, 319 N.E.2d 813).

One year later, in *People v. Wilkerson,* 87 Ill. 2d 151, 157, 57 Ill. Dec. 628, 429 N.E.2d 526 (1981), the supreme court summarized the three approaches for measuring harmless error:

> (1) focusing on the error to determine whether it might have contributed to the conviction . . . ; (2) examining the other evidence in the case to see if overwhelming evidence supports the conviction . . . ; (3) determining whether the evidence is cumulative or merely duplicates properly admitted evidence. . . .

See also People v. Warmack, 83 Ill. 2d 112, 128-129, 46 Ill. Dec. 141, 413 N.E.2d 1254 (1981), error is harmless when the appellate court "can safely conclude that a trial without [the] error would produce no different result"; *People v. Parmly,*

117 Ill. 2d 386, 111 Ill. Dec. 576, 512 N.E.2d 1213 (1987), error is harmless when court can say beyond a reasonable doubt that the jury would have convicted anyway or that the erroneous admission of the hearsay statement did not tip the scales against the defendant. In making a harmless error determination, the fact that the overruling of an objection in the presence of the jury amplifies the inadmissible evidence's probative value and thus its harmful effect is properly considered. *People v. Lewis,* 165 Ill. 2d 305, 209 Ill. Dec. 144, 651 N.E.2d 72 (1995); *People v. Hope,* 116 Ill. 2d 265, 108 Ill. Dec. 41, 508 N.E.2d 202 (1986). Recent cases employing the "no fair-minded jury could reasonably vote for acquittal" harmless error test of *Lindgren* supra or its equivalents also include *People v. Foster,* 119 Ill. 2d 69, 115 Ill. Dec. 557, 518 N.E.2d 82 (1987); *People v. Hayes,* 139 Ill. 2d 89, 151 Ill. Dec. 348, 564 N.E.2d 803 (1990).

Where the error, properly preserved, involves constitutional rights of the criminal defendant, a harmless error beyond a reasonable doubt test is applied following the dictates of *People v. Black,* 52 Ill. 2d 544, 555, 288 N.E.2d 376 (1972):

> In considering whether constitutional error constitutes harmless error beyond a reasonable doubt as required by *Chapman v. California* [(386 U.S. 18 (1966))], it is not enough that the erroneously admitted evidence be considered merely cumulative or that there be other evidence in the record sufficient to support the conviction [*Harrington v. California,* 395 U.S. 250 (1969); *Fahy v. Connecticut,* 375 U.S. 85 (1963)]. The inquiry of a court of review should not be as to the amount of untainted evidence as compared to the amount of tainted evidence. The focus should rather be upon the character and quality of the illegally obtained evidence as it relates to the other evidence bearing on the same issue and the court should appraise the possible impact upon the jury of the wrongfully obtained evidence. *Schneble v. Florida,* 405 U.S. 427 [(1972)].

Accord People v. Spicer, 79 Ill. 2d 173, 37 Ill. Dec. 279, 402 N.E.2d 169 (1979); *People v. Shields,* 143 Ill. 2d 435, 159 Ill. Dec. 40, 575 N.E.2d 538 (1991). Confrontation clause errors are subject to the harmless error test. *Lee v. Illinois,* 476 U.S. 530 (1986); *People v. Johnson,* 116 Ill. 2d 13, 106 Ill. Dec. 763, 506 N.E.2d 563 (1987). The harmless error beyond a reasonable doubt test is also applied to errors affecting constitutional rights not involving the admissibility of evidence, for example, reference by the prosecution to defendant's failure to testify. *People v. Tate,* 45 Ill. 2d 540, 259 N.E.2d 791 (1970). Sometimes the nature of the constitutional right is so basic to a fair trial that its infraction may never be considered harmless. *Chapman v. California,* 386 U.S. 18 (1966), effective assistance of counsel.

§104   Preliminary Questions of Admissibility

§104.1   *Weight and Credibility; An Overview*

The rules of evidence are administered by the trial judge. The admissibility of evidence, the assertion of a privilege, or the competency of witnesses often depends upon particular preliminary or foundation facts, which may be disputed. To submit factual issues of this kind generally to the jury, as they arise from time to time during the trial or at its conclusion, could only be hopelessly confusing, as well as beyond the probable capacity of the jurors. To illustrate, with respect to the admissibility of a statement asserted to be protected from disclosure by the lawyer-client privilege, §§505.1 to 505.7 infra, if the jurors heard the actual statement with instructions to erase it from their minds if they found it was not made knowingly in the presence of a third party, the jury would be incapable of so doing. It is somewhat like telling a little boy to go to the corner and not think of elephants. The result would be frustration of the policy underlying the privilege. Hence preliminary questions of fact as conditions precedent to admissibility or competency are generally decided by the court. McCormick, Evidence §53 (4th ed. 1992). The court, in making this determination, is not bound by rules of evidence except those with respect to privilege. 5 Wigmore, Evidence §1385 (Chadbourn rev. 1974); *accord,* Federal Rule of Evidence 104(a). *See also United States v. Matlock,* 415 U.S. 164 (1974), upholding the use of inadmissible hearsay on a motion to suppress evidence. Thus an affidavit is properly considered by the court in determining unavailability as a prerequisite to admissibility of a hearsay statement as former testimony. *Curt Bullock Builders v. H.S.S. Development, Inc.,* 261 Ill. App. 3d 178, 199 Ill. Dec. 698, 634 N.E.2d 751 (1994).

Some of the rules that exclude relevant evidence rest upon policy considerations having no immediate connection with credibility. Hence the evidence upon preliminary questions of fact, as well as the ultimate decision of such issues, is for the trial judge alone. Illustrations are: unlawful seizure of evidence, *People v. Brocamp,* 307 Ill. 448, 138 N.E. 728 (1923); the reasonableness of notice to the opponent to produce a document in his possession as a prerequisite to secondary evidence of its contents, *Barto v. Kellogg,* 289 Ill. 528, 124 N.E. 633 (1919), §1004.5 infra; and competency of witness on technical grounds, such as when the witness is also a juror, §605.3 infra.

Other rules that exclude relevant evidence rest upon policy considerations intimately connected with or overlapping credibility. While the judge in these cases also decides preliminary issues of fact, the evidence adduced thereon bears upon credibility as well, and, in the event of a ruling favorable to admissibility or competency, falls within the province of the jury in determining that question. Examples are: qualification of expert witnesses (§702.2 infra), *People v. Jennings,* 252 Ill. 534, 96 N.E. 1077 (1911); admissibility of dying declarations (§804.6 infra), *People v. White,* 251 Ill. 67, 95 N.E. 1036 (1911); and whether a confession was voluntary, *People v. Wagoner,* 8 Ill. 2d 188, 133 N.E.2d 24 (1956). In the interest of saving time, the practice of presenting the preliminary evidence to judge and jury simultaneously seems proper, except in cases in which a ruling against admissibility would allow the jury to hear prejudicial evidence. *People v. Wagoner* supra, voluntariness of confession should be determined out of the presence of the jury; if admitted, accused may present his evidence again before the jury. Clearly the jury should not be instructed to second-guess the favorable ruling of the court on admissibility or competency and to disregard the evidence if they find the evidence inadmissible or the witness incompetent; their function is to determine weight and credibility, not admissibility. To assist the jury in determining weight and credibility, any party may of course introduce relevant evidence.

In reaching a determination on a question of admissibility for the court alone, whether in a criminal or a civil case, the court should apply the standard for the burden of persuasion applicable generally in civil cases of more probably true than not true. *See Lego v. Twomey,* 404 U.S. 477 (1972).

The preliminary admissibility of evidence whose relevancy is conditioned upon fact is discussed in §104.2 infra.

§104.2 *Relevancy Conditioned on Fact; Connecting Up*

When the relevancy of a particular item of evidence depends upon the existence of a preliminary or connecting fact, if determination of such conditional relevancy was made solely by the court, the function of the jury would be unduly restricted. Accordingly, issues of relevancy depending upon preliminary facts such as authentication or connecting facts are treated differently. If relevancy depends upon facts of this kind, only a *prima facie* showing of their existence, that is, evidence sufficient to support a finding by a reasonable juror that the fulfillment of the condition is more probably true than not true is required as a prerequisite to admitting the evidence. This preliminary determination is made by the court. *Marvel Eng. v. Commercial Union Ins. Co.,* 118 Ill. App. 3d 844, 74 Ill. Dec. 272, 455 N.E.2d 545 (1983) (Illinois law on the question is the same as Federal Rule of Evidence 104(b)). *See also* Morgan, Basic Problems of Evidence 45-46 (1962); McCormick, Evidence §53 (4th ed. 1992). *Accord Huddleston v. United States,* 485 U.S. 681 (1988) interpreting Federal Rule of Evidence 104(b). This evidence, together with contrary evidence produced by the opponent, is then considered by the jury as part of the overall process of determining the facts of the case. *Scott v. Delany*, 87 Ill. 146 (1877), deed admissible in ejectment case on *prima facie* showing of execution and delivery, with final determination whether executed and delivered to be made by jury after hearing evidence pro and con; *Chicago & Joliet Elec. Ry. v. Spence*, 213 Ill. 220, 72 N.E. 796 (1904), X-ray properly admitted on *prima facie* showing of correctness, despite opposing evidence of inaccuracy; *Von Reeden v. Evans*, 52 Ill. App. 209 (1893), statement of defendant that he "knocked hell out of them up at Nokomis," properly admitted on basis of evidence tending to show that it referred to the assault in question, leaving to jury to decide on evidence both ways. When appropriate, the jury may be instructed to determine whether the evidence is relevant by deciding whether the condition is fulfilled, and to ignore or employ the evidence accordingly. *See* 1969 Draft of Federal Rules of Evidence 104(b), 46 F.R.D. 186 (1969). *See* §§602, 901, 902, and 1008 infra, for specialized application of the principle of conditional relevancy.

If the admissibility of evidence depends upon connecting facts, the order of proof is largely within the discretion of the trial judge, §611.1 infra. *Mitchell v. McEwen Assocs.*, 360 Ill. 278, 196 N.E. 186 (1935), agreement made by agent may be introduced prior to proof of agency. *See* §705.1 with respect to order of proof as to the basis of an expert witness's opinion. Evidence admitted upon a promise to connect it up should be excluded upon failure to establish the connection. *People v. Smith*, 254 Ill. 167, 98 N.E. 281 (1912); *Krengiel v. Lissner Corp., Inc.*, 250 Ill. App. 3d 288, 190 Ill. Dec. 222, 621 N.E.2d 91 (1993). As to motions to strike, *see* §103.3 supra.

§104.3 Hearing in Presence of Jury

It is usually within the court's discretion to determine whether the interests of justice require that the hearing of a preliminary matter be conducted outside the hearing of the jury. What is critical is the hearing of the jury, not the jury's presence; thus use of side bar conferences is sometimes appropriate. In exercising its discretion, the court must weigh the potential for prejudice derived from the jury's hearing the evidence against such trial concerns as waste of time caused by taking the same testimony twice and the dislike of juries in being excluded. Not infrequently the same evidence that is relevant to the issue of establishment of fulfillment of a condition precedent to admissibility is also relevant to weight or credibility, and time is saved by taking foundation proof in the presence of the jury. Much evidence on preliminary questions, though not relevant to jury issues, may be heard by the jury with no adverse effect. A great deal must be left to the discretion of the court, which will act as the interests of justice require.

When, however, the preliminary matter concerns the admissibility of a confession, the hearing must be conducted outside the jury's presence. *Jackson v. Denno,* 378 U.S. 368 (1964). Due regard for the right of an accused not to testify generally in the case suggests that hearings on other preliminary matters should also be conducted out of the presence of the jury where the accused is a witness and so requests. In the rare cases in which a matter usually decided prior to trial involving a constitutional right of the accused surfaces initially at trial, such as pretrial identification, search and seizure, or *Miranda* warnings, the interests of justice will call for identical treatment. *See Watkins v. Sowders,* 449 U.S. 341 (1981), stating that while judicial determination outside the presence of the jury of the admissibility of identification evidence may often be advisable, it is not constitutionally necessary.

With respect to claiming of privileges outside the presence of the jury, *see* §506.3 infra.

§104.4   Testimony by Accused as to Preliminary Matters

An accused, by testifying upon a preliminary matter, such as a motion to suppress, does not subject herself to cross-examination as to other issues in the case unless the accused herself injects such other issues into the hearing. *See* McCormick, Evidence §§26, 134 (4th ed. 1992).

While such testimony by the accused at a suppression hearing may not be used against him as evidence in chief at trial, *Simmons v. United States*, 390 U.S. 377 (1968), it may be admitted to impeach the defendant if he testifies. *Oregon v. Hass*, 420 U.S. 714 (1975); *Harris v. New York*, 401 U.S. 222 (1971).

With respect to the scope of cross-examination, *see also* §611.11 infra.

§105 Limited Admissibility

§105.1 Commentary

Evidence may be admissible for one purpose and not for another. *People v. Lucas*, 132 Ill. 2d 399, 139 Ill. Dec. 447, 548 N.E.2d 1003 (1989). The usual practice is to admit the evidence. *Joseph Taylor Coal Co. v. Dawes*, 220 Ill. 145, 77 N.E. 131 (1906), evidence that engineer lowered mine cage at excessive speed on other occasions admissible to show knowledge of defendant but not that speed was excessive on occasion in question; *Eizerman v. Behn*, 9 Ill. App. 2d 263, 132 N.E.2d 788 (1956), prior statement of witness admissible to impeach but not as substantive evidence. The opposing party is entitled, on request, to an instruction to the jury limiting their use of the evidence accordingly. Generally the court is under no duty to give a limiting instruction on its own. *People v. Gacho*, 122 Ill. 2d 221, 119 Ill. Dec. 287, 522 N.E.2d 1146 (1988); *People v. Garza*, 92 Ill. App. 3d 723, 48 Ill. Dec. 44, 415 N.E.2d 1328 (1981). However, in order to avoid plain error, §103.10 supra, the court may *sua sponte* give a limiting instruction or preferably inquire of counsel's desire as to one being given. *See People v. Tunstall*, 17 Ill. 2d 160, 161 N.E.2d 300 (1959), prior inconsistent statement bearing directly upon defendant's guilt. *See also People v. Garza,* 92 Ill. App. 3d 723, 48 Ill. Dec. 44, 415 N.E.2d 1328 (1981). Evidence admissible as to one party but not to another is similarly treated. *Consolidated Ice Mach. Co. v. Keifer,* 134 Ill. 481, 25 N.E. 799 (1890); *Tellone v. Worth Shore Dodge, Inc.,* 271 Ill. App. 3d 885, 208 Ill. Dec. 569, 649 N.E.2d 625 (1995); *People v. Taylor,* 66 Ill. App. 3d 907, 23 Ill. Dec. 764, 384 N.E.2d 558 (1978). Whenever evidence is admitted for a limited purpose, it is proper for the court to so advise the jury at the time the evidence is introduced as well as to include such an instruction in the instructions given at the conclusion of the case. *People v. Cruz,* 162 Ill. 2d 314, 205 Ill. Dec. 345, 643 N.E.2d 636 (1994); *People v. Bradford,* 106 Ill. 2d 492, 88 Ill. Dec. 615, 478 N.E.2d 1341 (1985). Evidence admissible for one purpose but not another may be considered generally unless a proper objection is made and a limiting instruction requested. *People v. Camp,* 128 Ill. App. 3d 223, 83 Ill. Dec. 414, 470 N.E.2d 540 (1984).

On occasion, however, the harm likely to result from improper use, despite the limiting instruction, is held to outweigh the proper use, requiring exclusion. *Bruton v. United States,* 391 U.S. 123 (1968), confession of a nontestifying codefendant implicating defendant, where it is exceedingly difficult for jurors who have heard such evidence to disregard it despite limiting instruction; *Nash v. United States,* 54 F.2d 1006, 1007 (2d Cir. 1932), such a limiting instruction is "a mental gymnastic which is beyond, not only their powers, but anybody else's." *Accord People v. Johnson,* 116 Ill. 2d 13, 106 Ill. Dec. 763, 506 N.E.2d 563 (1987); *People v. Hernandez,* 121 Ill. 2d 293, 117 Ill. Dec. 914, 521 N.E.2d 25 (1988); *People v. Burns,* 171 Ill. App. 3d 178, 121 Ill. Dec. 116, 524 N.E.2d 1164 (1988). Nevertheless, when the risk of prejudice is not as severe as it was in *Bruton,* the common practice is to admit evidence for a limited purpose and instruct the jury accordingly. McCormick, Evidence §59 (4th ed. 1992). *Accord Richardson v. Marsh,* 481 U.S. 200, 206 (1987) ("This accords with the almost invariable assumption of the law that jurors follow their instructions, which we have applied in many varying contexts"). *See*

§103.3 supra, discussing similar considerations in connection with curative instructions. *See also* §403.1. infra for a general discussion of the exclusion of relevant evidence by reason of the danger of unfair prejudice.

With respect to a confession of a codefendant in a joint trial, unless a hearsay exception exists applicable to the nondeclarant defendant's confession, *Lee v. Illinois,* 476 U.S. 530 (1986); *People v. Dixon,* 169 Ill. App. 3d 959, 120 Ill. Dec. 249, 523 N.E.2d 1160 (1988); *People v. Cathers,* 194 Ill. App. 3d 318, 140 Ill. Dec. 893, 550 N.E.2d 1018 (1989), the confession of the codefendant is admissible only if the confession is cleansed of all references to the nondeclarant defendant (i.e., redacted), and a proper limiting instruction is given. *People v. Duncan,* 124 Ill. 2d 400, 125 Ill. Dec. 265, 530 N.E.2d 423 (1988), discussing the *Richardson v. Marsh,* 481 U.S. 200 (1987) interpretation of *Bruton* supra. The improper admission of a codefendant's confession is subject to the harmless error test. *Lee v. Illinois* supra; *People v. Mahaffey* supra; *People v. Williams,* 196 Ill. App. 3d 851, 144 Ill. Dec. 1, 554 N.E.2d 1040 (1990). With respect to confessions of a codefendant and the use of redaction, *see People v. Cruz,* 121 Ill. 2d 321, 117 Ill. Dec. 907, 521 N.E.2d 18 (1988); *People v. Hernandez,* 121 Ill. 2d 293, 117 Ill. Dec. 914, 521 N.E.2d 25 (1988). A redacted confession, taken in conjunction with other evidence at trial, will nevertheless violate an accused's right to confrontation when an impermissible incriminating implication of defendant's involvement exists. *People v. Williams,* 182 Ill. 2d 171, 230 Ill. Dec. 890, 695 N.E.2d 380 (1998); *People v. Duncan,* 124 Ill. 2d 400, 125 Ill. Dec. 265, 530 N.E.2d 423 (1988). Thus a redaction by means of a blank or the word "delete" may run afoul of *Bruton.* Gray v. Maryland,—U.S.—, 118 S. Ct. 1151 (1998). With respect to interlocking confessions, *see People v. Mahaffey,* 128 Ill. 2d 388, 132 Ill. Dec. 366, 539 N.E.2d 1172 (1989); *People v. Lincoln,* 157 Ill. App. 3d 700, 109 Ill. Dec. 958, 510 N.E.2d 1026 (1987); *People v. Elston,* 158 Ill. App. 3d 652, 110 Ill. Dec. 533, 511 N.E.2d 710 (1987).

§106   Remainder of Related Writings, Recorded Statements, or Conversation

§106.1   Remainder of Related Writings or Recorded Statements

When a party introduces a writing or recorded statement or only part of a writing or recorded statement, an adverse party may require him to introduce at that time any other part or any other writing or recorded statement if otherwise admissible that in fairness ought to be considered contemporaneously. *Lawson v. G.D. Searle & Co.,* 64 Ill. 2d 543, 1 Ill. Dec. 497, 356 N.E.2d 779 (1976). The principle is one of completeness. The additional writing or recorded statement must be either part of the writing or recorded statement or in the nature of an addendum to the introduced exhibit, such as another part of former testimony of accused offered against her, *People v. Hicks,* 28 Ill. 2d 457, 192 N.E.2d 891 (1963); *Miller v. People,* 216 Ill. 309, 74 N.E. 743 (1905); a letter accompanying statement in evidence, *Morris v. Jamieson,* 205 Ill. 87, 68 N.E. 742 (1903); or favorable entries in business records when the opponent has offered unfavorable entries, *Boudinot v. Winter,* 190 Ill. 394, 60 N.E. 553 (1901). Of course the additional writing or recorded statement or part thereof to be admitted must relate to the same subject matter and tend to explain, qualify, or otherwise shed light on the meaning of the part already received. *People v. Patterson,* 154 Ill. 2d 414, 182 Ill. Dec. 592, 610 N.E.2d 16 (1992) (the writing was a separate statement, made at a different time, to a different audience, concerning a different subject matter); *People v. Andersch,* 107 Ill. App. 3d 810, 63 Ill. Dec. 551, 438 N.E.2d 482 (1982) (only relevant portions are admissible). *See generally* McCormick, Evidence §56 (4th ed. 1992). In short, the additional writing or recorded statement is admissible when necessary to prevent the jury from receiving a misleading impression as to the nature of the introduced statement. *People v. Weaver,* 92 Ill. 2d 545, 65 Ill. Dec.

944, 442 N.E.2d 255 (1982); *People v. Olinger*, 112 Ill. 2d 324, 97 Ill. Dec. 772, 493 N.E.2d 579 (1986). The burden falls on the party seeking to introduce the additional statement to specify what portion of the statement is necessary to prevent the jury from receiving a misleading impression. *Id.*

When oral testimony as to a conversation is introduced, it may be reversible error to refuse to allow the opposing party to introduce a tape recording of the same conversation; the declarant's demeanor and voice inflections may affect the jury's assessment of credibility. *People v. Williams*, 109 Ill. 2d 327, 93 Ill. Dec. 788, 487 N.E.2d 613 (1985). However, fairness does not mandate introduction of a tape recording of a conversation when offered by the same party who introduced the conversation. *People v. Rios*, 145 Ill. App. 3d 571, 99 Ill. Dec. 368, 495 N.E.2d 1103 (1986).

With respect to the admissibility of oral statements, *see* §106.2 infra.

The importance of bringing out such material at the time of introduction is apparent. First, it avoids the danger of mistaken first impressions when matters are taken out of context. Second, it avoids the inadequate remedy of requiring the adverse party to wait until a later point in the trial to repair his case. The principle of completeness applies with equal force to writings and recorded statements introduced for a limited purpose such as impeachment.

With respect to depositions, Supreme Court Rule 212(c) provides:

> If only a part of a deposition is read or used at the trial by a party, any other party may at that time read or use or require him to read any other part of the deposition that ought in fairness to be considered in connection with the part read or used.

Smith v. Rock Island, 22 Ill. App. 2d 389, 161 N.E.2d 369 (1959), additional portions of deposition must be explanatory of that originally introduced; *Tashes v. Lake Shore Harley Davidson*, 171 Ill. App. 3d 143, 121 Ill. Dec. 88, 524 N.E.2d

1136 (1988), additional statements must be necessary to either explain or modify the originally introduced statements.

The adverse party is of course under no obligation to require her opponent to introduce at that time other parts or related writings or recorded statements; the adverse party is free to develop the matter on cross-examination or as part of her own case.

§106.2   Remainder of Conversation or Document on Next Examination

Oral conversations, parts of written or recorded statements or in the nature of addenda thereto, and written or recorded statements neither part of the previously introduced written or recorded statement nor in the nature of addenda thereto may be introduced by an opposing party on his next examination of the same witness, whether cross or redirect, provided such evidence tends to explain, qualify, or otherwise shed light on the meaning of the evidence already received. *People v. Provo*, 409 Ill. 63, 97 N.E.2d 802 (1951); *In re W.D.*, 194 Ill. App. 3d 686, 141 Ill. Dec. 364, 551 N.E.2d 357 (1990), other parts of same conversation; *Barnes v. Northern Trust Co.*, 169 Ill. 112, 48 N.E. 31 (1897), letter to which letter in evidence was a reply; *People v. Perez*, 101 Ill. App. 3d 64, 56 Ill. Dec. 488, 427 N.E.2d 820 (1981), other parts of transcript of testimony at earlier hearing; *People v. Andersch*, 107 Ill. App. 3d 810, 63 Ill. Dec. 551, 438 N.E.2d 482 (1982), other parts of 21-page statement given to police; *People v. Nolan*, 291 Ill. App. 3d 879, 225 Ill. Dec. 841, 684 N.E. 2d 832 (1997), oral statements not included in written statement prepared by the police. Other parts of oral conversations, or written or recorded statements that do not concern the same subject matter, are not admissible. *People v. Ward*, 154 Ill. 2d 272, 181 Ill. Dec. 884, 609 N.E.2d 252 (1992); *People v. Collins*, 265 Ill. App. 3d 568, 201 Ill. Dec. 891, 637 N.E.2d 480 (1994); *Connelly v. General Motors Corp.*, 184 Ill. App. 3d 378, 132 Ill. Dec. 630, 540 N.E.2d 370 (1989).

See also §§611.14 and 613.3 infra. Statements that contradict rather than shed light are not included. *People v. Pietryzk,* 153 Ill. App. 3d 428, 106 Ill. Dec. 437, 505 N.E.2d 1228 (1987). In short, the additional portion of the oral conversation or writing or recorded statement is admissible when necessary to prevent the jury from receiving a misleading impression as to the nature of the introduced statement, *People v. Weaver,* 92 Ill. 2d 545, 65 Ill. Dec. 944, 442 N.E.2d 255 (1982); *People v. Olinger,* 112 Ill. 2d 324, 97 Ill. Dec. 772, 493 N.E.2d 579 (1986); *People v. Harris,* 236 Ill. App. 3d 574, 177 Ill. Dec. 284, 603 N.E.2d 65 (1992). *See also People v. Kaczmarek,* 243 Ill. App. 3d 1067, 184 Ill. Dec. 661, 613 N.E.2d 1253 (1993) (the opposing party may introduce the remainder or as much as is required to place that part originally offered in proper context so that a correct and true meaning is conveyed to the jury). The burden falls on the party seeking to introduce the additional evidence to specify what portion of the oral conversation, writing, or recorded statement is necessary to prevent the jury from receiving a misleading impression. *Id.* When the additional portion of the oral conversation, writing, or recorded statement is sought to be admitted through a different witness, while the current doctrine is in fact applicable, *People v. Nolan,* 291 Ill. App. 3d 879, 225 Ill. Dec. 841, 684 N.E. 2d 832 (1997); *People v. Pirrello,* 166 Ill. App. 3d 614, 117 Ill. Dec. 238, 520 N.E.2d 399 (1988), reference is sometimes made to the doctrine of "door opening," §103.4 supra.

Mere mention of a conversation or statement does not entitle the opponent to bring out its content. *People v. Crawford,* 23 Ill. 2d 605, 179 N.E.2d 667 (1962); *People v. Baker,* 290 Ill. 349, 125 N.E. 263 (1919). Moreover, the principle of completeness does not give an adverse party an automatic right on her next examination of the witness or on rebuttal to introduce an omitted part of a related writing or recorded statement or related conversation otherwise inadmissible on the ground that the opponent has "opened the door." *See* §103.4 supra. It is within the court's discretion, however, to permit introduction, in the interests of justice, of such evidence where necessary to refute or explain an unfavorable inference that might arise from the evidence originally admitted, *People v. Wright,* 261 Ill. App. 3d 772, 198 Ill. Dec. 376, 632 N.E.2d 706 (1994); *People v. Russell,* 177 Ill. App. 3d 40, 126 Ill. Dec. 472, 531 N.E.2d 1099 (1988) (citing Handbook); *Buczyna v. Cuomo & Son Cartage Co.,* 146 Ill. App. 3d 404, 100 Ill. Dec. 51, 496 N.E.2d 1116 (1986) (citing Handbook), provided that the probative value of such evidence is not substantially outweighed by the danger of unfair prejudice. *People v. Manning,* 182 Ill. 2d 193, 230 Ill. Dec. 933, 695 N.E.2d 423 (1998). *See also* §§103.4 supra and 403.1 infra. *See generally People v. Williams,* 146 Ill. App. 3d 767, 100 Ill. Dec. 399, 497 N.E.2d 377 (1986) (trial court was within its discretion in not allowing defendant to introduce other portions of statement made to police in absence of impeachment during cross-examination or evidence tending to imply that defendant had made damaging admissions or told a different story; on balance, a more liberal application by the trial court is to be preferred). The indication in *People v. Brown,* 249 Ill. App. 3d 986, 189 Ill. Dec. 773, 620 N.E.2d 1090 (1993), that the completeness doctrine always operates as an exception to the hearsay rule is incorrect and should not be followed. Admissibility lies in the discretion of the trial court. Moreover, evidence so introduced is admitted solely to explain, qualify, or otherwise shed light on the meaning of the evidence already received and not generally for all purposes.

ARTICLE II

Judicial Notice

§201   Nature of Judicial Notice

§201.1   An Overview

Judical notice is founded on the assumption that certain matters either are not or need not be within the area of controversies appropriately resolved by the production of evidence before the trier of fact at a trial.

Sometimes the doctrine of judicial notice arises by virtue of a particular fact, relevant to the determination of the case, itself not being the subject of reasonable controversy. This process is known as judicial notice of an adjudicative fact. Adjudicative facts are simply the facts of the particular case — the facts that normally go to the jury. Adjudicative facts are the "who did what, where, when, how, and for what reason." They relate to the parties, their activities, their properties, their businesses. *See* Advisory Committee's Note to Federal Rule of Evidence 201, 56 F.R.D. 183, 201-202 (1973). For adjudicative facts to be judicially noticed, a high degree of indisputability is an essential prerequisite. In some instances the particular fact may be beyond reasonable dispute because it is generally known and accepted. "Courts are presumed to be no more ignorant than the public generally, and will take judicial notice of that which everyone knows to be true." *Chicago v. Murphy*, 313 Ill. 98, 102, 144 N.E. 802 (1924). Or, if not widely known, the matter may be beyond controversy because verifiable from sources of such nature as to eliminate reasonable dispute. Judicial notice may be taken even though "the memory of the judge may be at fault, or the court may require instruction or information upon the point." *Rock Island v. Cuinely*, 126 Ill. 408, 414, 18 N.E. 753 (1888).

Another basis for judicial notice, not always recognized and labeled as such, is that the matter is better decided by the judge and better decided by him without the confining limitations of ordinary evidence and the rules governing its admission. Within this aspect fall most matters of law. Within it also fall the factual foundations of rules of decision, including social, scientific, economic, and often political factors, whether or not generally known or readily determinable. Both of these matters, collectively referred to as judicial notice of legislative facts, are discussed in §§203.1 to 203.5 infra. With respect to judicial notice of legislative facts a high degree of indisputability is not required.

From the foregoing remarks, it seems apparent that courts

may be expected to apply judicial notice in a more restricted fashion when the matter involved is an adjudicative fact, one relevant only to the particular case, than when the formulation, validity, or construction of a legal rule (i.e., legislative fact) is concerned. The correctness of this conclusion is illustrated in the following cases. In *222 E. Chestnut St. Corp. v. Board of Appeals*, 14 Ill. 2d 190, 152 N.E.2d 465 (1958), the court refused to take judicial notice that fumes and noise from a particular property rezoned as a parking lot would damage an adjoining apartment building so as to give the owner standing to object, while in *Gore v. Carlinville*, 9 Ill. 2d 296, 137 N.E.2d 368 (1956), the court took judicial notice of the odor and inflammable character of gasoline as affording a reasonable basis for zoning restrictions upon the location of filling stations.

Judicial notice, adjudicative and legislative, may also be taken by any court of appellate jurisdiction even if the taking of judicial notice was refused by the trial court or not requested below. 735 ILCS 5/8-1002; *May Department Stores v. Teamsters Union Local #743*, 64 Ill. 2d 153, 355 N.E.2d 7 (1976); *In re Ersch's Estate*, 29 Ill. 2d 576, 195 N.E.2d 149 (1964); *Lubershane v. Village of Glencoe*, 63 Ill. App. 3d 874, 20 Ill. Dec. 681, 380 N.E.2d 890 (1978). However, an appellate court will not take judicial notice of evidentiary material not presented below that is critical to a proper determination of the issues between the parties. *Vulcan Materials Co. v. Bee Constr.*, 96 Ill. 2d 159, 70 Ill. Dec. 465, 449 N.E.2d 812 (1983); *People v. Mehlberg*, 249 Ill. App. 3d 499, 188 Ill. Dec. 598, 618 N.E.2d 1168 (1993).

With respect to proceedings conducted pursuant to the Illinois Administrative Procedure Act, 5 ILCS 100/1-1 to 100/15-10, judicial notice is governed by *id.*, 10-40(c), which provides:

> Notice may be taken of matters of which the circuit courts of this State may take judicial notice. In addition, notice may be taken of generally recognized technical or scientific facts within

the agency's specialized knowledge. Parties shall be notified either before or during the hearing, or by reference in preliminary reports or otherwise, of the material noticed, including any staff memoranda or data, and they shall be afforded an opportunity to contest the material so noticed. The agency's experience, technical competence and specialized knowledge may be utilized in the evaluation of the evidence.

See Caterpiller Tractor Co. v. Illinois Pollution, 48 Ill. App. 3d 655, 6 Ill. Dec. 737, 363 N.E.2d 419 (1977) for procedures to be followed. *See also* §202.3 infra. Judicial notice may also be taken by a court on review of an administrative agency decision. *Bobber Auto Truck Plaza v. Department of Revenue*, 143 Ill. App. 3d 614, 97 Ill. Dec. 741, 493 N.E.2d 404 (1986).

Decisions on judicial notice are too numerous to permit citation except by way of illustration. They fall into reasonably defined categories, as treated in the following sections, based upon the preceding general observations.

§202   Adjudicative Facts

§202.1   Matters Generally Known

The courts take judicial notice of matters that are generally known in the territorial jurisdiction of the trial court and not subject to reasonable dispute. Universal knowledge is not required, generally known information being sufficient. *Owens v. Green*, 400 Ill. 380, 81 N.E.2d 149 (1948); *Chicago v. Williams*, 254 Ill. 360, 98 N.E. 666 (1912). For example, judicial notice may be taken that the Illinois and Mississippi rivers are navigable, *Sikes v. Moline Consumers' Co.*, 293 Ill. 112, 127 N.E. 342 (1920); *Brockschmidt v. Sanitary Dist.*, 260 Ill. 502, 103 N.E. 243 (1913), although not that the Kaskaskia River is navigable, *Sproul v. Springman*, 316 Ill. 271, 147 N.E. 131 (1925); that a letter mailed to Chicago would be delivered in Philadelphia in the usual course of the mail within one week, *Keogh v. Peck*, 316 Ill. 318, 147 N.E. 266 (1925); that an unprecedented rainfall occurred on or about a particular date, *Jacobi v. Mantle*, 16 Ill. 2d 142, 156 N.E.2d 582 (1959); that at 4:30 on July 30 daylight savings time was in effect, *People v. Cain*, 14 Ill. App. 3d 1003, 303 N.E.2d 756 (1973); that a large tractor and trailer are worth more than $125, *People v. Tassone*, 41 Ill. 2d 7, 241 N.E.2d 419 (1968); that water will not run uphill, *Bossler v. Countryside Gardens, Inc.*, 44 Ill. App. 3d 423, 3 Ill. Dec. 185, 358 N.E.2d 352 (1976); that 8 percent is a conservative, fair earning power of money during a certain time period, *In re Marriage of Smith*, 100 Ill. App. 3d 1126, 56 Ill. Dec. 716, 427 N.E.2d 1262 (1981); that a home that is indisputably in need of substantial repairs at the time of purchase is worth considerably less than a home that does not require such repairs, *Grass v. Homann*, 130 Ill. App. 3d 874, 85 Ill. Dec. 751, 474 N.E.2d 711 (1984); that many diseases are claimed to result from asbestos exposure, *Costello v. Unarco Indus., Inc.*, 129 Ill. App. 3d 736, 84 Ill. Dec. 880, 473 N.E.2d 96 (1984); but not of weather conditions not strikingly unusual existing approximately two months prior to trial, *Cook County Dept. of Envl. Control v. Tomar Indus.*, 29 Ill. App. 3d 751, 331 N.E.2d 196 (1975); nor in an action under the Fair Trade Act that plaintiff's brand of scotch whiskey was in fair and open competition, *Buckingham Corp. v. Vesolowski*, 16 Ill. App. 3d 719, 307 N.E.2d 699 (1973); nor that two members of a film cast were stars of the number one- and two-rated television programs, *Motion Picture Appeal Board, Ltd. v. City of Chicago*, 65 Ill. App. 3d 217, 21 Ill. Dec. 809, 382 N.E.2d 103 (1978); nor that current laws do not fully address sex discrimination in the labor force, *In re Marriage of Aud*, 142 Ill. App. 3d 320, 96 Ill. Dec. 615, 491 N.E.2d 894 (1986).

The matter judicially noticed must be generally known; it is insufficient that the judge is personally aware of the matter as an individual observer outside of court. 9 Wigmore, Evidence §2569 (Chadbourn rev. 1981). *See also* §605.2 infra.

§202.2   Accurate and Ready Determination

Although not generally known, matters may be so capable of verification as to be beyond reasonable controversy and hence proper subjects of judicial notice. *Rock Island v. Cuinely,* 126 Ill. 408, 18 N.E. 753 (1888); *Murdy v. Edgar,* 103 Ill. 2d 384, 83 Ill. Dec. 151, 469 N.E.2d 1085 (1984). Matters falling within this category are numerous and varied, as shown by the following.

Geographical Facts. *People ex rel. Lejcar v. Meyering,* 345 Ill. 449, 178 N.E. 80 (1931), distance between cities such as to permit accused to be at scene of both crime and alibi on same day; *Colligan v. Cousar,* 38 Ill. App. 2d 392, 187 N.E.2d 292 (1963), tavern on south side of Chicago was in close proximity to state line; *M.I.G. Inv., Inc. v. Marsala,* 92 Ill. App. 3d 400, 47 Ill. Dec. 265, 414 N.E.2d 1381 (1981), no place in Winnebago County is over 50 miles from Bonus Township in Boone County; *Curtis v. County of Cook,* 109 Ill. App. 3d 400, 65 Ill. Dec. 87, 440 N.E.2d 942 (1982), the existence and territorial boundaries of a municipality.

Historical events. *Dowie v. Sutton,* 227 Ill. 183, 81 N.E. 395 (1907), date of Boer War as fixing time when letter was written by testator; *In re Ersch's Estate,* 29 Ill. 2d 572, 195 N.E.2d 149 (1964), chaotic conditions in Poland during World War II.

Tables, statistics, and economic facts. *Worcester Natl. Bank v. Cheney,* 94 Ill. 430 (1880), population of county as shown by census returns; *Lacny v. Police Board of City of Chicago,* 291 Ill. App. 3d 397, 225 Ill. Dec. 602, 683 N.E. 2d 1265 (1997), Chicago is only municipality with over 500,000 people; *DiModica v. Department of Employment Security,* 164 Ill. App. 3d 445, 115 Ill. Dec. 511, 517 N.E.2d 1197 (1987), population of Freeport is approximately 25,000 people; *Sherman v. City of Springfield,* 111 Ill. App. 2d 391, 250 N.E.2d 537 (1969), mortality tables; *Island Lake Water Co. v. Illinois Commerce Comm.,* 65 Ill. App. 3d 853, 22 Ill. Dec. 445, 382 N.E.2d 835 (1978), yields of public utility bonds by reference to authoritative publication; *In re Marriage of Aschwanden,* 76 Ill. App. 3d 680, 32 Ill. Dec.

537, 395 N.E.2d 767 (1979), value of stock on a given day, *contra In re Marriage of Moody*, 119 Ill. App. 3d 1043, 75 Ill. Dec. 581 457 N.E.2d 1023 (1983) (incorrectly decided); *In re Marriage of Aud*, 142 Ill. App. 3d 320, 96 Ill. Dec. 615, 491 N.E.2d 894 (1986), census material; *In re Marriage of Ryman*, 172 Ill. App. 3d 599, 122 Ill. Dec. 646, 527 N.E.2d 18 (1988), the fair earning power of money or invested capital over a given period of time. Judicial notice, however, will not be taken of the value of specific real property. *In re Marriage of Holder*, 137 Ill. App. 3d 596, 91 Ill. Dec. 926, 484 N.E.2d 485 (1985).

Calendar. *Lange v. Massachusetts Mut. Life Ins. Co.*, 273 Ill. App. 356 (1934), day of week on which a date fell; *People v. Hawkins*, 284 Ill. App. 3d 1011, 221 Ill. Dec. 447, 675 N.E.2d 642 (1996), calendar dates and corresponding day of the week.

Court personnel. *Dyer v. Last*, 51 Ill. 179 (1869), incumbency as clerk of person signing jurat; *Vahle v. Brackenseick*, 145 Ill. 231, 34 N.E. 524 (1893), identity of judges of courts of record; *Ferris v. Commercial Natl. Bank*, 158 Ill. 237, 41 N.E. 1118 (1895), status of individuals as licensed attorneys.

Acts and records of court. A court will take judicial notice of its own acts and records in the same case, *Secrist v. Petty*, 109 Ill. 188 (1883); of facts established in prior proceeding in the same case, *In re Brown*, 71 Ill. 2d 151, 15 Ill. Dec. 744, 374 N.E.2d 209 (1978); of the authenticity of the record of another case in the same court including records of prior convictions, *People v. Davis*, 65 Ill. 2d 157, 2 Ill. Dec. 572, 357 N.E.2d 792 (1976) (overruling previous decisions); of an administrative decision even though it is subject to further administrative and judicial review, *People of Cook County v. Stanview Drive-In Theatre*, 100 Ill. App. 3d 624, 56 Ill. Dec. 121, 427 N.E.2d 201 (1981); of the condition of a Circuit Court docket, *Boston v. Rockford Memorial Hosp.*, 140 Ill. App. 3d 969, 95 Ill. Dec. 208, 489 N.E.2d 429 (1986); and of the records of proceedings in other courts at least where those proceedings involved the same parties and are determinations of the cause, *Walsh v. Union Oil*, 53 Ill. 2d 295, 291 N.E.2d 644 (1972). However, if contents are to be considered, then according to the traditional view the record in another case must be offered in evidence. *People ex rel. Zilm v. Carr*, 265 Ill. 220, 106 N.E. 801 (1914). Since the offer in evidence amounts to little more than directing the attention of the court to the record, resembling a request to take judicial notice as discussed in §202.3 infra, a disposition more recently to take judicial notice of matters involved in other cases is not surprising. *In re O'Malley*, 404 Ill. 257, 88 N.E.2d 881 (1949); *People ex rel. McDonough v. Chicago, M., St. P. & P. Ry.*, 354 Ill. 438, 188 N.E. 404 (1933). Of course, the matters involved in the other proceeding must comprise facts that are not subject to reasonable dispute. *Metropolitan Life Insurance v. American National Bank*, 288 Ill. App. 3d 760, 224 Ill. Dec. 511, 682 N.E. 2d 72 (1997); *Hastings v. Gulledge*, 272 Ill. App. 3d 861, 209 Ill. Dec. 600, 651 N.E.2d 778 (1995); *Filrep, S.A. v. Barry*, 88 Ill. App. 3d 935, 44 Ill. Dec. 45, 410 N.E.2d 1137 (1980). Moreover, if the facts are to be derived from the pleadings (not the record) of another case not involving the same parties and are not so proved, judicial notice cannot be taken. *Vulcan Materials Co. v. Bee Constr.*, 96 Ill. 2d 159, 70 Ill. Dec. 465, 449 N.E.2d 812 (1983). Similarly, judicial notice may not be taken of the contents of a book written by a trial prosecutor about the investigation and trial of the case. *People v. Sims*, 244 Ill. App. 3d 966, 184 Ill. Dec. 135, 612 N.E.2d 1011 (1993).

Governmental matters and public records. *Gooding v. Morgan*, 70 Ill. 275 (1873), public land surveys; *Rockford v. Mower*, 259 Ill. 604, 102 N.E. 1032 (1913), incumbents of public offices within territorial jurisdiction of court; *Chicago & Alton R. Co. v. Keegan*, 152 Ill. 413, 39 N.E. 33 (1894), genuineness of seal of state; *People v. Garrett*, 62 Ill. 2d 51, 339 N.E.2d 753 (1976), report and protocol of Cook County coroner; *Nordine v. Illinois Power Co.*, 32 Ill. 2d 421, 206 N.E.2d 709 (1965), orders and decision of Illinois Commerce Commission; *Department of Pub. Welfare v. Bohleber*, 21 Ill. 2d 587, 173 N.E.2d 457 (1961), reports and records of Department of Public Welfare; *Lubershane v. Village of Glencoe*, 63 Ill. App. 3d 874, 20 Ill. Dec. 681, 380 N.E.2d 890 (1978), recorded plot surveys; *In re W.S. Jr.,* 81 Ill. 2d 252, 42 Ill. Dec. 140, 408 N.E.2d 718 (1980), corporate existence of a theft victim; *Peacre v. Illinois Cent. Gulf R. Co.,* 89 Ill. App. 3d 22, 44 Ill. Dec. 196, 411 N.E.2d 102 (1980), orders and decisions of the Illinois Commerce Commission; *Swieton v. Landoch,* 106 Ill. App. 3d 292, 62 Ill. Dec. 181, 435 N.E.2d 1153 (1982), certified copy of deed filed with the Registrar of Titles; *Baker v. Illinois Dept. of Law Enforcement,* 124 Ill. App. 3d 964, 80 Ill. Dec. 277, 464 N.E.2d 1260 (1984), regulations of Illinois Department of Corrections. On the other hand, judicial notice can not be taken of the contents of a police report. *Vincent v. Williams,* 279 Ill. App. 3d 1, 216 Ill. Dec. 13, 664 N.E.2d 650 (1996) (not source of indisputable accuracy).

Scientific principles and authoritative treatises. Taking judicial notice of elementary principles of physics and other sciences is commonplace, *Woods v. New York, C. & St. L. Ry.,* 339 Ill. App. 132, 88 N.E.2d 740 (1949) (force of gravity), and requires no investigation. Simple mathematical calculations also fall within this category. *Thomas v. Price,* 81 Ill. App. 3d 542, 36 Ill. Dec. 810, 401 N.E.2d 651 (1980), time required to travel 60 feet at 50 miles per hour. Beyond these rudimentary matters, the extent to which judicial notice will be taken of scientific principles remains largely unexplored. Admittedly, the use of scientific experts produced by the parties as witnesses does not always afford a satisfactory resolution of scientific questions. Note Supreme Court Rule 215(d), providing for impartial medical experts, §706.1 infra dealing generally with court appointed experts, and the exasperation with expert witnesses expressed in *Opp v. Pryor,* 294 Ill. 538, 128 N.E. 580 (1920), and *Kemeny v. Skorch,* 22 Ill. App. 2d 160, 170, 159 N.E.2d 489 (1959). A greatly expanded use of judicial notice would go far in solving these problems. A welcome step in this direction is *Darling v. Charleston Community Memorial Hosp.,* 33 Ill. 2d 326, 211 N.E.2d 253 (1965), relating to judicial notice of the authenticity of learned treatises. *See* §705.2 infra. Of course, the scientific principle must either be generally known or readily verifiable from sources of indisputable accuracy. *See Murdy v. Edgar,* 103 Ill. 2d 384,

83 Ill. Dec. 151, 469 N.E.2d 1085 (1984), a score of 15 on the Michigan Alcoholic Screening Test does not meet the requirements of judicial notice; explanation of its relevance should have been introduced by way of expert testimony. *See also People v. David,* 180 Ill. App. 3d 749, 129 Ill. Dec. 488, 536 N.E.2d 172 (1989); *People v. Lee,* 256 Ill. App. 3d 856, 194 Ill. Dec. 939, 628 N.E.2d 436 (1993).

§202.3 *Procedural Aspects*

The theory and effective application of judicial notice of adjudicative facts not only renders the formal introduction of evidence before the trier of fact unnecessary, *Secrist v. Petty,* 109 Ill. 188 (1883), but also precludes the introduction of evidence of contrary tenor, *Nicketta v. National Tea Co.,* 338 Ill. App. 159, 87 N.E.2d 30 (1949); 8 Wigmore, Evidence §2567 (McNaughton rev. 1961), at least in civil cases. *See* infra. Of course, the party requesting judicial notice must supply the court, where appropriate, with the necessary information upon which to act. The court may take judicial notice *sua sponte. People v. Speight,* 222 Ill. App. 3d 766, 165 Ill. Dec. 213, 584 N.E.2d 392 (1991).

The party opposing the taking of judicial notice is entitled, upon timely request, to an opportunity to be heard as to the propriety of taking judicial notice and the tenor of the matter noticed. In the absence of prior notification, the request may be made after judicial notice has been taken. This procedure conforms to accepted standards of fairness and due process. Opportunity to be heard on the question of the propriety of taking judicial notice of adjudicative facts is afforded all parties, whether the proposal for taking judicial notice originates with the court or with a party. *See Nicketta v. National Tea Co.* supra; *Caterpillar Tractor Co. v. Illinois Pollution,* 48 Ill. App. 3d 655, 6 Ill. Dec. 373, 363 N.E.2d 419 (1977). If a party is not given prior notification, request for an opportunity to be heard may be made after judicial notice has been taken. *See People v. Speight,* supra.

Judicial notice, which may be taken at any stage of the proceeding, see §201.1 supra, must be taken where the specified requirements in either §202.1 or §202.2 are satisfied, if requested by a party and the court is supplied with the necessary information. Consistent with the adversary theory and avoidance of embarrassment to the court, a party is not entitled to complain of failure to take judicial notice unless she has requested it and brought appropriate materials to the attention of the court. *People ex rel. McCallister v. Keokuk & Hamilton Bridge Co.*, 287 Ill. 246, 122 N.E. 467 (1919); *Woods v. Village of LaGrange Park*, 287 Ill. App. 201, 4 N.E.2d 764 (1936). Similarly, a party is not entitled to complain that judicial notice was taken by the trial court unless an objection was interposed. *In Interest of A.T.*, 197 Ill. App. 3d 821, 144 Ill. Dec. 283, 555 N.E.2d 402 (1990). The decision of the trial judge should be made a matter of record, as in *Nicketta v. National Tea Co.* supra, thus rendering unnecessary such speculation in the reviewing court concerning the trial court's action as appeared in *Secrist v. Petty* supra. The provision of the Uniform Judicial Notice of Foreign Law Act, specifying notice to the adverse party as a prerequisite to asking that judicial notice be taken of matters of law, is consistent with these standards. 735 ILCS 5/8-1006.

If the matter is one that would fall within the province of the jury were judicial notice not taken, the court must ensure that the jury is aware that the particular fact has been judicially noticed. This may be accomplished at the time judicial notice is taken, as a direct result of the jury hearing counsel's request for judicial notice and the court's concurrence, or by the judge's advising the jury specifically at the time that he has judicially noticed the particular fact. In other situations it may be appropriate to include an instruction to the jury at the time they are formally instructed upon the law to the effect that a particular fact has been judicially noticed. *See generally* Illinois Pattern Jury Instruction — Civil 23.01, 50.02 (1994). Whether done at the time of taking judicial notice or at the formal instruction stage, in civil cases, if the fact is important, the court should advise the jury also that it must accept as conclusive any fact established. In criminal cases, it is even more critical that the court ensure that the jury is aware that it may, but is not required to, accept as conclusive against the criminal defendant the fact judicially noticed. *See* Federal Rule of Evidence 201(g).

§202.4   Establishment of Incontrovertible Adjudicative Facts Other than by Judicial Notice

In addition to the taking of judicial notice, other procedures may be invoked to establish matters of fact so conclusively as to remove them from the area of controversy in the case. Proof of the existence of matters thus established is neither necessary nor appropriate, and evidence of their nonexistence is inadmissible. The jury should be instructed accordingly. *See* Illinois Pattern Jury Instructions — Civil 50.01, 50.02 (1994).

Admission in pleadings.   An allegation in a pleading that is expressly admitted in an opposing pleading, *Regan v. Berent,* 392 Ill. 376, 64 N.E.2d 483 (1946), or that is not denied, 735 ILCS 5/2-610(b); *Laegeler v. Bartlett,* 10 Ill. 2d 478, 140 N.E.2d 702 (1957), is conclusively established for purposes of the particular case. The effect of superseded pleadings and pleadings in other cases is discussed in §802.11 infra.

Admission in open court.   Clear and unequivocal admissions based upon personal knowledge made in open court are binding. *People v. Green,* 17 Ill. 2d 35, 160 N.E.2d 814 (1959), confession; *Petersen v. General Rug & Carpet Cleaners, Inc.,* 333 Ill. App. 47, 77 N.E.2d 58 (1947), admission of ownership of vehicle by defendant in opening statement; *Tolbird v. Howard,* 43 Ill. 2d 357, 253 N.E.2d 444 (1969), testimony admitting that no consideration existed for note. With respect to testimony of a party as a judicial admission in open court, *see* §802.12 infra.

Stipulation.   Facts may be established by stipulation, even to the extent of the entire case for the state in a criminal proceeding. *People v. Malin,* 372 Ill. 422, 24 N.E.2d 349 (1939). While a stipulation is ordinarily binding, *People v. Gibson,* 287 Ill. App. 3d 878, 223 Ill. Dec. 234, 679 N.E.2d 419 (1997), the trial judge may, in her sound discretion, relieve a party from its effect upon application seasonably made and a showing that the matter is in fact untrue, violative of public policy, or the result of fraud. *Brink v. Industrial Commn.,* 368 Ill. 607, 15 N.E.2d 491 (1938); *Hudson v. Safeway Ins. Co.,* 106 Ill. App. 3d 391, 62 Ill. Dec. 283, 435 N.E.2d 1255 (1982).

Request to admit. Requests may be served to admit the genuineness of documents or the truth of matters of fact. Unless a sworn denial or statement of grounds for inability to admit or deny, or objections, are served within 28 days, the matters stand admitted. The admission is not effective in other proceedings. Supreme Court Rule 216(c); *Iversen v. Iversen,* 28 Ill. App. 2d 45, 169 N.E.2d 822 (1960).

Pretrial order. The provisions of a pretrial order control the subsequent course of the action unless modified by the trial judge. Supreme Court Rule 218(b).

§203 Legislative Facts

§203.1 Matters of Law

The manner in which and the extent to which courts take cognizance of matters of law is not, strictly speaking, a concern of the law of evidence but is treated here as a matter of convenience.

Pleading and proof of the general laws of Illinois or the nation, whether embodied in statute or court decision, are neither necessary nor appropriate. *Parrino v. Landon,* 8 Ill. 2d 468, 134 N.E.2d 311 (1956). But note Supreme Court Rule 133(a), requiring citation of the statute in alleging a breach of statutory duty.

Every court is required to take judicial notice of the common law and statutes of every state, territory, and other juris-diction of the United States. 735 ILCS 5/8-1003; *Rockford v. Gill,* 60 Ill. App. 3d 194, 17 Ill. Dec. 421, 376 N.E.2d 420 (1978), judicial notice taken of amendment to the Illinois Local Library Act. The Uniform Proof of Statutes Act provides that printed books or pamphlets purporting to be the session or other statutes of any of the United States or its territories or of a foreign jurisdiction and to have been published by its authority, or proved to be commonly recognized by its courts, shall be received as *prima facie* evidence. 735 ILCS 5/8-1001 to 5/8-1003. Every court of original jurisdiction is required to take judicial notice of all general ordinances of every munici-pal corporation within the State, all ordinances of every county within the State, all laws of a public nature enacted by any state or territory of the United States, and all rules of practice in force in the court from which a case has been transferred by change of venue or otherwise. Reviewing courts must take judicial notice of all matters of which the inferior court was required to take judicial notice, including the rules of practice of the latter. 735 ILCS 5/8-1001, 5/8-1002; *South Stickney Park Dist. v. Village of Bedford Park,* 131 Ill. App. 3d 205, 86 Ill. Dec. 402, 475 N.E.2d 616 (1985). Judicial notice may also be taken of administrative rules and regula-tions. *People v. Easterly,* 264 Ill. App. 3d 233, 201 Ill. Dec. 750, 636 N.E.2d 1182 (1994); *Acme Brick & Supply v. Department of Revenue,* 133 Ill. App. 3d 757, 88 Ill. Dec. 654, 478 N.E.2d 1380 (1985); *Sturm v. Block,* 72 Ill. App. 3d 306, 28 Ill. Dec. 553, 390 N.E.2d 912 (1979). A dispute as to the correct version of a statute will be resolved by taking judicial notice of the en-rolled bill in the office of the secretary of state, *Di Bella v. Cuccio,* 15 Ill. 2d 580, 155 N.E.2d 645 (1959), but judicial notice will not be taken of the contents of the legislative jour-nals to determine whether a bill was validly passed. *Worthy v. Bush,* 262 Ill. 560, 104 N.E. 904 (1914); *Illinois Central Ry. v. Wren,* 43 Ill. 77 (1867). A reviewing court may take judicial notice of statutes and constitutional provisions even if they were not raised before a lower tribunal and any argument thereon was consequently waived. *AFSCME, Council 31 v.*

Courts of Cook, 145 Ill. 2d 475, 164 Ill. Dec. 904, 584 N.E.2d 116 (1991).

Historically, as a matter of convenience to the court in view of the unavailability of source material and possible language differences, the common law required that ordinances, private statutes, and the laws of foreign states and nations be pleaded and proved, under the guise of the convenient fiction that they were "facts." *Illinois Central Ry. v. Ashline,* 171 Ill. 313, 49 N.E. 521 (1898). Only the law of a foreign nation continues today to be treated as a question of fact, although one to be decided by the court, 735 ILCS 5/8-1007; *Vrozos v. Sarantopoulos,* 195 Ill. App. 3d 610, 142 Ill. Dec. 352, 552 N.E.2d 1093 (1990), and in the absence of the proof will be taken to be the same as the local law. *Groome v. Freyn Eng. Co.,* 374 Ill. 113, 28 N.E.2d 274 (1940). The Uniform Judicial Notice of Foreign Law Act requires every court now to take judicial notice of the common law and statutes of every state, territory, and other jurisdiction of the United States. The court may inform itself as it deems proper and may call upon counsel for aid. The determination is by the court, not by the jury. Evidence of these laws is also admissible, but to enable a party to offer evidence or to ask the court to take judicial notice thereof, reasonable notice must be given the adverse party, in the pleadings or otherwise. 735 ILCS 5/8-1003 to 5/8-1009. However, with respect to the laws of a foreign country, the Act states that the provisions relating to judicial notice are not applicable. 735 ILCS 5/8-1007; *Atwood Vacuum Mach. Co. v. Continental Cas. Co. of Chicago,* 107 Ill. App. 2d 248, 246 N.E.2d 832 (1969). Failure to provide a discretionary measure of judicial notice as to foreign law is unfortunate. *See* Fed. R. Civ. P. 44.1; Fed. R. Crim. P. 26.1.

§203.2 Factual Bases of Judicial Rules

It is familiar doctrine that a case is decided by applying the law, as determined by the court, to the facts, as determined by the trier of fact. *See* Illinois Pattern Jury Instructions — Civil 1.01 (1994). The facts contemplated are the adjudicative facts of the particular case, as developed by the conventional process of producing evidence at the trial or as judicially noted within the rather limited categories suggested in §§201.2 and 201.3 supra. Another way in which facts enter most significantly into the judicial process is in the formulation of the rules of law themselves by the courts.

Many rules of law are predicated upon factual foundations. These factual foundations are commonly constructed by the process of judicial notice. Often they consist of patterns of human behavior, assumed to exist on the basis of casual observation, experience, and anecdote but without systematic or statistical observation. No judicial counterpart even of the legislative hearing exists. These assumptions are thus wide-ranging and far-reaching, without the cautious insistence upon certainty that characterizes judicial notice of adjudicative facts. *See, e.g., Molitor v. Kaneland Community Unit District,* 18 Ill. 2d 11, 163 N.E.2d 89 (1959), justifying the abolition of school district tort immunity on the ground, among others, that a tendency to reduce school bus accidents, rather than grave problems of finance, would result; *Patargias v. Coca-Cola Bottling Co.,* 332 Ill. App. 117, 74 N.E.2d 162 (1947), supporting a finding of negligence on the basis that bottles cannot be inspected with reasonable care at the rate of 264 per minute; *Donehue v. Duvall,* 41 Ill. 2d 377, 243 N.E.2d 222 (1968), noticing that small boys have a propensity to throw things at each other; *Borowitz v. Borowitz,* 19 Ill. App. 3d 176, 311 N.E.2d 292 (1974), women have recently become emancipated both socially and economically; *Hernandez v. Power Constr. Co.,* 73 Ill. 2d 90, 22 Ill. Dec. 503, 382 N.E.2d 1201 (1978), supreme court took judicial notice that it takes approximately two years longer to obtain a jury trial than a bench trial in Cook County; *J.I. Case Co. v. Industrial Commn.,* 36 Ill. 2d 386, 223 N.E.2d 847 (1966), metal is a conductor of electricity; *Lahman v. Gould,* 82 Ill. App. 2d 220, 226 N.E.2d 443 (1967), when periods of inflation and deflation exist. A significant case is *Nicketta v. National Tea Co.,* 338

Ill. App. 159, 87 N.E.2d 30 (1949), in which the court read the literature in the field, took judicial notice that trichinosis could not be contracted from properly cooked pork and affirmed the trial court's dismissal of a complaint for breach of warranty. *Cf. Beck v. Binks,* 19 Ill. 2d 72, 165 N.E.2d 292 (1960), in which the court refused to inform itself concerning the nature of naprapathy as a method of treating human ailments. Many of the rules of evidence are based upon like assumptions concerning human conduct. *Hawkins v. United States,* 358 U.S. 74 (1958), adverse testimony by spouse of the accused in a criminal prosecution is likely to destroy any marriage. *See also Trammel v. United States,* 445 U.S. 40 (1980).

§203.3 *Factual Aspects of Legislation*

Facts also enter importantly into the process of making law by legislative enactment and in the treatment accorded its product by the courts.

The validity of a statute not infrequently depends upon the reasonableness of the legislature's view of the factual basis upon which it is erected. This reasonableness is commonly tested by the courts against the factual background of their own developed by the broadest kind of judicial notice. Thus, to sustain statutory limit upon weights of vehicles, judicial notice was taken of injury to roads and bridges and danger to the public from vehicles of excessive weight. *People v. Linde,* 341 Ill. 269, 173 N.E. 361 (1930). Judicial notice was taken of economic conditions to sustain relief legislation. *Reif v. Barrett,* 355 Ill. 104, 188 N.E. 889 (1933). A legislative requirement that optometrists preserve records of examination for three years was upheld by taking judicial notice that spectacles may cause the eye to return to normal. *Klein v. Department of Registration,* 412 Ill. 75, 105 N.E.2d 758 (1952). Judicial notice was taken of Legislative Investigatory Commission Report in sustaining validity of statute concerning racetrack messenger service. *Finish Line Express, Inc. v. City of Chicago,* 72 Ill. 2d 131, 19 Ill. Dec. 626, 379 N.E.2d 290

(1978). And a statutory requirement that all work by a licensed journeyman plumber be supervised by a master plumber was held invalid on the ground that neither common knowledge and experience nor evidence submitted suggested a connection with considerations of public health. *Schroeder v. Binks,* 415 Ill. 192, 113 N.E.2d 169 (1953).

Judicial notice also plays a significant role in the construction and application of legislation. *Robertson Products Co. v. Nudelman,* 389 Ill. 281, 59 N.E.2d 655 (1945), determining incidence of retailers' occupation tax on sales of soap and similar supplies to hotels by taking judicial notice of practice of hotels to furnish these items to guests without thought of resale; *Brandt v. Keller,* 413 Ill. 503, 109 N.E.2d 729 (1953), abandoning earlier construction of Married Women's Act on basis, in part, of judicial notice that tort actions between spouses would not destroy domestic tranquility to any greater extent than other actions.

§203.4 *Procedural Aspects*

When legislative facts are the subject of judicial notice, whether in the formulation of a legal principle, or a ruling by the court or in the enactment of a legislative body, the law would stop growing if the lawmaking body,

> in thinking about questions of law and policy, were forbidden to take into account the facts they believe, as distinguished from facts which are clearly . . . within the domain of the indisputable. Facts most needed in thinking about difficult problems of law and policy have a way of being outside the domain of the clearly indisputable. [Davis, A System of Judicial Notice Based on Fairness and Convenience, in Perspectives of Law 82 (1964).]

To illustrate, consider *Hawkins v. United States,* 358 U.S. 74 (1958), where, in deciding whether to discard the common law privilege preventing one spouse from testifying against the other, the Court stated, "Adverse testimony given in criminal proceedings would, we think, be likely to destroy almost any marriage." *Id.* at 78. *See also Trammel v. United States,* 445 U.S. 40 (1980). While this conclusion is hardly "indisputable" (*see* Hutchins and Slesinger, Some Observations on the Law of Evidence — Family Relations, 13 Minn. L. Rev. 675 (1929)), the appropriateness of the taking of judicial notice in cases such as *Hawkins* is beyond question. As Morgan, Judicial Notice, 57 Harv. L. Rev. 269, 270-271 (1944), stated:

> In determining the content or applicability of a rule of domestic law, the judge is unrestricted in his investigation and conclusion. He may reject the propositions of either party or of both parties. He may consult the sources of pertinent data to which they refer, or he may refuse to do so. He may make an independent search for persuasive data or rest content with what he has or what the parties present. . . . [T]he parties do no more than to assist; they control no part of the process.

Accordingly, any limitations in the form of indisputability, any formal requirements of notice other than those already inherent in affording opportunity to hear and be heard and exchanging briefs, and any requirement of formal findings at any level would be inappropriate. When the court decides it is preferable to resort to the formal introduction of evidence with respect to legislative fact, it may so order. *See Borden's Farm Prods. Co. v. Baldwin,* 293 U.S. 194 (1934), cause remanded for the taking of evidence as to the economic conditions and trade practices underlying the New York Milk Control Law.

§203.5 Knowledge and Experience of Fact Finder in Considering Issues of Fact

Jurors, as well as judges, import into the judicial process a storehouse of experience, observation, and learning. This background presumably equips them to detect truth from falsehood, draw inferences, evaluate ordinary negligence situations, and otherwise function as jurors.

Jurors are properly instructed that they may consider the evidence in the light of their own observation and experience in the affairs of life. Illinois Pattern Jury Instructions — Civil 1.04 (1994); *Ottawa Gas Light & Coke Co. v. Graham,* 28 Ill. 73 (1862). Extending this principle to include an instruction that they might use their own knowledge of land values, as approved in *Kankakee Park Dist. v. Heidenreich,* 328 Ill. 198, 159 N.E. 289 (1927), seems questionable.

Argument based upon this area of general observation and experience is common, effective, and proper. Thus, arguing that an expert medical witness, whose testimony was contradicted on a factual matter, would not lie because he would risk conviction of perjury and loss of his license was upheld in *Perez v. Baltimore & O.R. Co.,* 24 Ill. App. 2d 204, 164 N.E.2d 209 (1960). *Cf. Herricks v. Chicago & E.I.R. Co.,* 257 Ill. 264, 100 N.E. 897 (1913), holding improper an argument that plaintiff might lose his other eye, in the absence of evidence to that effect, and *Goad v. Grissom,* 324 Ill. App. 123, 57 N.E.2d 514 (1944), holding it improper to read a newspaper article relating to the connection between the delicacy of female organs and the happiness of the possessor thereof.

As to the effect of admitting evidence on matters within knowledge of jury, *see* §702.4 infra.

In the process of determining adjudicative facts, the fact finder, whether judge or jury, employs nonevidence facts, facts that have not been formally proved. Thayer, Preliminary Treatise on Evidence 279-280 (1898), describes the reasoning process as follows: "In conducting a process of judicial reasoning, as of other reasoning, not a step can be taken without assuming something which has not been proved; and the capacity to do this with competent judgment and efficiency, is imputed to judges and juries as part of their necessary mental outfit."

Similarly, Professor Davis points out, A System of Judicial Notice Based on Fairness and Convenience, in Perspectives of Law 69, 73 (1964), that every case involves the use of hundreds or thousands of nonevidence facts. When a witness in an automobile accident case says "car," everyone, judge and jury included, furnishes, from nonevidence sources within himself, the supplementing information that the "car" is an automobile, not a railroad car, that it is self-propelled, probably by an internal combustion engine, that it may be assumed to have four wheels with pneumatic rubber tires, and so on.

The judicial process cannot construct every case from scratch, like Descartes creating a world based on the postulate *Cogito, ergo sum.* These items could not possibly be introduced into evidence, and no one suggests that they be. Nor are they appropriate subjects for any formalized treatment of judicial notice of facts. *See* Levin and Levy, Persuading the Jury with Facts Not in Evidence: The Fiction-Science Spectrum, 105 U. Pa. L. Rev. 139 (1956). Accordingly, the common fund of knowledge of jurors may obviate a claimed deficiency in the evidence. Thus *Pennell v. Baltimore & O.R. Co.,* 13 Ill. App. 2d 433, 142 N.E.2d 497 (1957), held that the jury could fix a life expectancy without the benefit of mortality tables.

Another aspect of the use of nonevidence facts is to appraise or assess the adjudicative facts of the case as illustrated by the following two cases. In *People v. Strook,* 347 Ill. 460, 179 N.E. 821 (1932), the Court held that venue in Chicago was not established by testimony that the crime was committed at 7956 South Chicago Avenue, since judicial notice would not be taken that the address was in Chicago, while in *People v. Pride,* 16 Ill. 2d 82, 156 N.E.2d 551 (1959), the Court held that venue was established in Chicago by testimony that the crime occurred at 8900 South Anthony Avenue, since judicial notice would be taken of the common practice of omitting the city when speaking of local addresses, and the witness was testifying in Chicago. In the latter case the court was fashioning a judicial rule for evaluating evidence.

Obviously, with respect to each of the foregoing, the formal procedures associated with the judicial notice of adjudicative facts are inappropriate.

ARTICLE III

Burdens of Proof and Presumptions

§301   Burden of Pleading and Proof in Civil Cases

§301.1   *Nature of Responsiblity for Elements*

In civil cases, the nature of the burden imposed upon a party charged with responsibility for a particular contested element is normally threefold: (1) the burden of pleading, §301.3 infra; (2) the burden of production as to the particular matter, referred to also as the burden of going forward, §301.4 infra; and (3) the burden of persuading the trier of fact of its existence, §301.6 infra. *Behnke v. Brookfield,* 366 Ill. 516, 9 N.E.2d 232 (1937); *Egbers v. Egbers,* 177 Ill. 82, 52 N.E. 285 (1898). To illustrate, in a typical contract action, plaintiff will have the burdens of (1) pleading the existence of the contract, (2) producing evidence of the existence of the contract, and (3) persuading the trier of fact of the contract's existence. The defendant bears the same three burdens with regard to the affirmative defense of payment.

The term burden of proof as frequently used includes both the concepts of burden of production and burden of persuasion. *Franciscan Sisters Health Care Corp. v. Dean,* 95 Ill. 2d 452, 69 Ill. Dec. 960, 448 N.E.2d 872 (1983); *Ambrose v. Thornton Township School Trustees,* 274 Ill. App. 3d 676, 211 Ill. Dec. 83, 654 N.E.2d 545 (1995). Analytical description is fostered and confusion avoided by separate reference to each burden.

§301.2 *Allocating the Elements*

In any given situation, the law recognizes certain elements as of consequence to the decision of the case. Examples of these elements in a contract action are offer, acceptance, consideration, and payment, and in a negligence action, negligence, proximate cause, and damage. Their presence or absence is properly to be considered in deciding the case. They constitute the substantive law. A plaintiff is not required to deal with every element that might conceivably affect the decision of the case. On the contrary, the elements are allocated between the parties, so that plaintiff is entitled to recover if she establishes certain selected elements, comprising a "cause of action," unless defendant establishes other elements called "affirmative defenses." *Noyes v. Gold,* 310 Ill. App. 1, 34 N.E.2d 1 (1941).

The cases dealing with problems of allocation do not generally disclose the fundamental reasons why a particular result is reached. *See* Cleary, Presuming and Pleading: An Essay on Juristic Immaturity, 12 Stan. L. Rev. 5 (1959). Nevertheless, the following factors, along with caution and convenience tending to place certain elements upon the party seeking relief, *People v. Orth,* 124 Ill. 2d 326, 125 Ill. Dec. 182, 530 N.E.2d 210 (1988), seem to underlie the decisions, with now one and now another being predominant but none alone being conclusive:

(1) *Policy* may dictate charging one side or the other with a particular element as a means of encouraging or discourag-

ing a given kind of litigation. An example is truth in actions for libel. *Ogren v. Rockford Star Printing Co.,* 288 Ill. 405, 123 N.E. 587 (1919). Observe that policy considerations are of prime importance in cases of complete absence of proof on the particular point, so that the allocation of the burden is decisive of the case. *See In re Estate of Moos,* 414 Ill. 54, 110 N.E.2d 194 (1953), burden on proponents to prove that testator did not revoke missing will retained in his possession.

(2) *Fairness* may suggest placing the burden of an element upon the party within whose control the evidence lies. Thus payment, *Department of Finance v. Schmidt,* 374 Ill. 351, 29 N.E.2d 530 (1940), and discharge in bankruptcy, *Martinez v. Cogan,* 320 Ill. App. 468, 51 N.E.2d 595 (1943), have long been regarded as affirmative defenses and are among those enumerated in the Code of Civil Procedure. 735 ILCS 5/2-613(d).

(3) *Probabilities* may be estimated and the burden placed upon the party who will benefit by a departure from the supposed norm. Payment mentioned above is illustrative.

In causes of action based on statute, if an exception appears in the enacting clause (i.e., the clause creating the right sued upon), the burden is on the party invoking the statute to negative the applicability of the exception; otherwise the exception is the responsibility of the opposite party. *Great Western R. Co. v. Hanks,* 36 Ill. 281 (1865); *Chicago, B. & Q.R. Co. v. Carter,* 20 Ill. 391 (1858). With respect to the burden of proof as to negative averments, *see Board of Trade v. Dow Jones & Co.,* 108 Ill. App. 3d 681, 64 Ill. Dec. 275, 439 N.E.2d 526 (1982).

Certain aspects of contract litigation are decided by similar mechanical tests. In insurance cases, plaintiff must bring himself within the general coverage of the policy; exceptions are affirmative defenses. *Sell v. Country Mut. Ins. Co.,* 23 Ill. App. 2d 497, 163 N.E.2d 547 (1960). Conditions precedent are allocated to plaintiff, conditions subsequent to defendant. *Scott v. Freeport Motor Cas. Co.,* 392 Ill. 332, 64 N.E.2d 542 (1946).

§301.3 Burden of Pleading

In civil cases, one of the useful functions served by the pleadings is to settle in advance of trial, in accordance with the substantive law, not only what matters are relevant to the merits but also which party is responsible for them. Thus the complaint sets forth the elements of plaintiff's cause of action — for example, in a negligence action negligence, proximate cause, and damage; the answer contains affirmative defenses; and so on. *Noyes v. Gold,* 310 Ill. App. 1, 34 N.E.2d 1 (1941). The accuracy of the blueprint of the trial thus created may, however, be distorted by the workings of presumptions. *See* §§302.1-302.11 infra.

Many civil cases, are, of course, tried without formal pleadings. Problems of allocation are nevertheless present, though not settled in advance of trial. Their solution is often misleadingly phrased in terms of presumptions. *See, e.g., In re Estate of Moos,* 414 Ill. 54, 110 N.E.2d 194 (1953), a proceeding to probate a lost will in which the burden was fixed on proponents to prove that the will was not revoked by saying that revocation was presumed. This usage, which adds to the confusion attending the subject of presumptions, should be discontinued.

§301.4 Burden of Production: Measure and Effect; Prima Facie Case

The burden of production, also called the burden of producing evidence or the burden of going forward, is satisfied by evidence that, viewed in the aspect most favorable to the burdened party, is sufficient to enable the trier of fact reasonably to find the issue for her. *Donoho v. O'Connell's, Inc.,* 13 Ill. 2d 113, 148 N.E.2d 434 (1958); *Offutt v. World's Columbian Exposition,* 175 Ill. 472, 51 N.E. 651 (1898); *Glover v. City of Chicago,* 106 Ill. App. 3d 1066, 62 Ill. Dec. 597, 436 N.E.2d 623 (1982). In the normal case where the burden of persuasion also rests upon the party with the burden of production, the burden of production is satisfied by the introduction of evidence that, viewed in the aspect most favorable to the burdened party, is sufficient to enable the trier of fact reasonably to find each element of the cause of action more probably to be true than not true. When the party thus burdened introduces such evidence as to each element of the cause of action, she is said to have presented a *"prima facie case."* *Ambrose v. Thornton Township School Trustees,* 274 Ill. App. 3d 676, 211 Ill. Dec. 83, 654 N.E.2d 545 (1995); *Anderson v. Department of Public Property,* 140 Ill. App. 3d 772, 95 Ill. Dec. 60, 489 N.E.2d 12 (1986). Failure to satisfy the burden of production requires a decision by the court as a matter of law on the particular issue adverse to the burdened party. *Olinger v. Great Atlantic & Pacific Tea Co.,* 21 Ill. 2d 469, 173 N.E.2d 443 (1961).

In its minimum aspect, the case so made is sufficient to support, but does not require, a finding in favor of the burdened party. While the opposite party is entitled to introduce contrary evidence, he is under no compulsion to do so and may submit the issue to the trier of fact on this evidence alone. No burden of producing evidence is cast upon him. *Caley v. Manicke,* 29 Ill. App. 2d 323, 173 N.E.2d 209 (1961), *rev'd on other grounds,* 24 Ill. 2d 390, 182 N.E.2d 206 (1962). *See also Leonardi v. Loyola University of Chicago,* 168 Ill. 2d 83, 212 Ill. Dec. 968, 658 N.E.2d 450 (1995), referring to the burden of proof as not shifting when proper reference is to the burden of production. However, the case made may be much stronger than that required to satisfy the minimum requirements. The testimony of witnesses that is not contradicted, impeached, or inherently improbable, by either internal or external circumstances, cannot arbitrarily be disregarded. *People v. Skelly,* 409 Ill. 613, 100 N.E.2d 915 (1951); *Coupon Redemption, Inc. v. Ramadan,* 164 Ill. App. 3d 749, 115 Ill. Dec. 760, 518 N.E.2d 285 (1987). A case thus constituted, and permitting only inferences favorable to the burdened party, imposes on the opponent the burden of producing evidence to meet it, and the absence thereof requires the court to rule for the burdened party as a matter of law. *Ryan v. Goldblatt Bros., Inc.*, 24 Ill. App. 2d 239, 164 N.E.2d 280 (1960), verdict directed for plaintiff on issue of liability; *Campbell v. Prudential Ins. Co.*, 16 Ill. App. 2d 65, 147 N.E.2d 404 (1958), verdict directed for defendant on uncontradicted affirmative defense.

At times the term *prima facie case* has also been applied to the situation where the introduction of evidence has in actuality shifted the burden of producing evidence as a matter of law by virtue of the weight of such evidence, *Egbers v. Egbers*, 177 Ill. 82, 52 N.E. 285 (1898), or as a result of a presumption, *McElroy v. Force*, 38 Ill. 2d, 528, 232 N.E.2d 708 (1967); *People v. Peeples*, 155 Ill. 2d 422, 186 Ill. Dec. 341, 616 N.E.2d 294 (1993). *See* 9 Wigmore, Evidence §2494 (Chadbourn rev. 1981). Sometimes the court simply misunderstands the concept. *Ambrose v. Thornton Township School Trustees*, 274 Ill. App. 3d 676, 211 Ill. Dec. 83, 654 N.E.2d 545 (1995) (upon establishment of *prima facie* case the burden of production shifts to the defendant to come forward with evidence; incorrect statement of law). Clarity would be enhanced if the term *prima facie case* were employed solely to refer to satisfaction of the burden of production as to each element of the cause of action or affirmative defense. For a discussion of the term *prima facie evidence, see* §302.8 infra.

In most situations the burdened party will satisfy her burden of producing evidence with the introduction of evidence less than sufficient to entitle her to a directed verdict as a matter of law if the opponent fails to introduce sufficient contrary evidence. However, the trier of fact may conclude that the burdened party has in fact satisfied her burden of persuasion. *See* §301.6 infra. In such instances, although neither party is aware of it, the practical effect is to shift the burden of production to the opposing party.

§301.5   Burden of Production: Exceptional Situations

Occasional departures from the normal treatment of the burden of producing evidence are found. Their common characteristic is a difficulty of proof on the part of the party burdened with overall responsibility for the element, due to the fact that evidence upon the matter lies within the control of the opposite party.

This group of cases consists of civil actions in which the burden of producing evidence is held to be satisfied by less evidence than would normally be required. In some, the fact that the element is negative in form and the added difficulty of proof occasioned thereby are emphasized. *Prentice v. Crane*, 234 Ill. 302, 84 N.E. 916 (1908), suit by heirs of grantor allegedly induced to convey by false representation that it was necesary in order to carry out a will; burden on plaintiffs to establish will never existed. In others, no problem of proving a negative is present, but the opposite party could easily produce evidence on the point. *Harper v. Fay Livery Co.*, 264 Ill. 459, 106 N.E. 273 (1914), question whether decedent was a passenger for hire of defendant; *Belding v. Belding*, 358 Ill. 216, 192 N.E. 917 (1934), question whether partners had agreed to increase share of partner now deceased; *Southwest Federal Sav. & Loan Assn. v. Cosmopolitan Natl. Bank*, 23 Ill. App. 2d 174, 161 N.E.2d 697 (1959), question whether defendant was interested as trustee or as individual. These cases are readily explicable by resort to the inference that evidence within the control of a party and not produced by him is unfavorable to his cause. *See* §302.6 infra. The possible impact of modern broad discovery procedure on this area remains largely unexplored.

Many of the cases cited above rely upon *Great Western Ry. v. Bacon*, 30 Ill. 347 (1863), an action for killing a mule on unfenced right-of-way, in which plaintiff was held not required to produce evidence that the owner of the land had not agreed to construct a fence, under a statutory provision relieving the railroad of the duty to fence if the owner agreed to do so. The case would seem better based on the factors that dictate the allocation of elements, §301.2 supra, rather than on any supposed inference as to the truth of a negative when facts are within the control of the opponent. It would be preferable to eliminate such departures completely through a reallocation of the burden of producing evidence.

§301.6   Burden of Persuasion: Incidence and Measure in Civil Cases

As has been seen, §301.4 supra, the burden of producing evidence may shift from party to party as the case progresses. The cases abound with statements to the effect that the burden of persuasion, unlike the burden of producing evidence, never shifts as a result of the introduction of evidence. *Caley v. Manicke*, 29 Ill. App. 2d 323, 173 N.E.2d 209 (1961), *rev'd on other grounds*, 24 Ill. 2d 390, 182 N.E.2d 206 (1962); *Egbers v. Egbers*, 177 Ill. 82, 52 N.E. 285 (1898). The correctness of this general proposition cannot be doubted. However, it must be taken as qualified to the extent that a particular presumption might provide for the shifting of the burden of persuasion. *See* §302.5 infra.

Civil Cases.   In the usual civil case the burden of persuasion requires that the trier of fact "be persuaded . . . that the proposition . . . is more probably true than not true." Illinois Pattern Jury Instructions — Civil 21.01 and Comment (1994). The phrase seems more likely to be meaningful to juries than the former term "preponderance" with which it is sometimes incorrectly and unfortunately stated to equate. *In re K. G.*, 288 Ill. App. 3d 728, 224 Ill. Dec. 534, 682 N.E. 2d 95 (1997); *People v. Hammerli*, 277 Ill. App. 3d 873, 214 Ill. Dec. 886, 662 N.E.2d 452 (1996); *People v. Wilhoite*, 228 Ill. App. 3d 12, 169 Ill. Dec. 561, 592 N.E.2d 48 (1991). Attempts at further refinement, definition, or qualification are believed to be unnecessary and undesirable. *Reivitz v. Chicago Rapid Transit Co.*, 327 Ill. 207, 158 N.E 380 (1927). Clear and convincing evidence constitutes a burden of persuasion greater than the general civil standard of more probably true than not true but less than the criminal standard of proof beyond a reasonable doubt. *Estate of Ragen*, 79 Ill. App. 3d 8, 34 Ill. Dec. 523, 398 N.E.2d 198 (1979). *Contra Matter of Jones*, 285 Ill. App. 3d 8, 220 Ill. Dec.

359, 673 N.E.2d 703 (1996), clear and convincing evidence leaves no reasonable doubt, obviously incorrectly equating clear and convincing with proof beyond a reasonable doubt. Clear and convincing evidence has been defined as evidence producing a firm belief or conviction as to the truth of the proposition. *See United States v. Montague,* 40 F.3d 1251 (D.C. Cir. 1994). Illinois Pattern Jury Instructions—Criminal 4.19 (1996) states that the "phrase 'clear and convincing evidence' means that degree of proof which, considering all the evidence in the case, produces the firm and abiding belief that it is highly probable that the proposition on which the defendant has the burden of proof is true." For a discussion of the various attempted definitions of the term "clear and convincing," as well as a discussion of whether the term should be defined in an instruction to the jury in a civil case, *see* Buckley, J., *concurring in part and dissenting in part,* in *Washington Courte v. Washington-Gulf,* 267 Ill. App. 3d 790, 205 Ill. Dec. 248, 643 N.E.2d 199 (1994).

Crime Involved.   The rule formerly was that facts in civil cases that amounted to a crime must be proved beyond a reasonable doubt. This rule has been repudiated, and the ordinary measure of proof is now held to be sufficient. *Sundquist v. Hardware Mut. Fire Ins. Co.,* 371 Ill. 360, 21 N.E.2d 297 (1939); *Moore v. Farmers Ins. Exch.,* 111 Ill. App. 3d 401, 67 Ill. Dec. 181, 444 N.E.2d 220 (1982).

Stability of Transaction.   The public interest in preserving the stability of transactions in certain cases not falling within the protection of the parol evidence rule requires a higher measure of proof, variously described as "clear and convincing," "strong and convincing," "unquestionable and free from reasonable doubt," and "evidence amounting to a certainty." *Christ v. Rake,* 287 Ill. 619, 122 N.E. 854 (1919), reformation; *Shipley v. Shipley,* 274 Ill. 506, 113 N.E. 906 (1916), lost deed; *Johnson v. Lane,* 369 Ill. 135, 15 N.E.2d 710 (1938), constructive trust; *Krueger v. Dorr,* 22 Ill. App. 2d 513, 161 N.E.2d 433 (1959), impeachment of notary's certificate.

Involuntary Commitment.   Clear and convincing evidence is required for establishing the need for mental treatment in an action for involuntary commitment rather than proof beyond a reasonable doubt. *In re Stephenson,* 67 Ill. 2d 544, 10 Ill. Dec. 507, 367 N.E.2d 1273 (1977).

Fraud.   In fraud cases, confusion is apparent. *Compare Barrett v. Shanks,* 382 Ill. 434, 47 N.E.2d 481 (1943), requiring proof "so strong as to produce a conviction," and *Regenold v. Baby Fold, Inc.,* 42 Ill. App. 3d 39, 355 N.E.2d 361 (1976), requiring clear and convincing proof to invalidate in adoption matters an irrevocable consent on grounds of fraud or duress, *with Racine Fuel Co. v. Rawlins,* 377 Ill. 375, 36 N.E.2d 710 (1941), approving an instruction that specified only the ordinary degree of proof. Unless a fraud case also involves a public interest in the stability of transactions as discussed *supra,* no reason is apparent why a greater measure of proof should be required.

Civil Conspiracy.   The quantum of proof required in a civil conspiracy to tortiously interfere with contract or business advantage is clear and convincing evidence. *P.A. Bergner & Co. of Ill. v. Lloyds Jewelers, Inc.,* 130 Ill. App. 3d 987, 86 Ill. Dec. 59, 474 N.E.2d 1256 (1984).

Unfit Parent.   Clear and convincing evidence is required to support a finding of parental unfitness under the Illinois Adoption Act, 750 ILCS 50/1; *Paul v. Steele,* 101 Ill. 2d 345, 78 Ill. Dec. 149, 461 N.E.2d 983 (1984); *Freeman v. Settle,* 75 Ill. App. 3d 799, 31 Ill. Dec. 78, 393 N.E.2d 1385 (1979).

Inheritance of Illegitimate.   An illegitimate child may inherit from his father only if paternity is established by clear and convincing evidence. 755 ILCS 5/2-2; *Estate of Ragen,* 79 Ill. App. 3d 8, 34 Ill. Dec. 523, 398 N.E.2d 198 (1979).

§301.7   *Motion for Directed Verdict; Judgment N.O.V.; New Trial Based Upon Weight of the Evidence*

Verdicts are to be directed at the close of the evidence and judgments n.o.v. entered, 735 ILCS 5/2-1202, only in those cases in which all of the evidence, when viewed in its aspect most favorable to the opponent, so overwhelmingly favors movant that no contrary verdict based on that evidence could ever stand. *Pedrick v. Peoria and E.R.R.,* 37 Ill. 2d 494, 229 N.E.2d 504 (1967), which includes but is not limited to total lack of evidence to prove an essential element of the case. *See Merlo v. Public Service Co.,* 381 Ill. 300, 45 N.E. 2d 665 (1942); *Peterson v. Ress Enterprises, Inc.,* 292 Ill. App. 3d 566, 226 Ill. Dec. 848, 686 N.E. 2d 631 (1997). Testimony that is physically impossible or so inherently improbable as to be contrary to the common experience of mankind is to be given no consideration. *Old Second Natl. Bank of Aurora v. Gould,* 75 Ill. App. 3d 839, 31 Ill. Dec. 49, 393 N.E.2d 1356 (1979); *Doran v. Lobell,* 67 Ill. App. 3d 634, 24 Ill. Dec. 323, 385 N.E.2d 90 (1978). In applying the *Pedrick* rule, a jury may not disregard the testimony of a witness who has not been impeached when that testimony is neither contradicted (either by positive testimony or by circumstances) nor inherently improbable. *Bazydlo v. Volant,* 164 Ill. 2d 207, 207 Ill. Dec. 311, 647 N.E.2d 273 (1995); *People ex rel. Brown v. Baker,* 88 Ill. 2d 81, 58 Ill. Dec. 875, 430 N.E.2d 1126 (1981); *Bucktown Partners v. Johnson,* 119 Ill. App. 3d 346, 75 Ill. Dec. 20, 456 N.E.2d 703 (1983). The same rule applies in a bench trial. *People v. Bavas,* 251 Ill. App. 3d 720, 191 Ill. Dec. 286, 623 N.E.2d 876 (1993).

As is immediately apparent, the *Pedrick* rule lacks an anchor, for no standard is provided for determining when a contrary verdict could not stand. McCormick, Evidence §338 at 433 (4th ed. 1992), states the test to be applied as follows: "[I]f there is substantial evidence opposed to the [motion for directed verdict], that is evidence of such quality and weight that reasonable and fair-minded men in the exercise of impartial judgment might reach different conclusions, the [motion] should be denied." This test was rejected in *Pedrick* on the basis of a surface incongruity in a trial judge's saying all reasonable men must agree that the proof established the presence or absence of due care when twelve jurors have just reached a contrary conclusion, and it being even more incongruous for reviewing courts to so state when the trial judge and jury reached the opposite result, when the trial and reviewing courts disagree, or the members of a reviewing court disagree among themselves that such is the case. Nevertheless, trial and reviewing courts, in deciding motions for directed verdicts at the close of the evidence and motions n.o.v., are probably in fact applying the reasonable person test under the elusive rubric known as the *Pedrick* rule.

A new trial may be granted if the verdict is against the manifest weight of the evidence. *Jardine v. Rubloff,* 73 Ill. 2d 31, 21 Ill. Dec. 868, 382 N.E.2d 232 (1978); *Mizowek v. De Franco,* 64 Ill. 2d 303, 1 Ill. Dec. 32, 356 N.E.2d 32 (1976); *Lau v. West Towns Bus Co.,* 16 Ill. 2d 442, 158 N.E.2d 63 (1959). Manifest weight means the clearly evident, plain, and indisputable weight of the evidence. *Aguinaga v. City of Chicago,* 243 Ill. App. 3d 552, 183 Ill. Dec. 648, 611 N.E.2d 1296 (1993); *Tharp v. Critton,* 135 Ill. App. 3d 796, 90 Ill. Dec. 454, 482 N.E.2d 161 (1985); *Gettemy v. Grgula,* 25 Ill. App. 3d 625, 323 N.E.2d 628 (1975). A verdict is contrary to the manifest weight of the evidence when the opposite conclusion is clearly apparent, i.e., the findings appear to be unreasonable, arbitrary, and not based on the evidence. *Bazydlo v. Volant,* 164 Ill. 2d 207, 207 Ill. Dec. 311, 647 N.E.2d 273 (1995); *Maple v. Gustafson,* 151 Ill. 2d 445, 177 Ill. Dec. 438, 603 N.E.2d 508 (1992); *O'Donnell v. Holy Family Hospital,* 289 Ill. App. 3d 634, 224 Ill. Dec. 825, 682 N.E. 2d 386 (1997); *Dupree v. County of Cook,* 287 Ill. App. 3d 135, 222 Ill. Dec. 504, 677 N.E.2d 1303 (1997). While it has been asserted that "contrary to the manifest weight of the evidence" may be alternatively defined as "after viewing the evidence in a light most favorable to victorious party, no rational trier of fact could concur with the decision," *Price v. Industrial Commission,* 278 Ill. App. 3d 848, 215 Ill. Dec. 543, 663 N.E.2d 1057 (1996), such definition is first not in fact a different way to say the same thing, and more importantly parallels the proper definition for motions for directed verdict and judgments n.o.v., supra, thus improperly declaring the two identical.

In a nonjury trial, 735 ILCS 5/2-1110 specifically requires the trial court to weigh the evidence when ruling on defendant's motion for judgment at the close of plaintiff's case. Instead of considering the evidence in the light most favorable to the plaintiff as in a jury trial, the court must consider the weight and quality of the evidence, which necessarily includes any favorable to the defendant, and pass on the credibility of the witnesses. *City of Evanston v. Ridgeview House, Inc.,* 64 Ill. 2d 40, 349 N.E.2d 399 (1976); *State Farm v. Best in the West Foods,* 282 Ill. App. 3d 470, 217 Ill. Dec. 764, 667 N.E.2d 1340 (1996). The trial court does not simply decide whether plaintiff has made out a *prima facie* case but must make a final determination and enter judgment for defendant if plaintiff has not met this burden of persuasion of more probably true than not. *Kokinis v. Kotrich,* 81 Ill. 2d 151, 40 Ill. Dec. 812, 407 N.E.2d 43 (1980); *Pacini v. Regopoulos,* 281 Ill. App. 3d 274, 216 Ill. Dec. 433, 665 N.E.2d 493 (1996); *Bau v. Sobut,* 50 Ill. App. 3d 732, 735, 8 Ill. Dec. 486, 365 N.E.2d 724 (1977). On review, the decision of the trial court will not be reversed unless it is contrary to the manifest weight of the evidence. *City of Evanston v. Ridgeview House, Inc.,* supra; *Hill v. Ben Franklin Sav. & Loan Assn.,* 177 Ill. App. 3d 51, 126 Ill. Dec. 462, 531 N.E.2d 1089 (1988). In a bench trial, error in the denial of a motion for a directed verdict at the close of the opponent's case in chief is waived if the moving party then proceeds to introduce evidence. 735 ILCS 5/2-1110; *Miller v. Racine Trust,* 65 Ill. App. 3d 207, 21 Ill. Dec. 747, 382 N.E.2d 41 (1978).

§302   Presumptions in Civil Cases

§302.1   *Definition and Nature*

Properly considered, a presumption is a rule of law that requires that the existence of a fact (the presumed fact) be taken as established when certain other facts (the basic facts) are established, unless and until a certain specified condition is fulfilled. *People v. Watts,* 181 Ill. 2d 133, 229 Ill. Dec. 542, 692 N.E.2d 315 (1998) (citing Handbook); *Trustees of*

Schools v. Lilly, 373 Ill. 431, 26 N.E.2d 489 (1940); *Brown v. Brown,* 329 Ill. 198, 160 N.E. 149 (1928); Morgan, Basic Problems in Evidence 32 (1962). Both the Thayer approach adopted in Federal Rule of Evidence 301, 65 F.R.D. 131, 142 (1975), and the Morgan approach proposed by the Federal Advisory Committee, 56 F.R.D. 183, 208 (1973), are aimed at providing criteria for the specific condition removing the requirement that the presumed fact be taken as established.

The Thayer bursting bubble approach may be stated as follows:

> When the basic fact (*A*) is established, the presumed fact (*B*) must be taken as established unless and until the opponent introduces evidence sufficient to support a finding by the trier of fact of the nonexistence of the presumed fact. Upon introduction of such evidence the presumption is overcome and disappears, without regard to whether it is believed. However, any inference that exits from fact *A* to fact *B* remains.

Under this approach, if a presumption would operate against a party already having the burden of production as to the presumed fact, the presumption has no effect. Notice also that under the Thayer bursting bubble approach the burden of persuasion remains throughout upon the originally burdened party. However, application of the presumption shifts the burden of production to the opposing party.

The Morgan approach to presumptions is described as follows:

> When fact *A* is established, the jury is instructed that it must find fact *B* unless and until the opponent persuades the jury that the nonexistence of fact *B* is more probably true than not true.

Pursuant to the Morgan approach, application of the presumption shifts both the burden of production and the burden of persuasion to the opposing party.

The unhappy confusion that surrounds the subject arises in no small degree from loose and imprecise terminology. A presumption involves a legally recognized relation between facts. A court that says, "Courts are presumed to be no more ignorant than the public generally," *Chicago v. Murphy,* 313 Ill. 98, 102, 144 N.E. 802 (1924), has in mind a supposedly correct proposition of legal reasoning, rather than a true presumption. Or, when a court says that, if a will is retained by the testator and cannot be found after her death, it is "presumed" to have been destroyed by her *animo revocandi, In re Estate of Moos,* 414 Ill. 54, 57, 110 N.E.2d 194 (1953), *see* §301.2 supra, it is in reality allocating the element of nonrevocation to proponents as a part of their case, unfortunately phrasing the result in terms of a presumption when none is concerned. Allocation of an element is also involved with respect to legislative enactments, including zoning ordinances that are "presumed" valid with the "presumption being overcome" only by clear and convincing evidence. *Tomasek v. City of Des Plaines,* 64 Ill. 2d 172, 354 N.E.2d 899 (1964); *Cosmopolitan Natl. Bank v. County of Cook,* 116 Ill. App. 3d 1089, 72 Ill. Dec. 564, 452 N.E.2d 817 (1983). Courts and laymen often use the term presumed as a synonym for an inference, *see* §302.2 infra, in such expressions as "Dr. Livingston, I presume." A court speaking of the "presumption" of sanity in a criminal case, *People v. Skeoch,* 408 Ill. 276, 96 N.E.2d 473 (1951); *People v. Spears,* 63 Ill. App. 3d 510, 20 Ill. 445, 380 N.E.2d 423 (1978), prior to statutory amendment in 1984 simply meant that sanity did not become an element of the state's case unless and until some evidence raised the issue, a matter the Criminal Code now treats in terms of a true affirmative defense requiring proof by clear and convincing evidence rather than a presumption. 720 ILCS 5/6-2(e). *See* §§303.1 to 303.4 infra. With respect to defining clear and convincing, *see* §301.6 supra. The persistent use of the term *presumption* to describe these nonpresumption situations must inevitably lead to difficulty, in view of the natural assumption that things of the same name have the same characteristics. It is an example of what is known in the field of logic as the fallacy of the transplanted category.

§302.2 Inferences and Permissive Presumptions; Res Ipsa Loquitur

While the words *inference* and *presumption* are sometimes used interchangeably, they are by no means the same thing. An inference is a conclusion as to the existence of a particular fact reached by considering other facts in the usual course of human reasoning. *Ohio Bld. Safety Vault Co. v. Industrial Bd.*, 277 Ill. 96, 115 N.E. 149 (1917). With respect to an inference, if fact *A* is established, fact *B* may be deduced from fact *A* through reasoning and logic. An inference is thus a deduction the fact finder may in its discretion draw but is not required to draw as a matter of law. An inference may be based upon another inference. *Leavitt v. Farwell Tower Ltd. Partnership*, 252 Ill. App. 3d 260, 192 Ill. Dec. 88, 625 N.E.2d 48 (1993). Under certain circumstances an inference may be so strong that no other may reasonably be drawn. However, this is because of the compelling nature of the particular factual circumstances rather than that, as is the case with a presumption, a rule of law requires the conclusion to be drawn. *Smith v. Tri-R Vending*, 249 Ill. App. 3d 654, 188 Ill. Dec. 808, 619 N.E.2d 172 (1993).

Running through the cases are references to presumptions that are merely permissive in the sense that the trier may reach the suggested conclusion but is not, as a matter of law, required to do so. *See, e.g., Bollenbach v. Blumenthal,* 341 Ill. 539, 173 N.E. 670 (1930), stating that the presumption or inference of negligence raised by *res ipsa loquitur* will support recovery; *Bullard v. Barnes,* 102 Ill. 2d 505, 82 Ill. Dec. 448, 468 N.E.2d 1228 (1984), holding that parents are entitled to a presumption of pecuniary injuries from loss of a child's society; *Berlinger's Inc. v. Beef Finest, Inc.,* 57 Ill. App. 3d 319, 14 Ill. Dec. 764, 372 N.E.2d 1043 (1978), referring to inference arising from failure to produce evidence in party's control as a presumption. The so-called permissive presumptions, not properly considered presumptions at all, should be considered as inferences, which they in fact are. *Cobb v. Mar-*

shall Field & Co., 22 Ill. App. 2d 143, 159 N.E.2d 520 (1959), *res ipsa loquitur.*

The limitation of the Code of Civil Procedure that the court shall instruct the jury "only as to the law of the case," 735 ILCS 5/2-1107(a), seems not to be regarded as precluding instructions calling attention to inferences that may be drawn in certain standardized and recurrent situations. *People v. Stone,* 349 Ill. 52, 181 N.E. 648 (1932), inference of larceny from recent unexplained possession of stolen property; *McCleod v. Nel-Co Corp.,* 350 Ill. App. 216, 112 N.E.2d 501 (1953), *res ipsa loquitur; Bullard v. Barnes* supra, inference of pecuniary damage to parents from loss of a child's society. *See* Illinois Pattern Jury Instructions — Civil 10.08 (1994), inference of due care by decedent from proof of careful habits; *id.,* 50.07, agency of driver from ownership of automobile. It may be that calling these matters presumptions at one time aided in escaping the application of the limitation of instruction only as to the law. If so, it is no longer necessary or useful.

To illustrate the confusion fostered by calling an inference a presumption, consider the doctrine of *res ipsa loquitur* dealt with in Illinois Pattern Jury Instructions — Civil 22.01 and B 22.01 (1994). *Res ipsa loquitur* requires the introduction of evidence sufficient to support a finding that: (1) the result must be caused by an agency or instrument that is, or has been, within the control or management of the defendant; (2) the result must not be due to any action on the part of the plaintiff; and (3) the result must be one that normally does not occur without negligence in the control or management of the agency or instrument. *Imig v. Beck,* 115 Ill. 2d 18, 104 Ill. Dec. 767, 503 N.E.2d 324 (1986); *Lynch v. Precision Machine Shop, Ltd.,* 93 Ill. 2d 266, 66 Ill. Dec. 643, 443 N.E.2d 569 (1982); *Kolakowski v. Voris,* 83 Ill. 2d 388, 47 Ill. Dec. 392, 415 N.E.2d 397 (1980); *Walker v. Rumer* 72 Ill. 2d 495, 21 Ill. Dec. 362, 381 N.E.2d 689 (1978); *Metz v. Central Ill. Elec. & Gas Co.,* 32 Ill. 2d 446, 207 N.E.2d 305 (1965). The Comment to Instruction 22.01 (1971) stated that "the presumption of negligence is a permissive presumption." *Res ipsa loquitur* is an inference, not a presumption of any type. *See* Prosser and Keeton,

Law of Torts §40 (5th ed. 1984). Properly understood, there is no such animal as a permissive presumption in a civil case. *Res ipsa loquitur* warrants, but does not compel, an inference of negligence. It does not affect the burden of persuasion, which remains upon the plaintiff. In other words, *res ipsa loquitur,* if applicable, is enough to take the case to the jury. The jury is at liberty to accept or reject the inference of negligence. The plaintiff is not entitled to a directed verdict even if the defendant offers no evidence to negate the inference unless the inference is so clear that no reasonable person could fail to accept it. *Imig v. Beck,* 115 Ill. 2d 18, 104 Ill. Dec. 767, 503 N.E.2d 324 (1986). Thus, unlike certain natural inferences that remain after the presumption has been rebutted, *see, e.g.,* Illinois Pattern Jury Instructions — Civil 50.07 (1994), *res ipsa loquitur* is always solely an inference and never a presumption. The foregoing has been recognized in the Comment to Instructions 22.01 and B 22.01 (1992), which states that the "presumption of negligence is not a true presumption. It is an instructed inference of fact and is circumstantial evidence to be considered by the jury. It does not vanish when defendant introduces evidence of his due care in managing the injuring instrumentality, but remains in the case."

Regarding application of *res ipsa loquitur* in medical or dental malpractice actions, 735 ILCS 5/2-1112, provides that the trial court must initially decide, before the doctrine may be applied, that it is more probably true than not true that "the medical result complained of would not have ordinarily occurred in the absence of negligence on the part of the defendant." With respect to *res ipsa loquitur* in medical malpractice actions, *see also Spidle v. Steward,* 79 Ill. 2d 1, 37 Ill. Dec. 326, 402 N.E.2d 216 (1980); *Walker v. Rumer,* 72 Ill. 2d 495, 21 Ill. Dec. 362, 381 N.E.2d 689 (1978).

§302.3 Conclusive Presumptions

A so-called presumption that cannot be rebutted by evidence is not a presumption but a rule of substantive law.

Thus the effect of saying that everyone is presumed to know the law is to preclude ignorance of the law as a defense. *People v. Player,* 377 Ill. 417, 36 N.E.2d 729 (1941); 720 ILCS 5/4-3. And the so-called presumption that only death terminates the ability of a woman to bear children excludes the raising of an issue of fact upon that question, *Hill v. Sangamon Loan & Trust Co.,* 295 Ill. 619, 129 N.E. 554 (1921). *See also* Illinois Pattern Jury Instructions—Civil 11.03 (1994), child under seven years old conclusively presumed to be incapable of contributory negligence. Thus so-called conclusive presumptions, sometimes referred to as irrebuttable presumptions, should be referred to only as rules of law and never as presumptions.

With respect to the question of due process raised by a conclusive presumption denying a party an opportunity to rebut, *see Usery v. Turner Elkhorn Mining Co.,* 428 U.S. 1 (1976); *NLRB v. Heyman,* 541 F.2d 796 (9th Cir. 1976).

§302.4   *Attack by Rebutting Basic Facts*

Two methods of attack are open to the party against whom a presumption is invoked: he may introduce evidence tending to disprove the existence of the basic facts on which the presumption depends, or he may offer evidence tending to disprove the presumed fact itself.

If the attack is solely by introducing evidence to disprove the basic facts, then an issue of fact is presented as to their existence. This issue should be presented to the jury under an instruction outlining the result that follows success or failure in proving the basic facts. *McNaghten v. Northwestern Mut. Life Ins. Co.,* 318 Ill. App. 390, 48 N.E.2d 200 (1943), under conflicting evidence whether the insured had been seen within seven years after disappearance, the jury was properly instructed to return verdict for plaintiff if they found the insured had not been seen within the seven years, under presumption of death based on seven years' absence without tidings. *Accord In re Estate of Kline,* 245 Ill. App. 3d

413, 184 Ill. Dec. 737, 613 N.E.2d 1329 (1993) (quoting Handbook).

§302.5 Attack by Rebutting Presumed Facts; Instructions

If a presumption is attacked by introducing evidence to disprove the existence of the presumed fact, the question arises whether the presumption continues to have any effect in the case. Different approaches have been suggested.

Thayer Bursting Bubble. According to the Thayer bursting bubble theory, a presumption vanishes entirely upon the introduction of evidence sufficient to support a finding of the nonexistence of the presumed fact. *Bollenbach v. Bloomenthal,* 341 Ill. 539, 173 N.E. 670 (1930); *Lohr v. Barkmann Cartage Co.,* 335 Ill. 335, 167 N.E. 35 (1929). *See also Franciscan Sisters Health Care Corp. v. Dean,* 95 Ill. 2d 452, 69 Ill. Dec. 960, 448 N.E.2d 872 (1983), dealing with a "strong" presumption discussed below. The bursting bubble is easy to apply, since the judge need only determine whether the requisite contrary evidence has been introduced. If she finds in the affirmative, no reference is made to the presumption in instructing the jury; if she finds in the negative, the jury is instructed to find the presumed fact if the basic facts are proved. However, if the presumption is found to have been rebutted, the bubble was burst, and any underlying inference remains to be considered by the trier of fact and is a proper subject for jury instruction. *See, e.g.,* Illinois Pattern Jury Instructions — Civil 50.08 (1994). Such an inference instruction when appropriate should advise the jury that if they decide in favor of the basic fact they may, but are not required to, infer the existence of the inferred fact. *See, e.g.,* Illinois Pattern Jury Instructions — Civil 50.08 (1994) and Graham, Presumptions in Civil Cases in Illinois, Do they Exist? 1977 S. Ill. L.J. 1 suggesting modifications to reflect the fact that solely an inference instruction is being given. Whether the party upon whom the burden of production was originally placed can reach the jury once the bubble has burst requires the court to determine whether a reasonable jury viewing all the evidence most favorable to the burdened party could find the existence of each element of the cause of action to be more probably true than not true. *See* §§301.4 and 301.7 supra.

To illustrate the Thayer bursting bubble theory, consider the presumption that a letter properly addressed, with proper postage, mailed in a proper location, and not returned, was duly received:

(1) If the basic fact of mailing is not disputed, and if sufficient evidence to rebut the presumed fact (i.e., non-receipt) is not introduced, the jury will be instructed to find receipt of the letter. Evidence as to the nonexistence of the presumed fact rebuts the presumption when it is sufficient to support a finding by a reasonable trier of fact that the nonexistence of the presumed fact is more probably true than not true.

(2) If the basic fact is disputed but evidence sufficient to rebut the presumption has not been introduced, the jury would be instructed as follows:

> If you find it is more probably true than not true that the letter properly addressed and stamped was mailed, and not returned, then you must find the letter was duly received. Conversely, if you do not find that it is more probably true than not true that the letter was properly addressed, stamped, mailed, and not returned, then you must find that the letter was not received.

(3) If the presumed fact is disputed and evidence as to the nonreceipt of the letter sufficient to rebut the presumption has been introduced, no instruction will be given on the presumption for the bubble has burst. The court may, however, give an inference instruction:

> If you find that the letter was properly addressed, stamped, mailed, and not returned you may, but are not required to, infer from these facts that the letter was duly received. If you do draw such an inference, then consider the inference together with all other evidence in the case in deciding whether plaintiff has

established that it is more probably true than not true that the letter was duly received.

Whether an inference instruction should be given rests in the discretion of the court. The importance of the question to the trial, as well as the likelihood of the jury realizing the propriety of drawing the permitted inference absent such an instruction, should, of course, be considered.

Morgan Shifting the Burden of Persuasion.   Supporters of the Morgan shifting burden of persuasion approach to presumptions assert that the bursting bubble theory accords too slight an effect to presumptions. An examination of presumptions discloses that they rest upon the same considerations of caution and convenience, policy, fairness, and probability that govern the allocation of the elements of the case originally. *See* §301.2 supra. Presumptions are an aspect of allocation working within the larger framework of the elements of the case. To hold that the sole effect of a presumption is that of requiring the opposite party to produce evidence sufficient to support a finding of the nonexistence of the presumed fact, wholly without regard to whether it is in fact believed, is argued by those supporting the Morgan approach to ignore the wisdom that underlies presumptions. For cases placing the burden of persuasion of more probably true than not true as to the nonexistence of the presumed fact upon the opposite party, *see Kavale v. Morton Salt Co.,* 329 Ill. 445, 160 N.E. 752 (1928); *Stephens v. Hoffman,* 275 Ill. 497, 114 N.E. 142 (1916); *Kennedy v. Modern Woodman,* 243 Ill. 560, 90 N.E. 1084 (1910); *Helbig v. Citizen's Ins. Co.,* 234 Ill. 251, 84 N.E. 897 (1908); *Bradshaw v. People,* 153 Ill. 156, 38 N.E. 652 (1894); *Bielunski v. Tousignant,* 17 Ill. App. 2d 359, 149 N.E.2d 801 (1958); *Sutherland v. Guccione,* 8 Ill. App. 2d 201, 131 N.E.2d 130 (1955). In addition, statutes sometimes specify the shifting burden of persuasion approach. *See* §302.6 infra.

Jury instructions under the Morgan approach will follow basically the form of those "directing a verdict," i.e., if you find *A, B,* and *C* (the basic facts) then you will find *D* (the presumed fact), unless from the evidence you find its nonexistence. *See, e.g.,* Illinois Pattern Jury Instructions—Civil 21.03 and B 21.03 (1994). In contrast to the simple jury instruction approach under the Thayer bursting bubble, consider the complexity associated with the recommended procedure for instructing the jury regarding a presumption given the Morgan shifting burden of persuasion effect when both the basic and presumed facts are in dispute:

Determination on Evidence of Both Basic and Presumed Facts.

When evidence as to the existence of the basic facts is such that reasonable minds would not necessarily agree whether their existence is more probable than not and evidence as to the nonexistence of the presumed fact is such that they would not necessarily agree that its nonexistence is more probable than not, the judge shall submit the matter to the jury with an instruction to find in favor of the existence of the presumed fact if they find from the evidence that the existence of the basic facts is more probable than not and unless they find the nonexistence of the presumed fact more probable than not, otherwise to find against the existence of the presumed fact. [Federal Rules of Evidence, 1969 Draft Rule 303(c)(3), 46 F.R.D. 161, 214 (1969).]

The strongest single argument in favor of the Thayer bursting bubble theory and against the Morgan approach is the paragraph quoted above. *See* Graham, Presumptions in Civil Cases in Illinois, Do They Exist? supra. It is ventured to say that not one juror in a hundred is able to understand such an instruction as presented at trial. In addition, a strong argument can be made that the above-quoted paragraph, by its very structure, if understood, results in a greater burden of persuasion being placed upon the party opposing the presumption than if the identical burden of persuasion has been initially placed on that party. The greater burden naturally flows from the court advising the trier of fact that they "must" find unless they find to the contrary. When told "must," the probative value of evidence needed to satisfy the burden of persuasion is most likely greater in practice than "more probably true than not true" constitutes if placed upon the opposing party in the first instance.

For support of the Morgan view, see Cleary, *Presuming and Pleading: An Essay on Juristic Immaturity*, 12 Stan. L. Rev. 5 (1959).

In some situations, when an element of the case rather than a presumption is involved, the rule on presumptions will not apply, *see* §301.2 supra; as to when placing the burden of persuasion on the opponent will be appropriate, *see* §301.6 supra.

Illinois Practice.   In spite of the support the Morgan theory has received from some commentators, the three most recent pronouncements by the supreme court clearly indicate that the basic approach in Illinois is application of the Thayer bursting bubble theory. *McElroy v. Force,* 38 Ill. 2d 528, 531-532, 232 N.E.2d 708 (1967):

> Presumptions "do not shift the burden of proof. Their only effect is to create the necessity of evidence to meet the *prima facie* case created thereby, and which, if no proof to the contrary is offered, will prevail.". . . Stated differently, the presence of a presumption in a case only has the effect of shifting to the party against whom it operates the burden of going forward and introducing evidence to meet the presumption. If evidence is introduced which is contrary to the presumption, the presumption will cease to operate.

Diederich v. Walters, 65 Ill. 2d 95, 102, 2 Ill. Dec. 685, 357 N.E.2d 1128 (1976), Illinois "generally" follows the Thayer theory of presumptions whereby a presumption "ceases to operate in the face of contrary evidence"; *Franciscan Sisters Health Care Corp. v. Dean,* 95 Ill. 2d 452, 462, 69 Ill. Dec. 960, 448 N.E.2d 872 (1983), "The prevailing theory regarding presumptions that Illinois follows and *Diederich* speaks about is Thayer's bursting-bubble hypothesis: once evidence is introduced contrary to the presumption, the bubble bursts and the presumption vanishes." *Accord Lehman v. Stephens,* 148 Ill. App. 3d 538, 101 Ill. Dec. 736, 499 N.E.2d 103 (1986); *People ex rel. Daley v. $53,263.00,* 159 Ill. App. 3d 114, 111 Ill. Dec. 351, 512 N.E.2d 740 (1987); *Barnes v. Brown,* 193 Ill. App. 3d 604, 140 Ill. Dec. 552, 550 N.E.2d 34 (1990).

Occasionally presumptions, due to unusually compelling considerations of policy, have been held to impose upon a party attacking a presumption a greater burden of production to burst the Thayer bubble than merely producing evidence sufficient to support a finding by a reasonable jury as to the nonexistence of the presumed fact. Thus it was said that the presumption that a deed was delivered to a grantee in possession of it could be overcome only by "clear and convincing" evidence, *Layton v. Layton,* 5 Ill. 2d 506, 126 N.E.2d 225 (1955); the presumption as to the validity of a zoning ordinance is overcome only by clear and convincing evidence, *LaSalle Natl. Bank v. County of DuPage,* 54 Ill. App. 3d 387, 12 Ill. Dec. 8, 369 N.E.2d 505 (1977); the presumption of undue influence in a fiduciary relationship by a beneficiary who procured the testator's will may be overcome only by clear and convincing evidence, *Schmidt v. Schwear,* 98 Ill. App. 3d 366, 53 Ill. Dec. 766, 424 N.E.2d 401 (1981), *Lamb v. Lamb,* 124 Ill. App. 3d 687, 80 Ill. Dec. 8, 464 N.E.3d 873 (1984), *In re Estate of Henke,* 203 Ill. App. 3d 975, 149 Ill. Dec. 36, 561 N.E.2d 314 (1990); the presumption of undue influence that arises when a "gift" is made by a client to his attorney is overcome only by clear and convincing evidence, *In re Schuyler,* 91 Ill. 2d 6, 61 Ill. Dec. 540, 434 N.E.2d 1137 (1982); the presumption that the sheriff's return of service establishes service is overcome only by clear and convincing evidence, *Mitchell v. Tatum,* 104 Ill. App. 3d 986, 60 Ill. Dec. 740, 433 N.E.2d 978 (1982); the presumption of undue influence when the client's attorney is a beneficiary in the client's will is overcome only by clear and convincing evidence, *Franciscan Sisters Health Care Corp. v. Dean,* 95 Ill. 2d 452, 69 Ill. Dec. 960, 448 N.E.2d 872 (1983); the presumption that the placing of title by a parent in a child is a gift is overcome only by clear and convincing evidence, *Nordlund v. Nordlund,* 116

Ill. App. 3d 223, 72 Ill. Dec. 86, 452 N.E.2d 18 (1983); the presumption of undue influence in fee arrangement between client and attorney entered into after the creation of a fiduciary relationship is overcome only by clear and convincing evidence, *Durr v. Beatty*, 142 Ill. App. 3d 443, 96 Ill. Dec. 623, 491 N.E.2d 902 (1986); the presumption that a gift was intended by creation of a statutory joint tenancy is overcome only by clear and convincing evidence, *Matter of Estate of Lewis*, 193 Ill. App. 3d 316, 140 Ill. Dec. 309, 549 N.E.2d 960 (1990); and the presumption that a child born during marriage is the offspring of the married couple could be overcome only by "clear and irrefragable" proof. *Orthwein v. Thomas*, 127 Ill. 554, 21 N.E. 430 (1889); *People ex rel. Davis v. Clark*, 99 Ill. App. 3d 979, 55 Ill. Dec. 319, 426 N.E.2d 294 (1981). (The presumption of paternity during marriage is now governed by statute, 750 ILCS 45/5; the presumption may be rebutted only by clear and convincing evidence). With respect to such "strong" presumptions, the finding of the basic fact requires a finding of the presumed fact unless the court itself finds that "clear and convincing" evidence has been introduced by the party opposing the presumption, which establishes the nonexistence of the presumed fact. *Franciscan Sisters Health Care Corp. v. Dean* supra; *Klaskin v. Klepak*, 126 Ill. 2d 376, 128 Ill. Dec. 526, 534 N.E.2d 971 (1989); *Idleman v. Raymer*, 183 Ill. App. 3d 938, 132 Ill. Dec. 265, 539 N.E.2d 828 (1989). In reaching this determination the court must weigh the evidence, including the credibility of witnesses. *Nemeth v. Banhalmi*, 125 Ill. App. 3d 938, 81 Ill. Dec. 175, 466 N.E.2d 977 (1984). If the court decides that considered alone "clear and convincing" evidence has been introduced by the party opposing the presumption, the bubble bursts and the presumption vanishes. Of course, any natural inference arising from the basic fact to the fact previously presumed remains to be considered in determining whether the originally burdened party has satisfied his burden of production and burden of persuasion. *Nemeth v. Banhalmi* supra. *See generally In re Estate of Woodruff*, 164 Ill. App. 3d 791, 115 Ill. Dec. 770, 518 N.E.2d 295 (1987); *In re Marriage of*

Pagano, 181 Ill. App. 3d 547, 130 Ill. Dec. 331, 537 N.E.2d 398 (1989). If the court decides that the presumption has not been rebutted by "clear and convincing evidence," then the jury is instructed to find the existence of the presumed fact if they find that the basic facts giving rise to the presumption have been proved. *Matter of Estate of Berry,* 170 Ill. App. 3d 454, 120 Ill. Dec. 659, 524 N.E.2d 689 (1988).

§302.6   Presumptions and Inferences: Statutory and Common Law Illustrations

Bailee, negligence of.   Proof by a bailor that goods were delivered to the bailee and not returned on demand, or that goods were delivered to the bailee in good condition and returned in a damaged condition, gives rise to a presumption of negligent loss or damage by the bailee. *Miles v. International Hotel Co.,* 289 Ill. 320, 124 N.E. 599 (1919); *Bielunski v. Tousignant,* 17 Ill. App. 2d 359, 149 N.E.2d 801 (1958). *See also* 810 ILCS 5/7-403(1)(b), discussed infra.

Continuation of condition.   Gaps in proof may often be bridged by the presumption that a condition, once proved to exist, continued. Though described as a presumption, it is properly an inference of the kind described in §302.2 supra, with its force varying according to circumstances. Illustrative applications are that bonds are still in the hands of the original holder, *Choisser v. People ex rel. Rude,* 140 Ill. 21, 29 N.E. 546 (1892); that a member of a benefit society continues in good standing, *Independent Order of Foresters v. Zak,* 136 Ill. 185, 26 N.E. 593 (1891); that insanity continues to exist, unless shown to be temporary in character, *Turley v. Turley,* 374 Ill. 571, 30 N.E.2d 64 (1940); that a person adjudicated unfit to stand trial remains unfit, *People v. Stribling,* 104 Ill. App. 3d 969, 60 Ill. Dec. 729, 433 N.E.2d 967 (1982); and that title or ownership continues, *Old Salem Chautauqua Assn. v. Assembly of God,* 16 Ill. 2d 470, 158 N.E.2d 38 (1959). Due regard must of course be had for the nature of the situation and the mandates of common sense. *Chicago, B. & Q.R. Co. v.*

Sierer, 13 Ill App. 261 (1883), proof that a frequently used gate was open on one day not sufficient to establish that it continued to be open on following day.

The inference may operate retroactively under appropriate circumstances. Thus meat shown to be in good condition could not have been spoiled at an earlier time, *Luetgert v. Volker*, 153 Ill. 385, 39 N.E. 113 (1894); and a man proved to be a bachelor must have been one at a prior date, *Gibson v. Brown*, 214 Ill. 330, 73 N.E. 578 (1905). However, proof that a woman was a married woman raises no inference that she was a married woman six years earlier. *Erskine v. Davis*, 25 Ill. 228 (1861).

Date of instrument. A document is presumed to have been executed upon the date it bears. *Holm v. Lynd*, 343 Ill. 645, 176 N.E. 57 (1931).

Death after seven years' absence. A person is presumed dead where (1) the person has disappeared or is continuously absent for seven years from his home without explanation, (2) those persons with whom he would likely communicate have not heard anything from him or about him, and (3) a diligent search has been made without obtaining information that he is alive. A diligent search is one that a reasonably prudent person would make in similar circumstances. It encompasses all of the places where information is likely to be obtained and extends to all of the people who would be likely to hear from the missing person. *Estate of Morrison v. Rosewell*, 92 Ill. 2d 207, 65 Ill. Dec. 276, 441 N.E.2d 68 (1982). Death at an earlier time may be inferred from the circumstances of the disappearance, for example, embarking upon a ship that was lost at sea. *Donovan v. Major*, 253 Ill. 179, 97 N.E. 231 (1912); *Whiting v. Nicholl*, 46 Ill. 230 (1867). The fact that the person was a fugitive from justice does not preclude the application of the presumption. *Blodgett v. State Mut. Life Assurance Co.*, 32 Ill. App. 2d 155, 177 N.E.2d 1 (1961).

Due care. The Illinois decisions have on occasion referred to the instinct of self-preservation as a factor to be considered in the evaluation of circumstantial evidence on the question of due care by a decedent, *Duffy v. Cortesi*, 2 Ill.

2d 511, 119 N.E.2d 241 (1954); *Lauer v. Elgin, J. & E. Ry.*, 305 Ill. App. 200, 27 N.E.2d 315 (1940), or by an amnesia victim, *Campbell v. Ragel*, 7 Ill. App. 2d 301, 129 N.E.2d 451 (1955). However, it seems clear that an inference, §302.2 supra, rather than a presumption is involved since such instinct for self-preservation does not operate to relieve plaintiff completely of the burden of establishing due care of the decedent. *Newell v. Cleveland, C., C. & St. L. Ry.*, 261 Ill. 505, 104 N.E. 223 (1914); *Overman v. Illinois Central R. Co.*, 34 Ill. App. 2d 30, 180 N.E.2d 213 (1962). For proving due care by evidence of careful habits, *see* §406.2 infra.

Failure to produce evidence.   Failure of a party to call a witness or to produce evidence within her control not equally available to an adverse party, it is sometimes said, gives rise to a "presumption" that the testimony or other evidence would be unfavorable to her. *Tepper v. Campo*, 398 Ill. 496, 76 N.E.2d 490 (1948). A witness is not considered equally available if likely to be biased against a party. *Tonarelli v. Gibbons*, 121 Ill. App. 3d 1042, 77 Ill. Dec. 408, 460 N.E.2d 464 (1984). Witnesses aware of material facts in a criminal case are considered available to both sides and thus it is improper for the prosecution to comment on the criminal defendant's failure to produce such a witness. *People v. Beller*, 54 Ill. App. 3d 1053, 12 Ill. Dec. 771, 370 N.E.2d 575 (1977). However, potential alibi witnesses injected into the case by the defendant are deemed unavailable to the prosecution, and comment with regard to the failure of such witnesses to testify is proper. *People v. Spenard*, 46 Ill. App. 3d 892, 5 Ill. Dec. 533, 361 N.E.2d 856 (1977). As an aspect of the techniques of evaluating and drawing inferences from facts, the principle is perfectly sound. It is of course an inference and not a presumption in the proper sense. Illinois Pattern Jury Instructions—Civil 5.01 (1992) concurs that such an inference does provide an appropriate basis for a jury instruction.

Identity of person of same name.   Persons of the same name may be presumed to be the same person. *Brown v. Metz*, 33 Ill. 339 (1864), grantee with same name as subsequent grantor; *People v. Buford,* 396 Ill. 158, 71 N.E.2d 340 (1947), accused who testified in own behalf with same name as person convicted in criminal record offered for impeachment; *People v. Keller,* 128 Ill. App. 3d 325, 83 Ill. Dec. 780, 470 N.E.2d 1200 (1984), invalid traffic ticket is sufficient proof of arrest for implied consent hearing. *Accord People v. Davis,* 95 Ill. 2d 1, 31, 69 Ill. Dec. 136, 151, 447 N.E.2d 353, 368 (1983), "identity of name gives rise to a rebuttable presumption of identity of person." Notice that in criminal cases the effect of a presumption differs. *See* §304.1 infra. In *Filkins v. O'Sullivan,* 79 Ill. 524 (1875), identity of the name of the special deputy serving summons and one of the plaintiffs was relied upon to invalidate the service. This application in the face of the opposing presumption of regularity of official conduct is open to question. *Cf. Richardson v. People,* 85 Ill. 495 (1877), name of judge approving bond same as surety, presumption not applied. In prosecutions for enhancement of punishment because of prior convictions, further proof is required of the identity of the accused with a person of the same name shown in a record of prior conviction. *People v. Casey,* 399 Ill. 374, 77 N.E.2d 812 (1948).

Mail, receipt of.   Mail, properly addressed and placed in the mails with postage prepaid, is presumed to have been received by the addressee. *Ashley Wire Co. v. Illinois Steel Co.,* 164 Ill. 149, 45 N.E. 410 (1896); *First Natl. Bank of Antioch v. Guerra Constr. Co.,* 153 Ill. App. 3d 662, 106 Ill. Dec. 582, 505 N.E. 1373 (1987). The efficiency of the post office has been supposed to be such that evidence of nonreceipt has at times not been regarded as evidence of the nonexistence of the presumed fact, which would destroy the presumption under the bursting bubble theory, but rather has been regarded as raising an issue as to the credibility of the evidence of mailing. *Talmage v. Union Central Ins. Co.,* 315 Ill. App. 623, 43 N.E.2d 575 (1942); *Loving v. Allstate Ins. Co.,* 17 Ill. App. 2d 230, 149 N.E.2d 641 (1958). However, *compare Chicago v. Supreme Sav. & Loan Assn.,* 27 Ill. App. 3d 589, 327 N.E.2d 5 (1975); *Winkfield v. American Continental Ins. Co.,* 110 Ill. App. 2d 156, 249 N.E.2d 174 (1969), indicating receipt of letter becomes an issue of fact, and *Liquorama Co. of Chicago v. American Natl. Bank & Trust,* 86 Ill. App. 3d 974, 41 Ill Dec. 951, 408 N.E.2d 373 (1980); *Mulholland v. State Farm Mut. Auto Ins. Co.,* 171 Ill. App. 3d 600, 122 Ill. Dec. 657, 527 N.E.2d 29 (1988), denial of receipt rebuts presumption. *See also Angelo v. Board of Review, Dept. of Labor,* 58 Ill. App. 3d 50, 15 Ill. Dec. 512, 573 N.E.2d 858 (1978), stating that common knowledge of capability of postal service negates any conclusion as a matter of law that item was received. Actual mailing of notice as authorized by statute creates a presumption of receipt treated in accordance with the foregoing. *M.S. Kaplan Co. v. Cullerton,* 49 Ill. App. 3d 374, 7 Ill. Dec. 220, 364 N.E.2d 381 (1977); *Winkfield v. American Continental Ins. Co.* supra.

Regularity of conduct.   Conduct that is open to two interpretations, one regular and one not, will be presumed to have been regular. Thus a charge of 10 percent has been presumed to be for money loaned when that rate was unlawful for any other purpose, *Sutphen v. Cushman,* 35 Ill. 186 (1864); a partner has been presumed to have signed the partnership name prior to the dissolution of the partnership, *Loehde v. Glos,* 265 Ill. 401, 106 N.E. 940 (1914); a state's attorney to have performed his office according to law, *In Interest of Vital,* 44 Ill. App. 3d 1030, 3 Ill. Dec. 603, 358 N.E.2d 1288 (1976); and the Attorney General will act to enforce statutes regulating lobbying. *Fuchs v. Bidwell,* 65 Ill. 2d 503, 3 Ill. Dec. 748, 359 N.E.2d 158 (1977).

Suicide.   Death from violent and external means is presumed not to have been suicide. *Wilkinson v. Aetna Life Ins. Co.,* 240 Ill. 205, 88 N.E. 550 (1909). In life insurance cases, this presumption properly finds application only if the policy is one of limited coverage insuring against accidental death. Plaintiff can make a *prima facie* case of loss within the terms of the policy by proving that death was due to causes that could be either accident or suicide, the presumption then becoming operative. If, however, the policy insures against death generally, suicide within the contestable period is an affirmative defense to be pleaded and proved as any affirmative defense, and invoking the presumption is neither necessary nor proper. The decision in *Kettlewell v. Prudential Ins. Co.,* 6 Ill. App. 2d 434, 128 N.E.2d 652 (1955), might well have been put more clearly on this latter basis. Failure to recognize the distinction between an accidental death policy and a general policy with a defense of suicide within the contestable period impairs the clarity also of *Kettlewell v. Prudential Ins. Co.,* 4 Ill. 2d 383, 122 N.E.2d 817 (1954).

Vehicle driven by owner. A motor vehicle is presumed to have been driven by the owner. *Robinson v. Workman,* 9 Ill. 2d 420, 137 N.E.2d 804 (1956); *Sutherland v. Guccione,* 8 Ill. App. 2d 201, 131 N.E.2d 130 (1955).

Vehicle driver agent of owner. The driver of a motor vehicle is presumed to be the agent of the owner, acting in the scope of his agency. *Parrino v. Landon,* 8 Ill. 2d 468, 134 N.E.2d 311 (1956); *Kavale v. Morton Salt Co.,* 329 Ill. 445, 160 N.E. 752 (1928). *See* Illinois Pattern Jury Instructions — Civil 50.07 (1994). But *see* §302.2 supra, suggesting classification as an inference.

Vehicle, ownership of. A vehicle is presumed to be owned by the person whose name appears thereon. *East St. Louis Connecting Ry. v. Altgen,* 210 Ill. 213, 71 N.E. 377 (1904), locomotive; *Robeson v. Greyhound Lines, Inc.,* 257 Ill. App. 278 (1930), bus.

Marital property. All property acquired by either spouse after the marriage and before a judgment of dissolution of marriage or declaration of invalidity of marriage is presumed to be marital property, regardless of whether title is held individually or by the spouses in some form of co-ownership such as joint tenancy, tenancy in common, tenancy by the entirety, or community property. 750 ILCS 5/503(b).

Uniform Commercial Code. With respect to the Uniform Commercial Code, 810 ILCS 5/1-201(31) defines *presumption* and *presumed* consistently with the bursting bubble theory. Where the Uniform Commercial Code contemplates a shift in the burden of persuasion, it employs the term *burden of establishing,* which is defined in 5/1-201(8) in terms equivalent to a Morgan shifting burden of persuasion approach. For illustrations *see* 5/3-115, 5/3-308(a), 5/7-403(1) and 5/8-105(3)(b) and (d). The Uniform Commercial Code also employs the terms *prima facie* and *prima facie evidence,* although neither is specifically defined. *See, e.g.,* 5/1-202, 5/4-103(c). It is assumed that the legislature intended that these terms be employed in accordance with their preferred usage, *see* §301.4 supra (*prima facie*) and §302.8 infra (*prima facie* evidence). *See generally* Bigham, Presumptions, Burden of Proof and the Uniform Commercial Code, 21 Vand. L. Rev. 177 (1968).

Undue influence: A presumption of undue influence arises when it is shown that: (1) a person in a fiduciary relationship with a testator receives a substantial benefit under the will; (2) the fiduciary is in a position of dominance over the testator; (3) the testator reposes trust and confidence in the fiduciary; and (4) the will is written by or its preparation is procured by the fiduciary. *Matter of Estate of Wills,* 203 Ill. App. 3d 574, 149 Ill. Dec. 66, 561 N.E.2d 344 (1990); *In re Estate of Berry,* 277 Ill. App. 3d 1088, 214 Ill. Dec. 705, 661 N.E.2d 1150 (1996). In addition, a presumption of undue influence arises where a party having a claim to the testator's bounty is excluded following the active participation of a beneficiary in procuring a will. *In re Estate of Hoover,* 155 Ill.2d 402, 185 Ill. Dec. 866, 615 N.E.2d 736 (1993); *In re Estate of Roeseler,* 287 Ill. App. 3d 1003, 223 Ill. Dec. 208, 679 N.E.2d 393 (1997).

§302.7   Presumptions as Evidence

It was once somewhat fashionable to treat a presumption as evidence to be weighed by the jury in determining the existence of a particular fact. However, it is now universally recognized that a presumption is a rule of law for the handling of evidence, not a species of evidence. *Diederich v. Walters,* 65 Ill. 2d 95, 2 Ill. Dec. 685, 357 N.E.2d 1128 (1976). It is impossible to weigh a presumption as evidence on the one hand against physical objects and personal observations.

Speck v. Sarver, 20 Cal. 2d 585, 594, 128 P.2d 16, 21 (1942) (Traynor, J.). The presumption as evidence doctrine never had a foothold in Illinois.

§302.8   Prima Facie *Evidence*

The term *prima facie evidence* has taken a foothold in Illinois. The term has been employed by the court with respect to common law presumptions, *McElroy v. Force,* 38 Ill. 2d 528, 232 N.E.2d 708 (1967) (the law may declare proof of one fact to be *prima facie* evidence of another) and by the legislature in many statutes. *See, e.g.,* 325 ILCS 325/33, order over seal of department *prima facie* proof that signature of director is genuine.

With respect to common law presumptions, the term *prima facie evidence* creates confusion similar to that surrounding the term *prima facie case. See* §301.4 supra. *Prima facie* evidence, used in similar fashion to the term *permissive presumptions,* signifying the introduction of evidence sufficient to satisfy one element of the *prima facie* case, should be discarded in favor of the term *burden of production.* With respect to legislative use, the term *prima facie evidence* should be interpreted merely to establish a presumption, i.e., the terms *presume, presumption,* and *prima facie evidence* should be treated synonymously. *See Chicago v. Hartz,* 71 Ill. 2d 333, 17 Ill. Dec. 1, 375 N.E.2d 1285 (1978) for discussion of *prima facie* responsibility in connection with a municipal ordinance concerning parking violations.

§302.9   *Conflicting Presumptions*

Where the court is faced with inconsistent presumptions, a solution of considerable appeal is to apply the presumption founded upon weightier considerations of social policy. If policy considerations are of equal weight, both presumptions are then disregarded. The principle is incorporated in Rule

301 (b) of the Revised Uniform Rules of Evidence approved in 1974 by the Commissioners on Uniform State Laws. *Accord* Morgan, Some Observations Concerning Presumptions, 44 Harv. L. Rev. 906, 932 n.41 (1936). The principal class of cases in which the problem has arisen is where rights are asserted under a second marriage but no direct evidence is available of a death or divorce terminating the first marriage before the second. Most courts say the presumption of the validity of a marriage is stronger than the presumption of continuance of life or continuance of marriage. McCormick, Evidence §345 (3d ed. 1984).

Another solution is to consider that the conflicting presumptions have disappeared with the facts upon which the respective presumptions are based simply being weighed as circumstances with all the other facts that may be relevant, thus giving no effect to the presumptions, 9 Wigmore, Evidence §2493 (Chadbourn rev. 1981). *Accord In re Marriage of Rosen,* 126 Ill. App. 3d 766, 81 Ill. Dec. 840, 467 N.E.2d 962 (1984), since presumption that property acquired after marriage is marital and presumption that property transferred from a parent to a child is a gift conflict, both will be treated as though they cancelled. When the conflicting presumptions involved are based upon probability or upon procedural convenience but not upon clear considerations of social policy, this solution is a fairly practical one. McCormick, Evidence §345 (Cleary ed. 1972).

§302.10   Constitutionality of Presumptions in Civil Cases

With respect to the constitutionality in a civil case of a Thayer type presumption, the Supreme Court in *Usery v. Turner Elkhorn Mining Co.,* 428 U.S. 1, 28 (1976), quoted with approval the standard articulated in *Mobile, J. & K.C.R. Co. v. Turnipseed,* 219 U.S. 35, 43 (1910):

> That a legislative presumption of one fact from evidence of another may not constitute a denial of due process of law or a

denial of the equal protection of the law it is only essential that there shall be some rational connection between the fact proved and the ultimate fact presumed, and that the inference of one fact from proof of another shall not be so unreasonable as to be a purely arbitrary mandate.

The foregoing standard applies to common law presumptions as well. *See Dick v. New York Life Ins. Co.*, 359 U.S. 437 (1959). Where a legislative presumption is being judged, significant weight is accorded the capacity of the legislature "to amass the stuff of actual experience and cull conclusions from it." *Usery v. Turner Elkhorn Mining Co.*, supra, quoting from *United States v. Gainey*, 380 U.S. 63, 67 (1965).

With respect to the constitutionality of the Morgan approach in civil cases, the Advisory Committee Note to Proposed Federal Rule of Evidence 301, 56 F.R.D. 183, 208-209 (1973) stated:

> In the opinion of the Advisory Committee, no constitutional infirmity attends . . . [the Morgan] view of presumptions. In *Mobile, J. & K.C.R. Co. v. Turnipseed*, 219 U.S. 35, 31 S. Ct. 136, 55 L. Ed. 78 (1910), the Court upheld a Mississippi statute which provided that in actions against railroads proof of injury inflicted by the running of trains should be *prima facie* evidence of negligence by the railroad. The injury in the case had resulted from a derailment. The opinion made the points (1) that the only effect of the statute was to impose on the railroad the duty of producing some evidence to the contrary, (2) that an inference may be supplied by law if there is a rational connection between the fact proved and the fact presumed, as long as the opposite part is not precluded from presenting his evidence to the contrary, and (3) that considerations of public policy arising from the character of the business justified the application in question. Nineteen years later, in *Western & Atlantic R. Co. v. Henderson*, 279 U.S. 639, 49 S. Ct. 445, 73 L. Ed. 884 (1929), the Court overturned a Georgia statute making railroads liable for damages done by trains, unless the railroad made it appear that reasonable care had been used, the presumption being against the railroad. The declaration alleged the death of plaintiff's husband from a grade crossing collision, due to specified acts of

negligence by defendant. The jury were instructed that proof of the injury raised a presumption of negligence; the burden shifted to the railroad to prove ordinary care; and unless it did so, they should find for plaintiff. The instruction was held erroneous in an opinion stating (1) that there was no rational connection between the mere fact of collision and negligence on the part of anyone, and (2) that the statute was different from that in *Turnipseed* in imposing a burden upon the railroad. The reader is left in a state of confusion. Is the difference between a derailment and a grade crossing collision of no significance? Would the *Turnipseed* presumption have been bad if it had imposed a burden of persuasion on defendant, although that would in nowise have impaired its "rational connection"? If *Henderson* forbids imposing a burden of persuasion on defendants, what happens to affirmative defenses?

Two factors serve to explain *Henderson*. The first was that it was common ground that negligence was indispensable to liability. Plaintiff thought so, drafted her complaint accordingly, and relied upon the presumption. But how in logic could the same presumption establish her alternative grounds of negligence that the engineer was so blind he could not see decedent's truck and that he failed to stop after he saw it? Second, take away the basic assumption of no liability without fault, as *Turnipseed* intimated might be done ("considerations of public policy arising out of the character of the business"), and the structure of the decision in *Henderson* fails. No question of logic would have arisen if the statute had simply said: a *prima facie* case of liability is made by proof of injury by a train; lack of negligence is an affirmative defense, to be pleaded and proved as other affirmative defenses. The problem would be one of economic due process only. While it seems likely that the Supreme Court of 1929 would have voted that due process was denied, that result today would be unlikely. See, for example, the shift in the direction of absolute liability in the consumer cases. Prosser, The Assault upon the Citadel (Strict Liability to the Consumer), 69 Yale L.J. 1099 (1960).

Any doubts as to the constitutional permissibility of a presumption imposing a burden of persuasion of the nonexistence of the presumed fact in civil cases is laid at rest by *Dick v. New York Life Ins. Co.,* 359 U.S. 437, 79 S. Ct. 921, 3 L. Ed. 2d 935 (1959). The Court unhesitatingly applied the North Dakota rule that the presumption against suicide imposed on defendant the burden of proving that the death of insured, under an accidental death clause, was due to suicide.

"Proof of coverage and of death by gunshot wound shifts the burden to the insurer to establish that the death of the insured was due to his suicide." 359 U.S. at 443, 79 S. Ct. at 925.

"In a case like this one, North Dakota presumes that death was accidental and places on the insurer the burden of proving that death resulted from suicide." *Id.* at 446, 79 S. Ct. at 927.

§302.11 *Application of Federal Presumptions in State Cases*

Illinois courts give effect to the federal law of presumptions under the same circumstances and to the same extent to which federal courts are required to give effect to state law of presumptions. Thus a presumption representing a fact relating to a cause of action or defense as to which federal law supplies the rule of decision is to be given effect in accordance with federal law. For a discussion of the extent to which a state may or must enforce federal law, *see* Wright, The Law of Federal Courts, §45 (4th ed. 1983).

§303 Burden of Pleading and Proof in Criminal Cases

§303.1 *Allocating the Elements*

In criminal cases, the pattern of allocation resembles that of civil cases to the extent that the prosecution need not, in the first instance, assume responsibility for every element that might bear upon the guilt of the accused. Thus, conformably to the treatment accorded statutes in civil cases, §301.2 supra, the state need not initially negative an exception that is not a part of the description of the offense but withdraws certain acts or persons from the operation of the statute. *People v. Sallis,* 328 Ill. 494, 160 N.E. 86 (1928), in prosecution for carrying concealed weapons, exemption of peace officers and the like. Similarly, matters arising after the date of the alleged crime need not be dealt with by the prosecution in the first instance. *People v. Scales,* 18 Ill. 2d 283, 164 N.E.2d 76 (1960). (*Contra* as to statute of limitations. *People v. Ross,* 325 Ill. 417, 156 N.E. 303 (1927).) At this point, however, the resemblance to civil cases ends. In Illinois the accused herself, with the exception of insanity and guilty but mentally ill, is never responsible for an affirmative defense in the same sense as is a defendant in a civil case.

The term *defense* is used loosely and often misleadingly in the criminal law. The cases speak of matters such as entrapment, *People v. Guagliata,* 362 Ill. 427, 200 N.E. 169 (1936), as defenses. The Criminal Code refers to numerous matters as "affirmative defenses," for example, ignorance or mistake of law or fact under certain circumstances, 720 ILCS 5/4-8, infancy, and intoxicated or drugged condition in specified situations, *id.* 5/6-1, 5/6-3, and 5/6-4; justifiable use of force or exoneration, i.e., compulsion, entrapment or necessity, *id.* 5/7-14. In a few instances statutes expressly impose upon an accused the burden of proving himself within an exemption or exception, as with unlawful use of weapons, *id.,* 5/24-2(h); and sales of securities, 815 ILCS 5/15. Yet none of these matters is in fact a true affirmative defense as the term is used in civil cases, and no case can be found approving a jury instruction to treat them as such. Even statutory language expressly imposing a burden of proof upon the accused does not create a true affirmative defense. *People v. Durand,* 307 Ill. 611, 139 N.E 78 (1923), mitigation or excuse in homicide cases; *People v. Williams,* 23 Ill. 2d 549, 179 N.E.2d 639 (1962), narcotics concentration within statutory exemption.

The maximum effect of such a so-called affirmative defense in a criminal case is to enable the accused to impose on the prosecution responsibility for an additional element that would not otherwise constitute a part of the State's case. *People v. Durand* supra, absence of mitigation or excuse for homicide; *People v. Dollen,* 53 Ill. 2d 280, 290 N.E.2d 879 (1972), *People v. Darnell,* 214 Ill. App. 3d 345, 158 Ill. Dec. 67, 573 N.E.2d 1252 (1990), entrapment; *People v. Seaberry,* 63 Ill. App. 3d 718, 20 Ill. Dec. 533, 380 N.E.2d 511 (1978), defendant did not act in heat of passion in prosecution for murder; *People v. Tackett,* 169 Ill. App. 3d 397, 119 Ill. Dec. 891, 523 N.E.2d 647 (1988), defendant did not produce sufficient evidence to raise necessity defense in connection with unlawful use of a weapon by a felon. Some matters traditionally called defenses do not even have this effect but merely designate particular kinds of disproof of the state's case. Thus in *People v. Pearson,* 19 Ill. 2d 609, 169 N.E.2d 252 (1960), the court pointed out that alibi, often described as a defense, is no more than disproof of the state's evidence placing the accused at the scene of the crime by the introduction of evidence showing the accused was in another place at the time the act was committed. *Accord People v. Fritz,* 84 Ill. 2d 72, 48 Ill. Dec. 880, 417 N.E.2d 612 (1981). *Cf. People v. Brown,* 52 Ill. 2d 94, 285 N.E.2d 1 (1972), misleadingly indicating defendant had to raise reasonable doubt as to presence at scene of crime, thus placing upon the state the burden of negating contention beyond a reasonable doubt.

With respect to fitness to stand trial, once a defendant raises a bona fide doubt as to her fitness to stand trial, the prosecution, as a matter of due process, must prove that defendant's fitness is more probably true than not true. *People v. McCullum,* 66 Ill. 2d 306, 5 Ill. Dec. 836, 362 N.E.2d 307 (1977).

A true affirmative defense exists in criminal cases with respect to guilty but mentally ill and with respect to insanity. If the defense of guilty but mentally ill is raised at trial, the defendant bears the burden of proving that he was mentally ill by a preponderance of the evidence, i.e., more probably true than not true. 725 ILCS 5/115–4(j). If the defense of insanity is raised at trial, the defendant bears the burden of proving insanity by clear and convincing evidence. 720 ILCS 5/6–2(e). With respect to defining clear and convincing, *see* §301.6 supra.

§303.2   Burden of Pleading

In criminal cases, written pleadings remain at an unsophisticated level. An indictment or information must, of course, set forth the *prima facie* elements of the crime, *People v. Edge,* 406 Ill. 490, 94 N.E.2d 359 (1950); *People v. Chiafreddo,* 381 Ill. 214, 44 N.E.2d 888 (1942), and in this respect resembles the complaint in a civil action. As regards the accused, however, all "defenses" remain available under the general plea of not guilty, although special pleas are permissible under appropriate circumstances. *People v. Ferguson,* 20 Ill. 2d 295, 170 N.E.2d 171 (1960). It follows that the defensive pleading in the usual case serves no function of allocation and that its informational aspects go no further than to serve notice that the prosecution is put to proof of all elements of its case.

The so-called affirmative defenses in criminal cases, indicated in §303.1 supra, amount to no more than imposing on the prosecution the responsibility for an additional element, injected into the case by the presentation of some evidence thereon, by either the state or the accused. In this respect the Criminal Code, 720 ILCS 5/3-2, is declaratory of the prior law, *People v. Durand,* 307 Ill. 611, 139 N.E 78 (1923), mitigation or excuse for homicide. *See* Joint Committee Comments on Illinois Criminal Code of 1961, §3-2, (1960).

With respect to disclosure to the prosecution of defenses the accused intends to offer, including so-called affirmative defense, e.g., entrapment, and nonaffirmative defenses such as alibi, *see* Supreme Court Rule 413(d).

§303.3   Burden of Producing Evidence

The prosecution in a criminal case has the burden of going forward, of producing evidence upon which a reasonable jury, after viewing the evidence in a light most favorable to the prosecution, could conclude that each element of the substantive offense charged has been established beyond a reasonable doubt. *People v. Campbell,* 146 Ill. 2d 363, 166 Ill.

Dec. 932, 586 N.E.2d 1261 (1992). Conversely, a criminal conviction will not be set aside unless the evidence is so improbable or unsatisfactory as to create a reasonable doubt as to defendant's guilt. *People v. Manning,* 182 Ill. 2d 193, 230 Ill. Dec. 933, 695 N.E.2d 423 (1998). If the prosecution fails to meet the burden, the court must enter a judgment of acquittal. 725 ILCS 5/115-4(k). Motions for a directed verdict of acquittal may be made by the defendant at the close of the prosecution's case or at the close of all the evidence. The trial court may reserve ruling on a motion made at the close of all the evidence until the jury has returned a verdict. *People v. Wallerstedt,* 77 Ill. App. 3d 677, 33 Ill. Dec. 179, 396 N.E.2d 568 (1979).

Curiously enough, in criminal prosecutions for doing without a license an act for which a license is required, there exists a solidly entrenched exception to the principle that the prosecution must meet a burden of producing evidence as to each element of the offense. In *Williams v. People,* 121 Ill. 84, 11 N.E. 881 (1887), a prosecution for unlicensed practice of medicine, the state was held not required to produce evidence that accused had not been engaged in practice for ten years prior to the passage of the licensing statute, under a grandfather clause exempting those persons from licensing. The case is readily explainable on the theory that the exception was an "affirmative defense." *See* discussion later in this section. However, later cases have consistently held that the state need not produce evidence of the absence of a license. *People v. Handzik,* 410 Ill. 295, 102 N.E.2d 340 (1951). Since the absence of a license is an essential element of the offense, to classify the holding of a license as an affirmative defense is inconsistent with basic principles of criminal law. The reason given for this result, namely, that the matter is peculiarly within the knowledge of the accused, does not bear examination in view of the fact that licenses are granted by public bodies who must be assumed to keep records of their actions.

A burden of producing evidence is placed on the accused in criminal cases with respect to so-called affirmative defenses that he wishes to inject into the case. The burden of producing evidence placed upon the accused in order to raise an affirmative defense is satisfied, according to the Criminal Code, by the production of "some" evidence, 720 ILCS 5/3-2(a). *See also* §§303.1 and 303.2 supra. Cases have variously described the required measure as "sufficient to raise a reasonable doubt," *People v. Brown,* 52 Ill. 2d 94, 285 N.E.2d 1 (1972), alibi discussed also in §303.1 supra; *People v. Scherzer,* 179 Ill. App. 3d 624, 128 Ill. Dec. 598, 534 N.E.2d 1043 (1989); compulsion, *People v. Kite,* 153 Ill. 2d 40, 178 Ill. Dec. 769, 605 N.E.2d 563 (1992); necessity, *People v. Redmond,* 59 Ill. 2d 328, 320 N.E.2d 321 (1974); insanity prior to it becoming a true affirmative defense; or as evidence "tending to prove" the defense, *People v. Munroe,* 15 Ill. 2d 91, 154 N.E.2d 225 (1958), insanity also prior to the 1984 statutory change; or simply as "some" evidence, *People v. Cross,* 63 Ill. App. 3d 628, 20 Ill. Dec. 281, 379 N.E.2d 1319 (1978), entrapment; *People v. Woods,* 81 Ill. 2d 537, 43 Ill. Dec. 733, 410 N.E.2d 866 (1980); *People v. McDowell,* 138 Ill. App. 3d 622, 92 Ill. Dec. 855, 485 N.E.2d 1098 (1985), self-defense; *People v. Gutknecht,* 121 Ill. App. 3d 839, 77 Ill. Dec. 201, 460 N.E.2d 60 (1984), intoxication. *See also People v. Spears,* 63 Ill. App. 3d 510, 20 Ill. Dec. 445, 380 N.E.2d 423 (1978), tracing various descriptions of the test once employed with respect to insanity. Any difference in most cases will be without significance in view of the essential inexactness of any attempt to describe the quantity or quality of evidence with precision. *Cf. People v. Redmund* supra, Justice Schaeffer dissenting. The result of raising a so-called affirmative defense is to place upon the prosecution the responsibility of proving the defendant guilty beyond a reasonable doubt as to that issue together with all other elements of the offense. 720 ILCS 5/3-2(b); *People v. Woods,* 81 Ill. 2d 537, 43 Ill. Dec. 733, 410 N.E.2d 866 (1980), prosecution must prove beyond a reasonable doubt that the defendant did not reasonably believe the force he executed was necessary to prevent imminent death or great bodily harm; *People v. Washington,* 154 Ill. App. 3d 648, 107 Ill. Dec. 332, 506 N.E.2d 1387 (1987), state must demonstrate beyond a reasonable doubt that the defendant was not entrapped.

Whether a particular burden of producing or going forward with evidence has been satisifed is a question for the court in the administration of the trial; it is not a proper subject of instruction to the jury. *People v. Pearson,* 19 Ill. 2d 609, 169 N.E.2d 252 (1960). Once the court determines that the burden of producing or going forward with evidence has been satisfied, since the prosecution must prove the negative of the contention beyond a reasonable doubt (i.e., the so-called affirmative defense is now an element in the case), the assertion in *People v. Schenzer,* 179 Ill. App. 3d 624, 128 Ill. Dec. 598, 534 N.E.2d 1043 (1989), that the court may remove the element from the case as a matter of law upon a determination that there is clear and convincing evidence of its nonexistence is highly questionable as it appears to sanction directing a verdict on an element of a crime against the criminal defendant.

§303.4   Burden of Persuasion: Incidence and Measure

In criminal cases the burden on the prosecution is to prove guilt beyond a reasonable doubt, 720 ILCS 5/3-1; *In re Winship,* 397 U.S. 358 (1970), which means proof of each essential element beyond a reasonable doubt. *People v. Sanford,* 24 Ill. 2d 365, 181 N.E.2d 118 (1962); *People v. Brannon,* 56 Ill. App. 3d 531, 16 Ill. Dec. 733, 375 N.E.2d 840 (1978). *See also* Illinois Pattern Jury Instructions—Criminal 2.03 (1996). If the accused raises a so-called affirmative defense by introducing "some evidence," §303.3 supra, that element is added to the case that the prosecution must prove beyond a reasonable doubt. 720 ILCS 5/3-2(b). These statutory provisions are declaratory of the prior law. *People v. Skeoch,* 408 Ill. 276, 96 N.E.2d 473 (1951); *People v. Fiorita,* 339 Ill. 78, 170 N.E. 690 (1930). If the true affirmative defense of guilty but mentally ill is raised at trial, the defendant bears the burden of proving that he was mentally ill by a preponderance of the evidence (i.e., more probably true than not true). 725 ILCS 5/115-4(j). If the true affirmative defense of insanity is raised at trial, the defendant bears the burden of proving insanity by clear and convincing evidence. 720 ILCS 5/6–2(e). With respect to defining clear and convincing, *see* §301.6 supra.

Attempts to elaborate upon the meaning of "reasonable doubt" have been prohibited by the supreme court as unnecessary and misleading. *People v. Edwards,* 55 Ill. 2d 25, 302 N.E.2d 306 (1973), attempting to define reasonable doubt is an exercise in futility; attorney admonished to refrain from doing so. Joint Committee Comments on Illinois Criminal Code of 1961, §3.1 (1960). *See also* Illinois Pattern Jury Instructions — Criminal 2.05 (1996) recommending that no instruction defining reasonable doubt be given. *Accord People v. Speight,* 153 Ill. 2d 365, 180 Ill. Dec. 97, 606 N.E.2d 1174 (1992), neither the court nor counsel should attempt to define the reasonable doubt standard for the jury. *See also People v. Failor,* 271 Ill. App. 3d 968, 208 Ill. Dec. 681, 649 N.E.2d 1342 (1995).

Circumstantial evidence alone is sufficient even to establish the commission of a crime. *People v. Williams,* 66 Ill. 2d 478, 363 N.E.2d 801, 6 Ill. Dec. 854 (1977). Proof of circumstances must be such that on the whole each element of the offense may be found by the trier of fact to exist beyond a reasonable doubt. *People v. Magnafichi,* 9 Ill. 2d 169, 137 N.E.2d 256 (1956). The jury need not be satisfied beyond a reasonable doubt as to each link in the chain of circumstances relied upon to establish guilt; it is sufficient if all the evidence, taken together, satisfies the jury beyond a reasonable doubt of the accused's guilt. *People v. Williams* supra. Ultimately, any verdict of guilty will be sustained on appeal if, after viewing all the evidence most favorably to the prosecution, any rational trier of fact could have found the essential elements of the crime beyond a reasonable doubt. *People v. Schott,* 145 Ill. 2d 188, 164 Ill. Dec. 127, 582 N.E.2d 690 (1991).

With respect to circumstantial evidence, *see* §§401.1 to 401.4 infra. As to the presumption of innocence, *see* §304.2 infra.

§304   Presumptions in Criminal Cases

§304.1   Definition and Nature; Instructions

A presumption that is irrebuttable (i.e., conclusive) is not permitted; nor is a presumption, sometimes called a "mandatory presumption," that shifts the burden of introducing evidence to the defendant. *People v. Watts*, 181 Ill. 2d 133, 229 Ill. Dec. 542, 692 N.E.2d 315 (1998) (a presumption that shifts the burden of production to the criminal defendant is unconstitutional; citing Handbook). *See also* Graham, Handbook of Federal Evidence §303.4 (4th ed. 1996). The only function of a presumption in a criminal case is that of an instructed inference advising the jury that they are permitted but not required (i.e. "may," not "must") to find the presumed fact. *See People v. Frazier*, 123 Ill. App. 3d 563, 79 Ill. Dec. 27, 463 N.E.2d 165 (1984); *People v. Marcotte*, 217 Ill. App. 3d 797, 160 Ill. Dec. 474, 577 N.E.2d 799 (1991).

Presumptions in criminal cases, whether recognized at common law or created by statute, and whether phrased in terms of "*prima facie* evidence," "presumed," or "presumption," should all be treated identically. If a presumed fact establishes guilt or is an element of the offense or negatives a defense, the court may submit the question of guilt or of the existence of the presumed fact to the jury only if a reasonable juror on the evidence as a whole, including the evidence of the basic facts, could find guilt or the presumed fact beyond a reasonable doubt. However, if the presumed fact has only a lesser effect, the question of its existence may be submitted to the jury provided the basic facts are supported by substantial evidence or are otherwise established, unless the court determines that a reasonable juror on the evidence as a whole could not find the existence of the presumed fact.

Whenever the existence of a presumed fact against the accused is submitted to the jury, the court may instruct the jury that if they find the basic fact to exist they may, but are not required to, infer the presumed fact. In addition, if the presumed fact establishes guilt, is an element of the offense, or negatives a so-called affirmative defense, the court must instruct the jury that its existence on all the evidence must be proved beyond a reasonable doubt. Under no circumstances is the judge permitted to direct the jury to find a presumed fact against an accused. *People v. Watts,* 181 Ill. 2d 133, 229 Ill. Dec. 542, 692 N.E.2d 315 (1998). *See also* Proposed Federal Rule of Evidence 303, 56 F.R.D. 183, 212 (1973); Rule 303(b), Revised Uniform Rules of Evidence (1974). *Cf.* Illinois Pattern Jury Instructions — Criminal 13.34 (1996), Inference Arising from Exclusive Possession of Recently Stolen Property (which is still probably in need of revision). However, due process requires that the court instruct the jury on the inference that arises from the basic fact to the presumed (i.e., "inferred"), fact, only if there is a sufficient rational connection between the basic fact and the fact to be inferred. Whether a sufficient rational connection exists between the basic fact and the fact to be inferred to warrant giving an instruction, or the particular instruction given, depends not only upon the natural strength of the logical inference, but also upon the wording of the instruction. Rational connection also varies depending on whether the fact to be inferred is an element of the offense, negates a so-called affirmative defense, or has a lesser effect.

Thus, for example, if the fact to be inferred is an element of a crime or negates a so-called affirmative defense, and if a sufficient rational connection exists, the jury may be instructed that if they find the basic fact beyond a reasonable doubt, they may, but are not required to, infer the inferred fact. A sufficient rational connection exists for giving such an instruction if the court determines that proof of the basic fact establishes the fact to be inferred to be more probably true than not true. *People v. Ward,* 194 Ill. App. 3d 229, 141 Ill. Dec. 162, 550 N.E.2d 1208 (1990). Imposing the more-probably-true-than-not-true threshold standard prevents the jury from giving excessive weight to an inference with little probative value, a distortion that may occur simply because the court has given an instruction concerning the inference. However, the existence of the fact to be inferred may be submitted for the jury's determination if, but only if, a reasonable juror on the evidence taken as a whole could find the inferred fact beyond a reasonable doubt. The jury must be instructed accordingly. *See People v. Hester,* 131 Ill. 2d 91, 136 Ill. Dec. 111, 544 N.E.2d 797 (1989).

The foregoing description of the nature and workings of a presumption in a criminal case operating against the accused does not comport with the definition of a presumption in a civil case. In criminal cases there can be no compelled finding of the presumed fact. Upon a finding of the basic fact, the trier of fact in a criminal matter may, but is not required to, find the presumed fact; the presumption is "may" rather than "must." Neither the burden of production nor the burden of persuasion ever shifts to the defendant. *People v. Watts,* 181 Ill. 2d 133, 229 Ill. Dec. 542, 692 N.E.2d 315 (1998). Thus a presumption employed in criminal cases operating against the accused corresponds to an inference in a civil case. *See* §302.2 supra. In the criminal context use of the term *instructed inference* rather than *presumption* would promote clarity.

The purpose of a presumption operating against the accused in a criminal case is to guide the jury by highlighting the propriety of drawing a factual inference they might otherwise be naturally less likely to draw. A jury's reluctance to draw the inference may arise simply because the jury is unaware that once having found particular facts to exist, they may infer an element of the offense such as intent or knowledge. In other cases, the reluctance to infer arises because the jury may be unaware, absent an instruction, that a particular fact naturally flows from certain other facts they have found to exist. This occurs, for example, with the presumption that illegal importation of narcotics may be inferred solely from possession of certain specified narcotic drugs by the defendant in this country. Encouraging the trier of fact to draw such factual inferences operates to the obvious benefit of the prosecution.

In practice presumptions rarely play a significant role in Illinois criminal trials. With respect to criminal statutes the

terms *presumption, presumed,* and *prima facie evidence,* with nota-
ble exceptions, not only appear relatively infrequently in the
criminal statute but in relatively minor sections. *See, e.g.,* 720
ILCS 5/11-20(2), Obscenity; 5/16-1.1, Theft by Lessee; 5/17-
1, Deceptive Practices; 5/24-1(d), Unlawful Use of Weapons;
5/24-5, Defacing Identification Mark on Firearms; 5/39-1,
Criminal Usury; 415 ILCS 105/7, Abandonment of Motor
Vehicle. 815 ILCS 515/3, Home Repair Fraud, which shifted
the burden of production and/or the burden of persuasion to
the criminal defendant, was declared unconstitutional in *People v. Watts,* 181 Ill. 2d 133, 229 Ill. Dec. 542, 692 N.E.2d 315
(1998). The breath alcohol presumption is, however, rather
common. The form of inference instruction that should be
given is discussed in *People v. Hester,* 131 Ill. 2d 91, 136 Ill. Dec.
111, 544 N.E.2d 797 (1989), where the Supreme Court approved the trial court's substitution of the word "may" for
"shall" in Illinois Pattern Jury Instructions—Criminal 23.30
(1996). *See also People v. Haas,* 203 Ill. App. 3d 779, 148 Ill. Dec.
667, 560 N.E.2d 1365 (1990). Another commonly occurring
presumption in criminal cases is the inference arising from
the possession of recently stolen property. An inference instruction with respect to possession of recently stolen property
does not infringe upon due process if (1) there is a rational
connection between possession of the recently stolen property and the offense charged, (2) the offense charged is more
likely than not to flow from the recent possession, and (3)
there is evidence corroborating the accused's guilt. *People v.
Housby,* 84 Ill. 2d 415, 50 Ill. Dec. 834, 420 N.E.2d 151 (1981);
People v. Jones, 105 Ill. 2d 342, 86 Ill. Dec. 453, 475 N.E.2d 832
(1985). *See also People v. Ferguson,* 204 Ill. App. 3d 146, 149 Ill.
Dec. 422, 561 N.E.2d 1118 (1990); *People v. Speed,* 106 Ill. App.
3d 890, 62 Ill. Dec. 686, 436 N.E.2d 712 (1982); *People v. Jones,*
64 Ill. App. 3d 1018, 21 Ill. Dec. 791, 382 N.E.2d 85 (1978). *See
generally People v. Houston,* 118 Ill. 2d 194, 113 Ill. Dec. 77, 514
N.E.2d 989 (1987). With respect to child abduction, 720 ILCS
5/10-5, *see People v. Patten,* 230 Ill. App. 3d 922, 172 Ill. Dec.
471, 595 N.E.2d 1141 (1992).

With respect to the constitutionality of the inference arising from possession of recently stolen property, *see* §304.3 infra. As to the presumption of identity of a person, *see* §302.6 supra.

§304.2   Presumption of Innocence

The presumption of innocence in criminal cases is not a presumption in the usual sense but rather a forceful way of saying that the prosecution must prove guilt beyond a reasonable doubt and that there is to be no inference against the defendant because of his arrest, indictment, or presence as a defendant in court. The continued existence of the presumption of innocence is recognized specifically in the Criminal Code of 1961, 720 ILCS 5/3-1; Joint Committee Comments on Illinois Criminal Code of 1961, §3-1 (1960). *See also* Illinois Pattern Jury Instructions — Criminal 2.03 (1996). If requested by the defendant, an instruction with respect to the presumption of innocence is required by the Due Process Clause of the Fourteenth Amendment, *Taylor v. Kentucky*, 436 U.S. 478 (1978).

§304.3   Constitutionality of Presumptions in Criminal Cases

With respect to the constitutionality of presumptions in criminal cases, the Advisory Committee's Note to proposed Federal Rule 301, 56 F.R.D. 181, 210-211 (1973) states:

> The rational connection requirments [between the basic fact and the presumed fact] survives in criminal cases, *Tot v. United States*, 319 U.S. 463, 63 S. Ct. 1241, 87 L. Ed. 1519 (1943), because the Court has been unwilling to extend into that area the greater-includes-the-lesser theory of *Ferry v. Ramsey*, 277 U.S. 88, 48 S. Ct. 443, 72 L. Ed. 796 (1928). In that case the Court sustained a Kansas statute under which bank directors were personally liable for deposits made with their assent and with knowledge of insolvency, and the fact of insolvency was prima facie evidence of

assent and knowledge of insolvency. Mr. Justice Holmes pointed out that the state legislature could have made the directors personally liable to depositors in every case. Since the statute imposed a less stringent liability, "the thing to be considered is the result reached, not the possibly inartificial or clumsy way of reaching it." *Id.* at 94, 48 S. Ct. at 444. Mr. Justice Sutherland dissented: though the state could have created an absolute liability, it did not purport to do so; a rational connection was necessary, but lacking, between the liability created and the prima facie evidence of it; the result might be different if the basis of the presumption were being open for business.

The Sutherland view has prevailed in criminal cases by virtue of the higher standard of notice there required. The fiction that everyone is presumed to know the law is applied to the substantive law of crimes as an alternative to complete unenforceability. But the need does not extend to criminal evidence and procedure, and the fiction does not encompass them. "Rational connection" is not fictional or artificial, and so it is reasonable to suppose that Gainey should have known that his presence at the site of an illicit still could convict him of being connected with (carrying on) the business, *United States v. Gainey,* 380 U.S. 63, 85 S. Ct. 754, 13 L. Ed. 2d 658 (1965), but not that Romano should have known that his presence at a still could convict him of possessing it, *United States v. Romano,* 382 U.S. 136, 86 S. Ct. 279, 15 L. Ed. 2d 210 (1965).

In his dissent in *Gainey,* Mr. Justice Black put it more artistically:

> It might be argued, although the Court does not so argue or hold, that Congress if it wished could make presence at a still a crime in itself, and so Congress should be free to create crimes which are called "possession" and "carrying on an illegal distillery business" but which are defined in such a way that unexplained presence is sufficient and indisputable evidence in all cases to support conviction for those offenses. *See Ferry v. Ramsey,* 277 U.S. 88, 48 S. Ct. 443, 72 L. Ed. 796. Assuming for the sake of argument that Congress could make unexplained presence a criminal act, and ignoring also the refusal of this Court in other cases to uphold a statutory presumption on such a theory, *see Heiner v. Donnan,* 285 U.S. 312, 52 S. Ct. 358, 76 L. Ed. 772, there is no indication here that Congress intended to adopt such a misleading method of draftsmanship, nor in my judgment could the statutory provisions if so con-

strued escape condemnation for vagueness, under the principles applied in *Lanzetta v. New Jersey,* 306 U.S. 451, 59 S. Ct. 618, 83 L. Ed. 888, and many other cases. 380 U.S. at 84, n.12, 85 S. Ct. at 766.

And the majority opinion in *Romano* agreed with him:

> It may be, of course, that Congress has the power to make presence at an illegal still a punishable crime, but we find no clear indication that it intended to so exercise this power. The crime remains possession, not presence, and with all due deference to the judgment of Congress, the former may not constitutionally be inferred from the latter. 382 U.S. at 144, 86 S. Ct. at 284.

The rule does not spell out the procedural aspects of its application. Questions as to when the evidence warrants submission of a presumption and what instructions are proper under varying states of fact are believed to present no particular difficulties.

The already complex situation with respect to the constitutionality of criminal presumptions was further complicated by the United States Supreme Court's confusing opinions in *County Court of Ulster County v. Allen,* 442 U.S. 140 (1979), and *Sandstrom v. Montana,* 442 U.S. 510 (1979), introducing the concepts of permissive and mandatory presumptions. The United States Supreme Court's opinion in *Francis v. Fanklin,* 471 U.S. 307 (1985), did nothing to clarify the situation. This confusion was carried forward by the Illinois Supreme Court in its discussion of the constitutionality of the inference arising from exclusive possession of recently stolen property in *People v. Housby,* 84 Ill. 2d 415, 50 Ill. Dec. 834, 420 N.E.2d (1981). *Cf.* excellent discussion in *People v. Embry,* 177 Ill. App. 3d 96, 126 Ill. Dec. 503, 531 N.E.2d 1130 (1988) (mandatory presumptions are unconstitutional). *See also People v. Ziltz,* 98 Ill. 2d 38, 74 Ill. Dec. 40, 455 N.E.2d 70 (1983); *People v. Frazier,* 123 Ill. App. 3d 563, 79 Ill. Dec. 27, 463 N.E.2d 165 (1984). *Accord People v. Atteberry,* 213 Ill. App. 3d 851, 157 Ill. Dec. 365, 572 N.E.2d 434 (1991), an instruction employing the term "prima facie" impermissibly shifted the burden of persuasion to the defendant. Fortunately the Illinois Supreme Court in *People v. Watts,* 181 Ill. 2d 133, 229 Ill. Dec. 542, 692 N.E.2d 315 (1998), clarified the situation when it correctly declared that 815 ILCS 515/3, Home Repair Fraud, which shifted the burden of production and/or the burden of persuasion to the criminal defendant, was unconstitutional.

The Illinois Supreme Court in *Housby* observed that a permissive presumption operating against the criminal defendant may be the subject of an inference instruction to the jury if:

> (i) there was a rational connection between his recent possession of property stolen in the burglary and his participation in the burglary; (ii) his guilt of burglary is more likely than not to flow from his recent, unexplained and exclusive possession of burglary proceeds; and (iii) there was evidence corroborating [defendant's] guilt. [84 Ill. 2d at 424.]

Accord People v. Lewis, 88 Ill. 2d 129, 164, 58 Ill. Dec. 895, 430 N.E.2d 1346 (1981). *See also People v. Mallette,* 131 Ill. App. 3d 67, 86 Ill. Dec. 240, 475 N.E.2d 237 (1985). As interpreted in *People v. Johnson,* 96 Ill. App. 3d 1123, 1125-1126, 52 Ill. Dec. 338, 442 N.E.2d 19 (1981), a presumption may be the subject of an inference instruction to the jury under the following circumstances:

> (1) there must be a rational connection between the basic facts that the prosecution proved and the ultimate fact presumed and the latter is more likely than not to flow from the former; (2) a permissive inference which requires the inference be supported by corroborating evidence of guilt is proper because the permissive inference may always be rejected by the fact finder and where there is corroborating evidence, the permissive inference is not the sole and sufficient basis for a guilty finding, it is unnecessary to establish that the inference follows beyond a reasonable doubt from the proved fact, for proof of the elements of the offense beyond a reasonable doubt may be done by resort to all the evidence, including the inference and (3) where the permissive inference is unsupported by corroborating

evidence, the leap from the proved fact to the presumed element must satisfy proof beyond a reasonable doubt because there is nothing else on which to rest the fact finder's guilty verdict.

Given the infrequent use of presumptions in criminal trials in Illinois, a full discussion of the constitutionality of criminal presumptions is inconsistent with the purpose of this Handbook. For further discussion of the constitutionality of criminal presumptions, *see* Graham, Presumptions—More Than You Ever Wanted to Know and Yet Were Too Disinterested to Ask, 17 Crim. L. Bull. 431 (1981).

ARTICLE IV
Relevancy and Its Limits

§401   Relevant Evidence

§401.1   *Definition of Relevant Evidence: Materiality and "Fact of Consequence"*

In *People v. Monroe,* 66 Ill. 2d 317, 5 Ill. Dec. 824, 362 N.E.2d 295 (1977), *In re Elias,* 114 Ill. 2d 321, 102 Ill. Dec. 314, 499 N.E.2d 1327 (1986), and *People v. Boclair,* 129 Ill. 2d 458, 136 Ill. Dec. 29, 544 N.E.2d 715 (1989), the Court adopted Rule 401 of the Federal Rules of Evidence, 65 F.R.D. 131, 142 (1975), which provides: " 'Relevant evidence' means evidence having any tendency to make the existence of any fact that is of consequence to the determination of the action more probable or less probable than it would be without the evidence." *Accord People v. Hope,* 168 Ill. 2d 1, 212 Ill. Dec. 909, 658 N.E.2d 391 (1995). Quoted with similar approval was the following segment of the Advisory Committee's Note to Rule 401:

> Problems of relevancy call for an answer to the question whether an item of evidence, when tested by the processes of legal reasoning, possesses sufficient probative value to justify receiving it in evidence. . . .
>
> Relevancy is not an inherent characteristic of any item of evidence but exists only as a relation between an item of evidence and a matter properly provable in the case. Does the item of evidence tend to prove the matter sought to be proved? Whether the relationship exists depends upon principles evolved by experience or science, applied logically to the situation at hand. . . .
>
> The rule uses the phrase "fact that is of consequence to the determination of the action" to describe the kind of fact to which proof may properly be directed. The language is that of California Evidence Code §210; it has the advantage of avoiding the loosely used and ambiguous word "material." Tentative Recommendation and a Study Relating to the Uniform Rules of Evidence (Art. I. General Provisions), Cal. Law Revision Comm'n, Rep., Rec. & Studies, 10-11 (1964). The fact to be proved may be ultimate, intermediate, or evidentiary; it matters not, so long as it is of consequence in the determination of the action. . . .

Accord People v. Free, 94 Ill. 2d 378, 69 Ill. Dec. 1, 447 N.E.2d 218 (1983); *People v. Johnson,* 114 Ill. 2d 170, 102 Ill. Dec. 342, 499 N.E.2d 1355 (1986); *People v. Lewis,* 165 Ill. 2d 305, 209 Ill. Dec. 144, 651 N.E.2d 72 (1995).

While the phraseology is slightly different, the concept of relevancy expressed in Federal Rule 401 comports with prior Illinois decisions. For example, in *Marut v. Costello,* 34 Ill. 2d 125, 128, 214 N.E.2d 768 (1966), the court stated, "Relevancy is established where a fact offered tends to prove a fact in controversy or renders a matter in issue more or less probable. To be probable, it must be tested in the light of logic, experience and accepted assumptions as to human behavior." Notice that the phrase "fact of consequence to the determination of the litigation" is employed in Federal Rule 401 in place of the common law term "material," a term that has proved ambiguous. *See* Federal Advisory Committee's Note *supra.* Use of the phrase "fact of consequence" in place of materiality also serves to make clear that the breadth of admissibility of relevant evidence extends to facts not in dispute. *People v. Cannon,* 49 Ill. 2d 162, 273 N.E.2d 829 (1971), identity of victims and fact they were deceased; *People v. Botulinski,* 392 Ill. 212, 64 N.E.2d 486 (1946), prosecutor not barred from proving a fact even if the defendant admits or stipulates to it; *Minnis v. Friend,* 360 Ill. 328, 196 N.E. 191 (1935), right to display personal injuries to the jury even if no controversy exists as to the existence, nature, and extent thereof; *People v. Chatman,* 110 Ill. App. 3d 19, 65 Ill. Dec. 778, 441 N.E.2d 1292 (1982), the prosecution may ask the victim to display the area where he was shot in spite of the defendant's offer to stipulate because the prosecution has the right to prove every element of the crime. Whether to admit evidence upon a point conceded by an opponent should be decided on the basis of trial concerns such as waste of time and considerations of unfair prejudice, §403.1 *infra.*

In addition, evidence that is essentially background in nature offered as an aid to understanding may be admitted even if not disputed. *See* Federal Advisory Committee's Note to Rule 401, 56 F.R.D. 183, 216 (1973). Such items include, for example, charts, photographs, views of real estate, and murder weapons. Similarly, a police officer may testify concerning investigatory procedures. *People v. Colts,* 269 Ill. App. 3d 679, 206 Ill. Dec. 220, 645 N.E.2d 225 (1993). *See also* §801.5 *infra.* Also included are the physical characteristics of a person as well as a person's personal and family history when stated in general terms, *see People v. Lewis,* 165 Ill. 2d 305, 209 Ill. Dec. 144, 651 N.E.2d 72 (1995), victim's gender, weight, and the fact that no needle marks were present is admissible, as is the testimony of a life-and-death witness given for the purpose of identifying the decedent indicating the victim left a spouse or children, if elicited in an incidental manner not causing the jury to believe such evidence is material. *People v. Salazar,* 126 Ill. 2d 424, 129 Ill. Dec. 1, 535 N.E.2d 766 (1988). Also admissible is an incidental reference to victim's personal traits, *People v. Williams,* 147 Ill. 2d 173, 167 Ill. Dec. 853, 588 N.E.2d 983 (1991), such as that the victim was returning home from church services immediately prior to the shooting. *People v. Williams,* 161 Ill. 2d 1, 204 N.E.2d 72, 641 N.E.2d 296 (1994). Evidence of family background is likely to be considered improper material where the victim is a spouse or family breadwinner but not usually where the victim is either a sibling or an adult child of a parent, that is, a dependent situation is usually absent with respect to such individuals. *See generally People v. Lewis* supra; *People v. Johnson,* 149 Ill. 2d 118, 171 Ill. Dec. 401, 594 N.E.2d 253 (1992); *People v. Holman,* 103 Ill. 2d 133, 82 Ill. Dec. 585, 469 N.E.2d 119 (1984); *People v. Bernette,* 30 Ill. 2d 359, 197 N.E.2d 436 (1964). *Compare People v. Grisset,* 288 Ill. App. 3d 620, 224 Ill. Dec. 389, 681 N.E.2d 1010 (1997) (not error to preclude witness on direct examination from testifying as to how long he had been living with his grandmother and testifying as to whether the witness was currently employed). Whether such improper material was elicited incidentally or dwelled upon during trial is to be considered in deciding whether its introduction in the absence of a sustained objection and instruction to disregard constitutes reversible error. *People v. Lewis* supra; *People v. Bernette* supra; *People v. Dukes,* 12 Ill. 2d 334, 146 N.E.2d 14 (1957). Similarly, in a civil case, evidence of proprietary interest or occupation is not improper if presented in passing and not unduly emphasized so as not to highlight a party's financial condition, *Lagoni v. Holiday Inn Midway,* 262 Ill. App. 3d 1020, 200 Ill. Dec. 283, 635 N.E.2d 622 (1994). Identical treatment is given to evidence of plaintiff's family circumstances. *Le Master v. Chicago Rock Island and Pacific R.R. Co.,* 35 Ill. App. 3d 1001, 343 N.E.2d 65 (1976) (family circumstances not elicited in manner so as to elicit special sympathy or compassion). On the other hand, as previously alluded to, testimony in a criminal case regarding the impact of the victim's death on the victim's family is improper. *People v. Kitchen,* 159 Ill. 2d 1, 201

Ill. Dec. 1, 636 N.E.2d 433 (1994); *People v. Del Vecchio,* 129 Ill. 2d 265, 135 Ill. Dec. 816, 544 N.E.2d 312 (1989). Finally, the term *fact of consequence* includes facts bearing circumstantially upon the evaluation of the probative value to be given to other evidence in the case, including the credibility of witnesses. Included in this category are demeanor, personal knowledge, impeachment, rehabilitation, and background biographical information concerning a witness.

The terms *material* (now *fact of consequence*), and *relevant* to a considerable extent were previously used interchangeably, and evidence that was objected to as immaterial was likely also to be objected to as irrelevant. However, considerable clarification is gained by distinguishing between the propriety of the proposition to be established and the propriety of the proof to establish it. To illustrate in a medical malpractice action, let's assume that the plaintiff wishes to introduce evidence that the doctor was drunk the night before the operation. If the plaintiff is asserting that the doctor failed to perform the procedure properly, such evidence is relevant. However if the plaintiff is only asserting that the procedure selected two weeks before the operation was not suitable, then evidence of drunkenness is irrelevant, as the condition of the doctor on the day of the operation is not of consequence. *Fact of consequence* then describes a proposition that is in the case, and *relevant* describes evidence that has a tendency to prove or disprove a proposition. *See Yamnitz v. William J. Diestelhorst Co.,* 251 Ill. App. 3d 244, 190 Ill. Dec. 593, 621 N.E.2d 1046 (1993) (citing Handbook). Whether a fact is of consequence is determined by the substantive law, within the framework of the pleadings. *Department of Transportation v. LaSalle National Bank,* 251 Ill. App. 3d 901, 191 Ill. Dec. 145, 623 N.E.2d 390 (1993) (citing Handbook); *Spencer v. Wandolowski,* 264 Ill. App. 3d 611, 201 Ill. Dec. 422, 636 N.E.2d 854 (1994). For example, evidence of contributory negligence by the parents of a plaintiff of tender years is properly excluded, since their negligence as a matter of law is not imputed to the child, *Romine v. City of Watseka,* 341 Ill. App 370, 91 N.E.2d 76 (1950), and in an action on a note, with no denial of execution in the answer, evidence of non-execution offered by defendant maker is properly excluded as not within the issue. *Bailey v. Valley Natl. Bank*, 127 Ill. 332, 19 N.E. 695 (1889). *See also Banovz v. Rantanen*, 271 Ill. App. 3d 910, 208 Ill. Dec. 617, 649 N.E.2d 977 (1995).

Relevancy is any tendency to render a proposition in the case more or less probable than it would be without the evidence, in the light of logic, experience, and accepted assumptions concerning human behavior. *People v. Newsome*, 291 Ill. 11, 125 N.E. 735 (1920), in prosecution for altering ballots, proper to admit prior statements by accused that it would be easy to alter ballots; *Buttita v. Lawrence*, 346 Ill. 164, 178 N.E. 390 (1931), in action for false representations as to value of worthless notes given in exchange for property, error to exclude evidence for defendant that property was worth little more than mortgage on it, since this would reduce probability that representations were made; *Fox v. Hopkins*, 343 Ill. App. 404, 99 N.E.2d 363 (1951), evidence of drunkenness properly admitted to prove negligence in failing to keep proper lookout and driving on wrong side; *Klavine v. Hair*, 29 Ill. App. 3d 483, 331 N.E.2d 355 (1975), evidence as to speed of car 300 yards prior to accident improperly excluded; *People v. Merritt*, 64 Ill. App. 3d 482, 21 Ill. Dec. 298, 381 N.E.2d 407 (1978), in prosecution for rape, statement of defendant that he was a "pimp" was relevant in light of his request that victim work as prostitute for him and statement after intercourse that now she really was a whore; *People v. Johnson*, 114 Ill. 2d 170, 102 Ill. Dec. 342, 499 N.E.2d 1355 (1986), the state must be permitted to make some explanation why a previously unidentified defendant was arrested and shown to the victim of a crime; *People v. Sadaka*, 174 Ill. App. 3d 260, 123 Ill. Dec. 738, 528 N.E.2d 283 (1988), evidence showing that defendant carried the telephone number of a known drug trafficker was relevant to establish knowledge of possession of heroin; *People v. Peeples*, 155 Ill. 2d 422, 186 Ill. Dec. 341, 616 N.E.2d 294 (1993), testimony concerning tabulations of African-Americans in jury venire composition in the third district relevant to discrimination. On the other hand, *see, e.g., People v. Hope,* 168 Ill. 2d 1, 212 Ill. Dec. 909, 658 N.E.2d 391 (1995), whether the police officer had seen newspaper articles or photos of the defendant was not relevant since the police officer was not a witness to the crime being asked to identify the defendant as the perpetrator; *People v. Lewis,* 165 Ill. 2d 305, 209 Ill. Dec. 144, 651 N.E.2d 72 (1995), fact that victim was pregnant has absolutely no relationship to defendant's guilt or innocence; *People v. Hope,* 116 Ill. 2d 265, 108 Ill. Dec. 41, 508 N.E.2d 202 (1986), fact that murder victim left a family has no relationship to guilt or innocence of accused; *People v. Stewart,* 105 Ill. 2d 22, 85 Ill. Dec. 241, 473 N.E.2d 840 (1984), names of persons portrayed in a photographic line-up were not relevant; *People v. Daniels,* 172 Ill. App. 3d 616, 122 Ill. Dec. 687, 527 N.E.2d 59 (1988), testimony as to therapy administered to alleged victim of sexual abuse standing alone is not relevant to defendant's guilt; *People v. Jones,* 219 Ill. App. 3d 795, 162 Ill. Dec. 156, 579 N.E.2d 970 (1991), failure of a person to identify anyone at a lineup does not make it more or less likely that the person correctly identified the defendant in a subsequent lineup; *People v. Shelton,* 293 Ill. App. 3d 747, 228 Ill. Dec. 133, 688 N.E.2d 831 (1997), improper to admit obituary notice with respect to the victim. As to when earlier driving of a party involved in an accident is relevant to what happened at the site of the collision, *see Spencer v. Wandolowski,* 264 Ill. App. 3d 611, 201 Ill. Dec. 422, 636 N.E.2d 854 (1994). The concept of relevancy must be kept separate from any issue as to sufficiency of evidence for any purpose such as to satisfy a burden of production, §§301.4, 303.3 supra. *People v. Peeples,* 155 Ill. 2d 422, 186 Ill. Dec. 341, 616 N.E.2d 294 (1993) (citing Handbook). As McCormick, Evidence §185 at 776 (4th ed. 1992), states, "[A] brick is not a wall."

Evidence may be either direct or circumstantial. *People v. Sherman,* 110 Ill. App. 3d 854, 65 Ill. Dec. 581, 441 N.E.2d 896 (1982). Direct evidence is evidence where the sole inference that must be made to establish a fact of consequence is the truth of the matter asserted. Testimony such as "I saw *X* shoot

B," is direct evidence as to a fact of consequence. Circumstantial evidence involves evidence offered to establish a fact of consequence where an inference in addition to the truth of the matter stated needs to be made. *Devine v. Delano,* 272 Ill. 166, 111 N.E. 742 (1916); *People v. Jenkins,* 117 Ill. App. 3d 33, 72 Ill. Dec. 614, 452 N.E.2d 867 (1983). Thus evidence that *X* fled the scene would be circumstantial evidence of the murderous act. *People v. Rhodes,* 85 Ill. 2d 241, 52 Ill. Dec. 603, 422 N.E.2d 605 (1981), circumstantial evidence is proof of certain facts from which a jury may infer other connected facts that reasonably follow according to the common experience of mankind. The inference to be drawn need not be the only conclusion logically to be drawn; it suffices that the suggested inference may reasonably be drawn therefrom. *Mort v. Walter,* 98 Ill. 2d 391, 75 Ill. Dec. 228, 457 N.E.2d 18 (1983). Questions of relevancy arise solely with respect to circumstantial evidence. McCormick, Evidence §185 (4th ed. 1992).

Evidence that is relevant is admissible except as otherwise provided by law. *People v. Peeples,* 155 Ill. 2d 422, 186 Ill. Dec. 341, 616 N.E.2d 294 (1993) (citing Handbook); *People ex rel. Noren v. Dempsey,* 10 Ill. 2d 288, 139 N.E.2d 780 (1957). Evidence that is not relevant is not admissible, §402.1 infra. The determination of relevancy rests with the sound discretion of the trial court and will be disturbed on review only if clearly abused. *People v. Boclair,* 129 Ill. 2d 458, 136 Ill. Dec. 29, 544 N.E.2d 715 (1989). In addition, relevant evidence may be excluded where it lacks sufficient probative value when considered in light of the danger of unfair prejudice, the likelihood of confusion of the issues, misleading the jury and considerations of undue delay, waste of time or the needless presentation of cumulative evidence, §403.1 infra. In considering the admissibility of the types of evidence discussed in the sections that follow, the determination of logical relevancy in practice frequently, albeit improperly, merges with the foregoing concerns comprising grounds for exclusion. *See, e.g., People v. Littlejohn,* 144 Ill. App. 3d 813, 98 Ill. Dec. 555, 494 N.E.2d 677 (1986), evidence of finding at fitness hearing is irrelevant on issue of insanity; *Elder on Behalf of*

Finney v. Finney, 256 Ill. App. 3d 424, 194 Ill. Dec. 896, 628 N.E.2d 393 (1993), because people argue and get mad is irrelevant as to whether they ever again had sexual relations with each other; *People v. Goodloe,* 263 Ill. App. 3d 1060, 201 Ill. Dec. 609, 636 N.E.2d 1041 (1994), prior inconsistent statement by person that she was drinking all day irrelevant on impairment because of the dearth of other evidence. Both aspects of admissibility are discussed together in each section as a matter of convenience to the reader.

§401.2 Demonstrative and Real Evidence: Definitions

The term *demonstrative* evidence is often used to describe means of proof other than the conventional giving of oral testimony and the use of ordinary documentary exhibits. Demonstrative evidence as thus employed is evidence from which the trier of fact may derive a relevant sense impression. However, the foregoing definition is so broad as to be of little assistance; analysis is fostered by treating separately its two component parts, real and demonstrative evidence.

Real evidence involves the production of some object that had a direct part in the incident, such as a murder weapon or a piece of exploding bottle, and includes the exhibition of injured parts of the body. Courts are to weigh the explanatory value of an object against its possible unfair prejudicial effect with no flat rule that a gruesome object may not be introduced, §403.1 infra. Demonstrative evidence, including such items as a model, map, photograph, X-ray, or demonstration, is distinguished from real evidence in that it has no probative value itself, but serves merely as a visual aid to the jury in comprehending the verbal testimony of a witness or other evidence. For further discussion of the independent probative value of a photograph, *see* §401.8 infra. Thus demonstrative evidence includes techniques using visual aids and demonstrations that may not be, in the strict sense, actually offered as evidence. *Cisarik v. Palos Community Hospital,* 144 Ill. 2d 339, 162 Ill. Dec. 59, 579 N.E.2d 873 (1991) (citing Handbook). *See generally Smith v. Ohio Oil Co.,* 10 Ill. App. 2d 67, 134 N.E.2d 526 (1956), holding skeleton properly admitted to illustrate medical testimony and distinguishing between "real" and "demonstrative" evidence.

The convincing power and appeal of evidence of this kind may be very great, and it has been termed the "most convincing and satisfactory class of proof." *Virgil v. New York, C. & St. L.R. Co.,* 347 Ill. App. 281, 106 N.E.2d 749 (1952).

§401.3   *Demonstrative and Real Evidence: Relevancy*

The relevancy aspects of demonstrative and real evidence are no different from other evidence: if its appearance or other physical characteristics render a proposition in issue more or less probable, the demonstrative or real evidence is relevant. The requirement is met by demonstrative evidence that promotes understanding of other relevant evidence. With respect to demonstrative evidence, the verbal testimony, which it aids in understanding, must of course itself be relevant to a fact of consequence in the litigation.

Real evidence may be direct, as when the condition of the object itself is an issue, *Virgil v. New York, C. & St. L.R. Co.,* 347 Ill. App. 281, 106 N.E.2d 749 (1952), angle cock itself offered issue as to whether it was defective at time of injury; or it may be circumstantial, affording inferences as to matters in issue, *Tudor Iron Works v. Weber,* 129 Ill. 535, 21 N.E. 1078 (1889), clothing worn by plaintiff, caught and torn by machinery at time of injury; *Burns v. West Chem. Prod., Inc.,* 12 Ill. App. 3d 947, 299 N.E.2d 455 (1973), shoe worn by truck driver on day injured at loading dock. The only showing required of direct evidence is that it is genuinely what it purports to be and, if essential to probative value, that its condition is unchanged. *See generally* §§901 and 902 infra. Circumstantial demonstrative evidence shares the problems of circumstantial evidence generally. More detailed treatment is given in connection with particular topics.

§401.4   Real Evidence: Tangible Objects

Tangible objects of almost every kind involved in an incident have been ruled properly admitted as tending to establish a fact of consequence. *Henry v. People,* 198 Ill. 162, 65 N.E. 120 (1902), buggy in which deceased was shot and clothes that he wore; *People v. Tilley,* 406 Ill. 398, 94 N.E.2d 328 (1950), preserved female organs of deceased in murder by abortion; *Ostendorf v. Brewer,* 51 Ill. App. 3d 1009, 367 N.E.2d 214, 9 Ill. Dec. 780 (1977), tractor gas tank involved in accident; *People v. Valentino,* 131 Ill. App. 3d 257, 86 Ill. Dec. 413, 475 N.E.2d 627 (1985), semen deposit; *People v. Jurczak,* 147 Ill. App. 3d 206, 101 Ill. Dec. 19, 497 N.E.2d 1332 (1986), victim's bloodstained clothing; *People v. Speirs,* 231 Ill. App. 3d 807, 173 Ill. Dec. 378, 596 N.E.2d 1257 (1992), display of tattoo on right arm of the defendant. The fact of consequence to which the object relates need not be in dispute. *See* §401.1 supra. Relevant real evidence may be excluded, however, on the grounds of unfair prejudice in accordance with §403.1 infra. Often evidence in the form of a tangible object is duplicative of other evidence and potentially excludable on this ground. *See* §403.1 infra. Nevertheless, in view of the present general acceptance of evidence of this nature, the exclusion of an object of undoubted relevance and probative value on either ground is unlikely. With respect to a controverted fact, exclusion is likely to be regarded as an abuse of discretion. *See Virgil v. New York, C. & St. L.R. Co.,* 347 Ill. App. 281, 106 N.E.2d 749 (1952).

The object must be proved to be genuinely what it purports to be. *People v. Berkman,* 307 Ill. 492, 139 N.E. 91 (1923), error to admit bullet not identified as one removed from victim. If probative value depends upon similarity of condition in a particular respect, that condition must be proved to be unchanged. *Chicago Terminal Transfer R. Co. v. Korando,* 129 Ill. App. 620 (1906), error to admit torn garment without showing condition same as immediately after accident; *Yohalem v. Matalone,* 225 Ill. App. 221 (1922), error to admit sample of beans without proof condition was same as at time of alleged breach of warranty; *Escher v. Norfolk & W.R. Co.,* 77 Ill. App. 3d 967, 33 Ill. Dec. 676, 397 N.E.2d 9 (1979), error to admit evidence as to condition of a door to a company locker room inspected over three years after incident. *Cf. Yedor v. Centre Properties, Inc.,* 173 Ill. App. 3d 132, 122 Ill. Dec. 916, 527 N.E.2d 414 (1988), proper to admit paper towels used to rub residual oil stain found on loading dock two days after Yedor's fall on basis of evidence that no vehicle could fit into location to have deposited oil in the interim. However, changes not impairing probative value do not require exclusion if pointed out to the trier of fact. *Geiken v. Chicago Great Western R. Co.,* 289 Ill. App. 45, 6 N.E.2d 690 (1937); *Ostendorf v. Brewer* supra, citing Handbook. *See* §901.2 infra for a full discussion of authentication of real evidence.

A photograph of property that the accused is alleged to have exerted unauthorized control over or to have otherwise obtained unlawfully is admissible in a prosecution for theft, retail theft, deceptive practice, robbery, armed robbery, burglary, or residential burglary if the photograph: (1) will serve the purpose of demonstrating the nature of the property; and (2) is otherwise admissible into evidence under all other rules of law governing the admissibility of photographs into evidence. The fact that it is impractical to introduce into evidence the actual property for any reason, including its size, weight, or unavailability, need not be established for the court to find a photograph of that property to be competent evidence. If a photograph is found to be competent evidence, it is admissible into evidence in place of the property and to the same extent as the property itself. 725 ILCS 5/115-9(a). With respect to procedural aspects of the statute, *see People v. Mikolajewski,* 272 Ill. App. 3d 311, 208 Ill. Dec. 443, 649 N.E.2d 499 (1995).

Instruments allegedly used in the commission of a crime and offered to prove that the accused committed the crime must be connected both with the accused and with the crime, thereby furnishing a link between the accused and the crime. *People v. Jones,* 22 Ill. 2d 592, 177 N.E.2d 112

(1961); *People v. Fair,* 45 Ill. App. 3d 301, 4 Ill. Dec. 15, 359 N.E.2d 848 (1977). *Accord People v. Yelliot,* 156 Ill. App. 3d 601, 108 Ill. Dec. 685, 509 N.E.2d 111 (1987) (gun never shown to be in the possession or control of the defendant improperly admitted); *People v. Maldonado,* 240 Ill. App. 3d 470, 181 Ill. Dec. 426, 608 N.E.2d 499 (1992) (rifle not linked to defendant, the shooting, or the crime scene improperly admitted); *People v. Fields,* 258 Ill. App. 3d 912, 197 Ill. Dec. 300, 631 N.E.2d 303 (1994) (screwdriver found on defendant improperly admitted because it was never connected with the crime). The connection may be circumstantial and has been held sufficiently shown with respect to burglary tools found in the building where the burglary occurred and accused was apprehended, *People v. Panczko,* 381 Ill. 625, 46 N.E.2d 28 (1943), or found in the vicinity of the crime bearing his fingerprints, *People v. Malmenato,* 14 Ill. 2d 52, 150 N.E.2d 806 (1958), or found in the building where the crime was committed and from which the accused fled, *People v. Santucci,* 24 Ill. 2d 93, 180 N.E.2d 491 (1962). Similarly, a knife that an expert testified could have inflicted the wound found with blood on it in a car loaned to the defendant has been held to be sufficiently connected, *People v. Owens,* 109 Ill. App. 3d 1150, 65 Ill. Dec. 593, 441 N.E.2d 908 (1982), as is a person's testimony that the accused shot him coupled with forensic evidence that the bullet discharged matched a bullet later used by the gunman in another crime for which the accused is on trial. *People v. Lawson,* 232 Ill. App. 3d 284, 173 Ill. Dec. 356, 596 N.E.2d 1235 (1992). Also, a gun belonging to the defendant's roommate that was one of 13 types of .22-caliber guns that could have fired the shots was found to be sufficiently connected. *People v. Hoffstetter,* 203 Ill. App. 3d 755, 148 Ill. Dec. 651, 560 N.E.2d 1349 (1990). Connection with respect to firearms has been held sufficiently shown by testimony that the gun was similar to that used by accused in the robbery and was identified ballistically as having shot a bystander, *People v. Ashley,* 18 Ill. 2d 272, 164 N.E.2d 70 (1960), and even by showing that it was suitable for use in committing the robbery and was in accused's possession when arrested, without further description of the weapon actually used. *People v. Fierer,* 124 Ill. 2d 176, 124 Ill. Dec. 855, 529 N.E.2d 972 (1988); *People v. Gambino,* 12 Ill. 2d 29, 145 N.E.2d 42 (1957). The fact that the witness is mistaken about the type of weapon used affects the weight of the testimony but not its admissibility. *People v. Ramsey,* 147 Ill. App. 3d 1084, 99 Ill. Dec. 962, 496 N.E.2d 1054 (1986). While possession furnishes a means of connecting the accused with the instrument, it is not essential. *People v. Jones,* 22 Ill. 2d 592, 177 N.E.2d 112 (1961). If an object is shown to be connected with a defendant, admissibility does not require a showing that the object was actually used in the offense charged as long as it is shown that the object is at least suitable for the commission of the crime. *People v. Sutherland,* 155 Ill. 2d 1, 182 Ill. Dec. 577, 610 N.E.2d 1 (1992); *People v. Free,* 94 Ill. 2d 378, 69 Ill. Dec. 1, 447 N.E.2d 218 (1983); *People v. Bridges,* 273 Ill. App. 3d 773, 210 Ill. Dec. 121, 652 N.E.2d 1097 (1995); *People v. Lee,* 242 Ill. App. 3d 40, 182 Ill. Dec. 858, 610 N.E.2d 727 (1993); *People v. Maldonado,* 240 Ill. App. 3d 470, 181 Ill. Dec. 426, 608 N.E.2d 499 (1992); *People v. Williams,* 220 Ill. App. 3d 297, 163 Ill. Dec. 277, 581 N.E.2d 228 (1991). *Compare People v. Smith,* 241 Ill. App. 3d 365, 182 Ill. Dec. 667, 610 N.E.2d 91 (1992), testimony that butcher knife found in vacant lot could have caused injury and that witness testified that the defendant had stated he had disposed of murder weapon was insufficient. Conversely, an object is not admissible where evidence such as a ballistic test establishes that the object connected to the defendant was not used in the commission of the offense. *People v. McQueen,* 115 Ill. App. 3d 833, 71 Ill. Dec. 233, 450 N.E.2d 921 (1983). *See also People v. Babiarz,* 271 Ill. App. 3d 153, 207 Ill. Dec. 681, 648 N.E.2d 137 (1995), error to admit nine millimeter handgun found in defendant's residence when bullets recovered from victim's body were .38/.357 caliber, citing Handbook.

Instrumentalities may be admitted if relevant other than as being used to commit a crime, such as possession of weapons as a reason to offer a bribe to an arresting officer. *People v. Wright,* 140 Ill. App. 3d 576, 95 Ill. Dec. 1, 488 N.E.2d 1344 (1986). Instrumentalities sufficiently shown to have been employed in the commission of the crime, not connected with the defendant, such as a bloody knife found at the scene of a murder, may be admitted for a purpose other than to show the defendant committed the crime. *People v. Lee,* 242 Ill. App. 3d 40, 182 Ill. Dec. 858, 610 N.E.2d 727 (1993); *People v. Case,* 246 Ill. App. 3d 566, 186 Ill. Dec. 411, 616 N.E.2d 601 (1993).

In *People v. Pulliam,* 176 Ill. 2d 261, 223 Ill. Dec. 610, 680 N.E.2d 343 (1997), the Illinois Supreme Court stated that a book found in the defendant's apartment two days after a murder, entitled "The Force of Sex," was improperly admitted in light of the absence of testimony that the defendant owned or had read the book and the fact that the apartment was unsecured for those two days. Obviously, *Pulliam* can't mean what it might seem to imply, for if it did, a gun found in the defendant's apartment three days after a murder would be inadmissible. The book in *Pulliam* should have been found inadmissible, if at all, solely on the basis of its probative value being substantially outweighed by the danger of unfair prejudice, misleading the jury, and confusion of the issues. *See* §403.1 infra.

Instrumentalities not used by the accused during the commission of the crime have on occasion been admitted as relevant to testimony concerning the details of an arrest. *People v. Washington,* 127 Ill. App. 3d 365, 82 Ill. Dec. 505, 468 N.E.2d 1285 (1984); *People v. LeBron,* 83 Ill. App. 3d 598, 39 Ill. Dec. 156, 404 N.E.2d 540 (1980); *People v. Upshire,* 62 Ill. App. 3d 248, 19 Ill. Dec. 523, 379 N.E.2d 38 (1978). *Contra People v. Wade,* 51 Ill. App. 3d 721, 9 Ill. Dec. 271, 366 N.E.2d 528 (1977), holding that reference to a gun found on defendant at the time of arrest was reversible error. *Accord People v. Sui Wing Eng,* 138 Ill. App. 3d 281, 93 Ill. Dec. 12, 485 N.E.2d 1222 (1985) (Jiganti, J., dissenting). *See also People v. Washington,* 127 Ill. App. 3d 365, 81 Ill. Dec. 505, 468 N.E.2d 1285 (1984), while the three guns were not used in the offense, they were closely and inextricably mixed up with the history of the guilty act itself. The prejudice of introduction into evidence of a weapon whose only connection to the incident was presence on the accused at the time of arrest seems clearly to outweigh its slight probative value. *Accord People v. Fierer,* 124 Ill. 2d 176, 124 Ill. Dec. 855, 529 N.E.2d 972 (1988).

Similarly, physical evidence, such as blood found upon an accused, must be sufficiently connected with both the accused and the crime. *People v. Allison,* 236 Ill. App. 3d 175, 177 Ill. Dec. 116, 602 N.E.2d 1288 (1992). *See also* §901.1 infra.

With respect to the introduction of a person other than the accused as evidence relevant to identification, *see People v. Ward,* 193 Ill. App. 3d 677, 140 Ill. Dec. 691, 550 N.E.2d 576 (1990).

§401.5   Real Evidence: Exhibiting Personal Injuries

Although an earlier decision discouraged the display of personal injuries to the jury as an attempt to excite sympathy, *Wagner v. Chicago, R.I. & P. Ry.,* 277 Ill. 114, 115 N.E. 201 (1917), the propriety of the practice is now firmly established. The absence of controversy as to the existence, nature, or extent of the injury is not controlling, §401.1 supra. *Minnis v. Friend,* 360 Ill. 328, 196 N.E. 191 (1935). Exhibition ordinarily has been permitted, either as a matter of right, *Stegall v. Carlson,* 6 Ill. App. 2d 388, 128 N.E.2d 352 (1955), or as a matter of discretion, *Howard v. Gulf, M. & O.R. Co.,* 13 Ill. App. 2d 482, 142 N.E.2d 825 (1957), with the discretion usually exercised in favor of exhibition. *See* §403.1 infra; *Burnett v. Caho,* 7 Ill. App. 3d 266, 285 N.E.2d 619 (1972), plaintiff properly permitted to remove his artificial eye while on witness stand; *Sparling v. Peabody Coal Co.,* 59 Ill. 2d 491, 322 N.E.2d 5 (1974), display of burns and scars on legs of plaintiff was proper. However, displaying an arm that had suffered additional subsequent injuries has been held error. *O'Hara v. Central Illinois Light Co.,* 319 Ill. App. 336, 49 N.E.2d 274 (1943).

Demonstrating the extent of impairment or disability resulting from injury is recognized as proper, *Vander Veen v. Yellow Cab Co.*, 89 Ill. 2d 91, 233 N.E.2d 68 (1967); *Tindall v. Chicago & N.W. Ry.*, 200 Ill. App. 556 (1916), or as a matter of right, *Villegas v. Kercher*, 111 Ill. App. 2d 282, 137 N.E.2d 92 (1956). Allowing the jurors to manipulate and test the strength of plaintiff's hand has, however, been held error, *Vance v. Monroe Drug Co.*, 149 Ill. App. 499 (1909), and referred to as being "frowned upon," *Hehir v. Bowers*, 85 Ill. App. 3d 625, 40 Ill. Dec. 918, 407 N.E.2d 149 (1980). Caution should be encouraged in permitting the injured person to perform certain acts or to be manipulated by a physician since such acts raise significant problems such as feigning, difficulty in conducting cross-examination, and the inducement of an undue emotional response by the trier of fact to manifestations of pain. *See* McCormick, Evidence §215 (4th ed. 1992).

Display of wounds has also been permitted in criminal cases. *People v. Smith*, 1 Ill. App. 3d 518, 275 N.E.2d 268 (1971). Thus it is proper in a trial for assault with intent to commit murder for the victim to open his shirt and lift his undershirt to show the jury the location of his wounds. *People v. Chatman*, 110 Ill. App. 3d 19, 65 Ill. Dec. 778, 441 N.E.2d 1292 (1982).

As to the admission of photographs of personal injuries, *see* §401.8 infra.

§401.6 Real Evidence: Exhibiting Child in Paternity Cases

In paternity cases, whether the child may be exhibited in court to demonstrate resemblance to the putative father is not settled. *Robnett v. People*, 16 Ill. App. 299 (1885), exhibition of child under four months of age error as prejudicial and uncertain; *Morrison v. People*, 52 Ill. App. 482 (1893), not error to exhibit child in case involving different races; *Benes v. People*, 121 Ill. App. 103 (1905), not error to permit relatrix to hold child of eight months while testifying.

The solution may well be to permit exhibition if, in the opinion of the trial judge, the child is old enough to possess settled features or other corporal indications. 1 Wigmore, Evidence §166 (3rd ed. 1940). While it could scarcely be said that inspecting the child would not be evidence but merely would enable the trier to understand and apply the evidence, as with views of real estate, §412.1 infra, nevertheless the same problem of judicial control exists, and a finding should not be permitted on the basis of inspection alone. *See Wistrand v. People*, 213 Ill. 72, 72 N.E. 748 (1904), jury cannot fix age of accused by inspecting him.

§401.7 Demonstrative Evidence: Maps, Models, Drawings, Charts, and Tangible Items

The propriety of permitting a witness to explain her testimony by visual illustration is established. *People v. Fisher*, 340 Ill. 216, 172 N.E. 743 (1930), blackboard demonstration by ballistics expert properly allowed. Unless the illustration is essential to an understanding of the testimony, it is largely cumulative in effect, and admission or exclusion rests technically within the discretion of the trial judge, §403.1 infra. *Smith v. Sanitary Dist. of Chicago*, 260 Ill. 453, 103 N.E. 254 (1913), not error to exclude graph of rainfall; *Department of Public Works v. Chicago Title & Trust Co.*, 408 Ill. 41, 95 N.E.2d 903 (1951), not error to admit colored contour maps; *Christopherson v. Hyster Co.*, 58 Ill. App. 3d 791, 137 Ill. Dec. 83, 374 N.E.2d 858 (1978), proper to exclude model of forklift made by taping cardboard together as prejudicially implying instability; *Little v. Tuscola Stone Co.*, 234 Ill. App. 3d 726, 175 Ill. Dec. 812, 600 N.E.2d 1270 (1992), not error to exclude a summary of two documents already in evidence because of concern over the jury giving the summarized information undue weight. In practice, however, the use of maps, models, drawings, and charts, properly authenticated, *see* §901.1 infra, is now almost universally permitted. *Burke v. Toledo, Peoria & Western Ry.*, 148 Ill. App. 3d 208, 101 Ill. Dec. 358,

498 N.E.2d 682 (1986) (courts favors use of demonstrative evidence). *See e.g., People v. Henenberg,* 55 Ill. 2d 5, 302 N.E.2d 27 (1973), model of human skull employed by pathologist to show cause of death; *People v. Williams,* 274 Ill. App. 3d 598, 210 Ill. Dec. 704, 653 N.E.2d 899 (1995), map depicting apartment accurately shown to reflect the layout on the day of the crime; *People v. Mitchell,* 78 Ill. App. 3d 458, 33 Ill. Dec. 823, 397 N.E.2d 156 (1979), plastic torso model employed as adjunct to testimony establishing cause of death; *Madigan v. Browning Ferris Indus.,* 61 Ill. App. 3d 842, 19 Ill. Dec. 67 378 N.E.2d 568 (1978), scaled architectural drawing of shopping center; *Farmer v. Crane,* 32 Ill. App. 3d 383, 336 N.E.2d 607 (1975), magnetic blackboard used by witness to aid his expression of the occurrence. With respect to courtroom demonstrations, *see* §401.10 infra.

Demonstrative evidence may also consist of tangible items or pictures thereof that are not contended themselves to have played a part in the incident but are instead offered for the purpose of rendering other evidence more understandable. McCormick, Evidence §212 (4th ed. 1992). Thus it is proper to admit a tiller crossbar made of fiberglass to demonstrate feasibility of a safer design, *Ogg v. City of Springfield,* 121 Ill. App. 3d 25, 76 Ill. Dec. 531, 458 N.E.2d 1331 (1984); and a photograph of a different portion of a gravel road to illustrate an expert's testimony of adequate compaction, *Herman v. Will Township,* 284 Ill. App. 3d 53, 219 Ill. Dec. 688, 671 N.E.2d 1141 (1996); and a peeled automobile steering column to demonstrate the process of peeling, *People v. Cook,* 279 Ill. App. 3d 718, 216 Ill. Dec. 239, 665 N.E.2d 299 (1996). A sufficient foundation establishing substantial similarity where appropriate is, of course, required. *People v. Chatman,* 102 Ill. App. 3d 692, 58 Ill. Dec. 315, 430 N.E.2d 257 (1981), two-by-four board established to be same dimensions as actual piece of wood no longer available; *Fedt v. Oak Lawn Lodge, Inc.,* 132 Ill. App. 3d 1061, 88 Ill. Dec. 154, 478 N.E.2d 469 (1985), a "Bosworth splint," an item of medical hardware, identical to the one inserted into the pelvis of the plaintiff; *People v. Seals,* 153 Ill. App. 3d 417, 106 Ill. Dec. 316,

505 N.E.2d 1107 (1987), .45 caliber handgun, identical to gun used in shooting that was not recovered, properly employed by police officer to explain casings found at the crime site; *People v. Madison,* 264 Ill. App. 3d. 481, 202 Ill. Dec. 338, 637 N.E.2d 1074 (1994), clear plastic bag containing three small bags of light brown sugar improperly employed in place of lost evidence which was described as having been dark brown chunks.

The effectiveness of visual presentation imposes certain limits on its use. The line of demarcation falls between explanation of testimony, which is entirely proper, and the reduction of testimony to graphic form in such manner as to confer upon it a disproportionate emphasis. *People v. Village of Camp Point,* 286 Ill. App. 3d 247, 221 Ill. Dec. 641, 675 N.E.2d 1371 (1997) (citing Handbook). Thus, when the witness illustrates his testimony with a blackboard drawing, *People v. Fisher* supra, or points out on a plat the manner in which a collision occurred, his testimony is clarified but is not likely to be regarded by the trier as being anything more than oral testimony. However, an exhibit that in effect sets forth graphically testimony about matters may be regarded as possessing undue weight and thus may be misleading to the jury, §403.1 infra, as in *Corning v. Dollmeyer,* 123 Ill. App. 188 (1905), plat of room bearing inscriptions describing conduct properly excluded; *Hatcher v. Quincy Horse Ry. & Carrying Co.,* 181 Ill. App. 30 (1913), plat of scene of accident with lines of vision inscribed, possibly to the point of being considered improperly as substantive evidence. *Compare People v. Village of Camp Point* supra. *Compare Yakstis v. William J. Diestelhorst Co.,* 61 Ill. App. 3d 833, 19 Ill. Dec. 90, 378 N.E.2d 591 (1978), witness permitted to employ photograph containing predrawn-in arrows to explain his testimony. A visual presentation employed for dramatic effect or emotional appeal rather than factual explanation should also be excluded. *Bugno v. Mount Sinai Hosp. Medical Center,* 201 Ill. App. 3d 245, 147 Ill. Dec. 1, 559 N.E.2d 1 (1990).

Mathematical accuracy is not required of a drawing, map, model, chart, or tangible item for use for illustrative pur-

poses either by a witness, *Brown v. Galesburg Pressed Brick &*
Tile Co., 132 Ill. 648, 24 N.E. 522 (1890), or in argument,
Lake St. El. R. Co. v. Burgess, 200 Ill. 628, 66 N.E. 215 (1903).
However, if the drawing, map, model, chart, or tangible item
does not aid in understanding by reason of such inaccuracies
(i.e., is misleading even after being explained), the exhibit
will properly be excluded. *Peterson v. Lou Bachrodt Chevrolet
Co.*, 76 Ill. 2d 353, 20 Ill. Dec. 444, 392 N.E.2d 1 (1979);
Nolan v. Elliott, 179 Ill. App. 3d 1077, 129 Ill. Dec. 288, 535
N.E.2d 1053 (1989); *Forest Preserve Dist. of DuPage County v.
Harris Trust & Sav. Bank*, 108 Ill. App. 2d 65, 247 N.E.2d 188
(1969). *Accord Slavin v. Saltzman*, 268 Ill. App. 3d 392, 205 Ill.
Dec. 776, 643 N.E.2d 1383 (1994), diagram of accident scene
not to scale properly excluded as misleading. Of course, if
essential matters depicted in the drawing, map, model,
chart, or tangible item are not supported by the proper foundation, introduction of the exhibit is error. *Cunningham v.
Cent. & S. Truck Lines, Inc.*, 104 Ill. App. 2d 247, 244 N.E.2d
412 (1968).

A young child may use anatomically correct dolls as testimonial aids at trial in the giving of testimony. *People v. Harris*,
187 Ill. App. 3d 832, 135 Ill. Dec. 291, 543 N.E.2d 859 (1989);
People v. Barger, 251 Ill. App. 3d 448, 191 Ill. Dec. 556, 624
N.E.2d 405 (1993). Moreover, testimony of witnesses concerning an alleged young victim's use of anatomically correct dolls to demonstrate sexual abuse during out-of-court
interviews is admissible. *People v. Mitchell*, 215 Ill. App. 3d
849, 159 Ill. Dec. 409, 576 N.E.2d 78 (1991); *People v. Roman*,
260 Ill. App. 3d 436, 197 Ill. Dec. 932, 632 N.E.2d 1 (1992);
People v. Giles, 261 Ill. App. 3d 833, 200 Ill. Dec. 630, 635
N.E.2d 969 (1994).

§401.8   Demonstrative Evidence: Photographs, Motion
Pictures, Videotapes

Still photographs, motion pictures, and videotapes are admissible in evidence when helpful to an understanding of a

fact of consequence in the litigation. *Baggett v. Ashland Oil & Refining Co.,* 92 Ill. App. 2d 433, 236 N.E.2d 243 (1968). Still photographs, motion pictures, and videotapes may be admitted in evidence when properly authenticated and relevant either to illustrate or corroborate the testimony of a witness, or to act as probative evidence of what the photograph depicts. *People v. Smith,* 152 Ill. 2d 229, 178 Ill. Dec. 335, 604 N.E.2d 858 (1992). The decision whether to admit or exclude photographic evidence is reserved for the discretion of the trial judge. *People v. Brown,* 172 Ill. 2d 1, 216 Ill. Dec. 733, 665 N.E.2d 1290 (1996); *People v. Kitchen,* 159 Ill. 2d 1, 201 Ill. Dec. 1, 636 N.E.2d 433 (1994); *Schaffner v. Chicago & N.W. Transp. Co.,* 129 Ill. 2d 1, 133 Ill. Dec. 432, 541 N.E.2d 643 (1989).

Foundation.   A sufficient foundation is laid for a still photograph, a motion picture, or a videotape by testimony of any person with personal knowledge of the photographed object *at a time relevant to the issues* that the photograph is a fair and accurate representation of the object at that time; the photographer is not required. *People v. Donaldson,* 24 Ill. 2d 315, 181 N.E.2d 131 (1962); *Brownlie v. Brownlie,* 357 Ill. 117, 191 N.E. 268 (1934); *Gaunt & Haynes, Inc. v. Moritz Corp.,* 138 Ill. App. 3d 356, 92 Ill. Dec. 880, 485 N.E.2d 1123 (1985) (citing Handbook); *People v. Hebel,* 174 Ill. App. 3d 1, 123 Ill. Dec. 592, 527 N.E.2d 1367 (1988) (citing Handbook); *Brooke Inns, Inc. v. S & R Hi-Fi and TV,* 249 Ill. App. 3d 1064, 188 Ill. Dec. 164, 618 N.E.2d 734 (1993); *People v. West,* 294 Ill. App. 3d 939, 229 Ill. Dec. 241, 691 N.E.2d 177 (1998). *Kooyumjjan v. Stevens,* 10 Ill. App. 2d 378, 368, 135 N.E.2d 146, 151 (1956), states, "The witness need not be the photographer, nor need he know anything of the time or condition of the taking, but he must have personal knowledge of the scene or object in question and testify that is correctly portrayed by the photograph." *Accord People v. Holman,* 103 Ill. 2d 133, 82 Ill. Dec. 585, 469 N.E.2d 119 (1984). Exclusion is proper in the absence of evidence that the object depicted in a photograph taken at the later date was then in the same condition as it was at the time relevant to the issues. *Casson v. Nash,* 74 Ill. 2d

164, 23 Ill. Dec. 571, 384 N.E.2d 365 (1978); *People v. Pope,* 138 Ill. App. 3d 726, 93 Ill. Dec. 249, 486 N.E.2d 350 (1985); *Maroldy v. Isaacson,* 189 Ill. App. 3d 785, 137 Ill. Dec. 83, 545 N.E.2d 736 (1989). *See also Slavin v. Saltzman,* 268 Ill. App. 3d 392, 205 Ill. Dec. 776, 643 N.E.2d 1383 (1994), improper to admit photographs of intersection taken six months after accident on foundation by witness that he had passed by intersection two or three times a month for several months before and after the accident but was not at the intersection the day of the accident.

Complete similarity of conditions is not required of a still photograph used in the same way as a map to illustrate physical relations. Motion pictures and videotapes are given identical treatment. *People v. Generally,* 170 Ill. App. 3d 668, 121 Ill. Dec. 300, 525 N.E.2d 106 (1988). Remoteness of time of taking the photograph from the time of the transaction is of no consequence if conditions have not changed. *People v. West,* 294 Ill. App. 3d 939, 229 Ill. Dec. 241, 691 N.E.2d 177 (1998); *Lake County Forest Preserve Dist. v. Vernon Hills Dev. Corp.,* 85 Ill. App. 3d 241, 40 Ill. Dec. 605, 406 N.E.2d 611 (1980); *Miller v. Pillsbury Co.,* 56 Ill. App. 2d 403, 206 N.E.2d 272 (1965). Changed conditions alone do not render the photograph inadmissible if, after the changes are explained, the trier of fact can understand the correct representation and will not be misled by the photograph. *Prochnow v. El Paso Golf Club, Inc.,* 253 Ill. App. 3d 387, 192 Ill. Dec. 614, 625 N.E.2d 769 (1993) (quoting Handbook); *Reid v. Sledge,* 224 Ill. App. 3d 817, 167 Ill. Dec. 541, 587 N.E.2d 1156 (1992). *See, e.g., Warner v. City of Chicago,* 72 Ill. 2d 100, 19 Ill. Dec. 1, 378 N.E.2d 502 (1978), photograph of accident site taken without snow present at time of incident properly admitted since it was made clear to jury that only nature of defect and not condition at time of occurrence was depicted; *Birnbaum v. Kirchner,* 337 Ill. App. 25, 85 N.E.2d 191 (1949), photographs taken during daytime when not raining properly admitted to show location of accident on rainy night; *Burke v. Toledo, Peoria & Western Ry.,* 148 Ill. App. 3d 208, 101 Ill. Dec. 358, 498 N.E.2d 682 (1986), photographs properly admitted after fact that bushes at corner of the cornfield had been removed was explained to jury; *Grieg v. Griffel,* 49 Ill. App. 3d 829, 7 Ill. Dec 499, 364 N.E.2d 660 (1977), whether dent upon the truck depicted in photograph taken immediately after accident was caused by accident itself was for jury to determine. *Cf. State Toll Highway Auth. v. Grand Mandarin,* 189 Ill. App. 3d 323, 136 Ill. Dec. 370, 544 N.E.2d 1145 (1989), videotape of property in condemnation action taken after abandonment and removal of equipment and fixtures properly excluded as likely to mislead the jury.

Similarly, photographs of a demonstration performed under conditions not precisely the same as those at the time of the occurrence are admissible if after the variations are explained the trier of fact will not be misled. *Saldana v. Wirtz Cartage Co.,* 74 Ill. 2d 379, 24 Ill. Dec. 523, 385 N.E.2d 664 (1978), motion picture of asphalt paving machine in operation. Of course, exclusion is proper if adequate evidence establishing the conditions alleged to exist at the time of the occurrence is not introduced. *Waite v. Chicago Transit Auth.,* 157 Ill. App. 3d 616, 110 Ill. Dec. 145, 510 N.E.2d 1176 (1987). Since the nature of a photograph makes difficult any separation of illustration from assertion, a change of conditions may make the picture so misleading as to require exclusion. *Chicago & E.I.R. Co. v. Crose,* 214 Ill. 602, 73 N.E. 865 (1905). *See, e.g., Amstar Corp. v. Aurora Fast Freight,* 141 Ill. App. 3d 705, 96 Ill. Dec. 31, 490 N.E.2d 1067 (1986), proper to exclude as misleading videotape of vantage point of driver taken from a car when the driver had been in the tractor of a semi. *See also* §401.10 infra.

Once a proper foundation has been introduced, it is highly unlikely that the probative value of the photograph will be overshadowed by the danger of unfair prejudice. *People v. Roy,* 49 Ill. 2d 114, 273 N.E.2d 363 (1971); *People v. Foster,* 76 Ill. 2d 365, 29 Ill. Dec. 449, 392 N.E.2d 6 (1979), relevant photographs were properly admitted in spite of fact they were gruesome. *See also* §403.1 infra. Moreover, the probative value of a photograph is often so great that its exclusion is likely to be error if a controverted situation is portrayed. *Lake Erie & W.R.*

Co. v. Wilson, 189 Ill. 89, 59 N.E. 573 (1901); *Casson v. Nash,* 54 Ill. App. 3d 783, 12 Ill. Dec. 760, 370 N.E.2d 564 (1977). *See also People v. Jenko,* 410 Ill. 478, 102 N.E.2d 783 (1952). On the other hand, there may arise situations where the incremental probative value of the photograph is so slight that its admission is error when considered in light of the inherent danger of unfair prejudice. *People v. Smith,* 152 Ill. 2d 229, 178 Ill. Dec. 335, 604 N.E.2d 858 (1992).

A still photograph, motion picture, or videotape may be excluded in the discretion of the trial court, if a matter ruled inadmissible is also depicted in the picture. *Schaffner v. Chicago & N.W. Transp. Co.,* 129 Ill. 2d 1, 133 Ill. Dec. 432, 541 N.E.2d 643 (1989), proper for trial judge to exclude photograph showing proper direction for traffic when fact that plaintiff was riding his bicycle the wrong direction on a one-way street had been precluded on pretrial motion.

Posed photographs. Posed still photographs, motion pictures, and videotapes are regarded with disfavor in light of the propensity of the trier of fact to be misled into conferring disproportionate emphasis. §403.1 infra; *People v. Whitlock,* 174 Ill. App. 3d 749, 124 Ill. Dec. 263, 528 N.E.2d 1371 (1988) (citing Handbook). *See, e.g., Ellis v. Flannigan,* 253 Ill. 397, 97 N.E. 696 (1912), improper to admit photograph of room with furniture arranged as witness testified it was when will was attested; *People v. Crowe,* 390 Ill. 294, 61 N.E.2d 348 (1945), proper to exclude photograph of accused standing beside trunk on which child allegedly stood when indecent liberties were taken; *Hammer v. Slive,* 35 Ill. App. 2d 447, 183 N.E.2d 49 (1962), not error to exclude photograph showing truck in disputed location as testified to by some witnesses; *French v. City of Springfield,* 65 Ill. 2d 74, 2 Ill. Dec. 271, 357 N.E.2d 438 (1976), error to admit motion pictures taken from driver's seat of car proceeding down street in view of preconditioning effect on jurors' minds to accept plaintiff's theory of accident; *People v. Jones,* 114 Ill. App. 3d 576, 70 Ill. Dec. 419, 449 N.E.2d 547 (1983), not error to exclude photograph creating a misleading impression as to the distance between a witness and the defendant at the scene of the crime; *J.L. Simmons Co. v. Firestone Tire & Rubber,* 126 Ill. App. 3d 859, 81 Ill. Dec. 627, 467 N.E.2d 327 (1981), photograph of objects arranged favorably to Firestone's theory of the case properly excluded. *Cf. Margevich v. Chicago & N.W. Ry.,* 1 Ill. App. 2d 162, 116 N.E.2d 914 (1953), discretionary with trial judge, *American State Bank v. County of Woodford,* 55 Ill. App. 3d 123, 13 Ill. Dec. 515, 371 N.E.2d 232 (1978), no abuse of discretion to admit posed motion pictures in light of other demonstrative evidence in case and jury view of scene, *People v. Bryant,* 202 Ill. App. 3d 1057, 148 Ill. Dec. 358, 560 N.E.2d 955 (1990), posed photographs depicting the crime scene, though not linking the defendant to the crime, were properly admitted to show physical facts as they existed prior to and after the time of the crime, and *People v. Sims,* 244 Ill. App. 3d 966, 184 Ill. Dec. 135, 612 N.E.2d 1011 (1993), no abuse of discretion to admit videotape reenacting disappearance of victim because defendant "opened the door" when he cross-examined state's witnesses about the videotape.

Enlarged and color photographs.   Enlarged photographs may be used. *Howard v. Illinois Trust & Sav. Bank,* 189 Ill. 568, 59 N.E. 1106 (1901), disputed document case. Color photographs are also permitted within the discretion of the court. *De Rosa v. Albert F. Amling Co.,* 84 Ill. App. 3d 64, 39 Ill. Dec. 180, 404 N.E.2d 564 (1980); *Hedrick v. Borden Co.,* 100 Ill. App. 2d 237, 241 N.E.2d 546 (1968); *Murphy v. Lindahl,* 24 Ill. App. 2d 461, 165 N.E.2d 340 (1960).

Motion Pictures and Videotapes.   Motion pictures are admissible on the same basis as still photographs. *Saldana v. Wirtz Cartage Co.,* 74 Ill. 2d 379, 24 Ill. Dec. 523, 385 N.E.2d 664 (1978), motion picture of an asphalt paving machine in operation. The same is true with respect to videotapes, *People v. Generally,* 170 Ill. App. 3d 668, 121 Ill. Dec. 300, 525 N.E.2d 106 (1988); *Missouri Portland Cement v. United Cement,* 145 Ill. App. 3d 1023, 99 Ill. Dec. 796, 496 N.E.2d 489 (1986), such as a 90-second excerpt from an actual 90-minute surgical procedure depicting fluid build-up in the plaintiff's lungs. *Barry v. Owens-Corning Fiberglas Corp.,* 282 Ill. App. 3d 199, 217 Ill. Dec. 823, 668 N.E.2d 8 (1996).

Animations.   Video animations are admissible provided a foundation of sufficient similarity is presented, subject to exclusion on the basis of misleading the jury or confusion of the issues, §403.1 infra. Video animations that go beyond illustration incorporating experimental elements raise additional concerns relating to similarity, §401.11 infra, as well as the reliability of the explanative theory being employed, §702.4 infra. *See generally* Graham, et al., Illinois Evidentiary Foundations 107 (2d ed. 1997).

Illustrative versus substantive.   Still photographs, motion pictures, and videotapes are sometimes admitted solely to "illustrate" the testimony of the witness and not as substantive evidence. *Brennan v. Leshyn,* 51 Ill. App. 2d 132, 201 N.E.2d 167 (1964). While one might rightly criticize the artificiality and theoretical unsoundness of such a distinction, McCormick, Evidence §214 (4th ed. 1992), it may serve to prevent the original writing rule, §1002.1 infra, from generally being applicable. *See* §1002.4 infra. However, where the fiction of illustrative purposes is not available, e.g., X-rays, *see* §401.9 infra, and automatic photograph of bank robber, the photograph will be admitted as substantive evidence. *See* Federal Advisory Committee's Note to Rule 1002, 56 F.R.D. 183, 342 (1973). *Accord People v. Hebel,* 174 Ill. App. 3d 1, 123 Ill. Dec. 592, 527 N.E.2d 1367 (1988), photographs are to be given substantive effect where an adequate foundation is laid. Moreover, *see generally People v. Smith,* 152 Ill. 2d 229, 178 Ill. Dec. 335, 604 N.E.2d 858 (1992), photographs may be admitted in evidence either to illustrate or corroborate the testimony of a witness, or to act as probative evidence of what the photograph depicts.

Personal injury action.   Still photographs, motion pictures, and videotapes of an injury may be admitted to the same extent that the injury itself might be exhibited, §401.5 supra. *Stach v. Sears, Roebuck & Co.,* 102 Ill. App. 3d 397, 57 Ill. Dec. 879, 429 N.E.2d 1242 (1981); *McNally v. Chauncy Body Corp.,* 315 Ill. App. 190, 42 N.E.2d 853 (1942). Similarly, photographs of relevant real evidence are also admissible. *Lundquist v. Nickels,* 238 Ill. App. 3d 410, 179 Ill. Dec. 150, 605 N.E.2d

1373 (1992), photograph depicting condition of motorcycle helmet following crash. In a wrongful death case, a decedent's photograph is admissible to show her prior state of well-being, *Fedt v. Oak Lawn Lodge Inc.*, 132 Ill. App. 3d 1061, 88 Ill. Dec. 154, 478 N.E.2d 469 (1985), *Exchange Natl. Bank v. Air Illinois, Inc.*, 167 Ill. App. 3d 1081, 118 Ill. Dec. 691, 522 N.E.2d 146 (1988) (videotape), or to show the decedent's state of health, his relationship to his family, and the services and instruction he provided his family, *Drews v. Gobel Freight Lines, Inc.*, 144 Ill. 2d 84, 161 Ill. Dec. 324, 578 N.E.2d 970 (1991) (videotapes). While admissibility of photographs depicting injuries is stated to be within the sound discretion of the court, the standard to be applied favors admissibility. *Darling v. Charleston Community Memorial Hosp.*, 50 Ill. App. 2d 253, 200 N.E.2d 149 (1964), competent photographic evidence may not be excluded merely because it might arouse feelings of horror or indignation in the jury. *See, e.g., Drews v. Gobel Freight Lines, Inc.*, 144 Ill. 2d 84, 161 Ill. Dec. 324, 578 N.E.2d 970 (1991), two morgue photographs showing multiple lacerations of decedent's face and throat and burns on right knee properly admitted in discretion of the court; *Bullard v. Barnes*, 102 Ill. 2d 505, 82 Ill. Dec. 448, 468 N.E.2d 1228 (1984), gruesome morgue photographs of decedent relevant as to pain and suffering were sufficiently probative to be admitted in discretion of the trial court; *Sparling v. Peabody Coal Co.*, 59 Ill. 2d 491, 322 N.E.2d 5 (1974), photograph of injured child's leg and feet showing scars and burns properly admitted over objection that evidence was cumulative with exhibition of injury; *De Rosa v. Albert F. Amling Co.*, 84 Ill. App. 3d 64, 39 Ill. Dec. 180, 404 N.E.2d 564 (1980), color photograph of injury properly admitted over objection that it was brutally graphic; *Lindsay v. Appleby*, 91 Ill. App. 3d 705, 46 Ill. Dec. 832, 414 N.E.2d 885 (1980), photograph of plaintiff's vehicle showing blood on white roof relevant to establish head injury sustained in the collision; *Parson v. City of Chicago*, 117 Ill. App. 3d 383, 72 Ill. Dec. 895, 453 N.E.2d 770 (1983), photograph of plaintiff prior to surgery admitted over objection that less prejudicial evidence as to the injuries and pain suffered existed — "it is an old cliche that a picture is worth a thousand words;" *Hartness v. Ruzich,* 155 Ill. App. 3d 878, 108 Ill. Dec. 494, 508 N.E.2d 1071 (1987), photographs admissible to show appearance of plaintiff before and after wreck to assist jury in assessing extent of disfigurement; *Barry v. Owens-Corning Fiberglas Corp.,* 282 Ill. App. 3d 199, 217 Ill. Dec. 823, 668 N.E.2d 8 (1996), 90-second videotape excerpt from an actual 90-minute surgical procedure depicting fluid build-up in the plaintiff's lungs. However, photographs of plaintiff who had undergone abdominal surgery on two prior occasions were properly excluded. *Eckley v. St. Therese Hosp.,* 62 Ill. App. 3d 299, 19 Ill. Dec. 642, 379 N.E.2d 306 (1978). Similarly, photographs taken during a surgical operation depicting the nature and extent of the injury have been properly excluded on the bases that incremental probative value was substantially outweighed by the danger of unfair prejudicial effect. *Pyskaty v. Oyama,* 266 Ill. App. 3d 801, 204 Ill. Dec. 328, 641 N.E.2d 552 (1994). The admission of photographs showing treatment, such as traction, is also within the discretion of the trial judge. *Herndobler v. Goodwin,* 310 Ill. App. 267, 34 N.E.2d 8 (1941), not error to admit; *Villegas v. Kercher,* 11 Ill. App. 2d 282, 137 N.E.2d 92 (1956), not error to exclude when treatment adequately described in evidence.

Still photographs, motion pictures, and videotapes depicting a day in the life of an impaired plaintiff are admissible if their probative value is not substantially outweighed by the danger of unfair prejudice, confusion, and misleading. *Cisarik v. Palos Community Hospital,* 144 Ill. 2d 339, 162 Ill. Dec. 59, 579 N.E.2d 873 (1991); *Roberts v. Sisters of Saint Francis,* 198 Ill. App. 3d 891, 145 Ill. Dec. 44, 556 N.E.2d 662 (1990). *Compare In re Marriage of Willis,* 234 Ill. App. 3d 156, 174 Ill. Dec. 633, 599 N.E.2d 179 (1992) (videotape of day in life of children should not be employed in custody proceeding). The still photographs, motion pictures, or videotapes must also satisfy the rule against hearsay if the actions of the plaintiff are considered assertive. *See* §§801.1-801.3 infra. Since *Cisarik v. Palos Community Hospital* supra fails to discuss that day-in-the-life videos can depict assertive conduct, the hearsay question has yet to be fully resolved. *Cf.* C.J. Miller dissenting. While it may be overly cautious to require that opposing counsel be given an opportunity to be present during the filming of a day in the life of an impaired plaintiff, the assertions in *Burke v. 12 Rothschild's Liquor Mart,* 209 Ill. App. 3d 192, 154 Ill. Dec. 80, 568 N.E.2d 80 (1991), that presence of opposing counsel would "add nothing" to the protection of authentication and that, by implication, the presence of counsel would not assist the determination of whether incremental probative value was substantially outweighed by trial concerns are clearly incorrect.

Still photographs, motion pictures, and videotapes, in the nature of surveillance films, are also admissible to show that injuries claimed are either nonexistent or not as severe as plaintiff asserts. *Carney v. Smith,* 240 Ill. App. 3d 650, 181 Ill. Dec. 306, 608 N.E.2d 379 (1992) (citing cases).

Still photographs, motion pictures, and videotapes in the nature of instructional material, such as an instructional videotape depicting proper medical procedures provided the defendant surgeon is not depicted, *Glassman v. St. Joseph Hospital,* 259 Ill. App. 3d 730, 197 Ill. Dec. 727, 631 N.E.2d 1186 (1994), or a videotape depicting gymnastic moves similar to those made by plaintiff but not involving plaintiff, *Montag v. Board of Education,* 112 Ill. App. 3d 1039, 68 Ill. Dec. 565, 446 N.E.2d 299 (1983), are admissible when sufficiently probative.

Criminal prosecutions. Generally, despite their gruesomeness and prejudicial effect on the jury, relevant photographs have been found admissible in the court's discretion, *People v. Fierer,* 124 Ill. 2d 176, 124 Ill. Dec. 855, 529 N.E.2d 972 (1988); *People v. Lefler,* 38 Ill. 2d 216, 230 N.E.2d 827 (1967), where they, for example, tend to prove the manner and cause of death, the nature, number, extent, and location of the wounds, the manner in which they were inflicted, the amount of force used, the position, condition, and location of the body, the willfulness of the act in question, to corroborate a defendant's confession, or to aid in understanding and to corroborate the testimony of a pathologist or other witness. *People v. Kidd,* 175 Ill. 2d 1, 221 Ill. Dec. 486, 675 N.E.2d

910 (1996); *People v. Brown,* 172 Ill. 2d 1, 216 Ill. Dec. 733, 665 N.E.2d 1290 (1996); *People v. Bounds,* 171 Ill. 2d 1, 215 Ill. Dec. 28, 662 N.E.2d 1168 (1995); *People v. Rissley,* 165 Ill. 2d 364, 209 Ill. Dec. 205, 651 N.E.2d 133 (1995); *People v. Kitchen,* 159 Ill. 2d 1, 201 Ill. Dec. 1, 636 N.E.2d 433 (1994); *People v. Scott,* 148 Ill. 2d 479, 171 Ill. Dec. 365, 594 N.E.2d 217 (1992); *People v. Lindgren,* 79 Ill. 2d 129, 37 Ill. Dec. 348, 402 N.E.2d 238 (1980); *People v. Owens,* 65 Ill. 2d 83, 2 Ill. Dec. 298, 357 N.E.2d 465 (1976); *People v. Stremmel,* 258 Ill. App. 3d 93, 197 Ill. Dec. 177, 630 N.E.2d 1301 (1994); *People v. Brown,* 253 Ill. App. 3d 165, 192 Ill. Dec. 26, 624 N.E.2d 1378 (1993). Photographs have accordingly been admitted as tending to prove that the defendant must have known that his actions created the strong probability of great bodily harm or death, *People v. Seaberry,* 63 Ill. App. 3d 718, 20 Ill. Dec. 533, 380 N.E.2d 511 (1978); to establish issues of self-defense and the defendant's mental state, *People v. Fierer,* 124 Ill. 2d 176, 124 Ill. Dec. 855, 529 N.E.2d 972 (1988) (photograph of body prior to autopsy clearly showing victim's wounds); to establish familiarity with guns to refute accidental discharge defense, *People v. Seuffer,* 144 Ill. 2d 482, 163 Ill. Dec. 805, 582 N.E.2d 71 (1991); to establish the amount of force exerted to overpower and subdue victims and that more than one person committed the offenses, *People v. Driskel,* 224 Ill. App. 3d 304, 166 Ill. Dec. 622, 586 N.E.2d 580 (1991); to establish an unusual cause of death, *People v. Newburg,* 53 Ill. 2d 228, 290 N.E.2d 592 (1972); *People v. Speck,* 41 Ill. 2d 177, 242 N.E.2d 208 (1969); and to corroborate a defendant's confession. *People v. Bounds,* 171 Ill. 2d 1, 215 Ill. Dec. 28, 662 N.E.2d 1168 (1995). A life photograph of a victim may be admitted as part of the *corpus delicti* of the murder as well as to corroborate testimony from a "life and death" witness even when the fact of the victim's death is not in dispute. *People v. Morgan,* 142 Ill. 2d 410, 154 Ill. Dec. 534, 568 N.E.2d 755 (1991); *People v. Smith,* 152 Ill. 2d 229, 178 Ill. Dec. 335, 604 N.E.2d 858 (1992); *People v. Tenner,* 157 Ill. 2d 341, 193 Ill. Dec. 105, 626 N.E.2d 138 (1993); *People v. Kitchen,* 159 Ill. 2d 1, 201 Ill. Dec. 1, 636 N.E.2d 433 (1994).

See also People v. Abernathy, 189 Ill. App. 3d 292, 136 Ill. Dec. 677, 545 N.E.2d 201 (1989) (videotape of victim as participant in choir concerts). *Cf. People v. Young,* 206 Ill. App. 3d 789, 151 Ill. Dec. 592, 564 N.E.2d 1254 (1990) (mother should have been cropped from photograph of victim to avoid unfair prejudice); *People v. McKay,* 279 Ill. App. 3d 195, 215 Ill. Dec. 825, 664 N.E.2d 222 (1996) (preferable if photograph had not depicted victim wearing a graduation gown).

By their very nature, the more gruesome the crime, the more gruesome the photographs that have been admitted. *See People v. Generally,* 170 Ill. App. 3d 668, 121 Ill. Dec. 300, 525 N.E.2d 106 (1988). However, although photographs have been admitted where they help the jury better understand medical testimony, *People v. Owens* supra, if the gruesome nature of the photographs is caused by the autopsy procedure itself, the photographs may be excluded by reason of their relatively slight probative value. *People v. Landry,* 54 Ill. App. 3d 159, 11 Ill. Dec. 588, 368 N.E.2d 1334 (1977); *People v. Lefler* supra. On the other hand, photographs possessing probative value will not be excluded merely because they show a surgical incision. *People v. Bennet,* 82 Ill. App. 3d 225, 37 Ill. Dec. 648, 402 N.E.2d 650 (1980); *People v. Smith,* 20 Ill. App. 3d 756, 314 N.E.2d 543 (1974). *Accord People v. Green,* 209 Ill. App. 3d 233, 154 Ill. Dec. 92, 568 N.E.2d 92 (1991), autopsy photographs that were descriptive of the pathologist's search for injuries and corroborated his testimony were properly admitted. Photographs are, of course, admissible in criminal prosecutions for other purposes as well. *See, e.g., People v. Bujdud,* 177 Ill. App. 3d 396, 126 Ill. Dec. 685, 532 N.E.2d 370 (1988), photograph of defendant wearing a gang sweater making a hand gesture relevant to show motive.

Photographs do not necessarily become cumulative merely because there is also oral testimony on the same subject. *People v. Henenberg,* 55 Ill. 2d 5, 302 N.E.2d 27 (1973); *People v. Benford,* 295 Ill. App. 3d 695, 230 Ill. Dec. 119, 692 N.E.2d 1285 (1998); *People v. Crayton,* 175 Ill. App. 3d 932, 125 Ill. Dec. 493, 530 N.E.2d 651 (1988). Moreover, even where a defendant stipulates to the facts to which the photograph is relevant, the photograph has been admitted on the theory that the prosecution has the right to prove each and every element. *People v. Morgan*, 142 Ill. 2d 410, 154 Ill. Dec. 534, 568 N.E.2d 755 (1991); *People v. Kubat*, 94 Ill. 2d 437, 69 Ill. Dec. 30, 447 N.E.2d 247 (1983); *People v. Foster*, 76 Ill. 2d 365, 29 Ill. Dec. 449, 392 N.E.2d 6 (1979); *People v. Starks*, 278 Ill. App. 3d 1035, 223 Ill. Dec. 313, 679 N.E.2d 764 (1997). *See also* §401.1 supra.

Occasionally photographs of the decedent should be excluded on the grounds that probative value is substantially outweighed by the danger of unfair prejudice. *People v. Garlick*, 46 Ill. App. 3d 216, 4 Ill. Dec. 746, 360 N.E.2d 1121 (1977), color photograph depicting the decedent's massive head wound should have been excluded where defendant admitted killing and raised defense of insanity; *People v. Cruz*, 164 Ill. App. 3d 802, 115 Ill. Dec. 795, 518 N.E.2d 320 (1987), defendant not shown to be a member of a gang at time depicted in film showing acts of gang violence; *People v. Szudy*, 262 Ill. App. 3d 695, 200 Ill. Dec. 462, 635 N.E.2d 801 (1994), trial judge excluded photograph depicting body's severe decomposition and skeletalization; *People v. Gonzalez*, 265 Ill. App. 3d 315, 202 Ill. Dec. 399, 637 N.E.2d 1135 (1994), photograph showing gunshot wound to the victim's penis was more prejudicial than probative in light of other evidence describing the wound. However, in all but the most unusual circumstances, if a photograph is relevant to establish any fact of consequence in the litigation, the photograph is admissible in spite of the fact that it may be of a gruesome nature, *People v. Shum*, 117 Ill. 2d 317, 111 Ill. Dec. 546, 512 N.E.2d 1183 (1987); *People v. Kubat* supra; *People v. Lindgren* supra; *People v. Foster* supra; *People v. Speck* supra, even when the photograph can be described as "disgusting." *People v. Rissley*, 165 Ill. 2d 364, 209 Ill. Dec. 205, 651 N.E.2d 133 (1995).

A "mug shot" from police files, along with the array from which it was picked, should not be shown to the jury unless relevant and sufficiently probative in light of the danger of unfair prejudice. *People v. Murdock*, 39 Ill. 2d 553, 237 N.E.2d

442 (1968); *People v. Hardy*, 70 Ill. App. 3d 351, 26 Ill. Dec. 212, 387 N.E.2d 1042 (1979); *People v. Janis*, 240 Ill. App. 3d 805, 181 Ill. Dec. 286, 608 N.E.2d 359 (1992). *See also* §§404.3 and 404.5 infra. "Mug shots" have been held to have been properly admitted when offered for the purpose of showing how the defendant was initially identified. *People v. Sims*, 285 Ill. App. 3d 598, 220 Ill. Dec. 698, 673 N.E.2d 1119 (1996) (witness had known person only as G-man); *People v. Davis*, 173 Ill. App. 3d 300, 123 Ill. Dec. 89, 527 N.E.2d 552 (1988) (police photograph book shown to jury); *People v. Cross*, 100 Ill. App. 3d 83, 55 Ill. Dec. 477, 426 N.E.2d 623 (1981); *People v. Smith*, 20 Ill. App. 3d 756, 314 N.E.2d 543 (1974). At the same time it is asserted that "mug shot" evidence tending to inform the jury of the commission by the defendant of an unrelated criminal act should not be admitted. *People v. Warmack*, 83 Ill. 2d 112, 46 Ill. Dec. 141, 413 N.E.2d 1254 (1980). How "mug shot" evidence is to be offered to establish how the defendant was initially linked to the commission of the offense without, in the usual case, raising the inference of an unrelated crime has not been adequately addressed. *See People v. Arman*, 131 Ill. 2d 115, 137 Ill. Dec. 5, 545 N.E.2d 658 (1989). "Mug shot" evidence is most frequently introduced in response to the defendant raising the suggestiveness of the identification procedure, *People v. Bradley*, 43 Ill. App. 3d 463, 2 Ill. Dec. 529, 357 N.E.2d 696 (1976); *People v. McGee*, 160 Ill. App. 3d 807, 112 Ill. Dec. 276, 513 N.E.2d 885 (1987), the defendant arguing mistaken identification, *People v. Hughes*, 257 Ill. App. 3d 633, 195 Ill. Dec. 566, 628 N.E.2d 1030 (1993), as well as simply to enhance the credibility of the witness's in-court identification, *see* §611.16 infra. *People v. Hemphill*, 230 Ill. App. 3d 453, 171 Ill. Dec. 759, 594 N.E.2d 1279 (1992). Where admitted, to the extent possible, the "mug shots" should be taped over or cut to delete all reference to booking information, *People v. Woodruff*, 62 Ill. App. 3d 949, 20 Ill. Dec. 74, 379 N.E.2d 907 (1978); *People v. Friedman*, 144 Ill. App. 3d 895, 98 Ill. Dec. 638, 494 N.E.2d 760 (1986), and be undated. *People v. Sims*, 285 Ill. App. 3d 598, 220 Ill. Dec. 698, 673 N.E.2d 1119 (1996). The photo-

graphs should not be referred to as either "mug shots" or "booking photographs." *See People v. Sledge,* 183 Ill. App. 3d 1035, 132 Ill. Dec. 506, 539 N.E.2d 1312 (1989); *People v. Taylor,* 244 Ill. App. 3d 806, 184 Ill. Dec. 67, 612 N.E.2d 943 (1993). *See also People v. Hughes,* 257 Ill. App. 3d 633, 195 Ill. Dec. 566, 628 N.E.2d 1030 (1993), photographs referred to as a "photo book" with all pages with words on them being removed. *Compare People v. Gonzalez,* 238 Ill. App. 3d 303, 179 Ill. Dec. 472, 606 N.E.2d 304 (1992), not improper for police officer to refer to photographs shown to the witness as having come from "area 2" headquarters. Unfortunately, even when such precautions are taken, it is extremely doubtful that the jury will not be aware from common knowledge of the source of the front and profile view photographs. *People v. Campbell,* 126 Ill. App. 3d 1028, 82 Ill. Dec. 39, 467 N.E.2d 1112 (1984). However, it has been suggested that the jury may very well assume, depending upon the facts of the case, that the "mug shot" was taken when the defendant was arrested for the offense for which he is on trial. *People v. Lewis,* 103 Ill. 2d 111, 82 Ill. Dec. 442, 468 N.E.2d 1222 (1984); *People v. Warmack,* 83 Ill. 2d 112, 46 Ill. Dec. 141, 413 N.E.2d 1254 (1980). *Cf. People v. Wilson,* 168 Ill. App. 3d 847, 119 Ill. Dec. 575, 523 N.E.2d 43 (1988); *People v. Smith,* 160 Ill. App. 3d 89, 111 Ill. Dec. 747, 512 N.E.2d 1384 (1987), implying that it is neither necessary nor helpful to alter "mug shots." Sometimes the risk of prejudice is simply ignored, albeit incorrectly. *See People v. Neely,* 184 Ill. App. 3d 1097, 133 Ill. Dec. 65, 540 N.E.2d 931 (1989). The discrepancy in the cases concerning the admissibility of "mug shots" in connection with the testimony of witnesses relating to an out-of-court photographic identification of the defendant, §611.16 infra, outlined in *People v. Wheeler,* 71 Ill. App. 3d 91, 27 Ill. Dec. 235, 388 N.E.2d 1284 (1979), may be ameliorated by admission of "mug shots" only on rebuttal when the necessity for introduction of such evidence on the question of identity can be more accurately evaluated. *People v. Maffioli,* 406 Ill. 315, 94 N.E.2d 191 (1950); *People v. Dean,* 99 Ill. App. 3d 999, 55 Ill. Dec. 304, 426 N.E.2d 279 (1981). It is preferable not to permit the "mug shots" to go to the jury room. *See People v. Taylor,* 143 Ill. App. 3d 252, 97 Ill. Dec. 352, 492 N.E.2d 1011 (1986). *See generally People v. Arman,* 171 Ill. App. 3d 232, 121 Ill. Dec. 147, 524 N.E.2d 1195 (1988) (Freeman, J., dissenting). With respect to providing "mug shots" to the jury when specifically requested, *see People v. Lash,* 252 Ill. App. 3d 239, 191 Ill. Dec. 751, 624 N.E.2d 1129 (1993). The erroneous admission of "mug shots" is subject to harmless error analysis. *People v. Arman* supra; *People v. Lash* supra.

Tangible personal property.   A photograph of property that the accused is alleged to have exerted unauthorized control over or to have otherwise obtained unlawfully is admissible in a prosecution for theft, retail theft, deceptive practice, robbery, armed robbery, burglary, or residential burglary if the photograph: (1) will serve the purpose of demonstrating the nature of the property; and (2) is otherwise admissible into evidence under all other rules of law governing the admissibility of photographs into evidence. The fact that it is impractical to introduce into evidence the actual property for any reason, including its size, weight, or unavailability, need not be established for the court to find a photograph of that property to be competent evidence. If a photograph is found to be competent evidence, it is admissible into evidence in place of the property and to the same extent as the property itself. 725 ILCS 5/115-9(a). With respect to procedural aspects of the statute, *see People v. Mikolajewski,* 272 Ill. App. 3d 311, 208 Ill. Dec. 443, 649 N.E.2d 499 (1995).

§401.9   Demonstrative Evidence: X-rays

X-rays are no different from ordinary photographs. However, the fact that the X-ray shows an image not visible to the unaided eye requires a different type of foundation proof to establish the correctness of the portrayal. *Stevens v. Illinois Central R. Co.,* 306 Ill. 370, 137 N.E. 859 (1923), suggests that correctness may be shown by comparison with what the witness saw through a fluoroscope or by proving skill in X-ray techniques, proper working condition and accuracy of equipment, manner of taking the picture, and correctness of result based on experience. Since an X-ray goes beyond mere illustration of the witness's testimony, it is admitted as substantive evidence. Accordingly, the Original Writing Rule applies, *see* Federal Advisory Committee's Note to Rule 1002, 56 F.R.D. 183, 342 (1973).

§401.10 Demonstrative Evidence: Courtroom and Recorded Demonstrations

Demonstrations in court, often employing models, in general are permissible for explanatory purposes but not for dramatic effect or emotional appeal. *Smith v. Ohio Oil Co.,* 10 Ill. App. 2d 67, 134 N.E.2d 526 (1956). The admissibility of courtroom demonstrations rests in the discretion of the court. *People v. Aliwoli,* 42 Ill. App. 3d 1014, 1 Ill. Dec. 609, 356 N.E.2d 891 (1976). The use by medical witnesses of a skeleton of a human foot, *Chicago & Alton Ry. Co. v. Walker,* 217 Ill. 605, 75 N.E. 520 (1905), or a plastic model of a human skeleton, *Smith v. Ohio Oil Co.* supra; *People v. Henenberg,* 55 Ill. 2d 5, 302 N.E.2d 27 (1973), to explain the nature of injuries or the cause of death has been sustained. Moreover, the exhibition of an injured eyeball that had been removed has been held not improper, *Seltzer v. Saxton,* 71 Ill. App. 229 (1896). The use of anatomically correct dolls as a testimonial aid by young children testifying as to sexual abuse is permitted. *People v. Carter,* 244 Ill. App. 3d 792, 185 Ill. Dec. 318, 614 N.E.2d 452 (1993). On the other hand, production of surgical instruments with a demonstration of operating techniques has been disapproved. *Winters v. Richerson,* 9 Ill. App. 2d 359, 132 N.E.2d 673 (1956). Similarly, a request to have a person put a nylon stocking cap over his face to show the difficulty of identification was properly refused. *People v. Rose,* 77 Ill. App. 3d 330, 32 Ill. Dec. 700, 395 N.E.2d 1081 (1979). Since the dividing line between proper and improper demonstrations is by no means a sharp one, considerable discretion must be left to the trial judge. *Smith v. Ohio Oil Co.* supra. With respect to demonstrating personal injuries, *see* §401.5 supra.

Involving a juror in the demonstration as an assistant or as a subject is improper as it may have the effect of converting the participant into a witness for the party conducting the demonstration; the juror may acquire knowledge that is not directly available to the other jurors, knowledge that is not subject to cross-examination by opposing counsel. *Schaffner v. Chicago & N.W. Transp. Co.,* 129 Ill. 2d 1, 133 Ill. Dec. 432, 541 N.E.2d 643 (1989).

A recording of an out of court demonstration reconstructing a relevant event such as the occurrence of an accident is admissible in the discretion of the court provided that the essential elements of the incident are substantially similar to those existing at the time of the event. *Wiedemann v. Industrial Erectors, Inc.,* 137 Ill. App. 3d 47, 91 Ill. Dec. 504, 483 N.E.2d 990 (1985). *See also* §401.8 supra dealing with photographs of a demonstration.

During final argument, considerable latitude is allowed in illustrating and explaining argument. *Caley v. Manicke,* 24 Ill. 2d 390, 182 N.E.2d 206 (1962), proper to itemize elements of claimed damages on chart. *See also Robinson v. Kathryn,* 23 Ill. App. 2d 5, 161 N.E.2d 477 (1959), error to permit plaintiff himself during final argument to reenact how he was riding motorcycle but suggesting propriety of attorney's making the demonstration, and §702.7 for discussion of propriety of "*per diem*" argument.

§401.11   Experiments

The results of experiments are substantive evidence, admissible to show cause and effect, characteristics, and the like. Illustrations are: determining whether visibility was sufficient to identify persons, *Hauser v. People,* 210 Ill. 253, 71 N.E. 416 (1904); whether defendant could see plaintiff's car in spite of presence of a hill, *Terrel v. Lovelace,* 65 Ill. App. 3d 332, 21 Ill. Dec. 841, 382 N.E.2d 135 (1978); ballistics test to identify firearm from which bullet was fired, *People v. Fisher,* 340 Ill. 216, 172 N.E. 743 (1930); contents of soft drink bottle, *Neubauer v. Coca-Cola Bottling Co. of Chicago,* 96 Ill. App. 2d 18, 238 N.E.2d 437 (1968).

Since an experiment to show cause and effect occurs under controlled conditions, with the possibility of varying conditions so as to produce a desired result, and since physical characteristics are commonly involved, insistence upon substantial similarity of essential conditions is usually strict. *R.A. Watson Orchards, Inc. v. New York, C. & St. L.R. Co.,* 250 Ill. App. 22 (1928), evidence of experiments to prove that locomotive sparks set fire to granulated cork held erroneously admitted for failure to show coal and cork used or atmospheric conditions were same; *Sansonetti v. Archer Laundry, Inc.,* 44 Ill. App. 3d 789, 358 N.E.2d 1142, 3 Ill. Dec. 457 (1977), reconstruction of accident involving scaffold excluded for failure substantially to duplicate conditions; *Illinois State Trust Co. v. Walker Mfg. Co.,* 73 Ill. App. 3d 585, 29 Ill. Dec. 513, 392 N.E.2d 70 (1979), tests of jack stand should have been excluded since conditions were not similar; *Kent v. Knox Motor Serv., Inc.,* 95 Ill. App. 3d 223, 50 Ill. Dec. 804, 419 N.E.2d 1253 (1981), proper to exclude experiment to determine extent of visibility prior to accident on grounds the conditions not shown substantially similar; *Amstar Corp. v. Aurora Fast Freight,* 141 Ill. App. 3d 705, 96 Ill. Dec. 31, 490 N.E.2d 1067 (1986), proper to exclude videotape of vantage point of driver taken from a car when driver had been in the tractor of a semi; *People v. Wills,* 153 Ill. App. 3d 328, 106 Ill. Dec. 207, 505 N.E.2d 754 (1987), proper to exclude videotape of test firing where weapon and physical position of the shooter were significantly altered. In *Handley v. Erb,* 314 Ill. App. 207, 41 N.E.2d 222 (1941), it was held error to admit evidence of experiment to determine visibility of rope stretched across street, because among other differences, the witness in the experiment knew of the presence of the rope, while defendant at time of accident did not. It may be suggested, however, that the physical characteristic of visibility was an important circumstance, properly determinable by a subject who knew of the presence of the rope and helpful in determining whether defendant should have seen it. Similarity of conditions was held sufficient in *Downing v. Metropolitan Life Ins. Co.*, 314 Ill. App. 222, 41 N.E.2d 297 (1941), experiments to determine whether insured could have reached trigger of gun by reaching over fence, in *Silverman v. General Motors Corp.*, 99 Ill. App. 3d 593, 54 Ill. Dec. 882, 425 N.E.2d 1099 (1981), experiment to determine what occurs when the brakes are applied in a car whose throttle has locked while the vehicle is travelling 80 m.p.h., and in *Barth v. International Harvester Co.*, 160 Ill. App. 3d 1072, 112 Ill. Dec. 479, 513 N.E.2d 1088 (1987), experiment to show that a truck could turn a 90-degree corner safely at a speed in excess of five miles per hour. Where the experiment does not seek to reenact the incident but only to deal with one aspect or principle directly involved, the requirement of substantial similarity relates solely to that aspect or principle. *Galindo v. Riddell, Inc.*, 107 Ill. App. 3d 139, 62 Ill. Dec 849, 437 N.E.2d 376 (1982); *Brennan v. Wisconsin Central Limited*, 227 Ill. App. 3d 1070, 169 Ill. Dec. 321, 591 N.E.2d 494 (1992); *Van Steemburg v. General Aviation, Inc.*, 243 Ill. App. 3d 299, 183 Ill. Dec. 496, 611 N.E.2d 1144 (1993).

Experiments not designed to recreate the incident, such as testing to determine the nature of a substance, often require no control or less stringent control over similarity of conditions.

Experiments are generally conducted out of court with the results being reported in court. Still photographs, motion pictures, or videotapes of the experiment are sometimes displayed to the jury. *Silverman v. General Motors Corp.*, 99 Ill. App. 3d 593, 54 Ill. Dec. 882, 425 N.E.2d 1099 (1981). With these experiments, establishing substantial similarity is facilitated by giving notice of the experiment to the adversary and providing for an opportunity to observe. Notice and opportunity to observe remove the most telling argument against admission of such experiments. "Your Honor, I wasn't there; how can I even begin to prepare for cross-examination?" When a litigant wishes actually to conduct an experiment before the trier of fact, the court must decide whether the confusion, delay, and potential misleading of the jury substantially outweigh its probative value, §403.1 infra. Of course the requirement of similarity of conditions must initially be satisfied. *Compare* discussion of posed photographic reenactment, §401.8 supra.

If conducted in court, involvement of a juror in the experiment as an assistant or as a subject is improper as it may have the effect of converting the participant into a witness for the party conducting the experiment; the juror may acquire knowledge that is not directly available to the other jurors, knowledge that is not subject to cross-examination by opposing counsel. *Schaffner v. Chicago & N.W. Transp. Co.*, 129 Ill. 2d 1, 133 Ill. Dec. 432, 541 N.E.2d 643 (1989).

The trial court's determination of admissibility of the experiment will not be reversed on appeal absent clear abuse of discretion. *Ford v. City of Chicago*, 132 Ill. App. 3d 408, 87 Ill. Dec. 240, 476 N.E.2d 1232 (1985); *People v. Haas*, 203 Ill. App. 3d 779, 148 Ill. Dec. 667, 560 N.E.2d 1365 (1990); *Halleck v. Coastal Building Maintenance Co.*, 269 Ill. App. 3d 887, 207 Ill. Dec. 387, 647 N.E.2d 618 (1995).

Distinguishing between an experiment and the use of demonstrative evidence is sometimes difficult. *See, e.g., Foster v. Devilbiss Co.*, 174 Ill. App. 3d 359, 124 Ill. Dec. 600, 529 N.E.2d 581 (1988), where an in-court experiment to establish that a piece of metal comprising a trigger guard could be easily bent was called a demonstration.

§401.12 Other Scientific Evidence

Scientific evidence in great variety has become so commonplace as scarcely to require discussion, and many instances of its use are found elsewhere in this volume. Its relevancy depends upon judicial acceptance of the scientific principle invoked and a showing of the propriety of its application in the particular case.

In determining whether a scientific principle, technique, or test is sufficiently reliable to be admitted, *People v. Baynes,* 88 Ill. 2d 225, 241, 58 Ill. Dec. 819, 430 N.E.2d 1070 (1981), *strongly implies,* and *People v. Jordan,* 103 Ill. 2d 192, 82 Ill. Dec. 925, 469 N.E.2d 569 (1984), *specifically states,* while *People v. Columbo,* 118 Ill. App. 3d 882, 74 Ill. Dec. 304, 455 N.E.2d 733 (1983), and *People v. Cohoon,* 120 Ill. App. 3d 62, 74 Ill. Dec. 556, 457 N.E.2d 998 (1983), *simply assume* that the test to be applied is that enunciated in *Frye v. United States,* 293 F. 1013, 1014 (D.C. Cir. 1923):

> Just when a scientific principle or discovery crosses the line between the experimental and demonstrable stages is difficult to define. Somewhere in this twilight zone the evidential force of the principle must be recognized, and while courts will go a long way in admitting expert testimony deduced from a well-recognized scientific principle or discovery, the thing from which the deduction is made must be sufficiently established to have gained general acceptance in the particular field in which it belongs.

A scientific principle, technique, or test may be established to have gained general acceptance in a variety of ways. When offered into evidence for the first time, expert testimony as to the underlying scientific principle and as to the validity of the technique or test applying that principle will be received. On the basis of its evaluation of the conflicting expert testimony the court must determine whether the scientific test is sufficiently reliable to be received into evidence. Application of the *Frye* standard calls for a judicial determination both that the court itself finds the scientific test reliable and that the test's reliability is generally accepted in the particular scientific field in which the test belongs. Newness alone is not a bar to admissibility, for every scientific technique that is eventually accepted must have its first day in court. Moreover, neither lack of absolute certainty nor lack of uniformity of expert opinion precludes a court from finding on the basis of expert witness testimony and other evidence admitted at trial that a scientific test is reliable and that the scientific test's reliability is, or clearly would be when brought to the attention of the appropriate experts, generally accepted in the particular scientific field in which the test belongs. *See also* §702.4 infra.

Traditionally, and not without reason, courts have been conservative in accepting new scientific principles, techniques, and tests, and at the early stages proof of their validity has been required. As validity is established by evidence, however, acceptance tends to move into the area of judicial notice, leaving for proof only such explanations as may be necessary for understanding by the trier of fact. A current development is the legislative disposition to recognize scientific evidence and to specify its effect by statute. *See, e.g.,* chemical tests of bodily substance for intoxication, 625 ILCS 5/11-501.2; blood tests for paternity, *id.,* 750 ILCS 45/1-45/26; radar speed detection (by implication), *id.,* 625 ILCS 5/11-601, 5/11-602.

In connection with the application of a scientific technique in the particular case, cognizance should be taken of the necessity of identifying specimens submitted to tests and showing that their condition was unchanged. A less stringent standard appears to prevail in civil cases than in criminal cases. *Woolley v. Hafner's Wagon Wheel, Inc.,* 22 Ill. 2d 413, 176 N.E.2d 757 (1961), error in civil case to exclude results of intoxication test of blood handled in ordinary laboratory routine because possibility of tampering was not eliminated. *Cf. People v. Norman,* 24 Ill. 2d 403, 182 N.E.2d 188 (1962), holding in a criminal case that the requirements were not satisfied as to a specimen of powder that lay on a laboratory desk for several days in an unsealed envelope. An illustration of sufficient compliance is *People v. Jones,* 19 Ill. 2d 131, 166 N.E.2d 20 (1960). *See also* §901.2 infra.

§401.13   Availability of Better Method or Device

Negligence actions. Evidence that a better method or device is available for use in connection with the operation in question is admissible in negligence cases for the same purpose and on the same theory as evidence of usage or practice. *See* §406.5 infra. *Stephen v. Duffy,* 237 Ill. 549, 86 N.E. 1082 (1909), method of exploding dynamite that would disclose a misfire of one charge; *Supolski v. Ferguson & Lange Foundry Co.,* 272 Ill. 82, 111 N.E. 544 (1916), practicability of enclosing equipment; *Wawryszyn v. Illinois Central R. Co.,* 10 Ill. App. 2d 394, 135 N.E.2d 154 (1956), use of different method to handle heavy freight; *Mullen v. Chicago Transit Auth.,* 33 Ill. App. 2d 103, 178 N.E.2d 670 (1961), use of protective device over electrically charged third rail by another railroad.

Products liability.   The feasibility of alternative methods or devices is relevant in an action alleging an unreasonably dangerous product due to a design defect. If a method or device represents a safer design alternative and was technologically feasible at the time, evidence of the method or device may be introduced. *Sutkowski v. Universal Marion Corp.,* 5 Ill. App. 3d 313, 281 N.E.2d 749 (1972). Plaintiff may introduce evidence of the availability of methods or devices although not adopted by the industry at the time. *Rivera v. Rockford Machine & Tool Co.,* 1 Ill. App. 3d 641, 274 N.E.2d 828 (1971). Evidence that defendant violated a relevant industry custom or usage, *Williams v. Brown Mfg. Co.,* 93 Ill. App. 2d 334, 236 N.E.2d 125 (1968), *rev'd on other grounds,* 45 Ill. 2d 418, 261 N.E.2d 305 (1970), or failed to comply with a regulation or standard operating like custom, *Moren v. Samuel M. Langston Co.,* 96 Ill. App. 2d 133, 237 N.E.2d 759 (1968), may also be admitted if tending to show manufacture of an unreasonably dangerous product. *Ruffiner v. Material Service Corp.,* 116 Ill. 2d 53, 106 Ill. Dec. 781, 506 N.E.2d 581 (1987); *Doyle v. White Metal Rolling & Stamping,* 249 Ill. App. 3d 370, 188 Ill. Dec. 339, 618 N.E.2d 909 (1993). Evidence of standards, regulations, usage, or customs is also admissible on behalf of the defendant to show lack of culpable conduct in a products liability action. *Rucker v. Norfolk & W.R. Co.,* 77 Ill. 2d 434, 33 Ill. Dec. 145, 396 N.E.2d 534 (1979), evidence of compliance with federal standards is admissible on issue of whether a product is defective as well as whether a defective condition is unreasonably dangerous. *See* §406.5 infra. *See* §407.1 for discussion of admissibility of subsequent remedial measures in relation to feasibility of precautionary methods.

§401.14   Admissibility of Similar Occurrences: General Considerations

In numerous situations the law recognizes the propriety of drawing inferences from happenings other than the one in issue. The process parallels the observational method of science. The validity of the inference and the admissibility of the evidence frequently depend upon the presence of a sufficient degree of similarity between the other happenings and the one in question. The similarity required should be consistent with the situation and the inference sought to be drawn. Once substantial similarity has been shown, variations go to the weight to be accorded the evidence, not to its admissibility. *Yassin v. Certified Grocers of Illinois,* 150 Ill. App. 3d 1052, 104 Ill. Dec. 52, 502 N.E.2d 315 (1986). Thus, when animal or human participation is involved in the other occurrences, the implicit assumption is that they were normal, average specimens, without any showing to that effect. On the other hand, when physical conditions are significant, as is often the case, any substantial variation will destroy the probative value, and this is so whether other instrumentalities or the same one are involved. For example, in *Bloomington v. Legg,* 151 Ill. 9, 37 N.E. 696 (1894), a horse ran away because its bridle caught on a projection on a watering fountain, resulting in the driver's death. Other occurrences of this nature that happened when the projections were different were held inadmissible; those happening after the projections were altered to the condition existing at the time of the accident in question were admissible. No concern was indicated as to the characteristics of any of the other horses or drivers. In *O.H. Jewell Filter Co. v. Kirk,* 200 Ill. 382, 65 N.E. 698 (1902), evidence that other filters worked satisfactorily, offered to show satisfactory performance of the one in question, was held properly excluded in the absence of a showing that the water to be treated and the use made of it were the same. No human participation was involved. And in *Moore v. Bloomington, D. & C.R. Co.*, 295 Ill. 63, 128 N.E. 721 (1920), a grade crossing collision with an automobile going south, evidence of collisions with automobiles going north, to show notice of a dangerous condition, was held improperly admitted. No concern for individual characteristics of the various drivers was indicated.

This difference in requirements of similarity of participants and of physical conditions is well calculated to promote the sensible use of evidence of other happenings, while at the same time minimizing the collateral issues necessarily involved. *See generally* §401.1 supra and §§403.1 and 607.2 infra.

§401.15   Admissibility of Similar Occurrences: Illustrative Uses

Cause and effect.   Evidence of similar happenings is admissible to prove the effect resulting from certain conditions. *Cooper v. Randall*, 59 Ill. 317 (1871), in action for damages to property from dust given off by mill, error to exclude evidence that mill threw dust on neighboring properties; *Nixon v. Chicago*, 212 Ill. App. 365 (1918), evidence of damage to other buildings as result of constructing tunnels properly admitted to prove that construction of tunnel damaged plaintiff's building. *Cf. Arnell v. Superior Mirror Co.*, 210 Ill. App. 486 (1918), in action by employee for silver nitrate poisoning, evidence of silver nitrate poisoning of employees in other factories held properly excluded as raising collateral issues. *See also* the following paragraph.

Dangerous condition; cause of accident; notice.   The negligence cases agree that evidence of other accidents occurring under substantially similar conditions is admissible to prove the probability that defendant had notice of the existence of a dangerous condition. *Wolczek v. Public Serv. Co.*, 342 Ill. 482,

174 N.E. 577 (1931); *Chicago v. Powers,* 42 Ill. 169 (1866); *Ficken v. Alton & Southern Railway Co.,* 291 Ill. App. 3d 635, 226 Ill. Dec. 187, 685 N.E.2d 1 (1996); *Simmons v. Aldi-Brenner Co.,* 162 Ill. App. 3d 238, 113 Ill. Dec. 594, 515 N.E.2d 403 (1987). While evidence of other accidents may also be relevant to establish notice on the part of the plaintiff, *see Belshaw v. Hillsboro Hotel, Inc.,* 229 Ill. App. 3d 480, 170 Ill. Dec. 628, 593 N.E.2d 170 (1992), such evidence is not admissible to the extent offered to establish character, e.g., lack of carefulness, for the inference that the plaintiff acted in conformity therewith. *See* §404.2 infra.

Unfortunately, some suggestion is found that the use of the evidence is limited to notice. *Wolczek v. Public Serv. Co.* supra; *Moore v. Bloomington, D. & C.R. Co.,* 295 Ill. 63, 128 N.E. 721 (1920); *Mobile & Ohio R. Co. v. Vallowe,* 214 Ill. 124, 73 N.E. 416 (1905); *Chicago v. Powers* supra. These cases did not, however, squarely involve the issue, and the suggestion that they put forth has been abandoned. The logic of *Bloomington v. Legg,* 151 Ill. 9, 13, 37 N.E. 696 (1894), as to both negligence and products liability cases, seems unassailable:

> Where an issue is made as to the safety of any machinery or work of man's construction which is for practical use, the manner in which it has served that purpose, when put to that use, would be a matter material to the issue, and ordinary experience of that practical use, and the effect of such use, bear directly upon such issue.

This view finds support in *Chicago v. Jarvis,* 226 Ill. 614, 80 N.E. 1079 (1907); *Shepard v. Aurora,* 5 Ill. App. 2d 12, 124 N.E.2d 584 (1955); *Linneen v. Chicago,* 310 Ill. App. 274, 34 N.E.2d 100 (1941); *Miller v. Rokita,* 131 Ill. App. 3d 774, 86 Ill. Dec. 850, 476 N.E.2d 26 (1985); and *Van Steemburg v. General Aviation, Inc.,* 243 Ill. App. 3d 299, 183 Ill. Dec. 496, 611 N.E.2d 1144 (1993). *Accord Bass v. Cincinnati, Inc.,* 180 Ill. App. 3d 1076, 129 Ill. Dec. 781, 536 N.E.2d 831 (1989), evidence of prior accidents is admissible to show that the common cause of the accidents is a dangerous or unsafe thing or condition; *Gowler v. Ferrell-Ross Co.,* 206 Ill. App. 3d 194, 150 Ill. Dec. 646, 563 N.E.2d 773 (1990), admission of evidence of either prior accidents or subsequent accidents is proper if, at the relevant times, the equipment involved was in substantially the same condition and the accidents were sufficiently similar.

When offered to establish the existence of a particular danger, sufficient similarity must be shown between the other accidents and the present accident, *Boersma v. Amoco Oil Co.,* 276 Ill. App. 3d 638, 213 Ill. Dec. 152, 658 N.E.2d 1173 (1995); *Trimble v. Olympic Tavern, Inc.,* 239 Ill. App. 3d 393, 180 Ill. Dec. 199, 606 N.E.2d 1276 (1993), which includes a sufficient showing that the condition or thing shown to be the common cause of danger in such earlier accidents must be the condition or thing contributing to the danger of the accident complained of, and that the instrumentality which caused the danger in the earlier accidents was in substantially the same condition at the time such other accidents occurred as it was at the time of the accident complained of. *Simmons v. Aldi-Brenner Co.,* 162 Ill. App. 3d 238, 113 Ill. Dec. 594, 515 N.E.2d 403 (1987).

Testimony as to reasonably similar occurrences is also admissible in products liability actions to establish that the cause of each accident was a dangerous or unsafe condition of a product. *Schaffner v. Chicago & N.W. Transp. Co.,* 129 Ill. 2d 1, 133 Ill. Dec. 432, 541 N.E.2d 643 (1989); *Rucker v. Norfolk & W. Ry.,* 77 Ill. 2d 434, 33 Ill. Dec. 145, 396 N.E.2d 534 (1979); *Doyle v. White Metal Rolling & Stamping,* 249 Ill. App. 3d 370, 188 Ill. Dec. 339, 618 N.E.2d 909 (1993); *Biehler v. White Metal Rolling & Stamping Corp.,* 65 Ill. App. 3d 1001, 22 Ill. Dec. 634, 382 N.E.2d 1389 (1979.) *See also* Prosser and Keeton, Law of Torts §103 (5th ed. 1984); *Hoppe v. Midwest Conveyor Co.,* 485 F.2d 1196 (8th Cir. 1973), the frequency or infrequency of use of the same product with or without mishap is relevant in the issue of defective design.

Evidence of a prior accident is also admissible to establish the generally hazardous nature of the accident site and the defendant's notice thereof. For this purpose evidence of both similar and dissimilar accidents is admissible although the proponent may not establish the details of dissimilar accidents when offered solely to show the generally hazardous conditions and the defendant's notice thereof. *Turgeon v. Commonwealth Edision Co.*, 258 Ill. App. 3d 234, 197 Ill. Dec. 194, 630 N.E.2d 1318 (1994); *Trimble v. Olympic Tavern, Inc.* supra; *Henderson v. Illinois Gulf R.R. Co.*, 114 Ill. App. 3d 754, 70 Ill. Dec. 595, 449 N.E.2d 942 (1983).

While earlier cases held a history of no accidents to be inadmissible, *Mobile & Ohio R. Co. v. Vallowe* supra, the evidence now is held admissible for the purpose of showing absence of notice, *Wolczek v. Public Serv. Co.* supra, and subject to problems regarding proof as evidence tending to establish that the condition was not dangerous. *Compare Van Holt v. National Railroad Passenger Corp.*, 283 Ill. App. 3d 62, 218 Ill. Dec. 762, 669 N.E.2d 1288 (1996) (lack of prior accidents is less probative than evidence of prior accidents and is properly excluded within discretion of the court in light of evidence of improper maintenance of taxi tunnel). Absence of similar accidents is also admissible in a products liability action. *Schaffner v. Chicago N.W. Transp. Co.*, 129 Ill. 2d 1, 133 Ill. Dec. 432, 541 N.E.2d 643 (1989), evidence of absence of accidents with bicycle quick-release mechanism; *Leischner v. Deere & Co.*, 127 Ill. App. 3d 175, 82 Ill. Dec. 120, 468 N.E.2d 182 (1984), evidence that no accidents of the type suffered were reported with respect to 64,000 automobiles was improperly excluded. The proponent of such evidence must show that the absence of such claims occurred when others were using the same product as the injured party under conditions substantially similar to those conditions present when the injury occurred. *McKenzie v. S.K. Hand Tool Corp.*, 272 Ill. App. 3d 1, 208 Ill. Dec. 918, 650 N.E.2d 612 (1995); *Connelly v. General Motors Corp.*, 184 Ill. App. 3d 378, 132 Ill. Dec. 630, 540 N.E.2d 370 (1989).

The reasonably similar occurrences or lack thereof may be either prior to or subsequent to the incident in question. *Bass v. Cincinnati, Inc.*, 180 Ill. App. 3d 1076, 129 Ill. Dec. 781, 536 N.E.2d 831 (1989).

Intent and motive.   As in the criminal cases, similar acts are admissible in civil cases to show intention or motive. Thus evidence that other Negro children were excluded from certain schools was admissible to prove that petitioners were excluded on account of race, *People v. Alton,* 179 Ill. 615, 54 N.E. 421 (1899), and proof of prior transactions was admissible to show that a note was given for "gambling" on the board of trade, *Gardner v. Meeker,* 169 Ill. 40, 48 N.E. 307 (1897).

Fraud cases.   The fraud cases follow the above pattern as regards intent. *Lockwood v. Doane,* 107 Ill. 235 (1883); *Blalock v. Randall,* 76 Ill. 224 (1875); *Smith v. National Life & Acc. Ins. Co.,* 286 Ill. App. 566, 4 N.E.2d 128 (1936). However, they show a disposition to go farther and to admit other instances of similar conduct to prove that the fraud occurred on the occasion in question. *Blalock v. Randall* supra. The latter holding runs counter to the general rule against circumstantial use of character evidence in civil cases, §404.2 infra, but may be justified as showing a scheme or plan, §404.5 infra. *Cf. Burroughs v. Comegys,* 17 Ill. App. 653 (1885), error to admit testimony that another person also found sand in oats purchased from defendant.

Other sales of property; offers.   Evidence of sales of other property has long been recognized as a proper method of proving fair cash market value. *Department of Public Works & Bldgs. v. Klehm,* 56 Ill. 2d 121, 306 N.E.2d 1 (1974); *White v. Hermann,* 51 Ill. 243 (1869). The other property sold must be similar in locality and character to that in question, *O'Hare v. Chicago, M. & N.R. Co.,* 139 Ill. 151, 28 N.E. 923 (1891), the sale not too remote in time, *St. Louis & Illinois Belt Ry. v. Guswelle,* 236 Ill. 214, 86 N.E. 230 (1908), and no change in conditions or marked fluctuations in values have occurred since the sale, *Department of Transp. v. Prombo,* 63 Ill. App. 3d 407, 20 Ill. Dec. 120, 379 N.E.2d 953 (1978). All told, similarity in material respects includes such characteristics as locality, character, time, proximity, market conditions, improvements, and mode of payment, which should be cash. Minor differences do not require exclusion of the evidence of other sales that would assist the jury; differences may be emphasized and explained to the jury. *People ex rel. Director of Finance v. Y.W.C.A.,* 74 Ill. 2d 561, 25 Ill. Dec. 649, 387 N.E.2d 305 (1979). While the determination of these preliminary questions is largely within the discretion of the trial judge, *Evanston v. Piotrowicz,* 20 Ill. 2d 512, 170 N.E.2d 569 (1960), his discretion is not uncontrolled; sales in a general farming area characterized by large tracts are not admissible to prove value in an area of specialized small acreage tracts on the fringe of change from semi-urban to urban, *Chicago v. Habecke,* 409 Ill. 425, 100 N.E.2d 616 (1951), and sales of subdivided lots are irrelevant to the value of unsubdivided land, *Waukegan Park Dist. v. First Natl. Bank,* 22 Ill. 2d 238, 174 N.E.2d 824 (1961), subdividing in this connection meaning improvement beyond mere platting, *Union Elec. Power Co. v. Sauget,* 1 Ill. 2d 125, 115 N.E.2d 246 (1953). Difference in size alone does not necessarily establish dissimilarity, nor does location within as contrasted with location outside corporate limits. *Chicago v. Harbecke* supra. Similarly, the existence of zoning dissimilarities does not per se render evidence of a sale incompetent. *Lake County Forest Preserve Dist. v. O'Malley,* 96 Ill. App. 3d 1084, 52 Ill. Dec. 117, 421 N.E.2d 980 (1981).

A sale of the property in question is admissible if not too remote in time and no substantial change in conditions or in market values has intervened. *Forest Preserve Dist. v. Krol,* 12 Ill. 2d 139, 145 N.E.2d 599 (1957); *Department of Conservation v. Aspegren Fin. Corp.,* 72 Ill. 2d 302, 21 Ill. Dec. 153, 381 N.E.2d 231 (1978); *Application of Busse,* 124 Ill. App. 3d 433, 79 Ill. Dec. 747, 464 N.E.2d 651 (1984).

The other sales must be voluntary. Prices paid under threat of condemnation, *Peoria Gaslight & Coke Co. v. Peoria Term. Ry.,* 146 Ill. 372, 34 N.E. 550 (1893), or under foreclosure, *West Skokie Drainage Dist. v. Dawson,* 243 Ill. 175, 90 N.E. 377 (1909), are not admissible. A trustee's sale under decree is not voluntary, *Forest Preserve Dist. v. Dearlove,* 337 Ill. 555, 169 N.E. 753 (1930), nor is a private sale induced by inability to pay upkeep charges. *Forest Preserve Dist. v. Eckhoff,* 372 Ill. 391, 24 N.E.2d 52 (1939).

Evidence proving a comparable sale must show the sale was for money and not wholly or partly for other consideration such as exchange of land. *Department of Business & Econ. Dev. v. Baumann,* 56 Ill. 2d 382, 308 N.E.2d 580 (1974).

Inadmissible sales cannot be brought out on cross-examination under the guise of testing the knowledge of the witness. *Forest Preserve Dist. v. Chilvers,* 344 Ill. 573, 176 N.E. 720 (1931); *Sanitary Dist. v. Corneau,* 257 Ill. 93, 100 N.E. 517 (1913).

Offers present collateral problems as to good faith and ability to pay that are not present in actual sales. Hence certain restrictions are found in this connection. An offer to buy the land in question is admissible on behalf of the owner, if made for cash, and with due regard for market values rather than for a particular need, by an offeror able to pay. *Chicago v. Harrison-Halsted Bldg. Corp.,* 11 Ill. 2d 431, 143 N.E.2d 40 (1957). In short, the offer must be *bona fide,* i.e., made in good faith, by a person of good judgment, who is acquainted with the value of real estate, possessing a sufficient ability to pay. *City of Chicago v. Anthony,* 136 Ill. 2d 169, 144, Ill. Dec. 93, 554 N.E.2d 1381 (1990); *County of St. Clair v. Wilson,* 284 Ill. App. 3d 79, 219 Ill. Dec. 712, 672 N.E.2d 27 (1996). Offers to buy similar property are admissible on behalf of the owner, subject to the same requirements, if evidence of sales is not available. *Chicago v. Lehmann,* 262 Ill. 468, 104 N.E. 829 (1914). Offers to sell would on principle seem to be admissible on behalf of a condemnor, if voluntary, in the absence of actual sales.

An offer to sell by the owner is admissible against her as an admission. *Springer v. Chicago,* 135 Ill. 552, 26 N.E. 514 (1891). An offer to purchase by a condemnor, however, being in the nature of an offer of compromise, is inadmissible. *Chicago v. Harrison-Halsted Bldg. Corp.* supra; §408.1 infra.

Rebuttal.   Evidence to the effect that a practice followed rendered the event in question impossible or unlikely may be rebutted by specific happenings indicating the contrary. *Stolp v. Blair,* 68 Ill. 541 (1873), evidence that plaintiff had loaned money to others without taking notes properly admitted to rebut inference that transaction of this kind with defendant was improbable; *Welter v. Bowman Dairy Co.*, 318 Ill. App. 305, 47 N.E.2d 739 (1943), finding of glass in other milk properly admitted to rebut inference that careful inspection procedures made presence of foreign substance in milk impossible.

Uniform Commercial Code. Under the Uniform Commercial Code, "course of performance" is admissible to determine the meaning of a contract. 810 ILCS 5/2-208(1). In addition, course of dealing and usage of trade may be relevant considerations. 810 ILCS 5/2-208(2) and 5/1-205. Such concepts are also relevant where the Uniform Commercial Code does not apply. *Beatrice Foods Co. v. Gallagher,* 47 Ill. App. 2d 9, 197 N.E.2d 274 (1964), course of dealings. Conversely, evidence of a course of performance under a contract that does not contain the same provisions as the contract in issue is irrelevant. *Dayan v. McDonald's Corp.,* 125 Ill. App. 3d 972, 81 Ill. Dec. 156, 466 N.E.2d 958 (1984).

§402 Admissibility of Relevant Evidence Only

§402.1 Relevant Evidence Generally Admissible; Irrelevant Evidence Inadmissible

The general rule that all relevant evidence is admissible unless otherwise provided by law states a touchstone of any rational system of justice. *People v. Cruz,* 162 Ill. 2d 314, 205 Ill. Dec. 345, 643 N.E.2d 636 (1994); *People v. Peeples,* 155 Ill. 2d 422, 186 Ill. Dec. 341, 616 N.E.2d 294 (1993) (citing Handbook); *People ex rel. Noren v. Dempsey,* 10 Ill. 2d 288, 139 N.E.2d 780 (1957). Relevant evidence will be inadmissible whenever applicable state or federal common law, statutes, promulgated rules, or either the Illinois or United States Constitution so require. Specific rules of evidence, both common law and statute, themselves call for exclusion of relevant evidence in various specific situations where the risk of confusion or prejudice is so great that the truth would probably be obscured. It other instances, considerations of policy require exclusion. *See, e.g.,* discussion in §§404-408 infra. The rules limiting the competency of witnesses (Article VI), excluding hearsay (Article VIII), requiring authentication or identification (Article IX), and requiring use of the original writing (Article X) are designed to protect the jury from testimony that may not be worthy of belief. The rules on privilege (Article V) reject highly relevant evidence because they protect relationships that are regarded as of sufficient social importance to justify some sacrifice of sources of facts that would aid in bringing out the truth. Illinois Supreme Court Rule 212(b), by requiring a showing of unavailability on the deponent, restricts use of relevant evidence dispositions. Statutory provisions similarly restrict the admissibility of relevant evidence. *See, e.g.,* §503 infra relating to privileges. *See also* the statutory provisions relating to lie detectors discussed in §403.2 infra.

In addition to these specific illustrations is the power of the court generally to exclude relevent evidence if its probative value is overshadowed by the danger of unfair prejudice, confusion of the issues, or waste of time. Such a power is necessary to facilitate the ascertainment of the truth and to keep the conduct of the trial within bounds. *See* §403.1 infra.

Constitutional considerations, of course, may require the exclusion of relevant evidence. To illustrate, evidence obtained by unlawful search and seizure, *Weeks v. United States,* 232 U.S. 283 (1914); *Katz v. United States,* 389 U.S. 347 (1967), and incriminating statements elicited from an accused in violation of right to counsel, *Massiah v. United States,* 377 U.S. 201 (1964), are not admissible.

Irrelevant evidence may not be admitted. *People v. Reddock,* 13 Ill. App. 3d 296, 300 N.E.2d 31 (1975), a hatchet not connected to both the defendant and the crime should not have been admitted into evidence; *In re Estate of Breault,* 34 Ill. App. 3d 56, 339 N.E.2d 340 (1975), *aff'd in part, rev'd in part,* 64 Ill. 2d 344, 1 Ill. Dec. 86, 356 N.E.2d 86 (1976), evidence of compensation for prior services irrelevant and improperly admitted with respect to reasonableness of current claim for different services.

§403   Exclusion of Relevant Evidence on Grounds of Prejudice or Confusion

§403.1   Exclusion of Relevant Evidence: Factors to be Considered; Standard Applied

Evidence that meets the standard of relevancy, §401.1 supra, may nevertheless be attended with disadvantages of sufficient importance to call for its exclusion. These disadvantages generally consist of unfair prejudice, confusion of the issues, misleading the jury, considerations of undue delay, waste of time, and the needless presentation of cumulative evidence. *See* Federal Rule of Evidence 403, 65 F.R.D. 131, 143 (1975). A particular item of evidence may involve more than one of them.

The admissibility of relevant evidence is favored; evidence that is relevant should be excluded only if its probative value is substantially outweighed by any of the foregoing factors alone or in combination. *See People v. Chambers,* 179 Ill. App. 3d 565, 128 Ill. Dec. 372, 534 N.E.2d 554 (1989); *People v. Kimbrough,* 138 Ill. App. 3d 481, 93 Ill. Dec. 82, 485 N.E.2d 1292 (1985). *See also* discussion infra. The burden is on the objecting party. In exercising its discretion in applying this standard, the court should consider the importance of the evidence to the issues under consideration, the availability of alternative means of proof, whether the point for which proof is offered is being disputed, §401.1 supra, and, where appropriate, the potential effectiveness of a limiting, §105.1 supra, or cautionary instruction. Obviously where either the probative value of the offered evidence or the importance of the fact sought to be proved is relatively slight, the likelihood of exclusion is enhanced. *People v. Cloutier,* 156 Ill. 2d 483,

190 Ill. Dec. 744, 622 N.E.2d 744 (1993); *People v. Enis,* 139 Ill. 2d 264, 151 Ill. Dec. 493, 564 N.E.2d 1155 (1990). *See also People v. Decker,* 126 Ill. App. 3d 428, 81 Ill. Dec. 666, 467 N.E.2d 366 (1984), evidence of actions in 1971 was too remote. In evaluating the incremental probative value of the evidence, the trial judge must assume that the evidence will be believed by the trier of fact.

Since all effective evidence is prejudicial in the sense of damaging the party against whom offered, only unfairly prejudicial evidence calls for exclusion, i.e., evidence having an undue tendency to suggest decision on an improper basis, commonly an emotional one, such as bias, sympathy, hatred, contempt, or horror. *People v. Lewis,* 165 Ill. 2d 305, 209 Ill. Dec. 144, 651 N.E.2d 72 (1995); *People v. Sutherland,* 155 Ill. 2d 1, 182 Ill. Dec. 577, 610 N.E.2d 1 (1992); *People v. Eyler,* 133 Ill. 2d 173, 139 Ill. Dec. 756, 549 N.E.2d 268 (1989) (all quoting Handbook while adopting definition). *See People v. Ward,* 154 Ill. 2d 272, 181 Ill. Dec. 884, 609 N.E.2d 252 (1992); *People v. Williams,* 147 Ill. 2d 173, 167 Ill. Dec. 853, 588 N.E.2d 983 (1991), improper to elicit information concerning crime victim's personal traits or familial relationships; *People v. Wilson,* 400 Ill. 603, 81 N.E.2d 445 (1948), improper to admit details of marital troubles years before alleged attempt on life of ex-wife; *Waugh v. Cender,* 29 Ill. App. 2d 408, 173 N.E.2d 860 (1961), improper to permit defendant's wife to describe injuries sustained by her in collision; *People v. Barnes,* 182 Ill. App. 3d 75, 130 Ill. Dec. 620, 537 N.E.2d 949 (1989), improper to cross-examine the defendant concerning personal vices or bad experiences; *People v. Gibson,* 197 Ill. App. 3d 162, 143 Ill. Dec. 142, 553 N.E.2d 1128 (1990), improper to permit police officer to testify to the existence of 20 prior contacts with the defendant; *People v. Brewer,* 245 Ill. App. 3d 890, 185 Ill. Dec. 917, 615 N.E.2d 787 (1993), proper to prohibit defendant from cross-examining accomplice witness as to possible sentence on grounds of unfair prejudice to the state through incidental disclosure of possible sentence facing the defendant himself. However, description of injuries by the physician does not preclude exhibition of the injuries themselves to the jury as being needlessly cumulative, *People v. Evans,* 25 Ill. 2d 194, 184 N.E.2d 836 (1962), nor does the introduction of three separate confessions made to different individuals constitute the needless presentation of cumulative evidence. *People v. Torres,* 54 Ill. 2d 384, 297 N.E.2d 142 (1973). For a case that perhaps reached an incorrect conclusion, *see Estate of Parks v. O'Young,* 289 Ill. App. 3d 976, 224 Ill. Dec. 905, 682 N.E. 2d 466 (1997), trial court properly excluded evidence detailed in an incident report indicating abusiveness to children and racial prejudice against blacks as unfairly prejudicial offered in litigation alleging that person committing such acts unlawfully caused the author of the incident report to be fired.

The concept of confusion of the issues refers to the probability that certain proof and the answering evidence that it provokes might distract the jury unduly causing the jury to lose sight of the main issues. Misleading the jury refers primarily to the possibility of the jury overvaluing the probative value of a particular item of evidence for any reason other than the emotional reaction associated with unfair prejudice. Exclusion of the results of lie detector tests and the imposition of the *Frye* test, *see* §702.4, with respect to scientific techniques and devices are illustrative. *See Gill v. Foster,* 157 Ill. 2d 304, 193 Ill. Dec. 157, 626 N.E.2d 190 (1993), hospital bill that did not distinguish between expenses caused by the alleged medical malpractice and hospital expenses that would nevertheless have been incurred is misleading; *People v. Schulz,* 154 Ill. App. 3d 358, 107 Ill. Dec. 288, 506 N.E.2d 1343 (1987), evidence from blood test that defendant was within 20 percent of population known as nonsecreters, improperly declared irrelevant on appeal, could in the court's discretion have been excluded as misleading. In addition, a jury may be misled by the sheer amount of time spent upon an issue into incorrectly believing the issue to be of major importance.

Occasionally evidence is excluded because of considerations of undue delay, waste of time, or needless presentation of cumulative evidence, Federal Rule of Evidence 403.

Concerns associated with improper use of trial time arise when an unsuitable amount of time will be consumed in clarifying a situation, when the evidence possesses only minimal probative value, or when the evidence will be available only after considerable delay. Evidence that in the context of the litigation is merely repetitious or time consuming may be excluded, but only if time considerations substantially outweigh the incremental probative value of the proffered evidence. The admission of cumulative evidence is within the discretion of the court. *Simmons v. City of Chicago,* 118 Ill. App. 3d 676, 74 Ill. Dec. 202, 455 N.E.2d 232 (1983); *Aguinaga v. City of Chicago,* 243 Ill. App. 3d 552, 183 Ill. Dec. 648, 611 N.E.2d 1296 (1993); *Boersma v. Amoco Oil Co.,* 276 Ill. App. 3d 638, 213 Ill. Dec. 152, 658 N.E.2d 1173 (1995); *Hubbard v. Sherman Hospital,* 292 Ill. App. 3d 148, 226 Ill. Dec. 393, 685 N.E. 2d 648 (1997). The trial court's discretion in this context includes limiting the number of expert witnesses, *Yassin v. Certified Grocers of Illinois,* 150 Ill. App. 3d 1052, 104 Ill. Dec. 52, 502 N.E.2d 315 (1986), or permitting several expert witnesses to testify. *Moore v. Anchor Organization for Health Maintenance,* 284 Ill. App. 3d 874, 220 Ill. Dec. 9, 672 N.E.2d 826 (1996) (five physicians for plaintiff on breach of standard of care).

In evaluating the incremental probative value of proffered evidence, the fact that the opponent has offered to stipulate or is not disputing the proposition for which the evidence is being offered must be considered. However, the fact that the proposition is not being disputed or the opponent has offered to stipulate is not determinative; the proponent of the evidence is entitled to have the court also consider the fair and legitimate weight that introduction of the evidence would have upon the trier of fact. *People v. Bounds,* 171 Ill. 2d 1, 215 Ill. Dec. 28, 662 N.E.2d 1168 (1995); *People v. Speck,* 41 Ill. 2d 177, 242 N.E.2d 208 (1968); *People v. Chatman,* 110 Ill. App. 3d 19, 65 Ill. Dec. 778, 441 N.E.2d 1292 (1982); *People v. Jones,* 236 Ill. App. 3d 244, 177 Ill. Dec. 549, 603 N.E.2d 619 (1992). *See also* §401.1 supra; 9 Wigmore, Evidence §2591 (Chadbourn rev. 1981). If the offer to stipulate or not to dispute does not cover all purposes for which the evidence is relevant, the evidence will not be excluded.

Where unfair surprise is asserted, a continuance is a more appropriate remedy than exclusion of the evidence. Accordingly, unfair surprise is not included as a factor to be considered in the foregoing balancing.

The fertility of the legal mind in attacking practical problems of proof presents situations of infinite variety. Some have recurred with sufficient frequency to evolve fairly definite rules, as is seen in later sections. In general, however, the variables that are present, not only in the disadvantages enumerated above but in the extent to which they outweigh or are outweighed by the proper aspects of the evidence, indeed the variations in the force of relevancy itself, make the entire area one in which the judgment of the trial judge ought to be disturbed only if the exercise of discretion was clearly abused. *People v. Childress,* 158 Ill. 2d 275, 198 Ill. Dec. 794, 633 N.E.2d 635 (1994); *People v. Gonzalez,* 142 Ill. 2d 481, 154 Ill. Dec. 643, 568 N.E.2d 864 (1991); *People v. Adams,* 25 Ill. 2d 568, 185 N.E.2d 676 (1962). "Where the confusion of issues will not be compensated by the assistance of useful evidence it is proper to exclude the evidence offered. Whether the offered evidence should be admitted where its admission will tend to confuse the issues is left to the sound discretion of the trial court." *Veer v. Hagemann,* 334 Ill. 23, 28, 165 N.E. 175 (1929).

A situation that raises the trial concerns of misleading the jury, confusion of the issues, and waste of time involves an attempt by the criminal defendant to establish that someone else committed the crime with which he is accused. Articulation of the application of the aforementioned trial concerns in such a situation is often avoided by the court in favor of employment of the rubric that such evidence will be excluded if too remote or speculative. *See, e.g., People v. Morgan,* 142 Ill. 2d 410, 154 Ill. Dec. 534, 568 N.E.2d 755 (1991); *People v. Creque,* 214 Ill. App. 3d 587, 158 Ill. Dec. 112, 573 N.E.2d 1297 (1991); *People v. Allgood,* 242 Ill. App. 3d 1082, 183 Ill. Dec. 479, 611 N.E.2d 1127 (1993). *See also* §403.2 infra.

With respect to comparing the probative value of relevant

evidence with the dangers associated with introduction of such evidence, no clear standard has been enunciated in the cases. Occasionally a statement is found to the effect that evidence is admissible only if its probative value outweighs the danger of unfair prejudice. *See, e.g., People v. Monroe,* 66 Ill. 2d 317, 5 Ill. Dec. 824, 362 N.E.2d 295 (1977); *People v. DeHoyos,* 64 Ill. 2d 128, 355 N.E.2d 19 (1976). However, a review of the many cases setting forth a standard as well as those decisions failing to enunciate any standard leads clearly to the conclusion that in actual practice probative evidence, when considered in light of the factors mentioned above, is not excluded unless substantially outweighed by trial concerns, including the danger of unfair prejudice. *See People v. Lewis,* 165 Ill. 2d 305, 329, 209 Ill. Dec. 144, 155, 651 N.E.2d 72, 83 (1995), relevant evidence may be "excluded if its prejudicial effect substantially outweighs its probative value"; *People v. Baynes,* 88 Ill. 2d 225, 244, 58 Ill. Dec. 819, 430 N.E.2d 1070 (1981), "the prejudicial effects [of admitting on stipulation the results of a lie detector test] substantially outweigh the probative value of admitting such testimony." *Accord Gill v. Foster,* 157 Ill. 2d 304, 193 Ill. Dec. 157, 626 N.E. 2d 190 (1993); *Estate of Parks v. O'Young,* 289 Ill. App. 3d 976, 224 Ill. Dec. 905, 682 N.E. 2d 466 (1997). *See generally People v. Kolep,* 29 Ill. 2d 116, 193 N.E.2d 753 (1963), photographs were not so gruesome and inflammatory so that probative value was far outweighed by prejudicial effect; *People v. Jenko,* 410 Ill. 478, 102 N.E.2d 783 (1952), spectacular exhibits having little probative value offered for the principal purpose of arousing prejudicial emotions should be excluded. *See also People v. Cannon,* 49 Ill. 2d 162, 273 N.E.2d 829 (1971); *People v. Lefler,* 38 Ill. 2d 216, 230 N.E.2d 827 (1967); *Baird v. Adeli,* 214 Ill. App. 3d 47, 157 Ill. Dec. 861, 573 N.E.2d 279 (1991); *People v. Chambers,* 179 Ill. App. 3d 565, 128 Ill. Dec. 372, 534 N.E.2d 554 (1989); *People v. Kimbrough,* 138 Ill. App. 3d 481, 93 Ill. Dec. 82, 485 N.E.2d 1292 (1985). *Compare People v. Petitt,* 245 Ill. App. 3d 132, 184 Ill. Dec. 766, 613 N.E.2d 1358 (1993) (probative value must substantially outweigh risk of unfair prejudice; incorrect standard).

With respect to exhibition of personal injuries, *see* §401.5 supra; with respect to photographs, *see* §401.8 supra.

§403.2 Lie Detectors, Truth Serums, Hypnosis, Probability Assessment, and Other Person Culprit; Nicknames

Illinois law is fragmentary on the subject of evaluation of the testimony of witnesses by use of the lie detector, so-called truth serums, hypnosis, and the like.

Two statutes deal with some aspects of the matter. In criminal cases the trial judge is prohibited from requiring, requesting, or suggesting in the course of the trial that the accused submit to a lie detector test or to questioning under drugs. 725 ILCS 125/8b (Div. XIII). In the course of any civil trial or pretrial proceeding he is prohibited from requiring either party to submit to a lie detector test and from requiring, requesting, or suggesting that either party submit to questioning under drugs. 735 ILCS 5/2-1104. The criminal statute does not deal with possible testing before trial, with psychiatric and similar examinations, or with the testing of witnesses generally other than the accused. The civil statute is silent as to requesting or suggesting a lie detector test to a party, as to psychiatric and similar examinations, and as to the testing of witnesses generally other than parties. *See generally People v. Melock*, 149 Ill. 2d 423, 174 Ill. Dec. 857, 599 N.E.2d 941 (1992).

In criminal cases, the results of lie detector or polygraph tests voluntarily taken are inadmissible on the question of guilt or innocence even if admissibility of the results had been stipulated by the parties, *People v. Gard*, 158 Ill. 2d 191, 198 Ill. Dec. 415, 632 N.E.2d 1026 (1994); *People v. Yarbrough*, 93 Ill. 2d 421, 67 Ill. Dec. 257, 444 N.E.2d 493 (1982); *People v. Baynes*, 88 Ill. 2d 225, 58 Ill. Dec. 819, 430 N.E.2d 1070 (1981), regardless of whether the person taking the lie detector or polygraph is a party or a witness. *People v. Gard* supra. The results of lie detector tests are not "reliable enough to be admitted. The prejudicial effects [on the integrity of the trial process] substantially outweigh the probative value of admitting such testimony." *People v. Baynes,* 88 Ill. 2d 225, 244, 58 Ill. Dec. 819, 430 N.E.2d 1070 (1981). *Accord People v. Taylor,* 101 Ill. 2d 377, 78 Ill. Dec. 359, 462 N.E.2d 478 (1984), exposure of potential juror to fact lie detector test was administered requires that juror be excused. Similarly evidence that a polygraph was offered to, or refused by, a defendant is inadmissible. *People v. Yarbrough,* 93 Ill. 2d 421, 67 Ill. Dec. 257, 444 N.E.2d 493 (1982); *People v. Eickhoff,* 129 Ill. App. 3d 99, 84 Ill. Dec. 300, 471 N.E.2d 1066 (1984). Nor are the results admissible at a death sentencing hearing, *People v. Pecoraro,* 175 Ill. 2d 294, 222 Ill. Dec. 341, 677 N.E.2d 875 (1997); *People v. Szabo,* 94 Ill. 2d 327, 68 Ill. Dec. 935, 447 N.E.2d 193 (1983), post-conviction proceedings, *People v. Hilliard,* 109 Ill. App. 3d 797, 65 Ill. Dec. 343, 441 N.E.2d 135 (1982), on a post-trial motion, *People v. Yarbrough,* 93 Ill. 2d 421, 67 Ill. Dec. 257, 444 N.E.2d 493 (1982), or at an administrative hearing, *Kaske v. City of Rockford,* 96 Ill. 2d 298, 70 Ill. Dec. 841, 450 N.E.2d 314 (1983). This prohibition may not be circumvented by reference to the accused having talked to a laboratory "technician," or "examiner," thereby avoiding use of the words "polygraph" and "lie detector." *People v. Mason,* 274 Ill. App. 3d 715, 210 Ill. Dec. 909, 653 N.E.2d 1371 (1995). Given the foregoing, it is logical to assume that the results of lie detector tests are inadmissible to establish truthfulness, or its converse, of witnesses in civil matters as well. The continued admissibility of lie detector results for other purposes in civil matters, such as to establish good faith when an insurer determines whether to make payment on a fire policy, *Moskos v. National Ben Franklin Ins. Co.,* 60 Ill. App. 3d 130, 17 Ill. Dec. 389, 376 N.E.2d 388 (1978), or to establish the lack of a conspiracy in the termination of an employee, *Alm v. General Tel. Co. of Ill.,* 27 Ill. App. 3d 876, 327 N.E.2d 523 (1975), or to establish the commission of an offense justifying termination of a police officer from the force, *Austin v. City of East Moline Bd. of Fire and Police Commrs.,* 7 Ill. App. 3d 537, 288 N.E.2d 113 (1972), is not necessarily inconsistent with *Baynes.* Nevertheless, the emerging trend is to find that polygraph results are insufficiently reliable for such purposes as well. *See, e.g., Manias v. Peoria County Sheriff's Dept.*, 109 Ill. App. 3d 700, 65 Ill. Dec. 253, 440 N.E.2d 1269 (1982); *Kaske v. City of Rockford*, 96 Ill. 2d 298, 70 Ill. Dec. 841, 430 N.E.2d 314 (1983); *Collura v. Board of Police Commrs.*, 135 Ill. App. 3d 827, 90 Ill. Dec. 436, 482 N.E.2d 143 (1985); *Elder v. Coronet Ins. Co.*, 201 Ill. App. 3d 733, 146 Ill. Dec. 978, 558 N.E.2d 1312 (1990).

Although the results of a polygraph test are inadmissible and constitute reversible error, *People v. Baynes*, 88 Ill. 2d 225, 58 Ill. Dec. 819, 430 N.E.2d 1070 (1981), and plain error requiring reversal in the absence of proper objection, *People v. Gard*, 158 Ill. 2d 191, 198 Ill. Dec. 415, 632 N.E.2d 1026 (1994), the admission of evidence *merely* that the defendant or a witness has taken such a test does not necessarily constitute reversible error. *See People v. Melquist*, 26 Ill. 2d 22, 185 N.E.2d 825 (1962); *People v. Flowers*, 14 Ill. 2d 406, 152 N.E.2d 838 (1958). The decision of whether to grant a mistrial is within the sound discretion of the trial court, and that determination will not be disturbed unless it appears that there was a manifest necessity for a mistrial, i.e., it must appear that the jury has been so influenced and prejudiced that it cannot be fair and impartial. *People v. Turner*, 240 Ill. App. 3d 340, 181 Ill. Dec. 68, 608 N.E.2d 141 (1992); *People v. Kuhfuss*, 241 Ill. App. 3d 311, 181 Ill. Dec. 730, 608 N.E.2d 1204 (1993). *See also People v. Thomas*, 123 Ill. App. 3d 857, 79 Ill. Dec. 278, 463 N.E.2d 832 (1984) (argument by prosecutor to jury that defendant lied on polygraph to explain why defendant not released is reversible error even though no evidence of the results of the polygraph was introduced in evidence).

Statements made by a person before, during, or after being administered a lie detector test are admissible. *People v. Sickley*, 114 Ill. App. 3d 167, 69 Ill. Dec. 894, 448 N.E.2d 612 (1983). When such statements are admitted, the defendant is entitled to introduce evidence of the fact of the polygraph examination and the surrounding circumstances, as well as the fact of the nonexistence of any results from that examination. *People v. Melock*, 149 Ill. 2d 423, 174 Ill. Dec. 857, 599

N.E.2d 941 (1992). The circumstances surrounding the taking of a lie detector test are also admissible when the issue is a confession's voluntariness where a limiting instruction is given to the jury, *People v. Triplett,* 37 Ill. 2d 234, 226 N.E.2d 30 (1967), and when relevant to voluntariness in the context of a motion to suppress. *People v. Avery,* 227 Ill. App. 3d 382, 169 Ill. Dec. 542, 592 N.E.2d 29 (1991). *See generally People v. Daniels,* 272 Ill. App. 3d 325, 208 Ill. Dec. 767, 650 N.E.2d 224 (1994). With respect to the question of voluntariness, *see* §§502.1 and 502.2 infra. As to the admissibility of the taking of a lie detector test by a person who did not testify at trial and who was not a defendant, *see People v. Poliquin,* 97 Ill. App. 3d 122, 52 Ill. Dec. 290, 421 N.E.2d 1362 (1981). As to the use of lie detectors to screen sexual abuse prosecutions, *see* §404.4 infra.

An agreement by the prosecution and the accused to dismiss pending charges if the accused took and passed a lie detector test is enforceable. *People v. Starks,* 106 Ill. 2d 441, 88 Ill. Dec. 35, 478 N.E.2d 350 (1985).

Statements made by a witness under the influence of truth serum or hypnosis are not admissible. *People v. Harper,* 111 Ill. App. 2d 204, 250 N.E.2d 5 (1969), the scientific reliability of neither hypnosis nor truth serum is sufficient to justify the test results of either; *People v. Smrekar,* 68 Ill. App. 3d 379, 24 Ill. Dec. 707, 385 N.E.2d 848 (1979), courts have uniformly ruled test results of hypnosis to be inadmissible. Nonverbal responses made to questioning while under hypnosis are similarly excluded. *People v. Duckett,* 133 Ill. App. 3d 639, 88 Ill. Dec. 742, 479 N.E.2d 355 (1985).

Whether a witness who has been hypnotized to refresh recollection may testify at trial is a more difficult question. In *People v. Wilson,* 116 Ill. 2d 29, 106 Ill. Dec. 771, 506 N.E.2d 571 (1987), the supreme court addressed the admissibility of testimony by a witness who had been hypnotized. Statements made while under the influence of hypnosis, while not specifically discussed in *Wilson,* are undoubtedly inadmissible. With respect to the admissibility of post-hypnotic testimony, after presenting the various positions taken in other jurisdictions, the supreme court in *Wilson* stated that it need not determine whether post-hypnotically induced testimony of a witness may ever be admitted as the question was not before the court. *See generally Rock v. Arkansas,* 483 U.S. 44 (1987) (a per se rule declaring post-hypnotic testimony of the criminal defendant inadmissible is unconstitutional). In *People v. Zayas,* 131 Ill. 2d 284, 137 Ill. Dec. 568, 546 N.E.2d 513 (1989), the supreme court held that, other than when performed upon a criminal defendant, the hypnotically induced testimony of a witness is always inadmissible. *See also Tardi v. Henry,* 212 Ill. App. 3d 1027, 157 Ill. Dec. 1, 571 N.E.2d 1020 (1991). As to prehypnotic recollection testified to by a witness in court, *Wilson* supra holds that the fact that the witness's confidence in his memory may be bolstered to some degree by the hypnosis itself does not require exclusion. The proponent of the witness must, however, establish the nature and extent of the witness's prehypnotic recall. *See People v. Wilson,* 254 Ill. App. 3d 1020, 193 Ill. Dec. 731, 626 N.E.2d 1282 (1993). In addition both parties may present expert testimony before the trier of fact explaining the potential effects of hypnosis on the prehypnotic recollection of the witness. *See also People v. Lampkin,* 251 Ill. App. 3d 361, 190 Ill. Dec. 632, 622 N.E.2d 42 (1993).

No Illinois case deals with the propriety of employing psychiatric and psychological techniques for evaluating witnesses generally. The matter is discussed in 3 Wigmore, Evidence §§997-999 (Chadbourn rev. 1970) and McCormick, Evidence §§206 (4th ed. 1992).

Statistical probability evidence is properly admitted where other evidence connects the accused to the crime, the statistical probabilities are based upon established facts and not estimates, and the scientific principles employed are found to be generally accepted as reliable. *People v. Alzoubi,* 133 Ill. App. 3d 806, 89 Ill. Dec. 202, 479 N.E.2d 1208 (1985) (expert testimony based upon HLA combinations that only 6 men out of 1000 would have the correct pattern for paternity); *People v. Henderson,* 83 Ill. App. 3d 854, 39 Ill. Dec. 8, 404 N.E.2d 392 (1980) (testimony concerning percentages of the population having a particular ABO classification of blood); *People v. Bush,* 103 Ill. App. 3d 5, 58 Ill. Dec. 482, 430 N.E.2d 514 (1981) (blood samples typed according to the ABO grouping system and, in some instances, the Esterase D (EsD) system); *People v. Redman,* 135 Ill. App. 3d 534, 90 Ill. Dec. 361, 481 N.E.2d 1272 (1985) (using ABO and PGM blood typing that 1 person in 100 could have been the source of the semen found in the car); *People v. Lipscomb,* 215 Ill. App. 3d 413, 158 Ill. Dec. 952, 574 N.E.2d 1345 (1991) (DNA identification showing that a likelihood of a match on all five bands in the black population was 1 in 6.8 billion); *People v. Miles,* 217 Ill. App. 3d 393, 160 Ill. Dec. 347, 577 N.E.2d 477 (1991) (DNA identification resulting in a statistical probability of a random match in the African-American community of 1 in 300,000). Care must be exercised in the manner of presentation to reduce the possibility of statistical probability evidence misleading the jury into overevaluation. *See People v. Harbold,* 124 Ill. App. 3d 363, 79 Ill. Dec. 830, 464 N.E.2d 734 (1984) (expert testimony that only 1 out of 500 persons in the population at large have the blood type in question is likely to be equated by the jury with a 1 out of 500 chance that the defendant is innocent). *See also People v. Phillips,* 159 Ill. App. 3d 483, 110 Ill. Dec. 873, 511 N.E.2d 1193 (1987); *People v. Linscott,* 159 Ill. App. 3d 71, 111 Ill. Dec. 8, 511 N.E.2d 1303 (1987); *People v. Case,* 246 Ill. App, 3d 566, 186 Ill. Dec. 411, 616 N.E.2d 601 (1993). *See generally People v. Moore,* 171 Ill. 2d 74, 215 Ill. Dec. 75, 662 N.E.2d 1215 (1996) (*Harbold* raised but not decided). *See also* §702.4 infra.

A defendant may establish any fact tending to show that the crime was committed by a person other than himself, but the right is not without limitations. *People v. Nitti,* 312 Ill. 73, 90, 143 N.E. 448 (1924); *People v. Enis,* 139 Ill. 2d 264, 151 Ill. Dec. 493, 564 N.E.2d 1155 (1990). A trial court may reject offered evidence if it has little probative value due to its remoteness, uncertainty, or if it is speculative in nature. *People v. Lewis,* 165 Ill. 2d 305, 209 Ill. Dec. 144, 651 N.E.2d 72 (1995); *People v. Howard,* 147 Ill. 2d 103, 167 Ill. Dec. 914, 588 N.E.2d 1044 (1991); *People v. Whalen,* 238 Ill. App. 3d 994,

178 Ill. Dec. 810, 605 N.E.2d 604 (1992). A close connection must be demonstrated between the third person and the commission of the offense. *People v. Maberry*, 193 Ill. App. 3d 250, 140 Ill. Dec. 323, 549 N.E.2d 974 (1990); *People v. Wilson*, 271 Ill. App. 3d 943, 208 Ill. Dec. 716, 649 N.E.2d 1377 (1995). The trial court has a wide scope of discretion; its ruling will not be reversed absent a clear showing of abuse of that discretion. *People v. King*, 61 Ill. App. 3d 49, 18 Ill. Dec. 371, 377 N.E.2d 856 (1978). With respect to other crimes, wrongs, or acts of another person offered by the defendant, *see* §404.5 infra.

Calling a criminal defendant by his or her nickname is not unfairly prejudicial unless the nickname has a pejorative connotation. In such circumstances, while it is not improper to refer to the defendant by such a negative nickname if witnesses knew and identified the defendant by that nickname, the nickname should be employed sparingly. *People v. Jones*, 295 Ill. App. 3d 444, 229 Ill. Dec. 773, 692 N.E.2d 762 (1998); *People v. Salgado*, 287 Ill. App. 3d 432, 222 Ill. Dec. 776, 678 N.E.2d 648 (1997).

§403.3 Intoxication as Evidence of Negligence

In order to avoid the unfair prejudicial effect often resulting from the mere mention of alcohol, a party may not introduce evidence of alcohol upon the issue of negligence unless the evidence is sufficient to support a jury determination of intoxication as defined in Illinois Pattern Jury Instructions — Civil 150.15 (1994). *Ballard v. Jones*, 21 Ill. App. 3d 496, 316 N.E.2d 281 (1974); *Hagopian v. First Venture, Ltd.*, 90 Ill. App. 3d 951, 46 Ill. Dec. 363, 414 N.E.2d 85 (1980); *Sandburg-Schiller v. Rosello*, 119 Ill. App. 3d 318, 74 Ill. Dec. 690, 456 N.E.2d 192 (1983); *Reuter v. Korb*, 248 Ill. App. 3d 142, 186 Ill. Dec. 731, 616 N.E.2d 1363 (1993), record must contain evidence that the individual consumed alcohol and behaved unusually or inappropriately, or evidence in the form of an opinion as to such individual's intoxication. Once such evidence has been introduced, the jury will be instructed to consider the evidence introduced as to intoxication in accordance with Illinois Pattern Jury Instructions — Civil 12.01 (1994). *French v. City of Springfield,* 5 Ill. App. 3d 368, 283 N.E.2d 18 (1972). Evidence as to drinking not sufficient to support a finding of intoxication is so highly prejudicial as to be treated as reversible error. *Miller v. Chicago Transit Auth.,* 3 Ill. App. 2d 223, 121 N.E.2d 348 (1959). The same results follow if intoxication is raised by insinuation. *Clark v. Rochford,* 79 Ill. App. 2d 336, 224 N.E.2d 679 (1967).

The admissibility of evidence of alcohol and cannabis when offered by the prosecution also requires evidence tying these facts to the inference of intoxication, i.e., that the defendant's mental or physical faculties were impaired as a result of the consumption. *People v. Gosse,* 119 Ill. App. 3d 733, 75 Ill. Dec. 339, 457 N.E.2d 129 (1983).

A lay witness possessing personal knowledge may express an opinion relating to intoxication. *Weaver v. Lovell,* 128 Ill. App. 2d 338, 262 N.E.2d 113 (1970). *See also* §§701.1 and 704.1 infra.

With respect to intoxication as relating to credibility, *see* §§607.5 and 701.7 infra.

§403.4   Taking Exhibits to Jury Room; Use in Closing; Reading of Testimony; Taking Notes; Answering Jury Questions

As to taking documentary exhibits to the jury room, the Code of Civil Procedure provides : "Papers read or received in evidence, other than depositions, may be taken by the jury to the jury room for use during the jury's deliberation." 735 ILCS 5/2-1107(d). While the statute applies only to civil cases, little actual difference is apparent between civil and criminal cases, and the statute suggests the approach is applicable to both. The practice of allowing nontestimonial written evidence to be taken to the jury room is supported by many of the same considerations underlying the Original

Writing Rule, §1002 infra. *See People v. Levato,* 330 Ill. 498, 161 N.E. 731 (1928), not error in confidence game prosecution to permit jury to take similar forged checks at another store; *Kavale v. Morton Salt Co.,* 329 Ill. 445, 160 N.E. 752 (1928), not error to send X-ray film to jury room; *People v. Clearlee,* 101 Ill. App. 3d 16, 56 Ill. Dec. 600, 427 N.E.2d 1005 (1981), not error to send police inventory slip to jury room. *Compare Merlo v. Parisi,* 255 Ill. App. 3d 53, 194 Ill. Dec. 193, 627 N.E.2d 309 (1993), in spite of 5/2-1107(d) trial court in its discretion may refuse to send a paper read or received in evidence to the jury room; *Gossard v. Kalra,* 291 Ill. App. 3d 180, 225 Ill. Dec. 725, 684 N.E.2d 410 (1997), voluminous documents such as medical records containing irrelevant information pertaining to unrelated medical problems may be barred from the jury room in the court's discretion.

The basis for excluding depositions from the room is that to admit them would confer an unfair advantage by allowing the deponent in effect to be present at the deliberations. The same reasoning precludes taking to the jury room other documents that are assertive or testimonial in character.

Subject to this salutary limitation, which seems sometimes recently to have been overlooked, the matter is committed largely to the discretion of the trial judge. *Compare Dunn v. People,* 172 Ill. 582, 50 N.E. 137 (1898), error to allow the jury to take written dying declaration; *Johnson v. N.K. Fairbank Co.,* 156 Ill. App. 381 (1910), proper to exclude from jury room a prior inconsistent written statement used to impeach; *Wilkinson v. Mullen,* 27 Ill. App. 3d 804, 327 N.E.2d 433 (1975), not error to preclude police report being taken to jury room, with *People v. Hauck,* 362 Ill. 266, 199 N.E. 821 (1935), not error to allow jury to take auditor's computation; *People v. Caldwell,* 39 Ill. 2d 346, 236 N.E.2d 706 (1968), written confessions of defendant may be taken to the jury room; *People v. Williams,* 97 Ill. 2d 252, 73 Ill. Dec. 360, 454 N.E.2d 220 (1983); not improper to send defendant's 30-page written confession to jury room during sentencing phase; *People v. Hudson,* 157 Ill. 2d 401, 193 Ill. Dec. 128, 626 N.E.2d 161 (1993), proper to send confession in the form of a signed transcript to jury room; *Stanton v. Pennsylvania R. Co.*, 32 Ill. App. 2d 406, 178 N.E.2d 121 (1961), not error to allow jury to take admission of party-opponent; *People v. Lee*, 243 Ill. App. 3d 1038, 184 Ill. Dec. 907, 614 N.E.2d 108 (1993), not error to allow prior inconsistent statement of witness *admissible substantively* to be taken to jury room.

The taking of nondocumentary exhibits to the jury room is left much to the discretion of the trial judge, that is, the trial court is to balance probative value against prejudicial effect. *People v. Williams*, 97 Ill. 2d 252, 73 Ill. Dec. 360, 454 N.E.2d 220 (1983). *See, e.g., People v. Ciucci*, 8 Ill. 2d 619, 137 N.E.2d 40 (1956), *aff'd*, 356 U.S. 571, *rehearing denied*, 357 U.S. 924 (1958), not error in murder case to allow rifle, cartridge cases, bullets, and bloodstained bed clothing to be taken to jury room; *Chicago v. Kimmel*, 31 Ill. 2d 202, 201 N.E.2d 386 (1964), proper for jury to take to jury room book alleged to be obscene; *Sparling v. Peabody Coal Co.*, 59 Ill. 2d 491, 322 N.E.2d 5 (1974), proper for photograph of burns and scars of feet and legs of plaintiff to be taken to jury room; *People v. Mireles*, 79 Ill. App. 3d 173, 34 Ill. Dec. 475, 398 N.E.2d 150 (1979), proper for wires found at scene of murder and photographs of deceased to go to jury room; *People v. Watson*, 107 Ill. App. 3d 691, 63 Ill. Dec. 522, 438 N.E.2d 453 (1982), proper to send clothes of three-year-old sexual abuse victim to jury room; *People v. Arnold*, 139 Ill. App. 3d 429, 94 Ill. Dec. 120, 487 N.E.2d 997 (1985), proper for jury to have two photographs of decedent with his family; *People v. Blommaert*, 184 Ill. App. 3d 1065, 133 Ill. Dec. 307, 542 N.E.2d 144 (1989), proper to permit graphic photographs of autopsy probative of cause of death and location of victim's wounds to accompany jury; *People v. Williams*, 228 Ill. App. 3d 981, 171 Ill. Dec. 148, 593 N.E.2d 968 (1992), not error to send bloodstained trunk carpet to jury room; *cf. People v. Kirkpatrick*, 413 Ill. 595, 110 N.E.2d 519 (1953), error to admit meat grinder claimed to have been stolen from market to go to jury room; *People v. Taylor*, 143 Ill. App. 3d 252, 97 Ill. Dec. 352, 492 N.E.2d 1011 (1986), probably error to let "mug shots" go to jury room; *People v. Burrell*, 228 Ill.

App. 3d 133, 170 Ill. Dec. 17, 592 N.E.2d 453 (1992), improper to send police officer's clothes with bloodstains and bullet holes to jury room. *See also O'Brien v. Hertl,* 238 Ill. App. 3d 217, 179 Ill. Dec. 393, 606 N.E.2d 225 (1992), not error to refuse to send photograph of ditch to jury room where the evidence was in strong conflict as to whether the correct ditch was portrayed. This discretion does not, however, extend to the taking of exhibits susceptible to use in such a way as to constitute in effect the production of evidence for the first time in the jury room. The liquor cases, in view of the possibility of sampling, illustrate the point. *People v. Elias,* 316 Ill. 376, 147 N.E. 472 (1925), error to permit jury to take seized liquor in prohibition prosecution; *Treolo v. Iroquois Auto Ins. Underwriters,* 348 Ill. 93, 180 N.E. 575 (1932), proper to exclude from jury room jug of wine found in wreckage of automobile. Where the tangible exhibit requires expert interpretation and exposition, the court should generally refuse to permit the exhibit to go to the jury room. *People v. McElroy,* 63 Ill. App. 2d 403, 211 N.E.2d 444 (1965), handwriting exemplars introduced and shown to jury during reception of evidence properly not permitted to go to jury room; *People v. Rhoden,* 101 Ill. App. 3d 223, 56 Ill. Dec. 746, 427 N.E.2d 1292 (1981), jury properly refused access to a magnifying glass with which to inspect fingerprint evidence; *People v. Elwell,* 48 Ill. App. 3d 828, 6 Ill. Dec. 195, 362 N.E.2d 830 (1977), error to permit vial containing deceased's blood to go to jury room.

Questions as to taking nondocumentary exhibits in criminal cases to the jury room have occasionally been resolved by reference to the right of confrontation, a reference that at best appears questionable. *People v. Clark,* 301 Ill. 428, 134 N.E. 95 (1922), error to send handwriting specimens to the jury room for the purpose, for the first time, and in the absence of the accused, of making comparisons; *People v. Elias* supra, error to send seized liquor to jury room, in view of possibility of sampling in absence of accused. With respect to the right of confrontation, *see* §807.1 infra.

Items that have not been introduced into evidence may

not be taken to the jury room. *People v. Williams,* 173 Ill. 2d 48, 218 Ill. Dec. 916, 670 N.E.2d 638 (1996); *Yates v. People,* 38 Ill. 527 (1865); *People v. Holcomb,* 370 Ill. 299, 18 N.E.2d 878 (1939); *People v. Thomas,* 199 Ill. App. 3d 79, 145 Ill. Dec. 344, 556 N.E.2d 1246 (1990); *Bieles v. Ables,* 234 Ill. App. 3d 269, 174 Ill. Dec. 685, 599 N.E.2d 469 (1992); *People v. Fields,* 258 Ill. App. 3d 912, 197 Ill. Dec. 300, 631 N.E.2d 303 (1994). The preferred procedure with respect to items containing inadmissible as well as admissible evidence is to have the admissible portions of the exhibit *published* to the jury. *Lawson v. G.D. Searle & Co.,* 64 Ill. 2d 543, 1 Ill. Dec. 497, 356 N.E.2d 779 (1976); *Fultz v. Peart,* 144 Ill. App. 3d 364, 98 Ill. Dec. 285, 494 N.E.2d 212 (1986).

Similarly, it is left to the discretion of the court whether testimony of a witness will be read or transcripts provided if requested by the jury. *People v. Williams,* 173 Ill. 2d 48, 218 Ill. Dec. 916, 670 N.E.2d 638 (1996); *People v. Flores,* 128 Ill. 2d 66, 131 Ill. Dec. 106, 538 N.E.2d 481 (1989); *People v. Autman,* 58 Ill. 2d 171, 317 N.E.2d 570 (1974); *People v. Walker,* 230 Ill. App. 3d 292, 171 Ill. Dec. 679, 594 N.E.2d 1199 (1992). *People v. Pierce,* 56 Ill. 2d 361, 364, 308 N.E.2d 577 (1974), states:

> The trial court will have a full knowledge of the case. It will know the charges against the accused, the witnesses and their supporting or defeating testimony and other evidence which may have been presented. It will be in a position to assess the request and judge whether a review of testimony, considering the circumstances, will be helpful or hurtful to the jury's proper deliberations. This question of review, like so many others which appear in the course of trial, is best entrusted to the trial court's sound discretion.

As to who has the burden on appeal to establish that the trial court understood that it had such discretion, *see People v. Washington,* 243 Ill. App. 3d 138, 183 Ill. Dec. 395, 611 N.E.2d 1043 (1993).

The use of exhibits to illustrate a closing argument is

proper as long as the exhibits are not misleading to the jury. *LeMaster v. Chicago Rock Island & Pac. R.R.*, 35 Ill. App. 3d 1001, 343 N.E.2d 65 (1976). The exhibits, like closing argument itself, cannot be based on facts not in evidence. *Martin v. Zucker*, 133 Ill. App. 3d 982, 88 Ill. Dec. 980, 479 N.E.2d 1000 (1985).

Members of the jury are entitled to take notes during the trial. The sheriff of the county in which the jury is sitting is charged with providing writing materials. Notes made by the jury are confidential; they must be destroyed by the sheriff after the verdict has been returned or a mistrial declared. 725 ICLS 5/115-4(n) and 705 ILCS 315/1(b).

A trial judge has discretion to answer or refrain from answering a question from the jury. This decision will not be disturbed absent abuse. *People v. Reid*, 136 Ill. 2d 27, 143 Ill. Dec. 239, 554 N.E.2d 174 (1990). However, a judge has a duty to give additional instruction where clarification is requested, the original instructions are incomplete, and the jurors are manifestly confused. *Id.* Additionally, where a jury has raised an explicit question on a point of law arising from facts over which there is doubt or confusion, the court should attempt to clarify the question in the minds of the jury members, even if the proper instructions were originally given to the jury. *Id.* On the other hand, a trial judge properly exercises his discretion and refuses to answer a jury's question where the given instructions sufficiently explain the relevant law in clear and common language which the jury could understand. *People v. Petty*, 160 Ill. App. 3d 207, 112 Ill. Dec. 72, 513 N.E.2d 486 (1987). Obviously, the judge is not required to answer a question from the jury if it involves ramifications the judge could not properly go into, *People v. Walker*, 33 Ill. App. 3d 681, 338 N.E.2d 449 (1975), or if the answer would not be useful to the jury. *People v. Jones*, 40 Ill. App. 3d 771, 353 N.E.2d 79 (1976). It is reversible error, however, if a trial judge refuses to answer a jury question in the erroneous belief that he has no discretion to respond to the inquiry. *People v. Queen*, 56 Ill. 2d 560, 310 N.E.2d 166

(1974). *See generally People v. Patten,* 240 Ill. App. 3d 407, 181 Ill. Dec. 278, 608 N.E.2d 351 (1992).

§404   Character Evidence Not Admissible to Prove Conduct: Exceptions; Other Crimes

§404.1   Character Evidence: An Overview

Character is the nature of a person, his disposition generally, or his disposition in respect to a particular trait such as honesty, peacefulness, or truthfulness. Reputation is the community estimate of him. Failure to make the distinction results in confusion that is compounded by the fact that reputation may enter as a method of proving character, §§405.1 and 608.1 infra.

Over the years, owing perhaps to the far greater frequency with which it is encountered in criminal cases, the concept of character has acquired strong moral overtones. Inquiry into the nature of the person has largely been confined to considerations of goodness and badness. As psychiatry and psychology progress and win increasing acceptance in the law, the concept seems to encompass a broadened view of human nature. Note, for example, the treatment of sexually dangerous persons. 725 ILCS 205/1.01 to 205/12.

This section deals with the basic question of when evidence of character or a trait of character is admissible for the purpose of proving that a person acted in conformity with it on a particular occasion, sometimes described as "circumstantial" use of character. Methods of proof are dealt with in §405.1 infra. The general rule is that character evidence is not admissible for the purpose of showing that a person acted in conformity therewith on a particular occasion. *Crose v. Rutledge,* 81 Ill. 266 (1876). An exception exists in criminal cases that allows an accused to offer evidence of a pertinent trait of his character, such as honesty or peacefulness, and allows the state to rebut such evidence once the accused has done so, *see* §404.3 infra. The admissibility of a similar exception with respect to evidence of a pertinent character trait of the victim of the crime offered by the accused, and a further exception made for prosecution proof of the character trait for peacefulness of the victim in a homicide case, is discussed in §404.4 infra. Evidence as to the character of a witness for truthfulness to impeach or bolster his credibility is addressed in §§607, 608, and 609 infra.

The admissibility of evidence to establish a pertinent character trait of an individual when such a character trait is an element of a charge, claim, or defense is discussed in §405.3 infra.

Evidence of other crimes, wrongs, or acts is, however, admissible for a purpose other than to prove character of a person in order to show that he acted in conformity therewith, such as proof of modus operandi, intent, identity, motive, or absence of mistake. *People v. Robinson,* 167 Ill. 2d 53, 212 Ill. Dec. 256, 656 N.E.2d 1090 (1995). *See* §404.5 infra.

§404.2 Character Evidence: Circumstantial Use in Civil Cases

The circumstantial use of character must be distinguished from character in issue, discussed in §405.3 infra. Character is used circumstantially when the inference suggested is that the person on a particular occasion was more likely than not to have acted in a manner inconsistent with her character.

Circumstantial use of character evidence is not permitted in civil cases. *Holtzman v. Hoy,* 118 Ill. 534, 8 N.E. 832 (1886), evidence of defendant's reputation for skill properly excluded in malpractice action; *Joseph Taylor Coal Co. v. Dawes,* 220 Ill. 145, 77 N.E. 131 (1906), evidence that defendant's engineer lowered mine cage at excessive speed on prior occasions admissible to show willfulness of violation but not to show excessive speed on occasion in question; *McBean v. Fox,* 1 Ill. App. 177 (1878), evidence of defendant's reputation for business integrity properly excluded in action of deceit; *Dixon v. Montgomery Ward & Co.,* 351 Ill. App. 75, 114 N.E.2d 44 (1953), error to admit evidence that same employee wired another furnace incorrectly for purpose of proving that he did so with furnace in question; *Plooy v. Paryani,* 275 Ill. App. 3d 1074, 212 Ill. Dec. 317, 657 N.E.2d 12 (1995), error to admit evidence of complaints and disputes same taxi driver had with other customers and drivers.

Circumstantial use of character evidence has been stated to be admissible in a civil case where the focus of the inquiry is essentially criminal. *See McCleary v. Board of Fire & Police Commission of the City of Woodstock,* 251 Ill. App. 3d 988, 190 Ill. Dec. 940, 622 N.E.2d 1257 (1993) (stated with no discussion).

Impeachment of a witness by attacking his character is treated in §§607, 608, and 609 infra. Careful habits testimony is discussed in §406.2 infra.

§404.3   Character Evidence of the Accused

In criminal cases the prosecution may not in the first instance introduce evidence of a pertinent character trait of the accused by evidence of other offenses or otherwise as part of the case in chief against him. *People v. Whiters,* 204 Ill. App. 3d 334, 149 Ill. Dec. 861, 562 N.E.2d 325 (1990). By longstanding tradition the unfair prejudice to the defendant in being portrayed as a "bad man" substantially outweighs any probative value the evidence might possess. *People v. Haas,* 293 Ill. 274, 127 N.E. 740 (1920); *People v. Randle,* 147 Ill. App. 3d 621, 101 Ill. Dec. 408, 498 N.E.2d 732 (1986) (citing Handbook). *Accord People v. Robinson,* 167 Ill. 2d 53, 212 Ill. Dec. 256, 656 N.E.2d 1090 (1995); *People v. Williams,* 161 Ill. 2d 1, 204 Ill. Dec. 72, 641 N.E.2d 296 (1994). *See generally People v. Richardson,* 123 Ill. 2d 322, 123 Ill. Dec. 908, 528 N.E.2d 612 (1988) (such evidence tends to persuade the jury that, on the basis of past conduct, defendant is a probable perpetrator of the crime, or to influence the jurors to convict simply because they find he is a bad person deserving of punishment). "The underlying rationale is that such evidence 'is objectionable "not because it has no appreciable probative value, but because it has too much." ' " *People v. Romero*, 66 Ill. 2d 325, 330, 5 Ill. Dec. 817, 819, 362 N.E.2d 288, 290 (1977), quoting *People v. Lehman*, 5 Ill. 2d 337, 342, 125 N.E.2d 506, 509 (1955). *See also People v. Hendricks*, 137 Ill. 2d 31, 148 Ill. Dec. 213, 560 N.E.2d 611 (1990). "The law distrusts the inference that because a man has committed other crimes he is more likely to have committed the current crime. And so, as a matter of policy, where the testimony has no value beyond that inference, it is excluded." *People v. Lehman*, 5 Ill. 2d 337, 342, 125 N.E.2d 506, 509 (1955). *Accord People v. Cruz*, 162 Ill. 2d 314, 205 Ill. Dec. 345, 643 N.E.2d 636 (1994).

The accused may, however, in the first instance, whether or not testifying at the trial, offer proof as to a pertinent trait of his character, *People v. Lewis*, 25 Ill. 2d 442, 185 N.E.2d 254 (1962); *Wistrand v. People*, 218 Ill. 323, 75 N.E. 891 (1905); *People v. Perez*, 209 Ill. App. 3d 457, 154 Ill. Dec. 250, 568 N.E.2d 250 (1991); *People v. Hall*, 159 Ill. App. 3d 1021, 112 Ill. Dec. 15, 513 N.E.2d 429 (1987); *People v. Bascomb*, 74 Ill. App. 3d 392, 30 Ill. Dec. 262, 392 N.E.2d 1130 (1979), and the prosecution may then offer evidence as to the same character trait by way of rebuttal. *People v. Holt*, 398 Ill. 606, 76 N.E.2d 474 (1948); *People v. Willy*, 301 Ill. 307, 133 N.E. 859 (1922). In both instances the evidence of pertinent character trait must be in the form of reputation testimony. *See* §405.1 infra. As to affirmative defenses, *see* §404.4 infra. Thus an accused may *not* introduce evidence that she has never been previously arrested, charged, prosecuted, or convicted of a crime. *People v. Flax*, 147 Ill. App. 3d 943, 101 Ill. Dec. 343, 498 N.E.2d 667 (1986). Logically, if character evidence of a pertinent trait is available to the accused, it should be equally available to the prosecution as part of its case in chief. That the rule is to the contrary has been explained as an amelioration of the "brutal rigors" of the early criminal law. Maguire, Evidence — Common Sense and Common Law 204 (1947).

The prosecution may not circumvent the foregoing by

simply eliciting testimony from the accused concerning his character on cross-examination and then argue that the accused's assertion of good character permits the prosecution to offer reputation testimony as to the character of the accused by way of rebuttal. *People v. Harris,* 224 Ill. App. 3d 649, 167 Ill. Dec. 165, 587 N.E.2d 47 (1992). *See also* §103.4 supra. Similarly, it is improper for the prosecution to introduce evidence of the use of an alias by the accused when indicative of prior criminal activity. *People v. Howard,* 147 Ill. 2d 103, 167 Ill. Dec. 914, 588 N.E.2d 1044 (1991); *People v. Daniels,* 237 Ill. App. 3d 986, 178 Ill. Dec. 543, 604 N.E.2d 1066 (1992).

This practice is sometimes incorrectly described as "putting his character in issue by the accused." Obviously, however, character does not become an actual issue in the case but is being used circumstantially, the suggested inference being that the accused acted consistently with his character. *See* §405.3 infra for situations where character is, in the strict sense, in issue.

The rationale precluding character evidence from being offered by the prosecution in the first instance also precludes the prosecution from offering evidence as to the character of a defense witness in the form of either reputation testimony or specific instances of conduct. The probative value of such evidence is substantially outweighed by the damage of unfair prejudice to the defendant arising from the jury improperly inferring guilt by association. *People v. Randle,* 147 Ill. App. 3d 621, 101 Ill. Dec. 408, 498 N.E.2d 732 (1986).

If the accused elects not to offer proof of a pertinent character trait, the prosecution may not comment thereon. *People v. Haas* supra.

It should be noted that when the accused becomes a witness, she is subject to impeachment as a witness, including attack upon her character for truth and veracity. *See* §§607, 608, and 609 infra. This is not a case of "putting character in issue."

With respect to cross-examination of the reputation witness, *see* §405.1 infra.

§404.4 Character Evidence as to Victim of Crime; Sexual Abuse

Evidence of a pertinent character trait of the victim of a crime is admitted circumstantially if offered in the first instance by the accused or following by the prosecution in order to rebut. Evidence of a pertinent character trait of the victim of a crime is not admissible when offered by the prosecution in the first instance. *People v. Lucas,* 151 Ill. 2d 461, 177 Ill. Dec. 390, 603 N.E.2d 460 (1992); *People v. Goodwin,* 98 Ill. App. 3d 726, 53 Ill. Dec. 790, 424 N.E.2d 425 (1981). Generally speaking, evidence of specific acts is not admissible for the purpose of showing character; proof must be by reputation. *People v. Allen,* 289 Ill. 218, 124 N.E. 329 (1919); *People v. Jiminez,* 115 Ill. App. 3d 1091, 72 Ill. Dec. 108, 452 N.E.2d 40 (1983). *See generally People v. Patterson,* 154 Ill. 2d 414, 182 Ill. Dec. 592, 610 N.E.2d 16 (1992) (evidence of a specific act of the victim offered by the accused would open up collateral issues; it would be unfair to allow a single act to prove character; and the state could not anticipate or rebut all such evidence). The foregoing rules were unfortunately apparently overlooked in *People v. Peeples,* 155 Ill. 2d 422, 473, 186 Ill. Dec. 341, 365, 616 N.E.2d 294, 318 (1993) where specific acts of the victim were admitted by the prosecution in the first instance as "character evidence, which was relevant to whether the victim would permit defendant to enter her apartment," a case that should be treated as an aberration. Evidence of a pertinent character trait of the victim of a crime will be excluded when the probative value of such evidence is substantially outweighed by the danger of unfair prejudice. *People v. Batac,* 259 Ill. App. 3d 415, 197 Ill. Dec. 370, 631 N.E.2d 373 (1994). *See also* §403.1 supra.

Accordingly, in a homicide or battery case, when the theory of self-defense is raised, that is, that the victim was the aggressor, *People v. Ciavirelli,* 262 Ill. App. 3d 966, 200 Ill. Dec. 271, 635 N.E.2d 610 (1994), the accused is entitled to prove that the alleged victim was reputed to be a violent and dangerous man. *People v. Ware,* 180 Ill. App. 3d 921, 129 Ill. Dec. 663, 536 N.E.2d 713 (1988). Of course the prosecutor is permitted to offer reputation evidence as to the same character trait in rebuttal. The accused must introduce "some evidence" thereon, *see* §303.1–303.3 supra, before being permitted to introduce evidence of the alleged victim's pertinent character trait. *People v. Allen,* 50 Ill. 2d 280, 278 N.E.2d 762 (1972) (defendant must introduce some evidence of self-defense prior to introducing reputation testimony as to the violent character of the victim). If this reputation was known to the accused, the knowledge is a factor to be considered in determining whether he reasonably apprehended bodily harm. *People v. Gibson,* 385 Ill. 371, 52 N.E.2d 1008 (1944); *People v. Berry,* 175 Ill. App. 3d 420, 124 Ill. Dec. 884, 529 N.E.2d 1001 (1988); *People v. Robinson,* 163 Ill. App. 3d 754, 114 Ill. Dec. 898, 516 N.E.2d 1292 (1987). Regardless of whether the accused knew of the reputation, however, it is admissible for the purpose of showing the character of the victim, for the suggested inference that the latter was more probably the aggressor. *People v. Brindley,* 369 Ill. 486, 17 N.E.2d 218 (1938); *People v. Berry* supra. In *People v. Lovings,* 275 Ill. App. 3d 19, 211 Ill. Dec. 769, 655 N.E.2d 1152 (1995), the court correctly refused on the ground of relevance to extend the foregoing principle to an armed robbery or robbery case to permit a defendant to question the complaining witness regarding past instances of violent behavior by the witness for the purpose of showing that the witness did not subjectively feel threatened by the defendant's actions.

Moreover, evidence of specific instances of conduct probative of the violent character of the alleged victim is admissible in such cases as well. *People v. Lynch,* 104 Ill. 2d 194, 83 Ill. Dec. 598, 470 N.E.2d 1018 (1984) (three prior convictions for battery); *People v. Robinson,* 163 Ill. App. 3d 754, 114 Ill. Dec. 898, 516 N.E.2d 1292 (1987) (prior threats and violence by victim against accused). *Compare People v. Trimble,* 131 Ill. App. 3d 474, 86 Ill. Dec. 592, 475 N.E.2d 971 (1985) (prior conviction for unlawful use of a weapon properly excluded as not sufficiently probative of violent character);

People v. Ware, 180 Ill. App. 3d 921, 129 Ill. Dec. 663, 536 N.E. 2d 713 (1988) (psychiatric report of victim prepared twelve days after the incident was insufficiently probative of violent character); *People v. Loggins,* 257 Ill. App. 3d 475, 195 Ill. Dec. 829, 629 N.E. 2d 137 (1993) (a question employing the word "aggressive" does not convey any specific acts of behavior for consideration). Evidence of specific instances of conduct of the victim may be excluded, however, where there is no conflict that the victim was not in fact the aggressor. *People v. Jackson,* 293 Ill. App. 3d 1009, 228 Ill. Dec. 319, 689 N.E.2d 191 (1997); *People v. Armstrong,* 273 Ill. App. 3d 531, 210 Ill. Dec. 430, 653 N.E.2d 17 (1995).

Finally, if the accused in a homicide or battery prosecution introduces evidence that the victim was the first aggressor, whether or not employing reputation testimony, the prosecution may offer in rebuttal reputation testimony as to the character trait of peacefulness of the victim. *People v. Knox,* 94 Ill. App. 2d 36, 236 N.E.2d 384 (1968), permitting such evidence offered by the prosecution to rebut defense cross-examination of state's witness suggesting that the deceased was violent. *Contra People v. Goodwin,* 98 Ill. App. 3d 726, 53 Ill. Dec. 790, 424 N.E.2d 425 (1981), if the character of deceased as a peaceful person has not been attacked by a defendant asserting self-defense, peaceful character is not admissible on rebuttal.

In rape cases where the issue of consent was raised, the traditional view had allowed the accused to show the unchaste character of the prosecutrix to support the inference that consent was probable. *People v. Collins,* 25 Ill. 2d 605, 186 N.E.2d 30 (1962); *People v. Cieslak,* 319 Ill. 221, 149 N.E. 815 (1925). The same principle had been applied to a charge of deviate sexual assault. *People v. Chaney,* 48 Ill. App. 3d 775, 6 Ill. Dec. 455, 362 N.E.2d 1375 (1977). Today, in prosecutions involving sexual penetration or other prohibited sexual conduct upon an adult or child victim, evidence of specific instances of prior sexual activity with someone other than the accused and the reputation of the alleged victim for chastity with persons other than the accused is prohibited by 725

ILCS 5/7(a) unless constitutionally required to be admitted. Section 5/115-7 provides as follows:

(a) In prosecutions for predatory criminal sexual assault of a child, aggravated criminal sexual assault, aggravated criminal sexual abuse, criminal sexual abuse, or criminal transmission of HIV; and in prosecutions for battery and aggravated battery, when the commission of the offense involves sexual penetration or sexual conduct as defined in Section 12-12 of the Criminal Code of 1961, and with the trial or retrial of the offenses formerly known as rape, deviate sexual assault, indecent liberties with a child, and aggravated indecent liberties with a child, the prior sexual activity or the reputation of the alleged victim or corroborating witness under Section 115-7.3 of this Code is inadmissible except (1) as evidence concerning the past sexual conduct of the alleged victim or corroborating witness under Section 115-7.3 of this Code with the accused when this evidence is offered by the accused upon the issue of whether the alleged victim or corroborating witness under Section 117-7.3 of this Code consented to the sexual conduct with respect to which the offense is alleged; or (2) when constitutionally required to be admitted.

(b) No evidence admissible under this Section shall be introduced unless ruled admissible by the trial judge after an offer of proof has been made at a hearing to be held in order to determine whether the defense has evidence to impeach the witness in the event that prior sexual activity with the defendant is denied. Such offer of proof shall include reasonably specific information as to the date, time and place of the past sexual conduct between the alleged victim or corroborating witness under Section 115-7.3 of this Code and the defendant. Unless the court finds that reasonably specific information as to date, time or place, or some combination thereof, has been offered as to prior sexual activity with the defendant, counsel for the defendant shall be ordered to refrain from inquiring into prior sexual activity between the alleged victim or corroborating witness under Section 115-7.3 of this Code and the defendant. The court shall not admit evidence under this Section unless it determines at the hearing that the evidence is relevant and the probative value of the evidence outweighs the danger of unfair prejudice. The evidence shall be admissible at trial to the extent an order made by the court specifies the evidence that may be admitted and areas with respect to which the alleged victim or corroborating witness under Section 115-7.3 of this Code may be examined or cross-examined.

See, e.g., People v. Newman, 123 Ill. App. 3d 43, 78 Ill. Dec. 612, 462 N.E.2d 731 (1984), cross-examination as to prostitution for the purpose of affecting general credibility is prohibited; *People v. Stengel*, 211 Ill. App. 3d 337, 155 Ill. Dec. 878, 570 N.E.2d 391 (1991), dating habits of alleged rape victim and the uniform she wore at work were not proper subjects of cross-examination; *People v. Land*, 241 Ill. App. 3d 1066, 182 Ill. Dec. 476, 609 N.E.2d 1010 (1993), prohibition extends to all reasons not just when offered on issue of consent; *People v. Hernadez-Valdez*, 260 Ill. App. 3d 644, 198 Ill. Dec. 698, 633 N.E.2d 160 (1994), evidence that the alleged rape victim was a virgin was improperly admitted. The prohibition precludes *anyone,* including the State, from introducing evidence of the victim's sexual history with someone other than the accused. *People v. Kemblowski*, 201 Ill. App. 3d 824, 147 Ill. Dec. 247, 559 N.E.2d 247 (1990).

Notice that evidence of prior sexual conduct and of prior conversations between the defendant and the victim or corroborating witness and of the reputation of the victim or corroborating witness concerning the past sexual conduct of the victim or corroborating witness with the accused, where relevant to the issue of consent, are not prohibited. 725 ILCS 5/115-7(a)(1); *People v. Halcomb*, 176 Ill. App. 3d 100, 125 Ill. Dec. 665, 530 N.E.2d 1074 (1988).

Evidence of specific instances of prior sexual activity with someone other than the accused and the reputation of the alleged victim or corroborating witness for chastity with persons other than the accused is also admissible when constitutionally required to be admitted, 725 ILCS 5/115-7(a)(2). Evidence of specific instances of conduct and reputation must be admitted when constitutionally required for a fair trial. Thus, for example, prior sexual conduct evidence possessing sufficient probative value tending to establish that a person other than the accused was the source of semen, injury, or other physical evidence is constitutionally required to be admitted. *See* Federal Rule of Evidence 412(b)(1)(A). In addition evidence of prior sexual conduct possessing sufficient probative value tending to establish bias, interest, ulterior motive to make a false charge, or prior pattern of behavior clearly similar to the conduct immediately in issue are each constitutionally required to be admitted. *People v. Sandoval,* 135 Ill. 2d 159, 142 Ill. Dec. 135, 552 N.E.2d 726 (1990). *See, e.g., People v. Gorney,* 107 Ill. 2d 53, 89 Ill. Dec. 830, 481 N.E.2d 673 (1985), evidence that complainant had offered to make a false allegation of rape against another person should be admitted if sufficiently probative; *People v. Gray,* 209 Ill. App. 3d 407, 154 Ill. Dec. 219, 568 N.E.2d 219 (1991), defendant improperly prohibited from cross-examining the alleged victim about her fear of pregnancy by another as a possible motive to falsely accuse the defendant. *See also People v. Alexander,* 116 Ill. App. 3d 855, 72 Ill. Dec. 338, 452 N.E.2d 591 (1983), the question of whether the rape shield statue would permit cross-examination of the complainant as to prior false allegations of rape was reserved on the ground that the defendant had not established that the complainant's prior allegations of rape were false. *Compare People v. Jones,* 264 Ill. App. 3d 556, 201 Ill. Dec. 172, 636 N.E.2d 604 (1993), allegation that victim suddenly feared disclosure of prior consensual sexual activity as motive to fabricate current rape complaint is, alone, absent a fear of pregnancy, insufficient to override rape shield statute, as a contrary result would permit introduction of alleged victim's prior sexual activity whenever a motive to lie is asserted. Also evidence of prior sexual conduct of a child sufficiently similar to fully account for the child's testimony evidencing unique sexual knowledge without having suffered the conduct for which the defendant is on trial is constitutionally required to be admitted. *People v. Hill,* 289 Ill. App. 3d 859, 225 Ill. Dec. 244, 683 N.E.2d 188(1997). *See also People v. Warren,* 162 Ill. App. 3d 430, 113 Ill. Dec. 658, 515 N.E.2d 467 (1987).

The admissibility of prior specific instances of prostitution of the alleged victim is not yet fully resolved. *See, e.g., People v. Buford,* 110 Ill. App. 3d 46, 65 Ill. Dec. 721, 441 N.E.2d 1235 (1982), in a close case involving a prior conviction of prostitution, when the defendant claims that the act involved was an act of prostitution, the rape shield statute held not to violate right of confrontation and to be harmless error in any event; *People v. Hughes,* 121 Ill. App. 3d 992, 77 Ill. Dec. 429, 460 N.E.2d 485 (1984), where question of showing the victim was a prostitute was avoided on ground that such evidence had in fact been permitted at trial; *People v. Weatherspoon,* 265 Ill. App. 3d 386, 202 Ill. Dec. 112, 637 N.E.2d 651 (1994), a questionable decision where exclusion of evidence of the victim's previously engaging in sexual activity to obtain drugs supporting contention that victim's shame over "prostituting for cocaine" underlied her false accusation found not to deny right of confrontation on the basis that the defendant was otherwise able to present his theory of the case to the jury. *See also People v. Ivory,* 139 Ill. App. 3d 448, 94 Ill. Dec. 158, 487 N.E.2d 1035 (1985); *People v. Newman,* 123 Ill. App. 3d 43, 78 Ill. Dec. 612, 462 N.E.2d 731 (1984), cross-examination inquiring about prostitution for the purpose of affecting general credibility is prohibited.

Section 115-7(a) has been held neither to constitute a denial of due process, *People v. Cornes,* 80 Ill. App. 3d 166, 35 Ill. Dec. 818, 399 N.E.2d 1346 (1980), nor to violate defendant's equal protection rights; *People v. Requena,* 105 Ill. App. 3d 831, 61 Ill. Dec. 636, 435 N.E.2d 125 (1982). *See also People v. Sandoval,* 135 Ill. 2d 159, 142 Ill. Dec. 135, 149, 552 N.E.2d 726, 740 (1990), right of confrontation not denied as defendant was seeking to impeach victim as to having lied on a collateral issue, i.e., whether victim had anal intercourse with someone other than the accused.

As provided in 725 ILCS 5/115-7(b), evidence of past sexual conduct between the alleged victim or corroborating witness and the accused may not be introduced unless ruled admissible upon an offer of proof made in camera to the trial judge. The purpose of the hearing is to determine whether the defendant has evidence to impeach the alleged victim or corroborating witness in the event that the prior sexual activity with the defendant is denied. The defendant must be able to offer reasonably specific information as to date, time, or place, or some combination thereof, as to the prior sexual conduct between the alleged victim or corroborating witness and the accused. Furthermore, such evidence is admissible only if the court finds that its probative value outweighs the danger of unfair prejudice.

A criminal defendant may not open the door himself and then seek to cross-examine the alleged victim or corroborating witness as to past sexual acts with others on the grounds of a need to explain. *People v. Todd,* 241 Ill. App. 3d 542, 181 Ill. Dec. 682, 608 N.E.2d 933 (1993). *See generally People v. Sandoval* supra (the concise and precise language of the statue barring all evidence of prior sexual activity of the victim not with the accused precludes any operation of the doctrine of door opening); *People v. Hooker,* 253 Ill. App. 3d 1075, 192 Ill. Dec. 926, 625 N.E.2d 1081 (1993) (the proper response for a trial court when faced with a situation in which one side improperly introduces sexual history evidence in contravention of the Illinois rape shield statute is not to allow the other side to offer rebuttal evidence, but rather to strike the original evidence and admonish the jury to disregard it).

Neither the police nor the state's attorney may require the alleged victim of sexual abuse to submit to a lie detector as a condition for proceeding with an investigation, charging, or prosecution. The victim upon request must be administered the lie detector test. However failure to submit to a lie detector may not "mitigate" against the prosecution. 725 ILCS 200/1.

> In a prosecution for an illegal sexual act perpetrated upon a victim, . . . testimony by an expert, qualified by the court relating to any recognized and accepted form of post-traumatic stress syndrome shall be admissible as evidence.

725 ILCS 115-7.2. *See People v. Roy,* 201 Ill. App. 3d 166, 146 Ill. Dec. 874, 558 N.E.2d 1208 (1990); *People v. Harp,* 193 Ill.

App. 3d 838, 141 Ill. Dec. 117, 550 N.E.2d 1163 (1990); *People v. Douglas,* 183 Ill. App. 3d 241, 131 Ill. Dec. 779, 538 N.E.2d 1335 (1989).

With respect to prior sexual activity with the accused, *see also* §404.6 infra.

§404.5 Other Crimes, Wrongs, or Acts Admitted for Another Purpose

As an aspect of the rule that the prosecution cannot introduce evidence of a character trait of the accused as part of its case in chief, §404.3 supra, evidence of the commission of other crimes, wrongs, or acts by her is inadmissible for the purpose of showing a disposition or propensity to commit crimes, thus suggesting the inference that she therefore committed the crime in question. *People v. McCarthy,* 132 Ill. 2d 331, 138 Ill. Dec. 292, 547 N.E.2d 459 (1989); *People v. Lampkin,* 98 Ill. 2d 418, 75 Ill. Dec. 260, 457 N.E.2d 50 (1983); *People v. Baptist,* 76 Ill. 2d 19, 27 Ill. Dec. 792, 389 N.E.2d 1200 (1979). The underlying rationale is that such evidence is objectionable "not because it has no appreciable probative value, but because it has too much." 1 Wigmore, Evidence §194 (3rd ed. 1940), quoted in *People v. Romero,* 66 Ill. 2d 325, 5 Ill. Dec. 817, 362 N.E.2d 288 (1977) and *People v. Lucas,* 151 Ill. 2d 461, 177 Ill. Dec. 390, 603 N.E.2d 460 (1992). The law simply distrusts permitting the trier of fact to draw the inference that because a man has committed other crimes he is more likely to have committed the current crime. *People v. Lehman,* 5 Ill. 2d 337, 125 N.E.2d 506 (1955). "Such evidence overpersuades the jury, which might convict the defendant only because it feels he or she is a bad person deserving punishment." *People v. Lindgren,* 79 Ill. 2d 129, 137, 37 Ill. Dec. 348, 402 N.E.2d 238 (1980). *Accord People v. Manning,* 182 Ill. 2d 193, 230 Ill. Dec. 933, 695 N.E.2d 423 (1998); *People v. Robinson,* 167 Ill. 2d 53, 212 Ill. Dec. 256, 656 N.E.2d 1090 (1995); *People v. Thingvold,* 145 Ill. 2d 441, 164 Ill. Dec. 877, 584 N.E.2d 89 (1991); *People v. McGee,* 286 Ill.

App. 3d 786, 222 Ill. Dec. 137, 676 N.E.2d 1341 (1997). *See also People v. Nichols,* 235 Ill. App. 3d 499, 176 Ill. Dec. 519, 601 N.E.2d 1217 (1992) (improper to imply that accused is well known to police).

Great inroads upon this rule of exclusion, however, occur because the rule allows evidence of other crimes, wrongs, or acts for purposes other than merely showing a disposition to commit such crimes. *People v. Illgen,* 145 Ill. 2d 353, 164 Ill. Dec. 599, 583 N.E.2d 515 (1991); *People v. Phillips,* 127 Ill. 2d 499, 131 Ill. Dec. 125, 538 N.E.2d 500 (1989); *Wernowsky v. Economy Fire & Cas. Co.,* 106 Ill. 2d 49, 87 Ill. Dec. 484, 477 N.E.2d 231 (1985). Wrongs or acts that are not criminal are included. *People v. Davis,* 260 Ill. App. 3d 176, 197 Ill. Dec. 389, 631 N.E.2d 392 (1994). Thus evidence of other crimes, wrongs, or acts is admissible for other purposes such as proof of motive, opportunity, intent, preparation, plan, knowledge, identity, or absence of mistake or accident. Accordingly, the commission of other crimes, wrongs, or acts may be proved to show:

Knowledge or specific intent. *Du Bois v. People,* 200 Ill. 157, 65 N.E. 658 (1902) (confidence game); *People v. Smith,* 18 Ill. 2d 547, 165 N.E.2d 333 (1960) (confidence game); *People v. Hobbs,* 297 Ill. 399, 130 N.E. 779 (1921) (abortion); *People v. Alexander,* 93 Ill. 2d 73, 66 Ill. Dec. 326, 442 N.E.2d 887 (1982) (intent to deprive owner of automobile); *People v. Tiller,* 94 Ill. 2d 303, 68 Ill. Dec. 916, 447 N.E.2d 174 (1982) (murder committed by an accomplice); *People v. Oaks,* 169 Ill. 2d 409, 215 Ill. Dec. 188, 662 N.E.2d 1328 (1996) (prior instance of injury to three-year-old boy diminished possibility that defendant did not knowingly inflict injury causing death); *People v. Johnson,* 174 Ill. App. 3d 726, 124 Ill. Dec. 248, 528 N.E.2d 1356 (1988) ("track marks" on defendant's arm to show knowledge of presence of syringe); *People v. McCarthy,* 132 Ill. 2d 331, 138 Ill. Dec. 292, 547 N.E.2d 459 (1989) (homicide was not committed under sudden passion); *People v. DeCesare,* 190 Ill. App. 3d 934, 138 Ill. Dec. 483, 547 N.E.2d 650 (1989) (guns and plastic bags as evidence of intent to distribute cocaine); *People v. Heredia,* 193 Ill. App. 3d 1073, 140 Ill. Dec. 898, 550 N.E.2d 1023 (1989) (prior acts of violence toward victim); *People v. Houston,* 288 Ill. App. 3d 90, 223 Ill. Dec. 471, 679 N.E.2d 1244 (1997) (telephone fraud).

Motive. *People v. Laures,* 289 Ill. 490, 124 N.E. 585 (1919) (adultery as motive for murder); *People v. Witherspoon,* 27 Ill. 2d 483, 190 N.E.2d 281 (1963) (arrest warrant as motive for shooting policeman); *People v. Gonzalez,* 104 Ill. 2d 332, 84 Ill. Dec. 457, 472 N.E.2d 417 (1984) (evidence of victim's gang membership admissible when relevant to defense theory); *People v. Stewart,* 105 Ill. 2d 22, 85 Ill. Dec. 241, 473 N.E.2d 840 (1984) (fact decedent had turned defendant in to police on prior occasion as motive for killing); *People v. Lucas,* 132 Ill. 2d 399, 139 Ill. Dec. 447, 548 N.E.2d 1003 (1989) (fact defendant resented the way his baby son had come between him and his wife as motive for killing child); *People v. Smith,* 141 Ill. 2d 40, 152 Ill. Dec. 218, 565 N.E.2d 900 (1990) (gang membership as showing motive for otherwise inexplicable act if linked to crime charged); *People v. Thingold,* 145 Ill. 2d 441, 164 Ill. Dec. 877, 584 N.E.2d 89 (1991) (insurance proceeds as motive for murder); *People v. Williams,* 161 Ill. 2d 1, 204 Ill. Dec. 72, 641 N.E.2d 296 (1994) (defendant's lack of income and assets as motive for defendant's agreement to commit murder-for-hire); *People v. Colon,* 162 Ill. 2d 23, 204 Ill. Dec. 656, 642 N.E.2d 118 (1994) (evidence relevant to show motive for shooting was gang rivalry); *People v. Enis,* 163 Ill. 2d 367, 206 Ill. Dec. 604, 645 N.E.2d 856 (1994) (filing of criminal sexual assault charges against defendant as motive for murder); *People v. Hendricks,* 145 Ill. App. 3d 71, 99 Ill. Dec. 20, 495 N.E.2d 85 (1986) (unprofessional conduct with models as motive to kill wife); *People v. Groleau,* 156 Ill. App. 3d 742, 109 Ill. Dec. 325, 509 N.E.2d 1337 (1987) (prior altercation between defendant and ex-wife who became the murder victim over child custody); *People v. Leaks,* 179 Ill. App. 3d 231, 128 Ill. Dec. 309, 534 N.E.2d 491 (1989) (prior robbery of victim by accused, followed by prior shooting of accused by victim as bearing on motive of accused to shoot victim); *People v. McFarland,* 259 Ill. App. 3d 479, 197 Ill. Dec. 524, 631 N.E.2d 746 (1994) (prior refusal to sell dope as motive for battery); *People v. Tomes,* 284 Ill. App. 3d 514, 219 Ill. Dec. 781, 672 N.E.2d 289 (1996) (prior assault of victim over failure to return security deposit as evidence of hostility in attempted first degree murder trial); *Reinneck v. Taco Bell Corp.,* 297 Ill. App. 3d 211, 231 Ill. Dec. 543, 696 N.E.2d 839 (1998) (prior discriminatory conduct or statements condoning or advocating discrimination to show current discriminatory motive).

As to gang membership, *see, e.g., People v. Patterson,* 154 Ill. 2d 414, 182 Ill. Dec. 592, 610 N.E.2d 16 (1992) (evidence of gang-related activity is admissible to show common purpose or design or to establish motive, when there is sufficient proof that membership or activity is related to the crime charged); *People v. Maldonado,* 240 Ill. App. 3d 470, 181 Ill. Dec. 426, 608 N.E.2d 499 (1992) (evidence of gang membership admissible to show motive provided substantial gang involvement established and accused is shown to be aware of facts alleged to give rise to motive, relying upon *People v. Easley,* 148 Ill. 2d 281, 170 Ill. Dec. 356, 592 N.E.2d 1036 (1992) and *People v. Smith,* 141 Ill. 2d 40, 152 Ill. Dec. 218, 565 N.E.2d 900 (1990)); *People v. Resendez,* 273 Ill. App. 3d 751, 210 Ill. Dec. 381, 652 N.E.2d 1357 (1995) (shooting was motivated by gang rivalry between Disciples and Latin Kings); *People v. Gonzalez,* 265 Ill. App. 3d 315, 202 Ill. Dec. 399, 637 N.E.2d 1135 (1995) (gang membership relevant to establish how defendant knew that pulling up "hoodies" indicated an intent to rob and/or murder); *People v. Abrams,* 260 Ill. App. 3d 566, 197 Ill. Dec. 853, 631 N.E.2d 1312 (1994) (evidence of defendant's gang membership admissible to explain why witness waited two years to disclose what she had seen); *compare People v. Mason,* 274 Ill. App. 3d 715, 210 Ill. Dec. 909, 653 N.E.2d 1371 (1995) (facts about gang rivalries, presentment, graffiti, tattoos, and drug sales improperly admitted where prosecution's theory asserted that victim and defendant were members of the same gang); *People v. Davis,* 287 Ill. App. 3d 46, 222 Ill. Dec. 541, 677 N.E.2d 1340

(1997); *People v. Jefferson*, 260 Ill. App. 3d 895, 197 Ill. Dec. 915, 631 N.E.2d 1374 (1994) (prosecution witness's gang membership properly excluded where completely unrelated to the crime and in no way relevant to the defense theory) and *People v. Negron*, 297 Ill. App. 3d 519, 231 Ill. Dec. 775, 697 N.E.2d 329 (1998) (evidence of gang membership improper in absence of evidence indicating the defendant was aware that a member of the same gang had been murdered.

Absence of good faith. *People v. Lewerenz*, 24 Ill. 2d 295, 81 N.E.2d 99 (1962) (sale of narcotics by physician).

Identity of object. *People v. Carter*, 38 Ill. 2d 496, 232 N.E.2d 692 (1968) (identification of weapon used in crime); *People v. Stewart*, 105 Ill. 2d 22, 85 Ill. Dec. 241, 473 N.E.2d 840 (1984) (gun that killed victim was taken during a robbery); *People v. Coleman*, 158 Ill. 2d 319, 198 Ill. Dec. 813, 633 N.E.2d 654 (1994) (killing of victim linked defendant to gun used to kill another victim).

Corroboration. *People v. King*, 109 Ill. 2d 514, 94 Ill. Dec. 702, 488 N.E.2d 949 (1986) (evidence of other robbery to show accuracy of confession against claim of coercion); *People v. Tellez*, 235 Ill. App. 3d 542, 176 Ill. Dec. 586, 601 N.E.2d 1284 (1992) (evidence of defendant's involvement in another killing properly admitted after defendant claimed his confession as to both killings was fabricated to support his undercover investigation).

Absence of mistake, inadvertance, or accident. *People v. Burgess*, 176 Ill. 2d 289, 223 Ill. Dec. 624, 680 N.E.2d 357 (1997) (prior incidents resulting in injury to same child to establish absence of accident); *People v. Lucas*, 132 Ill. 2d 399, 139 Ill. Dec. 447, 548 N.E.2d 1003 (1989) (prior incidents in which young child suffered similar injuries); *People v. Illgen*, 145 Ill. 2d 353, 164 Ill. Dec. 599, 583 N.E.2d 515 (1991) (prior assaults on the victim to negate accident); *People v. Parrott*, 244 Ill. App. 3d 424, 184 Ill. Dec. 278, 613 N.E.2d 305 (1993) (sexually explicit materials of prepubescent girls where defendant claims contact with young girls was inadvertent); *People v. Le Cour*, 273 Ill. App. 3d 1003, 210 Ill. Dec.

245, 652 N.E.2d 1221 (1995) (prior narcotics transactions to establish that conduct was not inadvertent and innocent).

Common design.   *People v. Rooney*, 355 Ill. 613, 190 N.E. 85 (1934) (extortion plan leading to murder); *People v. Bennet*, 9 Ill. App. 3d 1021, 293 N.E.2d 687 (1973) (another robbery in close proximity as to both time and place); *People v. Middleton*, 38 Ill. App. 3d 984, 350 N.E.2d 223 (1976) (similar sexual assaults on six other women by doctor to show plausibility of complainant's allegations, i.e., to establish existence of crime; *see also* sex crimes infra); *People v. Therriault*, 42 Ill. App. 3d 876, 1 Ill. Dec. 717, 356 N.E.2d 999 (1976) (two rapes occurring within five blocks of each other following similar pattern); *People v. Copeland*, 66 Ill. App. 3d 556, 23 Ill. Dec. 597, 384 N.E.2d 391 (1978) (two armed robberies within one mile two hours apart); *People v. Rodriguez*, 107 Ill. App. 3d 43, 62 Ill. Dec. 914, 437 N.E.2d 441 (1982) (other forged checks stolen in the same burglary as the forged checks referred to in the information); *People v. Willis*, 119 Ill. App. 3d 34, 74 Ill. Dec. 663, 456 N.E.2d 165 (1983) (two crimes committed to obtain gasoline for trip to Oklahoma); *People v. Dougherty*, 160 Ill. App. 3d 870, 112 Ill. Dec. 337, 513 N.E.2d 946 (1987) (prior payment comprising part of same bribery scheme); *People v. Davis*, 260 Ill. App. 3d 176, 197 Ill. Dec. 389, 631 N.E.2d 392 (1994) (prior instances where defendant approached men with questions concerning masturbation and homosexual acts).

Modus operandi.   *People v. Phillips*, 127 Ill. 2d 499, 131 Ill. Dec. 125, 538 N.E.2d 500 (1989) (two rapes where both women were placed in trunk of car and taken to same industrial park); *People v. Evans*, 125 Ill. 2d 50, 125 Ill. Dec. 790, 530 N.E.2d 1360 (1988) (offenses of murder and attempted rape each took place on a CHA elevator stopped between floors in the same apartment complex); *People v. Watson*, 98 Ill. App. 3d 296, 53 Ill. Dec. 694, 424 N.E.2d 329 (1981) (two rapes both involving a pistol, an automobile, and deviate sexual behavior); *People v. Curtis*, 141 Ill. App. 3d 827, 96 Ill. Dec. 320, 491 N.E.2d 134 (1986) (two robberies of the same store in identical manner two days apart); *People v. Matthews*,

137 Ill. App. 3d 870, 92 Ill. Dec. 592, 485 N.E.2d 403 (1985) (two rapes both involving robbery, oral sex, intercourse, and a small silver gun); *People v. Brewer,* 118 Ill. App. 3d 189, 73 Ill. Dec. 774, 454 N.E.2d 1023 (1983) (all victims were young children who were offered something in return for oral sex act).

The term *common design,* or its equivalents *common plan* and *common scheme,* and the term *modus operandi,* while often employed interchangeably, *see People v. Soler,* 228 Ill. App. 3d 183, 170 Ill. Dec. 81, 592 N.E.2d 517 (1992), in fact refer to separate concepts. *See People v. Barbour,* 106 Ill. App. 3d 993, 999-1000, 62 Ill. Dec. 641, 436 N.E.2d 667 (1982) ("The State (and, indeed, some of the authorities) have used 'common design' and *'modus operandi'* interchangeably but the concepts are quite distinguishable. A common design refers to a larger criminal scheme of which the crime charged is only a portion. *Modus operandi* means, literally, 'method of working,' and refers to a pattern of criminal behavior so distinctive that separate crimes are recognizable as the handiwork of the same wrongdoer. (*See generally* McCormick, Evidence sec. 190, at 448-49 (2d ed. 1972). A common design is frequently relevant to show the motive for the crime charged. *Modus operandi* is most useful in showing that the accused is the perpetrator of the crime charged."). *Accord People v. Bryan,* 159 Ill. App. 3d 46, 110 Ill. Dec. 969, 511 N.E.2d 1289 (1987); *People v. Rose,* 198 Ill. App. 3d 1, 144 Ill. Dec. 295, 555 N.E.2d 414 (1990); *People v. Tipton,* 207 Ill. App. 3d 688, 152 Ill. Dec. 665, 566 N.E.2d 352 (1990); *People v. Hall,* 235 Ill. App. 3d 418, 176 Ill. Dec. 185, 601 N.E.2d 883 (1992).

When offered by the prosecution, proof of *modus operandi* is admissible to establish identity only on a strong and persuasive showing of similarity. *People v. Robinson,* 167 Ill. 2d 53, 212 Ill. Dec. 256, 656 N.E.2d 1090 (1995); *People v. Cruz,* 162 Ill. 2d 314, 205 Ill. Dec. 345, 643 N.E.2d 636 (1994); *People v. Phillips,* 127 Ill. 2d 499, 131 Ill. Dec. 125, 538 N.E.2d 500 (1989); *People v. Tate,* 87 Ill. 2d 134, 57 Ill. Dec. 572, 429 N.E.2d 470 (1981). *See also People v. Harper,* 279 Ill. App. 3d 801, 216 Ill. Dec. 414, 665 N.E.2d 474 (1996). The similarities must be so striking that the two crimes appear distinctive and can be earmarked as the crime of a particular individual or group. *People v. Robinson,* supra (citing Handbook). *See also People v. Uzelac,* 179 Ill. App. 3d 395, 128 Ill. Dec. 645, 534 N.E.2d 1250 (1989); *People v. Williams,* 185 Ill. App. 3d 840, 133 Ill. Dec. 737, 541 N.E.2d 1175 (1989); *People v. Gibbs,* 226 Ill. App. 3d 1068, 169 Ill. Dec. 60, 590 N.E.2d 979 (1992); *People v. Harris,* 288 Ill. App. 3d 597, 224 Ill. Dec. 287, 681 N.E.2d 602 (1997). Nevertheless, the two crimes need not satisfy a test of exact rigorous identity, for some dissimilarity will always exist between independent crimes. *People v. Robinson,* supra; *People v. Cruz* supra; *People v. Maxwell,* 148 Ill. 2d 116, 170 Ill. Dec. 280, 592 N.E.2d 960 (1992). The inference that if the defendant committed one crime he may have committed the other "does not depend upon one or more unique features common to the charge and uncharged offenses, for features of substantial but lesser distinctiveness, although insufficient to raise the inference if considered separately, may yield a distinctive combination if considered together." *People v. Haston,* 69 Cal. 2d 233, 245-246, 70 Cal. Rptr. 419, 427, 444 P.2d 91, 99 (1968), quoted in *People v. Bullock,* 154 Ill. App. 3d 266, 270, 107 Ill. Dec. 380, 383, 507 N.E.2d 44, 47 (1987). *See also People v. Berry,* 244 Ill. App. 3d 14, 184 Ill. Dec. 534, 613 N.E.2d 1126 (1991). *Accord People v. Phillips,* 127 Ill. 2d 499, 131 Ill. Dec. 125, 538 N.E.2d 500 (1989) (there must be present some distinctive features that are not common to most offenses of that type); *People v. Kokoraleis,* 154 Ill. App. 3d 519, 107 Ill. Dec. 482, 507 N.E.2d 146 (1987) (crimes need not be identical but rather must possess distinctive features not common to most offenses of that type); *People v. Hayes,* 168 Ill. App. 3d 816, 119 Ill. Dec. 420, 522 N.E.2d 1279 (1988) (prior crime was substantially similar; the two crimes need not be identical); *People v. Howard,* 169 Ill. App. 3d 536, 120 Ill. Dec. 32, 523 N.E.2d 943 (1988) (the two crimes must possess distinctive features); *People v. Smith,* 236 Ill. App. 3d 1060, 177 Ill. Dec. 216, 602 N.E.2d 1388 (1992) (the totality of the similarities must reveal a distinctive combination which suggests the work of one person); *People v. Houston,* 240 Ill. App. 3d 754, 180 Ill. Dec. 924, 608

N.E.2d 46 (1992) (while unique features were absent, there was a sufficient number of substantial similarities to permit admission). Sufficient similarity may be established by evidence indicating that the perpetrator was, for example, using similar weapons, dressing the same, acting with the same number of people, and/or using a distinctive method of committing the particular offense. *People v. Phillips* supra; *People v. Bennett*, 281 Ill. App. 3d 814, 217 Ill. Dec. 230, 666 N.E.2d 899 (1996); *People v. Walker*, 253 Ill. App. 3d 93, 192 Ill. Dec. 1, 624 N.E.2d 1353 (1993). *See also People v. Patten*, 230 Ill. App. 3d 922, 172 Ill. Dec. 471, 595 N.E.2d 1141 (1992) (geographic proximity and similarity in execution). For a case illustrating the difficulty of determining whether the crimes are sufficiently distinctive as to be like a signature, McCormick, Evidence §190 (4th ed. 1992), *see People v. Johnson*, 107 Ill. App. 3d 156, 62 Ill. Dec. 909, 437 N.E.2d 436 (1982). Evidence of *modus operandi* is also admissible to prove that a crime was in fact committed, *People v. Rucheinski*, 224 Ill. App. 3d 118, 166 Ill. Dec. 548, 586 N.E.2d 506 (1991), and to prove intent. *People v. Miller*, 254 Ill. App. 3d 997, 193 Ill. Dec. 799, 626 N.E.2d 1350 (1993).

A less substantial showing of similarity is required when evidence of *modus operandi* is offered to negative inadvertence, accident, or other form of innocent intent. *People v. Oaks*, 169 Ill. 2d 409, 215 Ill. Dec. 188, 662 N.E.2d 1328 (1996); *People v. Illgen*, 145 Ill. 2d 353, 164 Ill. Dec. 599, 583 N.E.2d 515 (1991); *People v. Bartall*, 98 Ill. 2d 294, 74 Ill. Dec. 557, 456 N.E.2d 59 (1983); *People v. McKibbins*, 96 Ill. 2d 176, 70 Ill. Dec. 474, 449 N.E.2d 821 (1983). *Accord People v. Burgess*, 176 Ill. 2d 289, 223 Ill. Dec. 624, 680 N.E.2d 357 (1997); *People v. Cruz*, 162 Ill. 2d 314, 205 Ill. Dec. 345, 643 N.E.2d 636 (1994) (mere general areas of similarity suffice). When offered to prove intent or the corresponding absence of an innocent frame of mind, the commission of one crime increases the probability that a subsequent crime was done deliberately. *People v. Charles*, 238 Ill. App. 3d 752, 179 Ill. Dec. 771, 606 N.E.2d 603 (1992).

When offered by the defense, proof of another crime

indicating *modus operandi* is admissible if the evidence contains significant probative value to the defense and if a strong and persuasive showing of similarity between the two crimes is presented; a discretionary balancing test is not employed as unfair prejudice to the prosecution is not recognized. *People v. Tate*, 87 Ill. 2d 134, 57 Ill. Dec. 572, 429 N.E.2d 470 (1981); *People v. Cruz*, 162 Ill. 2d 314, 205 Ill. Dec. 345, 643 N.E.2d 636 (1994).

Common design, common plan, or *common scheme* refers to the introduction of other crimes, wrongs, or acts from which it can be inferred that the accused committed the crime in question or did so with the appropriate mental state. When not employed incorrectly as functionally interchangeable with *modus operandi,* as was done in *People v. Banks,* 161 Ill. 2d 119, 204 Ill. Dec. 107, 641 N.E.2d 331 (1994); *People v. Overlin,* 241 Ill. App. 3d 530, 181 Ill. Dec. 674, 608 N.E.2d 925 (1993) and *People v. Kimbrough,* 138 Ill. App. 3d 481, 93 Ill. Dec. 82, 485 N.E.2d 1292 (1985), *common design, common plan,* or *common scheme* refers to the notion of a series of crimes, wrongs, or acts employed usually to establish identity or *mens rea* with respect to the crime for which the accused is on trial, such as identification of the accused as having stolen the gun used in a shooting, that the accused had threatened to kill a witness to an armed robbery he is charged with having committed, or that the defendant was present when another was arrested previously for presenting forged checks as evidence of knowledge when that same person once again presented a forged check. *See generally People v. Denny,* 241 Ill. App. 3d 345, 181 Ill. Dec. 839, 608 N.E.2d 1313 (1993); *People v. Murdock,* 259 Ill. App. 3d 1014, 198 Ill. Dec. 254, 632 N.E.2d 313 (1994). In such instances, obviously, similarity of any kind is sometimes not required. Sometimes evidence of other crimes, wrongs, or acts is admitted under the rubric of *common design, common plan,* or *common scheme* under circumstances similar but not identical to *modus operandi,* such as where two armed robberies were committed within a mile of each other two hours apart. Less similarity will be required in such a case than with *modus operandi* in light of time and space proximity, as well as other connecting factors. What must be established in either instance is a "coherent pattern of connected behavior." Louisell & Mueller, Federal Evidence §140 at 262 (1985). *See, e.g., People v. Rooney,* 355 Ill. 613, 190 N.E. 85 (1934) (extortion plan leading to murder); *People v. Bennett,* 9 Ill. App. 3d 1021, 293 N.E.2d 687 (1973) (another robbery in close proximity as to both time and place); *People v. Therriault,* 42 Ill. App. 3d 876, 1 Ill. Dec. 717, 356 N.E.2d 999 (1976) (two rapes occurring within five blocks of each other following similar pattern); *People v. Copeland,* 66 Ill. App. 3d 556, 23 Ill. Dec. 597, 384 N.E.2d 391 (1978) (two armed robberies within one mile two hours apart); *People v. Rodriguez,* 107 Ill. App. 3d 43, 62 Ill. Dec. 914, 437 N.E.2d 441 (1982) (other forged checks stolen in the same burglary as the forged checks referred to in the information); *People v. Willis,* 119 Ill. App. 3d 34, 74 Ill. Dec. 663, 456 N.E.2d 165 (1983) (two crimes committed to obtain gasoline for trip to Oklahoma); *People v. Dougherty,* 160 Ill. App. 3d 870, 1112 Ill. Dec. 337, 513 N.E.2d 946 (1987) (prior payment comprising part of same bribery scheme).

Evidence of other crimes, wrongs, or acts has also been received as rebuttal to the defense of entrapment, *People v. Outten,* 13 Ill. 2d 21, 147 N.E.2d 284 (1958) (sale of narcotics); *People v. Placek,* 292 Ill. App. 3d 521, 226 Ill. Dec. 547, 685 N.E. 2d 1002 (1997) (delivery of controlled substance); to rebut the assertion of alibi, *People v. Romero,* 66 Ill. 2d 325, 5 Ill. Dec. 817, 362 N.E.2d 288 (1977); as rebuttal to evidence procured, invited, or acquiesced to by the defendant, *People v. McGee,* 268 Ill. App. 3d 582, 206 Ill. Dec. 324, 645 N.E.2d 329 (1994); and to explain reason for lengthy detention undermining defendant's claim of coerced confession. *People v. Gilliam,* 172 Ill. 2d 484, 218 Ill. Dec. 884, 670 N.E.2d 606 (1996). With respect to consciousness of guilt, *see People v. Jefferson,* 260 Ill. App. 3d 895, 197 Ill. Dec. 915, 631 N.E.2d 1374 (1994), and §801.3 infra.

With respect to the introduction of other crimes, wrongs, or acts evidence by the accused, *see* discussion supra. *See also People v. Cruz,* 162 Ill. 2d 314, 205 Ill. Dec. 345, 643 N.E.2d

636 (1994); *People v. Tate*, 87 Ill. 2d 134, 57 Ill. Dec. 572, 429 N.E.2d 470 (1981). *See also* §403.2 supra. With respect to admitting other crimes, wrongs, or acts evidence to establish that someone other that the accused did *not* commit the crime, *see People v. Taylor*, 264 Ill. App. 3d 197, 202 Ill. Dec. 217, 637 N.E.2d 756 (1994).

Testimony narrating the offense or laying a basis for identification is not excludable because of incidental disclosure of other offenses. *People v. Diekelmann*, 367 Ill. 372, 11 N.E.2d 420 (1937), taking indecent liberties disclosed in prosecution for kidnapping; *People v. Davis*, 14 Ill. 2d 196, 151 N.E.2d 308 (1958), witness in robbery case identified accused as man who robbed him before; *People v. Richardson*, 123 Ill. 2d 322, 123 Ill. Dec. 908, 528 N.E.2d 612 (1988), evidence establishing identification based upon same gun being used in both incidents; *People v. Schockey*, 66 Ill. App. 2d 245, 213 N.E.2d 107 (1966), witness testified that accused signed and cashed some of the checks later burglarized; *People v. Novak*, 94 Ill. App. 3d 1024, 50 Ill. Dec. 285, 419 N.E.2d 393 (1981), identification of blood on pants of defendant charged with murder when arrested for an unrelated offense; *People v. Brown*, 275 Ill. App. 3d 1105, 212 Ill. Dec. 441, 657 N.E.2d 642 (1995), fact defendant had appeared in court in Indiana under same false name on question of identity. Nonetheless, reference to the prior incident offered for the purpose of establishing a basis of identification should be confined to the details needed to show opportunity for identification and thus exclude, where context permits, the details of the crime. *People v. Butler*, 31 Ill. App. 3d 78, 334 N.E.2d 448 (1975). Determining where context permits without the testimony becoming artificial may be difficult. For example, in *People v. Andrade*, 279 Ill. App. 3d 292, 215 Ill. Dec. 859, 664 N.E.2d 256 (1996), it is stated that the government agent could have established a prior incident with defendant establishing a basis for identification without referring to the incident as a drug transaction, a questionable proposition given that the agent's only reason to have observed the defendant was the existence of a drug transaction. Similarly, references by the accused to periods spent in prison are admissible where relevant to establish defendant's intent. *People v. Chapin*, 84 Ill. App. 3d 788, 40 Ill. Dec. 573, 406 N.E.2d 579 (1980) (intimidation). *Cf. People v. Armstrong*, 175 Ill. App. 3d 874, 125 Ill. Dec. 409, 530 N.E.2d 567 (1988), where reference of the accused's prior prison record appears to be relevant to show intent solely by virtue of the prohibited "bad man" inference. With respect to disclosure of other offenses offered to show how the investigation unfolded and how the accused came into custody, *see* §801.5 infra. It naturally follows that evidence describing the circumstances of an accused's arrest that does not include a reference to an unrelated crime, wrong, or act is not excludable. *People v. Hayes*, 139 Ill. 2d 89, 151 Ill. Dec. 348, 564 N.E.2d 803 (1990).

As stated in *People v. Cross*, 96 Ill. App. 3d 268, 272, 51 Ill. Dec. 754, 758, 421 N.E.2d 262, 266 (1981): "The test of admissibility is whether the evidence of other crimes is so closely connected with the offense for which the accused is tried that it tends to prove guilt of that charge." Accordingly, evidence of other crimes has been admitted where necessary to explain the circumstances of the crime that would otherwise be unclear or improbable, *People v. Cole*, 29 Ill. 2d 501, 194 N.E.2d 269 (1963); *People v. Leaks*, 179 Ill. App. 3d 231, 128 Ill. Dec. 309, 534 N.E.2d 491 (1989); *People v. Turner*, 78 Ill. App. 3d 82, 33 Ill. Dec. 415, 396 N.E.2d 1139 (1979), to explain that the defendant is not as naive as the defendant claims, *People v. O'Toole*, 226 Ill. App. 3d 974, 169 Ill. Dec. 31, 590 N.E.2d 950 (1992), and to explain why defendant did not notify the authorities when discovering the victims' bodies because he was on parole and thought he would be blamed for their murders. *People v. Wiley*, 165 Ill. 2d 259, 209 Ill. Dec. 261, 651 N.E.2d 189 (1995). *See also People v. Lowry*, 231 Ill. App. 3d 788, 173 Ill. Dec. 339, 596 N.E.2d 1218 (1992) (prior drug sale set background for initial phone call). Moreover, where "the evidence of the act and the evidence of the crime charged are inextricably intertwined, the act is not extrinsic and the rule relating to 'other crimes' evidence is not implicated, simply because such evidence formed an integral and natural part of the witness's account of the circumstances surrounding the offenses for which the defendant was indicted. *People v. Baptist,* (1979) 76 Ill 2d 19, 27 Ill. Dec. 792, 389 N.E.2d 1200." *People v. Allen,* 184 Ill. App. 3d 438, 449, 132 Ill. Dec. 671, 678, 540 N.E.2d 411, 418 (1989). *Accord People v. Waller,* 195 Ill. App. 3d 376, 142 Ill. Dec. 1, 552 N.E.2d 351 (1990); *People v. Liberman,* 228 Ill. App. 3d 639, 170 Ill. Dec. 139, 592 N.E.2d 575 (1992); *People v. Manuel,* 294 Ill. App. 3d 113, 228 Ill. Dec. 472, 689 N.E.2d 344 (1997) (quoting Handbook). The term *res gestae,* discussed in § 803.2 infra, should not be employed to described the foregoing concepts as occurred in *People v. Rogers,* 264 Ill. App. 3d 740, 201 Ill. Dec. 133, 636 N.E.2d 565 (1992), amongst others as the concept of *res gestae* has been thoroughly repudiated. *Accord People v. Rogers id.* (Greiman J., specially concurring) (citing Handbook); *People v. Hill,* 278 Ill. App. 3d 871, 215 Ill. Dec. 492, 663 N.E.2d 503 (1996) (*res gestae* disavowed as it serves only to confuse the determination of evidence of other crimes).

Time and place proximity, without more, is an insufficient basis for permitting evidence of other crimes. *People v. Lindgren,* 79 Ill. 2d 129, 37 Ill. Dec. 348, 402 N.E.2d 238 (1980). It is thus improper to admit evidence of a crime wholly unrelated to the offense for which the accused is on trial even though it is argued that the separate and distinct crime forms a part of the narrative of the defendant's arrest for the present charge because it explains why the police appeared, *People v. Lindgren,* supra; *People v. Richardson,* 123 Ill. 2d 322, 123 Ill. Dec. 908, 528 N.E.2d 612 (1988); *People v. Groves,* 287 Ill. App. 3d 84, 222 Ill. Dec. 552, 677 N.E.2d 1351 (1997); *People v. Brown,* 275 Ill. App. 3d 1105, 212 Ill. Dec. 441, 657 N.E.2d 642 (1995); *People v. Cobbins,* 162 Ill. App. 3d 1010, 114 Ill. Dec. 227, 516 N.E.2d 382 (1987); *People v. Spiezio,* 105 Ill. App. 3d 769, 61 Ill. Dec. 482, 434 N.E.2d 837 (1982); *People v. Connors,* 82 Ill. App. 3d 32, 37 Ill. Dec. 771, 402 N.E.2d 773 (1980). Other crimes, proximately committed, may be relevant if additional reasons are present. *People v. Taylor,* 101 Ill. 2d 508, 79 Ill. Dec. 151, 463 N.E.2d 705

(1984) (time and place proximity plus common scheme); *People v. Wilson*, 46 Ill. 2d 376, 263 N.E.2d 856 (1970) (time and place proximity plus relevance to defendant's knowledge); *People v. Armstrong*, 41 Ill. 2d 390, 243 N.E.2d 825 (1968) (proximity plus common design or scheme); *People v. Hall*, 38 Ill. 2d 308, 231 N.E.2d 416 (1967) (proximity plus confession corroboration); *People v. McGuire*, 35 Ill. 2d 219, 220 N.E.2d 447 (1966) (proximity plus indication of resistance to arrest); *People v. Walls*, 33 Ill. 2d 394, 211 N.E.2d 699 (1965) (proximity plus issue of identity); *People v. Matthews*, 137 Ill. App. 3d 870, 92 Ill. Dec. 592, 485 N.E.2d 403 (1985) (proximity plus rebuttal of defendant's assertion of arbitrary arrest); *People v. Janes*, 138 Ill. App. 3d 558, 93 Ill. Dec. 216, 486 N.E.2d 317 (1985) (unrelated arrest led to discovery of victim's wallet at booking); *People v. Millighan*, 265 Ill. App. 3d 967, 203 Ill. Dec. 24, 638 N.E.2d 1150 (1994) (proximity plus identification of weapon).

Evidence admitted as relevant for a purpose other than to show a disposition to commit crimes may relate to a crime committed subsequent to the crime for which the defendant is on trial. *People v. Coleman*, 158 Ill. 2d 319, 198 Ill. Dec. 813, 633 N.E.2d 654 (1994); *People v. Bartall*, 98 Ill. 2d 294, 74 Ill. Dec. 557, 456 N.E.2d 59 (1983); *People v. Campbell*, 28 Ill. App. 3d 480, 328 N.E.2d 608 (1975); *People v. Mitchell*, 95 Ill. App. 3d 779, 51 Ill. Dec. 1, 420 N.E.2d 415 (1981); *People v. Gales*, 248 Ill. App. 3d 204, 188 Ill. Dec. 277, 618 N.E.2d 847 (1993). Subsequent conversations relating to proposed criminal activity relevant to show the full circumstances surrounding the transaction in question are also admissible. *People v. Mitchell*, 129 Ill. App. 3d 189, 84 Ill. Dec. 364, 472 N.E.2d 114 (1984). Similarly, evidence may be introduced as to the crime for which the defendant was placed under arrest when the offense charged is resisting arrest. *People v. Meyers*, 94 Ill. App. 2d 340, 236 N.E.2d 786 (1968); *People v. Hoppock*, 98 Ill. App. 3d 58, 53 Ill. Dec. 547, 423 N.E.2d 1351 (1981).

Evidence of other crimes may not be admitted for the sole purpose of bolstering the credibility of a prosecution witness. *People v. Romero*, 66 Ill. 2d 325, 5 Ill. Dec. 817, 362 N.E.2d 288

(1977); *People v. Thingvold,* 145 Ill. 2d 441, 164 Ill. Dec. 877, 584 N.E.2d 89 (1991).

Evidence of other crimes, wrongs, or acts may be admitted to attack credibility on the basis of interest, bias, corruption, or coercion as set forth in §607.7 infra. *People v. Rodriguez,* 267 Ill. App. 3d 942, 204 Ill. Dec. 509, 641 N.E.2d 939 (1994), stating that other crimes are not admissible to attack credibility, should be read to mean that impeachment by other crimes is not governed by the principles set forth in this section but rather by those set forth in §607.7 infra.

With respect to other sexual acts of the accused, see §404.6 infra. As to prior convictions for battery of a family member or for stalking, see § 404.7 infra.

The foregoing exposition is illustrative and not exclusive; evidence of other crimes, wrongs, or acts is admissible when relevant for any purpose other than to show a disposition to engage in such conduct. *People v. Evans,* 125 Ill. 2d 50, 125 Ill. Dec. 790, 530 N.E.2d 1360 (1988); *People v. Stewart,* 105 Ill. 2d 22, 85 Ill. Dec. 241, 473 N.E.2d 840 (1984). For example, evidence of other crimes, wrongs, or acts sometimes involves conduct by the accused directed on another occasion against the victim relevant to establish identity, intent, or *corpus delicti. See, e.g, People v. Bailey,* 167 Ill. 2d 210, 212 Ill. Dec. 608, 657 N.E.2d 953 (1995); *People v. West,* 137 Ill. 2d 558, 148 Ill. Dec. 196, 560 N.E.2d 594 (1990); *People v. McCarthy,* 132 Ill. 2d 331, 138 Ill. Dec. 292, 547 N.E.2d 459 (1989). Evidence of other crimes, wrongs, or acts has been admitted to show defendants' awareness of the effects of a given amount of physical force. *People v. Tainter,* 294 Ill. App. 3d 634, 229 Ill. Dec. 119, 691 N.E.2d 55 (1998). Evidence of other crimes allegedly confessed to by the accused as part of the accused's alleged confession to the current offense has been admitted to establish that the defendant actually confessed to and committed the current offense. *People v. Williams,* 285 Ill. App. 3d 394, 220 Ill. Dec. 748, 673 N.E.2d 1169 (1996). Evidence of other crimes, wrongs, or acts may be relevant where the accused raises the defense of insanity. Such evidence may nevertheless be excluded on the grounds of being substantially more prejudicial than probative, especially if such evidence is not purged of detailed reference to other crimes. *See People v. McMillen,* 281 Ill. App. 3d 247, 217 Ill. Dec. 143, 666 N.E.2d 812 (1996). *See also* §703.1 infra. Of course, evidence of other crimes, wrongs, or acts if not relevant is not admissible. *People v. Wydra,* 265 Ill. App. 3d 597, 202 Ill. Dec. 202, 637 N.E.2d 741 (1994), defendant's assault on former girlfriend's new boyfriend was not relevant to show intent to harm police officer.

Evidence of other offenses may thus be received, if relevant, for any purpose other than to show a mere propensity or disposition on the part of the defendant to commit the crime, provided, however, that the court may exclude the evidence if its incremental probative value is substantially outweighed by the risk that its admission will create a danger of undue prejudice to the accused. *See* §403.1 supra. *People v. Friedman,* 79 Ill. 2d 341, 38 Ill. Dec. 141, 403 N.E.2d 229 (1980); *People v. Weaver,* 92 Ill. 2d 545, 65 Ill. Dec. 944, 442 N.E.2d 255 (1982); *People v. Smith,* 141 Ill. 2d 40, 152 Ill. Dec. 218, 565 N.E.2d 900 (1990); *People v. Illgen,* 145 Ill. 2d 353, 164 Ill. Dec. 599, 583 N.E.2d 515 (1991); *People v. Robinson,* 167 Ill. 2d 53, 212 Ill. Dec. 256, 656 N.E.2d 1090 (1995); *People v. Manning,* 182 Ill. 2d 193, 230 Ill. Dec. 933, 695 N.E.2d 423 (1998); *People v. Harper,* 251 Ill. App. 3d 801, 191 Ill. Dec. 185, 623 N.E.2d 775 (1993). Evidence of other offenses offered by the accused is not subject to the same discretionary balancing test as a risk of unfair prejudice to the prosecution is not recognized. *People v. Cruz,* 162 Ill. 2d 314, 205 Ill. Dec. 345, 643 N.E.2d 636 (1994); *People v. Tate,* 87 Ill. 2d 134, 57 Ill. Dec. 572, 429 N.E.2d 470 (1981).

In exercising its discretion in applying this standard, the trial court should consider the importance of the fact of consequence for which the evidence is offered in the context of the litigation, the strength and length of the chain of inferences necessary to establish the fact of consequence, the availability of alternative means of proof, whether the fact of consequence for which the evidence is offered is being disputed, whether a party has agreed to stipulate to the existence of the fact of consequence, and, where appropriate, the potential effectiveness of a limiting instruction. *See People v. Robinson,* 167 Ill. 2d 53, 212 Ill. Dec. 256, 656 N.E.2d 1090 (1995), trial court did not abuse its discretion in permitting prosecution to admit two of eight other crimes. *See also Thompson v. Petit,* 294 Ill. App. 3d 1029, 229 Ill. Dec. 387, 691 N.E.2d 860 (1998). The probative value of the evidence itself must of course be considered in light of various factors, such as remoteness in time, the conclusiveness of proof of commission by the defendant, and where relevancy depends, upon the degree of resemblance between the other crime and the crime charged. *See People v. Robinson,* supra (trial court did not abuse its discretion in admitting crime occurring 13 years earlier as the accused had spent all but two of those years incarcerated). For example, similarity is often an important consideration with respect to identity or intent but rarely important with respect to evidence offered to prove motive. Moreover, the degree of similarity needed, when relevant at all, to establish intent, such as arises with respect to prior narcotics transactions, is less than the degree of similarity required of other crimes, wrongs, or acts offered to prove *modus operandi. People v. Cruz,* 162 Ill. 2d 314, 205 Ill. Dec. 345, 643 N.E.2d 636 (1994); *People v. Le Cour,* 273 Ill. App. 3d 1003, 210 Ill. Dec. 245, 652 N.E.2d 1221 (1995). In evaluating the incremental probative value of the evidence, the trial judge must assume that the evidence will be believed by the trier of fact. Obviously where either the probative value of the offered evidence or the importance of the fact sought to be proved is relatively slight, the likelihood of exclusion is enhanced. *People v. Stewart,* 105 Ill. 2d 22, 85 Ill. Dec. 241, 473 N.E.2d 840 (1984); *People v. Murray,* 254 Ill. App. 3d 538, 193 Ill. Dec. 589, 626 N.E.2d 1140 (1993). While remoteness of the other crime, wrong, or act is appropriately considered by the court in balancing incremental probative value versus the danger of unfair prejudice, remoteness alone tends not to result in exclusion. *See, e.g., People v. Illgen,* 145 Ill. 2d 353, 164 Ill. Dec. 599, 583 N.E.2d 515 (1991); *People v. Davis,* 260 Ill. App. 3d 176, 197 Ill. Dec.

389, 631 N.E.2d 392 (1994); *People v. Jendras*, 216 Ill. App. 3d 149, 159 Ill. Dec. 560, 576 N.E.2d 229 (1991); *People v. Burgos*, 184 Ill. App. 3d 474, 132 Ill. Dec. 716, 540 N.E.2d 456 (1989); *People v. Hanei*, 81 Ill. App. 3d 690, 38 Ill. Dec. 1, 403 N.E.2d 16 (1980). The fact the other crime is itself barred from prosecution by the statute of limitations is not preclusive. *People v. Peebles*, 114 Ill. App. 3d 684, 70 Ill. Dec. 356, 449 N.E.2d 230 (1983).

Trial courts should be cautious of the unfair prejudice that may arise if extensive detailed evidence of the other crime, wrong, or act is received. *See People v. McKibbins*, 96 Ill. 2d 176, 70 Ill. Dec. 474, 449 N.E.2d 821 (1983); *People v. Sykes*, 161 Ill. App. 3d 623, 113 Ill. Dec. 444, 515 N.E.2d 253 (1987). The jury should be apprised of the behavior; the jury should not be told that the behavior constituted the commission of a crime. *People v. Overton*, 281 Ill. App. 3d 209, 217 Ill. Dec. 84, 666 N.E.2d 753 (1996). Overall, the process of disclosure must be conducted in such a way as to prevent the other crime, wrong, or act evidence from becoming a feature of the case, i.e., presentation of the details of the other crime, wrong, or act should not be a trial within a trial. *People v. Bennett*, 281 Ill. App. 3d 814, 217 Ill. Dec. 230, 666 N.E.2d 899 (1996). *Accord People v. Robinson*, 167 Ill. 2d 53, 212 Ill. Dec. 256, 656 N.E.2d 1090 (1995), trial court should carefully limit evidence of other crimes to that which is relevant for the purpose it was admitted and thus curtail the risk of a "mini-trial."

Applying the foregoing standard, where the evidence of other offenses is central to the establishment of an element of the crime, i.e., extremely necessary and probative, the evidence is admissible in spite of its potentially prejudicial impact. *People v. Foster*, 76 Ill. 2d 365, 29 Ill. Dec. 449, 392 N.E.2d 6 (1979). Conversely, when, for example, there is no question as to where the defendant lived, for his identity, the introduction of evidence of the defendant's probation status to establish his address is reversible error. *People v. Pitts*, 257 Ill. App. 3d 949, 196 Ill. Dec. 225, 629 N.E.2d 770 (1994). The process of admitting evidence of another crime, wrong, or act should not become a feature of the case, i.e., become a mini trial within the trial; the trial court should carefully limit the details to what is necessary to illuminate the issue for which the other crime, wrong, or act is introduced. *People v. Nunley*, 271 Ill. App. 3d 427, 208 Ill. Dec. 93, 648 N.E.2d 1015 (1995).

The decision with respect to the admissibility of evidence of other crimes, wrongs, or acts will be overturned only if there exists a clear abuse of discretion. *People v. Illgen*, 145 Ill. 2d 353, 164 Ill. Dec. 599, 583 N.E.2d 515 (1991); *People v. Thingvold*, 145 Ill. 2d 441, 164 Ill. Dec. 877, 584 N.E.2d 89 (1991); *People v. Robinson*, 167 Ill. 2d 53, 212 Ill. Dec. 256, 656 N.E.2d 1090 (1995); *People v. Oaks*, 169 Ill. 2d 409, 215 Ill. Dec. 188, 662 N.E.2d 1328 (1996); *People v. Jenkins*, 209 Ill. App. 3d 249, 154 Ill. Dec. 122, 568 N.E.2d 122 (1991) (quoting Handbook); *People v. Sims*, 244 Ill. App. 3d 966, 184 Ill. Dec. 135, 612 N.E.2d 1011 (1993). Clear abuse of discretion will be found only where the court's decision is arbitrary, fanciful, or unreasonable, or where no reasonable man would take the view adopted by the trial court. *People v. Illgen*, 145 Ill. 2d 353, 164 Ill. Dec. 599, 583 N.E.2d 515 (1991). If the evidence of other crimes, wrongs, or acts is admitted in error, the high risk of prejudice ordinarily calls for reversal, *People v. Lindgren*, 79 Ill. 2d 129, 37 Ill. Dec. 348, 402 N.E.2d 238 (1980); *People v. Eveland*, 181 Ill. App. 3d 458, 130 Ill. Dec. 69, 536 N.E.2d 1280 (1989); *People v. Denny*, 241 Ill. App. 3d 345, 181 Ill. Dec. 839, 608 N.E.2d 1313 (1993), but not always as harmless error analysis applies. *People v. Richardson*, 123 Ill. 2d 322, 123 Ill. Dec. 908, 528 N.E.2d 612 (1988); *People v. King*, 293 Ill. App. 3d 739, 228 Ill. Dec. 127, 688 N.E.2d 825 (1997); *People v. Miller*, 254 Ill. App. 3d 997, 193 Ill. Dec. 799, 626 N.E.2d 1350 (1993); *People v. Foster*, 190 Ill. App. 3d 1018, 138 Ill. Dec. 311, 547 N.E.2d 478 (1989).

Evidence of "other" crimes cannot be admitted for any of the foregoing purposes unless it is first shown that the crime, wrong, or act actually took place and that the defendant committed it or participated in its commission. *People v. Thingvold*, 145 Ill. 2d 441, 164 Ill. Dec. 877, 584 N.E.2d 89 (1991); *People v. Brozan*, 163 Ill. App. 3d 73, 115 Ill. Dec. 83,

517 N.E.2d 285 (1987); *People v. Scott,* 13 Ill. App. 3d 620, 301 N.E.2d 118 (1973). While proof of other crimes, wrongs, or acts need not be beyond a reasonable doubt, *Wernowsky v. Economy Fire & Cas. Co.,* 106 Ill. 2d 49, 87 Ill. Dec. 484, 477 N.E.2d 231 (1985); *People v. MacRae,* 47 Ill. App. 3d 305, 5 Ill. Dec. 362, 361 N.E.2d 685 (1977); *People v. Smith,* 3 Ill. App. 3d 958, 279 N.E.2d 512 (1972), mere suspicion is insufficient. *People v. Sims,* 244 Ill. App. 3d 966, 184 Ill. Dec. 135, 612 N.E.2d 1011 (1993); *People v. Nearn,* 178 Ill. App. 3d 480, 127 Ill. Dec. 637, 533 N.E.2d 509 (1988); *People v. Miller,* 55 Ill. App. 3d 421, 13 Ill. Dec. 128, 370 N.E.2d 1155 (1977). With respect to the exact standard to be applied, in the federal court the debate between requiring a preliminary determinate by the court that the prior crime, wrong, or act was established by clear and convincing evidence or merely treating the question as one involving conditional relevancy, was resolved in *Huddleston v. United States,* 485 U.S. 681 (1988), where the United States Supreme Court decided as a matter of federal law that under Federal Rule of Evidence 404(b) a showing of clear and convincing evidence is *not* required; the introduction of evidence sufficient to support a finding of more probably true than not true, Federal Rule of Evidence 104(b), suffices. The exact standard to be applied in Illinois remains unclear. *See People v. Smith,* 141 Ill. 2d 40, 152 Ill. Dec. 218, 565 N.E.2d 900 (1990) (the evidence must, at least to a slight degree, tend to establish the motive relied on); *People v. Davis,* 248 Ill. App. 3d 886, 187 Ill. Dec. 660, 617 N.E.2d 1381 (1993) (implying without holding that evidence more than a mere suspicion in fact equates with evidence sufficient to support a finding of more probably true than not true). Notice that the Illinois Supreme Court in *People v. Thingvold,* 145 Ill. 2d 441, 164 Ill. Dec. 877, 584 N.E.2d 89 (1991), and once again in *People v. Oaks,* 169 Ill. 2d 409, 215 Ill. Dec. 188, 662 N.E.2d 1328 (1996), declined to refine the appropriate standard to be applied beyond the traditional less than reasonable doubt more than a mere suspicion test stated above. Adoption of the "evidence sufficient to support a finding" standard of Federal Rules of Evidence 104(b)

seems most in keeping with the overall thrust of Illinois decisions. While evidence of "other" crimes is usually introduced through the testimony of an occurrence witness, the existence of the "other" crimes may also be established through introduction of the defendant's own confession. *People v. Kokoraleis,* 132 Ill. 2d 235, 138 Ill. Dec. 233, 547 N.E.2d 202 (1989). A statement by an occurrence witness who later recants has been held to be sufficient. *People v. Johnson,* 264 Ill. App. 3d 1000, 202 Ill. Dec. 228, 637 N.E.2d 767 (1994) (prior statement and grand jury testimony). However, a police report of an investigation of an offense may *not* be employed to establish a prior crime, wrong, or act in a criminal prosecution. 725 ILCS 5/115-5(c). *See also People v. Gayton,* 293 Ill. App. 3d 442, 228 Ill. Dec. 229, 688 N.E.2d 1206 (1997). An acquittal of the accused after trial does not preclude the introduction of evidence with regard to the crime for which the defendant was acquitted at a subsequent trial for a different offense. *Dowling v. United States,* 493 U.S. 342 (1990).

Other crimes, wrongs, or acts meeting the foregoing requirements are admissible regardless of the fact that they may have occurred outside the jurisdiction of the trial court. *People v. Demeron,* 153 Ill. App. 3d 440, 106 Ill. Dec. 431, 505 N.E.2d 1222 (1987); *People v. Failor,* 271 Ill. App. 3d 968, 208 Ill. Dec. 681, 649 N.E.2d 1342 (1995).

When evidence of a crime, wrong, or act is admitted for a purpose other than showing a disposition to commit such crimes the limiting instruction contained in Illinois Pattern Jury Instructions—Criminal 3.14 (1996) should be given. *See People v. Illgen,* 145 Ill. 2d 353, 164 Ill. Dec. 599, 583 N.E.2d 515 (1991). The limiting instruction should be modified to reflect the particular purpose or purposes for which the other crime, wrong, or act evidence has been admitted. *People v. Leaks,* 179 Ill. App. 3d 231, 128 Ill. Dec. 309, 534 N.E.2d 491 (1989), under the facts of the case only motive and intent, not identity, should have been mentioned in limiting instruction. A limiting instruction should be given at the time the other crime, wrong, or act evidence is received if requested. In the absence of a request for an immediate limiting instruction, such an admonition as part of the jury instruction process at the conclusion of the case will suffice. *People v. Smith,* 18 Ill. 2d 547, 165 N.E.2d 333 (1960); *People v. Leaks* supra. The Illinois Supreme Court Committee on Pattern Jury Instructions in Criminal Cases recommends in the Committee Notes to Criminal 3.14 that a limiting instruction be given prior to the introduction of the crime, wrong, or act evidence, unless the defendant objects.

Evidence of other crimes, wrongs, or acts such as fraud is also admissible under similar circumstances in civil cases. *See, e.g., Hanchett v. Riverdale Distilling Co.,* 15 Ill. App. 57 (1885), common scheme; *Joseph Taylor Coal Co. v. Dawes,* 122 Ill. App. 389 (1905), *aff'd,* 220 Ill. 147, 77 N.E. 131 (1906), knowledge and intent; *Wernowsky v. Economy Fire & Cas. Co.,* 106 Ill. 2d 49, 87 Ill. Dec. 484, 477 N.E.2d 231 (1985), identity; *Mack v. First Security Bank of Chicago,* 158 Ill. App. 3d 497, 110 Ill. Dec. 537, 511 N.E.2d 714 (1987), motive. *See generally* McCormick, Evidence §197 (4th ed. 1992).

§404.6   Other Sexual Acts of the Accused

The common law of Illinois, as did the common law generally, struggled to resolve the question of when other sexual acts of the accused could be admitted when offered by the prosecution. The problem, of course, is that evidence of other sexual acts is evidence of a pertinent character trait of the accused which the prosecution is prohibited from establishing in its case in chief. *See* §§ 404.3 and 404.5 supra. On the other hand, evidence of other sexual acts is admissible when offered for a purpose other than merely showing a disposition or propensity to commit such crimes. *See* §404.5 supra. Illinois courts admitted other sexual acts between the same parties to show the relationship and familiarity of the parties and to corroborate the complaining witness's testimony concerning the offense charged, *People v. Morgan,* 152 Ill. App. 3d 97, 105 Ill. Dec. 303, 504 N.E.2d 172 (1987); *People v. Barlow,* 188 Ill. App. 3d 393, 136 Ill. Dec. 172, 544

N.E.2d 947 (1989); *People v. McCarthy,* 213 Ill. App. 3d 873, 157 Ill. Dec. 755, 572 N.E.2d 1219 (1991); *People v. Anderson,* 225 Ill. App. 3d 636, 167 Ill. Dec. 435, 587 N.E.2d 1050 (1992), even when the fact of a continuing relationship was not at issue. *People v. Cregar,* 172 Ill. App. 3d 807, 122 Ill. Dec. 613, 526 N.E.2d 1376 (1988); *People v. Harper,* 251 Ill. App. 3d 801, 191 Ill. Dec. 185, 623 N.E.2d 775 (1993); *People v. Failor,* 271 Ill. App. 3d 968, 208 Ill. Dec. 681, 649 N.E.2d 1342 (1995); *People v. Biggers,* 273 Ill. App. 3d 116, 209 Ill. Dec. 934, 652 N.E.2d 474 (1995). Other sexual acts were also admissible on the question of intent, *People v. Foster,* 195 Ill. App. 3d 926, 142 Ill. Dec. 371, 552 N.E.2d 1112 (1990), on the question of lack of consent, *People v. Weis,* 120 Ill. App. 3d 597, 76 Ill. Dec. 18, 458 N.E.2d 157 (1983), and on behalf of the defendant to show consent. *People v. Halcomb,* 176 Ill. App. 3d 100, 125 Ill. Dec. 665, 530 N.E.2d 1074 (1988). *See also* §404.4 supra. This limited exception to the rule barring evidence of other crimes, wrongs, or acts to show a disposition or propensity to commit crimes was once said not to extend to sex offenses with third persons. *People v. Rogers,* 324 Ill. 224, 154 N.E. 909 (1926). *See also* §404.4 supra. However, evidence of acts between the same parties, *and with third persons,* was subsequently admitted to show the relationship and familiarity of the parties, the intent with which the act was done, the defendant's design or course of conduct, and to corroborate the complainant's testimony as to the particular acts for which the defendant was on trial. *People v. Banks,* 161 Ill. 2d 119, 204 Ill. Dec. 107, 641 N.E.2d 331 (1994) (evidence of crimes committed on two other children was relevant to show defendant's motive, intent, and absence of mistake or accident in the manner in which he acted toward all three children that eventually caused the death of the victim). *See also People v. Bradley,* 128 Ill. App. 3d 372, 83 Ill. Dec. 701, 470 N.E.2d 1121 (1984); *People v. Tannahill,* 152 Ill. App. 3d 882, 105 Ill. Dec. 765, 504 N.E.2d 1283 (1987); *People v. Bayer,* 160 Ill. App. 3d 218, 112 Ill. Dec. 43, 513 N.E.2d 457 (1987); *People v. Johnson,* 239 Ill. App. 3d 1064, 180 Ill. Dec.

914, 608 N.E.2d 36 (1992). *See generally People v. Taggart,* 233 Ill. App. 3d 530, 174 Ill. Dec. 717, 599 N.E.2d 501 (1992) (book showing homosexual encounters of older male with young boys). *Cf. People v. Esterline,* 159 Ill. App. 3d 164, 111 Ill. Dec. 242, 512 N.E.2d 358 (1987); *People v. Daniels,* 172 Ill. App. 3d 616, 122 Ill. Dec. 687, 527 N.E.2d 59 (1988); *People v. Denny,* 241 Ill. App. 3d 345, 181 Ill. Dec. 839, 608 N.E.2d 1313 (1993), prior acts with third person are not admissible to show relationship or familiarity between the parties nor to establish lack of innocent intent. *See also People v. Woltz,* 228 Ill. App. 3d 670, 170 Ill. Dec. 502, 592 N.E.2d 1182 (1992), prior acts with third person not needed on issue of intent as "accident" not raised nor sufficiently similar to be admitted as *modus operandi* to show identity; *People v. Bobo,* 278 Ill. App. 3d 130, 214 Ill. Dec. 1057, 662 N.E.2d 623 (1996), prior acts with other students at other times and places were not needed to show intent, guilty knowledge, accident, or absence of mistake as these factors were shown by testimony concerning the act itself. Moreover, other sexual acts with third persons following the same *modus operandi* had been admitted to show that the crime charged was commited at all, *actus reus,* even if the question of identity of the defendant has not been raised, probably on the theory of a continuous plan (i.e., common design) to commit distinctively identical acts. *People v. Taylor,* 153 Ill. App. 3d 710, 106 Ill. Dec. 614, 506 N.E.2d 321 (1987); *People v. Partin,* 156 Ill. App. 3d 365, 109 Ill. Dec. 1, 509 N.E.2d 662 (1987); *People v. Clauson,* 182 Ill. App. 3d 268, 130 Ill. Dec. 719, 537 N.E.2d 1048 (1989); *People v. Brown,* 214 Ill. App. 3d 836, 158 Ill. Dec. 396, 574 N.E.2d 190 (1991); *People v. Guiterrez,* 238 Ill. App. 3d 339, 179 Ill. Dec. 540, 606 N.E.2d 372 (1992); *People v. Novak,* 242 Ill. App. 3d 836, 183 Ill. Dec. 555, 611 N.E.2d 1203 (1993). *See also* §404.4 supra. Obviously, the continued authority of *People v. Rogers,* supra, had been seriously questioned. Such crimes were also admitted on rebuttal, for example, to explain the absence of complaint in light of the response to prior complaints by other members of the victim's family. *People v. Manley,* 163 Ill. App. 3d 950, 114 Ill. Dec. 949, 516 N.E.2d 1343 (1987).

Effective January 1, 1998, 725 ILCS 5/115-7.3 provides:

Evidence in certain cases.

(a) This Section applies to criminal cases in which:

(1) the defendant is accused of predatory criminal sexual assault of a child, aggravated criminal sexual assault, criminal sexual assault, aggravated criminal sexual abuse, criminal sexual abuse, or criminal transmission of HIV;

(2) the defendant is accused of battery or aggravated battery when the commission of the offense involves sexual penetration or sexual conduct as defined in Section 12-12 of the Criminal Code of 1961; or

(3) the defendant is tried or retried for any of the offenses formerly known as rape, deviate sexual assault, indecent liberties with a child, or aggravated indecent liberties with a child.

(b) If the defendant is accused of an offense set forth in paragraph (1) or (2) of subsection (a) or the defendant is tried or retried for any of the offenses set forth in paragraph (3) of subsection (a), evidence of the defendant's commission of another offense or offenses set forth in paragraph (1), (2), (3) or subsection (a), or evidence to rebut that proof or an inference from that proof, may be admissible (if that evidence is otherwise admissible under the rules of evidence) and may be considered for its bearing on any matter to which it is relevant.

(c) In weighing the probative value of the evidence against undue prejudice to the defendant, the court may consider:

(1) the proximity in time to the charged or predicate offense;

(2) the degree of factual similarity to the charged or predicate offense; or

(3) other relevant facts and circumstances.

(d) In a criminal case in which the prosecution intends to offer evidence under this Section, it must disclose the evidence, including statements of witnesses or a summary of the substance of any testimony, at a reasonable time in advance of trial, or during trial if the court excuses pretrial notice on good cause shown.

(e) In a criminal case in which evidence is offered under this Section, proof may be made by specific instances of conduct, testimony as to reputation, or testimony in the form of an expert opinion, except that the prosecution may offer reputation testimony only after the opposing party has offered that testimony.

Section 115-7.3(b) provides in criminal cases only that evidence of a defendant's commission of an offense or offenses involving sexual abuse or child sexual abuse as defined in 5/115-7.3(a), otherwise admissible under the rules of evidence, may be considered for its bearing on any matter to which it is relevant. Section 115-7.3(c) imposes a discretionary balancing test, *see* §403.1 supra, while 5/115-7.3(d) imposes a notice requirement upon the prosecution. Finally, 5/115-7.3(e) provides that proof of the other offense or offenses may be made by specific instances of conduct, testimony as to reputation, or testimony in the form of an expert opinion, except that the prosecution may offer reputation testimony only after the opposing party has offered that testimony. Exactly how evidence of "defendant's commission of another offense or offenses," 5/115-7.3(b), is to be made in the form of "expert opinion" is unclear. With respect to expert testimony in sexual abuse and child sexual abuse, *see* §704.2 infra. Section 115-7.3 is modeled on Federal Rules of Evidence 413 and 414, discussed in Graham, Handbook of Federal Evidence §§ 413.1 and 414.1 (4th ed. 1996). *See also* §404.7 infra.

§404.7 Prior Conviction for Battery of Family Member or for Stalking

Effective January 1, 1998, 725 ILCS 5/115-20 provides:

Evidence of prior conviction.
(a) Evidence of a prior conviction of a defendant for domestic battery, aggravated battery committed against a family or household member as defined in Section 112A-3, stalking, aggravated stalking, or violation of an order of protection is admissible

in a later criminal prosecution for any of these types of offenses when the victim is the same person who was the victim of the previous offense that resulted in conviction of the defendant.

(b) If the defendant is accused of an offense set forth in subsection (a) or the defendant is tried or retried for any of the offenses set forth in subsection (a), evidence of the defendant's conviction for another offense or offenses set forth in subsection (a) may be admissible (if that evidence is otherwise admissible under the rules of evidence) and may be considered for its bearing on any matter to which it is relevant if the victim is the same person who was the victim of the previous offense that resulted in conviction of the defendant.

(c) In weighing the probative value of the evidence against undue prejudice to the defendant, the court may consider:

(1) the proximity in time to the charged or predicate offense;

(2) the degree of factual similarity to the charged or predicate offense; or

(3) other relevant facts and circumstances.

(d) In a criminal case in which the prosecution intends to offer evidence under this Section, it must disclose the evidence, including statements of witnesses or a summary of the substance of any testimony, at a reasonable time in advance of trial, or during trial if the court excuses pretrial notice on good cause shown.

(e) In a criminal case in which evidence is offered under this Section, proof may be made by specific instances of conduct as evidenced by proof of conviction, testimony as to reputation, or testimony in the form of an expert opinion, except that the prosecution may offer reputation testimony only after the opposing party has offered that testimony.

Section 5/115-20(b) provides in criminal cases only that evidence of a defendant's prior conviction for domestic battery, aggravated battery committed against a family or household member, stalking, aggravated stalking, or violation of an order of protection, otherwise admissible under the rules of evidence, may be considered for its bearing on any matter to which it is relevant. Section 115-20(c) imposes a discretionary balancing test, *see* §403.1 supra, while 5/115-20(d) imposes a notice requirement on the prosecution. Finally, 5/115-20(c) provides that proof of the prior conviction or violation may be made by specific instances of conduct, testimony as to reputation, or testimony in the form of an expert opinion, except that the prosecutor may offer reputation testimony only after the opposing party has offered that testimony. Exactly how evidence of a defendant's conviction or violation, 5/115-20(b), is to be made in the form of "expert opinion" is unclear. Section 115-20 is modeled on Federal Rules of Evidence 413 and 414, discussed in Graham, Handbook of Federal Evidence §§ 413.1 and 414.1 (4th ed. 1996). *See also* §404.6 supra.

§405 Methods of Proving Character

§405.1   *Proof of Pertinent Trait of Character by Reputation Testimony: Specific Instances Not Permitted on Direct or Cross-Examination*

Proof of a pertinent character trait used circumstantially in criminal cases, as outlined in §§404.3, 404.4 supra, is confined to evidence of reputation; neither specific instances, *People v. Flax,* 147 Ill. App. 3d 943, 101 Ill. Dec. 343, 498 N.E.2d 667 (1986), nor opinion testimony is permitted. Section 405.2 infra; *People v. Willy,* 301 Ill. 307, 133 N.E. 859 (1922). The reputation of the person testified to cannot be a general one for being law abiding but must be limited to the pertinent trait of character. *See* §§404.3 and 404.4 supra; *People v. Redola,* 300 Ill. 392, 133 N.E. 292 (1921); *People v. Hall,* 159 Ill. App. 3d 1021, 112 Ill. Dec. 15, 513 N.E.2d 429 (1987); *People v. Batinich,* 196 Ill. App. 3d 1078, 143 Ill. Dec. 678, 554 N.E.2d 613 (1990). To illustrate, reputation for honesty and integrity is pertinent where the charge is larceny or theft, *People v. Shockey,* 30 Ill. 2d 147, 195 N.E.2d 703 (1964), while the pertinent character traits in a prosecution for sexual abuse are morality and chastity. *People v. Petitt,* 245 Ill. App.

3d 132, 184 Ill. Dec. 766, 613 N.E.2d 1358 (1993). The reputation may be that in the neighborhood in which the person resides or among any group of her associates; the witness must, of course, indicate familiarity with it. *People v. Moretti*, 6 Ill. 2d 494, 129 N.E.2d 709 (1955); *People v. LaFiura*, 93 Ill. App. 3d 1099, 49 Ill. Dec. 404, 418 N.E.2d 48 (1981). The cases recognize that since good reputation for a pertinent character trait is unlikely to excite discussion, the fact that the witness has actually heard no discussion does not bar him from testifying to that reputation. *People v. Okopske*, 321 Ill. 32, 151 N.E. 507 (1926); *People v. Bascomb*, 74 Ill. App. 3d 392, 30 Ill. Dec. 262, 392 N.E.2d 1130 (1979); *People v. Thornton*, 61 Ill. App. 3d 530, 18 Ill. Dec. 734, 378 N.E.2d 198 (1978). The testimony must relate to reputation at or prior to the time of the act in question rather than at trial, *People v. Lucas*, 151 Ill. 2d 461, 177 Ill. Dec. 390, 603 N.E.2d 460 (1992); *People v. Reeves*, 360 Ill. 55, 195 N.E. 443 (1935), and the reputation witness must be shown to have adequate knowledge of the subject. *People v. McClelland*, 96 Ill. App. 2d 410, 238 N.E.2d 597 (1968). Reputation evidence may not be based upon specific instances of conduct. *People v. Lucas* supra. Whether an investigator hired to ascertain the pertinent character trait of a person will be permitted to testify rests in the discretion of the court. *People v. Bingham*, 75 Ill. App. 3d 418, 31 Ill. Dec. 228, 394 N.E.2d 430 (1979). Character evidence properly offered only in the form of reputation may be rebutted by the testimony of other witnesses also only in the form of reputation. The reputation witness is not limited to characterizing the reputation of the pertinent character trait as either "good" or "bad" but may employ terms such as "excellent" or "outstanding." *People v. Petitt*, 245 Ill. App. 3d 132, 184 Ill. Dec. 766, 613 N.E.2d 1358 (1993).

The trial judge is authorized to limit character witnesses to a reasonable number. *People v. Arnold*, 248 Ill. 169, 93 N.E. 786 (1911), each side properly limited to 25, though defense tendered an additional 1400 and the prosecution, 600.

Specific instances of relevant conduct of the person whose reputation has been testified to may not be brought out on either direct, *see, e.g., People v. Buehler,* 261 Ill. App. 3d 539, 201 Ill. Dec. 337, 636 N.E.2d 769 (1994) (improper to testify as to absence of a criminal record), or cross-examination of the character witness or on rebuttal. *People v. Celmars,* 332 Ill. 113, 163 N.E. 421 (1928). *See also People v. Perruquet,* 118 Ill. App. 3d 339, 73 Ill. Dec. 802, 454 N.E.2d 1051 (1983) (improper to inquire of defendant's arrests); *People v. Roberts,* 133 Ill. App. 3d 731, 88 Ill. Dec. 773, 479 N.E.2d 386 (1985) (character witness may not be questioned about specific acts of misconduct). *Accord People v. Hall,* 159 Ill. App. 3d 1021, 112 Ill. Dec. 15, 513 N.E.2d 429 (1987); *People v. West,* 246 Ill. App. 3d 1070, 186 Ill. Dec. 908, 617 N.E.2d 147 (1993). This latter limitation is predicated upon the impossibility of an accused's adequately preparing to defend against a variety of possible charges, *People v. Stanton,* 1 Ill. 2d 444, 115 N.E.2d 630 (1953), together probably with a desire to avoid collateral issues and some considerable doubt as to the probative value of such evidence in any event. The general rule is to the contrary. McCormick, Evidence §191 (4th ed. 1992). It is everywhere improper to inquire of a character witness as to whether the witness is aware that the person whose reputation has been testified to committed the act for which he or she is on trial as such inquiry assumes facts that are the subject of the litigation and destroys the presumption of innocence. *See People v. Nyberg,* 275 Ill. App. 3d 570, 211 Ill. Dec. 873, 656 N.E.2d 65 (1995); *People v. Graves,* 61 Ill. App. 3d 732, 18 Ill. Dec. 829, 378 N.E.2d 293 (1978). *See also* §611.21 infra.

On cross-examination of a witness who has testified as to the reputation of another with respect to a pertinent character trait, inquiry is of course proper with respect to with whom, where, and when the reputation was actually discussed and the nature of the relationship with the person about whom testifying. *People v. Greeley,* 14 Ill. 2d 428, 152 N.E.2d 825 (1958). Moreover, inquiry is also permitted as to whether the character witness has heard any rumors or reports that are inconsistent with his testimony. *People v. Greeley, id.* However, the contents of such rumors or reports cannot be disclosed in any way either by means of a question on cross-examination or as contradiction of the witness on rebuttal. *People v. Redmond,* 50 Ill. 2d 313, 278 N.E.2d 766 (1972); *People v. Lewis,* 25 Ill. 2d 442, 185 N.E.2d 254 (1962). *But cf. People v. Corder,* 91 Ill. App. 3d 392, 46 Ill. Dec. 851, 414 N.E.2d 904 (1980), and *see* McCormick, Evidence §191 (3d ed. 1984).

With respect to reputation testimony as to a witness's character for truthfulness or untruthfulness, *see* §608.1 infra.

§405.2   *Testimony in Form of Opinion Not Permitted*

In all cases in which evidence of character or pertinent trait of character is admissible circumstantially, proof may be made solely by testimony as to general reputation. Opinion testimony as to a pertinent character trait is not permitted. *People v. Moretti,* 6 Ill. 2d 494, 129 N.E.2d 709 (1955); *People v. Willy,* 301 Ill. 307, 133 N.E. 859 (1922); *People v. Goodwin,* 98 Ill. App. 3d 726, 53 Ill. Dec. 790, 424 N.E.2d 425 (1981); *People v. Sargent,* 207 Ill. App. 3d 631, 152 Ill. Dec. 631, 566 N.E.2d 318 (1990); Mauet, Reputation Evidence in Criminal Trial, 58 Chicago Bar Record, Sept., Oct. p.72 (1976). The current Illinois rule apparently rests upon the notion that opinion testimony is not sufficiently probative in light of its capacity to confuse and consume time and that introduction of opinion testimony might result in many trials becoming swearing contests between character witnesses. Why this should be true with regard to opinion but not with reputation is unclear. *See People v. Arnold,* 248 Ill. 169, 93 N.E. 786 (1911), where a total of 2,000 character witnesses were tendered by the two sides, in addition to the 50 allowed to testify.

Federal Rule of Evidence 405(a), 65 F.R.D. 131, 143 (1975), in addition to reputation testimony, also permits proof by testimony in the form of opinions based upon personal knowledge. In support of its position in favor of permitting opinion as well as reputation testimony, the Federal Advisory Committee's Note, 56 F.R.D. 183, 222 (1973), states:

> In recognizing opinion as a means of proving character, the rule departs from usual contemporary practice in favor of that of an earlier day. *See* 7 Wigmore §1986, pointing out that the earlier practice permitted opinion and arguing strongly for evidence based on personal knowledge and belief as contrasted with "secondhand, irresponsible product of multiplied guesses and gossip which we term 'reputation'." It seems likely that the persistence of reputation evidence is due to its largely being opinion in disguise. Traditionally character has been regarded primarily in moral overtones of good and bad: chaste, peaceable, truthful, honest. Nevertheless, on occasion nonmoral considerations crop up, as in the case of the incompetent driver, and this seems bound to happen increasingly. If character is defined as the kind of person one is, then account must be taken of varying ways of arriving at the estimate. These may range from the opinion of the employer who has found the man honest to the opinion of the psychiatrist based upon examination and testing. No effective dividing line exists between character and mental capacity, and the latter traditionally has been provable by opinion.

In fact, the current Illinois practice of permitting a witness who testifies as to the reputation of another for truthfulness or untruthfulness to state whether she would believe such a witness under oath, §608.3 infra; *People v. Lehner*, 326 Ill. 216, 157 N.E. 211 (1927), amounts to permitting the witness to give an opinion.

The rule barring opinion testimony as to a pertinent trait of character is unduly restrictive and contrasts unfavorably with the closely related subject of mental capacity. *See* §704.3 infra. *See also* §701.7 infra, discussing limited use of opinion evidence with regard to condition of persons. Permitting character testimony in the form of opinion deserves serious consideration.

§405.3   *Character as an Element: Specific Instances of Conduct*

Character is itself on infrequent occasions an element of a charge, claim, or defense in civil or criminal cases and thus, in the strict sense, is in issue. In a civil action, for example, for breach of promise to marry, the defense of unchastity of the plaintiff places in issue her character as to chastity, *Butler v. Eschleman,* 18 Ill. 44 (1856), and a charge of negligence in employing an incompetent person places in issue his character as to competency. *Consolidated Coal Co. v. Seniger,* 179 Ill. 370, 53 N.E. 733 (1899); *Western Stone Co. v. Whalen,* 151 Ill. 472, 38 N.E. 241 (1894).

While ill-fame apparently is not an element of the crime of maintaining a place of prostitution, 720 ILCS 5/11-117; *People v. Flagg,* 18 Ill. App. 548, 153 N.E.2d 116 (1958), reputation should be admissible at least to prove reason to know of the use of premises for that purpose. *See* §404.5 supra.

When character is in issue, it deserves searching inquiry and the most convincing proof. Hence, in addition to reputation testimony, proof by specific incidents is recognized as proper, despite the attendant disadvantages. *See* cases cited above. With respect to the admissibility of opinion testimony, *see* §405.2 supra.

§406   Habit and Routine Practice

§406.1   *An Overview*

While habit, in contrast to character, may be defined as a settled way of doing a particular thing, *see Chicago, R.I. & P.R. Co. v. Bell,* 70 Ill. 102 (1873), the dividing line between habit and character is far from distinct.

"Habit" is more specific than "character." Character is a generalized description of one's disposition, or of one's disposition in respect to a particular trait, such as honesty, temperance, or peacefulness. Evidence of a person's character or a trait of his character for the purpose of proving that he acted in conformity therewith on a particular occasion is not admissible in civil cases and admissible in criminal proceedings only in limited situations. *See* §404 supra. On the other hand, in both civil and criminal cases a person's habit or the routine practice of an organization is admitted as tending to establish that conduct on a particular occasion was in conformity therewith. Habit describes one's regular response to a repeated specific situation so that doing the habitual act becomes semi-automatic. The routine practice of an organization is comparable to habit of an individual. It is the notion of virtually invariable regularity that gives habit its probative force. *Alvarado v. Goepp,* 278 Ill. App. 3d 494, 214 Ill. Dec. 313, 663, N.E.2d 63 (1996) (quoting Handbook); *Knecht v. Radiac Abrasives, Inc.,* 219 Ill. App. 3d 979, 162 Ill. Dec. 434, 579 N.E.2d 1248 (1991) (invariably regular semiautomatic conduct constitutes a habit). *See also* McCormick, Evidence §195 (4th ed. 1992). Evidence that one is a "careful man" is lacking the specificity of the act becoming semi-automatic; it goes to character rather than habit. Accordingly, intemperate "habits" cannot be shown to prove drunkenness at the time of an accident.

In *Bradfield v. Illinois Central Gulf R.R.,* 115 Ill. 2d 471, 106 Ill. Dec. 25, 505 N.E.2d 331 (1987), the supreme court affirmed the admissibility of testimony that trains approaching a particular crossing over the prior couple of years did not whistle on the ground that the objection was not properly preserved. Nevertheless the tone of the opinion clearly signals an acceptance of Federal Rule of Evidence 406 permitting admissibility of evidence of both habit of a person and routine practice of an organization whether corroborated or not and regardless of the presence of eyewitnesses:

> Evidence of the habit of a person or the routine practice of an organization, whether corroborated or not and regardless of the presence of eyewitnesses, is relevant to prove that the conduct of

the person or organization on a particular occasion was in conformity with the habit or routine practice. [Fed. R. Evid. 406.]

Cf. Cairns v. Hansen, 170 Ill. App. 3d 505, 120 Ill. Dec. 757, 524 N.E.2d 939 (1988), still refusing to sanction the admissibility of habit testimony if competent eyewitness testimony is available on the basis that the Illinois Supreme Court has not yet clearly changed the rule.

§406.2   Careful Habits Testimony

The Illinois requirement, now abolished, *see* infra, that plaintiff in a negligence action plead and prove freedom from contributory negligence was applied to wrongful death actions. Accordingly, a plaintiff personal representative was confronted with a difficult problem of proof if there were no eyewitnesses to the occurrence. As a means of coping with the problem, case law evolved a procedure of allowing plaintiff to introduce evidence of careful habits of her decedent. *See also* §302.6 supra as to presumption of due care. However, the relief granted was equal in scope only to the dimension of the problem: there must have been no competent eyewitnesses. *Casey v. Chicago Ry.,* 269 Ill. 386, 109 N.E. 984 (1915).

The practice of admitting careful habits testimony was then expanded to include all similar situations in other than wrongful death actions. *See McElroy v. Force,* 38 Ill. 528, 232 N.E.2d 708 (1968). Thus where there were no eyewitnesses to an accident, or where the only eyewitnesses were silenced by death, amnesia, mental incompetency, or the Dead Man's Act, §606 infra, evidence of the plaintiff's habits for careful driving could be admitted on the issue of whether the plaintiff was in the exercise of due care immediately prior to and at the time of the accident. *McElroy v. Force* supra; *Casey v. Chicago Ry.* supra; *Eichorn v. Olson,* 32 Ill. App. 3d 587, 335 N.E.2d 774 (1975). The essential thrust was that in such situations, where no better evidence on the issue was available, habit evidence became admissible in order to give the plaintiff a fair chance to prove his freedom from contributory negligence. This rule of necessity based on hardship, however, did not extend beyond its own reason. Where there were available competent witnesses who had observed and could relate enough of the circumstances of the accident so as to form a sufficient basis from which the trier of fact might reasonably infer the exercise of or failure to exercise due care by the plaintiff, habit evidence, being unnecessary, was not admitted. *Plank v. Holman,* 46 Ill. 2d 465, 264 N.E.2d 12 (1970); *Quick v. Nagel,* 85 Ill. App. 3d 342, 40 Ill. Dec. 632, 406 N.E.2d 835 (1980); *Peltz v. Chicago Transit Auth.,* 31 Ill. App. 3d 948, 335 N.E.2d 74 (1975); *Driessens v. Verkruyse,* 46 Ill. App. 2d 87, 196 N.E.2d 353 (1964).

A party could, by tendering the name and address of an eyewitness in advance, foreclose the introduction of evidence of careful habits. *Moore v. Bloomington, D. & C.R. Co.,* 295 Ill. 63, 128 N.E. 721 (1920). The eyewitness must have been competent to testify on behalf of the party tendering him, *Hann v. Brooks,* 331 Ill. App. 535, 73 N.E.2d 624 (1947), but his veracity was immaterial in this respect. *Petro v. Hines,* 299 Ill. 236, 132 N.E. 462 (1921). Evidence of careful habits previously introduced would be stricken on motion if an eyewitness later testified, *Plank v. Holman* supra, or was tendered after becoming competent as a result of being dismissed as a defendant. *Hawthorne v. New York Cent. R. Co.,* 2 Ill. App. 2d 338, 119 N.E.2d 516 (1954). To qualify as an eyewitness, the observer must have been able to perceive circumstances from which decedent's behavior might reasonably be inferred. *Plank v. Holman,* supra, decedent's wife following behind in another automobile observed facts from which position of husband's car in relation to center line could be inferred; *Lauer v. Elgin, J. & E. Ry.,* 305 Ill. App. 200, 27 N.E.2d 315 (1940), brakeman on rear of train not in a position to know whether deceased passenger in automobile warned driver; *Bitner v. Central Ill. Light Co.,* 75 Ill. App. 3d 715, 31 Ill. Dec. 290, 394 N.E.2d 492 (1979), no witness observed the actual accident or decedent's actions leading up to the accident.

Careful habits when admissible could be given in the form of reputation testimony and, in practice but not in theory, opinion testimony; specific instances of conduct were inadmissible. *See* cases cited supra. With respect to cross-examination of the careful habits witness, *see* §405.1 supra.

As to the relationship of careful habits testimony and the Dead Man's Act, *see* §606.9 infra.

The decision of the Illinois Supreme Court in *Alvis v. Ribar*, 85 Ill. 2d 1, 52 Ill. Dec. 23, 421 N.E.2d 886 (1981), abolishing contributory negligence as a bar to plaintiff's recovery in favor of comparative negligence, removed the necessity of plaintiff's offering careful habits testimony in its case in chief in order to avoid a directed verdict.

§406.3 Habit of an Individual

Decisions have at times indicated the acceptance of habit testimony in other than the context of due care discussed in §406.2 supra. *Stolp v. Blair*, 68 Ill. 541 (1873), lending money to other persons without taking notes; *Thorp v. Goewey*, 85 Ill. 611 (1877), promptness of decedent in paying debts; *Sorenson v. Sorenson*, 189 Ill. 179, 59 N.E. 555 (1901), party affiliation to show how person voted; *Wolf v. Peoples Bank*, 255 Ill. App. 127 (1929), habit of decedent to consult banker or lawyer and otherwise be secretive on business matters, as bearing on execution of note. In most of these cases the element of necessity for the introduction for such habit testimony was strong. However, given the age of the foregoing cases and the emphasis upon the hardship aspect as a justification for the use of habit testimony to establish due care and the absence of competent eyewitnesses as described in §406.2 supra, it is likely but not without doubt that habit evidence is generally admissible for the purpose of inviting the inference that the person probably acted consistently with his habits. *See* Federal Rule of Evidence 406, 65 F.R.D. 131, 144 (1975), providing for the general admission of habits of an individual regardless of the presence of eyewitnesses. *Accord Bradfield v. Illinois Cent. Gulf R.R.,* 115 Ill. 2d 471, 106 Ill. Dec. 25, 505 N.E.2d 331 (1987), implying acceptance but not specifically adopting Federal Rule of Evidence 406. Federal Rule of Evidence 406 was specifically stated to present the proper formulation for the admissibility of evidence of the habit of an individual in *Taruc v. State Farm Mut. Auto. Ins. Co.,* 218 Ill. App. 3d 51, 161 Ill. Dec. 7, 578 N.E.2d 134 (1991) and stated to have been adopted in Illinois in *Alvarado v. Goepp,* 278 Ill. App. 3d 494, 215 Ill. Dec. 313, 663 N.E.2d 63 (1996). *Compare People v. West,* 102 Ill. App. 3d 50, 57 Ill. Dec. 701, 429 N.E.2d 599 (1981), evidence of habit is not admissible as proof of behavior, i.e., conformity with that habit on a specific occasion; *Cairns v. Hansen,* 170 Ill. App. 3d 505, 120 Ill. Dec. 757, 524 N.E.2d 939 (1988), still refusing to sanction the admissibility of habit testimony if competent eyewitness testimony is available on the basis that the Illinois Supreme Court has not clearly changed the rule.

In any event where habit testimony is offered, it will, of course, be necessary to establish a sufficient pattern of repeated responses so that the conduct of the person may be considered a habit, i.e., conduct that has become semiautomatic and invariably regular. *Hajian v. Holy Family Hospital,* 273 Ill. App. 3d 932, 210 Ill. Dec. 156, 652 N.E.2d 1132 (1995) (Nurse Zeller's testimony relating detailed and specific facts sufficiently established her habit to respond to patient and family requests). On the other hand, a question inquiring whether a person had on another occasion acted in a particular manner is obviously insufficient to establish a habit. *LeMaster v. Chicago Rock Island & Pacific R. Co.,* 35 Ill. App. 3d 1001, 343 N.E.2d 65 (1976). So is testimony that the witness had ridden with the driver every day over a certain period of time to show that the driver did not drink (temperance is a character trait, not a habit; character evidence is not admissible in civil cases, *see* §§404.1 and 404.2 supra). *Cairns v. Hansen,* 170 Ill. App. 3d 505, 120 Ill. Dec. 757, 524 N.E.2d 139 (1988). Similarly, testimony that a doctor "often" failed to have a treatment plan was too vague, general, and ambiguous to establish a habit. *Alvarado v. Goepp,* 278 Ill.

App. 3d 494, 215 Ill. Dec. 313, 663 N.E.2d 63 (1996). *Cf.* Proposed Federal Rules of Evidence 406(b), 56 F.R.D. 183, 223 (1973), providing for the admission of opinion testimony as to habit in addition to the introduction of specific instances of conduct sufficient in number to warrant a finding that the habit existed. *See also Bradfield v. Illinois Central Gulf R.R.*, 115 Ill. 2d 471, 106 Ill. Dec. 25, 30, 505 N.E.2d 331, 336 (1987) (J. Ryan, dissenting) ("The important point is, whether we consider habit evidence of an individual or custom evidence of an organization, the evidence must be sufficiently detailed and specific, and the situations involved must be similar enough to give rise to a reliable inference and not to speculation or conjecture").

§406.4   Routine Practice of an Organization

The operation of organizations depends to a large extent upon the establishing and following of routines, hence evidence of a routine practice of an organization is admissible as tending to prove that it was followed on the occasion in question. *Webb v. Pacific Mut. Life Ins. Co.*, 348 Ill. App. 411, 109 N.E.2d 258 (1952), office routine of mailing notices. However, evidence of existence of a routine standing alone has been stated to be insufficient to prove the doing of an act; some corroboration that the routine was then followed is also required. *Lynn v. Village of West City*, 36 Ill. App. 3d 561, 345 N.E.2d 172 (1976), proof of customary business practice in the mailing of correspondence insufficient absent proof that practice of mailing was followed with respect to item in question; *State Bank of East Moline v. Standaert*, 335 Ill. App. 519, 82 N.E.2d 393 (1948), general practice of bank at close of business day to send notice to secondary parties insufficient to prove sending of notice to defendant endorser. For example, corroboration exists when the secretary who prepared the mailing testifies that she remembers the item being picked up by the mail clerk, *Commonwealth Edison Co. v. Property Tax Appeal Bd.*, 86 Ill. App. 3d 414, 41 Ill. Dec. 590, 407 N.E.2d 1088

(1980); when the witness remembers preparing the document in question and taking it to the mailroom, *First Natl. Bank of Antioch v. Guerra Constr. Co.*, 153 Ill. App. 3d 662, 106 Ill. Dec. 582, 505 N.E.2d 1373 (1987); when defendant admits receiving other mailings, a copy of the item in question had been received by plaintiff's branch office, and no similar item sent out in same mailing was returned, *Tabor & Co. v. Gorenz*, 43 Ill. App. 3d 124, 1 Ill. Dec. 868, 356 N.E.2d 1150 (1976).

Any requirement of corroboration as a condition of admissibility should be eliminated, if it hasn't already been so, since it defeats the purpose of admitting evidence of routine practice in the first place and because it relates to sufficiency of the evidence rather than admissibility. *See* Federal Rule of Evidence 406, 65 F.R.D. 131, 144 (1975) specifically removing any then existing requirement of corroboration. *Accord Kolias v. State Farm Mut. Automobile Ins. Co.*, 148 Ill. App. 3d 1086, 102 Ill. Dec. 609, 500 N.E.2d 502 (1986), mailing need not be corroborated by direct testimony; given the routine nature of the job, the clerk could not be expected to remember the particular event in question. *See Webb v. Angell*, 155 Ill. App. 3d 845, 108 Ill. Dec. 347, 508 N.E.2d 508 (1987), evidence of routine practice admitted in apparent absence of corroboration. *See also* §406.1 supra. *See generally Bradfield v. Illinois Cent. Gulf R.R.*, 115 Ill. 2d 471, 106 Ill. Dec. 25, 505 N.E.2d 331 (1987), implying acceptance but not specifically adopting Federal Rule of Evidence 406. Federal Rule of Evidence 406 was specifically stated to present the proper formulation for the admissibility of evidence of the routine practice of an organization in *Taruc v. State Farm Mut. Auto. Ins. Co.*, 218 Ill. App. 3d 51, 161 Ill. Dec. 7, 578 N.E.2d 134 (1991).

The routine practice of an organization is established by what in effect is opinion testimony of a person with personal knowledge or by the introduction of specific instances of conduct sufficient in number to support a finding of routine practice. *See* cases cited supra; Proposed Federal Rule of Evidence 406(b), 56 F.R.D. 183, 223 (1973). *See also Bradfield v. Illinois Central Gulf R.R.*, 115 Ill. 2d 471, 166 Ill. Dec. 25, 30, 505 N.E.2d 331, 336 (1987) (J. Ryan, dissenting) ("The important point is, whether we consider habit evidence of an individual or custom evidence of an organization, the evidence must be sufficiently detailed and specific, and the situations involved must be similar enough to give rise to a reliable inference and not to speculation or conjecture"). *Accord Brennan v. Wisconsin Central Limited,* 227 Ill. App. 3d 1070, 169 Ill. Dec. 321, 591 N.E.2d 494 (1992). Opinion testimony saves time with respect to undisputed matters. Where in controversy, specific instances of conduct may be brought out upon cross-examination or be required in the discretion of the court to be disclosed as part of development of the witness's basis for his opinion. *See* §701.1 infra.

The following of a routine is the basis of entries in the regular course of business as an exception to the Hearsay Rule. *See* §803.10 infra.

§406.5   Usage, Practice, and Standards of Care in Negligence and Products Liability Actions

In negligence actions, a usage or practice in a trade or business, sometimes loosely called custom, may be introduced for the purpose of assisting the trier to fix the standard of care to which the defendant should be held. *Pressley v. Bloomington & N. Ry. & Light Co.,* 271 Ill. 622, 111 N.E. 511 (1916), evidence offered by plaintiff of customary and approved method of constructing high voltage lines admissible but error to admit evidence of "proper" construction; *Hauck v. First Natl. Bank of Highland Park,* 323 Ill. App. 300, 55 N.E.2d 565 (1944), evidence offered by defendent of practice of other banks in handling safe-deposit boxes properly admitted; *Turner v. Chicago Housing Auth.,* 11 Ill. App. 2d 160, 136 N.E.2d 543 (1956), evidence offered by plaintiff of customary and accepted method of constructing steps admissible but departure therefrom not sufficient alone to establish negligence; *Bridges v. Ford Motor Co.,* 104 Ill. App. 2d 26, 243 N.E.2d 559 (1968), evidence properly admitted as to custom with respect to application of paint by spray gun method and scheduling of work among crafts at construction site; *Santiago v. Package Mach. Co.*, 123 Ill. App. 2d 305, 260 N.E.2d 89 (1970), testimony that it was not industry practice to install interference bar safety device properly admitted; *McClure v. Suter*, 63 Ill. App. 3d 378, 20 Ill. Dec. 308, 379 N.E.2d 1376 (1978), evidence of swimming regulations at similar campground admitted as custom and usage; *Roach v. Springfield Clinic*, 223 Ill. App. 3d 597, 166 Ill. Dec. 48, 585 N.E.2d 1070 (1991), book containing standards for obstetricians and gynecologists should have been received. Similarly, evidence of this nature is also admissible as bearing on contributory negligence or freedom therefrom. *Campbell v. Chicago, R.I. & P. Ry.*, 243 Ill. 620, 90 N.E. 1106 (1910), usual practice for switchman to step on brake-beam; *Fowler v. Chicago Rys.*, 285 Ill. 196, 120 N.E. 635 (1918), usual and customary arrangement of driver's seat on wagon loaded with lumber. It must be emphasized that usage or practice does not in itself constitute a legal standard of conduct and that conformity with it does not necessarily constitute reasonable care or failure to conform negligence. *Hansell-Elcock Foundry Co. v. Clark*, 214 Ill. 399, 73 N.E. 787 (1905). Usage or practice may be relevant in other ways. *See Franey v. Union Stock Yard Transit Co.*, 235 Ill. 522, 85 N.E. 750 (1908), practice of shippers to enter pens admissible on degree of care required of defendant in keeping premises safe; *Fetterman v. Production Steel Co. of Illinois*, 4 Ill. App. 2d 403, 124 N.E.2d 637 (1954), usage in building trade of using scaffold erected by another admissible to prove plaintiff rightfully on defendant's scaffold.

Evidence of standards, safety rules, regulations, and codes are admissible to aid the finder of fact in deciding the standard of care in negligence actions. *Merchants Natl. Bank v. Elgin, J. & E.R.R.*, 49 Ill. 2d 118, 273 N.E.2d 809 (1971); *Darling v. Charleston Community Memorial Hosp.*, 33 Ill. 2d 326, 211 N.E.2d 253 (1965); *Grimming v. Alton & S. R.*, 204 Ill. App. 3d 961, 150 Ill. Dec. 283, 562 N.E.2d 1086 (1990); *Ruffiner v. Material Serv. Corp.*, 34 Ill. App. 3d 747, 89 Ill. Dec. 414, 480

N.E.2d 1157 (1985), standards, etc., are helpful to indicate what was feasible and what the defendant knew or should have known. They also are admissible in aid of determining willful and wanton conduct. *Tenenbaum v. City of Chicago,* 60 Ill. 2d 363, 325 N.E.2d 607 (1975). Such items promulgated subsequent to the relevant time may be admitted if shown to be intended to eliminate hazards existing at the relevant time, *Davis v. Marathon Oil Co.,* 64 Ill. 2d 380, 1 Ill. Dec. 93, 356 N.E.2d 1299 (1976), but not otherwise. *Murphy v. Messerschmidt,* 68 Ill. 2d 79, 11 Ill. Dec. 553, 368 N.E.2d 1299 (1977).

Evidence of standards promulgated by industry, trade, or regulating groups or agencies is admissible in a products liability action when relevant in determining whether a condition is unreasonably dangerous. *Moehle v. Chrysler Motors Corp.,* 93 Ill. 2d 299, 66 Ill. Dec. 649, 443 N.E.2d 575 (1982); *Rucker v. Norfolk & W. Ry.,* 77 Ill. 2d 434, 33 Ill. Dec. 145, 396 N.E.2d 534 (1979).

Evidence of standards may be relevant and admissible in negligence and products liability actions even though the standards have not been imposed by statute or promulgated by a regulatory body and thus are without the force of law. *Ruffiner v. Material Serv. Corp.,* 116 Ill. 2d 53, 106 Ill. Dec. 781, 506 N.E.2d 581 (1987).

For a similar discussion with respect to products liability, *see* 401.13 supra.

§407   Subsequent Remedial Measures

§407.1   *Commentary*

Subsequent remedial measures, whether a change, repair, or precaution, taken after an event may not be introduced as an admission of negligence or culpable conduct in connection with the event. The reasons are similar to those applicable to compromises. *See* §408.1 infra. First, the taking of remedial measures may be motivated by a desire to exercise the highest care and thus in fact not be an admission of negligence, and second, the taking of corrective steps should not be discouraged by allowing evidence thereof as the jury might view such corrective steps as an admission of negligence or culpable conduct. *Hodges v. Percival,* 132 Ill. 53, 23 N.E. 423 (1890). Finally, a strong public policy favors encouraging improvements to enhance public safety. *Schaffner v. Chicago & N.W. Transp. Co.,* 129 Ill. 2d 1, 133 Ill. Dec. 432, 541 N.E.2d 643 (1989). *See generally, Herzog v. Lexington Township,* 167 Ill. 2d 288, 212 Ill. Dec. 581, 657 N.E.2d 926 (1995). These same policy reasons also require the exclusion of evidence of subsequent remedial measures when offered to establish willful and wanton conduct, *Schaffner v. Chicago & N.W. Transp. Co.,* 129 Ill. 2d 1, 133 Ill. Dec. 432, 541 N.E.2d 643 (1989), as well as post manufacture, but preinjury, remedial measures in negligence actions. *Carrizales v. Rheem Manufacturing Co., Inc.,* 226 Ill. App. 3d 20, 168 Ill. Dec. 169, 589 N.E.2d 569 (1991).

Evidence of this kind may, however, be used for other purposes, such as proving ownership, feasibility of precautionary measures, or impeachment, *see* infra. *See, e.g., Taylorville v. Stafford,* 196 Ill. 288, 63 N.E. 624 (1902), driving down of stake after injury admissible to rebut testimony based on measurement taken after injury and contradicting plaintiff's testimony as to height at time of injury; *Kuhn v. Illinois Central R. Co.,* 111 Ill. App. 323 (1903), raising of stacks after suit brought and diminution of smoke damage thereby admissible to show that lowness of original stacks caused damage; *Kellems v. Schiele,* 297 Ill. App. 388, 17 N.E.2d 604 (1938), making of subsequent repairs admissible to show ownership of manhole. The evidence has also been admitted to prove control, *Larson v. Commonwealth Edison Co.,* 33 Ill. 2d 316, 211 N.E.2d 247 (1965); absence of causation and the absence of deliberate infliction of highly unreasonable risk of harm needed to support punitive damages, *Proctor v. Davis,* 275 Ill. App. 3d 593, 211 Ill. Dec. 831, 656 N.E.2d 23 (1995) (offered by defendant); authority to take precautions, *Unger v. Eichleay Corp.,*

244 Ill. App. 3d 445, 185 Ill. Dec. 556, 614 N.E.2d 1241 (1993); feasibility of alternate design or construction, *Sutkowski v. Universal Marion Corp.*, 5 Ill. App. 3d 313, 281 N.E.2d 749 (1972); defendant's knowledge of safe design in negligence action, *Moren v. Samuel M. Langston Co.*, 96 Ill. App. 2d 133, 237 N.E.2d 759 (1968); and that the cost of remedial change is slight in comparison to risk of injury, *Dallas v. Granite City Steel Co.*, 64 Ill. App. 2d 409, 211 N.E.2d 907 (1965).

With respect to product liability actions, *see Holmes v. Sahara Coal Co.*, 131 Ill. App. 3d 666, 86 Ill. Dec. 816, 475 N.E.2d 1383 (1985); *Millette v. Radosta*, 84 Ill. App. 3d 5, 39 Ill. Dec. 232, 404 N.E.2d 823 (1980); *Burke v. Illinois Power*, 57 Ill. App. 3d 498, 15 Ill. Dec. 670, 373 N.E.2d 1354 (1978), post-occurrence changes are admissible in product liability cases, an apparent overstatement. The preferred position applying the doctrine of subsequent remedial measures to post-occurrence changes in products liability cases was adopted in *Davis v. International Harvester Co.*, 167 Ill. App. 3d 814, 118 Ill. Dec. 589, 521 N.E.2d 1282 (1988). In addition post manufacture, but preinjury, remedial measures are inadmissible in product liability actions to prove liability. *Smith v. Black & Decker (U.S.), Inc.*, 272 Ill. App. 3d 451, 209 Ill. Dec. 135, 650 N.E.2d 1108 (1995). Evidence of a subsequent remedial measure offered to establish the feasibility of an alternative design in a products liability case is admissible. *Davis v. International Harvester Co.*, id.; *Holmes v. Sahara Coal Co.*, supra. Evidence of a subsequent remedial measure is inadmissible in product liability actions when offered to establish willful and wanton conduct including with respect to injuries caused by the continued sale of products not incorporating the subsequent remedial measure. *Schaffner v. Chicago & N.W. Transp. Co.*, 129 Ill. 2d 1, 133 Ill. Dec. 432, 541 N.E.2d 643 (1989). *Compare Collins v. Interroyal Corp.*, 126 Ill. App. 3d 244, 81 Ill. Dec. 389, 466 N.E.2d 1191 (1984). *See generally Smith v. Black & Decker (U.S.), Inc.* supra.

Subsequent remedial measures taken after an event by a nonparty may be introduced if relevant to the issues of negligence or culpable conduct. *McLaughlin v. Rush-Presbyterian,*

St. Lukes Med. Center, 68 Ill. App. 3d 546, 25 Ill. Dec. 63, 386 N.E.2d 334 (1979), there is no policy reason to exclude evidence of post-occurrence design changes in catheter by manufacturer in negligence action against hospital. Evidence of subsequent remedial measures taken by a nonparty are admissible when relevant to other issues as well. *Zavala v. St. Regis Paper Co.,* 256 Ill. App. 3d 736, 194 Ill. Dec. 908, 628 N.E.2d 405 (1993), relevant to establish that conduct of third party was proximate cause of injury. Similarly, subsequent remedial measures required by governmental authority are not excluded. *Millette v. Radosta,* 84 Ill. App. 3d 5, 39 Ill. Dec. 232, 404 N.E.2d 823 (1980), public policy underlying exclusion of evidence of subsequent remedial measures does not apply to recall of defective vehicles, since recall was mandated by the federal government and was thus not a voluntary act by a party to the lawsuit. *Accord Gaunt & Haynes, Inc. v. Moritz Corp.,* 138 Ill. App. 3d 356, 92 Ill. Dec. 880, 485 N.E.2d 1123 (1985) (order of Illinois Department of Transportation). This rationale was extended to permit admissibility of a post-occurrence discharge of an employee by the Chicago Transit Authority (CTA) following an inquiry required by the CTA's *own* internal policy in *Pearl v. Chicago Transit Auth.,* 177 Ill. App. 3d 499, 126 Ill. Dec. 754, 532 N.E.2d 439 (1988) (incorrectly decided).

Where a party offers evidence as to a subsequent remedial measure for a purpose other than as an admission of negligence or culpable conduct, admissibility will be affected by whether the purpose for which it is offered is being controverted. While evidence remains relevant if offered to establish an undisputed point, §401.1 supra, exclusion of such evidence on the basis of confusion of the issue, misleading the jury and the danger of unfair prejudice is required where the matter is uncontroverted. *See* §403.1 supra. For example, in a case where ownership of the offending instrumentality is admitted by defendant, little or no need appears for admitting evidence of subsequent repair to prove ownership, and the likelihood of an impermissible inference that fault has been admitted appears to be substantial. *Coshenet v. Holub,* 80

Ill. App. 3d 430, 35 Ill. Dec. 733, 399 N.E.2d 1022 (1980). *Accord Schaffner v. Chicago & N.W. Transp. Co.,* 129 Ill. 2d 1, 133 Ill. Dec. 432, 541 N.E.2d 643 (1989), evidence of subsequent replacement of railroad crossing was not justified as defendant did not dispute that replacement of the crossing was feasible; *Taake v. WHGK, Inc.,* 228 Ill. App. 3d 692, 170 Ill. Dec. 479, 592 N.E.2d 1159 (1992), evidence of subsequent remedial measure is admissible to prove ownership or feasibility of precautionary measures, if controverted. In *Herzog v. Lexington Township,* 167 Ill. 2d 288, 300–301, 212 Ill. Dec. 581, 587, 657 N.E.2d 926, 932 (1995), the Illinois Supreme Court stated that "evidence of subsequent remedial measures may be admissible for the purpose of proving ownership or control of property *where disputed by the defendant*" and "for the purpose of proving feasibility of precautionary measures *where disputed by the defendant*" (emphasis added), thus effectively imposing an if controverted "requirement." *See also* Federal Rule of Evidence 407. *Compare Lundquist v. Nickels,* 238 Ill. App. 3d 410, 179 Ill. Dec. 150, 605 N.E.2d 1373 (1992), placement of a rope between parking area and drop-off point properly admitted to demonstrate feasibility of such a safety measure at the site; incorrectly decided as feasibility clearly was not controverted.

In *Herzog v. Lexington Township,* 167 Ill. 2d 288, 301–303, 212 Ill. Dec. 581, 587–589, 657 N.E.2d 926, 931–934 (1995), the Illinois Supreme Court set forth guidelines for impeachment employing evidence of a subsequent remedial measure:

> Illinois has long recognized that subsequent remedial measures may also be used for impeachment purposes. (*See City of Taylorville v. Stafford* (1902), 196 Ill. 288, 63 N.E. 624.) However, the principles necessary for determining when the impeachment exception should apply have not been clearly articulated. The appellate court determined that because defendant's witnesses testified that the single, winding road sign present on the date of the accident was adequate, plaintiff should have been permitted to impeach this testimony with evidence those same individuals were responsible for placing additional signs on the roadway after the accident. We disagree.
>
> The flaw in the appellate court's reasoning is that the sole

value of the impeachment rests on the impermissible inference that the subsequent measures are admissible evidence of prior negligence. Defendant's witnesses testified only that the single sign present on the roadway was adequate. In order for the evidence of the subsequent signs to be considered impeaching, we must accept the premise that the conduct of placing additional signs contradicts the witnesses' testimony and supports the view that the original condition was unsafe. However, this premise directly contradicts the assumptions that support the general rule regarding subsequent remedial measures. Just as evidence of subsequent remedial measures is not considered sufficiently probative to be admissible to prove prior negligence, that evidence is not admissible for impeachment where the sole value of the impeachment rests on the same impermissible inference of prior negligence.

Allowing such evidence in these circumstances would swallow the general rule prohibiting the introduction of subsequent remedial measures and frustrate the policy considerations that support it. In every case, a defendant will dispute that his prior conduct was negligent. Once a defendant disputes his or her negligence at trial, a plaintiff could always seek to introduce evidence of subsequent remedial measures under the guise of impeachment. Thus, the general rule of excluding evidence of subsequent remedial measures would be swallowed by the impeachment exception. Furthermore, contrary to the policies supporting the general rule, parties to lawsuits would be discouraged from making improvements for fear that such actions would be used against them at trial.

Where the impeachment value rests on inferences other than the prior negligence, such evidence may be admitted where its probative value outweighs the prejudice to defendant. For example, this court first recognized that evidence of subsequent remedial measures may be admissible for the purpose of impeachment in *City of Taylorville v. Stafford* (1902), 196 Ill. 288, 63 N.E. 624. In that case, plaintiff was injured when she stumbled on a stake jutting up from a walkway. Defendant introduced evidence of a measurement of the stake taken after the accident that differed from plaintiff's measurement. This court found that plaintiff was properly permitted to attack this testimony with evidence that the difference in defendant's measurement was due to defendant's subsequent repair of the walkway. *Stafford*, 196 Ill. at 290–91, 63 N.E. 624.

Similarly, where the defendant goes beyond stating that the original condition was safe or adequate, and attempts to make exaggerated claims that the condition was the "safest possible," fairness may require that conduct inconsistent with these claims be admitted. (*See Muzyka v. Remington Arms Co.* (5th Cir. 1985), 774 F.2d 1309 (allowing impeachment of gun manufacturer with evidence of subsequent changes to safety mechanism where defendant repeatedly stated that mechanism was "safest" possible).) In such a situation, the defendant has gone beyond simply stating that he was not negligent prior to the accident and claimed that no greater care was possible. Any subsequent remedial measure taken by the defendant is directly impeaching of this claim without an inference of prior negligence. *See also Lewis v. Cotton Belt Route-St. Louis Southwestern Ry. Co.* (1991), 217 Ill. App. 3d 94, 159 Ill. Dec. 995, 576 N.E.2d 918 (allowing impeachment of defendant's witness who claimed that placing spotter was not "feasible" with evidence that a spotter was used later the same day).

Defendant's witnesses never made any exaggerated claims regarding the safety of the roadway or disputed that placing the additional signs on this roadway was possible. Defendant's witnesses only testified that the single, winding road sign was adequate and that traffic was capable of moving safely through the turns. Thus, plaintiff was not entitled to impeach this testimony with evidence of the additional signs defendant placed on the roadway after the accident.

Rulings on admissibility of subsequent remedial measures are exclusively within the province of the court. *See* §104.1 supra.

§408   Compromise and Offers to Compromise

§408.1   Commentary

Neither an offer to compromise a disputed liability claim of the opposing party nor an actual completed compromise is admissible as an admission of liability. *Hill v. Hiles*, 309 Ill.

App. 321, 32 N.E.2d 933 (1941). *Accord Plooy v. Paryani*, 275 Ill. App. 3d 1074, 212 Ill. Dec. 317, 657 N.E.2d 12 (1995), reversible error to permit testimony by plaintiff that defendant's investigator offered her $200 to settle her claim. The reasons assigned for exclusion are (1) irrelevancy, since the offer or compromise in reality involves a purchase of peace rather than an admission of liability, *Paulin v. Howser*, 63 Ill. 312 (1872), and (2) policy in that compromises, favored by public policy, would be discouraged by admitting the evidence, *Hill v. Hiles* supra; *Barkei by Barkei v. Delnor Hosp.*, 176 Ill. App. 3d 681, 126 Ill. Dec. 118, 531 N.E.2d 413 (1988); *Garcez v. Michel*, 282 Ill. App. 3d 346, 218 Ill. Dec. 31, 668 N.E.2d 194 (1996).

Either liability or amount must be disputed. Offers made to settle upon the amount to be paid where liability is admitted fall within the rule of exclusion. *Khatib v. McDonald*, 87 Ill. App. 3d 1087, 43 Ill. Dec. 266, 410 N.E.2d 266 (1980). *See also* Graham, Handbook of Federal Evidence §408.1 (4th ed. 1996). However, only the actual compromise or offer thereof is inadmissible. Admissions of fact are not excluded merely because they are made in the course of negotiations for settlement. *Domm v. Hollenbeck*, 142 Ill. App. 439 (1908), error in action for dog bite to exclude statement of defendant that dog was supposed to be kept tied, made during settlement negotiations; *Niehuss v. Merrill Lynch, Pierce, Fenner*, 143 Ill. App. 3d 444, 97 Ill. Dec. 483, 492 N.E.2d 1356 (1986), statement of manager of defendant's commodity office made during settlement negotiations properly admitted to impeach. *Accord Khatib v. McDonald* supra; *Sawicki v. Kim*, 112 Ill. App. 3d 641, 67 Ill. Dec. 771, 445 N.E.2d 63 (1983); *Skonberg v. Owens-Corning Fiberglas Corp.*, 215 Ill. App. 3d 735, 159 Ill. Dec. 359, 576 N.E.2d 28 (1991). *Cf.* Federal Rule of Evidence 408, 65 F.R.D. 131, 144 (1975), making all conduct and statements inadmissible if made in the course of compromise negotiations and defining compromise negotiations to include solely dispute as to amount.

Statements made in connection with compromise negotiations may be sheltered by the addition of phrases of qualification such as "without prejudice" or "hypothetically speaking."

McCormick, Evidence §266 (4th ed. 1992). The reasons underlying the rule of exclusion relating to compromise negotiations, however, do not require the exclusion of relevant evidence otherwise discoverable merely because it is first presented in a qualified fashion in the course of compromise negotiations. A party may not immunize from discovery or admissibility documents otherwise discoverable and/or admissible merely by offering them in a compromise negotiation. A party, by presenting a fact in such a manner during compromise negotiations, does not thereby prevent an opposing party from offering evidence of the fact at trial if the evidence was obtained from independent sources. Thus the subject matter disclosed in the course of compromise negotiations may be admissible, although the statement disclosing it would not. No "fruit of the poisonous tree" doctrine is intended.

If, for purposes of impeachment, proof is offered that the witness received or made a payment by way of compromise, a conflict develops between the principle that bias or prejudice may be shown and the policy of encouraging compromise. In *Fenberg v. Rosenthal*, 348 Ill. App. 510, 109 N.E.2d 402 (1952), the policy prevailed and the evidence was held properly excluded. It should be noted that proof that the witness made a claim, thus acting in a manner inconsistent with his testimony, was not precluded by this decision. *Cf. Chicago City Ry. v. Bundy*, 210 Ill. 39, 71 N.E. 28 (1904), plaintiff entitled to give her own version of conversation introduced by defendant, even though offer of compromise thereby is disclosed. *Cf. also* the final sentence of Federal Rule of Evidence 408, 65 F.R.D. 131, 144 (1975), which provides, "This rule also does not require exclusion when the evidence is offered for another purpose, such as proving bias or prejudice of a witness, negating a contention of undue delay, or proving an effort to obstruct a criminal investigation or prosecution." The Federal Advisory Committee's Note, 56 F.R.D. 183, 227-228 (1973) states:

> The final sentence of the rule serves to point out some limitations upon its applicability. Since the rule excludes only when

the purpose is proving the validity or invalidity of the claim or its amount, an offer for another purpose is not within the rule. The illustrative situations mentioned in the rule are supported by the authorities. As to proving bias or prejudice of a witness, see Annot. 161 A.L.R. 395, *contra, Fenberg v. Rosenthal,* 348 Ill. App. 510, 109 N.E.2d 402 (1952), and negativing a contention of lack of due diligence in presenting a claim, 4 Wigmore §1061. An effort to "buy off" the prosecution or a prosecuting witness in a criminal case is not within the policy of the rule of exclusion. McCormick §251, p.542.

However, recently resolution of the conflict has shifted with the principle that bias or prejudice may be shown prevailing. *Accord Batteast v. Wyeth Labs,* 137 Ill. 2d 175, 184, 148 Ill. Dec. 13, 17, 560 N.E.2d 315, 319 (1990) ("The Illinois position on this point is well established; if an extrajudicial agreement has the potential to bias a witness' testimony as to a relevant issue, disclosure is necessary to maintain the fairness and integrity of our judicial system."). Thus it is now clear that a witness may be cross-examined with respect to any bias or prejudice that may result from the terms of a loan-receipt agreement. *Reese v. Chicago, Burlington & Quincy R.R.,* 55 Ill. 2d 356, 303 N.E.2d 382 (1973). Since the terms of the loan-receipt agreement are relevant to the jury's assessment of credibility, disclosure is preferable to speculation. *Palmer v. AVCO Distrib. Corp.,* 82 Ill. 2d 211, 45 Ill. Dec. 377, 412 N.E.2d 959 (1980); *Eckley v. St. Therese Hospital,* 62 Ill. App. 3d 299, 19 Ill. Dec. 642, 379 N.E.2d 306 (1978). Similarly, if the settling defendant has agreed to testify against a remaining defendant, the terms of the settlement agreement may be disclosed. *Batteast v. Wyeth Labs* supra; *Boey v. Quaas,* 139 Ill. App. 3d 1066, 94 Ill. Dec. 345, 487 N.E.2d 1222 (1986). On the other hand, if the settling defendant did not believe he would be required to testify and had no further financial interest or exposure in the case as a result of a settlement agreed to by his insurance carrier, the trial court should prohibit the plaintiff from cross-examining the settling defendant regarding the settlement. *Uhr v. Lutheran General*

Hospital, 226 Ill. App. 3d 236, 168 Ill. Dec. 323, 589 N.E.2d 723 (1992); *Garcez v. Michel,* 282 Ill. App. 3d 346, 218 Ill. Dec. 31, 668 N.E.2d 194 (1996). *Contra* id. Cahill, J., dissenting, arguing that inquiry should be permitted to establish that witness was a former defendant that was dismissed when his employer settled with plaintiff. *Accord Banovz v. Rantanen,* 271 Ill. App. 3d 910, 208 Ill. Dec. 617, 649 N.E.2d 977 (1995), evidence of settlement properly excluded where the true extent of financial interest of the witness is already readily apparent to the trier of fact.

Where the witness whose interest in the outcome of the case resulting from a compromise agreement is also a party, evidence of the compromise agreement is not admissible if the true financial interest of witness is already readily apparent to the trier of fact in assessing credibility, *Casson v. Nash,* 74 Ill. 2d 164, 23 Ill. Dec. 571, 384 N.E.2d 365 (1978), but is admissible if the situation is otherwise. *Banovz v. Rantanen* supra. Where the witness is a third person whose interest in the outcome of the litigation is thus not readily apparent to the jury, the compromise agreement may be employed in the court's discretion on cross-examination to affect credibility if the witness retains a financial interest or has agreed to testify against a remaining defendant. *See McGrath v. Chicago & N.W. Transp. Co.,* 190 Ill. App. 3d 276, 137 Ill. Dec. 725, 546 N.E.2d 670 (1989); *See also Kenny v. Lakewood Eng. & Mfg. Co.,* 85 Ill. App. 3d 790, 41 Ill. Dec. 53, 407 N.E.2d 551 (1980); *Batteast v. Wyeth Laboratories, Inc.,* 172 Ill. App. 3d 114, 122 Ill. Dec. 169, 526 N.E.2d 428 (1988); *Lam v. Lynch Machinery Division of Lynch Corp.,* 178 Ill. App. 3d 229, 127 Ill. Dec. 419, 533 N.E.2d 37 (1988).

An actual compromise or an offer to compromise should not be admitted as evidence of inconsistent conduct nor as an inconsistent statement to impeach. *See* Graham, Handbook of Federal Evidence §408.1 (4th ed. 1996).

Evidence relating to a compromise or compromise negotiations is admissible when offered for a purpose other than to prove liability for or invalidity of a claim or its amount not relating to impeachment. *Lagoni v. Holiday Inn Midway,* 262

Ill. App. 3d 1020, 200 Ill. Dec. 283, 635 N.E.2d 622 (1994), evidence of settlement admissible to establish independence of evaluation by the participant; *Stathis v. Geldermann, Inc.,* 295 Ill. App. 3d 844, 229 Ill. Dec. 809, 692 N.E.2d 798 (1998), evidence of settlement negotiation admissible to explain that plaintiff had approved an earlier agreement only because he then believed he would be reimbursed the full amount of his investment.

A determination of whether a statement falls within the scope of the rule is exclusively for the court. *See* §104.1 supra.

§409 Payment of Medical and Similar Expenses

§409.1 *Commentary*

While evidence of payment or an offer to pay medical, hospital, or similar expenses may often be made from human impulses, under the broad definition of relevancy discussed in §401.1 supra, evidence of paying or offering to pay such expenses occasioned by an injury is relevant as having some tendency to be an admission of liability. In furtherance of the policy of encouraging assistance to an injured party, it being felt that assistance might be withheld if there were a risk of its use as an admission in a subsequent trial, the legislature enacted 735 ILCS 5/8-1901, which provides:

> The providing of, or payment for, medical, surgical, hospital, or rehabilitation services, facilities, or equipment by or on behalf of any person, or the offer to provide, or pay for, any one or more of the foregoing, shall not be construed as an admission of any liability by such person or persons. Testimony, writings, records, reports or information with respect to the foregoing shall not be admissible in evidence as an admission of any liability in any action of any kind in any court or before any commission, administrative agency, or other tribunal in this State,

except at the instance of the person or persons so making any such provision, payment or offer.

This statute implicitly disapproves the earlier decision in *Hanlon v. Lindberg,* 319 Ill. App. 1, 48 N.E.2d 735 (1945), where introduction of paying or promising to pay medical expenses of an injured party to prove liability was held proper. The statute precludes introduction of evidence of the reduction of a bill by a doctor, *Sawicki v. Kim,* 112 Ill. App. 3d 641, 67 Ill. Dec. 771, 445 N.E.2d 63 (1983), as well as the failure to submit a bill by a doctor or hospital. *Martin v. Zucker,* 133 Ill. App. 3d 982, 88 Ill. Dec. 980, 479 N.E.2d 1000 (1985).

No requirement is imposed that there be an actual dispute as to liability or amount at the time the furnishing of or offer to pay medical, hospital, or similar expense is made. Statements that accompany the offer or payment are not precluded from introduction into evidence by the statute. Moreover, evidence of furnishing or offering to pay the expenses is inadmissible only when offered to prove liability for the injury; it may be admitted if otherwise relevant to a fact of the consequence in the litigation.

A determination of whether evidence is barred by operation of the statute is exclusively for the court. *See* §104.1 supra.

§410   Inadmissibility of Pleas, Offers of Pleas, and Related Statements

§410.1   Commentary

Illinois Supreme Court Rule 402(f) provides:

If a plea discussion does not result in a plea of guilty, or if a plea of guilty is not accepted or is withdrawn, or if judgment on a plea of guilty is reversed on direct or collateral review, neither the plea discussion nor any resulting agreement, plea, or judgment shall be admissible against the defendant in any criminal proceeding.

Excluding, in any subsequent criminal proceeding against the same person, offers to plead guilty or *nolo contendere,* evidence of a plea of guilty later withdrawn, or a *nolo contendere* plea, and statements made in connection with and relevant to any of the foregoing, has as its purpose promotion of the disposition of criminal cases by plea bargaining. *People v. Friedman,* 79 Ill. 2d 341, 38 Ill. Dec. 141, 403 N.E.2d 229 (1980); *People v. Sexton,* 162 Ill. App. 3d 607, 114 Ill. Dec. 88, 515 N.E.2d 1359 (1987). If for any reason a plea of guilty is not subsequently entered or is later withdrawn, Rule 402(f) protects the defendant from use of the plea, offer, and related statements against her either as substantive evidence or for purposes of impeachment. *People v. Taylor,* 289 Ill. App. 3d 399, 224 Ill.Dec. 749, 682 N.E. 2d 310 (1997). In finding reversible error in the admissibility of a plea of guilty later withdrawn on a subsequent trial of the accused, the court in *People v. Haycraft,* 76 Ill. App. 2d 149, 153, 221 N.E.2d 317 (1966), stated:

> It is utterly inconsistent to permit a defendant to withdraw his guilty plea and then allow it, even inferentially, to be used against him. Once an accused has been permitted to withdraw his plea of guilty, he is entitled to all the privileges and presumptions that the law affords, including the presumption of innocence.

See also Kercheval v. United States, 274 U.S. 220 (1927).

The prohibition extends only to actions in which the person making the statement barred by Rule 402(f) is a defendant in any criminal proceeding. Thus any witness in a civil case and any witness in a criminal case other than the criminal defendant herself may be impeached by a statement given under any of the circumstances specified in Rule

402(f). Such statement is not being used "against the defendant in a criminal proceeding" when offered solely to impeach such witnesses.

The principle applies only to withdrawn pleas and offers, and *nolo contendere* pleas whether or not withdrawn. A guilty plea not withdrawn is generally admissible in a subsequent action arising out of the same facts, since an unwithdrawn plea of guilty admits all matters well pleaded in the indictment or information. Statements, made in conjunction with a plea of guilty not subsequently withdrawn, are similarly admissible. *People v. Chrisos,* 151 Ill. App. 3d 142, 104 Ill. Dec. 498, 502 N.E.2d 1158 (1986). Admission of the guilty plea must be distinguished from admission of the judgment of conviction resulting from it. The judgment constitutes an exception to the hearsay rule, §803.21 infra, admissible to prove any fact essential to sustain the judgment. A plea of guilty is not offered to prove the facts recited in the charge but to prove that the offender, not necessarily the defendant, admitted the facts. The plea of guilty may be admissible as an admission of a party, §802.2 infra, or as a declaration against interest of a nonparty, §804.7 infra, in situations where the judgment of conviction could not be shown because the offense was not sufficiently serious. For further discussion, *see* §§802.4 and 803.21 infra.

Supreme Court Rule 402(f) is intended to exclude related statements made in the course of or as a consequence of a plea of *nolo contendere* or plea bargaining that does not result in a plea of guilty or that results in a guilty plea later withdrawn. The standard to be followed by the court, §104.1 supra, in determining whether the related statement is to be excluded under Supreme Court Rule 402(f) was stated in *People v. Friedman,* 79 Ill. 2d 341, 38 Ill. Dec. 141, 403 N.E.2d 229 (1980), to be that set forth in *United States v. Robertson,* 582 F.2d 1356 (5th Cir. 1978): whether a statement is plea bargaining related depends upon, first, whether the accused exhibited an actual subjective expectation to negotiate a plea, and, second, whether this expectation was reasonable under the totality of the objective circumstances. For the court to find "actual" subjective expectation, the accused must have "exhibited" the expectation by expressing in some way the hope that a concession in exchange for his plea will come to pass. The mere hope of obtaining lenience is not enough. *People v. Sexton,* 162 Ill. App. 3d 607, 114 Ill. Dec. 88, 515 N.E.2d 1359 (1987). Nor is an inquiry to a police officer as to what type of arrangement might be made with the State's Attorney's Office, *People v. Victory,* 94 Ill. App. 3d 719, 50 Ill. Dec. 206, 419 N.E. 2d 73 (1981), or an inquiry to a police officer as to what would happen if the defendant pleaded no contest. *People v. Taylor,* 289 Ill. App. 3d 399, 224 Ill. Dec. 749, 682 N.E. 2d 310 (1997). An offer to "go easy" does not constitute a sufficiently definite concession, nor is a representation to report the defendant's cooperation to the state's attorney's office for appropriate consideration. *People v. Ramirez,* 244 Ill. App. 3d 136, 184 Ill. Dec. 524, 613 N.E.2d 1116 (1993). To have plea bargaining, a discussion seeking a concession in exchange for a plea must occur. *People v. Friedman* supra; *People v. Taylor* supra. Unconditional, unbargained for, volunteered admissions or confessions by the accused are thus outside the scope of exclusion. On the other hand, when the defendant expresses a desire to explore a plea in exchange for a concession, actual subjective expectation is clearly present. When such a preamble is not explicitly stated, the totality of the circumstances may nevertheless evidence an actual subjective expectation that plea negotiations had commenced. *People v. Tennin,* 123 Ill. App. 3d 894, 79 Ill. Dec. 64, 463 N.E. 2d 202 (1984). An accused's later account of her prior subjective mental impressions is not determinative. To prevent every admission from being vulnerable to subsequent challenge, the actual subjective expectation of the defendant that plea bargaining was in progress must have been "exhibited" by the defendant as reflected by the totality of the circumstances. *People v. Austin,* 123 Ill. App. 3d 788, 79 Ill. Dec. 103, 463 N.E.2d 444 (1984) (inquiry as to fate of women and whether the death penalty was applicable did not contain rudiments of negotiation). Nevertheless the conclusion in *People v. Tennin,* 123 Ill. App. 3d 894, 79 Ill. Dec. 64, 463 N.E.2d 202 (1984) and *People v. Ward,* 192 Ill. App. 3d

544, 139 Ill. Dec. 564, 548 N.E.2d 1120 (1989), that the statement "I want to make a deal" does not demonstrate a subjective expectation to negotiate a plea on the grounds that it does not adequately exhibit the rudiments of a negotiation, i.e., willingness to enter a plea of guilty *in return for a concession,* on the basis of a possible alternative motive such as seeking pretrial release without cash bond is overly narrow and should not be followed.

The related statement made in the course of plea bargaining may be made to either an attorney for the state or a police officer or investigator. *People v. Friedman* supra, adopting the position put forth in *United States v. Herman,* 544 F.2d 791 (5th Cir. 1977), and *United States v. Brooks,* 536 F.2d 1137 (6th Cir. 1976), that the statement may also be made to a police officer or investigator. The fact that the party to whom this statement was made is a law enforcement agent who did not have the actual authority to enter negotiation is not, standing by itself, necessarily sufficient to render the statement admissible. *People v. Hill,* 78 Ill. 2d 465, 36 Ill. Dec. 676, 401 N.E.2d 517 (1980); *People v. Hardiman,* 85 Ill. App. 3d 347, 40 Ill. Dec. 639, 406 N.E.2d 842 (1980). Circumstances surrounding the making of a statement to a law enforcement agent must be considered in determining whether the standard enunciated in *Friedman* was satisfied. *People v. Miller,* 94 Ill. App. 3d 725, 50 Ill. Dec. 211, 419 N.E.2d 78 (1981). A preamble explicitly demarcating the beginning of negotiations is not required. However, where such statement is made, it cannot be ignored as it is a clear indication of defendant's intent to pursue plea negotiations. In *Friedman* itself, defendant's statements to an investigator of the Attorney General concerning "making a deal" and of wishing to go to federal as opposed to state prison were plea-bargaining related statements inadmissible at trial.

A statement is not made in the course of plea discussions if made prior to any plea discussion commencing, if made subsequent to the agreement upon a plea bargain that did not call for the making of the statement, or if made after formalization of a negotiated plea agreement but before withdrawal from that agreement. *Hutto v. Ross,* 429 U.S. 28 (1976); *People v. Connery,* 296 Ill. App. 3d 384, 230 Ill. Dec. 689, 694 N.E.2d 658 (1998).

A plea of *nolo contendere* whether or not withdrawn, or an offer to plead *nolo contendere,* together with all statements made in connection therewith, is not admissible in a later civil or criminal action. An unwithdrawn plea of *nolo contendere,* while like a plea of guilty, constitutes an admission only for the purposes of the criminal case at hand. *Nolo contendere* pleas are used in order to avoid the effect on an impending civil case of a recorded plea of guilty; there is no admission usable in the civil case arising from a plea of *nolo contendere.* The plea of *nolo contendere* is recognized in 725 ILCS 5/113-4.1 as available only in prosecutions arising from the Illinois Income Tax Act, 35 ILCS 5/101 *et seq.* In addition, the question may arise in connection with a plea entered in another jurisdiction, in which case the rule of exclusion is similarly applied. *In re Eaton,* 14 Ill. 2d 338, 152 N.E.2d 850 (1958).

Statements made to probation officer by an accused during his pretrial services interview may not be employed as an admission of a party-opponent or to impeach at trial. *People v. Bennett,* 257 Ill. App. 3d 299, 195 Ill. Dec. 808, 629 N.E.2d 116 (1993) interpreting 725 ILCS 185/11.

With respect to the introduction of evidence of the lack of any plea bargaining, *see People v. Coleman,* 158 Ill. 2d 319, 198 Ill. Dec. 813, 633 N.E.2d 654 (1994), which, while raising the issue without explicitly stating a position, implies disapproval.

§411 Liability Insurance

§411.1 Commentary

Evidence that a defendant is insured against liability is irrelevant on the issue of fault, for a person by reason of being insured is felt to be no more likely to act negligently. The evidence is also excluded as being an invitation to the jury to share the resources of the insurer with the plaintiff, regardless of the merits of the case. *See Smithers v. Henriquez,* 368 Ill. 588, 15 N.E.2d 499 (1938); *Imparato v. Rooney,* 95 Ill. App. 3d 11, 50 Ill. Dec. 512, 419 N.E.2d 620 (1981) (citing Handbook). Similarly, evidence of lack of insurance is also excluded when offered upon the issue of negligence or otherwise wrongful conduct. However, an apparently inadvertent disclosure in a jury trial by a witness for plaintiff, with no indication of bad faith on the part of witness or counsel, whether as a result of an unresponsive answer on direct examination, *Williams v. Consumers Co.,* 352 Ill. 51, 185 N.E. 217 (1933); *Schaffer v. Dorsey,* 70 Ill. App. 2d 390, 217 N.E.2d 19 (1966); or on cross-examination, *Kelley v. Call,* 324 Ill. App. 143, 57 N.E.2d 501 (1944), does not require a mistrial. *See also Stenger v. Germanos,* 265 Ill. App. 3d 942, 203 Ill. Dec. 140, 639 N.E.2d 179 (1994) (identification of the defendant as an insurance broker did not result in prejudice). Nor is the disclosure fatal in a nonjury trial. *Rutherford v. Bentz,* 345 Ill. App. 532, 104 N.E.2d 343 (1952). On the other hand, an intentional disclosure of liability insurance may result in reversible error, *Imparato v. Rooney,* 95 Ill. App. 3d 11, 50 Ill. Dec. 512, 419 N.E.2d 620 (1981), if prejudice is shown. *Joynt v. Barnes,* 71 Ill. App. 3d 187, 27 Ill. Dec. 249, 388 N.E.2d 1298 (1979). In this regard "it has been noted that the mention of insurance is not quite the *bête noir* that it was a generation or more ago," *Milwaukee Mut. Ins. Co. v. Wessels,* 114 Ill. App. 3d 746, 750, 70 Ill. Dec. 550, 555, 449 N.E.2d 897, 902 (1983), and that it "seems likely today that in nearly all cases the jury will either be informed of the fact of insurance or will consciously assume that the defendant is so protected." *Kitsch v. Goode,* 48 Ill. App. 3d 260, 266, 6 Ill. Dec. 17, 22, 362 N.E.2d 446, 451 (1978) quoting McCormick, Evidence §201 at 481 (2d ed. 1972). *See generally Stenger v. Germanos* supra. Where the fact of insurance has been disclosed, Illinois Pattern Jury Instructions — Civil 2.13 (1994) should be given.

While not admissible on the question of liability, the exis-

RELEVANCY AND ITS LIMITS   §411.1

tence and extent of insurance coverage is discoverable. *People ex rel. Terry v. Fisher,* 12 Ill. 2d 231, 145 N.E.2d 588 (1957).

The existence of insurance may be shown in connection with issues other than fault, such as agency, ownership, or control, bias, or prejudice of a witness. *Pagano v. Leisner,* 5 Ill. App. 2d 223, 125 N.E.2d 301 (1955), taking out of liability insurance admissible upon issue of ownership of vehicle; *Allen B. Wrisley Co. v. Burke,* 203 Ill. 250, 67 N.E. 818 (1903); *Pinkerton v. Oak Park Natl. Bank,* 16 Ill. App. 2d 91, 147 N.E.2d 390 (1958), connection of witness with liability insurer admissible for impeachment by showing interest in case. With respect to identifying the preparer of a statement offered for impeachment as connected with an insurer for purpose of establishing bias or prejudice, *compare Yelm v. Masters,* 81 Ill. App. 2d 186, 225 N.E.2d 152 (1967), fact of preparation by insurer becomes relevant and may be established to show interest, *with Guardado v. Navarro,* 47 Ill. App. 2d 92, 197 N.E.2d 469 (1964), ordinarily possible to discredit statement without eliciting fact preparer worked for insurer and right to establish adverse interest may not be used as an excuse to insert prejudicial material. *See also Rubenstein v. Fred A. Coleman Co.,* 22 Ill. App. 2d 116, 159 N.E.2d 379 (1959), within discretion of trial judge to refuse to allow plaintiff to bring out on cross-examination of examining physician that he was paid by liability insurer, when defense counsel stated in open court that payment was made through him.

The question whether prospective jurors may be asked on *voir dire* examination as to connections with defendant's liability insurer has had an unusual history. Confronted on the one hand with the argument that plaintiff was entitled to jurors free from connection with defendant's insurer, and on the other hand with the argument that disclosure of insurance was highly prejudicial, the supreme court ruled that in the discretion of the trial court the inquiry might be made if in good faith for the purpose of safeguarding plaintiff's right to an impartial jury and not for the purpose of disclosing the existence of insurance. This nebulous standard resulted in a series of cases, ending with *Wheeler v. Rudek,* 397 Ill. 438, 74

N.E.2d 601 (1947), under which a practice evolved whereby defense counsel, by offering appropriate proof that no prospective juror is connected with the insurer, may make compliance with the good faith requirement impossible. *Compare Haymes v. Catholic Bishop of Chicago,* 41 Ill. 2d 336, 243 N.E.2d 203 (1968), inquiry of prospective jurors with respect to interest in or connection with liability insurance company upheld as not an abuse of discretion with specific reference being made to numerous liability insurance companies in Chicago, *with Leischner v. Daniel's Restaurant, Inc.,* 54 Ill. App. 3d 568, 12 Ill. Dec. 534, 370 N.E.2d 157 (1977), where court's refusal to permit inquiry with respect to employment by insurance company of prospective jurors or close friends, in spite of fact that three insurance companies had home offices in the city, was upheld on ground that general questions concerning place of employment of jurors or members of the family provided an adequate substitute.

§412   View by the Trier of Fact

§412.1   Commentary

Whether property that is the subject of litigation or the location where a relevant event occurred is viewed by the trier of fact has long been within the discretion of the trial judge, *Boner v. Peabody Coal Co.,* 142 Ill. 2d 523, 154 Ill. Dec. 662, 568 N.E.2d 883 (1991); *Springer v. Chicago,* 135 Ill. 552, 26 N.E. 514 (1891); *People v. Poole,* 123 Ill. App. 3d 375, 78 Ill. Dec. 691, 462 N.E.2d 810 (1984) (a trial judge is not required to permit a view), except that in proceedings under the Eminent Domain Act either party is entitled to a view as a matter of right, 735 ILCS 5/7-118. The court has discretion not only to permit a view of property and the scene of the occurrence but also to allow a view of any object, demonstration, or experiment, a view of which is relevant and otherwise admissible in evidence. *See People v. Durso*, 40 Ill. 2d 242, 239 N.E.2d 842 (1968); *Thomas v. Chicago Transit Auth.*, 115 Ill. App. 2d 476, 253 N.E.2d 492 (1969); McCormick, Evidence §216 (3d ed. 1984). A view may be appropriate in products liability actions where, for example, the witness can assume his actual position as he operated a piece of machinery, or in criminal proceedings where, for example, a witness may demonstrate the relevant positions and actions of persons or objects. *Cf. People v. Durso* supra, no useful purpose would be served by having jury observe car in which murder occurred. However, the alternative and frequently preferable procedure of employing photographs, motion pictures, or videotape should not be overlooked. *See People v. Gonzalez*, 294 Ill. App. 3d 205, 228 Ill. Dec. 766, 689 N.E.2d 1187 (1998).

In making their determination as to whether a view should be conducted under the particular circumstances, trial judges are not unmindful that the disruption and confusion often associated with taking the jury on a view often resembles that associated with taking a third grade class to a firehouse. Also relevant is whether the scene is adequately portrayed in photographs or by models, whether the scene is the same condition at the time of trial as it was at the relevant time, and whether the jury's travel to the scene would be burdensome, expensive, or time-consuming. *Boner v. Peabody Coal Co.* supra; *Lundquist v. Nickels*, 238 Ill. App. 3d 410, 179 Ill. Dec. 150, 605 N.E.2d 1373 (1992).

Changed conditions alone do not ordinarily preclude exercising discretion in favor of a view, *Osgood v. Chicago*, 154 Ill. 194, 41 N.E. 40 (1894), but discretion is not unlimited, and allowing a discretionary view of premises that had deteriorated greatly has been held in error. *Chicago v. Koff*, 341 Ill. 520, 173 N.E. 666 (1930).

Since a view cannot be incorporated in the record, it involves problems of control by the trial judge over the jury and by the reviewing court over the trial court. Accordingly it is said that a view is not evidence but is to enable the trier to understand and apply the evidence. *Boner v. Peabody Coal*

Co., 142 Ill. 2d 523, 154 Ill. Dec. 662, 568 N.E.2d 883 (1991); *Lundquist v. Nickels,* 238 Ill. App. 3d 410, 179 Ill. Dec. 150, 605 N.E.2d 1373 (1992); *Geohegan v. Union El. R. Co.,* 258 Ill. 352, 101 N.E. 577 (1913). Hence an essential finding cannot be based merely on a view. *Inlet Swamp Drainage Dist. v. Mehlhausen,* 291 Ill. 459, 126 N.E. 113 (1920), finding by trial judge on basis of view alone that water course was artificial; *Devon Bank v. Illinois Dept. of Transp.,* 95 Ill. App. 3d 690, 51 Ill. Dec. 191, 420 N.E.2d 605 (1981), facts gained from viewing property at issue cannot be considered in bench trial. Nor, despite a view, can a verdict on value stand that is not within the range of the testimony. *Chicago v. Koff* supra.

With respect to the procedure to be followed at a view, it is preferable for the judge to accompany the jury. Under such circumstances, in the discretion of the court, testimony may be received, demonstrations conducted, and experiments performed. *See* McCormick, Evidence §216 (4th ed. 1992); Cal. Code Civ. Proc. §651 (1976).

ARTICLE V

Privilege

§501 Description and Overview

§501.1   Commentary

The purpose of the ordinary rules of evidence is to promote the ascertainment of the truth. Another group of rules, however, is designed to permit the exclusion of evidence for reasons wholly unconnected with the quality of the evidence or the credibility of the witness. These reasons are found in the desire to protect an interest or relationship. The term *privilege* is used broadly herein to describe these latter rules of exclusion.

Since the effect of a privilege is to suppress the truth, privilege should be recognized only if the interest or relationship is of outstanding importance and would, beyond question, be harmed by denying the protection of privilege. *See People ex rel. Noren v. Dempsey,* 10 Ill. 2d 288, 139 N.E.2d 780 (1957). Moreover, privileges are strictly construed as an exception to the general duty to disclose. *In re Marriage of Daniels,* 240 Ill. App. 3d 314, 180 Ill. Dec. 742, 607 N.E.2d 1255 (1992). On the other hand, the Illinois Supreme Court has expressly *declined* to adopt a generalized public interest exception that would have permitted the prosecution's need to gather evidence to overcome a privilege and thus require disclosure. *People v. Knuckles,* 165 Ill. 2d 125, 209 Ill. Dec. 1, 650 N.E.2d 974 (1995) (lawyer-client).

The ordinary rules of evidence are invoked or waived by the parties in their capacity of litigants as an essential aspect of the adversary system. Privileges, on the contrary, are invoked or waived by their owners, who may or may not be parties to the litigation. The person asserting the privilege has the burden of showing facts that give rise to the privilege; a mere assertion of the privilege does not suffice. *People v. McNeal,* 175 Ill. 2d 335, 222 Ill. Dec. 307, 677 N.E.2d 841 (1997); *Consolidated Coal Co. v. Bucyrus-Erie Co.,* 89 Ill. 2d 103, 59 Ill. Dec. 666, 432 N.E.2d 250 (1982); *Krupp v. Chicago Transit Auth.,* 8 Ill. 2d 37, 132 N.E.2d 532 (1956). The existence of a privilege is a matter for the court. *See* §104.1 supra. An *in camera* examination of the disputed materials or communications by the court is a reasonable way to protect the privilege, if it exists, or to prevent groundless assertions of the privilege, if it does not. *In re Marriage of Decker,* 204 Ill. App. 3d 566, 150 Ill. Dec. 197, 562 N.E.2d 1000 (1990). The finding of the trial court is reviewed by applying the against manifest weight of the evidence standard. *People v. McNeal* supra.

All matters that are privileged against disclosure at trial are privileged against disclosure through any discovery proceeding. Supreme Court Rule 201(b) (2).

The more significant constitutional privileges, §502, those created by statute, §503, by court rule, §504, and by the common law, §505, are discussed in the sections that follow. This is followed in turn by a discussion of the procedural aspects governing all privileges, no matter what their source. *See* §§506.1 to 506.3 infra.

§502   Constitutional Privilege

§502.1   Self-Incrimination; Nature and Purpose

The privilege against self-incrimination is found in the Constitution of Illinois. "No person shall be compelled in any criminal case to give evidence against himself. . . ." Art. I, §10. The Fifth Amendment to the Constitution of the United States, containing substantially identical operative language, also applies to proceedings conducted by a state. *Malloy v. Hogan,* 378 U.S. 1 (1964). Both provisions have received the same general construction. *People ex rel. Hanrahan v. Power,* 54 Ill. 2d 154, 295 N.E.2d 472 (1973); *People v. Lynch,* 83 Ill. App. 3d 479, 39 Ill. Dec. 223, 404 N.E.2d 814 (1980).

The purpose of the provision is to protect a person against criminal punishment on her own evidence. *People v. Williams,* 40 Ill. 2d 522, 240 N.E.2d 645 (1968); *People v. Boyle,* 312 Ill. 586, 144 N.E. 342 (1924). Criminal punishment includes imprisonment, fine, forfeiture, and penalty, whether imposed in a criminal or a civil proceeding. *People ex rel. Akin v. Butler St. Foundry,* 201 Ill. 236, 66 N.E. 349 (1903); *Robson v. Doyle,* 191 Ill. 566, 61 N.E. 435 (1901). This privilege does not, however, extend to attorney disciplinary proceedings. *In re March,* 71 Ill. 2d 382, 17 Ill. Dec. 214, 376 N.E.2d 213 (1978), testimony taken under grant of use immunity, *see*

§501.17 infra, may be introduced in attorney disciplinary proceedings, which are not criminal in nature as punishment is not the objective. *Cf. Spevack v. Klein*, 385 U.S. 511 (1967). Nor does the privilege apply where the only consequence may be loss of employment. *Hoban v. Rochford*, 73 Ill. App. 3d 671, 29 Ill. Dec. 531, 392 N.E.2d 88 (1979). The privilege also does not extend to a probation revocation hearing that is a noncriminal proceeding. *People v. Bell*, 296 Ill. App. 3d 146, 230 Ill. Dec. 704, 694 N.E.2d 673 (1998). The privilege is not designed to protect another person. *People v. Schultz*, 380 Ill. 539, 44 N.E.2d 601 (1942). It does not extend to the testimony or statements of third parties called as witnesses at trial, *United States v. Nobles*, 422 U.S. 225 (1975), or to documents prepared by a person's accountant and given by the person himself to his attorney. *Fisher v. United States*, 425 U.S. 391 (1976). The privilege also does not extend to the voluntarily kept business records of a sole proprietorship, although the act of production itself if incriminating is protected. *Baltimore City Dept. of Social Serv. v. Bouknight*, 493 U.S. 549 (1990); *United States v. Doe*, 465 U.S. 605 (1984). *Cf. People v. Herbert*, 108 Ill. App. 3d 143, 63 Ill. Dec. 892, 438 N.E.2d 1255 (1982). However, the "act of production" doctrine does not extend to a corporation; the corporation must produce corporate documents. *Grand Jury Subpoena Duces Tecum 001144*, 164 Ill. App. 3d 344, 115 Ill. Dec. 471, 517 N.E.2d 1157 (1987). Nor does the privilege against self-incrimination prevent seizure of records of the defendant pursuant to a search warrant and subsequent admission at trial. *Andresen v. Maryland*, 427 U.S. 463 (1976).

The assertion by either the criminal defendant or a witness of the privilege against self-incrimination at a prior proceeding, such as before the grand jury, may not be employed to impeach testimony given at trial. *People v. Godsey*, 74 Ill. 2d 64, 23 Ill. Dec. 117, 383 N.E.2d 988 (1978), no basis exists to impeach with silence before the grand jury resulting from reliance upon the privilege against self-incrimination.

With respect to the trial court's exercise of discretion in advising a witness of his or her privilege against self-incrimination, *see People v. King*, 154 Ill. 2d 217, 181 Ill. Dec. 626, 608 N.E.2d 877 (1993); *People v. Radovick*, 275 Ill. App. 3d 809, 212 Ill. Dec. 2, 656 N.E.2d 235 (1995); *People v. Morley*, 255 Ill. App. 3d 589, 194 Ill. Dec. 281, 627 N.E.2d 397 (1994).

§502.2   Self-Incrimination; Proceedings Included

The constitutional language is very narrow, literally applied only "in any criminal case." However, the construction is that no person may be compelled to give evidence that may be used against him in a criminal proceeding.

> The constitutional exemption from compulsion in this regard extends to all proceedings sanctioned by law.
> Neither civil nor criminal courts, quasi-judicial tribunals, grand juries, commissioners, courts martial or inquisitors of any kind can compel a person to give evidence which may tend to convict him of a criminal offense. [*Kantner v. Clerk of the Circuit Court*, 108 Ill. App. 287, 301 (1903).]

The decisions of the supreme court support this broad view. *Lamson v. Boyden*, 160 Ill. 613, 43 N.E. 781 (1896), assumpsit to recover money lost as result of cornering the corn market; *Eggers v. Fox*, 177 Ill. 185, 52 N.E. 269 (1898), election contest; *People v. Argo*, 237 Ill. 173, 86 N.E. 679 (1908), grand jury investigation; *People ex rel. Keith v. Keith*, 38 Ill. 2d 405, 231 N.E.2d 387 (1967), commitment for mental treatment; *In re March*, 71 Ill. 2d 382, 376 N.E.2d 213, 17 Ill. Dec. 214 (1978), attorney disciplinary proceedings. *See also People v. Marcisz*, 32 Ill. App. 3d 467, 334 N.E.2d 737 (1975), privilege applies in criminal contempt proceedings. Although the privilege has been said to apply only to compelling disclosure in judicial proceedings, *People v. Fox*, 319 Ill. 606, 150 N.E. 347 (1926), this view now stands repudiated; the privilege affords one of the bases for excluding involuntary confessions, *People v. Miller*, 13 Ill. 2d 84, 148 N.E.2d 455 (1958).

§502.3 Self-Incrimination; Protected Disclosures

The privilege is against being compelled to give evidence against oneself or otherwise provide the State with evidence of a testimonial or communicative nature. *People ex rel. Bowman v. Woodward,* 63 Ill. 2d 382, 349 N.E.2d 57 (1976). Though compulsion may be involved, a purely physical, objective disclosure is not within the protection. *People v. Curran,* 286 Ill. 302, 121 N.E. 637 (1919), privilege not violated by requiring accused to stand for identification in court; *People v. Munziato,* 24 Ill. 2d 432, 182 N.E.2d 199 (1962), privilege not violated by compulsory weighing of vehicle for weight violation; *Schmerber v. California,* 384 U.S. 757 (1964), compulsory blood tests do not violate privilege; *Cardwell v. Lewis,* 417 U.S. 583 (1974), privilege not violated by paint scrapings from a car or by examination of tires; *People v. Warmack,* 73 Ill. App. 3d 783, 29 Ill. Dec. 777, 392 N.E.2d 334 (1979), making defendant wear certain clothing before the jury did not violate privilege. *See generally* Supreme Court Rule 413(a) providing disclosure to prosecution. *See also* §502.7 infra.

Compelling the giving of testimony is, of course, within the privilege, and the protection has been extended also to forbidding compulsory production of personal records containing assertions. *Lamson v. Boyden,* 160 Ill. 613, 43 N.E. 781 (1896); *United States v. Doe,* 465 U.S. 605 (1984). Extension of the privilege to preclude compulsory production of documents in the possession of a person that do not contain assertions by her, or of objects in her possession, while once countenanced, *People v. Zazove,* 311 Ill. 198, 142 N.E. 543 (1924), is no longer to be followed. *United States v. Nobles,* 422 U.S. 225 (1975); *People v. Ryan,* 25 Ill. 2d 233, 184 N.E.2d 853 (1962). The privilege not to produce documents where the act of production is itself incriminating does not extend to entities. *Grand Jury Subpoena Duces Tecum 001144,* 164 Ill. App. 3d 344, 115 Ill. Dec. 476, 517 N.E.2d 1157 (1987).

A required records exception to the privilege against self-incrimination was first recognized in *Shapiro v. United States,* 335 U.S. 1 (1948), and refined in *Grosso v. United States,* 390 U.S. 62 (1968) and *Baltimore City Dept. of Social Serv. v. Bouknight,* 493 U.S. 549 (1990). Essentially, the exception holds that where an individual is required by the government to keep records, those records are subject to disclosure if the following three factors exist: (1) the purpose of the record-keeping requirement must be essentially regulatory; (2) the records must be of a kind customarily kept; and (3) the records themselves must have assumed public aspects. *People v. Herbert,* 108 Ill. App. 2d 143, 63 Ill. Dec. 892, 438 N.E.2d 1255 (1982). Records that are required to be kept must be produced in spite of the fact that the act itself of production may be incriminating. *In re January, 1986 Grand Jury, No. 217,* 155 Ill. App. 3d 445, 108 Ill. Dec. 116, 508 N.E.2d 277 (1987).

With respect to silence on the part of an accused, *see* §802.7 infra.

A mental examination of an accused on the issue of sanity, over his objection, does not in itself violate his privilege against self-incrimination, *People v. Carpenter,* 13 Ill. 2d 470, 150 N.E.2d 100 (1958); *People v. Krauser,* 315 Ill. 485, 146 N.E. 593 (1925), since any statements by him are admissible only on the issue of insanity or drugged condition and not as an admission of guilt. 725 ILCS 5/115-6; *People v. Larson,* 47 Ill. App. 3d 9, 5 Ill. Dec. 390, 361 N.E.2d 713 (1977). *See also Estelle v. Smith,* 451 U.S. 454 (1981), testimony of psychiatrist may not be introduced at sentencing hearing in absence of waiver of privilege. The same principles are equally applicable when the issue is the accused's fitness to stand trial. 725 ILCS 5/104-14; *People v. Pulliam,* 176 Ill. 2d 261, 223 Ill. Dec. 610, 680 N.E.2d 343 (1997). In a proceeding to commit a person for mental treatment pursuant to the Mental Health and Developmental Disabilities Code, 405 ILCS 5/1-100 *et seq.* and the Guardianship and Advocacy Act, 20 ILCS 3955/1 *et seq.* the respondent may be required to submit to a mental examination, again provided that questions that might tend to expose the individual to criminal liability need not be answered. *See People ex rel. Keith v. Keith,* 38 Ill. 2d 405, 231 N.E.2d 387 (1967). In proceeding under the Sexually Dangerous Persons Act, 725 ILCS 205/1.01 *et seq.,* a defendant may be compelled to submit to a psychiatric examination, and because the proceedings are not criminal and because the defendant's statements may not be used in a subsequent criminal proceeding, he may be compelled to answer questions that might expose him to criminal liability. *People v. Allen,* 107 Ill. 2d 91, 89 Ill. Dec. 847, 481 N.E.2d 690 (1985).

With respect to disclosure to the prosecution of medical and scientific reports, Supreme Court Rule 413(c), such information may be required to be disclosed only if the defendant intends to call the expert concerned as a witness or to use the requested reports or materials at a hearing or trial. *People ex rel. Bowman v. Woodward* supra. Similarly, the defendant may be required to provide the prosecution with the names of witnesses she intends to call at trial, *Williams v. Florida,* 399 U.S. 78 (1970), as well as written or recorded statements of such persons relevant to the testimony and real evidence intended to be offered at trial.

§502.4 Self-Incrimination; Ordinary Witness and Accused

Fundamental differences between an ordinary witness and the accused in a criminal case must be noted.

The ordinary witness cannot refuse to take the stand and be sworn; he can claim the privilege only during examination and as questions are asked. *Pennsylvania Tank Line v. Jordan,* 341 Ill. 94, 173 N.E. 181 (1930). He may claim the privilege at the point where further answering would tend to incriminate him or constitute a link in a chain of evidence that might incriminate him, and "is not required to go on and answer questions until one is propounded the answer to which will of itself incriminate him. . . ." *Minler v. People,* 139 Ill. 363, 366, 29 N.E. 45 (1891), witness entitled to refuse to disclose to grand jury names of persons seen gambling, since link to own guilt might be disclosed; *Mallory v. Hogan,* 378

U.S. 1 (1964), *semble*. While it has been said that the circumstances of the case and the nature of the requested evidence must show reasonable grounds for apprehension, *People v. Schultz,* 380 Ill. 539, 44 N.E.2d 601 (1942); *People v. Mileris,* 103 Ill. App. 3d 589, 59 Ill. Dec. 307, 431 N.E.2d 1064 (1981) (court must determine if, under the particular facts, there is a real danger of incrimination), the court must remain aware that "in the deviousness of crime and its detection, incrimination may be approached and achieved by obscure and unlikely lines of inquiry." *People v. Burkert,* 7 Ill. 2d 506, 518, 131 N.E.2d 495 (1955). *Accord Heath by Heath v. Heath,* 143 Ill. App. 3d 390, 97 Ill. Dec. 615, 493 N.E.2d 97 (1986) (it must be apparent under all the circumstances that the answers cannot possibly have a tendency to incriminate the party claiming the privilege). *See also Hoffman v. United States,* 341 U.S. 479 (1951); McCormick, Evidence §139 (4th ed. 1992). Nevertheless, circumstances warranting application of the privilege are confined to those instances where the witness has reasonable cause to suspect the possibility of subsequent prosecution from a direct answer. *People v. Redd,* 135 Ill. 2d 252, 143 Ill. Dec. 802, 553 N.E.2d 316 (1990); *People v. Wiesneske,* 234 Ill. App. 3d 29, 175 Ill. Dec. 252, 599 N.E.2d 1266 (1992); *People v. Prater,* 158 Ill. App. 3d 330, 110 Ill. Dec. 655, 511 N.E.2d 842 (1987). However, the witness is not required to prove that the answer to a particular question would necessarily subject him to prosecution. *People v. Redd* supra; *People v. Lockett,* 260 Ill. App. 3d 266, 197 Ill. Dec. 498, 631 N.E.2d 720 (1993).

Neither an unreasonable fear of self-incrimination nor a mere reluctance to testify is grounds for asserting the privilege. *People v. Cooper,* 202 Ill. App. 3d 336, 147 Ill. Dec. 602, 559 N.E.2d 942 (1990). Once these conditions are met, the decision is up to the witness. *People v. Spain,* 307 Ill. 283, 138 N.E.2d 614 (1923). Whether the conditions are met, however, is for the court to decide, *People v. Redd,* 135 Ill. 2d 252, 143 Ill. Dec. 802, 553 N.E.2d 316 (1990); *People v. Baker,* 123 Ill. 2d 233, 122 Ill. Dec. 17, 526 N.E.2d 157 (1988); *People v. Prater* supra, as is whether to hold a hearing on the expanse of any privilege, *People v. Katsigiannis,* 171 Ill. App. 3d 1090, 122 Ill. Dec. 249, 526 N.E.2d 508 (1988).

Where it is clear that a witness such as a codefendant will assert her privilege against self-incrimination, the trial court may refuse to permit the witness to be called by any party including the criminal defendant. *People v. Meyers,* 35 Ill. 2d 311, 220 N.E.2d 297 (1966); *People v. Vera,* 277 Ill. App. 3d 130, 213 Ill. Dec. 752, 660 N.E.2d 9 (1995); *People v. Nally,* 134 Ill. App. 3d 865, 89 Ill. Dec. 630, 480 N.E.2d 1373 (1985); *People v. Cole,* 50 App. 3d 133, 7 Ill. Dec. 848, 365 N.E.2d 133 (1977). *See* §506.3 infra. *See also People v. Crawford Distrib. Co.,* 78 Ill. 2d 70, 34 Ill. Dec. 296, 397 N.E.2d 1362 (1979), not error to call witness who had advised of his intention to assert privilege in light of prior grant of immunity.

The privilege of an accused is spelled out by statute providing that the accused shall "only at his or her own request be deemed a competent witness, and the person's neglect to testify shall not create any presumption against the person, nor shall the court permit any reference or comment to be made to or upon such neglect." 725 ILCS 125/6. Thus the accused is privileged not to take the stand at all, and comment upon his election not to do so is error. *Griffin v. California,* 380 U.S. 609 (1965); *Austin v. People,* 102 Ill. 261 (1882); 725 ILCS 125/6. The line between what constitutes comment and what does not is sometimes a fine one. The standard in deciding whether the prosecutor's remarks violated defendant's right to remain silent is to ascertain if the reference was calculated to direct the jury's attention to defendant's failure to testify. *People v. Cruz,* 38 Ill. App. 3d 21, 347 N.E.2d 277 (1976). Employing the standard, it has nevertheless been held proper for a prosecutor to comment on the uncontradicted nature of the State's case, even where the only person who could have contradicted the State's evidence was the defendant himself, *People v. Withers,* 87 Ill. 2d 224, 57 Ill. Dec. 736, 429 N.E.2d 853 (1981); *People v. Mills,* 40 Ill. 2d 4, 237 N.E.2d 697 (1968), especially where motivated by a purpose of demonstrating the absence of any evidentiary basis for defense counsel's argument. *People v. Dixon,* 91 Ill. 2d 346, 63

Ill. Dec. 442, 438 N.E.2d 180 (1982). On the other hand, it has been held error to emphasize that the defense called only one witness who was not the accused, *People v. Morgan,* 20 Ill. 2d 437, 170 N.E.2d 529 (1960), to indicate, after listing the witnesses who testified, that no one else testified, *People v. Wollenberg,* 37 Ill. 2d 480, 229 N.E.2d 490 (1969), or to emphasize repeatedly the uncontradicted nature of the State's case. *People v. Johnson,* 102 Ill. App. 3d 122, 57 Ill. Dec. 788, 429 N.E.2d 905 (1981). With respect to the effect of improper comment, *see* §103.10 supra. Notice, however, that 725 ILCS 125/6 applies only to a criminal proceeding. Thus, for example, at a revocation proceeding, which is not a criminal proceeding, the defendant may be called as a witness. *People v. Neckopulos,* 284 Ill. App. 3d 660, 219 Ill. Dec. 904, 672 N.E.2d 757 (1996).

The accused is entitled on request to an instruction that she is not compelled to testify and that the fact that she did not testify cannot be used as the basis for an inference of guilt. *Carter v. Kentucky,* 450 U.S. 288 (1981).

Earlier Illinois decisions assumed, without squarely ruling, that the privilege against self-incrimination contained in the Constitution of Illinois applied to corporations. *Manning v. Mercantile Sec. Co.,* 242 Ill. 584, 90 N.E. 238 (1909); *People ex rel. Akin v. Butler St. Foundry,* 201 Ill. 236, 66 N.E. 349 (1903). Abandonment of this view indicated in *People v. Monroe,* 27 Ill. 2d 449, 189 N.E.2d 350 (1963), and *People v. Ryan,* 410 Ill. 486, 103 N.E.2d 116 (1952), crystallized in *People ex rel. Scott v. Pintozzi,* 50 Ill, 2d 115, 277 N.E.2d 844 (1972). Nor does the protection provided by the Fifth Amendment against self-incrimination apply to corporations, *George Campbell Painting Corp. v. Reid,* 392 U.S. 286 (1968), or to Subchapter S corporations. *Monarch Gas Co. v. Illinois Commerce Commn.,* 51 Ill. App. 3d 892, 9 Ill. Dec. 434, 366 N.E.2d 945 (1977). Moreover, the privilege does not extend to the *contents* of voluntarily prepared business records of a sole proprietorship. *United States v. Doe,* 465 U.S. 605 (1984). *Cf. People v. Herbert,* 108 Ill. App. 3d 143, 63 Ill. Dec. 892, 438 N.E.2d 1255 (1982). A corporation does not have a privilege not to produce documents even if the act of production is itself incriminating. *Grand Jury Subpoena Duces Tecum 001144,* 164 Ill. App. 3d 344, 115 Ill. Dec. 471, 517 N.E.2d 1157 (1987). In the prosecution of an officer of a corporation, the officer cannot claim a privilege as to corporate books and records, even though he is custodian thereof and they may tend to incriminate him personally. *People ex rel. Scott v. Pintozzi* supra; *People v. Ryan* supra; *People v. Munday,* 280 Ill. 32, 117 N.E. 286 (1917). However, the producer of corporate records may assert the privilege with respect to questions about the records. *People v. Monroe* supra.

With respect to organizations such as labor unions, political parties, and partnerships, an individual may not rely upon the privilege against self-incrimination to avoid producing the records of a collective entity in her possession in a representative capacity, even if these records might incriminate her personally. *Bellis v. United States,* 417 U.S. 85 (1974), partnership; *People v. Lynch,* 83 Ill. App. 3d 479, 39 Ill. Dec. 223, 404 N.E.2d 814 (1980), family-owned partnership; *United States v. White,* 322 U.S. 694 (1944), labor union; *United States v. Fleischman,* 339 U.S. 349 (1950), Joint Anti-Fascist Refugee Committee; *Rogers v. United States,* 340 U.S. 367 (1950), Communist Party of Denver; *In re Zisook,* 88 Ill. 2d 321, 58 Ill. Dec. 786, 430 N.E.2d 1037 (1981), professional corporation. The papers and effects protected by the privilege at most extend only to private property of the person claiming the privilege, or at least in his possession in a purely personal capacity. *United States v. White* supra. Whether a small family partnership possesses a privilege against self-incrimination is undecided. *Bellis v. United States* supra; *People v. Lynch* supra. *See generally,* McCormick, Evidence §§128, 129 (3d ed. 1984).

§502.5 Self-Incrimination; Claiming and Waiving the Privilege, Necessity of Warning

The privilege against self-incrimination of a witness is personal to him and cannot be claimed by either party for him,

Bolen v. People, 184 Ill. 338, 56 N.E. 408 (1900); *Eggers v. Fox,* 177 Ill. 185, 52 N.E. 269 (1898), although counsel for the witness may invoke the privilege on his behalf. *People v. Myers,* 35 Ill. 2d 311, 220 N.E.2d 297 (1966). Improper denial of a claim of privilege by a witness who is not a party cannot, therefore, be urged as error on appeal. *Samuel v. People,* 164 Ill. 379, 45 N.E. 728 (1897).

The privilege may of course be waived. An ordinary witness waives the privilege for purposes of the particular proceeding by failure to claim it. *People v. Nachowicz,* 340 Ill. 480, 172 N.E. 812 (1930); *People v. Cantu,* 79 Ill. App. 3d 279, 34 Ill. Dec. 633, 398 N.E.2d 308 (1979). An accused waives the privilege by electing to take the stand, *People v. Roberson,* 30 Ill. 2d 168, 195 N.E.2d 722 (1964); *People v. Kelley,* 24 Ill. App. 3d 1018, 322 N.E.2d 527 (1975), even for the limited purpose of exhibiting his teeth to the jury. *People v. Harris,* 46 Ill. 2d 395, 263 N.E.2d 35 (1970). The extent of waiver is discussed below.

Prior disclosure, even in the course of legal proceedings, has been held not to preclude a subsequent claim of privilege (*Samuel v. People* supra, signing affidavit to information; *People v. Rockola,* 339 Ill. 474, 171 N.E. 559 (1930), testifying before grand jury) unless occurring in the course of a single civil action. *Stadler v. Stone,* 412 Ill. 488, 107 N.E.2d 696 (1952), waiver by giving deposition without claim of privilege; *Loraitis v. Kukulka,* 1 Ill. 2d 533, 116 N.E.2d 329 (1954), defendant not entitled to refuse to give deposition because it might show him guilty of perjury in verifying answer. The applicable principle was stated in *People v. Walker,* 28 Ill. 2d 585, 588, 192 N.E.2d 819 (1963), quoting from 8 Wigmore, Evidence §2276 (3d ed. 1940): "His voluntary testimony before a coroner's inquest or a grand jury, or other preliminary and separate proceeding, e.g., in bankruptcy, is therefore not a waiver for the main trial; nor is his testimony at a first trial a waiver for a later trial." It should be observed, however, that the subsequent claim of privilege does not preclude use of the testimony already given. *See* §804.2 relating to former testimony and §802.1 relating to admissions of a party opponent. As to whether the defendant's display of his face or a tattoo constitutes an election to testify, *see People v. Alksnis,* 291 Ill. App. 3d 347, 225 Ill. Dec. 35, 682 N.E.2d 1112 (1997).

The privilege against self-incrimination is not waived by the filing of a complaint, interposing of a counterclaim, pleading an affirmative defense, or responding to an interrogatory unless the document amounts to an admission of guilt or furnishes clear proof of a crime. *10-Dix Bldg. Corp. v. McDannel,* 134 Ill. App. 3d 664, 89 Ill. Dec. 469, 480 N.E.2d 1212 (1985).

The extent of waiver by a witness who testifies without objection and by an accused who elects to take the stand have been measured by the same standard: waiver is co-extensive with the proper scope of cross-examination, a determination resting in the sound discretion of the court. *People v. Burris,* 49 Ill. 2d 98, 273 N.E.2d 605 (1971). This standard has been developed to the effect that it is proper on cross-examination of the defendant to develop all circumstances within the knowledge of the witness that explain, qualify, discredit, or destroy her direct testimony, although this may incidentally constitute new matter of aid to the cross-examiner's case. *People v. Williams,* 66 Ill. 2d 478, 6 Ill. Dec. 854, 363 N.E.2d 801 (1977); *Heath by Heath v. Heath,* 143 Ill. App. 3d 390, 97 Ill. Dec. 615, 493 N.E.2d 97 (1986). The practical application in *Williams* resulted in an extremely broad waiver by an accused person. *Cf.* McCormick, Evidence §134 (4th ed. 1992).

After relating a part of a transaction or conversation, the ordinary witness cannot refuse to disclose the whole. *Eggers v. Fox* supra; *People v. Nachowicz* supra.

The final sentence of Federal Rule of Evidence 608, 65 F.R.D. 131, 148 (1975), provides that the giving of testimony, whether by an accused or by any other witness, does not operate as a waiver of his privilege against self-incrimination when examined with respect to matters that relate only to credibility. The Federal Advisory Committee's Note to Rule 608, 56 F.R.D. 183, 269 (1973), states:

[W]hile it is clear that an ordinary witness cannot make a partial disclosure of incriminating matter and then invoke the privilege on cross-examination, no tenable contention can be made that merely by testifying he waives his right to foreclose inquiry on cross-examination into criminal activities for the purpose of attacking his credibility. So to hold would reduce the privilege to a nullity. While it is true that an accused, unlike an ordinary witness, has an option whether to testify, if the option can be exercised only at the price of opening up inquiry as to any and all criminal acts committed during his lifetime, the right to testify could scarcely be said to possess much vitality. In *Griffin v. California*, 380 U.S. 609, 85 S. Ct. 1229, 14 L. Ed. 2d 106 (1965), the Court held that allowing comment on the election of an accused not to testify exacted a constitutionally impermissible price, and so here. While no specific provision in terms confers constitutional status on the right of an accused to take the stand in his own defense, the existence of the right is so completely recognized that a denial of it or substantial infringement upon it would surely be of due process dimensions. *See Ferguson v. Georgia*, 365 U.S. 570, 81 S. Ct. 756, 5 L. Ed. 2d 783 (1961); McCormick §131; 8 Wigmore §2276 (McNaughton Rev. 1961). In any event, wholly aside from constitutional considerations, the provision represents a sound policy.

Since cross-examination of any witness as to acts of misconduct not resulting in a conviction to attack the credibility of a witness is prohibited in Illinois, *see* §608.1 infra, need to resort to assertion of the privilege against self-incrimination will occur infrequently, if at all. Of course, the same principle applies to prohibit cross-examination designed to bring out a prior assertion by the witness of his privilege against self-incrimination. *People v. Godsey*, 57 Ill. App. 3d 364, 15 Ill. Dec. 1, 373 N.E.2d 95 (1978). *See also* §§104.3 supra and 506.3 infra with respect to hearings outside presence of the jury.

Waiver is the intentional relinquishment of a known right. *People v. Shroyer*, 336 Ill. 324, 168 N.E. 336 (1929). Must the person be advised of her right to say nothing and warned that any statement may be used against her? No requirement of this nature is found with respect to an ordinary witness. With respect to an accused, *Miranda v. Arizona,* 384 U.S. 436 (1966), specifically requires that when an individual is first subject to police interrogation while in custody or otherwise deprived of his freedom in any significant way, he must immediately be warned that he has a right to remain silent, "and that 'anything said can be used against the individual in court.'"

§502.6 Self-Incrimination; Immunity and Grants Thereof; Finality of Conviction

Crime barred by limitations. Illinois has long recognized that a witness cannot refuse to disclose a crime to which the statute of limitations is a defense. *Weldon v. Burch,* 12 Ill. 374 (1851). Later decisions have impaired the effectiveness of this principle by requiring the party calling for the testimony to show that no prosecution is pending, *Lamson v. Boyden,* 160 Ill. 613, 43 N.E. 781 (1896), and that the running of the statute has not been tolled by absence from the state or concealment, *People v. Rockola,* 339 Ill. 474, 171 N.E. 559 (1930). *See generally People v. Taylor,* 287 Ill. App. 3d 800, 223 Ill. Dec. 138, 679 N.E.2d 82 (1997).

Promise of immunity. The giving of testimony in reliance upon a promise of immunity by the prosecutor or sheriff has been held to be a defense against prosecution. *People v. Martorano,* 359 Ill. 258, 194 N.E. 505 (1935); *People v. Bogolowski,* 326 Ill. 253, 157 N.E. 181 (1927). However, the power of the state's attorney to compel testimony by promising immunity has been denied, *People v. Rockola* supra, a result that may appear illogical but that is justified in terms of reluctance to recognize in state's attorneys the equivalent of a full pardoning power.

Grant of immunity under statute. On the theory that a bird in the hand is worth two in the bush, statutes began to appear authorizing the compulsion of self-incriminating testimony in return for a grant of immunity. Earlier statutes applied only to prosecutions involving special difficulties of proof without testimony of this nature, such as bribery or extortion. In 1953 a general immunity statute applicable to all crimes was enacted. Ill. R.S. 1961, c.38, §714.1. The statute provided for the entry of an order by the court granting immunity upon motion of the state's attorney and a showing that the person is a material witness for the prosecution whose testimony would tend to incriminate him, and the witness is then required to testify. A request must be forthcoming from the prosecution; the court had and has no power to grant immunity in order to secure testimony desired by the defense. *People v. Burrows,* 148 Ill. 2d 196, 170 Ill. Dec. 317, 592 N.E.2d 997 (1992); *People v. English,* 31 Ill. 2d 301, 201 N.E.2d 455 (1964); *People v. Frascella,* 81 Ill. App. 3d 794, 36 Ill. Dec. 907, 401 N.E.2d 1045 (1980). Under some special statutes that are still in effect, the assurance provided by a court order is absent, as in investigations under the Cigarette Tax Act, 35 ILCS 130/10a, with immunity arising simply by virtue of testifying at the instance of the Department of Revenue in response to a subpoena.

A statute that merely protects the witness from the use of her own disclosure against her leaves open the possibility of conviction on other evidence discovered as a result of the disclosures and is invalid as being an inadequate substitute for the constitutional privilege against self-incrimination. *People v. Argo,* 237 Ill. 173, 86 N.E. 679 (1908). The Fifth Amendment is, however, satisfied by immunity whereby a witness's compelled testimony or leads derived therefrom may not be used in her prosecution, known as *use immunity. Kastigar v. United States,* 406 U.S. 441 (1972). Use immunity must be granted before a witness may be compelled to testify as to incriminating matters. *Gardner v. Broderick,* 392 U.S. 273 (1968); *In re March,* 71 Ill. 2d 382, Ill. Dec. 214, 376 N.E.2d 213 (1978), use immunity must be given to an attorney before testimony may be compelled at a disciplinary proceeding. Possible exposure to prosecution under the laws of another jurisdiction does not in itself render an immunity statute invalid, *Brown v. Walker,* 161 U.S. 591 (1896); *People ex rel. Akin v. Butler St. Foundry,* 201 Ill. 236, 66 N.E. 349 (1903), only use immunity being required as between states or as between a state and the federal government. *Murphy v. Waterfront Commn.*, 378 U.S. 52 (1964). Use immunity is provided with respect to certain crimes by 725 ILCS 5/106-2.5. The present Illinois statute, 725 ILCS 5/106-1 to 5/106-3, goes further and grants transactional immunity that fully immunizes the person from prosecution by any agency of the state for any offense to which his compelled testimony relates. *People ex rel. Cruz v. Fitzgerald*, 66 Ill. 2d 546, 6 Ill. Dec. 888, 363 N.E.2d 835 (1977). Testimony given by a witness under a grant of immunity may not be used to impeach his credibility as a testifying defendant in a subsequent criminal trial. *New Jersey v. Portash*, 440 U.S. 450 (1979).

Final conviction. Removal of the possibility of incrimination by virtue of a final adjudication of guilt eliminates the privilege. To be final, sentence must have been imposed, *People v. Hartley*, 22 Ill. App. 3d 108, 317 N.E.2d 57 (1974), a motion for a new trial may not be pending, *id.*, and an appeal may neither pend nor be available as a matter of right. *People ex rel. Kunce v. Hogan*, 37 Ill. App. 3d 673, 346 N.E.2d 456 (1976). However, final conviction does not waive the privilege against self-incrimination where the conviction does not encompass all the witness's potential criminal liability with respect to the subject under consideration. *Orlove v. Jacobsen*, 79 Ill. App. 3d 1141, 34 Ill. Dec. 495, 398 N.E.2d 170 (1979); *People v. Prater* 158 Ill. App. 3d 330, 110 Ill. Dec. 665, 511 N.E.2d 842 (1987). Similarly, an acquittal that does not encompass all of the witness's potential criminal liability with respect to the subject matter under consideration does not waive the privilege. *People v. Thornton*, 120 Ill. App. 3d 983, 76 Ill. Dec. 496, 458 N.E.2d 1150 (1983).

§502.7 *Breath, Blood, and Similar Tests; Driving While Intoxicated*

Compulsory breath, urine, saliva, or other bodily substance tests do not violate any constitutional right of an individual merely because she objects to the tests. *Schmerber v. California*, 384 U.S. 757 (1966), blood test; *People v. Pruitt*, 16 Ill. App. 3d 930, 307 N.E.2d 142 (1974), hair sample. The absence of a formal consent does not taint such a search, given probable cause and the fact that such evidence dissipates over time. *See Cupp v. Murphy*, 412 U.S. 291 (1973). Blood may constitutionally be removed from a person when unconscious. *People v. Todd*, 59 Ill. 2d 534, 322 N.E.2d 447 (1975). Paint scrapings from a car and examination of a tire infringe no constitutionally protected right, *Cardwell v. Lewis*, 417 U.S. 583 (1974). The accused may be required to furnish handwriting samples, *People ex rel. Hanrahan v. Power*, 54 Ill. 2d 154, 295 N.E.2d 472 (1973), as well as voice exemplars. *United States v. Dionisio*, 410 U.S. 1 (1973).

In drunken driving cases evidence of the amount of alcohol and/or drugs in the blood as shown by chemical analysis of breath, blood, urine, saliva, or other bodily substance is by statute admissible in evidence. 625 ILCS 5/11-501.1, 11-501.2. The statute, *id.*, 11-501.1, provides for implied consent to the taking of a breath test. Refusal to submit to a chemical test is admissible in civil and criminal proceedings that are based on acts the motorist allegedly committed while driving under the influence of alcohol and/or drugs. 625 ILCS 5/11-501.2(c); *People v. Bugbee*, 201 Ill. App. 3d 952, 147 Ill. Dec. 381, 559 N.E.2d 554 (1990). A person who is dead, unconscious, or otherwise incapable of refusal, is deemed to have withdrawn his consent. The written results of chemical tests of blood conducted in the regular course of providing emergency medical services are admissible in criminal prosecutions for driving under the influence and reckless homicide. 625 ILCS 5/11-501.4. *See also People v. Lendabarker*, 215 Ill. App. 3d 540, 159 Ill. Dec. 70, 575 N.E.2d 568 (1991); *People v. Wilber*, 279 Ill. App. 3d 462, 216 Ill. Dec. 74, 664 N.E.2d 711 (1996). A computer generated printout constitutes a written result for purposes of 11-501.4. *People v. Ethridge*, 243 Ill. App. 3d 446, 183 Ill. Dec. 61, 610 N.E.2d 1305 (1993). Introduction of the actual blood serum is not required as part of the foundation. *People v. Ethridge, id.* The results of the tests on breath, blood, urine, saliva, and other bodily substances are admissible in a civil trial arising out of acts committed while driving under the influence of liquor. 625 ILCS 5/11-501.1, 11-501.2, should be consulted. *See also* §403.3 supra, with respect to intoxication as evidence of negligence. With respect to the foundational requirements for admissibility of the result of a breath test, *see People v. Orth,* 124 Ill. 2d 326, 125 Ill. Dec. 182, 530 N.E.2d 210 (1988); *People v. Caruso,* 201 Ill. App. 3d 930, 147 Ill. Dec. 372, 559 N.E.2d 545 (1990). It is not necessary that an expert witness be called to interpret the results of the chemical analysis in light of the statutory presumptions. *Wade v. City of Chicago Heights,* 216 Ill. App. 3d 418, 159 Ill. Dec. 228, 575 N.E.2d 1288 (1991). In criminal actions other than for driving under the influence, and in civil proceedings, evidence of intoxication based on chemical analysis of a person's blood may be admitted without complying with the statute. *People v. Murphy,* 108 Ill. 2d 228, 91 Ill. Dec. 653, 483 N.E.2d 1288 (1985); *Wade v. City of Chicago Heights,* 295 Ill. App. 3d 873, 230 Ill. Dec. 297, 693 N.E.2d 426 (1998); *Thomas v. Brandt,* 144 Ill. App. 3d 95, 98 Ill. Dec. 121, 493 N.E.2d 1142 (1986). Evidence of breath alcohol analysis made without complying with the statute is admissible in such cases as well. *People v. Keith,* 148 Ill. 2d 32, 169 Ill. Dec. 276, 591 N.E.2d 449 (1992).

§503   Statutory Privilege

§503.1   *Physician-Patient, Including Psychiatrist; Counselors*

The common law recognized no physician-patient privilege, with the possible exception of confidential communications to a psychotherapist. 47 Nw. U.L. Rev. 384 (1952). A statute, 735 ILCS 5/8-802, deals with the subject of physician-patient privilege:

> No physician or surgeon shall be permitted to disclose any information he or she may have acquired in attending any patient in a professional character, necessary to enable him or her professionally to serve the patient, except only (1) in trials for homicide when the disclosure relates directly to the fact or immediate circumstances of the homicide, (2) in actions, civil or criminal, against the physician for malpractice, (3) with the expressed consent of the patient, or in case of his or her death or disability, of his or her personal representative or other person authorized to sue for personal injury or of the beneficiary of an insurance policy on his or her life, health, or physical condition, (4) in all actions brought by or against the patient, his or her personal representative, a beneficiary under a policy of insurance, or the executor or administrator of his or her estate wherein the patient's physical or mental condition is an issue, (5) upon an issue as to the validity of a document as a will of the patient, (6) in any criminal action where the charge is either first degree murder by abortion, attempted abortion or abortion, (7) in actions, civil or criminal, arising from the filing of a report in compliance with the Abused and Neglected Child Reporting Act, (8) to any department, agency, institution or facility which has custody of the patient pursuant to State statute or any court order of commitment, (9) in prosecutions where written results of blood alcohol tests are admissible pursuant to Section 11-501.4 of the Illinois Vehicle Code or (10) in prosecutions where written results of blood alcohol tests are admissible under Section 5-11a of the Boat Registration and Safety Act.
>
> In the event of a conflict between the application of this Section and the Mental Health and Developmental Disabilities Confidentiality Act to a specific situation, the provisions of the Mental Health and Developmental Disabilities Confidentiality Act shall control.

The physician-patient privilege exists to encourage free disclosure between a doctor and a patient and to protect the patient from the embarrassment and invasion of privacy that arise from disclosure. *People v. Bates,* 169 Ill. App. 3d 218, 119 Ill. Dec. 919, 523 N.E.2d 675 (1988). The privilege applies not only to physicians and surgeons but also to nurses, hospital staff, and paramedics. *People v. Wilber,* 279 Ill. App. 3d 462, 216 Ill. Dec. 74, 664 N.E.2d 711 (1996). The physician-patient privilege does not apply to statements by the plaintiff made during an examination by a defense physician conducted pursuant to Supreme Court Rule 215(a), as the expectation of confidentiality is absent. *Salingue v. Overturf,* 269 Ill. App. 3d 1102, 207 Ill. Dec. 575, 647 N.E.2d 1068 (1995). Generally speaking in civil cases, and to a lesser extent in criminal cases, the exceptions enumerated leave little scope for the operation of the physician-patient privilege and render of slight practical importance such problems as when the relationship exists, the extent of matters within the privilege, and when and how the privilege is waived. As to whether the reference in §8-808(8) to custody applies to a person under arrest, *see People v. Maltibia,* 273 Ill. App. 3d 622, 210 Ill. Dec. 497, 653 N.E.2d 402 (1995).

When the patient's physical and mental condition is an issue, 5/8-802(4), disclosure must be had through formal discovery procedures; informal ex parte communications between the patient's physician and the patient's legal adversary are prohibited. *Petrillo v. Syntex Laboratories, Inc.,* 148 Ill. App. 3d 581, 102 Ill. Dec. 172, 499 N.E.2d 952 (1986); *Mondelli v. Checker Taxi Co.,* 197 Ill. App. 3d 258, 143 Ill. Dec. 331, 554 N.E.2d 266 (1990). All ex parte communications between defense counsel and a treating physician are prohibited, even if of a *de minimis* nature. *Burns v. Michelotti,* 237 Ill. App. 3d 923, 178 Ill. Dec. 621, 604 N.E.2d 1114 (1992). *Contra Mahan v. Louisville & Nashville R.R. Co.,* 203 Ill. App. 3d 748, 148 Ill. Dec. 821, 561 N.E.2d 127 (1990) (no violation if contact *de minimis*). Nevertheless the treating physician may be permitted to testify if the improper ex parte communication did not taint the treating physician's testimony. *Burns v. Michelotti* supra. Of course, if the trial court determines that the treating physician's testimony has been tainted then the treating physician will be barred from testifying. *Karsten v. McCray,* 157 Ill. App. 3d 1, 109 Ill. Dec. 364, 509 N.E.2d 1376 (1987); *Pourchot v. Commonwealth Edison Co.,* 224 Ill. App. 3d 634, 167 Ill. Dec. 320, 587 N.E.2d 589 (1992). The prohibition applies to ex parte communications not only to the patient's physician but also to other medical providers. *Lewis v. Illinois Central Railroad Co.,* 234 Ill. App. 3d 669, 175 Ill. Dec. 573, 600 N.E.2d 504 (1992). A communication is not ex parte when the plaintiff's attorney is present during discussions between the defense attorney and patient's medical provider. *Glassman v. St. Joseph Hospital,* 259 Ill. App. 3d 730, 197 Ill. Dec. 727, 631 N.E.2d 1186 (1994). Written communication exchanged between defense counsel and plaintiff's medical provider is similarly prohibited unless first approved by plaintiff's attorney. *Glassman v. St. Joseph Hospital* supra; *Natasi v. United Mine Workers of America Union Hospital,* 209 Ill. App. 3d 830, 153 Ill. Dec. 900, 567 N.E.2d 1358 (1991).

Where the liability of the defendant is vicarious, such as when the physician is employed by a defendant hospital, there is disagreement as to whether discovery is limited to formal discovery. *Compare Almgren v. Rush-Presbyterian-St. Luke's Medical Center,* 240 Ill. App. 3d 585, 181 Ill. Dec. 19, 608 N.E.2d 92 (1992) (all communications between doctor and defendant hospital are subject to court supervision), with *Ritter v. Rush-Presbyterian-St. Luke's Medical Center,* 177 Ill. App. 3d 313, 126 Ill. Dec. 642, 532 N.E.2d 327 (1988) (prevention of informal communications between doctor and defendant hospital would effectively prevent hospital from defending itself). *See also Testin v. Dreyer Medical Clinic,* 238 Ill. App. 3d 883, 179 Ill. Dec. 56, 605 N.E.2d 1070 (1992), plaintiff, by agreeing that defendant may confer with physicians alleged by plaintiff to have been negligent, for whom defendant is vicariously liable, does not hereby waive his physician-patient privilege as to other physicians for whom the defendant is vicariously liable who are not alleged by plaintiff to be negligent. A treating physician may consult his own attorney prior to being made a defendant and disclose otherwise confidential physician-patient matters, provided that to insure that the disclosures are not shared the attorney consulted does not represent another defendant sued by the plaintiff arising from the same incident. *Baylaender v. Method,* 230 Ill. App. 3d 610, 171 Ill. Dec. 797, 594 N.E.2d 1317 (1992).

In prosecutions where the written results of blood-alcohol tests are sought pursuant to 625 ILCS 5/11–501.4, disclosure must be conducted through the use of a subpoena *duces tecum* commanding that the records be delivered to the court for in camera inspection to determine admissibility. *See People ex rel. Fisher v. Cary,* 77 Ill. 2d 259, 32 Ill. Dec. 904, 396 N.E.2d 17 (1979). 735 ILCS 5/8–802(9) provides an exception in such cases for admissibility of the written results of the blood-alcohol test as well as the observations of the physician or other medical personnel and any information obtained from the defendant. *People v. Wilber,* 279 Ill. App. 3d 462, 216 Ill. Dec. 74, 664 N.E.2d 711 (1996). Statements made to physicians or other medical personnel including paramedics are also made admissible in criminal cases involving the use of alcohol by 735 ILCS 5/8–802(4) providing an exception applicable in criminal and civil cases wherein the patient's physical or mental condition is an issue. *People v. Wilber id.; People v. Krause,* 273 Ill. App. 3d 59, 209 Ill. Dec. 566, 651 N.E.2d 744 (1995).

No physician-patient privilege is created as a result of an examination by a physician, employed by an opponent, solely for the purpose of rendering a medical-legal opinion. *Moore v. Centreville Township Hospital,* 246 Ill. App. 3d 579, 186 Ill. Dec. 689, 616 N.E.2d 1321 (1993).

The privilege between psychiatrist and patient is now governed by 5/8-802 supra, to the extent not in conflict with the Mental Health and Developmental Disabilities Confidentiality Act, 740 ILCS 110/1-110/17. *See generally House v. SwedishAmerican Hosp.,* 206 Ill. App. 3d 437, 151 Ill. Dec. 467, 564 N.E.2d 922 (1990). The previous statute specifically governing the psychiatrist-patient privilege, Ill. R.S. 1979, c.51, §5.2, has now been repealed, P.A. 80-1508. 740 ILCS 110/10 states in pertinent part:

> (a) Except as provided herein, in any civil, criminal, administrative, or legislative proceeding, or in any proceeding preliminary thereto, a recipient, and a therapist on behalf and in the interest of a recipient, has the privilege to refuse to disclose and to prevent the disclosure of the recipient's record or communications.
>
> (1) Records and communications may be disclosed in a civil, criminal or administrative proceeding in which the recipient introduces his mental condition or any aspect of his services received for such condition as an element of his claim or defense, if and only to the extent the court in which the proceedings have been brought, or, in the case of an administrative proceeding, the court to which an appeal or other action for review of an administrative determination may be taken, finds, after in camera examination of testimony or other evidence, that it is relevant, probative, not unduly prejudicial or inflammatory, and otherwise clearly admissible; that other satisfactory evidence is demonstrably unsatisfactory as evidence of the facts sought to be established by such evidence; and that disclosure is more important to the interests of substantial justice than protection from injury to the therapist-recipient relationship or to the recipient or other whom disclosure is likely to harm. . . .

With respect to the privilege under the Mental Health and Developmental Disabilities Confidentiality Act supra being waived by the holder introducing his or her mental condition as an element in the case, *see Goldberg v. Davis,* 151 Ill. 2d 267, 176 Ill. Dec. 866, 602 N.E.2d 812 (1992), or in the interests of substantial justice, *D.C. v. S.A.,* 178 Ill. 2d 551, 227 Ill. Dec. 550, 687 N.E.2d 1032 (1997). Mental health services covered by the foregoing statute do not extend to alcohol treatment. *People v. Leggans,* 253 Ill. App. 3d 724, 193 Ill. Dec. 12, 625 N.E.2d 1133 (1993).

For an interesting discussion as to when a plaintiff who seeks personal injury damages introduces his or her mental condition as an element in the case, *see D.C. v. S.A.* 283 Ill. App. 3d 693, 219 Ill. Dec. 248, 670 N.E.2d 1136 (1996); *Maxwell v. Hobart Corp.,* 216 Ill. App. 3d 108, 159 Ill. Dec. 599, 576 N.E.2d 268 (1991).

The statutory privileges for communications made to physicians and psychiatrists by a witness must give way in a criminal prosecution to the defendant's rights of confrontation and due process. When a physician-patient or psychiatrist-patient privilege is asserted with respect to communications made by a witness called by the prosecution, the court must hold an *in-camera* hearing with the attorneys for both sides to determine, in light of the nature of the prosecution, those communications to be disclosed. *People v. Monk,* 174 Ill. App. 3d 528, 124 Ill. Dec. 172, 528 N.E.2d 1063 (1988); *People v. Votava,* 223 Ill. App. 3d 58, 165 Ill. Dec. 546, 584 N.E.2d 980 (1991); *People v. McMillan,* 239 Ill. App. 3d 467, 180 Ill. Dec. 516, 607 N.E.2d 585 (1993). Neither the name nor address of the patient is confidential information protected by the privilege. *Geisberger v. Willuhn,* 72 Ill. App. 3d 435, 28 Ill. Dec. 586, 390 N.E.2d 945 (1979).

With respect to a defendant who raises an insanity defense, the privilege is waived as to the testimony and reports of those experts identified by the defense as witnesses who will be called by the defense to testify on behalf of the defendant at trial, as well as to the notes and reports of other experts used by defense experts who will testify. *People v. Knuckles,* 165 Ill. 2d 125, 209 Ill. Dec. 1, 650 N.E.2d 974 (1995). The waiver of the privilege at one proceeding operates as a waiver of the privilege with respect to the same testimony at subsequent proceedings. *Novak v. Rathnam* supra; *People v. Phillips,* 128 Ill. App. 3d 457, 83 Ill. Dec. 717, 470 N.E.2d 1137 (1984). It has also been held that the criminal defendant does not have a privilege with respect to statements made to a psychiatrist appointed in anticipation of a possible insanity defense. *People v. English,* 31 Ill. 2d 301, 201 N.E.2d 455 (1964); *People v. Primmer,* 111 Ill. App. 3d 1046, 67 Ill. Dec. 593, 444 N.E.2d 829 (1983). A privilege does exist with respect to statements made by the defendant to a psychiatrist appointed under 725 ILCS 5/104-14 to determine competency to stand trial. *See also* §502.3 supra, for discussion of privilege against self-incrimination as applied to statements made to psychiatrists. As to court appointment of a psychiatrist, *see* §706.1 infra. As provided in 5/8-802(1), in trials for homicide there is no physician-patient privilege when the disclosure relates directly to the fact or immediate circumstances of the homicide. *People v. Bates,* 169 Ill. App. 3d 218, 119 Ill. Dec. 919, 523 N.E.2d 675 (1988), results of blood alcohol test not privileged in prosecution for reckless homicide.

The physician-patient privilege may be asserted in certain instances by a hospital to protect the records of its patients. *Parkson v. Central Du Page Hosp.,* 105 Ill. App. 3d 850, 61 Ill. Dec. 651, 435 N.E.2d 140 (1982). For example, a hospital may assert the physician-patient privilege of its patients with respect to medical records of nonparty patients sought in a civil malpractice action. *House v. Swedish American Hosp.,* 206 Ill. App. 3d 437, 151 Ill. Dec. 467, 564 N.E.2d 922 (1990). The exception in 5/8-802(2) relates solely to the records of the patient who brings the malpractice action. Disclosure of records of nonparty patients in a malpractice action may not be compelled over the hospital's assertion of its patient's physician-patient privilege, even if the names and identifying numbers of the patients are excluded from the request for disclosure. *Ekstrom v. Temple,* 197 Ill. App. 3d 120, 142 Ill. Dec. 910, 553 N.E.2d 424 (1990); *Glassman v. St. Joseph Hospital,* 259 Ill. App. 3d 730, 197 Ill. Dec. 727, 631 N.E.2d 1186 (1994).

With respect to grand jury subpoenas of confidential medical records, the confidential records themselves may be obtained only if the patient consents, *People v. Bickham,* 89 Ill. 2d 1, 59 Ill. Dec. 80, 431 N.E.2d 365 (1982), while the names of the patients may be obtained even if the nature of the medical facility providing the names inevitably discloses the treatment received. *People v. Florendo,* 95 Ill. 2d 155, 69 Ill.

Dec. 65, 447 N.E.2d 282 (1983) (abortion clinic). However, in the investigation and trials of homicides the holder of the privilege is required to disclose the information. 735 ILCS 5/8-810(a)(9). *See also People v. Wilson,* 164 Ill. 2d 436, 207 Ill. Dec. 417, 647 N.E.2d 910 (1994).

Confidentiality of statements made to rape-crisis counselors, 735 ILCS 5/8-802.1, is discussed in §611.15 infra. In addition, 735 ILCS 5/8-802.2 provides the following confidential communications privilege for statements made to personnel counseling victims of violent crimes:

(a) Purpose. This Section is intended to protect victims of violent crimes from public disclosure of statements they make in confidence to counselors of organizations established to help them. Because of the fear and trauma that often result from violent crimes, many victims hesitate to seek help even where it is available and may therefore lack the psychological support necessary to report the crime and aid police in preventing future crimes.

(b) Definitions. As used in this Act, "violent crimes" include, but are not limited to, any felony in which force or threat of force was used against the victim or any misdemeanor which results in death or great bodily harm to the victim.

(c) Confidentiality. Where any victim of a violent crime makes a statement relating to the crime or its circumstances during the course of therapy or consultation to any counselor, employee or volunteer of a victim aid organization, the statement or contents thereof shall not be disclosed by the organization or any of its personnel unless the maker of the statement consents in writing or unless otherwise directed pursuant to this Section.

If in any judicial proceeding, a party alleges that such statements are necessary to the determination of any issue before the court and written consent to disclosure has not been given, the party may ask the court to consider the relevance and admissibility of the statements. In such a case, the court shall hold a hearing in camera on the relevance of the statements. If the court finds them relevant and admissible to the issue, the court shall order the statements to be disclosed.

§503.2   Communications to Clergy

The status of communications to clergy is governed by statute.

> A clergyman or practitioner of any religious denomination accredited by the religious body to which he or she belongs, shall not be compelled to disclose in any court, or to any administrative board or agency, or to any public officer, a confession or admission made to him or her in his or her professional character or as a spiritual advisor in the course of the discipline enjoined by the rules or practices of such religious body or of the religion he or she professes, nor be compelled to divulge any information which has been obtained by him or her in such professional character or as such spiritual advisor. [735 ILCS 5/8-803.]

The broad language of the statute indicates a purpose to include not only confessions made in pursuance of church doctrine, *Snyder v. Poplett,* 98 Ill. App. 3d 359, 53 Ill. Dec. 761, 424 N.E.2d 396 (1981); *People v. Byers,* 11 Ill. App. 3d 277, 296 N.E.2d 621 (1973); *People v. Pecora,* 107 Ill. App. 2d 283, 246 N.E.2d 865 (1970), but also disclosures made in the course of spiritual counseling of the kind now widely practiced by denominations not recognizing the confession as an article of religious faith. Thus, for example, a clergyman privilege exists with respect to statements relating to sexual abuse made to a person who is both a Lutheran pastor and a clinical psychologist; the fact that counseling incorporated both spiritual and psychological principles did not negate the existence of the privilege. *People v. Burnidge,* 279 Ill. App. 3d 127, 216 Ill. Dec. 19, 664 N.E.2d 656 (1996). The privilege belongs to both the person making the statement and to the clergyman. *People v. Burnidge id.; People v. Diercks,* 88 Ill. App. 3d 1073, 44 Ill. Dec. 191, 411 N.E.2d 97 (1980). *Cf.* Proposed Fed. R. Evid. 506(c), providing that the privilege belongs solely to the communicant. Statements not made to the clergyman or practitioner in the person's professional character or as a spiritual advisor do not fall within this privilege. *People v. McNeal,* 175 Ill. 2d 335, 222 Ill. Dec. 307, 677 N.E.2d 841 (1997).

§503.3   Husband and Wife

As pointed out in §601.6 infra, the common law incompetency of husband and wife was long ago abolished, leaving only a privilege against disclosure of confidential communications between them.

The privilege is embodied in the following language applicable to civil cases: "[N]either may testify to any communication or admission made by either of them to the other or as to any conversation between them during marriage," excepting in actions between them or involving custody or support, health or welfare of children and matters in which one acted as agent for the other. 735 ILCS 5/8-801. A similar provision applies to criminal cases, with appropriate exceptions where the interests of their child or children or of any child or children in either spouse's care, custody, or control are directly involved, for crimes by one spouse against the other, *People v. Mulinax*, 67 Ill. App. 3d 936, 24 Ill. Dec. 214, 384 N.E.2d 1372 (1979), in the case of wife abandonment, where either is charged with child sexual abuse, *People v. Burton*, 102 Ill. App. 3d 148, 57 Ill. Dec. 645, 429 N.E.2d 543 (1981), or as to matters in which either has acted as agent of the other. 725 ILCS 5/115-16. The interests of a child are directly involved, and accordingly the communications are not privileged, in a prosecution for murder of an infant child in spite of the fact that the child is dead. *People v. Eveans*, 277 Ill. App. 3d 36, 214 Ill. Dec. 49, 660 N.E.2d 240 (1995). The exceptions do not extend to communications between the spouses during marriage when they are engaged in a joint criminal activity. *People v. Krankel*, 105 Ill. App. 3d 988, 61 Ill. Dec. 565, 434 N.E.2d 1162 (1982) (privilege applies.) However, if a spouse acts as an agent for the other during the joint criminal activity, i.e., as one entrusted with another's business, the "agent" exception of 725 ILCS 5/115-16 applies. *People v. Saunders*, 288 Ill. App. 3d 523, 223 Ill. Dec. 840, 680 N.E.2d 790 (1997). The privilege must give way to the defendant's constitutional right to confront witnesses against her. *People v. Foskey*, 136 Ill. 2d 66, 143 Ill. Dec. 257, 554 N.E.2d 192 (1990), privilege does not apply to letters written by defendant's wife to defendant while he was in jail in which defendant's wife admitted fabricating the entire case against him.

The marital privilege includes both oral and written conversations from one spouse to another that are intended to be a confidential communication. *People v. Foskey* supra. Nonverbal conduct is not included within the term *communication* unless the conduct is an expression clearly intended as a substitute for the spoken word. *People v. Simpson,* 39 Ill. App. 3d 661, 350 N.E.2d 517 (1976), *rev'd on other grounds,* 68 Ill. 2d 276, 12 Ill. 2d 234, 369 N.E.2d 1248 (1977), wife permitted to testify to observing husband come to a trailer about 5 a.m. with blood-stained clothing and with purse belonging to victim; *People v. Krankel,* 105 Ill. App. 3d 988, 61 Ill. Dec. 565, 434 N.E.2d 1162 (1982), wife permitted to testify that she observed her husband taking the grandmother's silverware; *People v. Krankel,* 131 Ill. App. 3d 887, 87 Ill. Dec. 75, 476 N.E.2d 777 (1985), defendant's actions in entering and leaving the victim's home, then pulling the wallet out of hiding, were not clear substitutes for speech and thus properly testified to by defendant's wife. *Accord People v. Rettig,* 88 Ill. App. 3d 888, 44 Ill. Dec. 7, 410 N.E.2d 1099 (1980); *People v. Murphy,* 241 Ill. App. 3d 918, 182 Ill. Dec. 221, 609 N.E.2d 755 (1992).

While neither statute employs the term *confidential* in describing communications that are privileged, *People v. Palumbo,* 5 Ill. 2d 409, 125 N.E.2d 518 (1955), construed the criminal statute as applying only to confidential communications and held that the wife of the accused could testify over objection to a conversation when confidentiality was destroyed by the presence of a third person; *People v. Sanders,* 99 Ill. 2d 262, 75 Ill. Dec. 682, 457 N.E.2d 1241 (1983), presence of child old enough to understand destroys confidentiality — a parent-child privilege is not recognized in Illinois; *People v. McNanna,* 94 Ill. App. 2d 314, 236 N.E.2d 767 (1968), statement in public tavern in presence of wife's sister not within privilege as not intended to be confidential. Statements made between husband and wife that are intended to be communicated to a third party are not confidential and therefore are not privileged. *People v. Layne,* 286 Ill. App. 3d 981, 222 Ill. Dec. 266, 677 N.E.2d 469 (1997). The party offering the statement has the burden of establishing that the statement was not confidential. *People v. Sanders* supra.

The confidential communications privilege during marriage extends to communications of parties who are separated but does not attach to communications between spouses after divorce. *People v. Dubanowski,* 75 Ill. App. 3d 809, 31 Ill. Dec. 403, 394 N.E.2d 605 (1979).

While the statutes fail to designate the person by whom the privilege may be asserted, the privilege has been held to belong only to the communicating spouse. *People v. Simpson* supra. Thus disclosure by the spouse receiving the communication does not waive the privilege. *People v. Gardner,* 105 Ill. App. 3d 103, 60 Ill. Dec. 951, 433 N.E.2d 1318 (1982). The statutes apply only to testimony by the other spouse, *Gannon v. People,* 127 Ill. 507, 21 N.E. 525 (1889); the testimony of an ordinary eavesdropper remains admissible as was generally the rule at common law. McCormick, Evidence §§74, 82 (4th ed. 1992). Thus, if a third person learns of the contents of one spouse's confidential letter to the other spouse by interception, through loss, or by misdelivery, that person may testify as to the letter's contents. *People v. Gardner,* 105 Ill. App. 3d 103, 60 Ill. Dec. 951, 433 N.E.2d 1318 (1982). For further discussion *see* §506.2 infra. As to electronic eavesdropping, however, *see* §503.8 infra.

Confidential statements between parents and children are *not* privileged. *People v. Sanders,* 99 Ill. 2d 262, 75 Ill. Dec. 682, 457 N.E.2d 1241 (1983).

§503.4 *Public Accountants*

"A public accountant shall not be required by any court to divulge information or evidence which has been obtained by him in his confidential capacity as a public accountant." 225 ILCS 450/27.

By analogy to other privileges for confidential communications, the client rather than the accountant should be regarded as the holder of the privilege. *See also* §505.6 infra. Nevertheless the language of the statute itself supports the contrary conclusion that the privilege inures to and can be claimed only by the accountant. *In re October 1985 Grand Jury No. 746,* 154 Ill. App. 3d 288, 107 Ill. Dec. 342, 507 N.E.2d 6 (1987). The privilege only protects information received by the accountant from the client in confidence. *In re October 1985 Grand Jury No. 746, id.* As to the scope of the concept of confidential communication, *see* §505.5 infra. Since a tax client provides information to his accountant with the understanding that it might be disclosed to a third party, a client's tax returns and the accountant's work papers used to prepare the return are not confidential and are thus not protected by the public accountant privilege. *In re October 1985 Grand Jury No. 746,* 124 Ill. 2d 466, 125 Ill. Dec. 295, 530 N.E.2d 453 (1988).

§503.5   Reporters

A court may not compel a person to disclose the source of any information obtained by a reporter during the course of her employment, unless upon having due regard to the nature of the proceedings, the merits of the claim or defense, the adequacy of the remedy otherwise available (if any), the relevancy of the source, and the possibility of establishing by other means that which it is alleged the source requested will tend to prove, the court finds (a) that the information sought does not concern matters or details in any proceeding required to be kept secret under the laws of Illinois or of the federal government; and (b) that all other available sources of information have been exhausted and disclosure of the information sought is essential to the protection of the public interest involved or, in libel or slander cases, the plaintiff's need for disclosure of the information sought outweighs the public interest in protecting the confidentiality of sources of information used by a reporter as part of the news-gathering process under the particular facts and circumstances of each particular case. 735 ILCS 5/8-901 to 5/8-909. *See generally In re Subpoena Duces Tecum v. Arya*, 226 Ill. App. 3d 848, 168 Ill. Dec. 432, 589 N.E.2d 832 (1992). For a discussion of the concept of exhaustion of all available sources, *see In re Special Grand Jury Investigation*, 104 Ill. 2d 419, 84 Ill. Dec. 490, 472 N.E.2d 450 (1984).

As to the special showing that must be made prior to a reporter being required to testify in a given matter as to information obtained as a reporter, not involving the disclosure of sources, *see People v. Palacio*, 240 Ill. App. 3d 1078, 180 Ill. Dec. 862, 607 N.E.2d 1375 (1993) (testimony sought must be specifically stated; a showing of necessity to the party's case made; and a showing made that no alternative source of the evidence exists).

§503.6 Testimony That Is Broadcast or Televised, or of Which Motion Pictures Are Taken

"No witness shall be compelled to testify in any proceeding conducted by a court, commission, administrative agency or other tribunal in this State if any portion of his or her testimony is to be broadcast or televised or if motion pictures are to be taken of him or her while he or she is testifying." 735 ILCS 5/8-701. Nothing in this statute protects a witness from being compelled to have his deposition audio-visually recorded for playback at trial.

§503.7 Compulsory Reports; Public Records; Research Data

Statutes governing various types of reports often contain provisions restricting their admissibility in evidence, as a matter of policy and in some instances to forestall attack on grounds of violating the privilege against self-incrimination.

People ex rel. Director of Pub. Health v. Calvo, 89 Ill. 2d 130, 59 Ill. Dec. 639, 432 N.E.2d 223 (1982).

The most commonly encountered of those reports are those involving motor vehicle accidents, required to be made to the Administrator of the Department of Law Enforcement, 625 ILCS 5/11-406, and under some circumstances to the police or sheriff, *id.,* 5/11-401(b). These reports are confidential except as to the identity of the person involved and as a basis for certification whether a report was filed. *Id.,* 5/11-412; *People v. Young,* 92 Ill. 2d 236, 65 Ill. Dec. 506, 441 N.E.2d 641 (1982). Cities may by ordinance require the filing of a copy of the report with a municipal department, subject to the same provisions against disclosure. *Id.,* 5/11-415. Statements made to an investigating officer are not privileged under the statute, *Ritter v. Nieman,* 329 Ill. App. 163, 67 N.E.2d 417 (1946), and the statute does not in terms apply to reports made by police officers. *Cf.* the provisions of the Unemployment Compensation Act rendering information obtained by the director confidential, 820 ILCS 405/1900, thus foreclosing testimony by an employee of the department that plaintiff in a personal injury action had stated he was able to work, *Smith v. Illinois Valley Ice Cream Co.,* 20 Ill. App. 2d 312, 156 N.E.2d 361 (1959). *See also Harvard v. Forbes,* 185 Ill. App. 3d 848, 133 Ill. Dec. 474, 541 N.E.2d 685 (1989), the Unemployment Compensation Act privilege is solely for the benefit of the claimant.

All information, except the original medical records pertaining to a patient, used by a committee of an accredited hospital, amongst others, in the course of internal quality control or of medical study for the purpose of reducing morbidity or mortality, or for improving patient care, is strictly confidential, not discoverable, and inadmissible in any court, except in connection with proceedings to decide a physician's services or staff privileges; it shall be used only for medical research and the evaluation and improvement of medical care. 735 ILCS 5/8-2101 to 5/8-2105. *See generally Jenkins v. Wu,* 102 Ill. 2d 468, 82 Ill. Dec. 382 468 N.E.2d 1162 (1984). The privilege encompasses voluntary experimental medical research studies. *Doe v. Illinois Masonic Medical Center,* 297 Ill.

App. 3d 240, 231 Ill. Dec. 411, 696 N.E.2d 707 (1998). Documents such as applications for staff privileges and educational transcripts are generated prior to the peer review process and are therefore not privileged. Nor does the privilege apply to actions taken as a result of the peer review process. *Richter v. Diamond,* 108 Ill. 2d 265, 91 Ill. Dec. 621, 483 N.E.2d 1256 (1985). The party asserting the privilege has the burden of establishing its applicability. *Dunkin v. Silver Cross Hosp.,* 215 Ill. App. 3d 65, 158 Ill. Dec. 35, 573 N.E.2d 848 (1991). Disclosure of any privileged information or data, whether proper or improper, does not waive or have any effect upon the confidentiality, nondiscoverability or nonadmissibility of that information or data. 735 ILCS 5/8-2102. *See generally Sakosko v. Memorial Hosp.,* 167 Ill. App. 3d 842, 118 Ill. Dec. 818, 522 N.E.2d 273 (1988); *Zajac v. St. Mary of Nazareth Hosp.,* 212 Ill. App. 3d 779, 156 Ill. Dec. 860, 571 N.E.2d 840 (1991). With respect to the scope and operation of the peer-review privilege, *see Willing v. St. Joseph Hosp.,* 176 Ill. App. 3d 737, 126 Ill. Dec. 197, 531 N.E.2d 824 (1988); *Menoski v. Shih,* 242 Ill. App. 3d 117, 183 Ill. Dec. 907, 612 N.E.2d 834 (1993); *Toth v. Jensen,* 272 Ill. App. 3d 382, 208 Ill. Dec. 428, 649 N.E.2d 484 (1995).

The particular statutes should be consulted. With respect to the application of privileges associated with the federal Freedom of Information Act, *see Marshall v. Elward,* 78 Ill. 2d 366, 35 Ill. Dec. 801, 399 N.E.2d 1329 (1980).

Illinois does *not* recognize a deliberative process governmental privilege. *People ex rel. Birkett v. City of Chicago,* 292 Ill. App. 3d 745, 226 Ill. Dec. 717, 686 N.E.2d 66 (1997).

§503.8 Wiretapping and Eavesdropping

By statute in Illinois the use of an eavesdropping device to hear or record an oral conversation unless the person does so "(1) with the consent of all of the parties to such conversation or (2) in accordance with Article 108A or 108B," or the use or divulgence of information gained thereby, is a criminal offense. An eavesdropping device is any device capable of being used to hear or record oral conversation, whether conducted in person, by telephone, or by other means. Evidence obtained in violation is inadmissible. Hearing aids, public broadcasts, necessary listening-in by telephone company employees without divulgence, and emergency communications are among the exemptions. 720 ILCS 5/14-1 to 5/14-9. The statute permits evidence to be introduced against a person, even if she has not consented to the eavesdropping, provided the eavesdropping was at the request of a state's attorney. 725 ILCS 5/108A-1 to 5/108A-11 and 5/108B-1 to 5/108B-14. *See also People v. Herrington,* 252 Ill. App. 3d 63, 191 Ill. Dec. 170, 623 N.E.2d 760 (1993); *People v. Henderson,* 129 Ill. App. 3d 611, 84 Ill. Dec. 751, 472 N.E.2d 1147 (1984); *People v. O'Dell,* 84 Ill. App. 3d 359, 39 Ill. Dec. 830, 405 N.E.2d 809 (1980); *People v. Knight,* 28 Ill. App. 3d 232, 327 N.E.2d 518 (1975).

The constitutionality of the eavesdropping statute was upheld against an attack by a nonconsenting party to the conversation on the grounds of unlawful search and seizure in *People v. Richardson,* 60 Ill. 2d 189, 328 N.E.2d 260 (1975).

§503.9   Social Worker

A social worker has a privilege to refuse to disclose any information:

acquired from persons consulting the social worker in a professional capacity, except that which may be voluntarily disclosed under the following circumstances:
  (a) In the course of formally reporting, conferring or consulting with administrative superiors, colleagues or consultants who share professional responsibility, in which instance all recipients of such information are similarly bound to regard the communication as privileged;
  (b) With the written consent of the person who provided the information;
  (c) In case of death or disability, with the written consent of a personal representative, other person authorized to sue,

or the beneficiary of an insurance policy on the person's life, health or physical condition;

(d) When a communication reveals the intended commission of a crime or harmful act and such disclosure is judged necessary by the licensed clinical social worker or licensed social worker to protect any person from a clear, imminent risk of serious mental or physical harm or injury, or to forestall a serious threat to the public safety; or

(e) When the person waives the privilege by bringing any public charges against the licensee.

225 ILCS 20/16. The privilege is also inapplicable if abused or neglected children are involved. Abused and Neglected Child Reporting Act, 325 ILCS 5/4. *See People v. Morton,* 188 Ill. App. 3d 95, 135 Ill. Dec. 619, 543 N.E.2d 1366 (1989). The privilege is limited to social workers who are registered under the Clinical Social Work and Social Work Practice Act, 225 ILCS 20/1 *et seq.* The burden rests upon the person asserting the privilege to establish the privilege, including compliance with the registration requirements. *In Interest of Westland,* 48 Ill. App. 3d 172, 6 Ill. Dec. 331, 362 N.E.2d 1153 (1977).

§504   Court Rule

§504.1   *Privilege Against Discovery; Preparation for Trial*

Supreme Court Rule 201(b)(2) recognizes that the usual privileges, such as attorney-client, husband-wife, and the like may be invoked against disclosure through discovery proceedings.

In addition, the rule recognizes a privilege as to certain matters in preparation for trial: "Material prepared by or for a party in preparation for trial is subject to discovery only if it does not contain or disclose the theories, mental impressions, or litigation plans of the party's attorney." *Id.*

The popular term *work product* is unduly optimistic as a description of matters included within the preparation privilege, as the privilege is in fact limited narrowly in order to effectuate the purposes of discovery. Operation of the "work product" privilege was outlined in *Monier v. Chamberlain,* 35 Ill. 2d 351, 221 N.E.2d 410 (1966). Memoranda made by counsel of his impression of a prospective witness as distinguished from verbatim statements of such witness, trial briefs, documents revealing a particular marshalling of the evidentiary facts for presentment at the trial, and similar material that reveals the attorney's "mental processes" in shaping his theory of his client's cause, are "privileged against disclosure" under Rule 201(b)(2). Material within this scope of the "work product" privilege as thus narrowly defined was once thought exempt from discovery. However, this absolute bar to discovery of memoranda of counsel based on interviews of a witness and revealing, as well, the impressions of counsel was lowered in *Consolidated Coal Co. v. Bucyrus-Erie Co.,* 89 Ill. 2d 103, 59 Ill. Dec. 666, 432 N.E.2d 250 (1982). Factual material contained in attorney notes and memoranda also revealing the attorney's impressions are discoverable if, but only if, the party seeking disclosure conclusively demonstrates the absolute impossibility of securing similar information from other sources. Other material, not disclosing such "mental processes" but containing relevant and material evidentiary details, must, under the discovery rules, remain subject to the truth-seeking process thereof and are discoverable under the circumstances spelled out in the rules. *See generally Waste Management, Inc. v. International Surplus Lines Ins. Co.,* 144 Ill. 2d 178, 161 Ill. Dec. 774, 579 N.E.2d 322 (1991).

Reports of expert witnesses are discoverable as statements by third parties who have knowledge of the facts involved in the controversy. *Department of Transp. v. Western Natl. Bank of Cicero,* 63 Ill. 2d 179, 347 N.E.2d 161 (1976).

Rule 201(b)(2) in terms recognizes the preparation privilege as applicable only to discovery and is silent as to its applicability upon trial. Some decisions hold that the privilege may be invoked at the trial. *Chicago v. Harrison-Halsted Bldg. Corp.*, 11 Ill. 2d 431, 143 N.E.2d 40 (1957); *Walker v. Struthers*, 273 Ill. 387, 112 N.E. 961 (1916); *Eizerman v. Behn*, 9 Ill. App. 263, 132 N.E.2d 788 (1956). *Contra Haskell v. Seigmund*, 28 Ill. App. 2d 1, 170 N.E.2d 393 (1960). *See also Kemeny v. Skorch*, 22 Ill. App. 2d 160, 159 N.E.2d 489 (1959). Since the purpose of the privilege is to afford conditions conducive to adequate legal advice and representation by insuring privacy, extending the privilege to disclosure upon trial appears more consistent with its purpose. *See* Cleary, *Hickman v. Jencks*, Jurisprudence in the Adversary System, 14 Vand. L. Rev. 865 (1961). *See also United States v. Nobles*, 422 U.S. 225 (1975), enunciating a qualified testimonial privilege in a federal criminal trial.

§505 Common Law Privilege

§505.1 Lawyer-Client; An Overview

The Illinois decisions accord full recognition to the common law privilege against disclosure of confidential communications between lawyer and client.

> It is essential to the ends of justice that clients should be safe in confiding to their counsel the most secret facts, and to receive advice in the light thereof, without peril of publicity. Disclosures made to this end should be as secret and inviolable as if the facts had remained in the knowledge of the client alone. [*Dickerson v. Dickerson*, 322 Ill. 492, 500, 153 N.E. 740 (1926).]

The privilege finds its justification in benefit conferred to the process of administration of justice; clients are to be encouraged to make full disclosure to their lawyers so that lawyers may advise and represent the clients as effectively as possible. *In re Marriage of Decker*, 153 Ill. 2d 298, 180 Ill. Dec.

17, 606 N.E.2d 1094 (1992). The essential elements relating to the lawyer-client privilege were stated in *People v. Adam,* 51 Ill. 2d 46, 48, 280 N.E.2d 205 (1972), to be as follows:

> (1) Where legal advice of any kind is sought (2) from a professional legal adviser in his capacity as such, (3) the communications relating to that purpose, (4) made in confidence (5) by the client, (6) are at his instance permanently protected (7) from disclosure by himself or by the legal adviser, (8) except the protection be waived. [Quoting from 8 Wigmore, Evidence §2292 (McNaughton rev. 1961).]

Accord People v. Williams, 97 Ill. 2d 252, 73 Ill. Dec. 360, 454 N.E.2d 220 (1983); *People v. Brown,* 275 Ill. App. 3d 1105, 212 Ill. Dec. 441, 657 N.E.2d 642 (1995).

The party asserting the privilege of lawyer-client has the burden of establishing that the communication was protected. *Cox v. Yellow Cab Co.,* 61 Ill. 2d 416, 337 N.E.2d 15 (1975); *Shere v. Marshall Field & Co.,* 26 Ill. App. 3d 728, 327 N.E.2d 92 (1975). *See* §104.1 supra. The presence of a lawyer-client relationship in which a client has communicated to the lawyer in a professional capacity is a sufficient showing unless the opposing party challenges the existence of the lawyer-client privilege in which event the proponent of the privilege must then prove the existence of the essential elements giving use to the privilege. *In re Marriage of Decker,* 153 Ill. 2d 298, 180 Ill. Dec. 17, 606 N.E.2d 1094 (1992).

§505.2   *Lawyer-Client; Existence of Relationship*

In order to be privileged, the communication must be made with a view to the relationship of lawyer and client. A mere casual friendly communication made to a lawyer, without contemplation of legal advice or representation, does not create the relationship. *Goltra v. Wolcott,* 14 Ill. 89 (1852). The relationship does not exist between the state's attorney and a person consulting him about an alleged crime committed against the person. *Granger v. Warrington,* 3 Gilm. 299 (1846). *See* §§505.9 to 505.10 infra, as to the privilege against disclosure of identity of an informer. What is required is a confidential communication, that is, one not intended to be disclosed to a third party other than in the process of rendition of legal services, made for the purpose of facilitating the rendition of professional legal services.

Disclosures made during negotiations for retaining an attorney are within the privilege although no employment of the attorney results. *Thorp v. Goewey,* 85 Ill. 611 (1877). The privilege should extend not only to lawyers but also to confidential communications with persons reasonably believed by the client to be authorized to practice law in any state or nation. *See* Proposed Federal Rule of Evidence 503(a)(2), 56 F.R.D. 183, 235 (1973). *Accord Powell v. Western Ill. Electric Co-op.,* 180 Ill. App. 3d 581, 129 Ill. Dec. 547, 563 N.E.2d 231 (1989) (lawyer licensed in Iowa).

The confidential communication may be made (1) between the client or her representative and her lawyer or her lawyer's representative, or (2) between her lawyer and the lawyer's representative, or (3) by the client or her lawyer to a lawyer representing another in a matter of common interest, or (4) between representatives of the client or between the client and a representative of the client, or (5) between lawyers representing the client. *See* McCormick, Evidence §91 (3d ed. 1984). A representative of a lawyer includes associates, paralegals, secretaries, file clerks, etc., as well as the lawyer's investigator, *People v. Knippenberg,* 66 Ill. 2d 276, 6 Ill. Dec. 46, 362 N.E.2d 681 (1977); *People v. Shiflet,* 125 Ill. App. 3d 161, 80 Ill. Dec. 596, 465 N.E.2d 942 (1984), an investigator employed by an insured's own insurance company obligated to defend, *People v. Ryan,* 30 Ill. 2d 456, 197 N.E.2d 15 (1964), and an independent investigator engaged by an insurance company to investigate an accident, *Lower v. Rucker,* 217 Ill. App. 3d 1, 159 Ill. Dec. 753, 576 N.E.2d 422 (1991), *contra Shere v. Marshall Field & Co.,* 26 Ill. App. 3d 728, 327 N.E.2d 92 (1975), but does not include a police officer's report, *People v. Wolff,* 19 Ill. 2d 318, 167 N.E.2d 197 (1960), or a report prepared by a private security police force hired by a corporation. *People v. Jenkins,* 18 Ill. App. 3d 52, 309 N.E.2d 397 (1974). A representative of a lawyer also includes a psychiatrist engaged by the defense necessary for the preparation of an insanity defense. *People v. Knuckles,* 165 Ill. 2d 125, 209 Ill. Dec. 1, 650 N.E.2d 974 (1995). Representatives of a lawyer should also include an expert hired to assist in the planning and conduct of a litigation but not one hired to testify at trial. *See* Federal Advisory Committee Note to Proposed Federal Rule of Evidence 503(a)(3), 56 F.R.D 183, 238 (1973). It also extends to law students authorized to appear in court for limited purposes under Illinois Supreme Court Rule 711. *People v. Williams,* 97 Ill. 2d 252, 73 Ill. Dec. 360, 454 N.E.2d 220 (1983).

The lawyer-client privilege applies not only to confidential communications from the client or her representative to the lawyer or her lawyer's representative, the lawyer-client privilege applies to confidential communications, including legal advice, from the lawyer or lawyer's representative to the client or her representative as well. *Midwesco-Paschen Joint Venture v. Imo Industries,* 265 Ill. App. 3d 654, 202 Ill. Dec. 676, 638 N.E.2d 322 (1994); *In re Marriage of Granger,* 197 Ill. App. 3d 363, 143 Ill. Dec. 651, 554 N.E.2d 586 (1990). *Contra Dalen v. Ozite Corp.,* 230 Ill. App. 3d 18, 171 Ill. Dec. 845, 594 N.E.2d 1365 (1992) (incorrectly decided).

§505.3   Lawyer-Client; Representatives of the Organization Client

For purposes of the lawyer-client privilege a client is defined as a person, public officer, or corporation, association, or other organization or entity, either public or private, who is rendered professional legal services by a lawyer, or who consults a lawyer with a view to obtaining professional legal services from him. Thus governmental units, *In re Sanitary Dist. Atty.,* 351 Ill. 206, 184 N.E. 332 (1933), and corporations possess a lawyer-client privilege.

An issue arises, however, as to who is a representative of a corporation, association, or other organization or entity whose communication is protected by the lawyer-client privilege. Illinois has adopted the "control group" test, thereby limiting the category of representatives with the lawyer-client privilege to those with authority to take part in the decision to seek and act upon legal advice for the client. *Day v. Illinois Power Co.,* 50 Ill. App. 2d 52, 199 N.E.2d 802 (1964), communications by employees who repair or replace ruptured gas lines not protected by privilege in that they had no authority to make any judgment or decision as to any action to be taken by the corporation on the advice of the attorney; *Shere v. Marshall Field & Co.,* 26 Ill. App. 3d 728, 327 N.E.2d 92 (1975), independent investigator not in control group; *Cox v. Yellow Cab Co.,* 16 Ill. App. 3d 665, 306 N.E.2d 738 (1974), taxi cab driver not within control group. *Cf. Upjohn Co. v. United States,* 449 U.S. 383 (1981), the control group test is inconsistent with the principles of the common law as interpreted in light of reason and experience, Fed. R. Evid. 501, in that it discourages the communication of relevant information by employees of the client to attorneys seeking to render legal advice to the client corporation. However, if the employee not within the control group is a defendant or may be herself charged with liability, statements of the employee to the organization's lawyers may be within the privilege, *Golminas v. Fred Tietelbaum Const. Co.,* 112 Ill. App. 2d 445, 251 N.E.2d 314 (1969), especially if the employee is not represented by her own counsel. Note should be taken of possible conflict of interest in the latter instance.

The concept of *control group* includes all persons in top management who have the ability to take part in the making of a final decision. In addition, the control group includes certain employees acting in an advisory capacity, *Consolidated Coal Co. v. Bucyrus-Erie Co.,* 89 Ill. 2d 103, 120, 59 Ill. Dec. 666, 432 N.E.2d 250 (1982):

We believe that an employee whose advisory role to top management in a particular area is such that a decision would not normally be made without his advice or opinion, and whose opinion in fact forms the basis of any final decision by those with actual authority, is properly within the control group. However, the individuals upon whom he may rely for supplying information are not members of the control group. Thus, if an employee of the status described is consulted for the purpose of determining what legal action the corporation will pursue, his communication is protected from disclosure. This approach, we think, better accommodates modern corporate realities and recognizes that decision making within a corporation is a process rather than a final act.

See also Archer Daniels Midland Co. v. Koppers Co., 138 Ill. App. 3d 276, 93 Ill. Dec. 91, 485 N.E.2d 1301 (1985); *Hyams v. Evanston Hospital*, 225 Ill. App. 3d 253, 167 Ill. Dec. 512, 587 N.E.2d 1127 (1992). Moreover, for the lawyer-client privilege to apply, the claimant must show that the communication originated in a confidence that it would not be disclosed, that it was made to a lawyer acting in his legal capacity for the purpose of securing legal advice or services, and that it remained confidential. *Consolidated Coal Co. v. Bucyrus-Erie Co.*, 89 Ill. 2d 103, 59 Ill. Dec. 666, 432 N.E.2d 250 (1982).

The burden of establishing facts showing that the person making the statement was within the control group and that the statement is otherwise privileged falls upon the proponent of the privilege. *Claxton v. Thackston*, 201 Ill. App. 3d 232, 147 Ill. Dec. 82, 559 N.E.2d 82 (1990); *Mlynarski v. Rush Presbyterian-St. Luke's Medical Center*, 213 Ill. App. 3d 427, 157 Ill. Dec. 561, 572 N.E.2d 1025 (1991). This determination is reviewed on appeal applying the *de novo* standard. *Midwesco-Paschen Joint Venture v. Imo Industries*, 265 Ill. App. 3d 654, 202 Ill. Dec. 676, 638 N.E.2d 322 (1994).

§505.4   Lawyer-Client; Matters Within Privilege

The communication, in order to fall within the privilege, must relate to matters actually or supposedly necessary for legal advice or representation. *People v. Marcofsky,* 219 Ill. App. 230 (1920), error to allow wife of accused, testifying for prosecution on charge of pandering, on cross-examination to claim privilege as to statement to lawyer representing her in divorce that she intended to initiate prosecution unless husband returned her earrings. Communications relating to legal advice or representation emanating from the lawyer fall within this privilege. *Newton v. Meissner,* 76 Ill. App. 3d 479, 31 Ill. Dec. 864, 394 N.E.2d 1241 (1979); *In re Marriage of Granger,* 197 Ill. App. 2d 363, 143 Ill. Dec. 651, 554 N.E.2d 586 (1990). *Contra Dalen v. Ozite Corp.,* 230 Ill. App. 3d 18, 171 Ill. Dec. 845, 594 N.E.2d 1365 (1992) (incorrectly decided). If the lawyer acts merely as a scrivener in preparing a deed or contract, with no legal advice asked or required, no privilege exists. *Debolt v. Blackburn,* 328 Ill. 420, 159 N.E. 790 (1928); *Dickerson v. Dickerson,* 322 Ill. 492, 153 N.E. 740 (1926). Purely business advice, when furnished by a lawyer, is not included within the privilege. *CNR Investments, Inc. v. Jefferson Trust & Sav. Bank,* 115 Ill. App. 3d 1071, 71 Ill. Dec. 612, 451 N.E.2d 580 (1983).

Information gained by the lawyer from sources other than the client is not within the privilege. *Chillicothe Ferry, Road & Bridge Co. v. Jameson,* 48 Ill. 281 (1868); *Swaim v. Humphreys,* 42 Ill. App. 370 (1891). The privilege has been held not to extend to letters written by an accused to other lawyers about other matters, the letters being offered by the prosecution as standards for handwriting comparison and not for their contents. *People v. Smith,* 318 Ill. 114, 149 N.E. 3 (1925). With respect to documents, if the document was subject to production in the hands of the client, it will remain subject to production when placed in the possession of the lawyer. *Johnson v. Frontier Ford, Inc.,* 68 Ill. App. 3d 315, 24 Ill. Dec. 908, 386 N.E.2d 112 (1979).

An accident report by an employee to an employer in a situation of a kind reasonably likely to result in litigation has been held to fall within the privilege, even though no litigation is actually pending and no attorney is yet engaged in the case. *Forslund v. Chicago Transit Auth.,* 9 Ill. App. 2d 290, 132

N.E.2d 801 (1956). However, mere routine reports are regarded as outside the privilege. *See Hruby v. Chicago Transit Auth.*, 11 Ill. 2d 255, 142 N.E.2d 81 (1957). Reports by an insured to his liability insurer fall within the privilege if the relationship contemplates retention of counsel and defense against claims, *People v. Ryan*, 30 Ill. 2d 456, 197 N.E.2d 15 (1964); *Chavez v. Watts*, 161 Ill. App. 3d 664, 113 Ill. Dec. 337, 515 N.E.2d 146 (1987); *Claxton v. Thackston*, 201 Ill. App. 3d 232, 147 Ill. Dec. 82, 559 N.E.2d 82 (1990); *Hyams v. Evanston Hospital*, 225 Ill. App. 3d 253, 167 Ill. Dec. 512, 587 N.E.2d 1127 (1992); *Rapps v. Keldermans*, 257 Ill. App. 3d 205, 195 Ill. Dec. 354, 628 N.E.2d 818 (1993), but not otherwise, *Boettcher v. Fournie Farms, Inc.*, 243 Ill. App. 3d 940, 184 Ill. Dec. 93, 612 N.E.2d 969 (1993), and the possibility exists that the insured might be made a defendant in a lawsuit arising from the incident, even though no lawsuit is then pending. *Exline v. Exline*, 277 Ill. App. 3d 10, 213 Ill. Dec. 491, 659 N.E.2d 407 (1995); *Lower v. Rucker*, 217 Ill. App. 3d 1, 159 Ill. Dec. 753, 576 N.E.2d 422 (1991).

The fact itself of consultation, *Hernandez v. Williams*, 258 Ill. App. 3d 318, 197 Ill. Dec. 980, 632 N.E.2d 49 (1994), or employment of the lawyer; the identity of the client, *People v. Doe*, 55 Ill. App. 3d 811, 13 Ill. Dec. 617, 371 N.E.2d 334 (1977), together with his address and occupation; the identity of the lawyer, *People v. Adam*, 51 Ill. 2d 46, 280 N.E.2d 205 (1972); the scope or object of the employment, and communications concerning logistical matters such as court dates, *People v. Brown*, 275 Ill. App. 3d 1105, 212 Ill. Dec. 441, 657 N.E.2d 642 (1995), are outside the scope of the privilege, except in the rare instances when application of the privilege is shown to be in the public interest, McCormick, Evidence §90 (4th ed. 1992), or will harm the client in some substantial way. *People v. Williams*, 97 Ill. 2d 252, 73 Ill. Dec. 360, 454 N.E.2d 220 (1983). *Accord Cesena v. DuPage County*, 201 Ill. App. 3d 96, 146 Ill. Dec. 1044, 558 N.E.2d 1378 (1990) (revealing client's name would cause the client to face potential criminal and civil liability). For example, where the address of the client is conveyed to a lawyer as a confidential communication, it need not be disclosed where the lawyer is not representing the client in a pending case. *Taylor v. Taylor*, 45 Ill. App. 3d 352, 3 Ill. Dec. 961, 359 N.E.2d 820 (1977), address of client protected from disclosure to ex-husband where conveyed in confidence to lawyer out of fear for client's safety. Similarly, disclosure of certain types of billing information containing explanation of legal fees may reveal the substance of confidential attorney-client discussions and thus fall within the attorney-client privilege. *People ex rel. Ulrich v. Stukel*, 294 Ill. App. 3d 193, 228 Ill. Dec. 447, 689 N.E.2d 319 (1997). With respect to fitness to stand trial, a lawyer may testify to her client's demeanor, but the lawyer may not base an assessment of the defendant's mental condition on privileged communications made by the client. *People v. Burgess*, 176 Ill. 2d 289, 223 Ill. Dec. 624, 680 N.E.2d 357 (1997).

§505.5 Lawyer-Client; Matters Intended to Be Disclosed, Presence of Other Persons

The protection extends only to confidential communications made to facilitate the rendition of professional legal services. *People v. Doe*, 59 Ill. App. 3d 627, 16 Ill. Dec. 868, 375 N.E.2d 975 (1978), suicide note left in open view in writer's room obviously not intended as confidential communication to an attorney. A communication is confidential if not intended to be disclosed to third persons other than those to whom disclosure is in furtherance of the rendition of professional legal services to the client or those reasonably necessary for the transmission of the communication. *People v. Harris*, 211 Ill. App. 3d 670, 156 Ill. Dec. 117, 570 N.E.2d 593 (1991). Thus matters intended to be disclosed by the attorney to third parties or made public are not within the privilege. *People v. Brown*, 275 Ill. App. 3d 1105, 212 Ill. Dec. 441, 657 N.E.2d 642 (1995); *People v. McDaniel*, 249 Ill. App. 3d 621, 188 Ill. Dec. 850, 619 N.E.2d 214 (1993); *Cesena v. DuPage County*, 201 Ill. App. 3d 96, 146 Ill. Dec. 1044, 558

N.E.2d 1378 (1990). Since disclosure is necessary to carry out the intention of a client depositing a deed with his attorney as escrowee, the attorney may testify to the circumstances and instructions that accompanied the delivery of the deed to her. *Spencer v. Burns*, 413 Ill. 240, 108 N.E.2d 413 (1952). *See also Dickerson v. Dickerson*, 332 Ill. 492, 153 N.E. 740 (1926), statements by the client concerning her marital status made for the purpose of meeting a title objection not within privilege; *Jackson v. Pillsbury*, 380 Ill. 554, 44 N.E.2d 537 (1942), since an attesting witness is expected to testify to the authenticity of the document the privilege does not include testimony as to the circumstances of execution by an attorney who signs as attesting witness; *People v. Werhollic*, 45 Ill. 2d 459, 259 N.E.2d 265 (1970), offer or acceptance of offer by person to state's attorney to become prosecution witness in return for leniency or immunity is not within privilege; *In re Marriage of Johnson*, 237 Ill. App. 3d 381, 178 Ill. Dec. 122, 604 N.E.2d 378 (1992), terms of negotiations between parties were not intended to be confidential. Nor does the privilege extend to the demeanor of the client as observed by the lawyer in a courtroom. *People v. Williams*, 97 Ill. App. 3d 252, 73 Ill. Dec. 360, 454 N.E.2d 220 (1983).

Since intent to disclose is of critical concern, the presence of an eavesdropper or person overhearing by accident does not destroy confidentiality, unless it is clear that the client knew that the communication was being overheard. As to testimony by the eavesdropper, *see* §506.2 infra; McCormick, Evidence §91 (4th ed. 1992). Of course, the presence of a third person ordinarily indicates a lack of intention that communications be confidential, and hence the privilege does not apply. *Champion v. McCarthy*, 228 Ill. 87, 81 N.E. 808 (1907). Similarly, if two persons consult an attorney together, neither can claim the privilege against the other in subsequent litigation that develops between them. *Lynn v. Lyerle*, 113 Ill. 128 (1885). The presence of an agent of the client in furtherance of the client's business or the presence of representatives of the lawyer does not destroy the privilege. *In re Estate of Busse*, 332 Ill. App. 258, 75 N.E.2d 36

(1947); *Manella v. First Natl. Bank & Trust Co.*, 173 Ill. App. 3d 431, 122 Ill. Dec. 109, 526 N.E.2d 368 (1988). However, the presence of a third person merely to support the client in a moment of need *does* serve to destroy the privilege. *People v. Doss*, 161 Ill. App. 3d 258, 112 Ill. Dec. 839, 514 N.E.2d 502 (1987).

§505.6 Lawyer-Client; Claiming and Waiving the Privilege

The privilege belongs to the client, not to the attorney. *People ex rel. Shufeldt v. Barker*, 56 Ill. 299 (1870); *Lanum v. Patterson*, 151 Ill. App. 36 (1909). The privilege may be claimed by the client, his guardian or conservator, the personal representative of a deceased client, or the successor, trustee, or similar representative of a corporation, association, or other organization, whether or not in existence. The privilege once attaching thus persists unless waived, *People v. Halluin*, 36 Ill. App. 3d 556, 344 N.E.2d 579 (1976), without regard to whether the lawyer-client relationship has been terminated. *People v. Ryan*, 30 Ill. 2d 456, 197 N.E.2d 15 (1964). The person who was the lawyer at the time of the communication may claim the privilege but only on behalf of the client. *In Re Marriage of Decker*, 153 Ill. 2d 298, 180 Ill. Dec. 17, 606 N.E.2d 1094 (1992). Her authority to do so is presumed in the absence of evidence to the contrary. McCormick, Evidence §92 (4th ed. 1992). Like all privileges, the lawyer-client privilege may be claimed by its owner, whether or not a party to the litigation.

A client may waive the lawyer-client privilege by voluntary disclosure. *Fossler v. Schriber*, 38 Ill. 172 (1865), client waived privilege by calling attorney to testify; *Turner v. Black*, 19 Ill. 2d 296, 166 N.E.2d 588 (1960), attorney properly permitted to testify to communications after client had testified to his versions thereof. *See also* §506.1 infra. However, testimony of an attorney elicited by the client on direct examination not revealing privileged communications does not waive the privilege. *Regan v. Garfield Ridge Trust & Savings Bank*, 220 Ill.

App. 3d 1078, 163 Ill. Dec. 605, 581 N.E.2d 759 (1991). Privileged information furnished voluntarily to the prosecution by an investigator for an attorney may be employed as the basis for issuance of a search warrant. *People v. Shiflet,* 125 Ill. App. 3d 161, 80 Ill. Dec. 596, 465 N.E.2d 942 (1984). With respect to waiver of the lawyer-client privilege by the assertion of an insanity defense, *see People v. Knuckles,* 226 Ill. App. 3d 714, 168 Ill. Dec. 680, 589 N.E.2d 1080 (1992).

§505.7   Lawyer-Client; Situations Where Inapplicable

The lawyer-client privilege does not apply:

(1) If the services of the lawyer were sought or obtained to enable or aid anyone to commit or plan to commit what the client knew or reasonably should have known to be a crime or fraud. *In re Marriage of Granger,* 197 Ill. App. 3d 363, 143 Ill. Dec. 651, 554 N.E.2d 586 (1990). The court may conduct an *in-camera* inspection of the communication to determine whether the exception to the privilege applies, *Radiac Abrasives v. Diamond Technology,* 177 Ill. App. 3d 628, 126 Ill. Dec. 743, 532 N.E.2d 428 (1988), provided that a factual basis has been established adequate to support a good faith belief by a reasonable person that the *in camera* review of the materials may reveal that the crime-fraud exception applies. *In re Marriage of Decker,* 153 Ill. 2d 298, 180 Ill. Dec. 17, 606 N.E.2d 1094 (1992) adopting the approach taken in *United States v. Zolin,* 491 U.S. 554 (1989). The party opposing the attorney-client privilege also bears the ultimate burden of showing applicability of the crime-fraud exception. *Id.* An attorney may be compelled to disclose client information found by the court to fall within the crime-fraud exception to the lawyer-client privilege. *Id.*

(2) As to a communication relevant to an issue of breach of duty by the lawyer to his client or by the client to her lawyer. *Sokol v. Mortimer,* 81 Ill. App. 2d 55, 225 N.E.2d 496 (1967), confidential communication of client may be testified to by attorney suing for fees.

(3) As to a communication relevant to an issue concerning an attested document to which the lawyer is an attesting witness. *Jackson v. Pillsbury*, 380 Ill. 554, 44 N.E.2d 537 (1942).

(4) As to a communication relevant to a matter of common interest between two or more clients if the communication was made by any of them to a lawyer retained or consulted in common, when offered in an action between any of the clients, McCormick, Evidence §91 (4th ed. 1992). The common interest doctrine applies to an insured and his insurer even though the insurer is not a party in the initial proceeding. *Waste Management, Inc. v. International Surplus Lines Insurance Company*, 144 Ill. 2d 178, 161 Ill. Dec. 774, 579 N.E.2d 322 (1991).

(5) As to a communication put at issue by a party who is the holder of the privilege. *Waste Management, Inc. v. International Surplus Lines Ins. Co.*, 203 Ill. App. 3d 172, 148 Ill. Dec. 496, 560 N.E.2d 1093 (1990), insured suing insurer for indemnity for settlement costs and defense fees.

While upon the death of the client, the privilege survives in favor of his estate in regard to claims by outsiders against the estate, *In re Estate of Busse*, 332 Ill. App. 258, 75 N.E.2d 36 (1947), it does not apply to a communication relevant to an issue between parties who claim through the same deceased client, regardless of whether the claims are by testate or intestate succession or by inter vivos transaction. Will contests involve peculiar considerations, since the question of who succeeds to the interests of the decedent depends upon the outcome of the contest. While it had been suggested that the attorney may not disclose facts that would tend to invalidate the will, *Champion v. McCarthy*, 228 Ill. 87, 81 N.E. 808 (1907), and that he may not disclose confidential communications, *McLean v. Barnes*, 285 Ill. 203, 120 N.E. 628 (1918), the actual holding of the cases that pass upon the point has been that neither side may assert the privilege. *Norton v. Clark*, 253 Ill. 557, 97 N.E. 1079 (1912); *Wilkinson v. Service*, 249 Ill. 146, 94 N.E. 50 (1911). *Accord Lamb v. Lamb*, 124 Ill. App. 3d 687, 80 Ill. Dec. 8, 464 N.E.2d 873 (1984) (quoting foregoing paragraph with approval). *See also Hitt v. Stephens,* 285 Ill. App. 3d 713, 221 Ill. Dec. 368, 675 N.E.2d 275 (1996).

§505.8 *Trade Secrets*

The concept of trade secrets includes such matters as confidential research development, commercial information, chemical and physical composition of substances employed, the mechanical structure of tools and machines, and such facts as names of customers, subjects and amounts of expense, and the like. 8 Wigmore, Evidence §242 (McNaughton rev. 1961). *See also ILG Indus., Inc. v. Scott,* 49 Ill. 2d 88, 273 N.E.2d 393 (1971); *Lincoln Towers Ins. Agency v. Farrell,* 99 Ill. App. 3d 353, 54 Ill. Dec. 817, 425 N.E.2d 1034 (1981). In short, information that improves competitive position and the value of which is substantially enhanced by secrecy is within the concept of trade secrets.

A trade secret privilege will not be permitted if its allowance would tend to conceal fraud or work injustice, a determination to be made by the court, §104.1 supra. In determining whether to honor the privilege, the court must balance the competing interests — the desirability of making available all relevant evidence versus protecting trade secrets from disclosure. *Bee Chemical Co. v. Service Coatings, Inc.,* 116 Ill. App. 2d 217, 253 N.E.2d 512 (1969). The process of balancing of interests may be done *in camera* to prevent general disclosure both to the public and to the adversary if the claim of privilege is sustained. Where disclosure is desirable, those protective measures that the interest of the holder of the privilege and of the parties and the furtherance of justice may require should be taken. Judicial ingenuity is required in fashioning such protective measures. Suggestions contained as possibilities in the Federal Advisory Committee's Note to Proposed Federal Rule of Evidence 508, 56 F.R.D. 183, 250 (1973), are making disclosure to counsel but not to the opposing client, swearing all present not to make further disclosure, and making disclosure only to the court. *Bee*

Chemical Co. v. Service Coatings, Inc. supra, formulae are to be given only to counsel for defendants and shown only to individual defendants and presidents of corporate defendants; formulae are to be used only for purposes of this case.

§505.9   *Identity of Informers; Testimony on Merits*

In order to encourage citizens to communicate information concerning crimes to law enforcement officials and in recognition that effective use of informers by law enforcement officials requires anonymity, the State is privileged to refuse disclosure of the identity of an informer. *People v. Woods,* 139 Ill. 2d 369, 152 Ill. Dec. 110, 565 N.E.2d 643 (1990); *People v. Mack,* 12 Ill. 2d 151, 145 N.E.2d 609 (1957); *People v. Taylor,* 269 Ill. App. 3d 772, 207 Ill. Dec. 193, 646 N.E.2d 1280 (1995); Supreme Court Rule 412(j)(ii). The privilege, based upon the assumption that the identity of the informer is not relevant to the issues in the case, applies also in civil matters, although rarely arising. It may be claimed by an appropriate representative of the State, usually the state's attorney. Where the State is not a party, it may be claimed by others, for example, a police officer.

No privilege applies when the identity of the informer has already been disclosed to those who would have cause to resent the communication, *Roviaro v. United States,* 353 U.S. 53 (1957). Under such circumstances no need for the privilege exists. If the state intends to call the informer at trial, the fact that he is an informer must, of course, be disclosed as a significant aspect of her credibility. Supreme Court Rule 412(j)(ii) supra. The privilege extends only to the identity of the informer; if the contents of a communication would not disclose the informant's identity, then the privilege is not applicable to the communication. *People v. Chaney,* 63 Ill. 2d 216, 347 N.E.2d 138 (1976).

Where it appears that the informer may be able to give testimony necessary to a fair determination of the issues of guilt or innocence in a criminal case or the determination of probable cause, *People v. Lewis,* 57 Ill. 2d 232, 311 N.E.2d 685 (1974); *People v. McBee,* 228 Ill. App. 3d 769, 170 Ill. Dec. 685, 593 N.E.2d 574 (1992), or a material issue on the merits in a civil case, and the State invokes the privilege, the State will be afforded an opportunity to show *in camera* facts relevant to this determination. The party opposing the privilege must thus demonstrate a need for disclosure, which need must amount to more than a mere desire to cross-examine. *Cochrane's of Champaign v. Liquor Control,* 285 Ill. App. 3d 28, 220 Ill. Dec. 755, 673 N.E.2d 1176 (1996); *People v. Sutton,* 260 Ill. App. 3d 949, 197 Ill. Dec. 867, 831 N.E.2d 1326 (1994). The showing will usually be made by affidavits, but the court may direct oral testimony to be taken. At the showing *in camera,* no counsel or party is permitted to be present. Otherwise the hearing itself would give the disclosure demanded. The court's task is to balance the State's interest in protecting the flow of information from informers against the individual's right to prepare and present his defense. Whether a proper balance requires disclosure must depend on the particular circumstances of each case, taking into consideration the crime charged, the possible defenses, the possible significance of the informer's testimony, and other relevant factors including role played by the informer, and whether the informer's life or safety would likely be jeopardized by disclosure of his identity. *People v. Woods* supra; *People v. Chaney* supra; *Roviaro v. United States* supra; *People v. Taylor* supra; *People v. Friend,* 177 Ill. App. 3d 1002, 127 Ill. Dec. 537, 533 N.E.2d 409 (1988). The degree of potential threat to the informant resulting from disclosure is a relevant consideration. *People v. Bufford,* 277 Ill. App. 3d 862, 214 Ill. Dec. 503, 661 N.E.2d 357 (1995).

Applying the foregoing test, disclosure of the identity of an informant who also participated in the commission of the offense for which defendant is charged is required. *People v. Lewis,* 57 Ill. 2d 232, 311 N.E.2d 685 (1974), informer sole participant other than accused and police officer making narcotics purchase. Other decisions have suggested disclosure of an informant's identity when the informant helps to set up the criminal occurrence or is a witness thereto. *People v. Woods* supra; *People v. Bufford,* 277 Ill. App. 3d 862, 214 Ill. Dec. 503, 661 N.E.2d 357 (1995); *People v. Herrera,* 238 Ill. App. 3d 284, 179 Ill. Dec. 435, 606 N.E.2d 267 (1992); *People v. Pearson,* 210 Ill. App. 3d 1079, 155 Ill. Dec. 723, 569 N.E.2d 1334 (1991). *See also People v. Beattie,* 31 Ill. 2d 257, 201 N.E.2d 396 (1964). Such disclosure is required even when the State does not intend to call the informant at trial. *People v. Woods* supra. Disclosure is not required of a tipster who merely gives information to the police, *see People v. Chaney* supra; *People v. Taylor* supra, or supplies information in support of issuance of search warrant. *People v. Friend,* 177 Ill. App. 3d 1002, 127 Ill. Dec. 537, 533 N.E.2d 409 (1988); *People v. Jackson,* 37 Ill. App. 3d 279, 345 N.E.2d 509 (1976). However, in the latter instance, if an issue arises as to the existence or reliability of the informer, disclosure may be required. *See* §505.10 infra. Moreover, where a witness who was an informer is clearly going to be called by the defense, the State must inform the court prior thereto that the witness was an informer and disclose the existence of any prior statement that might be used for impeachment purposes. *People v. Chaney* supra.

The procedure to be employed in making the foregoing determination as to whether an informant must be identified and produced in a given case and what happens if he is not produced when required involves a three step analysis. *People v. Holmes,* 135 Ill. 2d 198, 142 Ill. Dec. 172, 552 N.E.2d 763 (1990). First, the defendant must initially satisfy the *Roviaro* burden of establishing the relevance and materiality, i.e., importance, of the informant's testimony. Second, once the defendant meets this burden the state must produce the informant or establish his unavailability following the exertion of a reasonable good-faith effort by the state to locate and produce the informant. Third, where the state has made a reasonable good-faith effort to locate the informant, but cannot produce him, the defendant will prevail only if the defendant further proves by clear and convincing evidence that the unavailable informant's testimony would raise a reasonable doubt as to the state's case. *People v. Holmes* id.; *People v.*

Le Cour, 273 Ill. App. 3d 1003, 210 Ill. Dec. 245, 652 N.E.2d 1221 (1995).

If the court finds a reasonable probability that the informer can give the testimony and the State elects not to disclose her identity, the charges should be dismissed. In a civil case the court may make any order that justice requires. *See* Proposed Federal Rule of Evidence 510, 56 F.R.D. 183, 255 (1973).

With respect to the disclosure of the address of any witness where disclosure may be a threat to health and safety, *see* §607.6 infra. *See also People v. Gaytan,* 186 Ill. App. 3d 919, 134 Ill. Dec. 656, 542 N.E.2d 1163 (1989), Supreme Court Rule 412(j)(ii) extends to informant's address where identity is already known. With respect to the limited privilege for law enforcement investigatory files, *see In re Marriage of Daniels,* 240 Ill. App. 3d 314, 180 Ill. Dec. 742, 607 N.E.2d 1255 (1992).

A qualified privilege exists for the disclosure of secret surveillance locations. Disclosure is decided on a case-by-case basis, balancing the public interest in keeping the location secret against the defendant's interests in preparing a defense. The defendant must demonstrate a need for disclosure. Even if the privilege is found not to have been overcome, the defendant will be permitted to cross-examine the police officer's observations with respect to distance, weather, possible obstructions, etc. *People v. Criss,* 294 Ill. App. 3d 276, 228 Ill. Dec. 586, 689 N.E.2d 645 (1998).

§505.10   Identity of Informers; Legality of Obtaining Evidence

Where information from an informer is relied upon to legitimate a search and seizure without a warrant, or to issue a warrant for arrest or search, or search and seizure accompanying an arrest, *id.,* a conflict arises between the interests of the State in protecting the identity of its informer and in avoiding unfairness to the accused.

The objective is to provide a measure of protection against arbitrary police action without unnecessarily impairing the secrecy and thus future value and personal safety of the informant. If the court is not satisfied the information was received from an informer reasonably believed to be reliable or credible, it may require disclosure of his identity and his examination. The decision rests with the discretion of the trial court. *People v. Vauzanges,* 158 Ill. 2d 509, 199 Ill. Dec. 731, 634 N.E.2d 1085 (1994). On request of the State, the disclosure may in the court's discretion be made *in camera, McCray v. Illinois,* 386 U.S. 300 (1967), or the court may order disclosure to the defendant and the production of the informer in open court. *People v. Clifton,* 42 Ill. 2d 526, 250 N.E.2d 649 (1969). *See generally People v. Lesure,* 195 Ill. App. 3d 437, 114 Ill. Dec. 13, 552 N.E.2d 363 (1990). The trial court is motivated by different concerns in exercising its discretion with respect to production of an informant as opposed to disclosure of an informant's identity. When considering whether to order the production of the informant and/or the police file for an *in camera* examination or inspection, the trial court is concerned with the existence of the informant and with maintaining the integrity of the judicial process. Conversely, when determining whether to disclose the identity of the informant, the trial court is concerned with a defendant's need for disclosure in order to prepare his defense. *People v. Vauzanges* supra.

§505.11   Voting

A legal voter cannot be compelled to testify for whom she voted. *Eggers v. Fox,* 177 Ill. 185, 52 N.E. 269 (1898). While an illegal voter may refuse to testify on the ground of self-incrimination, if she testifies that she voted, she cannot then refuse to answer how she voted. *Stevenson v. Baker,* 347 Ill. 304, 179 N.E. 842 (1932).

§506   Waiver of Privilege by Voluntary Disclosure

§506.1   Commentary

A privilege persists unless waived. *People v. Halluin,* 36 Ill. App. 3d 556, 344 N.E.2d 579 (1976); *In re Busse's Estate,* 332 Ill. App. 258, 75 N.E.2d 36 (1947). With respect to all privileges for confidential matters or communications, no matter what their origin, the privilege is waived upon voluntary disclosure or consent to disclosure of any significant part of the privileged matter. *Gottemoller v. Gottemoller,* 37 Ill. App. 3d 689, 346 N.E.2d 393 (1976), written consent to psychiatrist to release records; *People v. Newbury,* 53 Ill. 2d 228, 290 N.E.2 592 (1972), calling and eliciting testimony of psychiatrist at trial by defendant waives privilege; *People v. Simpson,* 68 Ill. 2d 276, 12 Ill. Dec. 234, 369 N.E.2d 1248 (1977), repeating to third person content of privileged communication by holder of the privilege is waiver; *People v. O'Connor,* 37 Ill. App. 3d 310, 345 N.E.2d 520 (1976), partial disclosure of privileged communications held to constitute a waiver of the privilege; *People v. Diercks,* 88 Ill. App. 3d 1073, 44 Ill. Dec. 191, 411 N.E.2d 97 (1980), disclosure of communication to clergyman in presence of third party negates confidential nature. *Cf. Chavez v. Watts,* 161 Ill. App. 3d 664, 113 Ill. Dec. 337, 515 N.E.2d 146 (1987), disclosure by defendant's attorney in defendant's presence of investigator's summary of defendant's privileged communication did *not* waive privilege as the defendant himself did not waive privilege — a questionable decision. Failure to assert the privilege at trial also constitutes a waiver. *People v. Orange,* 121 Ill. 2d 364, 118 Ill. Dec. 1, 521 N.E.2d 69 (1988). Waiver does not, however, occur if such disclosure is itself a privileged communication. Waiver also does not occur by the calling of a person who is privy to the privileged communication by the party possessing the privilege if no privileged communications are revealed during direct examination. *Regan v. Garfield Ridge Trust & Savings,* 220 Ill. App. 3d 1078, 163 Ill. Dec. 605, 581 N.E.2d 759

(1991). Disclosure of a confidential communication does not constitute a waiver of other nondisclosed confidential communications between the same parties. *In re Estate of Hoover v. Hoover,* 226 Ill. App. 3d 422, 168 Ill. Dec. 499, 589 N.E.2d 899 (1992). The presence of an interpreter does not waive the privilege with respect to a communication that is otherwise privileged. 735 ILCS 5/8-911(b).

Waiver of a privilege is limited to the subject matter of the confidential communication that was voluntarily disclosed. *In re Marriage of Decker,* 153 Ill. 2d 298, 180 Ill. Dec. 17, 606 N.E.2d 1094 (1992). Thus voluntary disclosure of a confidential communication does not waive the privilege as to all nondisclosed communications that may have taken place about a different subject matter. *In re Estate of Hoover,* 226 Ill. App. 3d 422, 168 Ill. Dec. 499, 589 N.E.2d 899 (1992). Waiver with respect to the same subject matter includes the remainder of the disclosed communication and other communications on the same subject matter. *In re Grand Jury January 246,* 272 Ill. App. 3d 991, 209 Ill. Dec. 518, 651 N.E.2d 696 (1995). *Contra In re Grand Jury January 246, id.,* J. Greiman, dissenting, asserting that waiver does not extend to other communications or even another part of the disclosed communication.

The matter protected by the privilege, and thus subject to be waived, may vary according to the particular privilege under consideration. For example, with respect to lawyer-client, §§505.1 to 505.7 supra, only the content of communication is protected, not the identity of the client or lawyer. With respect to informers, §§505.9 to 505.10 supra, it is the identity of the informer rather than the content of communication that is protected. Such differences must be considered in determining whether disclosure or consent to disclosure of any significant part of the privileged matter has occurred. Thus testimony as to the fact of consultation with a lawyer should not be held to waive the privilege with respect to the contents of the communication.

The privilege extends solely to the confidential communication and not to the underlying event itself. Thus a person may disclose or testify as to an event without waiving a confidential communications privilege. Conversely, disclosure or testimony as to the content of the confidential communication constitutes a waiver. To illustrate, testimony by *A* that event *X* occurred does not waive a privilege while testimony by *B* that the witness *A* told him that he, *A,* had told *Z* in confidence that event *X* occurred does waive the privilege.

Calling of one psychiatrist by the defendant should not be held a waiver of the privilege with respect to other psychiatrists who examined her. *See* discussion, §503.1 supra, with respect to waiver of psychiatrist-patient privilege.

Waiver of a privilege based on the need to protect the confidentiality of communications operates as a waiver of the privilege with respect to the same testimony at subsequent proceedings. *Novak v. Rathnam,* 106 Ill. 2d 478, 88 Ill. Dec. 608, 478 N.E.2d 1334 (1985); *People v. Phillips,* 128 Ill. App. 3d 457, 83 Ill. Dec. 717, 470 N.E.2d 1137 (1984). However, waiver of the privilege of self-incrimination does not operate as a waiver of that privilege in another case. *People v. Stufflebeam,* 19 Ill. App. 3d 462, 311 N.E.2d 601 (1974).

With respect to waiver of a privilege, knowledge or lack of knowledge of the existence of the privilege appears to be irrelevant. 8 Wigmore, Evidence §2327 (McNaughton rev. 1961). As to whether inadvertent disclosure of confidential matters or communications constitutes a waiver, *see Dalen v. Ozite Corp.,* 230 Ill. App. 3d 18, 171 Ill. Dec. 845, 594 N.E.2d 1365 (1992) (after reviewing various approaches adopts a "balancing test").

§506.2   Privileged Matter Disclosed Under Compulsion or Without Opportunity to Claim Privilege

Evidence of a statement or other disclosure of privileged matter should not be admissible against the holder of the privilege if the disclosure was compelled erroneously. When disclosure is wrongfully compelled, although confidentiality cannot be restored, the remedy of excluding the evidence if later offered against the holder seems clearly appropriate. 8 Wigmore, Evidence §2270 (McNaughton rev. 1961). For an appraisal of the argument that the holder of the privilege should, in order to preserve the privilege, be required to stand firm and take the consequences, including a judgment for contempt, *see* Federal Advisory Committee's Note to Proposed Federal Rule of Evidence 512, 56 F.R.D. 183, 256-260 (1973).

The same remedy is given when disclosure is made without the holder's having an opportunity to claim the privilege. *People v. Knippenberg,* 66 Ill. 2d 276, 6 Ill. Dec. 46, 362 N.E.2d 681 (1977). Thus a third person may not testify to a confidential communication disclosed to him by a spouse to whom the confidential marital communication was made, *see* §502.3 supra. *People v. Simpson,* 68 Ill. 2d 276, 12 Ill. Dec. 234, 369 N.E.2d 1248 (1977). Neither could the spouse so testify. *Id.* The same rule would apply in the unlikely event a lawyer, physician, or clergyman made an unauthorized disclosure of a confidential communication. *See People v. Mudge,* 143 Ill. App. 3d 193, 97 Ill. Dec. 391, 492 N.E.2d 1050 (1986). Other illustrations include disclosure by a family member participating in group therapy, disclosure by a person used in transmission of a privileged communication, or privileged data improperly made available from a computer bank.

Another problem that arises frequently is in connection with eavesdroppers. Where, for example, electronic surveillance is employed or the communication was lost or misdelivered, the holder should not be held to have waived the privilege. However, in *People v. Simpson* supra, in dictum the court stated that in the foregoing situation the privilege is waived, citing solely to McCormick, §82 (Cleary ed. 1972), while failing to note that McCormick, *id.,* goes on to state that the position barring disclosure by such third persons is preferable. *But see People v. Simpson,* 129 Ill. App. 3d 822, 84 Ill. Dec. 949, 473 N.E.2d 350 (1984), adopting the waiver position of *Simpson* supra. Notice that where the parties know that another person could easily with the naked ear hear a communication, no privilege would attach, for an intent to have the communication be confidential is lacking. *Gannon v. People,* 127 Ill. 507, 21 N.E. 525 (1889), third person in room with husband and wife may testify to the communication with each other; *People v. Simpson,* 129 Ill. App. 3d 822, 84 Ill. Dec. 949, 473 N.E.2d 350 (1984), mother-in-law in living room 15 feet from defendant and his wife who were in their bedroom could testify.

§506.3   Comment Upon an Inference from Claim of Privilege; Claim of Privilege in Presence of Jury

Comment by the court or counsel with respect to a claim of privilege is ordinarily prohibited in order that the assertion of a privilege not be costly and that the policy reasons behind the privilege be given maximum effect. Comment with respect to the accused's not testifying is prohibited by statute, 725 ILCS 125/6, and also infringes his privilege against self-incrimination. *Griffin v. California,* 380 U.S. 609 (1965). The underlying policy considerations support application of this prohibition to all privileges, no matter their source. 8 Wigmore, Evidence §§2243, 2322, 2386 (McNaughton rev. 1961). These same policy considerations also require, to the extent practicable, that proceedings be conducted so as to facilitate assertion of any privilege outside the presence of the jury. *People v. Myers,* 35 Ill. 2d 311, 220 N.E.2d 297 (1966), court may refuse to call a codefendant where it is clear the codefendant will assert his privilege against self-incrimination; *People v. Godsey,* 57 Ill. App. 3d 364, 15 Ill. Dec. 1, 373 N.E.2d 95 (1978), improper on cross-examination to cause prior assertion of privilege against self-incrimination to be divulged to the jury; *People v. Crawford Distrib. Co.,* 65 Ill. App. 3d 790, 22 Ill. Dec. 525, 382 N.E.2d 1223 (1978), improper for prosecution to call witness who it knows will assert a privilege if the claim of privilege creates an innuendo prejudicial to the defendant. *See also* §§103.9 and 104.3 supra.

An exception exists: assertion of a Fifth Amendment privilege in a *civil* case is properly the subject of an adverse inference. *People v. $1,124,905 U.S. Currency,* 177 Ill. 2d 314, 226 Ill. Dec. 627, 685 N.E.2d 1370 (1997).

If, but only if, a party against whom the jury might draw an adverse inference from a claim of privilege requests, the court should instruct the jury that no inference is to be drawn therefrom. *See* Illinois Pattern Jury Instructions— Criminal 2.04 (1992). *See also Bruno v. United States,* 308 U.S. 287 (1939).

With respect to comment upon accused's failure to testify, *see also* §502.4 supra.

ARTICLE VI

Witness

§601   Competency of Witnesses

§601.1   An Overview

While originally at common law persons were declared incompetent to be witnesses for numerous reasons, almost all such reasons have long since been eliminated. All persons possessing the required minimum standard of mental capacity (§601.3 infra) and personal knowledge (§602.1 infra) who understand the moral duty to testify truthfully (§603.1 infra) are now competent witnesses, with the major exception arising in connection with the Dead Man's Act. *See* §606.1 infra. In short, the competency of a witness to testify regarding a particular matter requires a minimum capacity to observe, record, recollect, and recount in response to questions, an understanding of the moral duty to tell the truth, which includes an understanding of the difference between the truth and a lie or fantasy along with a declaration to tell the truth, combined with evidence sufficient to support a finding of actual personal knowledge of the matter. *Accord* 725 ILCS 5/115-14; *People v. Jones,* 123 Ill. 2d 387, 123 Ill. Dec. 944, 528 N.E.2d 648 (1988); *Swanigan v. Chicago Bd. of Education,* 173 Ill. App. 3d 784, 123 Ill. Dec. 392, 527 N.E.2d 1030 (1988); *Clark v. Otis Elevator Co.,* 274 Ill. App. 3d 253, 210 Ill. Dec. 576, 653 N.E.2d 771 (1995).

In determining competency, the court views the evidence in the light most favorable to the witness. When a witness's actual acquisition of personal knowledge has been questioned, the court may reject the testimony only when no reasonable juror could believe that the witness perceived what she claims to have perceived. When the mental capacity of a witness has been questioned, the ultimate issue is whether the witness is so bereft of her powers of observation, recordation, recollection, and narration as to be so untrustworthy as a witness as to make her testimony lack relevancy. Considering mental and physical capacity and actual acquisition of personal knowledge together, the test of competency has been characterized as requiring minimum credibility. 3 Weinstein's Evidence ¶601[01] (1988). Judges increasingly tend to resolve all doubts concerning the minimum credibility of a witness in favor of permitting the jury to hear the testimony and judge the credibility of the witness for itself. A witness found minimally credible is subject to cross-examination regarding her capacity and actuality of observation, recordation, recollection, and narration, as well as her ability to understand the duty to testify truthfully. A witness who is minimally credible may not be barred from testifying on the basis of the trial court finding that the witness is untrustworthy; the determination of credibility is exclusively within the province of the jury. *People v. Trail,* 197 Ill. App. 3d 742, 144 Ill. Dec. 171, 555 N.E.2d 68 (1990).

With respect to issues arising in connection with the competency as witnesses of the judge, a juror, or a lawyer in the instant litigation, *see* §605 infra; as to competency of witnesses and the Original Writing Rule, *see* §1004.1 infra. It should be noted that otherwise competent witnesses may be debarred from testifying by claims of privilege. *See* §§501-506 supra.

Matters once regarded as grounds of incompetency may survive in a limited way as techniques of impeachment. *See, e.g.,* proof of conviction of crime, §609 infra. *Cf.* religious beliefs, §610 infra.

§601.2 Determination of Competency

The principles governing objections to competency are similar to those governing objections to admissibility. Appropriate objection must be made in ample time. If grounds of general disqualification are known, objection must be made before any testimony is given. *People v. Moretti,* 6 Ill. 2d 494, 129 N.E.2d 709 (1955). If the disqualification is only as to certain matters, objection need not be made until the witness is asked concerning them. *People v. Sawhill,* 299 Ill. 393, 132 N.E. 477 (1921). A motion to strike will not lie if grounds of incompetency were known when the testimony was given. *Chicago Title & Trust Co. v. Sagola Lumber Co.,* 242 Ill. 468, 90 N.E. 282 (1909). A specific objection is a waiver of all grounds not specified. *Holland v. People's Bank & Trust Co.,* 303 Ill. 381, 135 N.E. 717 (1922).

The burden of proof is upon the objecting party to show incompetency. 725 ILCS 5/115-14(c); *People v. Williams,* 147 Ill. 2d 173, 167 Ill. Dec. 853, 588 N.E.2d 983 (1991); *Green by Fritz v. Jackson,* 289 Ill. App. 3d 1001, 224 Ill. Dec. 848, 682 N.E.2d 409 (1997); *People v. Jenkins,* 20 Ill. App. 3d 727, 315

N.E.2d 269 (1974). The trial judge determines the competency of a witness, §104.1 supra. *People v. Ballinger,* 36 Ill. 2d 620, 255 N.E.2d 10 (1967); *Schneiderman v. Interstate Transit Lines, Inc.,* 394 Ill. 569, 69 N.E.2d 293 (1946). Unless an abuse of discretion is shown, the trial court's determination of competency will be upheld. *People v. Garcia,* 97 Ill. 2d 58, 73 Ill. Dec. 414, 454 N.E.2d 274 (1983); *People v. Brown,* 52 Ill. 2d 94, 285 N.E.2d 1 (1972). A competency hearing may be conducted only upon an objection to competency; the trial court may not initiate such a hearing *sua sponte.* The competency hearing must be held outside the presence of the jury. 725 ILCS 5/115-14(c); *People v. Jones,* 123 Ill. 2d 387, 123 Ill. Dec. 944, 528 N.E.2d 648 (1988); *People v. Wespfahl,* 295 Ill. App. 3d 327, 229 Ill. Dec. 842, 692 N.E.2d 831 (1998). A preliminary examination outside the hearing of the jury may be conducted by the trial court alone, *People v. Garcia* supra, or counsel may be permitted to participate in the conduct of the *voir dire* examination in the discretion of the court. *People v. Seel,* 68 Ill. App. 3d 996, 25 Ill. Dec. 99, 386 N.E.2d 370 (1979). Counsel for the challenging party does not have a right to participate in the *voir dire* examination. *People v. Williams,* 147 Ill. 2d 173, 167 Ill. Dec. 853, 588 N.E.2d 983 (1991). In a criminal case, if the accused's lawyer is present the defendant does *not* have a constitutional right to attend the preliminary examination himself. *Kentucky v. Stincer,* 482 U.S. 730 (1987). Nor must the defendant's attorney be given the opportunity to directly question the witness. *People v. Rainge,* 211 Ill. App. 3d 432, 115 Ill. Dec. 918, 570 N.E.2d 431 (1991). Leading questions should not be employed unless necessary under the circumstances. *In Interest of E.S.,* 145 Ill. App. 3d 906, 99 Ill. Dec. 599, 495 N.E.2d 1334 (1986). Where a serious challenge to competency has not been made, the court in a jury trial may determine competency by observing at trial the witness's demeanor and ability to testify. *See People v. Ford,* 139 Ill. App. 3d 894, 94 Ill. Dec. 574, 488 N.E.2d 573 (1986). In a bench trial, the trial judge may determine the witness's competency either by preliminary inquiry or by observing the witness during testimony at trial. *People v. Campos,*

155 Ill. App. 3d 348, 108 Ill. Dec. 1, 507 N.E.2d 1342 (1987). A psychiatric examination of a witness in a criminal case, such as the principal witness in a murder case, *People v. Gersbachen*, 44 Ill. 2d 321, 255 N.E.2d 429 (1970); *People v. Nash*, 36 Ill. 2d 275, 222 N.E.2d 473 (1967), may be ordered to determine a witness's competency. Such a motion is addressed to the court's discretion; denial of such an examination is not easily disturbed on appeal. *People v. Gersbachen* supra; *People v. Nash*, 36 Ill. 2d 275, 222 N.E.2d 473 (1967). However, the court may not order a witness who is the victim of an alleged sex offense to submit to or undergo either a psychiatric or psychological examination, 725 ILCS 5/115-7.1. *People v. Williams*, 220 Ill. App. 3d 297, 163 Ill. Dec. 277, 581 N.E.2d 228 (1991) (statute is not unconstitutional). The disadvantage obviously placed upon the criminal defendant when 5/115-7.1 is considered along with 725 ILCS 5/115-7.2, which provides for the admissibility of "any recognized and accepted form of post-traumatic stress syndrome" in prosecutions for an illegal sexual act, was analyzed by the Illinois Supreme Court in *People v. Wheeler*, 151 Ill. 2d 298, 176 Ill. Dec. 880, 602 N.E.2d 826 (1992) with the court concluding that unless the victim consents to an examination by an expert chosen by the defendant, the prosecution may not introduce testimony from an *examining* expert that the victim of an alleged sexual assault suffers from a "recognized and accepted form of post-traumatic stress syndrome."

Mental capacity is discussed in §601.3 infra; moral capacity in §603.1 infra. As to timing of cross-examination with respect to mental capacity, *see* §611.1 infra.

In abuse and neglect proceedings, the determination of competency is governed by 705 ILCS 405/2-18(4)(d).

§601.3 *Mental Capacity*

A witness who has the capacity to observe, record, recollect, understand questions, communicate, and appreciate the obligation to speak truthfully is mentally competent, and any mental deficiency then goes only to the weight of her testimony. *People v. Ballinger,* 36 Ill. 2d 620, 255 N.E.2d 10 (1967); *Green by Fritz v. Jackson,* 289 Ill. App. 3d 1001, 224 Ill. Dec. 848, 682 N.E.2d 409 (1997); *People v. Brewer,* 118 Ill. App. 3d 189, 73 Ill. Dec. 774, 454 N.E.2d 1023 (1983); *People v. Ward,* 49 Ill. App. 3d 780, 7 Ill. Dec. 547, 264 N.E.2d 708 (1977). Thus an adjudication of feeble mindedness does not render a witness incompetent, *Oswald v. Civil Serv. Comm.,* 406 Ill. 506, 94 N.E.2d 311 (1950); *People v. Scott,* 108 Ill. App. 3d 607, 64 Ill. Dec. 201, 439 N.E.2d 130 (1980), nor does having been declared disabled in regard to his person or finances, *Green by Fritz v. Jackson,* 289 Ill. App. 3d 1001, 224 Ill. Dec. 848, 682 N.E.2d 409 (1997), nor does an adjudication of being a disabled person under the Probate Act, *Clark v. Otis Elevator Co.,* 274 Ill. App. 3d 253, 210 Ill. Dec. 576, 653 N.E.2d 771 (1995), nor does an adjudication of incompetency under the Mental Health Code, *People v. Cox,* 87 Ill. App. 2d 243, 230 N.E.2d 900 (1967), nor does having spent time in a mental institution for nervous disorders, *People v. Sykes,* 45 Ill. App. 3d 674, 4 Ill. Dec. 64, 359 N.E.2d 897 (1977), or post-traumatic depression, *People v. Makiel,* 263 Ill. App. 3d 54, 200 Ill. Dec. 602, 635 N.E.2d 941 (1994), nor does impaired mental capacity, *People v. Blair,* 146 Ill. App. 3d 186, 100 Ill. Dec. 1, 496 N.E.2d 1066 (1986). A witness suffering from mental impairment such as retardation, *People v. Williams,* 147 Ill. 2d 173, 167 Ill. Dec. 853, 588 N.E.2d 983 (1991); *People v. Spencer,* 119 Ill. App. 3d 971, 75 Ill. Dec. 479, 457 N.E.2d 473 (1983), Down's syndrome, *People v. Davis,* 223 Ill. App. 3d 580, 165 Ill. Dec. 818, 585 N.E.2d 214 (1992), or senility, *People v. Scott* supra, is not by virtue of such impairment automatically rendered incompetent. Sanity is not the test of competency. *People v. Cox,* 87 Ill. App. 2d 243, 230 N.E.2d 900 (1967). The ultimate question to be asked is whether the witness is so bereft of his powers of observation, recordation, recollection, or narration as to be undeniably untrustworthy as a witness, *People v. Davis,* 43 Ill. App. 3d 603, 357 N.E.2d 96 (1976), i.e., lacks minimum credibility. *See* §601.1 supra. Accordingly, evidence of the reputation of a witness for untruthfullness is not admissible on a determination of competency as such evidence goes to weight rather than admissibility. *People v. Mason,* 219 Ill. App. 3d 76, 161 Ill. Dec. 705, 578 N.E.2d 1351 (1991).

While the Illinois Supreme Court once indicated that children under six years of age are not competent, *People v. Wilson,* 401 Ill. 68, 81 N.E.2d 485 (1948), now the correct test is whether the child has the capacity described above. *People v. Garcia,* 97 Ill. 2d 58, 73 Ill. Dec. 414, 454 N.E.2d 274 (1983); *People v. Edwards,* 55 Ill. 2d 25, 302 N.E.2d 306 (1973); *People v. Brewer,* 127 Ill. App. 3d 306, 82 Ill. Dec. 468 N.E.2d 1242 (1984), not age but degree of intelligence and understanding of child determines competency; *People v. Kincaid,* 87 Ill. App. 3d 552, 42 Ill. Dec. 854, 409 N.E.2d 469 (1980); *People v. Edwards,* 224 Ill. App. 3d 1017, 167 Ill. Dec. 54, 586 N.E.2d 1326 (1992), it is not age but whether the child is sufficiently mature to receive correct impressions by his senses, to record, recollect, understand questions, narrate intelligently, and appreciate the moral duty to tell the truth that determines competency. *Accord* 725 ILCS 5/115-14 (age is not a disqualification). Thus, if the child is sufficiently mature and of sufficient intelligence to receive correct impressions by his senses, to record, recollect, understand questions, narrate intelligently, and appreciate the moral duty to tell the truth, which includes along with a declaration to tell the truth an understanding of the difference between the truth and a lie or fantasy, *People v. McNichols,* 139 Ill. App. 3d 947, 94 Ill. Dec. 375, 487 N.E.2d 1252 (1986); *People v. Ridgeway,* 194 Ill. App. 3d 881, 141 Ill. Dec. 603, 551 N.E.2d 790 (1990); *People v. Diaz,* 201 Ill. App. 3d 830, 146 Ill. Dec. 1029, 558 N.E.2d 1363 (1990); *People v. Puhl,* 211 Ill. App. 3d 457, 155 Ill. Dec. 934, 570 N.E.2d 447 (1991), §603.1 infra, the witness is competent. *People v. Barfield,* 187 Ill. App. 3d 257, 134 Ill. Dec. 874, 543 N.E.2d 157 (1989), child who states that you get in trouble with your friends when you tell a lie adequately understands the moral duty to tell the truth; *People v. Lawler,* 181 Ill. App. 3d 464, 130 Ill. Dec. 72, 536 N.E.2d 1283 (1989), ambivalent answers as to knowledge of truth and falsehood did not require that the child be found incompetent; *People v. Born,* 156 Ill. App. 3d 584, 108 Ill. Dec. 699, 509 N.E.2d 125 (1987), four years and eleven-month-old victim found competent to testify as to sexual abuse; *In Interest of A.M.C.,* 148 Ill. App. 3d 775, 102 Ill. Dec. 482, 500 N.E.2d 104 (1986), five-year-old competent even though she answered questions primarily by nodding or shaking her head; *People v. Robinson,* 94 Ill. App. 3d 304, 49 Ill. Dec. 879, 418 N.E.2d 899 (1981), competency of seven-year-old not determined by age; *People v. Miller,* 58 Ill. App. 3d 156, 15 Ill. Dec. 605, 377 N.E.2d 1077 (1978), four-year-old found to lack sufficient recollection of dates, times, places or other incidents. Children often are asked their names, where they go to school, how old they are, whether they know who the judge is, whether they know what a lie is, and whether they know what happens when one tells a lie. *Kentucky v. Stincer,* 482 U.S. 730 (1987). It is not necessary for the child to give perfect answers to questions asked during a competency determination for the child to be found competent. *People v. Barfield,* 187 Ill. App. 3d 257, 134 Ill. Dec. 874, 543 N.E.2d 157 (1989); *People v. Dempsey,* 242 Ill. App. 3d 568, 182 Ill. Dec. 784, 610 N.E.2d 208 (1993). Once a finding of competency has been made, the foregoing matters concerning mental capacity, *People v. Rainge,* 211 Ill. App. 3d 432, 155 Ill. Dec. 918, 570 N.E.2d 431 (1991), as well as any subsequent confusion or contradiction in the testimony goes only to credibility, not competency. *In Interest of A.M.C.,* 148 Ill. App. 3d 775, 102 Ill. Dec. 482, 500 N.E.2d 104 (1986); *People v. McNichols,* 139 Ill. App. 3d 947, 94 Ill. Dec. 375, 487 N.E.2d 1252 (1986). The recent trend has been toward an extremely broad standard of competency in which trial courts' decisions permitting very young children to testify have been upheld. *People v. Mack,* 216 Ill. App. 3d 239, 160 Ill. Dec. 69, 576 N.E.2d 1023 (1991).

In reviewing the sufficiency of the evidence, as on a motion to direct a verdict or for a new trial, the court may, of course, determine whether the jury could reasonably have believed a particular witness, in view of manifest deficiencies in his power of observation, recordation, recollection, or narration. In light of the trial court's opportunity to take into account the demeanor of the witness, review on appeal is limited to determining abuse of discretion. *People v. Williams,* 147 Ill. 2d 173, 167 Ill. Dec. 853, 588 N.E.2d 983 (1991). *Accord People v. Garcia,* 97 Ill. 2d 58, 73 Ill. Dec. 414, 454 N.E.2d 274 (1983), there is no rigid formula that is applicable to determining competency.

Of course, the fact of mental abnormality of any witness, either at the time of observing the facts or at the time of testifying, may be explored on cross-examination and established by extrinsic evidence as bearing on credibility. *Schneiderman v. Interstate Transit Lines, Inc.,* 394 Ill. 569, 69 N.E.2d 293 (1946); *People v. Friesland,* 130 Ill. App. 3d 595, 85 Ill. Dec. 905, 474 N.E.2d 865 (1985) (it is well established that evidence of a witness's mental condition is admissible to the extent that it relates to the credibility of the witness's testimony). *See also* McCormick, Evidence §44 (4th ed. 1992). *Contra Adams v. Ford Motor Co.,* 103 Ill. App. 2d 356, 243 N.E.2d 843 (1968), sustaining rejection of offer of records of prior commitments of witness to mental institution. The mental abnormality being inquired of must, of course, be relevant to attacking the witness's ability to perceive, record, recollect, or narrate. *People v. Helton,* 153 Ill. App. 3d 901, 106 Ill. Dec. 600, 506 N.E.2d 307 (1987). Discovery of mental health records will be required if a showing is made of the relevancy of the information sought to the witness's credibility, *People v. Dace,* 114 Ill. App. 3d 908, 70 Ill. Dec. 684, 449 N.E.2d 1031 (1983), *aff'd,* 104 Ill. 2d 96, 83 Ill. Dec. 573, 470 N.E.2d 993 (1984), but not otherwise. *People v. Walton,* 107 Ill. App. 3d 698, 63 Ill. Dec. 351, 437 N.E.2d 1273 (1982); *People v. Friesland* supra.

See generally Advisory Committee's Note to Federal Rule of Evidence 601, 56 F.R.D. 183, 262 (1973), stating that no mental qualification as to competency is specified. *See also People v. Seel,* 68 Ill. App. 3d 996, 25 Ill. Dec. 99, 386 N.E.2d 370 (1979), the modern tendency regarding competency is to permit a questionable witness to testify and to allow the credibility of the witness to be thoroughly explored on cross-examination.

§601.4　Effect of Alcohol or Drug Use

Habitual use of intoxicants or drug addiction similarly does not by itself make a witness incompetent to testify. *People v. Dixon,* 22 Ill. 2d 513, 177 N.E.2d 224 (1961); *People v. Whitlock,* 174 Ill. App. 3d 749, 124 Ill. Dec. 263, 528 N.E.2d 1371 (1988); 2 Wigmore, Evidence, §492 (Chadbourn rev. 1970). However, the supreme court has gone so far as to state that habitual users of narcotics become notorious liars and that their testimony is likely to be affected thereby. *People v. Perkins,* 26 Ill. 2d 230, 186 N.E.2d 330 (1962). The use of alcohol or drugs, relevant in assessing a witness's credibility, may be inquired of on cross-examination. *People v. Drumwright,* 48 Ill. App. 2d 392, 199 N.E.2d 282 (1964). *See* §607.5 infra.

With respect to intoxication as evidence of negligence, *see* §403.3 supra; as to opinion as to intoxication, *see* §701.7 infra.

§601.5　Religious Belief

Religious tests of qualifications for witnesses are abrogated by Section 3 of Article I of the Constitution of Illinois. *People v. Ballinger,* 36 Ill. 2d 620, 225 N.E.2d 10 (1967); *Hronek v. People,* 134 Ill. 139, 24 N.E. 861 (1890).

With respect to affirming by persons with conscientious scruples against taking an oath, *see* §603.1 infra.

As to inquiring into religious beliefs for purpose of impeachment, *see* §610.1 infra; as to dying declarations, *see* §804.6 infra.

§601.6　Husband and Wife

The original common law of Illinois imposed a strict incompetency on a spouse to testify for or against the other spouse or to testify to conversations or admissions or any knowledge gained through the marriage relationship. *Reeves v. Herr,* 59 Ill. 81 (1871).

The Code of Civil Procedure now provides:

> In all actions, husband and wife may testify for or against each other, provided that neither may testify as to any communication or admission made by either of them to the other or as to any conversation between them during marriage, except in actions between such husband and wife, and in actions where the custody, support, health or welfare of their children or children in either spouse's care, custody or control is directly in issue, and as to matters in which either has acted as agent for the other. [735 ILCS 5/8-801.]

A similar provision, with appropriate exception for crimes by one spouse against the other, prevails in criminal cases. 725 ILCS 5/115-16. The statutory language clearly has removed the incompetency generally.

Some confusion, however, has resulted from the language of the statutory proviso, "neither may testify as to any communication or admission made by either of them to the other or as to any conversation between them during marriage. . . ." For a time it was construed as a rule of limited incompetency, permitting any party to object to testimony by the wife as to conversations with her husband, *Dunn v. Heasley,* 375 Ill. 43, 30 N.E.2d 628 (1940), or even as to knowledge gained through the marriage relationship. *Heineman v. Hermann,* 385 Ill. 191, 52 N.E.2d 263 (1944). The construction unduly restricted the remedial purpose of the statute and was at variance with the trend of modern legislation on the subject. *See* 8 Wigmore, Evidence §2288 (McNaughton rev. 1961). This unfortunate situation was corrected by *People v. Palumbo,* 5 Ill. 2d 409, 125 N.E.2d 518 (1955), in which the statute was construed as eliminating the marital incompetency completely, leaving under the proviso only a husband-wife privilege against disclosure of confidential communications between them. The privilege is discussed in §503.3 supra.

§601.7   Conviction of Crime

The common law disqualification as a witness by reason of conviction of crime has been abolished in both civil and criminal cases. 735 ILCS 5/8-101; 725 ILCS 125/6.

As to proof of conviction for purposes of impeachment, *see* §609 infra.

§601.8   Parties and Interested Persons

The common law disqualification of parties and interested persons as witnesses has been abolished in both civil and criminal cases. 735 ILCS 5/8-101; 725 ILCS 125/6.

The removal of this disqualification is subject to important exceptions in civil cases by virtue of the Dead Man's Act, discussed in §606 infra.

§602   Personal Knowledge

§602.1   The Requirement of Personal Knowledge

Admissible testimony is limited to matters of which the witness has personal knowledge through her own senses, i.e., capacity, opportunity, actual acquisition and retention of matter related. *Accord People v. Enis,* 139 Ill. 2d 264, 151 Ill. Dec. 493, 564 N.E.2d 1155 (1990) (a witness may only testify as to facts within personal knowledge, citing Handbook); *Northern Ill. Gas Co. v. Vincent DiVito Constr.,* 214 Ill. App. 3d 203, 157 Ill. Dec. 825, 573 N.E.2d 243 (1991) (citing Handbook). "[A] witness who testifies to a fact which can be perceived by the senses must have had an opportunity to observe, and must have actually observed the fact." McCormick, Evidence §10 at 37 (4th ed. 1992). Accordingly, it is improper to permit a witness to testify to the sale price of corn known to him only from reports of other persons, *Carpenter v. First Natl. Bank of Joliet,* 119 Ill. 352, 10 N.E. 18 (1887); improper to permit a policeman who was not an eyewitness to testify to details of an accident learned from defendant's statement, *Bezouskas v. Kruger,* 298 Ill. App. 462, 19 N.E.2d 116 (1939); testimony that defendant did not forge an instrument is properly excluded when the witness has no personal knowledge of the facts, *People v. Rosenbaum,* 299 Ill. 93, 132 N.E. 433 (1921); and police officer's testimony as to reputation for truth and veracity was properly stricken in absence of establishment of adequate personal knowledge. *People v. Bambulas,* 42 Ill. 2d 419, 247 N.E.2d 873 (1969). Of course, an expert may express opinions based on facts of which he does not have personal knowledge. *Village of Westchester v. Williamson,* 61 Ill. App. 2d 25, 208 N.E.2d 879 (1965). *See* §§703, 705 infra with respect to the basis of an expert's opinion.

Loose reference to testimony unsupported by personal knowledge as an "opinion" or a "conclusion" leads to confusion with matters treated in later sections. It should also be noted that a witness testifying to an extrajudicial statement that is not hearsay or is admissible as an exception to the hearsay rule, Article VIII, is not required to have personal knowledge of the matter related in the statement. The witness testifying to such a statement admitted as nonhearsay or as a hearsay exception must, however, possess personal knowledge as to the fact of the statement itself. To be admitted pursuant to a hearsay exception other than an admission of a party, §802.1 infra, the declarant of the extrajudicial statement must be shown to have personal knowledge as to the matter related. Personal knowledge may appear from his statement or be inferable from the circumstances.

The requirement of personal knowledge is one of conditional relevancy, §104.2 supra. The proponent of the evidence must thus introduce evidence sufficient, if believed, to support a finding by a reasonable jury of personal knowledge; the evidence may consist of the testimony of the witness himself. *People v. Jennings,* 252 Ill. 534, 96 N.E. 1077 (1911), identification of accused. Testimony previously received may be stricken if it later becomes clear that personal knowledge was lacking. *See* §103.3 supra. Once sufficient evidence of personal knowledge has been introduced, the ultimate determination as to whether the witness does in fact possess personal knowledge of the matter related rests with the jury.

§602.2   Degree of Personal Knowledge Required: "I Believe" and Similar Expressions

Absolute certainty, either of observation, recordation, or recollection, is not required. *Barber v. Barber,* 368 Ill. 215, 13 N.E.2d 257 (1938). All that is required is an opportunity to observe and a belief that what is related depicts the recorded perception.

The use of certain phrases by a witness may give rise to uncertainty as to whether he is stating his best recollection based on personal observation or a conclusion that he has reached on the basis of data derived from other sources. The former is admissible, the latter not. Thus testimony according to the "best belief" of the witness is admissible when the subject is within his personal knowledge. *People v. Fryer,* 266 Ill. 216, 107 N.E. 134 (1914). Under similar circumstances, testimony prefaced with "I think" is admissible. *Abbott v. Church,* 288 Ill. 91, 123 N.E. 306 (1919). On the other hand, testimony that the witness had "probably" seen what he is testifying about, or testimony of his "impression," in the absence of any showing of actual knowledge or observation, has been held inadmissible. *Allen B. Wrisley Co. v. Burke,* 203 Ill. 250, 67 N.E. 818 (1903); *Rounds v. McCormick,* 11 Ill. App. 220 (1882).

§602.3   Substance of Conversations and Documents

If a conversation or parol evidence of the contents of a document is admissible, *see* §1004.2 infra, verbatim accuracy by a witness who heard the conversation or is familiar with the document is not required; the substance of the language may be stated. *Kirchner v. Morrison*, 320 Ill. 236, 150 N.E. 690 (1926); *Main v. McCarty*, 15 Ill. 441 (1854); *People v. Riley*, 99 Ill. App. 3d 244, 54 Ill. Dec. 474, 424 N.E.2d 1377 (1981) (citing Handbook).

With respect to characterization of the conversation or document, *see* §704.5 infra.

§603   Oath or Affirmation

§603.1   *Commentary*

Before testifying, a witness must declare that she will testify truthfully by oath or affirmation. *McKinney v. People*, 7 Ill. 540 (1845). As stated in *McKinney v. People* supra, the object of swearing the witness is twofold. The first and principal design is to affect the conscience of the witness to compel her to speak the truth. The second is that if the witness willfully falsifies the truth, she may then be punished for perjury. 5 ILCS 255/5. The form of declaration may be either by oath or affirmation. 5 ILCS 255/3 and 255/4. The requirement that a witness be administered an oath or affirmation may be waived by failure to object. *People v. Krotz*, 341 Ill. 214, 172 N.E. 135 (1930).

To be a competent witness the person must be capable of appreciating the moral duty to tell the truth. *Accord* 725 ILCS 5/115-14. Where such an objection is raised, usually in regard to the competency of a child, the customary practice is for the court to conduct a preliminary examination to determine if the witness in fact possesses the ability to appreciate the moral duty to tell the truth. *People v. Ballinger*, 36 Ill. 2d 620, 225 N.E.2d 10 (1967), a nine-year-old boy competent; *People v. Linkogle*, 54 Ill. App. 3d 830, 11 Ill. Dec. 467, 368

N.E.2d 1075 (1977), eight-year-old girl competent. The trial court's determination will not be upset absent an abuse of discretion. *People v. Brown,* 52 Ill. 2d 94, 285 N.E.2d 1 (1972).

See generally Advisory Committee's Note to Federal Rule of Evidence 601, 56 F.R.D 183, 262 (1973), providing that no moral qualification as to competency is specified.

§604   Interpreters

§604.1   Commentary

An interpreter is a person who aids a communication when at least one party to the communication has a hearing or speaking impairment or a language difficulty, 735 ILCS 5/8-911(a).

Interpreters may be employed when necessary in civil matters, 735 ILCS 5/8-1401; they must be made available when necessary in criminal proceedings, 725 ILCS 140/1, and in any proceeding when a deaf person is a party, a juror, or a witness. 725 ILCS 5/115-4(1); 735 ILCS 5/8-1402. An interpreter may also assist a deaf juror during deliberations. *Id. See also* 725 ILCS 5/115-14, stating that a witness is competent if, among other requirements, the witness is capable of expressing himself through the use of an interpreter. Whether an interpreter is necessary rests in the discretion of the court. *People v. Soldat,* 32 Ill. 2d 478, 207 N.E.2d 449 (1965); *People v. Bragg,* 68 Ill. App. 3d 622, 25 Ill. Dec. 214, 386 N.E.2d 485 (1979). If communication is otherwise privileged, that underlying privilege is not waived because of the presence of the interpreter, 735 ILCS 5/8-911(b). Where the interpreter is for a criminal defendant, 725 ILCS 140/1, or for a deaf person, 735 ILCS 5/8-1402, the interpreter's fee is paid from general county funds. When an interpreter is employed, the interpreter is to be administered an oath or affirmation. The requirement that the interpreter be administered an oath or affirmation is waived by failure to object. *People v. Delgado,* 10 Ill. App. 3d 33, 294 N.E.2d 84 (1973). The oath or affirmation of the interpreter is to make a "true translation," which requires that everything be translated. *Schnier v. People,* 23 Ill. 17 (1859). Failure of the interpreter to provide a true and comprehensible translation may result in reversible error. *People v. Harris,* 104 Ill. App. 3d 833, 60 Ill. Dec. 546, 433 N.E.2d 343 (1982); *People v. Starling,* 21 Ill. App. 3d 217, 315 N.E.2d 163 (1974).

To be employed as an interpreter the person must meet the qualifications for an expert witness, §702.2 infra, which in the case of an interpreter means that by reason of knowledge, skill, experience, training, or education the particular interpreter is capable of providing a true translation.

§605 Competency of Judge, Juror, or Lawyer as Witness

§605.1 Competency of Judge as Witness

According to the older view of the common law a judge was competent to testify in a trial over which he presided but in his discretion might decline to do so. A second view developed under which the judge was disqualified from testifying to material disputed facts but free to testify with respect to matters merely formal and undisputed. A third view provides for a blanket prohibition against testimony by the presiding judge. As McCormick, Evidence §68 (4th ed. 1992) states, the third view, for which support is growing, seems the expedient one. The reasons for automatically rendering the judge incompetent are obvious. The role of witness plainly destroys his image of impartiality, however impartial he may in fact be. Moreover, it must create problems concerning jury overvaluing of his testimony, ruling on objections to his testimony, the conduct of cross-examination, and the virtual impossibility of impeachment. While there appears to be no Illinois case on point, it has been stated that where a judge is potentially a witness he should recuse himself. *People v. Williams*, 37 Ill. 2d 617, 230 N.E.2d 194 (1967); *People v. Short*, 66 Ill. App. 3d 172, 22 Ill. Dec. 915, 383 N.E.2d 723 (1978). As to the special showing that must be made before the trial judge may be called as a witness, *see People v. Montgomery*, 162 Ill. 2d 109, 205 Ill. Dec. 143, 642 N.E.2d 1260 (1994); *People v. Reynolds*, 284 Ill. App. 3d 611, 220 Ill. Dec. 576, 673 N.E.2d 720 (1996); *People v. Palacio*, 240 Ill. App. 3d 1078, 180 Ill. Dec. 862, 607 N.E.2d 1375 (1993).

Federal Rule of Evidence 605, 65 F.R.D. 131, 147 (1975), provides that no objection need be made in order to preserve the objection to the presiding judge testifying as a witness, a position that is eminently sensible.

§605.2   Consideration by Court of Evidence Not Admitted at Trial

In a bench trial, it is improper for the trial judge to consider the facts within her personal knowledge or to conduct investigations or experiments that result in considering evidence that was not introduced at trial, *People v. Gilbert*, 68 Ill. 2d 252, 12 Ill. Dec. 142, 369 N.E.2d 849 (1977). *See, e.g. People v. Wallenberg*, 24 Ill. 2d 350, 181 N.E.2d 143 (1962), error for trial judge in commenting on the testimony to state that he knew by own private knowledge that there were no gas stations on the road in question; *People v. Thunberg*, 412 Ill. 565, 107 N.E.2d 843 (1952), improper for judge to read a confession not in evidence and to conduct private interview with witness and her parents; *City of Chicago v. Garrett*, 136 Ill. App. 3d 529, 91 Ill. Dec. 127, 483 N.E.2d 409 (1985), improper for judge to consult an independent expert and obtain books relative to the dispute; *People v. Kent*, 111 Ill. App. 3d 733, 67 Ill. Dec. 334, 444 N.E.2d 570 (1982), error for trial judge to consider personal knowledge of facts not in evidence in assessing the credibility of an expert witness. Reliance on information dehors the record will result in a reversal when the information considered relates to an important matter to the prejudice of a party. *People v. Jeffries,* 26 Ill. 2d 248, 186 N.E.2d 242 (1962); *People v. Banks,* 102 Ill. App. 3d 877, 58 Ill. Dec. 570, 430 N.E.2d 602 (1981). *See also People v. Cannon,* 150 Ill. App. 3d 1009, 104 Ill. Dec. 82, 502 N.E.2d 345 (1986).

With respect to the court considering improperly admitted evidence, *see* §103.6 supra; as to judicial notice of matters generally known, *see* §202.1 supra.

§605.3 Competency of Juror as Witness at Trial

The likelihood of a juror ever being called to testify in a case in which he is sitting is extremely small, since any prospective juror disclosing personal knowledge would undoubtedly be excused during the jury selection process. In the unlikely event that a juror is called as a witness, for reasons similar to when the trial judge is so called, §605.1 supra, the member of the jury should not be permitted to testify. McCormick, Evidence §68 (4th ed. 1992). *See also* Federal Rule of Evidence 606(a), 65 F.R.D. 131, 147 (1975). Of course the reasons barring a juror from being a witness do not prevent the questioning of jurors by the judge or counsel as part of the jury selection process.

§605.4 Competency of Jurors to Attack Validity of Verdict or Indictment

Jurors are prohibited from attacking their verdict by testifying directly or indirectly by means of affidavits or statements as to irregularities intrinsic to the manner in which a decision was reached. *People v. Tobe,* 49 Ill. 2d 538, 276 N.E.2d 294 (1971); *Sanitary Dist. of Chicago v. Cullerton,* 147 Ill. 385, 35 N.E. 723 (1893). The rationale for thus insulating the jury decision-making process is expressed in *McDonald v. Pless*, 238 U.S. 264, 267 (1915):

> Jurors would be harassed and beset by the defeated party in an effort to secure from them evidence of facts which might establish misconduct sufficient to set aside a verdict. If evidence thus secured could be thus used, the result would be to make what was intended to be a private deliberation, the constant subject to public investigation — to the destruction of all frankness and freedom of discussion and conference.

Accord Tanner v. United States, 483 U.S. 107 (1987). A juror may thus not attack her verdict, for example, on the grounds of a quotient verdict, or on the grounds that a fellow juror was intoxicated, that jury instructions were misinterpreted, or that there was speculation as to insurance. Similarly excluded as grounds of attack are internal discussions, arguments, mental and emotional reactions, votes, statements, even a statement purporting to relate to specific factual information that was incorrect, and juror intoxication. *People v. Hobley*, 182 Ill. 2d 404, 231 Ill. Dec. 321, 696 N.E.2d 313 (1998); *People v. Boclair*, 129 Ill. 2d 458, 136 Ill. Dec. 29, 544 N.E.2d 715 (1989); *Chalmers v. City of Chicago*, 88 Ill. 2d 532, 59 Ill. Dec. 76, 431 N.E.2d 361 (1982); *People v. Holmes*, 69 Ill. 2d 507, 14 Ill. Dec. 460, 372 N.E.2d 656 (1978), juror may not impeach his verdict by showing motive, method, or process by which verdict was reached (for example, by explaining basis of findings or by asserting that jury was mistaken). *Accord People v. Szymanski*, 226 Ill. App. 3d 115, 168 Ill. Dec. 34, 589 N.E.2d 148 (1992), a map made by a juror considered by others was neither an independent juror investigation nor the presentation of information not in evidence.

Jurors may, however, attack their verdict on the grounds that prejudicial extraneous influences or information were injected into or brought to bear upon the deliberation process. *People v. Hobley* supra. Thus a juror may testify as to the existence of extraneous prejudicial information brought to the jury's attention (e.g., a radio newscast, a newspaper account, a list of other charges pending against the defendant, or a photograph previously ruled inadmissible, *People v. Hobley,* 182 Ill. 2d 404, 231 Ill. Dec. 321, 696 N.E.2d 313 (1998); *People v. Eddington,* 117 Ill. App. 3d 953, 73 Ill. Dec. 248, 453 N.E.2d 1383 (1983); *People v. Hayes,* 70 Ill. App. 3d 811, 26 Ill. Dec. 817, 388 N.E.2d 818 (1979)), an outside influence that improperly had been brought to bear upon a juror (e.g., a threat to the safety of a member of his family or statements by nonmembers of the jury to the jury that the jury knows the accused is guilty and should hang him, *People v. Hobley,* 182 Ill. 2d 404, 231 Ill. Dec. 321, 696 N.E.2d 313 (1998)), an unauthorized view, or jury investigation. *See, e.g., People v. Spice,* 54 Ill. App. 3d 539, 12 Ill. Dec. 506, 370 N.E.2d 129 (1977), juror visit to scene was prejudicial; *Heaver v. Ward,* 68 Ill. App. 3d 236, 24 Ill. Dec. 930, 386 N.E.2d 134 (1979), juror's visit to scene of accident, making of a diagram and showing of the diagram together with a "Rules of Road" book to fellow jurors required reversal; *People v. Holmes,* 69 Ill. 2d 507, 373 N.E.2d 656, 14 Ill. Dec. 460 (1978), investigation by several jurors, i.e., going to a shoe store to inspect various heels of shoes, resulted in prejudicial error; *Waller v. Bagga,* 219 Ill. App. 3d 542, 162 Ill. Dec. 259, 579 N.E.2d 1073 (1991), statement by bailiff that plaintiff had divorced his wife for a younger woman was improper extraneous information. With respect to juror intoxication, while *Tanner v. United States,* 483 U.S. 107 (1987), declares intoxication intrinsic and thus not subject to juror attack in the federal court, *Landstrom v. Williamson,* 165 Ill. App. 3d 1087, 116 Ill. Dec. 89, 518 N.E.2d 711 (1987), states that while a showing of mere consumption is not enough, a case by case analysis is required if evidence of juror intoxication is presented, a questionable distinction.

A juror may also attack her verdict by affidavit asserting that the juror or a fellow juror had answered falsely on *voir dire* about a matter involving potential bias or prejudice. *Department of Pub. Works & Bldgs. v. Christensen,* 25 Ill. 2d 273, 184 N.E.2d 884 (1962); *People v. Thomas,* 296 Ill. App. 3d 489, 230 Ill. Dec. 790, 694 N.E.2d 1068 (1998); *Hockett v. Dawdy,*

180 Ill. App. 3d 491, 129 Ill. Dec. 400, 536 N.E.2d 84 (1989); *Davis v. International Harvester Co.,* 167 Ill. App. 3d 814, 118 Ill. Dec. 589, 521 N.E.2d 1282 (1988).

Testimony or an affidavit of a juror may be admitted to rebut a charge of extraneous influence or information, thereby supporting the verdict. *Smith v. Illinois Valley Ice Cream Co.,* 20 Ill. App. 2d 312, 156 N.E.2d 361 (1959). This principle does not extend to supporting the verdict by jurors' affidavits that they did not consider certain evidence or instructions. *People v. Duzan,* 272 Ill. 478, 112 N.E. 315 (1916).

Where extraneous influence or information was brought to bear on the jury deliberation process, the verdict will be set aside if the court determines in its discretion that the matter injected, if considered by the jury, was prejudicial. *Pekelder v. Edgewater Automotive,* 68 Ill. 2d 136, 11 Ill. Dec. 292, 368 N.E.2d 900 (1977); *Wade v. City of Chicago,* 295 Ill. App. 3d 873, 230 Ill. Dec. 297, 693 N.E.2d 426 (1998). Extraneous influence or information is presumptively prejudicial. *People v. Hobley,* 182 Ill. 2d 404, 231 Ill. Dec. 321, 696 N.E.2d 313 (1998); *People v. Mitchell,* 152 Ill. 2d 274, 178 Ill. Dec. 354, 604 N.E.2d 877 (1992); *People v. Harris,* 123 Ill. 2d 113, 122 Ill. Dec. 76, 526 N.E.2d 335 (1988). The burden rests with the prevailing party to establish that the extraneous influence or information was harmless. *People v. Hobley* supra; *People v. Mitchell* supra; *People v. Harris* supra; *People v. Rettig,* 50 Ill. 2d 317, 278 N.E.2d 781 (1972). *See also People v. Childs,* 159 Ill. 2d 217, 201 Ill. Dec. 102, 636 N.E.2d 534 (1994). *Compare Kelly v. HCI Heinz Construction Co.,* 282 Ill. App. 3d 36, 218 Ill. Dec. 112, 668 N.E.2d 596 (1996), stating that while extraneous influence or information during jury deliberations are presumptively prejudicial placing the burden on the prevailing party, such matters occurring at other times during the trial do not create a presumption of prejudice leaving the burden on the losing party, a distinction, if it exists, that appears insufficiently grounded in policy to be properly recognized. The actual effect of the extraneous information or influence of the minds of the jury cannot be proved. *People v. Hobley,*

182 Ill. 2d 404, 231 Ill. Dec. 321, 696 N.E.2d 313 (1998); *People v. Holmes,* 69 Ill. 2d 507, 14 Ill. Dec. 460, 372 N.E.2d 656 (1978). The claim of prejudice must be specific: "a claim of prejudice cannot be founded on mere conjecture." *People v. Lewis,* 60 Ill. 2d 152, 158, 330 N.E.2d 857 (1975). The standard to be applied by the court is whether the extraneous information or influence involved such a probability that prejudice resulted that the judgment is deemed inherently lacking in due process. *People v. Hobley* supra; *People v. Holmes* supra; *Hockett v. Dawdy,* 180 Ill. App. 3d 491, 129 Ill. Dec. 400, 536 N.E.2d 84 (1989). A verdict will not be set aside where it is obvious that no prejudice resulted. *People v. Mills,* 40 Ill. 2d 4, 237 N.E.2d 697 (1968); *People v. Walker,* 292 Ill. App. 3d 500, 226 Ill. Dec. 542, 685 N.E.2d 997 (1997); *Waller v. Bagga,* 219 Ill. App. 3d 42, 162 Ill. Dec. 259, 579 N.E.2d 1073 (1991).

The Criminal Code contains prohibitions against disclosure of proceedings of a grand jury, including the pendency of an indictment under circumstances that might promote escape, the vote of a member, and opinions expressed by a member. 725 ILCS 5/112-6. Accordingly, the affidavit of a grand juror will not be admitted to show that fewer than the required number voted to find an indictment. *Gitchell v. People,* 146 Ill. 175, 33 N.E. 757 (1893). No prohibition exists, however, against disclosure of testimony given before the grand jury for purposes of impeaching a witness in a subsequent trial or to prove him guilty of perjury, and either a member of the grand jury or any other person properly present may testify thereto. *People v. Goldberg,* 302 Ill. 559, 135 N.E. 84 (1922); *Bressler v. People,* 117 Ill. 422, 8 N.E. 62 (1886). In this regard, a court reporter must attend sessions of the grand jury. 725 ILCS 5/112-6(a).

§605.5 Competency of Lawyer to Party as Witness

Effective August 1, 1990, the Illinois Rules of Professional Conduct replaced the Illinois Code of Professional Responsibility. The relevant provisions of the Illinois Rules of Professional Conduct dealing with a lawyer being a witness state as follows:

Rule 3.7. Lawyer as Witness

(a) A lawyer shall not accept or continue employment in contemplated or pending litigation if the lawyer knows or reasonably should know that the lawyer may be called as a witness on behalf of the client, except that the lawyer may undertake the employment and may testify:

(1) if the testimony will relate to an uncontested matter;

(2) if the testimony will relate to a matter of formality and the lawyer reasonably believes that no substantial evidence will be offered in opposition to the testimony;

(3) if the testimony will relate to the nature and value of legal services rendered in the case by the lawyer or the firm to the client; or

(4) as to any other matter, if refusal to accept or continue the employment would work a substantial hardship on the client.

(b) If a lawyer knows or reasonably should know that the lawyer may be called as a witness other than on behalf of the client, the lawyer may accept or continue the representation until the lawyer knows or reasonably should know that the lawyer's testimony is or may be prejudicial to the client.

(c) Except as prohibited by Rule 1.7 or Rule 1.9, a lawyer may act as advocate in a trial in which another lawyer in the lawyer's firm may be called as a witness.

Rule 1.7. Conflict of Interest: General Rule

(a) A lawyer shall not represent a client if the representation of that client will be directly adverse to another client, unless:

(1) the lawyer reasonably believes the representation will not adversely affect the relationship with the other client; and

(2) each client consents after disclosure.

(b) A lawyer shall not represent a client if the representation of that client may be materially limited by the lawyer's responsibilities to another client or to a third person, or by the lawyer's own interest, unless:

(1) the lawyer reasonably believes the representation will not be adversely affected; and

(2) the client consents after disclosure.

(c) When the representation of multiple clients in a single matter is undertaken, the disclosure shall include explanation of the implications of the common representation and the advantages and risks involved.

Rule 1.9. Conflict of Interest: Former Client

(a) A lawyer who has formerly represented a client in a matter shall not thereafter:

(1) represent another person in the same or a substantially related matter in which that person's interests are materially adverse to the interests of the former client, unless the former client consents after disclosure; or

(2) use information relating to the representation to the disadvantage of the former client, unless:

(A) such use is permitted by Rule 1.6; or

(B) the information has become generally known.

The court has wide discretion in refusing or permitting an attorney to testify in favor of a client or when subpoenaed to testify by an opposing party. *People v. King,* 66 Ill. 2d 551, 6 Ill. Dec. 891, 363 N.E.2d 838 (1977); *Beneficial Development v. Highland Park,* 239 Ill. App. 3d 414, 179 Ill. Dec. 1005, 606 N.E.2d 837 (1992). It will be generally exercised to prevent such testimony, especially where other sources of the evidence are available. *People v. Gendron,* 41 Ill. 2d 351, 243 N.E.2d 208 (1968). *See also Serpico v. Urso,* 127 Ill. App. 3d 667, 82 Ill. Dec. 821, 469 N.E.2d 355 (1984); *People v. Wilson,* 271 Ill. App. 3d 943, 208 Ill. Dec. 716, 649 N.E.2d 1377 (1995), trial court was within its discretion in prohibiting the defendant from calling as a witness the state's attorney trying the case when another witness was available to testify; *Giraldi v. Community Consolidated School District # 62,* 279 Ill. App. 3d 679, 216 Ill. Dec. 272, 665, N.E.2d 332 (1996), trial court should have required party to forego impeachment by virtue of an omission in an oral statement when attorney could alone provide extrinsic evidence where witness had already been impeached on same point by omission in the witness's deposition. When no other witness is available, discretion will sometimes be exercised in favor of preventing the lawyer from testifying and sometimes not. The presence or absence of surprise appears significant. *See, e.g., People v. Hill,* 56 Ill. App. 3d 510, 14 Ill. Dec. 204, 371 N.E.2d 1257 (1978), where lawyer acts as own investigator, he may be prohibited from testifying as to existence of a prior inconsistent statement; *People v. Langdon,* 91 Ill. App. 3d 1050, 47 Ill. Dec. 573, 415 N.E.2d 578 (1980), permitting prosecuting attorney to testify as to impeaching statement, while acknowledging the justified reluctance of courts to permit such testimony and suggesting that it would have been preferable for the prosecuting attorney to seek to withdraw from the case; *Stach v. Sears, Roebuck & Co.,* 102 Ill. App. 3d 397, 57 Ill. Dec. 879, 429 N.E.2d 1242 (1981), attorney who had not formally withdrawn as counsel, but had turned file over to another firm years earlier, may testify; *People v. Jackson,* 105 Ill. App. 3d 750, 61 Ill. Dec. 57, 433 N.E.2d 1385 (1982), prosecuting attorney permitted to testify to prior inconsistent statement by a prosecution witness who gave affirmatively damaging testimony of surprise to the state; *Andrea Dumon, Inc. v. Pittway Corp.,* 110 Ill. App. 3d 481, 66 Ill. Dec. 148, 422 N.E.2d 574 (1982), an attorney may properly testify without withdrawing where an unanticipated development in a complex action makes the attorney's testimony necessary; *In re Marriage of Lee,* 135 Ill. App. 3d 509, 90 Ill. Dec. 245, 481 N.E.2d 1045 (1985), an attorney may testify to rebut testimony from opposing party that the attorney had threatened financial repercussions; *People v. Janes,* 138 Ill. App. 3d 558, 93 Ill. Dec. 216, 486 N.E.2d 317 (1985), prosecuting attorney improperly permitted to testify on rebuttal as to inconsistent statement when trial testimony came as no surprise: prosecuting attorney should have withdrawn before trial; *People v. McMurtry,* 279 Ill. App. 3d 865, 216 Ill. Dec. 390, 665 N.E.2d 450 (1996), defense attorney properly precluded from testifying as to witness's prior inconsistent statement (suggestion made that trial might have permitted inquiry on cross-examination as to the content of the statement; a suggestion that runs right into the face of the principle that prior inconsistent statements not acknowledged by the witness must be proven by extrinsic evidence if noncollateral, §613.3 infra). The trial court similarly possesses wide discretion in deciding whether to permit trial counsel to withdraw from the case and testify as a witness. *People v. Blake,* 179 Ill. App. 3d 249, 128 Ill. Dec. 233, 534 N.E.2d 415 (1989), withdrawal properly denied where it would work a substantial hardship on defendant and waste judicial resources.

Pursuant to Rule 3.7(c), a lawyer may act as an advocate in a trial in which another lawyer in the lawyer's firm is called as a witness. *Beneficial Development v. Highland Park,* 239 Ill. App. 3d 414, 179 Ill. Dec. 1005, 606 N.E.2d 837 (1992). *See also People v. Elston,* 222 Ill. App. 3d 956, 165 Ill. Dec. 462, 584 N.E.2d 896 (1991); *People v. Harvey,* 92 Ill. App. 3d 465, 47 Ill. Dec. 848, 415 N.E.2d 1161 (1980), assistant state's attorney not prosecuting the case permitted to testify in rebuttal establishing impeaching statement of defendant or defense witness.

Where an attorney for a party becomes a witness through no action of his own — such as after being compared in appearance to the person committing the offense charged by a witness who testifies inconsistently at trial—the better practice is to permit the attorney to testify. *People v. Chatman,* 105 Ill. App. 3d 276, 61 Ill. Dec. 156, 434 N.E.2d 309 (1982).

As to the special showing that must be made before a prosecuting attorney may be subpoenaed to testify by the criminal defendant, *see People v. Palacio,* 240 Ill. App. 3d 1078, 180 Ill. Dec. 862, 607 N.E.2d 1375 (1993). Where the criminal defendant telephones the prosecuting attorney, thereby precluding the opportunity for a third party to be present, the trial court may in its discretion refuse to permit the defendant to call the prosecuting attorney to testify on the basis of waiver. *People v. Wilson,* 271 Ill. App. 3d 943, 208 Ill. Dec. 716, 649 N.E.2d 1377 (1995).

§606   Dead Man's Act

§606.1   An Overview

Attention is directed to the organization of the sections of the Code of Civil Procedure that deal with the competency of parties and interested persons. 735 ILCS 5/8-201 to 5/8-601. Common law incompetency, as continued by statute, applies to cases in which the opposite party sues or defends as a representative of a person who is deceased or legally disabled, under §8-201, §§606.2 to 606.6 infra, with four exceptions, one of which incorporates §8-401, §606.6 infra. A fifth is added by §8-601, §606.8 infra. The continuation of incompetency is applied to cases of deceased partners, joint contractors, and contracting agents, under specified circumstances, by §8-301, §606.7 infra. Removal of incompetency by assignment or release is precluded by §8-501, §606.3 infra.

Section 8-201 of the statute is commonly called the "Dead Man's Act." Its purported purpose is to remove the temptation of the survivor to a transaction to testify falsely and to equalize the positions of the parties in regard to the giving of testimony. *Hoem v. Zia*, 159 Ill. 2d 193, 201 Ill. Dec. 47, 636 N.E.2d 479 (1994) (citing Handbook); *Fleming v. Fleming*, 85 Ill. App. 3d 532, 40 Ill. Dec. 676, 406 N.E.2d 879 (1980); *Kamberos v. Magnuson*, 156 Ill. App. 3d 800, 109 Ill. Dec. 491, 510 N.E.2d 112 (1987); *Overcast v. Bodart*, 266 Ill. App. 3d 428, 203 Ill. Dec. 425, 639 N.E.2d 984 (1994) (citing Handbook). Accordingly, the Dead Man's Act bars only that evidence that the decedent or person under a legal disability could have refuted. *Smith v. Haran*, 273 Ill. App. 3d 866, 210 Ill. Dec. 191, 652 N.E.2d 1167 (1995). The Dead Man's Act applies to testimony at trial and to motions for summary judgment. *Groce v. South Chicago Community Hospital*, 282 Ill. App. 3d 1004, 218 Ill. Dec. 453, 669 N.E.2d 596 (1996); *Rerack v. Lally*, 241 Ill. App. 3d 692, 182 Ill. Dec. 193, 609 N.E.2d 727 (1992). The Dead Man's Act manifests the cynical view that a party will lie when she cannot be directly contradicted and the unrealistic assumption that jurors, knowing the situation, will believe anything they hear in these circumstances. While motivated by the laudable desire to protect decedent's and legally disabled person's assets from attack based on perjured testimony, *Wells v. Enloe*, 282 Ill. App. 3d 586, 218 Ill. Dec. 425, 669 N.E.2d 368 (1996), the validity of this approach is questioned with vigor; the modern trend is to remove the disqualification. 2 Wigmore, Evidence §§578, 578a (Chadbourn rev. 1979). In any event, it is by far the most frequent source of controversy over the competency of witnesses. Without considering the effect of the vast amount of litigation generated by the Dead Man's Act, it is felt that the Act should be abrogated on the ground that this surviving relic of the common law disqualification of parties as witnesses leads to more miscarriages of justice than it prevents. *Accord Smith v. Haran*, 273 Ill. App. 3d 866, 878, 210 Ill. Dec. 191, 199, 652 N.E.2d 1167, 1175 (1995) ("Because there is room for disagreement in this area (*see, for example*, the dissent to this opinion) and because the Act generates so much controversy and litigation, many commentators have suggested that the time has come for the legislature to repeal or modify the Dead Man's Act, as have more than half the States. (*See, e.g.*, Kahn, Repeal of Dead Man's Act Advocated, 55 Ill. B.J. 430 (1967); Barnard, The Dead Man's Act Rears Its Ugly Head Again, 72 Ill. B.J. 420 (1984); Barnard, The Dead Man's Act is Alive and Well, 83 Ill. B.J. 248 (1995).)"). *See generally Matter of Estate of Rollins*, 269 Ill. App. 3d 261, 206 Ill. Dec. 774, 645 N.E.2d 1026 (1995), modern trend is to remove the disqualification of the Dead Man's Act because the unjust results of its application often outweigh its protections, citing Handbook.

Evidentiary rulings by the trial court are reviewed on appeal applying the clear abuse of discretion standard. *In re Estate of Hoover*, 155 Ill. 2d 402, 185 Ill. Dec. 866, 615 N.E.2d 736 (1993).

With respect to the Dead Man's Act and the Original Writing Rule, *see* §§606.6 and 1004.1 infra.

§606.2   *The Three Requirements*

The Dead Man's Act provides:

> In the trial of any action in which any party sues or defends as the representative of a deceased person or person under a legal disability, no adverse party or person directly interested in the action shall be allowed to testify on his or her own behalf to any conversation with the deceased or person under legal disability or to any event which took place in the presence of the deceased or person under legal disability. . . . [735 ILCS 5/8-201.]

Observe that three requirements are set forth and that all must be met in order to render the witness incompetent:

(1) the witness must be an adverse party or person directly interested in the action, §606.3 infra;

(2) he must seek to testify in his own behalf, §606.4 infra; and

(3) an adverse party suing or defending as a representative of a deceased or person under legal disability is protected as to any conversation with the deceased or person under legal disability and as to any event taking place in such person's presence, §606.5 infra.

The statute deals primarily with competency and not with the admissibility of evidence. Its effect is to render a witness incompetent as to certain matters, unless the situation falls within one of the exceptions. Here objections that a conversation with a deceased person is called for, and like objections, are inappropriate (except as to a deceased partner, joint contractor, or agent, §606.7 infra). The question is whether the witness is competent. *Creighton v. Elgin,* 387 Ill. 592, 56 N.E.2d 825 (1944), statement by deceased person admissible if proved by competent witness; *Belfield v. Coop,* 8 Ill. 2d 293, 134 N.E.2d 249 (1956), wire recording of conversation between testator and incompetent witness admissible if proved by competent witness; *Muka v. Estate of Muka,* 164 Ill. App. 3d

223, 115 Ill. Dec. 262, 517 N.E.2d 673 (1982), tape recording of decedent himself admissible if authenticated by competent witness. *See also In re Estate of Miller,* 189 Ill. App. 3d 171, 136 Ill. Dec. 504, 544 N.E.2d 1279 (1989), tape recordings of telephone messages from decedent were not admissible because the only person with personal knowledge of the dates of the messages was an adverse party. The statute does not prohibit the protected party from introducing evidence that serves to protect the estate or assets of the protected party. *Wells v. Enloe,* 282 Ill. App. 3d 586, 218 Ill. Dec. 425, 669 N.E.2d 368 (1996).

The burden of establishing to the court that the witness is incompetent to testify as to the testimony being offered rests on the objecting party. *Heller v. Jonathan Investments, Inc.,* 135 Ill. App. 3d 350, 90 Ill. Dec. 197, 481 N.E.2d 997 (1985). The right to object that an adverse party or interested person is barred by the Dead Man's Act belongs solely to the representative of the deceased person or person under legal disability. *In re Estate of Sewart,* 274 Ill. App. 3d 298, 210 Ill. Dec. 175, 652 N.E.2d 1151 (1995). Failure to object under the Dead Man's Act on the grounds of incompetency of a witness to offer certain testimony constitutes a waiver, §103.2 supra. *Matter of Estate of Netherton,* 62 Ill. App. 3d 55, 19 Ill. Dec. 185, 378 N.E.2d 800 (1978).

As to competency to testify to loss or destruction of documents, *see* §1004.1 infra.

§606.3   First Requirement — Witness an Adverse Party or Interested Person

Parties.   The Dead Man's Act disqualifies an adverse party from testifying on his own behalf against a protected party, 735 ILCS 5/8-201. *See, e.g., Hoem v. Zia,* 159 Ill. 2d 193, 201 Ill. Dec. 47, 636 N.E.2d 479 (1994).

Determining whether the witness is a party presents few problems. Motive in making him a party is immaterial if he is a proper party. *Sullivan v. Corn Prods. Co.,* 245 Ill. 9, 91 N.E.

643 (1910), defendant foreman of principal defendant incompetent although purpose in making him a party was to render him incompetent. If he is not a proper party, he cannot be disqualified by merely making him a party. *Northern Trust Co. v. Sanford,* 308 Ill. 381, 139 N.E. 603 (1923).

If a party is dismissed or a verdict is directed in her favor, her status as a party and incompetency resulting therefrom are terminated. *Hawthorne v. New York Cent. R. Co.,* 2 Ill. App. 2d 338, 119 N.E.2d 516 (1954). If the party is dismissed or a verdict directed in her favor after both parties have rested, the trial judge should reopen the case on request to permit her to testify. *See* §611.4 infra.

Whether a party is seeking to testify against a protected party and is thus an adverse party within the meaning of 5/8-201 is not determined on the basis of formal designation as plaintiff and defendant but by analysis of actual interests. In equity, parties have long been realigned according to interest in applying the Dead Man's Act. Thus, in a will contest, a defendant who is both a devisee and an heir, but would take more as heir, is adverse to her codefendants, the executors and other devisees, and incompetent to testify against them at the instance of plaintiff contestants. *Pyle v. Pyle,* 158 Ill. 289, 41 N.E. 999 (1895). Conversely, an heir who would take more as legatee is adverse to the other heirs. *Brownlie v. Brownlie,* 351 Ill. 72, 183 N.E. 613 (1932). The question in every case is whether the testimony of the party-witness will be of benefit to him as against the protected party. *See Dyer v. Martin,* 4 Scam. 146 (1842); *Herron v. Underwood,* 152 Ill. App. 3d 144, 105 Ill. Dec. 105, 503 N.E.2d 1111 (1987).

With the advent of liberal joinder provisions of the old Practice Act, formal alignment of parties as plaintiffs or defendants has lost its significance in law actions as well as in equity. *See Johnson v. Moon,* 3 Ill. 2d 561, 121 N.E.2d 774 (1954). Hence the equitable approach of aligning parties according to their actual interests must be adopted in all cases. Otherwise liberality in joinder would accomplish an unwarranted extension of the Dead Man's Act.

Similar reasoning applies to adversity of interests as between coparties. Thus in a tort action the testimony of a defendant is incompetent against an administrator codefendant, it being to his advantage to have the estate held liable. *Mernick v. Chiodini,* 12 Ill. App. 2d 249, 139 N.E.2d 784 (1957).

Interested persons. The Dead Man's Act also applies if the person seeking to testify in his own behalf against a protected party is "directly interested in the action," 735 ILCS 5/8-201. The test of interest is whether the witness will gain or lose as a direct result of the litigation. *Brownlie v. Brownlie* supra. To be disqualifying the interest must be of a pecuniary nature. *Herron v. Underwood,* 152 Ill. App. 3d 144, 105 Ill. Dec. 105, 503 N.E.2d 1111 (1987). Actual interest controls, rather than belief, understanding, or feeling. *Pyle v. Pyle* supra. However, "person directly interested in the action," or "interested person," as used throughout 5/8-201, does not include a person who is interested solely as executor, trustee, or in any other fiduciary capacity, whether or not she receives or expects to receive compensation for acting in that capacity, 735 ILCS 5/8-201(c). *Accord Herron v. Underwood,* 152 Ill. App. 3d 144, 105 Ill. Dec. 105, 503 N.E.2d 1111 (1987); *Estate of Ierulli v. First Natl. Bank of Peoria,* 167 Ill. App. 3d 595, 118 Ill. Dec. 372, 521 N.E.2d 654 (1988).

Interested persons have been held to include the following:

(1) A shareholder of a corporation that is a party. *Thrasher v. Pike County R.R.,* 25 Ill. 393 (1861).
(2) A member of a benefit association that is a party, members being subject to assessments. *Cronin v. Royal League,* 199 Ill. 228, 65 N.E. 323 (1902).
(3) Beneficiaries of a fund in an action to recover a pledge to the fund. *Cutwright v. Preacher's Aid Society,* 271 Ill. App. 168 (1933).
(4) The spouse of a person who is himself disqualified as a party or by interest. *In re Estate of Babcock,* 105 Ill. 2d 267, 85 Ill. Dec. 511, 473 N.E.2d 1316 (1985); *In re Estate of Teehan,* 287 Ill. App. 58, 4 N.E.2d 513 (1936); *Matter of Estate of Babcock,* 119 Ill. App. 3d 482, 74 Ill.

Dec. 950, 456 N.E.2d 671 (1983). Curiously, divorce has been held not to eliminate this interest. *Heineman v. Hermann,* 385 Ill. 191, 52 N.E.2d 263 (1944); *Hann v. Brooks,* 331 Ill. App. 535, 73 N.E.2d 624 (1947).

(5) A grantor who would be liable on a convenant of warranty. *Zimmer v. Zimmer,* 298 Ill. 586, 132 N.E. 216 (1921).

(6) All parties generally to will contests. *Lyman v. Kaul,* 275 Ill. 11, 113 N.E. 944 (1916); *Manning v. Mock,* 119 Ill. App. 3d 788, 75 Ill. Dec. 453, 457 N.E.2d 447 (1983); *Estate of Jones v. Altwood State Bank,* 159 Ill. App. 3d 377, 111 Ill. Dec. 509, 512 N.E.2d 1050 (1987).

(7) Living comaker of note, as to his authority to sign name of now deceased comaker. *Fredrich v. Wolf,* 383 Ill. 638, 50 N.E.2d 755 (1943).

(8) The principal in an action against his sureties. *Grommes v. St. Paul Trust Co.,* 147 Ill. 634, 35 N.E. 820 (1893). But principal, not a party, has been held competent where sureties sue to enjoin an action at law. *English v. Landon,* 181 Ill. 614, 54 N.E. 911 (1899).

(9) A lessee under a lease the validity of which, though not directly contested, depends upon the validity of a deed that is contested. *Miller v. Meers,* 155 Ill. 284, 40 N.E. 577 (1895).

The Dead Man's Act may not be circumvented by simply suing the beneficiary of the estate on the theory of a constructive trust. If the corpus under question is derived from the protected party, conversations with the protected party and events that took place in his presence cannot be testified to by an interested person. *Kamberos v. Magnuson,* 156 Ill. App. 3d 800, 109 Ill. Dec. 491, 510 N.E.2d 112 (1987).

Conversely, the following have been held not to be interested persons:

(1) Members of a church that is a legatee. *Adams v. First M.E. Church,* 251 Ill. 268, 96 N.E. 253 (1911).

(2) The servant of a defendant corporation in a negligence action, even though he may be liable over to the corporation, since a judgment is not binding upon him in the absence of vouching-in. *Feitl v. Chicago City Ry.*, 211 Ill. 279, 71 N.E. 991 (1904).

(3) Prospective heirs of a party or interested person. *Ackman v. Potter*, 239 Ill. 578, 88 N.E. 231 (1909); *Bernardi v. Chicago Steel Container Corp.*, 187 Ill. App. 3d 1010, 135 Ill. Dec. 436, 543 N.E.2d 1004 (1989) (son of defendant). *Borman v. Oetzell*, 382 Ill. 110, 46 N.E.2d 914 (1943), *contra*, is out of line with the other cases.

(4) Attorney who may in the future earn fees from client. *Britt v. Darnell*, 315 Ill. 385, 146 N.E. 510 (1925). *Heller v. Jonathan Investments, Inc.*, 135 Ill. App. 3d 350, 90 Ill. Dec. 197, 481 N.E.2d 997 (1985), attorney with no financial interest who had represented plaintiff in connection with a relative's estate.

(5) The agent of a party. *Johnson v. Matthews*, 301 Ill. App. 295, 22 N.E.2d 772 (1939).

(6) Former girlfriend of decedent with no financial interest in litigation. *Heller v. Jonathan Investments, Inc.* supra.

(7) Trustee possessing an emotional interest in outcome. *Herron v. Underwood*, 152 Ill. App. 3d 144, 105 Ill. Dec. 105, 503 N.E.2d 1111 (1987).

(8) Mother of claimant seeking workers' compensation is not directly interested. *Sohigro Serv. Co. v. Industrial Commission*, 172 Ill. App. 3d 47, 122 Ill. Dec. 424, 526 N.E.2d 683 (1988).

(9) Attorney who drafted will who owned land adjoining testator's who had expressed interest in purchasing the land. *In re Estate of Henke*, 203 Ill. App. 3d 975, 149 Ill. Dec. 36, 561 N.E.2d 314 (1990).

(10) Attorney for estate whose right to recover fees from estate was not contingent on successful defense. *In re Estate of Sewart*, 274 Ill. App. 3d 298, 210 Ill. Dec. 175, 652 N.E.2d 1151 (1995).

Of course the decedent whose death gives rise to protection of his interests is not himself an interested party. *Overcast v. Bodart,* 266 Ill. App. 3d 428, 203 Ill. Dec. 425, 639 N.E.2d 984 (1994) (deposition testimony of decedent properly admitted as admission of a party opponent).

Release of interest. At common law a person disqualified by interest could assign or release her interest and become competent. *Illinois Mut. Ins. Co. v. Marseilles Mfg. Co.,* 1 Gilm. 236 (1844), transfer of shares by shareholder of corporate party. However, 5/8-501 of the Code of Civil Procedure provides that no person who would be incompetent if a party may become competent by assigning or releasing her claim for the purpose of allowing her to testify, 735 ILCS 5/8-501. Whether an assignment or release was made for the purpose of allowing the person to testify is a question of fact for the court under all the circumstances. *Snyder v. Steele,* 304 Ill. 387, 136 N.E. 649 (1922). While the language of the section appears to be limited to persons who would be proper parties except for the assignment or release, it has been assumed to apply also to persons who would be disqualified by interest. *Albers Comm. Co. v. Sessel,* 193 Ill. 153, 61 N.E. 1075 (1901), shareholder of corporate party. A contrary construction would be a distinction so arbitrary as to be difficult to justify.

§606.4   Second Requirement — Testifying on Own Behalf

The Dead Man's Act renders a party or directly interested person incompetent to testify "on his or her own behalf" to any conversation with the deceased or person under legal disability or any event taking place in such person's presence, 735 ILCS 5/8-201.

Questions as to what constitutes testifying on his own behalf are necessarily involved with problems as to when the interests of the witness and of the protected party are adverse. *See* §606.3 supra. A witness directly interested in the action is not disqualified from testifying where his testimony is adverse

to his own economic interest. *Estate of Shanahan v. Bowen,* 59
Ill. App. 3d 269, 16 Ill. Dec. 635, 375 N.E.2d 508 (1978).

Due regard to the purpose of the statute requires that an
incompetent party not be permitted to testify for a co-party if
it would indirectly give the incompetent party the benefit of
her own testimony, although the statute does not specifically
so provide. *Sullivan v. Corn Prods. Co.,* 245 Ill. 9, 91 N.E. 643
(1910), defendant foreman, in action based on his negligence, incompetent to testify for defendant principal. Complete incompetency need not result, however, since there
may be aspects as to which the party's testimony would not
benefit her. For example, a defendant driver would not benefit from testifying to her nonagency for a codefendant joined
as master.

Severances should be granted liberally, with a view to making testimony available as fully as possible. If plaintiffs having
claims that are several, so that one plaintiff has no financial
interest in the claim of another, are incautious enough to
join against a protected defendant, severance should be allowed, rendering one plaintiff competent to testify for another. *See Braun v. Lawder,* 344 Ill. App. 423, 100 N.E.2d 348
(1951). Severance as to codefendants should likewise result
in competency of one defendant to testify for another, provided no benefit accrues to the witness. Regard should be
had for the possibility that one party may benefit through
principles of *res judicata* or collateral estoppel from an outcome favorable to a coparty, in the case of a defendant principal who is sued for the negligence of a defendant agent. *See
Blachek v. City Ice & Fuel Co.,* 311 Ill. App. 1, 35 N.E.2d 416
(1941).

§606.5 Third Requirement—Opposite Party Protected as to Conversation and Event in Presence of Deceased or Legally Disabled

The statute provides that when any party sues, *Coleman v.
Heidke,* 291 Ill. App. 3d 670, 225 Ill. Dec. 688, 684 N.E.2d 163

(1997); *Smith v. Haran,* 273 Ill. App. 3d 866, 210 Ill. Dec. 191, 652 N.E.2d 1167 (1995), or defends as the representative of a deceased person or person under legal disability, no adverse party or person directly interested in the action shall be allowed to testify on his own behalf to any conversation with the deceased or person under legal disability or to any event that took place in the presence of the deceased or person under legal disability, 735 ILCS 5/8-201. A "person under legal disability" means any person who is adjudged by the court in the pending civil action to be unable to testify by reason of mental illness, mental retardation, or deterioration of mentality. *Id.,* 5/8-201(a). With respect to determining the competency of a person to be a witness, *see* §§ 606.1-606.4 supra. *See also Green by Fritz v. Jackson,* 289 Ill. App. 3d 1001, 224 Ill. Dec. 848, 682 N.E.2d 409 (1997). Prior decisions such as *Chicago Title & Trust Co. v. Merchants Trust Co.,* 329 Ill. 334, 160 N.E. 597 (1928), and *Tompkins v. Tompkins,* 257 Ill. 557, 100 N.E. 965 (1913), requiring an independent adjudication of incompetency, are thus no longer to be followed.

An "event" is a happening or occurrence. *Manning v. Mock,* 119 Ill. App. 3d 788, 75 Ill. Dec. 453, 457 N.E.2d 447 (1983). Thus testimony that an event didn't occur such as that no other person had an ownership interest in a motel was not directed toward an event that took place in the presence of the decedent, nor is testimony that the defendant's wife continued to reside with the decedent (in comparison with the act of moving in together), an event within the meaning of the Dead Man's Act. *Hartman v. Townsend,* 169 Ill. App. 3d 111, 119 Ill. Dec. 731, 523 N.E.2d 199 (1988). Similarly, the failure of a person to give the decedent money at any time is not precluded; negative testimony is not an event that took place in the presence of the decedent. *Smith v. Haran,* 273 Ill. App. 3d 866, 210 Ill. Dec. 191, 652 N.E.2d 1167 (1995). *Contra* id. Justice Hartman, *concurring in part and dissenting in part. See also* infra and §606.6 infra.

Determination of the question whether the party seeking its protection falls within a category enumerated in the statute usually involves no particular difficulty. The critical factor is whether the party is suing or defending as a "representative" rather than in her own right. A "representative" is defined as an executor, administrator, heir or legatee of a deceased person and any guardian or trustee of any such heir or legatee, or a guardian or guardian ad litem for a person under legal disability. *Id.*, 5/8-201(b). A "devisee" is also included with the definition of a "representative" although no longer specifically mentioned in the statute. *Idleman v. Raymer,* 183 Ill. App. 3d 938, 132 Ill. Dec. 265, 539 N.E.2d 828 (1989) ("devisee" excluded by oversight). Thus heirs of a deceased grantee, defending a suit by the grantor to set aside the deed as heirs by inheritance from the grantee, defend in a representative capacity and are protected by the statute. *Campbell v. Campbell,* 368 Ill. 202, 13 N.E.2d 265 (1938). Similarly, a legatee who acquired an interest in a promissory as sole beneficiary of the will and retained one-half interest following a settlement of a will contest retains the benefit of the statute in an action to collect upon the promissory note. *Coleman v. Heidke,* 291 Ill. App. 3d 670, 225 Ill. Dec. 688, 684 N.E.2d 163 (1997). However, the grantee of a now deceased grantor, having acquired his interest by deed rather than by descent, is not protected. *Smith v. Pelz,* 384 Ill. 446, 51 N.E.2d 534 (1943); *Seaton v. Lee,* 221 Ill. 282, 77 N.E. 446 (1906). A surviving joint tenant takes by deed and is not within the statute. *Wurth v. Hosmann,* 410 Ill. 567, 102 N.E.2d 800 (1952). Nor is the assignee of the now deceased payee of a note protected, *Andrews v. Matthewson,* 332 Ill. App. 325, 75 N.E.2d 123 (1947); nor is the beneficiary of an insurance policy. *Ziarko v. Ziarko,* 318 N.E.2d 1, 22 Ill. App. 3d 520 (1974). A defendant sued individually to recover property claimed by plaintiff has been held, surprisingly, not entitled to invoke the statute on the ground that he claims the property as executor. *Kernott v. Behnke,* 311 Ill. App. 389, 36 N.E.2d 575 (1941).

Death of a party pending litigation has been held to entitle his representative to the protection of the statute, even to the extent of excluding testimony of an adverse party already completed. *Smith v. Billings,* 177 Ill. 446, 53 N.E. 81 (1899). A contrary result is indicated if the party dying has testified.

Brubaker v. Gould, 34 Ill. App. 2d 421, 180 N.E.2d 873 (1962). *See also Turner v. Black,* 19 Ill. 2d 296, 166 N.E.2d 588 (1960), and the second exception to §8-201(b), §606.6 infra.

Prior to amendment of the Dead Man's Act in 1973, whenever a protected party sued or defended, all other parties were declared by the Act incompetent generally to testify. However, the actual construction was less sweeping, to the effect that the party could not testify to her own advantage against the protected party. Questions then arose in multiple party situations as to whether a party competent against some adverse parties but not as against others could testify under a limiting instruction. *See* limited admissibility generally, §105.1 supra. As noted previously, an incompetent party was and still is precluded from testifying for a coparty if the testimony must be to her own benefit. *Sullivan v. Corn Prods. Co.,* 245 Ill. 9, 91 N.E. 643 (1910), §606.4 supra. However, if a party was competent as against one adverse party and not as against another, the injustice of precluding her from testifying at all was properly held to override the possibility that her testimony may be considered against the protected party, and she was entitled to testify under a limiting instruction. *Clark v. A. Bazzoni & Co.,* 7 Ill. App. 2d 334, 129 N.E.2d 435 (1955).

With the amendment to 5/8-201, general incompetency of the adverse party was removed. A party is now incompetent to testify only as to any conversation with the deceased or person under legal disability or to any event that took place in such person's presence, 735 ILCS 5/8-201. A statement that a particular subject was never discussed with the deceased or person under legal disability falls within the prohibition. *Matter of Estate of Osborn,* 234 Ill. App. 3d 651, 175 Ill. Dec. 315, 599 N.E.2d 1329 (1992). Acts growing out of conversation with the deceased also fall within the prohibition. *Manning v. Mock,* 119 Ill. App. 3d 788, 75 Ill. Dec. 453, 457 N.E.2d 447 (1983). However an adverse party is now not prohibited from testifying as to any conversation or event not with or in the presence of the deceased or legally disabled. *Matter of Estate of Netherton,* 62 Ill. App. 3d 55, 19 Ill. Dec. 185,

378 N.E.2d 800 (1978), an adverse party could testify to envelope in decedent's bureau drawer since its observation took place outside decedent's presence; *Bernardi v. Chicago Steel Container Corp.*, 187 Ill. App. 3d 1010, 135 Ill. Dec. 436, 543 N.E.2d 1004 (1989), adverse party properly permitted to testify as to his own version of conversations outside presence of deceased, the content of which was previously testified to by witnesses called by the deceased's estate; *Rerack v. Lally*, 241 Ill. App. 3d 692, 182 Ill. Dec. 193, 609 N.E.2d 727 (1992), in absence of evidence decedent observed the "event," plaintiff could testify that his vehicle was stopped for two minutes, that his foot was on the brake of his car continually, and that he heard no sound prior to accident's impact; *Moran v. Erickson*, 297 Ill. App. 3d 342, 231 Ill. Dec. 484, 696 N.E.2d 780 (1998), evidence as to the posted speed limit is not an event taking place in the decedant's presence. *See also* supra. Of course an adverse party or person directly interested may testify on behalf of the representative of the deceased or person under legal disability. *Bank of Viola v. Staley*, 131 Ill. App. 3d 531, 86 Ill. Dec. 731, 475 N.E.2d 1110 (1985).

§606.6   *Exceptions Provided in Section 8-201*

Section 8-201 of the statute enunciates four situations in which a party or interested person may testify in his own behalf despite the fact that the opposite party is within the group protected by the statute, 735 ILCS 5/8-201(a) to (d):

(a) If any person testifies on behalf of the representative to any conversation with the deceased or person under legal disability or to any event which took place in the presence of the deceased or person under legal disability, any adverse party or interested person, if otherwise competent, may testify concerning the same conversation or event. [735 ILCS 5/8-201(a).]

This exception is reflective of the policy of the Dead Man's Act not to disadvantage the living but rather to put the parties on an equal footing. *Morse v. Harding,* 34 Ill. App. 3d 1020, 341 N.E.2d 172 (1976).

Notice that the exception speaks of "any" person so called by the representative without reference to whether such a person is otherwise incompetent to testify on her own behalf as to the particular matter by virtue of 5/8-201(a). Thus, if an occurrence witness is called by the representative and testifies to a conversation with the deceased or person under legal disability or an event in such person's presence, the adverse party becomes competent to testify to the same conversation or event testified to by the occurrence witness. *Groark v. Anderson,* 222 Ill. App. 3d 880, 165 Ill. Dec. 289, 584 N.E.2d 468 (1991); *Idleman v. Raymer,* 183 Ill. App. 3d 938, 132 Ill. Dec. 265, 539 N.E.2d 828 (1989); *Fleming v. Fleming,* 85 Ill. App. 3d 532, 40 Ill. Dec. 676, 406 N.E.2d 879 (1980). *See also Goad v. Evans,* 191 Ill. App. 3d 283, 138 Ill. Dec. 523, 547 N.E.2d 690 (1989), admission in a pleading presented to the jury is equivalent to the calling of a witness. The calling of any witness by the representative renders the adverse party competent only as to the conversation or events so testified to by the representative's witness and not as to other conversations with or events in the presence of the deceased or legally disabled. *In re Estate of Deskins,* 128 Ill. App. 3d 942, 84 Ill. Dec. 252, 471 N.E.2d 1018 (1984), testimony of defendant as to dates of hospitalization, access to decedent's apartment, and showing of will to plaintiff at funeral did not make defendant competent as to discussions with decedent concerning the will; *Vazirzadeh v. Kaminski,* 157 Ill. App. 3d 638, 110 Ill. Dec. 65, 510 N.E.2d 1096 (1987), testimony by the decedent's wife to a conversation between her and her husband did not open door for the defendant to testify as to a conversation he had with the decedent; *Argianas v. Chestler,* 259 Ill. App. 3d 926, 197 Ill. Dec. 900, 631 N.E.2d 1359 (1994), introduction of a letter by protected party does not open door to testimony of past conversations with the deceased indicating that the letter was false. *Compare Haist v. Wu,* 235 Ill. App. 3d 799, 176 Ill. Dec. 229, 601 N.E.2d 927 (1992), after plaintiff's estate elicited possible diagnosis from doctor defendant incompetent to testify, defendant doctor properly permitted to detail actual advice given to the plaintiff; *Herron v. Anderson,* 254 Ill. App. 3d 365, 193 Ill. Dec. 484, 626 N.E.2d 1035 (1993), testimony by decedent's mother as to part of conversation she overheard between her deceased daughter and treating doctor permitted treating doctor to testify as to omitted part of same conversation. Decisions under a prior version of 5/8-201 involving testimony of a party, now any witness, are also illustrative. *Garrus v. Davis,* 234 Ill. 326, 84 N.E. 924 (1908), calling defendants in a will contest to identify letters did not render them competent as to the other matters; *Hann v. Brooks,* 331 Ill. App. 535, 73 N.E.2d 624 (1947), examining one defendant on issue of agency for another defendant; *DeYoung v. Ralley,* 329 Ill. App. 1, 67 N.E.2d 221 (1946), calling defendant to prove admission. However, the otherwise incompetent party is entitled under the principle of completeness to deny or explain fully the matters used in the questioning; *Perkins v. Brown,* 400 Ill. 490, 81 N.E.2d 207 (1948), in suit to set aside deed, after protected plaintiffs elicited from incompetent defendant that he received deed without paying for it, defendant properly allowed to explain entire transaction, including conversation with deceased grantor; *Blanchard v. Blanchard,* 191 Ill. 450, 61 N.E. 481 (1901), witness permitted to deny. *See also* §106 supra. Cross-examination of a witness called by the representative beyond the scope of direct examination, §611.11 infra, may not be used to invoke this exception since the witness is then not testifying on behalf of the representative. *Loeb v. Stern,* 198 Ill. 371, 64 N.E. 1043 (1902). Similarly the calling of a witness by the precluded party as an adverse witness does not invoke the exception. *Estate of Jones v. Atwood State Bank,* 159 Ill. App. 3d 377, 111 Ill. Dec. 509, 512 N.E.2d 1050 (1987); *Yetton v. Henderson,* 190 Ill. App. 3d 973, 137 Ill. Dec. 887, 546 N.E.2d 1000 (1989).

Conversation or transaction is construed liberally under the Act in both its earlier form and today. On the question of delivery of a deed, all aspects are included, *Newman v. Youngblood,* 394 Ill. 617, 69 N.E.2d 309 (1946), and in a wrongful death action, all details of the accident, *Van Meter v. Goldfarb,* 317 Ill. 620, 148 N.E. 391 (1925). *Cf. Pennington v.*

Rowley Bros. Co., 241 Ill. App. 58 (1926), holding that testimony by the administrator as to earnings of and support by decedent did not concern the transaction and hence defendant was not qualified; *Buczyna v. Cuomo & Son Cartage Co.,* 146 Ill. App. 3d 404, 100 Ill. Dec. 51, 496 N.E.2d 1116 (1986), holding that testimony, describing what police officer had observed at scene of accident long after the death of the decedent, did not remove the bar of the statute. Introduction by the protected party in an action for medical malpractice of a note prepared by the opposing party relating to a conversation with the decedent and a medical examination of the decedent, when accompanied by testimony of an expert called by the protected party as to the meaning of the foregoing note, thus providing a view of what happened, waives the protection of the statute. *Hoem v. Zia,* 159 Ill. 2d 193, 201 Ill. Dec. 47, 636 N.E.2d 479 (1994). Moreover, the existence of a rebuttable presumption that decedent paid $125,000 waives the protection of the statute and permits the opposing party to testify that no such payment was ever made. *Smith v. Haran,* 273 Ill. App. 3d 866, 210 Ill. Dec. 191, 652 N.E.2d 1167 (1995). In addition, where undue influence and fraud are asserted, testimony concerning the events of the day upon which a deed was signed waived the statute as to all connected incidents and conversations leading up to the signing of the deed. *Zorn v. Zorn,* 126 Ill. App. 3d 258, 80 Ill. Dec. 14, 464 N.E.2d 879 (1984). *Compare Manning v. Mock,* 119 Ill. App. 3d 788, 75 Ill. Dec. 453, 457 N.E.2d 447 (1983), testimony as to guiding the hand of the deceased in writing her signature did not open up testimony as to will's preparation and execution; *Vazirzadeh v. Kaminski,* 157 Ill. App. 3d 638, 110 Ill. Dec. 65, 510 N.E.2d 1096 (1987), testimony by the decedent's wife to a conversation between herself and her husband did not open door for the defendant to testify as to a conversation he had with the decedent. *See also* §606.5 supra.

A stipulation to the admissibility of a document that contains a reference to an event in the decedent's presence does not waive the protection of the Dead Man's Act. *Matters of*

Estate of Rollins, 269 Ill. App. 3d 261, 206 Ill. Dec. 774, 645 N.E.2d 1026 (1995).

The taking of a deposition of an adverse party or interested person by the representative does not itself make such person competent; only the calling of the witness at trial or introduction of the deposition at trial constitutes a waiver. *Pink v. Dempsey,* 350 Ill. App. 405, 113 N.E.2d 334 (1953).

In a citation proceeding in probate, 755 ILCS 5/16-1, the respondent becomes a witness of the court when examined by or at the instance of the court and is competent to testify. *In re Estate of Hill,* 30 Ill. App. 2d 243, 174 N.E.2d 233 (1961); *Wagner v. Wagner,* 17 Ill. App. 2d 307, 149 N.E.2d 770 (1958). Significantly, courts of review are insisting increasingly that trial courts exercise their discretion in favor of calling and examining respondents fully. *Id.*

With respect to the relationship of this exception and careful habit testimony, §406.2 supra, *see* §606.9 infra.

> (b) If the deposition of the deceased or person under legal disability is admitted in evidence on behalf of the representative, any adverse party or interested person, if otherwise competent, may testify concerning the same matters admitted in evidence. [735 ILCS 5/8-201(b).]

This exception merely extends to the introduction of deposition testimony of the deceased or legally disabled the same effect afforded the introduction of *viva voce* testimony on behalf of the representative. The taking of a deposition of a deceased or legally disabled person itself does not constitute a waiver; a waiver occurs only upon the introduction at trial on behalf of the representative. The incompetent party cannot qualify himself by offering the deposition; it must be introduced by the protected party. *Doggett v. Greene,* 254 Ill. 134, 98 N.E. 219 (1912). Testimony given by a party who later dies during the pendency of the action is the equivalent of a deposition. *Turner v. Black,* 19 Ill. 2d 296, 166 N.E.2d 588 (1960); *Brubaker v. Gould,* 34 Ill. App. 2d 421, 180 N.E.2d 873 (1962); *Vancuren v. Vancuren,* 348 Ill. App. 351, 109 N.E.2d 225 (1952).

(c) Any testimony competent under Section 8-401 of this Act, is not barred by this Section. [735 ILCS 5/8-201(c).]

This third exception is in effect contained in 5/8-401, which provides:

> Where in any action or preceeding, the claim or defense is founded on a book account or any other record or document, any party or interested person may testify to his or her account book, or any other record or document and the items therein contained; that the same is a book, record, or document of original entries, and that the entries therein were made by himself or herself, and are true and just; or that the same were made by a deceased person, or by a disinterested person, a non-resident person of the state at the time of the trial, and where made by such deceased or non-resident person in the usual course of trade, and of his or her duty or employment to the party so testifying; and thereupon the account book and entries or any other record or document shall be admitted as evidence in the cause. Where such book of original entries or any other record or document has been photographed, microphotographed, microfilmed, optical imaged, or otherwise reproduced either in the usual course of business, or pursuant to any statute of this State authorizing the reproduction of public records, papers or documents, and the reproduction, in either case, complies with the minimum standards of quality for permanent records approved by the State Records Commission, then such reproduction shall be deemed to be an original record, book or document for all purposes, including introduction in evidence in all courts or administrative agencies. [735 ILCS 5/8-401.]

The primary concern of the section is with the competency of witnesses, rather than with the types of books, records, and documents that are admissible. *House v. Beak,* 141 Ill. 290, 30 N.E. 1065 (1892). As structured, 5/8-401 is an exception to 5/8-201, rather than the reverse. Under 5/8-201(c), a party or interested person may give the specified foundation proof although otherwise incompetent under §8-201. *Accord McGlasson v. Housel,* 127 Ill. App. 360 (1906). Certified copies of public records are admissible as well. *In re*

Estate of Tunnell, 210 Ill. App. 3d 904, 155 Ill. Dec. 295, 569 N.E.2d 295 (1991).

The impact of 5/8-401 upon the types of books, records, and documents that are admissible is discussed in §§803.10 and 1001.4 infra.

(d) No person shall be barred from testifying as to any fact relating to the heirship of a decedent. [735 ILCS 5/8-201(d).]

Prior to the amendment to the Dead Man's Act in 1973, in litigation over the distribution of estates, the assumption that the only purpose of the statute was to protect the estate against the assaults of strangers led to some curious results. If controversy did not exist as to the persons who were to share but only as to the amount of the shares, no one could invoke the statute. *Pigg v. Carroll,* 89 Ill. 205 (1878), partition among heirs with disputes over advancements; *Mueller v. Rebhan,* 94 Ill. 142 (1879), contest of will devising property to heirs but in different shares. If, however, controversy existed as to the persons who were to share, the statute could be invoked. *In re Estate of Maher,* 210 Ill. 160, 71 N.E. 438 (1904), dispute as to status of woman claiming to be widow; *Pyle v. Pyle,* 158 Ill. 289, 41 N.E. 999 (1895), contest of will containing devises to persons not heirs. The distinction drawn by these cases was wholly unwarranted by the language of the statute, as in all these cases the parties seeking to invoke the statute were clearly within its terms. As to will contests, it was repudiated in *Joyal v. Pilotte,* 293 Ill. 377, 127 N.E. 741 (1920), overruling *Mueller v. Rebhan* supra, so that it then became clear that any party to any will contest may invoke the statute, regardless of the devolution of the property. *Cf. Schwebel v. Sheets,* 133 Ill. App. 3d 777, 88 Ill. Dec. 887, 479 N.E.2d 500 (1985), citing *Mueller* but not *Joyal.* In disputes over the shares of admitted heirs due to claimed advancements, however, decisions that the statute was inapplicable persisted, in effect reading into the statute an exception that was not there. *Alward v. Woodard,* 315 Ill. 150, 146 N.E. 154 (1925).

While the impact of 5/8-201(d) has yet to be fully interpreted, the exception was clearly drafted with the intent of making all witnesses competent to testify as to "heirship," both where the controversy includes who shall share and in disputes over the amount of the shares. In addition, no person is barred from testifying in a proceeding to establish the proper administration of an estate. *Matter of Estate of Bailey,* 97 Ill. App. 3d 781, 53 Ill. Dec. 104, 423 N.E.2d (1981), petitioner may testify to her marriage to decedent. The use of the term *heirship* in 5/8-201(d) indicates an intention to retain the statute's general applicability in will contests. *Joyal v. Pilotte* supra. The exception is inapplicable where heirship of the decedent is not being disputed. *Manning v. Mock,* 119 Ill. App. 3d 788, 75 Ill. Dec. 453, 457 N.E.2d 447 (1983).

§606.7 Deceased Partner, Joint Contractor, or Agent

Section 8-301 of the Code of Civil Procedure, 735 ILCS 5/ 8-301, extends the protection of the Dead Man's Act in a limited degree to surviving partners and joint contractors and to the principal of a deceased agent. The section provides:

> In any action or proceeding by or against any surviving partner or partners, or joint contractor or joint contractors, no adverse party or person adversely interested in the event thereof, shall, by virtue of Section 8-101 of this Act, be rendered a competent witness to testify to any admission or conversation by any deceased partner or joint contractor, unless some one or more of the surviving partners or joint contractors were also present at the time of such admission or conversation; and in every action or proceeding a party to the same who has contracted with an agent of the adverse party—the agent having since died—shall not be a competent witness as to any admission or conversation between himself or herself and such agent, unless such admission or conversation with the deceased agent was had or made in the presence of a surviving agent or agents of such adverse party, and then only except where the conditions are such that under the provisions of Sections 8-201 and 8-401 of this Act he or she would have been permitted to testify if the

deceased person had been a principal and not an agent. [735 ILCS 5/8-301.]

The incompetency under this section is only with regard to conversations with and admissions by the decedent. *Helbig v. Citizen's Ins. Co.*, 234 Ill. 251, 84 N.E. 897 (1908), plaintiff competent to testify that deceased agent of defendant delivered policy to him and that he paid agent the premium; *Lueth v. Goodknecht*, 345 Ill. 197, 177 N.E. 690 (1931), in action by surviving partner on note, defendent competent to testify regarding payment to deceased partner and contents of lost receipt.

If the opposite party sues or defends as surviving agent or joint contractor, the common law incompetency of parties and interested persons is continued, although only with regard to conversations and admissions as indicated in the preceding paragraph, unless a survivor was present. Joint tenants are not joint contractors as used in this section. *Anderson v. Lybeck*, 15 Ill. 2d 227, 154 N.E.2d 259 (1958).

If the opposite party is the principal of a since deceased agent with whom a party has contracted, the latter is incompetent to testify to admissions by or conversations with the agent unless in the presence of a surviving agent of the opposite party and then only if she would be competent had the principal died. A mere employee who was present and survives does not fulfill the requirement of a surviving agent. *Warszawa v. White Eagle Brewing Co.*, 299 Ill. App. 509, 20 N.E.2d 343 (1939).

The section does not, of course, preclude proof of conversations with or admissions by a deceased agent if made by a witness who is not a party. *Spitzer v. Bradshaw-Praeger & Co.*, 10 Ill. App. 2d 445, 135 N.E.2d 114 (1956).

§606.8 Settlement of Estates, Recording of Deeds, Attestation of Wills

With respect to the settlement of estates, recording of deeds, the attestation of wills, and the like, the provisions of

735 ILCS 5/8-201 are inapplicable to the extent provided in 735 ILCS 5/8-601:

> Nothing in this Article shall in any manner affect the laws now existing relating to the settlement of the estates of deceased persons, minors, persons under legal disability who have guardians, or to the acknowledgement or proof of deeds and other conveyances relating to real estate, in order to entitle the same to be recorded, or to the attestation of the execution of last wills or any other instrument required by law to be attested. [735 ILCS 5/8-601.]

§606.9   Relationship with Careful Habits Testimony

As discussed previously, §406.2 supra, in actions for wrongful death, evidence of careful habits of the deceased was traditionally admissible as a circumstance tending to prove freedom from contributory negligence, provided there were no eyewitness. *Casey v. Chicago Rys.*, 269 Ill. 386, 109 N.E. 984 (1915); *Reid v. Sledge*, 224 Ill. App. 3d 817, 167 Ill. Dec. 541, 587 N.E.2d 1156 (1992).

The relationship of careful habits testimony to the Dead Man's Act is illustrated by *Plank v. Holman*, 46 Ill. 2d 465, 264 N.E.2d 12 (1970). Plaintiff called a witness to testify to decedent's careful driving habits on plaintiff's case in chief. Defendants, barred by operation of 5/8-201, called decedent's wife as an adverse witness under Civil Practice Act §60, Ill. R.S. 1979, c.110, §60, now Code of Civil Procedure, 735 ILCS 5/2-1102, and elicited testimony relating circumstances from which decedent's behavior and operation of his automobile might reasonably be inferred, thereby making her an eyewitness. As a consequence of decedent's wife being an eyewitness, the court held that the careful habits testimony should have been stricken. Since in order to establish her husband's lack of contributory negligence, the decedent's wife would then have to testify on behalf of the representative of the deceased to events occurring in the presence of the decedent, i.e., the accident, defendants would become competent to testify as to the same events.

The decision of the Illinois Supreme Court in *Alvis v. Ribar*, 85 Ill. 2d 1, 52 Ill. Dec. 23, 421 N.E.2d 886 (1981), abolishing contributory negligence as a bar to plaintiff's recovery in favor of comparative negligence, removed the necessity of plaintiff's offering careful habits testimony in its case in chief in order to avoid a directed verdict.

With respect to the effect of eyewitnesses upon the admissibility of reconstruction testimony, *see* §703.2 infra. As to the effect of the adoption of comparative negligence on the foregoing, *see* §406.3 supra.

§607 Components of Credibility: Impeachment

§607.1 An Overview

Credibility is dependent upon the willingness of the witness to tell the truth and upon his ability to do so. His ability to tell the truth of an event as to which he purports to possess personal knowledge is the product, in turn, of the accuracy of his perception, his powers of recordation and recollection, and his capacity to communicate. Impeachment of a witness is often directed to more than one component of credibility. The objective or objectives being sought in any given situation may be to draw into question the accuracy of the witness's perception, recordation, recollection, or narration, or the witness's sincerity. Thus impeachment is designed to aid in ascertaining the degree of credit due a witness. *Brown v. Luehrs*, 1 Ill. App. 74 (1877), *aff'd*, 95 Ill. 195 (1880). With respect to perception, recordation, recollection, and narration, discrediting may often be accomplished by the simple means of a leading question. For example, a witness may be asked if it was not nighttime when the event occurred or whether he was over 400 feet away at the time. When the attack is upon sincerity, since a simple leading question will tend to be argumentative ("You wouldn't hesitate to lie to help a friend, would you?"), resort to a specific mode of impeachment is generally required, such as a prior conviction or prior inconsistent statement. Of course, with respect to certain modes of impeachment, e.g., particular contradiction and prior inconsistent statements, the attack also extends to personal knowledge. To illustrate, if the witness denies being 400 feet away, asserting instead that he was only 20 feet from the event, a prior inconsistent statement that he was 400 feet away constitutes an attack not only upon sincerity but also upon perception, recordation, and recollection.

The modes of impeachment discussed herein are (1) reputation for truth and veracity, §608.1 infra; (2) prior acts of misconduct, §608.4 infra; (3) prior convictions, §609 infra; (4) religious belief, §610.1 infra; (5) interest, bias, corruption, or coercion, §607.7 infra; (6) contradiction by extrinsic evidence, §607.8 infra; and (7) self-contradiction by his own prior inconsistent statements, §613 infra. The demeanor of the witnesses on the stand may of course always be considered in assessing credibility, 3A Wigmore, Evidence §946 (Chadbourn rev. 1970). Mental abnormality as bearing on credibility is addressed in §601.3 supra.

The accused in a criminal case, by taking the stand in her own behalf, becomes a witness and is subject to impeachment as to her credibility, although her character otherwise is not placed in issue. *See* §§404.3 and 405.3 supra. With respect to use for purposes of impeachment of a suppressed confession or admission, *see* §613.5 infra.

Matters brought out on cross-examination attacking credibility of a witness generally are a proper subject for rehabilitation upon redirect examination, §611.12 infra. However, in the interest of avoiding excessive collateral issues, certain limitations on rebutting attacks upon witnesses are recognized, §607.2 infra. For specific illustrations of such limitation *see* §608.1 infra, character for truthfulness, and §611.14 infra, prior consistent statements.

As to impeachment of an expert by learned treatise, *see*

§705.2 infra; with respect to scientific evaluation of witnesses, including lie detector and truth serum, *see* §403.3 supra.

Impeachment by a party of his own witness is discussed in §607.4 infra.

§607.2 *Collateral and Noncollateral Matters*

In general, any permissible kind of impeaching matter may be developed on cross-examination, since cross-examination has for one of its purposes the testing of the credibility of the witness, *People v. Collins,* 106 Ill. 2d 237, 87 Ill. Dec. 910, 478 N.E.2d 267 (1985); *People v. Mannen,* 46 Ill. App. 3d 61, 360 N.E.2d 563, 4 Ill. Dec. 627 (1977). The use of extrinsic evidence (i.e., evidence of testimony other than from the witness himself), to impeach is more restricted, due to considerations of confusion, undue consumption of time, and unfair prejudice raised by the introduction of so-called collateral matters. *See also* §403.1 supra. If a matter is considered collateral, the cross-examiner must accept the answer given by the witness on cross-examination, *People v. Collins* supra; *People v. Morgan,* 142 Ill. 2d 410, 154 Ill. Dec. 534, 568 N.E.2d 755 (1991); *People v. Hall,* 235 Ill. App. 3d 418, 176 Ill. Dec. 185, 601 N.E.2d 883 (1992); *People v. Davis,* 254 Ill. App. 3d 651, 193 Ill. Dec. 636, 626 N.E.2d 1187 (1993) (citing Handbook); extrinsic evidence may not be introduced, *Holton v. Memorial Hospital,* 176 Ill. 2d 95, 223 Ill. Dec. 429, 679 N.E.2d 1202 (1997); *Kincaid v. Ames Dept. Stores, Inc.,* 283 Ill. App. 3d 555, 219 Ill. Dec. 215, 670 N.E.2d 1103 (1996); *People v. Jackson,* 237 Ill. App. 3d 712, 178 Ill. Dec. 552, 604 N.E.2d 1075 (1992). If the matter is not collateral, extrinsic evidence may be introduced disputing the witness's denial of truth of the facts asserted in the cross-examiner's impeaching question. *People v. Steptore,* 51 Ill. 2d 208, 281 N.E.2d 642 (1972); *People vs. Pfanschmidt,* 262 Ill. 411, 104 N.E. 804 (1914); *People v. Reed,* 84 Ill. App. 3d 1030, 39 Ill. Dec. 930, 405 N.E.2d 1065 (1980).

A matter employed to contradict is noncollateral if the

matter is relevant in the litigation to establish a fact of consequence, that is, relevant for a purpose other than mere contradiction of the in-court testimony of the witness. *People v.
Thomas,* 217 Ill. App. 3d 698, 160 Ill. Dec. 506, 577 N.E.2d
831 (1991). Conversely, a matter is collateral if not relevant
for some purpose other than to contradict the in-court testimony of the witness. *See, e.g., People v. Morgan,* 142 Ill. 2d 410,
154 Ill. Dec. 534, 568 N.E.2d 755 (1991), whether conversation with defendant took place in mid-May or a few days
before Memorial Day was collateral in the case at hand;
Tzystuck v. Chicago Transit Auth., 124 Ill. 2d 226, 124 Ill. Dec.
544, 529 N.E.2d 525 (1988), whether bus was dented in accident was collateral to whether plaintiff ran into path of bus
or the bus veered into the plaintiff; *People v. Dennis,* 47 Ill. 2d
120, 265 N.E.2d 385 (1970), extrinsic evidence that witness
had previously eaten meal with the defendant in a restaurant, contradicting defendant's testimony that he had never
eaten with witness in restaurant, was improper impeachment
upon collateral matter; *People v. Schott,* 39 Ill. App. 3d 366,
350 N.E.2d 49 (1976), since it was collateral whether witness
had previously stated he was going to farmhouse where robbery occurred to buy LSD, where at trial he said he was going
to purchase a gun, extrinsic evidence prohibited; *O'Brien v.
Walker,* 49 Ill. App. 3d 940, 7 Ill. Dec. 372, 364 N.E.2d 533
(1977), when in 1973 witness moved to Tennessee collateral
as to accident occurring in 1970; *Derrico v. Clark Equip. Co.,* 91
Ill. App. 3d 4, 46 Ill. Dec. 232, 413 N.E.2d 1345 (1980),
inability to recall the time of a conversation was a collateral
matter; *People v. Buchanan,* 98 Ill. App. 3d 193, 53 Ill. Dec.
529, 423 N.E.2d 1333 (1981), whether defendant had said he
knew a person or his wife was collateral because such fact was
not relevant in the case for a purpose other than contradiction; *People v. Moore,* 105 Ill. App. 3d 264, 61 Ill. Dec. 147, 434
N.E.2d 300 (1981), statement by a police officer to the effect
that no one had identified the robber is collateral to the
issue of whom the victim may have identified. The suggestion
in *People v. Buckner,* 121 Ill. App. 3d 391, 77 Ill. Dec. 6, 459
N.E.2d 1102 (1984), that such collateral matters testified to

by a criminal defendant may be contradicted by the prosecution on rebuttal is incorrect and should not be followed. With respect to opening the door, *see* §103.4 supra.

In addition, matters bearing upon the credibility of the witness, such as bias, interest, corruption or coercion (*see* §607.7 infra), prior conviction impeachment (*see* §609 infra), or degree of competency of an expert witness, *People v. Dowwey*, 53 Ill. App. 3d 532, 11 Ill. Dec. 44, 368 N.E.2d 595 (1977), and want of capacity, opportunity, or actual acquisition and retention of personal knowledge, *People v. Lane*, 256 Ill. App. 3d 38, 195 Ill. Dec. 218, 628 N.E.2d 682 (1993); McCormick, Evidence §49 (4th ed. 1992), are not collateral and may be contradicted by other testimony. *Herget Natl. Bank of Pekin v. Johnson*, 21 Ill. App. 3d 1024, 316 N.E.2d 191 (1974). *Contra Holton v. Memorial Hospital*, 176 Ill. 2d 95, 223 Ill. Dec. 429, 679 N.E.2d 1202 (1997) (bias collateral; incorrectly decided, *see* Nickels, J., dissenting quoting Handbook and §607.7 infra). *Cf. People v. Jones*, 148 Ill. App. 3d 345, 101 Ill. Dec. 922, 499 N.E.2d 510 (1986) (prior inconsistent statement of witness, to the effect that witness had seen the victim being beaten by her mother before the victim accused the defendant of rape, which statement witness at trial denied making (coercion), is collateral; notice that testimony by a witness, directly on the issue of the beating, would have been noncollateral). *See also People v. Hutson*, 223 Ill. App. 3d 50, 165 Ill. Dec. 541, 584 N.E.2d 975 (1991), extrinsic evidence of neglect by mother of child allegedly physically abused by defendant boyfriend properly excluded as collateral on ground that such evidence is not relevant to establish any fact of consequence other than by contradiction; however, such evidence is not collateral and thus should have been admitted when offered as relevant to establish the motive of the mother in accusing the boyfriend to prove that she was testifying falsely.

Finally, a third category creating a test of necessity exists. A witness may also be contradicted as to a part of her testimony where as a matter of human experience she would not be mistaken if the thrust of her testimony were true. *People v.*

Collins, 106 Ill. 2d 237, 87 Ill. Dec. 910, 478 N.E.2d 267 (1985), after witness testified that she was with defendant on the day of the murder and that her first date with him was at a kung-fu movie three days before, it was proper for the theater manager to testify on rebuttal that no kung-fu movie was shown that day; *People v. Jackson,* 293 Ill. App. 3d 1009, 228 Ill. Dec. 319, 689 N.E.2d 191 (1997), after defendant testified that he had made 911 call following the altercation, the 911 tape itself was properly admitted to establish that someone else had in fact called 911; *People v. Williams,* 96 Ill. App. 3d 958, 52 Ill. Dec. 518, 422 N.E.2d 199 (1981), after defendant testified that a green Cadillac he owned was totaled in an accident in March, testimony placing accused in a green Cadillac in April was properly admitted in connection with an armed robbery committed in May. *Accord People v. Bollman,* 163 Ill. App. 3d 621, 114 Ill. Dec. 715, 516 N.E.2d 870 (1987); *People v. Byer,* 75 Ill. App. 3d 658, 31 Ill. Dec. 430, 394 N.E.2d 632 (1979). *See also* McCormick, Evidence §49 (4th ed. 1992).

Consider the following illustration. Bob is called to testify that the color of the traffic light facing Apple Street was red at the time of an automobile accident he witnessed at the corner of Apple and Main. On direct examination, Bob testifies that he was proceeding east on Apple Street heading toward the Piagano's Pizza Restaurant, which was located on the corner of Apple and Peach. On cross-examination counsel asks, "Isn't it true that Piagano's Pizza Restaurant is located on Apple three blocks east of Peach at Maple?" Although this question is permissible as potentially affecting the jury's assessment of Bob's power of recollection and concern for detail, if Bob continues to maintain that the restaurant is on Peach Street, extrinsic evidence may not be offered during the cross-examiner's case in chief as to the location of the restaurant. The matter is collateral, because the location of the restaurant is not relevant in the litigation other than to contradict the testimony of the witness. Even if Bob denied on cross-examination making a prior statement in which he allegedly said that the restaurant was on Apple and Maple, extrinsic evidence establishing the prior statement would be inadmissible because the matter remains collateral. On the other hand, the color of the traffic light is not collateral; the color of the traffic light is otherwise relevant in the case. Thus contradictory evidence that the light facing Apple Street was green is admissible. Similarly, if Bob denies on cross-examination having previously stated that the traffic light was green, extrinsic evidence establishing Bob's prior inconsistent statement is admissible.

Assuming Bob is then asked on cross-examination if he was wearing his glasses while driving, a yes answer may be contradicted by extrinsic evidence that his only pair of glasses was being repaired at the time of the accident. Evidence disputing the acquisition of personal knowledge by the witness of facts relevant in the case is not collateral. Similarly, if Bob denied on cross-examination that his wife was related to the plaintiff, extrinsic evidence of such a fact would be admissible. Evidence of partiality of the witness is not collateral. Extrinsic evidence offered to establish bias, interest, corruption, or coercion of the witness may be admitted following denial by the witness of a fact giving rise to such an inference when put to the witness on cross-examination. Finally, restructuring the initial illustration, if Piagano's Pizza Restaurant is in fact located on Birch Street, and its location on Birch in relation to Bob's location prior to leaving for the restaurant would naturally place Bob on Main, and not Apple, as he approached the intersection, extrinsic evidence of the location of the restaurant would be admissible on the ground that error as to the location of the restaurant brings into question the trustworthiness of Bob's entire testimony. Bob may have seen the light facing Main and not the light facing Apple.

Limitations on the introduction of extrinsic evidence are also noted in the sections discussing treatment of the various modes of impeachment. Moreover, extrinsic evidence on a noncollateral matter may be excluded on the basis that its probative value is substantially outweighed by the danger of unfair prejudice, confusion of the issues, misleading the jury, or by considerations of undue delay, waste of time, or needless presentation of cumulative evidence, §403.1 supra. *People v. Jackson,* 237 Ill. App. 3d 712, 178 Ill. Dec. 552, 604 N.E.2d 1075 (1992).

Application of the collateral-noncollateral distinction is best left largely to the discretion of the trial court. *People v. Collins,* 106 Ill. 2d 237, 87 Ill. Dec. 910, 478 N.E.2d 267 (1985); *People v. Breton,* 237 Ill. App. 3d 355, 177 Ill. Dec. 916, 603 N.E.2d 1290 (1992).

§607.3   Good-Faith Basis for Impeachment

A good-faith basis is required on the part of examining counsel as to the truth of the matter contained in leading questions propounded to a witness on cross-examination. *People v. Sanchez,* 240 Ill. App. 3d 533, 181 Ill. Dec. 404, 608 N.E.2d 477 (1992); *People v. Herrera,* 238 Ill. App. 3d 284, 179 Ill. Dec. 435, 606 N.E.2d 267 (1992). Innuendoes and insinuations of inadmissible or nonexistent matters are improper. *See, e.g. People v. Fiorita,* 339 Ill. 78, 170 N.E. 690 (1930), cross-examination implying that there was something irregular about witness's ownership of a car was improper; *People v. Judge,* 221 Ill. App. 3d 753, 164 Ill. Dec. 267, 582 N.E.2d 1211 (1991), cross-examination as to whether defendant became excited when he saw his 12-year-old girlfriend in a bathing suit was improper as unsupported in the record; *People v. Strong,* 151 Ill. App. 3d 28, 104 Ill. Dec. 247, 502 N.E.2d 744 (1986), cross-examination of defendant as to whether he had ever freebased or ever used cocaine was unsupported and thus improper; *People v. Littlejohn,* 144 Ill. App. 3d 813, 98 Ill. Dec. 555, 494 N.E.2d 677 (1986), on cross-examination of an expert for the accused raising an insanity defense improper to refer to unproven assertion that the accused had taught a seminar on psychiatric disorders; *People v. Curry,* 25 Ill. App. 3d 637, 323 N.E.2d 778 (1975), unsubstantiated cross-examination that defense witness had been in possession of a gun during the shooting was improper. This principle also requires good faith in laying the foundation for impeachment, with the intent and ability to follow up in the event of denial. *Gordon v. Checker Taxi Co.*, 334 Ill. App. 313, 79 N.E.2d 632 (1948), questions asked relating to plaintiff's treatment for prior injury improper since not followed up; *Khatib v. McDonald*, 87 Ill. App. 3d 1087, 43 Ill. Dec. 266, 410 N.E.2d 266 (1980), question implying prior lower back injury improper since counsel not prepared to follow up. While cross-examination raising implications of interest, bias, corruption, or coercion, *see* §607.7 infra, may normally be conducted without extrinsic evidence later being introduced, considerations of unfair prejudice and misleading of the jury, *see* §403.1 supra, may require the presentation of contradictory extrinsic evidence in the face of a witness's denial of misconduct. *People v. Nuccio*, 43 Ill. 2d 375, 253 N.E.2d 353 (1969) (prosecution impeachment of defense witness); *People v. Beringer*, 151 Ill. App. 3d 558, 104 Ill. Dec. 916, 503 N.E.2d 778 (1987) (same).

Returning to the illustration employed in §607.2 supra, counsel on cross-examination may not ask Bob, "Isn't it true that Piagano's is located on Birch?" without having a reasonable basis in fact for believing that Piagano's is in truth located on Birch and not Apple. Nor may counsel on cross-examination inquire of Bob whether his wife was related to the plaintiff absent a good-faith basis. Note that the requirement of a good-faith basis applies only when the cross-examiner is effectively asserting in the form of a question the truth of a factual statement included within the question. If the cross-examiner is merely inquiring whether something is or is not true, a good-faith basis is not required. Thus the question, "Your glasses were being repaired at the time of the accident, weren't they?" requires a good-faith basis, while the question, "Were you wearing your glasses at the time of the accident?" does not.

With respect to good faith in laying the foundation for impeachment by prior inconsistent statement, *see* §613.3 infra.

§607.4   Impeachment of a Party's Own Witness: Section 2-1102, Rule 238, Court's Witness Doctrine

In order to appreciate the current state of the law with respect to impeachment by a party of a witness called by the party to testify, a brief historical review is necessary.

According to the common law's voucher rule, a party could not impeach a witness whom he had called. *Chicago City Ry. v. Gregory*, 221 Ill. 591, 77 N.E. 1112 (1906). A witness called by both parties, however, could be impeached by either by prior statements inconsistent with testimony given for the other that were not admissible as substantive evidence. *People v. Van Dyke*, 414 Ill. 251, 111 N.E.2d 165 (1953). A witness cross-examined beyond the scope of direct was for this purpose called by both parties. *Joseph v. Peoria & P.U. Ry.*, 265 Ill. 563, 107 N.E. 141 (1914). Impeachment by prior inconsistent statement was also permitted of witnesses required by law to be called, such as was formerly the case with attesting witnesses to a will. *Thompson v. Owen*, 174 Ill. 229, 51 N.E. 1046 (1898). *See also* §903.1 infra with respect to attesting witnesses. A party taking a deposition was not by virtue of the taking precluded from impeaching the deponent. The use of the deposition, however, was equivalent to calling the deponent as a witness for purposes of impeachment. With respect to the introduction of a prior criminal conviction on direct examination of a witness, *see* §609.6 infra.

After prolonged and vigorous attack by commentators, *see, e.g.*, 3A Wigmore, Evidence §§896-903 (Chadbourn rev. 1970), it became generally recognized that the traditional rationale supporting the voucher rule did not withstand analysis and that a party should be able under appropriate circumstances to attack the credibility of her own witness at least by means of a prior inconsistent statement that is not admissible as substantive evidence. However, it was also recognized that a party should not be able to place a prior statement of her witness before the jury under the guise of impeachment, *People v. Johnson*, 333 Ill. 469, 165 N.E. 235 (1929); *Crespo v. John Hancock Mut. Life Ins. Co.*, 41 Ill. App.

3d 506, 354 N.E.2d 381 (1976), and that a jury, in spite of a limiting instruction, §105.1 supra, would likely give substantive effect to prior inconsistent statements employed by a party to impeach her own witness. In an attempt to accommodate both concerns, exceptions developed in the voucher rule, permitting impeachment of a party's own witness by prior inconsistent statements to the point where it was stated that the voucher rule was in the "process of erosion." *People v. Wesley*, 18 Ill. 2d 138, 163 N.E.2d 500 (1960).

Four exceptions developed pursuant to which a party could impeach a witness he had called. Of these exceptions, three limit the mode of impeachment to use of prior inconsistent statements not substantively admissible, and the fourth, the court's witness doctrine, permits impeachment by any mode. Each exception also permits leading questions, sometimes inarticulately referred to as cross-examination, to be asked.

(1) A party may call an adverse party or person treated as an adverse party and examine the witness in accordance with 5/2-1102 of the Code of Civil Procedure, 735 ILCS 5/2-1102, formerly §60, Ill. R.S. 1981, c.110, §60:

> Upon the trial of any case any party thereto or any person for whose immediate benefit the action is prosecuted or defended, or the officers, directors, managing agents or foreman of any party to the action, may be called and examined as if under cross-examination at the instance of any adverse party. The party calling for the examination is not concluded thereby but may rebut the testimony thus given by countertestimony and may impeach the witness by proof of prior inconsistent statements.

This section applies in civil actions, including disbarment proceedings. *In re Eaton*, 14 Ill. 2d 338, 152 N.E.2d 850 (1958).

The status of the witness is determined as of the time of his examination. *Bituminous Cas. Corp. v. Harrisburg*, 315 Ill. App. 243, 42 N.E.2d 971 (1942). Dismissed parties accordingly do not fall within 5/2-1102. *Zajac v. St. Mary of Nazareth Hosp.*,

212 Ill. App. 3d 779, 156 Ill. Dec. 860, 571 N.E.2d 840 (1991). To fall within 5/2-1102 the witness must perform some function of authority with the adverse party. *Arians v. Larkin Bank,* 253 Ill. App. 3d 1037, 192 Ill. Dec. 946, 625 N.E.2d 1101 (1993). Accordingly, the head of a department in a store with supervision of employees has been held to be a managing agent, *Dixon v. Montgomery Ward & Co.,* 351 Ill. App. 75, 114 N.E.2d 44 (1953), prior to the addition of foremen to the section, as has a district manager for an insurance company although able to sell competitor's policies, *Hildebrand v. Franklin Life Ins. Co.,* 118 Ill. App. 3d 861, 74 Ill. Dec. 280, 455 N.E.2d 553 (1980). On the other hand, an employee who is neither a supervisor nor a manager, *Skelton v. Chicago Transit Auth.,* 214 Ill. App. 3d 554, 158 Ill. Dec. 130, 573 N.E.2d 1315 (1991), an independent auditor of a party, *Jaffe v. Chicago Warehouse Lumber Co.,* 4 Ill. App. 2d 415, 124 N.E.2d 618 (1955), an independent insurance broker who sold the policy written by defendant company, *Yadro v. United States F. & G. Co.,* 4 Ill. App. 2d 477, 124 N.E.2d 370 (1955), the manager of a shoe store that had been sold by defendant to his son prior to trial, *Bansch v. Donnelly,* 77 Ill. App. 3d 922, 33 Ill. Dec. 342, 396 N.E.2d 869 (1979), an attorney for a party to an antenuptial agreement, *Fleming v. Fleming,* 85 Ill. App. 3d 532, 40 Ill. Dec. 676, 406 N.E.2d 879 (1980), and an expert witness retained to testify at trial, *Tokar v. Crestwood Imports, Inc.,* 177 Ill. App. 3d 422, 126 Ill. Dec. 697, 532 N.E.2d 382 (1988), have been held not to fall within any of the named categories. Refusal to permit the examination of a child who was not in the opinion of the trial judge mentally competent to testify has been upheld. *Stowers v. Carp,* 29 Ill. App. 2d 52, 172 N.E.2d 370 (1961). Finally, a defendant called by a codefendant falls within the category of witnesses included within §2-1102 when independent, negligent conduct is alleged against each. *Fornoff v. Parke Davis & Co.,* 105 Ill. App. 3d 681, 61 Ill. Dec. 438, 434 N.E.2d 793 (1982).

Following the examination, the side to which the witness presumably is friendly is entitled to examine as if on redirect, i.e., to explain or qualify the testimony given but not to bring out new matters. *Griffin v. Subram,* 238 Ill. App. 3d 712, 179 Ill. Dec. 728, 606 N.E.2d 560 (1992). With respect to redirect examination, *see* §611.12 infra. A coparty whose interests are adverse to the witness is entitled to cross-examine and to impeach him generally. *Cascio v. Bishop Sewer & Water Co.,* 2 Ill. App. 2d 378, 119 N.E.2d 531 (1954); *Algozino v. Welch Fruit Prods. Co.,* 345 Ill. App. 135, 102 N.E.2d 555 (1951).

The party calling the witness may impeach him but only by proof of a prior inconsistent statement or by contradiction. 735 ILCS 5/2-1102. This limitation of impeachment is the result of fears that other methods might be abused, as by calling the adverse party merely to lay a foundation for proof that he had been convicted of an infamous crime or bore a bad reputation for veracity.

Testimony of a party examined under 5/2-1102 should not be confused with extrajudicial admissions that are generally not admissible against coparties, §802.1 infra; the fact that testimony is given under 5/2-1102 does not render it inadmissible against a coparty, *Latham v. Rishel,* 384 Ill. 478, 51 N.E.2d 531 (1943).

The provision that the examining party may contradict testimony given under 5/2-1102 is declaratory of the law with regard to witnesses generally. *See* §§607.8 and 607.9 infra.

(2) Former Supreme Court Rule 238, amended effective April 1, 1982, *see* infra, made applicable to criminal as well as civil proceedings by Supreme Court Rule 433, permitted, upon a showing of surprise, impeachment of an occurrence witness by the calling party:

> If the court determines that a witness is hostile or unwilling, he may be examined by the party calling him as if under cross-examination. The party calling an occurrence witness, upon the showing that he called the witness in good faith and is surprised by his testimony, may impeach the witness by proof of prior inconsistent statements.

The mere giving of testimony damaging to the calling party did not alone make the witness hostile for the purpose of permitting leading questions under former Rule 238, *People v. Swimley,* 57 Ill. App. 3d 116, 14 Ill. Dec. 608, 372 N.E.2d 887 (1978), but if the damaging testimony came as a surprise to the calling party, impeachment of an occurrence witness by proof of a prior inconsistent statement was permitted. *People v. Johnson,* 82 Ill. App. 3d 338, 39 Ill. Dec. 205, 404 N.E.2d 796 (1980). *See* §611.9 infra. Use of an inconsistent statement to impeach an occurrence witness whose damaging testimony did not surprise the calling party may have constituted reversible error. *Seibutis v. Smith,* 83 Ill. App. 3d 1010, 39 Ill. Dec. 359, 404 N.E.2d 950 (1980). *See also McCoy v. Board of Fire & Police Commrs.,* 54 Ill. App. 3d 276, 11 Ill. Dec. 824, 369 N.E.2d 278 (1973), rejecting the practice of using impeachment of a hostile witness by means of contrary statements merely as a device for placing a prior statement of the witness before the jury under the guise of impeachment. Notice that the first sentence of former Rule 238, now Rule 238(b), while employing the term cross-examination, refers to concepts of unwillingness and hostility that are associated solely with the right to ask leading questions. *See* §611.9 infra. Whether a witness is hostile or unwilling is simply irrelevant in determining whether impeachment by the calling party of the witness with a prior inconsistent statement should be permitted.

(3) Former Supreme Court Rule 238 was promulgated to establish a more straightforward practice with respect to impeachment of occurrence witnesses by the calling party. The prior practice pursuant to which the calling party was permitted in the process of examining the witness in open court to disclose the contents of an alleged prior inconsistent statement under the guise of refreshing the witness's recollection or awakening her conscience, *People v. Wesley,* 18 Ill. 2d 138, 163 N.E.2d 500 (1960), continued to survive, however. *See, e.g., People v. Mager,* 35 Ill. App. 3d 306, 341 N.E.2d 389 (1976); *Walsh v. Dream Builders, Inc.,* 129 Ill. App. 2d 280, 264 N.E.2d 247 (1970). The difficulty of drawing a line at an early stage between the two practices is evident. *See also People*

v. Oates, 58 Ill. App. 3d, 16 Ill. Dec. 369, 374 N.E.2d 1144 (1978), approving trial court's decision that attempts to refresh recollection occur first outside the presence of the jury.

(4) With respect to the court's witness doctrine as applied in criminal proceedings, upon a showing by the prosecution or by defense counsel of reasons for doubting the veracity of a witness, the court could call the witness as a court's witness. *People v. R.D.,* 155 Ill. 2d 122, 184 Ill. Dec. 389, 613 N.E.2d 706 (1993); *People v. Dennis,* 47 Ill. 2d 120, 265 N.E.2d 385 (1970); *People v. Siciliano,* 4 Ill. 2d 581, 123 N.E.2d 725 (1955); *Carle v. People,* 200 Ill. 494, 66 N.E. 32 (1902), party must show that the testimony of the witness whose veracity cannot be vouched relates to direct issues in the case and is necessary to prevent a miscarriage of justice. A party might be unable to vouch for a witness's veracity by virtue of advanced knowledge that the witness's testimony in court will contradict a prior statement given to the calling party. *People v. Marino,* 44 Ill. 2d 562, 256 N.E.2d 770 (1970). *Contra People v. Bryant,* 100 Ill. App. 3d 17, 55 Ill. Dec. 152, 425 N.E.2d 1325 (1981), a party is unable to vouch for the credibility of a witness's testimony only when the testimony is unknown; if the party knows what the witness will relate, the party must either refrain from calling the witness or limit questions to the evidence it desires to elicit. If the reasons for doubting veracity first appeared during examination, the court could at that time call the witness as its own. *People v. Pastorino,* 91 Ill. 2d 178, 62 Ill. Dec. 172, 435 N.E.2d 1144 (1982); *People v. Williams,* 22 Ill. 2d 498, 177 N.E.2d 100 (1961). The effect was to open the witness to cross-examination and impeachment by either side, as well as to avoid association of the witness with the prosecution or defense in the minds of the jury. Impeachment by prior inconsistent statement was, however, permitted only if the witness's testimony was damaging to the examining party. *People v. Triplett,* 87 Ill. App. 3d 763, 42 Ill. Dec. 786, 409 N.E.2d 401 (1980); *People v. Rogers,* 187 Ill. App. 3d 126, 135 Ill. Dec. 65, 543 N.E.2d 300 (1989). This departure from the usual adversary procedure, justified on

the ground of avoiding a miscarriage of justice, once held to apply only to eyewitnesses, *People v. Robinson,* was expanded to apply to all witnesses. *People v. Pastorino* supra. While the court's witness doctrine had also been declared applicable in civil proceedings, *Hooper v. Mizyad,* 98 Ill. App. 3d 768, 54 Ill. Dec. 101, 424 N.E.2d 851 (1981), it was stated that it should be used sparingly in this context. *Crespo v. John Hancock Mut. Life Ins. Co.,* 41 Ill. App. 3d 506, 354 N.E.2d 381 (1976); *Uhr v. Lutheran General Hospital,* 226 Ill. App. 3d 236, 168 Ill. Dec. 323, 589 N.E.2d 723 (1992). *Contra Kubisz v. Johnson,* 29 Ill. App. 3d 381, 329 N.E.2d 815 (1975), not applicable in civil cases.

None of these devices — court's witness, 5/2-1102 (formerly §60), prior Rule 238, or refreshing recollection relating to examination of a party's own witness — comprised a scheme providing for the use of prior inconsistent statements where necessary, while precluding to the extent possible a party from impeaching his own witness with the set purpose of having the jury give practical substantive effect to the prior statement. In recognition of this fact there developed the *Tunstall* doctrine, barring the use of prior inconsistent statements bearing directly on defendant's guilt when likely to be given substantive effect by the trier of fact, *People v. Bryant,* 94 Ill. 2d 514, 69 Ill. Dec. 84, 447 N.E.2d 301 (1983); *People v. McKee,* 39 Ill. 2d 265, 235 N.E.2d 625 (1968); *People v. Tunstall,* 17 Ill. 2d 160, 161 N.E.2d 300 (1959); *People v. Kimbrough,* 131 Ill. App. 2d 36, 266 N.E.2d 804 (1975), but not otherwise. *People v. Bailey,* 60 Ill. 2d 37, 322 N.E.2d 804 (1975); *People v. Marino,* 44 Ill. 2d 562, 256 N.E.2d 770 (1970). For a full discussion of these four exceptions as well as the *Tunstall* doctrine, *see* Graham, Prior Inconsistent Statement—Impeachment and Substantive Admissibility: An Analysis of the Effect of Adopting the Proposed Illinois Rules of Evidence, 1978 Ill. L. Forum, 329, 351-356. *See also People v. King,* 109 Ill. 2d 514, 94 Ill. Dec. 702, 488 N.E.2d 949 (1986) (the *Tunstall* doctrine is not a per se prohibition but rather a desire to avoid introduction of impeachment material the jury is likely to misuse; the giving of cautionary and limiting instructions is properly considered). For a decision that recognizes that confusion arises from having so many different approaches existing simultaneously, *see People v. Smith,* 113 Ill. App. 305, 69 Ill. Dec. 339, 447 N.E.2d 556 (1983).

Preservation of the rule that prior statements of a witness are inadmissible hearsay has been sought by insistence upon the dual requirements of surprise and affirmative damage. Surprise, required expressly in former Rule 238, occurs when a witness called by a party testifies in an unanticipated manner. Affirmative damage results from testimony of the party's own witness that gives positive aid to an adversary's case; it does not result when a witness simply fails to testify as expected, thus disappointing the cross-examiner, or claims lack of recollection. *People v. Cruz,* 162 Ill. 2d 314, 205 Ill. Dec. 345, 643 N.E.2d 636 (1994) (quoting article supra and citing Handbook); *People v. Chitwood,* 36 Ill. App. 3d 1017, 344 N.E.2d 611 (1976); *People v. Lipscomb,* 19 Ill. App. 3d 114, 311 N.E.2d 257 (1974). Whether prior inconsistent statements should be exempted from the rule against hearsay is discussed in §801.9 infra.

Illinois decisions during this time period indicated a burgeoning acceptance of the dual requirements of surprise and affirmative damage. Affirmative damage, as well as surprise, was required before permitting impeachment by means of a prior inconsistent statement under former Rule 238 in *People v. Lipscomb* supra. *Accord People v. Jackson,* 105 Ill. App. 3d 750, 61 Ill. Dec. 57, 433 N.E.2d 1385 (1982) (citing Handbook); *McCray v. Illinois Cent. R.R.,* 12 Ill. App. 425, 436, 139 N.E.2d 817 (1956). Other decisions citing former Rule 238 have discussed surprise and affirmative damage in ultimately reaching a decision pursuant to one of the other exceptions being discussed, e.g., the court's witness rule or the refreshing recollection doctrine. For example, in *Walsh v. Dream Builders, Inc.,* 129 Ill. App. 3d 280, 264 N.E.2d 247 (1970), the court cited former Rule 238 in holding that a witness whose surprise lapse of memory at trial was merely disappointing and not affirmatively damaging to the party calling could nevertheless have his recollection refreshed. *See also People v.*

Mager, 35 Ill. App. 3d 306, 341 N.E.2d 389 (1976). Also consider *People v. Grant,* 38 Ill. App. 3d 62, 347 N.E.2d 244 (1976), witness who testifies surprisingly to affirmatively damaging facts may have his recollection refreshed. In *People v. Chitwood,* 36 Ill. App. 3d 1017, 344 N.E.2d 611 (1976), the court held that affirmative damage must also be proved before a court's witness can be impeached with a prior statement. The court concluded that the court's witness's denial that she had heard defendants admit the burglary was merely disappointing to the examiner's case and not damaging, since the prosecution was no worse off than if she had not testified. Thus, there was nothing to impeach in this testimony. On the other hand, her surprise testimony that the allegedly stolen tape recorder introduced into evidence by the State had been in the defendant's possession before the burglary was damaging to the prosecution, and it was proper to allow her testimony on this subject to be impeached by prior inconsistent statements. For an illustration of the problems that arise when surprise and affirmative damage are not required, *see People v. Tate,* 87 Ill. 2d 134, 57 Ill. Dec. 572, 429 N.E.2d 470 (1981), trial court permitted defendant to impeach a witness called by the defendant with a prior inconsistent statement in which the witness allegedly admitted committing the offense for which the accused was on trial.

In *People v. Pastorino,* 90 Ill. App. 3d 921, 927-928, 46 Ill. Dec. 332, 414 N.E.2d 54, 60 (1980), the court, citing *Chitwood* and the Handbook, described as follows the rules governing impeachment by the prosecution of a court's witness with a prior inconsistent statement:

> The testimony of a court's witness generally falls into two distinct categories. In one situation, for example, the State expects the witness to testify, in a manner consistent with his out-of-court statement, that the defendant admitted to the witness that the defendant had committed the crime. Instead, the witness fails to confirm his prior statement. The consequence of this is that the State is merely disappointed by the witness' testimony. By simply failing to confirm his prior statement, the witness is not placing

before the jury any new evidence which would be damaging to the State. Under these circumstances, the witness may not be impeached because there is no evidence on which to impeach him.

The second situation arises where instead of simply failing to confirm his prior statement, the witness presents the jury with new evidence, such as providing the defendant with an alibi. If the jury believes this testimony, the State would be affirmatively damaged rather than merely disappointed. Under these circumstances, the State should be allowed to impeach the witness with his prior inconsistent statement.

Accord People v. Bryant, 100 Ill. App. 3d 17, 55 Ill. Dec. 152, 425 N.E.2d 1325 (1981) (citing Handbook). Unfortunately, the Illinois Supreme Court in reversing *Pastorino,* 91 Ill. 2d 178, 62 Ill. Dec. 172, 435 N.E.2d 1144 (1982), did not incorporate the above-quoted language, instead merely stating that "a court's witness may be impeached as any other witness," 91 Ill. 2d at 191. However, the Illinois Supreme Court thereafter championed the cause of requiring affirmative damage in *People v. Weaver,* 92 Ill. 2d 545, 565, 65 Ill. Dec. 944, 442 N.E.2d 255, 262 (1982):

A court's witness, or any witness for that matter, cannot be impeached by prior inconsistent statements unless his testimony has damaged, rather than failed to support the position of the impeaching party. The reason for this is simple: No possible reason exists to impeach a witness who has not contradicted any of the impeaching party's evidence, except to bring inadmissible hearsay to the attention of the jury. Impeachment is supposed to cancel out the witness' testimony. It is only when the witness' testimony is more damaging than his complete failure would have been that impeachment is useful. *See* People v. Johnson (1929), 333 Ill. 469, 165 N.E. 235; People v. Chitwood (1976), 36 Ill. App. 3d 1017, 344 N.E.2d 611; McCormick, Evidence Sec. 36 (2d ed. 1972).

Given this historical perspective, we may now turn to the current state of the law.

Effective April 1, 1982, Supreme Court Rule 238 was amended to abolish the common law voucher rule.

Impeachment of Witnesses; Hostile Witnesses

(a)   The credibility of a witness may be attacked by any party, including the party calling him.

(b)   If the court determines that a witness is hostile or unwilling, he may be examined by the party calling him as if under cross-examination.

Rule 238(b) is a verbatim copy of the first sentence of former Rule 238. *See* §611.9 infra. Rule 238(a) is a verbatim copy of Rule 607 of the Federal Rules of Evidence.

Given the amendment to Rule 238, made applicable to criminal cases as well by Supreme Court Rule 433, providing in section (a) supra that the credibility of any witness, whether or not an occurrence witness, *People v. Spence,* 188 Ill. App. 3d 761, 136 Ill. Dec. 145, 544 N.E.2d 831 (1989), may be attacked by any party including the party calling the witness, *People v. Cruz,* 162 Ill. 2d 314, 205 Ill. Dec. 345, 643 N.E.2d 636 (1994) (including by prior inconsistent statement), the court's witness doctrine no longer serves a useful purpose, nor does 5/2-1102 (formerly §60) of the Code of Civil Procedure. The process of refreshing recollection in open court never served a useful purpose. In short, the question of impeachment by a party of a witness called by the party should be, but in practice is not always, governed by Rule 238(a) and only Rule 238(a).

Whether the surprise and affirmative damage requirements for prior inconsistent statement impeachment by the party calling the witness that, generally speaking, accompanied former Rule 238 were to be applied to Rule 238(a) and the relationship of Rule 238(a) to the *Tunstall* doctrine remained unsure for some time. It was suggested that the surprise and affirmative damage requirements for impeachment by a party of a witness called by that party with a prior inconsistent statement not substantively admissible are consistent with final abandonment of the voucher rule and should be maintained.

> With respect to impeachment of a party's own witness with a prior inconsistent statement not substantively admissible, in the absence of both surprise and affirmative damage impeachment of one's own witness is inappropriate. If the witness does not give affirmatively damaging testimony, i.e., testimony of positive aid to the adversary, the party simply does not need to attack his credibility. If the witness' testimony does not surprise the party, the litigant should not be permitted to impeach his testimony by placing before the jury the witness' prior statement because he could have refrained from eliciting the statement he seeks to impeach. The requirement of surprise would prevent the party from consciously introducing affirmatively damaging testimony under the only circumstances in which he would do so — when the potential effect on the jury of the prior inconsistent statement outweighs the affirmatively damaging effect of the elicited testimony. [Graham, Handbook of Federal Evidence ¶607.3 (3rd ed. 1991).]

A contrary position permitting impeachment by the calling party in the absence of both surprise and affirmative damage was sanctioned in *People v. Gonzalez,* 120 Ill. App. 3d 1029, 76 Ill. Dec. 393, 458 N.E.2d 1047 (1983) and *People v. Rader,* 178 Ill. App. 3d 453, 127 Ill. Dec. 356, 532 N.E.2d 1365 (1988). *See also People v. Williams,* 262 Ill. App. 3d 734, 200 Ill. Dec. 442, 635 N.E.2d 781 (1994).

On the other hand, *People v. Bradford,* 106 Ill. 2d 492, 88 Ill. Dec. 615, 478 N.E.2d 1341 (1985), imposed the requirement of affirmative damage, citing *People v. Weaver* supra, with respect to impeachment of a court's witness. *See also People v. McMurtry,* 279 Ill. App. 3d 865, 216 Ill. Dec. 290, 665 N.E.2d 250 (1996) (affirmative damage required, quoting *Weaver*); *People v. Chatmon,* 236 Ill. App. 3d 913, 178 Ill. Dec. 143, 604 N.E.2d 399 (1992) (affirmative damage required, citing *Weaver*); *People v. Villegas,* 222 Ill. App. 3d 546, 165 Ill. Dec. 69, 584 N.E.2d 248 (1991) (affirmative damage required, quoting *Weaver*); *People v. Bolden,* 152 Ill. App. 3d 631, 105 Ill.

Dec. 550, 504 N.E.2d 835 (1987); *People v. Amato,* 128 Ill. App. 3d 985, 84 Ill. Dec. 162, 471 N.E.2d 928 (1984) (affirmative damage required); *People v. Johnson,* 138 Ill. App. 3d 1, 93 Ill. Dec. 332, 486 N.E.2d 433 (1985) (affirmative damage required, quoting *Weaver*); *People v. Chevalier,* 159 Ill. App. 3d 341, 111 Ill. Dec. 460, 512 N.E.2d 1001 (1987); *People v. Spence,* 188 Ill. App. 3d 761, 136 Ill. Dec. 145, 544 N.E.2d 831 (1989) (affirmative damage present, surprise not required). *See also People v. Hastings,* 161 Ill. App. 3d 714, 113 Ill. Dec. 451, 515 N.E.2d 260 (1970), requiring affirmative damage but incorrectly finding it present with respect to a witness who testified at trial to not being an eyewitness to the murder, a statement inconsistent with prior declarations, on the ground that without the witness's testimony the prosecution had no case; disappointment is not affirmative damage. *See generally* opinions in *People v. Parker,* 229 Ill. App. 3d 844, 171 Ill. Dec. 517, 594 N.E.2d 369 (1992), where applying *Weaver* one Justice found affirmative damage present on the basis of the witness's supposed suggestion that the state fabricated information that the other two Justices found factually not to exist.

The Illinois Supreme Court in *People v. Cruz,* 162 Ill. 2d 314, 205 Ill. Dec. 345, 643 N.E.2d 636 (1994), quoting the earlier quoted passage from *People v. Weaver* supra and citing the Handbook, held that pursuant to Illinois Supreme Court Rule 238(a), a prior inconsistent statement that is not substantively admissible may be employed to impeach only if the requirement of affirmative damages is satisfied. The court noted that jurors find it difficult to consider prior inconsistent statements solely to determine credibility and not as substantive evidence and that the "court has repeatedly disapproved prosecutorial efforts to impart substantive character to prior inconsistent statements under the guise of impeachment." Id. at 364, 205 Ill. Dec. at 369, 643 N.E.2d at 660 quoting *People v. Bradford,* 106 Ill. 2d 492, 88 Ill. Dec. 615, 478 N.E.2d 1341 (1985) quoting *People v. Bryant,* 94 Ill. 2d 514, 69 Ill. Dec. 84, 447 N.E.2d 301 (1983). Finally, the court opined that the enactment of Section 5/115-10.1, *see* §801.9 infra, providing for the substantive admissibility of some but not all prior inconsistent statements, supports a rigorous enforcement of the affirmative damage requirement under Rule 238(a); the introduction of prior inconsistent statements not substantively admissible "under the guise of impeachment should be foreclosed," citing Handbook and Steigman, Prior Inconsistent Statements as Substantive Evidence in Ilinois, 72 Ill. B. J. 638, 642-643 (1984). In short, when a party seeks to impeach a witness it has called to testify by means of a prior inconsistent statement that is not admissible as substantive evidence, affirmative damage must be established; surprise need not be shown. *Compare People v. Barton,* 286 Ill. App. 3d 954, 222 Ill. Dec. 273, 677 N.E.2d 476 (1997) plain error for the prosecution to introduce prior trial testimony of a witness in which the witness stated the defendant was with her all evening and said nothing of a shooting accompanied by impeachment testimony elicited at the prior trial that the witness had told a police officer that the defendant had told her that he had fired a shot on the evening in question at a female who had fired a shot at him; the only plausible purpose the state had to introduce such testimony was to have the jury give substantive effect to the prior statement to the police, an argument ringing of the requirement of surprise.

For a discussion of impeachment of a witness with a prior statement who claims lack of recollection at trial of the subject matter of the prior statement, *see* §801.9 infra.

When impeachment by prior inconsistent statement of a party's own witness is permitted, the impeachment should conform to the requirements set forth in §§613.1-613.3 infra. For a discussion of collateralness with respect to prior inconsistent statement impeachment, *see* §607.2 supra.

Prior inconsistent written, recorded, or acknowledged statements are now admissible as substantive evidence in criminal cases. 725 ILCS 5/115-10.1. *See* §801.9 infra. Since the police and others can now be expected to take written or, even better, recorded statements from occurrence witnesses, the number of occasions when a prior inconsistent statement of a witness will be offered by the calling party solely to impeach will be drastically reduced. Moreover, since such instances of impeachment will involve alleged unacknowledged oral inconsistent statements not made substantively admissible by 5/115-10.1 because of the enhanced risk of fabrication and distortion, the dual requirements of surprise and affirmative damage should be strictly enforced. Now that the prosecution may protect itself against witnesses who change their testimony for trial by obtaining a written or recorded statement admissible as substantive evidence, all subterfuge techniques to place prior oral inconsistent statements before the jury under the guise of impeachment should be foreclosed once and for all.

Under Rule 238(a), a party calling a witness may ordinarily impeach the witness using other modes of impeachment, including by means of a prior conviction, *People v. Tate,* 87 Ill. 2d 134, 57 Ill. Dec. 572, 429 N.E.2d 470 (1981); *People v. Collins,* 106 Ill. 2d 237, 87 Ill. Dec. 910, 478 N.E.2d 267 (1985), or by virtue of bias or improper motive, *People v. Williams,* 147 Ill. 2d 173, 167 Ill. Dec. 853, 588 N.E.2d 983 (1991). *See also People v. Nitz,* 143 Ill. 2d 82, 157 Ill. Dec. 431, 572 N.E.2d 895 (1991), to lessen its prejudicial effect, prosecution may establish on direct that two of its witnesses did not come forward with evidence of the crime because they feared the defendant. However, the trial court in its discretion may preclude impeachment by prior conviction where the witness's testimony does not affirmatively damage the calling party. *People v. Johnson,* 197 Ill. App. 3d 74, 143 Ill. Dec. 761, 554 N.E.2d 696 (1990).

§607.5   *Alcohol or Drug Use as Affecting Credibility*

Use of drugs at the time of the events related by the witness is a proper subject of cross-examination. *People v. Collins,* 106 Ill. 2d 237, 87 Ill. Dec. 910, 478 N.E.2d 267 (1985); *People v. Castiglione,* 150 Ill. App. 3d 459, 103 Ill. Dec. 606, 501 N.E.2d 923 (1986); *People v. Adams,* 259 Ill. App. 3d 995, 197 Ill. Dec. 717, 631 N.E.2d 1176 (1993). Drunkenness at the time of the event related is also properly brought out on cross-examination. *People v. McGuire,* 18 Ill. 2d 257, 163 N.E.2d 832 (1960); *People v. Spreyne,* 256 Ill. App. 3d 505, 194 Ill. Dec. 754, 628 N.E.2d 251 (1993). Neither drug use nor drunkenness is collateral; the cross-examiner is not foreclosed by a denial of the witness and may prove the condition in question by other witnesses. *People v. Crump,* 5 Ill. 2d 251, 125 N.E.2d 615 (1955); *In Interest of C.L.,* 180 Ill. App. 3d 173, 128 Ill. Dec. 725, 534 N.E.2d 1330 (1989).

The question whether a witness is a narcotics addict at the time of testifying is also an important consideration in passing upon his credibility. *People v. Collins,* 106 Ill. 2d 237, 87 Ill. Dec. 910, 478 N.E.2d 267 (1985). Judicial notice has been taken of the adverse effects of drugs on the ability of a witness to observe, recollect, and narrate, *People v. Boyd,* 17 Ill. 2d 321, 161 N.E.2d 311 (1959), and of the fact that habitual users of narcotics become notorious liars. *People v. Lewis,* 25 Ill. 2d 396, 185 N.E.2d 168 (1962); *People v. Davis,* 43 Ill. App. 3d 603, 2 Ill. Dec. 119, 357 N.E.2d 96 (1976). Cross-examination of the witness with respect to habitual use of narcotics is proper, subject to a good-faith basis establishing a foundation showing narcotics addiction and ability to present extrinsic evidence. *People v. Crisp,* 242 Ill. App. 3d 652, 182 Ill. Dec. 206, 609 N.E.2d 740 (1992); *People v. Kegley,* 227 Ill. App. 3d 48, 169 Ill. Dec. 3, 590 N.E.2d 922 (1992); *People v. Novak,* 63 Ill. App. 2d 433, 211 N.E.2d 554 (1965); *People v. Crump* supra; *People v. Lewis* supra. *Contra People v. Smith,* 105 Ill. App. 3d 84, 60 Ill. Dec. 816, 433 N.E.2d 1054 (1982). The failure to produce extrinsic evidence when required can constitute reversible error. *Bailey v. City of Chicago,* 116 Ill. App. 3d 862, 72 Ill. Dec. 427, 452 N.E.2d 680 (1983). Failure to permit defense counsel to examine a witness's arm for the presence of needle marks and to exhibit same to the jury if found is reversible error. *People v. Strother,* 53 Ill. 2d 95, 290 N.E.2d 201 (1972). Introduction of evidence of narcotics addiction ultimately rests in the discretion of the trial court. *See People v. Mercado,* 244 Ill. App. 3d 1040, 185 Ill. Dec. 150, 614 N.E.2d 284 (1993) (cumulative). Evaluation of evidence as to actual use of narcotics and the extent of impairment, including whether expert testimony has been offered, is critical in assessing whether probative value is substantially outweighed by the danger of unfair prejudice. *See People v. Henderson,* 175 Ill. App. 3d 483, 124 Ill. Dec. 934, 529 N.E.2d 1051 (1988). Absent evidence establishing the effect narcotics have had upon the particular witness's ability to perceive, record and recollect, and narrate, evidence of narcotics addiction should be excluded. *See People v. Stiff,* 185 Ill. App. 3d 751, 134 Ill. Dec. 213, 542 N.E.2d 392 (1989). *Cf. People v. Accardo,* 195 Ill. App. 3d 180, 141 Ill. Dec. 821, 551 N.E.2d 1349 (1990), narcotics addiction may be shown as habitual users of narcotics become habitual liars; *People v. Tomes,* 284 Ill. App. 3d 514, 219 Ill. Dec. 781, 672 N.E.2d 289 (1996), drug addiction admissible to impeach honesty and integrity in general.

Proof of chronic alcoholism as affecting credibility was implicitly approved in *People v. Davis,* 43 Ill. App. 3d 603, 2 Ill. Dec. 119, 357 N.E.2d 96 (1976). Habitual glue sniffing is treated similarly. *People v. Stalions,* 139 Ill. App. 3d 1033, 94 Ill. Dec. 471, 488 N.E.2d 297 (1986). In such instances, as in the case of narcotics addiction, the evidence of addiction should be admitted only if other evidence, which may, but need not, consist of expert witness testimony, establishes the effect that the addiction had on the particular witness's ability to perceive, record, recollect, and narrate at the time in question. *People v. Collette,* 217 Ill. App. 3d 465, 160 Ill. Dec. 420, 577 N.E.2d 550 (1991).

With respect to opinion as to intoxication in negligence actions, *see* §403.3 supra and §701.7 infra; as to the effect of drug or alcohol use on the competency of a witness, *see* §601.4 supra.

§607.6   Occupation and Residence of the Witness

The occupation and related background of the witness are regarded as having value in determining the credit to be given her testimony and may be inquired into as a matter of right, *People v. Crane*, 302 Ill. 217, 134 N.E. 99 (1922), even though an illegal occupation is disclosed, such as gambling, *People v. White*, 251 Ill. 67, 95 N.E. 1036 (1911), or keeping a house of ill fame, *People v. Bond*, 281 Ill. 490, 118 N.E. 14 (1917), or being a drug dealer, *People v. Shinkle*, 160 Ill. App. 3d 1043, 112 Ill. Dec. 463, 513 N.E.2d 1072 (1987); *People v. Kegley*, 227 Ill. App. 3d 48, 169 Ill. Dec. 3, 590 N.E.2d 922 (1992), or being a prostitute, *People v. Hines*, 94 Ill. App. 3d 1041, 50 Ill. Dec. 312, 419 N.E.2d 420 (1981). The rationale is that if a witness is engaged in an unlawful or disreputable occupation, in justice and fairness she should not be permitted to appear before the jury as a person of high character engaged in a lawful and reputable occupation. *People v. Anderson*, 48 Ill. 2d 488, 272 N.E.2d 18 (1971). Inquiry into such matters should be considered collateral; extrinsic evidence disputing a negative answer on cross-examination should not be allowed. *See Esser v. McIntyre*, 267 Ill. App. 3d 611, 204 Ill. Dec. 902, 642 N.E.2d 803 (1994). *See also* §607.2 supra.

It is also proper to cross-examine a witness as to his place of residence, since such evidence affects the witness's credibility. *Roewe v. Lombardo*, 76 Ill. App. 2d 164, 221 N.E.2d 521 (1966). However, inquiry may not be made on cross-examination designed to elicit the fact that the witness resides in prison. *People v. Kosears*, 408 Ill. 179, 96 N.E.2d 539 (1951). As to impeachment by proof of conviction of a crime, *see* §609 infra. Of course the defendant may not be compelled to appear before the jury in prison garb. *Estelle v. Williams*, 425 U.S. 501 (1976).

While the United States Supreme Court in *Alford v. United States*, 282 U.S. 687, 693 (1930), and *Smith v. Illinois*, 390 U.S. 129, 132 (1968), has indicated that defense counsel has the right to obtain on cross-examination the place of residence of a prosecution witness, understandably various decisions, including *People v. Lewis*, 57 Ill. 2d 232, 311 N.E.2d 685 (1974), and *People v. Thibudeaux*, 98 Ill. App. 3d 1105, 54 Ill. Dec. 275, 424 N.E.2d 1178 (1981), have followed the suggestion made in *United States v. Varelli*, 407 F.2d 735, 750 n.11 (7th Cir.

1969), that "when there is a sufficient showing that the witness's life may be in jeopardy, one solution may be to require submission by the government of the relevant information to the district judge *in camera* for him to decide whether disclosure would present a real problem." *Accord Smith v. Illinois* supra, at 133-134 (White, J., concurring), "In *Alford v. United States* . . . the Court recognized that questions which tend merely to harass, annoy, or humiliate a witness may go beyond the bounds of proper cross-examination. I would place in the same category those inquiries which tend to endanger the personal safety of the witness." Where the witness has recently changed residence for reasons of safety, disclosure solely of his prior residence would seem to be a satisfactory compromise. *See People v. Jones,* 155 Ill. App. 3d 641, 108 Ill. Dec. 196, 508 N.E.2d 357 (1987). Of course the name of a witness called by the prosecution must always be disclosed. *Alford v. United States* supra. *See generally People v. Cooper,* 244 Ill. App. 3d 366, 185 Ill. Dec. 86, 614 N.E.2d 220 (1993).

With respect to the defendant's assumption of an assumed name, *see People v. Berlin,* 58 Ill. App. 3d 612, 16 Ill. Dec. 173, 374 N.E.2d 948 (1978).

§607.7   *Interest, Bias, Corruption, or Coercion*

Matters that may reasonably be expected to color the testimony of a witness or cause him to testify falsely are proper subjects of inquiry of any witness by any party. Statutes specifically provide that interest on the part of a witness, while no longer disqualifying, may be shown for the purpose of affecting credibility. 725 ILCS 125/6; 735 ILCS 5/8-101. Bias (in the sense of favor for proponent or hostility or prejudice against an opponent), corruption, and coercion fall within the same category under the case law. *See* 3A Wigmore, Evidence §945 (Chadbourn rev. 1970). Hence inquiry is properly permitted into such matters as the compensation being paid the witness by a party, *Chicago City Ry. v. Carroll,* 206 Ill. 318, 68 N.E. 1087 (1903), or whether a defense witness was afraid of the defendant because of prior physical abuse, *People v. Tenner*, 157 Ill. 2d 341, 193 Ill. Dec. 105, 626 N.E.2d 138 (1993), or that a party is also a defendant in a companion lawsuit, *Holton v. Memorial Hospital*, 176 Ill. 2d 95, 223 Ill. Dec. 429, 679 N.E.2d 1202 (1997), or the course of a love relationship with defendant, *People v. Ross*, 63 Ill. App. 3d 884, 20 Ill. Dec. 688, 380 N.E.2d 897 (1978), or refusal to give a party a statement, *Goretz v. Chicago & N.W. Ry.*, 19 Ill. App. 2d 261, 153 N.E.2d 486 (1958), or an attempt by witness to smuggle hacksaw blades to the defendant, *People v. Sievers*, 56 Ill. App. 3d 880, 14 Ill. Dec. 509, 372 N.E.2d 705 (1978), or the existence of a loan agreement, *Casson v. Nash*, 74 Ill. 2d 164, 23 Ill. Dec. 571, 384 N.E.2d 365 (1978), or as to statements made by the police that might have motivated the witness to give false testimony, *People v. Rogers*, 123 Ill. 2d 487, 123 Ill. Dec. 963, 528 N.E.2d 667 (1988), or that the house where the witness resided was owned by a drug dealer for whom the defendant worked, *People v. Kitchen*, 159 Ill. 2d 1, 201 Ill. Dec. 1, 636 N.E.2d 433 (1994), as well as financial interest in the outcome of the case. Moreover, foreclosing inquiry has been held error with regard to an attempt to obtain money from the accused on behalf of the prosecuting witness, *People v. Provenzano*, 305 Ill. 493, 137 N.E. 414 (1922); as to prosecution witness having been beaten by her husband after defendant had informed him she was having an extramarital affair, *People v. Coles*, 74 Ill. 2d 393, 24 Ill. Dec. 553, 385 N.E.2d 694 (1979); as to hostility to a party, *Blanchard v. Blanchard*, 191 Ill. 450, 61 N.E. 481 (1901); concerning compensation being paid witnesses by a party, *Kerfoot v. Chicago*, 195 Ill. 229, 63 N.E. 101 (1902); with respect to payment by a party for expenses and lost time, *Schuman v. Bader & Co.*, 227 Ill. App. 28 (1922); that a witness was coerced into giving her testimony, *People v. Robinson*, 163 Ill. App. 3d 754, 114 Ill. Dec, 898, 516 N.E.2d 1292 (1987); and as to witness being biased toward prosecution arising out of the state's help in paying for his move out of a home he wanted to leave near a public housing project, *People v. Greer*, 293 Ill. App. 3d 861, 228 Ill. Dec. 262, 689 N.E.2d 134 (1997).

Since a witness has the right to refuse to talk to or cooperate with opposing counsel prior to trial, it is not an abuse of discretion for the trial court to refuse to permit inquiry. *See People v. Peter*, 55 Ill. 2d 443, 303 N.E.2d 398 (1973); *People v. Defyn*, 222 Ill. App. 3d 504, 165 Ill. Dec. 41, 584 N.E.2d 220 (1991); *People v. Brown*, 87 Ill. App. 3d 368, 42 Ill. Dec. 586, 409 N.E.2d 81 (1980). Conversely, inquiry into the refusal to be interviewed or otherwise cooperate may be permitted in the trial court's discretion. *See People v. Timmons*, 114 Ill. App. 3d 861, 70 Ill. Dec. 762, 449 N.E.2d 1366 (1983); *People v. Williams*, 131 Ill. App. 3d 597, 86 Ill. Dec. 703, 475 N.E.2d 1082 (1985). *Compare People v. Allison*, 236 Ill. App. 3d 175, 177 Ill. Dec. 116, 602 N.E.2d 1288 (1992) (it is always error to refuse to permit cross-examination of a witness as to his refusal to talk to opposing counsel; harmless error analysis applied). *Contra People v. McCollum*, 239 Ill. App. 3d 593, 180 Ill. Dec. 346, 607 N.E.2d 240 (1992); *People v. Atteberry*, 213 Ill. App. 3d 851, 157 Ill. Dec. 365, 572 N.E.2d 434 (1991), reversible error to prohibit such cross-examination by defense counsel.

In criminal proceedings the defendant has a right to question a witness concerning any matter that goes to explain, qualify, modify, discredit, or destroy what she said on direct examination. *People v. Aughinbaugh*, 36 Ill. 2d 320, 223 N.E.2d 117 (1967); *People v. Morris*, 30 Ill. 2d 406, 197 N.E.2d 433 (1964). The fact that a witness has been arrested, charged, or convicted of a crime may be shown or inquired into whenever it would reasonably tend to indicate that her testimony might be influenced by interest, bias, corruption, or coercion to testify falsely, *People v. Triplett*, 108 Ill. 2d 453, 92 Ill. Dec. 454, 485 N.E.2d 9 (1985); *People v. Eddington*, 77 Ill. 2d 41, 31 Ill. Dec. 808, 394 N.E.2d 1185 (1979); *People v. Mason*, 28 Ill. 2d 396, 192 N.E.2d 835 (1963), without regard to whether the event would be available to impeach the witness's character for truthfulness, *People v. Lucas*, 151 Ill. 2d 461, 177 Ill. Dec. 390, 603 N.E.2d 460 (1992). In short, cross-examination is proper whenever the prosecution has sufficient "leverage" over the witness justifying the defendant's claim that the witness has an interest or bias, or that there is corruption or coercion that would tend to make the witness testify falsely. *People v. Driskell,* 213 Ill. App. 3d 196, 156 Ill. Dec. 914, 571 N.E.2d 894 (1991). To illustrate, the fact that the witness is *merely* the subject of an investigation as to a crime may not be explored on cross-examination, *People v. Fonza,* 217 Ill. App. 3d 883, 160 Ill. Dec. 829, 578 N.E.2d 8 (1991), nor that the witness is on probation where there is no evidence that a violation of probation is pending or threatened. *People v. Tayborn,* 254 Ill. App. 3d 381, 193 Ill. Dec. 849, 627 N.E.2d 8 (1993). Proof of conviction of a crime as bearing on character of the witness for veracity is treated in §609 infra.

Though the scope of cross-examination is generally within the trial court's discretion, the widest latitude should generally be allowed the defendant in cross-examination for the purpose of establishing interest, bias, corruption, or coercion. *People v. Gonzalez,* 104 Ill. 2d 332, 84 Ill. Dec. 457, 472 N.E.2d 417 (1984); *People v. Mason,* 28 Ill. 2d 396, 192 N.E.2d 835 (1963); *People v. Naujokas,* 25 Ill. 2d 32, 182 N.E.2d 700 (1962); *People v. Young,* 206 Ill. App. 3d 789, 151 Ill. Dec. 592, 564 N.E.2d 1254 (1990) (citing Handbook). Thus, for example, where charges are dropped in exchange for testimony, *People v. Barr,* 51 Ill. 2d 50, 280 N.E.2d 708 (1972); a prosecution witness promised immunity, *People v. Maggio,* 324 Ill. 516, 155 N.E. 373 (1927); a promise of leniency made, *People v. Norwood,* 54 Ill. 2d 253, 296 N.E.2d 852 (1973); the witness hoped that his testimony against the accused would be taken into consideration at his sentencing, *People v. Ramey,* 152 Ill. 2d 41, 178 Ill. Dec. 19, 604 N.E.2d 275 (1992); the witness is currently in custody even if a juvenile, *People v. Triplett,* 108 Ill. 2d 453, 92 Ill. Dec. 454, 485 N.E.2d 9 (1985); the witness had threatened the accused, *People v. Hobson,* 77 Ill. App. 3d 22, 32 Ill. Dec. 940, 396 N.E.2d 53 (1979); the witness has brought, *People v. Doran,* 256 Ill. App. 3d 131, 194 Ill. Dec. 763, 628 N.E.2d 260 (1993), or is contemplating a civil action against the accused, *People v. Crosser,* 117 Ill. App. 3d 24, 72 Ill. Dec. 604, 452 N.E.2d 857 (1983) *contra, People v. Marti-*

nez, 120 Ill. App. 3d 305, 75 Ill. Dec. 936, 458 N.E.2d 104 (1983) (contemplations not enough); the prosecution witness's husband was in litigation against the defendant's husband, *People v. Blommaert,* 184 Ill. App. 3d 1065, 133 Ill. Dec. 307, 541 N.E.2d 144 (1989); the defendant intended to show that the police officers were attempting to cover up a beating, *People v. Lenard,* 79 Ill. App. 3d 1046, 35 Ill. Dec. 104, 398 N.E.2d 1054 (1979); the defendant intended to show that witness's gang membership provided a motive to fabricate, *People v. Gonzalez,* 104 Ill. 2d 332, 84 Ill. Dec. 457, 472 N.E.2d 417 (1984); a witness offers to have charges dropped in exchange for restitution, *People v. Pizzi,* 94 Ill. App. 3d 415, 50 Ill. Dec. 30, 418 N.E.2d 1024 (1981); a witness had pending bond forfeitures, *People v. Richmond,* 84 Ill. App. 3d 1017, 40 Ill. Dec. 434, 406 N.E.2d 135 (1980); a witness had her bail eliminated and had no preliminary hearing date set, *People v. Betts,* 116 Ill. App. 3d 551, 71 Ill. Dec. 874, 451 N.E.2d 1028 (1983); witnesses were in fact illegal aliens, *People v. Austin,* 123 Ill. App. 3d 788, 79 Ill. Dec. 103, 463 N.E.2d 444 (1984); that charges had been stricken but could be reinstated, *People v. Morando,* 169 Ill. App. 3d 716, 120 Ill. Dec. 150, 523 N.E.2d 1061 (1988) and *In re Interest of T.S.,* 287 Ill. App. 3d 949, 223 Ill. Dec. 283, 679 N.E.2d 468 (1997); the witness had been suspended from the police force on 15 prior occasions, *People v. Phillips,* 95 Ill. App. 3d 1013, 51 Ill. Dec. 423, 420 N.E.2d 837 (1981); a prosecution witness has been charged with a crime, *People v. Wilkerson,* 87 Ill. 2d 151, 57 Ill. Dec. 628, 429 N.E.2d 526 (1981), including the nature of the crime charged, *People v. Rufus,* 104 Ill. App. 3d 467, 60 Ill. Dec. 190, 432 N.E.2d 1089 (1982); the witness may have been placed on probation for the present offense, *People v. Foley,* 109 Ill. App. 3d 1010, 65 Ill. Dec. 520, 441 N.E.2d 655 (1982); where the defendants claim there are incidents indicative of strong bias against the defendant on the part of the complaining witness, *People v. Coles,* 74 Ill. 2d 393, 24 Ill. Dec. 553, 385 N.E.2d 694 (1979); the defendant is prevented from inquiring of a police officer testifying to an oral confession the accused denies making, whether it was the police officer's duty to obtain confessions, *People v. Furby,* 228 Ill. App. 3d 1, 169 Ill. Dec. 360, 591 N.E.2d 533 (1992); the witness was a police officer under suspension for drug addiction, *People v. Adams,* 259 Ill. App. 3d 995, 197 Ill. Dec. 717, 631 N.E.2d 1176 (1993); or a prosecution witness could be charged with a probation violation, *People v. Ciavirelli,* 262 Ill. App. 3d 966, 200 Ill. Dec. 271, 635 N.E.2d 610 (1994), foreclosure of inquiry was held to be reversible error. Nevertheless the trial judge retains wide latitude to impose reasonable limits; "the Confrontation Clause guarantees an *opportunity* for effective cross-examination, not cross-examination that is effective in whatever way, and to whatever extent, the defense might wish." *People v. Jones,* 156 Ill. 2d 225, 244, 189 Ill. Dec. 357, 364, 620 N.E.2d 325, 332 (1993), quoting *Delaware v. Fensterer,* 474 U.S. 15, 20 (1985).

The latitude allowed on cross-examination is a matter within the sound discretion of the trial court and a reviewing court will not interfere unless there has been a clear abuse of discretion resulting in manifest prejudice to the criminal defendant. *People v. Kitchen,* 159 Ill. 2d 1, 201 Ill. Dec. 1, 636 N.E.2d 433 (1994); *People v. Collins,* 106 Ill. 2d 237, 87 Ill. Dec. 910, 478 N.E.2d 267 (1985).

Counsel for the defendant may so inquire without a good faith basis that any of the foregoing events has actually occurred, *People v. Ramey,* 152 Ill. 2d 41, 178 Ill. Dec. 19, 604 N.E.2d 275 (1992); *People v. Triplett,* 108 Ill. 2d 453, 92 Ill. Dec. 454, 485 N.E.2d 9 (1985); *People v. Tomes,* 284 Ill. App. 3d 514, 219 Ill. Dec. 781, 672 N.E.2d 289 (1996); *People v. Bland,* 228 Ill. App. 3d 1080, 170 Ill. Dec. 750, 593 N.E.2d 639 (1992); *People v. Freeman,* 100 Ill. App. 3d 478, 55 Ill. Dec. 846, 426 N.E.2d 1220 (1981); *People v. Baptiste,* 37 Ill. App. 3d 808, 347 N.E.2d 92 (1976), or that any expectation of favor, fear, or other mental state exists in the witness's mind. *People v. Ciavirelli,* 262 Ill. App. 3d 966, 200 Ill. Dec. 275, 635 N.E.2d 610 (1994). *See generally In re Interest of T.S.,* 287 Ill. App. 3d 949, 223 Ill. Dec. 283, 679 N.E.2d 468 (1997), defendant is not required to show beforehand that any promise of leniency had actually been made or that any expectations of special favor existed in the mind of the witness. While *People v. Lewis,* 229 Ill. App. 3d 874, 171 Ill. Dec. 562, 594 N.E.2d 414 (1992), concludes that foreclosure of inquiry is not error where the state demonstrates that defense counsel knew before trial that no "deals" had been made, such foreclosure improperly and unnecessarily impairs a criminal defendant's right to explore the possibility of self-interest. *See id.,* Justice Harrison dissenting. The prosecution, of course, may also do likewise. *People v. Hominick,* 177 Ill. App. 3d 18, 126 Ill. Dec. 422, 531 N.E.2d 1049 (1988), inquiry proper as to the fact that witness for the defense's half-sister had been charged with the same offense; *People v. Triplett,* 108 Ill. 2d 463, 92 Ill. Dec. 454, 485 N.E.2d 9 (1985), inquiry proper as to defense witness's prior arrests and charges to establish antiprosecutorial bias; *cf. People v. Hughes,* 168 Ill. App. 3d 758, 119 Ill. Dec. 416, 522 N.E.2d 1275 (1988), pendency of a single criminal charge is not sufficient to establish antiprosecutorial bias. *See generally People v. Rivera,* 145 Ill. App. 3d 609, 99 Ill. Dec. 353, 495 N.E.2d 1088 (1986), the right to explore bias on cross-examination is not a license to engage in speculative attacks on the witness — the facts must be within the witness's knowledge and cannot be so remote as to be mere conjecture.

Evidence offered to establish interest, bias, corruption, or coercion that is remote or uncertain may be excluded, *People v. Triplett* supra; *People v. Harris,* 262 Ill. App. 3d 35, 199 Ill. Dec. 479, 634 N.E.2d 318 (1994); *People v. Sykes,* 224 Ill. App. 3d 369, 166 Ill. Dec. 671, 586 N.E.2d 629 (1991); *People v. Hiller,* 92 Ill. App. 3d 322, 47 Ill. Dec. 889, 415 N.E.2d 1202 (1980), i.e., the evidence should be timely, unequivocal, and directly related, *People v. Merz,* 122 Ill. App. 3d 972, 78 Ill. Dec. 273, 461 N.E.2d 1380 (1984); *People v. Mendiola,* 171 Ill. App. 3d 936, 122 Ill. Dec. 32, 526 N.E.2d 172 (1988); *People v. Schnurr,* 206 Ill. App. 3d 522, 151 Ill. Dec. 674, 564 N.E.2d 1336 (1990). *Accord People v. Jones,* 240 Ill. App. 3d 1055, 180 Ill. Dec. 900, 608 N.E.2d 22 (1992), cross-examination concerning a civil suit is improper when there is no indication that any civil action was filed or contemplated; *People v. John-*

son, 239 Ill. App. 3d 1064, 180 Ill. Dec. 914, 908 N.E.2d 36 (1992), trial court within its discretion to bar cross-examination as to two criminal charges stricken with leave to reinstate in 1988 and 1989 on basis of remoteness and uncertainty; *People v. Coleman,* 222 Ill. App. 3d 614, 165 Ill. Dec. 151, 584 N.E.2d 330 (1991), not error to prohibit inquiry as to complainant's knowledge of the progress of the case or the nature of her communications with the state's attorney's office; *People v. Davis,* 193 Ill. App. 3d 1001, 140 Ill. Dec. 792, 550 N.E.2d 677 (1990), unrelated civil suit against a police officer charging dereliction of duty too remote and uncertain; *People v. Cameron,* 189 Ill. App. 3d 998, 137 Ill. Dec. 505, 546 N.E.2d 259 (1989), unrelated civil suit against police officer is "too remote and uncertain" to show bias; *People v. Johnson,* 173 Ill. App. 3d 998, 123 Ill. Dec. 542, 527 N.E.2d 1317 (1988), the fact that witness had previously made homosexual advances reported by the defendant is "too remote and uncertain" to give rise to the inference of interest or bias. Cross-examination that is unduly repetitive or harassing may be curtailed. *People v. Phillips,* 95 Ill. App. 3d 1013, 51 Ill. Dec. 423, 420 N.E.2d 837 (1981); *People v. Paisley,* 149 Ill. App. 3d 556, 102 Ill. Dec. 474, 500 N.E.2d 96 (1986).

There is authority that interest may be shown in the first instance by extrinsic evidence without preliminary inquiry on cross-examination. *Aurora v. Scott,* 82 Ill. App. 616 *aff'd,* 185 Ill. 539, 57 N.E. 440 (1898). Recent authority is, however, contrary. *People v. Woolridge,* 91 Ill. App. 3d 298, 46 Ill. Dec. 761, 414 N.E.2d 814 (1980), extrinsic evidence concerning personal injury action by defendant's brother resulting from incident with a law enforcement agent was not admissible as relating to possible bias in the absence of the laying of a proper foundation during the cross-examination of a different law enforcement agent. If extrinsic proof is offered in the form of prior statements of the witness manifesting hostility and the like, it too has been held to be subject to the same foundation requirements on cross-examination as self-contradicting statements. *Aneals v. People,* 134 Ill. 401, 25 N.E. 1022 (1890); *People v. Curtis,* 123 Ill. App. 2d 384, 259

N.E.2d 897 (1970). With respect to foundation requirements for impeachment by prior inconsistent statement, *see* §613.3 infra.

Matters in this area are not considered collateral within the rule precluding contradiction on collateral matters. *People v. Gonzalez*, 104 Ill. 2d 332, 84 Ill. Dec. 457, 472 N.E.2d 417 (1984); *Hirn v. Edgewater Hosp.*, 86 Ill. App. 3d 939, 42 Ill. Dec. 261, 408 N.E.2d 970 (1980); *People v. Garrett*, 44 Ill. App. 3d 429, 3 Ill. Dec. 197, 358 N.E.2d 364 (1976). *See* §607.2 supra. Hence the answers are not conclusive on the cross-examiner but may be contradicted by other testimony. *Blanchard v. Blanchard*, 191 Ill. 450, 61 N.E. 481 (1901). To the extent that *Holton v. Memorial Hospital*, 176 Ill. 2d 95, 223 Ill. Dec. 429, 679 N.E.2d 1202 (1997), is to the contrary, it is incorrect and should not be followed. *See* Nickels, J., id., dissenting, quoting Handbook; the extrinsic evidence in *Holton* of knowledge of a companion lawsuit should have been excluded as "remote or uncertain," *see* supra, or on the basis of unfair prejudice, misleading the jury, or confusion of the issues, *see* §403.1 supra. The cross-examiner is not limited to questioning the witness concerning his feelings toward the party but may also inquire into prior statements by the witness. *Phenix v. Castner*, 108 Ill. 207 (1883); *People v. Gonzalez*, 120 Ill. App. 3d 1029, 76 Ill. Dec. 393, 458 N.E.2d 1047 (1983). *Cf. People v. Fonza*, 217 Ill. App. 3d 883, 160 Ill. App. 3d 829, 578 N.E.2d 8 (1991) (where it is unclear whether a pending charge relates to the witness, the matter would be considered collateral).

While cross-examination raising implications of interest, bias, corruption, or coercion may normally be conducted without extrinsic evidence later being introduced, considerations of unfair prejudice and misleading of the jury, *see* §403.1 supra, may require the presentation of contradictory extrinsic evidence in the face of a witness's denial of misconduct. *People v. Nuccio*, 43 Ill. 2d 375, 253 N.E.2d 353 (1969) (prosecution impeachment of defense witness); *People v. Beringer*, 151 Ill. App. 3d 558, 104 Ill. Dec. 916, 503 N.E.2d 778 (1987) (same); *People v. Davidson*, 235 Ill. App. 3d 605,

176 Ill. Dec. 448, 601 N.E.2d 1146 (1992) (prosecution insinuation on cross-examination of defendant having committed other crimes); *Boersma v. Amoco Oil Co.*, 276 Ill. App. 3d 638, 213 Ill. Dec. 152, 658 N.E.2d 1173 (1995) (plaintiff's impeachment that defense expert doctor has testified on 56 occasions for the defendant's law firm).

Expert witnesses are considered further in §702 infra. For disclosure of compromise payment to show bias, *see* §408.1 supra.

§607.8   *Contradiction by Other Evidence*

The principle is recognized that a witness may be contradicted by evidence introduced by any party. *Wisniewski v. Shimashus,* 22 Ill. 2d 451, 176 N.E.2d 781 (1961). Contradictory evidence may not, however, relate solely to collateral matters. *People v. Pfanschmidt,* 262 Ill. 411, 104 N.E. 804 (1914); *People v. Abrams,* 260 Ill. App. 3d 566, 197 Ill. Dec. 853, 631 N.E.2d 1312 (1994). Illustrations of collateral matters are whether there was in fact a lumberyard in the city, after a witness testified that a sidewalk was built of defective materials from rafts since there was no lumberyard, *East Dubuque v. Burhyte,* 173 Ill. 553, 50 N.E. 1077 (1898); whether a witness struck in the same automobile accident, who appeared on crutches and testified he could not walk without them, could in fact walk without crutches, *People v. Allen,* 368 Ill. 368, 14 N.E.2d 397 (1938); and contradiction of defendant's alleged conduct in a lockup after altercation for which on trial. *People v. McGhee,* 20 Ill. App. 3d 915, 314 N.E.2d 313 (1974). *See also* §607.2 supra.

A large measure of discretion must of necessity be accorded the trial judge in applying this principle. Reversible error is likely to result only when allowing the contradicting evidence results in prejudice other than the mere contradiction, §403.1 supra. Thus contradiction that discloses or suggests the commission of other offenses has been a source of error. *Dalton v. People,* 224 Ill. 333, 79 N.E. 669 (1906), after accused charged with statutory rape stated on cross-examination that he had never been upstairs where offense allegedly occurred, error to admit evidence that he had taken another girl upstairs; *People v. Kirkwood*, 17 Ill. 2d 23, 160 N.E.2d 766 (1959), after accused charged with rape testified on cross-examination that he had never been at the scene of the crime, error to admit testimony of two women that he had attacked them in the vicinity. *Cf. People v. Feinberg*, 237 Ill. 348, 86 N.E. 584 (1908), after accused charged with receiving stolen pig iron testified on direct that he had never possessed any pig iron, proper to admit evidence that he had offered to sell pig iron at an earlier date; *People v. Bush*, 103 Ill. App. 3d 5, 58 Ill. Dec. 482, 430 N.E.2d 514 (1981), after accused indicated during cross-examination that he did not like knives, it was proper to admit evidence that accused displayed a butcher knife at a party. For discussion of introduction of evidence as opening door for rebuttal, *see* §103.4 supra.

§607.9 *Contradiction by Conduct of the Witness*

A witness may be impeached by proof that she acted in a manner contradictory to her testimony. *People v. Boston*, 309 Ill. 77, 139 N.E. 880 (1923), continued friendliness of prosecuting witness and parents toward accused charged with rape; *People v. Rainford*, 58 Ill. App. 2d 312, 208 N.E.2d 314 (1965), 13-year-old girl continuing to live at home of stepfather after alleged assault with intent to commit rape; *Vendo Co. v. Stoner*, 108 Ill. App. 3d 51, 63 Ill. Dec. 791, 438 N.E.2d 933 (1982), agreement not to proceed with collection efforts beyond the point already reached.

Inconsistent conduct relied upon for impeachment has been held to be subject to the foundation requirements applicable to prior inconsistent statements discussed in §613.3 infra. *People v. Boston* supra. As with contradiction generally, the impeaching evidence cannot relate to collateral matters. *See* §607.2 supra.

§607.10 Personal Knowledge: Mental Capacity; Expert Testimony

The capacity and actuality of a witness's perception, his ability to record and remember sense impressions, and his ability to comprehend questions and narrate are relevant to an assessment of the weight to be given to a witness's testimony. Each of these areas is a proper subject of cross-examination. *See, e.g., People v. Montes*, 263 Ill. App. 3d 680, 200 Ill. Dec. 571, 635 N.E.2d 910 (1994) (error to preclude cross-examination into police officer's comprehension of Spanish). None of these areas are considered collateral; extrinsic evidence is permissible. *See* §607.2 supra.

The mental capacity of a witness is a proper subject of cross-examination. With respect to a witness possessing minimum credibility and thus competence to testify, *see* §601.3 supra, an adversary is entitled to explore on cross-examination the effect that age, retardation, injury, or mental illness has had on the witness's ability to observe, record, recollect, and recount, as well as his ability to understand the duty to tell the truth. Such inquiry is non-collateral; extrinsic evidence may be introduced. Whether psychiatric testimony offered by a party relating to the credibility of a witness is admissible rests in the discretion of the court. Similarly, whether the court will order a psychiatric examination of the witness for the purpose of permitting full exploration of the credibility of the witness also rests in the court's discretion.

§608 Character of Witness for Truthfulness or Untruthfulness

§608.1 An Overview

Testimony can scarcely be considered apart from the individual who gives it. Consequently, the character of the witness is relevant under the definition of relevancy, §401.1 supra. However, the likelihood of confusion, prejudice, and undue consumption of time, expressed in §403.1 supra, plus the policy factor that excessive scrutiny may increase the reluctance of people to come forward and testify, all have resulted in rather stringent limitations upon inquiry into the character of the witness. *See* §§404.1 and 404.3 supra. As stated previously, §404.1 supra, character evidence is generally not admissible for the purpose of proving that a person acted in conformity therewith. However, this proposition is subject to several exceptions, one of which concerns character evidence bearing upon the credibility of a witness for truthfulness. Evidence of character of the witness affecting credibility is limited solely to character for truthfulness or untruthfulness. Moreover, the inquiry is allowed only if the credibility of the witness for truthfulness has been attacked. *Tedens v. Schumers,* 112 Ill. 263 (1884). *See also People v. Petitt,* 245 Ill. App. 3d 132, 184 Ill. Dec. 766, 613 N.E.2d 1358 (1993). Only reputation testimony is permitted, *People v. Willy,* 301 Ill. 307, 133 N.E. 859 (1922); opinion testimony is not permitted, *People v. Williams,* 139 Ill. 2d 1, 150 Ill. Dec. 544, 563 N.E.2d 431 (1990) (citing Handbook), including when the witness is a child. *People v. West,* 158 Ill. 2d 155, 198 Ill. Dec. 393, 632 N.E.2d 1004 (1994). For a discussion of the merits of opinion testimony, *see* §405.2 supra.

Inquiry with respect to specific acts of misconduct is barred on the ground that such examination is overly prejudicial in relation to its probative value. Specific acts of misconduct not resulting in a conviction thus may not be inquired of on cross-examination of a witness or of another witness who testifies concerning his character for truthfulness. *Knowles v. Panopoulos,* 66 Ill. 2d 585, 6 Ill. Dec. 858, 363 N.E.2d 805 (1977), only convictions and not arrests, indictments, charges, or actual commissions of offenses may be used to impeach. Specific prior instances of conduct are also inadmissible upon direct or redirect examination to support the testimony of the character witness as to the reputation of the principal witness for truthfulness or untruthfulness.

Prior convictions of any witness may be employed for purposes of impeachment as described in §609 infra.

The distinction between an accused who takes the stand, thus becoming subject to impeachment as a witness, and an accused who introduces evidence of his pertinent character trait, §404.3 supra, must be borne in mind.

§608.2 Reputation Testimony Relating to Truthfulness: When Permitted

Any witness, including the accused in a criminal case if he takes the stand, may be impeached by proof of reputation for untruthfulness. *People v. Nash,* 36 Ill. 2d 275, 222 N.E.2d 473 (1966); *People v. Melnick,* 274 Ill. 616, 113 N.E. 971 (1916); *People v. Clauson,* 261 Ill. App. 3d 373, 199 Ill. Dec. 119, 633 N.E.2d 915 (1994); *People v. Rosario,* 180 Ill. App. 3d 977, 129 Ill. Dec. 706, 536 N.E.2d 756 (1989); *People v. Bramlett,* 131 Ill. App. 3d 616, 86 Ill. Dec. 868, 476 N.E.2d 44 (1985). If the witness's character for truthfulness has been attacked by means of reputation testimony, his character for truthfulness may then be supported, but only by reputation testimony. *Tedens v. Schumers,* 112 Ill. 263 (1884). In addition, if the character of the witness for truthfulness has been attacked "otherwise" than by evidence of reputation testimony, reputation testimony in support also becomes admissible. Impeachment of the witness by means of a prior conviction, §609 infra, or a showing of corruption, are attacks on character; reputation testimony is admissible in rebuttal. 4 Wigmore, Evidence §§1106, 1107 (Chadbourn rev. 1972). If the character of the witness is attacked by means of irrelevant or incompetent evidence, such as the volunteering of an unresponsive answer by another witness that the witness is a dishonest and corrupt person, reputation testimony for truthfulness may be introduced in rebuttal. *Werdell v. Turzynski,* 128

Ill. App. 2d 139, 262 N.E.2d 833 (1970). However, a showing of interest, bias, or coercion does not constitute an attack upon character sufficient to permit evidence of a good reputation for truth and veracity. 4 Wigmore, Evidence §1107A (Chadbourn rev. 1972).

Supporting evidence of good reputation for truthfulness may also be admissible in situations where the witness has had her character for truthfulness assaulted upon cross-examination or by means of self-contradiction. With respect to cross-examination, the trial court must determine whether the net effect of the cross-examination constitutes a direct attack on the witness's character for truthfulness, McCormick, Evidence §47 (4th ed. 1992). This is often a difficult decision. If the court finds that a direct attack has occurred, reputation testimony for truthfulness becomes admissible. Where the witness is impeached by a prior inconsistent statement, courts should allow subsequent proof of reputation for truthfulness where the impeachment raises a question of character for truthfulness but not where such impeachment merely charges lack of memory or mistake. 4 Wigmore, Evidence §1108A (Chadbourn rev. 1972). While McCormick, Evidence §47 (4th ed. 1992) points out that whether contradiction constitutes a sufficient attack upon the character of the witness should depend upon the circumstances, prior cases have generally held that mere contradiction by other evidence is not enough. *Tedens v. Schumers* supra; *People v. Thomas,* 18 Ill. 2d 439, 164 N.E.2d 36 (1960); *People v. Krause,* 241 Ill. App. 3d 394, 182 Ill. Dec. 446, 609 N.E.2d 980 (1993).

Note that evidence of good reputation for truthfulness is not admissible in the first instance; it is admissible only after the character of the witness for truthfulness has been attacked by reputation evidence or "otherwise." *People v. Griffith,* 56 Ill. App. 3d 747, 14 Ill. Dec. 393, 372 N.E.2d 404 (1978); *People v. George,* 67 Ill. App. 3d 102, 23 Ill. Dec. 583, 384 N.E.2d 377 (1978); *People v. Doll,* 126 Ill. App. 3d 495, 81 Ill. Dec. 635, 467 N.E.2d 335 (1984); *Dodds v. Western Kentucky Navigation,* 297 Ill. App. 3d 702, 231 Ill. Dec. 898, 697 N.E.2d 452 (1998).

§608.3   Reputation Testimony Relating to Truthfulness: Basis, Belief Under Oath

The proper procedure is to ask the impeaching witness whether he knows the general reputation of the principal witness for truth and veracity in the neighborhood in which the latter lives or amongst those with whom the latter works or socializes. *People v. West*, 158 Ill. 2d 155, 198 Ill. Dec. 393, 632 N.E.2d 1004 (1994); *People v. Dorff*, 77 Ill. App. 3d 882, 33 Ill. Dec. 300, 396 N.E.2d 827 (1979); *In Interest of Brooks*, 63 Ill. App. 3d 328, 20 Ill. Dec. 39, 379 N.E.2d 872 (1978). *See also* §405.1 supra. The testimony must relate to reputation of the witness at the time of trial. It may not be based upon or stated to be personal opinion of the witness, *see* §405.2 supra, nor specific instances of the witness's alleged acts, *Brooke Inns, Inc. v. S & R Hi-Fi and TV*, 249 Ill. App. 3d 1064, 188 Ill. Dec. 164, 618 N.E.2d 734 (1993), but rather must be testimony as to reputation based upon having discussed the reputation with others, having heard it discussed by others, or of never having heard it discussed although he would have heard contrary comments had they existed. *People v. Clauson*, 261 Ill. App. 3d 373, 199 Ill. Dec. 119, 633 N.E.2d 915 (1994). *See* §405.1 supra. The reputation witness must be shown to have adequate knowledge. *Jackson v. Naffah*, 241 Ill. App. 3d 1043, 182 Ill. Dec. 424, 609 N.E.2d 958 (1993), conversation two years prior to the time of trial at Christmas party was inadequate. The reputation witness is not limited to characterizing the reputation for truthfulness or untruthfulness as either "good" or "bad" but may employ terms such as "excellent" or "outstanding." *See People v. Petitt*, 245 Ill. App. 3d 132, 184 Ill. Dec. 766, 613 N.E.2d 1358 (1993). Upon testifying as to knowledge of the witness's reputation for truthfulness or untruthfulness, the witness may, despite the rule excluding opinions, further be asked, "In view of that reputation, would you believe him under oath?" *People v. Lehner*, 326 Ill. 216, 157 N.E. 211 (1927); *Frye v. Bank of Illinois*, 11 Ill. 367 (1849). A question inquiring whether the witness would believe the person under oath is objectionable if it does not indicate clearly that the witness's opinion is based upon her knowledge of the other person's reputation. *People v. Bramlett,* 131 Ill. App. 3d 616, 86 Ill. Dec. 868, 476 N.E.2d 44 (1985).

§608.4   Cross-Examination of Reputation Witness: Specific Acts of Principal Witness

A witness who has testified to good reputation for truth and veracity of a witness cannot be cross-examined as to particular acts of misconduct by the principal witness, nor may extrinsic evidence of such acts be introduced in rebuttal. *People v. Hermens,* 5 Ill. 2d 277, 125 N.E.2d 500 (1955); *People v. Anderson,* 337 Ill. 310, 169 N.E. 243 (1929); *People v. West,* 246 Ill. App. 3d 1070, 186 Ill. Dec. 908, 617 N.E.2d 147 (1993). A character witness, whether testifying to truthfulness or untruthfulness, may be cross-examined concerning with whom, where, and when he actually discussed the reputation. *People v. Greeley,* 14 Ill. 2d 428, 152 N.E.2d 825 (1958); *People v. Doll,* 126 Ill. App. 3d 495, 81 Ill. Dec. 635, 467 N.E.2d 335 (1984). He may also be questioned about the nature and extent of his relationship with the person about whom he is testifying and regarding any bias, interest, corruption, or coercion in the outcome of the case. *People v. Sampson,* 1 Ill. 2d 399, 115 N.E.2d 627 (1953). A character witness may testify whether he has heard rumors or reports inconsistent with his testimony but may not state the content of the rumor. *People v. Greeley* supra.

§608.5   Cross-Examination: Specific Acts of the Witness

The credibility of any witness, including a reputation witness, may not be attacked upon cross-examination by questioning the witness concerning specific instances of her misconduct not leading to a conviction. *People v. Celmars,* 332 Ill. 113, 163 N.E. 421 (1928). Inquiry with respect to specific acts of misconduct is barred on the ground that such examination is regarded as overly prejudicial in relation to its probative value. *Cf. People v. Kirwan,* 96 Ill. App. 3d 221, 51 Ill. Dec. 809, 421 N.E.2d 317 (1981), after quoting previous sentence of Handbook and stating that complete prohibition may be the preferred rule, the court upheld the exclusion of evidence that prosecution witness lied under oath as a matter of discretion in light of the need for additional witnesses and other testimony attacking the witness's credibility. *See also Kelley v. American Motors Corp.,* 130 Ill. App. 3d 662, 85 Ill. Dec. 854, 474 N.E.2d 814 (1985), *Kirwan* might authorize such impeachment in some cases; *People v. McKinney,* 193 Ill. App. 3d 1012, 140 Ill. Dec. 719, 550 N.E.2d 604 (1990), appellate court need not decide whether cross-examination of defendant as to his prior statement that he would lie in court was proper. Cross-examination with respect to arrests, indictments, charges, or actual commission of offenses or bad acts is in fact clearly not permissible. *People v. Franklin,* 167 Ill. 2d 1, 212 Ill. Dec. 153, 656 N.E.2d 750 (1995); *People v. Lucas,* 151 Ill. 2d 461, 177 Ill. Dec. 390, 603 N.E.2d 460 (1992). Accordingly, it has been held improper to bring out that a witness lived with a woman other than his wife and did not support his family, *Chicago City Ry. v. Uhter,* 212 Ill. 174, 72 N.E. 195 (1904), or that the witness had committed forgery and was under indictment therefor, *People v. Moshiek,* 323 Ill. 11, 153 N.E. 720 (1926), and proper to foreclose inquiry into the chastity of a female witness, *People v. Brown,* 254 Ill. 260, 98 N.E. 535 (1912), and into a prior arrest, *People v. O'Dell,* 84 Ill. App. 3d 359, 39 Ill. Dec. 830, 405 N.E.2d 809 (1980), and into an uncharged crime, *People v. Olmos,* 67 Ill. App. 3d 281, 23 Ill. Dec. 946, 384 N.E.2d 853 (1978), and into the signing of W-4 forms under another name under the penalty of perjury, *People v. Turcios,* 228 Ill. App. 3d 583, 171 Ill. Dec. 87, 593 N.E.2d 907 (1992), and improper to permit inquiry as to the use of an assumed name during a prior arrest, *People v. McGee,* 286 Ill. App. 3d 786, 222 Ill. Dec. 137, 676 N.E.2d 1341 (1997). Extrinsic evidence of such misconduct is also barred. *Dimick v. Downs,* 82 Ill. 570 (1876), acts of adultery properly excluded; *Hoge v. People,* 117 Ill. 35, 6 N.E.

796 (1886), discharge for drunkenness improperly admitted; *Elliott v. Brown,* 349 Ill. App. 428, 111 N.E.2d 169 (1953), evidence improperly admitted to show that on a former occasion witness lied about an unrelated matter. *Cf. Wolf v. Peoples Bank,* 225 Ill. App. 127 (1929).

§609   Impeachment by Evidence of Conviction of Crime

§609.1   *An Historical Perspective*

The extent to which a witness and in particular the defendant in a criminal case may be impeached by evidence that he has been convicted of a crime has long been extremely controversial. To illustrate, Federal Rule of Evidence 609, F.R.D. 131, 148-149 (1975), engendered more debate in Congress than any other single federal rule, and the final result was a conference compromise settling the differences between the House and Senate versions. The focus of the dispute was whether to confine admissibility to convictions for a crime believed to be directly relevant to veracity, the so-called *crimen falsi,* or to admit proof of conviction for serious crimes of whatever nature, the latter being the orthodox rule. The orthodox rule is premised upon the assumption that a person with a criminal record has a bad general character, evidenced by his willingness to disobey the law, and that his bad general character would lead him to disregard his oath to testify truthfully. This rationale has been asserted to be tenuous, particularly where the conviction was for a crime of violence. Moreover, an accused with a criminal past faces a very serious dilemma under the orthodox rule. If he testifies and is impeached with prior convictions, he risks conviction upon the current charge simply because the jury thinks he is a bad man. *See People v. Williams,* 161 Ill. 2d 1, 204 Ill. Dec. 72, 641 N.E.2d 296 (1994) (evidence of a prior conviction tends to persuade the jury that, on the basis of past conduct, defendant is a probable perpetrator of the crime, or to influence jurors to convict simply because they feel he is a bad person deserving of punishment); *O'Bryan v. Sandrock,* 276 Ill. App. 3d 194, 213 Ill. Dec. 1, 658 N.E.2d 471 (1995) (society presumes that a person with a drug conviction is a notorious liar and that once an addict always an addict). The more similar the prior offense to the crime charged, the stronger the natural though impermissible inference likely to be drawn by the jury that, if the defendant did it before, he probably did it this time. This is true even though the jury will be given a limiting instruction that the prior conviction may be considered only insofar as it may affect the believability of the defendant and must not be considered as evidence of the defendant's guilt of the offense with which he is charged. *People v. Lawler,* 142 Ill. 2d 548, 154 Ill. Dec. 674, 568 N.E.2d 895 (1991); *People v. Chapman,* 262 Ill. App. 3d 439, 198 Ill. Dec. 877, 633 N.E.2d 718 (1992). If the defendant, in the alternative, chooses to remain silent, the jury may conclude that he is guilty despite instructions that no inference is to be drawn against him given his failure to testify. Illinois Pattern Jury Instructions — Criminal 2.04 (1996). On the other hand, in support of the use of prior convictions, it is asserted "that it would be misleading to permit the accused to appear as a witness of blameless life." McCormick, Evidence §42 at 153 (4th ed. 1992).

The recent history of the Illinois approach to the issue is illuminating. Prior to *People v. Montgomery,* 47 Ill. 2d 510, 268 N.E.2d 695 (1971), the conviction of a crime could be proved to affect credibility, *see* Ill. R.S. 1961, c.38, §155-1 and c.110, §8-101, provided the crime was infamous. *People v. Kirkpatrick,* 413 Ill. 595, 110 N.E.2d 519 (1953). The infamous crimes were defined as murder, rape, indecent liberties with a child, kidnapping, aggravated kidnapping, perjury, subornation of perjury, arson, burglary, robbery, sale of narcotic drugs, deviate sexual assault, incest, aggravated incest, forgery, bigamy, and theft if punishable by imprisonment in the penitentiary. Ill. R.S. 1961, c.38, §124-1 (now repealed). Convictions under the laws of another jurisdiction were treated the same as analogous local crimes, regardless of the classification as infamous or otherwise under the foreign law. *People v. Kirkpatrick* supra, conviction of transporting stolen car in interstate commerce, although infamous under federal law, analogous to receiving stolen property, not infamous under Illinois law, and hence erroneously admitted. Moreover, prior to *People v. Montgomery* supra, discretionary authority in the court with respect to permitting employment of a conviction was not recognized; the trial judge was required to admit evidence of a prior conviction for an infamous crime to impeach the credibility of a defendant whenever the prosecution saw fit to offer it. *People v. Buford,* 396 Ill. 158, 71 N.E.2d 340 (1947).

In *People v. Montgomery* supra, and again in *People v. Ray,* 54 Ill. 2d 377, 297 N.E.2d 168 (1973), the supreme court reached the conclusion that discretionary authority was conferred upon the court by Ill. R.S. 1961, c.38, §155-1, now 125 ILCS 125/6, and moreover that such discretion should be exercised in accordance with the 1971 draft of Federal Rule of Evidence 609(a), 51 F.R.D. 315, 393 (1971). *See* §609.2 for text of 1971 draft of Rule 609(a). Thus, under *People v. Montgomery* supra, the availability of a prior conviction becomes totally divorced from any consideration as to whether a particular crime is defined as infamous.

The general rule set forth in §609.2 infra applies to impeachment of all witnesses without regard to whether testifying in a criminal or civil proceeding. With respect to civil proceedings, *see Knowles v. Panopoulos,* 66 Ill. 2d 585, 6 Ill. Dec. 858, 363 N.E.2d 805 (1977); *Ashby v. Price,* 112 Ill. App. 3d 114, 67 Ill. Dec. 958, 445 N.E.2d 438 (1983); *Baldwin v. Huffman Towing Co.,* 51 Ill. App. 3d 861, 9 Ill. Dec. 469, 366 N.E.2d 980 (1977); *Pratt v. Bartol,* 55 Ill. App. 3d 884, 13 Ill. Dec. 642, 371 N.E.2d 359 (1977); *George S. May International Co. v. International Profit Associates,* 256 Ill. App. 3d 779, 195 Ill. Dec. 183, 628 N.E.2d 647 (1993). *See also Housh v. Bowers,* 271 Ill. App. 3d 1004, 208 Ill. Dec. 449, 649 N.E.2d 505

(1995) (reversible error to permit impeachment with drug conviction of plaintiff in negligence action where there was no evidence the driver had subsequent convictions, that driver had subsequently used or possessed drugs, or that the accident was related to drugs); *O'Bryan v. Sandrock*, 276 Ill. App. 3d 194, 213 Ill. Dec. 1, 658 N.E.2d 471 (1995) (reversible error to permit impeachment with drug conviction of plaintiff in negligence action where drug conviction occurred after the accident but 45 months prior to trial, citing *Housch*, supra).

For admissibility of prior convictions for purposes other than impeachment, *see* §404.5 supra.

As to preservation of error with respect to the use of the prior conviction to impeach, *see* §609.10 infra.

§609.2 The General Rule; An Overview

In *People v. Montgomery*, 47 Ill. 2d 510, 268 N.E.2d 695 (1971), the supreme court specifically stated that the provisions of the 1971 draft of Federal Rule of Evidence 609, 51 F.R.D. 315, 393 (1971), should be followed in future cases. The opinion at 268 N.E.2d at 698-700 sets forth in full both the text of the 1971 draft of Rule 609 and the Federal Advisory Committee's Note.

Impeachment by Evidence of Conviction of Crime

(a) General Rule. For the purpose of attacking the credibility of a witness, evidence that he has been convicted of a crime, except on a plea of *nolo contendere*, is admissible but only if the crime, (1) was punishable by death or imprisonment in excess of one year under the law under which he was convicted, or (2) involved dishonesty or false statement regardless of the punishment unless (3), in either case, the judge determines that the probative value of the evidence of the crime is substantially outweighed by the danger of unfair prejudice.

(b) Time Limit. Evidence of a conviction under this rule is not admissible if a period of more than 10 years has elapsed since the date of conviction or of the release of the witness from confinement, whichever is the later date.

(c) Effect of Pardon, Annulment, or Certificate of Rehabilitation. Evidence of a conviction is not admissible under this rule if (1) the conviction has been the subject of a pardon, annulment, certificate of rehabilitation, or other equivalent procedure, and (2) the procedure under which the same was granted or issued required a substantial showing of rehabilitation or was based on innocence.

(d) Juvenile Adjudications. Evidence of juvenile adjudications is generally not admissible under this rule. The judge may, however, allow evidence of a juvenile adjudication of a witness other than the accused if conviction of the offense would be admissible to attach the credibility of an adult and the judge is satisfied that admission in evidence is necessary for a fair determination of the issue of guilt or innocence.

(e) Pendency of Appeal. The pendency of an appeal therefrom does not render evidence of a conviction inadmissible. Evidence of the pendency of an appeal is admissible.

The Advisory Committee's comments to this Rule contain the following:

> The most significant feature of the rule is the requirement that the evidence of conviction be excluded if the judge determines that its probative value is outweighed by the danger of unfair prejudice. It is a particularized application of Rule 403(a). The provision finds its genesis in *Luck v. United States,* [121 U.S. App. D.C. 151] 348 F.2d 763 (D.C. Cir. 1965). Prior to that decision, slight latitude was recognized for balancing probative value against prejudice, though some authority allowed or required the trial judge to exclude convictions remote in point of time. Referring to 14 D.C. Code §305, the court said:
>
> > It says, in effect, that the conviction "may," as opposed to "shall," be admitted; and we think the choice of words in this instance is significant. The trial court is not *required* to allow impeachment by prior conviction every time a defendant takes the stand in his own defense. The statute, in our view, leaves room for the operation of a

sound judicial discretion to play upon the circumstances as they unfold in a particular case. There may well be cases where the trial judge might think that the cause of truth would be helped more by letting the jury hear the defendant's story than by the defendant's foregoing that opportunity because of the fear of prejudice founded upon a prior conviction. [Footnote omitted.] There may well be other cases where the trial judge believes the prejudicial effect of impeachment far outweighs the probative relevance of the prior conviction to the issue of credibility. This last is, of course, a standard which trial judges apply every day in other contexts; and we think it has both utility and applicability in this field. [Footnote omitted.]

In exercising discretion in this respect, a number of factors might be relevant, such as the nature of the prior crimes, [footnote omitted] the length of the criminal record, the age and circumstances of the defendant, and, above all, the extent to which it is more important to the search for truth in a particular case for the jury to hear the defendant's story than to know of a prior conviction. The goal of a criminal trial is the disposition of the charge in accordance with the truth. The possibility of a rehearsal of the defendant's criminal record in a given case, especially if it means that the jury will be left without one version of the truth, may or may not contribute to that objective. The experienced trial judge has a sensitivity in this regard which normally can be relied upon to strike a reasonable balance between the interests of the defendant and of the public. We think Congress has left room for that discretion to operate. 348 F.2d at 768.

The application of *Luck* has been refined and clarified in numerous subsequent decisions of the court which rendered it, notably in *Gordon v. United States,* [127 U.S. App. D.C. 343] 383 F.2d 936 (D.C. Cir. 1967). Pointing out that *Luck* placed on the accused the burden of demonstrating that the prejudice from his prior convictions "far outweigh" the probative relevance to credibility (p.939). Judge, now Chief Justice, Burger suggested in *Gordon* various factors to be considered in making the determination: the nature of the crime, nearness or remoteness, the subsequent career of the person, and whether the crime was similar to the one charged. It will be noted that subdivision (b) of the rule imposes a specific time limit and that subdivision (c) deals with aspects of rehabilitation; these provisions should be construed only as imposing outer limits upon the judge's determination and not as restricting his decision within them.

With regard to the types of crime potentially usable to impeach, the rule thus adopted in Illinois allows a crime that (1) was punishable by death or imprisonment in excess of one year under the law under which the witness was convicted, or (2) involved dishonesty or false statement regardless of the punishment. *People v. Schuning,* 106 Ill. 2d 41, 86 Ill. Dec. 922, 476 N.E.2d 423 (1985). "Punishable" means the punishment that may be imposed, not that which is actually imposed under the law under which convicted. *People v. Glover,* 71 Ill. App. 3d 570, 27 Ill. Dec. 871, 389 N.E.2d 1279 (1979). It is the law of the place of conviction rather than a comparable crime committed in Illinois that is relevant in determining the length of potential imprisonment. *Knowles v. Panopoulos,* 66 Ill. 2d 585, 6 Ill. Dec. 858, 363 N.E.2d 805 (1977); *People v. Blythe,* 17 Ill. App. 3d 768, 308 N.E.2d 675 (1974). A prior conviction based upon a plea of *nolo contendere* most likely may be employed to impeach. *See People v. Alexander,* 184 Ill. App. 3d 855, 133 Ill. Dec. 83, 540 N.E.2d 949 (1989). *Cf. People v. Helton,* 195 Ill. App. 3d 410, 142 Ill. Dec. 48, 552 N.E.2d 398 (1990), the exclusionary text of Rule 609 adopted in *Montgomery* supra indicates otherwise. The party seeking to employ the prior conviction bears the responsibility of presenting evidence that the prior conviction meets the requirements of *Montgomery. People v. Yost,* 78 Ill. 2d 292, 35 Ill. Dec. 755, 399 N.E.2d 1283 (1980). Discharge and dismissal upon a successful completion of a disposition of supervision is not considered a conviction. 730 ILCS 5/5-6-3.1(f); *People v. Miller,* 101 Ill. App. 3d 55, 56 Ill. Dec. 582, 427 N.E.2d 987 (1981); *People v. Schuning,* 106 Ill. 2d 41, 86 Ill. Dec. 922, 476 N.E.2d 423 (1985). Neither is treatment under a first offender statute, such as 720 ILCS 550/10; *People v. Du Montelle,* 71 Ill. 2d 157, 15 Ill. Dec. 770, 374 N.E.2d 205 (1978), nor sentence to probation without entering judgment with discharge to follow under 720 ILCS 570/410(a). *People v. De Savieu,* 120 Ill. App. 3d 420, 76 Ill. Dec. 104, 458 N.E.2d 504 (1983).

The rule requires the application of a balancing test in all cases where a prior conviction meeting the requirements of (a)(1) or (2) is offered for impeachment purposes. Such a conviction may be employed to impeach a witness unless the court determines that the probative value of admitting the evidence is substantially outweighed by its prejudicial effect to a party. Notice two points. First, it is the prejudicial effect to any party in a criminal or civil case, not merely the defendant, with which the rule is concerned. Second, the rule provides that the prior conviction is admissible unless the probative value is substantially outweighed by the prejudicial effect, thereby placing a burden of establishing inadmissibility upon the party opposing use of the conviction. *See also* §403.1 supra. Notice further that with respect to impeachment of prosecution witnesses by the defendant "it is difficult to conceive of a case in which the danger of unfair prejudice to the prosecution or its witnesses would substantially outweigh the probative value of evidence that such witnesses had been convicted of felonies or crimes involving dishonesty." *People v. Rollins,* 108 Ill. App. 3d 480, 491, 64 Ill. Dec. 3, 438 N.E.2d 1322 (1982). In *People v. Williams,* 161 Ill. 2d 1, 204 Ill. Dec. 72, 641 N.E.2d 296 (1994), the Illinois Supreme Court reminded trial courts of the importance of classifying the prior conviction properly under *Montgomery* and even more strongly emphasized the importance of conducting *Montgomery's* balancing test relating to probative value versus unfair prejudice. People v. Hester, 271 Ill. App. 3d 954, 208 Ill. Dec. 690, 649 N.E.2d 1351 (1995).

A conviction requires more than a finding of guilt or a plea of guilty; a conviction occurs only when sentence is imposed. *People ex rel. Grogan v. Lisinski,* 113 Ill. App. 3d 276, 68 Ill. Dec. 854, 446 N.E.2d 1251 (1983); *People v. Lashmett,* 126 Ill. App. 3d 340, 81 Ill. Dec. 656, 467 N.E.2d 356 (1984); *People v. Little,* 223 Ill. App. 3d 264, 165 Ill. Dec. 752, 585 N.E.2d 148 (1991).

Multiple convictions may be employed to impeach. *People v. Martinez,* 76 Ill. App. 3d 280, 32 Ill. Dec. 139, 395 N.E.2d 86 (1979); *People v. Hall,* 95 Ill. App. 3d 1057, 51 Ill. Dec. 595, 420 N.E.2d 1153 (1981) (eleven prior convictions). *See also* §609.4 infra.

A party may not contend that a prior conviction cannot be used to impeach on the ground that the conviction is invalid as a result of a guilty plea not taken in accordance with Supreme Court Rule 402, that rule being procedural only. Only failure to meet the constitutional requirements, i.e., that the defendant entered his plea of guilty voluntarily and understandingly, may be asserted. *People v. Burgin,* 74 Ill. App. 3d 58, 29 Ill. Dec. 694, 392 N.E.2d 251 (1979); *People v. Baker,* 78 Ill. App. 3d 411, 33 Ill. Dec. 450, 396 N.E.2d 1174 (1979).

The fact that the criminal defendant had a prior conviction is occasionally itself an element of the offense charged, such as the crime of unlawful possession of a weapon by a felon, 720 ILCS 5/24-1.1. *See People v. Gonzales,* 151 Ill. 2d 79, 175 Ill. Dec. 731, 600 N.E.2d 1189 (1992). Since under such circumstances the prosecution must prove the prior conviction beyond a reasonable doubt, it has been held that the prior conviction is automatically also admissible to impeach, i.e., the balancing test of *Montgomery* is inappropriate and thus need not be applied. *People v. Hester,* 271 Ill. App. 3d 954, 208 Ill. Dec. 690, 649 N.E.2d 1351 (1995). It is suggested that the two questions, substantive admissibility and impeachment, should be kept entirely separate, and that *Hester* should not be followed. Of course the fact that the jury will hear about the prior conviction in any event may properly be considered in assessing the danger of unfair prejudice in applying the discretionary balancing test of *Montgomery.*

§609.3   *Crimes of Dishonesty or False Statement*

The fact that the balancing test applies to both categories under the Illinois rule, discussed above in §609.2 supra, makes the question what is a crime of dishonesty or false statement of concern only if the crime was not punishable by imprisonment in excess of one year.

While it is fairly generally accepted that a conviction for a crime involving dishonesty or false statement is probative upon the issue of a witness's truthfulness, such convictions may be employed to impeach only if the balancing test of probative value versus prejudice is also satisfied. *See* §§609.2 supra and 609.4 infra.

The categories of specific offenses included within the phrase "dishonesty and false statement" have been subject to debate. The Report of the Conference Committee with respect to Federal Rule of Evidence 609 states:

> By the phrase "dishonesty and false statement" the Conference means crimes such as perjury or subornation of perjury, false statement, criminal fraud, embezzlement, or false pretense, or any other offense in the nature of *crimen falsi,* the commission of which involves some element of deceit, untruthfulness, or falsification bearing on the accused's propensity to testify truthfully. [Conference Report, H. Rept. No. 93-1597, reprinted at Congressional Record, H. 11930-11931 (Daily ed. Dec. 14, 1974).]

In view of the legislative history, the federal courts have ruled that "dishonesty or false statement" in fact means only crimes of false statement, i.e., *crimen falsi,* to the exclusion of such crimes as theft and robbery. Graham, Handbook of Federal Evidence §609.4 (4th ed. 1996). Whether Illinois in adopting a similar prior draft of Federal Rule 609 would follow this lead remained an open question for some time. *Compare People v. Clay,* 45 Ill. App. 3d 145, 3 Ill. Dec. 843, 359 N.E.2d 482 (1977), petty larceny, shoplifting; *Pratt v. Bartoli,* 55 Ill. App. 3d 884, 13 Ill. Dec. 642, 371 N.E.2d 359 (1977), misdemeanor theft, are crimes of dishonesty, *with People v. Vaughn,* 56 Ill. App. 3d 700, 14 Ill. Dec. 195, 371 N.E.2d 1248 (1978), petty larceny not crime of dishonesty, and *Knowles v. Panopoulos* supra, criminal trespass to a vehicle not a crime of dishonesty. The Illinois Supreme Court resolved this conflict in *People v. Spates,* 77 Ill. 2d 193, 32 Ill. Dec. 333, 395 N.E.2d 563 (1979), declaring generally that dishonesty and false statement includes any misdemeanor that has as its basis lying, cheating, deceiving, or stealing and specifically that theft falls within the foregoing definition. *Accord People v. Malone,* 78 Ill. 2d 34, 34 Ill. Dec. 311, 397 N.E.2d 1377 (1979). *See also People v. Poliquin,* 97 Ill. App. 3d 122, 52 Ill. Dec. 290, 421 N.E.2d 1362 (1981), armed robbery involves dishonesty; *People v. Burba,* 134 Ill. App. 3d 228, 88 Ill. Dec. 916, 479 N.E.2d 936 (1985), burglary involves dishonesty; *People v. Walker,* 157 Ill. App. 3d 133, 109 Ill. Dec. 408, 510 N.E.2d 29 (1987), possession of a controlled substance involves dishonesty; *People v. Elliot,* 274 Ill. App. 3d 901, 211 Ill. Dec. 174, 654 N.E.2d 636 (1995), violation of bail bond shows an indifference to the administration of justice.

Crimes of violence do not involve dishonesty or false statement. *People v. Stover,* 89 Ill. 2d 189, 59 Ill. Dec. 678, 432 N.E.2d 262 (1982), obstructing a police officer does not involve dishonesty or false statement; *People v. Williams,* 161 Ill. 2d 1, 204 Ill. Dec. 72, 641 N.E.2d 296 (1994), crimes of violence have little or no direct bearing on honesty and veracity.

In determining whether a crime involves dishonesty or false statement, the particular facts surrounding the conviction need not be looked at. *Knowles v. Panopoulos,* 66 Ill. 2d 585, 6 Ill. Dec. 858, 363 N.E.2d 805 (1977).

§609.4 *Application of the Discretionary Balancing Test*

The rule adopted in Illinois, §609.2 supra, provides that certain convictions may be used to impeach a witness, unless the court determines that the probative value of admitting this evidence is substantially outweighed by the danger of unfair prejudice. *People v. Montgomery,* 47 Ill. 2d 510, 268 N.E.2d 695 (1971), §609.2 supra, in discussing the exercise of discretion by the trial court, cited with approval the Advisory Committee's Note to the 1971 draft of Rule 609, 51 F.R.D. 315, 393 (1971), which stated:

> The trial court is not *required* to allow impeachment by prior conviction every time a defendant takes the stand in his own

defense. The [rule] ... leaves room for the operation of a sound judicial discretion to play upon the circumstances as they unfold in a particular case. There may well be cases where the trial judge might think that the cause of truth would be helped more by letting the jury hear the defendant's story than by the defendant's foregoing that opportunity because of the fear of prejudice founded upon a prior conviction.

In exercising discretion in this respect, a number of factors might be relevant, such as the nature of the prior crimes, [footnote omitted] the length of the criminal record, the age and circumstances of the defendant, and, above all, the extent to which it is more important to the search for truth in a particular case for the jury to hear the defendant's story than to know of a prior conviction. The goal of a criminal trial is the disposition of the charge in accordance with the truth. The possibility of a rehearsal of the defendant's criminal record in a given case, especially if it means that the jury will be left without one version of the truth, may or may not contribute to that objective. The experienced trial judge has a sensitivity in this regard which normally can be relied upon to strike a reasonable balance between the interests of the defendant and of the public.

In addition, *People v. Montgomery* supra states that also to be considered in making this determination are the nearness or remoteness in time of the conviction, the subsequent career of the person, and, very importantly, whether the crime was similar to the one charged. *Accord People v. Redd,* 135 Ill. 2d 252, 143 Ill. Dec. 802, 553 N.E.2d 316 (1990). Also important to the assessment of the probative value of the impeachment are the nature of the prior crime and the centrality of the credibility issue in the trial at hand. *See* McCormick, Evidence §42 (4th ed. 1992). In short, the following factors should be considered: (1) the nature of the prior crime; (2) the length of the defendant's criminal record; (3) the defendant's age and circumstances; (4) the likelihood that the defendant would not testify; (5) the nearness or remoteness of the prior crime; (6) the defendant's subsequent career; (7) whether the prior crime was similar to the one charged; (8) the centrality of the issue of credibility; and (9) the need for defendant's testimony. *See People v. Williams,* 161 Ill. 2d 1, 204 Ill. Dec. 72, 641 N.E.2d 296 (1994); *People v. Shelton,* 264 Ill. App. 3d 768, 201 Ill. Dec. 243, 636 N.E.2d 675 (1993); *People v. Rogers,* 264 Ill. App. 3d 740, 201 Ill. Dec. 133, 636 N.E.2d 565 (1992); *People v. Medreno,* 99 Ill. App. 3d 449, 54 Ill. Dec. 723, 425 N.E.2d 588 (1981); *People v. Ramey,* 70 Ill. App. 3d 327, 26 Ill. Dec. 572, 388 N.E.2d 196 (1979). *Compare O'Bryan v. Sandrock,* 276 Ill. App. 3d 194, 213 Ill. Dec. 1, 658, N.E.2d 471 (1995) (fact case is "hotly contested" and therefore the credibility of the plaintiff is central held not properly considered in determining admissibility of the prior conviction but only relevant to whether any claimed error was reversible or harmless; incorrectly decided).

Exactly how each factor is to be assessed and balanced pursuant to the prescribed standard cannot be stated with precision; it must be left to the sensitivity of the trial judge to strike a reasonable balance, Federal Advisory Committee's Note to 1971 draft, supra. In this regard, while the mere fact that the prior conviction is for the same crime as the offense now charged has been held not to mandate suppression, *People v. Flaugher,* 232 Ill. App. 3d 864, 174 Ill. Dec. 194, 598 N.E.2d 391 (1992) (citing Handbook); *People v. Pryor,* 171 Ill. App. 3d 865, 130 Ill. Dec. 812, 537 N.E.2d 1141 (1989); *People v. Medreno* supra; *People v. Evans,* 92 Ill. App. 3d 874, 48 Ill. Dec. 346 416 N.E.2d 377 (1981), use of similar convictions for purposes of impeachment should certainly not be encouraged. *See People v. Williams,* 161 Ill. 2d 1, 204 Ill. Dec. 72, 641 N.E.2d 296 (1994), convictions for the same crime should be admitted sparingly; *People v. Adams,* 281 Ill. App. 3d 339, 217 Ill. Dec. 100, 666 N.E.2d 769 (1996), probative value of prior conviction for aggravated battery is minimal in comparison to risk of unfair prejudice where current charge is also aggravated battery. *See generally People v. Hawkins,* 243 Ill. App. 3d 210, 183 Ill. Dec. 421, 611 N.E.2d 1069 (1993). *See* the interesting suggestion in *People v. Moore,* 65 Ill. App. 3d 712, 22 Ill. Dec. 420, 382 N.E.2d 810 (1978), that where the offenses are similar the nature of the prior offense not be disclosed to the jury discussed in §609.6 infra. In evaluating the danger of unfair prejudice, the trial court must keep in mind that such danger is greater when the prosecution seeks to impeach the defendant with a prior conviction than when the defendant wishes to do the same to a prosecution witness. *People v. Smith,* 105 Ill. App. 3d 84, 60 Ill. Dec. 816, 433 N.E.2d 1054 (1982); *People v. Pruitt,* 165 Ill. App. 3d 947, 117 Ill. Dec. 516, 520 N.E.2d 867 (1988). *Accord People v. Walker,* 157 Ill. App. 3d 433, 109 Ill. Dec. 408, 510 N.E.2d 29 (1987) (it is difficult to conceive of a case requiring exclusion where the defendant seeks to impeach a prosecution witness with a prior conviction).

It is not necessary that the record contain an affirmative statement concerning the factors considered by the court in reaching its determination, *People v. Washington,* 55 Ill. 2d 521, 304 N.E.2d 276 (1973); *People v. Owens,* 58 Ill. App. 3d 37, 15 Ill. Dec. 502, 373 N.E.2d 848 (1978); *People v. Thibudeaux,* 98 Ill. App. 3d 1105, 54 Ill. Dec. 275, 424 N.E.2d 1178 (1981); *People v. Turner,* 186 Ill. App. 3d 849, 134 Ill. Dec. 589, 542 N.E.2d 935 (1989); *People v. Wright,* 218 Ill. App. 3d 764, 161 Ill. Dec. 444, 578 N.E.2d 1090 (1991) (trial court is not required to specify and evaluate factors on the record), provided the record shows that the court actually applied the balancing test, *People v. Redd,* 135 Ill. 2d 252, 143 Ill. Dec. 802, 553 N.E.2d 316 (1990); *People v. Williams,* 289 Ill. App. 3d 24, 224 Ill. Dec. 133, 681 N.E.2d 115 (1997); *People v. Jennings,* 279 Ill. App. 3d 406, 216 Ill. Dec. 62, 664 N.E.2d 699 (1996); *People v. Bramlett,* 276 Ill. App. 3d 201, 213 Ill. Dec. 40, 658 N.E.2d 510 (1995); *O'Bryan v. Sandrock,* 276 Ill. App. 3d 194, 213 Ill. Dec. 1, 658 N.E.2d 471 (1995); *People v. Elliot,* 274 Ill. App. 3d 901, 211 Ill. Dec. 174, 654 N.E.2d 636 (1995); *People v. Bassett,* 84 Ill. App. 3d 133, 39 Ill. Dec. 534, 404 N.E.2d 1125 (1980), as it is assumed that the trial court gave the relevant factors appropriate consideration. *People v. Marron,* 145 Ill. App. 3d 975, 99 Ill. Dec. 722, 496 N.E.2d 297 (1986). *See generally People v. Redd* supra. Failure to give the relevant factors the appropriate consideration is, of course, error. *People v. McGee,* 286 Ill. App. 3d 786, 222 Ill. Dec. 137, 676 N.E.2d 1341 (1997), trial court improperly concluded that the prior conviction may be employed to impeach simply because it was not similar. The federal courts, however, have declared that the practice of articulating the factors considered is desirable. McCormick, Evidence §42 (4th ed. 1992). Overall, the trial court is afforded "wide latitude" in exercising its discretion in determining whether the probative value of the evidence of the prior conviction is substantially outweighed by the danger of unfair prejudice. *People v. Poliquin,* 97 Ill. App. 3d 122, 52 Ill. Dec. 290, 421 N.E.2d 1362 (1981); *People v. Tribett,* 98 Ill. App. 3d 663, 53 Ill. Dec. 897, 424 N.E.2d 688 (1981); *People v. Chapman,* 262 Ill. App. 3d 439, 198 Ill. Dec. 877, 633 N.E.2d 718 (1992). Reversal for abuse of discretion, while rare, is possible. *See In re Holmes,* 174 Ill. App. 3d 1081, 124 Ill. Dec. 480, 529 N.E.2d 300 (1988).

The fact that the prior conviction does not relate directly to dishonesty does not alone mean the conviction lacks probative value for impeachment. *People v. Warfel,* 67 Ill. App. 3d 620, 24 Ill. Dec. 408, 385 N.E.2d 175 (1979), prior conviction for rape met discretionary balancing test; *People v. Pryor,* 171 Ill. App. 3d 865, 130 Ill. Dec. 812, 537 N.E.2d 1141 (1989), and *People v. Daily,* 79 Ill. App. 3d 928, 34 Ill. Dec. 932, 398 N.E.2d 923 (1979), conviction for delivery of controlled substances admissible to impeach; *People v. Powell,* 139 Ill. App. 3d 701, 93 Ill. Dec. 894, 487 N.E.2d 719 (1985), conviction for deviate sexual assault is a serious felony conviction probative of veracity; *People v. Davis,* 193 Ill. App. 3d 1001, 140 Ill. Dec. 792, 550 N.E.2d 677 (1990), conviction for aggravated battery admissible to impeach. Such crimes, while not directly relating to dishonesty, indicate a disposition on the defendant's part "to place the advancement of individual self-interest ahead of principle or the interest of society, and such proof may suggest a willingness to do so again on the witness stand." *People v. Nelson,* 31 Ill. App. 3d 934, 938, 335 N.E.2d 79 (1975). *Accord In re Holmes,* 174 Ill. App. 3d 1081, 124 Ill. Dec. 480, 529 N.E.2d 300 (1988). *Contra People v. Elliot,* 274 Ill. App. 3d 901, 211 Ill. Dec. 174, 654 N.E.2d 636 (1995) (prior conviction for pure act of violence can not be employed to impeach; an incorrect statement).

Employment of the discretionary balancing test of *Montgomery* has resulted in multiple convictions for similar prior convictions being admitted to impeach. *People v. Blair,* 102 Ill. App. 3d 1018, 58 Ill. Dec. 42, 429 N.E.2d 1375 (1981). There is apparently no limit. *People v. McKibbins,* 96 Ill. 2d 176, 70 Ill. Dec. 474, 449 N.E.2d 821 (1983), all 20 theft convictions may be employed to impeach. *See also* §609.2 supra.

In *People v. Williams,* 161 Ill. 2d 1, 204 Ill. Dec. 72, 641 N.E.2d 296 (1994), the Illinois Supreme Court, in responding to its undoubtedly correct impression that the prosecution has been allowed to introduce "virtually all types of convictions [punishable by death or imprisonment in excess of one year] for the purported reason of impeaching a testifying defendant," *see* infra, opined that the true "focus of *Montgomery* was on crimes which bear upon the defendant's truthfulness as a witness," *see* infra. In the process the Illinois Supreme Court rejected the rationale that a prior conviction for a serious crime indicates a disposition on the defendant's part "to place the advancement of individual self-interest ahead of principle or the interest of society, and such proof may suggest a willingness to do so again on the witness stand." *People v. Nelson,* 31 Ill. App. 3d 934, 938, 335 N.E.2d 79, 83 (1975). *Accord In re Holmes,* 174 Ill. App. 3d 1081, 124 Ill. Dec. 480, 529 N.E.2d 300 (1988). *Williams, id* at 40-42, 204 Ill. Dec. at 88-89, 641 N.E.2d at 312-13 states:

> When presented with arguments that certain felonies have no direct relation to credibility, some courts employ the rationale that a felony of any type evinces a disrespect for societal order and thus adversely affects the defendant's veracity; or, stated another way, that prior felonious conduct establishes a disposition to place self-interest ahead of the interest of society, and may suggest a willingness to do so again on the witness stand. *See* 10 Loy. U. Chi. L.J. at 348-51.
>
> In our view, the increasingly mechanical application of these premises does not comport with the principles expressed in *Montgomery,* or in the authorities on which the *Montgomery* court relied in adopting Rule 609 as the rule to be applied in this

State. Arguably, all criminal conduct, from the most serious felony to misdemeanors such as reckless or disorderly conduct, criminal trespass, resisting a peace officer, and numerous others, evinces a disrespect for society. The *Montgomery* rule does not, however, allow for the admission of evidence of any and all prior crimes. The focus of *Montgomery* was on crimes which bear upon the defendant's truthfulness as a witness. . . .

The State disputes that the trial court admitted the evidence as probative of defendant's propensity toward deadly violence as "entirely speculative" and "highly doubtful," but offers no other reasonable interpretation of the court's remarks. The State's obscure suggestion that the trial judge could have been referring to any number of factors, such as that this was a capital case and a contract murder, escapes our comprehension. Moreover, the State has provided us with no insight as to the relation between the conviction and defendant's testimonial credibility. At trial, the State merely argued that defendant's criminal history was "relevant" and noted that voluntary manslaughter is a felony. On appeal, the State relies on the previously discussed argument that the conviction evinced a disrespect for societal order and thus adversely affected defendant's veracity.

We do not hold that there are no circumstances under which a voluntary manslaughter conviction may be admitted at a murder trial. However, we fail to see the relationship required by *Montgomery* between defendant's conviction and his testimonial credibility in this case. Rather, it clearly appears that the conviction was offered and admitted as relevant to the question of defendant's guilt of Valerie's murder. Such purpose contravenes the principles articulated in *Montgomery*. So long as the *Montgomery* rule remains the law in the State, we cannot countenance its further erosion.

Under the rationale of *Montgomery*, evidence of defendant's conviction of voluntary manslaughter should not have been admitted at trial.

The Illinois Supreme Court in rejecting the state's argument that the rationale for the admissibility of a prior conviction for a serious crime is that it "evinced a disrespect for societal order and thus adversely affected defendant's veracity," failed to provide an alternative rationale to assess whether a prior conviction for a serious crime not involving "dishonesty or false statement," the other prong of *Montgomery, see* §609.2 supra, comports with the "focus of *Montgomery* . . . on crimes which bear upon the defendant's truthfulness as a witness."

Failure to suggest an alternative rationale for the admissibility under *Montgomery* of prior convictions for crimes punishable by death or imprisonment in excess of one year is not surprising. As stated, by Justice Oliver Wendell Holmes, while a member of the Massachusetts Supreme Court, in *Gertz v. Fitchburg R.R. Co.,* 137 Mass. 77, 78 (1884),

> [W]hen it is proved that a witness has been convicted of a crime the *only* ground for disbelieving him which such proof affords is the general readiness to do evil which the conviction may be supposed to show. It is from that general disposition *alone* that the jury is asked to infer a readiness to lie in a particular case, and thence that he has lied in fact. The evidence has no tendency to prove that he was mistaken, but only that he has perjured himself, and it reaches that conclusion solely through the general proposition that he is a bad character and unworthy of credit. [Emphasis added.]

In short *Williams* did not overrule the *Montgomery* prong permitting admissibility to affect the credibility of witnesses of prior convictions for serious crimes not involving dishonesty or false statement. *Accord People v. Bramlett,* 276 Ill. App. 3d 201, 213 Ill. Dec. 40, 658 N.E.2d 510 (1995); *id.,* Justice Steigmann, specially concurring; *People v. Fomond,* 273 Ill. App. 3d 1053, 210 Ill. Dec. 346, 652 N.E.2d 1322 (1995), *Williams* is not contrary to *Montgomery* that evidence of past felonies of a defendant may be employed to impeach. *Williams* was in fact reversed because the trial judge had improperly admitted prior conviction as substantive evidence of guilt. *People v. Woodard,* 276 Ill. App. 3d 242, 212 Ill. Dec. 878, 658 N.E.2d 55 (1995), On the other hand, the Illinois Supreme Court expressly rejected what Justice Holmes described as the *only* rationale for admitting such evidence to impeach.

It can certainly be argued that actual application of a

discretionary balancing test by a trial court employing the number of highly varied and difficult-to-evaluate factors cutting in both directions involved in assessing probative value on credibility as enumerated in *Montgomery* and *Williams* supra, to be weighed against the notion of unfair prejudice arising from the prohibited bad man inference drawn by the jury in spite of a contrary limiting instruction, is extremely unlikely to result in uniform, predictable, reasoned, and equitable decisions. In addition, in actual fact everyone involved understands that concern by the accused that the prohibited bad man inference is likely to arise if the accused testifies at trial and is impeached with a prior conviction, *see* §609.1, impacts upon plea bargaining, trial strategy, and the likely outcome at trial. In short, discretionary balancing, incredibly difficult if not impossible to be done justly even if considered in the abstract, is further complicated by the practical reality of the ever present, although impermissible, bad man inference. In response, as noted in *Williams*, 161 Ill. 2d at 38-39, 204 Ill. Dec. at 87-88, 641 N.E.2d at 311-312, it is not surprising that trial judges and appellate courts, in almost all cases, simply permit impeachment: "We have herein examined the origin and rationale of the *Montgomery* rule because a review of case law since *Montgomery* reveals a regression toward allowing the State to introduce evidence of virtually all types of felony convictions for the purported reason of impeaching a testifying defendant."

It thus appears that while the Illinois Supreme Court in *Williams* was unhappy with the impeachment of criminal defendants under *Montgomery* with prior convictions punishable by death or imprisonment not involving dishonesty or false statement, it was not so unhappy that it is willing to eliminate such impeachment completely. While modification of *Montgomery* to permit impeachment solely with prior convictions involving dishonesty of false statements, the second prong of *Montgomery* discussed in §609.3 supra (that is, crimes involving *crimen falsi*, which should be construed, contrary to current Illinois law, to be limited to crimes involving active misrepresentation and thus excluding theft), naturally flowed from the *Williams* opinion, the court stopped short of abandonment, *id* at 41, 204 Ill. Dec. at 89, 641 N.E.2d at 313; "[s]o long as the *Montgomery* rule remains the law in this State, we cannot countenance its further erosion." *Accord People v. Bramlett,* 276 Ill. App. 3d 201, 213 Ill. Dec. 40, 658 N.E.2d 510 (1995) (in *Williams* the Illinois Supreme Court was expressing concern about the indiscriminate admission of all prior felonies for impeachment purposes absent application of the critical balancing test mandated by *Montgomery*). *See also* supra. The court deplored the situation while at the same time adding confusion by retaining such impeachment simultaneously with declaring unacceptable that only rationale that supports impeachment by a crime punishable by death or impeachment in excess of one year not involving dishonesty or false statement. The Illinois Supreme Court in removing the only viable rationale left a discretionary balancing test with no anchor.

Not surprisingly, lower courts experienced difficulty functioning under *Williams. See O'Bryan v. Sandrock,* 276 Ill. App. 3d 194, 213 Ill. Dec. 1, 658 N.E.2d 471 (1995) (drug conviction has little, if any, relation to veracity and is thus only remotely probative, if at all, of truthfulness). *See generally People v. Jennings,* 279 Ill. App. 3d 406, 412, 216 Ill. Dec. 62, 67, 664 N.E.2d 699, 704 (1996) ("No matter how the *Montgomery* test is applied, and no matter what *Williams* is taken to mean").

The mess caused by *Williams* is illustrated by *People v. McKay,* 279 Ill. App. 3d 195, 215 Ill. Dec. 825, 664 N.E.2d 222 (1996) where the court after beginning, not surprisingly, by acknowledging inconsistent interpretations of *Williams* opines that while *Williams* does not limit felonies referred to in the first prong of *Montgomery* to crimes of dishonest conduct, the felony must somehow bear some relationship to the defendant's testimonial credibility. Not surprisingly once again, the court in *McKay* concludes that the state failed to provide an explanation of the relationship between aggravated battery and testimonial credibility, rejecting along the way that the recency of the prior conviction provides such a relationship. *McKay* is not surprising for the simple reason that the true and only anchor for the first prong of *Montgomery,* as previously bemoaned, was expressly rejected in *Williams.*

Interestingly, in *People v. Elliot,* 274 Ill. App. 3d 901, 211 Ill. Dec. 174, 654 N.E.2d 636 (1995), Justice Wolfson set out to give meaning to *Williams* by attempting to describe those crimes having a sufficient bearing on truthfulness of a witness to be considered under *Montgomery,* and those that do not. *Elliot* concludes that crimes of violence may not be considered at all under *Montgomery* because they possess no element of dishonest conduct, thereby incorrectly eliminating the prong for *Montgomery* dealing with crimes punishable by death or imprisonment in excess of one year, a position *Williams* clearly did not endorse. Moreover, *Elliot* fails to suggest a rationale for the admissibility of prior convictions involving an element of dishonesty as a bearing on "honesty or veracity" after rejecting, in reliance on *Williams,* the anchor that such a crime shows a disposition to place advancement of individual self-interest ahead of principle or the interest of society. In fact, *Elliot* goes on in apparent disregard of *Williams* to include that violation of bail bond bears directly on believability as demonstrating an indifference to the administration of justice in general and to the specific promise to appear in court. In short, *Elliot* fails to provide an anchor for *Williams.* This is not unexpected as not even Justice Wolfson can make a silk purse out of a sow's ear.

In *People v. Williams,* 173 Ill. 2d 48, 218 Ill. Dec. 916, 670 N.E.2d 638 (1996), "*Williams II,*" the Illinois Supreme Court recognizing the "confusion" brought about by *Williams,* confirmed that *Montgomery* in all its majesty is in fact alive and well in Illinois.

The court commenced by recalling that *Williams* declared that "lower courts were mechanically applying the *Montgomery* rule to allow impeachment of a testifying defendant with virtually all types of felony convictions," and that the Illinois Supreme Court in *Williams* was "concerned with the lack of emphasis lower courts had placed on the third prong of the *Montgomery* rule, that is, the balancing test" emphasizing "the importance of conducting the balancing test of probative value versus unfair prejudice before admitting prior convictions for impeachment purposes." 173 Ill. 2d at 81, 218 Ill. Dec. at 932-933, 670 N.E.2d at 654-655. The first two prongs of the *Montgomery* rule are that for purposes of attacking a witness's credibility by admitting a prior conviction, evidence of a prior conviction is admissible only if (1) the crime was punishable by death or imprisonment in excess of one year, or (2) the crime involved dishonesty or false statement regardless of punishment. All three prongs of *Montgomery* rule result from the incorporation of the 1971 draft of Rule 609 of the Federal Rules of Evidence as set forth in full in §609.2 supra.

The court, 173 Ill. 2d at 82, 218 Ill. Dec. at 933, 670 N.E.2d at 655, continued:

> Following this court's decision in *Williams,* there has been confusion in the appellate court regarding whether *Williams* modified or changed the rule established in *Montgomery. See People v. Bramlett,* 276 Ill. App. 3d 201, 213 Ill. Dec. 40, 658 N.E.2d 510 (1995); *People v. Elliot,* 274 Ill. App. 3d 901, 211 Ill. Dec. 174, 654 N.E.2d 636 (1995); *People v. Fomond,* 273 Ill. App. 3d 1053, 21 Ill. Dec. 346, 652 N.E.2d 1322 (1995); *People v. Maxwell,* 272 Ill. App. 3d 57, 208 Ill. Dec. 841, 650 N.E.2d 298 (1995). We hold that *Williams* does not alter the three-prong rule set forth in *Montgomery.* Rather, this court in *Williams* was expressing concern about the indiscriminate admission of all prior felony convictions for impeachment purposes absent application of the critical balancing test mandated by *Montgomery.*
>
> To be sure, there is a language in *Williams* to the effect that this court no longer approved of the common rationale that a witness's prior felony conviction may itself evince disrespect for social order and therefore supply a proper basis for impeachment. *Williams,* 161 Ill. 2d at 39, 204 Ill. Dec. 72, 641 N.E.2d 296. It has been noted that this discussion in *Williams* could be construed as eliminating the first part of the *Montgomery* test, leaving as eligible grounds for impeachment only convictions for offenses that involve dishonesty or false statement and that thus qualify under the second part of *Montgomery. See Bramlett,* 276 Ill. App. 3d at 211–213, 213 Ill. Dec. 40, 658 N.E.2d 510 (Steigmann, J., specially concurring); *Fomond,* 273 Ill. App. 3d at 1068, 21 Ill. Dec. 346, 652 N.E.2d 1322; *Maxwell,* 272 Ill. App. 3d at 61,

208 Ill. Dec. 841, 650 N.E.2d 298; *see also* M. Graham, Cleary & Graham's Handbook of Illinois Evidence §609.4, at 82–87 (Supp. 1996). We now wish to make clear our continued adherence to the three-part test set forth in *Montgomery.*

Williams II, albeit obliquely, not only confirms the vitality of the *Montgomery* prong permitting admissibility for purposes of impeachment of a prior conviction punishable by death or imprisonment in excess of one year subject to discretionary balancing, *Williams II* restores the rationale for such impeachment, i.e., "disrespect for social order." The continued vitality of the first prong of *Montgomery* is evidenced by the fact that *Williams II* upholds impeachment of a criminal defendant on trial for first degree murder, attempted murder, and aggravated battery with a firearm, with a prior conviction for voluntary manslaughter following application by the trial court of the discretionary balancing test, the third prong of the *Montgomery* rule, i.e., the prior conviction is admissible to impeach unless the trial court determines that the probative value of the evidence is substantially outweighed by the danger of unfair prejudice. *Accord People v. McGee,* 286 Ill. App. 3d 786, 222 Ill. Dec. 137, 676 N.E.2d 1341 (1997). In short, *Williams II* sanctions the use of a prior convict for voluntary manslaughter to impeach a criminal defendant on trial for murder and aggravated battery with a firearm.

It is suggested that impeachment of the criminal defendant with a serious prior conviction is a very important component of the criminal justice system as we know it, thereby making complete elimination a very significant alteration of the balance between the state and the accused. Since this is a step the Illinois Supreme Court in *Williams II* has stated it is unwilling to take, consideration should be given to the adoption of the "mere fact" method of prior conviction impeachment, discussed in §609.6 infra. *See also People v. Fomond,* 273 Ill. App. 3d 1053, 210 Ill. Dec. 346, 652 N.E.2d 1322 (1995); *People v. Bramlett,* 276 Ill. App. 3d 201, 213 Ill. Dec. 40, 658 N.E.2d 510 (1995) (Justice Steigmann, specially concurring). Under the mere fact method as employed in other states, the discretionary balancing test is eliminated, all prior serious convictions may be employed to impeach, as may all convictions involving dishonesty or false statement. On the other hand, the chance of unfair prejudice arising in the form of the "bad man" inference is drastically reduced by virtue of the fact that under the mere fact method disclosure by the accused on direct examination is limited to the mere fact of conviction, that is, the date, court, and, most importantly, the nature of the offense are *not* disclosed. On cross-examination, the prosecution is not permitted to question the accused as to the previously disclosed conviction. Thus, in *Williams II* the jury would never learn that the defendant's prior conviction was for aggravated battery. This procedure also greatly reduces emphasis on the prior conviction by the trier of the fact. Moreover, the mere fact method is uniform, predictable, reasoned, and equitable, in that every accused and every similar prior conviction is treated the same.

Where the prior conviction is of a co-indictee, co-conspirator, codefendant, or accomplice called by the State as a witness who was separately tried or who pleaded guilty to the same offense, the fact of conviction may be employed by the defendant for purposes of impeachment, provided the rule is satisfied. *People v. Sullivan,* 72 Ill. 2d 36, 17 Ill. Dec. 827, 377 N.E.2d 17 (1978). However, the State on its own should not disclose that the State's witness has been convicted or pled guilty to the same offense for which the defendant is being charged. *People v. Baker,* 16 Ill. 2d 364, 158 N.E.2d 1 (1959); *People v. Burch,* 22 Ill. App. 3d 950, 317 N.E.2d 136 (1974). Introduction by the prosecution of the fact of conviction or plea to the same offense is reversible error, where the witness has not testified at trial directly establishing the defendant's guilt. *People v. Sullivan* supra. *See* §609.6 infra with respect to disclosure of prior conviction on direct examination.

As to use of pleas of guilty as prior inconsistent statements for purpose of impeachment, *see* §802.4 infra. With respect to deciding admissibility prior to trial, *see* §103.9 supra.

§609.5   Witness's Gratuitous Comments

On direct examination or gratuitously in the course of cross-examination, the witness may make representations regarding the existence or nature of prior convictions, thereby asserting or implying the absence of further convictions. In either event, other prior convictions of the witness become admissible as rebuttal evidence regardless of whether such convictions would otherwise be admissible to impeach. *People v. Bey,* 42 Ill. 2d 139, 246 N.E.2d 287 (1969); *People v. Nastasio,* 30 Ill. 2d 51, 195 N.E.2d 144 (1964); *People v. Brown,* 61 Ill. App. 3d 180, 18 Ill. Dec. 565, 377 N.E.2d 1201 (1978). *Cf. People v. Brown* supra, mere mention of a single conviction on direct does not sufficiently imply the absence of further convictions to open door. *See also* §103.4 supra.

§609.6   Method of Establishing Conviction: Direct and Cross-Examination

In civil matters, a conviction "may be proven like any fact not of record, either by the witness himself or herself (who shall be compelled to testify thereto) or by any other witness cognizant of such conviction . . . or by any other competent evidence." 735 ILCS 5/8-101. In criminal cases, while the statute is silent as to the method of proof, 725 ILCS 125/6, by decision convictions of witnesses other than the accused may be proved on cross-examination as well as by introducing the record of conviction, usually in the form of a certified copy, §902.2 infra. *People v. Roche,* 389 Ill. 361, 59 N.E.2d 866 (1945). However, if the accused herself testifies and does not disclose the prior conviction on direct, while she of course becomes subject to impeachment as a witness, in order to encourage her to take the stand by avoiding the prejudice to a defendant who is compelled to testify before a jury as to his prior convictions, *People v. Bey,* 42 Il. 2d 139, 246 N.E.2d 287 (1969), and because the state has ample opportunity to obtain the public record, convictions of the accused are provable only by public record on rebuttal and may not be brought out on cross-examination, either directly, *People v. Coleman*, 158 Ill. 2d 319, 198 Ill. Dec. 813, 633 N.E.2d 654 (1994); *People v. Madison*, 56 Ill. 2d 476, 309 N.E.2d 11 (1974); *People v. Halkens*, 386 Ill. 167, 53 N.E.2d 923 (1944); *People v. Nelson*, 275 Ill. App. 3d 877, 212 Ill. Dec. 276, 656 N.E.2d 1110 (1995); *People v. Depper*, 256 Ill. App. 3d 179, 196 Ill. Dec. 154, 629 N.E.2d 699 (1994); *People v. Smith*, 241 Ill. App. 3d 365, 182 Ill. Dec. 667, 610 N.E.2d 91 (1992), or by questions as to occupation and residence that disclose confinement in the penitentiary. *State v. Kosears*, 408 Ill. 179, 96 N.E.2d 539 (1951). Improper inquiry on cross-examination constitutes reversible error only if the error deprived the defendant of substantial justice or influenced the determination of guilt, i.e., the error may, and most often will, be deemed harmless. *See People v. Nelson*, supra; *People v. Madison*, supra. The public record consists of the original or a certified copy of the docket sheet showing the caption, the return of the indictment in open court by the grand jury, the indictment and arraignment of the defendant, the impaneling of the jury and its verdict or the waiver of the jury, and the final judgment of the court. *People v. Lane*, 400 Ill. 170, 79 N.E.2d 65 (1948); *People v. Moore*, 72 Ill. App. 3d 462, 28 Ill. Dec. 940, 391 N.E.2d 139 (1979); *People v. Lindsey*, 148 Ill. App. 3d 751, 102 Ill. Dec. 158, 499 N.E.2d 715 (1986). An exception to the rule prohibiting cross-examination of the accused concerning a prior conviction exists when the accused introduces the subject during her own direct examination. *People v. Coleman*, 158 Ill. 2d 319, 198 Ill. Dec. 813, 633 N.E.2d 654 (1994); *People v. Chrisos*, 151 Ill. App. 3d 142, 104 Ill. Dec. 498, 502 N.E.2d 1158 (1986); *People v. Johnson*, 206 Ill. App. 3d 318, 151 Ill. Dec. 255, 564 N.E.2d 232 (1990). *See also* §103.4 supra.

As part of the process of impeachment on cross-examination by means of a prior conviction of a witness other than the defendant, or in anticipation of impeachment on direct examination, the witness may be asked if he was the person convicted of the particular offense. In the process of questioning, in the court's discretion any matters appearing in the public record may be inquired into including the court, date, nature of offense, and sentence received. *People v. Enoch,* 146 Ill. 2d 44, 165 Ill. Dec. 719, 585 N.E.2d 115 (1991) (quoting Handbook); *People v. Denny,* 241 Ill. App. 3d 345, 181 Ill. Dec. 839, 608 N.E.2d 1313 (1993). *Cf. People v. Pruitt,* 165 Ill. App. 3d 947, 117 Ill. Dec. 516, 520 N.E.2d 867 (1988), disclosure of sentence received is improper. If a prior conviction is proved by certified copy of the public record of conviction, care must be taken to delete irrelevant and prejudicial surplusage, such as reference to other charges or the details of the nature of the crime of which the witness was convicted. *People v. Dudley,* 217 Ill. App. 3d 230, 160 Ill. Dec. 156, 576 N.E.2d 1110 (1991).

If the witness admits that he was so convicted, the impeachment has been completed. *People v. Enoch* supra, citing Handbook. If, however, the witness fails to admit the conviction in any respect, for example, by specifically denying or by claiming a lack of recollection, the State must introduce the public record, thereby establishing a conviction. *People v. Wallenberg,* 24 Ill. 2d 350, 181 N.E.2d 143 (1962). Where the conviction is not specifically denied, identity of name of the person convicted and the witness gives rise to an inference of identity that alone is sufficient. *People v. Buford,* 396 Ill. 158, 71 N.E.2d 340 (1947); *People v. Davis,* 95 Ill. 2d 1, 69 Ill. Dec. 136, 447 N.E.2d 353 (1983) (identity of names gives rise to a "rebuttable presumption" of identity; an unfortunate choice of terms, *see* §304.1 supra). *See also People v. Hall,* 145 Ill. App. 3d 873, 99 Ill. Dec. 644, 495 N.E.2d 1379 (1986); *People v. Gregory,* 264 Ill. App. 3d 569, 201 Ill. Dec. 823, 637 N.E.2d 412 (1993). In addition, where neither the fact of conviction nor identity is specifically denied, judicial notice of both the fact of conviction and identity is proper. *People v. Davis,* 65 Ill. 2d 157, 2 Ill. Dec. 572, 357 N.E.2d 792 (1976); *People v. Scott,* 278 Ill. App. 3d 468, 215 Ill. Dec. 347, 663 N.E.2d 97 (1996). Where, however, the witness denies either the fact of a conviction or that he was the person convicted, or asserts that more than ten years have elapsed since the release of the witness from confinement, formal proof of conviction, identity, or confinement is required, *People v. Reid*, 179 Ill. 2d 297, 228 Ill. Dec. 179, 688 N.E.2d 1156 (1997); *People v. Davis* (1983) supra, *People v. Davis* (1976) supra, *People v. Strange*, 125 Ill. App. 3d 43, 80 Ill. Dec. 504, 465 N.E.2d 616 (1984) (date of release), although when a conviction is offered for purpose of impeachment, identity need not be established beyond a reasonable doubt. *People v. Buford* supra. Failure to introduce such proof on rebuttal will result in reversal. *People v. Hope*, 11 Ill. App. 3d 460, 297 N.E.2d 366 (1973). Where there is evidence that a witness has also used other names, evidence of a conviction under either name is admissible. *People v. Buford* supra. Proof of identity may consist of testimony by the arresting officer on the prior conviction, by the presiding judge at the trial, by the parole counselor, correction officer, or the like, by comparison of fingerprint records, or by photographic comparison. *See People v. Langdon*, 73 Ill. App. 3d 881, 29 Ill. Dec. 585, 392 N.E.2d 142 (1979); *People v. Malone*, 78 Ill. 2d 34, 34 Ill. Dec. 311, 397 N.E.2d 1377 (1979). Establishing identity, a matter to be determined by the court alone, *see* §104.1 supra, may be decided *in camera* to reduce possible prejudice to the defendant. *People v. Malone* supra.

Inquiry on either direct, *People v. DeHoyos*, 64 Ill. 2d 128, 355 N.E.2d 19 (1976); *People v. Cruz*, 162 Ill. 2d 314, 205 Ill. Dec. 345, 643 N.E.2d 636 (1994), cross-examination, or redirect into related matters, such as length of time served, fact pardoned or paroled, name of victim, aggravating circumstances, or guilt or innocence is improper. *People v. DeHoyos*, 64 Ill. 2d 128, 355 N.E.2d 19 (1976); *Gallagher v. People*, 211 Ill. 158, 71 N.E. 842 (1904); *People v. Fox*, 177 Ill. App. 3d 602, 126 Ill. Dec. 787, 532 N.E.2d 472 (1988); *People v. Butler*, 63 Ill. App. 3d 132, 19 Ill. Dec. 831, 379 N.E.2d 703 (1978). *Cf. People v. Denny*, 241 Ill. App. 3d 345, 181 Ill. Dec. 839, 608 N.E.2d 1313 (1993), court has discretion to permit inquiry into additional details. However, the permitting of protestations on behalf of the convicted person is likely to be considered a harmless charity on appeal. *Trice v. Illinois Cent. Gulf R.R.*, 127 Ill. App. 3d 1019, 82 Ill. Dec. 810, 469 N.E.2d 344

(1984). The criminal defendant has been permitted to testify that he entered a plea of guilty to the prior offense, *People v. Seider*, 98 Ill. App. 3d 175, 53 Ill. Dec. 413, 423 N.E.2d 1217 (1981); *People v. Taylor*, 68 Ill. App. 3d 680, 24 Ill. Dec. 955, 386 N.E.2d 159 (1979); *People v. Belvedere*, 72 Ill. App. 3d 998, 28 Ill. Dec. 649, 390 N.E.2d 1239 (1979). *Cf.* subdivision (c) of the rule, §609.8 infra, for rehabilitation procedure and pardons based on innocence. *See also* infra.

In *People v. DeHoyos*, 64 Ill. 2d 128, 355 N.E.2d 19 (1976), the Illinois Supreme Court recognized the common practice to permit the party who calls a witness with a criminal record to prove the record on direct examination. 3A Wigmore, Evidence §900 (Chadbourn rev. 1970). The process was declared not to constitute impeachment of one's own witness, §607.4 supra, but rather to be "anticipatory" disclosure designed to reduce the prejudicial effect of the evidence on the witness's credibility. The prosecution is required by Supreme Court Rule 412(a)(vi) to furnish the defendant in advance of trial any records of the defendant's prior convictions that are in the prosecution's possession. If the criminal defendant chooses to disclose her prior conviction on her direct examination, then details of the prior conviction otherwise admissible that are not disclosed may be explored on cross-examination. *People v. Adams*, 106 Ill. App. 3d 467, 62 Ill. Dec. 231, 435 N.E.2d 1203 (1982). Of course, details of the prior conviction that would not be admissible if the fact of the prior conviction was first raised on cross-examination do not become admissible on cross-examination by virtue of anticipatory disclosure of the prior conviction on direct. *People v. Boclair*, 129 Ill. 2d 458, 136 Ill. Dec. 29, 544 N.E.2d 715 (1989); *People v. Cruz*, 162 Ill. 2d 314, 205 Ill. Dec. 345, 643 N.E.2d 636 (1994). Where, however, the introduction on direct examination may create a danger of unfair prejudice to a party; for example, where there is evidence of a past association between the prosecution witness and the criminal defendant, the conviction may not be disclosed on direct examination if its prejudicial effect substantially outweighs its probative value. *People v. DeHoyos* supra. Given the characterization of such disclosure as "anticipatory," a representation by the adverse party claiming unfair prejudice that such conviction will not be employed upon cross-examination of the witness should be a factor of considerable significance in assessing the necessity and therefore probative value of the prior conviction in assessing credibility.

If disclosure of the prior conviction on direct examination follows a denial of a motion at trial to preclude use of the conviction to impeach, disclosure on direct examination does not waive error with respect to such ruling. *People v. Spates,* 77 Ill. 2d 193, 32 Ill. Dec. 333, 395 N.E.2d 563 (1979). *See generally People v. Williams,* 161 Ill. 2d 1, 204 Ill. Dec. 72, 641 N.E.2d 296 (1994), where the Illinois Supreme Court appears to have assumed without discussion that it was not necessary to renew an objection to the admissibility of a prior conviction ruled admissible before trial to impeach prior to anticipatory disclosure of such conviction by the criminal defendant on direct examination to preserve error on appeal. Anticipatory disclosure in the absence of a pretrial or trial ruling permitting admissibility to impeach constitutes a waiver of the right to raise error on appeal. *People v. Williams,* 161 Ill. 2d 1, 204 Ill. Dec. 328, 641 N.E.2d 296 (1994). *See also* §103.9 supra and §609.10 infra.

As part of the process of "anticipatory" disclosure, it is common practice for a witness to testify to having pled guilty to the prior offense, thereby suggesting his willingness to "own up" to what he has done leading to the further inference that he is innocent of the current charges. *People v. Williams* supra; *People v. Seider* supra, *People v. Taylor* supra, *People v. Belvedere* supra. However in *People v. Coleman,* 158 Ill. 2d 319, 198 Ill. Dec. 813, 633 N.E.2d 654 (1994), the Illinois Supreme Court stated that when the accused discloses that he had pled guilty to a prior offense, he is asserting that he possessed a desire to tell the truth, thereby opening the door to cross-examination as to the details of the prior offense to establish that the accused in fact pled guilty because the evidence against him was overwhelming. *Coleman* never mentioned the "own up" rationale. It is suggested that *Coleman* was improperly decided, that the true rationale is "own up," and that permitting cross-examination as to the details of the conviction under the "door opening" "tell the truth" rationale will most often effectively preclude the accused from disclosing that he had pled guilty to the prior offense, that is, the price to be paid appears too high. In *People v. Williams* supra, the Illinois Supreme Court appears to at least recognize and acknowledge, if not completely embrace, the "own up" rationale when it states, *id* at 35, 204 Ill. Dec. at 86, 641 N.E.2d at 310, that "it is apparent from the record that defense counsel's strategy in his examination of defendant concerning the manslaughter conviction was to raise the inferences that: defendant is a person who, when guilty of wrongdoing, does not deny his guilt . . ."

Recently it has been suggested that prejudice is reduced when references to the nature of the conviction and the length of sentence are deleted. *People v. Bradshaw,* 100 Ill. App. 3d 45, 55 Ill. Dec. 370, 426 N.E.2d 345 (1981); *People v. Mitchell,* 98 Ill. App. 3d 398, 53 Ill. Dec. 867, 424 N.E.2d 658 (1981); *People v. Slaughter,* 84 Ill. App. 3d 88, 39 Ill. Dec. 467, 404 N.E.2d 1058 (1980). This procedure, known as the *mere fact method,* has substantial merit and should be further encouraged. While the probative value of a conviction not involving dishonesty or false statement may depend to some degree on the nature of the offense, *see People v. Bradshaw* supra, it is suggested that the balancing of probative value against prejudice clearly favors use of the mere fact method. The mere fact method is particularly compelling when the prior conviction and current charged offense are similar. *See People v. Williams,* 137 Ill. App. 3d 736, 92 Ill. Dec. 336, 484 N.E.2d 1191 (1985); *People v. Williams,* 230 Ill. App. 3d 761, 172 Ill. Dec. 445, 595 N.E.2d 1115 (1992); *People v. Fomond,* 273 Ill. App. 3d 1053, 210 Ill. Dec. 346, 652 N.E.2d 1322 (1995). Disclosure on direct examination provides the defendant opportunity to keep the nature of the prior offense from being disclosed to the jury. The defendant need only admit on direct the "mere fact" of conviction, i.e., "Have you ever been convicted of an offense punishable in excess of one year?" Answer: "Yes." "How many times?" Answer:

"Twice." *People v. Moore,* 65 Ill. App. 3d 712, 22 Ill. Dec. 420, 382 N.E.2d 810 (1978). The comment in *People v. Jennings,* 279 Ill. App. 3d 406, 216 Ill. Dec. 62, 664 N.E.2d 699 (1996), that the date and place for conviction in addition be the subject of inquiry goes beyond the "mere fact" method of conviction as employed in other jurisdictions and is unnecessary, although harmless. For further discussion of the mere fact method, *see* Graham, Handbook of Federal Evidence §609.6 (4th ed. 1996). *See generally People v. Gil,* 240 Ill. App. 3d 151, 181 Ill. Dec. 124, 608 N.E.2d 197 (1992) (Illinois law does not require use of the "mere fact" method under any circumstances). Use of the mere fact method is left to the discretion of the trial court. *People v. Jennings,* supra. *Compare People v. Atkinson,* 288 Ill. App. 3d 102, 223 Ill. Dec. 493, 679 N.E.2d 1266 (1997), abuse of discretion to name a prior *similar* offense; *but see* Green, J., id., dissenting, stating that the Illinois Supreme Court does not require application of the mere fact method. For a well-presented endorsement of the mere fact method, *see* Justice Steigmann specially concurring in *People v. Kunze,* 193 Ill. App. 3d 708, 140 Ill. Dec. 648, 550 N.E.2d 284 (1990). The mere fact method appears to be slowly finding acceptance at the trial court. *See, e.g., People v. Gapski,* 283 Ill. App. 3d 937, 219 Ill Dec. 228, 670 N.E.2d 1116 (1996).

A limiting instruction may be given to the jury stating that the prior conviction may be considered only insofar as it may affect the believability of the witness and must not be considered as evidence of the defendant's guilt of the offense for which he is charged. *People v. Lawler,* 142 Ill. 2d 548, 154 Ill. Dec. 674, 578 N.E.2d 895 (1991); *People v. Chapman,* 262 Ill. App. 3d 439, 198 Ill. Dec. 877, 633 N.E.2d 718 (1992). While a limiting instruction need not to be given at the time the evidence is presented, it has been suggested that giving a limiting instruction at such time is the better practice. *People v. Scott,* 278 Ill. App. 3d 468, 215 Ill. Dec. 347, 663 N.E.2d 97 (1996). As to the effectiveness of a limiting instruction, *see People v. Woodard,* 276 Ill. App. 3d 242, 212 Ill. Dec. 878, 658 N.E.2d 55 (1995) (the court does not doubt the jury's ability to properly follow the trial court's instructions). *See also* §105.1 supra.

As correctly stated in *People v. Elliot,* 274 Ill. App. 3d 901, 211 Ill. Dec. 174, 654 N.E.2d 636 (1995), the Illinois Supreme Court in *People v. Williams,* 161 Ill. 2d 1, 204 Ill. Dec 72, 641 N.E.2d 296 (1994), discussed in §609.4 supra, did not indicate approval or disapproval of the "mere fact" procedure. *See also* Green, J., dissenting in *People v. Atkinson,* 288 Ill. App. 3d 102, 223 Ill. Dec. 493, 679 N.E.2d 1266 (1997). It is respectfully suggested that given the theoretical and practical difficulties and realities associated with *Montgomery* discretionary balancing, as reflected in *Williams* and *Williams II,* §609.4 supra, it is time for the court to fully consider adoption of the "mere fact" procedure.

§609.7   Conviction as to Which More Than Ten Years Have Elapsed

Evidence of a conviction is not admissible if a period of more than ten years has elapsed since the date of the conviction or of the release of the witness from the confinement imposed for that conviction, whichever is the later date. *See* subdivision (b) of the rule, adopted in *People v. Montgomery,* 47 Ill. 2d 510, 268 N.E.2d 695 (1971), §609.2 supra. *See also People v. Bynum,* 257 Ill. App. 3d 502, 196 Ill. Dec. 179, 629 N.E.2d 724 (1994). The ten year period commences with the date of conviction itself. *See People v. Hawkins,* 243 Ill. App. 3d 210, 183 Ill. Dec. 421, 611 N.E.2d 1069 (1993). As to the date of a conviction, *see* §609.2 supra. Like the rule generally, subdivision (b) applies to witnesses other than to the accused, as well as to the accused who elects to testify, *People v. Stewart,* 54 Ill. App. 3d 76, 11 Ill. Dec. 677, 369 N.E.2d 131 (1977), in criminal and civil cases regardless of which party calls the witness to testify. *People v. Gandy,* 227 Ill. App. 3d 112, 169 Ill. Dec. 165, 591 N.E.2d 45 (1992) (prosecution witness). Where probation had been revoked, the ten-year period runs from the date of release from prison and not the date of conviction. *People v. Owens*, 58 Ill. App. 3d 37, 15 Ill. Dec. 502, 373 N.E.2d 848 (1978). The party proposing to employ the conviction must establish the fact of confinement and the date of release; it will not be assumed that a person sentenced served at least the minimum period. *People v. Yost*, 65 Ill. App. 386, 21 Ill. Dec. 846, 382 N.E.2d 140 (1978).

In *People v. Ray*, 54 Ill. 2d 377, 297 N.E.2d 168 (1973), the Illinois Supreme Court quoted from the 1969 version of Federal Rule of Evidence 609(b), 46 F.R.D. 161, 296 (1969), which makes reference to the ten-year period also running from the date of expiration of parole or probation. The reference in *Ray* to the earlier draft was referred to as an "inadvertent mistake" in *People v. Yost* supra. On appeal, the supreme court in *People v. Yost*, 78 Ill. 2d 292, 35 Ill. Dec. 755, 399 N.E.2d 1283 (1980), acknowledged that the reference in *Ray* supra, to parole on probation was a "regrettable inadvertency" and that Rule 609(b) as adopted in *Montgomery* supra, i.e., ten years from date of conviction or release, whichever is the later date, is controlling. Moreover, in *Yost*, the supreme court confirmed that the party proposing to employ a conviction must establish the fact of confinement and the date of release and further that it will not be assumed that a person served at least the minimum term or any portion of the sentence. With respect to a retrial, the ten-year provision is applied as if the trial was occurring when it initially did. *People v. Reddick*, 123 Ill. 2d 184, 122 Ill. Dec. 1, 526 N.E.2d 141 (1988).

§609.8 *Effect of a Pardon, Annulment, or Certification of Rehabilitation*

Evidence of a conviction is not admissible if (1) the conviction has been the subject of a pardon, annulment, certificate of rehabilitation, or other equivalent procedure, and (2) the procedure under which the same was granted or issued requires a substantial showing of rehabilitation or was based on innocence. *See* subdivision (c) of the rule, adopted in *People v. Montgomery,* 47 Ill. 2d 510, 268 N.E.2d 691 (1971), §609.2 supra. The terms *annulment* and *certificate of rehabilitation,* not used in Illinois, were included because they are used in some other states, and out-of-state convictions are admissible under the rule. Illinois does employ the terms *pardon, commutation,* and *reprieve.* 730 ILCS 5/3-3-13.

For a conviction to be inadmissible under this provision, the procedure, whatever called, must have required a substantial showing of rehabilitation of the person convicted. Thus none of the following is sufficient alone to bar use of the conviction for purposes of impeachment: a certificate showing a sentence has been satisfactorily completed, 730 ILCS 5/5-5-5; pardon not based upon a finding of innocence, *Freeman v. Chicago Transit Auth.,* 33 Ill. 2d 103, 210 N.E.2d 191 (1965); parole successfully completed, *People v. Andrae,* 295 Ill. 445, 129 N.E. 178 (1920). A pardon, annulment, or equivalent procedure, if based upon a finding of innocence, also makes the conviction inadmissible. *See* subdivision (c) of the adopted rule supra.

§609.9 Juvenile Adjudications

Juvenile adjudications are not admissible to impeach a witness, with the sole exception that evidence of a juvenile adjudication of a witness other than the defendant may be employed in a criminal case for purposes of attacking the credibility of a witness on the basis of either bias, interest, or willingness to disobey the law if (1) the conviction would be admissible if an adult, and (2) its admission in evidence is necessary to a fair determination of guilt or innocence. Subdivision (d) of the rule, adopted in *People v. Montgomery,* 47 Ill. 2d 510, 268 N.E.2d 691 (1971), §609.2 supra. *See also* 705 ILCS 405/1-10; *Davis v. Alaska,* 415 U.S. 308 (1974); *People v. Triplett,* 108 Ill. 2d 453, 92 Ill. Dec. 454, 485 N.E.2d 9 (1985); *People v. Norwood,* 54 Ill. 2d 253, 296 N.E.2d 852 (1973); *People v. Sharrod,* 271 Ill. App. 3d 684, 208 Ill. Dec. 219, 648 N.E.2d 1141 (1995); *People v. Massie,* 137 Ill. App. 3d 723, 92 Ill. Dec.

358, 484 N.E.2d 1213 (1985). Thus when the criminal defendant is the witness, his other juvenile adjudications are never admissible to impeach. *People v. Sneed,* 274 Ill. App. 3d 287, 210 Ill. Dec. 887, 653 N.E.2d 1349 (1995); *People v. Kerns,* 229 Ill. App. 3d. 938, 172 Ill. Dec. 144, 595 N.E.2d 207 (1992). With respect to a witness other than the accused, the importance of the juvenile's testimony must be balanced against the public policy of preserving the anonymity of a juvenile's record. *People v. Eatherly,* 78 Ill. App. 3d 777, 34 Ill. Dec. 77, 397 N.E.2d 533 (1979), not error to bar impeachment with juvenile conviction where person was neither only witness nor a crucial witness essential to the prosecution. A juvenile adjudication is admissible for the inference that the juvenile is predisposed to testify favorably to the prosecution in order to obtain leniency only upon a showing that the witness might receive favorable treatment. *People v. Harrell,* 112 Ill. App. 3d 241, 68 Ill. Dec. 48, 445 N.E.2d 496 (1983).

People v. McClendon, 146 Ill. App. 3d 1004, 100 Ill. Dec. 671, 497 N.E.2d 849 (1986), holds that 705 ILCS 405/1-10 supplants Rule 609(d) as adopted in *Montgomery* and that all juvenile adjudications are freely admissible to impeach. *McClendon* is incorrect and should not be followed. Section 1-10 provides for impeachment of a witness with a juvenile adjudication "only . . . pursuant to the rules of evidence for criminal trials." Thus Rule 609(d) continues. The inappropriateness of *McClendon* as a matter of policy if not statutory construction is patent. No reason exists why a juvenile adjudication offered to impeach credibility as a prior conviction should be automatically admissible while an adult conviction for the same offense requires discretionary balancing. Finally, *McClendon* read literally would permit a juvenile adjudication for a crime punishable by imprisonment for one year or less not involving dishonesty or false statement to be employed freely when impeachment of an adult who was convicted of the identical offense is prohibited. *McClendon* was specifically abandoned in *People v. Kerns,* 229 Ill. App. 3d 938, 172 Ill. Dec. 144, 595 N.E.2d 207 (1992) (quoting Handbook), in favor of the conclusion that Rule 609(d) is to be applied.

§609.10 Pendency of Appeal; Preservation of Error for Appeal

The pendency of an appeal from a conviction does not render the conviction inadmissible; evidence of the pendency of the appeal is itself admissible. Subdivision (e) of the rule adopted in *People v. Montgomery*, 47 Ill. 2d 510, 268 N.E.2d 691 (1971), §609.2 supra; *People v. Bey*, 42 Ill. 2d 139, 246 N.E.2d 287 (1969). A conviction reversed on appeal prior to the litigation at hand may not be used for impeachment. *People v. Shook*, 35 Ill. 2d 597, 221 N.E.2d 290 (1966). Employment of a conviction to impeach that is subsequently reversed on appeal will not normally be considered error. *People v. Miller*, 27 Ill. App. 3d 788, 327 N.E.2d 253 (1975). However, where the ground of reversal for the conviction was constitutional error, the appropriate standard is constitutional harmless error. *People v. Martin-Trigona*, 129 Ill. App. 3d 212, 84 Ill. Dec. 548, 472 N.E.2d 508 (1984), where a prior conviction used to impeach is reversed because of an uncounseled conviction, the standard for determining whether that error is reversible is whether use of the conviction was harmless beyond a reasonable doubt. *See also* §103.10 supra.

Luce v. United States, 469 U.S. 38 (1984), provides that in federal court error with respect to a ruling on a motion in limine permitting use of a prior conviction to impeach is preserved for appeal only if the defendant actually testifies at trial. Absent the defendant's actual testimony, the degree of harm caused by the error is said to be wholly speculative and impossible to measure. The position of *Luce* requiring a defendant to testify to preserve error was adopted in *People v. Hartfield*, 137 Ill. App. 3d 679, 92 Ill. Dec. 281, 484 N.E.2d 1136 (1985), *People v. Redman*, 141 Ill. App. 3d 691, 95 Ill. Dec. 866, 490 N.E.2d 958 (1986), *People v. Helton*, 195 Ill. App. 3d 410, 142 Ill. Dec. 48, 552 N.E.2d 398 (1990), *People v. Gil*, 240 Ill. App. 3d 151, 181 Ill. Dec. 124, 608 N.E.2d 197 (1992), *People v. Bynum*, 257 Ill. App. 3d 502, 196 Ill. Dec. 179, 629 N.E.2d 724 (1994), and *People v. Steward*, 295 Ill. App. 3d 735, 230 Ill. Dec. 307, 693 N.E.2d 436 (1998). *Contra People v. Smith*, 73 Ill. App. 3d 577, 29 Ill. Dec. 790, 392 N.E.2d 347 (1979).

As to whether it is necessary to obtain a ruling at trial as to the admissibility of a prior conviction to impeach in light of an earlier ruling on a motion in limine, *see* §§103.9 and 609.6 supra.

§610   Religious Beliefs or Opinions

§610.1   Commentary

Evidence with respect to the religious beliefs or opinions of a witness is not admissible for the purpose of enhancing or impairing the witness's credibility by virtue of the nature of the beliefs. *People v. Baseer*, 90 Ill. App. 3d 866, 46 Ill. Dec. 283, 414 N.E.2d 5 (1980); *Starks v. Schlensky*, 128 Ill. App. 1 (1906). Prohibition of such inquiry is in accord with Section 3 of Article I of the Constitution of 1970 abolishing religious qualifications for witnesses. *See* §601.1 supra. However, evidence of religious affiliation may be admitted for other purposes, such as to show bias where the witness's church is a party to the litigation. McCormick, Evidence §46 (4th ed. 1992). *See also People v. Nevitt*, 135 Ill. App. 3d 423, 142 Ill. Dec. 854, 553 N.E.2d 368 (1990), evidence of the witness's religious conviction was admissible to show the witness was interested in protecting the religious organization's reputation.

As to dying declarations, *see* §804.6 infra.

§611   Mode and Order of Interrogation and Presentation

§611.1   An Overview

It is the responsibility of the court to control the mode and order of interrogating witnesses and the presentation of evidence so as to foster the ascertainment of truth, avoid needless consumption of time, and at the same time protect witnesses from harassment or undue embarrassment. The normal pattern with respect to opening statements and closing arguments, §611.2 infra, and the presentation of evidence at trial, §611.3 infra, assists counsel and the court in conducting the trial in an orderly manner. Introduction of evidence after a party rests is discussed in §611.4 infra.

While denial of the right to open and close, which includes *voir dire*, presentation of evidence, and final argument, has been held error, §611.2 infra, with respect to presentation of evidence, as long as each party is afforded the opportunity to present her own evidence and to meet that of her opponent, she is scarcely in a position to complain of deviation or lack thereof from the normal pattern. On some occasions, it may be difficult to ascertain where a particular item of evidence neatly fits within the normal pattern. *Chillicothe Ferry, Road & Bridge Co. v. Jameson,* 48 Ill. 281 (1868). Instances of counsel's deliberate attempt to depart from this general scheme are regarded unfavorably, however, and include offering evidence in rebuttal, which was merely cumulative of plaintiff's case in chief, properly excluded, *Pepe v. Caputo,* 408 Ill. 321, 97 N.E.2d 260 (1951); attempting to establish a new ground of liability in rebuttal rejected, *Grayson v. Pennsylvania R. Co.,* 349 Ill. App. 408, 111 N.E.2d 185 (1953); proving an affirmative defense on cross-examination of a witness for plaintiff barred, *Horner v. Bell,* 336 Ill. App. 581, 84 N.E.2d 672 (1949). *Cf. Kupcikevicius v. Fitzgibbons,* 41 Ill. App. 3d 405, 354 N.E.2d 434 (1976), testimony in rebuttal by doctor that might have been admitted in case in chief permitted since it also tended to rebut, subject to being "connected up"; *Mitchell v. Shermane McEwen Assoc.,* 360 Ill. 278, 196 N.E. 186 (1935), agreement made by agent may be introduced prior to proof of agency. *See also* §705.1 infra, with respect to "connecting up" and expert witness testimony. Evidence admitted upon a promise to connect it up should be excluded upon failure to establish the connection. *People v.*

Smith, 254 Ill. 167, 98 N.E. 281 (1912). As to motions to strike, *see* §103.3 supra. The trial court may alternatively in its discretion reserve ruling as to the admissibility of the evidence offered "subject to connection" pending introduction at trial of the necessary foundational evidence. *Myers v. Williams,* 160 Ill. App. 3d 707, 112 Ill. Dec. 600, 513 N.E.2d 1209 (1987).

While ordinarily cross-examination is deferred until completion of the direct examination, cross-examination of a witness as to his qualifications or competency prior to giving his principal testimony, sometimes described as *voir dire,* may avoid exposing the jury to inadmissible evidence if the witness proves to be unqualified or incompetent. Hence cross-examination as to qualifications or competency should be permitted at this time if requested. *People v. Sawhill,* 299 Ill. 393, 132 N.E. 477 (1921), qualifications of witness as expert accountant; *People v. Karpovich,* 288 Ill. 268, 123 N.E. 324 (1919), competency of child. Similar considerations surround the conducting of *voir dire* examination with respect to preliminary questions of admissibility generally.

In summary, the entire matter of order of presentation of evidence and mode of witness examination must and does rest largely in the discretion of the trial judge. *People v. Waller,* 67 Ill. 2d 381, 10 Ill. Dec. 517, 367 N.E.2d 1283 (1977); *United States Wringer Co. v. Cooney,* 214 Ill. 520, 73 N.E. 803 (1905). Abuse of discretion is likely to arise only if opportunity is denied to impeach witnesses, to support the credibility of impeached witnesses, or to meet new points raised by the opponent. *Rock Island v. Starkey,* 189 Ill. 515, 59 N.E. 971 (1901).

Incorporated in the commentary following are references to specific objections to both the form of the question and unresponsiveness of the answer. These objections form a discrete area sometimes referred to collectively as trial objections. *See* §611.9, 611.18 to 611.26 infra. Trial courts are vested with considerable discretion in ruling upon trial objections. *Department of Pub. Works v. Finks,* 10 Ill. 2d 15, 139 N.E.2d 267 (1956). Objections of this nature, as well as objections generally, are subject to the rules and procedures outlined in §103 supra.

§611.2   Order of Presentation: Voir Dire, Opening Statements, and Closing Arguments

The right to open and close, including *voir dire*, arguments, and the presentation of evidence, §611.3 infra, is regarded as a substantial advantage. It is a matter of right and is not discretionary with the trial judge. *Liptak v. Security Benefit Assn.*, 350 Ill. 614, 183 N.E. 564 (1932). The parties proceed in all stages of the proceeding, including *voir dire* selection of jurors, opening statement and closing argument, the offering of evidence, and the examination of witnesses in the order in which they appear in the pleadings. Supreme Court Rule 233. However, a defendant who admits plaintiff's entire case and relies only on an affirmative defense has the right. *Liptak v. Security Benefit Assn.* supra. In consolidated cases, third party proceedings, and all other cases not otherwise provided for, the court designates the order of proceeding. *Id.*

The opening statement by the plaintiff in civil cases, Supreme Court Rule 235, and by the prosecution in criminal cases, Supreme Court Rule 432, the parties with the burden of proof, shall be made as soon as the jury is empanelled. The attorney for the defendant may follow immediately with an opening statement; an opening statement may not be made at any other time, except in the discretion of the court. *Id.* The purpose of an opening statement is to apprise the jury of the nature of the party's case and the evidence to sustain it. *People v. Fuerback,* 66 Ill. App. 2d 452, 214 N.E.2d 330 (1966). The opening statement should be brief and general rather than detailed. *People v. Platter,* 89 Ill. App. 3d 803, 45 Ill. Dec. 48, 412 N.E.2d 181 (1980). It should contain an outline of the facts that a party in good faith intends to prove and should not be a long, narrative, evidentiary recitation, *People v. Hampton,* 78 Ill. App. 3d 238, 33 Ill. Dec. 784, 397 N.E.2d 117 (1979), or counsel's argument to the jury, *People v. Hardy,* 70 Ill. App. 3d 238, 33 Ill. Dec. 784, 387 N.E.2d 1042 (1979). Its scope and latitude is largely within the discretion of the trial court. *People v. Cobbins,* 162 Ill. App. 3d 1010, 114 Ill. Dec. 227, 516 N.E.2d 382 (1987). When a statement by counsel that certain evidence will be introduced is followed by a failure to introduce such evidence, there may be reversible error. *People v. Smith,* 141 Ill. 2d 40, 152 Ill. Dec. 218, 565 N.E.2d 900 (1990); *People v. Weinger,* 101 Ill. App. 3d 857, 51 Ill. Dec. 244, 428 N.E.2d 924 (1981).

The closing argument consists of the opening final argument of the plaintiff-prosecutor, the defendant's closing argument, and a rebuttal argument of the plaintiff-prosecutor. The rebuttal argument is limited to responding to arguments made by the defendant. If defendant waives closing argument, the plaintiff-prosecutor has no right to offer further argument. However, the court may in its discretion permit further argument, if, for example, counsel by inadvertence has omitted something she intended to state. *Cunningham v. People,* 210 Ill. 410, 71 N.E. 389 (1904).

Either party may waive his right to make an opening statement, *Pietsch v. Pietsch,* 245 Ill. 454, 92 N.E. 325 (1910), or closing argument, *Lovas v. Independent Breweries Co.,* 199 Ill. App. 60 (1916) (abstract).

With respect to selection of prospective jurors, *see* 705 ILCS 305/1 *et seq.* In criminal cases, *see also* 725 ILCS 5/115-4; in civil cases, 735 ILCS 5/2-1106. In both civil and criminal cases *voir dire* is to be conducted in accordance with Supreme Court Rule 234, made applicable in criminal cases by Supreme Court Rule 431. The court in the exercise of its discretion may refuse to permit counsel directly to examine a prospective juror. 725 ILCS 5/115-4(f), at one time mandating a right of direct examination in criminal cases, was declared unconstitutional in *People v. Jackson,* 69 Ill. 2d 252, 13 Ill. Dec. 667, 371 N.E.2d 602 (1977). In response to the supreme court's action, 5/115-4(f) was amended to state: "After examination by the court the jurors may be examined, passed upon, accepted and tendered by opposing counsel as provided by Supreme Court rules." Supreme Court Rule 234 does not in fact provide for the passing upon, acceptance, and tendering of juries, thus leaving the process to be followed very much up in the air. The purpose of *voir dire* is to enable counsel to exercise peremptory challenges and challenges for cause. *See generally People v. Pasch,* 152 Ill. 2d 133, 178 Ill. Dec. 38, 604 N.E.2d 294 (1992). If a prospective juror has a physical impairment, the court must consider such juror's ability to perceive and appreciate the evidence when considering a challenge for cause. 725 ILCS 5/115-4(d); 735 ILCS 5/2-1105.1. The goal is to select an impartial jury. *People v. Buie,* 238 Ill. App. 3d 260, 179 Ill. Dec. 447, 606 N.E.2d 279 (1992). *Voir dire* should not be employed as a vehicle for pre-educating and indoctrinating prospective jurors with a particular theory or defense or empanelling a jury with particular predispositions. *People v. Phillips,* 99 Ill. App. 3d 362, 54 Ill. Dec. 823, 425 N.E.2d 1040 (1981).

§611.3   Order of Presentation: Evidence Introduced at Trial

Plaintiff's case in chief.   In the usual case, the plaintiff in a civil case or a prosecutor in a criminal matter must initially present his case in chief, i.e., introduce facts sufficient to establish each controverted element of the claim asserted or offense charged, known as a *prima facie* case. *See* §301.4 supra. For further details, *see* McCormick, Evidence §4 (4th ed. 1992).

Defendant's denials and affirmative defenses.   The defendant then presents the witnesses and the documents and other tangible evidence in support of her case. Documents authenticated by defendant during cross-examination of plaintiff's witnesses are offered into evidence at this time. *People v. Crawford Distrib. Co.,* 65 Ill. App. 3d 790, 22 Ill. Dec. 525, 382 N.E.2d 1223 (1978). At this stage the defendant will produce evidence not only in denial of the plaintiff-prosecutor's claim, but also in support of any affirmative defenses that the defendant has pleaded or, in a criminal case, has given appropriate notice of. Supreme Court Rule 413(d). *See* §§303.1 to 303.3 supra. *See also* McCormick, Evidence §4 (4th ed. 1992).

Plaintiff's rebuttal; defendant's surrebuttal.   The plaintiff is next entitled to present his case in rebuttal. Plaintiff may not present at this stage witnesses who merely support

WITNESS   §611.3

the allegations of the complaint, but is confined to testimony
that is directed to explain, qualify, modify, discredit, or destroy the evidence of the defendant, *People v. Waller,* 67 Ill. 2d
381, 367 N.E.2d 1283, 10 Ill. Dec. 517 (1977); *Brown v. Sexner,*
85 Ill. App. 3d 139, 39 Ill. Dec. 947, 405 N.E.2d 1082 (1980);
Martin v. Allstate Ins. Co., 92 Ill. App. 3d 829, 48 Ill. Dec. 316,
416 N.E.2d 347 (1981) (contradictory or explanatory evidence in reply to issue raised by opponent is admissible on
rebuttal); *People v. Biro,* 260 Ill. App. 3d 1012, 201 Ill. Dec.
371, 636 N.E.2d 803 (1994) (evidence as to prior disclosure
by the accused of other crimes tended to establish trusting
relationship refuting assertion that accused disclosed to the
same person that he had committed the murders only as a
joke); *People v. Mischke,* 278 Ill. App. 3d 252, 214 Ill. Dec. 876,
662 N.E.2d 442 (1995) (evidence contradicting defendant's
statement that he had told police he thought gun was un-
loaded), unless the court in its discretion permits him to
depart from the regular order of proof. *See* McCormick, Evidence §4 (4th ed. 1992). In the court's discretion, evidence
introduced tending to refute is admissible in rebuttal even if
it would also have been admissible as part of plaintiff's case
in chief, *Hoem v. Zia,* 159 Ill. 2d 193, 201 Ill. Dec. 47, 636
N.E.2d 479 (1994); *People v. Lucas,* 132 Ill. 2d 399, 139 Ill.
Dec. 447, 548 N.E.2d 1003 (1989); *People v. Daugherty,* 43 Ill.
2d 251, 253 N.E.2d 389 (1969); *People v. Williams,* 209 Ill.
App. 3d 709, 154 Ill. Dec. 388, 568 N.E.2d 388 (1991); *People
v. Williams,* 223 Ill. App. 3d 692, 166 Ill. Dec. 166, 585 N.E.2d
1188 (1992), and even if repetitive of matters actually intro-
duced during the case in chief. *People v. Daugherty* supra;
People v. Williams, supra; *People v. Moss,* 54 Ill. App. 3d 769, 12
Ill. Dec. 466, 370 N.E.2d 89 (1977). *See generally Prorskevitch v.
Chicago & A. Ry.,* 232 Ill. 136, 83 N.E. 545 (1908); *Sandwich v.
Colan,* 141 Ill. 430, 31 N.E. 416 (1892); *Chillicothe Ferry Road
& Bridge Co. v. Jameson,* 48 Ill. 281 (1868). Evidence in rebut-
tal is limited to noncollateral matters. *People v. Mischke,* supra;
People v. Westbrook, 262 Ill. App. 3d 836, 200 Ill. Dec. 59, 635
N.E.2d 398 (1992); *Hall v. Northwestern Univ. Med. Clinics,* 152
Ill. App. 3d 716, 105 Ill. Dec. 496, 504 N.E.2d 781 (1987);

People v. Burnett, 35 Ill. App. 3d 109, 341 N.E.2d 86 (1975). *See* §607.2 supra for discussion of collateral and noncollateral matters; as to opening the door, *see* §103.4 supra. If new points are brought out during rebuttal, refutation by the defendant is called either surrebuttal or rejoinder. *People v. Perez,* 209 Ill. App. 3d 457, 154 Ill. Dec. 250, 568 N.E.2d 250 (1991). Like rebuttal, *State Toll Highway Auth. v. Grand Mandarin,* 189 Ill. App. 3d 323, 136 Ill. Dec. 370, 544 N.E.2d 1145 (1989), the scope and extent of surrebuttal, as well as whether new matters may be introduced, rests in the sound discretion of the court. *People v. Lucas* supra; *Levin v. Welsh Brothers Motor Serv., Inc.,* 164 Ill. App. 3d 640, 115 Ill. Dec. 680, 518 N.E.2d 205 (1987); *People v. Torres,* 198 Ill. App. 3d 1066, 145 Ill. Dec. 123, 556 N.E.2d 741 (1990). Evidence on rebuttal and surrebuttal should be confined to the purpose for which relevant and thus to the extent possible avoid the unnecessary introduction of the risk of unfair prejudice. *People v. Cortes,* 181 Ill. 2d 249, 229 Ill. Dec. 918, 692 N.E.2d 1129 (1998).

Defendant's counterclaim.   Where the defendant has interposed a counterclaim, the defendant's case in chief with respect to the counterclaim is normally presented together with defendant's evidence in opposition to plaintiff's main case and in support of defendant's affirmative defenses. Plaintiff presents her opposition and affirmative defenses to the counterclaim when she presents rebuttal evidence.

§611.4   Introduction of Evidence After Parties Rest

The court's discretion discussed in the preceding section extends to reopening a case for the taking of further evidence after a party or even both parties have rested. In considering a motion to reopen proofs, the court should take into account various factors, including the existence of an excuse for the failure to introduce the evidence at trial, e.g., whether it was inadvertence or calculated risk; whether the adverse party will be surprised or unfairly prejudiced by the new evidence; whether the evidence is of utmost importance to the movant's case; and whether there are the most cogent reasons to deny the request. *Hollembaek v. Dominick's Finer Foods,* 137 Ill. App. 3d 773, 92 Ill. Dec. 382, 484 N.E.2d 1237 (1985); *People v. Watkins,* 238 Ill. App. 3d 253, 179 Ill. Dec. 422, 606 N.E.2d 254 (1992); *Affatato v. Jewel Companies, Inc.,* 259 Ill. App. 3d 787, 198 Ill. Dec. 78, 632 N.E.2d 137 (1994). *See, e.g., People v. Fox,* 48 Ill. 2d 239, 269 N.E.2d 720 (1971), involving a request to reopen a case for the making of a motion to strike certain testimony; *People v. Pastorino,* 91 Ill. 2d 178, 62 Ill. Dec. 172, 435 N.E.2d 1144 (1982), involving the calling of someone as a court's witness after both sides had rested; *People v. Smith,* 149 Ill. App. 3d 145, 102 Ill. Dec. 712, 500 N.E.2d 605 (1986), affirming denial of defendant's request to recall the victim where testimony would have been merely cumulative; *People v. Faulkner,* 64 Ill. App. 3d 453, 21 Ill. Dec. 243, 381 N.E.2d 321 (1978), involving reserving a ruling on motion for a directed verdict while permitting prosecution to reopen to introduce evidence as to the value of a stolen automobile essential to prove an element of the crime; *People v. Robbins,* 21 Ill. App. 3d 317, 315 N.E.2d 198 (1974), involving admission of exhibits after closing of a party's case; and *Schutt v. Terminal R.R. Assn.,* 79 Ill. App. 2d 69, 76, 223 N.E.2d 264 (1967), involving an attempt to recall a witness for further cross-examination after close of the case. The discretion may be exercised in favor of reopening the case even after argument and instruction, and the opposite party seems not to be in a position to complain unless he is denied the opportunity to meet the additional evidence. *Crothers v. LaSalle Inst.,* 68 Ill. 2d 399, 12 Ill. Dec. 590, 370 N.E.2d 213 (1977); *People v. Cross,* 40 Ill. 2d 85, 237 N.E.2d 437 (1968); *Indiana, D. & W. Ry. v. Hendrian,* 190 Ill. 501, 60 N.E. 902 (1901); *Bolen v. People,* 184 Ill. 338, 56 N.E. 408 (1900). Particularly in nonjury cases, liberality in favor of reopening is encouraged, with a view to affording the fullest possible hearing. *People ex rel. Boos v. St. Louis, I.M. & S. Ry.,* 278 Ill. 25, 115 N.E. 854 (1917); *In re Marriage of Suarez,* 148 Ill. App. 3d 849, 102 Ill. Dec. 85, 499 N.E.2d 642 (1986); *In re Marriage of Phillips,* 229 Ill. App. 3d 809, 171 Ill. Dec. 501, 594

N.E.2d 353 (1992). The additional evidence need not be allowed absent a showing of diligence, *McGlaughlin v. Pickerel*, 381 Ill. 574, 46 N.E.2d 368 (1943), and should not be allowed when deliberately withheld in an attempt to deprive the opponent of the opportunity to meet it. *Herricks v. Chicago & E.I.R. Co.*, 257 Ill. 264, 100 N.E. 897 (1913). While motions to reopen are generally made by one of the parties, there is no prohibition against the trial court's taking such action on its own motion where a sound basis for the action appears on the record. *Bank of Illmo v. Simmons*, 142 Ill. App. 3d 741, 97 Ill. Dec. 4, 492 N.E.2d 207 (1986). The court's discretion in allowing or denying a party to reopen his or her case is reviewed on appeal applying the clear abuse of discretion test. *People v. Smith*, 278 Ill. App. 3d 343, 214 Ill. Dec. 914, 662 N.E.2d 480 (1996).

For the information of the court and to preserve possible error for review, the nature of the additional evidence sought to be introduced should be disclosed. *Gunderson v. First Natl. Bank*, 296 Ill. App. 111, 16 N.E.2d 306 (1938). *See* §103.7 supra.

Of course, the court possesses similar discretion to permit the recalling of a witness by a party who has not yet rested, *People v. Clark*, 178 Ill. App. 3d 848, 127 Ill. Dec. 892, 533 N.E.2d 974 (1989); *People v. Thompson*, 57 Ill. App. 3d 134, 14 Ill. Dec. 773, 372 N.E.2d 1052 (1978), or to deny such a request, *People v. Edens*, 174 Ill. App. 3d 1033, 124 Ill. Dec. 636, 529 N.E.2d 617 (1988), and to permit or deny examination as to new matter. *People v. Mahon*, 77 Ill. App. 3d 413, 32 Ill. Dec. 569, 395 N.E.2d 950 (1979). It is, however, error to deny the request when the denial will manifestly prejudice a party. *People v. Gray*, 209 Ill. App. 3d 407, 154 Ill. Dec. 219, 568 N.E.2d 219 (1991).

§611.5   Direct Examination

During the presentation by a party of her evidence in any one of the stages described in §611.2 supra, the party seeks to elicit from witnesses testimony establishing certain facts and to introduce documentary and other tangible evidence, properly authenticated. §§901-902 infra. To facilitate the presentation of testimony, witnesses may be subpoenaed to appear at trial, *see* §611.6 infra, and exhibits may be required to be produced. *See* §611.7 infra.

The process of eliciting facts from a witness called by a party is termed direct examination. Leading questions, i.e., questions suggesting the answer, are generally not permitted upon direct examination. *See* §611.9 infra.

§611.6   *Attendance of Witnesses at Trial: Witness Fees*

The right to produce witnesses on one's behalf at trial is basic to our system of justice. *Regan v. Regan,* 53 Ill. App. 3d 50, 11 Ill. Dec. 1, 368 N.E.2d 552 (1977). Witnesses, including physicians and surgeons, may be compelled to appear at trial by service of a subpoena; attendance of a party may be compelled by service of a notice to appear. The subpoena is a writ commanding the witness to appear and testify in a designated cause or matter at a specified time and place. Subpoenas are issued by the clerk at the request of either party in both civil and criminal cases. 735 ICLS 5/2-1101; 725 ILCS 125/7. Many administrative agencies are authorized to issue subpoenas by special statutes that should be consulted.

The right "to have process to compel the attendance of witnesses in his behalf" is guaranteed by the Constitution of Illinois to persons accused of crime. Art. I, §8. However, refusal to subpoena witnesses is not a ground for complaint without a showing that their testimony would have been material to the defense. *People v. Robinson,* 22 Ill. 2d 162, 174 N.E.2d 820 (1961).

In criminal cases the subpoena is directed to the sheriff or coroner of any county in the State, 725 ILCS 125/7, while in civil cases it is directed to the witness himself. *Chicago & Aurora R. Co. v. Dunning,* 18 Ill. 494 (1857). The fact that the subpoena in civil cases is directed to the witness is the basis for the conclusion that it may be served by any person or by mail. *Id.* The inference would then seem to be that service in criminal cases could be made only by one of the officers to whom the writ is directed, but the contrary has been held. *Ferriman v. People,* 128 Ill. App. 230 (1906). *See also People v. Ryan,* 410 Ill. 486, 103 N.E.2d 116 (1952). Confirmation of the availability of service by mail, registered or certified return receipt requested, in civil cases is now found in Illinois Supreme Court Rule 237(a). The salutary principle thus appears to be that the witness is bound to obey, regardless of how the subpoena comes to his hands, in both civil and criminal cases.

Historically the requirement of tender seems never to have applied to witnesses for the State in criminal cases, 8 Wigmore, Evidence §2201 (McNaughton rev. 1961); the constitutional guaranty of compulsory process, Constitution of Illinois, Art. I, §8, may demand its rejection as regards witnesses for the accused. Supreme Court Rule 237(a) specifically provides in civil proceedings for the tendering of the witness fee and mileage allowance with service of the subpoena. The requirement of tender has been eliminated in some administrative proceedings. *Department of Revenue v. Wakeford Hardware Co.,* 2 Ill. App. 2d 66, 118 N.E.2d 627 (1954).

Witnesses attending trial or a deposition are entitled to $20.00 per day plus $.20 per mile each way for necessary travel. 705 ILCS 35/4.3. *Lee v. Hyster Co.,* 156 Ill. App. 3d 214, 108 Ill. Dec. 890, 509 N.E.2d 586 (1987), expert witnesses are entitled to fees. With respect to professional fees to be paid a physician or surgeon attending a deposition, *see* Illinois Supreme Court Rule 204(c). *See also Tzytuck v. Chicago Transit Auth.,* 124 Ill. 2d 226, 124 Ill. Dec. 544, 529 N.E.2d 525 (1988), and §702.3 infra.

In the event that a party has subpoenaed an expert witness, including but not limited to physicians or medical providers, and the expert witness appears in court, and a conflict arises between the party subpoenaing the expert witness and the expert witness over the fees charged by the expert witness, the trial court must be advised of the conflict. The trial court must conduct a hearing subsequent to the testimony of the expert witness and determine the reasonable fee to be paid to the expert witness. 735 ILCS 5/2-1101.

The Uniform Act to Secure the Attendance of Witnesses from Within or Without a State in Criminal Proceedings is in effect in Illinois. 725 ILCS 220/1 to 220/6. The Act, which deals with compelling the attendance of witnesses residing in another state at trial in Illinois and vice versa, has been held to apply only to material witnesses. *People v. Nash*, 36 Ill. 2d 275, N.E.2d 473 (1966). Both the court in Illinois and the court in the country where the witness is found must review the facts presented and determine whether the witness must be compelled to travel and testify. A witness will be so compelled, i.e., is material, only if both courts make the qualitative judgment that the witness's testimony is necessary to the proceeding. *People v. Burt*, 168 Ill. 2d 49, 212 Ill. Dec. 893, 658 N.E.2d 375 (1995). Its validity was sustained in *New York v. O'Neill*, 359 U.S. 1 (1959), against attack on federal grounds.

For writ of *habeas corpus ad testificandum* to procure the attendance of a prisoner whose testimony is desired, *see* 735 ILCS 5/10-135 and 5/10-136.

Illinois Supreme Court Rule 237(b) provides that upon service of only a notice, a party or person who at the time of the trial is an officer, director, or employee of a party may be compelled to appear at trial, thus eliminating the necessity of serving a subpoena and the tendering of fees and mileage. If the party or person designated is a nonresident of the county, the court may order the payment of reasonable expenses in connection with the court appearance. Failure of a nonresident party to appear following service of notice may be excused in the discretion of the court. *O'Brien v. Walker*, 49 Ill. App. 3d 940, 7 Ill. Dec. 372, 364 N.E.2d 533 (1977).

With respect to compelling the appearance of expert witnesses at trial, *see* §702.3 infra; to attendance of witnesses at depositions, *see* Illinois Supreme Court Rule 204. If a party wishes to depose an expert, Illinois Supreme Court Rule 203, in conjunction with Rule 204, unless otherwise agreed, permits the taking of the deposition only in the county where the expert resides, is employed, or transacts business. The statutory mileage and *per diem* fees *are* applicable. *Lee v. Hyster Co.,* 156 Ill. App. 3d, 108 Ill. Dec. 890, 509 N.E.2d 586 (1987).

With respect to exclusion and separation of witnesses, *see* §615.1 infra.

§611.7   Production of Exhibits at Trial

The subpoena *duces tecum* may be employed to compel witnesses to attend trial and bring with them books, documents, and other exhibits for use in evidence. Pursuant to Supreme Court Rule 237(b), the same result may be obtained from a party by means of a notice to produce.

With respect to issuance of a subpoena *duces tecum* in civil cases, by specific statutory provision no court order is required for issuance of the writ. 735 ILCS 5/2-1101. In criminal cases the practice reflected in the cases is to obtain an order. The reason for this difference is not apparent, as the person to whom the writ is directed can in any case protect himself against an improper writ by motion to quash, vacate, or amend. The statute in criminal cases, 725 ILCS 125/7, empowers the clerk to issue subpoenas without restriction as to kind and could well be construed to include subpoenas *duces tecum.*

If the witness chooses to disobey the writ and to test its validity in contempt proceedings, she incurs the risk of punishment only if it is held valid; if the subpoena is found part good and part bad the witness may not be held in contempt. *People v. Lurie,* 39 Ill. 2d 331, 235 N.E.2d 637 (1968).

A subpoena *duces tecum* must not be so broad in its demands and general in its terms as to amount to an unreasonable search and seizure. The items demanded ought to be described with sufficient particularity to enable compliance without unnecessary hardship. *Larson v. Commonwealth Edison Co.,* 33 Ill. 2d 316, 211 N.E.2d 247 (1965), request for plans, progress reports, etc., concerning construction and alteration on Units 7 and 8 of an electric generating plant and the barrier wall between was sufficiently definite. The permissible number of items and the time interval covered by them is measured by the scope of the problem under investigation and the nature of the inquiry. *People v. Allen,* 410 Ill. 508, 103 N.E.2d 92 (1952), grand jury investigation of gambling conspiracy. Items requested by subpoena *duces tecum* for production at trial must be relevant; irrelevant items requested may be deleted upon preliminary inspection by the court. *People v. Hartgraves,* 31 Ill. 2d 375, 202 N.E.2d 33 (1964).

Also available is a court order for a party in civil cases to produce books or writings in his possession, 735 ILCS 5/8-402, subject to the same limitations mentioned in the preceding paragraph. *Red Star Laboratories Co. v. Pabst,* 359 Ill. 451, 194 N.E. 734 (1935). This statutory provision, enacted as a companion piece to abolition of the privilege of a party not to testify, should be regarded as generally doing away with the common law privilege of a party not to produce documents in his possession, extending to subpoenas *duces tecum* as well as to orders thereunder. 8 Wigmore, Evidence §2219 (McNaughton rev. 1961).

With respect to a notice to produce, Illinois Supreme Court Rule 237(b) provides that upon notice, a party or an officer, director, or employee of a party may be required to appear at trial and produce documents or tangible things. *Cox v. Yellow Cab Co,* 16 Ill. App. 3d 665, 306 N.E.2d 738 (1974), statement of former employee in possession of employer properly sought by notice directed to employer. If a party fails to comply with the notice, an order may be entered providing for sanctions authorized in Rule 219(c).

Documents or tangible things requested to be produced at trial by means of any of the foregoing procedures do not thereby become admissible on behalf of the producing party. The document or tangible thing so requested is admissible solely if admissible without reference to the request. *Scully v. Morrison Hotel Corp.,* 118 Ill. App. 2d 254, 254 N.E.2d 852 (1969).

Police reports are subject to a subpoena *duces tecum* served on behalf of the criminal defendant prior to a preliminary hearing but subsequent to charging of the accused, i.e., when it becomes clear with what offenses an accused will be finally charged. Such subpoenaed material must be sent directly to the court, which then determines the relevance of the materials produced, whether they are subject to a claim of privilege, and whether the subpoena is unreasonable or oppressive. *People ex rel. Fisher v. Carey,* 77 Ill. 2d 259, 32 Ill. Dec. 904, 396 N.E.2d 17 (1979).

See also §612.1 infra, relating to documents used to refresh recollection.

§611.8   Form of Testimony on Direct: Viva Voce and Affidavit

The ordinary mode of introducing evidence on disputed issues at trial is by answers of a witness in open court in response to nonleading questions by counsel. This method tends to keep the witness within the bounds of relevancy and the exclusionary rules of evidence and is designed to afford opportunity to object to inadmissible evidence before it is given. A straight narrative by the witness, on the other hand, possesses the advantages of naturalness and freedom from interruption. The extent to which testimony tends to fall in one pattern or the other depends largely on the extent to which questions are specific or general, a matter much within the discretion of the trial judge. *Chicago, R.I. & P.R. Co. v. Bell,* 70 Ill. 102 (1873); *Mayville v. French,* 246 Ill. 434, 92 N.E. 919 (1910). This discretion sensibly permits the adoption of a course best suited to the characteristics of the particular witness.

With respect to leading questions, *see* §611.9 infra; as to narrative questions, *see* §611.20 infra.

In many preliminary stages prior to trial not involving the resolution of a disputed issue going to the merits of the case, the procedure either by statute or by established practice is to supply evidence by affidavit. Illustrative of the many instances of this practice are motions for continuance under

Supreme Court Rule 231; motions for summary judgment, 735 ILCS 5/2-1005; motions for involuntary dismissal, 735 ILCS 5/2-619; special appearances to contest jurisdiction, 735 ILCS 5/2-301; applications for change of venue, 735 ILCS 5/2-1001(b); showing basis for questioning prospective jurors on *voir dire* examination, *Wheeler v. Rudek,* 397 Ill. 438, 74 N.E.2d 601 (1947); and establishing unavailability as a prerequisite to admissibility under a hearsay exception, *Curt Bullock Builders v. H.S.S. Development, Inc.,* 261 Ill. App. 3d 178, 199 Ill. Dec. 698, 634 N.E.2d 751 (1994) (quoting Handbook). With respect to the content of such affidavits relating to motions under the Code of Civil Procedure, *see* Supreme Court Rule 191. In addition, the Code of Civil Procedure provides that the trial judge may, except in applications for change of venue on grounds of prejudice, require evidence to be given in the form of testimony by witnesses in lieu of affidavit. 735 ILCS 5/2-1103.

§611.9 Trial Objection: Leading Questions; Direct and Redirect Examination

There is general agreement that asking leading questions of one's own witness is improper. *People v. Cobb,* 186 Ill. App. 3d 898, 134 Ill. Dec. 664, 542 N.E.2d 1171 (1989). The vice lies in substituting the suggestions of counsel for the actual testimony of the witness. "The test of a leading question is whether it suggests the answer thereto by putting into the mind of the witness the words or thought of such answer." *People v. Schladweiler,* 315 Ill. 553, 556, 146 N.E. 525 (1925). Examples of leading questions are found in *Cannon v. People,* 141 Ill. 270, 30 N.E. 1027 (1892), in which after witness testified, "All I heard him say was, 'Keep still,' " the question was asked, "Did you hear him say, 'Don't?' "; and in *Ogren v. Rockford Star Printing Co.,* 288 Ill. 405, 123 N.E. 587 (1919), in which witness was handed newspaper report of meeting at which plaintiff spoke and asked if plaintiff spoke those words. A question may be leading because of its form, e.g., "Didn't he . . . ?", its detail, the examiner's emphasis on certain words, the tone used by the examiner in asking the whole question, or by the examiner's nonverbal conduct. Generally, questions that may be answered either "Yes" or "No" are considered leading, but not always. The question, "Did you see what happened?", is not leading. Merely using the term "whether or not," or another form of alternative, does not of itself keep a question from being leading. *Peebles v. O'Gara Coal Co.,* 239 Ill. 370, 88 N.E. 166 (1909). On the other hand, a witness can scarcely be examined without calling attention to the subject matter on which her testimony is sought, and a question so doing is not considered leading. *People v. Elliott,* 272 Ill. 592, 112 N.E. 300 (1916); *Swartwout v. Evans,* 41 Ill. 376 (1866). Thus the determination of whether a question is leading is often difficult and obviously does not by and large offer a profitable area of appellate review. *Peebles v. O'Gara Coal Co.* supra; *People v. Hirschmann,* 175 Ill. App. 3d 150, 124 Ill. Dec. 779, 529 N.E.2d 760 (1988).

Whether leading is harmful depends on the circumstances, including the nature of the witness and the context within which the question is asked. For example, leading may be necessary if any testimony at all is to be elicited from an unwilling witness or from a witness whose recollection is exhausted. Hence the propriety of questions that are admittedly leading is peculiarly within the competency of the trial judge and largely entrusted to his discretion. *Maguire v. People,* 219 Ill. 16, 76 N.E. 67 (1905). Reversal of a judgment on appeal requires a finding that the trial court abused its discretion and that such abuse resulted in substantial injury to the litigant. *People v. Luigs,* 96 Ill. App. 3d 700, 52 Ill. Dec. 98, 421 N.E.2d 961 (1981). Reversals for abuse of this discretion are rare. 3 Wigmore, Evidence §770 (Chadbourn rev. 1970).

Sustaining an objection to a leading question may be more or less an empty gesture. Effective enforcement requires foreclosing all further inquiry into the subject, or permitting counsel to return to it only after an exploration of other matters has reduced the effect of the communication of the answer to the witness. These measures are available to the trial judge. 3 Wigmore, Evidence §770 (Chadbourn rev. 1970). The fact that they are seldom invoked may well lead to the conclusion that the rule against leading questions is lacking in true substance and operates merely to create a false sense of spontaneity that the examiner might otherwise destroy by use of leading questions. *See* Cleary, Evidence as a Problem in Communicating, 5 Vand. L. Rev. 277, 287 (1952). Counsel generally refrain from propounding leading questions on direct examination not only because of the desire to avoid having opposing counsel's objections sustained before the jury but also from a desire to enhance the witness's persuasiveness by having the witness testify in a natural manner in response to nonleading questions.

Leading questions of one's own witness are recognized as proper in the following particular situations:

(1)   Undisputed preliminary or inconsequential matters. *Cannon v. People* supra. Leading questions focus the witness's attention upon a topic; leading upon a point about which no controversy exists is harmless and saves time.

(2)   A witness who is hostile or unwilling. *See* Supreme Court Rule 238(b); *People v. Gallery,* 336 Ill. 580, 168 N.E. 650 (1929). Thus a witness who demonstrates recalcitrance by giving damaging testimony, or by answering unsurely or reluctantly, i.e., a witness hostile in fact, may be led. *Jensen v. Chicago & W. Indiana R. Co.,* 94 Ill. App. 3d 915, 50 Ill. Dec. 470, 419 N.E.2d 578 (1981). However, the fact of giving damaging answers in the absence of recalcitrance does not permit counsel to lead. *See Martin v. Brennan,* 54 Ill. App. 3d 421, 12 Ill. Dec. 104, 369 N.E.2d 601 (1977); *Curtis v. Goldenstein,* 125 Ill. App. 3d 562, 80 Ill. Dec. 730, 465 N.E.2d 1367 (1984). An unwilling witness is one who shows himself or herself by demeanor or testimony to be reticent, deceptive, evasive, or uncooperative. Whether an ordinary witness is hostile or unwilling should be determined *after*

the witness has taken the stand and responded to questions. *Uhr v. Lutheran General Hospital,* 226 Ill. App. 3d 236, 168 Ill. Dec. 323, 589 N.E.2d 723 (1992); *Mazzone v. Holmes,* 197 Ill. App. 3d 886, 145 Ill. Dec. 416, 557 N.E.2d 186 (1990). *Accord Zajac v. St. Mary of Nazareth Hosp.,* 212 Ill. App. 3d 779, 156 Ill. Dec. 860, 571 N.E.2d 840 (1991), Rule 238 only applies to witnesses who prove hostile or unwilling *while on the witness stand* (emphasis in original). *See also* infra as to a witness hostile in law.

(3)   A witness who is frightened, nervous, or upset while testifying, frequently a child sexual assault victim. *People v. Luigs,* 96 Ill. App. 3d 700, 52 Ill. Dec. 98, 421 N.E.2d 961 (1981), question to a 12-year-old rape victim, "When you say he entered you, do you mean his penis entered?" was a proper question to clarify her testimony; *People v. Spencer,* 119 Ill. App. 3d 971, 75 Ill. Dec. 479, 457 N.E.2d 473 (1983), a witness who cannot speak may be examined using leading questions. *See also People v. Ridgeway,* 194 Ill. App. 3d 881, 141 Ill. Dec. 603, 551 N.E.2d 790 (1990); *People v. C.H.,* 237 Ill. App. 3d 462, 177 Ill. Dec. 906, 603 N.E.2d 1280 (1992) (citing Handbook).

(4)   A witness whose recollection is exhausted. *See* infra. *See also* §607.4 supra and §612.1 infra.

(5)   In impeaching a party's own witness when permitted. *See* §607.4 supra as to when such impeachment is permitted.

(6)   A child witness or an adult with communication problems, either physical or mental.

Some witnesses are automatically considered hostile so that leading questions are permitted without a prior in-court showing that leading questions are in fact necessary for the orderly development of the witness's testimony. Code of Civil Procedure 5/2-1102, 735 ILCS 5/2-1102, discussed in §607.4 supra, defines hostile in law witnesses to include "any [adverse] party . . . or any person for whose immediate benefit the action is prosecuted or defended, or the officers, directors, managing agents, or foreman of any party to the action. . . ." The category of witnesses considered sufficiently adverse under 5/2-1102 includes a defendant called by a codefendant in an action alleging independent negligent conduct by each. *Fornoff v. Parke Davis & Co.*, 105 Ill. App. 3d 681, 61 Ill. Dec. 438, 434 N.E.2d 793 (1982). Whether a witness is to be considered automatically hostile is determined as of the time of her examination. *Bituminous Cas. Corp. v. Harrisburg*, 315 Ill. App. 243, 42 N.E.2d 971 (1942); *Hildebrand v. Franklin Life Ins. Co.*, 118 Ill. App. 3d 861, 74 Ill. Dec. 280, 455 N.E.2d 553 (1983). For further discussion of leading questions to hostile in fact and hostile in law witnesses *see* Graham, Examination of a Party's Own Witness Under the Federal Rules of Evidence: A Promise Unfulfilled, 54 Tex. L. Rev. 917 (1976) and §607.4 supra.

A party may refresh the recollection of a witness by either a leading question or by showing a writing to the witness. Thus a witness who testifies that he cannot recall anything else discussed during a particular conversation may either (1) be asked the leading question "Do you recall whether you discussed the acquisition of XYZ Company?" or (2) be shown a document that might refresh his recollection regarding any discussion concerning the acquisition of XYZ Company, and then be questioned once again whether he recalls anything else discussed during the conversation. To the extent *People v. Shatner*, 174 Ill. 2d 133, 220 Ill. Dec. 346, 673 N.E.2d 258 (1996), indicates that the response "I don't remember telling her" is an inadequate foundation in that it fails to sufficiently establish that memory was exhausted so as to permit refreshing recollection, the decision should not be followed as the purpose of the follow-up leading question or the showing of a document to the witness in the attempt to refresh recollection is in fact to determine if the witness has no recollection, i.e., recollection is exhausted, or in the alternative that the witness's recollection can be refreshed, i.e., recollection was not exhausted. *See also* §803.9 dealing with recorded recollection.

If the witness states that his recollection has been refreshed, the witness may testify as to what it is he then recalls. With respect to documents used to refresh recollection, *see also* §612.1 infra; as to refreshing recollection on cross-examination, *see* §611.11 infra.

Many courts allow the party to seek to refresh the recollection of a witness only if the witness testifies that her recollection is exhausted and that she cannot recall the matter forming the subject of the inquiry. Thus if a witness replies in an absolute fashion that nothing else happened, there is authority for the proposition that refreshment of recollection is not permissible. Other decisions, however, reach the sensible position that refreshing recollection is proper even if the witness gives a definite albeit unanticipated answer. McCormick, Evidence §9 at 34 (4th ed. 1992). Counsel can sometimes avoid having to face the issue by incorporating lack of recollection in the question asked, such as, "Do you recall whether anything else was said?" Where such a question would be inconvenient as a matter of form, counsel must fall back on a general instruction to the witness to respond to questions such as, "Was anyone else present?" with the answer, "I don't recall."

The process of refreshing recollection must be conducted so as to prevent inadmissible evidence from being suggested to the jury by any means. *See* §103.9 supra. *See also Reed v. Northwestern Publishing Co.*, 124 Ill. 2d 495, 125 Ill. Dec. 316, 530 N.E.2d 474 (1988). *See also Pruett v. Norfolk and Western Railway Co.*, 261 Ill. App. 3d 29, 198 Ill. Dec. 322, 632 N.E.2d 652 (1994), leading questions in open court to refresh recollection on cross-examination disclosing privileged information properly prohibited. When refreshment of recollection is through a writing, this mandate is accomplished easily by counsel handing the writing to the witness accompanied by a request to the witness to read the writing to himself. The witness is then asked whether his recollection has been refreshed. If the answer is yes, counsel repeats the initial question. If the witness, however, states that his recollection has not been refreshed, it is improper for counsel to read the writing aloud before the trier of fact.

When refreshing recollection is by means of a leading question, counsel may not employ a leading question incorporating the content of the anticipated testimony before the trier of fact if the matter under consideration is of significance in the litigation. For example, when the prosecution seeks to refresh the recollection of a witness it has called regarding a statement bearing directly on the guilt of the defendant, the prosecutor may not use the substance of the statement in her question. Accordingly a question such as, "Didn't the defendant tell you, on July 4 at the Ace Bar and Grill, that he shot Mary Jane?" propounded in open court to refresh recollection, is objectionable. The proper procedure is either to reduce the oral statement to writing and proceed as set out above or to excuse the jury and attempt to refresh the witness's recollection by means of the leading question. Only if the witness states that his recollection has been refreshed may the witness be once again asked what the defendant said to him during their conversation on July 4. On the other hand, when the witness cannot recall a preliminary or relatively unimportant matter, such as which direction Main Street runs, a leading question in open court incorporating the answer may be employed. Similarly, leading questions are also proper to refresh recollection that suggest that something else may have occurred, without directly stating the substance of the occurrence. Thus, following the answer, "Not that I now recall" to the question, "Was anything else said?", the question, "Was anything said concerning the proposed Acme merger?" is proper.

With respect to redirect examination, leading questions may be necessary in order to focus the witness's attention upon the subject matter on which his testimony is desired. *Cruz v. Gulf M. & O. Ry.*, 7 Ill. App. 2d 209, 129 N.E.2d 272 (1955). The court possesses similar discretion in permitting leading questions in the eliciting of rebuttal testimony for the same reason. *People v. Taylor*, 132 Ill. App. 2d 473, 270 N.E.2d 628 (1971).

For a discussion of leading questions upon cross-examination, *see* §611.10 infra.

Nonleading questions do not suggest the desired response to the witness. Specific nonleading questions such as, "How many lanes of traffic are there on Main Street at the point of the accident?" tend to keep the witness within the bounds of relevancy and admissibility. They also allow the opponent an opportunity to object to inadmissible evidence before it is given. A narrative answer in response to a general nonleading question, such as, "Please tell the jury what you observed at the time of the robbery," possesses the advantages of naturalness and freedom from interruption. The extent to which testimony tends to be confined or free-flowing depends largely on the extent to which the nonleading question is specific or general, a matter largely left to the discretion of the examining attorney and, if an objection is made, the trial judge. This discretion sensibly permits the adoption of a course best suited to the particular witness's characteristics, considered in light of testimony to be given in the context of the litigation. In either case, the testimony is that of the witness, not a mere assent to the suggestion of the attorney who called the witness to the stand.

§611.10 Cross-Examination: An Overview

Cross-examination is a matter of right, *People v. Crawford,* 23 Ill. 2d 605, 179 N.E.2d 667 (1962); *People v. Del Prete,* 364 Ill. 376, 4 N.E.2d 484 (1936), and constitutes an important aspect of due process, *People ex rel. Bernat v. Bicek,* 405 Ill. 510, 91 N.E.2d 588 (1950); *Kurrack v. American District Telegraph Co.,* 252 Ill. App. 3d 885, 192 Ill. Dec. 520, 625 N.E.2d 675 (1993) (citing Handbook). The right of the criminal defendant to conduct cross-examination is protected by the confrontation clause. *Lee v. Illinois,* 476 U.S. 530 (1986). The right is not, however, without qualifications. For example, if the witness dies before the right to cross-examine can be exercised, it has been held that his testimony on direct should nevertheless be allowed to stand, in view of the possibility of attacking it by other evidence. *Bruner v. Battell,* 83 Ill.

317 (1876). A preferable approach is to allow the testimony to stand in the absence of a showing that loss of cross-examination has resulted in actual injury. *See Kubin v. Chicago Title & Trust Co.,* 307 Ill. App. 12, 29 N.E.2d 859 (1940). With respect to cross-examination on statements admitted pursuant to a hearsay exception, *see* §806.

Leading questions are permitted on cross-examination; the reasons for objecting to leading questions when propounded to one's own witness generally do not apply. *See* §611.9 supra; *In re Mitgang,* 385 Ill. 311, 52 N.E.2d 807 (1944). However, if the witness is partial to the cross-examining party, there is the same danger in leading questions as on direct, and the court has discretion to prohibit their use. One circumstance in which a prohibition upon the use of leading questions on cross-examination will usually be appropriate is where the witness was called by an opponent and automatically regarded and treated as hostile pursuant to 5/2-1102 of the Code of Civil Procedure, 735 ILCS 5/2-1102, on direct examination, and then cross-examined by her own or other friendly counsel. *Fornoff v. Parke Davis & Co.,* 105 Ill. App. 3d 681, 61 Ill. Dec. 438, 434 N.E.2d 793 (1982). For further discussion *see* §607.4 supra.

The term *cross-examination* in common parlance refers to the right to lead a witness and to employ modes of impeachment, such as prior conviction, partiality, and prior inconsistent statement, in an attempt to "destroy" the testimony of the witness. While the cross-examination of a particular witness may well be destructive in nature, as the examining counsel employs leading questions and modes of impeachment in an attempt to minimize the trier of fact's assessment of the weight to be accorded the witness's testimony given during direct examination by discrediting the witness or his testimony, cross-examination is in fact much more. Counsel on cross-examination may (1) attempt to elicit disputed facts from the witness favorable to his case, (2) have the witness repeat those facts testified to on direct favorable to the cross-examiner, (3) have the witness testify to nondisputed facts essential to presentation of his theory of the case, (4) attempt to have the witness qualify or modify his testimony with respect to unfavorable versions of disputed facts given on direct examination, (5) establish that the witness's testimony is not harmful to the advocate's case on the critical points under dispute, and/or (6) ask questions to the witness designed primarily to keep the cross-examiner's theory of the case before the trier of fact. Whether the cross-examiner chooses to attempt to elicit favorable facts from a witness called by an opponent, ask questions designed to discredit the witness or his testimony, or possibly both, depends upon various factors including the importance of the testimony of the witness in the context of the litigation considered in light of the realistic possibilities for a successful destructive cross-examination given the ammunition available. Cross-examination is also sometimes much less. It is less in that on cross-examination leading questions are sometimes prohibited and certain kinds of impeachment will not always be allowed.

§611.11   Scope of Cross-Examination

The scope of cross-examination is limited to the subject matter of direct examination and matters affecting the credibility of the witness. *People v. Van Dyke,* 414 Ill. 251, 111 N.E.2d 165 (1953); *Stafford v. Fargo,* 35 Ill. 481 (1864); *People v. Hosty,* 146 Ill. App. 3d 876, 100 Ill. Dec. 356, 497 N.E.2d 334 (1986) (citing Handbook). The limited scope of the cross-examination rule serves to preserve the usual order of proof on plaintiff's case in chief. *Cuellar v. Hout,* 168 Ill. App. 3d 416, 118 Ill. Dec. 867, 522 N.E.2d 322 (1988), cross-examination beyond the scope of direct examination designed to place the party's theory of the case before the jury is improper. *See also* §611.3 supra. The limitation to the scope of direct examination is, however, construed liberally to allow inquiry into whatever tends to explain, qualify, modify, discredit, or destroy the testimony on direct, *People v. Gacho,* 122 Ill. 2d 221, 119 Ill. Dec. 287, 522 N.E.2d 1146 (1988); *People v. Williams,* 66 Ill. 2d 478, 6 Ill. Dec. 854, 363 N.E.2d

801 (1977); *People v. Aughinbaugh,* 36 Ill. 2d 320, 223 N.E.2d 117 (1967); *People v. Gordon,* 247 Ill. App. 3d 891, 187 Ill. Dec. 245, 617 N.E.2d 453 (1993), as well as inferences therefrom, *Crosby v. De Land Special Drainage Dist.,* 367 Ill. 462, 11 N.E.2d 937 (1937), even if the inquiry may incidentally constitute new matter that aids the cross-examiner's case. *People v. Enis,* 139 Ill. 2d 264, 151 Ill. Dec. 493, 564 N.E.2d 1155 (1990); *People v. Williams,* supra; *People v. Winston,* 106 Ill. App. 3d 673, 62 Ill. Dec. 355, 435 N.E.2d 1327 (1982). *Accord Bell v. Hill,* 271 Ill. App. 3d 224, 207 Ill. Dec. 714, 648 N.E.2d 170 (1995), scope of cross-examination is not limited to actual material discussed during direct examination but to the subject matter of direct examination. To illustrate, a witness in a will contest who testifies that testator was incompetent may on cross-examination be asked concerning business dealings between witness and testator, *Roe v. Taylor,* 45 Ill. 485 (1867), while one who testifies only to a single transaction with testator cannot be asked as to testator's falling into uncontrollable rages, *Larabee v. Larabee,* 240 Ill. 576, 88 N.E. 1037 (1909); a defendant who testifies that he went to Alabama to help a sick relative may be cross-examined as to whether he was out on bond and forfeited the bond by failing to return, *People v. Wallace,* 114 Ill. App. 3d 242, 70 Ill. Dec. 32, 448 N.E.2d 910 (1983); a doctor testifying to what he found during an autopsy may be cross-examined as to what he did not find, *Kurrack v. American District Telegraph Co.,* 252 Ill. App. 3d 885, 192 Ill. Dec. 520, 625 N.E.2d 675 (1993). Questions designed solely to humiliate or harass a witness are improper. *People v. Sparkman,* 68 Ill. App. 3d 865, 25 Ill. Dec. 75, 386 N.E.2d 346 (1979). Of course, questions inquiring of irrelevant matters are improper. *People v. Harris,* 182 Ill. 2d 114, 230 Ill. Dec. 957, 695 N.E.2d 447 (1998); *People v. Sandoval,* 135 Ill. 2d 159, 142 Ill. Dec. 135, 552 N.E.2d 726 (1990).

Inquiry is, of course, permitted on cross-examination into matters affecting the credibility of the witness. *Bailey v. Beall,* 251 Ill. 577, 96 N.E. 567 (1911), error to foreclose inquiry into interest of attorney who appeared as witness; *People v. Davis,* 70 Ill. App. 3d 454, 26 Ill. Dec. 886, 388 N.E.2d 887

(1979), error to foreclose inquiry as to whether witness had reported accident the day it occurred; *People v. Outlaw,* 75 Ill. App. 3d 626, 31 Ill. Dec. 339, 394 N.E.2d 541 (1979), proper to cross-examine alibi witness concerning surrounding circumstances and whether witness had ever told the same story previously; *Selby v. Danville Pepsi-Cola Bottling,* 169 Ill. App. 3d 427, 119 Ill. Dec. 941, 523 N.E.2d 697 (1988), proper to permit cross-examination into matters showing bias of an expert. The widest latitude should be allowed the criminal defendant in cross-examination designed to establish bias. *People v. Barr,* 51 Ill. 2d 50, 280 N.E.2d 708 (1972). Failure to provide sufficient latitude to the criminal defendant to cross-examine constitutes a denial of the constitutional right to confront witnesses. *People v. Maldonado,* 193 Ill. App. 3d 1062, 140 Ill. Dec. 886, 550 N.E.2d 1011 (1989). As to impeachment generally, *see* §§607, 608, and 609 supra. The defendant who takes the stand and testifies in his own behalf in a criminal case thereby subjects himself to such cross-examination. *People v. Burris,* 49 Ill. 2d 98, 273 N.E.2d 605 (1971).

The fact that the scope of cross-examination as thus defined is not susceptible to being determined with exactness, *People v. Jones,* 174 Ill. App. 3d 737, 124 Ill. Dec. 255, 528 N.E.2d 1363 (1988) (citing Handbook), together with the practical necessity of curbing interminable and pointless inquiries, *Spring Valley v. Gavin,* 182 Ill. 232, 54 N.E. 1035 (1899), and to preclude repetitive or unduly harassing questioning, *People v. Frieberg,* 147 Ill. 2d 326, 168 Ill. Dec. 108, 589 N.E.2d 508 (1992); *People v. Bunch,* 159 Ill. App. 3d 494, 111 Ill. Dec. 359, 512 N.E.2d 748 (1987), combine to make reviewing courts reluctant to disturb decisions of trial judges, absent a clear showing of abuse of discretion resulting in manifest prejudice to a party. *People v. Frieberg* supra; *People v. Coles,* 74 Ill. 2d 393, 24 Ill. Dec. 553, 385 N.E.2d 694 (1979); *People v. McKinney,* 260 Ill. App. 3d 539, 197 Ill. Dec. 822, 631 N.E.2d 1281 (1994); *Kurrack v. American District Telegraph Co.,* 252 Ill. App. 3d 885, 192 Ill. Dec. 520, 625 N.E.2d 675 (1993) (citing Handbook); *People v. Hurley,* 62 Ill. App. 3d 243, 19 Ill. Dec. 569, 379 N.E.2d 84 (1978). However, if actual harm is apparent or likely, a reversal may be had. *Muscarello v. Peterson,* 20 Ill. 2d 548, 170 N.E.2d 564 (1960), error to deny questioning designed to develop prior statements inconsistent with answer to hypothetical question on direct; *Tenenbaum v. City of Chicago,* 60 Ill. 2d 363, 325 N.E.2d 607 (1975), error to prohibit cross-examination as to statements made in deposition and on the source of plaintiff's refreshed recollection; *Babcock v. Chesapeake & Ohio R. Co.,* 83 Ill. App. 3d 919, 38 Ill. Dec. 841, 404 N.E.2d 265 (1979), error to foreclose inquiry of plaintiff as to knowledge and notice bearing on question of contributory negligence; *People v. Coleman,* 205 Ill. App. 3d 567, 150 Ill. Dec. 883, 563 N.E.2d 1010 (1990), error to preclude cross-examination of the alleged child victim of sexual abuse concerning prior inconsistent statements that no abuse occurred and that someone other than the defendant did it. Complaints that cross-examination exceeded the scope of direct are usually disposed of by saying the matter is largely within the discretion of the trial judge, *People v. Provo,* 409 Ill. 63, 97 N.E.2d 802 (1951), unless cross-examination is used to bring out or emphasize evidence that is inadmissible on other grounds. *People v. Smith,* 413 Ill. 218, 108 N.E.2d 596 (1952), error to cross-examine accused as to ammunition not shown to be connected with murder; *People v. King,* 276 Ill. 138, 114 N.E. 601 (1916), error to cross-examine witness for accused as to other crimes. *See also Champion v. Knasiak,* 25 Ill. App. 3d 192, 323 N.E.2d 62 (1974), error to require witness to comment on asserted inconsistencies between his testimony and that of another witness; *Ryan v. Monson,* 33 Ill. App. 2d 406, 179 N.E.2d 449 (1961), error to ask witness whether other witness's testimony was true or false; *People v. Coleman,* 222 Ill. App. 3d 614, 165 Ill. Dec. 151, 584 N.E.2d 330 (1991), not error to prohibit inquiry as to complainant's knowledge of the progress of the case or the nature of her communications with the state's attorney's office.

With respect to cross-examination as to a proper subject matter, the extent of cross-examination is subject to the broad discretion of the trial court. *People v. Kellas,* 72 Ill. App. 3d 445, 28 Ill. Dec. 9, 389 N.E.2d 1382 (1979). Unduly harassing, embarrassing or repetitive cross-examination of a witness is subject to similar control by the court. *People v. Thompson*, 75 Ill. App. 3d 901, 31 Ill. Dec. 220, 394 N.E.2d 422 (1979). Broad discretion also exists in the court with respect to whether to recall a witness for the purpose of further cross-examination. *Chew v. Graham*, 122 Ill. App. 3d 461, 77 Ill. Dec. 951, 461 N.E.2d 574 (1984).

As to cross-examination of expert witnesses, *see* §705.2 infra; as to the scope of rebuttal, *see* §611.3 supra. When a witness's recollection is refreshed on cross-examination, the procedures employed in refreshing recollection on direct examination must be followed. *See* §611.9 supra and §612.1 infra. *See also People v. Shatner*, 174 Ill. 2d 133, 220 Ill. Dec. 346, 673 N.E.2d 258 (1996); *Reed v. Northwestern Publishing Co.*, 124 Ill. 2d 495, 125 Ill. Dec. 316, 530 N.E.2d 474 (1988).

Cross-examination of a party may in the court's discretion be permitted to exceed the scope of direct examination, in which case inquiry should be conducted as if on direct examination. McCormick, Evidence §25 (4th ed. 1992). Thus leading questions would not be permitted, §611.9 infra, and impeachment, including by inconsistent statement, would be only as described in §607.4 supra. Under such circumstances, the party originally calling the witness may then proceed to cross-examine the witness with respect to those matters raised beyond the scope of direct. *Joseph v. Peoria & P.U. Ry.*, 265 Ill. 563, 107 N.E. 141 (1914).

Use of the scope of testimony voluntarily given as a measurement of the extent of waiver of the privilege against self-incrimination is discussed in §502.5 supra; the scope of cross-examination of an accused testifying as to a preliminary matter is discussed in §104.4 supra. With respect to the components of credibility, *see* §§607.1 to 607.9 supra.

§611.12   *Redirect Examination; Recross-Examination*

The function of redirect is to meet new factual aspects or impeaching matter brought out on cross-examination. The witness may be asked questions designed to explain apparent inconsistencies between statements made on direct and cross-examination, *Dietz v. Big Muddy Coal & Iron Co.,* 263 Ill. 480, 105 N.E. 289 (1914); to explain the making of an alleged prior inconsistent statement, §613.3 infra, *People v. Hicks,* 28 Ill. 2d 457, 192 N.E.2d 891 (1963); *People v. McMullen,* 82 Ill. App. 3d 1042, 38 Ill. Dec. 308, 403 N.E.2d 539 (1980); *People v. Hanson,* 83 Ill. App. 3d 1108, 39 Ill. Dec. 210, 404 N.E.2d 801 (1980), even if the witness fails to specifically recall the prior statement, *Senase v. John,* 96 Ill. App. 3d 164, 51 Ill. Dec. 546, 420 N.E.2d 1104 (1981); to correct inadvertent mistakes made on cross-examination, *People v. Washington,* 327 Ill. 152, 158 N.E. 386 (1927); to bring out circumstances repelling unfavorable inferences raised on cross-examination, *Wilson v. People,* 94 Ill. 299 (1880); *People v. Davis,* 92 Ill. App. 3d 426, 48 Ill. Dec. 174, 416 N.E.2d 69 (1981), such as, for example, bringing out the reason and content of an argument referred to generally upon cross-examination, *People v. Miller,* 58 Ill. App. 3d 156, 15 Ill. Dec. 605, 373 N.E.2d 1077 (1978), or bringing out why the witness had not referred to the defendant in his earlier statement, *People v. Coleman,* 223 Ill. App. 3d 975, 166 Ill. Dec. 312, 586 N.E.2d 270 (1992); or asserting that his testimony on direct was not a lie to help a friend, *People v. Tingle,* 279 Ill. App. 3d 706, 216 Ill. Dec. 323, 665 N.E.2d 383 (1996); to elicit an explanation showing why the witness recalls a particular event, *People v. Puente,* 98 Ill. App. 3d 936, 54 Ill. Dec. 25, 424 N.E.2d 775 (1981); to bring out prior consistent statements, §611.13 infra; to bring out information tending to lessen the effect of cross-examination establishing bias, *People v. Lewis,* 97 Ill. App. 3d 982, 53 Ill. Dec. 353, 423 N.E.2d 1157 (1981); to rebut an inference of recent fabrication by explaining the delay in coming forward with the information, *People v. Groleau,* 156 Ill. App. 3d 742, 109 Ill. Dec. 325, 509 N.E.2d 1337 (1987); to remove or correct unfavorable inferences as to the credibility of a witness left by the preceding cross-examination, *People v. Thompkins,* 121 Ill. 2d 401, 117 Ill. Dec. 927, 521 N.E.2d 38 (1988); to bring out other relevant aspects of a transaction, *Morton v. Zwierzykowski*, 192 Ill. 328, 61 N.E. 413 (1901), such as to present the fact of a citizen complaint in response to a suggestion by the defendant of fabrication by the police of the charge in order to conclude an unproductive investigation, *People v. Marino*, 80 Ill. App. 3d 657, 36 Ill. Dec. 71, 400 N.E.2d 491 (1980), or within the limits stated in §106.2 supra, of a conversation or document brought out in part on cross-examination. *Chicago City Ry. v. Lowitz*, 218 Ill. 24, 75 N.E. 755 (1905); *Darling v. Charleston Community Memorial Hosp.*, 50 Ill. App. 2d 253, 200 N.E.2d 149 (1964); *People v. Lewis*, 52 Ill. App. 3d 477, 10 Ill. Dec. 257, 367 N.E.2d 710 (1977); *People v. Hicks* supra. In order to accomplish these objectives, questions directed to the specific topics on which testimony is desired will often be necessary. Hence some questions that would be objectionable as leading if asked on direct, *see* §611.9 supra, are permissible. *Cruz v. Gulf, M. & O.R. Co.*, 7 Ill. App. 2d 209, 129 N.E.2d 272 (1955). Ultimately, the scope of redirect examination and the form of the question rest in the discretion of the court. *People v. Tingle*, 279 Ill. App. 3d 706, 216 Ill. Dec. 323, 665 N.E.2d 383 (1996) (quoting Handbook). Relevant evidence may be excluded on redirect examination if its probative value is substantially outweighed by the danger of unfair prejudice. *See* §403.1 supra. *See also People v. Chambers*, 179 Ill. App. 3d 565, 128 Ill. Dec. 372, 534 N.E.2d 554 (1989).

A witness may not be asked, however, on redirect, whether her testimony on direct examination was the truth, since the answer is not rehabilitating, *People v. Tingle*, 279 Ill. App. 3d 706, 216 Ill. Dec. 323, 665 N.E.2d 383 (1996); *Highland Park v. Block*, 48 Ill. App. 3d 241, 6 Ill. Dec. 285, 362 N.E.2d 1107 (1977); nor may a witness be permitted merely to repeat on redirect statements made upon direct examination. *Schmitt v. Chicago Transit Auth.*, 34 Ill. App. 2d 67, 179 N.E.2d 838 (1962). *See* §611.23 infra. In addition, a suggested explanation in the form of leading questions as to an inconsistency developed on cross-examination is impermissible. *People v. Torczak*, 96 Ill. App. 2d 373, 238 N.E.2d 626 (1968), objection as leading to question, "Sandy, could it have been 6:30 that you saw Dennis?" properly sustained.

While redirect is usually confined to meeting matters brought out on cross-examination, the trial judge has discretion to permit the development of new matters at this stage, *Springfield v. Dalbey,* 139 Ill. 34, 29 N.E. 860 (1891); *Myers v. Arnold,* 83 Ill. App. 3d 1, 38 Ill. Dec. 228, 403 N.E.2d 316 (1980), subject, of course, to allowance of appropriate recross-examination thereon, 6 Wigmore, Evidence §1897 (Chadbourn rev. 1976).

The function of recross-examination is to respond to testimony elicited during redirect examination. *People v. Williams,* 161 Ill. 2d 1, 204 Ill. Dec. 72, 641 N.E.2d 296 (1994); *People v. Franklin,* 135 Ill. 2d 78, 142 Ill. Dec. 152, 552 N.E.2d 743 (1990) (citing Handbook). Inquiry merely repeating material developed during cross-examination is improper. The scope and extent of recross examination rests in the discretion of the trial court. *Johns-Manville Prods. Corp. v. Industrial Commn.,* 78 Ill. 2d 171, 35 Ill. Dec. 540, 399 N.E.2d 606 (1980); *Diaz v. Kelley,* 275 Ill. App. 3d 1058, 212 Ill. Dec. 456, 657 N.E.2d 657 (1995).

§611.13   *Corroboration of Witness: Rebutting Attacks; An Overview*

In the interest of avoiding excessive collateral issues, certain limitations on corroboration of testimony on direct examination or to rebut attacks upon a witness are recognized. Corroboration with its limitations is discussed generally throughout this Handbook. *See,* e.g., reputation testimony for truthfulness, §608 supra; collateral and noncollateral matters, §607.2 supra; redirect examination, §611.12 supra; rebuttal testimony, §611.3 supra; explain or deny alleged self-contradiction, §613.3 infra. Certain specific instances of corroboration are discussed in the sections that follow: prior consistent statements, §611.14 infra; prompt complaint in rape prosecutions, §611.15 infra; and prior identification testimony, §611.16 infra.

§611.14   Corroboration of Witness: Prior Consistent Statements

A witness cannot be corroborated on direct examination by proof of prior statements consistent with his testimony. *People v. Williams,* 147 Ill. 2d 173, 167 Ill. Dec. 853, 588 N.E.2d 983 (1991); *People v. Shum,* 117 Ill. 2d 317, 111 Ill. Dec. 546, 512 N.E.2d 1183 (1987); *People v. Emerson,* 97 Ill. 2d 487, 74 Ill. Dec. 11, 455 N.E.2d 41 (1983); *People v. Rogers,* 81 Ill. 2d 571, 44 Ill. Dec. 254, 411 N.E.2d 223 (1980). *See People v. Montgomery,* 254 Ill. App. 3d 782, 193 Ill. Dec. 703, 626 N.E.2d 1254 (1993), jury is likely to enhance unfairly a witness's credibility simply because the statement was repeated. Moreover, when a witness is impeached by means of a prior inconsistent statement or by a showing of failure to speak when it is natural to do so, if a consistent statement does not disprove, explain, or qualify the failure to speak or making of the inconsistent statement, it is not admissible on redirect examination. *People v. Williams,* 147 Ill. 2d 173, 167 Ill. Dec. 853, 588 N.E.2d 983 (1991) (citing Handbook); *People v. DePoy,* 50 Ill. 2d 433, 240 N.E.2d 616 (1968); *People v. Ruffin,* 406 Ill. 437, 94 N.E.2d 433 (1950); *People v. Steffens,* 131 Ill. App. 3d 141, 86 Ill. Dec. 392, 475 N.E.2d 606 (1985); *People v. Chandler,* 231 Ill. App. 3d 110, 172 Ill. Dec. 874, 596 N.E.2d 153 (1992); *People v. West,* 263 Ill. App. 3d 1041, 201 Ill. Dec. 516, 636 N.E.2d 948 (1994); *People v. Bobiek,* 271 Ill. App. 3d 239, 207 Ill. Dec. 704, 648 N.E.2d 160 (1995). *Cf.* 4 Wigmore, Evidence §1126 (Chadbourn rev. 1972). *Contra People v. Torres,* 53 Ill. App. 3d 171, 10 Ill. Dec. 766, 368 N.E.2d 361 (1977), incorrectly decided.

However, to rebut an express or implied charge on cross-examination that the witness is motivated or has been influenced to testify falsely or that his testimony is a recent fabrication, evidence is admissible that he told the same story *before* the motive or influence came into existence or *before* the time of the alleged fabrication. *People v. Emerson,* 97 Ill. 2d 487, 74 Ill. Dec. 11, 455 N.E.2d 41 (1983); *People v. Titone,* 115 Ill. 2d 413, 105 Ill. Dec. 923, 505 N.E.2d 300 (1987); *People v. Shum,* 117 Ill. 2d 317, 111 Ill. Dec. 546, 512 N.E.2d 1183 (1987); *People v. Henderson,* 142 Ill. 2d 258, 154 Ill. Dec. 785, 568 N.E.2d 1234 (1990); *People v. Williams,* 147 Ill. 2d 173, 167 Ill. Dec. 853, 588 N.E.2d 983 (1991); *People v. Patterson,* 154 Ill. 2d 414, 182 Ill. Dec. 592, 610 N.E.2d 16 (1992); *People v. Thomas,* 278 Ill. App. 3d 276, 214 Ill. Dec. 950, 662 N.E.2d 516 (1996); *People v. Randall,* 283 Ill. App. 3d 1019, 219 Ill. Dec. 395, 671 N.E.2d 60 (1996); *Accord Tome v. United States,* 513 U.S. 150 (1995). *Cf. People v. Harris,* 123 Ill. 2d 113, 122 Ill. Dec. 76, 526 N.E.2d 335 (1988), incorrectly impliedly converting the requirement of "implied or express *charge* of improper motive" to a requirement of "proof" of the improper motive but then inexplicably permitting introduction of a prior consistent statement in the absence of such "proof." *Cf. also People v. Nicholls,* 236 Ill. App. 3d 275, 177 Ill. Dec. 626, 603 N.E.2d 696 (1992) permitting introduction of a prior inconsistent statement to rebut a charge of fabrication without discussing whether the prior inconsistent statement predates the initiation of the alleged fabrication. *See also People v. Smith,* 242 Ill. App. 3d 668, 182 Ill. Dec. 216, 609 N.E.2d 750 (1992) (query that police officer had changed original uncertainty to a determination of intoxication is an implied charge of recent fabrication). There must, of course, be an express or implied charge levied during cross-examination of the witness; the mere introduction of contradictory evidence does not suffice. *Moore v. Anchor Organization for Health Maintenance,* 284 Ill. App. 3d 874, 220 Ill. Dec. 9, 672 N.E.2d 826 (1996). Moreover, the impeachment of a witness on an issue which was not the subject of the witness's prior consistent statement cannot be used to create a back-door under the guise of an implied charge of recent fabrication through which the witness's prior consistent statement becomes admissible. *People v. West,* 263 Ill. App. 3d 1041, 201 Ill. Dec. 516, 636 N.E.2d 948 (1994). A charge of recent fabrication is *not* made simply by questioning a witness as to whether the witness went "over his testimony" or "rehearsed his testimony" with opposing counsel. *People v. Lambert,* 288 Ill. App. 3d 450, 224 Ill. Dec. 360, 681 N.E.2d 675 (1997). *Contra People v. Askew,* 273 Ill. App. 3d 798, 210 Ill. Dec. 65, 652 N.E.2d 410 (1995) (question inquiring if the witness rehearsed testimony with counsel amounts to a charge of recent fabrication).

The party seeking to introduce the prior consistent statement has the burden of establishing that the statement predates the alleged creation of the improper influence, motive, or recent fabrication. *People v. Deavers,* 220 Ill. App. 3d 1057, 163 Ill. Dec. 26, 580 N.E.2d 1367 (1991); *People v. Antczak,* 251 Ill. App. 3d 709, 190 Ill. Dec. 788, 622 N.E.2d 818 (1993) (quoting Handbook). Charges of improper motive, improper influence, or recent fabrication are to be treated separately. Accordingly, a prior consistent statement is admissible to rebut a charge of recent fabrication even if the prior consistent statement is inadmissible to rebut a separate charge of improper motive because the prior consistent statement was made during the time the improper motive is alleged to exist. *People v. Antczak* supra; *People v. Lambert,* 288 Ill. App. 3d 450, 224 Ill. Dec. 360, 681 N.E.2d 675 (1997). *Contra People v. Grisset,* 288 Ill. App. 3d 620, 224 Ill. Dec. 389, 681 N.E.2d 1010 (1997) (prior consistent statements are admissible to rebut a claim of recent fabrication only if those prior statements were made before the motive to testify falsely arose; incorrectly decided; charge of recent fabrication may exist under circumstances in which a charge of improper motive is either not factually present or not asserted; cases cited do not support proposition). Other attacks on the credibility of a witness, such as lack of recollection or mistake, do not trigger the right to introduce prior consistent statements. *See People v. Hayes,* 139 Ill. 2d 89, 151 Ill. Dec. 348, 564 N.E.2d 803 (1990); *Moore v. Anchor Organization for Health Maintenance* supra.

To illustrate, assume that John, while standing on the sidewalk, witnessed an automobile accident involving a car driven by Mary and a truck driven by Bill. The factual issue in dispute is the color of the traffic light at the intersection facing both parties. At trial, John testifies that the light facing Mary was green. On cross-examination, Bill's attorney brings out that four weeks after the accident John met Mary for the first time at her lawyer's office, that they dated thereafter, and that they are now engaged to be married. On redirect examination, John may testify that one day after the accident he told his best friend Tim that the light facing the car driven by the woman was green. However, John may not testify that two weeks after John and Mary were engaged he told his mother that the light facing Mary was green. *See People v. Harris,* 123 Ill. 2d 113, 122 Ill. Dec. 76, 526 N.E.2d 335 (1988), quoting illustration.

Once a person has come in contact with the police, circumstances surrounding plea negotiations, a grant of immunity, or the actuality of conviction must be taken into consideration in determining whether the motive or influence had already come into existence. *Compare People v. Green,* 125 Ill. App. 3d 734, 81 Ill. Dec. 44, 466 N.E.2d 630 (1984) (statement not admissible if made after investigation had centered on declarant as a prime suspect); *People v. Henderson,* 142 Ill. 2d 258, 154 Ill. Dec. 785, 568 N.E.2d 1234 (1990) (motive to protect brother predated witness's statement to police), *with People v. King,* 165 Ill. App. 3d 464, 116 Ill. Dec. 329, 518 N.E.2d 1309 (1988) (motive to fabricate had not yet arisen even though declarant had been told he was a suspect); *People v. Ashford,* 121 Ill. 2d 55, 117 Ill. Dec. 171, 520 N.E.2d 332 (1988) (statement made to police at most showed a desire to be released in the absence of any promise of leniency of favorable treatment; if statement in fact admitted in error it was harmless); *People v. Eichelberger,* 189 Ill. App. 3d 1020, 137 Ill. Dec. 520, 546 N.E.2d 274 (1989) (statement made to witness's lawyer who could not make any concession to the witness for the statement, at time when witness knew the police were investigating him and that a grand jury indictment was pending properly admitted); *People v. Gonzalez,* 265 Ill. App. 3d 315, 202 Ill. Dec. 399, 637 N.E.2d 1135 (1994) (prior written statement to Assistant State's Attorney properly admitted after defendant cross-examined witness as to prior inconsistent statement, and implied that the witness's trial testimony was motivated by expectations of leniency arising from plea agreement reached only two weeks earlier); *People v. Askew,* 273 Ill. App. 3d 798, 210 Ill. Dec. 65, 652 N.E.2d 1041 (1995) (cross-examination focused on motive to fabricate engendered by plea agreement relating to his testimony against codefendants, which his prior consistent statement predated). On balance, it appears that a statement to a police officer or a government attorney will be admitted as a prior consistent statement to rebut an implied or express change of improper motive or influence arising from plea bargaining when made under circumstances indicating that neither a suggestion of a plea bargain nor a threat by the police existed at the time of the making of the prior consistent statement. *See generally People v. Lambert,* 288 Ill. App. 3d 450, 224 Ill. Dec. 360, 681 N.E.2d 675 (1997).

In addition, a prior statement that corroborates the witness may be admitted if it serves to explain, qualify, or modify a fragment thereof introduced by the opposite party for purposes of impeachment, *see* §106.1 supra; *People v. Harris,* 123 Ill. 2d 113, 122 Ill. Dec. 76, 526 N.E.2d 335 (1988); *People v. Hicks,* 28 Ill. 2d 457, 192 N.E.2d 891 (1963); *People v. Williams,* 274 Ill. App. 3d 598, 210 Ill. Dec. 704, 653 N.E.2d 899 (1995); *Smith v. City of Rock Island,* 22 Ill. App. 2d 389, 161 N.E.2d 369 (1959), or if it is otherwise related to and supportive of a denial or explanation offered in response to impeachment of a witness by an alleged self-contradiction, whether an inconsistent statement or failure to speak when natural to do so. *People v. Pendleton,* 185 Ill. App. 3d 768, 134 Ill. Dec. 207, 542 N.E.2d 386 (1989); *People v. Morrow,* 104 Ill. App. 3d 995, 60 Ill. Dec. 747, 433 N.E.2d 985 (1982); *People v. Rodriguez,* 58 Ill. App. 3d 562, 16 Ill. Dec. 129, 374 N.E.2d 904 (1978). However, a prior consistent statement that does not directly corroborate the witness's response to the alleged attempted impeachment by self-contradiction will not be admitted, i.e., the foregoing may not be employed as a subterfuge to admit a prior consistent statement that is otherwise inadmissible. *People v. Emerson,* 97 Ill. 2d 487, 74 Ill. Dec. 11, 455 N.E.2d 41 (1983); *People v. Ciavirelli,* 262 Ill. App. 3d 966, 200 Ill. Dec. 271, 635 N.E.2d 610 (1994). *Cf. Interest of Brooks,* 63 Ill. App. 3d 328, 20 Ill. Dec. 39, 379 N.E.2d 872 (1978), where the court enters into a misleading discussion of the hearsay rule in connection with the admissibility of a statement that could have been admitted as a prior consistent statement. *See also* §613 infra.

Prior consistent statements are admitted solely for rehabilitative purposes and not as substantive evidence; a limiting instruction must be given. *People v. Lambert,* 288 Ill. App. 2d 450, 224 Ill. Dec. 360, 681 N.E.2d 675 (1997). *Compare* id., Doyle, J., dissenting (failure to give a limiting instruction was harmless error).

Where admissible, the prior consistent statement may be testified to by either the witness herself or any other person with personal knowledge of the statement. *People v. Wurster,* 83 Ill. App. 3d 399, 38 Ill. Dec. 702, 403 N.E.2d 1306 (1980); 4 Wigmore, Evidence §1123 (Chadbourn rev. 1972).

With respect to prompt complaint in a rape case on direct examination, *see* §611.15 infra.

§611.15 Corroboration of Witness: Prompt Complaint in Rape Case; Child Sexual Abuse

In rape cases, the fact that the prosecuting witness made complaint of the offense without inconsistent or unexplained delay is admissible on direct examination to corroborate her testimony, but the name of the accused or details cannot be disclosed. *Stevens v. People,* 158 Ill. 111, 41 N.E. 856 (1895). The evidence is permitted on the basis that it is entirely natural that the victim of a forcible rape would speak out regarding it, *People v. Damen,* 28 Ill. 2d 464, 193 N.E.2d 25 (1963), in an expression of indignation at the injury inflicted. *People v. De Frates,* 395 Ill. 439, 70 N.E.2d 591 (1947). Accordingly, if proof of complaint were not permitted, it is felt the jury might naturally assume that no complaint occurred, *People v. Damen* supra, to the detriment of the prosecution's case. *People v. Secret*, 72 Ill. 2d 371, 21 Ill. Dec. 207, 381 N.E.2d 285 (1978). While either the victim or someone hearing the complaint may testify to its making, if the victim fails for any reason to so testify and become subject to cross-examination concerning the statement, the fact of making the complaint is inadmissible. *People v. Furlong*, 392 Ill. 247, 64 N.E.2d 460 (1946); *People v. Lewis*, 252 Ill. 281, 96 N.E. 1005 (1911). The admissibility of a prompt complaint does not generally extend to crimes other than rape; *People v. Romano*, 306 Ill. 502, 138 N.E. 169 (1923); *People v. Goebel*, 161 Ill. App. 3d 113, 112 Ill. Dec. 664, 514 N.E.2d 60 (1987), not admissible in prosecution for indecent liberties, former Ill. R.S. 1983, c.38, §11-4(a)(2) and (a)(3); *People v. Woith*, 126 Ill. App. 3d 817, 81 Ill. Dec. 743, 467 N.E.2d 614 (1984), nor in prosecution for contributing to the sexual delinquency of a child, former Ill. R.S. 1983, c.38, §11-5; *People v. Gillman*, 91 Ill. App. 3d 53, 46 Ill. Dec. 518, 414 N.E.2d 240 (1980), but is admissible in prosecution for sexual intercourse with a child under 16 years of age, former *id.*, §11-4(a)(1); *People v. Darby*, 58 Ill. App. 3d 294, 15 Ill. Dec. 794, 374 N.E.2d 229 (1978); *People v. Russell*, 177 Ill. App. 3d 40, 126 Ill. Dec. 472, 531 N.E.2d 1099 (1988). The foregoing offenses are now addressed in 720 ILCS 5/12-12 to 5/12-16. The doctrine of prompt complaint applies to crimes under these statutes regardless of whether the victim is a female or a male. *People v. Tipton*, 222 Ill. App. 3d 657, 165 Ill. Dec. 131, 584 N.E.2d 310 (1991).

Under the doctrine of prompt complaint, only the fact of complaint is admissible; details of the incident, including identification of the defendant, are prohibited. *People v. Holveck*, 141 Ill. 2d 84, 152 Ill. Dec. 237, 565 N.E.2d 919 (1990); *People v. Damen* supra; *People v. Robinson*, 73 Ill. 2d 192, 22 Ill. Dec. 688, 383 N.E.2d 164 (1978); *People v. Witte*, 115 Ill. App. 3d 20, 70 Ill. Dec. 619, 449 N.E.2d 966 (1983) (*citing* Handbook); *People v. Laremont*, 174 Ill. App. 3d 201, 123 Ill. Dec. 704, 528 N.E.2d 249 (1988); *People v. Duplessis*, 248 Ill. App. 3d 195, 188 Ill. Dec. 522, 618 N.E.2d 1092 (1993). While there is not a fixed time limit within which the complaint must be made, *People v. Morrow*, 104 Ill. App. 3d 995, 60 Ill. Dec. 747, 433 N.E.2d 985 (1982), it must be made without inconsistent or unexplained delay. *People v. Davis*, 10 Ill. 2d 430, 140 N.E.2d 675 (1957); *People v. Fuelner*, 104 Ill. App. 3d 340, 60 Ill. Dec. 87, 432 N.E.2d 986 (1982); *People v. Denny*, 241 Ill. App. 3d 345, 181 Ill. Dec. 839, 608 N.E.2d 1313 (1993); *People v. Jones*, 273 Ill. App. 3d 377, 210 Ill. Dec. 92, 652 N.E.2d 1068 (1995). *See People v. Robinson*, 94 Ill. App. 3d 304, 49 Ill. Dec. 879, 418 N.E.2d 899 (1981), 16-hour delay did not destroy promptness. Whether an earlier complaint was to be reasonably expected necessarily depends upon the circumstances in which the complainant found herself. *People v. Secret*, 72 Ill. 2d 371, 21 Ill. Dec. 207, 381 N.E.2d 285 (1978); *People v. Houck*, 50 Ill. App. 3d 274, 8 Ill. Dec. 338, 365 N.E.2d 576 (1977). It is not always necessary for a rape victim to make an outcry to the very first stranger she meets after the rape. *People v. Barbour*, 106 Ill. App. 3d 993, 62 Ill. Dec. 641, 436 N.E.2d 667 (1982). Even bypassing a relative in favor of disclosure to a nonrelative does not destroy admissibility if there is a good reason for the nondisclosure. *People v. Williams*, 146 Ill. App. 3d 767, 100 Ill. Dec. 399, 497 N.E.2d 377 (1986). In addition, the complaint must be voluntary and spontaneous and thus not made as a result of a series of questions. *People v. Lawler*, 142 Ill. 2d 548, 154 Ill. Dec. 674, 568 N.E.2d 895 (1991); *People v. Taylor*, 48 Ill. 2d 91, 268 N.E.2d 865 (1971); *People v. Harris*, 134 Ill. App. 3d 705, 89 Ill. Dec. 446, 480 N.E.2d 1189 (1985), statement is inadmissible if it would not have been made but for the declarant's being questioned. However, the single question "what happened," *People v. Hood*, 59 Ill. 2d 315, 319 N.E.2d 802 (1974), "what's wrong," *People v. Evans*, 173 Ill. App. 3d 186, 122 Ill. Dec. 950, 527 N.E.2d 448 (1988), or "did he rape you," *People v. Barbour* supra, does not disqualify the assertion.

A complaint in a rape case may also meet the requirements of an excited utterance. *See* §803.3 infra; *People v. Poland*, 22 Ill. 2d 175, 174 N.E.2d 804 (1961). In such event, the entire content of the excited utterance, which may include details of the occurrence and identification of the defendant, becomes admissible. *People v. Collier,* 66 Ill. App. 3d 1007, 23 Ill. Dec. 703, 384 N.E.2d 497 (1978). Statements of the victim of a rape made at a time too remote to qualify as an excited utterance may nevertheless meet the requirements of a prompt complaint. *People v. Damen* supra.

Statements given to rape-crisis personnel are made confidential by operation of 735 ILCS 5/8-802.1. Under the statute no rape-crisis counselor may disclose any confidential communication or be examined as a witness in any case as to a confidential communication without the consent of victim, except that consent is not required if failure to disclose is likely to result in a clear, imminent risk of serious physical injury or death of the victim or another person:

(a) Purpose.   This Section is intended to protect victims of rape from public disclosure of statements they make in confidence to counselors of organizations established to help them. On or after July 1, 1984, "rape" means an act of forced sexual penetration or sexual conduct, as defined in Section 12-12 of the Criminal Code of 1961, as amended, including acts prohibited under Sections 12-13 through 12-16 of the Criminal Code of 1961, as amended. Because of the fear and stigma that often results from those crimes, many victims hesitate to seek help even where it is available at no cost to them. As a result they not only fail to receive needed medical care and emergency counseling, but may lack the psychological support necessary to report the crime and aid police in preventing future crimes.

(b) Definitions.   As used in this Act:

(1) "Rape crisis organization" means any organization or association the major purpose of which is providing information, counseling, and psychological support to victims of any or all of the crimes of aggravated criminal sexual assault, criminal sexual assault, sexual relations between siblings, criminal sexual abuse and aggravated criminal sexual abuse.

(2) "Rape crisis counselor" means a person who is a psychologist, social worker, employee, or volunteer in any organization or association defined as a rape crisis organization

under this Section, who has undergone 40 hours of training and is under the control of a direct services supervisor of a rape crisis organization.

(3) "Victim" means a person who is the subject of, or who seeks information, counseling, or advocacy services as a result of an aggravated criminal sexual assault, criminal sexual assault, sexual relations within families, criminal sexual abuse, aggravated criminal sexual abuse, sexual exploitation of a child, indecent solicitation of a child, public indecency, exploitation of a child, or an attempt to commit any of these offenses.

(4) "Confidential communication" means any communication between a victim and a rape crisis counselor in the course of providing information, counseling, and advocacy. The term includes all records kept by the counselor or by the organization in the course of providing services to an alleged victim concerning the alleged victim and the services provided.

(c) Waiver of Privilege.

(1) The confidential nature of the communication is not waived by: the presence of a third person who further expresses the interests of the victim at the time of the communication; group counseling; or disclosure to a third person with the consent of the victim when reasonably necessary to accomplish the purpose for which the counselor is consulted.

(2) The confidential nature of counseling records is not waived when: the victim inspects the records; or in the case of a minor child less than 12 years of age, a parent or guardian whose interests are not adverse to the minor inspects the records; or in the case of a minor victim 12 years or older, a parent or guardian whose interests are not adverse to the minor inspects the records with the victim's consent.

(3) When a victim is deceased or has been adjudged incompetent by a court of competent jurisdiction, the victim's guardian or the executor or administrator of the victim's estate may waive the privilege established by this Section, unless the guardian, executor, or administrator has an interest adverse to the victim.

(4) A minor victim 12 years of age or older may knowingly

waive the privilege established in this Section. When a minor is, in the opinion of the Court, incapable of knowingly waiving the privilege, the parent or guardian of the minor may waive the privilege on behalf of the minor, unless the parent or guardian has been charged with a violent crime against the victim or otherwise has any interest adverse to that of the minor with respect to the waiver of the privilege.

(d) Confidentiality.   Except as provided in this Act, no rape crisis counselor shall disclose any confidential communication or be examined as a witness in any civil or criminal proceeding as to any confidential communication without the written consent of the victim or a representative of the victim as provided in subparagraph (c).

(e) A rape crisis counselor may disclose a confidential communication without the consent of the victim if failure to disclose is likely to result in a clear, imminent risk of serious physical injury or death of the victim or another person. Any rape crisis counselor or rape crisis organization participating in good faith in the disclosing of records and communications under this Act shall have immunity from any liability, civil, criminal, or otherwise that might result from the action. In any proceeding, civil or criminal, arising out of a disclosure under this Section, the good faith of any rape crisis counselor or rape crisis organization who disclosed the confidential communication shall be presumed.

(f) Any rape crisis counselor who knowingly disloses any confidential communication in violation of this Act commits a Class C misdemeanor.

The constitutionality of the privilege created by 5/8-802.1 was upheld in *People v. Foggy,* 149 Ill. App. 3d 599, 102 Ill. Dec. 925, 500 N.E.2d 1026 (1986). Statements made to personnel counseling victims of violent crimes are made confidential by operation of 735 ILCS 5/8-802.2:

(a) Purpose.   This Section is intended to protect victims of violent crimes from public disclosure of statements they make in confidence to counselors of organizations established to help them. Because of the fear and trauma that often results from violent crimes, many victims hesitate to seek help even where it is available and may therefore lack the psychological support necessary to report the crime and aid police in preventing future crimes.

(b) Definitions. As used in this Act, "violent crimes" include, but are not limited to, any felony in which force or threat of force was used against the victim or any misdemeanor which results in death or great bodily harm to the victim.

(c) Confidentiality. Where any victim of a violent crime makes a statement relating to the crime or its circumstances during the course of therapy or consultation to any counselor, employee or volunteer of a victim aid organization, the statement or contents thereof shall not be disclosed by the organization or any of its personnel unless the maker of the statement consents in writing or unless otherwise directed pursuant to this Section.

If in any judicial proceeding, a party alleges that such statements are necessary to the determination of any issue before the court and written consent to disclosure has not been given, the party may ask the court to consider the relevance and admissibility of the statements. In such a case, the court shall hold a hearing in camera on the relevance of the statements. If the court finds them relevant and admissible to the issue, the court shall order the statements to be disclosed.

With respect to the confidential communications privileges for physicians, psychiatrists, and personnel counseling victims of violent crimes, *see also* §503.1 supra.

Between 1983 and 1988, Ill. R.S. 1983, c.38, §115-10 (as amended in 1984) provided that in a prosecution for a sexual act perpetrated upon a child under the age of 13, including prosecutions for rape, deviate sexual conduct, deviate sexual assault, contributing to the delinquency of a child, and indecent liberties with a child, now known by the label criminal sexual assault and criminal sexual abuse, 720 ILCS 5/12-12 to 5/12-16, testimony by such child that she complained of such act to another and testimony by the person to whom the child complained that such complaint was made in order to corroborate the child's testimony was admissible not only to corroborate but as an exception to the hearsay rule. *See, e.g., People v. Bradley,* 172 Ill. App. 3d 545, 122 Ill. Dec. 523, 526 N.E.2d 916 (1988); *People v. Bailey,* 177 Ill. App. 3d 679, 126 Ill. Dec. 962, 532 N.E.2d 587 (1988); *People v. Baggett,* 185 Ill. App. 3d 1007, 133 Ill. Dec. 828, 541 N.E.2d 1266 (1989).

Effective January 1, 1988, Ill. R.S. 1989, c.38, §115-10 was amended to eliminate the statutory prompt complaint hearsay exception discussed above. Presumably the common law prompt complaint corroborative doctrine as applied to children remains. In its place, 725 ILCS 5/115-10 now provides a comprehensive hearsay exception applicable in sexual and physical abuse prosecutions for acts perpetrated upon or against a child or institutionalized severely or profoundly mentally retarded person:

(a) In a prosecution for a physical or sexual act perpetrated upon or against a child under the age of 13, or a person who was an institutionalized severely or profoundly mentally retarded person as defined in Section 2-10.1 of the Criminal Code of 1961 at the time the act was committed, including but not limited to prosecutions for violations of Sections 10-1, 10-2, 10-3, 10-3.1, 10-4, 10-5, 10-6, 10-7, 11-6, 11-9, 11-11, 11-15.1, 11-17.1, 12-4.7, 12-5, 12-6, 12-6.1, 12-7.1, 12-7.3, 12-7.4, 12-10, 12-11, 12-21.5, 12-21.6, and 12-31 of the Criminal Code of 1961, the following evidence shall be admitted as an exception to the

(1) testimony by such child or institutionalized severely or profoundly mentally retarded person, of an out-of-court statement made by such child or institutionalized severely or profoundly mentally retarded person, that he or she complained of such act to another; and

(2) testimony of an out-of-court statement made by such child or institutionalized severely or profoundly mentally retarded person, describing any complaint of such act or matter or detail pertaining to any act which is an element of an offense which is the subject of a prosecution for a sexual or physical act perpetrated upon or against a child or institutionalized severely or profoundly mentally retarded person.

(b) Such testimony shall only be admitted if:

(1) The court finds in a hearing conducted outside the presence of the jury that the time, content, and circum-

stances of the statement provide sufficient safeguards of reliability; and

(2) The child or institutionalized severely or profoundly mentally retarded person either:

(A) Testifies at the proceeding; or

(B) Is unavailable as a witness and there is corroborative evidence of the act which is the subject of the statement.

(c) If a statement is admitted pursuant to this Section, the court shall instruct the jury that it is for the jury to determine the weight and credibility to be given the statement and that, in making the determination, it shall consider the age and maturity of the child, or the intellectual capabilities of the institutionalized severely or profoundly mentally retarded person, the nature of the statement, the circumstances under which the statement was made, and any other relevant factor.

(d) The proponent of the statement shall give the adverse party reasonable notice of his intention to offer the statement and the particulars of the statement.

For a comprehensive discussion of 5/115-10, *see* Graham, Indicia of Reliability and Face to Face Confrontation: Emerging Issues in Child Sexual Abuse Prosecutions, 40 U. Miami L. Rev. 19 (1985). *See also* §803.23 infra and Federal Rule of Evidence 807. With respect to whether a designated victim's testimony must be clear and convincing or be substantially corroborated, *see People v. Schott,* 145 Ill. 2d 188, 164 Ill. Dec. 127, 582 N.E.2d 690 (1991) (answered "No"). With respect to the comprehensive hearsay exception made applicable by 735 ILCS 5/8-2601 to civil proceedings involving child abuse or an unlawful sexual act, *see* §803.23 infra.

In proceedings under the Juvenile Court Act, out-of-court statements made by a minor relating to any allegation of abuse or neglect are admissible as an exception to the rule against hearsay; but if uncorroborated and not subject to cross-examination the statement alone is not sufficient to sustain a finding of abuse or neglect. 705 ILCS 405/2-18(4)(c). *See In Interest of K.L.M.,* 146 Ill. App. 3d 489, 100 Ill. Dec. 197, 496 N.E.2d 1262 (1986).

*§611.16   Corroboration of Witness: Prior Identification of a
            Person After Perceiving Him; Police Officer or
            Other Witnesses' Testimony*

When a witness testifies and is subject to cross-examination, his prior statement identifying a person after perceiving him — usually at a lineup, a one-on-one viewing often called a showup, in a photograph, or at a prior hearing — is admissible at common law on direct examination to corroborate the witness's courtroom identification but not as substantive evidence. *People v. Sterling,* 341 Ill. 112, 173 N.E. 139 (1930); *People v. Coleman,* 17 Ill. App. 3d 421, 308 N.E.2d 364 (1974). There is no requirement that the witness first be impeached. *People v. Panczko,* 86 Ill. App. 3d 409, 41 Ill. Dec. 490, 407 N.E.2d 988 (1980). The theory is that courtroom identification is so unconvincing as practically to impeach itself, thus justifying the corroboration. *People v. Rogers,* 81 Ill. 2d 571, 44 Ill. Dec. 254, 411 N.E.2d 223 (1980); *People v. Jones,* 293 Ill. App. 3d 119, 227 Ill. Dec. 646, 687 N.E.2d 1128 (1997). *Accord* 4 Wigmore, Evidence §1130 (Chadbourn rev. 1972). The circumstances of the prior identification may be considered by the trier of fact in determining the weight to be accorded. *People v. Thompson,* 406 Ill. 555, 94 N.E.2d 349 (1950). As to constitutional requirements of identification, *see* §611.17 infra.

A problem area had arisen with respect to the testimony of police officers or others, *People v. Pavone,* 44 Ill. App. 3d 998, 3 Ill. Dec. 578, 358 N.E.2d 1263 (1976), state's attorney, relating the prior identification. Testimony of a witness, usually a police officer, as to the prior identification of the accused as the perpetrator by another person falls within the definition of hearsay when offered to prove the truth of the matter asserted. *People v. Canale,* 52 Ill. 2d 107, 285 N.E.2d 133 (1972); *People v. Denham,* 41 Ill. 2d 1, 241 N.E.2d 415 (1968). Where the testimony of the police officer or other witness elicited by the prosecution during its case in chief was utilized as a substitution for an in-court identification or to bolster a weak case, introduction of the hearsay testimony constituted reversible error. *People v. Harrison,* 25 Ill. 2d 407, 185 N.E.2d 244 (1962); *People v. Townsend,* 111 Ill. App. 2d 316, 250 N.E.2d (1969). However, where the person making the identification also testified and made a positive identification, *People v. Coleman* supra, or where identification was supported by other corroborative circumstances, the admission of the police officer or other witness hearsay testimony previously was held to be harmless error. *People v. Robinson,* 73 Ill. 2d 192, 22 Ill. Dec. 688, 383 N.E.2d 164 (1978); *People v. Canale* supra; *People v. Morano,* 69 Ill. App. 3d 580, 25 Ill. Dec. 940, 387 N.E.2d 816 (1979); *People v. Johnson,* 73 Ill. App. 3d 431, 29 Ill. Dec. 890, 392 N.E.2d 587 (1979); *People v. Overton,* 44 Ill. App. 3d 490, 358 N.E.2d 393 (1976). In response to such harmless error ruling on appeal, the State often offered testimony of a police officer or other witness to corroborate the identification testimony of the in-court witness. Concerned with this practice, the Illinois Supreme Court set forth in *People v. Rogers,* 81 Ill. 2d 571, 579, 44 Ill. Dec. 254, 411 N.E.2d 223, 227 (1980), several rules to be followed:

> If a third person were to testify that he saw or heard *A* identify *B* as the person who committed the offense, that would obviously and clearly be hearsay testimony and would not be admissible. However, if *A* testifies that he previously identified *B* and his veracity is tested by cross-examination, the reason for excluding the third person's testimony has been removed. The third person should then be permitted to testify that he heard or saw *A* identify *B* because both *A* and the third person would be subject to cross-examination concerning the out-of-court identification. Evidence of such out-of-court identification by both *A* and the third person should be admissible but should be used only in corroboration of in-court identifications and not as substantive evidence. Before the third person is permitted to testify as to *A*'s identification of *B*, *A* should first testify as to his out-of-court identification.

Notice, however, that the rules set forth in *Rogers* related only to a witness who made a positive in-court identification and thus failed to address admissibility of police officer or other witness testimony offered as a substitute for an in-court identification or to bolster a weak one. There still remained problems associated with the prosecution's routinely offering police officer or other witness testimony as a substitute for in-court identification or to bolster a weak one in the hope that any error perceived on appeal will be considered harmless. *See People v. Grier,* 90 Ill. App. 3d 840, 46 Ill. Dec. 203, 413 N.E.2d 1316 (1980); *People v. McCreary,* 123 Ill. App. 3d 880, 79 Ill. Dec. 114, 463 N.E.2d 455 (1984). *See also People v. Rodriguez,* 291 Ill. App. 3d 55, 225 Ill. Dec. 653, 684 N.E. 2d 128 (1997), *citing Rogers* while unexplicably ignoring Section 5/115-12 infra.

In response, the legislature enacted c.38, §115-12, effective January 1, 1984, now 725 ILCS 5/115-12, which provides that "a statement is not rendered inadmissible by the hearsay rule if (a) the declarant testifies at the trial or hearing, and (b) the declarant is subject to cross-examination concerning the statement, and (c) the statement is one of identification of a person made after perceiving him." Thus, provided the declarant testify at trial and be subject to cross-examination concerning the prior statement of identification of a person made after perceiving him, the prior statement of identification, testified to by the declarant or another witness, including a police officer, is now admissible as an exception to the hearsay rule as substantive evidence, *People v. Beals,* 162 Ill. 2d 497, 205 Ill. Dec. 498, 643 N.E.2d 789 (1994), without regard to whether the statement of prior identification corroborates a positive in-court identification by the declarant, is offered as a substitute for an inability to make an in-court identification, or to bolster a weak in-court identification on the part of the declarant. *United States v. Fosher,* 568 F.2d 207 (1st Cir. 1978) (weak identification); *United States v. Lewis,* 565 F.2d 1248 (2d Cir. 1977) (inability to identify). *See also People v. Bell,* 132 Ill. App. 3d 354, 87 Ill. Dec. 247, 476 N.E.2d 1239 (1985) (testimony of police officer admissible following introduction of a positive identification by the witness made at a preliminary hearing as former testimony); *People v. Page,* 163 Ill. App. 3d 959, 115 Ill. Dec. 15, 516 N.E.2d 1371 (1987) (both person making the prior identification and person testifying to the identification must be available for cross-examination); *People v. Gonzalez,* 292 Ill. App. 3d 280, 226 Ill. Dec. 406, 685 N.E. 2d 661 (1997) (testimony of police officer admissible after witness to crime testified that she was unable to make an in-court identification). Similarly, the declarant's prior statement of identification is admissible as substantive evidence when testified to by a witness to the identification, such as a police officer, even when the declarant at trial denies making or repudiates the identification and denies that the defendant was involved in the crime. *Niemoth v. Kohls,* 171 Ill. App. 3d 54, 121 Ill. Dec. 37, 524 N.E.2d 1085 (1988) (quoting Handbook); *People v. Lemons,* 192 Ill. App. 3d 997, 140 Ill. Dec. 149, 549 N.E.2d 800 (1989) (quoting Handbook). *Contra People v. Davis,* 137 Ill. App. 3d 769, 92 Ill. Dec. 243, 484 N.E.2d 1098 (1985) (inconsistent identification admissible under 725 ILCS 5/115-10.1 only (*see* §801.9 infra) and not 5/115-12; incorrectly decided). In *People v. Lewis,* 165 Ill. 2d 305, 342, 209 Ill. Dec. 144, 162, 651 N.E.2d 72, 90 (1995), citing this Handbook, the Illinois Supreme Court states:

> Born out of this court's decision in *People v. Rogers* (1980), 81 Ill. 2d 571, 44 Ill. Dec. 254, 411 N.E.2d 223, the rule [section 115-12] is designed to permit the use of prior *consistent* out-of-court statements as corroborative or substantive evidence of a witness's prior identity of a defendant.

It is extremely difficult to ascertain the true meaning of the foregoing sentence as it speaks of a prior statement corroborating a "prior identity" [identification] while Section 115-12 addresses the admissibility of a prior statement to establish that the defendant committed the offense. The statement seems to have one too many priors. In any event, given its context if not its ambiguity, *Lewis* should not be read as holding that only prior *consistent* statements of identification are admissible under 725 ILCS 5/115-12. *See also People v. Gonzalez,* 292 Ill. App. 3d 280, 226 Ill. Dec. 406, 685 N.E. 2d

661 (1997) (*Davis* expressly *not* followed; *Lewis* interpreted to adopt position expressed in this Handbook that Section 115-12 permits the introduction of a prior identification even where the witness is unable to identify the defendant in open court).

A statement of identification made any time prior to trial, even on the day of trial, is admissible; it need not be made substantially closer in time to the event. *People v. Arteman,* 150 Ill. App. 3d 750, 103 Ill. Dec. 938, 502 N.E.2d 85 (1986). Finally, a prior statement of identification of a declarant who at trial claims lack of recollection of the out-of-court identification, and/or of the identity of the perpetrator of the crime is also admissible as substantive evidence under 5/115-12 and under Rule 801(d)(1)(C) of the Federal Rules of Evidence, from which §115-12 is taken. *Accord People v. Flores,* 128 Ill. 2d 66, 131 Ill. Dec. 106, 538 N.E.2d 481 (1989); *United States v. Owens,* 484 U.S. 554 (1988). Section 115-12 embraces statements of identification made at a lineup, showup, or photo session as well as statements made after perceiving the accused again at a prior hearing, trial, or at the grand jury. *People v. Robinson,* 163 Ill. App. 3d 991, 114 Ill. Dec. 928, 516 N.E.2d 1322 (1987) (quoting Handbook). With respect to whether the prior statement of identification of a declarant testifying as to a lack of recollection of the subject matter of the statement should be admitted as substantive evidence, *see* Graham, Handbook of Federal Evidence §801.13 (4th ed. 1996). Only prior statements of identification are included in §115-12; the fact the witness had not identified anyone prior to identifying the defendant is not included. *People v. Hayes,* 139 Ill. 2d 89, 151 Ill. Dec. 348, 564 N.E.2d 803 (1990). Whether a police officer can testify that the witness stated that he or she was positive of the identification was left undecided in *Hayes* supra, although a negative answer appears implied.

The possibility of harmless error when evidence of prior identification is improperly admitted, such as when the person making the prior identification does not testify, still persists. *People v. Colon,* 162 Ill. 2d 23, 204 Ill. Dec. 656, 642

N.E.2d 118 (1994) (hearsay identification is reversible error only when it serves as a substitute for courtroom identification or when it is used to strengthen or corroborate a weak identification; if, however, the testimony is merely cumulative or is supported by a positive identification and by other corroborative circumstances, it constitutes harmless error).

In *People v. Shum*, 117 Ill. 2d 317, 111 Ill. Dec. 546, 512 N.E.2d 1183 (1987), the court held that a police officer may testify to corroborate the in-court identification of the victim that the victim had told him that her attacker was "Keith." The decision is unfortunate as is *People v. Williams*, 263 Ill. App. 3d 1098, 202 Ill. Dec. 561, 638 N.E.2d 207 (1994), and *People v. Thomas*, 296 Ill. App. 3d 489, 230 Ill. Dec. 790, 694 N.E.2d 1068 (1998), which relies upon *Shum* and should not be followed. A prior statement of identification must follow perception of the perpetrator again at a time following the incident. Under the court's view, any time a victim identifies an assailant, the statement of identification will be admissible provided the declarant is subject to cross-examination at trial. Thus if a rape victim five days later told her mother it was Bob Smith who raped her, the statement would be admissible. The purpose of the rule permitting introduction of a prior statement of identification is to permit evidence of an identification made after recognizing the assailant on subsequent observation prior to trial. It is not intended to permit introduction of hearsay statements of the victim advising friends, relatives, or the police that it was Bob Smith who raped her. *Accord Swafford v. State*, 533 So. 2d 270 (Fla. 1988).

Composite drawings or sketches of suspects identified by the complainant as accurate portrayals of the perpetrator of the offense are considered hearsay. *People v. Rogers* supra. Where the eyewitness testifies and authenticates the sketch or drawing at trial, classification of the sketch as hearsay is extremely questionable. *See United States v. Moskowitz*, 581 F.2d 14 (2d Cir.), *cert. denied*, 439 U.S. 871 (1978). In any event, admission of such sketches or drawings, whether authenticated by the complaining witness or a police officer, is treated identically with that of police officer testimony as to eyewitness pretrial identification discussed above. *People v. Rogers* supra; 725 ILCS 5/115-12.

§611.17   Corroboration of Witness: Prior Identification of a Person After Perceiving Him; Constitutional Considerations

With respect to prior identification of the criminal defendant, various constitutional safeguards must be satisfied before an out-of-court identification may be introduced at trial. Initially, with respect to prior corporal identifications, whether at a lineup or a showup, if conducted at or after the instigation of adversary judicial criminal proceedings — whether by way of formal charge, preliminary hearing, indictment, information, or arraignment—the accused is entitled to the presence of counsel. *Moore v. Illinois*, 434 U.S. 220 (1977); *Kirby v. Illinois*, 406 U.S. 682 (1972); *Gilbert v. California*, 388 U.S. 263 (1967); *United States v. Wade*, 388 U.S. 218 (1967). Failure to provide counsel renders the pretrial identification inadmissible. *Gilbert v. California* supra. *See also People v. Santiago*, 53 Ill. App. 3d 694, 11 Ill. Dec. 671, 369 N.E.2d 125 (1977), counsel need not be provided at lineup occurring prior to commencement of adversary proceeding. In-court identification of the defendant where counsel was not provided as required will be excluded unless the prosecution establishes by clear and convincing evidence that the in-court identification was based upon observation of the suspect other than the lineup or showup. *United States v. Wade* supra. Among the factors to be considered in making this determination are the prior opportunity to observe the alleged criminal act, the existence of any discrepancy between any pre-lineup description and the defendant's actual description, any identification prior to lineup of another person, the identification by picture of the defendant prior to the lineup, failure to identify the defendant on a prior occasion, and the lapse of time between the alleged act and the lineup identification. *Id.* The right to counsel announced in

Wade and *Gilbert* attaches only to corporal identifications; there is no requirement of defense counsel when the witness views police or prosecution photographs. *United States v. Ash,* 413 U.S. 300 (1973).

With respect to lineups, showups, and photographic identification, the requirements of due process must also be met before the prior identification may be admitted. As to photographic identification, *see People v. Calvillo,* 170 Ill. App. 3d 1070, 121 Ill. Dec. 6, 524 N.E.2d 1054 (1988). The pretrial identification procedure, of course, may not be suggestive unless required by the exigencies of the circumstances. *Stovall v. Denno,* 388 U.S. 293 (1967), victim in hospital who might not live properly shown accused singly. However, admission into evidence of testimony concerning a suggestive identification not required by the exigencies of the circumstances, e.g., stationhouse showup, *Neil v. Biggers,* 409 U.S. 188 (1972); the exhibiting of a single photograph instead of an array, *Simmons v. United States,* 390 U.S. 377 (1968), and *Manson v. Brathwaite,* 432 U.S. 98 (1977); staging of a lineup with people of different height, wearing different clothing, *Foster v. California,* 394 U.S. 440 (1969), does not violate due process as long as the identification possesses, in light of the totality of the circumstances, sufficient aspects of reliability so that there is not a very substantial likelihood of misidentification. *Neil v. Biggers* supra; *Manson v. Brathwaite* supra; *People v. Hamilton,* 54 Ill. App. 3d 215, 11 Ill. Dec. 923, 369 N.E.2d 377 (1977); *People v. Thornton,* 61 Ill. App. 3d 530, 18 Ill. Dec. 734, 378 N.E.2d 198 (1978). Factors to be considered in determining reliability include the opportunity of the witness to view the criminal at the time of the crime, the witness's degree of attention, the accuracy of her prior description of the criminal, the level of certainty demonstrated at the confrontation, and the time between the crime and the confrontation. *People v. Simpson,* 172 Ill. 2d 117, 216 Ill. Dec. 671, 665 N.E.2d 1228 (1996); *People v. Enis,* 163 Ill. 2d 367, 206 Ill. Dec. 604, 645 N.E.2d 856 (1994); *People v. Richardson,* 123 Ill. 2d 322, 123 Ill. Dec. 908, 528 N.E.2d 612 (1988); *People v. Williams,* 118 Ill. 2d 407, 113 Ill. Dec. 923, 515

N.E.2d 1230 (1987); *People v. Bragg,* 277 Ill. App. 3d 468, 213 Ill. Dec. 731, 659 N.E.2d 1378 (1995); *People v. Favors,* 254 Ill. App. 3d 876, 193 Ill. Dec. 714, 626 N.E.2d 1265 (1993). In addition, the Illinois courts also consider whether the witness was acquainted with the suspect prior to the crime, *People v. Blumenshine,* 42 Ill. 2d 508, 250 N.E.2d 152 (1969); *People v. Graham,* 179 Ill. App. 3d 496, 128 Ill. Dec. 777, 534 N.E.2d 1382 (1989), and whether the witness was under any pressure to make a certain identification. *People v. Enis* supra. Against these factors is to be weighed the corrupting effect of the suggestive identification itself. *Neil v. Biggers* supra. The criminal defendant bears the burden of establishing a denial of due process. *People v. Johnson,* 45 Ill. 2d 38, 257 N.E.2d 3 (1970); *People v. Hartzol,* 222 Ill. App. 3d 631, 165 Ill. Dec. 112, 584 N.E.2d 291 (1991).

If the pretrial identification is excluded by application of the foregoing standard, an in-court identification will also not be permitted if the pretrial procedure was so impermissibly suggestive as to give rise to a very substantial likelihood of irreparable misidentification. *Simmons v. United States* supra; *Neil v. Biggers* supra. *See also People v. Slim,* 127 Ill. 2d 302, 130 Ill. Dec. 250, 537 N.E.2d 317 (1989); *People v. Miller,* 254 Ill. App. 3d 997, 193 Ill. Dec. 799, 626 N.E.2d 1350 (1993). In Illinois the principle is stated in the affirmative: where a pretrial identification is held to be suggestive, an in-court identification may nevertheless be admitted if it is shown by clear and convincing evidence to be of independent origin arising from an earlier uninfluenced observation of the defendant. *People v. Williams,* 118 Ill. 2d 407, 113 Ill. Dec. 923, 515 N.E.2d 1230 (1987); *People v. Cohoon,* 104 Ill. 2d 295, 84 Ill. Dec. 443, 472 N.E.2d 403 (1984); *People v. McTush,* 81 Ill. 2d 513, 43 Ill. Dec. 728, 410 N.E.2d 861 (1980) (citing Handbook); *People v. Green,* 282 Ill. App. 3d 510, 217 Ill. Dec. 973, 668 N.E.2d 158 (1996); *People v. Westbrook,* 262 Ill App. 3d 836, 200 Ill. Dec. 59, 635 N.E.2d 398 (1992). Similarly, an in-court identification will not be prohibited as the fruit of an unlawful arrest when the victim's independent recollections of the defendant preceded the lineup identification following the unlawful arrest. *United States v. Crews*, 445 U.S. 463 (1980); *People v. Payne*, 102 Ill. App. 3d 950, 58 Ill. Dec. 11, 429 N.E.2d 1344 (1981).

While the United States Supreme Court, in *Stovall v. Denno* supra, stated the practice of showing suspects singly to persons for the purpose of identification has been widely condemned, the Illinois Supreme Court believes that prompt on-the-scene identification of a single suspect is common in the apprehension of offenders and is necessary. *People v. Lippert*, 89 Ill. 2d 171, 59 Ill. Dec. 819, 432 N.E.2d 605 (1982); *People v. McKinley*, 69 Ill. 2d 145, 13 Ill. Dec. 13, 370 N.E.2d 1040 (1977); *People v. Manion*, 67 Ill. 2d 564, 10 Ill. Dec. 547, 367 N.E.2d 1313 (1977); *People v. Elam*, 50 Ill. 2d 214, 278 N.E.2d 76 (1972). *See also People v. Hughes*, 259 Ill. App. 3d 172, 198 Ill. Dec. 192, 632 N.E.2d 251 (1994). In *People v. Young*, 46 Ill. 2d 82, 87, 263 N.E.2d 72, 75 (1970), the court went so far as to state: "Indeed, in our opinion, police officers who failed, in circumstances like these, to determine at once whether or not the victim of the crime could identify the men in custody as the men who had committed the crime, would be subject to criticism," and in *People v. Elam*, 60 Ill. 2d 214, 218, 278 N.E.2d 76, 78 (1972), that it "fosters the desirable objectives of fresh, accurate identifications which may lead to the immediate release of an innocent suspect and at the same time enable the police to resume the search for the fleeing offender while the trail is fresh."

§611.18 Trial Objections: An Overview; Lack of Foundation

In the process of examining witnesses, occasions arise when the party opposing the examination, whether it be direct, cross, redirect, or recross, feels that the question itself being propounded by counsel is improper for one reason or another. If the witness is on direct or redirect examination, the question may, for example, be leading, call for a narrative answer, be compound, be repetitive, call for speculation on the part of the witness, or simply be unintelligible. Questions propounded on cross-examination or recross may suffer from the deficiency of being compound, repetitive, unintelligible, or of calling for speculation. In addition, questions on cross-examination or recross may be argumentative, may assume facts either not in evidence or in dispute, or may misquote the prior testimony of the witness. Occasionally the difficulty is not with the question but with the fact that the witness's answer is not responsive. Together the foregoing deficiencies may be referred to as trial objections. Trial objections thus focus primarily on the form of the question or unresponsiveness of the answer rather than the content of the answer itself. *See* §§611.9 and 611.19 to 611.26 infra.

Whenever a preliminary factual finding is required by either the court alone, §104.1 supra, or in connection with a matter of conditional relevancy, §104.2 supra, opposing counsel may object that the evidence presented fails to support introduction of the evidence being offered, i.e., the evidence lacks a sufficient foundation to be admitted. *People v. Lewis,* 165 Ill. 2d 305, 209 Ill. Dec. 144, 651 N.E.2d 72 (1995) (citing Handbook). The objection "lack of foundation," involving a preliminary determination of fact in connection with the admissibility of evidence thus falls outside the scope of trial objections. The objection "lack of foundation" may be employed at trial with respect to at least each of the following:

(1) Competency of a lay witness.
(2) Qualifications of an expert witness.
(3) Introduction of opinion testimony.
(4) Personal knowledge.
(5) Unavailability in connection with a hearsay exception.
(6) Satisfaction of the requirements of a hearsay exception.
(7) Authentication or identification.
(8) Admissibility of evidence other than the original writing.
(9) The existence or waiver of a privilege.

(10) Admissibility of extrinsic evidence as to a prior inconsistent statement.

(11) Relevancy.

Accord People v. Lewis, 165 Ill. 2d 305, 209 Ill. Dec. 144, 651 N.E.2d 72 (1995) (citing Handbook).

Counsel objecting to the introduction of evidence on the grounds of lack of sufficient foundation will, if requested, frequently be given an opportunity to cross-examine the witness at the time of offer limited solely to the question of the foundation's sufficiency. This process is referred to as *voir dire.* If opposing counsel is successful in his objection to the adequacy of the foundation for the testimony of the witness or the introduction of an item of evidence, inadmissible evidence will never come to the attention of the trier of fact.

Occasionally counsel opposing an examination of a witness believes something is improper in the questioning process but can't put a label on it. Counsel in such situations have been known to rise and state, "Your Honor, I object; he can't do that." A more acceptable method of accomplishing the same objective is merely to object. If there is something amiss, the court may simply sustain the objection. If the court does not perceive any irregularity or itself can't put a label on it, counsel when asked to state the ground of the objection frequently responds as follows: If the witness is on direct examination, opposing counsel asserts either "form of the question" or "lack of foundation," whichever is felt to more nearly approximate what she has in mind. If the witness is on cross-examination, counsel generally asserts "form of the question." It is not uncommon for counsel conducting the examination to issue the telling retort: "Your Honor, this is cross-examination." Given the imprecise nature of trial objections and the determination of preliminary questions of admissibility, §104 supra, and thus the broad discretion placed in the trial court in this area, judges will frequently reply, "Counsel, lay additional foundation," "Counsel, rephrase the question," or simply "Counsel, move along."

Persistent asking of questions after an objection has been

sustained in violation of the court's ruling may result in the granting of a new trial. *People v. Thomas,* 261 Ill. App. 3d 366, 199 Ill. Dec. 43, 633 N.E.2d 839 (1994).

§611.19   Trial Objection: Unresponsive Answers; No Question Pending

An answer that is not responsive to the question should be stricken on motion of the questioner, whether on direct or cross-examination. *Math v. Chicago City Ry.,* 243 Ill. 114, 90 N.E. 235 (1909), witness, asked on cross-examination about his testimony at prior trial as foundation for impeachment, attempted instead to relate what happened; *People v. Peter,* 55 Ill. 2d 443, 303 N.E.2d 398 (1973), police officer, on cross-examination asked who else was assigned to case, stated that Officer Mortemer corroborated him; *People v. Roth,* 19 Ill. 2d 195, 166 N.E.2d 578 (1960), accused in conspiracy case, asked on direct whether he had conspired with alleged co-conspirators against victim, answered, "Never conspired with anybody"; *People v. Yonder,* 44 Ill. 2d 376, 256 N.E.2d 321 (1969), response to question on direct examination as to residence of witness, answered by statement by witness that she was in protective custody, was properly stricken as not responsive; *People v. Phillips,* 186 Ill. App. 3d 668, 134 Ill. Dec. 468, 542 N.E.2d 814 (1989), answer to question on cross-examination as to date of conversation disclosing contents of conversation was unresponsive. The objection, however, does not extend to statements of the witness, either in answer to a question or concerning a matter involved in the litigation, made as part of an argument between the witness and counsel. *People v. Burris,* 49 Ill. 2d 98, 273 N.E.2d 605 (1971). Nor is the objection available to defense counsel when the criminal defendant on direct examination volunteers an alibi defense. *People v. Colts,* 269 Ill. App. 3d 679, 206 Ill. Dec. 220, 645 N.E.2d 225 (1993).

The motion is available only to the questioner, unresponsiveness not being a matter of concern to the opposite party if the answer is otherwise admissible. *Hester v. Goldsbury,* 64 Ill. App. 2d 66, 212 N.E.2d 316 (1965); *Barnett v. Chicago City Ry.,* 167 Ill. App. 87 (1912). If the answer is otherwise admissible, sustaining an objection by opposing counsel would be both fruitless and time-wasting, for examining counsel could simply ask a question designed to elicit the exact same information. However, in order to prevent a witness from continuing to give an unresponsive answer, opposing counsel may object on the ground that there is no question pending before the witness, that the answer is being volunteered, or that the witness is providing a narrative. *See People v. Cortes,* 181 Ill. 2d 249, 229 Ill. Dec. 918, 692 N.E.2d 1129 (1998). The objection is predicated upon the notion that in the absence of a pending question, it is impossible to predict and therefore to object in advance to inadmissible evidence. *See also* §611.20 infra discussing narrative answers. The court in its discretion may admonish a witness not to volunteer answers not responsive to questions posed. *People v. Kukulski,* 358 Ill. 601, 193 N.E. 504 (1934); *People v. Gonzalez,* 238 Ill. App. 3d 303, 179 Ill. Dec. 472, 606 N.E.2d 304 (1992).

For discussion of motions to strike generally, *see* §103.3 supra.

§611.20 Trial Objection: Questions Too Broad or Calling for Narrative Answer; Compound Questions

A question that is too broad or general permits the witness to give a narrative answer that may include irrelevant or otherwise objectionable testimony such as hearsay or inadmissible opinion. Since opposing counsel cannot discern from the broad general question what testimony is being sought, he cannot frame a proper objection on such grounds prior to hearing the witness's answer, at which point the jury has also heard the inadmissible matter. While a motion to strike would be granted under such circumstances, *see* §103.3 supra, its effectiveness in having the jury disregard what it heard is suspect. Illustrative of too broad or general questions calling for a narrative response are "Tell us everything that was said that night," and "How did the accident happen?" In *Franklin v. Randolph,* 130 Ill. App. 2d 801, 267 N.E.2d 337 (1971), the question asked in *Kozlowski v. City of Chicago,* 113 Ill. App. 513 (1904), "What has been the effect of the injury on your health?" was characterized as objectionable as quite broad.

The use of questions calling for a narrative response versus specific nonleading questions in any given situation rests very much in the discretion of the court. Generally speaking, when hearsay or other inadmissible evidence is unlikely to be included in a response, judges will usually permit narrative questions. When hearsay or other inadmissible evidence is likely to be forthcoming, while the alternative of instructing the witness not to include specified matter in response to a narrative question is available, specific nonleading questions providing the opponent an opportunity to object before an answer is given are more appropriate. Witnesses are frequently examined in the narrative form, being interrupted at appropriate junctures with specific inquiries to establish additional material or to more fully develop facts included in the witness's answer. Specific inquiries may be desirable for other purposes, such as to ensure the presentation of facts in a desirable order, to establish the witness's personal knowledge, to give the witness more confidence in the courtroom, to supplement the testimony with demonstrative evidence, to lay a foundation for the introduction of evidence whether it be documentary or real, or to establish the competency of a lay or expert witness.

A question is objectionable as compound if it contains two or more questions. A compound question increases the risk of inaccuracy, since the witness may be confused by the question. Moreover, the answer of the witness may be ambiguous if it is hard to determine which question is being answered. To illustrate, the question, "Did you go to the store or did you go to the park?" is a compound question to which an intelligible yes or no answer could not be made. There are no reported Illinois decisions discussing this objection.

§611.21 Trial Objection: Questions Assuming Facts Either Not in Evidence or in Dispute

A question that assumes a fact not in evidence is objectionable in that it presents before the jury facts that have not been proved. *See* §103.9 supra. The danger inherent in such questioning is that the jury will ignore the denial and presume the accuracy of the impeaching insinuation contained in the question. *People v. Enis,* 139 Ill. 2d 264, 151 Ill. Dec. 493, 564 N.E.2d 1155 (1990) (citing Handbook). *See also Gabosch v. Tullman,* 21 Ill. App. 3d 908, 316 N.E.2d 226 (1974), counsel, without ever introducing the measurement in evidence, effectively conveyed to the jury by his questions that a measurement had been taken that would place the plaintiff in a certain position at the time of the accident. Similarly, a question that assumes a fact in dispute is calculated to suggest the adoption of the assumption by the witness. *Bartimus v. Paxton Community Hosp.,* 120 Ill. App. 3d 1060, 76 Ill. Dec. 418, 458 N.E.2d 1072 (1983). Moreover, the answer may leave it unclear whether the witness actually did adopt the assumption, leaving the true purport of the answer unclear. Close to the classic illustration is the question, "When did you first begin to quarrel with your wife about going with other men?" *Balswic v. Balswic,* 179 Ill. App. 118 (1912). Questions of this sort are objectionable. *Meyer v. Krohn,* 114 Ill. 574, 2 N.E. 495 (1885). If the witness has previously testified to the fact, the reasons for the objection do not exist. Nor is it objectionable to assume the existence of a fact not in dispute. *Erie & Pacific Despatch v. Cecil,* 112 Ill. 180 (1884).

On cross-examination, the use of questions assuming a fact in dispute or not in evidence is also prohibited. *People v. Moretti,* 6 Ill. 2d 494, 129 N.E.2d 709 (1955); *Pepe v. Caputo,* 408 Ill. 321, 97 N.E.2d 260 (1951); *People v. Aguirre,* 291 Ill. App. 3d 1028, 226 Ill. Dec. 169, 684 N.E.2d 1372 (1997); *People v. Montgomery,* 254 Ill. App. 3d 782, 193 Ill. Dec. 703, 626 N.E.2d 1254 (1993); *People v. Erp,* 134 Ill. App. 3d 397, 89 Ill. Dec. 383, 480 N.E.2d 865 (1985); *People v. Giangrande,*

101 Ill. App. 3d 397, 56 Ill. Dec. 911, 428 N.E.2d 503 (1981). Questions assuming a fact not in evidence on cross-examination often begin with such phrases as "Did you know," "Have you heard," or "Would it surprise you if I told you." Many of these questions will also be objectionable on the ground of relevancy. Questions merely insinuating the existence of facts not proved are also objectionable. *People v. Nuccio,* 43 Ill. 2d 375, 253 N.E.2d 353 (1969); *People v. Skorka,* 147 Ill. App. 3d 976, 101 Ill. Dec. 283, 498 N.E.2d 607 (1986); *People v. Barnett,* 34 Ill. App. 3d 174, 340 N.E.2d 116 (1975). This prohibition does not, however, extend to assuming that the witness's answer is untrue for the purpose of putting various questions to show that fact, *Briggs v. People,* 219 Ill. 330, 76 N.E. 499 (1905), as such questions do not thereby assume that the witness has testified to a fact that he has not testified to.

The court in its discretion may accept a representation of counsel that a fact assumed or insinuated on cross-examination to be true will be connected up later in the trial through the introduction of admissible evidence. McCormick, Evidence, §58 (4th ed. 1992); *People v. Nuccio,* 43 Ill. 2d 375, 253 N.E.2d 353 (1969). Failure to introduce evidence establishing the facts previously assumed or insinuated may constitute reversible error. With respect to the "connecting up" of matters raised on direct examination, *see* §104.2 supra.

The assumption of facts in the cross-examination of an expert witness is treated in §705.2 infra.

§611.22   *Trial Objection: Misquoting a Witness in a Question*

A question that misstates the testimony of the witness as part of a subsequent question is improper. *Briggs v. People,* 219 Ill. 330, 76 N.E. 499 (1905). In *Berger v. United States,* 295 U.S. 78 (1935), the prosecutor took testimony to the effect that one Godly had threatened the witness and made it appear in a question that the witness had admitted threatening the prosecutor. Misquoting the prior testimony of the witness creates confusion similar to the assuming of facts not in evidence or in dispute, discussed in §611.21 supra.

§611.23 Trial Objection: Question Is Argumentative

A question is argumentative if asked for the purpose of persuading the trier of fact, rather than to elicit information. *People v. Clay,* 27 Ill. 2d 27, 187 N.E.2d 719 (1963), after a witness had stated that he did not know the nature of the object he saw passing hands, a subsequent question inquiring if it was a box, a newspaper, or just persons shaking hands was argumentative. Questions are also argumentative if they call for an argument in answer to an argument contained in a question. Thus, for example, the question, "Are you lying now or were you lying then?" is argumentative, as is the question to an informer who says she had not been paid, "In other words, you did it for the good of the country, is that correct?" *People v. Clay* supra. Finally, a question is argumentative if it merely invokes the witness's assent to the questioner's inferences from or interpretation of facts proved or assumed. McCormick, Evidence §7 (4th ed. 1992). *See, e.g., People v. Williams,* 161 Ill. 2d 1, 204 Ill. Dec. 72, 641 N.E.2d 296 (1994), question to the defendant asking him whether he would tell the truth on the witness stand even if it would result in his going to prison was improperly argumentative; *County of Cook v. Colonial Oil Corp.,* 15 Ill. 2d 67, 153 N.E.2d 844 (1958), question stating to an expert witness that certain of his experiences were of no help in determining market value held argumentative; *Kelley v. Cross,* 79 Ill. App. 2d 342, 223 N.E.2d 555 (1967), a question to the witness stating that the witness does not recall how the accident really happened declared argumentative; *People v. Starks,* 116 Ill. App. 3d 384, 71 Ill. Dec. 931, 451 N.E.2d 1298 (1983), question to the defendant inquiring whether if the defendant "did shoot him in cold blood" he "would come right in here and tell us about it" is improper; *People v. Colts,* 269 Ill. App. 3d 679, 206 Ill. Dec. 220, 645 N.E.2d 225 (1995), question to the defendant, "So you are a pimp?" is a highly improper attempt to highlight defendant's immorality.

Whether a particular question is argumentative is often not easily determined. The relationship between counsel and the witness, volume, tone of voice, inflection, emphasis, and gestures all affect the determination. Everything considered, it is thus not surprising that what is an argumentative question in one court is often considered perfectly proper cross-examination in another.

§611.24   Trial Objection: Question Is Repetitive; Asked and Answered

A question is objectionable if the witness has previously asked and has already answered a substantially similar question by the same counsel. *People v. Abrams,* 260 Ill. App. 3d 566, 197 Ill. Dec. 853, 631 N.E.2d 1312 (1994). Such a question, being repetitive, has the tendency to unduly emphasize the testimony. *People v. Santucci,* 24 Ill. 2d 93, 180 N.E.2d 491 (1962). The objection asked and answered frequently arises on redirect, *Gabosch v. Tullman,* 21 Ill. App. 3d 908, 316 N.E.2d 226 (1974), on recross-examination, *People v. Jackson,* 28 Ill. 2d 37, 190 N.E.2d 823 (1963), or on surrebuttal, *People v. Owens,* 46 Ill. App. 3d 978, 5 Ill. Dec. 321, 361 N.E.2d 644 (1977), when counsel attempts to have the witness repeat a favorable answer to obtain emphasis. On cross-examination repetition is more frequently allowed for its effect on credibility. *People v. Moses,* 11 Ill. 2d 84, 142 N.E.2d 1 (1957). However, even on cross-examination, if the question has been asked and fully answered, the objection will be sustained. *People v. Hardy,* 70 Ill. App. 3d 351, 26 Ill. Dec. 212, 387 N.E.2d 1042 (1979); *People v. Meeks,* 11 Ill. App. 3d 973, 297 N.E.2d 705 (1973).

§611.25 Trial Objection: Question Calls for Conjecture, Speculation, or Judgment of Veracity

A question addressed to a witness lacking personal knowledge of the event is objectionable if it asks the witness to guess or surmise what occurred. *People v. Cloutier,* 156 Ill. 2d 483, 190 Ill. Dec. 744, 622 N.E.2d 774 (1993) (since expert specifically disclaimed recall, any opinion as to percentage of victims of forced sex not suffering injury to genitalia would have been speculative and uncertain); *People v. Enis,* 139 Ill. 2d 264, 151 Ill. Dec. 493, 564 N.E.2d 1155 (1990) (improper to ask witness to speculate about matters beyond his personal knowledge). Thus a question asking the witness what "probably" occurred or asking for her "impression," is objectionable as calling for speculation or conjecture. *Allen B. Wrisley Co. v. Burke,* 203 Ill. 250, 67 N.E. 818 (1903); *Rounds v. McCormick,* 11 Ill. App. 220 (1882).

With respect to a question calling for opinion testimony of a lay witness, §701.1 infra, if the witness's opinion is not based upon personal knowledge, §602 supra, or is based upon ambiguous matters, the question is objectionable as calling for speculation that is sometimes confusingly couched in terms of calling for a conclusion of the witness as to an ultimate issue. *People v. Hamilton,* 268 Ill. 390, 109 N.E. 329 (1915), testimony that accused acted as if he had something on his mind condemned as a conclusion; *American Car & Foundry Co. v. Hill,* 226 Ill. 227, 80 N.E. 784 (1907), what other employees were aiming to do inadmissible as a conclusion. *Cf. Pfiester v. Western Union Tel. Co.,* 282 Ill. 69, 118 N.E. 407 (1918), testimony by plaintiff that he would have accepted telegraphic offer if delivered held admissible. *See also* §704.1 infra.

Similarly, if the basis of an expert's opinion includes so many varying or uncertain factors that he is required to guess or surmise in order to reach an opinion, the expert's opinion is objectionable as speculation or conjecture, *Dyback v. Weber,* 114 Ill. 2d 232, 102 Ill. Dec. 386, 500 N.E.2d 8 (1986); *People v. Sargeant,* 292 Ill. App. 3d 508, 226 Ill. Dec. 501, 685

N.E. 2d 956 (1997); *Coffey v. Brodsky,* 165 Ill. App. 3d 14, 116 Ill. Dec. 16, 518 N.E.2d 638 (1987); *Mote v. Montgomery Ward & Co.,* 125 Ill. App. 3d 839, 81 Ill. Dec. 7, 466 N.E.2d 593 (1984). Alternatively stated, an expert may not guess, surmise, or conjecture based upon matters that have not been shown to be factual, *Baird v. Adeli,* 214 Ill. App. 3d 47, 157 Ill. Dec. 861, 573 N.E.2d 279 (1991); *Zavala v. Powermatic, Inc.,* 260 Ill. App. 3d 963, 198 Ill. Dec. 181, 632 N.E.2d 240 (1994), or upon matters with which she is not familiar even after proper application of Rule 703, discussed in §703.1 infra. *Tierney v. Community Memorial General Hospital,* 268 Ill. App. 3d 1050, 206 Ill. Dec. 279, 645 N.E.2d 284 (1994). *Accord Damron v. Micor Distributing, Ltd.,* 276 Ill. App. 3d 901, 213 Ill. Dec. 297, 658 N.E.2d 1318 (1995) (when experts fail to take into consideration their party's actions, base their opinions on facts that are not in evidence, ignore significant factors, or base their opinions on what might have happened, the court will hold that the experts' opinions are based on mere speculation and conjecture). It is also improper to ask an expert what someone else might have done differently if aware of a certain fact. *Casey v. Penn,* 45 Ill. App. 3d 573, 4 Ill. Dec. 346, 360 N.E.2d 93 (1977). *See also* §705.2 infra.

A question that requires the witness to comment on the veracity of another witness, a matter exclusively within the province of the trier of fact, is improper. *People v. Kokoraleis,* 132 Ill. 2d 235, 138 Ill. Dec. 233, 547 N.E.2d 202 (1989); *People v. Enis,* 139 Ill. 2d 264, 151 Ill. Dec. 493, 564 N.E.2d 1155 (1990) (citing Handbook); *People v. Martin,* 271 Ill. App. 3d 346, 208 Ill. Dec. 70, 648 N.E.2d 992 (1995); *Grant v. Petroff,* 291 Ill. App. 3d 795, 226 Ill. Dec. 24, 684 N.E. 2d 1020 (1997). Such questions are also considered improper because they force the witness to call the opponent's witnesses liars, thereby demeaning and ridiculing the witness herself before the jury. *People v. Barnes,* 182 Ill. App. 3d 75, 130 Ill. Dec. 620, 537 N.E.2d 949 (1989); *People v. Robinson,* 219 Ill. App. 3d 235, 161 Ill. Dec. 908, 579 N.E.2d 579 (1991). *See, e.g., Champion v. Knasiak,* 25 Ill. App. 3d 192, 323 N.E.2d 62 (1974), cross-examination asking for comment on inconsistency between his testimony and that of another witness; *Ryan v. Monson,* 33 Ill. App. 2d 406, 179 N.E.2d 449 (1961), improper to ask witness to characterize other witness's testimony as true or false; *People v. Best,* 97 Ill. App. 3d 1083, 53 Ill. Dec. 616, 424 N.E.2d 29 (1981); *People v. Tribett,* 98 Ill. App. 3d 663, 53 Ill. Dec. 897, 424 N.E.2d 688 (1981); *People v. Andras,* 241 Ill. App. 3d 28, 181 Ill. Dec. 237, 608 N.E.2d 310 (1992), question to the criminal defendant inquiring whether the prosecution witnesses are lying is improper; *People v. Hyche,* 91 Ill. App. 3d 559, 47 Ill. Dec. 26, 414 N.E.2d 1142 (1980), question to criminal defendant inquiring whether prosecution witnesses were mistaken is improper. It is also improper to ask the witness whether she can explain why another witness testified as to a particular fact. *People v. Adams,* 111 Ill. App. 3d 658, 67 Ill. Dec. 298, 444 N.E.2d 534 (1982). The suggestion that while a witness may not be asked whether another's testimony is true or false, a witness may be asked whether another witness is mistaken or whether his testimony is at variance as articulated in *Bass. v. Washington Kinney Co.,* 119 Ill. App. 3d 713, 75 Ill. Dec. 295, 457 N.E.2d 85 (1983), and that it is not an abuse of discretion to permit a question asking a witness whether other witnesses were telling untruthful things about her, *People v. Turner,* 128 Ill. 2d 540, 132 Ill. Dec. 390, 539 N.E.2d 1196 (1989), implies a difference not rising to a distinction and should not be encouraged. On the other hand, inquiring of the criminal defendant as to whether prosecution witnesses were lying is "not necessarily inappropriate" where the defendant's defense is that the police framed him by providing information about the murders and causing him to repeat these facts in his statements. *People v. Kokoraleis,* 132 Ill. 2d 235, 138 Ill. Dec. 233, 547 N.E.2d 202 (1989). Nevertheless, a witness may not be asked on direct or redirect examination to tell the jury whether the witness's own testimony is the truth. *People v. Loggins,* 257 Ill. App. 3d 475, 195 Ill. Dec. 829, 629 N.E.2d 137 (1993). It is, of course, improper to attempt to impeach a witness with an inconsistent statement made by another for which the testifying witness is not responsible. *J.L. Simmons Co. v. Firestone Tire & Rubber Co.,* 108 Ill. 2d 106, 90 Ill. Dec. 955, 483 N.E.2d 273 (1985).

§611.26   Trial Objection: Question Is Ambiguous, Imprecise, Unintelligible, or Calls for a Vague Answer

In the interrogation of a witness, questions should be intelligibly phrased, concise, and clear in meaning. Neither the witness, the court, nor counsel should have to guess what a question is supposed to mean. If the question cannot be understood, it is objectionable as being ambiguous, imprecise, unintelligible, or calling for a vague answer. *People v. Ward,* 19 Ill. App. 3d 833, 313 N.E.2d 314 (1974), the question whether the defendant was "acting like he was crazy" was held improper as being ambiguous, imprecise, and calling for a vague answer; *People v. Harrison,* 25 Ill. 2d 407, 185 N.E.2d 244 (1962), the question whether "that is a dark neighborhood" was held improper on the ground that the term neighborhood was too indefinite.

§611.27   Instructing the Jury; Jury Poll

In both civil cases, Supreme Court Rule 239, and criminal cases, Supreme Court Rule 451, the court is required to give the applicable Illinois Pattern Jury Instructions if the court determines that the jury should be instructed on the subject, unless the court determines that the instruction does not accurately state the applicable law. The burden of preparing jury instructions is primarily upon the parties. 735 ILCS 5/2-1107. The trial court is under no general obligation to give a jury instruction not requested by counsel or to rewrite an instruction that was tendered. *People v. Kubat,* 94 Ill. 2d 437, 69 Ill. Dec. 30, 447 N.E.2d 247 (1983); *People v. Parks,* 65 Ill. 2d 132, 357 N.E.2d 487, 2 Ill. Dec. 320 (1976). Failure to tender a proper instruction bars asserting failure to give the instruction on appeal. Supreme Court Rule 366(b)(2)(i); *People v. Alvine,* 173 Ill. 2d 273, 219 Ill. Dec. 546, 671 N.E.2d 713 (1996); *People v. Tannenbaum,* 82 Ill. 2d 177, 47 Ill. Dec. 714, 415 N.E.2d 1027 (1980). Failure to object to an instruction tendered by an opponent, *People v. Pickett,* 54 Ill. 2d 280, 296 N.E.2d 856 (1973), to the actual instruction given in response to counsel's request, *People v. Pastorino,* 91 Ill. 2d 178, 62 Ill. Dec. 172, 435 N.E.2d 1144 (1982); *People v. Edwards,* 135 Ill. App. 3d 671, 90 Ill. Dec. 430, 482 N.E.2d 137 (1985), or to an instruction otherwise given by the court, *People v. Roberts,* 75 Ill. 2d 1, 25 Ill. Dec. 675, 387 N.E.2d 331 (1979), each also constitutes a waiver of the right to raise error on appeal. Accordingly, waiver of the right to raise error on appeal occurs when a party either fails to object to a challenged instruction or fails to offer his own instruction at trial. *People v. Almo,* 108 Ill. 2d 54, 90 Ill. Dec. 885, 483 N.E.2d 203 (1985); *People v. Milestone,* 283 Ill. App. 3d 682, 219 Ill. Dec. 386, 671 N.E.2d 51 (1996). Objections to jury instructions made at trial will be considered waived if not included in the post-trial motion. *People v. Huckstead,* 91 Ill. 2d 536, 65 Ill. Dec. 232, 440 N.E.2d 1248 (1982); *People v. Hamilton,* 283 Ill. App. 2d 854, 219 Ill. Dec. 301, 670 N.E.2d 1189 (1996). *See also* §103.8 supra.

The form and procedure required in tendering and objecting to jury instructions is provided in Supreme Court Rule 239 supra for civil cases and Supreme Court Rule 451 supra with respect to criminal matters. The original written instructions given by the court to the jury are taken by the jury to the jury room. 735 ILCS 5/2-1107(b); Supreme Court Rule 451(c) supra.

In criminal cases failure to tender, to object, or to preserve error will not prevent review of "substantial defects" in jury instructions "if the interests of justice require," Supreme Court Rule 451(c) supra; *People v. Underwood,* 72 Ill. 2d 124, 19 Ill. Dec. 12, 378 N.E.2d 513 (1978); *People v. Thurman,* 104 Ill. 2d 326, 84 Ill. Dec. 454, 472 N.E.2d 414 (1984), preservation not required to correct grave errors or in cases so close factually that fundamental fairness requires proper instructions. Instructional errors are subject to the harmless error test. *People v. Scott,* 148 Ill. 2d 479, 171 Ill. Dec. 365, 594 N.E.2d 217 (1992). *See generally People v. Alvine,* 173 Ill. 2d 273, 219 Ill. Dec. 546, 671 N.E.2d 713 (1996). *See also* §103.10 supra.

The court is not permitted in its instructions to the jury either to sum up the evidence or to comment to the jury upon the weight of the evidence or the credibility of the witness. *See generally* Illinois Pattern Jury Instructions — Criminal 1.01 (1996). *Cf.* Standard 107 of the Federal Rules of Evidence, 1 Weinstein's Evidence ¶107[01](1988).

With respect to requiring the jury to answer a special interrogatory, 735 ILCS 5/2-1108 states that, "The jury may be required by the court, and must be required on request of any party, to find specially upon any material question or questions of fact submitted to the jury in writing." The function of the special interrogatory is to require the jury's determination as to one or more specific issues of ultimate fact as a check upon the deliberations of the jury. *Sommese v. Maling Bros., Inc.,* 36 Ill. 2d 263, 222 N.E.2d 468 (1967). Thus special interrogatories test the general verdict against the jury's conclusions as to the ultimate controlling facts. *Wise v. Wise,* 22 Ill. App. 2d 54, 159 N.E.2d 500 (1959). Whether a fact is an ultimate fact depends upon its effect on the issue that the jury is required to resolve. To be an ultimate fact, the fact must be one that controls the general verdict. *Department of Transp. v. Bryant,* 63 Ill. App. 3d 483, 20 Ill. Dec. 486, 380 N.E.2d 464 (1978). Special interrogatories on a fact that is not controlling should not be submitted to a jury. *Wicks v. Cuneo-Henneberry Co.,* 319 Ill. 344, 150 N.E. 276 (1925).

An inconsistent finding to a special interrogatory controls a general verdict. *North Shore Sanitary Dist. v. Schulik,* 12 Ill. 2d 309, 146 N.E.2d 25 (1957). The rationale of this policy is that a jury more clearly understands a particularized special interrogatory than a composite of all of the questions in a case, and therefore a special finding upon which a jury presumably has more intensively focused its attention should prevail over an inconsistent general verdict. *Borries v. Z. Frank, Inc.,*

37 Ill. 2d 263, 226 N.E.2d 16 (1967). Inconsistency exists only when the special findings are clearly and absolutely irreconcilable with the general verdict. *Wicks v. Cuneo-Henneberry Co.,* 319 Ill. 344, 150 N.E. 276 (1925); *Devine v. Federal Life Ins. Co.,* 250 Ill. 203, 95 N.E. 174 (1911). Where an examination of the jury findings reveals that a reasonable hypothesis consistent with the general verdict exists, the special findings are not absolutely irreconcilable. *Devine v. Federal Life Ins. Co.* supra; *Smith v. McCarthy,* 33 Ill. App. 176 (1889). Thus, if the special findings do not cover all the issues submitted to the jury and are not solely determinative of the case, a reasonable hypothesis consistent with the general verdict exists. *Finnegan v. Davis,* 68 Ill. App. 3d 118, 24 Ill. Dec. 813, 385 N.E.2d 1103 (1979); *Calcese v. Cunningham Cartage, Inc.,* 25 Ill. App. 3d 1094, 322 N.E.2d 620 (1975); *Legerski v. Nolan,* 132 Ill. App. 2d 51, 265 N.E.2d 696 (1971); *Cohen v. Sager,* 2 Ill. App. 3d 1018, 278 N.E.2d 453 (1971).

Where the jury's answer to a special interrogatory is inconsistent with a general verdict, a judgment consistent with the special finding must be entered unless the jury's verdict to the special interrogatory is so contrary to the overwhelming weight of the evidence that it will not be permitted to stand, *Pedrick v. Peoria & E.R.R.,* 37 Ill. 2d 494, 229 N.E.2d 504 (1967); §301.7 supra, or is against the manifest weight of the evidence. Where the special finding must be set aside upon application of the *Pedrick* rule, a judgment on the general verdict may be entered. Where the special finding is against the manifest weight of the evidence, a new trial must be granted. *Borries v. Z. Frank, Inc.,* 37 Ill. 2d 263, 226 N.E.2d 16 (1967); *Leonard v. Pacific Intermountain Express Co.,* 37 Ill. App. 3d 995, 347 N.E.2d 359 (1976); *Zygadlo v. McCarthy,* 17 Ill. App. 3d 454, 308 N.E.2d 167 (1974).

After the jury has returned a verdict, counsel, in civil and criminal cases, *Bianchi v. Mikhail,* 266 Ill. App. 3d 767, 204 Ill. Dec. 21, 640 N.E.2d 1370 (1994), has a right to have a poll of the jury. *People v. Herron,* 30 Ill. App. 3d 788, 332 N.E.2d 623 (1975), right to poll described as substantial. The purpose of the jury poll is to determine whether the verdict has in fact been freely reached (i.e., was not the product of force or coercion), and remains unanimous. *People v. Preston,* 60 Ill. App. 3d 162, 17 Ill. Dec. 300, 376 N.E.2d 299 (1978); *People v. Smith,* 53 Ill. App. 3d 395, 11 Ill. Dec. 10, 368 N.E.2d 561 (1977). When a jury is polled, each juror should be questioned individually as to whether the announced verdict is his own. The specific form of question to be asked each juror rests in the court's discretion provided that the question asked does not hinder a juror's expression of dissent. *People v. Williams,* 97 Ill. 2d 252, 73 Ill. Dec. 360, 454 N.E.2d 220 (1983); *People v. Gunn,* 237 Ill. App. 3d 508, 178 Ill. Dec. 521, 604 N.E.2d 1044 (1992). The often used question "Was this then and is this now your verdict?" was specifically approved in *People v. Kellogg,* 77 Ill. 2d 524, 34 Ill. Dec. 163, 397 N.E.2d 835 (1979). The trial court in determining whether the jury verdict is unanimous and freely assented to hears the juror's response and observes the juror's demeanor and tone of voice. However, the trial court must also be careful not to make the polling process another arena for deliberations. If a juror indicates some hesitancy or ambivalence in his answer, then the trial court must ascertain the juror's present intent by affording the juror the opportunity to make an unambiguous reply as to his present state of mind. Once the trial court determines that a juror dissents from the verdict, then the proper remedy is for the trial court to either direct the jury to retire for further deliberations or to continue to poll the jury until the process is completed, *People v. Chandler,* 88 Ill. App. 644, 44 Ill. Dec. 314, 411 N.E.2d 283 (1980); *Bianchi v. Mikhail,* 266 Ill. App. 3d 767, 204 Ill. Dec. 21, 640 N.E.2d 1370 (1994) (failure to complete polling improperly isolates dissenting juror) and then discharge them. *People v. Kellogg,* 77 Ill. 2d 524, 34 Ill. Dec. 163, 397 N.E.2d 835 (1979); *People v. Lark,* 127 Ill. App. 3d 927, 83 Ill. Dec. 121, 469 N.E.2d 728 (1984). A trial judge's determination of the voluntariness of a juror's assent to the verdict will not be set aside unless it is clearly unreasonable. *People v. Cabrera,* 116 Ill. 2d 474, 108 Ill. Dec. 397, 508 N.E.2d 708 (1987).

§612 Documents Used to Refresh Recollection

§612.1 Commentary

A party may refresh the recollection of a witness either by a leading question or by showing a document to the witness. Requirements applicable generally with regard to refreshing recollection are discussed in §611.9 supra. Matters discussed infra relate solely to refreshment of recollection by means of a document.

A witness may refresh her memory by referring to a document while testifying when unable to recall relevant facts. *People v. Griswold*, 405 Ill. 533, 92 N.E.2d 91 (1950); *People v. Nickson*, 58 Ill. App. 3d 470, 16 Ill. Dec. 29, 374 N.E.2d 804 (1978). The document itself need not be admissible in evidence; all that is required is for the witness to state the facts from her own recollection after inspecting it. *Scovill Mfg. Co. v. Cassidy*, 275 Ill. 462, 114 N.E. 181 (1916); *People v. Van Dyk*, 40 Ill. App. 3d 275, 352 N.E.2d 327 (1976). The memorandum need not have been prepared by the witness, or at her direction. *Northern Ill. Gas Co. v. Vincent DiVito Constr.*, 214 Ill. App. 3d 203, 157 Ill. Dec. 825, 573 N.E.2d 243 (1991); *People v. Cross*, 100 Ill. App. 3d 83, 55 Ill. Dec. 477, 426 N.E.2d 623 (1981). The document need not have been made at or near the time of the event, *cf.* §803.9; and the Original Writing Rule, §1002 infra, does not apply. *In Interest of Thomas*, 65 Ill. App. 3d 136, 22 Ill. Dec. 236, 382 N.E.2d 556 (1978). Thus anything may be used for this purpose, the only question being whether it genuinely is calculated to revive the witness's recollection. *People v. Olson*, 59 Ill. App. 3d 643, 16 Ill. Dec. 660, 375 N.E.2d 533 (1978). Illustrations are: a photograph, *People v. Lindsey*, 17 Ill. App. 3d 137, 308 N.E.2d 111 (1974); an earlier deposition of the witness, *Beringer v. Lackner*, 331 Ill. App. 591, 73 N.E.2d 620 (1947); a pleading, *Dunlap v. Berry*, 5 Ill. 327 (1843); a newspaper article, *Clifford v. Drake*, 110 Ill. 135 (1884); a police report, *People v. Shatner*,

174 Ill. 2d 133, 220 Ill. Dec. 346, 673 N.E.2d 258 (1996); *Rigor v. Howard Liquors, Inc.,* 10 Ill. App. 3d 1004, 295 N.E.2d 491 (1973); and a hospital report, *Tenenbaum v. City of Chicago,* 60 Ill. 2d 363, 325 N.E.2d 607 (1975).

There is a real possibility that the witness will testify from what purports to be a revived present memory when his testimony is actually a reflection, conscious or unconscious, of what he has read rather than what he remembers. The court has considerable discretion to reject such testimony by finding that the document does not in fact revive the witness's recollection. *People v. Black,* 84 Ill. App. 3d 1050, 40 Ill. Dec. 322, 406 N.E.2d 23 (1980); *City of Crystal Lake v. Nelson,* 5 Ill. App. 3d 358, 283 N.E.2d 239 (1972). In reaching this determination the court may initially require the witness to read the writing to himself and surrender possession of it before responding to any questions. A finding that his memory is not revived may, however, pave the way for admission of the writing under the hearsay exception for recorded past recollection, §803.9 infra. In practice, however, in almost all instances a question as to whether the witness's recollection has in fact been refreshed is treated as a matter going to the weight of the witness's testimony. *Corrales v. American Cab Co.,* 170 Ill. App. 3d 907, 120 Ill. Dec. 741, 524 N.E.2d 923 (1988).

Opposing counsel has the right to inspect the document referred to while testifying, to cross-examine regarding it, *Tenenbaum v. City of Chicago,* 60 Ill. 2d 363, 325 N.E.2d 607 (1975); *Justice v. Pennsylvania R.R.,* 41 Ill. App. 2d 352, 191 N.E.2d 72 (1963); *Lebajo v. Department of Public Aid,* 210 Ill. App. 3d 263, 155 Ill. Dec. 70, 569 N.E.2d 70 (1991), and to show the document to the jury, 3 Wigmore, Evidence §762 (Chadbourn rev. 1970), all of which serve to afford protection against an abuse. Neither inspection of the document nor its employment upon cross-examination makes the document admissible on behalf of the proponent of the witness.

A witness may also refer to documents to refresh her recollection prior to taking the stand. *People v. Griswold,* 405 Ill. 533, 92 N.E.2d 91 (1950). An opponent possesses the same rights with regard to documents so consulted as with those consulted on the stand. *People v. Scott,* 29 Ill. 2d 97, 112, 193 N.E.2d 814 (1963). *Accord* 3 Wigmore, Evidence §762 (Chadbourn rev. 1970). *Cf. Cole v. Brundage,* 36 Ill. App. 3d 782, 344 N.E.2d 583 (1976), and *Aetna Ins. Co. v. 3 Oak Wrecking & Lumber Co.,* 65 Ill. App. 3d 618, 21 Ill. Dec. 919, 382 N.E.2d 283 (1978), relying on Rule 612 of the Federal Rules of Evidence, and *Goldman v. United States,* 316 U.S. 129 (1942), declaring that it is within the court's discretion whether a writing reviewed before testifying to refresh recollection must be produced for inspection at trial and that such discretion is necessary to prevent wholesale exploration of an opposing party's files during trial.

An assertion of privilege, usually lawyer-client, §§505.1 to 505.7 supra, may be made with respect to the document referred to whether before or at trial. *See People v. White,* 8 Ill. App. 2d 428, 131 N.E.2d 803 (1956), allowing the claim. An argument in favor of waiver under these circumstances seems, however, to have merit. If a claim of privilege is successfully asserted as reason for not allowing access to opposing counsel, to insure fairness the court may make any order justice requires. If the claim of privilege is known in advance, one obvious solution is simply to forbid the witness to refresh his recollection at trial from the document.

If it is claimed that the document reviewed on the stand or prior to testifying contains matters not related to the subject matter of the testimony, the court should examine the document *in camera,* excise any portions not so related, and order delivery of the remainder to the party entitled thereto. If a document is not produced or delivered as ordered by the court, the court may make any order justice requires, including striking the testimony, contempt, dismissal, or finding issues against the offender. In criminal cases when the prosecution elects not to comply, the order should be one striking the testimony or, if the court in its discretion determines that the interests of justice so require, declaring a mistrial. *See* Federal Rule of Evidence 612, 65 F.R.D. 131, 150 (1975).

A document used to refresh recollection should not be confused with recorded past recollection (an exception to the hearsay rule discussed in §803.9 infra), or with refreshing recollection with leading questions, §611.9 supra. Similarly, refreshing recollection of a witness on direct examination with a document discussed supra should not be confused with the use of a prior inconsistent written statement to impeach. *See* §613.1 infra.

With respect to the use of a document to refresh the recollection of a witness on cross-examination for any purpose such as to the making of an alleged prior inconsistent statement by another witness, *see People v. Lavas,* 113 Ill. App. 3d 196, 68 Ill. Dec. 791, 446 N.E.2d 1188 (1983) (permitting refreshing recollection on cross-examination is discretionary with the court); *Moran v. Erickson,* 297 Ill. App. 3d 342, 231 Ill. Dec. 484, 696 N.E.2d 780 (1998) (hospital record properly employed on cross-examination to refresh recollection, the contents of the record not mentioned). *See also People v. Shatner,* 174 Ill. 2d 133, 220 Ill. Dec. 346, 673 N.E.2d 258 (1996), assuming without discussion that refreshing recollection is permitted on cross-examination. *Contra Munjal v. Baird & Warner, Inc.,* 138 Ill. App. 3d 172, 92 Ill. Dec. 809, 485 N.E.2d 855 (1985) (refreshing recollection on cross-examination is improper; only inconsistent statement impeachment is permitted).

§613   Prior Statements of Witness

§613.1   *Prior Inconsistent Statements of Witness: An Overview*

A witness may be impeached by proof that she made a statement outside of court contradicting her in-court testimony or failed to speak under circumstances where it would have been natural to relate the matters testified to in court if true. The rationale is that a witness who testifies one way at trial while speaking inconsistently prior to trial is blowing hot and cold thereby raising doubts as to the truthfulness of both statements. McCormick, Evidence §34 at 114 (4th ed. 1992). In other words, prior inconsistent statement impeachment tends to cancel out the witness's testimony. *People v. Cruz*, 162 Ill. 2d 314, 205 Ill. Dec. 345, 643 N.E.2d 636 (1994).

A prior statement of a witness may be employed for purposes of impeachment only if inconsistent with the witness's in-court testimony. *See also* §613.2 infra. *See People v. Chatmon*, 236 Ill. App. 3d 913, 178 Ill. Dec. 143, 604 N.E.2d 399 (1992) (witness must testify concerning his or her knowledge, or lack of it, about the subject matter before impeachment is allowed). The prior statement must be that of the witness being impeached; it cannot be a statement made by another person. *Contra People v. Buie*, 238 Ill. App. 3d 260, 179 Ill. Dec. 447, 606 N.E.2d 279 (1992) (incorrectly decided). *See People v. Pendleton*, 256 Ill. App. 3d 983, 195 Ill. Dec. 41, 628 N.E.2d 505 (1993). An inconsistent statement by a witness meeting the definition of hearsay, §801.1 infra, is admissible as substantive evidence if the statement meets the requirements of a hearsay exception, §§801.9, 802, 803, and 804 infra. Most importantly, prior inconsistent written, recorded, or acknowledged statements are also admissible as substantive evidence in criminal cases, 725 ILCS 5/115-10.1, provided the requirement of a preliminary foundation on cross-examination, discussed in §613.3 infra, is satisfied. *People v. Hallbeck*, 227 Ill. App. 3d 59, 169 Ill. Dec. 52, 590 N.E.2d 971 (1992). *See* §801.9 infra. Otherwise, its effect is limited to impairing the credibility of the witness. *People v. Morgan*, 28 Ill. 2d 55, 190 N.E.2d 755 (1963); *Smith v. Pelz*, 384 Ill. 446, 51 N.E.2d 534 (1943). *Accord People v. Cruz*, 162 Ill. 2d 314, 205 Ill. Dec. 345, 643 N.E.2dd 636 (1994) (the purpose of impeachment by use of a prior inconsistent statement "is to destroy credibility of the witness and *not* to establish the truth of the impeaching material"). With respect to the giving of a limiting instruction, *see* §613.3 infra.

A prior inconsistent statement should not be confused with an admission of a party, §802 infra, that, being a hearsay exception and substantive evidence, requires no preliminary foundation on cross-examination. *Brown v. Calumet River Ry.,* 125 Ill. 600, 18 N.E. 283 (1888); *Kane v. Wehner,* 312 Ill. App. 391, 39 N.E.2d 51 (1941).

A requirement emanated from *Queen Caroline's Case,* 129 Eng. Rep. 976 (1820), that cross-examining counsel show or disclose to the witness an inconsistent writing prior to examining the witness concerning its contents. Adopted in Illinois in *Illinois Central R.R. v. Wade,* 206 Ill. 523, 69 N.E. 565 (1903), it was abolished in England long ago by statute. This requirement, which has not been followed by trial courts in actual practice, should be formally discarded in favor of surprise; the truth-seeking process is better served by cross-examination without first providing the witness a warning. Adequate protection against unwarranted insinuation as to the existence of a prior statement is provided by requiring disclosure of the contents of the prior statement upon request to opposing counsel.

As with contradiction generally, the impeaching evidence cannot relate to collateral matters. *People v. Schott,* 39 Ill. App. 3d 266, 350 N.E.2d 49 (1976), collateral where witness had previously stated he was going to farmhouse where robbery occurred to buy LSD when at trial he said he was going to purchase a gun. *See* §607.2 supra.

The traditional foundation requirement, discussed in §613.3 infra, must precede the introduction of extrinsic proof of prior inconsistent statements admitted solely for purposes of impeachment unless the interests of justice otherwise require.

The use of prior statements to refresh recollection is discussed in §§611.9 and 612.1 supra. The use of prior statements to corroborate a witness is addressed in §611.14 supra. *See* §801.9 infra for a discussion of impeachment of a witness who at trial claims lack of recollection of the subject matter of his prior statement.

With respect to the admissibility of prior inconsistent statements as an exception to the hearsay rule, *see* §801.9 infra, and as to the use of suppressed or inadmissible evidence to impeach the criminal defendant if he testifies at trial, including his silence in the face of police accusation, *see* §502.5 supra and §802.7 infra.

§613.2   Prior Inconsistent Statements of Witness: Requirement of Inconsistency

Prior inconsistent statements are not limited to those that are directly contradictory; it is sufficient if the inconsistency has a reasonable tendency to discredit the testimony of the witness, i.e., "the inconsistency is great enough to contravene the witness's direct testimony." *Ogg v. City of Springfield,* 121 Ill. App. 3d 25, 39, 76 Ill. Dec. 531, 540, 458 N.E.2d 1331, 1340 (1984). *See, e.g., In re Lane,* 127 Ill. 2d 90, 129 Ill. Dec. 101, 535 N.E.2d 866 (1989) (citing Handbook); *People v. Flores,* 128 Ill. 2d 66, 131 Ill. Dec. 106, 538 N.E.2d 481 (1989); *Van Steemburg v. General Aviation, Inc.,* 243 Ill. App. 3d 299, 183 Ill. Dec. 496, 611 N.E.2d 1144 (1993), where a witness claims to be unable to recollect a matter which would be expected to be recalled if true, a prior statement of it is inconsistent and thus admissible as a contradiction; *People v. Davis,* 106 Ill. App. 3d 260, 62 Ill. Dec. 40, 435 N.E.2d 838 (1982), testimony that defendant had left for Milwaukee on the evening of the 17th is inconsistent with statement that he had been in Milwaukee on the 17th. The suggestion of a more rigorous test of inconsistency, i.e., "materially inconsistent," made in *Keller v. State Farm Ins. Co.,* 180 Ill. App. 3d 539, 129 Ill. Dec. 510, 536 N.E.2d 194 (1989), and *Tarin v. Pellonari,* 253 Ill. App. 3d 542, 192 Ill. Dec. 584, 625 N.E.2d 739 (1993), is incorrect and should be disregarded. Whether the prior statement is sufficiently inconsistent to be employed to impeach rests in the discretion of the trial court. *People v. Salazar,* 126 Ill. 2d 424, 129 Ill. Dec. 1, 535 N.E.2d 776 (1988); *People v. Johnson,* 251 Ill. 2d 227, 182 Ill. Dec. 1, 609 N.E.2d 304 (1993). Where the discrepancy between the witness's testimony and prior statement is slight and the subject matter is collateral or otherwise insignificant, the court in the exercise of discretion may preclude cross-examination. *People v. Batchelor,* 202 Ill. App. 3d 316, 147 Ill. Dec. 608, 559 N.E.2d 948 (1990); *People v. Brooks,* 172 Ill. App. 3d 417, 122 Ill. Dec. 161, 526 N.E.2d 420 (1988).

The inconsistency may consist of omitting from the prior statement a significant matter that would reasonably be expected to be mentioned if true. *People v. Zurita,* 295 Ill. App. 3d 1072, 230 Ill. Dec. 409, 693 N.E.2d 887 (1998), witness who testified to defendant drawing a gun and lifting his arm in a shooting motion may be impeached with his prior statement to police not mentioning the defendant as the shooter; *Carroll v. Krause,* 295 Ill. App. 552, 15 N.E.2d 323 (1938), witness who testified car had only one headlight properly impeached by showing failure to mention that fact in testimony at inquest. The inconsistency may consist of failure to speak of a matter entirely when it is shown that the witness had an opportunity to make a statement and that a person would reasonably be expected under the circumstances to make a statement. *People v. Conley,* 187 Ill. App. 3d 234, 134 Ill. Dec. 855, 543 N.E.2d 138 (1989), witness for defendant who testified that another person committed the offense properly impeached with failure to volunteer the information to the police; *People v. Knott,* 224 Ill. App. 3d 236, 166 Ill. Dec. 521, 586 N.E.2d 479 (1991), alibi witness properly impeached with fact that with notice of the circumstances the witness failed to give the exculpatory evidence to the police; *People v. Jennings,* 254 Ill. App. 3d 14, 193 Ill. Dec. 232, 626 N.E.2d 265 (1993), alibi witness who is a friend or member of defendant's family may be impeached regarding failure to give information to the police; *People v. Colts,* 269 Ill. App. 3d 679, 206 Ill. Dec. 220, 645 N.E.2d 225 (1993), defendant properly impeached with fact that he had failed to speak about his alibi defense to private parties prior to its assertion at trial. *Accord People v. Nemecek,* 277 Ill. App. 3d 243, 213 Ill. Dec. 876, 660 N.E.2d 133 (1995); *People v. Berry,* 264 Ill. App. 3d 773, 205 Ill. Dec. 190, 642 N.E.2d 1307 (1994); *People v. Andras,* 241 Ill. App. 3d 28, 181 Ill. Dec. 237, 608 N.E.2d 310 (1992). *See* §802.7 infra. *Cf. People v. McKinney,* 193 Ill. App. 3d 1012, 140 Ill. Dec. 719, 550 N.E.2d 604 (1990), not reasonable to expect person who acts accidentally or negligently to immediately acknowledge such action. The inconsistency may also consist of a photograph, sketch, or identikit picture previously adopted by the witness as an accurate portrayal of an individual differently described or identified by that witness in court. *People v. Johnson,* 109 Ill. App. 3d 511, 65 Ill. Dec. 137, 440 N.E.2d 992 (1982). There must be unequivocal testimony from the police artist that the drawing not only was a representation prepared at the direction of the witness, but that the witness, after having had an opportunity to view the completed sketch, adopted it as an accurate portrayal of the suspect. *People v. Yates,* 98 Ill. 2d 502, 75 Ill. Dec. 188, 456 N.E.2d 1369 (1983). The statement of another may be adopted by silent acquiescence on the part of the witness under circumstances that would normally call for a denial if untrue. *Clark v. A. Bazzoni & Co.,* 7 Ill. App. 2d 334, 129 N.E.2d 435 (1955). While it had previously been held that an opinion inconsistent with testimony is inadmissible unless the subject is a proper one for opinion evidence, because the opinion itself is inadmissible, *Pienta v. Chicago City Ry.,* 284 Ill. 246, 120 N.E. 1 (1918) (who was to blame for accident), the rationale of the decisions was recognized as unsound in *People v. Edwards,* 55 Ill. 2d 25, 302 N.E.2d 306 (1973), citing 3A Wigmore, Evidence §1041 (Chadbourn rev. 1970). Recollection of a matter at trial is inconsistent with a prior assertion of lack of recollection of the same subject matter. *Contra Keller v. State Farm Ins. Co.,* 180 Ill. App. 3d 539, 129 Ill. Dec. 510, 536 N.E.2d 194 (1989) (incorrectly decided). Professed lack of recollection at trial of a matter which would be expected to be recalled if true is inconsistent with a prior statement upon the subject. *In re Lane,* 127 Ill. 2d 90, 129 Ill. Dec. 101, 535 N.E.2d 866 (1989) (citing Handbook); *People v. Flores,* 128 Ill. 2d 66, 131 Ill. Dec. 106, 538 N.E.2d 481 (1989); *People v. Lee,* 243 Ill. App. 3d 745, 184 Ill. Dec. 46, 612 N.E.2d 922 (1993); *People v. Zurita,* 295 Ill. App. 3d 1072, 230 Ill. Dec. 409, 693 N.E.2d 887 (1998).

Earlier versions of changed deposition transcripts, shown to reflect accurately the original testimony at the deposition, as well as withdrawn or superseded answers to interrogatories, if inconsistent with trial testimony, may be employed to impeach. *La Salle National Bank v. 53rd-Ellis Currency Exchange,* 249 Ill. App. 3d 415, 188 Ill. Dec. 533, 618 N.E.2d 1103 (1993); *Palumbo v. Kuiken,* 201 Ill. App. 3d 785, 147 Ill. Dec. 206, 559 N.E.2d 206 (1990).

A prior statement of a witness who is unavailable to testify as a witness at trial even if physically present, for example, by asserting a privilege, *see* §804.1 infra, is not inconsistent and thus may not be employed to impeach. *People v. Redd,* 135 Ill. App. 3d 252, 143 Ill. Dec. 802, 553 N.E.2d 316 (1990). With respect to hearsay statements, see §806.1 infra.

§613.3   *Prior Inconsistent Statements of Witness: Foundation Requirement*

Before proof of an inconsistent statement for impeachment purposes is admitted, proper foundation must ordinarily be laid during cross-examination. *People v. Powell,* 53 Ill. 2d 465, 292 N.E.2d 409 (1973). This traditional foundation consists of directing the attention of the witness to the time, place, and circumstances of the statement and its substance. *People v. Bradford,* 106 Ill. 2d 492, 88 Ill. Dec. 615, 478 N.E.2d 1341 (1985); *People v. Perri,* 381 Ill. 244, 44 N.E.2d 857 (1942); *Brooke Inns, Inc. v. S & R Hi-Fi and TV,* 249 Ill. App. 3d 1064, 188 Ill. Dec. 164, 618 N.E.2d 734 (1993); *People v. Hood,* 229 Ill. App. 3d 202, 170 Ill. Dec. 916, 593 N.E.2d 805 (1992). The purpose of the requirement is to afford an opportunity to deny, correct, or explain and to avoid placing the witness in a bad light through misapprehension, inattention, or lack of recollection. *People v. Smith,* 78 Ill. 2d 298, 35 Ill. Dec. 761, 399 N.E.2d 1289 (1980); *Aneals v. People,* 134 Ill. 401, 25 N.E. 1022 (1890); *In Interest of A.M.,* 274 Ill. App. 3d 702, 210 Ill. Dec. 832, 653 N.E.2d 1294 (1995), purpose of foundation requirement is to avoid unfair surprise and give the witness an opportunity to explain; *People v. McDonald,* 276

Ill. App. 3d 466, 213 Ill. Dec. 230, 658 N.E.2d 1251 (1995), purpose of foundation requirement is to provide an opportunity to explain the inconsistency prior to the introduction of extrinsic evidence. The cross-examiner does not herself have to provide the witness the opportunity to correct or explain; the opportunity for the witness to correct or explain the apparent inconsistency on redirect examination suffices. *See* §611.12 supra. The opportunity to correct or explain includes the right to introduce other parts of the statement that qualify or explain the inconsistency, and the right to explain why the inconsistent statement, if acknowledged, was made. *People v. Hicks,* 28 Ill. 2d 457, 192 N.E.2d 891 (1963); *People v. Cowper,* 145 Ill. App. 3d 1074, 99 Ill. Dec. 868, 496 N.E.2d 729 (1986). *See, e.g., People v. Williams,* 262 Ill. App. 3d 734, 200 Ill. Dec. 442, 635 N.E.2d 781 (1994), witness explained that prior inconsistent statement was made because of fear for his and his family's safety. A prior statement that corroborates the witness may be admitted if it serves to explain or modify a fragment thereof introduced by the opposite party for purposes of impeachment. *See* §106.1 supra; *People v. Hicks,* 28 Ill. 2d 457, 192 N.E.2d 891 (1963); *Smith v. City of Rock Island,* 22 Ill. App. 2d 389, 161 N.E.2d 369 (1959). *See also In re Estate of Sewart,* 274 Ill. App. 3d 298, 210 Ill. Dec. 175, 652 N.E.2d 1151 (1995) (once impeached by her deposition testimony, witness should have been allowed to refer to her deposition on redirect to clarify). It is also admissible if it is otherwise related to and supportive of a denial or explanation offered in response to impeachment of a witness by an alleged self-contradiction, whether the latter is an inconsistent statement or failure to speak when natural to do so. *People v. Cowper* supra; *People v. Morrow,* 104 Ill. App. 3d 995, 60 Ill. Dec. 747, 433 N.E.2d 985 (1982); *People v. Rodriguez,* 58 Ill. App. 3d 562, 16 Ill. Dec. 129, 374 N.E.2d 904 (1978). However, a prior consistent statement that does not directly corroborate the witness's response to the alleged attempted impeachment by self-contradiction will not be admitted, i.e., the foregoing may not be employed as a subterfuge to admit a prior consistent statement that is otherwise inadmissible. *People v. Emerson,* 97 Ill. 2d 487, 74 Ill. Dec. 11, 455 N.E.2d 41 (1983). *See* §611.14 supra.

Strict adherence to the traditional formula for the foundation question is not always required, for a functional test is applied. Thus, if the rationale of the foundation rule is satisfied, that is, to provide the witness an opportunity otherwise to deny, correct, or explain, a sufficient foundation will have been laid. *People v. Henry,* 47 Ill. 2d 312, 265 N.E.2d 876 (1970), witness alerted to the substance of the statement and the identity of the person to whom it was allegedly made; *People v. Cobb,* 97 Ill. 2d 465, 74 Ill. Dec. 1, 455 N.E.2d 31 (1983), substance of statement and identity of person to whom it was made was an adequate foundation in spite of the absence of particular recitation of time and place in light of the critical nature of the alleged inconsistent statement; *In Interest of A.M.,* 274 Ill. App. 3d 702, 210 Ill. Dec. 832, 653 N.E.2d 1294 (1995), witness recalled conversation even though foundation question did not contain time, place, or circumstance; *Boyce v. Risch,* 276 Ill. App. 3d 274, 212 Ill. Dec. 800, 657 N.E.2d 1145 (1995), witness was advised of the person to whom the statement was made and that the subject matter of the conversation was the accident. Where the witness has not been alerted to the content of the prior statement, the purpose of the foundation required will not be found to have been satisfied. *People v. Smith,* 78 Ill. 2d 298, 35 Ill. Dec. 761, 399 N.E.2d 1289 (1980), general question to witness whether while in jail he had discussed defendant's case was found to be an inadequate foundation; *People v. Escobedo,* 151 Ill. App. 3d 69, 104 Ill. Dec. 603, 502 N.E.2d 1263 (1986), cross-examination inquiring of witness as to whether witness understood terms such as "false charges" did not alert witness to fact that the cross-examiner was asserting that the prior statement of witness that she was sorry she brought charges against the defendant meant that such charges were false; *People v. Galindo,* 95 Ill. App. 3d 927, 51 Ill. Dec. 359, 420 N.E.2d 773 (1981), cross-examination inquiring whether the witness had given a statement to the

Chicago police did not apprise the witness of the content of the prior statement. Similarly, where the identity of the person to whom the statement was allegedly made was not specified, the foundation requirement has been held not to have been satisfied. *People v. Coleman,* 124 Ill. App. 3d 285, 79 Ill. Dec. 802, 464 N.E.2d 706 (1984).

Failure to lay a proper foundation on cross-examination of the witness precludes introduction of extrinsic evidence of the prior inconsistent statement. *People v. Hallbeck,* 227 Ill. App. 3d 59, 169 Ill. Dec. 52, 590 N.E.2d 971 (1992). The trial court possesses discretion to permit recalling of the witness to perfect the foundation. *People v. Henry* supra; *People v. Powell,* 53 Ill. 2d 465, 292 N.E.2d 409 (1973). *Contra People v. Neumann,* 148 Ill. App. 3d 362, 101 Ill. Dec. 899, 499 N.E.2d 487 (1986) (witness may *not* be recalled, for to do so would unfairly highlight the attempted impeachment; incorrectly decided, as matter was properly within trial court's discretion). Where a proper foundation was not laid originally because counsel was not then aware of the prior inconsistent statement, failure to permit the witness to be recalled *may* constitute reversible error. *People v. Suerth,* 97 Ill. App. 3d 1005, 53 Ill. Dec. 381, 423 N.E.2d 1185 (1981). Moreover, where the alleged inconsistent statement is critical to the defendant, failure to permit the witness to be recalled *will* constitute reversible error. *People v. Cobb,* 97 Ill. 2d 465, 74 Ill. Dec. 1, 455 N.E.2d 31 (1983).

A good-faith basis for inquiry regarding a prior inconsistent statement is required: innuendoes or insinuations of a nonexistent statement are improper. *People v. Fiorita,* 339 Ill. 78, 170 N.E. 690 (1930); *Boyce v. Risch,* 276 Ill. App. 3d 274, 212 Ill. Dec. 800, 657 N.E.2d 1145 (1995); *Sutton v. Overcash,* 251 Ill. App. 3d 737, 191 Ill. Dec. 230, 623 N.E.2d 820 (1993). Counsel must be prepared and able to follow up with extrinsic proof if required. *People v. Olinger,* 112 Ill. 2d 324, 97 Ill. Dec. 772, 493 N.E.2d 579 (1986); *People v. Sanders,* 357 Ill. 610, 192 N.E. 697 (1934), *People v. Struberg,* 61 Ill. App. 3d 521, 18 Ill. Dec. 727, 378 N.E.2d 191 (1978). *See also* §§607.1 to 607.3 supra. As to the effect of a curative instruction, *see*

§103.3 supra. Protection against unwarranted insinuations is provided in part by requiring prior disclosure of the contents of the statement to opposing counsel on request.

If the witness denies making the statement, states that he cannot remember making it, *People v. Shatner*, 174 Ill. 2d 133, 220 Ill. Dec. 346, 673 N.E.2d 258 (1996), does not know if he made it, or gives any other equivocal answer not amounting to an admission such as "I might have" or "If it's in there I must have said it," the prior statement, if noncollateral, *see* §607.2 supra, must be proved, *People v. Moore*, 54 Ill. 2d 33, 294 N.E.2d 297 (1973); *People v. Williams*, 252 Ill. App. 3d 704, 192 Ill. Dec. 599, 625 N.E.2d 754 (1993); *People v. Villegas*, 222 Ill. App. 3d 546, 165 Ill. Dec. 69, 584 N.E.2d 248 (1991) (citing Handbook); *People v. Brooks*, 175 Ill. App. 3d 136, 124 Ill. Dec. 751, 529 N.E.2d 732 (1988); *Bradford v. City of Chicago*, 132 Ill. App. 3d 317, 87 Ill. Dec. 229, 476 N.E.2d 1221 (1985), i.e., admissible evidence must be introduced sufficient to support a finding that the statement was made. *See People v. Hood*, 229 Ill. App. 3d 202, 170 Ill. Dec. 916, 593 N.E.2d 805 (1992), proof of the witness's statement must be substantially verbatim. Failure to prove the prior statement will result in the cross-examination being stricken and the jury being instructed to disregard. *People v. Cox*, 100 Ill. App. 3d 272, 55 Ill. Dec. 725, 426 N.E.2d 1050 (1981). Failure to prove the prior statement will result in reversible error when the circumstances show sufficient prejudice. *Walter v. Maxwell City, Inc.*, 117 Ill. App. 3d 571, 73 Ill. Dec. 92, 453 N.E.2d 917 (1983); *People v. Green*, 118 Ill. App. 3d 227, 73 Ill. Dec. 695, 454 N.E.2d 792 (1983); *People v. Redman*, 135 Ill. App. 3d 534, 90 Ill. Dec. 361, 481 N.E.2d 1272 (1985); *Hackett v. Equipment Specialists, Inc.*, 201 Ill. App. 3d 186, 147 Ill. Dec. 412, 559 N.E.2d 752 (1990); *People v. Adams*, 283 Ill. App. 3d 520, 218 Ill. Dec. 805, 669 N.E.2d 1331 (1996). The prior statement must be proved through the introduction of *admissible* evidence sufficiently establishing its existence; proof through the introduction of the inadmissible statement of another asserting the prior statement was made is precluded. *People v. Shatner*, 174 Ill. 2d 133, 220 Ill Dec. 346, 673 N.E.2d

258 (1996) (detective's written statement). With respect to the situation where the impeaching party is prohibited by the court from introducing the extrinsic proof *see People v. Pasch,* 152 Ill. 2d 133, 178 Ill. Dec. 38, 604 N.E.2d 294 (1992).

If the witness admits making the statement, extrinsic evidence is not required. *Kyowski v. Burns,* 70 Ill. App. 3d 1009, 26 Ill. Dec. 769, 388 N.E.2d 770 (1979). The party calling the witness is entitled on redirect to have him make such explanation as he can, *People v. Hicks,* 28 Ill. 2d 457, 192 N.E.2d 891 (1963); *People v. Frugoli,* 334 Ill. 324, 166 N.E. 129 (1929); *People v. Hanson,* 83 Ill. App. 3d 1108, 39 Ill. Dec. 210, 404 N.E.2d 801 (1980); *People v. Haynes,* 62 Ill. App. 3d 199, 19 Ill. Dec. 509, 379 N.E.2d 24 (1978); show the circumstances under which made, *People v. Gammons,* 130 Ill. App. 2d 120, 264 N.E.2d 866 (1970); to explain why he made the inconsistent statement, *People v. Hallom,* 265 Ill. App. 3d 896, 202 Ill. Dec. 897, 638 N.E.2d 765 (1994); or to introduce portions of the other conversation, document, or testimony tending to explain, qualify, or otherwise shed light on the inconsistency. *People v. Andersch,* 107 Ill. App. 3d 810, 63 Ill. Dec. 551, 438 N.E.2d 482 (1982); *People v. Perez,* 101 Ill. App. 3d 64, 56 Ill. Dec. 488, 427 N.E.2d 820 (1981); *People v. McMullen,* 82 Ill. App. 3d 1042, 38 Ill. Dec. 308, 403 N.E.2d 539 (1980). *See* §§106.1 and 106.2 supra. The fact that the witness admits having made the statement does not preclude the introduction of extrinsic evidence. *People v. Williams,* 22 Ill. 2d 498, 177 N.E.2d 100 (1961), disclaiming contrary suggestions in earlier cases. *Accord People v. King,* 109 Ill. 2d 514, 94 Ill. Dec. 702, 488 N.E.2d 949 (1986); *People v. Bradford,* 106 Ill. 2d 492, 88 Ill. Dec. 615, 478 N.E.2d 1341 (1985). Conversely, the trial court is not required to allow introduction of evidence of the prior inconsistent statement when admitted to have been made by the witness. The matter rests in the discretion of the trial court. *People v. Davis,* 254 Ill. App. 3d 651, 193 Ill. Dec. 636, 626 N.E.2d 1187 (1993).

The assertion in *Rigor v. Howard Liquors, Inc.,* 10 Ill. App. 3d 1004, 295 N.E.2d 491 (1973), and *Vancil v. Fletcher,* 90 Ill. App. 2d 277, 232 N.E.2d 789 (1967), that if the witness's answer at trial is equivocal, it is counsel's *option* to offer the impeaching statement if she desires, is misleading, having been made in connection with approval of the introduction of extrinsic proof. Since extrinsic evidence may be introduced even where the making of the statement is admitted, *People v. Williams* supra, the court's assertion serves no purpose and should be ignored. In summary, if the witness's answer is equivocal, extrinsic evidence *must* be introduced; if the witness admits making the prior statement, extrinsic statements may still be proved at the examiner's option. *Cf. Gillespie v. Chrysler Motors Corp.*, 135 Ill. 2d 363, 142 Ill. Dec. 777, 553 N.E.2d 291 (1990), not necessary to decide if it is error to fail to introduce extrinsic evidence when witness's answer is equivocal.

Questions to the impeaching witness presenting extrinsic proof should state the time, place, and circumstances of the prior statement and the subject matter of the statement but not its contents, a departure from the rule against leading questions, *see* §611.9 supra, designed to avoid bringing out incompetent matters that might result if the conversation were asked for generally. *Elgin, J. & E. Ry. v. Lawlor*, 132 Ill. App. 280, *aff'd*, 229 Ill. 621, 82 N.E. 407 (1907).

Where a prior inconsistent statement is admitted solely to impeach the witness, the jury upon request will be cautioned at the time the statement is introduced and/or given a limiting instruction when the court charges the jury as to the law that they are to consider the statement only as affecting the credibility of the witness. *People v. Cruz*, 162 Ill. 2d 314, 205 Ill. Dec. 345, 643 N.E.2d 636 (1994); *People v. Bradford*, 106 Ill. 2d 492, 88 Ill. Dec. 615, 478 N.E.2d 1341 (1985). *See also* §105.1 supra. Where neither a cautionary nor limiting instruction is requested by counsel, if the prior inconsistent statement is extremely damaging if considered by the jury as substantive evidence and the proponent of such evidence case is weak, the court, to avoid plain error, must *sua sponte* give such an instruction but not otherwise. *See* §103.10 supra. In the absence of plain error, if no request is made to have the jury advised that the prior inconsistent statement was admitted solely to impeach, the statement may be considered as substantive evidence by the jury. *See* §801.8 infra.

With respect to introduction of extrinsic proof on a collateral issue, *see* §§613.1 and 607.2 supra.

§613.4   Prior Conduct of Witness

A witness may be impeached by proof that he acted in a manner contradictory to his testimony. *See* §607.9 supra. *People v. Boston,* 309 Ill. 77, 139 N.E. 880 (1923), continued friendliness of prosecuting witness and parents toward accused charged with rape. As with contradiction generally, the extrinsic evidence may not be introduced relating solely to collateral matters. *See* §607.2 supra.

Inconsistent conduct relied upon for impeachment has been held to be subject to foundation requirements similar to prior inconsistent statements. *People v. Boston,* 309 Ill. 77, 139 N.E. 880 (1923). *See also* §613.3 supra.

§613.5   Use of Suppressed Statements and Illegally Seized Evidence to Impeach

If a defendant's confession is suppressed, for example, because of failure to give *Miranda* warnings or for failure to provide her a lawyer upon request, the State may still employ the confession for purposes of impeachment as a prior inconsistent statement of the defendant, *Michigan v. Harvey,* 494 U.S. 344 (1990); *Oregon v. Hass,* 420 U.S. 714 (1975); *Harris v. New York,* 401 U.S. 222 (1971); *People v. Byers,* 50 Ill. 2d 210, 278 N.E.2d 65 (1972), provided the statement is shown otherwise to have been voluntarily made. *People v. Peterson,* 74 Ill. 2d 478, 23 Ill. Dec. 554, 384 N.E.2d 348 (1979); *People v. Moore,* 54 Ill. 2d 33, 294 N.E.2d (1973). The suppressed admission or confession may be employed to impeach not only if inconsistent with the direct testimony of defendant but also if inconsistent with answers given by defendant to questions asked on cross-examination within the scope of defendant's direct examination. *United States v. Havens*, 446 U.S. 620 (1980). However, a suppressed admission or confession may not be employed to impeach inconsistent testimony given on direct examination at trial by a defense witness other than the accused. *James v. Illinois*, 493 U.S. 307 (1990), defense witness's testimony that at time defendant's hair was black improperly impeached with defendant's suppressed confession where the defendant stated that his hair was "reddish." Statement obtained in violation of *Miranda* rights may be admitted, if voluntary, as substantive evidence in civil proceedings, *Federal Kemper Life Assurance Co. v. Eichwedel*, 266 Ill. App. 3d 88, 203 Ill. Dec. 207, 639 N.E.2d 246 (1994).

Silence of an accused following the giving of *Miranda* warnings is inadmissible even for purposes of impeachment of the defendant. *Doyle v. Ohio*, 426 U.S. 610 (1976); *Wainwright v. Greenfield*, 474 U.S. 284 (1986); *People v. Szabo*, 94 Ill. 2d 327, 68 Ill. Dec. 935, 447 N.E.2d 193 (1983); *People v. Gagliani*, 210 Ill. App. 3d 617, 155 Ill. Dec. 353, 569 N.E.2d 534 (1991); *People v. Johnson*, 42 Ill. App. 3d 194, 355 N.E.2d 577 (1976). Harmless error analysis, §103.10 supra, does apply. *People v. Nitz*, 143 Ill. 2d 82, 157 Ill. Dec. 431, 572 N.E.2d 895 (1991). In contrast, prearrest silence not induced by governmental action may be employed to impeach the defendant. *Jenkins v. Anderson*, 447 U.S. 231 (1980). Notice also that *Doyle* does not apply to impeachment of the criminal defendant by means of assertive statements made subsequent to the giving of *Miranda* warnings manifestly inconsistent with the accused's testimony at trial. *Anderson v. Charles*, 447 U.S. 404 (1980); *People v. Purrazzo*, 95 Ill. App. 3d 886, 51 Ill. Dec. 47, 420 N.E.2d 461 (1981), statement made to police that he had shot wife in self-defense could be employed to impeach the defendant's trial testimony that his wife had been killed accidentally when their dog jumped on his arm, causing his weapon to discharge.

Following *Doyle*, the Illinois Supreme Court decided three cases dealing with comment by the prosecution on defendant's failure to include in a pretrial statement given to a police officer facts testified to by the defendant at trial. The three cases apply to impeachment by failure to speak when natural to do so with respect to situations arising both prior to and following the giving of *Miranda* warnings. The first decision, *People v. Rehbein,* 74 Ill. 2d 435, 24 Ill. Dec. 835, 386 N.E.2d 39 (1978), held that such impeachment was proper and did not constitute impermissible comment on defendant's right to remain silent. The second, *People v. Green,* 74 Ill. 2d 444, 25 Ill. Dec. 1, 386 N.E.2d 272 (1979), concluded that reference to defendant's post-*Miranda* silence violated *Doyle.* The third case, *People v. Beller,* 74 Ill. 2d 514, 25 Ill. Dec. 383, 386 N.E.2d 857 (1979), reconciled *Queen, Rehbein, Green,* and *Doyle.* According to *Beller,* where a defendant's earlier statement, whether prior to or following the giving of *Miranda* warnings, and in-court testimony or other statements are directly contradictory (i.e., manifestly inconsistent), the prosecution may properly impeach the defendant by means of the earlier statement, *Anderson v. Charles* supra, and derives no added advantage by commenting directly that when the defendant made the first statement he failed to make the contradictory second statement. *Accord People v. Craddock,* 163 Ill. App. 3d 1039, 115 Ill. Dec. 1, 516 N.E.2d 1357 (1987); *People v. Gil,* 240 Ill. App. 3d 151, 181 Ill. Dec. 124, 608 N.E.2d 197 (1992); *People v. Jones,* 240 Ill. App. 3d 213, 181 Ill. Dec. 193, 608 N.E.2d 266 (1992); *People v. Mischke,* 278 Ill. App. 3d 252, 214 Ill. Dec. 876, 662 N.E.2d 442 (1995). *See generally People v. Frieberg,* 147 Ill. 2d 326, 168 Ill. Dec. 108, 589 N.E.2d 508 (1992). *See also People v. Huddleston,* 243 Ill. App. 3d 1012, 184 Ill. Dec. 885, 614 N.E.2d 86 (1993) (defendant's prior statement to police that he was at his mother's house all evening was inconsistent with his trial testimony and properly used to impeach his testimony as to being other places that evening); *People v. Little,* 223 Ill. App. 3d 264, 165 Ill. Dec. 752, 585 N.E.2d 148 (1991) (where a defendant claims that he gave an exculpatory statement to the police when he was arrested, he may be impeached with evidence that he did not do so). However, where the inconsistency, if it exists, is not manifest, the defendant's silence may be prompted by reasons underlying the privilege against self-incrimination. Such silence is "insolubly ambiguous" and comment by the prosecution violates *Doyle*. *People v. Chriswell,* 133 Ill. App. 3d 458, 88 Ill. Dec. 568, 478 N.E.2d 1176 (1985). Thus, if the defendant gives a partial explanation regarding an incident and then testifies at trial to a more complete version without discussing the earlier statement, the witness may not be cross-examined to reveal this omission, nor is comment proper upon the defendant's earlier silence as to such greater details. *In Interest of S.L.C.,* 75 Ill. App. 3d 473, 31 Ill. Dec. 485, 394 N.E.2d 687 (1979). Similarly a post-arrest statement that the situation got out of hand is not manifestly inconsistent with trial testimony that the incident started as a practical joke. *People v. Smith,* 157 Ill. App. 3d 465, 109 Ill. Dec. 647, 510 N.E.2d 515 (1987). Nor is subsequent testimony by the accused that he saw a person pass a brown paper bag to a woman manifestly inconsistent with a post-arrest statement that he was at the gas station to purchase gas and cigarettes but did not commit the armed robbery. *People v. Louisville,* 241 Ill. App. 3d 772, 182 Ill. Dec. 148, 609 N.E.2d 682 (1992). And a general denial of guilt is not inconsistent with an alibi defense offered for the first time at trial. *People v. Ridley,* 199 Ill. App. 3d 487, 145 Ill. Dec. 608, 557 N.E.2d 378 (1990). For a decision where the court could not agree whether the partial explanation following the giving of *Miranda* warnings was sufficiently inconsistent, *see People v. Brooks,* 129 Ill. App. 3d 64, 84 Ill. Dec. 276, 471 N.E.2d 1042 (1984). *See also People v. Gagliani,* 210 Ill. App. 3d 617, 155 Ill. Dec. 353, 569 N.E.2d 534 (1991) discussed with approval in *People v. Frieberg,* 147 Ill. 2d 326, 168 Ill. Dec. 108, 589 N.E.2d 508 (1992), where a statement by the defendant simply denying knowledge of the incident, including how his fingerprints got into the victim's house, was held to be improper impeachment of trial testimony that he had engaged in consensual sexual intercourse with the victim in her house on the night in question, a decision that can possibly be explained on the basis of the state pursuing a line of questions highlighting the accused's opportunity to tell his trial story to the police following his arrest. For a decision that failed to address the directly contradictory requirement where the accused remained silent when asked about certain burglaries while denying the commission of others, *see People v. Foster,* 199 Ill. App. 3d 372, 145 Ill. Dec. 387, 556 N.E.2d 1289 (1990).

Following the Illinois Supreme Court's decision in *Beller,* supra, the United States Supreme Court in *Fletcher v. Weir,* 455 U.S. 603 (1982), held that post-arrest silence *prior* to the giving of *Miranda* warnings may be employed to impeach the defendant. *Beller* had held that such silence could not be employed to impeach the defendant relying upon *Doyle,* supra. *People v. Holmes,* 274 Ill. App. 3d 612, 211 Ill. Dec 200, 654 N.E.2d 662 (1995), concluded that *Beller* is no longer the law. Nevertheless, *Holmes,* supra, went on to conclude that generally a defendant's silence during police interrogation cannot be used for impeachment purposes because it is so ambiguous that it lacks the requisite inconsistency with his later exculpatory testimony at trial, citing *United States v. Hale,* 422 U.S. 171 (1975). The net result is that while *Beller* may have died, impeachment by silence post-arrest prior to *Miranda* warnings remains inadmissible to impeach.

Silence of an accused following the giving of *Miranda* warnings is inadmissible when offered to show proper police procedures. *People v. Flaugher,* 232 Ill. App. 3d 864, 174 Ill. Dec. 194, 598 N.E.2d 391 (1992). With respect to silence of the criminal defendant under other circumstances, *see* §802.7 infra.

With respect to illegally seized evidence, in order to facilitate making of a motion to suppress and to enhance the enforcement of constitutional rights, admissions made in connection with the motion to suppress may not be employed by the prosecution in its case in chief. *Simmons v. United States,* 390 U.S. 377 (1968). They may, however, be employed for impeachment purposes. *People v. Mulero,* 176 Ill. 2d 444, 223 Ill. Dec. 893, 680 N.E.2d 1329 (1997); *People v. Sturgis,* 58 Ill. 2d 211, 317 N.E.2d 545 (1974). Moreover, the illegally seized evidence is itself admissible to impeach the testimony of the defendant. *Walder v. United States,* 347 U.S. 62 (1954). However, where the cross-examination has too tenuous a connection to any subject opened on direct examination, impeachment with tainted evidence will not be permitted. *People v. Williams,* 205 Ill. App. 3d 1001, 151 Ill. Dec. 191, 564 N.E.2d 168 (1990).

§614   Calling and Interrogation of Witness by the Court

§614.1   *Calling of Witness by the Court*

Courts should rarely call *sua sponte* nonexpert witnesses to testify. Calling of such witnesses *sua sponte* by the court is generally an unwarranted intrusion into the adversary system that should be undertaken only when clearly required in the interests of justice. Instances where the action may be warranted may arise from situations such as custody matters where a special obligation is placed upon the court to protect the interests of a nonparty. On occasion, also, calling by the court may be justified to avoid any tendency by the jury to associate a witness with the party who calls him.

In practice the courts' exercise of their inherent discretion to call witnesses arises almost exclusively in connection with the court's witness doctrine, discussed in §607.4 supra. Pursuant to the court's witness doctrine, upon request and a showing by the prosecution or defendant of reasons for doubting the veracity of a witness whose testimony is crucial, the court may call the witness as its own, thereby making the witness subject to cross-examination, impeachment, and leading questions by either side. *People v. Williams,* 22 Ill. 2d 498, 177 N.E.2d 100 (1961), *Carle v. People,* 200 Ill. 494, 66 N.E. 32 (1902). In theory, this practice serves to avoid association of the witness with either side in the minds of the jury and may not be used merely as a device for placing before the jury a prior statement under the guise of impeachment. *People v. Johnson*, 333 Ill. 469, 165 N.E. 235 (1929).

With respect to court-appointed experts, *see* §706.1 infra.

§614.2 Interrogation by the Court; Ruling on Objections

The trial judge may ask questions of witnesses. He must, however, avoid conveying to the jury his views regarding the merits of the case, the veracity of the witness, or the weight of the evidence, *People v. Falaster,* 173 Ill. 2d 220, 218 Ill. Dec. 902, 670 N.E.2d 624 (1996); *People v. Harris,* 123 Ill. 2d 113, 122 Ill. Dec. 76, 526 N.E.2d 335 (1998); *People v. Trefonas,* 9 Ill. 2d 92, 136 N.E.2d 817 (1956); *People v. Rush,* 250 Ill. App. 3d 530, 190 Ill. Dec. 1, 620 N.E.2d 1262 (1993), or his impatience or hostility toward counsel, *People v. Santucci,* 24 Ill. 2d 93, 180 N.E.2d 491 (1962); *People v. Moriarity,* 33 Ill. 2d 606, 213 N.E.2d 516 (1966); *People v. Brown,* 172 Ill. 2d 1, 216 Ill. Dec. 733, 665 N.E.2d 1290 (1996), or indicate bias or prejudice against either party. *People v. Williams,* 173 Ill. 2d 48, 218 Ill. Dec. 916, 670 N.E.2d 638 (1996). *Accord People v. Sykes,* 224 Ill. App. 3d 369, 166 Ill. Dec. 671, 586 N.E.2d 629 (1991) (questioning must be fair and impartial, without showing prejudice or bias). If the question is an improper one, the embarrassing position of counsel is obvious. Similarly, the trial judge must not exhibit in any manner a hostile or favorable attitude to a party or a witness as this is very apt to influence the jury in arriving at its verdict. *People v. Marino,* 414 Ill. 445, 111 N.E.2d 534 (1953); *People v. Gilbert,* 12 Ill. 2d 410, 147 N.E.2d 44 (1957). *See also Holton v. Memorial Hospital,* 176 Ill. 2d 95, 223 Ill. Dec. 429, 679 N.E.2d 1202 (1997), trial judge improperly told jury that defendant had lied at the behest of his attorneys; *People v. Rega,* 271 Ill. App. 3d 17, 207 Ill. Dec. 674, 648 N.E.2d 130 (1995), trial judge improperly referred to the defense presented as "poppycock" and displayed hostility to defense lawyers.

Avoidance of these hazards confines him largely to brief questioning designed to elucidate a point, aid an embarrassed witness, facilitate the progress of the trial, or clarify issues that seem obscure. *People v. Williams* supra; *People v. Falaster* supra. *People v. Wright,* 42 Ill. 2d 457, 248 N.E.2d 78 (1969); *People v. Boone,* 180 Ill. App. 3d 98, 128 Ill. Dec. 661, 534 N.E.2d 1266 (1988); *People v. Bradley,* 128 Ill. App. 3d 372, 83 Ill. Dec. 701, 470 N.E.2d 1121 (1984). *See also People v. Costello,* 95 Ill. App. 3d 680, 51 Ill. Dec. 178, 420 N.E.2d 592 (1981), trial court may question witness to clarify what seems obscure or ambiguous; *People v. Nevitt,* 135 Ill. 2d 423, 142 Ill. Dec. 854, 553 N.E.2d 368 (1990); *People v. Cleveland,* 140 Ill. App. 3d 462, 94 Ill. Dec. 883, 488 N.E.2d 1276 (1986); *Norman v. American Natl. Fire Ins. Co.,* 198 Ill. App. 3d 269, 144 Ill. Dec. 568, 555 N.E.2d 1087 (1990), to elicit truth, to resolve ambiguities, to clarify relevant testimony, or to expedite the trial. Thus the trial judge may act to ensure that evidence essential to the proper disposition of a case is not inadvertently omitted. *People v. Murray,* 194 Ill. 2d 653, 141 Ill. Dec. 290, 551 N.E.2d 283 (1990); *People v. Walter,* 90 Ill. App. 3d 687, 46 Ill. Dec. 102, 413 N.E.2d 542 (1980); *People v. Martinez,* 76 Ill. App. 3d 658, 32 Ill. Dec. 177, 395 N.E.2d 124 (1979). A trial judge may remind the prosecutor of the necessity to prove additional elements, *People v. Franceschini,* 20 Ill. 2d 126, 169 N.E.2d 244 (1960); *People v. Walter,* 90 Ill. App. 3d 687, 46 Ill. Dec. 102, 413 N.E.2d 542 (1980); *People v. Sykes,* 224 Ill. App. 3d 369, 166 Ill. Dec. 671, 586 N.E.2d 629 (1991); examine witnesses to clarify material issues or eliminate confusion, *People v. Bradley,* 128 Ill. App. 3d 372, 83 Ill. Dec. 701, 470 N.E.2d 1121 (1984); *People v. Wells,* 106 Ill. App. 3d 1077, 62 Ill. Dec. 662, 436 N.E.2d 688 (1982), and advise counsel on the proper phrasing of questions, *People v. Clay,* 27 Ill. 2d 27, 187 N.E.2d 719 (1963); *People v. Galan,* 151 Ill. App. 3d 481, 104 Ill. Dec. 356, 502 N.E.2d 853 (1986), but may not interject to advise counsel on matters of trial strategy. *Yetton v. Henderson,* 190 Ill. App. 3d 973, 137 Ill. Dec. 887, 546 N.E.2d 1000 (1989). An extended cross-examination by the judge was condemned in *People v. Rongetti,* 331 Ill. 581, 163 N.E. 373 (1928). The single question to a witness called by the court *sua sponte* as to whether the accused was with the witness during the commission of the crime was condemned in *In Interest of R. S.,* 117 Ill. App. 3d 698, 72 Ill. Dec. 834, 453 N.E.2d 139 (1983). The danger of prejudice arising from the trial judge's asking questions is, of course, significantly lessened when the case is tried without a jury. *People v. Palmer,* 27 Ill. 2d 311, 189 N.E.2d 265 (1963); *People v. Nevitt,* 174 Ill. App. 3d 326, 123 Ill. Dec. 762, 528 N.E.2d 307 (1988). It is also improper for the trial court on its own initiative to object to questions posed by counsel to the point of giving the appearance of partisanship. *Pavilon v. Kaferly,* 204 Ill. App. 3d 235, 149 Ill. Dec. 549, 561 N.E.2d 1245 (1990).

Similarly, attempts at judicial humor during trial are ill-advised and inappropriate to the performance of judicial duties. *People v. Bernatowicz,* 413 Ill. 181, 108 N.E.2d 479 (1952); *People v. Merz,* 122 Ill. App. 3d 972, 78 Ill. Dec. 273, 461 N.E.2d 1380 (1984).

Overall, trial judges were reminded in *People v. Falaster,* 273 Ill. App. 3d 694, 210 Ill. Dec. 562, 653 N.E.2d 467 (1995), to question sparingly since any time the trial judge intervenes it is likely to be viewed by a party or parties as unwarranted interference and to lead at least one of the parties to feel that the trial judge is unfairly favoring the opponent.

In ruling on objections in open court, the judge must be sure not to appear to be offering an opinion as to the evidence. *People v. Smallwood,* 224 Ill. App. 3d 393, 166 Ill. Dec. 678, 586 N.E.2d 636 (1991), remark by judge that witness had already identified the defendant is not an improper comment.

With respect to the trial judge admonishing a witness to testify truthfully, *see People v. King,* 154 Ill. 2d 217, 181 Ill. Dec. 626, 608 N.E.2d 877 (1993); *People v. Sowewimo,* 276 Ill. App. 3d 330, 212 Ill. Dec. 702, 657 N.E.2d 1047 (1995); *People v. Morley,* 225 Ill. App. 3d 589, 194 Ill. Dec. 281, 627 N.E.2d 397 (1994).

With respect to *ex parte* communications between the trial judge and the jury, *see People v. Childs,* 159 Ill. 2d 217, 201 Ill. Dec. 102, 636 N.E.2d 534 (1994); *People v. Danielly,* 274 Ill. App. 3d 358, 210 Ill. Dec. 671, 653 N.E.2d 866 (1995).

For a trial judge's comments to constitute reversible error, defendant must demonstrate that the comments constituted a material factor in the conviction or were such that an effect on the jury verdict was the probable result. *People v. Brown,* 172 Ill. 2d 1, 216 Ill. Dec. 733, 655 N.E.2d 1290 (1996).

The examination of witnesses in citation proceedings is treated in §606.6 supra.

§614.3   Objections to Calling of Witness or Interrogation

A specific objection is required to preserve for appeal any alleged error with respect to the court calling or interrogating a witness. However, the objection need not be made contemporaneously with the calling or interrogation if the jury is present. *See* Federal Rule of Evidence 614, 65 F.R.D. 131, 151 (1975). Thus counsel is relieved of the embarrassment attendant upon objecting to the court's action in the presence of the jury. The objection can be made at the next available opportunity when the jury is absent, or preferably at the first reasonable opportunity for a side bar conference. *See People v. Westpfahl,* 295 Ill. App. 3d 327, 229 Ill. Dec. 842, 692 N.E.2d 831 (1998). Objections so made should be considered timely, §103.3 supra. The foregoing is far superior to the vague position adopted in *People v. Garrett,* 276 Ill. App. 3d 702, 213 Ill. Dec. 195, 658 N.E.2d 1216 (1995), that the waiver rule is not rigidly applied when the trial judge's conduct is the basis of the objection.

§615   Exclusion and Separation of Witness

§615.1   Commentary

If a witness hears the testimony of another before she herself takes the stand, she finds it much easier deliberately to shape her own story accordingly, or in all honesty she may be influenced subconsciously. Hence the sequestration of witnesses has long been recognized as a powerful and easily applied instrument of truth. 6 Wigmore, Evidence §§1837-1842 (Chadbourn rev. 1976).

After long adherence to the view that allowance of a motion to exclude witnesses was in the discretion of the trial court and that a denial thereof was not an abuse of discretion in the absence of a showing of prejudice, the supreme court basically shifted its position in *People v. Dixon,* 23 Ill. 2d 136, 177 N.E.2d 206 (1961). Taking cognizance of the practical impossibility of showing prejudice as a result of denial, the court ruled that a motion to exclude should normally be allowed and that a denial would not be sustained unless the record disclosed a sound reason for it. The ruling does not extend to excluding a natural party from the trial. *North Shore Marine, Inc. v. Engel,* 81 Ill. App. 3d 530, 36 Ill. Dec. 588, 401 N.E.2d 269 (1980); *Kopplin v. Kopplin,* 330 Ill. App. 211, 71 N.E.2d 180 (1946). The decision left the door open to the trial judge to permit one or more witnesses to remain for good reason. Exclusion does not extend to either rebuttal witnesses or witnesses called to impeach credibility.

Good reason generally exists to permit an officer or employee of a party that is not a natural person designated as its representative by its attorney or an investigation agent of the prosecution to remain in the courtroom. *People v. Leemon,* 66 Ill. 2d 170, 5 Ill. Dec. 250, 361 N.E.2d 573 (1977); *People v. Miller,* 26 Ill. 2d 305, 186 N.E.2d 317 (1962). The presence of other witnesses may also be essential to the presentation of the case. An obvious example of a witness whose presence may be essential is an expert witness. As discussed in §§703.1 and 705.1 infra, he is permitted to base an opinion on the testimony he has heard at trial. *See Friedman v. Park Dist. of Highland Park,* 151 Ill. App. 3d 374, 104 Ill. Dec. 329, 502 N.E.2d 826 (1986), permitting an expert witness to remain is within the court's discretion. Moreover, it is reasonable to give counsel the benefit of her expert's assistance while an expert for the other party is testifying. Similar assistance may be needed in connection with other technical matters with which counsel lacks sufficient familiarity to try the case on her own. Discretion also exists to permit a support person, such as a parent of a minor child victim witness who will also testify, to remain in court.

While the usual order is one of exclusion from the courtroom, the court may take futher measures designed to prevent communication between witnesses, such as ordering them separated, *Noone v. Olehy*, 297 Ill. 160, 130 N.E. 476 (1921), or prohibiting a witness from reading the trial transcript of another witness.

In child sexual abuse prosecutions, "where the alleged victim of the offense is a minor under 18 years of age, the court may exclude from the proceedings, while the victim is testifying, all persons, who, in the opinion of the court, do not have a direct interest in the case, except the media." 725 ILCS 5/115-10.2.

If a witness violates an order of exclusion or separation, the traditional view has been that the trial judge may in her discretion either preclude the witness from testifying, *Harrisburg School Dist. No. 3. v. Steapleton*, 195 Ill. App. 3d 1020, 142 Ill. Dec. 726, 553 N.E.2d 76 (1990), or nevertheless permit him to testify absent a showing of prejudice. *People v. Farnsley*, 53 Ill. 2d 537, 293 N.E.2d 600 (1973); *People v. Miller*, 254 Ill. App. 3d 997, 193 Ill. Dec. 799, 626 N.E.2d 1350 (1993); *People v. Bodeman*, 105 Ill. App. 3d 39, 60 Ill. Dec. 902, 433 N.E.2d 1140 (1982); *People v. Byer*, 75 Ill. App. 3d 658, 31 Ill. Dec. 430, 394 N.E.2d 632 (1979). Effectuation of the policy underlying exclusion and separation should limit the exercise of this discretion to permit the witness to testify to cases in which presence in court was accidental and the absence of prejudice affirmatively appears. *People v. Bridgeforth*, 51 Ill. 2d 52, 281 N.E.2d 617 (1972), a witness in court with the consent, connivance, procurement, or knowledge of the appellant or counsel should not be permitted to testify. Other potential remedies include holding the witness in contempt, declaring a mistrial, or instructing the jury to weigh credibility of the witness in light of the witness's presence in court or discussions with other witnesses. If the opposing party fails to object to the testimony of the witness who remains in the courtroom after having been excluded, the propriety of the testimony may not be raised for the first time on appeal. *People v. Miller*, 30 Ill. 2d 110, 195 N.E.2d 694 (1964).

With respect to a witness who has begun to testify, it is common practice for many courts to instruct the witness not to discuss his testimony with anyone during a recess. This practice is particularly prevalent when the recess occurs during cross-examination. *Stocker Hinge Mfg. Co. v. Darnel Indus., Inc.*, 61 Ill. App. 3d 636, 18 Ill. Dec. 489, 377 N.E.2d 1125 (1978). The practice of barring discussion with anyone including counsel during a short recess may constitutionally be applied to any witness, including the criminal defendant. *Perry v. Leeke*, 488 U.S. 272 (1989) (15-minute recess between direct and cross-examination). Nevertheless, it appears that a blanket prohibition on contact between the criminal defendant and counsel is unacceptable in Illinois no matter when or how brief the recess in the criminal defendant's testimony. *See People v. McDonald*, 276 Ill. App. 3d 466, 213 Ill. Dec. 230, 658 N.E.2d 1251 (1995); *People v. Abrams*, 260 Ill. App. 3d 566, 197 Ill. Dec. 853, 631 N.E.2d 1312 (1994). It is very clear, in any event, that where the witness is the criminal defendant and the recess is overnight, prohibiting consultation constitutes a denial of the accused's right to the assistance of counsel guaranteed by the Sixth Amendment. *Geders v. United States*, 425 U.S. 80 (1976); *People v. Noble*, 42 Ill. 2d 425, 248 N.E.2d 96 (1969). However, such denial of the right to assistance of counsel will not be found to have occurred if defense counsel fails to object to the court's instruction not to confer with the accused during the recess, overnight or otherwise. *People v. Knox*, 241 Ill. App. 3d 205, 181 Ill. Dec. 586, 608 N.E.2d 659 (1993).

ARTICLE VII
Opinion and Expert Testimony

§701   Opinion Testimony by Lay Witnesses

§701.1   *An Overview*

Implicit in the cases dealing with opinions is the recognition that the making of an intelligent decision on a contested issue of fact requires the trier of fact to be supplied with data that is useful in resolving the issue. This sensible policy applies equally whether the data consist of matters observed by an ordinary witness or specialized technical information supplied by an expert.

Accordingly, it seems clear that testimony that merely tells the jury to decide an issue in a particular way is, as a general proposition, useless and perhaps confusing. Illustrations are: on the issue whether plaintiff, suing for attorneys' fees, was employed by defendant, testimony by plaintiff that he was so employed, *Town of Evans v. Dickey,* 117 Ill. 291, 7 N.E. 263 (1886); on the issue whether a road was public, testimony that it was public, *Commissioners of Big Lake Drainage Dist. v. Commissioners of Highways,* 199 Ill. 132, 64 N.E. 1094 (1902);

on the issue whether the witness signed in the presence of the testator, testimony that he signed in the presence of the testator, *Snyder v. Steele,* 287 Ill. 159, 122 N.E. 520 (1919); and on the issue of negligence the impression of the witness that the driver of the car did not see the truck, *Freeding-Skokie Roll-Off Serv. v. Hamilton,* 108 Ill. 2d 217, 91 Ill. Dec. 178, 483 N.E.2d 524 (1985). Obviously these were all situations in which more detailed data, readily understood by a trier of fact, could and should have been supplied. Unfortunately, the soundness of excluding the evidence in cases of this kind led to generalizations that witnesses should state "facts" rather than "opinions" and that opinions on ultimate issues should not be allowed. The result was to deprive triers of fact of useful and needed assistance, especially when specialized technical information was necessary in evaluating facts. *See, e.g., Gillette v. Chicago,* 396 Ill. 619, 72 N.E.2d 326 (1947), in action to recover cost of necessary protection of building against injury from construction of subway, proper to exclude expert testimony that measures taken were necessary to protect building.

Nevertheless, even when the rule against opinions was in full flower, the courts recognized that a witness might gain an accurate total impression although unable to account for details, *People v. Williams,* 62 Ill. App. 3d 966, 20 Ill. Dec. 200, 379 N.E.2d 1268 (1978), or that a mere recounting of details would not accurately convey the total impression received by the witness. *People v. Burton,* 6 Ill. App. 3d 879, 286 N.E.2d 792 (1972). Thus, in a prosecution for destroying property by means of dynamite, witnesses familiar with the odor were held properly permitted to testify to having smelled dynamite after the explosion. "Most persons would probably find it difficult to describe the odor of a rose, whiskey, beer or limburger cheese, but this difficulty could scarcely be regarded as affecting the value of their testimony that they were familiar with and recognized the particular odor." *People v. Reed,* 333 Ill. 397, 401, 164 N.E. 847 (1929). Similarly, a witness was properly permitted to summarize his sensory impressions with the opinion that the defendant "attempted to slit [his] throat." *People v. Sprinkle,* 74 Ill. App. 3d 456, 30 Ill. Dec. 439, 393 N.E.2d 94 (1979).

As stated by the Illinois Supreme Court in *Freeding-Skokie Roll-Off Serv. v. Hamilton,* 108 Ill. 2d 217, 91 Ill. Dec. 178, 483 N.E.2d 524 (1985), a lay opinion is now admissible as helpful to "a clear understanding of his testimony or a determination of a fact in issue," Federal Rule of Evidence 701(b), whenever the witness cannot adequately communicate to the jury the facts upon which the opinion is based. *Accord People v. Novak,* 163 Ill. 2d 93, 205 Ill. Dec. 471, 643 N.E.2d 762 (1994), Illinois courts refer to Rule 701 of the Federal Rules of Evidence in considering the admissibility of lay witness opinion testimony. As summarized by the Illinois Supreme Court in *People v. Novak,* 163 Ill. 2d 93, 102, 205 Ill. Dec. 471, 476, 643 N.E.2d 762, 767 (1994):

> Lay witness opinion testimony is admissible where the facts could not otherwise be adequately presented or described to the fact finder in such a way as to enable the fact finder to form an opinion or reach an intelligent conclusion. Lay witnesses may relate their opinions or conclusions on what they observed because it is sometimes difficult to describe a person's mental or physical condition, character, or reputation, or the emotions manifest by his or her acts; or things that occur and can be observed, including speed, appearance, odor, flavor, and temperature.

Opinions interpreting an event that can be interpreted equally well by the trier of fact are not helpful. Thus it has been held improper for a mother to testify what her daughter meant by "wriggle his thing," *People v. Linkogle,* 54 Ill. App. 3d 830, 11 Ill. Dec. 467, 368 N.E.2d 1075 (1977); and it has also been held improper for a witness to testify that, when the defendant said "have some of this," he meant sex and not a drink. *People v. Brown,* 200 Ill. App. 3d 566, 146 Ill. Dec. 346, 558 N.E.2d 309 (1990).

A clear line between fact and opinion is impossible to draw. In a sense all testimony to matters of fact is the conclusion of the witness formed from observed phenomena and mental impressions. Witnesses who are accustomed in speaking to include opinions in describing events often find any line difficult to draw. It is more helpful to the jury to hear such a witness speak naturally than to have him harried by objections that he is improperly giving his opinion. *See* McCormick, Evidence §11 (4th ed. 1992).

Modern practice requires that prior to testifying to her opinion, the witness must first lay a foundation establishing personal knowledge of the facts that form the basis of the opinion, §602 supra. *People v. Robinson,* 102 Ill. App. 3d 884, 58 Ill. Dec. 23, 429 N.E.2d 1356 (1981). Thus the testimony must be based on concrete facts perceived from the witness's own senses, and cannot be based on the statements of others. *People v. Novak,* 163 Ill. 2d 93, 205 Ill. Dec. 471, 643 N.E.2d 762 (1994) (witness may not testify as lay witness concerning training methods since witness did not see any of the exercising allegedly administered by the defendant). If the basis of the opinion includes so many varying or uncertain factors that the lay witness is required to guess or surmise in order to reach an opinion, the opinion is objectionable as speculation or conjecture. *City of Evanston v. City of Chicago,* 279 Ill. App. 3d 255, 215 Ill. Dec. 894, 664 N.E.2d 291 (1996). In addition, where relevancy requires, a foundation must be laid as to the witness's personal knowledge of facts to which the observed facts are being compared. Thus a witness may not testify that something smelled like dynamite unless it is sufficiently established that the witness from prior experience knows what dynamite smells like. The opinion of the witness must also be rationally based on the witness's perception, *see* Federal Rule of Evidence 701(a), meaning only that it must be one that a lay person could normally form from observed facts. *People v. Burton,* 6 Ill. App. 3d 879, 286 N.E.2d 792 (1972). A lay witness will not be permitted to opine with respect to area of specialized knowledge beyond that ordinarily possessed by the average person. *See* §702.1 infra. *See also Burns v. Michelotti,* 237 Ill. App. 3d 923, 178 Ill. Dec. 621, 604 N.E.2d 1144 (1992), a nurse, unqualified to perform an intubation, was improperly permitted to opine that a doctor did not use undue force. Finally, testimony of a lay witness in the form of an opinion may be introduced only if helpful to a clear understanding of his testimony or the determination of a fact in issue. *Kolstad v. Rankin,* 179 Ill. App. 3d 1022, 128 Ill. Dec. 768, 534 N.E.2d 1373 (1989). Notice that the standard is one of "helpfulness" not "necessity." *See* Federal Rule of Evidence 701, 65 F.R.D. 131, 151 (1975).

Because the distinction between fact and opinion is so frequently impossible to delineate, specific application of the general principles stated above is left much to the discretion of the trial court. The closer the subject of the opinion approaches critical issues, the more likely it is that the court will require more concrete details from the witness, either alone or prior to the offering of an opinion, conveying the total picture more accurately than the mere recitation of the witness' opinion. *See Scheibel v. Groeteka,* 183 Ill. App. 3d 120, 131 Ill. Dec. 680, 538 N.E.2d 1236 (1989), plaintiff conveyed facts perceived in detail prior to testifying that the driver of the other car could have stopped. The court may insist that loaded words like "murdered," "stolen," or "assaulted" be avoided in a shorthand rendering. Obviously an opinion amounting to no more than a belief that the plaintiff or the defendant ought to win is inadmissible; such opinions are not helpful to a clear understanding of the testimony or in the determination of a fact in issue. *See Freeding-Skokie Roll-Off Serv. v. Hamilton,* 108 Ill. 2d 217, 91 Ill. Dec. 178, 483 N.E.2d 524 (1985). *See also* §704.1 infra.

Specific illustrations relating to the admissibility of lay witness opinion testimony are contained in §§701.2 to 701.8 infra. Note that the specific illustrations, while common, are not exclusive but illustrative only. *See, e.g., Kolstad v. Rankin,* 179 Ill. App. 3d 1022, 128 Ill. Dec. 768, 534 N.E.2d 1373 (1989) (lay witnesses properly permitted to testify that the noise disturbed them); *People v. Holveck,* 141 Ill. 2d 84, 152 Ill. Dec. 237, 565 N.E.2d 919 (1990) (lay witness may not testify as to the meaning of another witness's testimony). The admissibility of lay opinions upon the ultimate issue is addressed in §704.1 infra. With respect to opinions contained in admissions, *see* §802.1 infra; in statements admitted pursuant to hearsay exceptions, *see* §803.1 infra; and in prior inconsistent statements, *see* §613.2 supra.

For a discussion of expert witness opinion testimony, *see* §§702-706 infra.

§701.2   *Value of Personal Property*

In an early case the supreme court said, "Every one is presumed to have some idea of the value of property which is in almost universal use, and it is not necessary to show that a witness is a drover or butcher, before he is allowed to give an opinion of the value of a cow. If it were a steam engine, or a diamond ring, it might be different." *Ohio & M.R.R. v. Irvin,* 27 Ill. 178, 180 (1862). Consistent with this view, a housewife has been held qualified to testify to the value of household goods, *Brenton v. Sloan's United Storage & Van Co.,* 315 Ill. App. 278, 42 N.E.2d 945 (1942); *Martin v. McIntosh,* 37 Ill. App. 3d 526, 346 N.E.2d 450 (1976); an owner of a dog killed by an automobile may testify as to the dog's value, *Demeo v. Manville,* 68 Ill. App. 3d 843, 25 Ill. Dec. 443, 386 N.E.2d 917 (1979); and an owner of lost clothing may opine as to its value, *Magee v. Walbro, Inc.,* 171 Ill. App. 3d 774, 121 Ill. Dec. 668, 525 N.E.2d 975 (1988). Actual knowledge of values has been required in the case of an automobile, *Bangert v. Emmco Ins. Co.,* 349 Ill. App. 257, 110 N.E.2d 528 (1953), and automobile parts, *People v. Butman,* 357 Ill. 506, 192 N.E. 564 (1934). *Contra Adams v. Ford Motor Co.,* 103 Ill. App. 2d 356, 243 N.E.2d 843 (1968), requirements for qualifying a witness's testimony as to value of truck are no more stringent; *Bangert v. Emmco Ins. Co.* supra, specifically not followed. *Accord People v. Adams,* 156 Ill. App. 3d 444, 108 Ill. Dec. 786, 509 N.E.2d 482 (1987), owner of car was competent to testify as to value of his car.

Occasionally the situation is in fact "different," i.e., no presumption of some idea of the value of property arises, and the lay witness's familiarity with the value of the property must be affirmatively established. *See, e.g., State Farm v. Best in the West Foods,* 282 Ill. App. 3d 470, 217 Ill. Dec. 764, 667 N.E.2d 1340 (1996), store manager not shown to have personal knowledge of value of inventory; *Schultz v. Steinhagen,* 198 Ill. App. 3d 672, 144 Ill. Dec. 748, 555 N.E.2d 1267 (1990), witness lacked personal knowledge of the value of tools, equipment, and parts inventory employed in motorcycle repair and service business.

§701.3   *Value of Real Estate*

As viewed by the common law, value of real estate is regarded as essentially factual in nature, hence there is an emphasis upon knowledge of specific instances of comparable real estate value rather than upon development of expertise. As a result, while the witness testifying to value may in fact be a professional appraiser, the admissibility of the witness's opinion has traditionally been governed by principles applicable to opinions of lay witnesses. Knowledge of values has to be actual, not hearsay, and a valuation witness cannot testify on the basis of facts stated hypothetically, *Elmhurst v. Rohmeyer,* 297 Ill. 430, 130 N.E. 761 (1921), or on the basis of a list of sales furnished him, *Chicago & W.I.R. Co. v. Heidenreich,* 254 Ill. 231, 98 N.E. 567 (1912). Familiarity with the property in question, plus knowledge of real estate values in the vicinity, qualifies a witness, whether or not a professional appraiser, to give an opinion on value. *Trustees of Schools v. Kirane,* 5 Ill. 2d 64, 124 N.E.2d 886 (1955). Either experience in appraising for loans, engaging in the real estate business, owning property in the vicinity, or assessing for taxation has been held to satisfy the requirement of knowledge of values. *Crystal Lake Park Dist. v. Consumers Co.,* 313 Ill. 395, 145 N.E. 215 (1924); *Department of Pub. Works & Bldgs. v. Oberlaender,* 42 Ill. 2d 410, 247 N.E.2d 888 (1969). For proving value by other sales and bona fide offers to purchase, *see* §401.15 supra. With respect to treating witnesses possessing expert qualifications with respect to real estate valuation as experts, *see* infra.

An initial laying of a foundation detailing the factors on which an opinion is based is not only permitted, *Chicago v. Equitable Life Soc.,* 8 Ill. 2d 341, 134 N.E.2d 296 (1956), but required, *Chicago v. Giedraitis,* 14 Ill. 2d 45, 150 N.E.2d 577 (1958). If an improper factor is disclosed, the opinion will be stricken. *Id.* Improper factors have been held to include income from a business conducted on the property, in contrast to rental income, *Chicago v. Central Natl. Bank,* 5 Ill. 2d 164, 125 N.E.2d 94 (1955); possible future rentals, *Chicago v. Giedraitis* supra; the usefulness of the property to a condemnor, *Village of Oak Park v. Hulbert,* 307 Ill. 270, 138 N.E. 678 (1929); danger and inconvenience of crossing highway, *Department of Pub. Works & Bldgs. v. Griffin,* 305 Ill. 585, 137 N.E. 523 (1922); and the probability of rezoning the property, *Oak Brook Park Dist. v. Oak Brook Dev. Co.,* 170 Ill. App. 3d 221, 120 Ill. Dec. 448, 524 N.E.2d 213 (1988). Cross-examination on the factors relied on is a matter of right. *Chicago v. Equitable Life Soc.* supra.

Ownership of real estate usually indicates knowledge of the price paid for the land, income generated from it, and potential uses such that the owner on that basis alone is likely to have a reasonable idea of value. *American Natl. Bank & Trust Co. v. City of North Chicago,* 155 Ill. App. 3d 920, 108 Ill. Dec 534, 508 N.E.2d 1111 (1987); *Department of Transp. v. Harper,* 64 Ill. App. 3d 732, 21 Ill. Dec. 516, 381 N.E.2d 843 (1978). However, the owner will not be permitted to testify as to value where special circumstances exist, such as acquisition by inheritance or by dissolution of marriage, that affirmatively indicate that the owner is unfamiliar with facts that give the property value. *American Natl.* supra; *Hill v. Ben Franklin Sav. & Loan Assn.,* 177 Ill. App. 3d 51, 126 Ill. Dec. 462, 531 N.E.2d 1089 (1988); *In re Marriage of Vucic,* 216 Ill. App. 3d 692, 159 Ill. Dec. 737, 576 N.E.2d 406 (1991); *Department of Transportation v. White,* 264 Ill. App. 3d 145, 201 Ill. Dec. 772, 636 N.E.2d 1204 (1994).

When the landlord breaches the implied warranty of inhabitability, both the tenant and the landlord may testify in the form of an opinion as to diminution in value occasioned by the breach. *Glasoe v. Trinkle,* 107 Ill. 2d 1, 88 Ill. Dec. 895, 479 N.E.2d 915 (1985).

In eminent domain proceedings, each party is entitled to develop her own theory of the highest and best use of the property, and witnesses may give value opinions accordingly. *County of Cook v. Holland,* 3 Ill. 2d 36, 119 N.E.2d 760 (1954). This use does not include the one proposed by the condemnor, *Department of Pub. Works & Bldgs. v. Watson,* 346 Ill. 304, 178 N.E. 465 (1931), but may be a future reasonably anticipated use, although the property is not presently devoted thereto. *Illinois Light & Power Co. v. Bedard,* 343 Ill. 618, 175 N.E. 851 (1931), adaptability to golf course not too speculative. Value is fixed as of the time of the filing of the petition, *Chicago v. Farwell,* 286 Ill. 415, 121 N.E. 795 (1919), and the opinion should be phrased in terms of fair cash market value, rather than "worth." *Peoria, B. & C. Traction Co. v. Vance,* 234 Ill. 36, 84 N.E. 607 (1908). Land and improvements cannot be valued separately. *Chicago v. Giedraitis* supra.

Property without a market value in the ordinary sense is occasionally encountered. Witnesses familiar with property of the kind involved, even though unfamiliar with values generally, may then express opinions based on factors such as productiveness, capabilities, location, and volume of business done. The cases have generally concerned condemnations of portions of railroad property. *Sanitary Dist. of Chicago v. Pittsburgh, Ft. W. & C. Ry.,* 216 Ill. 575, 75 N.E. 248 (1905).

Evidence as to the fair market value of the improved property must be confined to the value of the improved property as a whole; it is error to admit evidence of the separate values of land and the improvements. *Department of Pub. Works & Bldgs. v. Lotta,* 27 Ill. 2d 455, 189 N.E.2d 238 (1963); *County of St. Clair v. Wilson,* 284 Ill. App. 3d 79, 219 Ill. Dec. 712, 672 N.E.2d 27 (1996). In order to avoid misleading and confusing the jury, it is also error to permit an appraisal witness to state underlying figures. *Department of Transp. v. Quincy Coach House, Inc.,* 64 Ill. 2d 350, 356 N.E.2d 13, 1 Ill. Dec. 13 (1976).

The rule against an opinion on an ultimate issue appears

never to have been applied to opinions of value, and of course does not now apply. *See* §704.1 infra.

Consideration should be given to treating witnesses possessing expert's qualifications with respect to real estate valuation, §702.2 infra, as expert witnesses rather than as lay witnesses. *Accord City of Chicago v. Anthony,* 136 Ill. 2d 169, 144 Ill. Dec. 93, 354 N.E.2d 1381 (1990); *County of St. Clair v. Wilson,* 284 Ill. App. 3d 79, 219 Ill. Dec. 712, 672 N.E.2d 27 (1996); *Department of Transportation v. Beeson,* 137 Ill. App. 3d 908, 92 Ill. Dec. 700, 485 N.E.2d 511 (1985), valuation witnesses should be treated as experts thus making Federal Rules of Evidence 703 and 705 applicable by virtue of *Wilson v. Clark,* 84 Ill. 2d 186, 49 Ill. Dec. 308, 417 N.E.2d 1322 (1981). *See* §703.1 infra. *See generally Department of Conservation v. Dorner,* 192 Ill. App. 3d 333, 139 Ill. Dec. 364, 548 N.E.2d 749 (1989); *Illinois State Toll Highway Authority v. Heritage Standard Bank and Trust Co.,* 250 Ill. App. 3d 665, 189 Ill. Dec. 272, 619 N.E.2d 1321 (1993). The Illinois Supreme Court in *City of Chicago v. Anthony,* 136 Ill. 2d 169, 144 Ill. Dec. 93, 554 N.E.2d 1381 (1990), held Federal Rules of Evidence 703 and 705 applicable to an expert witness testifying as to valuation in an eminent domain proceeding. The circuit court in its discretion must determine whether the underlying facts, data, or opinions are of a type reasonably relied upon by experts in the particular field. Such determinations will not be disturbed unless there has been an abuse of discretion. *City of Chicago* supra. *Accord Department of Transportation v. First National Bank,* 241 Ill. App. 3d 601, 182 Ill. Dec. 86, 609 N.E.2d 389 (1993) (trial court within its discretion must determine whether comparable sales were reasonably relied upon by expert in condemnation case).

§701.4   Speed

A witness familiar with the speed of vehicles may testify to the speed of an observed vehicle, and, if unable to give the speed in miles per hour, may state it as fast or slow. *Watkins v.*

Schmitt, 172 Ill. 2d 193, 216 Ill. Dec. 822, 665 N.E.2d 1379 (1996); *Peterson v. Lou Bachrodt Chevrolet Co.,* 76 Ill. 2d 353, 29 Ill. Dec. 444, 392 N.E.2d 1 (1979); *Jumer v. Henneberry,* 61 Ill. App. 3d 422, 18 Ill. Dec. 692, 377 N.E.2d 1328 (1978); *Forney v. Calvin,* 35 Ill. App. 3d 32, 340 N.E.2d 603 (1975). An opinion that the speed was too fast or too slow is generally inadmissible as not helpful to the jury. *See Delany v. Badame,* 49 Ill. 2d 168, 274 N.E.2d 353 (1971). While the witness must have observed the vehicle, the extent of observation goes to weight and not to admissibility. *Fuhry v. Chicago City Ry.,* 239 Ill. 548, 88 N.E. 221 (1909); *Conway v. Tamborini,* 68 Ill. App. 2d 190, 215 N.E.2d 303 (1966). Adequate observation is not excluded by the fact that darkness prevailed, *Birnbaum v. Kirchner,* 337 Ill. App. 25, 85 N.E.2d 191 (1949), or that witness was a passenger in back seat of another vehicle. *Wright v. Callaghan,* 50 Ill. App. 2d 157, 200 N.E.2d 56 (1964). The fact that the witness does not drive is admissible as going to weight. *Wright v. Callaghan* supra.

With respect to stopping distances, *see* §702.5 infra.

§701.5 Nature of Substances

Nonexperts may testify to the nature of substances observed by them with which they are familiar, and the testimony is not limited to a statement of the detailed characteristics observed but may take the form of a conclusion as to what the substance was. *People v. Ward,* 154 Ill. 2d 272, 181 Ill. Dec. 884, 609 N.E.2d 252 (1992) (citing Handbook). *See, e.g., People v. Korak,* 303 Ill. 438, 135 N.E. 764 (1922), substance on clothing appeared to be of same character as seminal discharge; *People v. Reed,* 333 Ill. 397, 164 N.E. 847 (1929), witnesses smelled dynamite after explosion; *People v. Preston,* 341 Ill. 407, 173 N.E. 383 (1930); *People v. Crabtree,* 162 Ill. App. 3d 658, 114 Ill. Dec. 52, 515 N.E.2d 1323 (1987), stains were bloodstains; *People v. Singletary,* 73 Ill. App. 3d 239, 29 Ill. Dec. 177, 391 N.E.2d 440 (1979), noise was a gun shot; *People v. Canity,* 100 Ill. App. 3d 135, 55 Ill. Dec. 445, 426

N.E.2d 591 (1981), "flicking" sound came from a knife, even though witness never saw a knife; *People v. Steffens,* 131 Ill. App. 3d 141, 86 Ill. Dec. 392, 475 N.E.2d 606 (1985), dents on car had been there for some time. A nonexpert may also testify as to the condition of things including causation when rationally based on perception and helpful. See *Altszyler v. Horizon House Condominium Assoc.,* 175 Ill. App. 3d 93, 124 Ill. Dec. 723, 529 N.E.2d 704 (1988), rainwater caused sidewalk to sink.

§701.6   *Identity and Physical Condition of Persons; Age*

Identity is a proper subject of lay testimony, and the witness may state that he identifies the person as the one in question. Identification testimony and constitutional requirements are discussed in §§611.16 and 611.17 supra. *See* §901.6 infra for voice identification. When helpful to the trier of fact and based upon personal knowledge, a lay witness may identify a person as being the individual appearing in a photograph or motion picture. *People v. Starks,* 119 Ill. App. 3d 21, 74 Ill. Dec. 760, 456 N.E.2d 262 (1983).

Intoxication is a proper subject of lay testimony, and the witness may state the fact of intoxication, *Aurora v. Hillman,* 90 Ill. 61 (1878), based upon observation, *Grant v. Paluch,* 61 Ill. App. 2d 247, 210 N.E.2d 35 (1965); *O'Brien v. Hertl,* 238 Ill. App. 3d 217, 179 Ill. Dec. 393, 606 N.E.2d 225 (1992), or experience, *People v. Lawson,* 85 Ill. App. 3d 376, 41 Ill. Dec. 401, 407 N.E.2d 899 (1980). Testimony that witness had been in contact with persons who had been drinking and could identify smell of alcohol sufficient foundation to testify that alcohol was smelled in vomit, *Logue v. Williams,* 111 Ill. App. 2d 237, 250 N.E.2d 159 (1969). However, it is not sufficient that the witness had talked to the person on the telephone. *Watson v. Fischbach,* 6 Ill. App. 3d 166, 284 N.E.2d 720 (1972), *rev'd on other grounds,* 54 Ill. 2d 498, 301 N.E.2d 303 (1973). *See also* §403.3 supra.

Condition of health, ability to work, suffering, possession of mental faculties, hearing, eyesight, and unconsciousness after an accident of oneself or of another person are all proper subjects of lay testimony. *Lauth v. Chicago Union Traction Co.,* 244 Ill. 244, 91 N.E. 431 (1910); *Chicago City Ry. v. Van Vleck,* 143 Ill. 480, 32 N.E. 262 (1892). Nervousness of another has been held to be a proper description of appearance by a nonexpert, *People v. Hauke,* 335 Ill. 217, 167 N.E. 1 (1929), as has the rendering of an opinion as to fear, upset state, or excitement of another, *People v. Hamilton,* 268 Ill. 390, 109 N.E. 329 (1915); *Dimick v. Downs,* 82 Ill. 570 (1876); *Law v. Central Ill. Pub. Serv. Co.,* 86 Ill. App. 3d 701, 41 Ill. Dec. 728, 408 N.E.2d 74 (1980), as has lay witness opinion of mental condition and capacity as bearing upon a defendant's fitness to stand trial, *People v. Bleitner,* 189 Ill. App. 3d 971, 137 Ill. Dec. 487, 546 N.E.2d 241 (1989), as has lay witness opinion as to sanity, *People v. Baker,* 253 Ill. App. 3d 15, 192 Ill. Dec. 564, 625 N.E.2d 719 (1993), as has deliriousness and disorientation of another, *Zoerner v. Iwan,* 250 Ill. App. 3d 576, 189 Ill. Dec. 191, 619 N.E.2d 892 (1993), to the extent exhibited and thus based upon physical manifestations, *Zoerner v. Iwan* supra, but testimony that an accused acted as if he had something on his mind more than usual has been condemned as a conclusion, *People v. Hamilton,* 268 Ill. 390, 109 N.E. 329 (1915), a result perhaps justified by the potential for prejudicial speculation as to what the "something" was, and that testimony that someone's conduct was "unusual" was improperly admitted on the ground of unhelpfulness to the jury. *People v. Hobley,* 159 Ill. 2d 272, 202 Ill. Dec. 256, 637 N.E.2d 992 (1994). *See* §403.1 supra. As to mental capacity, *see* §704.3 infra.

Age of another person is a proper subject of lay testimony. *People v. Claussen,* 367 Ill. 430, 11 N.E.2d 959 (1937). The individual himself, even if a minor, may also testify to his own age. *People v. Pennell,* 315 Ill. 124, 145 N.E. 606 (1924). Age may be proved by a birth certificate, 410 ILCS 535/25(2), (6). While a bartender is entitled to rely on a birth date on a driver's license, 235 ILCS 5/6-16(a), a driver's license, being hearsay, is not itself admissible as evidence of the age of the possessor. *Cochrane's of Champaign v. Liquor Control,* 285 Ill. App. 3d 28, 220 Ill. Dec. 755, 673 N.E.2d 1176 (1996). *Compare* id., Cook, J., dissenting, there should be no problems with proving age from a valid driver's license.

§701.7 State of Mind or Emotion

A witness may testify directly to her own mental or emotional state, if relevant. *People v. Weil,* 244 Ill. 176, 91 N.E. 112 (1910), testimony by complaining witness that he believed and relied upon representations; *Pfiester v. Western Union Tel. Co.,* 282 Ill. 69, 118 N.E. 407 (1918), testimony by plaintiff that he would have accepted telegraphic offer if delivered; *People v. Spranger,* 314 Ill. 602, 145 N.E. 706 (1924), testimony of accused that he did not intend to kill deceased; *People v. Lemcke,* 80 Ill. App. 3d 298, 35 Ill. Dec. 611, 399 N.E.2d 677 (1980), testimony of defendant as to his lack of intent to arouse or satisfy his sexual desires improperly excluded; *West Shore Associates v. American Wilbert,* 269 Ill. App. 3d 175, 206 Ill. Dec. 489, 645 N.E.2d 494 (1994), motive in requesting examination of books and records. *Cf. Hoehn v. Chicago, P. & St. L. Ry.,* 152 Ill. 223, 38 N.E. 549 (1894); *Rubinstein v. Fred A. Coleman Co.,* 22 Ill. App. 2d 116, 159 N.E.2d 379 (1959). Of course, the mental or emotional state may be irrelevant, as in *Flower v. Brumbach,* 131 Ill. 646, 23 N.E. 335 (1890), evidence of defendant as to what he intended by representations in letter properly excluded in action of deceit.

The state of mind or emotion of another person is not, in the nature of things, susceptible of firsthand knowledge. *Law v. Central Illinois Public Service Co.,* 86 Ill. App. 3d 701, 41 Ill. Dec. 728, 408 N.E.2d 74 (1980); *Zoerner v. Iwan,* 250 Ill. App. 3d 576, 189 Ill. Dec. 191, 619 N.E.2d 892 (1993). *Compare* §701.6 supra. Hence testimony directly upon the state in question has been excluded. *American Car & Foundry Co. v. Hill,* 226 Ill. 227, 80 N.E. 784 (1907), what other employees were aiming to do. *See also* §611.25 supra. The existence of a state of mind or emotion may, however, be proved by circumstances that would produce it, e.g., knowledge may be proved by evidence of what the person was told. A state of mind or emotion may also be proved by external manifestations of the person from which the state may be inferred. In the latter connection a shorthand description of a manner or of a variety of acts, difficult to describe in detail, has been allowed. *Sprague v. Craig,* 51 Ill. 288 (1869), testimony that plaintiff in action for breach of promise to marry appeared from her conduct sincerely attached to defendant; *People v. Peter,* 220 Ill. App. 3d 626, 163 Ill. Dec. 177, 581 N.E.2d 128 (1991), testimony that a flash of panic was observed to cross defendant's face when he picked up the canister. On the other hand, in *People v. Hamilton,* 286 Ill. 390, 109 N.E. 329 (1915), testimony that the accused acted as if he had something on his mind more than usual was not permitted as calling for a conclusion. Similarly, a witness will not be permitted to testify as to the meaning of another witness's testimony. *People v. Holveck,* 141 Ill. 2d 84, 152 Ill. Dec. 237, 565 N.E.2d 919 (1990).

A lay witness is not permitted to testify as to what another witness meant by making a remark, that is, such testimony is frequently stated not to be helpful, *People v. Taylor,* 264 Ill. App. 3d 197, 202 Ill. Dec. 217, 637 N.E.2d 756 (1994) ("the drops get the draws"); *People v. Williams,* 264 Ill. App. 3d 278, 201 Ill. Dec. 198, 636 N.E.2d 630 (1993) ("died like a bitch"); *People v. Brown,* 200 Ill. App. 3d 566, 146 Ill. Dec. 346, 558 N.E.2d 309 (1990) ("have some of this"); *People v. Linkogle,* 54 Ill. App. 3d 830, 11 Ill. Dec. 467, 368 N.E.2d 1075 (1977) ("wriggle his thing"), unless the lay witness has special knowledge and familiarity with the remark which would be of help to the trier of fact in interpreting the remark. *People v. Williams* supra; *People v. Stamps,* 108 Ill. App. 3d 280, 63 Ill. Dec. 919, 438 N.E.2d 1282 (1982). However, in general, if not in all of the foregoing cited instances, admitting the testimony would in fact aid the trier of fact in determining questions at issue, *see* §702.4 infra. It thus would be preferable to introduce the evidence as that of an expert qualified by experience, *see* §702.2 infra. As to expert witness testimony, *see*

§702.6. infra. In short, it is suggested that current Illinois law in this area is unduly restrictive, in that, helpful testimony is being kept from the trier of fact.

With respect to mental capacity, *see* §704.3 infra. The admissibility of declarations of the person indicating an existing state of mind or emotion as an exception to the hearsay rule is treated in §§803.4 to 803.7 infra.

§701.8 Relations of Time and Space

The difficulty encountered by a witness in expressing his impression of time and spatial relationships, particularly those involving motion, sensibly has been recognized in cases that permit the giving of shorthand summaries. *Central Ry. v. Allmon,* 147 Ill. 471, 35 N.E. 725 (1893), plaintiff could not have jumped from buggy in time to avoid streetcar; *Casey v. Kelly-Atkinson Constr. Co.,* 240 Ill. 416, 88 N.E. 982 (1909), sufficient time to fasten crane after foreman's attention was called to approaching storm and before storm struck; *Rost v. F.H. Noble & Co.,* 316 Ill. 357, 147 N.E. 258 (1925), possible to see a man from certain location; *People v. Grundeis,* 413 Ill. 145, 108 N.E.2d 483 (1952), accused was within hearing range of conversation; *Bobalek v. Atlass,* 315 Ill. App. 514, 524, 43 N.E.2d 584 (1942), "He turned so quick to avoid hitting him we had to turn"; *Scheibel v. Groeteka,* 183 Ill. App. 2d 120, 131 Ill. Dec. 680, 538 N.E.2d 1236 (1989), defendant could have stopped his vehicle.

However, *cf.* the following decisions unfortunately indicating approval of exclusion: *Chicago, M. & St. P. Ry. v. O'Sullivan,* 143 Ill. 48, 32 N.E. 398 (1892), whether deceased could have heard locomotive blowing off steam; *Brink's Chicago City Express Co. v. Kinnare,* 168 Ill. 643, 48 N.E. 446 (1897), whether driver could have stopped in time if he had seen child; *Chicago City Ry. v. Lowitz,* 218 Ill. 24, 75 N.E. 755 (1905), whether possible for motorman to see passenger alighting at rear; *Stefan v. Elgin, J. & E. Ry.,* 2 Ill. App. 2d 300, 120 N.E.2d 52 (1954), whether plaintiff had time to get out of car before train struck; *Diaz v. Kelley,* 275 Ill. App. 3d 1058, 212 Ill. Dec. 456, 657 N.E..2d 657 (1995), whether the accident happened so fast that the defendant had no time to stop the truck.

If the opinion or inference is rationally based upon the perceptions of the witness and is helpful, i.e., the facts could not otherwise be adequately presented or described to the fact finder, *People v. Novak,* 163 Ill. 2d 93, 205 Ill. Dec. 471, 643 N.E.2d 762 (1994); *Freeding-Skokie Roll-Off Service v. Hamilton,* 108 Ill. 2d 217, 91 Ill. Dec. 178, 483 N.E.2d 524 (1985), such an expression of relationship by a lay witness is admissible even if it embraces an ultimate issue of fact unless phrased in terms of unexplored legal criteria. *See* §704.1 infra.

§702   Testimony by Experts

§702.1   An Overview

The admissibility of expert testimony requires that three preliminary determinations be made by the court. *See* §104 supra. First, can expert testimony be of assistance to the trier of fact in understanding the evidence or determining a fact in issue? The court may be required, as an aspect of this inquiry, to determine whether a sufficiently reliable field of scientific, technical, or other specialized knowledge has been developed. *See* §702.4 infra. Second, the court must also determine whether the witness called is properly qualified to give the testimony sought. *See* §702.2 infra. The witness may be qualified as an expert on the basis of knowledge, skill, experience, training, or education. *See generally People v. Novak,* 163 Ill. 2d 93, 205 Ill. Dec. 471, 643 N.E.2d 762 (1994); Buford by Buford v. Chicago Housing Auth., 131 Ill. App. 3d 235, 86 Ill. Dec. 926, 476 N.E.2d 427 (1985). Finally, the opinion of an expert must be supported by an adequate foundation of facts, data or opinions, including facts, data, and opinions reasonably relied upon, §703.1 infra. Absence of such a foundation requires the striking of an expert's opinion as based on conjecture or speculation.

Expert testimony is not limited to scientific or technical areas, but rather includes all areas of specialized knowledge. All that is required is that the testimony of a qualified witness assist the trier of fact. *Chem-Pac, Inc. v. Simborg*, 145 Ill. App. 3d 520, 99 Ill. Dec. 389, 495 N.E.2d 1124 (1986) (quoting Handbook). Expert testimony is subject to exclusion on the grounds that its probative value is substantially outweighed by unfair prejudice, confusion, misleading, or waste of time. *Wakeford v. Rodehouse Restaurants,* 223 Ill. App. 3d 31, 165 Ill. Dec. 529, 584 N.E.2d 963 (1991). Determination of the limits of expert testimony rests in the sound discretion of the court.

When scientific, technical, or other specialized knowledge is of assistance to enable the trier to evaluate facts intelligently, the traditional method of supplying data of this nature is the introduction of an opinion of an expert witness. *People v. Jennings,* 252 Ill. 534, 96 N.E. 1077 (1911). Federal Rule of Evidence 702, 65 F.R.D. 131, 152 (1975), provides that expert testimony may be "in the form of an opinion or otherwise." Accordingly, an expert may, but need not, testify in the form of an opinion; she may instead give an exposition of relevant scientific or other principles, permitting the trier of fact to draw its own inference or conclusion from the evidence presented, or she may combine the two. The indisputable logic of the foregoing conforms to actual practice.

Expert witnesses frequently express an opinion in response to a question such as "Do you have an opinion to a reasonable degree of [scientific, medical, or other technical] certainty as to . . . ?" While the expert usually replies to follow-up questions indicating his opinion in absolute terms such as "did" or "was caused," less than absolute certainty is permissible. Thus, opinions expressed in terms such as "could," "most probably," or "is similar to" are properly received. *See* §704.2 infra. The term "reasonable degree of . . . certainty" refers to conformity with a generally accepted explanative theory used to derive the probabilities expressed by the expert as to his opinion. *Boose v. Digate,* 107 Ill. App. 2d 418, 246 N.E.2d 50 (1969); *Redmon v. Sooter,* 1 Ill. App. 3d 406, 274 N.E.2d 200 (1971); *Dabros by Dabros v. Wang,* 243 Ill. App. 3d 258, 183 Ill. Dec. 465, 611 N.E.2d 1113 (1993). *See also Hajian v. Holy Family Hospital,* 273 Ill. App. 3d 932, 210 Ill. Dec. 156, 652 N.E.2d 1132 (1995). While questions to an expert designed to elicit an opinion as to a fact of consequence, including an expression of his estimate of probabilities of the facts expressed in the opinion, are frequently couched in terms of reasonable certainty, courts have apparently not yet seen fit to mandate such phraseology. *See Dominguez v. St. John's Hospital,* 260 Ill. App. 3d 591, 197 Ill. Dec. 947, 632 N.E.2d 16 (1994), failure to employ terminology is of no consequence when the testimony of a qualified expert reveals that it is grounded on recognized medical thought. *Accord Plooy v. Paryani,* 275 Ill. App. 3d 1074, 212 Ill. Dec. 317, 657 N.E.2d 12 (1995).

The Illinois Supreme Court in *People v. Enis,* 139 Ill. 2d 264, 289, 151 Ill. Dec. 493, 503, 564 N.E.2d 1155, 1165 (1990), cautioned against the overuse of expert testimony:

> We caution against the overuse of expert testimony. Such testimony, in this case concerning the unreliability of eyewitness testimony, could well lead to the use of expert testimony concerning the unreliability of other types of testimony and, eventually, to the use of experts to testify as to the unreliability of expert testimony. So-called experts can usually be obtained to support most any position. The determination of a lawsuit should not depend upon which side can present the most or the most convincing expert witness.

Nevertheless the infatuation with expert witness testimony marches on unabated.

The expansion of judicial notice in this area may foretell a willingness to accept scientific and technical treatises as a substitute for, adjunct to, or check upon opinions of experts. *See* §202.3 supra and §705.2 infra.

The expert, whose function is to supply scientific or technical data, or other specialized knowledge, should be distinguished from the lay witness who is required to have some specific background of experience in order to render his observations significant, i.e., rationally based on the perception of the witness. *See* §701.1 supra. An example of the latter is the witness to speed. *See* §701.4 supra.

Comparison by expert witness is discussed in §901.4 infra. The basis of an expert's opinion is treated in §§703.1 and 705.1 infra.

An expert witness originally retained by a party may nevertheless be subpoenaed to testify by an opposing party. *People v. Speck,* 41 Ill. 2d 177, 242 N.E.2d 208 (1968).

An expert retained by a party is not an agent of that party; the expert's statements are not an admission of a party-opponent, §§802.8 and 802.9 infra. *Taylor v. Kohli,* 162 Ill. 2d 91, 204 Ill. Dec. 766, 642 N.E.2d 467 (1994).

With respect to the weight to be accorded expert testimony, *see In re Glenville,* 139 Ill. 2d 242, 152 Ill. Dec. 90, 565 N.E.2d 623 (1990); *Outboard Marine v. Liberty Mutual Ins. Co.,* 283 Ill. App. 3d 630, 219 Ill. Dec. 62, 670 N.E.2d 740 (1996).

§702.2 *Qualifications of Experts*

A witness may be qualified as an expert by reason of knowledge, skill, experience, training, or education. *Accord People v. Miller,* 173 Ill. 2d 167, 219 Ill. Dec. 43, 670 N.E.2d 721 (1996) (practical experience, scientific study, education, training, or research). A witness qualifies as an expert by virtue of any one such factor, or upon a combination of any of the five factors. Specific degrees, certificates of training, or memberships in professional organizations are not required; qualification of an expert on the basis of experience alone is proper. *People v. Novak,* 163 Ill. 2d 93, 205 Ill. Dec. 471, 643 N.E.2d 762 (1994); *Lee v. Chicago Transit Authority,* 152 Ill. 2d 432, 178 Ill. Dec. 699, 605 N.E.2d 493 (1992); *In re Interest of*

V.Z., 287 Ill. App. 3d 552, 223 Ill. Dec. 62, 678 N.E.2d 1070 (1997); *Leahy Realty v. American Snack Foods,* 253 Ill. App. 3d 233, 192 Ill. Dec. 801, 625 N.E.2d 956 (1993); *Duffy v. Midlothian Country Club,* 135 Ill. App. 3d 429, 90 Ill. Dec. 237, 481 N.E.2d 1037 (1985). Neither is extensive formal training or the publication of material in the field necessary. *People v. Cole,* 170 Ill. App. 3d 912, 120 Ill. Dec. 744, 524 N.E.2d 926 (1988); *People v. Douglas,* 183 Ill. App. 3d 241, 131 Ill. Dec. 779, 538 N.E.2d 1335 (1989). Included within the category of experts are persons sometimes called "skilled" experts, such as bankers or landowners testifying as to land value. The local carpenter, plumber, bricklayer, etc., may be added to the list of experts qualified on the basis of skill. *Schaffner v. Chicago & N.W. Transp. Co.,* 129 Ill. 2d 1, 133 Ill. Dec. 432, 541 N.E.2d 643 (1989), a contractor or builder may testify as an expert on matters relating to construction; *Stanley v. Board of Education of City of Chicago,* 9 Ill. App. 3d 963, 293 N.E.2d 417 (1973), training and experience; *Becker v. Aquaslide 'N' Dive Corp.,* 35 Ill. App. 3d 479, 341 N.E.2d 369 (1975), university professor of aquatics and swimming permitted to testify. *Nowakowski v. Hoppe Tire Co.,* 39 Ill. App. 3d 155, 349 N.E.2d 578 (1976), study or experience or combination of both; *Boyle v. Manley,* 263 Ill. App. 3d 200, 200 Ill. Dec. 675, 635 N.E.2d 1014 (1994), 30 year employee of Marine Division of Chicago Park District qualified as an expert on boat mooring. Thus no matter how obtained, if the expert witness possesses specialized knowledge that will assist the trier of fact, he may testify thereto in the form of an opinion or otherwise. *Taylor v. Carborundum Co.,* 107 Ill. App. 2d 12, 246 N.E.2d 898 (1969); *People v. Oberlander,* 109 Ill. App. 2d 469, 248 N.E.2d 805 (1969); *People v. Jackson,* 145 Ill. App. 3d 626, 99 Ill. Dec. 472, 495 N.E.2d 1207 (1986); *Bartsch v. Gordon N. Plumb, Inc.,* 138 Ill. App. 3d 188, 92 Ill. Dec. 862, 485 N.E.2d 1105 (1985). *Accord* Rule 702 of the Federal Rules of Evidence:

> If scientific, technical, or other specialized knowledge will assist the trier of fact to understand the evidence or to determine a fact in issue, a witness qualified as an expert by knowledge, skill,

experience, training, or education may testify thereto in the form of an opinion or otherwise.

The degree and manner of knowledge and experience required of an alleged expert is directly related to the complexity of the subject matter and the corresponding likelihood of error by one insufficiently familiar therewith. *People v. Park*, 72 Ill. 2d 203, 20 Ill. Dec. 586, 380 N.E.2d 795 (1978). Thus in *People v. Palmer*, 351 Ill. 319, 184 N.E. 205 (1933), prior ownership and marketing of hogs was sufficient practical experience and special knowledge to render an opinion as to value of a pregnant sow; in *People v. Calderon*, 98 Ill. App. 3d 657, 53 Ill. Dec. 880, 424 N.E.2d 671 (1981), a police officer with six years' experience investigating gang crimes may give his opinion on characteristics of gangs; in *People v. Free*, 94 Ill. 2d 378, 69 Ill. Dec. 1, 447 N.E.2d 218 (1983), psychopharmacologist with research experience with PCP qualified to give an opinion as to defendant's ability to act intentionally as it relates to defense of voluntary intoxication; in *McClure v. Suter*, 63 Ill. App. 3d 378, 20 Ill. Dec. 308, 379 N.E.2d 1376 (1978), owner of campground who had made inquiries qualified to testify as to swimming regulations at similar campgrounds; in *People v. Rhodes*, 81 Ill. App. 3d 339, 36 Ill. Dec. 556, 401 N.E.2d 237 (1980), witness qualified to give opinion as to fingerprint comparison on basis of training by F.B.I., 50 hours of in-service training, knowledge of current literature, and having compared five to six thousand fingerprints over last five years; in *O'Dell v. Dowd*, 102 Ill. App. 3d 189, 57 Ill. Dec. 650, 429 N.E.2d 548 (1981), registered engineer may testify to cause of tire failure; in *Fontanne v. Federal Paper Bd. Co.*, 105 Ill. App. 3d 306, 61 Ill. Dec. 178, 434 N.E.2d 331 (1982), a high school dropout with specialized training and experience was qualified to testify as an accident reconstruction expert; in *J.L. Simmons Co. v. Firestone Tire & Rubber*, 126 Ill. App. 3d 859, 81 Ill. Dec. 627, 467 N.E.2d 327 (1984), vocational counselor may testify that person was unemployable; in *Gordon v. Chicago Transit Auth.*, 128 Ill. App. 3d 493, 83 Ill. Dec. 743, 470 N.E.2d 1163 (1984), public transit security officer qualified to testify that the crime would not have happened if cab door of train had been closed; in *Buford by Buford v. Chicago Housing Auth.*, 131 Ill. App. 3d 235, 86 Ill. Dec. 926, 476 N.E.2d 427 (1985), a mechanical engineer can testify as to metal fatigue even though he was not familiar with elevator design; in *Ryan v. E.A.I. Constr. Corp.*, 158 Ill. App. 3d 449, 110 Ill. Dec. 924, 511 N.E.2d 1244 (1987), a contractor or builder may testify as to proper mode of doing construction work, conformity with plans and specifications, and adequacy of safeguards; in *Lively v. Kostoff*, 167 Ill. App. 3d 384, 118 Ill. Dec. 272, 521 N.E.2d 554 (1988), a doctor who had not personally examined the defendant could testify that the defendant was suffering from a degree of intoxication from alcohol; in *In re Estate of Hoover*, 155 Ill. 2d 402, 185 Ill. Dec. 866, 615 N.E.2d 736 (1993), Illinois law does not require an expert witness to physically examine or personally know the patient in order to render an opinion; in *People v. Sadaka*, 174 Ill. App. 3d 260, 123 Ill. Dec. 738, 528 N.E.2d 283 (1988), special drug enforcement agent with 17 years of experience qualified to testify as to "street value" of heroin; in *People v. Hayes*, 20 Ill. 2d 319, 169 N.E.2d 760 (1960), a police officer with 15 years' experience with stolen auto parts was qualified to testify that certain stolen auto parts were worth more than $50; in *State v. Aister*, 318 Ill. 230, 149 N.E. 297 (1925), prior drinking of liquor qualified a witness to testify that a certain beverage contained more than .5 percent alcohol on the basis of its taste; in *Webster Mfg. Co. v. Mulvanny*, 168 Ill. 311, 48 N.E. 168 (1897), steamfitters with some experience in running engines (but not to any great extent) were competent to testify to the cause of an explosion in a steam pipe connecting a steam engine with a boiler; and in *Keating v. People*, 160 Ill. 480, 43 N.E. 724 (1896), a paying teller of a bank was qualified to render an opinion of the genuineness of a bank note. *See generally People v. Lowitzki*, 285 Ill. App. 3d 770, 221 Ill. Dec. 66, 674 N.E.2d 859 (1996); *People v. McDarrah*, 175 Ill. App. 3d 284, 124 Ill. Dec. 827, 529 N.E.2d 808 (1988).

In contrast, *see People v. Fiorita*, 339 Ill. 78, 170 N.E. 690 (1930), a police employee is not qualified as a ballistics expert merely by engaging in identification of guns for several months where he had no other experience or education; *Penrod v. Merrill Lynch, Pierce, Fenner & Smith, Inc.,* 68 Ill. App. 3d 75, 24 Ill. Dec. 464, 385 N.E.2d 376 (1979), college teacher of economics, finance, investments, and insurance is not qualified to render opinion as expert regarding stockbroker activities; *People v. Owens,* 155 Ill. App. 3d 990, 108 Ill. Dec. 511, 508 N.E.2d 1088 (1987), testimony of police officer that he had studied "blood splatter technique" is not sufficient alone to establish qualifications; *People v. Huddleston,* 176 Ill. App. 3d 18, 125 Ill. Dec. 606, 530 N.E.2d 1015 (1988), police officer who had never before performed test to determine stippling patterns of gunpowder grains, had received no training, and did not understand test was not qualified; *Cleveringa v. J. I. Case Co.,* 230 Ill. App. 3d 831, 172 Ill. Dec. 523, 595 N.E.2d 1193 (1992), practical knowledge and frequent use of a machine does not alone qualify the user as an expert on either design or manufacture. Nor is a person qualified to render an opinion as to which parent should have custody of minor children on the basis solely of having taken courses in psychology. *Baty v. Baty,* 83 Ill. App. 3d 113, 38 Ill. Dec. 516, 403 N.E.2d 747 (1980). Nor is a person qualified to render an opinion on the cause and origin of a fire in the absence of any training or prior experience. *Bloomgren v. Fire Ins. Exchange,* 162 Ill. App. 3d 594, 115 Ill. Dec. 88, 517 N.E.2d 290 (1987). Similarly, a crime-scene technician is not qualified to render an opinion about the number of persons present at the time of the murder. *People v. Groth,* 105 Ill. App. 3d 244, 61 Ill. Dec. 128, 434 N.E.2d 65 (1982). Moreover, a former professional football player with a degree in mechanical engineering is not qualified to give an opinion that the rear rim of a football helmet did not cause a cervical injury. *Galindo v. Riddell, Inc.,* 107 Ill. App. 3d 139, 62 Ill. Dec. 849, 437 N.E.2d 376 (1982). Note also that police officers are not assumed, by virtue of their position alone, to possess the requisite expertise to identify heroin, *People v. Sanford,* 24 Ill. 2d 365, 181 N.E.2d 118 (1962), or cannabis, *People v. Park,* 72 Ill. 2d 203, 20 Ill. Dec. 586, 380

N.E. 795 (1978). For an interesting discussion of whether a particular subject matter falls within the expert's expertise, *see Broussard, Etc. v. Huffman Mfg. Co.,* 108 Ill. App. 3d 356, 63 Ill. Dec. 854, 438 N.E.2d 1217 (1982). *See also Levin v. Welsh Brothers Motor Serv., Inc.,* 164 Ill. App. 3d 640, 115 Ill. Dec. 680, 518 N.E.2d 205 (1987).

In some situations, a person will be permitted to testify as an expert witness only if licensed in the particular field. *See People v. West,* 264 Ill. App. 3d 176, 201 Ill. Dec. 807, 636 N.E.2d 1239 (1994) (arson investigators); 225 ILCS §445/2(h)(4), 3, 4. *See also* 730 ILCS 5/5-2-5, permitting only a clinical psychologist possessing specified qualifications including a doctorate in psychology to testify on a defendant's fitness, insanity, or mental illness. With respect to physicians, *see* §702.4 infra.

While the party offering the expert has the burden of establishing the expert's scientific, technical, or other specialized knowledge, *People v. Novak,* 163 Ill. 2d 93, 205 Ill. Dec. 471, 643 N.E.2d 762 (1994); *People v. Free,* 94 Ill. 2d 378, 69 Ill. Dec. 1, 447 N.E.2d 218 (1983); *People v. Groth,* 105 Ill. App. 3d 244, 61 Ill. Dec. 128, 434 N.E.2d 65 (1982) (citing Handbook); 2 Wigmore, Evidence §560 (Chadbourn rev. 1979), the sufficiency of qualifications is not a matter of arbitrary or fixed tests but rests largely in the sound discretion of the trial judge, §104.1 supra. *People v. Novak,* supra; *Lee v. Chicago Transit Authority,* 152 Ill. 2d 432, 178 Ill. Dec. 699, 605 N.E.2d 493 (1992); *Schaffner v. Chicago & N.W. Transp. Co.,* 129 Ill. 2d 1, 133 Ill. Dec. 432, 541 N.E.2d 643 (1989); *Hardward State Bank v. Cotner,* 55 Ill. 2d 240, 302 N.E.2d 257 (1973); *Curt Bullock Builders v. H.S.S. Development, Inc.,* 225 Ill. App. 3d 9, 167 Ill. Dec. 12, 586 N.E.2d 1284 (1992). The trial court's determination is subject to reversal only if it constitutes a gross abuse of discretion. *People v. Free* supra; *Hardward State Bank v. Cotner* supra; *People v. Fiorita,* 339 Ill. 78, 170 N.E. 690 (1930); *Natural Educational Music Co. v. Rieckhoff,* 292 Ill. App. 3d 260, 226 Ill. Dec. 88, 684 N.E.2d 1084 (1997).

If an opposing party believes that the witness lacks either

sufficient qualifications or sufficient foundation for her opinion, the court may permit a *voir dire* examination into such matters. *People v. Sawhill,* 299 Ill. 393, 132 N.E. 477 (1921); *Geving v. Fitzpatrick,* 56 Ill. App. 3d 206, 14 Ill. Dec. 175, 371 N.E.2d 1228 (1978). In this manner, if the witness is not qualified or a sufficient basis is lacking, *see* §611.25 supra and §705.1 infra, the witness's testimony may be stricken without the trier of fact being exposed to the inadmissible opinion of the witness. While considered a salutary procedure, the permitting of such preliminary cross-examination rests in the court's discretion and does not exist as a matter of right. *Payne v. Murphy Hardware Co.,* 62 Ill. App. 3d 803, 19 Ill. Dec. 945, 379 N.E.2d 817 (1978). *Contra People v. Hanna,* 120 Ill. App. 3d 602, 75 Ill. Dec. 793, 457 N.E.2d 1352 (1983) (*voir dire* on qualification is a matter of right). The opportunity to cross-examine the expert witness on *voir dire* or thereafter as to her qualifications does not reduce in any way the burden of the proponent of the expert to establish the expert's qualifications. *People v. Park,* 72 Ill. 2d 203, 20 Ill. Dec. 586, 380 N.E.2d 795 (1978).

§702.3   Compensation of Experts; Compelling Testimony

The expert may be compelled to testify at trial by a party, whether as to observed facts or in the form of an expert opinion, without payment or compensation other than ordinary witness fees. *Dixon v. People,* 168 Ill. 179, 48 N.E. 108 (1897). *See* §611.6 supra. An agreement to pay special compensation for the giving of testimony would thus seem to lack consideration. However, time spent in preparation would no doubt support a contract to pay therefor, since preparation is not compellable in the absence of compensation. *See* 8 Wigmore, Evidence §2203 (McNaughton rev. 1961). In practice nonstatutory witness fees are paid to an expert witness testifying at a deposition by the party retaining the expert for the purpose of rendering an opinion. *Tzystuck v. Chicago Transit Auth.,* 124 Ill. 2d 226, 124 Ill. Dec. 544, 529 N.E.2d 525

(1988). Expert witness fees for experts, such as a treating physician, who were not retained for the purpose of rendering an opinion, incurred in connection with a deposition, are the responsibility of the party taking the deposition. *Tzystuck* supra. Nonstatutory witness fees incurred in connection with trial testimony of any expert witness are presumably the responsibility of the party requiring the expert witness to appear at the trial. The fact that an expert has conferred with a party and been paid for his or her expert advice does *not* render the expert incompetent to testify for the opposing party. *People v. Speck,* 41 Ill. 2d 177, 242 N.E.2d 208 (1968). The party calling the expert at trial should, of course, be prohibited from revealing to the jury that the expert was first consulted by the opponent. *Akers v. Atchison, Topeka & Santa Fe Ry.,* 187 Ill. App. 3d 950, 135 Ill. Dec. 371, 543 N.E.2d 939 (1989).

§702.4   *Assist Trier of Fact; Common Knowledge of Jurors; Reliability—***Frye;** *When Required*

Expert testimony is admissible whenever it will assist the trier of fact to understand the evidence or to determine a fact in issue. *Accord* Federal Rule of Evidence 702, cited with approval in *Leonard v. Pitstick Dairy Lake & Park,* 124 Ill. App. 3d 580, 79 Ill. Dec. 740, 464 N.E.2d 644 (1984).

At one time expert testimony was limited to fields where only persons of "skill and experience in it are capable of forming a correct judgment as to any facts connected therewith. . . ." *People v. Jennings,* 252 Ill. 534, 549, 96 N.E. 1077 (1911), upholding admission of fingerprint evidence. This restriction was often stated conversely: expert testimony would be excluded if upon matters reasonably regarded as within the knowledge and experience of jurors and hence involving no need of expert assistance. *Ficht v. Niedert Motor Serv. Inc.,* 34 Ill. App. 2d 360, 181 N.E.2d 386 (1962); *Hays v. Place,* 350 Ill. App. 504, 113 N.E.2d 178 (1953). The effect given the admission of testimony of this nature was not uniform. It was ruled reversible error, as in *Chicago & Northwestern Ry. v. Ingersoll,* 65 Ill. 399 (1872), and *Hoffman v. Ernest Tosetti Brewing Co.,* 257 Ill. 185, 100 N.E. 531 (1913). Admission was in other cases held harmless because the jury would not be misled by opinions within their own knowledge and experience, *Illinois Steel Co. v. Mann,* 197 Ill. 186, 64 N.E. 328 (1902), or because the evidence was cumulative and not of sufficient importance to require reversal. *Wawryszyn v. Illinois Central R.R.,* 10 Ill. App. 2d 394, 135 N.E.2d 154 (1956).

Today the admissibility of expert testimony is to be determined solely on the basis of assisting the trier of fact. Even as to matters of common knowledge and experience of jurors, where helpful to comprehension or explanation, expert testimony is permitted. *Thacker v. UNR Industries, Inc.,* 151 Ill. 2d 343, 177 Ill. Dec. 379, 603 N.E.2d 449 (1992); *People v. Albanese,* 104 Ill. 2d 504, 85 Ill. Dec. 441, 473 N.E.2d 1246 (1984); *Merchants Natl. Bank of Aurora v. Elgin, J. & E. Ry.,* 49 Ill. 2d 118, 273 N.E.2d 809 (1971); *Van Hold v. National Railroad Passenger Corp.,* 283 Ill. App. 3d 62, 218 Ill. Dec. 762, 669 N.E.2d 1288 (1996) (citing Handbook). Thus expert testimony is admissible if it would aid the triers of fact, even if they might have a general knowledge of the subject matter. *People v. Gilliam,* 172 Ill. 2d 484, 218 Ill. Dec. 884, 670 N.E.2d 606 (1996); *Hernandez v. Power Construction Co.,* 73 Ill. 2d 90, 22 Ill. Dec. 503, 382 N.E.2d 1201 (1978); *Anderson v. Chesapeake & Ohio Ry.,* 147 Ill. App. 3d 960, 101 Ill. Dec. 262, 498 N.E.2d 586 (1986); *People v. Hendricks,* 145 Ill. App. 3d 71, 99 Ill. Dec. 20, 495 N.E.2d 85 (1986); *Binge v. J.J. Borders Constr. Co.,* 95 Ill. App. 3d 238, 50 Ill. Dec. 788, 419 N.E.2d 1237 (1981) (citing Handbook). *See, e.g., People v. Oaks,* 169 Ill. 2d 409, 215 Ill. Dec. 188, 662 N.E.2d 1328 (1996), whether injuries causing death of three-year-old, including extensive eye and brain hemorrhaging, were accidental or intentional was knowledge not common to lay persons; People v. Cooper, 97 Ill. App. 3d 222, 52 Ill. Dec. 676, 422 N.E.2d 885 (1981), whether a wound is self-inflicted is not a question of such common experience that layman may not be assisted by the opinion of a doctor; *Leonard v. Pitstick Dairy Lake & Park,* 124 Ill. App. 3d 580, 79 Ill. Dec. 740, 464 N.E.2d 644 (1984), an expert opinion is helpful as to whether surface diving into a lake by a teenage boy was dangerous; *Pease v. Ace Hardware Home Center,* 147 Ill. App. 3d 546, 101 Ill. Dec. 161, 498 N.E.2d 343 (1986), comprehension and understanding of the jury would have been aided by expert testimony on the feasibility and availability of alternative product designs; *People v. Abdelmassih,* 217 Ill. App. 3d 544, 160 Ill. Dec. 536, 577 N.E.2d 861 (1991), police officer may render opinion that the presence of various drugs and drug paraphernalia indicates that the drugs were for sale and not for personal use (*accord People v. King,* 218 Ill. App. 3d 248, 161 Ill. Dec. 90, 578 N.E.2d 217 (1991); *People v. Stone,* 244 Ill. App. 3d 881, 185 Ill. Dec. 159, 614 N.E.2d 293 (1993); *contra People v. Brown,* 232 Ill. App. 3d 885, 174 Ill. Dec. 316, 598 N.E.2d 948 (1992) (jury is capable of making such a distinction without expert assistance)). The proper test is stated by 7 Wigmore, Evidence §1923 (Chadbourn rev. 1978):

> The true test of the admissibility of such testimony is not whether the subject matter is common or uncommon, or whether many persons or few have some knowledge of the matter; but it is whether the witnesses offered as experts have any peculiar knowledge or experience, not common to the world, which renders their opinions founded on such knowledge or experience any aid to the court or the jury in determining the questions at issue.

Accord People v. Novak, 163 Ill. 2d 93, 205 Ill. Dec. 471, 643 N.E.2d 762 (1994) (through education, training, experience, or a combination of each, the witnesses possessed knowledge that is *not common to the average citizen,* which knowledge in adddition aided the jury in reaching its conclusion) (emphasis added).

Where the area of proposed expert testimony relates to a matter of common knowledge but offers no aid to the trier of fact in determining questions at issue, the expert's opinion will not be received. *People v. Hall,* 157 Ill. 2d 324, 193 Ill. Dec. 98, 626 N.E.2d 131 (1993); *People v. Mack,* 128 Ill. 2d 231, 131 Ill. Dec. 551, 538 N.E.2d 1107 (1989). *See, e.g., People v. Gilliam,* 172 Ill. 2d 484, 218 Ill. Dec. 884, 670 N.E.2d 606 (1996), whether a defendant might falsely confess to protect his family; *Hernandez v. Power Constr. Co.,* 73 Ill. 2d 90, 22 Ill. Dec. 503, 382 N.E.2d 1201 (1978), whether guardrails could prevent one from falling off a scaffold; *Ray v. Cock Robin, Inc.,* 10 Ill. App. 3d 276, 293 N.E.2d 488 (1973), *aff'd,* 57 Ill. 2d 19, 310 N.E.2d 9 (1974), whether the placement of tables close to a busy street was dangerous, and whether guardrails, barriers or blockades would have provided some degree of protection; *People v. Enis,* 139 Ill. 2d 89, 151 Ill. Dec. 493, 564 N.E.2d 1155 (1990) (extended discussion), expert testimony relating to the trustworthiness of eyewitness identification, a matter not beyond their common knowledge, is not of sufficient assistance to the jury to be admitted; *In re Interest of M.B.C.,* 125 Ill. App. 3d 512, 80 Ill. Dec. 821, 466 N.E.2d 273 (1984), minister with counseling experience is not in a better position to judge parental fitness than average person in the community; *People v. Perry,* 147 Ill. App. 3d 272, 101 Ill. Dec. 659, 498 N.E.2d 1167 (1986), opinion of expert on child abuse as to whether a sleeping mother could have accidentally rolled over onto her child and suffocated him was not of special assistance to the jury, was not within the witness's expertise, and thus should not have been received; *Stringham v. United Parcel Serv., Inc.,* 181 Ill. App. 3d 312, 130 Ill. Dec. 81, 536 N.E.2d 1292 (1989), opinion as to the causal relation of a particular state of intoxication and the accident properly excluded as of little assistance to the jury; *People v. Cox,* 197 Ill. App. 3d 1028, 145 Ill. Dec. 518, 557 N.E.2d 288 (1990), fact that complaint of rape by a person showing emotion is more credible is within the range of knowledge of the average person; *Fetzer v. Wood,* 211 Ill. App. 3d 70, 155 Ill. Dec. 626, 569 N.E.2d 1237 (1991), expert testimony as to the value of life based upon what society would pay to prevent loss of life is overly speculative and misleading; *People v. Sims,*

265 Ill. App. 3d 352, 202 Ill. Dec. 577, 638 N.E.2d 223 (1994), expert testimony that gangs have resulted in students not feeling safe, even if beyond the knowledge of average citizen, not helpful in determining a particular defendant's state of mind. Similarly, expert testimony pertaining to the credibility of a witness is inadmissible where it does not present a concept beyond the knowledge of the average person. *See, e.g., People v. Masor,* 218 Ill. App. 3d 884, 161 Ill. Dec. 530, 578 N.E.2d 1176 (1991), susceptibility to entrapment is not beyond common experience of the average fact finder; *People v. Elder,* 219 Ill. App. 3d 223, 161 Ill. Dec. 872, 579 N.E.2d 420 (1991), whether the defendant was acting in sudden and intense passion as a result of serious provocation was not difficult to comprehend and understand and thus not assisted by expert testimony; *People v. Lambrecht,* 231 Ill. App. 3d 426, 172 Ill. Dec. 688, 595 N.E.2d 1358 (1992), jury would be able to determine the question of the defendant's predisposition on its own; *People v. Wilson,* 246 Ill. App. 3d 311, 186 Ill. Dec. 226, 615 N.E.2d 1283 (1993), expert testimony about the problems child victims of sex abuse have remembering and describing incidents was already well known by jury and being a generalization would have no direct bearing on credibility of the children in the case at hand. The trial court possesses a wide area of discretion in determining whether the testimony of the expert will be of aid to the trier of fact in understanding the evidence or determining a fact in issue. *Brendel v. Hustava,* 97 Ill. App. 3d 792, 53 Ill. Dec. 119, 423 N.E.2d 503 (1981).

In determining whether a scientific principle, technique, or test is sufficiently reliable to be admitted, *People v. Baynes,* 88 Ill. 2d 225, 241, 58 Ill. Dec. 819, 430 N.E.2d 1070 (1981), strongly implies, *People v. Eyler,* 133 Ill. 2d 173, 139 Ill. Dec. 756, 549 N.E.2d 268 (1989), and *People v. Zayas,* 131 Ill. 2d 284, 137 Ill. Dec. 568, 546 N.E.2d 513 (1989), specifically state, and *People v. Columbo,* 118 Ill. App. 3d 882, 74 Ill. Dec. 304, 455 N.E.2d 733 (1983), and *People v. Cohoon,* 120 Ill. App. 3d 62, 75 Ill. Dec. 556, 457 N.E.2d 998 (1983), simply assume that the test to be applied is that enunciated in *Frye v. United States,* 293 F. 1013, 1014 (D.C. Cir. 1923):

> Just when a scientific principle or discovery crosses the line between the experimental and demonstrable stages is difficult to define. Somewhere in this twilight zone the evidential force of the principle must be recognized, and while courts will go a long way in admitting expert testimony deduced from a well-recognized scientific principle or discovery, the thing from which the deduction is made must be sufficiently established to have gained general acceptance in the particular field in which it belongs.

Imposition of the *Frye* test serves to (1) ensure that a minimal reserve of experts exist who can critically examine the validity of a scientific determination in a particular case, (2) promote a degree of uniformity of decision, (3) avoid the interjection of a time consuming and often misleading determination of the reliability of a scientific technique into the litigation, (4) assure that scientific evidence introduced will be reliable, *People v. Knox,* 121 Ill. App. 3d 579, 76 Ill. Dec. 942, 459 N.E.2d 1077 (1984), and thus relevant, (5) provide a preliminary screening to protect against the natural inclination of the jury to assign significant weight to scientific techniques presented under circumstances where the trier of fact is in a poor position to place an accurate evaluation upon reliability, and (6) impose a threshold standard of reliability, in light of the fact that cross-examination by opposing counsel is unlikely to bring inaccuracies to the attention of the jury.

When offered into evidence for the first time, expert testimony as to the underlying scientific principle and as to the validity of the technique or test applying that principle will be received. *See People v. Todd,* 154 Ill. 2d 57, 180 Ill. Dec. 676, 607 N.E.2d 1189 (1992) (at a minimum expert should opine that test is generally accepted). On the basis of its evaluation of the conflicting expert testimony, the court must determine whether the scientific test is sufficiently reliable to be received into evidence. Application of the *Frye* standard calls for a judicial determination both that the court itself finds the scientific test reliable and that the test's reliability is generally accepted in the particular scientific field in which the test belongs. Newness alone is not a bar to admissibility, for every scientific technique that is eventually accepted must have its first day in court. Moreover, neither lack of absolute certainty nor lack of uniformity of expert opinion precludes a court from finding on the basis of expert witness testimony and other evidence admitted at trial that a scientific test is reliable and that the scientific test's reliability is, or clearly would be when brought to the attention of the appropriate experts, generally accepted in the particular scientific field in which the test belongs. *See People v. Hendricks,* 145 Ill. App. 3d 71, 99 Ill. Dec. 20, 495 N.E.2d 85 (1986). *See also* §401.12 supra. The determination as to whether the *Frye* test has been satisfied is committed to the discretion of the trial court, reviewed on appeal for abuse. *People v. Eyler,* 133 Ill. 2d 173, 139 Ill. Dec. 756, 549 N.E.2d 268 (1989); *People v. Heaton,* 266 Ill. App. 3d 469, 203 Ill. Dec. 710, 640 N.E.2d 630 (1990). *Compare People v. Watson,* 257 Ill. App. 3d 915, 196 Ill. Dec. 89, 629 N.E.2d 634 (1994) (applying *de novo* standard on appeal).

The distinction suggested in *People v. Milone,* 43 Ill. App. 3d 385, 2 Ill. Dec. 63, 356 N.E.2d 1350 (1976), bite-mark comparison, and *People v. Columbo,* 118 Ill. App. 3d 882, 74 Ill. Dec. 304, 455 N.E.2d 733 (1983), handprint measurements, that *Frye* does not apply to comparison testimony not involving intermediate mechanical stages is ill-advised, inconsistent with the application of *Frye* to fingerprints, ballistics, tool marks, etc., and unnecessary to permit introduction of novel evidence when *Frye* is interpreted to include the notion of the clear prospect of general scientific acceptability when brought to the attention of the appropriate scientific community. Rejection of the distinction in favor of application of *Frye* in *People v. Ferguson,* 172 Ill. App. 3d 1, 122 Ill. Dec. 266, 526 N.E.2d 525 (1988) is to be commended. Similarly, the rejection of *Frye* in connection with hypnotically refreshed testimony, §403.2 supra, in *People v. Cohoon*, 120 Ill. App. 3d 62, 75 Ill. Dec. 556, 457 N.E.2d 998 (1983), on the ground that it involves eyewitness testimony and not expert opinion is ill-conceived. Note that *Frye* was applied to hypnotically refreshed testimony in *People v. Zayas*, 131 Ill. 2d 284, 137 Ill. Dec. 568, 546 N.E.2d 513 (1989).

Once the particular scientific principle, technique, or test has been judicially determined after an evaluation of expert testimony to be reliable and to have received general acceptance by the appropriate scientific community as being reliable, the validity of the principle, technique, or test is either assumed in subsequent litigation or established through judicial notice, §202.4 supra. *See People v. Thomas*, 137 Ill. 2d 500, 148 Ill. Dec. 751, 561 N.E.2d 57 (1990); *People v. Johnson*, 262 Ill. App. 3d 565, 199 Ill. Dec. 931, 634 N.E.2d 1285 (1994). In addition, the admissibility of the results of scientific tests is sometimes provided for by statute.

With respect to the application of the *Frye* test to specific scientific principles, techniques, or tests, *see, e.g., Heideman v. Kelsey*, 19 Ill. 2d 258, 166 N.E.2d 596 (1960), rejecting medical testimony claiming to determine competency of testator by appearance of signature; *People v. Eyler*, 133 Ill. 2d 173, 139 Ill. Dec. 756, 549 N.E.2d 268 (1989), accepting superglue enhancement of fingerprint identification; *People v. Driver*, 62 Ill. App. 3d 847, 20 Ill. Dec. 7, 379 N.E.2d 840 (1978), splatter characteristics of human blood indicated not to be a subject capable of expert evaluation; *compare People v. Owens*, 155 Ill. App. 3d 990, 108 Ill. Dec. 511, 508 N.E.2d 1088 (1987), inadequate evidence of reliability of splatter analysis; *contra People v. Knox*, 121 Ill. App. 3d 579, 76 Ill. Dec. 942, 459 N.E.2d 1077 (1984), evidence of blood splatter characteristics admitted; *People v. Perroni*, 14 Ill. 2d 581, 153 N.E.2d 578 (1958), expert testimony concerning matching of tool marks is proper on same basis as expert testimony relating to fingerprint identification; *People v. Johnson*, 114 Ill. 2d 170, 102 Ill. Dec. 342, 499 N.E.2d 1355 (1986); *People v. Cole*, 170 Ill. App. 3d 912, 120 Ill. Dec. 744, 524 N.E.2d 926 (1988), both neutron activation analysis and atom absorption analysis are admissible to determine gunshot residue; *People v. Jordan,* 103 Ill. 2d 192, 82 Ill. Dec. 925, 469 N.E.2d 569 (1984), forensic odontologist may testify that pursuant to the "pink tooth" theory strangulation was a possible cause of death; *People v. Newell,* 77 Ill. App. 3d 577, 33 Ill. Dec. 66, 396 N.E.2d 291 (1979), expert may testify upon analysis of small amount of substance that entire contents was cannabis, the fact that only a portion was tested going to weight rather than admissibility; *People v. Prather,* 138 Ill. App. 3d 32, 92 Ill. Dec. 619, 485 N.E.2d 430 (1985), expert may testify as to effects of caffeine and phenylpropanolamine upon the body; *People v. Cruz,* 162 Ill. 2d 314, 205 Ill. Dec. 345, 643 N.E.2d 636 (1994), evidence as to the trailing of either a man or an animal by a bloodhound should never be admitted in evidence in any case (quoting *People v. Pfanschmidt,* 262 Ill. 411, 104 N.E.804 (1914)) (an attempt to distinguish *Cruz* because the tracking dog was a highly trained German shepherd was rejected in *People v. LeFler,* 294 Ill. App. 3d 305, 228 Ill. Dec. 788, 689 N.E.2d 1209 (1998)); *People v. Acri,* 277 Ill. App. 3d 1030, 214 Ill. Dec. 761, 662 N.E.2d 115 (1996), uncorroborated canine alerts in the field of arson investigation have not been generally accepted; *People v. Shaw,* 278 Ill. App. 3d 939, 215 Ill. Dec. 700, 664 N.E.2d 97 (1996), bite mark comparison evidence as well as tool mark comparison of marks made by braces is admissible; *Duran by Duran v. Cullinan,* 286 Ill. App. 3d 1005, 222 Ill. Dec. 465, 677 N.E.2d 999 (1997), epidemiological studies and the extrapolation technique of plaintiff's expert relating to birth defects following administration of birth control pills during pregnancy were generally accepted.

HGN test result satisfies *Frye* and may be admitted to determine whether a person is alcohol-impaired. *People v. Buening,* 229 Ill. App. 3d 538, 170 Ill. Dec. 542, 592 N.E.2d 1222 (1992); *People v. Hood,* 265 Ill. App. 3d 232, 202 Ill. Dec. 618, 638 N.E.2d 264 (1994); *People v. Wiebler,* 266 Ill. App. 3d 336, 203 Ill. Dec. 597, 640 N.E.2d 24 (1994); *People v. Rose,* 268 Ill. App. 3d 174, 205 Ill. Dec. 574, 643 N.E.2d 865 (1994); *compare People v. Kirk,* 289 Ill. App. 3d 326, 224 Ill. Dec. 452, 681 N.E.2d 1073 (1997) (in spite of foregoing authority HGN test result held improperly admitted because a *Frye* hearing was not held below to determine admissibility).

A neat illustration is afforded by comparing *People v. Berkman,* 307 Ill. 492, 139 N.E.91 (1923), classifying ballistics identification as remarkable, absurd, preposterous, and inadmissible, *with People v. Fisher,* 340 Ill. 216, 172 N.E. 743 (1930), holding the same evidence admissible following a carefully laid testimonial foundation of the techniques followed. *See also* discussion of lie detector and truth serum, §403.2 supra.

With respect to DNA, both the Restriction Fragment Length Polymorphism (RFCP) method, *People v. Hickey,* 178 Ill. 2d 256, 227 Ill. Dec. 428, 687 N.E.2d 910 (1997); *People v. Miller,* 173 Ill. 2d 167, 219 Ill. Dec. 43, 670 N.E.2d 721 (1996), and the Polymerase Chain Reaction (PCR) method, *People v. Pope,* 284 Ill. App. 3d 695, 220 Ill. Dec. 309, 672 N.E.2d 1321 (1996), satisfy the *Frye* general acceptance test. Moreover, the FBI method of calculating the statistical probability of a random match as derived from the product rule meets the *Frye* standard as well. *People v. Hickey* supra; *People v. Miller* supra; *People v. Pope* supra. *Accord People v. Almighty Four Hundred,* 287 Ill. App. 2d 123, 222 Ill. Dec. 533, 677 N.E.2d 1332 (1997); *People v. Dalcollo,* 282 Ill. App. 3d 944, 218 Ill. Dec. 435, 669 N.E.2d 378 (1996) (in light of findings of FBI exhaustive worldwide population survey as suggested by NRC Report and recognition by scientists that the "ceiling principle" does not create a corresponding reduction in random probability match calculations, FBI's calculation of statistical probabilities as derived from the product rule is generally accepted in the scientific community). Questions as to whether generally accepted procedures were in fact followed in the case at hand go to weight to be given by the trier of fact to the evidence. *People v. Pope* supra. With respect to reliance by the expert on DNA tests performed by other experts, *see* §703.1 infra.

With respect to the admissibility of evidence in the form of expert witness testimony of the behavior reactions of victims, *see e.g., People v. Douglas,* 183 Ill. App. 3d 241, 131 Ill. Dec. 779, 538 N.E.2d 1335 (1989) (rape-trauma syndrome admissible); *People v. Minnis,* 118 Ill. App. 3d 345, 74 Ill. Dec. 179,

455 N.E.2d 209 (1983) (battered-woman syndrome admissible); *People v. Ridgeway*, 194 Ill. App. 3d 881, 141 Ill. Dec. 603, 551 N.E.2d 790 (1990) (child sexual abuse syndrome admissible); *People v. Roy*, 201 Ill. App. 3d 166, 146 Ill. Dec. 874, 558 N.E.2d 1208 (1990) (post-traumatic syndrome admissible). *See also* §704.2 infra.

In addition, the results of the application of a particular scientific principle, technique, or test are admissible only if the person conducting the procedure is shown to be a properly qualified expert in the particular field, *see* §702.2 supra, and a sufficient foundation is introduced that the procedure was properly conducted with respect to the matter at hand. *People v. Hood*, 265 Ill. App. 3d 232, 202 Ill. Dec. 618, 638 N.E.2d 264 (1994). Questions raised with respect to the actual procedures employed in the conducting of the particular scientific process, technique, or test are ordinarily properly considered by the trier of fact as going to the weight of the evidence. *People v. Pope* supra. However, if the procedures employed are shown to give an unreliable result, the trial court may exclude the evidence entirely. *People v. Mehlberg*, 249 Ill. App. 3d 499, 188 Ill. Dec. 598, 618 N.E.2d 1168 (1993); *People v. Lipscomb*, 215 Ill. App. 3d 413, 158 Ill. Dec. 952, 574 N.E.2d 1345 (1991).

In *Daubert v. Merrell Dow Pharmaceuticals, Inc.*, 509 U.S. 579 (1993), the United States Supreme Court, pursuant to its supervisory power over the federal courts, declared that the *Frye* "general acceptance" test did not survive adoption of the Federal Rules of Evidence. At the same time the Supreme Court imposed a requirement that with respect to "scientific" evidence the trial judge under Federal Rules of Evidence 702 and 104(a) must act as a gatekeeper screening "scientific" evidence to ensure reliability-validity. While not providing a definitive checklist, the United States Supreme Court declared the following appropriately considered in determining whether "scientific" evidence possesses the requisite reliability-validity: (1) Is the theory or technique testable and has it been tested?; (2) Has the theory or technique been subject to peer review publication?; (3)

What is the known or potential error rate of the scientific technique and are there standards controlling the technique's operation; and (4) Has the technique received widespread acceptance? *Daubert* didn't address the role of the trial judge with respect to expert witness testimony under Federal Rule of Evidence 702 presenting "technical, or other specialized knowledge" rather than "scientific" evidence. *Daubert* leaves many other questions unanswered as well. *See* Chief Justice Rehnquist concurring and dissenting, 509 U.S. at 598. *See also* Graham, Handbook of Federal Evidence §702.5 (4th ed. 1996). It is suggested that many theoretical and practical arguments support Illinois retaining adherence to *Frye. See People v. Watson,* 257 Ill. App. 3d 915, 196 Ill. Dec. 89, 629 N.E.2d 634 (1994) (*Frye* test applicable until ceased to be recognized by Illinois Supreme Court). In fact, it is very likely that the federal courts will be returning to what amounts to a *Frye* test within the next few years. *See* Graham, The *Daubert* Dilemma: At Last a Viable Solution?, 179 F.R.D. 1 (1998).

Under certain circumstances the testimony of an expert witness is not only permitted but is required. *See Suich v. H & B Printing Machinery, Inc.,* 185 Ill. App. 3d 863, 133 Ill. Dec. 768, 541 N.E.2d 1206 (1989) (expert witness testimony is only required where the matter is *clearly* outside the common knowledge and experience of the average jury). For example, except in those situations where the physician's conduct is so grossly negligent or the treatment so common that a layman could readily appraise it, *Purtill v. Hess,* 111 Ill. 2d 229, 95 Ill. Dec. 305, 489 N.E.2d 867 (1986); *Walker v. Rumer,* 72 Ill. 2d 495, 21 Ill. Dec. 362, 381 N.E.2d 689 (1978); *Duffin v. Seibring,* 154 Ill. App. 3d 821, 107 Ill. Dec. 777, 507 N.E.2d 930 (1977) (expert testimony is required only in instances where a layman cannot readily discern the appropriate standard of care; citing Handbook); *Estate of Sewart v. Taff,* 236 Ill. App. 2d 177, 177 Ill. Dec. 105, 602 N.E.2d 1277 (1991) (expert witness has not been required in *some* cases involving anesthesia, tonsillectomy, x-rays, and injections), or where evidence of standard of care was otherwise introduced,

Walski v. Tiesenga, 72 Ill. 2d 249, 21 Ill. Dec. 201, 381 N.E.2d 279 (1978), the plaintiff in a medical malpractice action must establish through the use of expert testimony that the defendant physician was negligent in his treatment and that the injuries suffered by the plaintiff were the result of such negligence. *Borowski v. Von Solbrig,* 60 Ill. 2d 418, 328 N.E.2d 301 (1975); *Stogsdill v. Manor Convalescent Home, Inc.,* 35 Ill. App. 3d 634, 343 N.E.2d 589 (1976); *Ciolino v. Bernstein,* 231 Ill. App. 3d 68, 172 Ill. Dec. 804, 596 N.E.2d 83 (1992). *Accord Purtill v. Hess,* 111 Ill. 2d 229, 95 Ill. Dec. 305, 489 N.E.2d 867 (1986) (negligent diagnosis and treatment of rectovaginal fistular); *Walski v. Tiesenga,* 72 Ill. 2d 249, 21 Ill. Dec. 201, 381 N.E.2d 279 (1978) (failure to identify left recurrent laryngeal nerve during surgery); *Estate of Sewart v. Taff,* 236 Ill. App. 3d 1, 177 Ill. Dec. 105, 602 N.E.2d 1277 (1991) (diagnosis of brain death); *Thompson v. Webb,* 138 Ill. App. 3d 629, 93 Ill. Dec. 225, 486 N.E.2d 326 (1985) (diagnosis of cancer). In addition, a lay witness may not opine regarding the condition of her injury to her health or the need for medical treatment. *Branum v. Slezak Construction Co., Inc.,* 289 Ill. App. 3d 948, 225 Ill. Dec. 88, 682 N.E.2d 1165 (1997). Similarly, expert testimony is required where a drug manufacturer's liability for a prescription drug is based upon a failure to provide an adequate warning. *Northern Trust Co. v. Upjohn Co.,* 213 Ill. App. 3d 390, 157 Ill. Dec. 566, 572 N.E.2d 1030 (1991). *See also Baltus v. Weaver Division of Kidde & Co.,* 199 Ill. App. 3d 821, 145 Ill. Dec. 810, 557 N.E.2d 580 (1990), detailing when expert witness testimony is required to establish that a product is unreasonably dangerous. On the other hand, expert testimony, while admissible and helpful, is not necessary to show asbestos exposure as a result of the likelihood of visible indoor dust traveling significant distances from its source. *Thacker v. UNR Industries, Inc.,* 151 Ill. 2d 343, 177 Ill. Dec. 379, 603 N.E.2d 449 (1992).

In order to testify as an expert witness as to the standard of care in a given school of medicine, it was once required that the witness be licensed therein. *Dolan v. Galluzzo,* 77 Ill. 2d 279, 32 Ill. Dec. 900, 396 N.E.2d 13 (1979), in malpractice action against podiatrist, only a podiatrist is qualified to testify as to the standard of care. The purpose of the rule was to prevent professionals licensed in one "school of medicine" from having their actions judged by someone licensed in another "school of medicine." *Bartimus v. Paxton Community Hosp.*, 120 Ill. App. 3d 1060, 76 Ill. Dec. 418, 458 N.E.2d 1072 (1983). Similar concerns were incorporated into 735 ILCS 5/8-2501 which since 1985 has required that in any case in which the standard of care given by a medical professional is at issue, the court apply the following factors to determine if a witness qualifies as an expert witness and can testify on the issue of the appropriate standard of care:

(a)   Relationship of the medical specialties of the witness to the medical problem or problems and the type of treatment administered in the case;

(b)   Whether the witness has devoted a substantial portion of his or her time to the practice of medicine, teaching, or university-based research in relation to the medical care and type of treatment at issue which gave rise to the medical problem of which the plaintiff complains;

(c)   Whether the witness is licensed in the same profession as the defendant; and

(d)   Whether, in the case against a nonspecialist, the witness can demonstrate a sufficient familiarity with the standard of care practiced in this State.

Thus, it is proper to permit a person possessing an M.D. and expert in teaching medical students in the same "school of medicine" to testify in spite of the absence of a license to practice medicine in any State. *Witherell v. Weimer*, 148 Ill. App. 3d 32, 101 Ill. Dec. 679, 499 N.E.2d 46 (1986). Statutes requiring persons to be licensed to practice a given specialty do not prevent persons not so licensed but other wise qualified from testifying in Illinois courts. *Poelker v. Warrensburg Latham School District*, 251 Ill. App. 3d 270, 190 Ill. Dec. 487, 621 N.E.2d 940 (1993). A physician in Illinois is licensed to practice medicine in all of its branches. *Gill v. Foster,* 157 Ill. 2d 304, 193 Ill. Dec. 157, 626 N.E.2d 190 (1993).

Ultimately it must be shown that the expert is both properly qualified and familiar with the method, procedures, and treatments ordinarily observed by other physicians in either the defendant's community or a similar community. *Purtill v. Hess,* 111 Ill. 2d 229, 95 Ill. Dec. 305, 489 N.E.2d 867 (1986); *Wodziak v. Kash,* 278 Ill. App. 3d 901, 215 Ill. Dec. 388, 663 N.E.2d 138 (1996); *Senderak v. Mitchell,* 282 Ill. App. 3d 881, 218 Ill. Dec. 209, 668 N.E.2d 1041 (1996). If the particular method, procedure, or treatment is subject to a minimum uniform standard, an expert is qualified if he or she is familiar with that standard. *Purtill v. Hess id., Netto v. Goldenberg,* 266 Ill. App. 3d 174, 203 Ill. Dec. 798, 640 N.E.2d 948 (1994). By hearing evidence on the expert's qualifications and comparing the medical problem and the type of treatment in the case to the experience and background of the expert, the court can evaluate whether the witness has demonstrated a sufficient familiarity with the standard of care practiced in the case. The foundational requirements provide the court with the information necessary to determine whether an expert has expertise in dealing with the plaintiff's medical problem and treatment. *See Hubbard v. Sherman,* 292 Ill. App. 3d 148, 226 Ill. Dec. 393, 685 N.E.2d 648 (1997), expert failed to demonstrate that experience in practice imparted the requisite knowledge of standard of care applicable to emergency room physicians. *Accord Northern Trust Co. v. Upjohn Co.,* 213 Ill. App. 3d 390, 157 Ill. Dec. 566, 572 N.E.2d 1030 (1991). Whether the expert is qualified to testify is not dependent on whether he is a member of the same specialty or subspecialty as the defendant, *Gill v. Foster* supra, but, rather, whether the allegations of negligence concern matters within his knowledge and observation. *Jones v. O'Young,* 154 Ill. 2d 39, 180 Ill. Dec. 330, 607 N.E.2d 224 (1992) (infectious disease specialist could testify as to standard of care of plastic surgeon, orthopedic surgeon, and general surgeon in treating plaintiff's infectious disease). With respect to testimony on causation in medical matters, *see also* §704.2 intra.

Applying the foregoing standard, it has been determined that a pediatrician was properly barred from testifying as to the standard of care for either obstetrics or gynecology, *Thomas v. University of Chicago Lying-In Hosp.*, 221 Ill. App. 3d 919, 164 Ill. Dec. 519, 583 N.E.2d 73 (1991); an emergency specialist from testifying as to the standard of care for either obstetrics or gynecology, *Northern Trust Co. v. Upjohn Co.*, 213 Ill. App. 3d 390, 157 Ill. Dec. 566, 572 N.E.2d 1030 (1991); and an occupational therapist from testifying as to the standard of care of a physical therapist, *Novey v. Kishwaukee Community Health Services Center,* 176 Ill. App. 3d 674, 126 Ill. Dec. 132, 531 N.E.2d 427 (1988). On the other hand, a surgeon may testify as to the standard of care of a radiologist, *Gill v. Foster* supra; an internist, being more specialized, was properly permitted to testify as to the standard of care of a general family practitioner, *Benison v. Silverman,* 233 Ill. App. 3d 689, 175 Ill. Dec. 87, 599 N.E.2d 1101 (1992); an orthopedic surgeon could properly testify as to the standard of care for surgical technicians, *Kniceley v. Migala,* 237 Ill. App. 3d 72, 177 Ill. Dec. 773, 603 N.E.2d 843 (1992); a general dentist could properly testify as to whether periodontist negligently read X-rays, *Rosenberg v. Miller,* 247 Ill. App. 3d 1023, 187 Ill. Dec. 285, 617 N.E.2d 493 (1993); an ophthalmologist as to whether an optometrist should have referred a patient for further treatment, *Moss v. Miller,* 254 Ill. App. 3d 174, 192 Ill. Dec. 889, 625 N.E.2d 1044 (1993); and a doctor could properly testify as to the standard of care for nurses, *Wingo by Wingo v. Rockford Memorial Hospital,* 292 Ill. App. 3d 896, 226 Ill. Dec. 939, 686 N.E.2d 722 (1997). *See generally Smock v. Hale,* 197 Ill. App. 3d 732, 144 Ill. Dec. 177, 555 N.E.2d 74 (1990); *Gorman v. Shu-Fang Chen, M.D., Ltd.,* 231 Ill. App. 3d 982, 173 Ill. Dec. 471, 596 N.E.2d 1350 (1992); *Hoem v. Zia,* 239 Ill. App. 3d 601, 179 Ill. Dec. 986, 606 N.E.2d 818 (1992).

The use of the Physician's Desk Reference (PDR) to establish the standard of care was approved in *Ohligschlager v. Proctor Community Hosp.,* 55 Ill. 2d 411, 303 N.E.2d 392 (1973). *See also Witherell v. Weimer,* 148 Ill. App. 3d 32, 101 Ill. Dec. 679, 499 N.E.2d 46 (1986). *Cf. Mielke v. Condell Memorial*

Hosp., 124 Ill. App. 3d 42, 79 Ill. Dec. 78, 463 N.E.2d 216 (1984) (standard of care not adequately established by PDR and package insert).

The situation with respect to other malpractice claims is similar; expert witness testimony is required to establish the standard of care, except in the situation in which the malpractice is so grossly apparent that a layman would have no difficulty recognizing it. *Barth v. Reagan,* 139 Ill. 2d 399, 151 Ill. Dec. 534, 564 N.E.2d 1196 (1990); *Gray v. Hallett,* 170 Ill. App. 3d 660, 121 Ill. Dec. 283, 525 N.E.2d 89 (1988) (lawyer malpractice).

While it has been held that a physician may not testify at trial regarding his or her opinion of a patient's prognosis or the permanency of the injury without having conducted a recent examination, *Henricks v. Nyberg, Inc.,* 41 Ill. App. 3d 25, 353 N.E.2d 273 (1976), recent decisions have held that the time interval between a physician's last examination of plaintiff and the trial goes to weight and not admissibility. *Marchese v. Vincelette,* 261 Ill. App. 3d 520, 199 Ill. Dec. 81, 633 N.E.2d 877 (1994); *Housh v. Bowers,* 271 Ill. App. 3d 1004, 208 Ill. Dec. 449, 649 N.E.2d 505 (1995). *See also Knight v. Lord,* 271 Ill. App. 3d 581, 207 Ill. Dec. 917, 648 N.E.2d 617 (1995).

In any action, whether in tort, contract, or otherwise, in which the plaintiff seeks damages for injuries or death by reason of medical, hospital, or other healing art malpractice, under 735 ILCS 5/2-622, the plaintiff's attorney or the plaintiff, if the plaintiff is proceeding pro se, must file an affidavit, attached to the original and all copies of the complaint, declaring one of the following:

> 1. That the affiant has consulted and reviewed the facts of the case with a health professional who the affiant reasonably believes: (i) is knowledgeable in the relevant issues involved in the particular action; (ii) practices or has practiced within the last 6 years or teaches or has taught within the last 6 years in the same area of health care or medicine that is at issue in the particular action; and (iii) is qualified by experience or demonstrated com-

petence in the subject of the case; that the reviewing health professional has determined in a written report, after a review of the medical record and other relevant material involved in the particular action that there is a reasonable and meritorious cause for the filing of such action; and that the affiant has concluded on the basis of the reviewing health professional's review and consultation that there is a reasonable and meritorious cause for filing of such action. If the affidavit is filed as to a defendant who is a physician licensed to treat human ailments without the use of drugs or medicines and without operative surgery, a dentist, a podiatrist, or a psychologist, or a naprapath, the written report must be from a health professional licensed in the same profession, with the same class of license, as the defendant. For affidavits filed as to all other defendants, the written report must be from a physician licensed to practice medicine in all its branches. In either event, the affidavit must identify the profession of the reviewing health professional. A copy of the written report, clearly identifying the plaintiff and the reasons for the reviewing health professional's determination that a reasonable and meritorious cause for the filing of the action exists, must be attached to the affidavit. The report shall include the name and the address of the health professional. . . .

Expert testimony in terms of possibilities or probabilities related specifically to the matter at hand is proper. *Beloit Foundry v. Industrial Commn.*, 62 Ill. 2d 535, 343 N.E.2d 504 (1976); *People v. Johnson*, 114 Ill. 2d 170, 102 Ill. Dec. 342, 499 N.E.2d 1355 (1986); *Boatmen's National Bank v. Martin*, 223 Ill. App. 3d 740, 166 Ill. Dec. 306, 585 N.E.2d 1328 (1992). Thus, medical testimony that conditions of employment might have resulted in injury is admissible, *County of Cook v. Industrial Commn.*, 69 Ill. 2d 10, 12 Ill. Dec. 716, 370 N.E.2d 520 (1977), as is medical testimony that plaintiff's fistulae may have been caused by the tearing of minute and obstructed adhesions which defendant could not have seen while performing surgery, *Carter v. Johnson*, 247 Ill. App. 3d 291, 187 Ill. Dec. 52, 617 N.E.2d 260 (1993), as is medical testimony that there was a 70 percent to 80 percent chance that plaintiff already had Stage IV lymphoma, *Creighton v.*

Thompson, 266 Ill. App. 3d 61, 203 Ill. Dec. 195, 639 N.E.2d 234 (1994), as is expert witness testimony that a part's non-compliance with design specification was a possible cause of the accident, *McKenzie v. S.K. Hand Tool Corp.*, 272 Ill. App. 3d 1, 208 Ill. Dec. 918, 650 N.E.2d 612 (1995), as is medical testimony as to various possible causes of an injury. *Conners v. Poticha*, 293 Ill. App. 3d 944, 228 Ill. Dec. 441, 689 N.E.2d 313 (1997). Microscopic analysis establishing a possibility that two hairs came from same source is admissible. *People v. Columbo*, 118 Ill. App. 3d 882, 74 Ill. Dec. 304, 455 N.E.2d 733 (1983). The product rule and statistical probabilities may be employed in connection with probabalistic identification expert testimony based upon the electrophoresis of blood samples. *People v. Stanley*, 246 Ill. App. 3d 393, 186 Ill. Dec. 295, 615 N.E.2d 1352 (1993). However, an expert may not testify as to the unreliability of eyewitness testimony based on statistical averages; it would be inappropriate for the jury to conclude on such a basis that all eyewitness testimony is unreliable. *People v. Enis*, 139 Ill. 2d 89, 151 Ill. Dec. 493, 564 N.E.2d 1155 (1990). With respect to the sufficiency of evidence concerning blood, hair, and paint comparisons to support a conviction, *see People v. Gomez*, 215 Ill. App. 3d 208, 158 Ill. Dec. 709, 574 N.E.2d 822 (1991). As to the importance of maintaining the distinction between admissibility and sufficiency of evidence, *see generally McKenzie v. S.K. Hand Tool Corp.* supra.

In addition to expert testimony on the applicable standard of care, state licensing regulations, the hospital's bylaws, and accreditation standards and regulations are admissible, but they do not conclusively determine the standard of care. *Darling v. Charleston Community Memorial Hosp.*, 33 Ill. 2d 326, 211 N.E.2d 253 (1965); *Andrews v. Northwestern Memorial Hosp.*, 184 Ill. App. 3d 486, 132 Ill. Dec. 707, 540 N.E.2d 447 (1989).

The admissibility of expert testimony is subject to considerations of unfair prejudice, confusion of the issue, and misleading of the jury as set forth in §403.1 supra.

§702.5 *Stopping Distance and Speed*

A properly qualified reconstruction expert or accidentologist may testify as to the feet per second travelled by a car moving at a certain hourly speed and to the distance required to stop a vehicle of the kind in question under existing conditions. *Young v. Patrick*, 323 Ill. 200, 153 N.E. 623 (1926); *Jamison v. Lambke*, 21 Ill. App. 3d 629, 316 N.E.2d 93 (1974). The propriety of evidence of this kind obviously requires that the expert's basis include careful and precise consideration of the various elements to be considered, *Deaver v. Hickox*, 81 Ill. App. 2d 79, 224 N.E.2d 468 (1967), including evidence of skid marks. *Young v. Patrick* supra.

In *Watkins v. Schmitt*, 172 Ill. 2d 216 Ill. Dec. 822, 665 N.E.2d 1379 (1996), the Illinois Supreme Court held that a reconstruction expert was properly barred from opining as to the speed of cement truck that left 124 feet of skid marks because such testimony would not be of assistance to the trier of fact, i.e., not beyond the ken of the average juror. The correct procedure, in accordance with *Watkins,* properly criticized by the separate opinion concurring and dissenting, is for the witness to testify on personal knowledge as to the existence of the 124 feet of skid marks, leaving it to the trier of fact to infer speed unaided by expert testimony. While three eyewitnesses testified in *Watkins* as to the speed of the cement truck, the decision to bar the expert witness opinion testimony as to speed was not made on that basis. *See* §703.2 infra. What unstated reasons prompted the Illinois Supreme Court to reach its decision remains a mystery. Concern with opening a flood gate to accident reconstruction testimony as to speed is a strong possibility. *See also Rinesmith v. Sterling,* 293 Ill. App. 3d 344, 227 Ill. Dec. 709, 687 N.E.2d 1191 (1997), trial court within its discretion in deeming expert testimony as to speed inadmissible.

With respect to the admissibility of reconstruction testimony generally, *see* §703.2 infra; as to testimony relating to speed of an observed vehicle, *see* §701.4 supra.

§702.6   Meaning of Language

In the absence of a technical or trade meaning, *City of Alton v. Unknown Heirs,* 95 Ill. App. 3d 107, 54 Ill. Dec. 252, 424 N.E.2d 1155 (1981) (professor of landscape architecture may render an opinion on the meanings of the terms *common* and *promenade* in an 1818 plat); *American College of Surgeons v. Lumbermens Mut. Cas. Co.,* 142 Ill. App. 3d 680, 96 Ill. Dec. 719, 491 N.E.2d 1179 (1986) (terms of group insurance agreement), expert opinion has been held not admissible as to the meaning of language in private documents. *Wolf v. Schwill,* 282 Ill. 189, 118 N.E. 414 (1918); *Clarke v. Shirk,* 170 Ill. 143, 48 N.E. 182 (1897).

The meaning of language in a statute is a question of law for the court, and expert testimony is properly excluded. *National Fire Ins. Co. v. Hanberg,* 215 Ill. 378, 74 N.E. 377 (1905).

In libel actions, testimony as to the witness's understanding of the meaning of the words has been held inadmissible if the purpose is merely to prove the meaning generally ascribed to the words, *Tiernan v. East Shore Newspapers, Inc.,* 1 Ill. App. 2d 150, 116 N.E.2d 896 (1953), but admissible if the witness is a customer whose lost patronage is an element of damages. *Lion Oil Co. v. Sinclair Refining Co.,* 252 Ill. App. 92 (1929).

An expert witness may testify as to what another witness meant by making a remark. *See United States v. Daly,* 842 F.2d 1380 (2d Cir. 1988) (meaning of the term "capo" in relation to structure of organized crime). With respect to lay witness testimony, *see* §701.7 supra.

§702.7   Damages and Benefits; Present Discounted Value, Per Diem Argument

As a result of application of the old rule against opinions on the ultimate issue, evidence of damages has sometimes been restricted to data from which the amount may be computed. *Springfield & N.E. Traction Co. v. Warrick*, 249 Ill. 470, 94 N.E. 933 (1911). Absurd extremes are found in cases of benefits and damages from public improvements holding that the witness cannot directly state the amount of benefits or damages, although he may give market value before and after. *Okaw Drainage Dist. v. Two Mile Slough Drainage Dist.*, 398 Ill. 174, 75 N.E.2d 333 (1947); *Village of Marissa v. Jones*, 327 Ill. 180, 158 N.E. 389 (1927). *Cf. Illinois Cent. R. Co. v. Chicago*, 169 Ill. 329, 48 N.E. 492 (1897). With abrogation of the rule barring opinions on the ultimate issue, §704.1 infra, such a restriction may no longer be imposed.

When an actuary or economist testifies to the present discounted value of future lost earnings, it had been said that actual figures as reflected in the proof projected into the future should not be used and that the expert witness instead should describe to the jury the mechanical process, using neutral figures. *Binge v. J.J. Borders Constr. Co.*, 95 Ill. App. 3d 238, 50 Ill. Dec. 788, 419 N.E.2d 1237 (1981). Application of the neutral figures to the facts at hand was then a matter of argument. *Allendorf v. Elgin, J. & E. R.R.*, 8 Ill. 2d 164, 133 N.E.2d 288 (1956). The theory is that use of figures in evidence creates a danger of the jury accepting such figures as proof of contribution and life and work expectancy when they are only being used by the expert for purposes of computation. In short, there was a perceived danger of misleading the jury, §403.1 supra. Moreover, use of actual figures ran afoul of the then existing rule against opinions on the ultimate issue, §704.1 infra. However, probably in recognition that the use of an actual figure is more informative to the jury, when actuaries and economists provide such testimony, failure to employ nominal figures was later found to be harmless error. *Allendorf v. Elgin, J. & E.R.R.* supra; *LeMaster v. Chicago Rock Island & Pacific R.R.*, 35 Ill. App. 3d 1001, 343 N.E.2d 65 (1976). In *Baird v. Chicago, Burlington & Q.R. Co.*, 63 Ill. 2d 463, 349 N.E.2d 413 (1976), the supreme court may have in fact abandoned the requirement altogether in its approval of economic testimony projecting plaintiff's wage loss in actual dollar figures over his lifetime, including testimony establishing that a projected trend of wage increase would overshadow any interest return on investments. In any event, in *Richardson v. Chapman*, 175 Ill. 2d 98, 221 Ill. Dec. 818, 676 N.E. 2d 621 (1997), the Illinois Supreme Court referring to the abandonment of the rule against testimony on the ultimate issue as removing the underpinning of *Allendorf, see* §704.1 infra, and citing this Handbook declared that *Allendorf* should no longer be followed.

Life expectancy tables are admissible as an aid in assessing damages, but are not conclusive. *Balzekas v. Looking Elk*, 254 Ill. App. 3d 529, 193 Ill. Dec. 925, 627 N.E.2d 84 (1993).

With respect to damages for pain and suffering, it is improper for counsel to suggest that the jury calculate damages by placing a dollar value upon each minute, hour, or day as to which pain and suffering was or will be experienced. *Caley v. Manicke*, 24 Ill. 2d 390, 182 N.E.2d 206 (1962), such argument presents an illusion of certainty. However, placing a monetary value on pain and suffering per year of life expectancy, where accompanied with advice that such calculation is only a suggestion, appears to be permitted as avoiding the illusion of certainty. *Watson v. City of Chicago*, 124 Ill. App. 3d 348, 80 Ill. Dec. 117, 464 N.E.2d 1100 (1984); *Johnson v. Chicago Transit Auth.*, 11 Ill. App. 3d 16, 295 N.E.2d 573 (1973); *Fortner v. McDermott*, 1 Ill. App. 3d 358, 272 N.E.2d 503 (1971). The matter is one concerning the propriety of argument rather than the admissibility of evidence.

With respect to admissibility of summaries *see* §1006 infra.

§703   Bases of Opinion Testimony by Experts

§703.1   Reasonably Relied Upon Facts, Data, or Opinions

An expert may base his opinion upon (1) the scientific, technical, or other specialized knowledge that makes the witness an expert, §702.1 supra, including facts, data, or opinions contained in a learned treatise recognized as reliable authority, *Lawson v. G.D. Searle & Co.*, 64 Ill. 2d 543, 1 Ill. Dec. 497, 356 N.E.2d 779 (1976); *People v. Bradney*, 170 Ill. App. 3d 839, 121 Ill. Dec. 306, 525 N.E.2d 112 (1988); *People v. Lopez*, 228 Ill. App. 3d 1061, 170 Ill. Dec. 758, 593 N.E.2d 647 (1992); *People v. Contreras*, 246 Ill. App. 3d 502, 186 Ill. Dec. 204, 615 N.E.2d 1261 (1993), *see also* §705.1 infra, (2) firsthand observation of facts or data perceived by him before trial, *Skanlon v. Manning, Maxwell, & Moore, Inc.*, 127 Ill. App. 2d 145, 262 N.E.2d 146 (1970), (3) facts, data, or opinions introduced in evidence at trial, and (4) facts, data, or opinions not admitted into evidence when such facts, data, or opinions are of a type reasonably relied upon by experts in the field in forming opinions or inferences upon the subject. *See* §705.1 infra with respect to disclosure of the basis of an expert's opinion, the form of the expert's testimony, including hypothetical questions, and reliance on testimony heard at trial.

The Illinois Supreme Court in *Wilson v. Clark*, 84 Ill. 2d 186, 49 Ill. Dec. 308, 417 N.E.2d 1322 (1981), specifically adopted without reservation Rule 703 of the Federal Rules of Evidence:

Bases of Opinion Testimony by Experts

The facts or data in the particular case upon which an expert bases an opinion or inference may be those perceived by or made known to the expert at or before the hearing. If of a type reasonably relied upon by experts in the particular field in forming opinions or inferences upon the subject, the facts or data need not be admissible in evidence.

The Federal Advisory Committee's Note to Federal Rule 703, 56 F.R.D. 183, 283-284 (1973), states as follows:

Facts or data upon which expert opinions are based may, under the rule, be derived from three possible sources. The first is the firsthand observation of the witness, with opinions based thereon traditionally allowed. A treating physician affords an example, Rheingold, The Basis of Medical Testimony, 15 Vand. L. Rev. 473, 489 (1962). Whether he must first relate his observations is treated in Rule 705. The second source, presentation at the trial, also reflects existing practice. The technique may be the familiar hypothetical question or having the expert attend the trial and hear the testimony establishing the facts. Problems of determining what testimony the expert relied upon, when the latter technique is employed and the testimony is in conflict, may be resolved by resort to Rule 705. The third source contemplated by the rule consists of presentation of data to the expert outside of court and other than by his own perception. In this respect the rule is designed to broaden the basis for expert opinions beyond that current in many jurisdictions and to bring the judicial practice into line with the practice of the experts themselves when not in court. Thus a physician in his own practice bases his diagnosis on information from numerous sources and of considerable variety, including statements by patients and relatives, reports and opinions from nurses, technicians and other doctors, hospital records, and X rays. Most of them are admissible in evidence, but only with the expenditure of substantial time in producing and examining various authenticating witnesses. The physician makes life-and-death decisions in reliance upon them. His validation, expertly performed and subject to cross-examination, ought to suffice for judicial purposes. Rheingold, supra, at 531; McCormick §15. A similar provision is California Evidence Code §801(b).

The rule also offers a more satisfactory basis for ruling upon the admissibility of public opinion poll evidence. Attention is directed to the validity of the techniques employed rather than to relatively fruitless inquiries whether hearsay is involved. *See* Judge Feinberg's careful analysis in *Zippo Mfg. Co. v. Rogers Imports, Inc.,* 216 F. Supp. 670 (S.D.N.Y. 1963). *See also* Blum et al., The Art of Opinion Research: A Lawyer's Appraisal of an Emerging Service, 24 U. Chi. L. Rev. 1 (1956); Bonynge, Trademark Surveys and Techniques and Their Use in Litigation, 48 A.B.A.J. 329 (1962); Zeisel, The Uniqueness of Survey Evidence, 45 Cornell L.Q. 322 (1960); Annot., 76 A.L.R.2d 919.

If it be feared that enlargement of permissible data may tend to break down the rules of exclusion unduly, notice should be taken that the rule requires that the facts or data "be of a type reasonably relied upon by experts in the particular field." The language would not warrant admitting in evidence the opinion of an "accidentologist" as to the point of impact in an automobile collision based on statements of bystanders, since this requirement is not satisfied. See Comment, Cal. Law Rev. Comm'n, Recommendation Proposing an Evidence Code 148-150 (1965).

Under Federal Rule 703 an expert may base her opinion on firsthand observation of facts or data perceived by her before trial, on presentation at the trial, as by the familiar hypothetical question or by having the expert attend the trial and hear the testimony establishing the facts relied on, or presentation of facts, data, or opinions to the expert outside the court other than by her own direct perception. The facts, data, or opinions need not be admitted or even admissible in evidence if of a type reasonably relied upon by experts in the field. An opportunity to cross-examine the presenter of facts, data, or opinions reasonably relied upon by the expert need not be provided. To the extent *Dugan v. Weber*, 175 Ill. App. 3d 1088, 125 Ill. Dec. 598, 530 N.E.2d 1007 (1988), implies the contrary it is incorrect and should not be followed. However, the opportunity to discover such facts, data, or opinions in advance of trial is apparently required. *Lebrecht v. Tuli*, 130 Ill. App. 3d 457, 85 Ill. Dec. 517, 473 N.E.2d 1322 (1984), facts, data, or opinions relied upon by expert witness in changing his opinion at trial from that given at his deposition did not fall within *Wilson v. Clark* supra. Federal Rule 703 thus brings judicial practice into line with the practice of experts themselves when not in court. For example, a physician in his own practice bases his diagnosis on information from a variety of sources, such as hospital records, X-ray reports, statements by patients, and reports and opinions from nurses and technicians. *Hatfield v. Sandoz-Wander, Inc.*, 124 Ill. App. 3d 780, 80 Ill. Dec. 122, 464 N.E.2d 1105 (1984) (deposition testimony of doctors and pharmacists). Most of these could be presented in the form of admissible evidence, but only through a time-consuming process of authentication. As the Federal Advisory Committee's Note states: "The physician makes life-and-death decisions in reliance upon them. His validation, expertly performed and subject to cross-examination, ought to suffice for judicial purposes." Under Federal Rule 703, the question whether facts, data, or opinions are of a type reasonably relied upon is a preliminary one for the court. *See* §104.1 supra. The trial court's determination will be disturbed on appeal only if there has been an abuse of discretion. *City of Chicago v. Anthony,* 136 Ill. 2d 169, 144 Ill. Dec. 93, 554 N.E.2d 1381 (1990).

There are several reasons why the procedure embodied in Federal Rules 703 and 705 is preferred to more traditional rules. First, the two are designed to bring the judicial practice into line with the practice of the experts themselves when not in court, so that facts, data, or opinions on which an expert would normally rely outside the trial setting may serve as the basis of an expert in-court opinion even when those facts, data, or opinions are inadmissible to prove the truth of the facts asserted therein. Also, in many situations rules 703 and 705 obviate the need for a long and time-consuming process of authentication. In addition, the rules eliminate the time-consuming process of posing long hypothetical questions. *Melecosky v. McCarthy Bros. Co.,* 115 Ill. 2d 209, 104 Ill. Dec. 798, 503 N.E.2d 355 (1986).

The requirement that the facts, data, or opinions be of a type reasonably relied upon by experts in the field provides a check on the trustworthiness of the opinion and its foundation. In determining whether reliance by the expert is reasonable, the court should be satisfied both that such items are of the type customarily relied upon by experts in the field, and that such items are sufficiently trustworthy to make such reliance reasonable. *Accord City of Chicago v. Anthony,* 136 Ill. 2d 169, 144 Ill. Dec. 93, 554 N.E.2d 1381 (1990); *Van Steemburg v. General Aviation, Inc.,* 243 Ill. App. 3d 299, 183 Ill. Dec. 496, 611 N.E.2d 1144 (1993); *Aguinaga v. City of Chicago,* 243 Ill. App. 3d 552, 183 Ill. Dec. 648, 611 N.E.2d 1296 (1993). *See, e.g., Matter of Village of Bridgeview,* 139 Ill. App. 3d 744, 94 Ill. Dec. 232, 487 N.E.2d 1109 (1985), the question is whether the information upon which the expert bases his opinion is considered reliable; *People v. Murphy*, 157 Ill. App. 3d 115, 109 Ill. Dec. 311, 509 N.E.2d 1323 (1987), statement of defendant's mother giving subjective interpretation of defendant's action and mental state was the kind of inherently unreliable statement that the hearsay rule was designed to exclude; *Connelly v. General Motors Corp.*, 184 Ill. App. 3d 378, 132 Ill. Dec. 630, 540 N.E.2d 370 (1989), reliance on the evidence must be both customary in the expert's field and reasonable; *Bloome v. Wiseman, Shaikewitz et al.*, 279 Ill. App. 3d 469, 216 Ill. Dec. 197, 664 N.E.2d 1125 (1996), letters from other attorneys opining that no malpractice occurred are not reasonably relied upon by an expert in the field of legal malpractice. The burden of persuasion should be placed upon the proponent of the expert witness's opinion. *Cf. Johnson v. Commonwealth Edison Co.*, 133 Ill. App. 3d 472, 88 Ill. Dec. 449, 478 N.E.2d 1057 (1985).

A statement by the witness that she, and experts generally, customarily finds facts, data, or opinions of a given type reliable in forming an opinion is highly influential but should not be considered binding upon the court. To allay the fear that enlargement of the permissible basis might break down the rules of exclusion unduly, the Advisory Committee's Note to Federal Rule 703, supra, stresses the reasonable reliance requirement. The Note cites an example of an opinion of "an accidentologist" concerning the point of impact, based on statements of bystanders, as a situation when the requirement is not satisfied. While a standard as to trustworthiness of facts, data, or opinions relied upon by the expert is not specified in Federal Rule 703, the foregoing example contained in the Advisory Committee's Note indicates that reliance is reasonable only if the facts, data, or opinions possess trustworthiness in excess of that possessed by the ordinary hearsay statement. Trustworthiness similar to that possessed by a hearsay statement admissible pursuant to any hearsay exception is apparently contemplated. For example, statements of subjective symptoms made to an examining physician are sufficiently trustworthy to be reasonably relied on, *Melecosky v. McCarthy Bros. Co.*, 115 Ill. 2d 209, 104 Ill. Dec. 798, 503 N.E.2d 355 (1986), as is information furnished the physician by other doctors and nurses. *Walters v. Yellow Cab Co.,* 265 Ill. App. 3d 331, 201 Ill. Dec. 842, 637 N.E.2d 431 (1994). *Compare Hatfield v. Sandoz-Wander, Inc.,* 124 Ill. App. 3d 780, 80 Ill. Dec. 122, 464 N.E.2d 1105 (1984), no evidence offered that experts relied upon had personal knowledge of matters stated; *In re Marriage of Hazard,* 167 Ill. App. 3d 61, 117 Ill. Dec. 770, 520 N.E.2d 1121 (1988), expert witness may not rely on reports of other persons when the standards of the profession require the expert to conduct a personal interview; *Dugan v. Weber,* 175 Ill. App. 3d 1088, 125 Ill. Dec. 598, 530 N.E.2d 1007 (1988), a report prepared in preparation for litigation by a defense expert after examination of the plaintiff is not sufficiently trustworthy to be relied upon by another defense expert; *Chicago & Illinois Midland v. Crystal Lake,* 225 Ill. App. 3d 653, 167 Ill. Dec. 696, 588 N.E.2d 337 (1992), appraiser improperly relied on letter from engineering firm in the absence of a separate feasibility study; *People v. Ramey,* 237 Ill. App. 3d 1001, 179 Ill. Dec. 207, 606 N.E.2d 39 (1992), doctor may not rely on investigator's report that family members said victim was "junkie" for several years in opining that the victim was a drug abuser.

The fact that the opinion relied upon was formed in contemplation of litigation is not alone disqualifying. *Kurrack v. American District Telegraph Co.,* 252 Ill. App. 3d 885, 192 Ill. Dec. 520, 625 N.E.2d 675 (1993), lung tissue analysis reasonably relied upon. Evidence indicating the unreliability of facts, data, or opinions reasonably relied upon by the expert offered to impeach is of course admissible. *Johnson v. Commonwealth Edison Co.,* 133 Ill. App. 3d 472, 88 Ill. Dec. 449, 478 N.E.2d 1057 (1985).

The concept of trustworthiness similar to that possessed by statements admissible pursuant to a hearsay exception is best explored by means of an illustration. Assume the issue being disputed is the cause of a fire in a warehouse leading to significant property damage and the death of a firefighter. In a criminal proceeding against Bob Jones, the prosecution calls to the stand a member of the arson squad of the local fire department, who testifies that he arrived on the scene about 20 minutes after the first firefighter arrived. The arson expert is prepared to testify that the fire was deliberately set. In support of his opinion, he relies upon certain oral statements made to him by a firefighter on the scene describing his observations during the first few minutes fighting the fire. These oral statements of another firefighter relating matters of personal knowledge are of a type reasonably relied upon by experts in the field, i.e., they are customarily relied upon, and the statements, by virtue of being statements made pursuant to a business duty to report, are sufficiently trustworthy to make such reliance reasonable. In addition, the arson expert relied upon the results of certain laboratory tests conducted upon material removed by firefighters from the wreckage. Once again, since these laboratory tests were conducted in the regular course of a regularly conducted business activity, the results of the test are reasonably relied upon by the arson expert. Finally, the arson expert also relies upon two statements. The first, made to him by a firefighter on the scene, relates that ten minutes after he arrived a bystander calmly reported seeing a man run out of the building shortly before it caught fire. The second is a statement by another firefighter that he had seen Bob Jones standing at the corner watching the fire and that Bob Jones is rumored among the firefighters to be a professional arsonist. While both of the foregoing statements may be of a type customarily relied upon by experts in the field, neither is sufficiently trustworthy to make such reliance reasonable. The statement by a bystander, a person under no business duty to report, possessing no indicia of trustworthiness beyond that possessed by hearsay statements at large, may not reasonably be relied upon by the expert. A statement by a member of the expert's organization reporting a rumor, a statement not based upon personal knowledge of the underlying facts, is similarly a hearsay statement not sufficiently trustworthy to be reasonably relied upon even if of a type customarily relied upon by experts in the field. *Compare People v. Washington*, 127 Ill. App. 3d 365, 88 Ill. Dec. 505, 468 N.E.2d 1285 (1984), police officer's opinion as to gang membership of accused inadmissible when based on information from single unnamed informant, *with People v. Jackson,* 145 Ill. App. 3d 626, 99 Ill. Dec. 472, 495 N.E.2d 1207 (1986), police officer's opinion of gang membership of accused admissible when based on five years of experience with gangs, observation, infiltration, and information from arrestees and other observers.

Care should be exercised in interpreting the reasonable reliance provision of Federal Rule 703 and *Wilson v. Clark* to ensure that statements that are indistinguishable in terms of trustworthiness from the unadulterated hearsay statements made by a bystander to an accidentologist (referred to in the Advisory Committee's Note to Rule 703 as a situation where the requirement is not satisfied) are not included. Illustrative of this danger is *Matter of Scruggs,* 151 Ill. App. 3d 260, 104 Ill. Dec. 448, 502 N.E.2d 1108 (1986), statement of a public housing project manager that respondent had opened her apartment door in the nude held to be reasonably relied on by a clinical psychologist testifying as to respondent's mental illness. The danger was correctly recognized in *Dugan v. Weber,* 175 Ill. App. 3d 1088, 125 Ill. Dec. 598, 530 N.E.2d 1007 (1988), where the trial court was held to have properly precluded a defense expert by relying upon a report of a physical examination of the plaintiff prepared by another defense expert in anticipation of litigation.

For most practical purposes, the effect of Federal Rule 703 is the same as if an additional exception to the rule against hearsay had been created in reliance upon the critical faculties of the particular profession. While for most practical purposes admissibility to form the basis of an expert's opinion is equivalent to having the evidence admitted for its truth under a hearsay exception, differences remain. First, what constitutes proper argument to the trier of fact as to the existence of the fact relied upon by the expert differs. More important, evidence admitted solely under Federal Rule 703 will *not* support a *prima facie* case, *see Smith v. United States,* 353 F.2d 838 (D.C. Cir. 1965), *cert. denied,* 382 U.S. 974 (1966); *People v. Anderson,* 113 Ill. 2d 1, 99 Ill. Dec. 104, 495 N.E.2d 485 (1986); *Mayer v. Baisier,* 147 Ill. App. 3d 150, 100 Ill. Dec.

649, 497 N.E.2d 827 (1986); *Beltz v. Griffin,* 244 Ill. App. 3d 490, 184 Ill. Dec. 178, 612 N.E.2d 1054 (1993) (quoting Handbook), or a motion for summary judgment, *see Groce v. South Chicago Community Hospital,* 282 Ill. App. 3d 1004, 218 Ill. Dec. 453, 669 N.E.2d 596 (1996). For all purposes, Federal Rule 703 creates an exception to the Original Writing Rule and the requirements of authentication in court with respect to facts, data, or opinions reasonably relied upon by the testifying expert. *See also* §705.2 infra. Since facts, data, or opinions reasonably relied upon by an expert witness not otherwise admitted in the case may be considered by the trier of fact only in assessing the appropriate weight, if any, to be accorded the expert's opinion and not for their truth, a limiting instruction to the jury to such an effect may be appropriate under certain circumstances. As the foregoing discussion makes clear, *Wilson v. Clark,* 84 Ill. 2d 186, 49 Ill. Dec. 308, 417 N.E.2d 1322 (1981), in adopting Federal Rule 703, did not create an additional exception to the hearsay rule. *People v. Pasch,* 152 Ill. 2d 133, 178 Ill. Dec. 38, 604 N.E.2d 294 (1992); *Mielke v. Condell Memorial Hosp.,* 124 Ill. App. 3d 42, 79 Ill. Dec. 78, 463 N.E.2d 216 (1984); *Beltz v. Griffin,* 244 Ill. App. 3d 490, 184 Ill. Dec. 178, 612 N.E.2d 1054 (1993) (citing Handbook); *People v. Almighty Four Hundred,* 287 Ill. App. 3d 123 222 Ill. Dec. 533, 677 N.E.2d 1332 (1997). *See also* §803.11 infra. The contrary suggestion in *Mohler v. Blanchette,* 106 Ill. App. 3d 545, 62 Ill. Dec. 189, 435 N.E.2d 1161 (1982), and *People v. Murphy,* 157 Ill. App. 3d 115, 109 Ill. Dec. 311, 509 N.E.2d 1323 (1987), is incorrect and should be disregarded. *See Walski v. Tiesenga,* 72 Ill. 2d 249, 21 Ill. Dec. 201, 381 N.E.2d 279 (1978), stating that it is unnecessary to decide whether and under what circumstances medical treatises may be admitted as substantive evidence. *Cf.* Federal Rule of Evidence 803(18), 65 F.R.D. 131, 157 (1975), creating a limited hearsay exception for learned treatises. *See Roach v. Springfield Clinic,* 157 Ill. 2d 29, 191 Ill. Dec. 1, 623 N.E.2d 246 (1993), stating that the question of Illinois adopting Federal Rule of Evidence 803(18) was not properly before the court and accordingly would not be addressed. *Accord Lewis v. Stoval,* 272 Ill. App. 3d 467, 209 Ill. Dec. 101, 650 N.E.2d 1074 (1995) (at this time statements in scientific and medical treatises are hearsay and inadmissible as substantive proof of the statements contained therein citing *Roach* id.). *See also* §705.1 infra.

While only the terms *facts* or *data* appear in Federal Rule 703, opinions not in evidence, even those not admissible, may also form the basis of an expert's opinion if reasonably relied upon by experts in the particular field. Federal Advisory Committee's Note to Rule 703 supra; *People v. Ward,* 61 Ill. 2d 559, 338 N.E.2d 171 (1975). *Accord People v. Pasch,* 152 Ill. 2d 133, 178 Ill. Dec. 38, 604 N.E.2d 294 (1992) (expert may reasonably rely upon other expert's findings and conclusions). Facts, data, or opinions reasonably relied upon under Federal Rule 703, may be disclosed to the jury to assist the jury in evaluating the expert's opinion by considering its bases. *People v. Ward* supra. This is true even if the facts, data, or opinions have not themselves been admitted and thus may not be considered for their truth. *People v. Scott,* 148 Ill. 2d 479, 171 Ill. Dec. 365, 594 N.E.2d 217 (1992); *People v. Anderson,* 133 Ill. 2d 1, 99 Ill. Dec. 104, 495 N.E.2d 485 (1986); *People v. Lang,* 113 Ill. 2d 407, 101 Ill. Dec. 597, 498 N.E.2d 1105 (1986). Thus, for example, facts, data, or opinions contained in a learned treatise reasonably relied on by the expert witness may be disclosed on direct examination to the trier of fact. *Piano v. Davison,* 157 Ill. App. 3d 649, 110 Ill. Dec. 35, 510 N.E.2d 1066 (1987). Similarly, a doctor may reasonably rely on inadmissible medical records in rendering an opinion, and disclose the contents of such records to the jury. *See Wingo by Wingo v. Rockford Memorial Hospital,* 292 Ill. App. 3d 896, 226 Ill. Dec. 939, 686 N.E.2d 722 (1997), obstetrical nurse may rely upon deposition of another to obtain an understanding of the facts of the case. *See generally* the excellent opinion of Justice Chapman dissenting in *Schuchman v. Stackable,* 198 Ill. App. 3d 209, 144 Ill. Dec. 493, 555 N.E.2d 1012 (1990) (expert medical witness may read to the jury from articles reasonably relied upon; majority opinion declaring such practice improper is clearly incorrect). In

Kochan v. Owens-Corning Fiberglass Corp., 242 Ill. App. 3d 781, 182 Ill. Dec. 814, 610 N.E.2d 683 (1993), *Schuchman* was appropriately limited with the court concluding that reasonable reliance does not permit an expert to act as a mere conduit by reading the opinions of other experts contained in published material for the purpose of showing that other experts agree with his opinion; the content of the published material to be read to the jury must be reasonably relied upon as a basis for the expert's opinion, and not merely to corroborate that opinion. *See infra. See also People v. Pasch,* 152 Ill. 2d 133, 178 Ill. Dec. 38, 604 N.E.2d 294 (1992), nontestifying medical expert's findings and conclusions reasonably relied upon were properly disclosed to the jury.

Facts, data, or opinions reasonably relied on by an expert witness, including learned treatises, *see* supra, are *not* by virtue thereof substantive evidence; reasonably relied on facts, data, or opinions constitute substantive evidence only if otherwise admitted into evidence. *City of Chicago v. Anthony,* 136 Ill. 2d 169, 144 Ill. Dec. 93, 554 N.E.2d 1381 (1990); *People v. Anderson* supra; *People v. Lang* supra; *Groce v. South Chicago Community Hospital,* 282 Ill. App. 3d 1004, 218 Ill. Dec. 453, 669 N.E.2d 596 (1996); *Giraldi v. Community Consolidated School District #62,* 279 Ill. App. 3d 679, 216 Ill. Dec. 272, 665 N.E.2d 332 (1996); *Mayer v. Baisier,* 147 Ill. App. 3d 150, 100 Ill. Dec. 649, 497 N.E.2d 827 (1986). The trial court on request should instruct the jury that such facts, data, or opinions, not otherwise admitted, may be considered "solely as a basis for the expert opinion and not as substantive evidence." *United States v. Sims,* 514 F.2d 147, 149-150 (9th Cir. 1975). *Accord City of Chicago v. Anthony,* 136 Ill. 2d 169, 144 Ill. Dec. 93, 554 N.E.2d 1381 (1990); *People v. Pasch* supra; *People v. Anderson* supra; *People v. Lang* supra; *Giraldi v. Community Consolidated School District #62,* 279 Ill. App. 3d 679, 216 Ill. Dec. 272, 665 N.E.2d 332 (1996); *Henry v. Brenner,* 138 Ill. App. 3d 609, 93 Ill. Dec. 401, 486 N.E.2d 934 (1985). An expert witness may be precluded from disclosing reasonably relied on facts, data, or opinions when in spite of the availability of a limiting instruction their probative value in explaining the expert's opinion pales beside their likely prejudicial impact or their tendency to create confusion. *People v. Anderson* supra; *People v. P.T.*, 233 Ill. App. 3d 386, 174 Ill. Dec. 533, 599 N.E.2d 79 (1992); *Kochan v. Owens-Corning Fiberglass Corp.*, 242 Ill. App. 3d 781, 182 Ill. Dec. 814, 610 N.E.2d 683 (1993); *Bass v. Cincinnati Inc.*, 281 Ill. App. 3d 1019, 217 Ill. Dec. 557, 667 N.E.2d 646 (1996); *Doe v. Lutz,* 281 Ill. App. 3d 630, 218 Ill. Dec. 80, 668 N.E.2d 564 (1996). *See People v. Chambers,* 259 Ill. App. 3d 631, 197 Ill. Dec. 595, 631 N.E.2d 817 (1994), prosecution expert on sanity should not have been permitted to detail defendant's criminal past in light of the prejudicial impact of the evidence and its marginal value to the crux of the experts's disagreement. *See also* discussion infra and §403.1 supra. If certain facts, data, or opinions are excluded from consideration by the expert, the expert may still render an opinion if an adequate basis nevertheless remains.

Although Federal Rule 703 is aimed at permitting experts to base opinions on reliable hearsay and other facts that might not be admissible, a prosecution witness could not base an opinion on evidence that had been seized from a defendant in violation of the Fourth Amendment. Application of the "fruit of the poisonous tree doctrine" mandates such a result. *Wong Sun v. United States,* 371 U.S. 471 (1963). Similarly, where policy considerations, such as those surrounding privileges, *see* Article V supra, and subsequent remedial measures, payment of medical expenses, etc., *see* §§407-411 supra, require that certain matters not be admitted at trial, that policy should not be thwarted by allowing the same evidence to come in the "back door" in the form of the basis of an expert's opinion. Thus it is improper for a state's expert to rely upon an inadmissible confession of the defendant in opining that a fire was intentionally set. *People v. Sifuentes,* 248 Ill. App. 3d 248, 188 Ill. Dec. 73, 618 N.E.2d 643 (1993). Similarly, it is improper for a state's expert in opining as to the defendant's blood-alcohol level to rely upon medical records that were inadmissible by virtue of failure to provide written test results in violation of then-existing 625 ILCS 5/11-

501.4. *People v. Solis,* 275 Ill. App. 3d 346, 211 Ill. Dec. 571, 655 N.E.2d 954 (1995). Nor do the concerns expressed in the Dead Man's Act, §606.1 supra, fall away in the face of the reasonable reliance provision of Rule 703. *Estate of Justus v. Justus,* 243 Ill. App. 3d 737, 183 Ill. Dec. 832, 612 N.E.2d 89 (1993). Moreover, care must be exercised to prevent the defendant from unjustifiably placing his statements before the jury free of cross-examination. *See United States v. McCollum,* 732 F.2d 1419 (9th Cir. 1984). Accordingly, an expert witness will not be permitted to rely solely upon self-serving statements of a criminal defendant asserting an insanity defense that would allow the accused to tell his story without the possibility of cross-examination. *People v. Britz,* 123 Ill. 2d 446, 124 Ill. Dec. 15, 528 N.E.2d 703 (1988); *People v. Chambers* supra. *See also People v. Sims,* 167 Ill. 2d 483, 212 Ill. Dec. 931, 658 N.E.2d 413 (1995) (question whether statements by defendant to psychiatrist, relied upon by a mitigation expert in death penalty case, were properly excluded was raised but not decided). Where the accused raises the defense of insanity based in part on his statements made to a psychiatrist, *People v. Murphy,* 147 Ill. App. 3d 122, 100 Ill. Dec. 693, 497 N.E.2d 871 (1986), while it is true that contradictory voluntary statements obtained in violation of the accused's *Miranda* rights may be admitted to rebut, *People v. Finkey,* 105 Ill. App. 3d 230, 61 Ill. Dec. 81, 434 N.E.2d 18 (1982), the mere fact that accused was capable of asserting his *Miranda* rights may not be employed to show sanity. *People v. Anderson,* 113 Ill. 2d 1, 99 Ill. Dec. 104, 495 N.E.2d 485 (1986).

An expert may not testify as a summary expert or mere conduit by relying on facts, data, or opinions reasonably relied on by experts in the particular field but without himself providing additional input. *See* Graham, Handbook of Federal Evidence §703.1 n.12 (4th ed. 1996). *See also Rock v. Pickleman,* 214 Ill. App. 3d 368, 158 Ill. Dec. 569, 574 N.E.2d 682 (1991), (Rakowski, J., concurring). Similarly, an expert may not rely on an opinion of another expert that merely corroborates and thus reinforces an opinion that had been independently arrived at by the testifying expert. *Kochan v.*

Owens-Corning Fiberglass Corp., 242 Ill. App. 3d 781, 182 Ill. Dec. 814, 610 N.E.2d 683 (1993). *See also Kim v. Nazarian,* 216 Ill. App. 3d 818, 159 Ill. Dec. 758, 576 N.E.2d 427 (1991); *Bloome v. Wiseman, Shaikewitz et al.,* 279 Ill. App. 3d 469, 216 Ill. Dec. 197, 664 N.E.2d 1125 (1996).

In *People v. Sassu,* 151 Ill. App. 3d 199, 104 Ill. Dec. 387, 502 N.E.2d 1047 (1986), the concept of reasonable reliance was employed to sanction the admissibility of an oral report from a Canadian forensic laboratory regarding the amount of marijuana in the victim's blood as testified to by the chief toxicologist for the Cook County Medical Examiner. Since the Canadian forensic laboratory report was an evaluative finding offered against the accused in a criminal case, the Sixth Amendment right of confrontation and 725 ILCS 5/ 115-5(c), §803.13 infra, require exclusion. *See* Federal Rule of Evidence 803(8)(C). *See also United States v. Oates,* 560 F.2d 45 (2d Cir. 1977). The concept of reasonable reliance in *Wilson v. Clark* should not be employed to do indirectly what is prohibited from being done directly. Reasonable reliance does not include an expert summarizing the literature for the general purpose of educating the jury when the expert had not conducted the tests and could not testify concerning test methods and procedures. *Mielke v. Condell Memorial Hosp.,* 124 Ill. App. 3d 42, 79 Ill. Dec. 78, 463 N.E.2d 216 (1984). Reasonable reliance does not include an expert relying solely on self-serving statements of a criminal defendant. *People v. Britz* supra. Nor does reasonable reliance extend to statements made to the testifying expert constituting an opinion on the merits of the case. *Denny v. Burpo,* 124 Ill. App. 3d 73, 79 Ill. Dec. 520, 463 N.E.2d 1074 (1984), opinions on the merits of the case are not ordinarily relied upon in nontrial situations.

As stated in the Federal Advisory Committee's Note supra, Federal Rule 703 also offers a more satisfactory basis for ruling upon the admissibility of public opinion poll evidence. *See Antry v. Educational Labor Relations Bd.,* 195 Ill. App. 3d 221, 141 Ill. Dec. 945, 552 N.E.2d 313 (1990), survey admissible if done in adherence to generally accepted survey principles and if utilization of the results is done in a statistically correct manner; *Galindo v. Riddell, Inc.,* 107 Ill. App. 3d 139, 62 Ill. Dec. 849, 437 N.E.2d 376 (1982), expert improperly permitted to rely upon a survey that was not shown to have employed methods generally accepted in the scientific community to produce statistically accurate results. *Cf. Bradley v. Booz, Allen & Hamilton, Inc.,* 67 Ill. App. 3d 156, 23 Ill. Dec. 839, 384 N.E.2d 746 (1978), employing questionable interpretation of the existing state of mind exception to the hearsay rule, *see* §803.4 infra, as part of double-level hearsay analysis to admit results of survey. The concept of reasonably relied upon facts, data, or opinions also provides a more satisfactory basis upon which to permit cross-examination of an expert witness as to the significance of certain additional facts appearing in hospital or medical records not themselves admitted in evidence. *Levenson v. Lake-to-Lake Dairy Coop.,* 76 Ill. App. 3d 526, 32 Ill. Dec. 20, 394 N.E.2d 1359 (1979).

Prior to the full incorporation of Federal Rule 703 in *Wilson v. Clark* supra, the concept of "reasonably relied upon by experts in the particular field" had first been applied by the Illinois Supreme Court in *People v. Ward,* 61 Ill. 2d 559, 338 N.E.2d 171 (1975), to expert medical opinion as to an accused's sanity based in large part on medical or psychological records compiled by others that were not admitted into evidence, and then by the lower courts in *People v. Cooper,* 64 Ill. App. 3d 880, 21 Ill. Dec. 634, 381 N.E.2d 1178 (1978); *People v. Sharkey,* 60 Ill. App. 3d 257, 17 Ill. Dec. 465, 376 N.E.2d 464 (1978); *People v. Espinoza,* 54 Ill. App. 3d 36, 11 Ill. Dec. 871, 369 N.E.2d 325 (1977), to expert medical psychiatric testimony at commitment proceedings; in *Clemons v. Alton & Southern R. Co.,* 56 Ill. App. 3d 328, 12 Ill. Dec. 875, 370 N.E.2d 679 (1978); *Smith v. Williams,* 34 Ill. App. 2d 677, 339 N.E.2d 10 (1975), to psychiatric reports relied upon by medical expert witnesses, not made under their supervision, in personal injury actions; in *People v. Brannon,* 59 Ill. App. 3d 531, 16 Ill. Dec. 733, 375 N.E.2d 840 (1978), in connection with the testing of a standard for comparison purposes; in *Chiero v.*

Chicago Osteopathic Hosp., 74 Ill. App. 3d 166, 29 Ill. Dec. 646, 392 N.E.2d 203 (1979), to medical records reasonably relied upon by the expert in a medical malpractice action; in *Montefusco v. Cecon Constr. Co.,* 74 Ill. App. 3d 319, 30 Ill. Dec. 235, 392 N.E.2d 1103 (1979), to calculations and test results dealing with wind resistance reasonably relied upon by an expert in testifying that if roof had been installed as per specifications it would have withstood the wind load placed on it; in *People v. Mello,* 87 Ill. App. 3d 506, 42 Ill. Dec. 657, 409 N.E.2d 152 (1980), to a laboratory blood test relied upon by a doctor to render an opinion as to intoxication; and in *Matter of Germich,* 103 Ill. App. 3d 626, 59 Ill. Dec. 335, 431 N.E.2d 1092 (1981), to intake reports of staff relied on by a psychiatrist in diagnosing mental illness.

Subsequent to *Wilson v. Clark* supra, the concept of "reasonably relied upon by experts in the particular field" has been applied to statements of an injured plaintiff made during an interview to a vocational counselor, *J.L. Simmons Co. v. Firestone Tire & Rubber Co.,* 108 Ill. 2d 106, 90 Ill. Dec. 955, 483 N.E.2d 273 (1985); to sales of property relied upon by a real estate appraiser expressing an opinion on value, *Department of Transp. v. Beeson,* 137 Ill. App. 3d 908, 92 Ill. Dec. 700, 485 N.E.2d 511 (1985); to economic data from census information relied upon by an expert in arriving at a real estate evaluation, *Matter of Village of Bridgeview,* 139 Ill. App. 3d 744, 94 Ill. Dec. 232, 487 N.E.2d 1109 (1985); to sign income earned on comparable property in determining value of subject property, *City of Chicago v. Anthony,* 174 Ill. App. 3d 288, 123 Ill. Dec. 753, 528 N.E.2d 298 (1988); to a statement of a radiologist to a doctor on the effect of retained pantopaque dye, *Lebrecht v. Tuli,* 130 Ill. App. 3d 457, 85 Ill. Dec. 517, 473 N.E.2d 1322 (1985); to deposition testimony of defendant doctors relied upon by nontreating expert witness testifying for the defense, *Thome v. Palmer,* 141 Ill. App. 3d 92, 95 Ill. Dec. 435, 489 N.E.2d 1163 (1986); to opinion of a psychiatrist based upon examination of defendant and various records that defendant suffered from a treatable personality disorder and not a mental disease in spite of fact that psychiatrist had not reviewed reports made during 15 years of hospitalization, *People v. Wright*, 111 Ill. 2d 128, 95 Ill. Dec. 787, 490 N.E.2d 640 (1986); to statements of criminal defendant made to examining, nontreating physician testifying on his behalf on the question of insanity, *People v. Anderson*, 131 Ill. 2d 1, 99 Ill. Dec. 104, 495 N.E.2d 485 (1986); to observations of nurses, social workers, and other hospital personnel as well as evaluation by other psychiatrists in rendering an opinion as to whether an individual was likely to cause serious harm to others in the near future, *People v. Lang*, 113 Ill. 2d 407, 101 Ill. Dec. 597, 498 N.E.2d 1105 (1986); to statements of subjective symptoms made to an examining physician testifying as to the plaintiff's pain and disability, *Melecosky v. McCarthy Bros. Co.*, 115 Ill. 2d 209, 104 Ill. Dec. 798, 503 N.E.2d 355 (1986); to psychiatric history relied upon by state expert testifying as to the mental state of the accused at the time of the offense, *People v. Scott*, 148 Ill. 2d 479, 171 Ill. Dec. 365, 594 N.E.2d 217 (1992); to nontestifying expert's findings and conclusions relied upon by a testifying expert as to a patient's sanity, *People v. Pasch*, 152 Ill. 2d 133, 178 Ill. Dec. 38, 604 N.E.2d 294 (1992); to statements of a subordinate relating to research as to type of tire capable of making a particular impression as well as reference to a "tire guide" manual, *People v. Sutherland*, 155 Ill. 2d 1, 182 Ill. Dec. 577, 610 N.E.2d 1 (1992); to bona fide offers to purchase real estate in opining as to value, *County of St. Clair v. Wilson*, 284 Ill. App. 3d 79, 219 Ill. Dec. 712, 672 N.E.2d 27 (1996); and to the findings of another geneticist based upon his conducting of a test to validate the independence of a database employed by an expert on DNA analysis; *People v. Almighty Four Hundred*, 287 Ill. App. 3d 123, 222 Ill. Dec. 533, 677 N.E.2d 1332 (1997). *Cf. People v. Maisonet*, 138 Ill. App. 3d 716, 93 Ill. Dec. 176, 486 N.E.2d 277 (1985), expert witness may not rely upon hearsay statement that defendant and the other assailant were members of the same gang; *In re Marriage of Hazard*, 167 Ill. App. 3d 61, 117 Ill. Dec. 770, 520 N.E.2d 1121 (1988), expert witness may not rely on reports of other persons when the standards of the profession require the expert to conduct a personal interview; *Curt Bullock Builders v. H.S.S. Development, Inc.,* 225 Ill. App. 3d 9, 167 Ill. Dec. 12, 586 N.E.2d 1284 (1992), no showing made that the particular surveys considered by plaintiff's experts were of the kind reasonably relied upon by experts in the field.

Where the facts, data, or opinions reasonably relied upon by the expert were based upon an electronic, mechanical, or similar device, it must be established that the particular device produces a reliable result when properly employed and operated and that the device was properly employed and operated in the manner at hand. *People v. Bynum,* 257 Ill. App. 3d 502, 196 Ill. Dec. 179, 629 N.E.2d 724 (1994); *People v. Payne,* 239 Ill. App. 3d 698, 180 Ill. Dec. 481, 607 N.E.2d 375 (1993); *Martin v. Thompson,* 195 Ill. App. 3d 43, 141 Ill. Dec. 739, 551 N.E.2d 1082 (1990).

In *Rock v. Pickleman,* 214 Ill. App. 3d 368, 158 Ill. Dec. 569, 574 N.E.2d 682 (1991), plaintiff's expert at trial was permitted to rely on another expert's opinion contained in a letter solicited by plaintiff's counsel (i.e., prepared in anticipation of litigation), the court treating the matter as analogous to a patient's statements made to an examining physician approved in *Melecosky v. McCarthy Bros. Co.,* 115 Ill. 2d 209, 104 Ill. Dec. 798, 503 N.E.2d 355 (1986). However, the justification for use of a patient's statement to an examining physician rests in great part upon practical necessity and the usual availability of the plaintiff as a witness at trial. Extension of *Melecosky* to encompass all statements made specifically for purposes of litigation is totally unwarranted, as such statements by virtue of the circumstances of their creation lack adequate assurance of trustworthiness. *See generally Palmer v. Hoffman,* 318 U.S. 109 (1943). *Contrast People v. Lipscomb,* 215 Ill. App. 3d 413, 158 Ill. Dec. 952, 574 N.E.2d 1345 (1991), where findings made employing proper procedures for DNA under identification were correctly held to have been reasonably relied on by an expert rendering an opinion in court. Notice that the facts, data, or opinions relied on in *Lipscomb* were created in the ordinary course of an investigatory process, *see* arson investigation illustration supra, and that the opinion itself, as in the illustration, was provided by an expert witness in court subject to cross-examination. *See* Graham, Handbook of Federal Evidence §803.8 (4th ed. 1996) and *United States v. Oates,* 560 F.2d 45 (2d Cir. 1977) for discussion of the admissibility in federal court of investigatory police reports under the public records hearsay exception. With respect to an expert testifying as a summary expert or mere conduit, *see* supra and §705.1 infra.

In summary, the concept of "reasonable reliance" under *Wilson v. Clark* supra was well stated in *Lovelace v. Four Lakes Dev. Co.,* 170 Ill. App. 3d 378, 120 Ill. Dec. 424, 427-428, 523 N.E.2d 1335, 1338-1339 (1988):

> However, evidence which is substantively inadmissible may nevertheless be admissible for the limited purpose of explaining the basis for an expert's opinion. (*People v. Anderson,* 113 Ill. 2d at 11-12, 99 Ill. Dec. 104, 495 N.E.2d 485; *see also People v. Lang* (1986), 113 Ill. 2d 407, 465-67, 101 Ill. Dec. 597, 498 N.E.2d 1105.) The determinative factor is whether the facts or data constitute information on which the expert "reasonably relies" as a basis for his opinion. (*People v. Anderson,* 113 Ill. 2d at 9, 99 Ill. Dec. 104, 495 N.E.2d 485.) The *Anderson* court also noted that the trial court has the authority to exclude information of its "probative value in explaining the expert's opinion pales beside its likely prejudicial impact or its tendency to create confusion." (113 Ill. 2d at 12, 99 Ill. Dec. 104, 495 N.E.2d 485.) It is therefore not enough for the proponent of the evidence to establish the expert's subjective reliance on it in forming his opinion; his reliance must also be reasonable. *See, e.g., People v. Murphy* (1987), 157 Ill. App. 3d 115, 119, 109 Ill. Dec. 311, 509 N.E.2d 1323 (holding inadmissible "inherently unreliable" hearsay statements of the defendant's mother regarding the defendant's violent conduct immediately before he killed the victim); *People v. Maisonet* (1985), 138 Ill. App. 3d 716, 719, 93 Ill. Dec. 176, 486 N.E.2d 277 (holding that hearsay reports that two crimes were connected and gang related were not of a type ordinarily and reasonably relied upon by police investigators where there was no indiction that the source of the information was reliable); *Henry v. Brenner* (1985), 138 Ill. App. 3d 609, 615, 93 Ill. Dec. 401, 486 N.E.2d 934 (recognizing the potential for abuse and conclud-

ing that disclosure of the facts underlying the opinion should depend upon necessity and trustworthiness as do "all exceptions to the hearsay rule"); *Hatfield v. Sandoz-Wander, Inc.* (1984), 124 Ill. App. 3d 780, 788, 80 Ill. Dec. 122, 464 N.E.2d 1105 (holding that an expert physician's out-of-court conversations with other physicians regarding the adequacy of defendant's product warnings was not information of the type reasonably relied upon by experts in his field where there was no testimony establishing that the other physicians had read the warnings). *But see In re Scruggs* (1986), 151 Ill. App. 3d 260, 263, 104 Ill. Dec. 448, 502 N.E.2d 1108 (holding the hearsay statement of a building manager that the patient had answered her door in the nude and left her keys in the building office admissible and concluding that the "unreliability of the . . . anecdotal statements . . . does not act to bar their admission, but rather acts merely as a caution as to the reliability of [the expert's] opinion").

Where the issue was the admission or exclusion of an expert's entire opinion testimony, the Illinois Supreme Court adopted the position that the trial court should liberally allow the expert to determine what materials are reasonably relied upon by those in his field. (*Melecosky v. McCarthy Brothers Co.* (1986), 115 Ill. 2d 209, 216, 104 Ill. Dec. 798, 503 N.E.2d 355, citing *Mannino v. International Mfg. Co.* (6th Cir. 1981), 650 F.2d 846, 853; *People v. Murphy*, 157 Ill. App. 3d at 125, 109 Ill. Dec. 311, 509 N.E.2d 1323 (McNamara, P.J., dissenting).) It is the opponent's responsibility to then challenge the sufficiency or reliability of the basis for the expert's opinion during cross-examination, and the determination of the weight to be given the expert's opinion is left to the finder of fact. (*Melecosky*, 115 Ill. 2d at 216-17, 104 Ill. Dec. 798, 503 N.E.2d 355.) We do not believe that the *Melecosky* ruling should be applied where, as here, the issue is not the admissibility of the expert's opinion testimony, but the propriety of allowing the expert to disclose substantively inadmissible underlying facts to explain his opinion. Such an extension of *Melecosky* would allow the proponent of otherwise inadmissible evidence to summarily circumvent its exclusion if he is able to find an expert to rely upon it in forming his opinion. (*See Henry v. Brenner*, 138 Ill. App. 3d at 615, 93 Ill. Dec. 401, 486 N.E.2d 934.) Under these circumstances, we believe the more appropriate position is that suggested by Professor Graham: "[t]he proponent of the evidence should be required to satisfy the court both that such items are of the type customarily relied upon by experts in the field, *and that such items are sufficiently trustworthy to make such reliance reasonable.*" (Emphasis in original.) (Graham, Expert Witness Testimony and the Federal Rules of Evidence: Insuring Adequate Assurance of Trustworthiness, 1986 U. Ill. L. Rev. 43, 75; *see also Melecosky*, 115 Ill. 2d at 218, 104 Ill. Dec. 798, 503 N.E.2d 355 (Ryan, J., dissenting).) In the instant case plaintiff has not demonstrated that Heffernan's reliance on the disputed evidence was customary in his field or reasonable.

§703.2 Expert Reconstruction Testimony

The propriety of expert testimony in reconstructing an incident, usually an automobile or airplane accident, generally has involved over the years an interplay of various competing considerations including (1) the Dead Man's Act, 735 ILCS 5/8-201, *see* §606 supra, (2) the admissibility of careful habits testimony in the absence of an eyewitness, *see* §406.3 supra, (3) admissibility of an opinion on an ultimate issue, considered in §704.1 infra, which itself is not a bar to such expert testimony, *Miller v. Pillsbury Co.*, 33 Ill. 2d 514, 211 N.E.2d 733 (1965), and (4) a general uneasiness with the reliability of reconstruction testimony.

Where there are no competent eyewitnesses "expert testimony on reconstruction of an . . . accident should be admissible where it is necessary to rely on knowledge and application of principles of physics, engineering and other sciences beyond the ken of the average juror." *Miller v. Pillsbury Co., id.* at 516, 211 N.E.2d at 735.

Reconstruction testimony, however, could not be used as a substitute for eyewitness testimony where such was available: "Whether it may be used in addition to eyewitness testimony is determined by whether it is necessary to rely on knowledge and application of principles of science beyond the ken of the average juror." *Plank v. Holman*, 46 Ill. 2d 465, 471, 264 N.E.2d 12, (1970). Accordingly, expert reconstruction testimony was not admissible if directly contradictory of credible, even if conflicting, eyewitness testimony as to an observed fact. *Palmer v. Craig*, 246 Ill. App. 3d 323, 186 Ill. Dec. 237, 615 N.E.2d 1294 (1993); *Olson v. Bell Helmets, Inc.*, 195 Ill. App. 3d 20, 141 Ill. Dec. 732, 551 N.E.2d 1075 (1990); *Whitman v. Lopatkiewicz*, 152 Ill. App. 3d 332, 105 Ill. Dec. 374, 504 N.E.2d 243 (1987); *National Bank of Bloomington v. Pickens*, 8 Ill. App. 3d 58, 289 N.E.2d 64 (1972). *See, e.g., Peterson v. Lou Bachrodt Chevrolet Co.*, 76 Ill. 2d 353, 29 Ill. Dec. 444, 392 N.E.2d 1 (1979) (testimony as to speed of automobile, even though conflicting, is not matter beyond ken of the average juror) followed in *Colonial Trust & Sav. Bank v. Kasmar*, 190 Ill. App. 3d 967, 138 Ill. Dec. 57, 546 N.E.2d 1112 (1989); *Lee v. Grand Trunk Western Ry.*, 143 Ill. App. 3d 500, 97 Ill. Dec. 491, 492 N.E.2d 1364 (1986) (court properly excluded expert reconstruction testimony as to whether train could stop in time in light of sufficient eyewitness and scientific testimony available to jury); *Levin v. Walsh Bros. Motor Serv.*, 164 Ill. App. 3d 640, 115 Ill. Dec. 680, 518 N.E.2d 205 (1987) (court in its discretion could exclude expert reconstruction testimony as to matters otherwise in evidence in the form of eyewitness testimony, photographs and other data). *Cf. Albee v. Emrath*, 53 Ill. App. 2d 910, 11 Ill. Dec. 608, 269 N.E.2d 62 (1977), reconstruction testimony may be admitted where testimony of eyewitness is unclear, unconvincing, or contradictory; *Turney v. Ford Motor Co.*, 94 Ill. App. 3d 678, 50 Ill. Dec. 85, 418 N.E.2d 1079 (1981), expert reconstruction testimony admitted in products liability action to rebut eyewitness testimony of plaintiff.

Testimony of an eyewitness would not preclude expert reconstruction testimony where the eyewitness lacks personal knowledge as to the matter addressed. *See, e.g., People v. Wolfe*, 114 Ill. App. 3d 841, 70 Ill. Dec. 633, 449 N.E.2d 980 (1983), there was no eyewitness testimony as to speed at the moment the car began to skid; *People v. McDermott*, 141 Ill. App. 3d 996, 96 Ill. Dec. 88, 490 N.E.2d 1293 (1985), no eyewitness could establish either speed at impact or lane in which accident occurred; *Galowich v. Beech Aircraft Corp.*, 209 Ill. App. 3d 128, 154 Ill. Dec. 46, 568 N.E.2d 46 (1991), while eyewitnesses saw the plane crash, none observed the cause. *See also Seward v.*

Griffin, 116 Ill. App. 3d 749, 72 Ill. Dec. 305, 452 N.E.2d 558 (1983), testimony of expert as to "second impact" injuries and his explanation of change in velocity was merely incidentally contradictory to the testimony of eyewitnesses.

Expert reconstruction testimony was admissible when eyewitness testimony was available, however, whenever such expert testimony would aid triers of fact in their understanding of the issues even though they might have a general knowledge of the subject matter. *See, e.g., Jamison v. Lambke,* 21 Ill. App. 3d 629, 316 N.E.2d 93 (1974), testimony of expert witness as to minimum braking distance and feet traveled per second at 25 m.p.h.; *Finfrock v. Eaton Asphalt Co.,* 41 Ill. App. 3d 1020, 355 N.E.2d 214 (1976), and *Fakhoury by Fakhoury v. Vapor Corp.,* 154 Ill. App. 3d 531, 107 Ill. Dec. 386, 507 N.E.2d 50 (1987), minimum and maximum braking distance; *Coffey v. Hancock,* 122 Ill. App. 3d 442, 77 Ill. Dec. 677, 461 N.E.2d 64 (1984), expert witness testimony as to significance of skid marks originally introduced by opposing party; *Ketchum v. Dura-Bond Concrete, Inc.,* 179 Ill. App. 3d 820, 128 Ill. Dec. 759, 534 N.E.2d 1364 (1989), interplay of physical forces that caused the collisions was beyond the average juror's ken; *People v. Reding,* 191 Ill. App. 3d 424, 138 Ill. Dec. 689, 547 N.E.2d 1310 (1989), expert testimony that rusty nail used in rear assembly of motorcycle did not contribute to the collision. *Cf. McGrath v. Rohdo,* 53 Ill. 2d 56, 289 N.E.2d 619 (1972), the driving actions of parties at the time of the accident involve a factual determination that does not necessitate expert evidence to supplement the eyewitness testimony available; *Ralston v. Plogger,* 132 Ill. App. 90, 87 Ill. Dec. 386, 476 N.E.2d 1378 (1985), testimony of a police officer as to location of point of impact improperly admitted. With respect to police officer testimony on point of impact, *see generally Loseke v. Mables,* 217 Ill. App. 3d 521, 160 Ill. Dec. 471, 577 N.E.2d 796 (1991).

As the foregoing indicates, lack of clarity in the approach of the decisions placed the matter very much in the discretion of the trial court. *Accord Peterson v. Lou Brachrodt Chevrolet Co.,* 61 Ill. App. 3d 698, 19 Ill. Dec. 117, 378 N.E.2d 618

(1978), there appears to be a certain amount of confusion as to when reconstruction testimony may be received when eyewitness testimony is available; *Augenstein v. Pulley,* 191 Ill. App. 3d 664, 138 Ill. Dec. 724, 547 N.E.2d 1345 (1989) (quoting Handbook while referring to it as a "calculated understatement of the degree of confusion" and concluding with the statement that expert reconstruction testimony should be treated the same as any other expert witness testimony). *See also Dotto v. Okan,* 269 Ill. App. 3d 808, 207 Ill. Dec. 190, 646 N.E.2d 1277 (1995) (the rule barring a reconstruction expert from testifying merely because there are eyewitnesses to the occurrence is an anachronism that must be allowed to rest in peace rather than be resurrected). The trend, however, was to interpret liberally the requirement that the jury be assisted in acquiring knowledge beyond that which they would ordinarily have when testified to by a qualified expert in spite of the presence of an eyewitness. *See, e.g., Augenstein v. Pulley* supra; *Robles v. Chicago Transit Authority,* 235 Ill. App. 3d 121, 176 Ill. Dec. 171, 601 N.E.2d 869 (1992); *People v. Rushton,* 254 Ill. App. 3d 156, 193 Ill. Dec. 827, 626 N.E.2d 1378 (1993). It was clear, moreover, that if expert reconstruction testimony was permitted on behalf of one party, such testimony must be permitted to be introduced by the opposing party as well. *Kelly v. American Motors Corp.,* 130 Ill. App. 3d 662, 85 Ill. Dec. 854, 474 N.E.2d 814 (1985).

It is safe to say that an uneasiness felt with reconstruction testimony generally has caused Illinois courts to view critically (1) the expert witness's qualifications, especially if the expert is a police officer qualified as an expert on the basis solely of experience, *Deaver v. Hickox,* 81 Ill. App. 2d 224, N.E.2d 468 (1967); *Thurmond v. Monroe,* 235 Ill. App. 3d 281, 176 Ill. Dec. 350, 601 N.E.2d 1048 (1992), and in particular if the expert had little actual experience, *Wade v. City of Chicago Heights,* 295 Ill. App. 3d 873, 230 Ill. Dec. 297, 693 N.E.2d 426 (1998); (2) the reliability of the scientific and technical basis of the expert's testimony considered in light of the evidence of physical facts introduced in the case, *Abramson v. Levinson,* 112 Ill. App. 2d 42, 250 N.E.2d 796 (1969); *Pritchett v. Steinker*

Trucking Co., 108 Ill. 2d 371, 247 N.E.2d 923 (1969), *see* §611.25 for discussion of objection to expert testimony on grounds of guess, surmise or conjecture, and §702.5 relating to stopping distance and speed; (3) the helpfulness of the expert testimony to the trier of fact; and (4) the sufficiency of the physical data upon which the expert bases her opinion. *People v. Ethridge,* 243 Ill. App. 3d 446, 183 Ill. Dec. 61, 610 N.E.2d 1305 (1993).

After acknowledging what was referred to as the unnecessary confusion about whether expert reconstruction testimony may be admitted where there is also an eyewitness, the Illinois Supreme Court in *Zavala v. Powermatic, Inc.,* 167 Ill. 2d 542, 546, 212 Ill. Dec. 889, 892, 658 N.E.2d 371, 374 (1995), adopted the straightforward principle that "expert reconstruction testimony is proper, even where there is an eyewitness, if what the expert offers is 'knowledge and application of principles of science beyond the ken of the average juror.' (*See Plank,* 46 Ill. 2d at 471, 264 N.E.2d 12; *see also Miller v. Pillsbury Co.* (1965), 33 Ill. 2d 514, 516, 211 N.E.2d 733.) The principle contains no hidden subtleties. Whether to admit expert reconstruction testimony, eyewitness or not, turns on the usual concerns of whether expert opinion testimony is appropriate generally." In short, as with the introduction of expert witness testimony generally, expert reconstruction testimony is admissible when of assistance to the trier of fact in understanding the evidence or in determining a fact of consequence. *See* §701.1 supra. Accordingly, in *Zavala,* id at 546, 212 Ill. Dec. at 892, 658 N.E.2d at 374, the expert reconstruction testimony was found to have been properly admitted in spite of the presence of an eyewitness: "Caulfield's testimony was appropriate in this case. Caulfield possessed expertise in 'human factors engineering,' a study of the relationship of a man to machinery, including human motor coordination and reaction time. His opinion as to how the accident happened focused on human factors and the nature of the reamer's operation. The information imparted by Caulfield was certainly 'beyond the ken of the average juror' and was proper notwithstanding Zavala's own testimony."

Following *Zavala,* the Illinois Supreme Court was called upon in *Watkins v. Schmitt,* 172 Ill. 2d 193, 216 Ill. Dec. 822, 665 N.E.2d 1379 (1996), to determine whether a police officer was improperly barred from testifying as to his calculations of speed based upon the presence of 124 feet of skid marks in light of presence of three eyewitnesses to testify as to the speed of the cement truck. The court recognized that under *Zavala* the appropriate test is whether the testimony of the expert witness would assist the trier of fact in understanding the evidence or in determining a fact of consequences, i.e., beyond the ken of the average juror. Nevertheless, relying upon its decision in *Peterson v. Lou Bachrodt Chevrolet Co.,* 76 Ill. 2d 353, 29 Ill. Dec. 444, 392 N.E.2d 1 (1979), that the speed of an automobile is not a matter beyond the ken of the average juror, i.e., jurors can evaluate eyewitness testimony as to speed, the supreme court concluded that expert testimony of speed calculations should not be admitted. The court continued by holding that the police officer could testify on personal knowledge that the cement truck left 124 feet of skid marks, thus leaving the jury on its own to draw an inference as to speed. As correctly pointed out by Justice Heiple, specially concurring in part and dissenting in part, 172 Ill. 2d at 212, 216 Ill. Dec at 1388, 665 N.E.2d at 1389:

> We have here a matter of physics involving weight, mass, measured skid marks, weather, pavement friction and surface conditions; all of which lend themselves to scientific analysis from an expert relative to the speed of the cement truck. While eyewitnesses to a moving vehicle can and should be allowed to testify as to its speed, the reliability of such testimony is problematical. To deny the supplementation of such testimony with the testimony of a qualified scientific expert interferes with the truthseeking function of a trial.

The majority of the Illinois Supreme Court's unwillingness, for whatever unstated reason, to permit accident reconstruction testimony as to speed, to be introduced in the ordinary automobile accident case where eyewitnesses testify, has clearly muddied the clear waters of *Zavala* that the presence of eyewitnesses is not a relevant consideration. For further discussion *see* §702.5 supra.

Hopefully, *Watkins* will at a minimum be restricted to its facts, i.e., speed. This seems to have happened in *Morrison v. Reckamp*, 294 Ill. App. 3d 1015, 229 Ill. Dec. 351, 691 N.E.2d 824 (1998), where the interpretation of tire imprints and markings to determine whether a vehicle was skidding or sliding at the time the imprints were made was held to be expert testimony needed to explain scientific principles to a jury, to enable the jury to make factual determinations, citing *Watkins*. *Rinesmith v. Sterling*, 293 Ill. App. 3d 344, 227 Ill. Dec. 709, 687 N.E.2d 1191 (1997), is also encouraging in this regard: (1) trial court acted within its discretion in deeming expert testimony as to speed inadmissible; and (2) trial court erred in excluding expert testimony as to whether a normally skilled driver of a tractor trailer hauling heavy steel coils would have attempted to stop rather than swerve around a deer on Interstate Highway 57.

§704   Opinion on Ultimate Issue

§704.1   *An Overview*

An expert or a lay witness will not be precluded from testifying in the form of an opinion upon the ultimate issue on the ground that the testimony invades the province of the jury. *Zavala v. Powermatic, Inc.*, 167 Ill. 2d 542, 212 Ill. Dec. 889, 658 N.E.2d 371 (1995); *People v. Harris* 132 Ill. 2d 366, 138 Ill. Dec. 620, 547 N.E.2d 1241 (1989); *Merchants Natl. Bank of Aurora v. Elgin, J. & E.R.R.*, 49 Ill. 2d 118, 273 N.E.2d 809 (1971); *Miller v. Pillsbury Co.*, 33 Ill. 2d 514, 211 N.E.2d 733 (1965). Since the trier of fact is not required to accept the opinion of the witness, the evidence does not usurp the province of the jury. *Zavala v. Powermatic, Inc.*, supra; *Merchants National Bank of Aurora v. Elgin, J. & E.R.R.*, supra. *See, e.g., Clifford-Jacobs Forging Co. v. Industrial Commn.*, 19 Ill. 2d 236, 166 N.E.2d 582 (1960), expert witness may testify that the injury "did cause" the condition; *Johnson v. Ward*, 6 Ill. App. 3d 1015, 286 N.E.2d 637 (1972), expert testimony permitted that a bent automobile A-frame was the cause of an accident; *Kobrand Corp. v. Foremost Sales Promotions, Inc.*, 8 Ill. App. 3d 418, 291 N.E.2d 61 (1972), expert opinion admitted in a fair trade suit that plaintiff's gin was in competition with other brands; *Coleman v. Illinois Cent. R.R.*, 13 Ill. App. 3d 442, 300 N.E.2d 297 (1973), *rev'd on other grounds*, 59 Ill. 2d 13, 319 N.E.2d 228 (1974), expert testimony introduced that a railroad grade crossing was inadequately protected; *In re Marriage of Sieck*, 78 Ill. App. 3d 204, 33 Ill. Dec. 490, 396 N.E.2d 1214 (1979), psychologist permitted to testify in child custody proceeding that child would be better off with the father; *People v. Scott*, 256 Ill. App. 3d 844, 194 Ill. Dec. 959, 628 N.E.2d 456 (1993), police officer may testify that what he witnessed was a drug transaction; *Pyskaty v. Oyama*, 266 Ill. App. 3d 801, 204 Ill. Dec. 328, 641 N.E.2d 552 (1994), treating doctor should have been permitted to testify that she had used the word "neglected" in her report in referring to the natural history of a perirectal abscess left untreated; *Wade v. City of Chicago Heights*, 295 Ill. App. 3d 873, 230 Ill. Dec. 297, 693 N.E.2d 426 (1998), police officer may testify that failure to use warning signs and channelization devices proximately caused the accident. Any question concerning the propriety of a lay witness expressing an opinion on a ultimate issue as well was put to rest in *Freeding-Skokie Roll-Off Serv. v. Hamilton*, 108 Ill. 2d 217, 91 Ill. Dec. 178, 483 N.E.2d 524 (1985), citing Federal Rule of Evidence 704. *Accord People v. Harris* supra. *Contra City of Evanston v. City of Chicago*, 279 Ill. App. 3d 255, 215 Ill. Dec. 894, 664 N.E.2d 291 (1996) (a nonexpert witness may not testify on an ultimate fact; incorrectly decided). Similarly, in *People v. West*, 234 Ill. App. 3d 578, 174 Ill. Dec. 419, 598 N.E.2d 1356 (1992), *rev'd on other grounds, People v. West*, 158 Ill. 2d 155, 198 Ill. Dec. 393, 632 N.E.2d 1004

(1994), it was incorrectly held error for the victim's mother to explain what "wiggled his thing" meant on the basis of usurping the jury's function. An expert witness may testify in terms of probabilities or possibilities. *Buford by Buford v. Chicago Housing Auth.*, 131 Ill. App. 3d 235, 86 Ill. Dec. 926, 476 N.E.2d 427 (1985). *See also* §704.2 infra.

A lay witness or expert witness may express an opinion on an ultimate issue even when the ultimate issue falls generally within the common knowledge or experience of the jury. *See* §702.4 supra. An expert may also express an opinion on the ultimate issue based upon an examination of voluminous documents. *People v. Albanese*, 102 Ill. 2d 54, 79 Ill. Dec. 608, 464 N.E.2d 206 (1984). The sole test is whether the opinion of a lay or expert witness on the ultimate issue will assist the trier of fact to understand the evidence or to determine a fact in issue. *Perschall v. Metropolitan Life Ins. Co.*, 113 Ill. App. 3d 233, 68 Ill. Dec. 664, 446 N.E.2d 570 (1983) (citing Handbook); *Carlson v. City Construction Co.*, 239 Ill. App. 3d 211, 179 Ill. Dec. 568, 606 N.E.2d 400 (1992). The modern trend is firmly in accord. Wigmore dismissed the common law ultimate issue rule as "a mere bit of empty rhetoric," 3 Wigmore, Evidence, §1920 (Chadbourn rev. 1970). *See American College of Surgeons v. Lumbermens Mut. Cas. Co.*, 142 Ill. App. 3d 680, 96 Ill. Dec. 719, 491 N.E.2d 1179 (1986) (quoting Handbook). *See also* Federal Rule of Evidence 704, 65 F.R.D. 131, 152 (1975).

The fact that an opinion or inference is not objectionable because it embraces the ultimate issue does not mean, however, that all opinions embracing the ultimate issue must be admitted, for the criterion of helpfulness is applicable to both lay and expert witnesses alike. *See* §§701.8, 702.1, and 702.4 supra. Thus an opinion that plaintiff should win or an opinion that plaintiff was "negligent" would be rejected as not helpful to the trier of fact. *See, e.g., First Natl. Bank of Evanston v. Sousanes*, 96 Ill. App. 3d 1047, 52 Ill. Dec. 507, 422 N.E.2d 188 (1981), an opinion as to whether a lease is breached is not helpful to the jury; *McCormick v. McCormick*, 180 Ill. App. 3d 184, 129 Ill. Dec. 579, 536 N.E.2d 419

(1988), legal opinion that a person acted imprudently in his duties as a cotrustee is properly excluded as not helpful; *C.L. Maddox, Inc. v. Royal Ins. Co. of Am.*, 208 Ill. App. 3d 1042, 153 Ill. Dec. 791, 567 N.E.2d 749 (1991), an opinion that the insured was "entitled" to recover under the policy was improperly admitted; *Coyne v. Robert H. Anderson & Assocs.*, 215 Ill. App. 3d 104, 158 Ill. Dec. 750, 574 N.E.2d 863 (1991), expert testimony as to person's legal duties under a construction contract improperly admitted, as the jury was clearly able to make a decision on its own; *Mache v. Mache*, 218 Ill. App. 3d 1069, 161 Ill. Dec. 607, 578 N.E.2d 1253 (1991), an opinion that undue influence was exerted regarding the transfer of funds was a legal opinion not touching on matters beyond the understanding or comprehension of the court; *Swanigan v. Smith*, 294 Ill. App. 3d 263, 228 Ill. Dec. 578, 689 N.E.2d 637 (1998), an opinion that it is unreasonable to leave an 18-month-old child in a room unattended will not aid the jury in understanding. Moreover, prejudice, confusion, and misleading the jury are to be avoided. *See* §403.1 supra.

Opinions phrased in terms of inadequately explored legal criteria should similarly be excluded as not helpful and possibly misleading. Employing the illustration referred to in the Federal Advisory Committee's Note to Rule 704, 56 F.R.D. 83, 284 (1973), a question asked of an expert witness whether she believed the testator had the testamentary capacity to make a will presupposes that both the expert and the trier of fact are familiar with the elements comprising the legal standard. Thus it is preferable, both in terms of effectiveness and the avoidance of an objection, to ask instead whether the testator had the mental capacity to appreciate the nature and extent of his property and the natural objects of his bounty and to formulate a rational scheme of distribution. *Heideman v. Kelsey*, 7 Ill. 2d 601, 131 N.E.2d 531 (1956); *Powell v. Weld*, 410 Ill. 198, 101 N.E.2d 581 (1951). *See also Laff v. John O. Butler Co.*, 64 Ill. App. 603, 21 Ill. Dec. 314, 381 N.E.2d 423 (1978), proper to prohibit witness from offering opinion as to who was the "owner" of a formula for a dental product. However, once the elements of testamentary capacity are fully explored, the expert should be permitted to express an opinion in terms of testamentary capacity itself when helpful to jury understanding. *People v. Ward,* 61 Ill. 2d 559, 338 N.E.2d 171 (1975), permitting expert witness to rely upon and read to the jury a letter of another expert stating that defendant was "legally sane"; *Perschall v. Metropolitan Life Ins. Co.,* 113 Ill. App. 3d 233, 237, 68 Ill. Dec. 66; 446 N.E.2d 570 (1983), doctor properly permitted to testify that plaintiff was "totally disabled" on the basis that plaintiff possessed "the inability due to illness or injury to perform any gainful occupation for which [plaintiff] had education, training and experience" even though that was the definition of "total disability" stated in the insurance policy.

Of course, an expert witness may not be asked by a party to render an opinion as to questions that are matters of law for the court, *Johnson v. Equipment Specialists, Inc.,* 58 Ill. App. 3d 133, 15 Ill. Dec. 491, 373 N.E.2d 837 (1978); *Selby v. Danville Pepsi-Cola Bottling,* 169 Ill. App. 3d 427, 119 Ill. Dec. 941, 523 N.E.2d 697 (1988), including statutory interpretation, *Magee v. Huppin-Fleck,* 279 Ill. App. 3d 81, 215 Ill. Dec. 849, 664 N.E.2d 246 (1996), to advise the jury to decide the question in a particular way, to offer a speculative opinion upon an unsubstantiated basis, *see* §611.25 supra and §705.1 infra, or to testify as to whether another witness is telling the truth, *see* §611.25 supra. *People v. Pertz,* 242 Ill. App. 3d 864, 183 Ill. Dec. 77, 610 N.E.2d 1321 (1993). *Accord Town of the City of Bloomington v. Bloomington Township,* 233 Ill. App. 3d 724, 174 Ill. Dec. 516, 599 N.E.2d 62 (1992) (opinion on question of law improper unless foreign law).

Determining whether an opinion on the ultimate issue involves a pure question of law or unexplored legal criteria with respect to a mixed fact and law question on the one hand (and is therefore inadmissible) or conversely is of help to the trier of fact in understanding the evidence or in determining a fact in issue is sometimes extremely difficult. As to the question of unexplored legal criteria with respect to a mixed fact and law question, roughly speaking if the phrase used by the expert witness has a legal meaning that is obviously different than its common meaning and the common meaning is clearly being employed, the testimony is usually admitted. When the two meanings are not clearly different in the minds of the trier of fact, since the legal meaning will involve unexplored legal criteria, such as occurs with the terms *fraud, discriminate,* and *manipulate,* the testimony is usually found inadmissible. If, however, the criteria underlying the legal meaning are explored so that the legal meaning is now clear to the trier of fact, such as may occur with *testamentary capacity, unreasonably dangerous,* and *deviation from accepted medical practice,* then the opinion testimony of the expert once again is usually admitted. Finally, if the common meaning and the legal meaning are the same, the testimony is usually found admissible. *Chicago Title and Trust Co. v. Brescia,* 285 Ill. App. 3d 671, 221 Ill. Dec. 709, 676 N.E.2d 230 (1996), expert could testify who was "in charge of" the work for purposes of the Structural Work Act, but could not define the term "in charge of" since the term is one of common usage and understanding and that any attempt to provide the jury with a specific definition could only lead to confusion and error, citing *Larson v. Commonwealth Edison Co.,* 33 Ill. 2d 316, 211 N.E.2d 247 (1965). For an excellent discussion of the problem of expert witness testimony upon the ultimate issue, *see* Comment, The Admissibility of Expert Witness Testimony: Time to Take the Final Leap? 42 U. Miami L. Rev. 831 (1988). *See also United States v. Unruh,* 855 F.2d 1363 (9th Cir. 1988); *United States v. Scop,* 846 F.2d 135 (2d Cir. 1988); *United States v. Fogg,* 652 F.2d 551 (5th Cir. 1981).

§704.2   *Medical Testimony on Cause and Effect; Prognosis; Sexual Abuse*

Earlier cases involving expert testimony on medical cause and effect illustrate the difficulty previously experienced in making scientific or technical knowledge available to the trier in intelligible and useful form within the framework of the common law rule against opinions on ultimate issues. The result of the refining process of a number of decisions was that, if there was no dispute that injury was sustained, then the expert was permitted to give an opinion that a particular condition or death resulted therefrom, *People v. Fedora*, 393 Ill. 165, 65 N.E.2d 447 (1946), but if dispute existed as to the fact of injury or the manner of sustaining it, the expert was limited to testifying that the hypothetically stated facts were sufficient from a medical point of view to cause and bring about the condition, or that the condition might or could result from and be caused by the hypothetical facts, *Fellows-Kimbrough v. Chicago City Ry.*, 272 Ill. 71, 111 N.E. 499 (1916). In the latter situation, even though the expert in fact held very positive and definite views, he was limited to expressing them in a form so lacking in those qualities as to deprive his testimony of much of its force and even invite attack as speculative and conjectural.

A happy resolution was reached in *Clifford-Jacobs Forging Co. v. Industrial Commn.*, 19 Ill. 2d 236, 166 N.E.2d 582 (1960), wherein the court observed that the refinements developed had resulted "in an absence of a real determination of the issue" and suggested that the witness might give her opinion on the assumed facts in any form including "did" cause. Testimony of an expert in terms of "might" or "could," or "possibly" remains admissible. *People v. Sargeant*, 292 Ill. App. 3d 508, 226 Ill. Dec. 501, 685 N.E.2d 956 (1997); *Granberry by Granberry v. Carbondale*, 285 Ill. App. 3d 54, 220 Ill. Dec. 284, 672 N.E.2d 1296 (1996); *Damron v. Micor Industries, Ltd.*, 276 Ill. App. 3d 901, 213 Ill. Dec. 297, 658 N.E.2d 1318 (1995); *Hajian v. Holy Family Hospital*, 273 Ill. App. 3d 932, 210 Ill. Dec. 156, 652 N.E.2d 1132 (1995); *McKenzie v. S.K. Handtool Corp.*, 272 Ill. App. 3d 1, 208 Ill. Dec. 918, 650 N.E.2d 612 (1995). *See also Wilsonville v. SCA Servs., Inc.*, 86 Ill. 2d 1, 55 Ill. Dec. 499, 426 N.E.2d 824 (1981), expert may testify upon a reasonable degree of scientific certainty that it was "entirely possible" but not "certain" that specific waste material might explode. The shift in emphasis from invading the province of the trier to a determination of whether the opinion or inference will assist the trier of fact is now firmly established. *See* §§701.1, 702.1, and 702.4 supra.

Medical expert testimony as to causation need not be based on absolute certainty, *Norwick v. Union Starch & Refining Co.*, 1 Ill. App. 3d 92, 272 N.E.2d 674 (1971), *rev'd on other grounds*, 54 Ill. 2d 93, 296 N.E.2d 321 (1973), but only upon a reasonable degree of medical and scientific certainty. *Redmon v. Sooter*, 1 Ill. App. 3d 406, 274 N.E.2d 200 (1971); *Hajian v. Holy Family Hospital*, 273 Ill. App. 3d 932, 210 Ill. Dec. 156, 652 N.E.2d 1132 (1995). *See also Frankenthal v. Grand Trunk Western Ry.*, 120 Ill. App. 3d 409, 76 Ill. Dec. 130, 458 N.E.2d 530 (1983) (whether death caused by heart attack or by train crash). Adoption of Federal Rules of Evidence 703 and 705, see §703.1 supra and §705.1 infra, did not eliminate or alter the requirement that causation be testified to by the medical expert in terms of a reasonable degree of medical or scientific certainty. *Collins by Collins v. Straka*, 164 Ill. App. 3d 355, 115 Ill. Dec. 461, 517 N.E.2d 1147 (1987). It is proper for an expert, based upon a reasonable degree of medical certainty in the sense of general acceptance of the validity of the explanatory theory relied upon, *People v. Williams*, 209 Ill. App. 3d 709, 154 Ill. Dec. 388, 568 N.E.2d 388 (1991), to testify to an opinion in terms of percentages, *Wise v. St. Mary's Hosp.*, 64 Ill. App. 3d 587, 21 Ill. Dec. 482, 381 N.E.2d 809 (1978) (proper for medical expert to offer opinion that there was a 50 percent chance that plaintiff's leg would have required amputation regardless of care); in terms of "could or might," *Robinson v. Chicago Transit Auth.*, 69 Ill. App. 3d 1003, 26 Ill. Dec. 539, 388 N.E.2d 163 (1979) (opinion in such terms was not speculative); in terms of "possibility" or "probability," *Presswood v. Morris*, 70 Ill. App. 3d 513, 26 Ill. Dec. 843, 388 N.E.2d 844 (1979); *Sears Roebuck & Co. v. Industrial Commn.*, 79 Ill. 2d 59, 37 Ill. Dec. 341, 402 N.E.2d 231 (1980) (expert may testify in terms of probability as to cause of heart attack and such testimony is not objectionable as being inconclusive or speculative); *Plooy v. Paryani*, 275 Ill. App. 3d 1074, 212 Ill. Dec. 317, 657 N.E.2d 12 (1995) (medical expert may state causation as a probability if the expert can relate the statistic to plaintiff's medical condition); or in terms of "consistent with," *Dupree v. County of Cook*, 287 Ill. App. 3d 135, 222 Ill. Dec. 504, 677 N.E.2d 1303 (1997). Clearly, however, something more than mere guess, surmise, conjecture, or speculation is required. *See* §611.25 supra and §705.1 infra. *Simon v. Lumbermens Mut. Cas. Co.*, 53 Ill. App. 3d 380, 10 Ill. Dec. 749, 368 N.E.2d 344 (1977). *See also* §403.1 supra. As to the necessity of expert testimony on cause and effect, *see* §702.4 supra.

Similar treatment is afforded expert witness testimony as to the prognosis of future recovery from current medical problems. *Jeffers v. Weinger*, 132 Ill. App. 3d 877, 87 Ill. Dec. 742, 477 N.E.2d 1270 (1985) (medical expert may testify that the probability of future loss of plaintiff's foot is less than 1 percent); *Roman v. City of Chicago*, 134 Ill. App. 3d 14, 89 Ill. Dec. 58, 479 N.E.2d 1064 (1985), plaintiff's doctor properly permitted to testify that plaintiff's arthritis in her ankle will cause her to need surgery, probably within the next ten years.

Testimony on causation and prognosis in medical matters is admissible when offered by a qualified expert who is not a licensed physician. *See, e.g., Greenberg v. Michael Reese Hosp.*, 83 Ill. 2d 282, 47 Ill. Dec. 385, 415 N.E.2d 390 (1980) (proper for expert in radiation treatment to testify as to standard of care for X-ray treatment by a hospital); *Valiulis v. Scheffels*, 191 Ill. App. 3d 775, 138 Ill. Dec. 668, 547 N.E.2d 1289 (1989) (neuropsychologist was qualified to testify concerning multiple sclerosis); *Nicholas v. City of Alton*, 107 Ill. App. 3d 404, 63 Ill. Dec. 108, 437 N.E.2d 757 (1982) (witness with Ph.D. in toxicology and pharmacology qualified to render expert opinion on causal connection between decedent's tear-gas exposure and death); *Kinsey v. Kolber* 103 Ill. App. 3d 933, 59 Ill. Dec. 559, 431 N.E.2d 1316 (1982) (clinical psychologist qualified to testify that individual suffered brain damage in automobile accident).

"In a prosecution for an illegal sexual act perpetrated upon a victim, . . . testimony by an expert, qualified by the court relating to any recognized and accepted form of post-traumatic stress syndrome shall be admissible as evidence." 725 ILCS 5/115-7.2. *See People v. Douglas,* 183 Ill. App. 3d 241, 131 Ill. Dec. 779, 538 N.E.2d 1335 (1989); *People v. Roy,* 201 Ill. App. 3d 166, 146 Ill. Dec. 874, 558 N.E.2d 1208 (1990). The expert witness need not be a behavioral psychologist, psychiatrist, or physician if otherwise qualified. *People v. Petitt,* 245 Ill. App. 3d 132, 184 Ill. Dec. 766, 613 N.E.2d 1358 (1993) (clinical psychologist); *People v. Turner,* 241 Ill. App. 3d 236, 181 Ill. Dec. 655, 608 N.E.2d 906 (1993) (police officer); *People v. Wasson,* 211 Ill. App. 3d 264, 155 Ill. Dec. 710, 569 N.E.2d 1321 (1991) (therapist without an advanced degree). It is proper for an expert to testify that based upon traditional post-traumatic stress syndrome analysis the symptoms exhibited by a victim of rape or child sexual abuse are consistent with having been sexually abused. *People v. Wheeler,* 151 Ill. 2d 298, 176 Ill. Dec. 880, 602 N.E.2d 826 (1992) (rape trauma syndrome); *People v. Leggans,* 253 Ill. App. 3d 724, 193 Ill. Dec. 12, 625 N.E.2d 1133 (1993) (child sexual abuse syndrome). *See also People v. Land,* 178 Ill. App. 3d 251, 127 Ill. Dec. 439, 533 N.E.2d 57 (1988); *People v. Harp,* 193 Ill. App. 3d 838, 141 Ill. Dec. 117, 550 N.E.2d 1163 (1990). If an adequate basis is otherwise present, it is not required that the expert either treated or counseled the victim. *People v. Eiskant,* 253 Ill. App. 3d 773, 192 Ill. Dec. 863, 625 N.E.2d 1018 (1993). The fact that many of the victim's symptoms may be caused by something other than rape or child sexual abuse goes to weight not admissibility. *People v. Eiskant, id.* Child Sexual Abuse Accommodation Syndrome is also a recognized and accepted form of post-traumatic stress syndrome. *People v. Pollard,* 225 Ill. App. 3d 970, 168 Ill. Dec. 61, 589 N.E.2d 175 (1992); *People v. Wasson* supra. *Cf. People v. Nelson,* 203 Ill. App. 2d 1038, 149 Ill. Dec. 161, 561 N.E.2d 439 (1990), where, following an exhaustive discussion of the literature and the approach of other jurisdictions, the court held that the introduction of post-traumatic stress syndrome evidence is limited to rebuttal if the victim's credibility is first attacked—which appears to restrict such evidence to explaining aspects of the victim's behavior, such as initial denial, delayed reporting, recantation or inconsistencies, generally referred to as Child Sexual Abuse Accommodation Syndrome (i.e., opinion evidence that the child victim's overall symptoms are consistent with having been sexually abused appears precluded). *Nelson* was modified in *People v. Dempsey,* 242 Ill. App. 3d 568, 182 Ill. Dec. 784, 610 N.E.2d 208 (1993), permitting evidence of Child Sexual Abuse Accommodation Syndrome to be admitted also in the prosecution's case-in-chief, but only where the defendant, through cross-examination of the prosecution's witnesses, has first attacked the credibility of the victim by introducing evidence of initial denial, delayed reporting, recantation, inconsistencies, or other means of impeachment which may be explained in part by evidence of the Child Sexual Abuse Accommodation Syndrome. To the extent that *People v. Simpkins,* 297 Ill. App. 3d 668, 231 Ill. Dec. 748, 697 N.E.2d 302 (1998), holds that expert witness opinion evidence explaining recantation by a victim of sexual abuse, which is the most significant part of the Child Sexual Abuse Accommodation Syndrome, is an improper comment on the credibility of a witness and does not aid the jury in reaching its conclusion, it is incorrect and should not be followed. In fact, such evidence is more trustworthy and probative than "post-traumatic stress syndrome" evidence, the admissibility of which is provided for in 725 ILCS 5/115-7.2. *See* infra.

Expert testimony that either the complainant had been raped or the child sexually abused or that either victim's in-court testimony is truthful, however, should be disallowed if based upon post-traumatic stress syndrome. *See People v. Eiskant,* 253 Ill. App. 3d 773, 192 Ill. Dec. 863, 625 N.E.2d 1018 (1993). *Contra People v. Smith,* 236 Ill. App. 3d 35, 177 Ill. Dec. 492, 603 N.E.2d 562 (1992) (in bench trial not error to permit child psychologist to testify that child was telling the truth); *People v. Coleman,* 205 Ill. App. 3d 567, 150 Ill. Dec. 883, 563 N.E.2d 1010 (1990) (in jury trial expert opinion that child had been sexually abused permitted). *See also* §702.4 supra. On the other hand, expert testimony based upon a physical medical examination that the victim was sexually assaulted is admissible. *People v. Harris,* 132 Ill. 2d 366, 138 Ill. Dec. 620, 547 N.E.2d 1241 (1989). Expert testimony as to the typical characteristics of a child-abuse perpetrator is not admissible, *People v. Bradley,* 172 Ill. App. 3d 545, 122 Ill. Dec. 523, 526 N.E.2d 916 (1988), even when offered by an accused to establish that he does not meet a pedophile profile. *People v. Wheeler,* 216 Ill. App. 3d 609, 159 Ill. Dec. 266, 575 N.E.2d 1326 (1991); *People v. Edwards,* 224 Ill. App. 3d 1017, 167 Ill. Dec. 54, 586 N.E.2d 1326 (1992).

For an argument that expert testimony by a psychiatrist or psychologist as to consistency, truthfulness, or actuality of abuse has *not* been shown to be sufficiently trustworthy to be admitted at this time, *see* Askowitz & Graham, The Reliability of Expert Psychological Testimony in Child Sexual Abuse Prosecutions, 15 Cardozo L. Rev. 2027 (1994).

A properly qualified expert may testify for the defendant concerning the basis and pitfalls of post-traumatic stress syndrome evidence including testimony concerning psychological conditions other than sexual abuse that exhibit identical symptoms and the effect of interview techniques employed upon the evaluation of the child's allegations, *People v. Petitt,* 245 Ill. App. 3d 132, 184 Ill. Dec. 766, 613 N.E.2d 1358 (1993). Moreover, similar testimony is admissible on behalf of the accused with respect to evaluating evidence of sexual abuse of other children introduced by the prosecution, *see* §404.5 supra. *People v. Petitt* supra.

Although the court may not order a witness who is a victim of an alleged sex offense to submit to or undergo either a psychiatric or psychological examination, 725 ILCS 5/115-7.1, nevertheless, unless the victim consents to an examination by an expert chosen by the defendant, the prosecution may not introduce testimony from an examining expert that the victim of an alleged sexual assault suffers from a "recognized and accepted form of post-traumatic stress syndrome." *People v. Wheeler,* 151 Ill. 2d 298, 176 Ill. Dec. 880, 602 N.E.2d 826 (1992).

§704.3   *Mental Capacity*

As might be expected, the restrictive common law opinion rule caused serious impairment of communications between witness and trier, particularly in the testamentary cases. Realistic recognition of the limited observational and descriptive powers of lay witnesses resulted in permitting them to describe a testator as "funny," "queer," or "strange," *American Bible Soc. v. Price,* 115 Ill. 623, 5 N.E. 126 (1886), although not all the cases reached so sensible a result, *e.g., Bundy v. West,* 297 Ill. 238, 130 N.E. 709 (1921), sustaining striking of testimony that testator was as bright as the common run of men. The ultimate issue rule resulted in the exclusion of opinions, whether expert or lay, directed to capacity to make a will, *Wetzel v. Firebaugh,* 251 Ill. 190, 95 N.E. 1085 (1911), even though testamentary capacity was broken down into its elements and a separate question put as to each. *Baddeley v. Watkins,* 293 Ill. 394, 127 N.E. 725 (1920). The semantic shift to the vaguer abstraction of soundness of mind was sufficient, however, to satisfy the amenities, and opinions phrased in the latter term were allowable. *Simpson v. Anderson,* 305 Ill. 172, 137 N.E. 88 (1922).

Here again, as with medical testimony on cause and effect, §704.2 supra, a shift occurred away from undue concern over invading the province of the jury in the direction of making useful opinions available to the trier of fact. Thus a witness may be asked for an opinion in a separate question as to each element to be considered in determining testamentary capacity. *Heideman v. Kelsey,* 7 Ill. 2d 601, 131 N.E.2d 531 (1956); *Powell v. Weld,* 410 Ill. 198, 101 N.E.2d 581 (1951); *Trojcak v. Hafliger,* 7 Ill. App. 3d 495, 288 N.E.2d 82 (1972). *See also* Illinois Pattern Jury Instruction — Civil 200.05 (1992). This approach avoids the initial expression on the basis of inadequately explored legal criteria of an opinion as to testamentary capacity itself. *See* §704.1 supra.

Mental condition and capacity is a proper subject for both expert and lay witness opinion testimony. The psychiatric expert witness may give an opinion based upon her own observations or upon the observations, data, and opinions of others. *See* §703.1 supra. The lay witness, too, may give his opinion, although it can be based only upon his own observations, which he is required first to state in sufficient detail to show knowledge of the mental condition of the person in question (§701.1 supra). *People v. Wright,* 111 Ill. 2d 128, 95 Ill. Dec. 787, 490 N.E.2d 640 (1985); *Walker v. Struthers,* 273 Ill. 387, 112 N.E. 961 (1916); *Estate of Veronico,* 78 Ill. App. 3d 379, 33 Ill. Dec. 371, 396 N.E.2d 1095 (1979); *People v. Robinson,* 102 Ill. App. 3d 884, 58 Ill. Dec. 23, 429 N.E.2d 1356 (1981); *People v. Stack,* 244 Ill. App. 3d 166, 184 Ill. Dec. 583, 613 N.E.2d 1175 (1993) (citing Handbook); *In re Estate of Roeseler,* 287 Ill. App. 3d 1003, 223 Ill. Dec. 208, 679 N.E.2d 393 (1997). *See also People v. Chavez,* 265 Ill. App. 3d 451, 201 Ill. Dec. 880, 637 N.E.2d 469 (1994) (witness failed to relate any facts or circumstances on which to base lay witness opinion that the defendant was mentally slow). Observations that are too remote in time to the moment in question may not be relied on. *People v. Lowitzki,* 285 Ill. App. 3d 770, 221 Ill. Dec. 66, 674 N.E.2d 859 (1996). However, an attesting witness to a will may express his opinion without the laying of a foundation therefor. *Both v. Nelson,* 31 Ill. 2d 511, 202 N.E.2d 494 (1964).

Clearly, an opinion as to testamentary capacity, absent an initial proper separation into the elements of testamentary capacity, is impermissible on the grounds of inadequately explored legal criteria. On the other hand, an opinion as to soundness of mind or memory, *Powell v. Weld* supra, or as to sanity or insanity, *Garrus v. Davis,* 234 Ill. 326, 84 N.E. 924 (1908); *People v. Dunigan,* 96 Ill. App. 3d 799, 52 Ill. Dec. 247, 421 N.E.2d 1319 (1981); *People v. Chatman,* 145 Ill. App. 3d 648, 99 Ill. Dec. 332, 495 N.E.2d 1067 (1986); *People v. Baker,* 253 Ill. App. 3d 15, 192 Ill. Dec. 564, 625 N.E.2d 719 (1993), has been held permissible once a proper foundation has been laid. Considering that expression of an opinion as to soundness of mind or sanity closely resembles if it does not equate to an expression of an opinion as to testamentary capacity, it would certainly seem that an expression of an opinion directly as to testamentary capacity, if (1) coupled with adequate foundation exploring the legal criteria and (2) helpful to the trier of fact, should also be permitted. *See also* §704.1 supra.

A similar approach to other areas of mental capacity is indicated.

§704.4 Negligence and Products Liability

With respect to opinions by lay and expert witnesses relating to the issue of negligence, confusion has existed in the cases with respect to the propriety of a witness employing terms such as "safe," "reasonable," "adequate," or "good practice." *See, e.g., Gundlach v. Schott,* 192 Ill. 509, 61 N.E. 332 (1901), proper to give opinion that operating machine with twisted belt was not reasonably safe for operator; *Merchants Natl. Bank of Aurora v. Elgin, J. & E.R.R.,* 49 Ill. 2d 118, 273 N.E.2d 809 (1971), expert witness permitted to testify that railroad crossing was very inadequately protected; *Borowski v. Von Solbrig,* 60 Ill. 2d 418, 328 N.E.2d 301 (1975), expert witness in medical malpractice action permitted to testify as to whether defendant's conduct met accepted standards of medical care; *Tripp v. Bureau Serv. Co.,* 62 Ill. App. 3d 998, 19 Ill. Dec. 660, 397 N.E.2d 324 (1978), witness expert as a railroad fireman permitted to testify that plaintiff could not have done anything to prevent accident; *Pozzi v. McGee Associates, Inc.,* 236 Ill. App. 3d 390, 177 Ill. Dec. 130, 602 N.E.2d 1302 (1992), expert witness permitted to opine as to OSHA regulation violations to establish standard of care in Structural Work Act case. *Contra Keefe v. Armour & Co.,* 258 Ill. 28, 101 N.E. 252 (1913), error to admit testimony that method of testing tank was not reasonably safe; *Wawryszyn v. Illinois Cent. R.R.,* 10 Ill. App. 2d 394, 135 N.E.2d 154 (1956), improper but not reversible error to admit testimony that method of loading heavy freight on dolly was not good practice; *Prill v. Illinois State Motor Serv.,* 16 Ill. App. 2d 202, 147

N.E.2d 681 (1958), error to admit testimony that safer practice was for mechanic to drive vehicle into garage. These latter cases may be accounted for by the earlier bar against opinions upon the ultimate issue. *See* §704.1 supra. *See also Allen v. Yancy,* 57 Ill. App. 2d 50, 206 N.E.2d 452 (1965), opinion that party not responsible is as much a conclusion on the ultimate issue as statement that party is not negligent.

With respect to lay witnesses' testimony, triers of fact are able generally to evaluate negligence situations on the basis of their own experience, observation, and learning. *See* §203.5 supra. In such cases, an opinion phrased in terms of negligence itself, involving not only the formulation of a legal standard by the witness, but also one substantially immune to exploration, seems calculated to confuse or mislead rather than assist the trier (§403.1 supra). *See Freeding-Skokie Roll-Off Serv. v. Hamilton,* 108 Ill. 2d 217, 91 Ill. Dec. 178, 483 N.E.2d 524 (1985), improper for a lay witness to testify to his impression that the driver of the car did not see the truck. Hence phrasing in more factual terms is desirable. Expressions such as "safe," "dangerous," "reasonable," and "good practice" appear appropriate, in that, where based on the perception of the witness, such terms do tend to assist the trier of fact in understanding the testimony of the witness.

Some negligence cases, however, involve technical considerations beyond the reach of the ordinary person and require a framework of special knowledge for proper evaluation of the facts. The question then arises as to what form an expert opinion may properly assume. In such cases, if a proper foundation is laid presenting to the trier of fact the specialized knowledge possessed by the expert witness, consistent with opinions as to testamentary capacity, it seems proper that the expert witness be permitted then to testify as to his opinion in terms of negligence if such an opinion will itself be of assistance to the trier of fact, rather than be limited to euphemisms such as good practice, accepted standards of care, and the like. *Williams v. Morris,* 237 Ill. 254, 86 N.E. 729 (1908), proper to give opinion that method used to raise floor bearing heavy weight was negligent and careless;

McCallister v. del Castillo, 18 Ill. App. 3d 1041, 310 N.E.2d 474 (1974), proper in medical malpractice action for expert to testify that what had occurred constituted negligence; *Chiero v. Chicago Osteopathic Hosp.,* 74 Ill. App. 3d 166, 29 Ill. Dec. 646, 392 N.E.2d 203 (1979), proper in medical malpractice action for expert to testify that no professional negligence was involved; *Baylie v. Swift & Co.,* 283 Ill. App. 3d 421, 219 Ill. Dec. 94, 670 N.E.2d 772 (1996), proper for expert to opine that defendant should have warned as to the danger of calcium stearate. As to medical malpractice cases, *see generally Nika v. Danz,* 199 Ill. App. 3d 296, 145 Ill. Dec. 255, 556 N.E.2d 873 (1990).

Similarly, in a products liability action, it has been held proper for an expert witness to testify that the product, a forage blower, was unreasonably dangerous, *Kerns v. Engelke,* 54 Ill. App. 3d 323, 12 Ill. Dec. 270, 369 N.E.2d 1284 (1977), and that failure to equip a grinding machine with a guard resulted in an unreasonably dangerous condition on the machine, *Crump v. Universal Safety Equip. Co.,* 79 Ill. App. 3d 202, 34 Ill. Dec. 513, 398 N.E.2d 188 (1979). *See Baltus v. Weaver Division of Kiddie & Co.,* 199 Ill. App. 3d 821, 145 Ill. Dec. 810, 557 N.E.2d 580 (1990), detailing when expert witness testimony is required to establish that a product is unreasonably dangerous. *See also Anderson v. Chesapeake & Ohio Ry.,* 147 Ill. App. 3d 960, 101 Ill. Dec. 262, 498 N.E.2d 586 (1986) (proper in a railroad crossing case for an expert to testify that a crossing is "ultrahazardous").

Dealing with the problem in terms of availability of better devices or methods is treated in §401.13 supra; usage, practice, and standards are discussed in §406.5 supra.

With respect to the Structural Work Act, *see* §704.2 supra.

§704.5 Characterization of Conversations and Documents

While verbatim accuracy by a witness who heard a conversation or is familiar with a document as to which parol evidence is admissible is not required, *see* §602.3 supra, and

§1004.2 infra, a conclusory statement as to the effect of the language, is, however, objectionable. *Helm v. Cantrell,* 59 Ill. 524 (1871), defendant admitted liability; *Bragg v. Geddes,* 93 Ill. 39 (1879), from what was said, there was a partnership; *Anderson v. Augustana College,* 300 Ill. 72, 132 N.E. 826 (1921), letter contained agreement to devise property. Similarly, testimony as to the meaning of another witness's testimony is inadmissible. *People v. Holveck,* 141 Ill. 2d 84, 152 Ill. Dec. 237, 565 N.E.2d 919 (1990).

§705   Examination of Expert Witnesses

§705.1   *Direct Examination of Experts: Disclosure of Basis; Hypothetical Questions*

The Illinois Supreme Court in *Wilson v. Clark,* 84 Ill. 2d 186, 49 Ill. Dec. 308, 417 N.E.2d 1322 (1981), adopted without reservation Rule 705 of the Federal Rules of Evidence and thereby drastically altered the common law with respect to disclosure requirements regarding the basis of expert witness testimony and the necessity to employ a hypothetical question when the basis of the expert's opinion includes matters not within the expert's personal knowledge.

Prior to *Wilson v. Clark* supra, an expert witness could, of course, state an opinion upon facts personally known to her, thus supplying both the factual basis and the scientific or technical information required to evaluate it. *Louisville, New Albany & Chicago Ry. v. Shires,* 108 Ill. 617 (1884). However, before offering the opinion, the expert was required to testify as to those facts personally known to her upon which her opinion was based. Prior disclosure of the basis of the expert's opinion was required as a safeguard of reliability. *People v. Driver,* 62 Ill. App. 3d 847, 20 Ill. Dec. 7, 379 N.E.2d 840 (1978); *People v. O'Neal,* 118 Ill. App. 2d 116, 254 N.E.2d 559 (1969). With respect to *voir dire* of the expert as to the basis, *see* §702.2 supra. As part of this disclosure, it was proper for the expert to state that she relied upon findings contained in authoritative literature. *Lawson v. G.D. Searle & Co.,* 64 Ill. 2d 543, 1 Ill. Dec. 497, 356 N.E.2d 779 (1976); *Rivera v. Rockford Mach. & Tool Co.,* 1 Ill. App. 3d 641, 274 N.E.2d 828 (1971). *See generally* the excellent opinion of Justice Chapman dissenting in *Schuchman v. Stackable,* 198 Ill. App. 3d 209, 144 Ill. Dec. 493, 555 N.E.2d 1012 (1990) (expert medical witness may read to the jury from articles reasonably relied upon; majority opinion declaring such practice improper is clearly incorrect). *See also* §703.1 supra, with respect generally to facts, data, or opinions reasonably relied upon in the field. Authoritative literature is admitted as forming part of the basis of the expert's testimony; authoritative literature is not admissible as substantive evidence because of the absence of a learned treatise hearsay exception. *See Costa v. Dresser Industries, Inc.,* 268 Ill. App. 3d 1, 205 Ill. Dec. 33, 642 N.E.2d 898 (1994). *See also* §703.1 supra. *Compare* Federal Rule of Evidence 803(18).

Where the expert's basis included facts not personally known, if the evidence of such facts admitted at trial was not in conflict, an expert who had heard it could be asked for an opinion based thereon. Thus, where the expert's opinion was based solely upon exhibits that had been admitted into evidence and other facts as to which the witness had personal knowledge, a hypothetical question was not required. *Peterson v. Lou Bachrodt Chevrolet Co.,* 76 Ill. 2d 353, 29 Ill. Dec. 444, 392 N.E.2d 1 (1979), hypothetical question not required to expert who relied solely upon brake shoe from braking system and two photographs of system, both admitted into evidence. However, this practice was improper if the evidence as to any fact relied upon was in conflict, since the expert would then be required to weigh the evidence, which is not his function. *Maton Bros. v. Central Illinois P.S. Co.,* 356 Ill. 584, 191 N.E. 321 (1934).

Where all or some of the facts not personally known to the expert were in conflict, the required procedure was to give an opinion to a hypothetical question containing an assumed state of facts. *Decatur v. Fisher,* 63 Ill. 241 (1872). Whether to permit an expert witness to answer a hypothetical question based upon facts that have not yet been adduced in evidence upon a representation of counsel that such facts will be produced and thus connected up rests within the sound discretion of the trial court. *Leonardi v. Loyola University of Chicago,* 168 Ill. 2d 83, 212 Ill. Dec. 968, 658 N.E.2d 450 (1995). Evidence so admitted upon an assurance that it will later be connected up will be excluded upon failure to establish the connection. *Coriell v. Industrial Commission,* 83 Ill. 2d 105, 46 Ill. Dec. 166, 413 N.E.2d 1279 (1980); *Leonardi v. Loyola University of Chicago,* supra; *Granberry by Granberry v. Carbondale,* 285 Ill. App. 3d 54, 220 Ill. Dec. 284, 672 N.E.2d 1296 (1996). The practice of permitting an expert witness to answer a hypothetical question based upon facts that had not yet been adduced in evidence upon a representation of counsel that they subsequently would be produced, while within the discretion of the court, was asserted to be "not desirable" and strongly to be discouraged. *Jamison v. Lambke,* 21 Ill. App. 3d 629, 316 N.E.2d 93 (1974); *Gibson v. Healy Bros. & Co.,* 109 Ill. App. 3d 342, 248 N.E.2d 771 (1969).

A hypothetical question of an assumed state of facts had to include those basic facts, data, and opinions not in dispute and the version of disputed ones favorable to the proponent of the question, *Granberry by Granberry v. Carbondale,* 285 Ill. App. 3d 54, 220 Ill. Dec. 284, 672 N.E.2d 1296 (1996); *Kane v. Northwest Special Recreation Assn.,* 155 Ill. App. 3d 624, 108 Ill. Dec. 96, 508 N.E.2d 257 (1987), which would reasonably appear to have a bearing upon the opinion. *Sanitary Dist. of Chicago v. Industrial Commn.,* 343 Ill. 236, 175 N.E. 372 (1931); *Lange v. Coca-Cola Bottling Co. of Chicago,* 105 Ill. App. 2d 99, 245 N.E.2d 35, *rev'd on other grounds,* 44 Ill. 2d 73, 254 N.E.2d 467 (1969). There must have been, of course, an evidentiary basis, (which now includes the concept of reasonable reliance, §703.1 supra), for each element included in the hypothetical question. *Leonardi v. Loyola University of Chicago,* 168 Ill. 2d 83, 212 Ill. Dec. 968, 658 N.E.2d 450 (1995);

Gus T. Handage & Son Painting Co. v. Industrial Commn., 33 Ill. 2d 201, 210 N.E.2d 448 (1965); *Dodson v. Shaw*, 113 Ill. App. 3d 1063, 69 Ill. Dec. 728, 448 N.E.2d 188 (1983); *Carter v. Johnson*, 247 Ill. App. 3d 291, 187 Ill. Dec. 52, 617 N.E.2d 260 (1993). *Accord Buford by Buford v. Chicago Housing Auth.*, 131 Ill. App. 3d 235, 86 Ill. Dec. 926, 476 N.E.2d 427 (1985) (facts assumed must be within the realm of direct or circumstantial evidence supportable by the facts or reasonable inferences that can be drawn therefrom); *Coriell v. Industrial Commn.*, 83 Ill. 2d 105, 46 Ill. Dec. 166, 413 N.E.2d 1279 (1980), proponent of hypothetical question may include only the elements of his theory that appear in the evidence. While there was no requirement that all pertinent facts, data, or opinions in the case be included in the hypothetical, *Wirth v. Industrial Commn.*, 57 Ill. 2d 475, 312 N.E.2d 593 (1974); *Johns-Manville Prods. v. Industrial Commn.*, 78 Ill. 2d 171, 35 Ill. Dec. 540, 399 N.E.2d 606 (1979), the court possessed discretion to require that additional facts be added to the original question if it deemed such facts essential to providing an adequate basis for a helpful answer. *Spilotro v. Hugi*, 93 Ill. App. 3d 837, 49 Ill. Dec. 239, 417 N.E.2d 1066 (1981). *See also* McCormick Evidence §14 (4th ed. 1992). In the alternative, the court in its discretion could leave it to counsel opposing the examination to employ a hypothetical question supplying the omitted facts on cross-examination and ask the expert whether his opinion would be modified by them. *Leonardi v. Loyola University of Chicago*, 168 Ill. 2d 83, 212 Ill. Dec. 968, 658 N.E.2d 450 (1995); *Wirth v. Industrial Commn.* supra; *Kane v. Northwest Special Recreation Assn.*, 155 Ill. App. 3d 624, 108 Ill. Dec. 96, 508 N.E.2d 257 (1987); *Hebeler v. Holland Co.*, 207 Ill. App. 3d 391, 152 Ill. Dec. 353, 565 N.E.2d 1035 (1991); *People v. Jackson*, 243 Ill. App. 3d 1026, 184 Ill. Dec. 893, 614 N.E.2d 94 (1993). *See also* §705.2 infra. Following a recitation of assumed facts, the form of the hypothetical question posed to the expert was usually similar to that approved in *Northern Trust Co. v. Skokie Valley Community Hosp.*, 81 Ill. App. 3d 1110, 1120-1121, 37 Ill. Dec. 153, 401 N.E.2d 1246 (1980):

"Doctor, assuming those facts, I would ask you whether or not you have an opinion based upon a reasonable degree of medical and surgical certainty whether or not the resuscitative efforts provided to the infant by the obstetrician were in conformance with the accepted standard of care to be expected of a reasonably competent obstetrician practicing in a community hospital in the Chicago-land area in 1967?"

An objection based on failure to include necessary facts but failing to specify them was insufficient. *Goldberg v. Capitol Freight Lines,* 382 Ill. 283, 47 N.E.2d 67 (1943). The same was true of an objection based on inclusion of facts not in evidence but failing to specify them, *Smith v. Illinois Valley Ice Cream Co.,* 20 Ill. App. 2d 312, 156 N.E.2d 361 (1959), as well as an objection raising grounds different from those asserted on appeal, *Johns-Manville Prods. v. Industrial Commn.,* 78 Ill. 2d 171, 35 Ill. Dec. 540, 399 N.E.2d 606 (1979). If the court determined upon objection that the expert depended upon facts neither admitted at trial nor reasonably relied upon by an expert in the field, the expert's opinion was stricken. *See Matter of Estate of Stuhlfauth,* 88 Ill. App. 3d 974, 43 Ill. Dec. 930, 410 N.E.2d 1063 (1980).

The hypothetical question had been under constant attack for a long time prior to the Illinois Supreme Court's decision in *Wilson v. Clark* infra. 2 Wigmore, Evidence §686 (Chadbourn rev. 1979) states, "the hypothetical question, misused by the clumsy and abused by the clever, has in practice led to intolerable obstruction of truth." It had been attacked as encouraging partisan bias, affording an opportunity for summing up in the middle of the case, and being complex and time-consuming. Ladd, Expert Testimony, 5 Vand. L. Rev. 414, 426-427 (1952). *Borowski v. Von Solbrig,* 60 Ill. 2d 418, 328 N.E.2d 301 (1975), hypothetical question to plaintiff doctor ran 72 pages, objections and rulings 27 pages. In response to such attacks, the Illinois Supreme Court abandoned the hypothetical question requirement.

Wilson v. Clark, 84 Ill. 2d 186, 49 Ill. Dec. 308, 417 N.E.2d

1332 (1981), declared Rule 705 of the Federal Rules of Evidence applicable in Illinois. Federal Rule 705 provides:

Disclosure of Facts or Data Underlying Expert Opinion

The expert may testify in terms of opinion or inference and give reasons therefor without prior disclosure of the underlying facts or data, unless the court requires otherwise. The expert may in any event be required to disclose the underlying facts or data on cross-examination.

The Federal Advisory Committee's Note to Federal Rule 705, 56 F.R.D. 183, 285-286 (1973), states as follows:

The hypothetical question has been the target of a great deal of criticism as encouraging partisan bias, affording an opportunity for summing up in the middle of the case, and as complex and time consuming. Ladd, Expert Testimony, 5 Vand. L. Rev. 414, 426-427 (1952). While the rule allows counsel to make disclosure of the underlying facts or data as a preliminary to the giving of an expert opinion, if he chooses, the instances in which he is required to do so are reduced. This is true whether the expert bases his opinion on data furnished him at second-hand or observed by him at firsthand.

The elimination of the requirement of preliminary disclosure at the trial of underlying facts or data has a long background of support. In 1937 the Commissioners on Uniform State Laws incorporated a provision to this effect in their Model Expert Testimony Act, which furnished the basis for Uniform Rules 57 and 58. Rule 4515, N.Y. CPLR (McKinney 1963), provides:

Unless the court orders otherwise, questions calling for the opinion of an expert witness need not be hypothetical in form, and the witness may state his opinion and reasons without first specifying the data upon which it is based. Upon cross-examination, he may be required to specify the data. . . .

See also California Evidence Code § 802; Kansas Code of Civil Procedure §§ 60-456, 60-457; New Jersey Evidence Rules 57, 58.

If the objection is made that leaving it to the cross-examiner to bring out the supporting data is essentially unfair, the answer is that he is under no compulsion to bring out any facts or data except those unfavorable to the opinion. The answer assumes that the cross-examiner has the advance knowledge which is essential for effective cross-examination. This advance knowledge has been afforded, though imperfectly, by the traditional foundation requirement. Rule 26(b)(4) of the Rules of Civil Procedure, as revised, provides for substantial discovery in this area, obviating in large measure the obstacles which have been raised in some instances to discovery of findings, underlying data, and even the identity of the experts. Friedenthal, Discovery and Use of an Adverse Party's Expert Information, 14 Stan. L. Rev. 455 (1962).

These safeguards are reinforced by the discretionary power of the judge to require preliminary disclosure in any event.

The necessity of a hypothetical question in eliciting testimony of an expert witness not possessing personal knowledge of all material facts is thus eliminated. In its place, Federal Rule 705 permits the opinion or inference of an expert to be given in court without prior disclosure of the underlying facts, data, or opinions unless the court requires otherwise. *People v. Whitefield,* 140 Ill. App. 3d 433, 94 Ill. Dec. 840, 488 N.E.2d 1087 (1986); *People v. Angelly,* 167 Ill. App. 3d 477, 118 Ill. Dec. 238, 521 N.E.2d 306 (1988); *Loitz v. Remington Arms Co.,* 177 Ill. App. 3d 1034, 127 Ill. Dec. 262, 532 N.E.2d 1091 (1988); *Patel v. Brown Machine Co.,* 264 Ill. App. 3d 1039, 201 Ill. Dec. 902, 637 N.E.2d 491 (1994). A bare bones foundation may well satisfy the court under Federal Rule 705.

For example, one can envision the following dialogue immediately after the expert had been qualified as an orthopedic surgeon:

Q. Doctor, do you have an opinion based upon a reasonable degree of medical certainty as to the extent of permanent disability suffered by the plaintiff as a result of this automobile accident?

A. Yes.

Q. What is your opinion?

A. She is totally permanently disabled.

Q. Thank you, doctor, that is all.

[Reprinted from Hearings on Proposed Rules of Evidence Before the Special Subcomm. on Crim. Justice of the House Comm. on the Judiciary, 93d Cong., 1st Sess. 355-356 (Supp. 1973).]

Of course, a full presentation developing in detail the expert witness's qualifications, basis, opinions and reasoning is permissible upon direct examination. Facts, data, and opinions contained in learned treatises established as a reliable authority are included. *In re Marriage of Gunn,* 233 Ill. App. 3d 165, 174 Ill. Dec. 381, 598 N.E.2d 1013 (1992). Facts, data, and opinions not themselves admitted into evidence may be included in such disclosure if the requirements of Federal Rule 703 are satisfied. *Poelker v. Warrensburg Latham School District,* 251 Ill. App. 3d 270, 190 Ill. Dec. 487, 621 N.E.2d 940 (1993); *Henry v. Brenner,* 138 Ill. App. 3d 609, 93 Ill. Dec. 401, 486 N.E.2d 934 (1985); *Mielke v. Condell Memorial Hosp.,* 124 Ill. App. 3d 42, 79 Ill. Dec. 78, 463 N.E.2d 216 (1984); *People v. Rhoades,* 73 Ill. App. 3d 288, 29 Ill. Dec. 249, 391 N.E.2d 512 (1979). The necessity of making the expert appear to the jury to be extremely well qualified, with the opinion of the expert understandable and persuasive, almost invariably results in counsel posing additional questions that further qualify the expert and elicit her basis before requesting her opinion. This is not to say, however, that counsel may not have his expert witness hold back some information to unleash on unsuspecting opposing counsel during cross-examination. Facts, data, and opinions forming the basis of an expert's opinion, not disclosed on direct examination, may be developed on cross-examination. *Lebrecht v. Tuli,* 130 Ill. App. 3d 457, 85 Ill. Dec. 517, 473 N.E.2d 1322 (1985); *People v. Whitefield,* 140 Ill. App. 3d 433, 94 Ill. Dec. 840, 488 N.E.2d 1087 (1986); *People v. Torry,* 212 Ill. App. 3d 759, 156 Ill. Dec. 847, 571 N.E.2d 827 (1991). If the testimony of the witness or other evidence reveals that the expert basis for her opinion is inadequate, the expert's opinion may be stricken as based upon conjecture or speculation. *See Zavala v. Powermatic, Inc.,* 167 Ill. 2d 542, 212 Ill. Dec. 889, 658 N.E.2d 371 (1995); *Dyback v. Weber,* 14 Ill. 2d 232, 102 Ill. Dec. 386, 500 N.E.2d 8 (1986); *Aguilera v. Mount Sinai Hospital Medical Center,* 293 Ill. App. 3d 967, 229 Ill. Dec. 65, 691 N.E.2d 1 (1998); *Murphy v. General Motors Corp.,* 285 Ill. App. 3d 278, 219 Ill. Dec. 863, 672 N.E.2d 371 (1996); *Tierney v. Community Memorial General Hospital,* 268 Ill. App. 3d 1050, 206 Ill. Dec. 279, 645 N.E.2d 284 (1994). *Accord Damron v. Micor Distributing, Ltd.,* 276 Ill. App. 3d 901, 213 Ill. Dec. 297, 658 N.E.2d 1318 (1995) (when experts fail to take into consideration their party's actions, base their opinions on facts that are not in evidence, ignore significant factors, or base their opinions on what might have happened, the court will hold that the experts' opinions are based on mere speculation and conjecture); *People v. Jakupcak,* 275 Ill. App. 3d 830, 212 Ill. Dec. 119, 656 N.E.2d 442 (1995) (expert improperly classified collision as in line when in fact it was angular). *See also* §611.25 supra. If the cross-examiner believes that the witness lacks either sufficient qualifications or sufficient foundation for her opinion, the court in its discretion may permit a *voir dire* examination into such matters. In this manner, if the witness is not qualified or a sufficient basis is lacking, the witness's testimony may be stricken without the trier of fact being exposed to the inadmissible opinion of the witness.

Federal Rule 705 adopted in *Wilson v. Clark* places a heavy burden on the cross-examiner who must be sufficiently informed about the subject matter to be able to bring out the underlying facts in a manner exposing any weakness inherent in the expert's opinion. The discovery rules in civil cases and to a lesser degree in criminal cases serve to provide the cross-examiner with advance knowledge of the nature of the expert's opinion and its bases. In addition, the cross-examiner may also have the assistance of his own expert in the courtroom. *See* §615.1 supra. Where the cross-examiner has for one reason or another not been provided with the necessary information to conduct an effective cross-examination, a situation most likely to occur in criminal cases, the court may exercise its discretion under Federal Rule 705 and require that a full foundation be established on direct examination.

If the basis of an expert's opinion includes so many varying or uncertain factors that she is required to guess or surmise in order to reach an opinion, the expert's opinion is objectionable as speculation or conjecture. *Dyback v. Weber,* 114 Ill. 2d 232, 102 Ill. Dec. 386, 500 N.E.2d 8 (1986); *Department of Pub. Works v. Finks,* 10 Ill. 2d 15, 139 N.E.2d 267 (1956); *Marshall v. Osborn,* 213 Ill. App. 3d 134, 156 Ill. Dec. 708, 571 N.E.2d 492 (1991); *Rodrian v. Seiber,* 194 Ill. App. 3d 504, 141 Ill. Dec. 585, 551 N.E.2d 772 (1990). *See also Masinelli v. McDonald,* 251 Ill. App. 3d 398, 190 Ill. Dec. 824, 622 N.E.2d 854 (1993) reconstruction testimony is inadmissible when based upon an inspection of premises no longer in substantially the same condition as immediately after the event; *People v. Pertz,* 242 Ill. App. 3d 864, 183 Ill. Dec. 77, 610 N.E.2d 1321 (1993), reliance by expert upon truth of defendant's out of court statements in opining as to the accused's mental state made the opinion mere speculation. *Compare Valiulis v. Scheffels,* 191 Ill. App. 3d 775, 138 Ill. Dec. 668, 547 N.E.2d 1289 (1989), testimony by economist as to future economic loss was not impermissibly speculative. Similarly, an expert witness may not guess, surmise, or conjecture based upon matters that have not been shown to exist. *Harris Trust & Savings Bank v. Otis Elevator,* 297 Ill. App. 3d 383, 231 Ill. Dec. 401, 696 N.E.2d 697 (1998); *Baird v. Adeli,* 214 Ill. App. 3d 247, 157 Ill. Dec. 861, 573 N.E.2d 279 (1991); *Wilson v. Bell Fuels, Inc.,* 214 Ill. App. 3d 868, 158 Ill. Dec. 406, 574 N.E.2d 200 (1991). Expert testimony based substantially upon unreliable or inaccurate facts, data, or opinions will also be precluded. *In re Marriage of Talty,* 252 Ill. App. 3d 80, 191 Ill. Dec. 451, 623 N.E.2d 1041 (1993). An expert also may not testify as a summary expert or mere conduit by relying on facts, data, or opinions reasonably relied on by experts in the particular field but without providing additional input himself. *See* Graham, Handbook of Federal Evidence §703.1 n.12 (4th ed. 1996). *See also Glassman v. St.*

Joseph Hospital, 259 Ill. App. 3d 730, 197 Ill. Dec. 727, 631 N.E.2d 1186 (1994). In addition, an expert may not rely on an opinion of another expert that merely corroborates and thus reinforces an opinion that had been independently arrived at by the testifying expert. *Kochan v. Owens-Corning Fiberglass Corp.,* 242 Ill. App. 3d 781, 182 Ill. Dec. 814, 610 N.E.2d 683 (1993). *See also Kim v. Nazarian,* 216 Ill. App. 3d 818, 159 Ill. Dec. 758, 576 N.E.2d 427 (1991).

While the hypothetical question is no longer required, if one is posed by counsel upon direct or cross-examination and permitted by the court, it must comply with the common law requirements set forth above. *Leonardi v. Loyola University of Chicago,* 262 Ill. App. 3d 411, 199 Ill. Dec. 13, 633 N.E.2d 809 (1993). Facts, data, and opinions reasonably relied upon by the expert under Federal Rule 703 may be included in the hypothetical question where appropriate.

The qualification for an expert witness is discussed in §702.2 supra; as to subject matter of expert testimony, *see* §§702.4 to 702.7 supra; on whether a learned treatise is substantive evidence, *see* §703.1 supra.

§705.2   Cross-Examination of Experts, Including by Learned Treatise

On cross-examination, counsel may probe the witness's qualifications, experience and sincerity, weaknesses in his basis, the sufficiency of his assumptions, and the soundness of his opinion. The expert may thus be cross-examined about matters which explain, qualify, modify, discredit, destroy, or otherwise shed light upon the witness's direct examination. *Tzystuck v. Chicago Transit Authority,* 124 Ill. 2d 226, 124 Ill. Dec. 544, 529 N.E.2d 525 (1988); *Hulman v. Evanston Hospital Corp.,* 259 Ill. App. 3d 133, 197 Ill. Dec. 319, 631 N.E.2d 322 (1994). An expert witness may be cross-examined with respect to testimony given in another case if in the discretion of the trial court the probative value of such cross-examination is not substantially outweighed by the risk of confusing or misleading the jury through interjecting of another lawsuit into the case. *Pappas v. Fronczak,* 249 Ill. App. 3d 42, 188 Ill. Dec. 308, 618 N.E.2d 878 (1993).

O'Brien v. Meyer, 196 Ill. App. 3d 457, 143 Ill. Dec. 322, 554 N.E.2d 257 (1989) held that under the facts of the case it was improper to permit a doctor to be impeached by the failure to pass a general licensing examination in Illinois having passed such an examination elsewhere, based upon the danger of misleading the jury; under the facts of the case a problematic decision obviously made with an eye to preventing a flood of this type of questioning in future cases. *O'Brien* was distinguished in *McCray v. Salah Uddin Shams, M.D., S.C.,* 224 Ill. App. 3d 999, 167 Ill. Dec. 184, 587 N.E.2d 66 (1992) (trial court erred in prohibiting cross-examination as to doctor's failure to ever pass the board-certification examination in internal medicine; testimony as a specialist was not involved in *O'Brien*), and in *Kurrack v. American District Telegraph Co.,* 252 Ill. App. 3d 885, 192 Ill. Dec. 520, 625 N.E.2d 675 (1993) (proper to permit cross-examination of doctor offered as expert in preventive medicine and occupational medicine in area of lung disease as to doctor's failure to pass board certification examination in internal medicine). *See also Creighton v. Thompson,* 266 Ill. App. 3d 61, 203 Ill. Dec. 195, 639 N.E.2d 234 (1994) (cross-examination properly permitted concerning restrictions imposed by licensing agency upon doctor, in that he was unable to practice medicine without supervision). In *Gossard v. Kalra,* 291 Ill. App. 3d 180, 225 Ill. Dec. 725, 684 N.E.2d 410 (1997), *O'Brien* was followed and *Creighton* and *Kurrack* distinguished on the ground that the expert being cross-examined had, following earlier failures, subsequently acquired board certification. *See generally People v. Charleston,* 132 Ill. App. 3d 769, 87 Ill. Dec. 636, 477 N.E.2d 762 (1985), expert may be asked whether he made an error in a blood test presented in another case. However, an expert may not be asked whether he had made an error in concluding that a defendant in another case was insane, *People v. Fierer,* 260 Ill. App. 3d 136, 197 Ill. Dec. 755, 631 N.E.2d 1214 (1994), on basis that blood tests are objectively verifiable while a finding of insanity is largely subjective, an arguably unhelpful distinction.

As part of the process, opposing counsel may require the expert to disclose the facts, data, and opinions underlying the expert's opinion, including those not admitted in evidence reasonably relied upon by the expert. *Neal v. Nimmagadda,* 279 Ill. App. 3d 834, 216 Ill. Dec. 364, 665 N.E.2d 424 (1996); *Halleck v. Coastal Building Maintenance Co.,* 269 Ill. App. 3d 887, 207 Ill. Dec. 387, 647 N.E.2d 618 (1995); *Roberts v. Sisters of Saint Francis,* 198 Ill. App. 3d 891, 145 Ill. Dec. 44, 556 N.E.2d 662 (1990). *See also* §703.1 supra. The expert may also be cross-examined with respect to material reviewed by the expert but upon which the expert did not rely. *Leonardi v. Loyola University of Chicago,* 168 Ill. 2d 83, 212 Ill. Dec. 968, 658, N.E.2d 450 (1995); *Piano v. Davison,* 157 Ill. App. 3d 649, 110 Ill. Dec. 35, 510 N.E.2d 1066 (1987); *People v. Aliwoli,* 238 Ill. App. 3d 602, 179 Ill. Dec. 515, 606 N.E.2d 347 (1992); *Halleck v. Coastal Building Maintenance Co.* supra. In short, on cross-examination an expert may be examined as to what facts, data, or opinions he reviewed, which he relies upon, and which he disregarded or simply did not utilize. *Leonardi v. Loyola University of Chicago* supra; *People v. Pasch,* 152 Ill. 2d 133, 178 Ill. Dec. 38, 604 N.E.2d 294 (1992). Facts, data, or opinions supported by the evidence, *Wirth v. Industrial Commn.,* 57 Ill. 2d 475, 312 N.E.2d 593 (1974), including reasonable reliance by an expert under Federal Rule 703, *see* §703.1 supra, may be varied in questions asked on cross-examination designed to develop a potentially different opinion of the expert than would prevail if the trier believed a contrary version of disputed facts. *Granberry by Granberry v. Carbondale,* 285 Ill. App. 3d 54, 220 Ill. Dec. 284, 672 N.E.2d 1296 (1996) (quoting Handbook); *Swaw v. Klompein,* 168 Ill. App. 3d 705, 119 Ill. Dec. 408, 522 N.E.2d 1267 (1988); *Spilotro v. Hugi,* 93 Ill. App. 3d 837, 49 Ill. Dec. 239, 417 N.E.2d 1066 (1981). *See also People v. Scott,* 148 Ill. 2d 479, 171 Ill. Dec. 365, 594 N.E.2d 217 (1992), expert for defense may be cross-examined as to what weight, if any, the defense expert accorded to facts, data, or opinions that had been reasonably relied upon by the state's expert witnesses. *See generally People v.*

Pasch, 152 Ill. 2d 133, 178 Ill. Dec. 38, 604 N.E.2d 294 (1992) (C.J. Miller, concurring) (cross-examination of an opponent's expert employing facts, data, or opinions reasonably relied upon by the cross-examiner's testifying expert is proper). On the other hand, facts, data, or opinions neither reviewed by the expert, properly authenticated and admitted in evidence, nor actually reasonably relied upon by another expert in testimony at trial, may not be employed in such manner to impeach the expert's opinion itself. *See Fleeman v. Fischer*, 244 Ill. App. 3d 753, 184 Ill. Dec. 519, 613 N.E.2d 836 (1993). *See* infra with respect to the employment of facts outside the record to test the extent of expertise and fairness. Because in many instances the opposing party has not had a chance to present his case in chief at that point, the question on cross-examination may, at the discretion of the trial court, include facts not yet in evidence if there is an assurance by counsel that such facts will later be established. *Needy v. Sparks*, 51 Ill. App. 3d 350, 9 Ill. Dec. 70, 366 N.E.2d 327 (1977). The party whose witness is being examined may be protected from a failure to supply those facts by the trial court's either reserving ruling on the issue until the close of evidence or admitting the testimony subject to a later motion to strike if the missing evidence is not supplied. *Coriell v. Industrial Commn.*, 83 Ill. 2d 105, 46 Ill. Dec. 166, 413 N.E.2d 1279 (1980). A hypothetical question incorporating a contrary version of disputed facts supported by the evidence and/or other facts in evidence or employed subject to later introduction into evidence, *Leonardi v. Loyola University of Chicago*, 168 Ill. 2d 83, 212 Ill. Dec. 968, 658 N.E.2d 450 (1995); *Granberry by Granberry v. Carbondale*, 285 Ill. App. 3d 54, 220 Ill. Dec. 284, 672 N.E.2d 1296 (1996), may be employed upon cross-examination in the court's discretion. *Johns-Manville Prods. v. Industrial Commn.*, 78 Ill. 2d 171, 35 Ill. Dec. 540, 399 N.E.2d 606 (1980). If opposing counsel establishes on cross-examination that the witness lacks either sufficient qualifications or sufficient foundation for her opinion, or that the scientific principle, technique, or test employed has not been generally accepted, *see* §702.4 supra, the opinion of the expert will be stricken. *Kleiss v. Cassida,* 297 Ill. App. 3d 165, 231 Ill. Dec. 700, 696 N.E.2d 1271 (1998); *People v. Thill,* 297 Ill. App. 3d 7, 231 Ill. Dec. 604, 696 N.E.2d 1175 (1998); *Aguilera v. Mount Sinai Hospital Medical Center,* 293 Ill. App. 3d 967, 229 Ill. Dec. 65, 691 N.E.2d 1 (1998); *Wassmann v. Ritchason,* 63 Ill. App. 3d 770, 20 Ill. Dec. 813, 380 N.E.2d 1022 (1978). In most instances, however, cross-examination as to such matters goes to its weight rather than its admissibility. *People v. Cole,* 170 Ill. App. 3d 912, 120 Ill. Dec. 744, 524 N.E.2d 926 (1988). The inquiry, of course, must test the expert's credibility. *Neal v. Nimmagada,* 279 Ill. App. 3d 834, 216 Ill. Dec. 364, 665 N.E.2d 424 (1996).

Counsel is also permitted to test the extent of expertise and fairness of the expert by inquiring into what changes of conditions would affect her opinion, *People v. Pasch,* 152 Ill. 2d 133, 178 Ill. Dec. 38, 604 N.E.2d 294 (1992); *Levenson v. Lake-to-Lake Dairy,* 76 Ill. App. 3d 526, 32 Ill. Dec. 20, 394 N.E.2d 1359 (1979), and in conducting such an inquiry, subject to the requirements discussed in §403.1, the cross-examiner is not limited to facts finding support in the record, *Kenna v. Calumet, H. & S.E.R. Co.,* 284 Ill. 301, 120 N.E. 259 (1918); *People v. Fields,* 170 Ill. App. 3d 1, 120 Ill. Dec. 285, 523 N.E.2d 1196 (1988). For example, an expert witness testifying as to the defendant's insanity based on a "single discrete episode" may be cross-examined as to other incidents of the accused's violent conduct. *People v. Buggs,* 112 Ill. 2d 284, 97 Ill. Dec. 669, 493 N.E.2d 332 (1986). *See generally People v. Pasch* supra, an expert testifying as to insanity may be cross-examined as to whether a nontestifying expert's findings and conclusions would alter his opinion; under facts of case such findings and conclusions had been reasonably relied upon by another testifying expert, the significance of which was not discussed in the majority opinion. *See also Jager v. Libretti,* 273 Ill. App. 3d 960, 210 Ill. Dec. 144, 652 N.E.2d 1120 (1995), relying upon *People v. Pasch* supra in support of cross-examination of expert from emergency room records and ambulance reports not reviewed by the testifying expert, if truly done for purpose of impeachment and not to slip hearsay into the trial; the significance of the records being cross-examined from being ordinary business records reasonably relied upon by experts, which presumably could have been admitted as substantive evidence at trial, was not discussed. However, it is improper to inquire of the expert whether her opinion differs from another expert's opinion not expressed in a learned treatise if the other expert's opinion has not itself been admitted in evidence or reasonably relied upon by a testifying expert. *Adamaitis v. Hesser,* 56 Ill. App. 2d 349, 206 N.E.2d 311 (1965); *Hirn v. Edgewater Hosp.,* 86 Ill. App. 3d 939, 42 Ill. Dec. 261, 408 N.E.2d 970 (1980) (expert properly asked whether opinion of another expert expressed at trial altered his view). *Accord Piano v. Davison,* 157 Ill. App. 3d 649, 110 Ill. Dec. 35, 510 N.E.2d 1066 (1987). *See generally People v. Pasch,* 152 Ill. 2d 133, 178 Ill. Dec. 38, 604 N.E.2d 294 (1992) (C.J. Miller, concurring).

Inquiry into compensation is a matter of right. *Chicago v. Van Schaach,* 330 Ill. 264, 161 N.E. 486 (1928). Prior employment by the same party may be brought out, *McMahon v. Chicago City Ry.,* 239 Ill. 334, 88 N.E. 223 (1909), as well as referrals from the same attorney, *Davis v. Gulf, Mobile & Ohio R.R.,* 130 Ill. App. 2d 988, 272 N.E.2d 240 (1971). An expert can be questioned about fee arrangements, prior testimony for the same party, and financial interest in the outcome of the case, *Sears v. Rutishauser,* 102 Ill. 2d 402, 80 Ill. Dec. 758, 466 N.E.2d 210 (1984). *See also Golden v. Kishwaukee Community Health Services Center,* 269 Ill. App. 3d 37, 206 Ill. Dec. 314, 645 N.E.2d 319 (1994) (fact that expert witness had performed significant economic services for defendant's insurance company in reviewing claims was a proper subject of cross-examination, but mere fact that expert witness is insured by the same mutual insurance company insuring the defendant may be precluded from inquiry within the discretion of the trial court). It is also within the court's discretion to permit cross-examination as to how many times the expert has testified in court within a given period of time and whether on such occasions he testified only on behalf of plaintiffs or defendants. *See Wilson v. Chicago Transit Auth.,* 159 Ill. App. 3d 1043, 112 Ill. Dec. 29, 513 N.E.2d 443 (1987).

The Illinois Supreme Court in *Trower v. Jones,* 121 Ill. 2d 211, 117 Ill. Dec. 136, 520 N.E.2d 297 (1988), recognized the importance of bringing to the jury's attention facts by which the jury may reasonably discount the credibility of an expert witness by permitting cross-examination of an expert witness regarding annual income derived from services relating to serving as an expert witness and the frequency with which the witness's testimony in prior cases has been for "people suing doctors." *See also Pruett v. Norfolk and Western Railway Co.,* 261 Ill. App. 3d 29, 198 Ill. Dec. 322, 632 N.E.2d 652 (1994), expert may be cross-examined concerning the frequency of his testimony for plaintiffs or defendants and the annual income earned from such testimony. The frequency of prior testimony alone is relevant information bearing upon the witness's familiarity with the courtroom and potential persuasiveness as a witness. *Aguinaga v. City of Chicago,* 243 Ill. App. 3d 552, 183 Ill. Dec. 648, 611 N.E.2d 1296 (1993). *See generally Dotto v. Okan,* 269 Ill. App. 3d 808, 207 Ill. Dec. 190, 646 N.E.2d 1277 (1995) (we recognize that expert witnesses are hired guns and not ordinarily disinterested witnesses). The fact that the expert is a treating doctor does not affect the right of the opposing party to cross-examine in the foregoing manner. *Aguinaga v. City of Chicago, id.* For further discussion, *see* Graham, Impeaching the Professional Expert Witness by a Showing of Financial Interest, 53 Ind. L.J. 35 (1977). *Accord Moore v. Centreville Township Hospital,* 246 Ill. App. 3d 579, 186 Ill. Dec. 689, 616 N.E.2d 1321 (1993) (quoting article).

While the precise scope of cross-examination rests within the discretion of the trial court, *Sears v. Rutishauer* supra, and will not be disturbed on appeal absent abuse of that discretion, *Leonardi v. Loyola University of Chicago,* 168 Ill. 2d 83, 212 Ill. Dec. 968, 658 N.E.2d 450 (1995); *Sweeney v. Max A.R. Matthews & Company,* 46 Ill. 2d 64, 264 N.E.2d 170 (1970), this discretion should not be applied in a narrow or restricted manner, especially with respect to experts who deal in opinions as to matters normally not in the common knowledge and experience of laymen. *People v. Buggs,* 112 Ill. 2d 284, 97 Ill.

Dec. 669, 493 N.E.2d 332 (1986) (wide latitude and broad scope of inquiry). *Accord Muscarello v. Peterson,* 20 Ill. 2d 548, 170 N.E.2d 564 (1960); *Moss v. Miller,* 254 Ill. App. 3d 174, 192 Ill. Dec. 889, 625 N.E.2d 1044 (1993); *Montefelice v. Terminal R.R. Assn. of St. Louis,* 100 Ill. App. 3d 858, 56 Ill. Dec. 290, 427 N.E.2d 370 (1981); *Chicago v. Avenue State Bank,* 4 Ill. App. 3d 235, 281 N.E.2d 66 (1972). There is an "ever-increasing importance of bringing to the jury's attention facts by which the jury may reasonably discount the credibility of an expert's testimony." *Trower v. Jones,* 121 Ill. 2d 211, 217, 117 Ill. Dec. 136, 139, 520 N.E.2d 297, 300 (1988). Accordingly, counsel must be given the widest latitude during cross-examination to develop circumstances that explain, qualify, discredit, or destroy the witness's direct testimony, even though those circumstances may not have been raised on direct examination, *Leonardi v. Loyola University of Chicago,* 168 Ill. 2d 83, 212 Ill. Dec. 968, 658 N.E.2d 450 (1995); *People v. Franklin,* 135 Ill. 2d 78, 142 Ill. Dec. 152, 552 N.E.2d 743 (1990), including circumstances that demonstrate any interest, bias, or motive of the expert witness to testify. *Sanchez v. Black Brothers Co.,* 98 Ill. App. 3d 264, 53 Ill. Dec. 505, 423 N.E.2d 1309 (1981). Similarly, on closing argument it is proper when supported by the evidence for counsel to assert that a given expert is a "high-priced" expert and a "hired-gun doctor." *Moore v. Centreville Township Hospital,* 246 Ill. App. 3d 579, 186 Ill. Dec. 689, 616 N.E.2d 1321 (1993). The scope of cross-examination is not without its limits. For example, it is proper to preclude cross-examination as to discharge and postoperative care in a case alleging wrongful removal of thyroid, *Neal v. Nimmagada,* 279 Ill. App. 3d 834, 216 Ill. Dec. 364, 665 N.E.2d 424 (1996). *See also Mazzone v. Holmes,* 197 Ill. App. 3d 886, 145 Ill. Dec. 416, 557 N.E.2d 186 (1990), proper for trial court to preclude cross-examination of defendant's expert in a malpractice case regarding involvement of the expert himself as a defendant in malpractice cases.

Views of recognized authorities, expressed in treatises or periodicals written for professional colleagues, may be employed upon cross-examination of an expert witness if the author's competency as a reliable authority is established by an admission of the expert witness or by other expert testimony or by judicial notice. *Darling v. Charleston Community Memorial Hosp.,* 33 Ill. 2d 326, 211 N.E.2d 253 (1965); *People v. Anderson,* 93 Ill. App. 3d 646, 48 Ill. Dec. 931, 417 N.E.2d 663 (1981); *Toppel v. Redondo,* 247 Ill. App. 3d 211, 187 Ill. Dec. 195, 617 N.E.2d 403 (1993). Frequently statements contained in a learned treatise, periodical, or pamphlet employed on cross-examination are established as a reliable authority by the testimony of a witness expert in the profession, art, or trade of the author, testifying as to the author's standing as an authority. 6 Wigmore, Evidence §1694 (Chadbourn rev. 1976). The burden of establishing that the authority is reliable is upon the party offering the item. *People v. Behnke,* 41 Ill. App. 3d 276, 353 N.E.2d 684 (1976), cross-examiner held to have failed to establish that the item was by a reliable authority on grounds that item was written with a view toward litigation and not established as being written for professional colleagues.

With respect to the taking of judicial notice, 4 Weinstein's Evidence ¶803(18)[02] (1984) suggests that a court might take judicial notice of learned treatises admitted in the course of other litigation; as to judicial notice of the content of learned treatises, *see* §202.2 supra.

§706   Court-Appointed Experts

§706.1   *Commentary*

Expert testimony under the adversary system has proved to be highly partisan in nature sufficiently often to be characterized as "generally discredited and regarded as the most unsatisfactory part of judicial administration." *Opp v. Pryor,* 294 Ill. 538, 545, 128 N.E. 580 (1920). While no statute or court rule provides generally for court appointment of experts, in an effort to remedy this situation and to promote settlements, the Illinois Supreme Court has, by Rule 215(d), provided for physical or mental examination when in issue by an impartial medical expert who is a member of a panel of physicians chosen for their special qualifications by the Administrative Office of the Illinois Courts. *See People ex rel. Aldworth v. Dutkanych,* 112 Ill. 2d 505, 98 Ill. Dec. 16, 493 N.E.2d 1037 (1986). Other specific provisions for court-appointed experts are found in 725 ILCS 5/115-6, defense of insanity; *id.,* 725 ILCS 205/4, sexually dangerous persons; 405 ILCS 5/3-804, commitment of mentally ill; 750 ILCS 45/11, blood test in paternity action; 405 ILCS 5/1-100 *et seq.,* Mental Health and Developmental Disabilities Code; and 20 ILCS 3955/1 *et seq.,* Guardianship and Advocacy Act. With respect to the inherent power of the court to call expert witnesses, *see* McCormick, Evidence §17 (Cleary ed. 1972).

As a matter of constitutional due process, a criminal defendant is entitled to have a reasonable fee paid on her behalf for the hiring of an expert witness whenever necessary to establish crucial issue in the case. *People v. Watson,* 36 Ill. 2d 228, 221 N.E.2d 645 (1966); *People v. Glover,* 49 Ill. 2d 78, 273 N.E.2d 367 (1971). In order to secure the appointment of an expert witness the criminal defendant must establish both indigence and that appointment of an expert witness is necessary to prove a crucial issue in the case. While preferable, where feasible the criminal defendant's appointed attorney should in advance petition the court, identifying the expert wished to be employed and providing an estimate of the reasonable fees involved, failure to conform will not preclude the subsequently revealed necessary expert from receiving a reasonable fee. *People v. Kinion,* 97 Ill. 2d 322, 73 Ill. Dec. 528, 454 N.E.2d 625 (1983); *People v. Lawson,* 163 Ill. 2d 187, 206 Ill. Dec. 119, 644 N.E.2d 1172 (1994). With respect to identifying what is or is not a crucial issue in the case, *see People v. Lawson* supra (fingerprint and shoe prints); *People v. Evans,* 271 Ill. App. 3d 495, 208 Ill. Dec. 42, 648 N.E.2d 964 (1995) (battered woman syndrome), and in particular *People v. Keene,* 169 Ill. 2d 1, 214 Ill. Dec. 194, 660 N.E.2d 901

(1996) (pathologist). As to the requirement that a psychiatrist be provided to a criminal defendant where insanity has been raised or where future dangerousness is suggested as an aggravating factor of sentencing, *see Ake v. Oklahoma,* 470 U.S. 68 (1985). A mitigation expert is not required to be appointed in death case, *People v. Burt,* 168 Ill. 2d 49, 212 Ill. Dec. 893, 658 N.E.2d 375 (1995). These requirements preclude the grant of a blank check on the county treasury to a defendant who can afford to hire his own experts. They also prevent the hiring of unneeded experts, experts whose opinions might not be relevant to any of the issues in the case, and so-called experts who really might not be experts. *People v. Sims,* 244 Ill. App. 3d 966, 184 Ill. Dec. 135, 612 N.E.2d 1011 (1993). Although 725 ILCS 5/113-3(d) provides for the payment of up to $250 to the defendant for the hiring of necessary expert witnesses, indigent defendants in *all* criminal cases are entitled to have necessary expert witnesses paid reasonable fees even when in excess of $250. *People v. Kinion* supra; *People v. Evans* supra.

The jury should not be advised of the court-appointed status of the expert witness. *Morrison v. Picket,* 103 Ill. App. 3d 643, 59 Ill. Dec. 636, 432 N.E.2d 2 (1981). For an interesting discussion of the problem associated with disclosure of the fact of court appointment to the jury, *see* Saltzburg, The Unnecessarily Expanding Role of the American Trial Judge, 64 Va. L. Rev. 1 (1978).

ARTICLE VIII
Hearsay

§801   Definition of Hearsay

§801.1   An Overview

Article VIII discusses hearsay in the traditional manner of a definition, §§801.1 to 801.9 infra, subject to certain exceptions under which a hearsay statement is not required to be excluded either (1) by virtue of the adversary system, §802 infra, dealing with admissions, (2) because the out-of-court declarant is subject to cross-examination in court, §611.16 and §801.9, or (3) based on a determination of reliability of and necessity for the hearsay statement, exceptions either without regard to the availability of the declarant as a witness, §803 infra, or only if the declarant is unavailable, §804 infra. Also addressed is the question of hearsay within hearsay, §805 infra, and of attacking and supporting the credibility of the hearsay declarant, §806 infra. Confrontation and due process concerns associated with the admission of hearsay are discussed in §807 infra.

Hearsay has been defined as follows:

> Hearsay evidence is testimony in court or written evidence, of a statement made out of court, such statement being offered as an assertion to show the truth of matters asserted therein, and thus resting for its value upon the credibility of the out-of-court asserter.

People v. Carpenter, 28 Ill. 2d 116, 121, 190 N.E.2d 738 (1963). *See also People v. Rogers,* 81 Ill. 2d 571, 44 Ill. Dec. 254, 411 N.E.2d 223 (1980). *Accord* McCormick, Evidence §246 (Cleary ed. 1972); 5 Wigmore, Evidence §1361 (Chadbourne rev. 1974); 6 Wigmore, Evidence §1766 (Chadbourne rev. 1976). The out-of-court asserter, referred to as a declarant, is the person who made the statement. Thus evidence generated instantaneously by a machine, such as a computer record of traced telephone call numbers, *People v. Holowko,* 109 Ill. 2d 187, 93 Ill. Dec. 344, 486 N.E.2d 877 (1985), is not hearsay. *Accord People v. Casey,* 225 Ill. App. 3d 82, 167 Ill. Dec. 242, 587 N.E.2d 511 (1992). A statement that is hearsay is not admissible unless the statement satisfies an exception to the rule against hearsay recognized by the common law of Illinois or an exception provided by statute. *See* §801.9 and §§802-805 infra. *See, e.g., In re Marriage of Noble,* 192 Ill. App. 3d 501, 139 Ill. Dec. 133, 548 N.E.2d 518 (1989), report of court-appointed investigator is admissible as a hearsay exception in a contested custody proceeding pursuant to 750 ILCS 5/605. Out-of-court statements that are not hearsay or that fall within a hearsay exception must, of course, still meet other requirements for admissibility, such as relevance, authenticity, and, when the contents of a document are sought to be proved, the Original Writing Rule, §1002 infra.

To illustrate the distinction between admissible testimony and that which is barred by the Hearsay Rule, consider the example of witness *A* testifying that *B* told him that event *X* occurred. *People v. Carpenter* supra: "If *A*'s testimony is offered for the purpose of establishing that *B* said this, it is clearly admissible — if offered to prove that event *X* occurred, it is clearly inadmissible, for the only probative value rests in *B*'s knowledge — and *B* is not present to be cross-examined." Of course, documentary evidence and recorded statements of a witness may also be hearsay. *Douglas v. Chicago Transit Auth.,* 3 Ill. App. 3d 318, 279 N.E.2d 44 (1972), police report. Thus, if the relevance of the statement depends upon the truth of the matter asserted or the declarant's belief in the truth or falsity of the matter asserted, the out-of-court statement is hearsay. Conversely, to the extent that an out-of-court statement is relevant simply because of the fact it was said, the statement is not barred by the Hearsay Rule. *See, e.g., People v. Poe,* 121 Ill. App. 3d 457, 76 Ill. Dec. 752, 459 N.E.2d 667 (1984), testimony that the witness spoke to the defendant over the telephone at a given time offered as an alibi is not hearsay; *People v. Gaurige,* 168 Ill. App. 3d 855, 119 Ill. Dec. 447, 522 N.E.2d 1306 (1988), tape recording of 911 telephone call not hearsay when offered to show that the declarant's voice demonstrated that he was frantic and fearful.

Examples of hearsay are: on issue of whether stock had been purchased, testimony of witness that his agent reported to him that the stock was purchased, *Hately v. Kiser*, 253 Ill. 288, 97 N.E. 651 (1912); on question of whether structure damage was caused by overloading, letter addressed to tenant of a party concerning distribution of loads, *Kane v. City of Chicago*, 392 Ill. 172, 64 N.E.2d 506 (1946); testimony of police officer as to what defendant told him the plaintiff was doing at time of accident, *Redding v. Schroeder*, 54 Ill. App. 2d 306, 203 N.E.2d 616 (1964); description of car and occupants received by police officer over the radio, *People v. Marquis*, 54 Ill. App. 3d 209, 11 Ill. Dec. 918, 369 N.E.2d 372 (1977); statement by maintenance man that tenant in apartment 203 responded to the defendant's knock on the apartment door with the statement "Get away from my door. I don't know who you are," *People v. Hall*, 90 Ill. App. 3d 1073, 46 Ill. Dec. 479, 414 N.E.2d 201 (1980); statement made to contractor that a beam was not level, *Hemenover v. DePatis*, 86 Ill. App. 3d 586, 42 Ill. Dec. 9, 408 N.E.2d 387 (1980); statement of a witness, who was not called to testify at trial, made at a lineup and identifying someone other than defendant, offered by defendant to establish that the state's witnesses called at trial incorrectly identified defendant, *People v. Dean*, 99 Ill. App. 3d 999, 55 Ill. Dec. 304, 426 N.E.2d 279 (1981); statement of company employees to supervisor that a particular person did not telephone on a given date, *Country Cas. Ins. Co. v. Wilson*, 144 Ill. App. 3d 28, 98 Ill. Dec. 225, 494 N.E.2d 152 (1986).

The presence or absence in court of the declarant of the out-of-court statement is, under the Illinois Supreme Court decisions, irrelevant to a determination as to whether the out-of-court statement is hearsay. *People v. Lawler*, 142 Ill. 2d 548, 154 Ill. Dec. 674, 568 N.E.2d 895 (1991) (quoting Handbook). *See also Moran v. Erickson*, 297 Ill. App. 3d 342, 231 Ill. Dec. 484, 696 N.E.2d 780 (1998); People v. Velasco, 216 Ill. App. 3d 578, 159 Ill. Dec. 147, 575 N.E.2d 954 (1991). *See* §801.9 infra. Contrary statements in cases such as *In Interest of C.L.*, 180 Ill. App. 3d 173, 128 Ill. Dec. 725, 534 N.E.2d 1330

(1989); *People v. Bonds,* 87 Ill. App. 3d 805, 43 Ill. Dec. 228, 410 N.E.2d 228 (1980); *People v. Mosley,* 71 Ill. App. 3d 808, 28 Ill. Dec. 197, 390 N.E.2d 364 (1979); *People v. Olmos,* 67 Ill. App. 3d 281, 23 Ill. Dec. 946, 384 N.E.2d 853 (1978); *People v. Smith,* 64 Ill. App. 3d 1045, 21 Ill. Dec. 934, 382 N.E.2d 298 (1978), must be regarded as incorrect as being inconsistent with *People v. Lawler* supra and *People v. Spicer,* 79 Ill. 2d 173, 37 Ill. Dec. 269, 402 N.E.2d 179 (1969). The implication in dictum to the contrary at one stage of the opinion in *People v. Rogers,* 81 Ill. 2d 571, 44 Ill. Dec. 254, 411 N.E.2d 223 (1980), may be treated as an oversight and disregarded when considered in light of the holding that testimony of an in-court witness relating a positive prior out-of-court identification was admitted solely as corroborative and not substantive evidence. *See also People v. Bonds* supra. With respect to the general lack of significance of the opposing party's presence when the statement was made in applying the definition of hearsay, *see* §801.7 infra.

Conduct, such as shopping, does not become hearsay because it is observed by means of a video camera or recorded on videotape any more than conduct becomes hearsay when observed by someone looking through a window or using a mirror. *See People v. Tharpe-Williams,* 286 Ill. App. 3d 605, 221 Ill. Dec. 914, 676 N.E.2d 717 (1997).

In deciding whether a statement falls within the definition of hearsay, it is irrelevant whether the statement was self-serving or disserving at the time of either being made or offered. *People v. Vanda,* 111 Ill. App. 3d 551, 67 Ill. Dec. 373, 444 N.E.2d 609 (1982). *See also People v. Nyberg,* 275 Ill. App. 3d 570, 211 Ill. Dec. 873, 656 N.E.2d 65 (1995) (Wolfson, J., specially concurring). Similarly, it is irrelevant whether the witness testifying to the out-of-court statement was a participant in the conversation. *Contra Starnawski v. License Appeal Commn.,* 101 Ill. App. 3d 1050, 57 Ill. Dec. 422, 428 N.E.2d 1102 (1981); *Singh v. Air Illinois, Inc.,* 165 Ill. App. 3d 923, 117 Ill. Dec. 501, 520 N.E.2d 852 (1988) (incorrectly decided).

The term *matters asserted* as employed in the definition of hearsay includes both matters directly expressed and matters the declarant necessarily implicitly intended to express. When the declarant necessarily intended to express the inference for which the statement is offered, the statement is tantamount to a direct assertion and therefore is hearsay. The declarant necessarily intends to assert (i.e., implicitly asserts) matters forming the foundation for matters directly expressed in the sense that such additional matters must be assumed to be true to give meaning to the matters directly expressed in the context in which the statement was made. *People v. Thomas,* 178 Ill. 2d 215, 227 Ill. Dec. 410, 687 N.E.2d 892 (1997) ("implicit assertion" citing Handbook); *People v. Camp,* 128 Ill. App. 3d 223, 83 Ill. Dec. 414, 470 N.E.2d 540 (1984) (citing Handbook). To illustrate, the question "Do you think it will stop raining in one hour?" contains the implicit assertion that it is currently raining. The fact that it is currently raining is a necessary foundation fact that must be assumed true for the question asked to make sense. *Cf. People v. Camp* supra where the declaration "Are you all right to drive the car?" was stated not to presuppose that the defendant was unable to drive as an implicit fact that must be true. It is suggested that the construction of the operative principle in *Camp* is unduly narrow, as the court's opinion itself later demonstrates, and should not be followed. The fact that a particular matter was being asserted by the declarant may not be avoided merely by a reference to conduct of others following the making of the statement where the matter asserted by the declarant is clearly being inferred. *People v. Colon,* 249 Ill. App. 3d 141, 188 Ill. Dec. 497, 618 N.E.2d 1067 (1993) (fact that person was asked to make identification followed by evidence that the accused was then arrested is hearsay).

With respect to a witness testifying in court, four risks must be considered in evaluating the trustworthiness of the witness's testimony. These risks are (1) perception, in the sense of capacity and actuality of observation through any of the senses, (2) recordation and recollection (sometimes called memory), (3) narration (sometimes called ambiguity), and (4) sincerity (sometimes called fabrication). To encourage the witness to testify to the best of her ability regarding each of the four risks, and to expose inaccuracies in the witness's testimony, a witness possessing minimum credibility is required to testify at trial as to a matter within her personal knowledge (1) under oath or affirmation, (2) in person, so that the trier of fact may observe the witness's demeanor, and (3) subject to contemporaneous cross-examination. Each of the four risks associated with evaluating the accuracy of a witness's in-court testimony is present as well when an out-of-court statement is offered to prove the truth of the matter asserted. Thus the trier of fact must evaluate risks of perception, recordation and recollection, narration, and sincerity when determining the trustworthiness of a hearsay statement. When the statement offered for the truth of the matter asserted was made out of court, however, the trier of fact, when ascertaining inaccuracies, does not have the benefit of having the declarant before it, under oath, and subject to contemporaneous cross-examination. Hearsay is excluded because of the absence of these tests for ascertaining trustworthiness. *Marshall v. Chicago & G.E. Ry.*, 48 Ill. 475 (1868). Of the three, inability to conduct cross-examination is the essential factor underlying the rule excluding hearsay. *People v. Holman*, 103 Ill. 2d 133, 82 Ill. Dec. 585, 469 N.E.2d 119 (1984); *Grand Liquor Co. v. Department of Revenue*, 67 Ill. 2d 195, 10 Ill. Dec. 472, 367 N.E.2d 1238 (1977); *People v. Carpenter*, 28 Ill. 2d 116, 190 N.E.2d 738 (1963).

The definition of hearsay, along with the four risks discussed relating to the trustworthiness of a hearsay statement, is depicted in the following "Stickperson Hearsay" diagrams. Stickperson Hearsay Diagram 1 portrays the hearsay risks associated with an oral statement of an out-of-court declarant. Diagram 2 portrays the hearsay risks associated with the introduction of a written or recorded statement of an out-of-court declarant.

To illustrate the use of the Stickperson Hearsay diagram as a means of understanding the definition of hearsay, consider in-court testimony by Mickey that Marilyn either said the following in his presence, wrote the following in a letter, or

STICKPERSON HEARSAY

Diagram 1

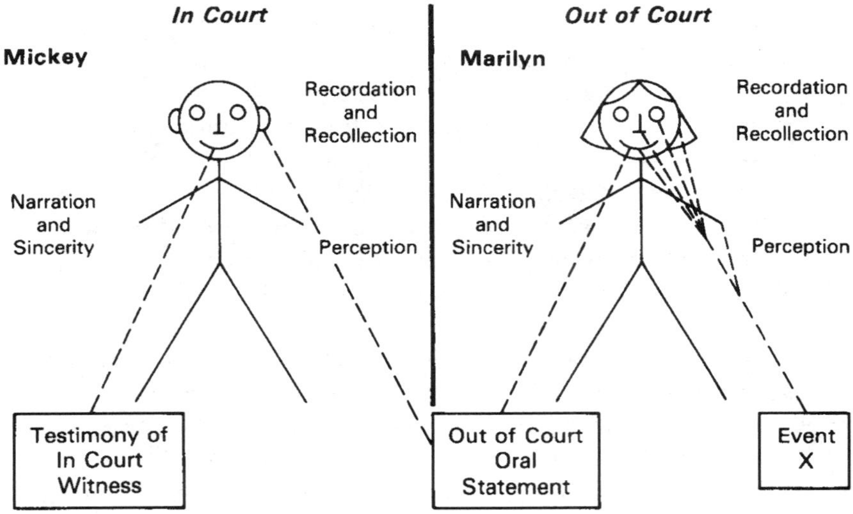

recorded the following on a tape: "I saw the car go through a red light." Marilyn's declaration is a statement, i.e., it is oral or written conduct intended by Marilyn as an assertion. Marilyn is the declarant. Diagram 1 represents Mickey testifying in court, under oath, subject to contemporaneous cross-examination, repeating the contents of an out-of-court conversation with Marilyn, during which she described, in detail, what she had previously perceived — referred to in the diagram as Event X. In the illustration, Event X corresponds to the car actually going through a red light. Diagram 2 represents Mickey authenticating in court a written or recorded statement of Marilyn detailing the same Event X. Thus the testimonial risks associated with in-court testimony (Mickey), and the hearsay risks associated with an out-of-court statement (Marilyn), can be appreciated by beginning at the left of either diagram and following the dashed lines of Mickey and then Marilyn. The dashed lines of Mickey represent the risks associated with an in-court declarant testi-

STICKPERSON HEARSAY

Diagram 2

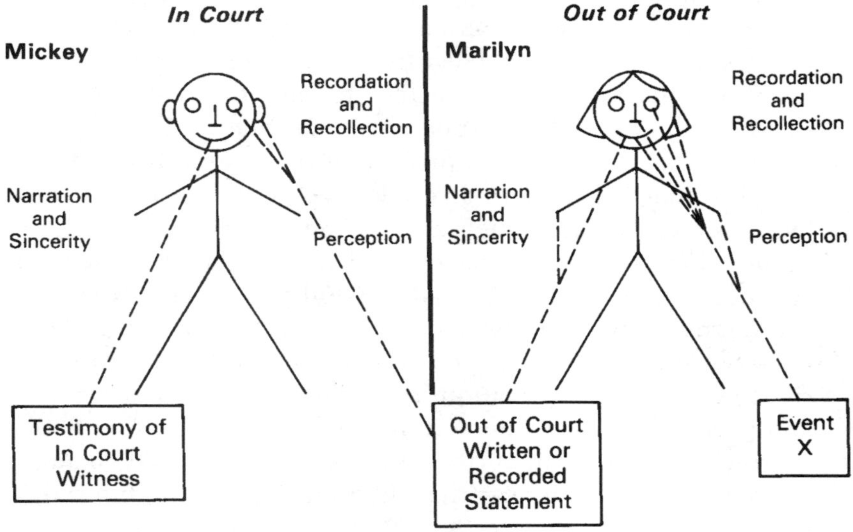

fying as to a fact of which he has personal knowledge, in this case the *making* of the oral, written, or recorded statement by Marilyn. The dashed lines of Marilyn represent the hearsay risks associated with an out-of-court declarant's hearsay statement — the oral, written, or recorded statement of Marilyn that the car went through a red light, relevant in the context of the litigation only when offered to prove the truth of the matter asserted, i.e., that the car actually went through a red light.

In both Diagram 1 and Diagram 2, testimony of Mickey repeating or authenticating a statement by Marilyn, which is relevant without regard to the truth of the matter asserted, is represented by movement from the left of the diagram along the dashed lines to the vertical line. Thus, returning to the illustration, if a fact of consequence in the litigation concerns whether following an accident in which Marilyn is hurt, Marilyn is still capable of coherent speech, relevancy of her out-of-court statement concerning the color of the traffic light does not depend upon the matter asserted in the statement being true. Marilyn's statement, authenticated by Mickey, the relevance of which depends solely upon the fact that it was said, and not the truth of its content, is not hearsay. Mickey is in court, under oath, and subject to cross-examination as to his testimony that Marilyn made the statement. On the other hand, testimony of Mickey repeating or authenticating a statement by Marilyn offered to prove that the matter asserted is true, i.e., that the car went through a red light, is represented by movement from the left side of the diagram, along the dashed lines, through Mickey's head to the right of the vertical line, through Marilyn's head to Event X at the right side of the diagram. Thus Marilyn's statement, when offered to prove that the car went through a red light, possesess all four hearsay risks, i.e., sincerity, narration, recordation and recollection, and perception. The statement is hearsay.

Now let us assume further that Marilyn, injured in an accident involving the car that she said went through a red light, ultimately died as a result of the injuries she sustained. In the hospital prior to her death she said to Mickey "I love you." When the statement is offered in evidence to establish damages in an action for wrongful death, Marilyn's statement is hearsay. The statement is hearsay because both the risks of narration and sincerity are present. The statement is relevant to establish damages only if Marilyn was truthful in her expression of her feelings for Mickey, i.e., the statement is being offered in evidence to prove the truth of the matter asserted. Turning to the diagrams, the relevance of the statement "I love you" requires movement beyond the dashed lines of Mickey along the dashed line of Marilyn leading into her head. Since Marilyn's statement is relevant only if she believed the statement to be true, i.e., Marilyn really loved Mickey, the two hearsay risks of narration and sincerity are present.

In summary, if relevance of the statement requires movement beyond the dashed lines of Mickey along the dashed lines of Marilyn, either into her head alone (belief—two hearsay risks) or further down the other side (Event X—

four hearsay risks), the statement is hearsay. Such statement is offered to prove the truth of the matter asserted. Thus any time a statement's relevance depends upon movement along the dashed lines of the diagram from the in-court testimony of Mickey to the right of the vertical line (i.e., the statement must either be believed by the declarant to be true or in fact be true in order to be relevant in the context of the particular litigation), the statement is hearsay. Conversely, to the extent that the statement is relevant simply because Mickey repeats his personal knowledge of the making of the oral statement (Diagram 1), or authenticates the written or recorded assertion of Marilyn (Diagram 2), because movement proceeds from the in-court testimony of Mickey, along the dashed lines, only to the vertical line, the statement of Marilyn is not hearsay. Such a statement is not being offered to prove the truth of the matter asserted, but is offered solely for the fact it was said.

A statement is hearsay if its relevance depends upon the declarant's belief in the falsity of the statement, as well as if relevance depends upon the declarant's belief that the matter being asserted is true. In either case the risks of narration and sincerity are present. Risks of perception and recordation and recollection may be present as well. To highlight the hearsay nature of a statement offered to show belief in falsity, assume that Able is charged with an offense in Chicago. The police talk to Able's wife, who tells them that Able was with her in Miami on the date and time in question. The prosecution is prepared to prove that her statement is false. The prosecution desires to offer Mrs. Able's statement to support its argument that she knew her husband was guilty, and that in response to such knowledge she lied to protect him. The wife's statement is relevant for the purpose offered by the prosecution only if she knew her statement was false. Because determining whether she knew the statement was false brings into issue her perception, recordation and recollection, narration, and sincerity regarding the statement placing the two of them in Miami at the critical moment, the statement is hearsay. *See People v. Shaw*, 278 Ill.

App. 3d 939, 215 Ill. Dec. 700, 664 N.E.2d 97 (1996), false exculpatory statement shifting blame is probative of consciousness of guilt. Conversely, when the relevancy of the statement does not depend upon the declarant believing the statement to be false but rather the statement is relevant because the content of the statement itself tends to establish a fact of consequence when shown by independent evidence to be false, the statement is not hearsay. *People v. Buffman,* 260 Ill. App. 3d 505, 201 Ill. Dec. 351, 636 N.E.2d 783 (1994) (quoting Handbook).

Determining whether a statement offered at trial for a particular purpose is hearsay thus involves solely a search for the presence of hearsay risks (belief — two hearsay risks, or Event X — four hearsay risks). If such hearsay risks are present the statement is hearsay. *No assessment of the magnitude of hearsay risks present is undertaken with respect to the statement for the purpose offered.* Magnitude of hearsay risks bears solely upon whether the hearsay statement is felt sufficiently trustworthy to be admitted pursuant to an exception to the rule against hearsay.

Under the definition of hearsay, when a statement offered to prove the truth of the matter asserted is made other than by the declarant while testifying at the trial or hearing, the statement is hearsay, regardless of whether the out-of-court declarant is available to testify or actually testifies at the trial or hearing at which the out-of-court statement is offered. Thus the definition of hearsay applies to all statements not made under oath at the trial or hearing, and thus not made subject to contemporaneous cross-examination before the trier of fact. When the out-of-court declarant also testifies at trial, cross-examination or direct and redirect examination provides an opportunity for the party opposing the truth of the out-of-court statement to explore the truth of the assertion before the trier of fact. Nevertheless, the Hearsay Rule and its common law exceptions do not provide for general admissibility of prior statements of in-court witnesses. With respect to the admissibility of certain prior inconsistent statements pursuant to a statutory exception to the Hearsay Rule, *see* §801.9 infra. Similarly as to the statutory exception for prior statements of identification, *see* §611.16 supra. With respect to the admissibility of prior consistent statements solely to rebut, *see* §611.14 supra.

§801.2 *Nonverbal Conduct Intended as an Assertion*

Nonverbal conduct may on occasion clearly be the equivalent of an assertive statement, that is, done for the purpose of deliberate communication, and thus classified as hearsay. *People v. Barger*, 251 Ill. App. 3d 448, 191 Ill. Dec. 556, 624 N.E.2d 405 (1993) (quoting Handbook; gestures and actions of child describing event using anatomically correct dolls). Nodding, pointing, and the sign language of the mute are as plainly assertions as are spoken words. *People v. Reeves*, 360 Ill. 55, 195 N.E. 443 (1935), error to admit testimony that person now deceased pointed at accused as being involved in crime; *People v. Higgs*, 11 Ill. App. 3d 1032, 298 N.E.2d 283 (1973), error to admit fact that members of a crowd attacked the defendant when offered to establish that the defendant shot the deceased.

§801.3 *Nonverbal Conduct Not Intended as an Assertion*

Whether nonverbal conduct not intended as an assertion is hearsay has long been a controversy among commentators. The controversy, however, has only rarely been the subject of judicial decision, frequently because the hearsay question has not been perceived. When the issue is whether an event happened, evidence of conduct from which may be inferred the actor's belief, from which in turn may be inferred the happening of the event, bears at least a superficial resemblance to an out-of-court statement by the actor that he believed the event occurred. An analysis in terms of the principal dangers that the hearsay rule is designed to guard against, i.e., lack of opportunity to test by cross-examination the actuality and accuracy of his perceptions, recollection and recordation, narration, and sincerity, leads, however, to a rejection of the analogy between such an inference, sometimes called "implied assertion," and an express assertion. When a person acts without intending to communicate a belief, his veracity is not involved. Furthermore, there is frequently a guarantee of the trustworthiness of the inference to be drawn because the actor has based his actions on the correctness of his belief. Consider, for example, a person who is observed opening an umbrella, offered for the inference that it is raining. While the inference to be drawn from such nonverbal conduct is the same as is the case of a direct assertion that it is raining, the fact remains that the intent to assert is absent, and thus the danger believed to be inherent in hearsay with respect to sincerity is absent. While the risk of insincerity is removed, the objection still remains that the accuracy of the actor's perception, recordation and recollection, and narration are untested by cross-examination as to the possibility of honest mistake. However, risks of error in these respects are more sensibly factors to be used in evaluating weight and credibility rather than grounds for exclusion. *People v. Jackson*, 203 Ill. App. 3d 1, 148 Ill. Dec. 422, 560 N.E.2d 1019 (1990) (citing Handbook).

Where the question of nonverbal conduct not intended as an assertion has been considered, Illinois decisions reach varying results. *Compare Wohl v. Yelen*, 22 Ill. App. 2d 455, 161 N.E.2d 339 (1959), actions of alleged agent in dealing with property, but not his extrajudicial declarations of existence of agency, admissible to prove agency, *with People v. Bush*, 300 Ill. 532, 133 N.E. 201 (1921), on issue whether prosecuting witness had venereal disease, error to admit evidence that institution in which she was placed did not segregate her, as was done with venereal cases. *People v. Bush id.*, might be explainable on the basis that the court may have felt that an implicit intent to assert as described in §801.1 supra was present. Recent authority, however, clearly recognizes that nonverbal conduct not intended as an assertion is not hearsay. *People v. Jackson,* 203 Ill. App. 3d 1, 148 Ill. Dec. 422, 560 N.E.2d 1019 (1990), post-incident behavior of child sexual abuse victim was not hearsay. In most instances the admissibility of nonverbal conduct as the basis for various inferences has been incorrectly treated as an admission. *See* §802.1 infra.

Fabrication or suppression of evidence. The destruction, suppression, or fabrication of evidence, or attempts thereat, constitute an admission. *See, e.g., Chicago City Ry. v. McMahon,* 103 Ill. 485 (1882); *People v. Albanese,* 104 Ill. 2d 504, 85 Ill. Dec. 441, 473 N.E.2d 1246 (1984), fabrication of exculpatory evidence. So does refusal to take a field test for sobriety. *People v. Townes,* 130 Ill. App. 3d 844, 86 Ill. Dec. 137, 474 N.E.2d 1334 (1985). So does any attempt to conceal or, by threat or otherwise, to suppress evidence or otherwise obstruct an investigation. *People v. Gacho,* 122 Ill. 2d 221, 119 Ill. Dec. 287, 522 N.E.2d 1146 (1988). Similarly treated is the coaching of a witness to speak a half-truth. *Holton v. Memorial Hospital,* 274 Ill. App. 3d 868, 211 Ill. Dec. 369, 655 N.E.2d 29 (1995). Proof of destruction, suppression, refusal, or fabrication gives rise to an inference of consciousness of guilt or having a weak case admissible on the general question of liability. Such inference is not, however, sufficient alone to support a finding of liability. *People v. Spaulding,* 309 Ill. 292, 141 N.E. 196 (1923); *Lubbers v. Norfolk & W. Ry.,* 118 Ill. App. 3d 705, 73 Ill. Dec. 937, 454 N.E.2d 1186 (1983). For a full discussion *see* McCormick, Evidence §265 (4th ed. 1992).

Flight; resistance to arrest. Flight, in the sense of leaving or concealment under circumstances indicating consciousness of guilt and a purpose of evading arrest, is an admission. *People v. Autman,* 393 Ill. 262, 65 N.E.2d 772 (1946). *Cf. People v. Henry,* 52 Ill. 2d 558, 288 N.E.2d 385 (1972), flight found admissible as circumstances tending to show consciousness of guilt without any reference being made to an admission. The inference of guilt that may be drawn from flight depends upon knowledge by the suspect that the offense has been committed and that he is or may be suspected. *People v. Lewis,* 165 Ill. 2d 305, 209 Ill. Dec. 144, 651 N.E.2d 72 (1995) (citing cases). Resisting arrest is also an admission. *Jamison v.*

People, 145 Ill. 357, 34 N.E. 486 (1893). It is also true of a letter written by the defendant expressing a desire to escape from jail. *People v. Gacho,* 122 Ill. 2d 221, 119 Ill. Dec. 287, 522 N.E.2d 1146 (1988). Evidence of attempts or threats to commit suicide is admissible, on the same theory, as a form of flight. *People v. Duncan,* 261 Ill. 339, 103 N.E. 1043 (1914); *People v. O'Neil,* 18 Ill. 2d 461, 165 N.E.2d 319 (1960). Consciousness of guilt also includes an attempt to intimidate a witness, *People v. Frazier,* 107 Ill. App. 3d 1096, 63 Ill. Dec. 692, 438 N.E.2d 623 (1982), "waste" a witness, *People v. Woods,* 122 Ill. App. 3d 176, 77 Ill. Dec. 576, 460 N.E.2d 880 (1984), a refusal to submit to a blood sampling, *People v. Edwards,* 241 Ill. App. 3d 839, 182 Ill. Dec. 428, 609 N.E.2d 962 (1993), an attempt to escape, *In Interest of L.F.,* 119 Ill. App. 3d 406, 74 Ill. Dec. 925, 456 N.E.2d 646 (1983), as well as the use of an alias. *People v. Coleman,* 158 Ill. 2d 319, 198 Ill. Dec. 813, 633 N.E.2d 654 (1994).

Silence.   The failure to speak or act may be offered as the basis for an inference that conditions were such as not to evoke speech or action in a reasonable person. A familiar example is the failure of other passengers on a train to complain, offered for the inference that the temperature of the train was too low. *Silver v. New York Central Ry.,* 329 Mass. 14, 105 N.E.2d 923 (1952). *See also People v. Thomas,* 222 Ill. App. 3d 1051, 165 Ill. Dec. 596, 584 N.E.2d 1030 (1991) (fact that witness heard no conversation concerning drugs properly admitted as not hearsay because testimony in court was not offered to prove truth of any matter *asserted* in the out-of-court conversation). *Cf. People v. Lester,* 145 Ill. App. 3d 720, 99 Ill. Dec. 543, 495 N.E.2d 1278 (1986) (court failed to discuss concept with respect to testimony that nobody said anything about an accident).

For the reasons previously stated, nonverbal conduct not intended as an assertion should not be classified as hearsay. *Accord* Federal Rule of Evidence 801, 65 F.R.D. 131, 153 (1975); McCormick, Evidence §250 (4th ed. 1992).

Of course, the court must still be satisfied of the relevancy of the proffered proof. The inference as to the belief to be drawn from the conduct and, furthermore, that the facts were in accordance with the belief may be too slight in comparison with the possibility of prejudice, that exclusion as specified in §403.1 supra is proper. Moreover, when nonverbal conduct is at issue, it is not always perfectly clear whether an assertion was intended by the person making the statement. If evidence of conduct is offered on the theory that it is not intended as an assertion and hence not hearsay, the burden of showing that an assertion is intended should be on the party objecting to the evidence. The question of intention to assert is a preliminary one for the court. *See* §104.1 supra.

§801.4 Oral or Written Conduct Not Intended as an Assertion

Considerations present with respect to nonverbal nonassertive conduct, *see* §801.3 supra, also support the position that oral or written conduct not intended as an assertion is not hearsay. Examples of such conduct are screams of pain, outbursts of laughter, singing a song, or uttering or writing an expletive. Of course, any of the foregoing may be intended as an assertion. *See, e.g., People v. Nitti,* 312 Ill. 73, 143 N.E. 448 (1924), defendant, when accused of murder, responded "bullshit," by which, the court said, he meant to characterize the accusation as "absurd or fanciful."

§801.5 Statements Offered Other Than to Prove the Truth of the Matter Asserted; Verbal Acts; Circumstantial Evidence

Hearsay does not encompass all extrajudicial statements but only those offered for the purpose of proving the truth of matters asserted in the statement. *See* §801.1 supra. Therefore, when the mere making of the statement is the significant fact, hearsay is not involved. Conversely, when the mere making of the statement is not relevant and significance of the statement lies solely in its substantive content, hearsay is involved. *People v. Edwards,* 144 Ill. 2d 108, 161 Ill. Dec. 788, 579 N.E.2d 336 (1991); *People v. Nyberg,* 275 Ill. App. 3d 570, 211 Ill. Dec. 873, 656 N.E.2d 65 (1995).

In one group of extrajudicial statements thus falling outside the category of hearsay, the statement itself — the verbal act — has legal significance. Thus testimony by an agent as to a statement by the principal granting her authority to act as agent is not hearsay and does not fall within the prohibition against proving agency by the extrajudicial declarations of the agent. *Digman v. Johnson,* 18 Ill. 2d 424, 164 N.E.2d 34 (1960). Other illustrations are statements constituting contracts, *Lundberg v. Church Farm, Inc.,* 151 Ill. App. 3d 452, 104 Ill. Dec. 309, 502 N.E.2d 806 (1986); proof of loss statement in prosecution for insurance fraud, *People v. Buffman,* 260 Ill. App. 3d 505, 201 Ill. Dec. 351, 636 N.E.2d 783 (1994); statements offered as evidence of publication of slander; as well as statements constituting a crime such as an offer to perform sexual intercourse for money, 720 ILCS 5/11-14.

Also included in the group of statements comprising operative legal acts are assertions that relate to and characterize an otherwise relevant act. *Grebe v. Vacek & Co.,* 203 Ill. App. 2d 79, 243 N.E.2d 438 (1968), contemporaneous statements as to why a check in the amount of $500 was made and delivered, not hearsay. *See also* §801.6 infra.

In another group falling outside the category of hearsay, a statement made by one person that becomes known to another is offered for the purpose of showing the latter's state of mind as a circumstance under which the latter acted and as bearing upon his conduct. *People v. Peterson,* 171 Ill. App. 3d 730, 121 Ill. Dec. 639, 525 N.E.2d 946 (1988). Thus a law enforcement official's explanation for being at the scene of a crime that he proceeded to a particular location in response to a radio call is not hearsay. A statement is also not hearsay when offered for the purpose of showing that the listener was placed on notice or had knowledge. *Kochan v. Owens-Corning Fiberglass Corp.,* 242 Ill. App. 3d 781, 182 Ill. Dec. 814, 610

N.E.2d 683 (1993). For example, in a negligence action to recover damages for personal injury sustained in a fall, a statement to a customer of a food store by the manager that the floor in aisle 2 is wet is not hearsay when it is offered to show the unreasonableness of the customer's conduct in skipping down aisle 2. The same statement if offered to show the floor was wet, of course, is hearsay. Similarly, threats made to the defendant bearing on the reasonableness of her apprehension of danger, or which conversely provide a reason for conduct, are not hearsay when offered for such purpose. In each of the foregoing situations the fact that the statement was made is relevant for its effect on the listener without regard to the truth of the matter asserted. *Heller v. Jonathan Investments, Inc.*, 135 Ill. App. 3d 350, 90 Ill. Dec. 197, 481 N.E.2d 997 (1985) (statement is not hearsay when offered as evidence of the state of mind that ensued in another person in consequence of hearing the statement); *Halleck v. Coastal Building Maintenance Co.*, 269 Ill. App. 3d 887, 207 Ill. Dec. 387, 647 N.E.2d 618 (1995) (statement as to when other employees would arrive is not hearsay as bearing on whether person hearing statement then waxed the floor). *Accord Lundberg v. Church Farm, Inc.*, 151 Ill. App. 3d 452, 104 Ill. Dec. 309, 502 N.E.2d 806 (1986) (quoting Handbook); *People v. Sanchez*, 189 Ill. App. 3d 1011, 137 Ill. Dec. 514, 546 N.E.2d 268 (1989) (quoting Handbook); *People v. Seesengood*, 266 Ill. App. 3d 351, 203 Ill. Dec. 400, 639 N.E.2d 959 (1994); *People v. Shoultz*, 289 Ill. App. 3d 392, 224 Ill. Dec. 885, 682 N.E.2d 446 (1997) (quoting Handbook). Statements relevant for their effect on the listener are subject to exclusion on the ground of unfair prejudice. *See* §403.1 supra. *Accord People v. Groleau*, 156 Ill. App. 3d 742, 109 Ill. Dec. 325, 509 N.E.2d 1337 (1987). A limiting instruction to the effect that the statement is being admitted for the limited purpose of its effect on the listener and not for the truth of the statement's contents is appropriate. *People v. Williams*, 233 Ill. App. 3d 1005, 175 Ill. Dec. 19, 599 N.E.2d 1033 (1992).

Accordingly, in a libel action, evidence that the defamatory matter was told to defendant by another is not hearsay if offered for the purpose of proving that defendant did not maliciously invent the story, *Spolek Denni Hlasatel v. Hoffman,* 204 Ill. 532, 68 N.E. 400 (1903); statement by police officer to defendant in presence of plaintiff that defendant was not driving properly not hearsay when offered to show plaintiff had knowledge of defendant's inability to drive as affecting the reasonableness of plaintiff's conduct, *Smith v. Solfest,* 65 Ill. App. 3d 779, 22 Ill. Dec. 441, 382 N.E.2d 831 (1978); statement made to defendant that decedent was a "killer" was not hearsay when offered to show the state of mind of the defendant at the time of the shooting, *People v. Ortiz,* 65 Ill. App. 3d 525, 21 Ill. Dec. 939, 382 N.E.2d 303 (1978); statement by friend of defendant's brother that vehicle defendant was borrowing was a family car is not hearsay when offered to show the effect of the statement on the reasonableness of her belief that the vehicle was not stolen, *People v. Canamore,* 88 Ill. App. 3d 639, 44 Ill. Dec. 323, 411 N.E.2d 292 (1980); statements relating to proposed narcotics transactions were not hearsay when offered to establish the reasonableness of the defendant's belief that the decedents were armed and dangerous in support of his claim of self-defense, *People v. Kline,* 90 Ill. App. 3d 1008, 46 Ill. Dec. 419, 414 N.E.2d 141 (1980) (quoting Handbook); statement made to witness by decedent's son that decedent's death was made to appear to be suicide was not hearsay when offered to show state of mind of the witness when he talked with the police, *People v. Cooper,* 97 Ill. App. 3d 222, 52 Ill. Dec. 676, 422 N.E.2d 885 (1981); statement to the effect that the narcotics business is lucrative was not hearsay when offered to show the effect of such statements on defendant's state of mind in connection with an entrapment defense, *People v. Husted,* 97 Ill. App. 3d 160, 52 Ill. Dec. 753, 422 N.E.2d 962 (1981); contents of telephone conversation stating that someone was trying to get into caller's apartment was not hearsay when offered for the purpose of showing why person receiving the telephone call went outside and observed defendant in the parking lot, *People v. Canity,* 100 Ill. App. 3d 135, 55 Ill. Dec. 445, 426 N.E.2d 591 (1981) (citing Handbook); statement made to the defendant, "Are you all right to drive the car?" was not hearsay when offered to show that when the defendant, having heard the question, chose to drive, he possessed a reckless state of mind, *People v. Camp*, 128 Ill. App. 3d 223, 83 Ill. Dec. 414, 470 N.E.2d 540 (1984); statement by little boy as to who had inflicted observed bruises was not hearsay when offered to show why the person hearing the statement approached the defendant, *People v. Jones*, 140 Ill. App. 3d 660, 95 Ill. Dec. 20, 488 N.E.2d 1363 (1986); statement of counselor, working secretly for the police, to defendant that defendant's involvement with the police "turned [her] on" was not hearsay when offered as bearing on the truth or falsity of the defendant's subsequent confessions, *People v. Britz*, 112 Ill. 2d 314, 97 Ill. Dec. 768, 493 N.E.2d 575 (1986); statement to person that credit card was bad not hearsay when offered to explain why person stopped the police, *People v. Turner*, 179 Ill. App. 3d 510, 128 Ill. Dec. 159, 534 N.E.2d 179 (1989) (citing Handbook); statements made to defendant were not hearsay to extent relevant to her compulsion defense, *People v. Quick*, 236 Ill. App. 3d 446, 177 Ill. Dec. 272, 603 N.E.2d 53 (1992); statement to nurse that declarant's father was unconscious was not hearsay when offered to show notice in medical malpractice case, *Lassai v. Holy Cross Hospital*, 224 Ill. App. 3d 330, 166 Ill. Dec. 610, 586 N.E.2d 568 (1991); statement by police officer to accused that his umbrella was found at crime scene was not hearsay when offered to explain why defendant confessed, *People v. Murdock*, 259 Ill. App. 3d 1014, 198 Ill. Dec. 254, 632 N.E.2d 313 (1994) (citing Handbook); statement by defendant's sister to defendant that she had seen the victim draw a gun on other students was not hearsay when offered to show the defendant's state of mind in support of self-defense claim, *People v. Sims*, 265 Ill. App. 3d 352, 202 Ill. Dec. 577, 638 N.E.2d 223 (1994); and statement to the defendant by police officers that a four year old had said that the defendant had beaten her was not hearsay when offered on question of whether defendant's subsequent confession was voluntary or coerced. *People v. Williams*, 274 Ill. App. 3d 598, 210 Ill. Dec. 704, 653 N.E.2d

899 (1995). *Cf. People v. Williams,* 181 Ill. 2d 297, 229 Ill. Dec. 898, 692 N.E.2d 1109 (1998), statement of police officer admitted to show his state of mind and why he acted as he did prior to being killed is not hearsay; *Gass v. Carducci,* 37 Ill. App. 2d 181, 185 N.E.2d 285 (1962), statements by husband of defendant as to condition of car door admitted as circumstantial evidence of knowledge of condition by wife; *Fleming v. Fleming,* 85 Ill. App. 3d 532, 40 Ill. Dec. 676, 406 N.E.2d 879 (1980), statements by decedent admitted to show knowledge of party to enable her to have entered a valid antenuptial agreement; *People v. Ingram* 91 Ill. App. 3d 1074, 47 Ill. Dec. 564, 415 N.E.2d 569 (1980), statement of witness that he would refuse to testify for $200 worth of drugs held not hearsay; and *People v. Jackson,* 145 Ill. App. 3d 626, 99 Ill. Dec. 472, 495 N.E.2d 1207 (1986), statement of witness, offered to show why witness told victim to go home, held not hearsay. Since the relevance of the statements in each of the last five cases depends upon the truth of the assertion as representing the declarant's state of mind and not upon the effect the statement had on the listener, the statement is hearsay. *See also People v. Szudy,* 262 Ill. App. 3d 695, 200 Ill. Dec. 462, 635 N.E.2d 801 (1994) (confusing discussion). With respect to admissibility of such hearsay statements, *see* §§803.4–803.7 infra.

In *People v. Simms,* 143 Ill. 2d 154, 157 Ill. Dec. 483, 572 N.E.2d 947 (1991), the supreme court stated that a police officer *may* recount the steps taken in the investigation of a crime, and may describe the events leading up to the defendant's arrest, where such testimony is necessary and important to fully explain the prosecution's case to the trier of fact. *Accord People v. Lewis,* 165 Ill. 2d 305, 209 Ill. Dec. 144, 651 N.E.2d 72 (1995); *People v. Hayes,* 139 Ill. 2d 89, 151 Ill. Dec. 348, 564 N.E.2d 803 (1990). The court also stated that a police officer *may* testify about his conversations with others, such as victims or witnesses, when such testimony is not offered to prove the truth of the matter asserted by the other, but is used to show the investigative steps taken by the officer. Testimony by a police officer, if relevant to describing the process of the investigation, is admissible, even if such testimony suggests that a nontestifying witness implicated the defendant. *Id.; People v. Morgan*, 142 Ill. 2d 410, 154 Ill. Dec. 534, 568 N.E.2d 755 (1991); *People v. Gacho*, 122 Ill. 2d 221, 119 Ill. Dec. 287, 522 N.E.2d 1146 (1988); *People v. Sims*. 285 Ill. App. 3d 598, 220 Ill. Dec. 698, 673 N.E.2d 1119 (1996); *People v. Flores*, 265 Ill. App. 3d 484, 194 Ill. Dec. 729, 628 N.E.2d 226 (1993). Similarly, testimony regarding the issuance of a warrant for arrest may be presented when it occurs as part of the narrative of the steps taken in the course of investigation. *People v. Bounds*, 171 Ill. 2d 1, 215 Ill. Dec. 28, 662 N.E.2d 1168 (1995) (a questionable decision, *see* infra). However, ordinarily, *see* infra, the content of the statement made by the third person itself is *not* admissible. *People v. Jones*, 153 Ill. 2d 155, 180 Ill. Dec. 68, 606 N.E.2d 1145 (1992); *People v. Morgan* supra; *People v. Gacho* supra; *People v. Henderson*, 142 Ill. 2d 258, 154 Ill. Dec. 785, 568 N.E.2d 1234 (1990); *People v. Miller*, 225 Ill. App. 3d 92, 168 Ill. Dec. 217, 589 N.E.2d 619 (1992); *People v. Trotter*, 254 Ill. App. 3d 514, 193 Ill. Dec. 553, 626 N.E.2d 1104 (1993); *People v. Byron*, 269 Ill. App. 3d 449, 206 Ill. Dec. 748, 645 N.E.2d 1000 (1995); *People v Rodriguez*, 275 Ill. App. 3d 274, 211 Ill. Dec. 639, 655 N.E.2d 1022 (1995); *People v. Topps*, 227 Ill. App. 3d 183, 227 Ill. Dec. 183, 687 N.E.2d 106 (1997). *Accord People v. Smith*, 177 Ill. 2d 53, 226 Ill. Dec. 425, 685 N.E.2d 880 (1997), fact jury would conclude that police began looking for defendant as a result of what nontestifying witnesses told them is not disqualifying as long as the testimony does not gratuitously reveal the substance of the codefendant's statements. *See, e.g., People v. Stout*, 110 Ill. App. 3d 830, 66 Ill. Dec. 496, 443 N.E.2d 19 (1982), affidavits submitted in support of search warrant were hearsay and under the circumstances should not have been admitted to show police officer's state of mind; *People v. Williams*, 159 Ill. App. 3d 612, 112 Ill. Dec. 1, 513 N.E.2d 415 (1987), improper for police officer to testify that upon arrival at scene a person at the scene said that the child who was beaten was upstairs; *People v. Pryor*, 131 Ill. App. 3d 865, 130 Ill. Dec. 812, 537 N.E.2d 1141 (1989), improper for police officer to testify that a passing citizen told him that a black man attempted to sell marijuana and to state the description of the black man provided by the citizen. *See also People v. O'Toole*, 226 Ill. App. 3d 974, 169 Ill. Dec. 31, 590 N.E.2d 950 (1992), proper for police officer to state that as a result of a conversation with a particular person an undercover sting operation was set up but not as to what was said in the conversation; *People v. Craddock*, 210 Ill. App. 3d 791, 155 Ill. Dec. 283, 569 N.E.2d 283 (1991), courts have recognized that police may testify to the fact that a conversation was held with a nontestifying witness for the purpose of explaining either police procedure or why the police acted as they did, but that testimony as to the content or substance of that conversation is improper hearsay; *People v. Cameron*, 189 Ill. App. 3d 998, 137 Ill. Dec. 505, 546 N.E.2d 259 (1989), proper for police officer to testify that an informant advised that the accused would be at a tavern to pick up a package but not that the package would contain cocaine, quoting McCormick, Evidence §249 at 734 (3d ed. 1984) that the "need for the evidence is slight, the likelihood of misuse great." The foregoing may be accomplished, i.e., disclosure of the fact but not content of the conversation, by having the police officer testify to having acted upon a "tip" or upon "information received." *See People v. Batson*, 225 Ill. App. 3d 157, 167 Ill. Dec. 280, 587 N.E.2d 549 (1992). *See generally People v. Johnson*, 68 Ill. App. 3d 836, 25 Ill. Dec. 371, 386 N.E.2d 642 (1979), quoting McCormick, Evidence §248 at 587 (Cleary ed. 1972), that if the policeman goes beyond stating that he acted "upon information received," and "becomes more specific by repeating definite complaints of a particular crime by the accused, this is so likely to be misused by the jury as evidence of the fact asserted that it should be excluded as hearsay." It has been suggested by Justice Egan, specially concurring in *People v. Singletary*, 273 Ill. App. 3d 1076, 1089, 210 Ill. Dec. 357, 366, 652 N.E.2d 1333, 1342 (1995), with much force, that the practice of offering the content of inadmissible hearsay statements made to the police in the course of their investigation "persists because some prosecutors are ever confident that we will write off the error as harmless." Moreover, in spite of the foregoing, admissibility of the content of the statement is nevertheless still sometimes incorrectly sanctioned. *See People v. Bell,* 273 Ill. App. 3d 439, 210 Ill. Dec. 164, 652 N.E.2d 1140 (1995); *People v. Williams,* 274 Ill. App. 3d 598, 210 Ill. Dec. 704, 653 N.E.2d 899 (1995). Failure of the Illinois Supreme Court in *People v. Pulliam,* 176 Ill. 2d 261, 223 Ill. Dec. 610, 680 N.E.2d 343 (1997), hopefully because of oversight, to mention that the content of statements offered to show investigative steps should not have been permitted is particularly unfortunate.

This limited admissibility of investigatory background as stated above is still nevertheless unfortunately overly broad. Investigatory steps taken by a police officer are rarely more than marginally relevant at best, while the risk of jury misuse of the information at great expense to the accused is substantial. *See, e.g., Sanborn v. Commonwealth,* 754 S.W.2d 534, 541 (Ky. 1988) ("Prosecutors should, once and for all, abandon the term 'investigative hearsay' as a misnomer, an oxymoron. The rule is that a police officer may testify about information furnished to him only where it tends to explain the action that was taken by the police officer as a result of this information *and* the taking of that action is an issue of the case. Such information is then admissible, not to prove the facts told to the police officer, but only to prove why the police officer then acted as he did. It is admissible *only if* there is an issue about the police officer's action."); *United States v. Martin,* 897 F.2d 1368, 1373-1374 (6th Cir. 1990) (Merritt, C.J., concurring and dissenting) ("[N]o court has explained why investigative background . . . is necessary or even helpful to jurors in a criminal trial. Jurors need not revisit the government's preliminary investigative processes, especially when such low-value evidence comes at such a high price to the accused. For prosecutors determined to present such low-value evidence, they should at least have to produce the out-of-court declarant for cross-examination, or demonstrate his or her unavailability. No such effort was made here. . . . Had Martin claimed some form of investigatory or prosecutorial misconduct, such as lack of probable cause, then the majority's argument would have greater force. *Cf. Tennessee v. Street,* 471 U.S. 409, 105 S. Ct. 2078, 85 L. Ed. 2d 425 (1985) (accomplice's written confession admissible only to rebut defendant's claim that his confession was coerced). Otherwise, it is difficult to see what value the out-of-court statements would retain, except to inform jurors that an out-of-court declarant not subject to cross-examination believed Martin was a food-stamp trafficker."). *Accord People v. McCray,* 273 Ill. App. 3d 396, 402, 210 Ill. Dec. 438, 442, 653 N.E.2d 25, 29 (1995) ("We do not hold that circumstances of the arrest evidence is inadmissible in every case. It may be admitted when relevant to the charge on trial. For example, when relevant for identification of the defendant (*People v. Gonzalez* (1991), 142 Ill. 2d 481, 154 Ill. Dec. 643, 568 N.E.2d 864); or to rebut claims that the police unjustifiably targeted the defendant (*People v. Johnson* (1986), 114 Ill. 2d 170, 102 Ill. Dec. 342, 499 N.E.2d 1355); or to rebut the defendant's alibi (*People v. Connor* (1988), 177 Ill. App. 3d 532, 126 Ill. Dec. 835, 532 N.E.2d 520)."). *See also People v. Lewis,* 165 Ill. 2d 305, 209 Ill. Dec. 144, 651 N.E.2d 72 (1995), error, but harmless to disclose, that defendant was in custody in California and extradited for trial; *People v. Brock,* 262 Ill. App. 3d 485, 198 Ill. Dec. 894, 633 N.E.2d 735 (1994), proper to admit police officer testimony that deceased witness had identified accused at a line-up as no specific detail of the conversation was elicited; clearly a decision that illustrates the hypocrisy of admissibility for the limited purpose of investigatory background.

Investigatory background may be of significant relevance when there is an important issue about subsequent police officer conduct, such as when the accused is charged with resisting arrest, *People v. Cordero,* 244 Ill. App. 3d 390, 184 Ill. Dec. 364, 613 N.E.2d 391 (1993), in which circumstance the content of the statement is admissible and a limiting instruction should be given. *See, e.g., People v. Simms,* 143 Ill. 2d 154, 157 Ill. Dec. 483, 572 N.E.2d 947 (1991) (content of third-party statement that defendant had confessed admitted to explain why police continued to question the defendant); *People v. Malave,* 230 Ill. App. 3d 556, 172 Ill. Dec. 54, 595 N.E.2d 117 (1992) (content of statement admitted to explain why detective confronted defendant with his suspicions); *People v. Godina,* 223 Ill. App. 3d 205, 165 Ill. Dec. 344, 584 N.E.2d 523 (1991) (content of statements to police officer detailing defendant's arrest out of town was not hearsay when offered to explain the police officer's decision not to do a parafin test upon the accused's return to the city); *People v. Gully,* 151 Ill. App. 3d 795, 104 Ill. Dec. 431, 502 N.E.2d 1091 (1986) (content of "anonymous" telephone call admitted to explain why defendant's picture was included in array of photographs shown to victim). *See also People v. Louisville,* 241 Ill. App. 3d 772, 182 Ill. Dec. 148, 609 N.E.2d 682 (1992), and *People v. Townsend,* 275 Ill. App. 3d 200, 211 Ill. Dec. 599, 655 N.E.2d 982 (1995) (content of police communication admissible to show that police officer had probable cause for the arrest). *Compare People v. Jones,* 153 Ill. 2d 155, 180 Ill. Dec. 68, 606 N.E.2d 1145 (1992) (substance of out-of-court conversation at a crime scene properly admitted where the substance of the conversation is not relevant to establish the commission of the crime for which the defendant is on trial, i.e., substance related to car stripping which placed accused at scene; it did not tend to establish the accused committed the armed robbery for which on trial, but solely to establish how the police came to learn of the accused). *See also People v. Williams,* 289 Ill. App. 3d 24, 224 Ill. Dec. 133, 681 N.E.2d 115 (1997) (content of statement that a man with a gun was threatening another admitted to explain why police stopped defendant); *compare id.,* McNulty, J. dissenting (details were not necessary to explain officer's actions). *See generally People v. Williams,* 181 Ill. 2d 297, 229 Ill. Dec. 898, 692 N.E.2d 1109 (1998), with respect to shooting death of police officer 911 tape properly admitted for the limited purpose of understanding the manner in which the police conducted their investigation, to show the continuity of the police conduct, the effect of the conversations on the listeners' states of mind and why the listeners acted as they did, to show the declarants' states of mind and why the declarants acted as they did, and to show the actual time in which all the events took place, even though cumulative of oral testimony covering same issues; to the extent the statements reflected the *declarant's* state of mind and future conduct the statements are in fact hearsay admissible under the current state of mind exception, *see* §§803.4–803.7 infra.

A related situation is presented if the police officer in describing his or her investigatory steps is prepared to state that the accused was arrested as the result of an investigation of another crime or that the police officer took certain action such as arresting the defendant as a consequence of having spoken to someone concerning another crime. Evidence of the investigation of another crime is not admissible merely to show how the current investigation unfolded and how the accused came into custody. *People v. Lewis*, 165 Ill. 2d 305, 209 Ill. Dec. 144, 651 N.E.2d 72 (1995); *People v. Richardson*, 123 Ill. 2d 322, 123 Ill. Dec. 908, 528 N.E.2d 612 (1988). Reference by the police officer to having spoken to someone concerning another crime is similarly inadmissible, even if the content is excluded, when offered to explain the course of the current investigation. *People v. Bass*, 220 Ill. App. 3d 230, 162 Ill. Dec. 855, 580 N.E.2d 1274 (1991). *See also* Egan, J., specially concurring. Evidence of the existence of another crime is not admissible unless such evidence specifically connects the defendant with the crime for which he is being tried. *People v. Lewis*, 165 Ill. 2d 305, 209 Ill. Dec. 144, 651 N.E.2d 72 (1995); *People v. Overton*, 281 Ill. App. 3d 209, 217 Ill. Dec. 84, 666 N.E.2d 753 (1996). Evidence of the existence of another crime is also admissible when the accused opens the door to its admission such as by asserting that the police had unjustifiably targeted him, *People v. Johnson*, 114 Ill. 2d 170, 102 Ill. Dec. 342, 499 N.E.2d 1355 (1986), or when relevant to show resistance to arrest. *People v. Sustak*, 15 Ill. 2d 115, 153 N.E.2d 849 (1958).

Extremely difficult analytical questions concerning the rule against hearsay sometimes arise when out-of-court statements are offered as circumstantial evidence relating to mechanical traces, character of establishments, personal knowledge otherwise established, and the state of mind of the declarant. *See, e.g., People v. Reed,* 108 Ill. App. 3d 984, 64 Ill. Dec. 469, 439 N.E.2d 1277 (1982). Nevertheless, it is clear that the concept of whether evidence is circumstantial or direct is irrelevant in applying the hearsay definition. *Accord Waechter v. Carson Pirie Scott & Co.,* 170 Ill. App. 3d 370, 120 Ill. Dec. 437, 523 N.E.2d 1348 (1988). The only question to be asked is whether the out-of-court statement is being offered to prove the truth of the matter asserted. *See* §801.1 supra. If the relevance of the statement depends upon the truth of the matter asserted or the declarant's belief in the truth or falsity of the matter asserted, the out-of-court statement is hearsay. Therefore, since a declarant must believe the truth of a statement offered to show insanity for the statement to be relevant, the statement is properly classified as hearsay. Calling such a statement not hearsay as circumstantial evidence of insanity as was done in *People v. Vanda,* 111 Ill. App. 3d 551, 67 Ill. Dec. 373, 444 N.E.2d 609 (1982), is incorrect as is the conclusion that the request of a person knocking on a door of an apartment to see Nick is not hearsay when offered to characterize the use of the apartment for drugs. *People v. Casas,* 234 Ill. App. 3d 847, 176 Ill. Dec. 100, 601 N.E.2d 798 (1992). Conversely, where such a statement is relevant without regard to its truth or the declarant's belief in its truth or falsity, such as when a statement in the form of a logo is offered for comparison purposes, *People ex rel. Hartigan v. Organization,* 147 Ill. App. 3d 826, 101 Ill. Dec. 273, 498 N.E.2d 597 (1986), the statement is not hearsay. As to the admissibility of statements indicating then-existing state of mind, *see* §803.4 infra. For a full discussion see Graham, "Stickperson Hearsay": A Simplified Approach to Understanding the Rule Against Hearsay, 1982 Ill. L. Rev. 887.

Finally, prior statements of a witness admitted for their effect upon the credibility of the witness are not being offered for their truth but solely for the fact said. *People v. Spaulding,* 68 Ill. App. 3d 663, 25 Ill. Dec. 198, 386 N.E.2d 469 (1979).

§801.6 Statements Offered Other Than to Prove the Truth of the Matter Asserted; Basis for Nonasserted Inference

If a statement, although assertive in form, is offered as a basis for inferring something other than the truth of the matter asserted, the statement is sometimes argued to fall outside the definition of hearsay. The argument is based on the assumption of a reduced sincerity hearsay risk similar to that present with respect to nonverbal conduct not intended as an assertion at all. *See* §801.3 supra. However, the argument is fallacious. Since the truth of the matter actually asserted in the statement must be accepted for the statement to be relevant, a reduction of the sincerity risk is not present and the statement is thus properly classified as hearsay. For a full discussion, *see* Graham, "Stickperson Hearsay:" A Simplified Approach to Understanding the Rule Against Hearsay, 1982 Ill. L. Rev. 887. Most common law authority is in accord. The leading English case was *Wright v. Doe D. Tatham*, 5 Cl. & F. 670 (H.L. 1838). In that case, letters written to a testator and offered by the proponents of his will were of a kind that would not likely have been written to a mentally defective person; the inference suggested was that the writers believed him to be sane, which in turn justified the inference that he was sane. The House of Lords ruled the letters inadmissible hearsay as "implied assertions." *Contra* McCormick, Evidence §250 (4th ed. 1992).

Sometimes statements offered for a different inference also characterize an act. *Brand v. Henderson*, 107 Ill. 141 (1883), statements made at time of future contract to show it was a gambling transaction; *Quinn v. Eagleston*, 108 Ill. 248 (1883), statements of owner of land indicating absence of intention to dedicate right of way; *Rush v. Collins*, 366 Ill. 307, 8 N.E.2d 659 (1937), statements by party claiming prescriptive easement showing that his use of alley was adverse; *In re Cronholm Estate*, 38 Ill. App. 2d 141, 186 N.E.2d 534 (1962), statement of disposition indicating lack of donative intent in establishing joint bank account. *See also* §801.5 supra.

Note that in each of the situations under discussion the

inference of the state of mind of the declarant is inferred from the statement, not asserted by it.

§801.7 Statements Not Made in Presence of Opposite Party

On occasion, whether the party against whom a statement is offered was present when the statement was made has a bearing upon admissibility. Thus an oral statement relied upon as notice cannot have been effective as such unless made in the presence of the person sought to be charged with notice, *see* §801.5 supra, and the presence of the person is essential if it is claimed that she admitted the truth of an oral statement by failing to deny it. *See* §802.7 infra. In general, however, the presence or absence of the party against whom an extrajudicial statement is offered has no bearing upon either its status as hearsay or its admissibility, and an objection so phrased betrays a basic lack of understanding of the nature of hearsay. The presence of the defendant is equally irrelevant when a prior statement of a witness is offered to impeach the declarant. *People v. King,* 109 Ill. 2d 514, 94 Ill. Dec. 702, 488 N.E.2d 949 (1986).

The frequently heard objection in criminal cases that the statement was made outside the presence of the defendant has now been put firmly to rest. *People v. Carpenter,* 28 Ill. 2d 116, 190 N.E.2d 738 (1963), objection of not in presence of defendant is not recognized in the law; the presence or absence of the defendant, except where an admission by silence is asserted, is irrelevant to a determination of hearsay.

§801.8 Hearsay Admitted Without Objection

Under general principles, §103 supra, a party who does not make a timely objection cannot complain of the admission of hearsay. For a discussion of plain error, *see* §103.10 supra. Similarly, a statement that is hearsay for one purpose but not another may be considered by the trier of fact generally unless a hearsay objection is interposed and a limiting instruction requested. *People v. Camp,* 128 Ill. App. 3d 223, 83 Ill. Dec. 414, 470 N.E.2d 540 (1984). The question remains, however, of the weight and probative value of hearsay so admitted. The almost infinite variety that hearsay assumes precludes any answer except that it will be "considered and given its natural probative effect." *Town of Cicero v. Industrial Comm.,* 404 Ill. 487, 495, 89 N.E.2d 354 (1950). *Accord People v. Williams,* 139 Ill. 2d 1, 150 Ill. Dec. 544, 563 N.E.2d 431 (1990); *People v. Collins,* 106 Ill. 2d 237, 87 Ill. Dec. 910, 478 N.E.2d 267 (1985); *Jackson v. Board of Review of Department of Labor,* 105 Ill. 2d 501, 86 Ill. Dec. 500, 475 N.E.2d 879 (1985); *People v. Akis,* 63 Ill. 2d 296, 347 N.E.2d 733 (1976). Depending on the apparent trustworthiness of the hearsay, it may receive full credit, as in *Town of Cicero v. Industrial Comm.* supra, medical opinion of cause of death by coroner's physician based on hearsay; or none, *First Natl. Bank v. Illinois Natl. Bank,* 19 Ill. 2d 385, 167 N.E.2d 223 (1960), self-serving statement seeking to characterize disputed transaction as loan.

§801.9   Prior Inconsistent Statements

Subject to restrictions with respect to collateral matters, §607.2 supra, a witness may be impeached by extrinsic proof that he made a statement out of court inconsistent with his in-court testimony. The prior statement has to be inconsistent, *see* §613.2 supra, and a proper foundation has to be laid during cross-examination of the witness. *See* §613.3 supra. Under the Illinois decisions a prior inconsistent statement is hearsay for which no common law hearsay exception exists. Hence, absent a statutory hearsay exception, a prior inconsistent statement is not admitted as substantive evidence but rather is admitted solely for its impeaching effect upon the credibility of the witness. *People v. Gant,* 58 Ill. 2d 178, 317 N.E.2d 564 (1974); *People v. Collins,* 49 Ill. 2d 179, 274 N.E.2d 77 (1971); *Smith v. Pelz,* 384 Ill. 446, 51 N.E.2d 534 (1943). Of course, prior inconsistent statements of a witness are not to be confused with an admission of a party, §802 infra, which, as a hearsay exception, is regarded as substantive evidence and requires no preliminary foundation on cross-examination. *Brown v. Calumet River Ry.*, 125 Ill. 600, 18 N.E. 283 (1888); *Kane v. Wehner,* 312 Ill. App. 391, 39 N.E.2d 51 (1941). If a witness confronted with her prior statement acknowledges both its making and the truth of its contents, the prior statement becomes the witness's in-court testimony and is thus not hearsay. If the court finds that lack of recollection displayed by a witness called by the prosecution is feigned, the court may treat the witness's feigned lack of recollection as an adoption of the truth of the witness's prior statement. *People v. Jenkins,* 104 Ill. App. 3d 522, 60 Ill. Dec. 272, 432 N.E.2d 1171 (1982); *People v. Amato,* 128 Ill. App. 3d 985, 84 Ill. Dec. 162, 471 N.E.2d 928 (1984).

Critics of the common law prohibition against substantive use of a prior inconsistent statement have long contended that the declarant at trial is under oath, that his demeanor may be observed and his credibility tested by cross-examination and that the timing of cross-examination is not critical. *See, e.g., De Carlo v. United States,* 6 F.2d 364 (2d Cir. 1925) (Judge Learned Hand); McCormick, Evidence, §251 (4th ed. 1992). Federal Rule of Evidence 801(d)(1)(A), 65 F.R.D. 131, 153-154 (1975), accepts the arguments of such critics only to the extent of permitting substantive use of prior inconsistent statements of a witness who testifies at trial and is subject to cross-examination if the prior statement was given under oath subject to the penalty of perjury at a trial, hearing, or other proceeding, or in a deposition. The rationale behind the very limited departure from the common law through exemption from operation of the Hearsay Rule by the definition of such prior inconsistent statements as "not hearsay" of Rule 801(d)(1)(A) is that expressed by the Report of the House Committee on the Judiciary:

(1) unlike in most other situations involving unsworn or oral statements, there can be no dispute as to whether the prior statement was made; and (2) the context of a formal proceed-

ing, an oath, and the opportunity for cross-examination [in most instances] provide firm additional assurances of the reliability of the prior statement. [H.R. Rep. No. 650, 93d Cong., 1st Sess. 13 (1973).]

In spite of criticism extended against the limitation of prior inconsistent statements to impeachment, the Supreme Court of Illinois has consistently refused to alter the common law approach. *People v. Collins* supra; *People v. Gant* supra; *People v. Bailey*, 58 Ill. 2d 178, 317 N.E.2d 564 (1974). *See People v. Spicer,*79 Ill. 2d 173, 37 Ill. Dec. 279, 402 N.E.2d 169 (1979), for a detailed statement of reasons underlying the court's position. For further discussion, see Graham, Prior Inconsistent Statements — Impeachment and Substantive Admissibility: An Analysis of the Effect of Adopting the Proposed Illinois Rules of Evidence, 1978 Ill. L. Forum 329.

In light of the Illinois Supreme Court's unwillingness to alter the common law rule, in 1984 the legislature adopted 725 ILCS 5/115-10.1, *applicable in criminal cases only,* providing for the substantive admissibility of certain prior inconsistent statements:

Admissibility of Prior Inconsistent Statements

In all criminal cases, evidence of a statement made by a witness is not made inadmissible by the hearsay rule if
(a) the statement is inconsistent with his testimony at the hearing or trial, and
(b) the witness is subject to cross-examination concerning the statement, and
(c) the statement —
(1) was made under oath at a trial, hearing, or other proceeding, or
(2) narrates, describes, or explains an event or condition of which the witness had personal knowledge, and
(A) the statement is proved to have been written or signed by the witness, or
(B) the witness acknowledged under oath the making of the statement either in his testimony at the hear-

ing or trial in which the admission into evidence of the prior statement is being sought or at trial, hearing, or other proceeding, or

(C) the statement is proved to have been accurately recorded by a tape recorder, videotape recording, or any other similar electronic means of sound recording.

Nothing in this Section shall render a prior inconsistent statement inadmissible for purposes of impeachment because such statement was not recorded or otherwise fails to meet the criteria set forth herein.

Subsection (c)(1) incorporates Rule 801(d)(1)(A) of the Federal Rules of Evidence. *See People v. Rivera,* 166 Ill. 2d 279, 209 Ill. Dec. 767, 652 N.E.2d 307 (1995) (prior trial testimony). Subsection (c)(1) includes statements made by a witness under oath before the grand jury, *People v. Sims,* 285 Ill. App. 3d 598, 220 Ill. Dec. 698, 673 N.E.2d 1119 (1996), that is, an "other proceeding," including grand jury statements in which the witness acknowledges having made prior statements and verifies that such prior statements are true and correct, thus making the prior statements current grand jury testimony. *People v. Coleman,* 187 Ill. App. 3d 541, 135 Ill. Dec. 172, 543 N.E.2d 555 (1989). Subsection (c)(2) extends admissibility to prior inconsistent statements felt to possess sufficient assurance of certainty of making and accuracy of reporting. Prior inconsistent statements proved to have been written or signed by the witness are included, subsection (c)(2)(A), *People v. Willis,* 274 Ill. App. 3d 551, 211 Ill. Dec. 109, 654 N.E.2d 571 (1995), as are prior inconsistent statements proved to have been accurately recorded, subsection (c)(2)(C). The actual written or signed statement or the actual recording must itself be offered into the evidence; an inadequate foundation is presented by evidence from a witness as to what the unproduced writing or recording states. *People v. Kinsloe,* 281 Ill. App. 3d 799, 217, Ill. Dec. 203, 666 N.E.2d 872 (1996). Prior oral statements acknowledged by the witness to have been made during her current testimony or at an earlier trial, hearing, or other proceeding are also included, subsection (c)(2)(B); *People v. Hastings,* 161 Ill. App. 3d 714, 113 Ill. Dec. 451, 515 N.E.2d 260 (1987); *People v. Sambo,* 197 Ill. App. 3d 574, 144 Ill. Dec. 41, 554 N.E.2d 1080 (1990); *People v. Chatmon,* 236 Ill. App. 3d 913, 178 Ill. Dec. 143, 604 N.E.2d 399 (1992); *People v. Zuritai,* 295 Ill. App. 3d 1072, 230 Ill. Dec. 409, 693 N.E.2d 887 (1998). Unacknowledged oral statements are not included. *People v. Grano,* 286 Ill. App. 3d 278, 221 Ill. Dec. 727, 676 N.E.2d 248 (1996). Unacknowledged oral statements are the most likely not to have been made and the most likely, if made, to have been unfairly obtained. A witness's testimony that he could "not exactly" remember, although he was sure he told the truth, is not an acknowledgment. *People v. Denny,* 221 Ill. App. 3d 298, 163 Ill. Dec. 685, 581 N.E.2d 839 (1991); *People v. Posedel,* 214 Ill. App. 3d 170, 157 Ill. Dec. 838, 573 N.E.2d 256 (1991). With respect to the necessity that the witness acknowledge making a specific statement, i.e., the content of the statement, rather than simply acknowledging having made a statement, *see People v. McDonald,* 276 Ill. App. 3d 466, 213 Ill. Dec. 230, 658 N.E.2d 1251 (1995), Wolfson, J., dissenting. A prior inconsistent statement to be admissible under subsection (c)(2) must, in addition, "narrate, describe, or explain an event or condition of which the witness had personal knowledge." Presence of the declarant in court subject to cross-examination concerning the prior inconsistent statement provides an adequate opportunity to expose and counteract any impropriety, such as coercion, deception, or subtle influence, that may have occurred in the taking of the statement. No additional assurance of trustworthiness is required. *People v. Carlos,* 275 Ill. App. 3d 80, 211 Ill. Dec. 799, 655 N.E.2d 1182 (1995) (citing Handbook). The determination of inconsistency follows that now employed with respect to prior statements offered solely to impeach. *See* §613.2 supra. *Accord People v. Thomas,* 220 Ill. App. 3d 298, 163 Ill. Dec. 12, 580 N.E.2d 1353 (1991) (omission of fact from prior written and signed statement of a witness subject to cross-examination was substantively admissible). *See also People v. Salazar,* 125 Ill. 2d 424, 129 Ill. Dec. 1, 535 N.E.2d 766 (1988) (court need not make a quantitative or mathematical analysis to find entire statement inconsistent); *People v. Morales,* 281 Ill. App. 3d 695, 217 Ill. Dec. 170, 666 N.E.2d 839 (1996) (witness's entire prior statement about what the defendant had said was inconsistent with witness's trial testimony that such conversation never took place). If only part of a statement is inconsistent, only such part is admissible under 5/115-10.1. *People v. Bush,* 227 Ill. App. 3d 81, 169 Ill. Dec. 65, 590 N.E.2d 984 (1992). Section 115-10.1 may not be employed by the state to admit what are generally consistent statements even though some inconsistencies exist in the hope of corroborating and bolstering the witness. *People v. Mitchell,* 225 Ill. App. 3d 708, 168 Ill. Dec. 3, 588 N.E.2d 1247 (1992). To the extent *People v. Fields,* 285 Ill. App. 3d 1020, 221 Ill. Dec. 273, 675 N.E.2d 180 (1996), is inconsistent, it is incorrect and should not be followed. The preliminary foundation requirement on cross-examination prior to the introduction of extrinsic proof, *see* §613.3 supra, applies to prior inconsistent statements admitted as substantive evidence under 5/115-10.1. *People v. Hallbeck,* 227 Ill. App. 3d 59, 169 Ill. Dec. 52, 590 N.E.2d 971 (1992).

Sections 115-10.1(c)(2)(A) and (C) both require that the statement be "proved" to have been made whenever the witness refuses to acknowledge that he made it. Introduction of evidence sufficient to support a jury finding that the witness made the out-of-court statement, *see* §104.2 supra, is inadequate. Rather, the litigant offering as substantive evidence a prior inconsistent statement that the witness has not admitted making must initially satisfy the court that it is more probably true than not true that the statement was in fact made. *See* §104.1 supra. While the statute requires that the proponent prove that it is more probably true than not true that the statement alleged to be that of the declarant was the exact statement the declarant wrote, signed, or spoke, the proponent of the prior statement should not be required to bear this burden of proof regarding other contested matters relating to the statement. The special problems of distortion through subtle wording variations, complete omissions, fabricated additions followed by uncritical signing, subtle influence, or appeal to the declarant's desire to please another person, etc., are to be resolved and can be adequately resolved by the jury after it has heard such allegations presented by the in-court declarant and explored during the cross-examination of the person who obtained the prior statement. The jury, consistent with its traditional function, is assigned the task of judging the credibility of each witness and of deciding what in fact occurred when the prior statement was allegedly made. However, if the declarant asserts that a prior statement was made involuntarily, the proponent of the statement should be required to convince the judge that it is more probably true than not true that the statement had not been the product of coercion.

The requirement that the witness have had personal knowledge of the event or condition the prior inconsistent statement narrates, describes, or explains, subsection (c)(2), has two very important consequences. First, only a witness with personal knowledge of the subject matter of a prior inconsistent statement can be examined about whether the statement is truthful. Second, the requirement excludes from evidence all prior statements of a witness that merely narrate a third person's declaration unless the witness also has personal knowledge of the facts underlying the third person's statement. *People v. Saunders,* 220 Ill. App. 3d 647, 162 Ill. Dec. 827, 580 N.E.2d 1246 (1991) (personal knowledge does not refer to knowledge acquired by being told something; it refers to that which has been seen by the witness). Thus a witness's prior statement that he heard a criminal defendant make an incriminating admission would be inadmissible as substantive evidence unless the witness had personal knowledge of the incriminating conduct itself. *People v. Coleman,* 187 Ill. App. 3d 541, 135 Ill. Dec. 172, 543 N.E.2d 555 (1989); *People v. Cooper,* 188 Ill. App. 3d 971, 136 Ill. Dec. 498, 544 N.E.2d 1273 (1989); *People v. Hubbard,* 276 Ill. App. 3d 98, 212 Ill. Dec. 814, 657 N.E.2d 1159 (1995); *People v. Morales,* 281 Ill. App. 3d 695, 217 Ill. Dec. 170, 666 N.E.2d 839 (1996). *See generally People v. Williams,* 264 Ill. App. 3d 278, 201 Ill. Dec. 198, 636 N.E.2d 630

(1993). The personal knowledge requirement excludes from evidence those statements most open to fabrication by the declarant while concurrently assuring the opportunity for effective cross-examination. Coupled with strong guarantees that the prior inconsistent statement was actually made, cross-examination of a witness with personal knowledge of the underlying facts can be expected to test effectively the reliability of the prior statement. The determination of whether the out-of-court statement was from personal knowledge is made from the face of the statement and not from the later testimony in court of the recanting witness; otherwise it would be too easy for a turncoat witness, whether or not intimidated (*see* discussion infra), to preclude admissibility. *People v. Fauber,* 266 Ill. App. 3d 381, 203 Ill. Dec. 769, 640 N.E.2d 689 (1994). On the other hand, where a non-recanting witness testifies in court that the prior inconsistent statement was not based upon personal knowledge, and the prior inconsistent statement does not on its face provide either a statement of personal knowledge nor any facts from which personal knowledge may be inferred, it is an error to admit the prior inconsistent statement under 725 ILCS 5/115-10.1. *Contra People v. Rodriguez,* 291 Ill. App. 3d 55, 225 Ill. Dec. 653, 684 N.E.2d 128 (1997) (witness in court stated that she did not see defendant get into another vehicle having already entered the house and was relying on being told of such fact later by the victim, prior statement to police that "All I know is that [defendant] got into the car and went after them" properly admitted relying upon *Fauber* super; incorrectly decided).

The following illustration demonstrates the functioning of the requirement of personal knowledge. Assume that in a bank robbery prosecution the prosecution calls a friend of the accused to the stand. The friend testifes that he saw the defendant at a local bar on the night of the offense, that the defendant did not say anything to him at that time, that he appeared in normal health, and that he was not carrying anything. Assume further that the prosecution possesses a written statement by the friend that concerns the night in question. While on the stand, the friend admits having written and signed the statement, though he denies its factual accuracy. Under subsection (c)(2) imposing a requirement of personal knowledge, a prior inconsistent statement contained in the friend's written declaration to the effect that the defendant admitted robbing the bank would not be admissible as substantive evidence, since the friend had no personal knowledge of the underlying subject matter of his prior inconsistent statement, i.e., that the defendant in fact robbed the bank. *People v. Coleman,* 187 Ill. App. 3d 541, 135 Ill. Dec. 172, 543 N.E.2d 555 (1989). Conversely, a prior inconsistent statement in the friend's out-of-court declaration to the effect that when the defendant entered the bar he was very sweaty and out of breath, was wearing a torn shirt, and was carrying a brown paper bag, would be substantively admissible "first-hand hearsay" since the friend's prior inconsistent statement sufficiently demonstrates his personal knowledge of the underlying event or condition related. The requirement of personal knowledge was apparently overlooked in *People v. Saver,* 177 Ill. App. 3d 870, 127 Ill. Dec. 117, 532 N.E.2d 946 (1988); *People v. Fields,* 285 Ill. App. 3d 1020, 221 Ill. Dec. 273, 675 N.E.2d 180 (1996).

Section 115-10.1 is the embodiment of a proposal for the substantive admissibility of prior inconsistent statements set forth in Graham, Employing Inconsistent Statements for Impeachment and as Substantive Evidence: A Critical Review and Proposed Amendments of Federal Rules of Evidence 801(d)(1)(A), 613 and 607, 75 Mich. L. Rev. 1565 (1977). For a detailed explanation of 5/115-10.1, including its legislative history, *see* Judge Steigmann, Prior Inconsistent Statements as Substantive Evidence in Illinois, 72 Illinois Bar Journal 638 (1984). *See also People v. Hubbard,* 276 Ill. App. 3d 98, 212 Ill. Dec. 814, 657 N.E.2d 1159 (1995) (personal knowledge requirement). The constitutionality of §115.10.1 was upheld in *People v. Orange,* 121 Ill. 2d 364, 118 Ill. Dec. 1, 521 N.E.2d 69 (1988); *People v. Rolfingsmeyer,* 101 Ill. 2d 137, 77 Ill. Dec. 787, 461 N.E.2d 410 (1984). *People v. Morales,* 281 Ill. App. 3d 695, 217 Ill. Dec. 170, 666 N.E.2d 839 (1996). With respect to whether a statement admitted pursuant to 5/115-10.1 is insufficient alone as a matter of law to establish guilt beyond a reasonable doubt, *see People v. Bailey,* 265 Ill. App. 3d 262, 202 Ill. Dec. 546, 638 N.E.2d 192 (1994) (indicating question should be answered in the negative). *Compare People v. Curtis,* 296 Ill. App. 3d 991, 231 Ill. Dec. 380, 696 N.E.2d 372 (1998) (prior inconsistent statement treated same as any other substantive evidence in determining whether evidence is sufficient to sustain a conviction; specifically disagreeing with other cases to the extent actually contrary).

In spite of the plain language, clear meaning, and consistently correct interpretation by Illinois Appellate Courts, the Illinois Supreme Court unfortunately muddied the waters as to the proper interpretation of the requirement of personal knowledge contained in 725 ILCS 5/115-10.1(c)(2) in *People v. Thomas,* 178 Ill.2d 215, 227 Ill. Dec. 410, 687 N.E.2d 892 (1997). In *Thomas,* the Illinois Supreme Court commences by outlining correctly the proper interpretation of "personal knowledge" as stated above, ultimately concluding that the defendant had waived any error, "if error," that occurred when the trial court admitted a handwritten statement of the witness in which she asserts that the defendant had confessed to the murder, which she denied at trial to be true. The Illinois Supreme Court then went on to consider the admissibility of that portion of the handwritten statement given to the police, once again the truth of which being denied at trial, wherein the witness stated that following the original admission the co-defendant, in a state of excitement, got into an argument with the defendant over why he had told the witness about the murder. The court found this statement to fall within the hearsay exception for an excited utterance, *see* §803.3 infra, as well as the hearsay exception for a co-conspirator's statement, *see* §802.10 infra. In deciding that the co-defendant's [Ricky] statement is admissible as multiple-level hearsay when incorporated into the prior inconsistent statement made to the police by the witness [Rhonda], the Illinois Supreme Court opined as follows with respect to the requirement of personal knowledge, 5/115-10.1(c)(2), 178 Ill. 2d at 238, 227 Ill. Dec. at 420-21, 687 N.E.2d at 902-03:

> Assuming but not deciding that the personal knowledge required under the statute must be from observing the event, Rhonda witnessed the argument between defendant and Ricky and her statement described and narrated that event. Thus, Rhonda's prior inconsistent hearsay statement was admissible under the statute. As both Ricky's and Rhonda's statements come under exceptions to the rule excluding hearsay, the trial judge did not need to give the limiting instruction on the use of Rhonda Powers' statement.

Clearly the event is not the argument but the murder. The subject matter of the prior inconsistent statement is that co-defendant Ricky acknowledged the murder in arguing with the defendant. Personal knowledge of the existence of the statement is already required under the rubric of authentication, see §901.1 infra. Personal knowledge in section 10.1(c)(2) on its face as well as in its legislative history refers to personal knowledge of the content of the prior inconsistent statement, i.e., the murder. Under the Illinois Supreme Court's analysis with respect to the co-defendant's statement, the confession of the defendant should have been admitted under section 10.1(c)(2) as well. If the Illinois Supreme Court does not like the result mandated by the personal knowledge requirement of section 10.1(c)(2), the proper course of conduct is to so state in its opinion and/or in its annual message to the legislature ask the legislature to remove the personal knowledge requirement from the statute. The proper course of conduct is not to deliberately misinterpret the plain meaning, legislative history, and consistent prior lower court interpretation of section 10.1(c)(2).

An extremely difficult question, not addressed by the language of 5/115-10.1, is the situation of a witness who after having given a prior statement to the police claims not to recall at trial the subject matter of the prior statement. In some instances such lack of recollection is real. However, in a majority of instances the expressed lack of recollection is feigned, most often as a result of intimidation of the witness by or on behalf of the accused.

When a witness testifies at trial to a lack of recollection as to a particular subject, two technical issues arise with respect to whether a prior statement of the witness relating to that subject may be admitted under 5/115-10.1, provided, of course, the remaining requirements of the statutes are satisfied. First, whether current lack of recollection and the prior statement are inconsistent. Second, whether a witness who testifies to a lack of current recollection as to the subject matter of a prior statement is at trial "subject to cross-examination concerning the statement" as required by subsection (b).

On the one hand, it can be argued that loss of memory and a prior statement are simply not incompatible; they do not evidence inconsistent belief, only a lack of current recollection. Moreover, and probably more important, if the witness claims a lack of recollection, whether true or feigned, the rationale underlying the requirement of inconsistency is arguably defeated. Substantive admissibility of prior inconsistent statements rests on the notion that "the requirement that the statement be inconsistent with the testimony given assures a thorough exploration of both versions while the witness is on the stand." Advisory Committee Notes to Rule 801(d)(1)(A) of the Federal Rules of Evidence. *See also* §804.1 infra where unavailability is defined as including testimony to a lack of memory of the subject matter of the prior statement. If the witness asserts a lack of recollection of the underlying event, however, there are not two versions to be explored. Any examination of the witness is arguably a formality at best. The witness who claims not to recall the event cannot testify concerning the truth or falsity of the prior statement. Thus, not only is a prior statement about a particular event not inconsistent with trial testimony confessing a lack of recollection, the witness is arguably not subject to the meaningful cross-examination by the defendant as to the subject matter of the statement that 5/115-10.1(b) contemplates.

On the other hand, a witness is often moved to assert lack

of recollection at trial to avoid giving damaging testimony even though she does recall the event if, for example, she is intimidated by the defendant or his associates, she is a friend of the defendant, or the witness simply wishes to avoid peer or community castigation as a "squealer." 3A Wigmore, Evidence §1043 at 1061 (Chadbourn Rev. 1970), expresses well the concern of courts with his observation that "the unwilling witness often takes refuge in a failure to remember, and the astute liar is sometimes impregnable unless his flank can be exposed to an attack of this sort." No one wants to reward witness intimidation. Such reward would befall the criminal defendant if the prior statement of a witness feigning lack of recollection is denied substantive admissibility. Nevertheless, a criminal defendant should not be convicted for one crime on the strength of untrustworthy evidence admitted solely because the defendant may have committed another crime, i.e., intimidated a witness.

The legislative history to 5/115-10.1 supports the position that the purpose of the statute can be too easily thwarted by a false claim of lack of recollection and thus that prior statements of the witness otherwise meeting the requirements of the statute are admissible. *See* the article by Judge Steigmann supra. The position taken by the federal courts in interpreting Rule 801(d)(1)(C), dealing with statements of prior identification is in accord. *See* §611.16 supra. This position was adopted by the Illinois Supreme Court in *People v. Flores,* 128 Ill. 2d 66, 131 Ill. Dec. 106, 538 N.E.2d 481 (1989). In *Flores* the court held (1) that where a witness claims to be unable to recollect a matter, a prior statement of it is inconsistent, and (2) that a witness's failure to recall the content of prior grand jury testimony does not destroy the opportunity for effective cross-examination, citing *United States v. Owens,* 484 U.S. 554 (1988). *See People v. Wheatley,* 187 Ill. App. 3d 371, 135 Ill. Dec. 24, 543 N.E.2d 259 (1989), lack of recollection as to subject matter of prior testimony given at the defendant's brother's trial. *See also People v. Howell,* 218 Ill. App. 3d 789, 161 Ill. Dec. 461, 578 N.E.2d 1107 (1991); *People v. Steele,* 265 Ill. App. 3d 584, 202 Ill. Dec. 194, 637 N.E.2d 733 (1994). It is suggested that rather than the court simply sanctioning blanket substantive admissibility in disregard of the requirements of the statute based upon a valid concern that the judicial system is being subverted by the defendant, the legislature should respond to the dilemma by enacting a statute providing a hearsay exception for prior statements of a witness claiming lack of recollection at trial possessing sufficient assurance of certainty of making and adequate circumstantial guarantees of trustworthiness. *See* the "other hearsay" exception of Rule 804(b)(5) of the Federal Rules of Evidence. *See generally* Graham, Witness Intimidation: The Law's Response (1985).

Section 5/115-10.1 may not be employed to introduce the prior statement of a witness who is unavailable to testify as a witness at trial even if physically present, for example, by asserting a privilege, *see* §804.1 infra. The prior statement is not inconsistent with the witness's testimony at trial. Moreover, the witness is not subject to cross-examination concerning the statement. *People v. Redd,* 135 Ill. 2d 252, 142 Ill. Dec. 802, 553 N.E.2d 316 (1990).

The opinion rule is not applicable to prior inconsistent statements admitted as substantive evidence under Section 5/115-10.1. *See* §803.1 infra. *Contra People v. Costello,* 224 Ill. App. 3d 500, 166 Ill. Dec. 784, 586 N.E.2d 742 (1992) (incorrectly decided).

§802 Hearsay Exceptions: Admissions by Party-Opponent

§802.1 An Overview

Relevant admissions of a party, whether consisting of a statement or conduct, are admissible when offered by the opponent as an exception to the Hearsay Rule. *Gillson v. Gulf, M. & O.R. Co.,* 42 Ill. 2d 193, 246 N.E.2d 269 (1968). Lack of opportunity to cross-examine is deprived of significance by the incongruity of a party objecting to his own statement on the ground that he was not subject to cross-examination by himself at the time. Hence it is apparent that the acceptance of admissions in evidence is rather a product of the adversary system than an exception to the Hearsay Rule resting on circumstantial guarantees of trustworthiness. Nevertheless, admissions in Illinois are treated as hearsay exceptions. Obviously an out-of-court statement of a party offered by that party does not fall within the admission exception. *People v. Patterson,* 154 Ill. 2d 414, 182 Ill. Dec. 592, 610 N.E.2d 16 (1992); *People v. Tye,* 141 Ill. 2d 1, 152 Ill. Dec. 249, 565 N.E.2d 931 (1990) (citing Handbook); *People v. Woods,* 292 Ill. App. 3d 172, 226 Ill. Dec. 57, 684 N.E.2d 1053 (1997) (citing Handbook); *People v. Nyberg,* 275 Ill. App. 3d 570, 211 Ill. Dec. 873, 656 N.E.2d 65 (1995); *People v. Berry,* 172 Ill. App. 3d 256, 122 Ill. Dec. 243, 526 N.E.2d 502 (1988).

In the nature of things, the statement is usually damaging to the party against whom offered, or else it would not be offered. However, the cases lay down no requirement that the statement be against interest either when made or when offered, and the theory of the exception is not based thereon. *Matter of Estate of Lewis,* 193 Ill. App. 3d 316, 140 Ill. Dec. 309, 549 N.E.2d 960 (1990) (citing Handbook); *Nastasi v. UMWA Union Hosp.,* 209 Ill. App. 3d 830, 153 Ill. Dec. 900, 567 N.E.2d 1358 (1991); *Overcast v. Bodart,* 266 Ill. App. 3d 428, 203 Ill. Dec. 425, 639 N.E.2d 984 (1994) (citing Handbook). *See generally People v. Aguilar,* 265 Ill. App. 3d 105, 202 Ill. Dec. 485, 637 N.E.2d 1221 (1994) (citing Handbook and containing an excellent discussion of the separate concept of "admission" used in the context of an incriminating statement not amounting to a "confession" with which an "admission of a party-opponent" is sometimes confused). The oft-encountered label, "admissions against interest," *Good v. Blount Construction Co. of Blount, Inc.,* 262 Ill. App. 3d 206, 199 Ill. Dec. 302, 633 N.E.2d 1293 (1994); *Dietrich v. Jones,* 172 Ill. App. 3d 201, 122 Ill. Dec. 191, 526 N.E.2d 450 (1988); *Kristensen v. Gerhardt F. Meyne Co.,* 104 Ill. App. 3d 1075, 60 Ill. Dec. 812, 433 N.E.2d 1050 (1982); *Grass v. Hill,* 94 Ill. App. 3d

709, 50 Ill. Dec. 139, 418 N.E.2d 1133 (1981); *Breslin v. Bates,* 14 Ill. App. 3d 941, 303 N.E.2d 807 (1973), is inaccurate, serves only to confuse, and should be abandoned. *Cf.* declarations against interest, §804.7 infra. Similarly to the extent that *People v. Ervin,* 297 Ill. App. 3d 586, 231 Ill. Dec. 796, 697 N.E.2d 350 (1998), and *People v. Rodriguez,* 291 Ill. App. 3d 55, 225 Ill. Dec. 653, 684 N.E.2d 128 (1997), conclude in reliance on *People v. Stewart,* 105 Ill. 2d 22, 85 Ill. Dec. 241, 473 N.E.2d 840 (1984), that an admission of a party opponent must infer "guilt" in some significant way rather than merely be relevant, it is incorrect and should not be followed. *See* excellent discussion distinguishing an "admission" from a "confession" in *Aguilar* supra.

Admissions are substantive evidence, as contrasted with mere impeaching statements, and no preliminary foundation need be laid by examining the party concerning an admission. *Brown v. Calumet River Ry.,* 125 Ill. 600, 18 N.E. 283 (1888); *Security Sav. & Loan Assn. v. Commissioner of Sav. & Loan Assns.* 77 Ill. App. 3d 606, 33 Ill. Dec. 95, 396 N.E.2d 320 (1979) (citing Handbook). As to impeaching statements, *see* §§607, 613, 801.9 supra.

Firsthand knowledge of the matter admitted is not required. *Waugh v. Cender,* 29 Ill. App. 2d 408, 173 N.E.2d 860 (1961); *Susemiehl v. Red River Lumber Co.,* 306 Ill. App. 430, 28 N.E.2d 743 (1940), *aff'd,* 376 Ill. 138, 33 N.E.2d 211 (1941); McCormick, Evidence §255 (4th ed. 1992). "The reason for this rule is that when a person speaks . . . it is to be supposed that he has made an adequate investigation." *Waugh v. Cender* supra; *Campen v. Executive House Hotel, Inc.,* 105 Ill. App. 3d 576, 61 Ill. Dec. 358, 434 N.E.2d 511 (1982). *Cf.* §803.1 infra, stating that the requirement of personal knowledge, §612 supra, is applicable to hearsay exceptions contained in §§803 and 804 infra. An admission of a party-opponent is admissible without reference to the availability or unavailability of the person making the admission. *Security Sav. & Loan Assn. v. Commissioner of Sav. & Loan Assns.,* 77 Ill. App. 3d 606, 33 Ill. Dec. 95, 396 N.E.2d 320 (1979). Thus, the death of a party does not make the party's admissions inadmissible. *In re*

Estate of Rennick, 181 Ill. 2d 395, 229 Ill. Dec. 939, 692 N.E.2d 1150 (1998) (citing Handbook). The statement must, of course, be relevant. *County of Cook v. Vulcan Materials Co.,* 16 Ill. 2d 385, 158 N.E.2d 12 (1959), error in eminent domain proceeding to admit balance of sheets of respondent not purporting to list property in question at market value. Admissions in the form of an opinion are competent, even if the opinion is a conclusion of law. *Campen v. Executive House Hotel, Inc.,* 105 Ill. App. 3d 576, 61 Ill. Dec. 358, 434 N.E.2d 511 (1982); McCormick, Evidence §256 (4th ed. 1992). *Ferry v. Checker Taxi Co.,* 165 Ill. App. 3d 744, 117 Ill. Dec. 382, 520 N.E.2d 733 (1988), to the extent contrary, is incorrect. The opinion rule, designed to elicit more concrete and informative answers, is a rule of preference as to the form of testimony. Since out-of-court statements are not made under circumstances in which alternative forms of expressions may be secured, this aspect of the opinion rule is simply inapplicable. *See also* §613.2 supra.

Statements of intent made by a party offered as an admission are admissible to prove the doing of the act intended. *Moran v. Erickson,* 297 Ill. App. 3d 342, 231 Ill. Dec. 484, 696 N.E.2d 780 (1998); *People v. Howell,* 53 Ill. App. 3d 465, 11 Ill. Dec. 138, 368 N.E.2d 689 (1977). *See also* §803.5 infra.

A statement made by defendant to a private investigator after defendant has obtained counsel, taken without notice to defendant's counsel, is illegally obtained and may not be employed even for purposes of impeachment. *Bruske v. Arnold,* 44 Ill. 2d 132, 254 N.E.2d 453 (1969), relying upon Illinois Supreme Court Rules governing discovery and Canon 9 of the Canons of Ethics, which bars opposing counsel from communicating with a party represented by counsel.

A statement made by a defendant while asleep, i.e., a "dream" statement, does not carry the necessary indicia of trustworthiness to be admissible. *People v. Kidd,* 147 Ill. 2d 510, 169 Ill. Dec. 258, 591 N.E.2d 431 (1992).

With respect to guilty pleas, *see* §410.1 supra and §§802.4, 803.21 infra. Judicial and evidentiary admissions are discussed in §§802.11 and 802.12 infra.

§802.2   Statements of Party Made in Individual Capacity

A party's own statement in his individual capacity may be offered by an opposing party as an admission. As with all admissions by a party-opponent, the statement need not relate to a matter as to which the party had personal knowledge; it need not be against interest when made; it may contain opinions or conclusions of law; and it may be offered whether or not the party testifies. If the party does testify, no foundation need be laid preliminary to its introduction in evidence, §613.3 supra. *See generally* McCormick, Evidence §256 (4th ed. 1992); *Guthrie v. Van Hyfte,* 36 Ill. 2d 252, 222 N.E.2d 492 (1967); *Breslin v. Bates,* 14 Ill. App. 3d 941, 303 N.E.2d 807 (1973). The statement may be relevant as either direct evidence or circumstantial evidence. *People v. Armstrong,* 111 Ill. App. 3d 471, 67 Ill. Dec. 237, 444 N.E.2d 276 (1983), statement made by defendant to police officer, "what's in it for me if I confess?"

With respect to corroboration required of a criminal defendant's statement to establish the corpus delecti, *see People v. Howard,* 147 Ill. 2d 103, 167 Ill. Dec. 914, 588 N.E.2d 1044 (1991); *People v. Curry,* 296 Ill. App. 3d 559, 230 Ill. Dec. 661, 694 N.E.2d 630 (1998).

With respect to statements of a party in a representative capacity, *see* §§802.8 and 802.9 infra.

§802.3   Mental Competency of Party

Although it has been stated broadly that an infant cannot make an admission, *Knights Templar Indem. Co. v. Crayton,* 209 Ill. 550, 70 N.E. 1066 (1904), other authorities disagree. *Reed v. Kabureck,* 229 Ill. App. 36 (1923), admissibility in tort case depends upon whether infant defendant was old enough to be liable; *Chicago City Ry. Co. v. Tuohy,* 196 Ill. 410, 63 N.E. 997 (1902), admission of six-year-old boy to playmates admitted; *Hardman v. Helene Curtis Indus. Inc.,* 48 Ill. Ap. 2d 42, 198

N.E.2d 681 (1964), admission of child nine years of age admissible. *But see Stowers v. Carp,* 29 Ill. App. 2d 52, 172 N.E.2d 370 (1961), upholding order not to take discovery deposition of six-year-old plaintiff.

Modern authorities treat absence of mental capacity of a party as going solely to the weight to be given an admission of a party-opponent and not to its admissibility; no requirement of mental capacity is imposed. McCormick, Evidence §255 (4th ed. 1992). *Accord* §803.1 infra, discussing the absence of a requirement of mental capacity with respect to the declarant of a hearsay statement pursuant to other hearsay exceptions.

§802.4   Plea of Guilty; Crimes Punishable in Excess of One Year, Minor Crimes Including Traffic Offenses

The introduction into evidence of a guilty plea not later withdrawn differs in theory, though perhaps not in result, from the introduction of a judgment resulting from it. The judgment constitutes a hearsay exception when offered to prove any fact essential to sustain the judgment. *See* §803.21 infra. The plea of guilty is offered not to prove that essential facts have been previously found to exist but rather to prove that the offender admitted facts constituting guilt. Thus a plea of guilty may be admissible as an admission of a party or possibly as a declaration against interest of a nonparty, §804.7 infra.

A question is raised whether a plea of guilty may be introduced either as an admission of a party-opponent or a declaration against interest, in situations in which the judgment of conviction could not be shown because the crime of which convicted was a minor offense. The rationale supporting exclusion of judgments of conviction for minor offenses was succinctly stated in *Smith v. Andrews,* 54 Ill. App. 2d 51, 62, 203 N.E.2d 160, 166 (1965):

Defendants in traffic cases are frequently unrepresented by counsel, and the proceedings are relatively informal. In view of the comparatively modest penalty a defendant faces on a judgment of conviction, the charge is rarely contested with the vigor that characterizes the adversary system at its best.

However, in spite of such compelling reasoning, equally applicable to pleas of guilty, a plea of guilty to a traffic offense has been admitted in subsequent civil proceedings as an admission. *Hartigan v. Robertson*, 87 Ill. App. 3d 732, 42 Ill. Dec. 751, 409 N.E.2d 366 (1980); *Cogdill v. Durham*, 43 Ill. App. 3d 940, 3 Ill. Dec. 6, 358 N.E.2d 6 (1976); *Miyatovich v. Chicago Transit Auth.*, 112 Ill. App. 2d 437, 251 N.E.2d 345 (1969). In addition to a plea of guilty, a stipulation to facts leading to a conviction and an order of supervision followed by an order of expungement have also been held admissible in a subsequent civil case as an admission of a party opponent. *Batterton v. Thurman*, 105 Ill. App. 3d 798, 61 Ill. Dec. 577, 434 N.E.2d 1174 (1982); *People v. Powell*, 107 Ill. App. 3d 418, 63 Ill. Dec. 336, 437 N.E.2d 1258 (1982); *People v. Chavez*, 134 Ill. App. 3d 598, 89 Ill. Dec. 525, 480 N.E.2d 1268 (1985). The driver's explanation for pleading guilty, if any, may also be considered by the jury. *Barnes v. Croston*, 108 Ill. App. 2d 182, 247 N.E.2d 1 (1969). The net result is that defendants, properly advised, permit a judgment to the traffic offense to be entered against them after a plea of not guilty, or by simply forfeiting bond, *Nunley v. Mares*, 114 Ill. App. 3d 779, 70 Ill. Dec. 517, 449 N.E.2d 864 (1983), while those ignorant of the consequences simply plead guilty. A judgment of conviction to a traffic offense following a plea of not guilty is not admissible as an exception to the hearsay rule. *Hengels v. Gilski*, 127 Ill. App. 3d 894, 83 Ill. Dec. 101, 469 N.E.2d 708 (1984). *See* §802.21 infra. *See also* Graham, Admissibility in Illinois of Convictions and Pleas of Guilty to Traffic Offenses in Related Civil Cases, 2 S. Ill. L. J. 209 (1979). This inequitable result might well be corrected by recognizing *nolo* pleas, or by resort to §403.1 supra.

Support for the rationale for the exclusion of a plea of guilty to a crime punishable only as a misdemeanor is found in *People v. Stover*, 89 Ill. 2d 189, 59 Ill. Dec. 678, 432 N.E.2d 262 (1982), where the court held that a plea of guilty to an offense not admissible to impeach under *Montgomery, see* §609.4 supra, may not be employed to impeach as a prior inconsistent statement.

With respect to withdrawn pleas, *nolo contendere,* etc., *see* §410.1 supra.

§802.5   *Persons in Privity or Jointly Interested*

At common law, statements by a person in privity with a party are receivable in evidence as an admission of the party. Thus a statement by a person since deceased is admissible generally against her estate. *In re Estate of Rennick,* 181 Ill. 2d 395, 229 Ill. Dec. 939, 692 N.E.2d 1150 (1998); *Patten v. Knowe,* 354 Ill. 156, 188 N.E. 173 (1933). *See also Overcast v. Bodart,* 266 Ill. App. 3d 428, 203 Ill. Dec. 425, 639 N.E.2d 984 (1994), stating that the discovery deposition, Illinois Supreme Court Rule 212(a), of original defendant in personal injury action is admissible as an admission of a party opponent against his estate, and correctly stating that *Abel v. General Motors Corp,* 155 Ill. App. 3d 208, 108 Ill. Dec. 28, 507 N.E.2d 1369 (1987), which held that only an evidence deposition, Illinois Supreme Court Rule 212(b), is admissible at trial upon the death of a deponent, was incorrectly decided. Since, however, an action for wrongful death is an entirely new right, rather than one that survives the death of the decedent, *Ohnesorge v. Chicago City Ry.,* 259 Ill. 424, 102 N.E. 819 (1913), no privity would appear to exist between decedent and her personal representative in an action for the wrongful death of the decedent, and statements of the decedent would seem to be admissible only upon meeting the requirements of declaration against interest, §804.7 infra, and not as admissions. The same would seem to be true as to death claims under the Worker's Compensation Act, but in *Republic Iron & Steel Co. v. Industrial Commn.,* 302 Ill. 401, 134 N.E. 754 (1922), statements of the deceased were held admissible against claimant, apparently as admissions. *See generally Rowe v. State Bank of Lombard,* 247 Ill. App. 3d 686, 187 Ill. Dec. 312, 617 N.E.2d 520 (1993).

Admissions by an insured are admissible against his estate but are not admissible against any other beneficiary unless the insured has reserved the right to change the beneficiary. *Bernard v. Metropolitan Life Ins. Co.,* 316 Ill. App. 655, 45 N.E.2d 518 (1942). The distinction rests upon tenuous grounds, as sufficient privity would seem to exist in any case, and admissibility would have seemed properly to be denied only if the beneficiary acquired his rights for value without notice.

Other illustrations of admissions by a person in privity with a party, admissible against the party are: admissions by a predecessor in title made prior to the transfer of title, *First Natl. Bank v. Strang,* 138 Ill. 347, 27 N.E. 903 (1891); admissions by principal during course of guaranteed business offered against guarantor of surety, *Scovill Mfg. Co. v. Cassidy,* 275 Ill. 462, 114 N.E. 181 (1916); statement of the then owner of property offered against person who inherited the property under the owner's will, *Oak Brook Park Dist. v. Oak Brook Dev. Co.,* 170 Ill. App. 3d 221, 120 Ill. Dec. 448, 524 N.E.2d 213 (1988).

An admission by one jointly interested is also receivable against others similarly interested. *Lowe v. Huckins,* 356 Ill. 360, 190 N.E. 683 (1934). However, since a will must stand or fall as a whole, an admission by one of several legatees or devisees is not admissible except in the unusual event of all interests being joint. *Belfield v. Coop,* 8 Ill. 2d 293, 134 N.E.2d 249 (1956).

Many of the statements of persons in privity or jointly interested treated as admissions will frequently also qualify as representative admissions, §§802.8, 802.9 infra; as declarations against interest, §804.7 infra; or as another hearsay exception. McCormick, Evidence §260 (4th ed. 1992).

§802.6 Manifestation of Adoption or Belief in Truth of Statement; Words or Conduct

A party may by words or conduct adopt as her own the statements of another person. *Pagel v. Yates,* 128 Ill. App. 3d

897, 84 Ill. Dec. 180, 471 N.E.2d 946 (1984), defendant adopted as his own a statement made by the United States Trotting Association in speaking to plaintiff. However, the party's words or conduct asserted to be a manifestation of assent to the truth of the statement may be susceptible to more than one interpretation. *People v. Hoffstetter,* 203 Ill. App. 3d 755, 148 Ill. Dec. 651, 560 N.E.2d 1349 (1990), conversation was too vague to be admitted. The mere fact that the party declares that she has heard that another person has made a given statement is not, standing alone, sufficient to justify a finding of adoption of the truth of such statement. McCormick, Evidence §261 (4th ed. 1992). Whether a party has manifested her assent to the truth of another person's statement is a question of conditional relevancy, §104.2 supra. The burden of proof is on the proponent to show that adoption was intended.

To illustrate, if the contested matter in a civil action for damages is whether a visiting child tripped over her shoelaces or was pushed down the stairs by defendant homeowner's dog, a statement by the homeowner, after talking to his son, such as "I am very sorry. My dog jumped on your little girl," would be an admission. On the other hand, the statement "My son said that he thinks my dog may have jumped on your little girl," does not indicate approval of the reported assertion and is thus not an admission. The statement of the homeowner is merely the reporting of another's assertion. It is not a manifestation of adoption or belief in the truth of its content.

A question arises whether documents supporting a proof of loss under a life insurance policy, such as a death certificate or affidavit by the attending physician, are admissible against the beneficiary in an action on the policy. While some cases have ruled in favor of admissibility, *Modern Woodmen v. Davis,* 184 Ill. 236, 56 N.E. 300 (1900); *Ziolkowski v. Continental Cas. Co.,* 263 Ill. App. 31 (1931), the argument for adoption is weak, especially when the documents are required to be furnished by the terms of the policy. Nor is any basis for agency apparent. *Contra Kannen v. Metropolitan Life*

Ins. Co., 310 Ill. App. 524, 34 N.E.2d 732 (1941), proper to exclude death certificate furnished in compliance with terms of policy.

Silence as acquiescence in a statement is treated in §802.7 infra.

§802.7 Manifestation of Adoption or Belief in Truth of Statement; Silence

Manifestation of belief in the truth of a statement may occur by silence, that is, a failure to respond when natural to do so.

Civil cases. The failure of a party in a civil case to deny a statement made in his presence under circumstances that would normally call forth a denial is recognized as an admission. *Dill v. Widman,* 413 Ill. 448, 109 N.E.2d 765 (1953), failure of widow, when will was read, to deny statement therein that full provision had been made for her by postnuptial contract. To illustrate further, *compare Wheeler v. City of LeRoy,* 296 Ill. 579, 130 N.E. 330 (1921), failure of 13-year-old plaintiff to deny father's statement, while being treated for serious injuries soon after accident, that plaintiff would not have been hurt if he had not been cutting up, not an admission under circumstances, *with Breslin v. Bates,* 14 Ill. App. 3d 941, 303 N.E.2d 807 (1973), failure of defendant to deny excessive speed when confronted in the hospital is an admission by silence. While an admission by silence does not normally extend to failure to answer letters, *Razor v. Razor,* 149 Ill. 621, 36 N.E. 963 (1894), it has been applied to failure to object to accounts rendered by mail during a course of dealing, *Bailey v. Bensely,* 87 Ill. 556 (1877), and to a letter stating entire amount of commission due, *Larson v. R.W. Borrowdale Co.,* 53 Ill. App. 2d 104, 203 N.E.2d 77 (1964).

Criminal cases: Silence under circumstances naturally calling for a denial has also been recognized as admissible in criminal cases, *Ackerson v. People,* 124 Ill. 563, 16 N.E. 847 (1888). Admissibility, however, was not based on an exception to the hearsay rule but rather on the theory that silence was offered only "to show the significance of the reaction of the accused." *People v. Homer,* 8 Ill. 2d 268, 133 N.E.2d 284 (1956). Today silence is treated under the admission of a party-opponent exception to the rule against hearsay. *People v. Cihak,* 169 Ill. App. 3d 606, 120 Ill. Dec. 64, 523 N.E.2d 975 (1988); *People v. Childrous,* 196 Ill. App. 3d 38, 142 Ill. Dec. 511, 552 N.E.2d 1252 (1990). Circumstances naturally calling for a denial do not extend to casual conversations among many people. *People v. Harbold,* 124 Ill. App. 3d 363, 79 Ill. Dec. 830, 464 N.E.2d 734 (1984). *See also People v. Sneed,* 274 Ill. App. 3d 287, 210 Ill. Dec. 887, 653 N.E.2d 1349 (1995), the statement overheard by the accused might have appeared to the accused as a joke, as well as it being unclear as to whether the statement even was referring to the accused.

Evidence must be introduced sufficient to support a finding, *see* §104.2 supra, that in light of the totality of the circumstances, a statement was made that the defendant heard, understood, had an opportunity to deny, contradict, or object, and in which the defendant by his silence acquiesced. In addition the court alone must determine that it is more probably true than not true, *see* §104.1 supra, that the statement was such that under the circumstances it would naturally be expected that an innocent person would deny, contradict, or object to the truth of the statement in some form if he believed it to be untrue. *People v. Bush,* 29 Ill. 2d 367, 194 N.E.2d 308 (1964); *People v. Cihak* supra; *People v. Miller,* 128 Ill. App. 3d 574, 83 Ill. Dec. 802, 470 N.E.2d 1222 (1984); *People v. Goswami,* 237 Ill. App. 3d 532, 178 Ill. Dec. 497, 604 N.E.2d 1020 (1992); *People v. Davis,* 254 Ill. App. 3d 651, 193 Ill. Dec. 636, 626 N.E.2d 1187 (1993); *People v. Sneed,* 274 Ill. App. 3d 287, 210 Ill. Dec. 887, 653 N.E.2d 1349 (1995). *See also United States v. Sears,* 663 F.2d 896 (9th Cir. 1981). The burden of proof belongs to the prosecution. *People v. Brown,* 171 Ill. App. 3d 391, 121 Ill. Dec. 518, 525 N.E.2d 576 (1988).

In addition to the inherently ambiguous nature of the inference itself, *United States v. Hale,* 422 U.S. 171 (1975), other considerations raise doubts as to the propriety of applying the rule in criminal cases, especially when an accusation to the defendant is made under the auspices of law enforcement personnel. Silence may be motivated by prior experience or the advice of counsel. *People v. Rush,* 65 Ill. App. 3d 596, 22 Ill. Dec. 310, 382 N.E.2d 630 (1978). Treating silence as an admission also affords unusual opportunity to manufacture evidence. Moreover, the accused would effectively be compelled to speak, either at the time or upon the trial, by way of explaining her reasons for remaining silent, which to say the least, crowds her privilege against self-incrimination uncomfortably. *See* §§501.2 to 501.6 supra. *See generally People v. Bennett,* 413 Ill. 601, 110 N.E.2d 175 (1953), error to admit evidence that accused, who had earlier denied guilt, remained silent when a prepared statement was read aloud in his presence by the state's attorney, as the defendant may be restrained by fear, doubt of his rights, instructions given to him by counsel, or reasonable belief that it would be better or safer for him if he kept silent. Thus, while pre-arrest silence not induced by government action may be employed to *impeach* the criminal defendant, *Jenkins v. Anderson,* 447 U.S. 231 (1980); *People v. Manley,* 222 Ill. App. 3d 896, 165 Ill. Dec. 298, 584 N.E.2d 477 (1991); silence in the face of a pre-arrest statement should be received as an admission only with extreme caution, *People v. Deberry,* 46 Ill. App. 3d 719, 5 Ill. Dec. 309, 361 N.E.2d 632 (1977). *Contra People v. Goswami,* 237 Ill. App. 3d 532, 178 Ill. Dec. 497, 604 N.E.2d 1020 (1992), *Miranda* supra changed the law with respect to warning defendants of their right to remain silent, thus negating statements in *Bennett* supra.

Obviously, once the *Miranda* warnings have been given advising the defendant of his right to remain silent, the defendant's failure to speak may no longer possibly be considered an admission, nor may his silence be employed for purposes of impeachment. *Doyle v. Ohio,* 426 U.S. 610 (1976), use of a criminal defendant's silence even for impeachment purposes after he was arrested and received *Miranda* warnings was a violation of the due process clause of the Fourteenth Amendment; *Wainwright v. Greenfield,* 474 U.S. 284

(1986), unfair to break the promise given to an arrested person that his silence will not be used against him, by using that defendant's silence to overcome his plea of insanity; *People v. Tyllas,* 96 Ill. App. 3d 1, 51 Ill. Dec. 211, 420 N.E.2d 625 (1981), it is error for evidence to be introduced that the defendant remained silent after being given *Miranda* warnings; *People v. Szabo,* 94 Ill. 2d 327, 68 Ill. Dec. 935, 447 N.E.2d 193 (1983), defendant's silence following *Miranda* rights cannot be used to impeach exculpatory testimony of the defendant at trial. *Accord People v. Johnson,* 170 Ill. App. 3d 828, 121 Ill. Dec. 488, 525 N.E.2d 546 (1988). The defendant, by raising his cooperation with the police, or the police officer's failure to reduce a confession to writing, may open the door, *see* §103.4 supra, to evidence of the defendant's silence upon being given the *Miranda* warnings. *Doyle v. Ohio* supra; *People v. Mendez,* 53 Ill. App. 3d 1038, 11 Ill. Dec. 758, 369 N.E.2d 212 (1977).

Following *Doyle,* the Illinois Supreme Court decided three cases dealing with comment by the prosecution as to defendant's failure to include in a pretrial statement given to a police officer facts testified to by the defendant at trial. The three cases apply to impeachment by failure to speak when natural to do so with respect to situations arising prior to and following the giving of *Miranda* warnings. The first decision, *People v. Rehbein,* 74 Ill. 2d 435, 24 Ill. Dec. 835, 386 N.E.2d 39 (1978), held that such impeachment was proper and did not constitute impermissible comment on defendant's right to remain silent. The second, *People v. Green,* 74 Ill. 2d 444, 25 Ill. Dec. 1, 386 N.E.2d 272 (1979), concluded that reference to defendant's post-*Miranda* silence violated *Doyle.* The third case, *People v. Beller,* 74 Ill. 2d 514, 25 Ill. Dec. 383, 386 N.E.2d 857 (1979), reconciled *Rehbein, Green,* and *Doyle.* According to *Beller,* when a defendant's earlier statement, whether prior to or following the giving of *Miranda* warnings, and in-court testimony or other statement are directly contradictory and manifestly inconsistent, the prosecution may properly impeach the defendant by means of the earlier statement, *Anderson v. Charles,* 447 U.S. 404 (1980), and derives no added advantage by commenting directly that when the defendant made the first statement he failed to make the contradictory second statement. *Accord People v. Frieberg,* 147 Ill. 2d 326, 168 Ill. Dec. 108, 589 N.E.2d 508 (1992); *People v. Craddock,* 163 Ill. App. 3d 1039, 115 Ill. Dec. 1, 516 N.E.2d 1357 (1987); *People v. Mischke,* 278 Ill. App. 3d 252, 214 Ill. Dec. 876, 662 N.E.2d 442 (1995). However, where the inconsistency is not manifest, the defendant's silence may be prompted by reasons underlying the privilege against self-incrimination. Such silence is "insolubly ambiguous"; comment by the prosecution violates *Doyle. People v. Chriswell,* 133 Ill. App. 3d 458, 88 Ill. Dec. 568, 478 N.E.2d 1176 (1985). Thus, if the defendant gives a partial explanation regarding an incident and then testifies at trial to a more complete version without discussing the earlier statement, the witness may not be cross-examined to reveal the omission nor is comment proper upon the defendant's earlier silence as to such greater detail. *In Interest of S.L.C.,* 75 Ill. App. 3d 473, 31 Ill. Dec. 485, 394 N.E.2d 687 (1979). Similarly, a post-arrest statement that the situation got out of hand is not manifestly inconsistent with trial testimony that the incident started as a practical joke. *People v. Smith,* 157 Ill. App. 3d 465, 109 Ill. Dec. 647, 510 N.E.2d 515 (1987). On the other hand, the statement of defendant after waiving *Miranda* rights of having "screwed" the complainant without mentioning that the complainant consented may be employed to impeach defendant's trial testimony as to consent, *People v. Henson,* 58 Ill. App. 3d 42, 15 Ill. Dec. 506, 373 N.E.2d 852 (1978); statements of defendant after waiving *Miranda* rights explaining incident but failing to mention provocative attempt of victim to cut defendant with broken bottle testified to at trial may be employed to impeach, *People v. Trumbull,* 67 Ill. App. 3d 262, 23 Ill. Dec. 935, 384 N.E.2d 842 (1978); statement of defendant when arrested that he had stabbed his victim while under the influence of drugs and alcohol may be impeached by the absence of any mention of self-defense raised at trial. *People v. Graves,* 142 Ill. App. 3d 885, 97 Ill. Dec. 81, 492 N.E.2d 517 (1986). For a decision where the court could not agree whether the partial explantion following the giving of *Mi-*

randa warnings was sufficiently inconsistent, *see People v. Brooks,* 129 Ill. App. 3d 64, 84 Ill. Dec. 276, 471 N.E.2d 1042 (1984).

Following the Illinois Supreme Court's decision in *Beller,* supra, the United States Supreme court in *Fletcher v. Weir,* 455 U.S. 603 (1982), held that post-arrest silence *prior* to the giving of *Miranda* warnings may be employed to impeach the defendant. *Beller* had held that such silence could not be employed to impeach the defendant relying upon *Doyle,* supra. Not surprisingly, *People v. Homes,* 274 Ill. App. 3d 612, 211 Ill. Dec. 200, 654 N.E.2d 662 (1995), concluded that *Beller* is no longer the law. Nevertheless, *Homes,* supra, went on to conclude that generally a defendant's silence during police interrogation cannot be used for impeachment purposes because it is so ambiguous that it lacks the requisite inconsistency with his later exculpatory testimony at trial, citing *United States v. Hale,* 422 U.S. 171 (1975). The net result is that while *Beller* may have died, impeachment by silence post-arrest prior to *Miranda* warnings remains inadmissible to impeach.

See also §613.5 supra.

§802.8   Statements by Persons Authorized to Speak; Guardians

Statements by a person authorized by a party to make a statement concerning the subject matter are admissions. The authority of the agent to speak as to a subject matter, which may be express or implied, must be established at trial. *Merchants' Dispatch Transp. Co. v. Leysor,* 89 Ill. 43 (1878), general agent of railroad with authority to adjust claims; *Lake Shore & M.S. Ry. v. Baltimore & O. & C.R.R.,* 149 Ill. 272, 37 N.E. 91 (1894), president of corporation; *Rose v. Chicago,* 317 Ill. App. 1, 45 N.E.2d 717 (1942), president of corporation; *Kutzler v. Booth,* 27 Ill. App. 3d 768, 327 N.E.2d 63 (1975), vice president of corporation; *Quincy Trading Post, Inc. v. Department of Revenue,* 12 Ill. App. 3d 725, 298 N.E.2d 789

(1973), statements by general manager, bookkeeper, and used car manager of automobile dealer; *Chmieleski v. Venture Stores, Inc.,* 106 Ill. App. 3d 312, 62 Ill. Dec. 422, 436 N.E.2d 4 (1982), evidence did not demonstrate that employee of insurance carrier was an agent authorized to make a statement on behalf of the insured; *Cornell v. Langland,* 109 Ill. App 3d 472, 65 Ill. Dec. 130, 440 N.E.2d 985 (1982), the pro manager of a golf course authorized to make decisions concerning safety has authority to speak concerning the length of a particular golf hole. An interpreter is an agent of a party unless circumstances negate the inference of agency. *United States v. Da Silva,* 725 F.2d 828 (2d Cir. 1983). This point was apparently overlooked in *People v. Gomez,* 141 Ill. App. 3d 935, 96 Ill. Dec. 254, 491 N.E.2d 68 (1986).

The fact of authorization and the subject matter of authority may not be established by the alleged agent's out-of-court statements. *Jones v. Beker,* 260 Ill. App. 3d 481, 198 Ill. Dec. 214, 632 N.E.2d 273 (1994); *C.L. Maddox, Inc. v. Royal Ins. Co. of Am.,* 208 Ill. App. 3d 1042, 153 Ill. Dec. 791, 567 N.E.2d 749 (1991); *Kapelski v. Alton & S.R.R.,* 36 Ill. App. 3d 37, 343 N.E.2d 207 (1976); *Halbeck v. Illinois Bankers Life Assurance Co.,* 318 Ill. App. 296, 47 N.E.2d 721 (1943). Authorization to make a statement concerning the subject matter may, however, be established by the acts or conduct of the principal or her statements to the agent or a third party. *Merchants Natl. Bank of Peoria v. Nichols & Shephard Co.,* 663 Ill. 41, 79 N.E. 38 (1906).

Along with statements to other persons, statements by the authorized person to the principal himself are also included. McCormick, Evidence §259 (4th ed. 1992). Accordingly, a party's books or records are usable against him without regard to any intent to disclose to third persons. 5 Wigmore, Evidence §1557 (Chadbourn rev. 1974).

It has been stated that a guardian of an infant may not make admissions, including statements contained in pleadings, binding on a minor. *Knights Templar Indem. Co. v. Crayton,* 209 Ill. 550, 70 N.E. 1066 (1904); *Anderson v. Anderson,* 39 Ill. App. 2d 141, 187 N.E.2d 746 (1963).

Neither a statement, report, nor deposition of an expert constitutes an admission of a party-opponent of the party retaining the expert. *Taylor v. Kohli,* 162 Ill. 2d 91, 204 Ill. Dec. 766, 642 N.E.2d 467 (1994). Thus a medical report of a physician engaged by a party to conduct physical examinations of the other party does not come within the exception to the hearsay rule for an admission of a party-opponent. *Smith v. Central Illinois Public Service Co.,* 176 Ill. App. 3d 482, 125 Ill. Dec. 872, 531 N.E.2d 51 (1988). *See also* §802.9 infra.

§802.9   Statements by Agent or Servant Concerning Matter Within Scope of His Agency or Employment; Attorneys

Whether a statement of an agent or servant concerning a matter within the scope of her employment, made during the existence of the relationship, is an admission of her employer has been decided at common law by applying the traditional agency test of whether the particular statement was authorized by the principal. *People v. Cruz,* 162 Ill. 2d 314, 205 Ill. Dec. 345, 643 N.E.2d 636 (1994) (citing Handbook). Not surprisingly, courts generally decide that damaging statements were not within the scope of authority, even of relatively high level employees. *Hodgerson v. St. Louis, C. & St. P.R.R.,* 160 Ill. 430, 43 N.E. 614 (1896), statement by right-of-way agent as to intended use of track, properly excluded; *Baier v. Selke,* 211 Ill. 512, 71 N.E. 1074 (1904), error to admit statement of foreman as to cause of plaintiff employee's injury; *Fortney v. Hotel Rancroft, Inc.,* 5 Ill. App. 2d 327, 125 N.E.2d 544 (1955), error to admit statement of defendant's hotel clerk that he had let men who allegedly assaulted plaintiff into his room.

Obviously the difficulty with applying the strict agency principles is that agents or servants are very rarely authorized to make damaging statements. *Miller v. J.M. Jones Co.,* 225 Ill. App. 3d 799, 167 Ill. Dec. 385, 587 N.E.2d 654 (1992). The truck driver is hired to drive, not to talk. *Taylor v. Checker Cab*

Co., 34 Ill. App. 3d 413, 339 N.E.2d 769 (1975). However, as a result of the fact that it also seemed unreasonable to deny admission to inculpatory statements by the driver about the driving he was hired to do in light of the probable reliability of such statements, courts often looked for another basis for admissibility, such as an excited utterance. *Taylor v. Checker Cab Co.* supra.

This strict view, which requires authority to make the statement, is contrary to the general present trend in the direction of admitting the statement of the agent if made concerning matters within the scope of his employment. In recognition of the reliability and reasonableness of admitting such statements, Federal Rule of Evidence 801(d)(2)(D), 65 F.R.D. 131, 154 (1975), declares statements of an agent or servant concerning a matter within the scope of his agency or employment to be admissions if made during the existence of the relationship. Authority to speak under the Federal Rule is no longer of concern; all that is required is that the statement concern a matter within the scope of the agency or employment and that the agent or servant still be employed at the time of making the statement. *Halleck v. Coastal Building Maintenance Co.,* 269 Ill. App. 3d 887, 207 Ill. Dec. 387, 647 N.E.2d 618 (1995). *Accord Werner v. Botti, Marinaccio & DeSalvo,* 205 Ill. App. 3d 673, 151 Ill. Dec. 41, 563 N.E.2d 1147 (1990) (statement of agent made in the exercise of his duties and pertaining to matters within the scope of his authority is admissible as an admission against the principal). Representative of the broader, better, and clearly current view is *Troop v. St. Louis Union Trust Co.,* 25 Ill. App. 2d 143, 166 N.E.2d 116 (1960), proper to admit statement of pump man as to manner of pumping oil; *Ogg v. City of Springfield,* 121 Ill. App. 3d 25, 76 Ill. Dec. 531, 458 N.E.2d 1331 (1983), deposition of employee pertaining to his duties is admissible; *County Treasurer v. Ford Motor Co.,* 166 Ill. App. 3d 373, 116 Ill. Dec. 795, 519 N.E.2d 1010 (1988), statement of employee acting within scope of his duties as to valuation of property; *Oakleaf of Illinois v. Oakleaf & Associates, Inc.,* 173 Ill. App. 3d 637, 123 Ill. Dec. 288, 527 N.E.2d 926 (1988), statement of employee concerning problems his employer had with another entity is admissible; *Roberts v. Norfolk and Western Ry. Co.*, 229 Ill. App. 3d 706, 171 Ill. Dec. 324, 593 N.E.2d 1144 (1992), statement of train engineer that he was not aware of another train in the area. *Accord Miller v. J.M. Jones Co.*, 225 Ill. App. 3d 799, 167 Ill. Dec. 385, 587 N.E.2d 654 (1992) (the present trend is to admit the statement if it concerns matters within the scope of the agent's employment; citing Handbook); *Bafia v. City International Trucks, Inc.*, 258 Ill. App. 3d 4, 196 Ill. Dec. 121, 629 N.E.2d 666 (1994) (while agents or employees are seldom given authority to make damaging statements, such statements will be admitted if they concern matters within scope of agency or employment); *Halleck v. Coastal Building Maintenance Co.*, 269 Ill. App. 3d 887, 207 Ill. Dec. 387, 647 N.E.2d 618 (1995) (quoting and following Handbook statement of the "broader, better, and clearly current view"). *See generally Rinchich v. Village of Bridgeview*, 235 Ill. App. 3d 614, 176 Ill. Dec. 504, 601 N.E.2d 1202 (1992), after quoting Handbook adopts and endorses approach taken in Federal Rule of Evidence 801(d)(2)(D). *Accord Edwards v. Alton & Southern Railway Co.*, 275 Ill. App. 3d 529. 212 Ill. Dec. 55, 656 N.E.2d 208 (1995), after citing Handbook states that scope of employment is broader and better view. On the other hand, the strict view that the agent or servant must have authority to speak concerning the matter related continues to have its adherents. *See, e.g., Waechter v. Carson Pirie Scott & Co.*, 170 Ill. App. 3d 370, 120 Ill. Dec. 437, 523 N.E.2d 1348 (1988), customer service clerk not shown to be authorized to speak concerning the previous condition of an escalator. *Compare Halleck v. Coastal Building Maintenance Co.*, 269 Ill. App. 3d 887, 207 Ill. Dec. 387, 647 N.E.2d 618 (1995) distinguishing *Waechter* on questionable grounds. Statements by employees of railroads made to the railroad at its request should be admitted against the railroad as admissions of a party-opponent thus avoiding consideration of application of the hearsay exception for business records, §803.10 infra, as occurred in *Ficken v. Alton & Southern Railway Co.*, 255 Ill. App. 3d 1047, 193 Ill. Dec. 51, 625 N.E.2d 1172 (1993), and

Amos v. Norfolk & Western Railway Co., 191 Ill. App. 3d 637, 138 Ill. Dec. 866, 548 N.E.2d 96 (1989).

An attorney may, of course, act as an ordinary agent and as such make admissions admissible against her principal. *See* §802.8 supra. *Haskell v. Siegmund,* 28 Ill. App. 2d 1, 170 N.E.2d 393 (1960), admission of insurance coverage by claims attorney of insurer. In addition, an attorney has authority in general to make admissions for the client in all matters relating to the progress and trial of an action. *Allen v. United States F. & G. Co.,* 269 Ill. 234, 109 N.E. 1035 (1915), pleadings and stipulations; *People v. Cruz,* 162 Ill. 2d 314, 205 Ill. Dec. 345, 643 N.E.2d 636 (1994), admission by State's Attorney during argument; *Dora Township v. Indiana Ins. Co.,* 67 Ill. App. 3d 31, 23 Ill. Dec. 801, 384 N.E.2d 595 (1979), admission of fact at hearing of motion for summary judgment; *Fearon v. Mobil Joliet Ref. Corp.,* 131 Ill. App. 3d 1, 86 Ill. Dec. 335, 475 N.E.2d 549 (1984), report included in affidavit of attorney filed with the court; *Standard Management Realty Co. v. Johnson,* 157 Ill. App. 3d 919, 109 Ill. Dec. 918, 510 N.E.2d 986 (1987), admission of fact during opening statement; *People v. Accardo,* 195 Ill. App. 3d 180, 141 Ill. Dec. 821, 551 N.E.2d 1349 (1990), statement of attorney at sentencing hearing. But in *McNealy v. Illinois Cent. R.R.,* 43 Ill. App. 2d 460, 193 N.E.2d 879 (1963), answers to interrogatories under name of plaintiff's attorneys, not under oath, the contents of which plaintiff had no knowledge, were not considered admissions. Moreover, it is within the discretion of the trial court to refuse to treat as an admission a statement by a State's Attorney made during trial argument in another case. *People v. Cruz* supra. In addition, the contents of a report prepared following an examination of the plaintiff by a defense physician conducted pursuant to Supreme Court Rule 215(a) is not an admission of the defendant. *Smith v. Central Ill. Pub. Serv. Co.,* 176 Ill. App. 3d 482, 125 Ill. Dec. 872, 531 N.E.2d 51 (1988).

Statements by agents or servants of the government, including an Assistant State's Attorney, are not admissible as admissions of a party-opponent when offered by the defendant in a criminal case. *People v. McDaniel,* 164 Ill. 2d 173, 207 Ill. Dec. 304, 647 N.E.2d 266 (1995).

Statements contained in an expert witness's report are not by virtue of that fact alone admissions of a party opponent. *See Brown v. Kidd,* 217 Ill. App. 3d 860, 161 Ill. Dec. 97, 578 N.E.2d 224 (1991). Similarly, an expert's discovery deposition may not be introduced as an admission of a party-opponent as the act of hiring an expert in preparation for trial does not make the expert an agent or servant of the party. *Taylor v. Kohli,* 162 Ill. 2d 91, 204 Ill. Dec. 766, 642 N.E.2d 467 (1994) (an expert witness is more accurately described as an independant contractor). *See also* §802.8 supra.

With respect to judicial and evidentiary admissions, *see* §§802.11 and 802.12 infra.

§802.10   Statements by Co-Conspirators

A statement of one co-conspirator is admissible against the others as an admission if made during the course of and in furtherance of the conspiracy. The acts and declarations of each member in furtherance of the common design made during the course of the conspiracy are admissible against all, *People v. Schmitt,* 131 Ill. 2d 128, 137 Ill. Dec. 12, 545 N.E.2d 665 (1989); *People v. Davis,* 46 Ill. 2d 554, 264 N.E.2d 140 (1970); *People v. Small,* 318 Ill. 437, 150 N.E. 435 (1926), even when not made in the person's presence. *People v. Unes,* 143 Ill. App. 3d 716, 97 Ill. Dec. 874, 493 N.E.2d 681 (1986); *People v. Pintos,* 172 Ill. App. 3d 1096, 122 Ill. Dec. 814, 527 N.E.2d 312 (1988). Statements in furtherance of the common design are those that had the effect of advising, encouraging, aiding, or abetting. *People v. Miller,* 128 Ill. App. 3d 574, 83 Ill. Dec. 802, 470 N.E.2d 1222 (1984); *People v. Howard,* 209 Ill. App. 3d 159, 154 Ill. Dec. 56, 568 N.E.2d 56 (1991). The common design includes subsequent efforts at concealment if proximate in time to the commission of the principal crime. *People v. Pace,* 225 Ill. App. 3d 415, 167 Ill. Dec. 642, 587 N.E.2d 1257 (1992);

People v. Eddington, 129 Ill. App. 3d 745, 84 Ill. Dec. 887, 473 N.E.2d 103 (1984); *People v. Columbo,* 118 Ill. App. 3d 882, 74 Ill. Dec. 304, 455 N.E.2d 733 (1983); *People v. Link,* 10 Ill. App. 3d 1000, 56 Ill. Dec. 394, 427 N.E.2d 589 (1981). Conversely, statements that narrate past occurrences not in furtherance of any objective of the conspiracy are not within the co-conspirator hearsay exception. *People v. Byron,* 164 Ill. 2d 279, 207 Ill. Dec. 453, 647 N.E.2d 946 (1995). *Accord Krulewitch v. United States,* 336 U.S. 440 (1949). Thus a statement made after arrest does not fall within the hearsay exception. *People v. Cart,* 102 Ill. App. 3d 173, 57 Ill. Dec. 655, 429 N.E.2d 553 (1981). As to the meaning of "concealment phrase," *see People v. Parmly,* 117 Ill. 2d 386, 111 Ill. Dec. 576, 512 N.E.2d 1213 (1987). To the extent *People v. Byron* supra opines that *People v. Parmly* supra indicates that concealment will never serve as a basis for admissibility under the co-conspirator hearsay exception, it misstates the holding of *Parmly* and is incorrect as a matter of policy. *See Grunewald v. United States,* 353 U.S. 391 (1957) (statements made in concealment phase fall within the scope of co-conspirator hearsay exception if in furtherance of main objectives of conspiracy, but not otherwise). *Accord People v. Thomas,* 178 Ill. 2d 215, 227 Ill. Dec. 410, 687 N.E.2d 892 (1997), the course of a conspiracy includes subsequent attempts at concealment of the crime where sufficiently proximate in time to the offense. A statement meeting the requirements of the co-conspirator's exception is admissible even if a conspiracy is not charged. *People v. White,* 122 Ill. App. 3d 24, 77 Ill. Dec. 498, 460 N.E.2d 802 (1984).

Provided that the declarant and the defendant are members of the conspiracy, the declarant's statement otherwise meeting the requirements of the co-conspirator hearsay exception may be testified to by anyone, including an undercover police officer, an informer, or a member of the conspiracy now cooperating with the prosecution. *People v. Swerdlow,* 269 Ill. App. 3d 1097, 207 Ill. Dec. 547, 647 N.E.2d 1040 (1995); *People v. Columbo,* 118 Ill. App. 3d 882, 74 Ill. Dec. 304, 455 N.E.2d 733 (1983).

There must be independent evidence apart from the co-conspirator's statement establishing defendant's and declarant's participation in the conspiracy. *People v. Steidl,* 142 Ill. 2d 204, 154 Ill. Dec. 616, 568 N.E.2d 837 (1991); *Alm v. General Tel. Co. of Illinois,* 27 Ill. App. 3d 876, 327 N.E.2d 523 (1975); *People v. Childrous,* 196 Ill. App. 3d 38, 142 Ill. Dec. 511, 522 N.E.2d 1252 (1990); *People v. Roppo,* 234 Ill. App. 3d 116, 174 Ill. Dec. 890, 599 N.E.2d 974 (1992). Independent evidence may consist of the defendant's own statements, *People v. Pintos,* 172 Ill. App. 3d 1096, 122 Ill. Dec. 814, 527 N.E.2d 312 (1988), or the in-court testimony of a co-conspirator. *See generally People v. Ervin,* 297 Ill. App. 3d 586, 231 Ill. Dec. 796, 697 N.E.2d 350 (1998). Gang membership when relevant is alone generally insufficient. *See People v. Jackson,* 281 Ill. App. 3d 759, 217 Ill. Dec. 185, 666 N.E.2d 854 (1996). The independent evidence may be direct or circumstantial, *People v. Soteras,* 153 Ill. App. 3d 449, 106 Ill. Dec. 343, 505 N.E.2d 1134 (1987); *People v. Saldana,* 146 Ill. App. 3d 328, 99 Ill. Dec. 896, 496 N.E.2d 757 (1986), hearsay evidence may be considered. Whether the sufficiency of the foundation establishing the independent evidence is a question solely for the judge, §104.1 supra, or one in which both judge and jury participate, §104.2 supra, and the applicable standard of proof, have given rise to differing views. *See* McCormick, Evidence §53 (4th ed. 1992). The clear weight of Illinois authority, however, supports a determination by the judge alone as to whether a conspiracy exists, whether the defendant and declarant were members of it, and whether the statement was made during the course of and in furtherance of the conspiracy applying the more probably true than not true (preponderance) burden of persuasion. *See, e.g., People v. Huminsky,* 184 Ill. App. 3d 595, 132 Ill. Dec. 814, 540 N.E.2d 554 (1989); *People v. Howard,* 209 Ill. App. 3d 159, 154 Ill. Dec. 56, 568 N.E.2d 56 (1991); *People v. Roppo,* 234 Ill. App. 3d 116, 174 Ill. Dec. 890, 599 N.E.2d 974 (1992); *People v. Martinez,* 278 Ill. App. 3d 218, 214 Ill. Dec. 907, 662 N.E.2d 473 (1996). *Cf. Alm v. General Tel. Co. of Illinois* supra, indicating that question is for court applying the clear and convincing evidence standard, §301.6 supra, and *People v. Gray,* 85 Ill. App. 3d 726, 43 Ill. Dec. 493, 410 N.E.2d 493 (1980); *People v. Abrego,* 142 Ill. App. 3d 973, 97 Ill. Dec. 200, 492 N.E.2d 636 (1986); *People v. Ervin,* 226 Ill. App. 3d 833, 168 Ill. Dec. 557, 589 N.E.2d 957 (1992), providing that the State is required to present no more than a prima facie case of conspiracy. *See generally People v. Steidl* supra employing the phrase "prima facie evidentiary showing" without providing a definition.

In *Bourjaily v. United States,* 483 U.S. 171 (1987), the United States Supreme Court pursuant to its supervisory power over the federal courts held as a matter of interpretation of Rule 801(d)(2)(E) of the Federal Rules of Evidence that determining the admissibility of a statement of a co-conspirator is solely a matter for the court, and that the court in making its determination must apply the more probably true than not true (preponderance) standard of proof. In *Bourjaily,* the Supreme Court also held that in reaching a determination as to whether there is a conspiracy and that the defendant and the declarant participated in the conspiracy, the content of the co-conspirator's statement itself *may* be considered. Whether the existence of the conspiracy and the defendant's and the declarant's participation therein can be established to be more probably true than not true based *solely* upon the content of the conspirator's statement sought to be admitted was expressly left undecided.

The impact of *Bourjaily* on federal criminal prosecutions may be substantial. Consideration of the content of the co-conspirator's statement in determining its admissibility, even if some undefined and probably undefinable quantum of independent evidence is required, will significantly ease the government's burden in many of its more difficult cases, cases very often involving drug trafficking. Assume, for example, that an informant or co-conspirator now cooperating with the prosecution testifies that *A* told him that cocaine was being shipped to *X,* the defendant, by truck. Such a statement, in context, if considered alone, would most likely support a finding by the court that it is more probably true than not true that a conspiracy existed and that *A* and *X* were participants in the conspiracy. If in addition some quantum of independent evidence was available, even the slightest such evidence of *X*'s participation in the conspiracy would cement the court's determination. Given the ease with which the prosecution will be able to satisfy the court as to the admissibility of the co-conspirator's statement given that the content of the statement may now be considered in the federal court, prior concern that the jury not be exposed to the content of the co-conspirator's statement lest it ultimately be excluded because of the absence of an adequate evidentiary foundation all but completely disappears.

The wisdom of *Bourjaily* is, however, extremely suspect both as a matter of construction of the Federal Rules of Evidence and as a matter of policy. *See* Blackmun, J., dissenting, 483 U.S. at 185. In addition to the agency rationale and real world perspective arguments asserted by the dissenters, it is important to keep in mind that evidence complying with a Federal Rule of Evidence, including Federal Rule of Evidence 104(a), is subject to exclusion by operation of Federal Rule of Evidence 403. In fact the independent evidence requirement of Federal Rule of Evidence 801(d)(2)(E) represented a determination at common law made over many years that the introduction of a statement of a co-conspirator was very likely to substantially mislead the jury into overvaluing its probative value unless the existence of the conspiracy and the declarant's and defendant's participation therein were established to be more probably true than not true by independent evidence. In short, abandonment of the independent evidence was ill advised and thus should not be emulated in Illinois. *Contra People v. Melgoza,* 231 Ill. App. 3d 510, 172 Ill. Dec. 591, 595 N.E.2d 1261 (1992) (Illinois Supreme Court should adopt *Bourjaily*). As to the confrontation clause, *see* §807.1 infra. *See also People v. Pintos,* 172 Ill. App. 3d 1096, 122 Ill. Dec. 814, 527 N.E.2d 312 (1988).

With respect to order of proof, *see United States v. Stanchich,* 550 F.2d 1294 (2d Cir. 1977); *United States v. James,* 590 F.2d 575 (5th Cir. 1979); and *People v. Goodman,* 81 Ill. 2d 278, 41 Ill. Dec. 793, 408 N.E.2d 215 (1980), it is preferable but not mandatory for the independent evidence of conspiracy to be introduced prior to the admission of the co-conspirator's declaration.

§802.11 Judicial and Evidentiary Admissions: Superseded and Alternative Pleadings

Judicial admissions must be distinguished from ordinary evidentiary admissions.

Judicial admissions are binding upon the party making them; they may not be controverted at trial or in a motion for summary judgment. *In re Estate of Rennick,* 181 Ill. 2d 395, 229 Ill. Dec. 939, 692 N.E.2d 1150 (1998); *Rosbottom v. Hensley,* 61 Ill. App. 2d 198, 209 N.E.2d 655 (1965); *Giamanco v. Giamanco,* 111 Ill. App. 3d 1017, 67 Ill. Dec. 606, 444 N.E.2d 1090 (1982). Judicial admissions are not evidence at all, but rather have the effect of withdrawing a fact from contention. *Pryor v. American Central Transport, Inc.,* 260 Ill. App. 3d. 76, 196 Ill. Dec. 361, 629 N.E.2d 1205 (1994). The purpose of the rule is to remove the temptation to commit perjury. *In re Estate of Rennick* supra. Included within this category are admissions in the pleadings, *State Security Ins. Co. v. Linton,* 67 Ill. App. 3d 480, 23 Ill. Dec. 811, 384 N.E.2d 718 (1979), including documents attached to and made part of the pleading, *Bank of Chicago v. Park National Bank,* 227 Ill. App. 3d 167, 213 Ill. Dec. 762, 660 N.E.2d 19 (1995); admissions made in an earlier hearing in the same case conducted prior to remand, *Dauen v. Board of Fire and Police Commissioners,* 275 Ill. App. 3d 487, 212 Ill. Dec. 104, 656 N.E.2d 427 (1995); written admissions filed in court, *Giamanco v. Giamanco* supra; admissions in court, *Dora Township v. Indiana Ins. Co.,* 67 Ill. App. 3d 31, 23 Ill. Dec. 801, 384 N.E.2d 595 (1979); stipulations of fact; and admissions pursuant to requests to admit, *see* §202.4 supra, if made in the same case. *Keeven v. City of Highland,* 294 Ill. App. 3d 345, 228 Ill. Dec. 599, 689 N.E.2d 658 (1998) (citing Handbook). *See generally Dremco v. Hartz Construction Co.,* 261 Ill. App. 3d 531, 199 Ill. Dec. 88,

633 N.E.2d 884 (1994). Sworn statements contained in a mechanics act lien claim have also been treated as a judicial admission. *Braun-Skiba, Ltd. v. LaSalle National Bank,* 279 Ill. App. 3d 912, 216 Ill. Dec. 425, 665 N.E.2d 485 (1996). Whether a statement made by an attorney during opening statement, witness examination, closing argument, or at any other point during the trial will be held to be a judicial admission depends on the meaning of the particular statement in light of circumstances of the case. *Lowe v. Kang,* 167 Ill. App. 3d 772, 118 Ill. Dec. 552, 521 N.E.2d 1245 (1988). Statements by an attorney at trial should be treated as a judicial admission only if deliberate, clear, and unequivocal concerning a concrete fact. *See* §802.12 infra. *See generally Williams v. Cahill,* 258 Ill. App. 3d 822, 196 Ill. Dec. 331, 629 N.E.2d 1175 (1994).

Ordinary evidentiary admissions, on the other hand, may be controverted, *Ayers v. Metcalf,* 39 Ill. 307 (1866), or explained. *In re Estate of Rennick,* 181 Ill. 2d 395, 229 Ill. Dec. 939, 692 N.E.2d 1150 (1998) (citing Handbook); *Green by Fritz v. Jackson,* 289 Ill. App. 3d 1001, 24 Ill. Dec. 848, 682 N.E.2d 409 (1997); *Haskell v. Siegmund,* 28 Ill. App. 2d 1, 170 N.E.2d 393 (1960). Within this category fall the pleadings in another case, *Chambers v. Appel,* 392 Ill. 294, 64 N.E.2d 511 (1946); *Robbins v. Butler,* 24 Ill. 387 (1860); *Firstmark Standard Live v. Superior Bank,* 271 Ill. App. 3d 435, 208 Ill. Dec. 409, 649 N.E.2d 465 (1995); *Anfinsen Plastic Molding Co. v. Konen,* 68 Ill. App. 3d 355, 24 Ill. Dec. 904, 386 N.E.2d 108 (1979); *Alan Wood Steel Co. v. Capital Equip. Enter.,* 39 Ill. App. 3d 48, 349 N.E.2d 627 (1976); even if the former case was dismissed, *Mey v. Gulliman,* 105 Ill. 272 (1882); *Bartsch v. Gordon N. Plumb, Inc.,* 38 Ill. App. 3d 188, 92 Ill. Dec. 862, 485 N.E.2d 1105 (1985); admissions, including pleas of guilty, in another case, *Green by Fritz v. Jackson,* 289 Ill. App. 3d 1001, 224 Ill. Dec. 848, 682 N.E.2d 409 (1997); *Firstmark Standard Life Insurance Co. v. Superior Bank FSB,* 271 Ill. App. 3d 435, 208 Ill. Dec. 409, 649 2d 465 (1995) (citing Handbook); superseded or withdrawn pleadings in the same case, *Bartlow v. Chicago, B. & Q.R. Co.,* 243 Ill. 332, 90 N.E. 721 (1910); *Daub v.*

Englebach, 109 Ill. 267 (1884); *In re Marriage of O'Brien,* 247 Ill. App. 3d. 745, 187 Ill. Dec. 416, 617 N.E.2d 873 (1993); *B. Kreisman & Co. v. First Arlington Natl. Bank,* 91 Ill. App. 3d 847, 47 Ill. Dec. 757, 415 N.E.2d 1070 (1980); *Kleb v. Wendling,* 67 Ill. App. 3d 1016, 24 Ill. Dec. 434, 385 N.E.2d 346 (1978); stipulation as to admissibility, *People v. Sclafani,* 166 Ill. App. 3d 605, 117 Ill. Dec. 248, 520 N.E.2d 409 (1988); as well as ordinary oral or written admissions of a party-opponent. An admission as to a fact or the genuineness of a document made in response to a request to admit does not constitute an admission for any other purpose and may not be used against the party in any other proceeding. Illinois Supreme Court Rule 216(e). With respect to the testimony of a party-opponent, *see* §802.12 infra.

Where the original pleading is verified it remains part of the record upon the filing of an amended pleading. Thus the unequivocal admissions of a party based upon personal knowledge contained in the verified pleading remain as judicial admissions unless the amended pleading discloses that such admissions were made through mistake or inadvertence. *In re Marriage of O'Brien,* 247 Ill. App. 3d 745, 187 Ill. Dec. 416, 617 N.E.2d 873 (1993); *Rynn v. Owens,* 181 Ill. App. 3d 232, 129 Ill. Dec. 909, 536 N.E.2d 959 (1989); *Robins v. Lasky,* 123 Ill. App. 3d 194, 78 Ill. Dec. 655, 462 N.E.2d 774 (1984). Allegations in a verified pleading, subsequently amended, stating legal conclusions, not being based upon personal knowledge, are treated as ordinary evidentiary admissions. *See Winnetka Bank v. Mandas,* 202 Ill. App. 3d 373, 147 Ill. Dec. 621, 559 N.E.2d 961 (1990). Admissions made in an unverified pleading subsequently amended are ordinary evidentiary admissions subject to being controverted. *Chavez v. Watts,* 161 Ill. App. 3d 664, 113 Ill. Dec. 337, 515 N.E.2d 146 (1987); *Good v. Blount Construction Co. of Blount, Inc.,* 262 Ill. App. 3d 206, 199 Ill. Dec. 302, 633 N.E.2d 1293 (1994).

The Code of Civil Procedure permits a pleader who is in doubt as to which of two or more statements of fact is true to plead them alternatively, regardless of consistency. 735 ILCS 5/2-613(b). When this is done, an admission in one alternative in the pleadings in the case does not nullify a denial in another alternative as a matter of pleading. *McCormick v. Kopmann*, 23 Ill. App. 2d 189, 161 N.E.2d 720 (1959); *Downs v. Exchange Natl. Bank*, 24 Ill. App. 2d 24, 163 N.E.2d 858 (1959). Since the purpose of alternative pleading is to enable the party to meet the uncertain contingencies of proof, unverified alternative pleadings are not admissible either as admissions or for purpose of impeachment. *Illinois Cas. Co. v. Turpen*, 84 Ill. App. 3d 288, 39 Ill. Dec. 556, 405 N.E.2d 4 (1980); *Alley v. Champion*, 75 Ill. App. 3d 878, 31 Ill. Dec. 533, 394 N.E.2d 735 (1979); *King v. Corsin*, 32 Ill. App. 3d 461, 335 N.E.2d 561 (1975). The same principle is applicable with respect to inconsistent allegations in an unverified answer to a complaint and those contained in a third party complaint filed in the same action. *Malauskas v. Tishman Constr. Corp.*, 81 Ill. App. 3d 759, 36 Ill. Dec. 875, 401 N.E.2d 1013 (1980); *Tuttle v. Fruehauf Div. of Fruehauf Corp.*, 122 Ill. App. 3d 835, 78 Ill. Dec. 526, 462 N.E.2d 645 (1984).

With respect to pleas of guilty, *see* §802.4 supra; as to pleas of *nolo contendere, see* §410.1 supra. Testimony of a party as a judicial admission is discussed in §802.12 infra.

§802.12   Testimony or Interrogatory of a Party as a Judicial Admission

Illinois cases have recognized that the testimony of a party at the trial of the action, adverse to her cause, may be binding upon her as a judicial admission in the same case. Satisfactory application of the principle would require that the matter be within her personal knowledge, *Tennes v. Tennes*, 320 Ill. App. 19, 50 N.E.2d 132 (1943), without reasonable chance of mistake, and that the admission be clear and unequivocal. *Gauchas v. Chicago Transit Auth.*, 57 Ill. App. 2d 346, 206 N.E.2d 752 (1965). *Accord In re Estate of Rennick*, 181 Ill. 2d 395, 229 Ill. Dec. 939, 692 N.E.2d 1150 (1998), judicial admission is a deliberate, clear, unequivocal statement of a party about a concrete fact within the party's peculiar knowledge; *Brummet v. Farel,* 217 Ill. App. 3d 264, 160 Ill. Dec. 278, 576 N.E.2d 1232 (1991), a judicial admission is not present when the party's testimony is inadvertent, uncertain, amounts to an estimate or opinion, or relates to a matter as to which the party could easily have been mistaken, such as swiftly moving events preceding a collision in which the party was injured; *Burns v. Michelotti,* 237 Ill. App. 3d 923, 178 Ill. Dec. 621, 604 N.E.2d 1144 (1992), a judicial admission is a clear and unequivocal statement made without reasonable chance of mistake about a matter within the speaker's personal knowledge. The term "peculiar knowledge" means that the information must be without question within the realm of information actually known to the declarant; the fact that others may also be in a position to have actual knowledge of the same information does not affect whether the declarant's statement is a judicial admission. *Eidson v. Audrey's CTL, Inc.,* 251 Ill. App. 3d 193, 190 Ill. Dec. 468, 621 N.E.2d 921 (1993). Such an admission must be given meaning consistent with its context and considered in relation to the testimony of other witnesses and their opportunity to observe the facts testified to. *McCormack v. Haan,* 20 Ill. 2d 75, 169 N.E.2d 239 (1960). Otherwise, the result is to penalize honest mistake and confusion. *See generally Trapkus v. Edstrom's Inc.,* 140 Ill. App. 3d 720, 95 Ill. Dec. 119, 489 N.E.2d 340 (1986). Statements by an attorney on behalf of the client at trial are treated similarly. *See Standard Management Realty Co. v. Johnson,* 157 Ill. App. 3d 919, 109 Ill. Dec. 918, 510 N.E.2d 986 (1987); *Doyle v. White Rolling and Stamping,* 249 Ill. App. 3d 370, 188 Ill. Dec. 339, 618 N.E.2d 909 (1993); *Dauen v. Board of Fire & Police Commissioners,* 275 Ill. App. 3d 487, 212 Ill. Dec. 104, 656 N.E.2d 427 (1995).

Application has not always been wholly consistent with these standards. To illustrate, holding that the admission was binding are *Tennes v. Tennes* supra, testimony of defendant driver that he fell asleep; *Huber v. Black & White Cab Co.,* 18 Ill. App. 2d 186, 151 N.E.2d 641 (1958), testimony of guest plaintiff that host defendant was driving carefully; *Waugh v. Cender,* 29 Ill. App. 2d 408, 173 N.E.2d 860 (1961), testimony of defendant that he did not know at time of occurrence that his cab struck plaintiff's intestate but knew it now. Significantly, in none of these cases was any effort made to introduce contrary evidence and all could well rest upon the weight of the evidence without ascribing a "binding" effect to the testimony of the party.

More recent cases have applied the standard with greater precision. *McCormack v. Haan* supra, the testimony of the guest plaintiff as to manner in which host drove into protected highway was not unequivocal and testimony of persons in other car was sufficient to support verdict for plaintiff; *Gauchas v. Chicago Transit Auth.* supra, answer of witness on cross-examination when viewed in context and in light of other testimony cannot be taken to mean she remembered nothing concerning the accident; *Corneiler v. School Dist. 152 1/2,* 62 Ill. App. 3d 549, 19 Ill. Dec. 372, 378 N.E.2d 1247 (1978), testimony that left front tire left pavement would not be treated as conclusive; *Bishop v. Crowther,* 92 Ill. App. 3d 1, 47 Ill. Dec. 594, 415 N.E.2d 599 (1980), testimony of plaintiff that the ladder seemed reasonably safe before he climbed it was not a "concrete fact" and therefore not a judicial admission; *Stambaugh v. International Harvester Co.,* 106 Ill. App. 3d 1, 61 Ill. Dec. 888, 435 N.E.2d 729 (1982), testimony by plaintiff that he had securely fastened a cap of the gas tank held not a judicial admission in light of testimony of other farmers that a securely fastened cap may nevertheless blow off; *Thomas v. Northington,* 134 Ill. App. 3d 141, 88 Ill. Dec. 956, 479 N.E.2d 976 (1985), statement by defendant made without certitude that his truck was five to six feet behind the plaintiff not binding where other witnesses testified to varying distances; *Deichmiller v. Industrial Commn. of Illinois,* 147 Ill. App. 3d 66, 100 Ill. Dec. 474, 497 N.E.2d 452 (1986), testimony that claimant would have passed journeyman plumber examination was a nonbinding subjective opinion and not a binding "concrete fact"; *International Harvester v. Industrial Commn.,* 169 Ill. App. 3d 809, 120 Ill. Dec. 392, 523 N.E.2d 1303 (1988), testimony of claimant that his condition remained unchanged was not a judicial admission in light of contradictory medical testimony; *Arnold v. Consolidated Railroad,* 227 Ill. App. 3d 600, 169

Ill. Dec. 738, 592 N.E.2d 225 (1992), statement by driver that he doubted he could have avoided the accident if he had seen the motorcycle sooner is not properly treated as binding; *Hack v. Multimedia Cablevision, Inc.*, 297 Ill. App. 3d 255, 231 Ill. Dec. 398, 696 N.E.2d 694 (1998), injured person's statement of which medical expenses were caused by the accident was an opinion, not a concrete fact, and thus not binding. *Cf. Tolbird v. Howard*, 43 Ill. 2d 357, 253 N.E.2d 444 (1969), testimony that no consideration existed for issuance of promissory note held a judicial admission; *Hartke v. Conn.*, 102 Ill. App. 3d 96, 57 Ill. Dec. 768, 429 N.E.2d 885 (1981), testimony of party that at the time another person signed a document he was acting as his agent was a deliberate, clear, and unequivocal judicial admission; *Dayan v. McDonald's Corp.*, 125 Ill. App. 3d 972, 81 Ill. Dec. 156, 466 N.E.2d 958 (1984), deliberate and unequivocal testimony on cross-examination of plaintiff concerning certain manuals removed from contention the issue of what McDonald's quality, service, and cleanliness standards were. Whether a party's testimony should ever be treated as a judicial admission is highly questionable.

Testimony at either an evidentiary or discovery deposition is admissible as either an evidentiary or judicial admission, regardless of whether the declarant is available or unavailable. *In re Estate of Rennick*, 181 Ill. 2d 395, 229 Ill. Dec. 939, 692 N.E.2d 1150 (1998) (properly admitted against deceased estate). Thus, testimony at either an evidence or discovery deposition in the same case meeting the foregoing standard is treated as a judicial admission. *Albright v. Parr*, 126 Ill. App. 3d 464, 81 Ill. Dec. 648, 467 N.E.2d 348 (1984); *Hansen v. Ruby Constr. Co.*, 164 Ill. App. 3d 884, 115 Ill. Dec. 829, 518 N.E.2d 354 (1987); *Arnold v. Consolidated Railroad*, 227 Ill. App. 3d 600, 169 Ill. Dec. 738, 592 N.E.2d 225 (1992), statements that are deliberate, detailed, and unequivocal relating to a concrete fact within the personal knowledge of the party are binding. The legal effect of uncontradicted admissions made at deposition may be tested by summary judgment proceedings. *Young v. Pease*, 114 Ill. App. 3d 120, 69 Ill. Dec. 868, 448 N.E.2d 586 (1983); *Hansen v. Ruby Constr. Co.*, 155

Ill. App. 3d 475, 108 Ill. Dec. 140, 508 N.E.2d 301 (1987). *See generally Pryor v. American Central Transport, Inc.,* 260 Ill. App. 3d 76, 196 Ill. Dec. 361, 629 N.E.2d 1205 (1994), testimony at a discovery deposition is usually held to be an evidentiary admission. Supreme Court Rule 201(j), stating that disclosure of matters obtained by the discovering party may be contradicted, does not impact upon whether matters testified to at a deposition may constitute a judicial admission. *Contra Trapkus v. Edstrom's Inc.,* 140 Ill. App. 3d 720, 95 Ill. Dec. 119, 489 N.E.2d 340 (1986). Identical treatment is accorded affidavits of a party submitted to the court. *In re Marriage of Smith,* 265 Ill. App. 3d 249, 202 Ill. Dec. 738, 638 N.E.2d 384 (1994).

Affidavits filed with the court are also subjected to the foregoing standard in determining whether statements contained therein are judicial or evidentiary admissions. *Williams Nationlease, Ltd. v. Motter,* 271 Ill. App. 3d 594, 207 Ill. Dec. 914, 648 N.E.2d 614 (1995).

Statements made by a party in response to an interrogatory are given identical treatment. *Hack v. Multimedia Cablevision, Inc.,* 297 Ill. App. 3d 255, 231 Ill. Dec. 398, 696 N.E.2d 694 (1998); *Brummet v. Farel,* 217 Ill. App. 3d 264, 160 Ill. Dec. 278, 576 N.E.2d 1232 (1991).

§803   Hearsay Exceptions: Availability of Declarant Immaterial

§803.1   An Overview

Exceptions to the general rule excluding hearsay other than admissions, §802 supra, are separated into two categories: those exceptions that are not affected by the availability or unavailability of the declarant, §803 infra, and those exceptions that require that the declarant be unavailable before the hearsay statement may be admitted, §804 infra. *See also* §902.1 infra. The legislature has created three hearsay exceptions applicable in criminal cases when the declarant of the out-of-court statement is subject to cross-examination concerning the subject matter of the statement. Prior statements of identification, 725 ILCS 5/115-12, *see* §611.16 supra, statements of complaint of sexual abuse by a child, *id.*, 5/115-10, *see* §611.15 supra, and certain prior inconsistent statements, *id.*, 5/115-10.1, *see* §801.9 supra, may now be received not only to corroborate or impeach but as substantive evidence as well. The Illinois supreme court in *People v. Redd*, 135 Ill. 2d 252, 143 Ill. Dec. 802, 553 N.E.2d 316 (1990), specifically refused to adopt the "other reliable" hearsay exception contained in Federal Rule of Evidence 804(b)(5), and it implicitly rejected Federal Rule of Evidence 803(24) as well, now collectively referred to as Federal Rule of Evidence 807.

Each exception discussed in §§803 and 804 specifies requirements considered to be sufficient guarantees of trustworthiness to justify introduction, absent an opportunity to conduct cross-examination of the declarant before the trier of fact. Those hearsay statements that have been considered so trustworthy as to be admissible without requiring imposition of the time and expense associated with production of an available declarant and to be admissible even if the declarant testifies are addressed in §803 infra. The exceptions, discussed under §804 infra, require that the declarant be unavailable, thereby manifesting a recognition that in such instances the live testimony of the declarant is preferable, but that it is better to permit the evidence pursuant to one of those exceptions than to deprive the factfinder of the evidence. The basis for the distinction between hearsay exceptions contained in §§803 and 804 is largely historical. For a suggestion that the unavailability requirements associated with most of the hearsay exceptions found in §804 infra derive from considerations similar to those underlying the confrontation clause of the Sixth Amendment, *see* Graham, The Confrontation Clause, the Hearsay Rule and Lack of Recollection of the In-Court Witness, 56 Texas L. Rev. 151 (1978). For further developments in this area, *see* §807.1 infra.

A statement qualifying as an exception to the Hearsay Rule, §803 or §804 infra, must of course satisfy other provisions in these rules before it is admissible. Thus, for example, a statement that qualifies as an exception to the Hearsay Rule must be relevant, §401.1 supra; be based on personal knowledge, §602 supra, *People v. Poland,* 22 Ill. 2d 175, 174 N.E.2d 804 (1961); *People v. Alvarez,* 186 Ill. App. 3d 541, 134 Ill. Dec. 391, 542 N.E.2d 737 (1989); be properly authenticated, §§901 and 902 infra; and meet the requirements of the Original Writing Rule, §1002 infra, where the content of writing is being proved, before it can be admitted into evidence. With the exception of a declaration against interest, §804.7 infra, hearsay statements falling within a hearsay exception are admissible whether or not self-serving when made or offered. Statements meeting the requirements of a hearsay exception are admissible even if made by a person who is incompetent to be a witness at trial for reasons not relating to personal knowledge, §602.1 supra. *See People v. Smith,* 152 Ill. 2d 229, 178 Ill. Dec. 335, 604 N.E.2d 858 (1992); *People v. Merideth,* 152 Ill. App. 3d 804, 105 Ill. Dec. 126, 503 N.E.2d 1132 (1987); *People v. Hart,* 214 Ill. App. 3d 512, 158 Ill. Dec. 103, 573 N.E.2d 1288 (1991).

Evidence offered as falling within a hearsay exception is subject to considerations outlined in §403.1 supra. Thus, even though the evidence meets the requirements of an exception, the court may still exclude the evidence on the grounds of unfair prejudice or confusion of the issues.

The opinion rule, §§701, 702, and 704 supra, save possibly in one instance, is not applicable to the admissibility of hearsay statements. McCormick, Evidence §18 (4th ed. 1992); *Burnett v. Caho,* 7 Ill. App. 3d 266, 285 N.E.2d 619 (1972), statement "If the boys had stood on the wire it wouldn't have flew up and hit me in the face" permitted as an excited utterance, §803.3 infra. The instance mentioned involves opinions contained in certain business and public records. *See* §§803.10 to 803.13 infra.

Questions arising with respect to multiple-level hearsay are addressed in §805 infra, while attacking and supporting the credibility of the declarant is discussed in §806 infra. *See* §807 infra for application of the confrontation clause to evidence admitted pursuant to a hearsay exception.

With respect to requirements for admissibility of an admission, *see* §802.1 supra.

§803.2 Res Gestae

The phrase *res gestae* has hung like a dark cloud over important areas of the law of evidence in Illinois. A concept employed to justify admitting evidence of the gentle character of the horses pulling plaintiff's wagon when it fell into an excavation, *Smith v. Taggart,* 21 Ill. App. 538 (1886), and to justify admitting evidence that the accused, after raping the complaining witness, then proceeded to rape her companion, *People v. Crocker,* 25 Ill. 2d 52, 183 N.E.2d 161 (1962), can scarcely constitute a satisfying explanation for admitting or excluding hearsay. Such expressions as "The rule is, that the *res gestae* generally remains with the *locus in quo,*" *Chicago & E.I.R. Co. v. Chancellor,* 165 Ill. 438, 443, 46 N.E. 269 (1897), serve to illuminate the nonsense for which the phrase has been responsible in connection with hearsay. Professor Morgan, A Suggested Classification of Utterance Admissible as *Res Gestae,* 31 Yale L.J. 229 (1922), argues that seven distinct concepts are encompassed within the term *res gestae.*

Nothing short of complete abandonment of *res gestae* as an explanation of admissibility permits rational analysis of exceptions of the hearsay rule, including that for excited utterances. *People v. Hill,* 278 Ill. App. 3d 871, 215 Ill. Dec. 492, 663 N.E.2d 503 (1996) (citing handbook); *People v. Giles,* 261 Ill. App. 3d 833, 202 Ill. Dec. 630, 635 N.E.2d 969 (1994) (quoting Handbook). *See* §803.3 infra. Although the *res gestae* concept was rejected outright in *People v. Poland,* 22 Ill. 2d 175, 174 N.E.2d 804 (1961), as not only failing to contribute to an understanding of the problems but as inhibiting any reasonable analysis, *accord Rockford Clutch Div. v. Industrial Commn.,* 37 Ill. 2d 62, 224 N.E.2d 830 (1967); *People v. Tye,*

141 Ill. 2d 1, 152 Ill. Dec. 249, 565 N.E.2d 931 (1990), the term continues to appear. *Perzovsky v. Chicago Transit Auth.*, 23 Ill. App. 3d 896, 320 N.E.2d 433 (1974), *res gestae* admissible that illustrates an act; *Grebe v. Vacek & Co.*, 103 Ill. App. 2d 79, 243 N.E.2d 438 (1968), statement as to why check delivered admitted as *res gestae; Perkins v. Chicago Transit Auth.*, 60 Ill. App. 2d 431, 208 N.E.2d 867 (1965), declaration of agent admissible against principal if part of *res gestae; People v. Miller*, 58 Ill. App. 3d 156, 15 Ill. Dec. 605, 373 N.E.2d 1077 (1978), statement by four-year-old to mother concerning indecent liberties within *res gestae.*

It is trusted that *res gestae* will finally receive the burial the Illinois Supreme Court thought it was providing in *People v. Poland* supra, *Rockford Clutch Div. v. Industrial Commn.* supra, and *People v. Tye* supra. *Accord People v. Dennis*, 181 Ill. 2d 87, 229 Ill. Dec. 552, 692 N.E.2d 325 (1998) (Illinois has abandoned the concept of *res gestae*); Kellman v. Twin Orchard Country Club, 202 Ill. App. 3d 968, 148 Ill. Dec. 291, 560 N.E.2d 888 (1990) (*res gestae* is no longer a term recognized by the Illinois courts); *People v. Rogers*, 264 Ill. App. 3d 740, 201 Ill. Dec. 133, 636 N.E.2d 565 (1992) (P. J. Greiman, specially concurring) (stating the "hope that this concurring opinion can be the equivalent of a stake in the heart of *res gestae* and that the coffin lid may be securely fastened"; Amen); *Lubeznik v. HEALTHCHICAGO, INC.*, 268 Ill. App. 3d 953, 206 Ill. Dec. 9, 644 N.E.2d 777 (1994) (*res gestae* is no longer in use); *People v. Hill*, 278 Ill. App. 3d 871, 215 Ill. Dec. 492, 663 N.E.2d 503 (1996) (*res gestae* disavowed as it serves only to confuse the determination of the admissibility of out-of-court statements or evidence of other crimes).

§803.3   Excited Utterance

A statement relating to a startling event or condition made while the declarant was under the stress of excitement caused by the event or condition is admissible as a hearsay exception. Many decisions have ruled in favor of the admissibility of an apparently spontaneous declaration made under the influence of a startling event. *Quincy Horse Ry. Co. v. Gnuse*, 137 Ill. 264, 27 N.E. 190 (1891), statement of driver concerning circumstances of injury, made while plaintiff was still under car; *Muren Coal & Ice Co. v. Howell*, 217 Ill. 190, 75 N.E. 469 (1905), statement of deceased almost immediately after mine accident; *Perkins v. Chicago Transit Auth.*, 60 Ill. App. 2d 431, 208 N.E.2d 867 (1965), collision of motor vehicles is a startling event. The exception is premised on the notion that the excitement caused by the event or condition temporarily stills the capacity for reflection, thus producing statements free of conscious fabrication, *People v. Pointer*, 93 Ill. App. 3d 1064, 49 Ill. Dec. 357, 418 N.E.2d 1 (1981) (citing Handbook); *People v. Damen*, 28 Ill. 2d 464, 193 N.E.2d 25 (1963); 6 Wigmore, Evidence §1745 (Chadbourn rev. 1976), and is recognized in spite of the fact a startling event often also impairs accurate observation. McCormick, Evidence §272 (4th ed. 1992).

The requirements for admissibility under this exception are: (1) the occurrence of an event or condition sufficiently startling to produce a spontaneous and unreflecting statement; (2) absence of time to fabricate; and (3) a statement relating to the circumstances of the occurrence. *People v. Smith*, 152 Ill. 2d 229, 178 Ill. Dec. 335, 604 N.E.2d 858 (1992); *People v. Shum*, 117 Ill. 2d 317, 111 Ill. Dec. 546, 512 N.E.2d 1183 (1987); *People v. Robinson*, 73 Ill. 2d 192, 22 Ill. Dec. 688, 383 N.E.2d 164 (1978). Determination of satisfaction of these requirements is for the court, §104.1 supra. The statement may be that of a bystander; it need not be made by a participant. An excited utterance made by a party is admissible even if self-serving. *People v. Watson*, 107 Ill. App. 3d 691, 63 Ill. Dec. 522, 438 N.E.2d 453 (1982); *Walczak v. General Motors Corp.*, 34 Ill. App. 3d 773, 340 N.E.2d 684 (1976). An excited utterance of an incompetent witness is admissible. *People v. Cherry*, 88 Ill. App. 3d 1048, 44 Ill. Dec. 155, 411 N.E.2d 61 (1980). Cases interpreting these three requirements have naturally employed a totality of circumstances approach. *See People v. Jarvis*, 158 Ill. App. 3d 415, 110 Ill.

Dec. 636, 511 N.E.2d 813 (1987); *People ex rel. Hatch v. Elrod,* 190 Ill. App. 3d 1004, 138 Ill. Dec. 643, 547 N.E.2d 1264 (1989). Nevertheless, the implication in *People v. Smith* supra that the absence of satisfaction of one of the three requirements for admissibility, e.g., that the statement be related to the startling event, would not preclude admissibility is an overstatement and should not be followed.

If the statement relates to the startling event, it matters not, for example, that the statement contains an opinion, *see* §803.1 supra, or provides details of the event or condition or accuses someone of committing a crime. *See, e.g., People v. Meras,* 284 Ill. App. 3d 157, 219 Ill. Dec. 579, 671 N.E.2d 746 (1996), beating done by same persons as the night before. As to prompt complaint in rape cases, *see* §611.15 supra. The scope of subject matter covered by the concept of "relate" is illustrated in the Federal Advisory Committee's Note to Federal Rule of Evidence 803(2), 56 F.R.D. 183, 305 (1973): *Sanitary Grocery Co. v. Snead,* 67 App. D.C. 129, 90 F.2d 374 (1937), slip-and-fall case sustaining admissibility of clerk's statement, "That has been on the floor for a couple of hours," and *Murphy Auto Parts Co. v. Ball,* 101 U.S. App. D.C. 416, 249 F.2d 508 (1957), upholding admission, on issue of driver's agency, of his statement that he had to call on a customer and was in a hurry to get home. *See also People v. Robinson,* 233 Ill. App. 3d 278, 174 Ill. Dec. 411, 598 N.E.2d 1348 (1992), statement regarding ownership of a bag lying on the seat of an Oldsmobile did not "relate" to opening of the trunk of a Nissan.

The fact that the declarant is an unidentified bystander does not affect admissibility. *People v. McNeal,* 88 Ill. App. 3d 20, 43 Ill. Dec. 480, 410 N.E.2d 480 (1980); *Moore v. Bellamy,* 183 Ill. App. 3d 110, 131 Ill. Dec. 658, 538 N.E.2d 1214 (1989). Nor does such a fact cause the statement to run afoul of the confrontation clause. *People v. Ingram,* 162 Ill. App. 3d 257, 113 Ill. Dec. 945, 515 N.E.2d 1252 (1987). *Contra Flath v. Madison Metal Servs.,* 212 Ill. App. 3d 367, 156 Ill. Dec. 496, 570 N.E.2d 1218 (1991), where out-of-court declarant is unidentified and unknown, there is no factual basis for determining that the exception is satisfied; the decision is overly broad and thus incorrect.

Some latitude exists as regards the permissible lapse of time between event and statement. In *People v. Jackson,* 9 Ill. 2d 484, 138 N.E.2d 528 (1956), a lapse of an hour between a stabbing and a declaration was held to require exclusion, in *People v. Jones,* 105 Ill. 2d 342, 86 Ill. Dec. 453, 475 N.E.2d 832 (1985), statement made eight hours after an event containing less detail than earlier statement improperly admitted, and in *Peterson v. Cochran & McCluer Co.,* 308 Ill. App. 348, 31 N.E.2d 825 (1941), a declaration one-half minute after a fall on a stairway was held properly excluded. On the other hand, in *Zwierzycki v. Metropolitan Life Ins. Co.,* 316 Ill. App. 345, 45 N.E.2d 76 (1942), exclusion of a statement made by the insured after walking two blocks after being fatally shot was held erroneous, and in *Interest of Hatfield,* 72 Ill. App. 3d 249, 28 Ill. Dec. 286, 390 N.E.2d 453 (1979), admission of a statement made five minutes after a break-in and robbery was held properly admitted considering declarant's nervous and distraught condition. The proper question is whether the statement was made while the excitement of the event predominated. Lapse of time is but one factor to be considered by the court in evaluating the totality of the circumstances in the particular case. Other factors include the nature of the event, the mental and physical condition of the declarant, the distance travelled from the scene before making the declaration, the presence or absence of self-interest, the influences of intervening occurrences, and the nature and circumstances of the statement itself. *People v. House,* 141 Ill. 2d 323, 152 Ill. Dec. 572, 566 N.E.2d 259 (1990) (citing Handbook); *People v. Nevitt,* 135 Ill. 2d 423, 142 Ill. Dec. 854, 553 N.E.2d 368 (1990) (quoting Handbook); *People v. Sommerville,* 193 Ill. App. 3d 161, 140 Ill. Dec. 443, 549 N.E.2d 1315 (1990); *People v. Wofford,* 156 Ill. App. 3d 238, 109 Ill. Dec. 187, 509 N.E.2d 1026 (1987). *See, e.g., People v. Smith,* 152 Ill. 2d 229, 178 Ill. Dec. 335, 604 N.E.2d 858 (1992), statement of four-year-old witness found huddled in corner ten minutes after observing a murder properly admitted; *People v. Gacho,* 122 Ill. 2d 221, 119 Ill. Dec. 287, 552

N.E.2d 1146 (1988), statement made after 6½ hours in car trunk suffering from multiple gunshot wounds accompanied by a dead man was properly admitted; *People v. Sanchez*, 105 Ill. App. 3d 488, 492, 61 Ill. Dec. 242, 434 N.E.2d 395 (1982), statement of victim made in emergency room 45 minutes after shooting was properly admitted as an excited utterance in light of fact that victim was "shivering," "shaking," "groaning," and in "great pain"; *People v. Chatman*, 110 Ill. App. 3d 19, 65 Ill. Dec. 778, 441 N.E.2d 1292 (1982), statement by four-year-old son of shooting victim made 18 hours after the incident was admissible where the boy was found in an uninhabited area lying among the weeds and leaves in an emotionally distraught condition; *People v. Witte*, 115 Ill. App. 3d 20, 70 Ill. Dec. 619, 449 N.E.2d 966 (1983), 17 minutes expiring between intercourse and declaration by victim who was crying, screaming, near shock, and hysterical does not defeat admissibility (citing Handbook); *People v. Washington*, 127 Ill. App. 3d 365, 82 Ill. Dec. 505, 468 N.E.2d 1285 (1984), statement of severely wounded man made after ten minutes properly admitted in discretion of trial court in spite of fact that during the same time period the declarant made a telephone call and went up to a third floor department; *People v. Smith*, 127 Ill. App. 3d 622, 83 Ill. Dec. 27, 469 N.E.2d 634 (1984), fact that declarant had five minutes before been stabbed in the back and finger and appeared in great pain permitted admission of statement as an excited utterance that identified his aunt's killer; *People v. Fenderson*, 157 Ill. App. 3d 537, 109 Ill. Dec. 611, 510 N.E.2d 479 (1987), statement of victim made approximately one-half hour after the victim had come out of dazed condition properly admitted; *People v. Meras*, 284 Ill. App. 3d 157, 219 Ill. Dec. 579, 671 N.E.2d 746 (1996), statement made only minutes after beating and immediately after victim gained consciousness while lying in a pool of blood was properly admitted. *But see, e.g., People v. Patterson*, 154 Ill. 2d 414, 182 Ill. Dec. 592, 610 N.E.2d 16 (1992), statement by defendant made after one hour of an interview with police was not spontaneous; *People v. Walton*, 43 Ill. App. 3d 74, 1 Ill. Dec. 849, 356 N.E.2d 1131 (1976), statement of rape complainant to doctor in a hospital one and a half hours after incident did not constitute an excited utterance; *People v. Gibson,* 99 Ill. App. 3d 1068, 55 Ill. Dec. 35, 425 N.E.2d 1208 (1981), statements made by defendant three hours after heated discussion and shooting were properly excluded even assuming defendant was in a state of intoxication; *People v. Van Scyoc,* 108 Ill. App. 3d 339, 64 Ill. Dec. 166, 439 N.E.2d 95 (1982), statements of four- and five-year-old occurrence witnesses made three to four hours after event when neither upset nor startled were improperly admitted; *People v. Woith,* 126 Ill. App. 3d 817, 81 Ill. Dec. 743, 467 N.E.2d 614 (1984), statement, made by victim of indecent liberties who finished doing some dishes before walking to cousin's house, was improperly admitted; *People v. Newell,* 135 Ill. App. 3d 417, 90 Ill. Dec. 327, 481 N.E.2d 1238 (1985), statement made 20 minutes after shooting by declarant who had placed the telephone call was properly excluded; *People v. Lopez,* 152 Ill. App. 3d 667, 105 Ill. Dec. 577, 504 N.E.2d 862 (1987), identification of the accused in the back of a police wagon 1½ hours after incident cannot be characterized as spontaneous and unreflective; *People v. Crayton,* 175 Ill. App. 3d 932, 125 Ill. Dec. 493, 530 N.E.2d 651 (1988), statement made by burn victim as to who started fire was improperly admitted in light of 7½ hour time lapse; *People v. Green,* 179 Ill. App. 3d 1, 128 Ill. Dec. 902, 535 N.E.2d 413 (1988), statement made two hours after being taken to hospital when declarant was alert, responsive, and speaking without trouble properly excluded.

Also included in circumstances to be taken into account is whether the statement was volunteered or in response to a question. *People v. Smith,* 152 Ill. 2d 229, 178 Ill. Dec. 335, 604 N.E.2d 858 (1992), fact that four-year-old declarant was prompted by police officer did not destroy spontaneity; *People v. Nevitt,* 135 Ill. 2d 423, 142 Ill. Dec. 854, 553 N.E.2d 368 (1990), mother's question "what's wrong?" to three-year-old son elicited an unreflective response; *People v. Gacho,* 122 Ill. 2d 221, 119 Ill. Dec. 287, 522 N.E.2d 1146 (1988), inquiring, "Who did this?" does not make statement inadmissible; *People v. Damen* supra, question, "What happened?" did not destroy spontaneity; *People v. Meras,* 284 Ill. App. 3d 157, 219 Ill. Dec. 579, 671 N.E.2d 746 (1996), question "Who did this to you?" did not destroy spontaneity. On the other hand, persistent questioning destroys spontaneity. *People v. Zwart,* 151 Ill. 2d 37, 175 Ill. Dec. 711, 600 N.E.2d 1169 (1992) (three prior interviews); *People v. Sommerville,* 193 Ill. App. 3d 161, 140 Ill. Dec. 443, 549 N.E.2d 1315 (1990) (repetitious responses each following successive questions). The more detailed and suggestive the questioning, the more likely the statement will be excluded. *People v. Merideth,* 152 Ill. App. 3d 804, 105 Ill. Dec. 126, 503 N.E.2d 1132 (1987). The key question to ask is whether the statement would have been made if the question had not been asked. *People v. Lawler,* 194 Ill. App. 3d 547, 141 Ill. Dec. 612, 551 N.E.2d 799 (1990). *See, e.g., People v. Jarvis,* 158 Ill. App. 3d 415, 110 Ill. Dec. 636, 511 N.E.2d 813 (1987), declarant would have otherwise disclosed who shot him; *People v. Watts,* 139 Ill. App. 3d 837, 94 Ill. Dec. 200, 487 N.E.2d 1077 (1985), complainant would have told mother of rape even if not asked if she had been raped. *Cf. People v. Lawler,* 142 Ill. 2d 548, 154 Ill. Dec. 674, 568 N.E.2d 895 (1991), statements consisting merely of the adoptions by alleged rape victim of assertions made to her by her father were properly excluded; *Kellman v. Twin Orchard Country Club,* 202 Ill. App. 3d 968, 148 Ill. Dec. 291, 560 N.E.2d 888 (1990), a statement solicited by the questioner by means of specific leading questions was properly excluded. While relevant, the fact that the declarant may have previously spoken to another person is not per se dispositive. *People v. House,* 141 Ill. 2d 323, 152 Ill. Dec. 572, 566 N.E.2d 259 (1990).

Courts are generally liberal in applying the excited utterance hearsay exception to children of tender years. *In re Marriage of Theis,* 121 Ill. App. 3d 1092, 77 Ill. Dec. 608, 460 N.E.2d 912 (1984); *People v. Lewis,* 147 Ill. App. 3d 249, 101 Ill. Dec. 661, 498 N.E.2d 1169 (1986). *Accord People v. Nevitt,* 135 Ill. 2d 423, 142 Ill. Dec. 854, 553 N.E.2d 368 (1990) (as long as five hours); *People v. Chatman,* 110 Ill. App. 3d 19, 65 Ill. Dec. 778, 441 N.E.2d 1292 (1982) (18 hours); *People v. McNichols,* 139 Ill. App. 3d 947, 94 Ill. Dec. 375, 487 N.E.2d 1252 (1986) (4 hours); *People v. Merideth,* 152 Ill. App. 3d 804, 105 Ill. Dec. 126, 503 N.E.2d 1132 (1987) (7½ hours); *People v. Phillips,* 159 Ill. App. 3d 483, 110 Ill. Dec. 873, 511 N.E.2d 1193 (1987) (15 hours); *People v. Hatfield,* 161 Ill. App. 3d 401, 112 Ill. Dec. 909, 514 N.E.2d 572 (1987) (later in morning of occurrence to mother and five hours later still to social worker); *People v. Fisher,* 169 Ill. App. 3d 785, 119 Ill. Dec. 760, 523 N.E.2d 368 (1988) (two to four hours for a 35-month-old child); *People v. White,* 198 Ill. App. 3d 641, 144 Ill. Dec. 722, 555 N.E.2d 1241 (1990) (45 minutes after sexual assault in bed of four-year-old girl; extended discussion); *People v. Williams,* 274 Ill. App. 3d 598, 210 Ill. Dec. 704, 653 N.E.2d 899 (1995) (statement to grandmother by four year old upon awakening lying on a gurney 12 hours after senseless beating). Liberality has reached the point where a three-day delay with respect to a two-year-old was found not preclusive. *People v. Wright,* 234 Ill. App. 3d 880, 176 Ill. Dec. 119, 601 N.E.2d 817 (1992). Nevertheless there is a limit. *People v. Zwart,* 151 Ill. 2d 37, 175 Ill. Dec. 711, 600 N.E.2d 1169 (1992) (five weeks destroyed spontaneity); *People v. Velasco,* 216 Ill. App. 3d 578, 159 Ill. Dec. 147, 575 N.E.2d 954 (1991) (nine days is too long). *Compare People v. March,* 250 Ill. App. 3d 1062, 189 Ill. Dec. 456, 620 N.E.2d 424 (1993) (several weeks not preclusive with a two year old: incorrectly decided). Rather than continuing the distortion of the excited utterance hearsay exception in child physical and sexual abuse cases, resort should be had to the various statutory hearsay exceptions applicable in child physical and sexual abuse prosecutions now provided by 725 ILCS 5/115-10, discussed in §611.15 supra and §§803.8 and 803.23 infra. *See* Graham, Indicia of Reliability and Face to Face Confrontation: Emerging Issues in Child Sexual Abuse Prosecutions, 40 U. Miami L. Rev. 19 (1985).

Early cases held that the happening of the exciting event could not be proved by the statement, extrinsic proof being required. *Frederick v. Industrial Commn.,* 329 Ill. 490, 160 N.E. 845 (1928); *Selz-Schwab & Co. v. Industrial Commn.,* 326 Ill. 120, 156 N.E. 763 (1927). Later cases, however, have treated the event as satisfactorily proved by circumstances consistent with its having happened, plus a recital of it in the declaration. *Morris v. Central West Cas. Co.,* 351 Ill. 40, 183 N.E. 595 (1932), witness found deceased standing at rear of truck, with tail gate down, holding his knee, and deceased stated that tail gate hurt his leg; *People v. Poland* 22 Ill. 2d 175, 174 N.E.2d 804 (1961), immediately after witness heard commotion and shots declarant appeared and made statement about shooting; *People v. Cherry,* 88 Ill. App. 3d 1048, 44 Ill. Dec. 155, 411 N.E.2d 61 (1980), excited utterance by four-year-old girl that her daddy had shot her mommy; *People v. Leonard,* 83 Ill. 2d 411, 47 Ill. Dec. 353, 415 N.E.2d 358 (1980), witness's testimony narrating a nearly contemporaneous struggle over a weapon was sufficient circumstantial evidence to corroborate the existence of an event sufficiently startling to support introduction of the declaration "He's got a gun" (citing Handbook); *People v. Merideth,* 152 Ill. App. 3d 804, 105 Ill. Dec. 126, 503 N.E.2d 1132 (1987), circumstances consistent with sexual abuse of four-year-old found present in testimony of observer describing actions of defendant and child in close proximity to the alleged abuse; *People v. Fisher,* 169 Ill. App. 3d 785, 119 Ill. Dec. 760, 523 N.E.2d 368 (1988), mother upon hearing child's statement about sexual abuse examined vaginal area and observed redness; *People v. Babbington,* 286 Ill. App. 3d 724, 222 Ill. Dec. 122, 676 N.E.2d 1326 (1997), in light of the absence of corroborating circumstantial evidence, statement that men were trying to break into the declarant's room should have been excluded. *Accord People v. M.S.,* 247 Ill. App. 3d 1074, 188 Ill. Dec. 53, 618 N.E.2d 623 (1993). McCormick, Evidence §297 (3d ed. 1984), states that the generally prevailing practice is to go one step further and permit introduction where the only evidence of the existence of the startling event or condition is the content of the statement itself.

In determining the admissibility of a hearsay statement as an excited utterance, the presence of a motive on the part of the declarant to fabricate, sometimes called "bad faith," is *not* properly considered. *See* Graham, Handbook of Federal Evidence §803.2 (4th ed. 1996). Similarly, the trial court may not deny admissibility because the court is in doubt as to whether the out-of-court statement was in fact made. *See, e.g., United States v. Satterfield,* 572 F.2d 687 (9th Cir. 1978); *United States v. Katsougrakis,* 715 F.2d 769 (2d Cir. 1983). Accordingly, *In re the Marriage of L.R.,* 202 Ill. App. 3d 69, 147 Ill. Dec. 439, 559 N.E.2d 779 (1990), denying admissibility to an excited utterance by a child in a custody case on the basis of the in-court witness's motive to fabricate, is incorrect and should not be followed. Similarly unfortunate is the statement in *People v. House,* 141 Ill. 2d 323, 152 Ill. Dec. 572, 566 N.E.2d 259 (1990), that lack of motive to fabricate is a factor properly utilized in determining admissibility. The motives of the out-of-court declarant and the in-court witness are properly considered as going to the weight, not the admissibility, of the statement.

§803.4 Mental or Emotional State; Then-Existing Mental, Emotional or Physical Condition, Overview

A statement expressing the declarant's then-existing state of mind, emotion, sensation, or physical condition, such as intent, plan, motive, design, mental feeling, pain, and bodily health, is admissible as a hearsay exception.

Under certain circumstances a statement meeting the requirements of this hearsay exception has been argued by some, usually incorrectly, *e.g., Lundberg v. Church Farm, Inc.,* 151 Ill. App. 3d 452, 104 Ill. Dec. 309, 502 N.E.2d 806 (1986); *Caponi v. Larry's 66,* 236 Ill. App. 3d 660, 176 Ill. Dec. 649, 601 N.E.2d 1347 (1992), to be properly classified as not hearsay, for example, as a statement offered for a different inference, §801.6 supra; McCormick, Evidence §249 (4th ed. 1992), or as relating to or characterizing an otherwise ambiguous act, §801.5 supra. Whether a particular statement disclosing a then-existing state of mind is or is not classed as hearsay is unimportant practically, since declarations of this nature are admissible in any event as a hearsay exception. *People v. Mayor of Alton,* 179 Ill. 615, 54 N.E. 421 (1899), declarations of mayor admissible to prove why children were excluded from certain schools; *Swanson v. Chicago City Ry.,* 242 Ill. 388, 90 N.E. 210 (1909), declaration of conductor admissible to show knowledge of presence of boys; *People v. Osborne,* 278 Ill. 104, 115 N.E. 890 (1917), declarations of accused admissible to prove intent to kill in connection with assault; *Carpenter's Union v. Citizens' Comm.,* 333 Ill. 225, 164 N.E. 393 (1928), declarations of employers admissible to show reason for discharging employees; *People v. Hampton,* 44 Ill. 2d 41, 253 N.E.2d 385 (1969), statement by members identifying defendant as their leader admissible as declaration of intent and mental state; *Rizzo v. Rizzo,* 95 Ill. App. 3d 636, 51 Ill. Dec. 141, 420 N.E.2d 555 (1981), and *In re Marriage of Deckard,* 246 Ill. App. 3d 427, 186 Ill. Dec. 270, 615 N.E.2d 1327 (1993), statements of children expressing desires admitted in a custody dispute; *Associates Corp. of N. Am. v. Industrial Commn.,* 167 Ill. App. 3d 988, 118 Ill. Dec. 647, 522 N.E.2d 102 (1988), statement of decedent that he was under pressure and concerned with losing his job; *People v. Fonza,* 217 Ill. App. 3d 883, 160 Ill. Dec. 829, 578 N.E.2d 8 (1991), statement concerning declarant's feeling as to his brother's violent death. Of course, the declarant's then-existing state of mind must itself be relevant. *People v. Cloutier,* 178 Ill. 2d 141, 227 Ill. Dec. 448, 687 N.E.2d 930 (1997); *People v. Floyd,* 103 Ill. 2d 541, 83 Ill. Dec. 335, 470 N.E.2d 293 (1984); *People v. Kinnett,* 287 Ill. App. 3d 709, 223 Ill. Dec. 296, 679 N.E.2d 481 (1997).

Then-existing mental state includes the current belief of the declarant that a matter asserted is true. Assume a declarant says "My brakes are bad," or "I know my brakes are bad." Such statements indicate the current belief of the declarant, i.e., state of mind, that his brakes are bad. Both statements are thus admissible under this hearsay exception as proof that he believed his brakes are bad. Of course, as more fully developed in §803.6 infra, the statement of current belief is not admissible to prove the fact believed, i.e., his brakes are in fact bad. *See People v. Coleman,* 116 Ill. App. 3d 28, 71 Ill. Dec. 819, 451 N.E.2d 973 (1983); *People v. Floyd,* 117 Ill. App. 3d

168, 72 Ill. Dec. 725, 453 N.E.2d 30 (1983); *People v. Olinger,* 112 Ill. 2d 324, 97 Ill. Dec. 772, 493 N.E.2d 579 (1986).

While the hearsay exception requires that the declarant describe a mental, emotional, or physical conditon or sensation existing at the time of the statement, the inference of continuity in time broadens the evidentiary effect. Accordingly, the then-existing mental, emotional, or physical condition or sensation may be inferred to exist into the future and to have existed in the past. With respect to the length of time covered by the inference of continuity, McCormick, Evidence §274 at 232 (4th ed. 1992), suggests that because:

> the duration of states of mind or emotion varies with the particular attitudes or feelings at issue and with the cause, it is reasonable to require that the statement mirror a state of mind, which in light of all the circumstances, including proximity in time, is reasonably likely to have been the same condition existing at the material time.

Determining questions involving continuity of inference rests very much in the discretion of the court. *People v. Berry,* 172 Ill. App. 3d 256, 122 Ill. Dec. 243, 526 N.E.2d 502 (1988).

A witness may testify to her own mental or emotional state without raising any question of hearsay. *See* §801.1 supra. *See generally People v. Keefe,* 209 Ill. App. 3d 744, 153 Ill. Dec. 825, 567 N.E.2d 1052 (1991).

With respect to intent offered to prove the act intended, *see* §803.5 infra. Will cases are discussed in §803.6 infra. As to particular situations in which an accompanying act has been required, *see* §803.7 infra.

The disturbing indication that this hearsay exception requires that the declarant be unavailable, *see People v. Coleman,* 116 Ill. App. 3d 28, 71 Ill. Dec. 819, 451 N.E.2d 973 (1983); *People v. Silvestri,* 148 Ill. App. 3d 380, 102 Ill. Dec. 563, 500 N.E.2d 456 (1986); *Laughlin v. France,* 241 Ill. App. 3d 185, 180 Ill. Dec. 662, 607 N.E.2d 962 (1993); *People v. Davis,* 254 Ill. App. 3d 651, 193 Ill. Dec. 636, 626 N.E.2d 1187 (1993); *People v. Curtis,* 262 Ill. App. 3d 876, 200 Ill. Dec. 521, 635

N.E.2d 860 (1994), is incorrect, ill-advised and accordingly should not be followed, as is the indication that there needs to be a reasonable probability that the statement is truthful. *People v. Gayfield,* 261 Ill. App. 3d 379, 199 Ill. Dec. 123, 633 N.E.2d 919 (1994). *Accord People v. Nyberg,* 275 Ill. App. 3d 570, 211 Ill. Dec. 873, 656 N.E.2d 65 (1995) (Wolfson, J., specially concurring).

§803.5   Mental or Emotional State; Intent as Proof of Doing Act Intended

The question arises whether a declaration of intent, since it is not excluded by the Hearsay Rule, §803.4 supra, may be admitted as proof that the intended act was done. The argument for admissibility is that persons who intend to do an act are more likely to do the act than are persons without the intent, and therefore the evidence of intent is relevant, §401.1 supra. At this point, however, some logical difficulty arises. The declaration of intent as evidence is subject to two weaknesses: (1) the trustworthiness of the declarant, and (2) the possibility of change of mind or supervening events to defeat the plan. A simple declaration by the declarant that he had done the act would be subject only to the first weakness, (along with the minor risks of perception and recordation and recollection), yet it would be excluded by the Hearsay Rule. Consequently, to allow the declaration of intent as proof of the doing of the intended act is to admit evidence that is arguably inferior to that excluded by the Hearsay Rule. However, notice that admissibility of a declaration of having done a past act, extended to its logical extent, would effectively destroy the Hearsay Rule. *See* §803.6 infra.

Despite this logical dilemma, when the issue is squarely presented, declarations of intent to prove the doing of the intended act are found admissible. *Mutual Life Ins. Co. v. Hillmon,* 145 U.S. 285 (1892); *People v. Bartall,* 98 Ill. 2d 294, 74 Ill. Dec. 557, 456 N.E.2d 59 (1983). Examination of the cases discloses that the offered evidence usually possesses very substantial convincing power, and often the necessity to resort to such declarations of intent is great. *See, e.g., City of Streator v. Industrial Commn.*, 92 Ill. 2d 353, 66 Ill. Dec. 71, 442 N.E.2d 497 (1982), suicide note is admissible to show state of mind and such other things as proof of state of mind tends to establish; *Lee v. Central Natl. Bank & Trust Co. of Rockford*, 56 Ill. 2d 394, 308 N.E.2d 604 (1974), letter of intent to marry and enter antenuptial agreement admissible to prove that prior to marriage the couple subsequently entered into an oral antenuptial agreement; *Painter v. People*, 147 Ill. 444, 35 N.E. 64 (1893), threats by accused admissible to prove he committed the crime; *Riggs v. Powell*, 142 Ill. 453, 32 N.E. 482 (1892), declarations by deceased of intention to provide well for wife admissible to prove he gave note to her and his endorsement was not forged; *Campbell v. People*, 16 Ill. 17 (1854), once self-defense raised, uncommunicated threats by deceased admissible to prove he was aggressor; *Kennedy v. Four Boys Labor Service, Inc.*, 276 Ill. App. 3d 248, 212 Ill. Dec. 785, 657 N.E.2d 1130 (1995), statement of intent to terminate the plaintiff relevant to accompany of letter of termination dated the next day; *People v. Jones*, 84 Ill. App. 3d 896, 40 Ill. Dec. 411, 406 N.E.2d 112 (1980), testimony of witnesses that decedent told them that he was going to meet the defendant the next day to purchase an automobile; *People v. Fletcher*, 59 Ill. App. 3d 310, 17 Ill. Dec. 49, 375 N.E.2d 1333 (1978), police officer's radio transmission stating observation of automobile relevant to show act of stopping automobile triggered defendant's motive for kidnapping and murder. *Contra People v. King*, 276 Ill. 138, 114 N.E. 601 (1916), threats by third person to kill victim properly excluded. *Compare People v. Floyd*, 103 Ill. 2d 541, 83 Ill. Dec. 335, 470 N.E.2d 293 (1984), statement of victim concerning her fear of harm was not relevant under facts of case other than to infer that her husband was guilty of murder.

The hearsay exception providing for admissibility of statements of intent as tending to prove the doing of the act intended applies only to statements of intent by a declarant to prove her own future conduct, not the future conduct of another person. *People v. Reddock,* 13 Ill. App. 3d 296, 300 N.E.2d 31 (1973), deceased's statements to his sister admissible to show his intent to accompany defendant on a trip and that he left on the mission, but not admissible to show any intent on part of defendant to go on a trip; *People v. Silvestri,* 148 Ill. App. 3d 980, 102 Ill. Dec. 563, 500 N.E.2d 456 (1986), victim's statement is admissible to show her intention of meeting the defendant on the 13th floor, but not admissible to show any intent on the part of the defendant to meet the victim on the 13th floor. *Contra Mutual Life Ins. Co. v. Hillmon* supra. One may question whether making such a distinction is a feat so subtle as to be in practice beyond the compass of ordinary minds. *See* Justice Traynor dissenting in *People v. Alcalde,* 24 Cal. 2d 177, 148 P.2d 627 (1944).

§803.6   Mental or Emotional State; Statements of Memory or Belief to Prove Fact Remembered or Believed, Exception in Will Cases

Since a declaration of intent is admissible as proof of the doing of the act intended, it may be argued that a declaration of the happening of a past event discloses a current state of mind from which the happening of the event that produced the state of mind may be inferred. Such a result would accomplish the effective destruction of the Hearsay Rule, which generally excludes narratives of past events, and is rejected on the basis of the presence of hearsay risks, §801.1 supra, and the lack of circumstantial guarantees of trustworthiness with respect to such statements. *In re Estate of Holmgren,* 237 Ill. App. 3d 839, 178 Ill. Dec. 569, 604 N.E.2d 1092 (1992), statement of declarant that he owes ten more payments to his parents for a boat is not admissible to prove the declarant, rather than his parents, is the owner of the boat. *See generally People v. Lawler,* 142 Ill. 2d 548, 154 Ill. Dec. 674, 568 N.E.2d 895 (1991).

One exception based upon necessity and expediency is recognized: a statement of opinion or belief is admissible to prove the facts remembered or believed if it relates to the execution, revocation, identification, or terms of the declarant's will. *Burton v. Wylde*, 261 Ill. 397, 103 N.E. 976 (1914), subsequent declarations of testator admissible to show whether he intended to revoke will by mutilation; *Cantway v. Cantway*, 315 Ill. 244, 146 N.E. 148 (1925), subsequent declarations of testator admissible to prove contents of lost will.

§803.7 Mental or Emotional State; No Necessity for Accompanying Act

As has been seen, a declaration of intent is admissible to prove intent, and also generally to prove the doing of the intended act, §803.5 supra. Thus, when the declaration is admissible on either theory, no problem of admissibility should arise. Unfortunately, however, a considerable number of early cases engrafted upon admissibility the further requirement that the declaration be contemporaneous, or nearly so, with a related act. This restriction, originating with the ill-advised concept of *res gestae*, §803.2 supra, seems to have arisen in part by converting the admissibility of a statement accompanying and qualifying an act, §801.5 supra, into an unjustified requirement that the declaration actually accompany the act, and in part from confusing the weight of evidence with its admissibility. The cases in question arise from the following situations:

Destination or purpose of journey. *Chicago & E.I.R. Co. v. Chancellor*, 165 Ill. 438, 46 N.E. 269 (1897), on issue whether deceased was a passenger, error to admit declaration of intent to take train, made an hour earlier; *Foster v. Shepherd*, 258 Ill. 164, 101 N.E. 411 (1913), on issue whether deceased was pretending to be a burglar in order to frighten defendant, who claimed killing in self-defense, error to admit declaration by deceased 2½ hours earlier that he intended to spend the night with his mother; *Boyer Chemical*

Laboratory v. Industrial Comm., 366 Ill. 635, 10 N.E.2d 389 (1937), on issue whether sales manager killed in highway accident had finished vacation and returned to service of employer, declarations of intention to call on customers inadmissible because not contemporaneous with act of departing on journey.

Suicide.   *Siebert v. People*, 143 Ill. 571, 32 N.E. 431 (1892), declarations by deceased of intent to commit suicide, offered by accused charged with murder by poisoning, excluded because not accompanied by an act; *Greenacre v. Filby*, 276 Ill. 294, 114 N.E. 536 (1916), a dram shop action for death of deceased killed by train while lying on track, proper to exclude declarations showing preoccupation with suicide for two years, as not connected with any act at time in question; *Treat v. Merchant's Life Assn.*, 198 Ill. 431, 64 N.E. 992 (1902), error to exclude declarations of insured indicating intent to commit suicide, made at time of taking out policy; *Nordgren v. People*, 211 Ill. 425, 71 N.E. 1042 (1904), in murder by poisoning case, error to exclude declarations by deceased of intent to commit suicide coupled with proof of possession of poison.

Domicile.   *Malzenbaugh v. People*, 194 Ill. 108, 62 N.E. 546 (1902), error to exclude declarations of intent to change domicile to Texas if so connected with act of going to Texas as to qualify it.

Under modern authority a declaration of intention is admissible without reference to the occurrence of a contemporaneous, or nearly so, related act. *Quick v. Michigan Millers Mut. Ins. Co.*, 122 Ill. App. 2d 314, 250 N.E.2d 819 (1969), expression of intent by owner to junk car admissible without reference to presence of an accompanying or related act. *Accord* Federal Rule of Evidence 803(3), 65 F.R.D. 131, 154 (1975).

§803.8   Statements for Purpose of Medical Diagnosis or Treatment; Sexual Abuse Prosecutions

Treating physicians.   Statements describing medical history, or past or present symptoms, pain, or sensations are admissible as an exception to the hearsay rule, if made by a person for purposes of medical diagnosis or treatment. The assumption underlying the exception is that the desire for proper diagnosis or treatment outweighs any motive to falsify. *Greinke v. Chicago City Ry.*, 234 Ill. 564, 85 N.E. 327 (1908). The statement may be made by either a patient or someone with an interest in his well-being. *Welter v. Bowman Dairy Co.*, 318 Ill. App. 305, 47 N.E.2d 739 (1943), statement by mother of sick baby admitted. *Contra Behles v. Chicago Transit Auth.*, 346 Ill. App. 220, 104 N.E.2d 635 (1952), statement must be made by patient himself, incorrectly decided. *See also* discussion of sexual abuse prosecutions infra. If made for purposes of medical diagnosis or treatment, the statement may be addressed to anyone thought to be associated with providing such services, including a physician, nurse, or ambulance attendant. *People v. Winfield,* 160 Ill. App. 3d 893, 112 Ill. Dec. 423, 513 N.E.2d 1032 (1987), nurse (quoting Handbook). Such persons are sometimes collectively referred to as treating physicians. Statements made for purposes of medical diagnosis or treatment are admissible even if made after the filing of the action. *Ryan v. Monson,* 33 Ill. App. 2d 406, 179 N.E.2d 449 (1961).

Examining physicians. Evidence of such statements, including those of pain, subjective symptoms, medical history, and physical demonstrations capable of simulation, are not admissible under this hearsay exception if made to a physician examining for the purpose of testifying, referred to as an examining physician. *People v. Hester,* 39 Ill. 2d 489, 237 N.E.2d 466 (1968). The examining physician's testimony is thus admissible as substantive evidence solely to the extent that the examining physician is testifying to observable, purely objective conditions, *Greinke v. Chicago City Ry.* supra; *Jensen v. Elgin, J. & E. Ry.*, 24 Ill. 2d 383, 182 N.E.2d 211 (1962); *Hastings v. Abernathy Taxi Assn.*, 16 Ill. App. 3d 671, 306 N.E.2d 498 (1973), even though the patient has testified that the responses that he made to the physician are true. *Shaughnessy v. Holt,* 236 Ill. 485, 86 N.E. 256 (1908). Of course, prior to the adoption of Federal Rule 703, if evidence of facts contained in such statements was otherwise introduced into evidence, the examining physician was permitted to give her opinion in response to a hypothetical question. *Shockley v. Industrial Commn.*, 75 Ill. 2d 189, 25 Ill. Dec. 798, 387 N.E.2d 674 (1979); *Brumley v. Federal Barge Lines, Inc.*, 78 Ill. App. 3d 799, 33 Ill. Dec. 609, 396 N.E.2d 1333 (1979). The foregoing of course remains true now that the requirement of a hypothetical question has been abolished, §705.1 supra. *Mathieu v. Venture Stores, Inc.*, 144 Ill. App. 3d 783, 98 Ill. Dec. 684, 494 N.E.2d 806 (1986). With the adoption of Federal Rule 703 in *Wilson v. Clark*, 84 Ill. 2d 186, 49 Ill. Dec. 308, 417 N.E.2d 1322 (1981), the examining physician may now testify as to facts, data, or opinions forming the basis of her opinion, whether or not admitted or admissible in evidence, if of a type reasonably relied upon by experts in the particular field. *People v. Anderson*, 113 Ill. 2d 1, 99 Ill. Dec. 104, 495 N.E.2d 485 (1986) (statements of criminal defendant made to nontreating, examining physician testifying on his behalf as to his insanity); *Melecosky v. McCarthy Bros. Co.*, 115 Ill. 2d 209, 104 Ill. Dec. 798, 503 N.E.2d 355 (1986) (nontreating examining physician may reasonably rely on subjective symptoms related by the plaintiff). See §703.1 supra. *See also* §705.1 supra with respect to disclosure of basis. *Cf.* Federal Rule of Evidence 803(4), 65 F.R.D. 131, 154-155 (1975), eliminating the distinction between examining and treating physicians. The rationale of Federal Rule 803(4) supports a determination that subjective symptoms related by a plaintiff to a nontreating examining physician are reasonably relied on, i.e., are of the type customarily relied on by experts in the field, and that such items are sufficiently trustworthy to make such reliance reasonable. *Melecosky v. McCarthy Bros. Co.* supra. An expert psychiatrist or psychologist testifying on behalf of the defendant on the question of insanity is permitted to rely upon and disclose defendant's self-serving statements, *People v. Gacy*, 103 Ill. 2d 1, 82 Ill. Dec. 391, 468 N.E.2d 1171 (1984); *People v. Anderson* supra, provided the expert is not relying solely upon the defendant's statements. *People v. Britz,* 123 Ill. 2d 446, 124 Ill. Dec. 15, 528 N.E.2d 703 (1988).

Statements of causation. While statements to physicians as to the cause of an injury or condition were originally excluded, *Illinois Cent. R. Co. v. Sutton,* 42 Ill. 438 (1867), more recent decisions sensibly recognized that cause may be a factor in such medical diagnosis or treatment and accordingly that such statements are admissible as falling within the guarantee of truthfulness. *Shell Oil Co. v. Industrial Commn.,* 2 Ill. 2d 590, 119 N.E.2d 224 (1954); *Jensen v. Elgin, J. & E. Ry.* supra. In fact, in one instance the supreme court has sanctioned, on the basis of the relevancy of the cause of an external source of the condition to be treated, part of a statement arguably going far beyond. *People v. Gant,* 58 Ill. 2d 178, 181, 317 N.E.2d 564, 566-567 (1974), physician permitted to testify patient said "she was sitting on the couch when a man entered the room behind her, threatened her, and apparently something hit her on the head, and at the same time a gun went off." *See also In re Marriage of Theis,* 121 Ill. App. 3d 1092, 77 Ill. Dec. 608, 460 N.E.2d 912 (1984), identity of molester of three-year-old child was relevant to treatment in light of possibility of repeated occurrence at home.

The admissibility of statements as to causation extends only to those of inception or general character of the cause of external source of the injury insofar as reasonably pertinent to medical diagnosis or treatment. Statements of fault would not qualify. *Shell Oil Co. v. Industrial Commn.* supra; McCormick, Evidence §277 (4th ed. 1992). Thus a patient's statement that he was struck by an automobile would be admissible but not his statement that the car was driven through a red light. Federal Advisory Committee's Note to Federal Rule of Evidence 803(4), 56 F.R.D. 183, 306 (1973). *See also Healy v. City of Chicago,* 109 Ill. App. 2d 6, 248 N.E.2d 679 (1969), patient's statement that he fell as a result of slipping on ice admissible. With respect to *People v. Gant* supra, only that part of the statement relating to being hit on the head is clearly admissible. However, while the segment of the statement concerning a gun going off seems to tend to prove that the object striking her was a gun, the nature of the object is at best only marginally relevant to medical diagnosis or treatment; the statement as to a threat seems irrelevant.

Statement to lay witnesses. Statements of medical history, or past or present symptoms, pain, or sensations made to lay witnesses are not admissible pursuant to this hearsay exception unless made for purposes of medical diagnosis or treatment. *See* Advisory Committee's Note to Federal Rule of Evidence 803(4), 56 F.R.D. 183, 306 (1973). To illustrate, a statement by a wife to her husband advising what the husband should tell a physician concerning a sick child is a statement for purposes of medical diagnosis or treatment. However, the lay witness may testify in the form of an opinion as to the state of health, hearing, or eyesight of another, the ability of another to work or walk, and whether the other appears to be suffering pain, is conscious or unconscious, or is in possession of his mental facilities, intoxicated, excited, calm, etc. *Lauth v. Chicago Union Traction Co.,* 244 Ill. 244, 91 N.E. 431 (1910); *West Chicago St. R. Co. v. Kennelly,* 170 Ill. 508, 48 N.E. 996 (1897). While this distinction is indeed tenuous, *see* 6 Wigmore, Evidence §1719 (Chadbourn rev. 1976), many of these statements made to a lay witness will qualify under the hearsay exception for then-existing mental or emotional state, §803.4 supra. *See also* §701.7 supra.

Sexual abuse prosecutions. In sexual abuse prosecutions "statements made by the victim to medical personnel for purposes of medical diagnosis or treatment including descriptions of the cause of symptom, pain or sensations, or the inception or general character of the cause or external source thereof insofar as reasonably pertinent to diagnosis or treatment shall be admitted as an exception to the hearsay rule." 725 ILCS 5/115-13. The apparent purpose of adopting the substance of Federal Rule of Evidence 803(4) but limiting adopting its application to sexual abuse prosecutions, regardless of whether the victim is a child, was implicitly to adopt the position taken in several cases that in *child* sexual abuse prosecutions statements of the *child* victim identifying the perpetrator are admissible under this hearsay exception as reasonably pertinent to medical diagnosis or treatment of emotional and psychological injuries and as reasonably pertinent to preventing a recurrence of the injury. *See United States v. Renville,* 779 F.2d 430 (8th Cir. 1985). *Accord People v. Morgan,* 259 Ill. App. 3d 770, 197 Ill. Dec. 765, 631 N.E.2d 1224 (1994). Such a contention had been rejected in *People v. Taylor,* 153 Ill. App. 3d 710, 106 Ill. Dec. 614, 506 N.E.2d 321 (1987). The statement is admissible when made by the victim to medical personnel solely for the purpose of medical diagnosis, that is, no treatment was contemplated. *People v. Falaster,* 173 Ill. 2d 220, 218 Ill. Dec. 902, 670 N.E.2d 624 (1996); *People v. Roy,* 201 Ill. App. 3d 166, 146 Ill. Dec. 874, 558 N.E.2d 1208 (1990); *People v. Balle,* 234 Ill. App. 3d 804, 176 Ill. Dec. 90, 601 N.E.2d 788 (1992). Moreover, an investigation function on the part of the person to whom the statement is made is not incompatible with a diagnostic purpose being present as well. *People v. Falaster,* 173 Ill. 2d 220, 218 Ill. Dec. 902, 670 N.E.2d 624 (1996); *People v. Simpkins,* 297 Ill. App. 3d 668, 231 Ill. Dec. 748, 697 N.E.2d 302 (1998). The constitutionality of the statute under the confrontation clause, §807.1 infra, was upheld in *People v. Roy* supra on the basis that the hearsay exception for statements made for the purpose of medical diagnosis or treatment is firmly rooted. Section 115-13 is to be liberally construed in accordance with legislative intent to encompass all statements that are reasonably pertinent to diagnosis or treatment including the identity of the perpetrator. *People v. Falaster,* 173 Ill. 2d 220, 218 Ill. Dec. 902, 670 N.E.2d 624 (1996) (in a family setting, child victim's identification of family member as sex offender is closely related to diagnosis and treatment); *People v. Rushing,* 194 Ill. App. 3d 444, 139 Ill. Dec. 403, 548 N.E.2d 788 (1989) (name of perpetrator and the fact that the defendant threatened to kill victim's parents if she told anyone was within hearsay exception). *Accord People v. White,* 198 Ill. App. 3d 641, 144 Ill. Dec. 722, 555 N.E.2d 1241 (1990); *People v. Roy,* 201 Ill. App. 3d 166, 146 Ill. Dec. 874, 558 N.E.2d 1208 (1990); *People v. Denny,* 241 Ill. App. 3d 345, 181 Ill. Dec. 839, 608 N.E.2d 1313 (1993); *People v. Park,*

245 Ill. App. 3d 994, 185 Ill. Dec. 883, 615 N.E.2d 753 (1993); *People v. March*, 250 Ill. App. 3d 1062, 189 Ill. Dec. 456, 620 N.E.2d 424 (1993). *Compare People v. Falaster*, 273 Ill. App. 3d 694, 210 Ill. Dec. 562, 653 N.E.2d 467 (1995); *People v. Morgan*, 259 Ill. App. 3d 770, 197 Ill. Dec. 765, 631 N.E.2d 1224 (1994), apparently limiting admissibility of the identity of the perpetrator to situations in which the alleged child sexual abuse was committed by a family member. *Contra People v. Hall*, 235 Ill. App. 3d 418, 176 Ill. Dec. 185, 601 N.E.2d 883 (1992); *People v. Perkins*, 216 Ill. App. 3d 389, 159 Ill. Dec. 686, 576 N.E.2d 355 (1991); *People v. Hudson*, 198 Ill. App. 3d 915, 145 Ill. Dec. 22, 556 N.E.2d 640 (1990) (statement may not include identity of the alleged perpetrator); *People v. Cassell*, 283 Ill. App. 3d 112, 218 Ill. Dec. 512, 669 N.E.2d 655 (1996) (fact victim was dragged from apartment admissible but not the identity of the person who did so). Since 725 ILCS 5/115-13 refers solely to "statements made by the victim to medical personnel," statements made to medical personnel by someone with an interest in the victim's well being are not admissible. *People v. Roy*, 201 Ill. App. 3d 166, 146 Ill. Dec. 874, 558 N.E.2d 1208 (1990); *People v. Giles*, 261 Ill. App. 3d 833, 200 Ill. Dec. 630, 635 N.E.2d 969 (1994). Amending 5/115-13 to admit such statements seems in order. *See also* discussion under "treating physicians" supra.

While the motives underlying the statute are clearly praiseworthy, such expansion is nevertheless a distortion of the rationale underlying the hearsay exception. Since children who make such statements are not usually seeking treatment or prevention from the health care professional, the basic guarantee of trustworthiness that buttresses the exception is often missing. Moreover, defining the class of health care professionals, i.e., "medical personnel," to whom such statements are admissible is not without difficulty. Are social workers included? *United States v. De Noyer*, 811 F.2d 436 (8th Cir. 1987) says "Yes." What about high school guidance counselors? Finally, to the extent expansion converts treatment into prevention, the rationale would extend to statements made to parents, police officers, and others as well. It is suggested that a better approach to determining the admissibility of accusatory statements of the victims of child sexual abuse would have been by reference to the hearsay exception specifically provided in 725 ILCS 5/115-10 for such purpose. *See* §611.15 supra and §803.23 infra. Extension of the exception to adult victims of sexual abuse is even more questionable.

§803.9 Recorded Recollection

A record or memorandum is admissible as an exception to the Hearsay Rule if the proponent can show that the testifying witness once had personal knowledge of the matter, *Roeseke v. Pryor,* 152 Ill. App. 3d 771, 105 Ill. Dec. 642, 504 N.E.2d 927 (1987); *Barker v. Eagle Food Centers, Inc.,* 261 Ill. App. 3d 1068, 199 Ill. Dec. 922, 634 N.E.2d 1276 (1994), that the record or memorandum was prepared or adopted by her when it was fresh in her memory, *Salcik v. Tassone,* 236 Ill. App. 3d 548, 177 Ill. Dec. 723, 603 N.E.2d 793 (1992) (lapse of three months was too long), and that it accurately reflected her knowledge. In addition, it must also be shown that the witness currently lacks independent recollection of the occurrence and that the record or memorandum fails to refresh the current recollection. *People v. Unes,* 143 Ill. App. 3d 716, 97 Ill. Dec. 874, 493 N.E.2d 681 (1986); *Dexheimer v. Industrial Commission,* 202 Ill. App. 3d 437, 147 Ill. Dec. 694, 559 N.E.2d 1034 (1990); *Medina v. City of Chicago,* 238 Ill. App. 3d 385, 179 Ill. Dec. 658, 606 N.E.2d 490 (1992). Thus the witness may testify either that she remembers making an accurate recording of the event in question that she now no longer sufficiently remembers or, if the witness has entirely forgotten the situation in which the recording was made, that she recalls from the circumstances that she would not have written or adopted such description of the facts unless that description truly described her observations at the time. The involvement of many persons in the process of observation and recording is permitted. *Diamond Glue Co. v. Weitzychowski,* 227 Ill. 338, 81 N.E. 392 (1907); *People v. Andrews,*

101 Ill. App. 3d 808, 57 Ill. Dec. 368, 428 N.E.2d 1048 (1981); *Wilsey v. Schlawin,* 35 Ill. App. 3d 892, 342 N.E.2d 417 (1976).

While it has been stated that the witness must lack "any" independent recollection of the occurrence, *see, e.g., Wilsey v. Schlawin* supra, the weight of modern authority describes the requirement as a lack of sufficient present recollection to enable a witness to testify fully and accurately, McCormick, Evidence, §282 (4th ed. 1992), a standard probably currently applied in practice. *Cf. People v. Harrison,* 384 Ill. 207, 51 N.E.2d 172 (1943), witness must state that he can recall nothing further than that he had accurately reduced the whole transaction to writing.

Memoranda or records admitted as past recollection recorded may be read to the jury or admitted as an exhibit. *People v. Olson,* 59 Ill. App. 3d 643, 16 Ill. Dec. 660, 375 N.E.2d 533 (1978); *People v. Skidmore,* 56 Ill. App. 3d 862, 14 Ill. Dec. 527, 372 N.E.2d 723 (1978).

Police reports, *People v. Strausberger,* 151 Ill. App. 3d 832, 104 Ill. Dec. 503 N.E.2d 832 (1987); *Taylor v. City of Chicago,* 114 Ill. App. 3d 715, 70 Ill. Dec. 398, 449 N.E.2d 272 (1983); *Wilkinson v. Mullen,* 27 Ill. App. 3d 804, 327 N.E.2d 433 (1975); medical and hospital records, *Wilson v. Parker,* 132 Ill. App. 2d 5, 269 N.E.2d 523 (1971); forensic chemist's report, *People v. Unes,* 143 Ill. App. 3d 716, 97 Ill. Dec. 874, 493 N.E.2d 681 (1986); and stenographic statements of the defendant, *People v. Lykins,* 65 Ill. App. 3d 808, 22 Ill. Dec. 544, 283 N.E.2d 1242 (1978), being records or memoranda, may be admitted if the requirements of past recollection recorded are satisfied. *Cf.* the limitations on use of police reports, §803.13 infra, and hospital and medical records as business records, §803.11 infra. It will be observed that compliance with the recorded recollection requirement requires the presence of the declarant in court.

A memorandum or record satisfying the requirements for past recollection recorded may be admitted for the purpose of establishing the making of a prior inconsistent statement of a witness. *People v. Andrews,* 101 Ill. App. 3d 808, 57 Ill. Dec. 368, 428 N.E.2d 1048 (1981), police report. Past recollection recorded may be employed in connection with double-level hearsay. *Minor v. City of Chicago,* 101 Ill. App. 3d 823, 57 Ill. Dec. 410, 428 N.E.2d 1090 (1981), hospital record, admitted as past recollection of an intern, contained statements of plaintiff pertinent to medical diagnosis or treatment. *Accord Loughnane v. City of Chicago,* 188 Ill. App. 3d 1078, 136 Ill. Dec. 626, 545 N.E.2d 150 (1989). With respect to double-level hearsay, *see* §805.1 infra. Memoranda or records satisfying the requirements of recorded recollection are subject to application of the Original Writing Rule, §1002 infra. *See Dayan v. McDonald's Corp.,* 125 Ill. App. 3d 972, 81 Ill. Dec. 156, 466 N.E.2d 958 (1984) (where the original record or memorandum is unavailable, a copy thereof or a report subsequently transcribed therefrom may be introduced). *But see* the use of a memorandum to refresh recollection, §612.1 supra.

Consider the following illustration from T. Mauet, Fundamentals of Trial Techniques 193-194 (3rd ed. 1992):

Elements:

    a. Exhibit is relevant.
    b. Witness has no full or accurate present recollection of the facts.
    c. Witness had firsthand knowledge of facts when they occurred.
    d. Witness made a record of the facts at or near the time the facts occurred.
    e. Record was accurate and complete when made.
    f. Record is in the same condition now as when made.

Example:

Witness has testified that he recorded the serial numbers of every automobile on a dealership lot on a certain date.

Q. Mr. Doe, how many cars did you see on the lot that day?
A. About 300.
Q. Did each car have a serial number?
A. Yes.

Q. Can you tell the jury what the serial numbers on the cars were?

A. No, sir, I can't possibly remember them.

Q. Did you make any record of those serial numbers?

A. Yes, sir, I made a list.

Q. When did you make that list?

A. I made it at the time I was on the dealership lot.

Q. Was the list you made accurate and complete?

A. Yes, sir.

Q. Mr. Doe, would that list refresh your recollection as to what those serial numbers were?

A. No, I couldn't possibly remember them, even if I reviewed the list.

> *Step 1.* Have exhibit marked.
> *Step 2.* Show exhibit to opposing counsel.
> *Step 3.* Ask permission to approach the witness.
> *Step 4.* Show the exhibit to witness.
> *Step 5.* Establish foundation:

Q. I show you what has been marked Plaintiff's Exhibit #1. Do you recognize it?

A. Yes.

Q. What is it?

A. That's the list I made of the serial numbers on the cars I saw at the car dealership.

Q. Is the record in the same condition now as when you made it?

A. Yes, nothing on it has been changed.

> *Step 6.* Offer exhibit in evidence.
> *Step 7.* Have exhibit marked in evidence.
> *Step 8.* Have witness mark exhibit.
> *Step 9.* Ask permission to show/read exhibit to jury.
> *Step 10.* Show/read exhibit to jury.

§803.10 Business Records

The theory upon which entries in the regular course of business are admissible as an exception to the Hearsay Rule is that since their purpose is to aid in the proper transaction of the business and they are useless for that purpose unless accurate, the motive for following a routine of accuracy is great and the motive to falsify nonexistent. *See Chicago & Alton R. Co. v. American Strawboard Co.*, 190 Ill. 268, 60 N.E. 518 (1901); *Ocasio-Morales v. Fulton Mach. Co.*, 10 Ill. App. 3d 719, 295 N.E.2d 329 (1973). Under this view, it makes no difference whether the records are those of a party or of a third person authorized by the business to generate the record on the business's behalf. *Argueta v. Baltimore & Ohio Chicago Terminal Railroad Co.*, 224 Ill. App. 3d 11, 166 Ill. Dec. 428, 586 N.E.2d 386 (1991), ultrasonic test reports prepared by third party as part of railroad routine testing of spindle pins; *Ramsey v. Greenwald*, 91 Ill. App. 3d 855, 47 Ill. Dec 150, 414 N.E.2d 1266 (1980), a party's business records of a self-serving character are admissible.

Illinois Supreme Court Rule 236 ("Rule 236(a)"), applicable in civil cases, and substantially identical to 725 ILCS 5/115-5(a) ("5/115-5(a)"), applicable in criminal cases, provides for the admission as a hearsay exception of records of regularly conducted activities of any business. Any writing or record, whether in the form of an entry in a book or otherwise, made as a memorandum or record of any act, transaction, occurrence, or event, is admissible as evidence of the act, transaction, occurrence, or event, if made in the regular course of any business and if it was the regular course of the business to make such a memorandum or record at the time of such an act, transaction, occurrence, or event or within a reasonable time thereafter. *People ex rel. Schacht v. Main Ins. Co.*, 114 Ill. App. 3d 334, 70 Ill. Dec. 72, 448 N.E.2d 950 (1983); *People v. Morrow*, 256 Ill. App. 3d 392, 195 Ill. Dec. 86, 628 N.E.2d 550 (1993). The term *business* is defined in both Rule 236(a) and 5/115-5(a) to include business, profession, occupation, and calling of every kind. All other circumstances of the making of the writing or record, including lack of personal knowledge by the entrant or maker, may be shown to affect its weight but do not affect its admissibility. *Preski v. Warchol Constr. Co.*, 111 Ill. App. 3d 641, 67 Ill. Dec. 621, 444 N.E.2d 1105 (1982). If the source of information or the method or circumstances of preparation, however, indicate lack of trustworthiness, the court may exclude the record. *Eastman v. Department of Pub. Aid,* 178 Ill. App. 3d 993, 128 Ill. Dec. 276, 534 N.E.2d 458 (1989); *Neal v. Whirl Air Flow Corp.,* 43 Ill. App. 3d 266, 1 Ill. Dec. 891, 356 N.E.2d 1173 (1976); *Windmiller v. McCartney,* 108 Ill. App. 2d 264, 247 N.E.2d 63 (1969). The motivation of the declarant and whether the record was made in anticipation of litigation are factors appropriately considered by the court in making this determination. *People ex rel. Schacht v. Main Ins. Co.* supra, summaries prepared after the event for the purpose of litigation are not admissible; *Kelly v. HCI Heinz Construction Co.,* 282 Ill. App. 3d 36, 218 Ill. Dec. 112, 668 N.E.2d 596 (1996), medical records of a treating doctor prepared in anticipation of litigation are not made in the regular course of business. *See also People v. Morrow,* 256 Ill. App. 3d 392, 195 Ill. Dec. 86, 628 N.E.2d 550 (1993), fact copy of document prepared by another in the ordinary cause of business was in the hands of the defendant, who had a motive to falsify, made copy of document inadmissible. *See generally People v. Smith,* 141 Ill. 2d 40, 152 Ill. Dec. 218, 565 N.E.2d 900 (1990); *In re N.W.,* 293 Ill. App. 3d 794, 228 Ill. Dec. 157, 688 N.E.2d 855 (1997). Statements made in anticipation of litigation, such as railroad accident investigation reports, are admissible business records when offered against the party who prepared them. *Ficken v. Alton & Southern Railway Co.,* 255 Ill. App. 3d 1047, 193 Ill. Dec. 51, 625 N.E.2d 1172 (1993); *Amos v. Norfolk & Western Railway Co.,* 191 Ill. App. 3d 637, 138 Ill. Dec. 866, 548 N.E.2d 96 (1989). The modern trend necessarily tends to be more liberal as to the admission of business records as business gets more complicated and transactions are broken down into various operations so that no particular person can identify any particular operation. *Birch v. Drummer Township,* 139 Ill. App. 3d 397, 94 Ill. Dec. 41, 487 N.E.2d 798 (1985); *Agrico Chem. Corp. v. Forreston Fertilizer Co.,* 32 Ill. App. 3d 986, 337 N.E.2d 76 (1975). Thus neither the fact that the identity of the person creating the record is unknown nor the fact that the record contains certain unexplained alterations requires exclusion. *Progress Printing Corp. v. Jane Byrne Political Committee,* 235 Ill. App. 3d 292, 176 Ill. Dec. 357, 601 N.E.2d 1055 (1992). Similarly, the fact that a business record was not in fact used or relied upon does not affect admissibility but only weight. *Compare People v. Berberena,* 265 Ill. App. 3d 1033, 203 Ill. Dec. 279, 639 N.E.2d 599 (1994).

The Original Writing Rule, §1002 infra, is applicable to writings and records admitted pursuant to the business record hearsay exceptions. *Kerbis v. Kerbis,* 38 Ill. App. 3d 866, 350 N.E.2d 1 (1976).

Both Illinois Supreme Court Rule 236(b) and 725 ILCS 5/ 115-5(c) state that they do not permit the introduction of police accident or investigation reports. Section 115-5(c)(1), applicable in criminal cases, includes hospital and medical business records as well. The admissibility of medical and hospital writings and records, being both public and nonpublic in nature, is discussed in §803.11 infra; police accident and investigative reports, being public in nature, are addressed in §803.13 infra, following a discussion of the public records hearsay exception, §803.12 infra.

No small confusion once existed from the erroneous assumption that the rules for admissibility of entries in the regular course of business were codified by Section 3 of the Evidence Act, Ill. R.S. 1981, c.51, §3, now Code of Civil Procedure, 735 ILCS 5/8-401, and that such records were to be admissible only in conformity with the statute. *See National Malleable Castings Co. v. Iroquois Steel Co.,* 333 Ill. 588, 165 N.E. 199 (1929); *Trainor v. German-American Sav. Assn.,* 204 Ill. 616, 68 N.E. 650 (1903); *Rude v. Siebert,* 22 Ill. App. 2d 477, 161 N.E.2d 39 (1959); *Secco v. Chicago Transit Auth.,* 6 Ill. App. 2d 266, 127 N.E.2d 266 (1955). In fact, the essential and apparent purpose of 5/8-401 is only to enable parties incompetent to testify under the Dead Man's Act, 735 ILCS 5/8-201, *see* §606 supra, nevertheless to testify to the extent required for admission of their own books and records. The specifications in 5/8-401 as to the showings required and the types of records admissible are limited to this situation. For the text of 5/ 8-401 and further comments, *see* §606.6 supra.

Types of Records. An occasional early case had indicated that only conventional commercial account books were admissible, *Baltimore & Ohio Southwestern Ry. v. Tripp,* 175 Ill. 251, 51 N.E. 833 (1898), engine inspection record properly excluded as not a "book of account," and moreover admissibility was confined to books of original entry; *McCormick v. Elston,* 16 Ill. 204 (1854), journal but not ledger is admissible. This limitation, if in fact it ever properly existed, was long since discarded in favor of admitting any writing or record in the form of an entry or otherwise, of any act, transaction, occurrence, or event if made in the regular course of any business. *Chicago & Alton R. Co. v. American Strawboard Co.,* 190 Ill. 268, 60 N.E. 518 (1901), business inventory record; *Pittsburgh, C., C. & St. L. Ry. v. Chicago,* 242 Ill. 178, 89 N.E. 1022 (1909), records of movements and history of equipment; *National Malleable Castings Co. v. Iroquois Steel Co.,* 333 Ill. 588, 165 N.E. 199 (1929), railroad record of car weights; *Secco v. Chicago Transit Auth.,* 6 Ill. App. 2d 266, 127 N.E.2d 266 (1955), school record of pupil's attendance, under Municipal Court of Chicago Rule 5, later Rule 70, now Rule 236(a) with some modifications; *Matter of Estate of Severson,* 107 Ill. App. 3d 634, 62 Ill. Dec. 903, 437 N.E.2d 430 (1982), record to prove parentage in Church Book for a parish in Norway in late 1800s.

Opinions. Entries, it has been said, must be factual in character and not consist of "opinions" or "conclusions." *See Wright v. Upson,* 303 Ill. 120, 135 N.E. 209 (1922), which seems to insist upon this requirement to an unwarranted extreme in the case of hospital records, discussed specifically in §803.11 infra. This is contrary to the Federal Rule of Evidence 803(6), 65 F.R.D. 131, 155 (1975), and to the trend of authority generally. McCormick, Evidence §287 (4th ed. 1992). It is also inconsistent with the recent adoption by the supreme court of Federal Rule of Evidence 703. *See* §703.1 supra. One surmises that the winds of change are blowing if they have not already blown. *Accord People ex rel. Schacht v. Main Ins. Co.,* 122 Ill. App. 3d 826, 78 Ill. Dec. 551, 462 N.E.2d 670 (1984); *Birch v. Drummer Township,* 139 Ill. App. 3d 397, 94 Ill. Dec. 41, 487 N.E.2d

798 (1985); *Amos v. Norfolk & Western Railway Co.*, 191 Ill. App. 3d 637, 138 Ill. Dec. 866, 548 N.E.2d 96 (1989), business records containing opinions are admissible under Rule 236(a). *Contra Kelly v. HCI Heinz Construction Co.*, 282 Ill. App. 3d 36, 218 Ill. Dec. 112, 668 N.E.2d 596 (1996), records of routine, ministerial, objective, and nonevaluative matters are admissible but opinions should be presented in the form of live testimony subject to cross-examination and not in the form of a medical record.

Who must be called. If all persons who participated in the furnishing of information and the making of entries must be called as witnesses, then the hearsay exception for records of regularly conducted activities goes no farther than the one for recorded recollection. *See* §803.9 supra. A number of earlier decisions required all participants to be called, departing from the requirements for recorded recollection only to the extent of dispensing with the testimony of participants shown to be unavailable. *People v. Small*, 319 Ill. 437 150 N.E. 435 (1926); *Wright v. Upson*, 303 Ill. 120, 135 N.E. 209 (1922); *Trainor v. German-American Sav. Loan & Bldg. Assn.*, 204 Ill. 616, 68 N.E. 650 (1903); *Stettauer v. White*, 98 Ill. 72 (1881). In conformity with more recent authority, under both Rule 236(a) and 725 ILCS 5/115-5(a), business records are admissible upon the testimony of the custodian of the writing or record or other person familiar with the business and its mode of operation, identifying the writing or record and establishing that a routine was followed producing accuracy; neither the original entrant nor an individual possessing personal knowledge of the event need be produced. *Lecroy v. Miller*, 272 Ill. App. 3d 925, 209 Ill. Dec. 439, 651 N.E.2d 617 (1995); *People v. Morrow*, 256 Ill. App. 3d 392, 195 Ill. Dec. 86, 628 N.E.2d 550 (1993); *Ford Motor Credit Co. v. Neiser*, 196 Ill. App. 3d 515, 143 Ill. Dec. 387, 554 N.E.2d 322 (1990); *People v. Shiflet*, 125 Ill. App. 3d 161, 80 Ill. Dec. 596, 465 N.E.2d 942 (1984); *People v. Clark*, 108 Ill. App. 3d 1071, 64 Ill. Dec. 835, 440 N.E.2d 387 (1982); *Agrico Chem. Corp. v. Forreston Fertilizer Co.*, 32 Ill. App. 3d 986, 337 N.E.2d 76 (1975). Therefore, and most important, the custodian or other witness need not have personal knowledge of the matter recorded, nor is it a requirement that a custodian called to testify have been the custodian of the records when they were made. *Nussbaum Trucking v. Illinois Commerce Commn.*, 99 Ill. App. 3d 741, 55 Ill. Dec. 56, 425 N.E.2d 1229 (1981). Thus it is sensibly recognized that the dependability of regular entries rests upon proof of a routine of making accurate records, rather than upon the testimony of each participant that he himself was accurate. Lack of personal knowledge of the entrant or maker may be shown to affect the weight to be given to the record but does not effect its admissibility. *Easley v. Apollo Detective Agency, Inc.*, 69 Ill. App. 3d 920, 26 Ill. Dec. 313, 387 N.E.2d 1241 (1979).

The person testifying as to the routine producing accuracy must, of course, be testifying as to the procedures of the business. Accordingly, a person receiving a document from a business could not solely by virtue thereof lay a sufficient foundation for admitting the document as a business record of the issuing business. *People v. Morrow*, 256 Ill. App. 3d 392, 195 Ill. Dec. 86, 628 N.E.2d 550 (1993); *International Harvester Credit Corp. v. Helland*, 151 Ill. App. 3d 848, 104 Ill. Dec. 833, 503 N.E.2d 548 (1986); *Pell v. Victor J. Andrew High School*, 123 Ill. App. 3d 423, 78 Ill. Dec. 739, 462 N.E.2d 858 (1984). An exception exists when the business receiving the information, acting in the regular course of business, integrates the information received into the business's records, relies on it in its day-to-day operations, and surrounding circumstances indicate trustworthiness. Under such limited circumstances, admissibility through the testimony of the receiving custodian is warranted. *See United States v. Parker*, 749 F.2d 628 (11th Cir. 1984).

Laying a foundation. A sufficient foundation for admitting records of regularly conducted business activities may be established through testimony of the custodian of the record or another person familiar with the business and its mode of operation. The custodian identifies the record, establishing that it is a record made at or near the time in the regular course of a regularly conducted business activity by, or from information transmitted by, a person within the business with personal knowledge. After identifying the witness as the custodian of the record, and after the witness identifies the record, counsel lays a sufficient foundation by eliciting a positive response to each of the following questions:

(1) "Was it the regular course of business to make this record?"
(2) "Was this record kept in the regular course of business?"
(3) "Was the record made at or near the time of the matter recorded?" and
(4) "Was this record made by a person within the business with knowledge of, or made from information transmitted by a person within the business with knowledge of the acts, events, conditions, opinions, or diagnosis appearing in it?"

Consider the following illustration from T. Mauet, Fundamentals of Trial Techniques 189-190 (3rd ed. 1992):

Elements:

a. Record is relevant.
b. Record is a "memorandum, report, record or data compilation in any form."
c. Witness is the "custodian or other qualified witness."
d. Record was "made by a person with knowledge" of the facts or was "made from information transmitted by a person with knowledge" of the facts.
e. Record was "made at or near the time" of the "acts, events, conditions, opinions, or diagnoses" appearing on it.
f. Record was made as part of "the regular practice of that business activity."
g. Record was "kept in the course of a regularly conducted business activity."

The following example shows how easily the required technical elements of [the business record hearsay exception] can be met.

Example:

Q. Mr. Doe, please state your occupation.
A. I'm the records keeper of the XYZ Corporation.
Q. What does your job involve?
A. I collect, keep, and maintain all the company records according to our indexing system.

>   *Step 1.* Have exhibit marked.
>   *Step 2.* Show exhibit to opposing counsel.
>   *Step 3.* Ask permission to approach the witness.
>   *Step 4.* Show exhibit to witness.
>   *Step 5.* Establish foundation:

Q. Mr. Doe, I am showing you what has been marked Plaintiff's Exhibit #1. Do you recognize it?
A. Yes, it's one of our records.
Q. Was that record made by a person with knowledge of, or made from information transmitted by a person with knowledge of, the acts and events appearing on it?
A. Yes.
Q. Was the record made at or near the time of the acts and events appearing on it?
A. Yes.
Q. Is it the regular practice of the XYZ Corporation to make such a record?
A. Yes.
Q. Was that record kept in the course of a regularly conducted business activity?
A. Yes.

>   *Step 6.* Offer exhibit in evidence.
>   *Step 7.* Have exhibit marked in evidence.
>   *Step 8.* Have witness mark/explain exhibit.
>   *Step 9.* Ask permission to show/read exhibit to jury.
>   *Step 10.* Show/read exhibit to jury.

The record must be made in the regular course of business to make such records, rather than a merely casual entry. *Kibbe v. Bancroft,* 77 Ill. 18 (1875), casual entry made in old account book that had not been used for many years excluded. However, a record made in response to an event that has never occurred before may still qualify as a record made in the regular course of business. *Newark Elec. Corp. v. City of Chicago,* 130 Ill. App. 2d 1021, 264 N.E.2d 868 (1970), not abuse of discretion to permit introduction of record indicating compilation and computation of water damage caused by flooding; *Birch v. Drummer Township,* 139 Ill. App. 3d 397, 94 Ill. Dec. 41, 487 N.E.2d 798 (1985), safety report of traffic signs prepared before accident, while never before made, is admissible if made in the regular course of business; *Tie Sys. v. Telcom Midwest,* 203 Ill. App. 3d 142, 148 Ill. Dec. 438, 560 N.E.2d 1080 (1990), list of missing files prepared after discovery of customer cancellation of maintenance agreements properly admitted.

The record must have been made at or near the time of the event recorded, a requirement given a practical, flexible, and liberal interpretation. *See Taluzek v. Illinois Central Gulf Railroad Co.,* 255 Ill. App. 3d 72, 193 Ill. Dec. 816, 626 N.E.2d 1367 (1993) (two weeks); *Amos v. Norfolk & Western Railway Co.,* 191 Ill. App. 3d 637, 138 Ill. Dec. 866, 548 N.E.2d 96 (1989) (up to one month). Ultimately the question depends upon whether the time span between the event recorded and the entry is so great as to suggest a danger of inaccuracy by lapse of memory.

Once a writing or record has been shown to comply with either Rule 236(a) or 5/115-5(a), it may be admitted into evidence and, in the court's discretion, be either read to or handed to the jury. A witness is, however, not permitted to testify as to the contents of the document or provide a summary thereof; the document "speaks for itself." *Smith v. Williams,* 34 Ill. App. 3d 677, 339 N.E.2d 10 (1975); *Topps v. Unicorn Insurance Co.,* 271 Ill. App. 3d 111, 207 Ill. Dec. 758, 648 N.E.2d 214 (1995). *But see* §1006 with respect to summaries of voluminous documents.

Computer Records. Business records generated by a computer are admissible in evidence without testimony of the persons who made the entries in the regular course of a regularly conducted business activity if it is shown that (1) the electronic computing equipment is recognized as standard; (2) the entries are made in the regular course of business at or reasonably near the time of the happening of the event recorded; (3) the particular computer produces an accurate record when properly employed and operated; (4) the particular computer was properly employed and operated in the manner at hand; and (5) the foundation testimony satisfies the court that the sources of information, method and time of preparation were such as to indicate its trustworthiness and justify its admission. *Grand Liquor Co. v. Department of Revenue*, 67 Ill. 2d 195, 10 Ill. Dec. 472, 367 N.E.2d 1238 (1977); *People v. Morrow*, 256 Ill. App. 3d 392, 195 Ill. Dec. 86, 628 N.E.2d 550 (1993); *People v. Turner*, 233 Ill. App. 3d 449, 174 Ill. Dec. 558, 599 N.E.2d 104 (1992); *Eastman v. Department of Pub. Aid*, 178 Ill. App. 3d 993, 128 Ill. Dec. 276, 534 N.E.2d 458 (1989); *People v. Hendricks*, 145 Ill. App. 3d 71, 99 Ill. Dec. 20, 495 N.E.2d 85 (1986); *Victory Memorial Hosp. v. Rice*, 143 Ill. App. 3d 621, 97 Ill. Dec. 635, 493 N.E.2d 117 (1986). *See generally People v. Friedland*, 202 Ill. App. 3d 1094, 148 Ill. Dec. 415, 560 N.E.2d 1012 (1990), computer records improperly admitted in the absence of testimony as to what type of computer system was used by the bank and whether that system was recognized as standard and in the absence of testimony to establish that the sources of information, method, and time of preparation indicated trustworthiness. Computer-generated records, such as tracing records of telephone call numbers, being created without the assistance of a person, are not hearsay. *People v. Holowko*, 109 Ill. 2d 187, 93 Ill. Dec. 344, 486 N.E.2d 877 (1985). *See* §801.1 supra. While the mere retrieval of computer-generated computer records does not make the record hearsay, the record is hearsay if the retrieval process itself incorporates a purposeful selection from various sources. *People v. Houston*, 288 Ill. App. 3d 90, 223 Ill. Dec. 471, 679 N.E.2d 1244 (1997); *People v. Casey*, 225 Ill. App. 3d 82, 167 Ill. Dec.

242, 587 N.E.2d 511 (1992). Thus a certified copy of computer records indicating all medical payments made over time by the Department of Public Aid is properly admitted. *In re Estate of Huffman*, 265 Ill. App. 3d 225, 202 Ill. Dec. 589, 638 N.E.2d 235 (1994); *In re Estate of Zander*, 242 Ill. App. 3d 774, 183 Ill. Dec. 233, 611 N.E.2d 86 (1993). *See also* §§901.2 and 1001.2 infra.

Business Duty.   Since the guarantee of accuracy of regular entries rests upon a duty to make an accurate record, all persons who participate in the initial furnishing of information must possess personal knowledge, §602 supra, of matters related, and all persons furnishing and recording information must be under a duty to do so. *See, e.g., Pennsylvania Co. v. McCaffrey*, 173 Ill. 169, 50 N.E. 713 (1898), and *Paliokaitis v. Checker Cab Co.*, 324 Ill. App. 21, 57 N.E.2d 216 (1944), police record of accidents compiled by investigation not based on personal knowledge of police, properly excluded. *See also Johnson v. Lutz*, 253 N.Y. 124, 170 N.E. 517 (1930). While both Rule 236(a) and 5/115-5(a) are less clear in this respect than might be desired, the premise underlying the rule makes any other construction unlikely. In addition, if a statement made by a person not under a duty to report is not hearsay or meets the requirements of a hearsay exception, and if the person recording the information is under a duty to do so, the statement would be admissible. *See also* §805 infra.

The following illustrates the foregoing principles:

(1) If a security guard at Universal Studios observed an accident and filed an accident report because he was under a business duty to observe and record, if the report was also made in the regular course of business by following proper procedures at the proper times, the hearsay exception is satisfied.

(2) Assume that the security guard, instead of preparing the report, transmitted his observations over his car radio to headquarters and the person at headquarters took notes of the radio transmission. The notes were then typed into a formal report by a third person. Provided each person was

performing his assigned duty in the regular course of a regularly conducted business activity, the hearsay exception is satisfied.

(3) Now assume that ten minutes after the accident, the security guard spoke to a nonparty eyewitness who calmly described how the accident occurred. Although the security guard was under a business duty to record the statement, the matter reported was not transmitted by an individual with a business duty to report. Under such circumstances, the business record hearsay exception extends only to the point of admitting the statement of the occurrence witness for the fact the statement was said, but not as proof of the truth of the facts stated. Because the statement of the occurrence witness is only relevant when offered for the truth of the matter asserted, the statement will be excluded as hearsay. If the security guard was not under a business duty to record the particular statement made by the occurrence witness, the record prepared containing the statement would not be admissible even to establish that the statement was made.

(4) Finally, if the occurrence witness's statement as to which there was a business duty to record is not hearsay or satisfies the requirements of any hearsay exception, then the statement will be admitted. The business record hearsay exception permits introduction of the occurrence witness's statement for the fact it was said while the hearsay exception would provide for admissibility for the truth of the matter stated. Thus a statement of a nonparty eyewitness made to the security guard while the declarant was still under the stress of the excitement caused by the accident, §803.3 supra, that the truck went through a red light would be admissible double-level hearsay. *See also* §805.1 infra.

§803.11   *Medical and Hospital Records*

725 ILCS 5/115-5(c) ("5/115-5(c)") states that it does not permit the introduction of business records in any form of hospital or medical business in criminal proceedings. Illinois

Supreme Court Rule 236(b) ("Rule 236(b)"), which contained a similar exclusion of medical records, was amended effective August 1, 1992, to eliminate the exclusion thus making hospital and medical records admissible in civil proceedings. *See* Illinois Supreme Court Rule 1.

Supreme Court Rule 236(a) was adopted from old Municipal Court of Chicago Rule 5, which was a counterpart of the former Federal Business Records Act, now superseded by Federal Rule of Evidence 803(6), 65 F.R.D. 131, 155 (1975). As applied to medical records, the federal statute, by reason of its ambiguities and insufficiencies, had produced a variety of inconsistent results, as the Illinois Rules Committee noted in its Committee Comments to Supreme Court Rule 236, and for that reason hospital or medical and police accident or investigative records were excluded from the coverage of the rule. The committee pointed out, however, that the admissibility of the records was not affected. In other words, in the two areas of medical records and police reports, rules of general admissibility would have to be mapped out on a case-by-case basis. *Casey v. Penn,* 45 Ill. App. 3d 573, 4 Ill. Dec. 346, 360 N.E.2d 93 (1977). *Accord People v. Jackson,* 41 Ill. 2d 102, 242 N.E.2d 160 (1968), county jail inmate card containing notation of defendant's condition as good, outside purview of medical exclusion and thus admissible pursuant to Supreme Court Rule 236; *Thomas J. Douglas & Co. v. Industrial Commn.,* 35 Ill. 2d 100, 219 N.E.2d 486 (1966), army records showing long history of psychiatric trouble should have been admitted as public record. *Contra People v. Aristotle,* 131 Ill. App. 2d 175, 268 N.E.2d 227 (1971), a record within medical record exclusion of Supreme Court Rule 236(b), is properly refused admission; *People v. Gargano,* 10 Ill. App. 3d 957, 295 N.E.2d 342 (1975), admission of hospital records offered by criminal defendant barred by 725 ILCS 5/115-5(c); *People v. Staten,* 89 Ill. App. 3d 1113, 45 Ill. Dec. 493, 412 N.E.2d 1075 (1980), medical records offered by the prosecution through testimony of custodian were improperly received in evidence.

The leading common law decision on the admissibility of hospital records is *Wright v. Upson,* 303 Ill. 120, 135 N.E. 209

(1922), a will contest, holding it error to admit hospital records made by two or more nurses, some of whom did not testify and were not shown to be dead or outside the jurisdiction, a requirement then considered by some of the case law to apply to business records generally. The records showed the physical and mental condition of the testatrix, as well as food, treatment, and medications. The court also pointed out that, in any event, many of these entries were conclusions and indicated that no part should have been admitted. While conceding that a hospital record might be admissible against the surgeon, the court saw no reason why any party to the will contest in question should be bound by it. It is difficult to acknowledge that *Wright* continued to represent the state of the law of admissibility of hospital records in Illinois for nearly 70 years. The requirement of calling or accounting for all persons making entries has virtually disappeared from the law of evidence everywhere, as applied to business records generally. Illinois Supreme Court Rule 236(a); McCormick, Evidence §292 (4th ed. 1992). However, it continued to be applied to hospital records. *Khatib v. McDonald,* 87 Ill. App. 3d 1087, 43 Ill. Dec. 266, 410 N.E.2d 266 (1980); *Wilson v. Clark,* 80 Ill. App. 3d 194, 35 Ill. Dec. 585, 399 N.E.2d 651 (1980); *Casey v. Penn* supra; *Slater v. Missionary Sisters of Sacred Hearts,* 20 Ill. App. 3d 464, 314 N.E.2d 715 (1974); *Messina v. Zody,* 13 Ill. App. 3d 566, 300 N.E.2d 851 (1973). No reason for continuing it with respect to hospital records was advanced, and none is apparent.

The result of such a foundation requirement with respect to who must be called was to permit medical and hospital records to be admitted as a business record exception only under circumstances in which such evidence would be cumulative of the in-court testimony of the entrant possessing personal knowledge. *Martin v. Zucker,* 133 Ill. App. 3d 982, 88 Ill. Dec. 980, 479 N.E.2d 1000 (1985) (citing Handbook); *Smith by Smith v. Victory Memorial Hosp.,* 167 Ill. App. 3d 618, 118 Ill. Dec. 142, 521 N.E.2d 210 (1988). The objection to opinions in the form of diagnoses or recitals of the patient's condition is equally outmoded. The rule against opinions as it once was conceived has been revised so as to admit opinions that may be helpful to the trier of fact, and this attitude needed to be extended to hospital records. *See generally* as to hospital records, McCormick, Evidence §293 (4th ed. 1992).

The Illinois Supreme Court amended Rule 236(b) effective August 1, 1992, to eliminate the exclusion, thus making hospital and medical records admissible in civil proceedings. *Herron v. Anderson,* 254 Ill. App. 3d 365, 193 Ill. Dec. 484, 626 N.E.2d 1035 (1993). Unfortunately, hospital and medical records remain inadmissible as business records in criminal proceedings. 725 ILCS 5/115-5(c).

Certain medical or hospital records are made admissible by statute. 725 ILCS 5/115-5.1 provides that a certified copy of coroner's protocol autopsy report is admissible as *prima facie* evidence of facts, findings, opinions, diagnosis, and conditions stated therein, including the cause of death. *See Heitz v. Hogan,* 134 Ill. App. 3d 352, 89 Ill. Dec. 299, 480 N.E.2d 185 (1985); *People v. Campos,* 227 Ill. App. 3d 434, 169 Ill. Dec. 598, 592 N.E.2d 85 (1992); *People v. Harper,* 279 Ill. App. 3d 801, 216 Ill. Dec. 414, 665 N.E.2d 474 (1996). The autopsy report is made self-authenticating by statute; all parties are given the right to examine the preparer of the report. *See Affatato v. Jewel Companies, Inc.,* 259 Ill. App. 3d 787, 198 Ill. Dec. 78, 632 N.E.2d 137 (1994). 625 ILCS 5/11-501.4 provides that the written results of chemical tests of blood conducted in the regular course of providing emergency medical services are admissible in criminal prosecutions for driving under the influence and reckless homicide. *See People v. Lendabarker,* 215 Ill. App. 3d 540, 159 Ill. Dec. 70, 575 N.E.2d 568 (1991); *People v. Menssen,* 263 Ill. App. 3d 946, 201 Ill. Dec. 669, 636 N.E.2d 1101 (1994). 820 ILCS 305/16 provides that in proceeding before the Industrial Commission, records kept by a hospital, certified to as true and correct by the superintendent or other officer in charge, showing the medical and surgical treatment given an injured employee in such hospital, shall be admissible, without any further proof, as evidence of the medical and surgical matters stated there. In addition, a medical report or letter of a doctor of the injured employee may be admitted in evidence before the Industrial Commission as an exception to the Hearsay Rule. *United Elec. Coal Co. v. Industrial Commn.*, 93 Ill. 2d 415, 67 Ill. Dec. 76, 444 N.E.2d 115 (1982); *Fefferman v. Industrial Commn.*, 71 Ill. 2d 325, 16 Ill. Dec. 935, 375 N.E.2d 1277 (1978).

Medical and hospital records, like other business records, may be employed to refresh a witness's recollection. *LeMaster v. Chicago Rock Island & Pacific R. Co.*, 35 Ill. App. 3d 1001, 343 N.E.2d 65 (1976); *Hall v. Checker Taxi Co.*, 109 Ill. App. 2d 445, 248 N.E.2d 721 (1969). In addition, such records are admissible as past recollection recorded, §803.9 supra; *Wilson v. Parker*, 132 Ill. App. 2d 5, 269 N.E.2d 523 (1971); *Healy v. City of Chicago*, 109 Ill. App. 2d 6, 248 N.E.2d 679 (1969); *Wolfe v. City of Chicago*, 78 Ill. App. 2d 337, 223 N.E.2d 231 (1966). Statements contained in medical and hospital reports inconsistent with the in-court testimony of the maker of the report may be employed to impeach. *Jones v. Lukas*, 122 Ill. App. 2d 162, 258 N.E.2d 147 (1970). Such statements may also constitute admissions of a party-opponent. *Smith by Smith v. Victory Memorial Hosp.*, 167 Ill. App. 3d 618, 118 Ill. Dec. 142, 521 N.E.2d 210 (1988).

With respect to computer printouts, *see* §803.10 supra and §§901.10 and 1001.2 infra.

Police reports are discussed in §803.13 infra.

§803.12   Public Records

Records kept by a public officer dealing with her official activities and reasonably necessary for the performance of the duties of the office are admissible to prove the matters recorded. *See, e.g., Board of Educ. of Community High School Dist. No. 94 v. Regional Bd. of School Trustees of Du Page County*, 242 Ill. App. 3d 229, 184 Ill. Dec. 437, 613 N.E.2d 754 (1993) (school report cards). *People v. Hester*, 88 Ill. App. 3d 391, 43 Ill. Dec. 638, 410 N.E.2d 638 (1980), a public record is a record required by statute or authorized to be maintained by the nature of the office evidencing matters properly required to be maintained and recorded. The hearsay exception exists at common law, and no rule or statute making the records admissible is needed. *Bell v. Bankers Life & Gas. Co.*, 327 Ill. App. 321, 64 N.E.2d 204 (1945), record of Cook County Bureau of Public Welfare showing age of deceased pensioner; *Carlin v. Chicago & W.I.R. Co.*, 297 Ill. 184, 130 N.E. 371 (1921), record of copies of letters written by Department of Public Works of City of Chicago; *In re Ersch's Estate*, 29 Ill. 2d 572, 195 N.E.2d 149 (1964), document received from Polish authorities as to change of name of a city properly admitted; *People ex rel. Person v. Miller*, 56 Ill. App. 3d 450, 13 Ill. Dec. 920, 371 N.E.2d 1012 (1977), record of social services department as to arrearages in child support payments by defendant; *Department of Pub. Aid v. Estate of Wall*, 81 Ill. App. 3d 394, 36 Ill. Dec. 798, 401 N.E.2d 639 (1980), certificate of Director of Illinois Department of Public Aid presenting list compiled from records on file with the Department indicating payments made; *People v. Black*, 84 Ill. App. 3d 1050, 40 Ill. Dec. 322, 406 N.E.2d 23 (1980), decal upon breathalyzer, indicating that the machine was tested and certified as accurate, affixed by the Department of Health as required by statute; *Loughnane v. City of Chicago*, 188 Ill. App. 3d 1078, 136 Ill. Dec. 626, 545 N.E.2d 150 (1989), certified weather reports. Official reports of a statistical nature are also admissible. *People v. Chicago, B. & Q.R. Co.*, 300 Ill. 399, 133 N.E. 325 (1921), reports of State Tax Commission showing ratio of assessed value to market value in different counties; *People ex rel. Wenzel v. Chicago & N.W. Ry.*, 28 Ill. 2d 205, 190 N.E.2d 780 (1963), ratio study of Department of Revenue. In addition, matters observed pursuant to duty imposed by law as to which matter there was a duty to report are within the exception. *People v. Dolgin*, 415 Ill. 434, 114 N.E.2d 389 (1953), sustaining the admission of a letter from the manufacturer of a tax stamp meter setting forth the counterfeit-detection code, contained in the files of the Department of Revenue; *People v. Rockman*, 144 Ill. App. 3d 801, 98 Ill. Dec. 566, 494 N.E.2d 688 (1986), license plates and car registration transfer application. However, public records concerning causes and effects, involving the exercise of judgment and discretion, expressing opinions, or drawing conclusions have been held not admissible. *Barker v. Eagle Food Containers, Inc.*, 261 Ill. App. 3d 1068, 199 Ill. Dec. 922, 634 N.E.2d 1276 (1994); *Bloomgren v. Fire Ins. Exchange*, 162 Ill. App. 3d 594, 115 Ill. Dec. 88, 517 N.E.2d 290 (1987); *Lombard Park Dist. v. Chicago Title & Trust Co.*, 105 Ill. App. 2d 371, 245 N.E.2d 298 (1969). *Contra People v. Rudi*, 94 Ill. App. 3d 856, 50 Ill. Dec. 538, 419 N.E.2d 646 (1981), report of federal Food and Drug Administration containing conclusions and opinions on cause and effect, admitted under the public record hearsay exception. In this regard, *see* Rule 803(8)(C) of the Federal Rules of Evidence, 65 F.R.D. 131, 155 (1975), providing for the admissibility of evaluative reports, which include conclusions or opinions as well as factual findings. *Beech Aircraft Corp. v. Rainey*, 488 U.S. 153 (1988). A hearsay exception is provided by 725 ILCS 5/115-5.1, in both civil and criminal cases for public records of the coroner's medical or laboratory examiner summarizing the results of an autopsy. *See Heitz v. Hogan*, 134 Ill. App. 3d 352, 89 Ill. Dec. 299, 480 N.E.2d 185 (1985); *People v. Harper*, 279 Ill. App. 3d 801, 216 Ill. Dec. 414, 665 N.E.2d 474 (1996). The records of the coroner are admissible as *prima facie* evidence of the facts, findings, opinions, diagnosis, and conditions stated therein, including the cause of death. *People v. Campos*, 227 Ill. App. 3d 434, 169 Ill. Dec. 598, 592 N.E.2d 85 (1992). The autopsy report is made self-authenticating by statute; all parties are given the right to examine the preparer of the report. *Affatato v. Jewel Companies, Inc.*, 259 Ill. App. 3d 787, 198 Ill. Dec. 78, 632 N.E.2d 137 (1994). However, a coroner's verdict is not admissible in a negligence action to establish a fact in controversy. 735 ILCS 5/8-2201, 55 ILCS 5/3-3031.

The hearsay exception for public records is based upon the assumption that public officers will perform their duties, that they lack motive to falsify, and that public inspection to which many such records are subject will disclose inaccuracies. *Lane v. Bommelmann*, 17 Ill. 95 (1855); *People ex rel. Wenzel v. Chicago & N.W. Ry.* supra; *Steward v. Crissell*, 289 Ill.

App. 3d 66, 224 Ill. Dec. 419, 681 N.E.2d 1040 (1997) (citing Handbook); 5 Wigmore, Evidence §1632 (Chadbourn rev. 1974). In addition, the disruptive effect of bringing public officials into court to testify about matters that have generally been accurately reported and recorded is avoided. Use of the record serves the public convenience by saving time and the expenditure of public money. In fact, the record is likely to be more reliable than the official's often hazy recollection. If the source of information or the method or circumstances of preparation indicate lack of trustworthiness, the court may bar admissibility. *People v. Graney,* 234 Ill. App. 3d 497, 174 Ill. Dec. 790, 599 N.E.2d 574 (1992) (quoting Handbook). *See, e.g., People v. Smith,* 141 Ill. 2d 40, 152 Ill. Dec. 218, 565 N.E.2d 900 (1990), public records prepared with an eye toward litigation will be excluded when offered by the preparing party; *People v. Kautz,* 272 Ill. App. 3d 444, 209 Ill. Dec. 594, 651 N.E.2d 772 (1992), public record of weight tickets from a police scale inadmissible where an adequate foundation was not presented establishing that the scales were properly tested for accuracy. The party opposing admissibility has the burden of establishing that the public record lacks trustworthiness. *Steward v. Crissell,* 289 Ill. App. 3d 66, 224 Ill. Dec. 419, 681 N.E.2d 1040 (1997).

Notice that the definition of business as contained in the hearsay exception for business records, Supreme Court Rule 236 and 725 ILCS 5/115-5(a), §803.10 supra, is broad enough to encompass public records. *In re Guardianship of Smith,* 109 Ill. App. 3d 786, 65 Ill. Dec. 300, 441 N.E.2d 92 (1982), records of Department of Mental Health admissible under Supreme Court Rule 236 to show person was a resident at a developmental center.

The public records hearsay exception imposes no requirement regarding regularity or contemporaneousness, other than to the extent lack of either bears upon an overall assessment of lack of trustworthiness. The absence of specific requirements of regularity and contemporaneousness results from the fact that public records are generally authenticated by means of a certified copy of the record, §902.2 infra.

Specific requirements would add substantial complexity to the process of self-authentication, while providing little additional guarantee of trustworthiness. Moreover, in some instances the presence of the custodian of the record would undoubtedly be required. Finally, the use of a compared copy, §1005.1 infra, would effectively be precluded.

As to the duty of the public employee to record, and the admissibility of computer records, *see* §803.10 supra. With respect to medical or hospital records, *see* §803.11 supra; as to police accident or investigative reports, *see* §803.13 infra. Vital statistics are discussed in §803.14 infra.

Public records may, of course, be used to refresh a witness's recollection, §612 supra; *Hall v. Checker Taxi Co.,* 109 Ill. App. 2d 445, 248 N.E.2d 721 (1969); they may also be admitted upon a proper foundation as past recollection recorded, §803.9 supra. *Wilkinson v. Mullen,* 27 Ill. App. 3d 804, 327 N.E.2d 433 (1975).

As to proof of public records by certified copies, *see* §902.2 infra. For a discussion of privilege in connection with public records, *see* §503.7 supra; as to the admissibility of judgments of conviction, *see* §803.21 infra; as to authentication of public records, *see* §§901.8, 902.2 to 902.4 and 1005.1 infra. With respect to the Original Writing Rule, *see* §1005.1 infra.

§803.13   Police Reports

Supreme Court Rule 236(b), relating to civil cases, states that it does not permit the admission of police accident reports. 725 ILCS 5/115-5(c), provides with respect to criminal cases that it did not permit any writing or record made by anyone during an investigation of an alleged offense or during any investigation relating to pending or anticipated litigation of any kind.

Civil Cases.   Police reports in civil cases are actually governed solely by the common law; some decisions state incorrectly that admissibility is barred by Supreme Court Rule 236(b) supra. *Hall v. Checker Taxi Co.,* 109 Ill. App. 2d 445,

248 N.E.2d 721 (1969); *Kelly v. Chicago Transit Auth.,* 69 Ill. App. 2d 316, 217 N.E.2d 560 (1966). This error is of no consequence, since such reports are also excluded by the common law. *Wilkinson v. Mullen,* 27 Ill. App. 3d 804, 327 N.E.2d 433 (1975); *Moore v. Daydif,* 7 Ill. App. 2d 534, 130 N.E.2d 119 (1955); *Smith v. Johnson,* 2 Ill. App. 2d 315, 120 N.E.2d 58 (1954).

Criminal Cases. 725 ILCS 5/115-5(c) specifically provides that it does not permit the introduction of a writing or record relating to a police investigation. The exclusion from the hearsay exception extends to all writings or records made by anyone, including persons other than the police, *People v. Casey,* 225 Ill. App. 3d 82, 167 Ill. Dec. 242, 587 N.E.2d 511 (1992), during the investigation of an alleged offense, whether at the scene of the crime, at the apprehension of the accused, or elsewhere. *People v. Smith,* 141 Ill. 2d 40, 152 Ill. Dec. 218, 565 N.E.2d 900 (1990); *People v. Holowko,* 124 Ill. App. 3d 426, 79 Ill. Dec. 909, 464 N.E.2d 813 (1984) *rev'd on other grounds,* 109 Ill. 2d 387, 93 Ill. Dec. 344, 486 N.E.2d 877 (1985). The exclusion encompasses reports relating to a police investigation of the specific offense for which the accused is on trial as well as police investigation reports of other events relevant to the current trail. *People v. Gayton,* 293 Ill. App. 3d 442, 228 Ill. Dec. 229, 688 N.E.2d 1206 (1997). Prison incident reports also fall within the exclusion, *People v. Smith* supra, including when offered in probation revocation proceedings, *In re N.W.,* 293 Ill. App. 3d 794, 228 Ill. Dec. 157, 688 N.E.2d 855 (1997), but are admissible in the aggravation stage of a sentencing hearing where hearsay is not inadmissible per se. *People v. Westbrook,* 262 Ill. App. 3d 836, 200 Ill. Dec. 59, 635 N.E.2d 590 (1992). Since no other hearsay exception will usually be available, such statements will generally be inadmissible. *People v. Marselle,* 20 Ill. App. 3d 1012, 314 N.E.2d 21 (1974), reaching identical conclusion interpreting Supreme Court Rule 236 supra. A potential for grave confrontation clause questions would exist if such records were admitted against the criminal defendant without accounting for the availability of the out-of-court declarant. *People v. Smith* supra (citing Handbook); *People v. Smith,* 38 Ill. 2d 13, 230 N.E.2d 188 (1967). *See generally* §807.1 infra. If, however, the report is not investigative in nature, e.g., a report of observations made by police officers and other law enforcement personnel made at the scene of the crime or apprehension of the accused, but records routine activities, i.e., ministerial, objective nonevaluative matters made in a nonadversarial setting; the limitation is not applicable, and the writing or record may be admitted as a hearsay exception pursuant to 5/115-5(a), discussed in §803.10 supra. *See also People v. Lacey,* 93 Ill. App. 2d 430, 235 N.E.2d 649 (1968), introduction of police radio logs; *People v. Hawthorne,* 60 Ill. App. 3d 776, 18 Ill. Dec. 182, 377 N.E.2d 335 (1978), county jail address records admitted pursuant to the common law exception for public records, §803.12 supra; *People v. White,* 167 Ill. App. 3d 439, 118 Ill. Dec. 281, 521 N.E.2d 563 (1988), logbook entry of police department to establish accuracy of intoxilyzer machine; *People v. Tsombanidis,* 235 Ill. App. 3d 823, 176 Ill. Dec. 426, 601 N.E.2d 1124 (1992), DEA chemical analysis of drug evidence (*contra United States v. Oates,* 560 F.2d 45 (2d Cir. 1977)). Similarly, investigative reports produced by a machine, such as computer-generated telephone tracing records, are admissible; a computer-generated record made without a human declarant falls outside the definition of hearsay. *People v. Holowko,* 109 Ill. 2d 387, 93 Ill. Dec. 344, 486 N.E.2d 877 (1985); *People v. Houston,* 288 Ill. App. 3d 90, 223. Ill. Dec. 471, 679 N.E.2d 1244 (1997). *See also* §801.1 supra.

Ordinarily §115-5(c) would preclude admission of laboratory reports of forensic laboratories. *See United States v. Oates,* 560 F.2d 45 (2d Cir. 1977). However, with respect to laboratory reports dealing with controlled substances, such a report is admissible unless the accused demands the testimony of the person who conducted the laboratory analysis and prepared the report. 725 ILCS 5/115-15, provides:

(a) In any criminal prosecution for a violation of either the Cannabis Control Act or the Illinois Controlled Substances Act, a laboratory report from the Department of State Police, Division of Forensic Services and Identification, that is signed and sworn to by the person performing an analysis and that states (1) that the substance that is the basis of the alleged violation has been weighed and analyzed, and (2) the person's finding as to the contents, weight, and identify of the substance, and (3) that it contains any amount of a controlled substance or cannabis is *prima facie* evidence of the contents, identity, and weight of the substance. Attached to the report shall be a copy of a notarized statement by the signer of the report giving the name of the signer and stating (i) that he or she is an employee of the Department of State Police, Division of Forensic Services and Identification, (ii) the name and location of the laboratory where the analysis was performed, (iii) that performing the analysis is a part of his or her regular duties, and (iv) that the signer is qualified by education, training, and experience to perform the analysis. The signer shall also allege that scientifically accepted tests were performed with due caution and that the evidence was handled in accordance with established and accepted procedures while in the custody of the laboratory.

(b) The State's Attorney shall serve a copy of the report on the attorney of record for the accused, or on the accused if he or she has no attorney, before any proceeding in which the report is to be used against the accused other than at a preliminary hearing or grand jury hearing when the report may be used without having been previously served upon the accused.

(c) The report shall not be *prima facie* evidence of the contents, identity, and weight of the substance if the accused or his or her attorney demands the testimony of the person signing the report by serving the demand upon the State's Attorney within seven days from the accused or his or her attorney's receipt of the report.

In both civil and criminal cases, police reports may be employed to refresh the witness's recollection, §612.1 supra, and as past recollection recorded, §803.9 supra. *People v. Strausberger,* 151 Ill. App. 3d 832, 104 Ill. Dec. 970, 503 N.E.2d 832 (1987); *Wilsey v. Schlawin,* 35 Ill. App. 3d 892, 342 N.E.2d 417 (1976); *Wilkinson v. Mullen,* 27 Ill. App. 3d 804, 327 N.E.2d 433 (1975). As a matter of practice in criminal cases, police officers almost invariably find their recollection capable of refreshment, making resort to past recollection re-corded unnecessary. *People v. Griswold,* 405 Ill. 533, 92 N.E.2d 91 (1950). Statements contained in a police report inconsis-tent with the maker of the report's in-court testimony may be employed to impeach, §§613.2 and 801.9 supra. *Black v. De-Witt,* 55 Ill. App. 2d 220, 204 N.E.2d 820 (1965); *People v. Garrett,* 216 Ill. App. 3d 348, 159 Ill. Dec. 662, 576 N.E.2d 331 (1991). Statements of a declarant contained in a police re-port, however, may *not* be employed as an inconsistent state-ment when made by someone other than the maker of the police report to impeach the in-court testimony of such a declarant. *People v. Gagliani,* 210 Ill. App. 3d 617, 155 Ill. Dec. 353, 569 N.E.2d 534 (1991). Such statements, when prepared by private police officers such as railroad police, may also constitute admissions of a party-opponent. *Poltrock v. Chicago & N.W. Transp. Co.,* 151 Ill. App. 3d 250, 104 Ill. Dec. 540, 502 N.E.2d 1200 (1986).

With respect to the admissibility of official reports of law enforcement officials in summary suspension of impaired driver proceedings, 625 ILCS 5/2-118.1, *see People v. Gafford,* 218 Ill. App. 3d 492, 161 Ill. Dec. 225, 578 N.E.2d 583 (1991).

§803.14   Records of Vital Statistics

The statute dealing with vital statistics, 410 ILCS 535/1 *et seq.,* requiring birth and death certificates and specifying their contents, places strict limitations on their contents and provides that they "shall be considered as *prima facie* evidence of facts therein stated." With respect to the term *prima facie evidence, see* §302.8 supra. In recognition that the public offi-cer may lack personal knowledge of the matters stated, the statute has been narrowly construed. The term *facts* in the language quoted above has been interpreted to exclude opin-ions, factual findings, or conclusions. *People v. Fiddler,* 45 Ill. 2d 181, 258 N.E.2d 359 (1970), opinions of examining physi-cians as to cause of death contained in certificate of death not admissible; *Henninger v. Inter-Ocean Cas. Co.,* 217 Ill. App. 542

(1920), a physician's death certificate inadmissible to prove that an abrasion was caused by a garter belt; *Plano Foundry Co. v. Industrial Commn.,* 356 Ill. 186, 190 N.E. 255 (1934), a coroner's death certificate inadmissible to prove the cause of death. The statute has been limited also by holding it applicable only to matters specifically permitted by the statute to be included. *Alfaro v. Meagher,* 27 Ill. App. 3d 292, 326 N.E.2d 545 (1975), certificate of death inadmissible to establish residence of decedent; *In re Estate of Nowak,* 130 Ill. App. 2d 573, 264 N.E.2d 307 (1970), coroner's certificate not admissible to establish marriage of deceased and person stated therein to be spouse; *Howard v. Illinois Trust & Sav. Bank,* 189 Ill. 568, 59 N.E. 1106 (1901), physician's birth certificate inadmissible to prove that child is second child of mother. Still further limitation results from insisting upon strict compliance with provisions governing the source of information. Thus the requirement that information in a death certificate be obtained from the nearest of kin or person best qualified, over his signature, is not satisfied by information obtained from hospital records, *Hodge v. Globe Mut. Life Ins. Co.,* 274 Ill. App. 31 (1934), or given by telephone, *In re Estate of Schultz,* 316 Ill. App. 540, 45 N.E.2d 577 (1942), *rev'd on other grounds,* 384 Ill. 148, 51 N.E.2d 140 (1943). On the other hand, a birth certificate has been held admissible to prove that the child was born out of wedlock. *People ex rel. Ashford v. Ziemann,* 110 Ill. App. 3d 34, 65 Ill. Dec. 741, 441 N.E.2d 1255 (1982).

With respect to the current status of coroners' autopsy protocol reports, *see* §803.12 supra.

§803.15 *Absence of Business or Public Record or Entry*

Failure to record or include a matter that would ordinarily be included in a business or public record, offered to prove the nonoccurrence or nonexistence of the matter, is recognized by common law as a hearsay exception. McCormick, Evidence §287 (4th ed. 1992); *People v. Love,* 310 Ill. 585, 142 N.E. 204 (1923), certification of Secretary of State prepared in accordance with statute admitted to show failure to file documents required by Securities Law; *Easley v. Apollo Detective Agency, Inc.,* 69 Ill. App. 3d 920, 26 Ill. Dec. 313, 387 N.E.2d 1241 (1979), business records of prior employees admitted to establish that they contained no notation of anyone from Apollo ever having called. While in many instances such a failure will not be hearsay, §801.1 supra, in order to assure uniform admissibility, the common law hearsay exception was developed. The writing or record must, of course, have been kept in accordance with the requirements imposed with respect to business or public records, and the matter itself must be shown to be of a kind of which a writing or record was regularly made and preserved. If the source of information or other circumstances indicate lack of trustworthiness, admission may be denied.

A certification as to lack of record of entry, §902.2 infra, should be admitted to prove the absence of a public record. 5 Wigmore, Evidence §1677 (Chadbourn rev. 1974). The Original Writing Rule, §1002 infra, requiring the production of the writing itself when its contents are sought to be proved, does *not* apply to testimony that a record has been examined and found not to contain any reference to a designated matter but does apply if evidence of the record itself is offered. *Leischner v. Deere & Co.,* 127 Ill. App. 3d 175, 82 Ill. Dec. 120, 468 N.E.2d 182 (1984). If the record itself is not offered in evidence, the opposing party must be afforded an opportunity to examine the record. *Tipsord v. Unarco Indus., Inc.,* 188 Ill. App. 3d 895, 136 Ill. Dec. 423, 544 N.E.2d 1198 (1989).

§803.16   Records of Religious Organizations; Birth Certificates

Statements contained in regularly kept records of religious organizations concerning facts of personal or family history, including such matters as birth, marriage, divorce, death, legitimacy, ancestry, and relationship by blood or marriage, constitutes a hearsay exception of somewhat uncertain dimension. To illustrate, records of baptism, although admissible to prove the fact, date, and place of baptism, are not admissible as proof of the date of birth of the child except, inferentially, that he was born prior to being baptized. *Daily v. Grand Lodge,* 311 Ill. 184, 192 N.E. 478 (1929). Guarantees of trustworthiness are found in the solemn nature of the sacrament, lack of personal interest of the church official, the duty under church law or usage to make the record, and the moral nature of the act. *Daily v. Grand Lodge* supra. A baptismal record has also been held admissible to prove that the child was adopted rather than natural. *In re Estate of Curby,* 334 Ill. App. 212, 78 N.E.2d 835 (1948). *Cf.* Rule 803(11) of the Federal Rules of Evidence, 65 F.R.D. 131, 156 (1975).

A birth certificate is admissible as a hearsay exception to establish the fact, date, and place of birth of the child as well as other matters such as the age of the mother but apparently not the name of the father. *See Ashford v. Ziemann,* 99 Ill. 2d 353, 76 Ill. Dec. 805, 459 N.E.2d 940 (1984).

§803.17   Statement in Ancient Document

A hearsay exception is provided for 30-year-old documents affecting title, if authenticated as provided in §901.9 infra. While the ancient document exception was applied in *Lunger v. Sechrest,* 186 Ill. App. 521 (1914), to a marriage certificate, the supreme court decisions have in fact limited it to documents affecting real property. *Reuter v. Stuckart,* 181 Ill. 529, 54 N.E. 1014 (1899); *Smith v. Rankin,* 20 Ill. 14 (1858). The 30-year-old document only affects real property if it is in fact an official document, i.e., one commissioned under official authority or ratified as an official document by reason of having been recorded and relied on by the general public, for example, in the ascertaining of property lines. *People v. Village of Camp Point,* 286 Ill. App. 3d 247, 221 Ill. Dec. 641, 675 N.E.2d 1371 (1997). *But see* 7 Wigmore, Evidence §2145 (Chadbourn rev. 1978), indicating that the reasons for the rule extend to ancient documents generally. *See also Matter of*

Estate of Severson, 107 Ill. App. 3d 634, 62 Ill. Dec. 903, 437 N.E.2d 430 (1982), admitting record in Church Book for a parish in Norway relating matters occurring in the late 1800s to prove parentage as a business record under Supreme Court Rule 236, §803.10 supra.

Cf. Federal Rule of Evidence 901(b)(8), 65 F.R.D. 131, 161 (1975), applying the ancient document concept to documents in existence 20 years or more without regard to subject matter.

§803.18   Market Reports and Mortality Tables

The Uniform Commercial Code, 810 ILCS 5/2-724 provides for the admissibility of "reports in official publications or trade journals or in newspapers or periodicals of general circulation published as the reports of such [established commodity] market." *Nash v. Classen,* 163 Ill. 409, 45 N.E. 276 (1896), commodity price quotations in the evening newspaper; *Pass v. Briggs & Turevas,* 231 Ill. App. 214 (1923), trade journal market quotations; *Bushness v. Curtis,* 236 Ill. App. 89 (1925), published market report of stock exchange; *Alimissis v. Nanos,* 171 Ill. App. 3d 1005, 121 Ill. Dec. 826, 525 N.E.2d 1133 (1988), published stock market quotations.

Mortality and annuity tables, shown to be or recognized as standard authorities, are admissible to show expectancy of life. *Henderson v. Harness,* 184 Ill. 520, 56 N.E. 786 (1900), value of life estate; *Avance v. Thompson,* 387 Ill. 77, 55 N.E.2d 57 (1944), permanent personal injury; *Hann v. Brooks,* 331 Ill. App. 535, 73 N.E.2d 624 (1947), wrongful death; *Sherman v. City of Springfield,* 111 Ill. App. 2d 391, 250 N.E.2d 537 (1969), life expectancy table judicially noticed. *See also* §201.3 supra. For the instructions required to be given as to the proper use of mortality tables in cases of permanent personal injury or death, *see* Illinois Pattern Jury Instructions — Civil 31.13 and 34.04 (1994).

The rationale of this hearsay exception, trustworthiness based upon general reliance by the public or a segment thereof, would also extend to items such as city and telephone directories. 6 Wigmore, Evidence §§1702-1706 (Chadbourn rev. 1976).

§803.19 Reputation Concerning Personal or Family History

A hearsay exception exists for reputation generally accepted among the family based upon more than occasional and casual conversation as a means of proving family history, *Harland v. Eastman,* 107 Ill. 535 (1883); deaths and residences, *Stumpf v. Osterhage,* 111 Ill. 82 (1884); and illegitimacy, *Champion v. McCarthy,* 228 Ill. 87, 81 N.E. 808 (1907). Reputation in the community and amongst the person's associates is admissible to establish death, *Ringhouse v. Keever,* 49 Ill. 470 (1869), and marriage in civil cases other than criminal conversation. *Miller v. White,* 80 Ill. 580 (1875). To be admissible, the reputation must have arisen prior to the controversy. *Sugrue v. Crilley,* 329 Ill. 458, 160 N.E. 847 (1928).

With respect to statements of pedigree, *see* §804.8 infra; as to statements by a witness as to his own age, *see* §701.6 supra.

§803.20 Reputation as to Character

Implicit in the traditional acceptance of reputation testimony to prove character, *see* §405 supra, is the admissibility of such reputation testimony as an exception to the Hearsay Rule. *See* Federal Rule of Evidence 803(21), 65 F.R.D. 131, 157 (1975).

§803.21 Judgment of Previous Conviction

Evidence of a final judgment, entered after trial or upon a plea of guilty (but not upon a plea of *nolo contendere*), adjudging a person guilty of a "serious" crime is admissible when offered against the person convicted who is a party in a subsequent civil suit as a hearsay exception to prove any fact essential to sustain the judgment. *Smith v. Andrews,* 54 Ill. App. 2d 51, 203 N.E.2d 160 (1965). The exception has been held to apply as well when the prior conviction is of a person who is not a party in the subsequent civil suit. *In re Marriage of Engelbach,* 181 Ill. App. 3d 563, 130 Ill. Dec. 305, 537 N.E.2d 372 (1989), in custody dispute fact that the wife's new husband had been convicted of criminal sexual abuse and assault. The pendancy of an appeal may be shown but does not affect admissibility. *McCottrell v. Benson,* 32 Ill. App. 2d 367, 178 N.E.2d 144 (1961). Neither a judgment of acquittal nor a dismissal is included within this exception. The exception does not apply to the use of civil judgments in a subsequent litigation. *Ruane v. Amore,* 287 Ill. App. 3d 465, 222 Ill. Dec. 570, 677 N.E.2d 1369 (1997).

While Illinois decisions have not as of yet fully defined which criminal matters are sufficiently "serious," Federal Rule of Evidence 803(22), 65 F.R.D. 131, 157 (1975), provides that the crime must be punishable by death or imprisonment in excess of one year for the judgment of conviction to constitute a hearsay exception. The purpose of this limitation to serious offenses is to exclude lesser offenses where the motivation to defend vigorously may be lacking. An Illinois decision has determined that a judgment of conviction following a plea of not guilty to a traffic offense is not admissible, *Hengels v. Gilski,* 127 Ill. App. 3d 894, 910, 83 Ill. Dec. 101, 469 N.E.2d 708 (1984):

> A traffic court conviction will often result from expediency, convenience and compromise; the constitutional safeguards are often perfunctory and the defendant's opportunity and motive to defend vigorously are often lacking. We do not believe that such a traffic court conviction possesses the adequate assurance of reliability necessary to justify its admission into evidence at a later civil trial based upon the same facts. To hold otherwise, we believe, could conceivably turn a mechanical and summary traffic court hearing into the cornerstone of a significant civil action filed after the conclusion of the criminal proceedings.

Accord Wine v. Bauerfreund, 155 Ill. App. 3d 19, 107 Ill. Dec. 491, 507 N.E.2d 155 (1987). *Contra O'Dell v. Dowd,* 102 Ill. App. 3d 189, 57 Ill. Dec. 650, 429 N.E.2d 548 (1981). *See also* §802.4 supra. On the other hand, a judgment of conviction following a plea of not guilty to a misdemeanor battery is admissible. *Thornton v. Paul,* 74 Ill. 2d 132, 23 Ill. Dec. 541, 384 N.E.2d 335 (1978).

The judgment of conviction to a sufficiently "serious" offense may be after trial, *Smith v. Andrews* supra, disapproving previous suggestions to the contrary in *Gould v. County M.I. Cas. Corp.,* 37 Ill. App. 2d 265, 185 N.E.2d 603 (1962), or after a plea of guilty. A judgment based upon a plea of *nolo contendere* is not admissible, nor is a judgment entered upon forfeiture of a bond posted for a traffic ticket. *Nunley v. Mares,* 114 Ill. App. 3d 779, 70 Ill. Dec. 517, 449 N.E.2d 864 (1983).

The person convicted has been held entitled to attempt to rebut such evidence by offering whatever explanation she may have as to either the circumstances surrounding the conviction, *Barnes v. Croston,* 108 Ill. App. 3d 182, 247 N.E.2d 1 (1969), or the underlying event. *Smith v. Andrews* supra; *In re Marriage of Engelbach,* 181 Ill. App. 3d 563, 130 Ill. Dec. 305, 537 N.E.2d 372 (1989). However, the risk of misleading or confusing the jury may afford a basis for limiting such attempts. *See* §403.1 supra.

With respect to introduction of a plea of guilty as an admission of a party or a declaration against interest of a nonparty, *see* §802.4 supra and §804.7 infra; as to withdrawn pleas, pleas of *nolo contendere,* etc., *see* §410.1 supra.

§803.22 Receipt or Paid Bills as Evidence of Payment and Reasonableness

An offshoot of the declaration against interest hearsay exception, §804.7 infra, but not requiring unavailability, is the hearsay exception for a receipt given by a third person as *prima facie* evidence of the fact of payment. *People v. Davis,*

269 Ill. 256, 110 N.E. 9 (1915). Payment constitutes, in addition, *prima facie* proof that the charge was reasonable. *Wicks v. Cuneo-Henneberry Co.,* 319 Ill. 344, 150 N.E. 276 (1926), paid medical bill; *Byalos v. Matheson,* 328 Ill. 269, 159 N.E. 242 (1927), receipted repair bill; *Chicago, Burlington & Quincy R.R. v. Ommen,* 130 Ill. App. 2d 713, 264 N.E.2d 535 (1970), paid bill for repair to damage of railroad cars; *Almgren v. Engelland,* 94 Ill. App. 3d 475, 50 Ill. Dec. 66, 418 N.E.2d 1060 (1981), written receipt for $10,000 from assignment of interest; *Smith v. Champaign-Urbana City Lines, Inc.,* 116 Ill. App. 2d 289, 252 N.E.2d 381 (1969), paid automobile repair bill; *Flynn v. Cusentino,* 59 Ill. App. 3d 262, 16 Ill. Dec. 560, 375 N.E.2d 433 (1978), paid hospital and doctor bills.

A receipt or paid bill is often employed at trial as a convenient means to establish both the reasonableness of the charge and the fact of payment under circumstances in which no real dispute as to either item exists. Testimony as to the fact of payment is, of course, admissible; a notation of payment on the bill or a receipt is not necessary. *Saunders v. Wilson,* 114 Ill. App. 2d 380, 253 N.E.2d 89 (1969). Testimony as to payment is sufficient even if it indicates that payment was made by a third party, *Flynn v. Cusentino,* 59 Ill. App. 3d 262, 16 Ill. Dec. 560, 375 N.E.2d 433 (1978); an insurance company, *Ross v. Cortes,* 95 Ill. App. 3d 772, 51 Ill. Dec. 432, 420 N.E.2d 846 (1981); or was made by someone who was not identified by the witness testifying to payment at trial; *Elberts v. Nussbaum,* 97 Ill. App. 3d 381, 52 Ill. Dec. 831, 422 N.E.2d 1040 (1981). Payment may also be established by business record, §803.10 supra; *Smith v. Champaign-Urbana City Lines, Inc.* supra. An unpaid bill does not qualify as proof of its own reasonableness. *Cooper v. Cox,* 31 Ill. App. 2d 51, 175 N.E.2d 651 (1961), medical bill.

§803.23   Sexual and Physical Abuse of Child or Institutionalized Mentally Retarded Person; Elder Adults

The legislature has provided a comprehensive hearsay exception applicable in sexual and physical abuse prosecutions for acts perpetrated upon or against a child under the age of 13 or institutionalized severely or profoundly mentally retarded person. 725 ILCS 5/115-10, provides:

(a) In a prosecution for a physical or sexual act perpetrated upon or against a child under the age of 13, or a person who was an institutionalized severely or profoundly mentally retarded person as defined in Section 2-10.1 of the Criminal Code of 1961 at the time the act was committed, including but not limited to prosecutions for violations of Sections 12-13 through 12-16 of the Criminal Code of 1961, and to prosecutions or violations of Sections 10-1, 10-2, 10-3, 10-3.1, 10-4, 10-5, 10-6, 10-7, 11-6, 11-9, 11-11, 11-15.1, 11-17.1, 11-18.1, 11-19.1, 11-19.2, 11-20.1, 11-21, 12-1, 12-2, 12-3, 12-3.2, 12-4, 12-4.1, 12-4.2, 12-4.3, 12-4.7, 12-5, 12-6, 12-6.1, 12-7.1, 12-7.3, 12-7.4, 12-10, 12-11, 12-21.5, 12-21.6, and 12-32 of the Criminal Code of 1961 the following evidence shall be admitted as an exception to the hearsay rule:
　(1) testimony by such child or institutionalized severely or profoundly mentally retarded person, of an out-of-court statement made by such child or institutionalized severely or profoundly mentally retarded person, that he or she complained of such act to another; and
　(2) testimony of an out-of-court statement made by such child or institutionalized severely or profoundly mentally retarded person, describing any complaint of such act or matter of detail pertaining to any act which is an element of an offense which is the subject of a prosecution for a sexual or physical act perpetrated upon or against a child or institutionalized severely or profoundly mentally retarded person.
(b) Such testimony shall only be admitted if:
　(1) The court finds in a hearing conducted outside the presence of the jury that the time, content, and circumstances of the statement provide sufficient safeguards of reliability; . . .

Section 115-10 creates a wholly new hearsay exception in cases of physical or sexual abuse against a child or institutionalized severely or profoundly mentally retarded person. The section is not merely an extension of the doctrine of prompt complaint. *See* §611.15 supra. Accordingly cases decided under either the doctrine of prompt complaint or prior 5/115-10, *see* §611.16 supra, are *not* to be looked to as persuasive authority, a point overlooked in *People v. Robertson,* 168 Ill. App. 3d 132, 118 Ill. Dec. 784, 522 N.E.2d 239 (1988). *Accord People v. Kelley,* 185 Ill. App. 3d 43, 133 Ill. Dec. 259, 540 N.E.2d 1125 (1989); *People v. Anderson,* 225 Ill. App. 3d 636, 167 Ill. Dec. 435, 587 N.E.2d 1050 (1992); *Hannigan v. Hoffmeister,* 240 Ill. App. 3d 1065, 181 Ill. Dec. 323, 608 N.E.2d 396 (1992), promptness is *not* a requirement.

Section 115-10 applies to an out-of-court statement complaining of, or describing complaining of, a physical or sexual act in a prosecution for a physical or sexual act, including but not limited to those offenses where the physical or sexual nature of the act is an element of the offense. *People v. Pinta,* 210 Ill. App. 3d 1071, 155 Ill. Dec. 644, 569 N.E.2d 1255 (1991) (battery prosecution). Whether Section 115-10 permits the admissibility of statements by the victim describing acts of physical or sexual abuse perpetrated on the same victim not constituting the crime charged, i.e., other crimes, wrongs, or acts, *see* §404.5 supra, is disputed. *Compare People v. Jahn,* 246 Ill. App. 3d 689, 186 Ill. Dec. 213, 615 N.E.2d 1270 (1993); *People v. Edwards,* 224 Ill. App. 3d 1017, 167 Ill. Dec. 54, 586 N.E.2d 1326 (1992); and *People v. Schmitt,* 204 Ill. App. 3d 820, 149 Ill. Dec. 913, 562 N.E.2d 377 (1990), upholding admissibility on various theories under the particular facts, with *People v. Anderson,* 225 Ill. App. 3d 636, 167 Ill. Dec. 435, 587 N.E.2d 1050 (1992); and *People v. Kinnett,* 287 Ill. App. 3d 709, 223 Ill. Dec. 296, 679 N.E.2d 481 (1997), declaring that Section 115-10 only applies to physical or sexual acts for which the accused is currently on trial thus excluding sexual acts constituting other crimes, wrongs, or acts of evidence against the same victim; cases admitting such evidence distinguished in *Kinnett* on their facts.

Section 115-10 applies to children under the chronological age of 13; the fact that the person may have a functional age below 13 does not make the statute applicable. *People v. Velasco,* 216 Ill. App. 3d 578, 159 Ill. Dec. 147, 575 N.E.2d 954 (1991). The child must be under the age of 13 at the time the statement was made. *People v. Bridgewater,* 259 Ill. App. 3d 344, 197 Ill. Dec. 557, 631 N.E.2d 779 (1994); *People v. E.Z.,*

262 Ill. App. 3d 29, 199 Ill. Dec. 226, 633 N.E.2d 1022 (1994). The statute applies solely to statements describing offenses against the victim declarant; it does not extend to statements describing offenses against another victim. *People v. Zwart,* 151 Ill. 2d 37, 175 Ill. Dec. 711, 600 N.E.2d 1169 (1992); *People v. Peck,* 285 Ill. App. 3d 14, 220 Ill. Dec. 897, 674 N.E.2d 440 (1996); *People v. Embry,* 249 Ill. App. 3d 780, 188 Ill. Dec. 882, 619 N.E.2d 246 (1993).

The legislature has also provided a comprehensive hearsay exception applicable in civil proceedings involving child abuse or an unlawful sexual act. 735 ILCS 5/8-2601 provides:

Section 8-2601. (a) An out-of-court statement made by a child under the age of 13 describing any act of child abuse or any conduct involving an unlawful sexual act performed in the presence of, with, by, or on the declarant child, or testimony by such of an out-of-court statement made by such child that he or she complained of such acts to another, is admissible in any civil proceeding, if: (1) the court conducts a hearing outside the presence of the jury and finds that the time, content, and circumstances of the statement provide sufficient safeguards of reliability; and (2) the child either: (i) testifies at the proceeding; or (ii) is unavailable as a witness and there is corroborative evidence of the act which is the subject of the statement.

(b) If a statement is admitted pursuant to this Section, the court shall instruct the jury that it is for the jury to determine the weight and credibility to be given to the statement and that, in making its determination, it shall consider the age and maturity of the child, the nature of the statement, the circumstances under which the statement was made, and any other relevant factors.

(c) The proponent of the statement shall give the adverse party reasonable notice of an intention to offer the statement and the particulars of the statement.

Under both statutes, the out-of-court statement of the child may be testified to either by the child or someone who heard the child's statement personally. *People v. Mitchell,* 155 Ill. 2d 344, 185 Ill. Dec. 528, 614 N.E.2d 1213 (1993); *In re Marriage of Rudd,* 293 Ill. App. 3d 367, 227 Ill. Dec. 861, 688

N.E.2d 342 (1997); *People v. Petitt,* 245 Ill. App. 3d 132, 184 Ill. Dec. 766, 613 N.E.2d 1358 (1993). The fact that multiple witnesses testify to multiple prior statements is not alone error, although caution should be exercised in the introduction of such repetitive evidence. *People v. Anderson,* 225 Ill. App. 3d 636, 167 Ill. Dec. 435, 587 N.E.2d 1050 (1992); *People v. Byron,* 269 Ill. App. 3d 449, 206 Ill. Dec. 748, 645 N.E.2d 1000 (1995). Concern has also been expressed that testimony by multiple witnesses to the child's prior statements is unnecessary and thus misleading, *see* §403.1 supra, when the child actually testifies to the alleged occurrence in court. *People v. Barger,* 251 Ill. App. 3d 448, 191 Ill. Dec. 556, 624 N.E.2d 405 (1993) (Cook, J., specially concurring). *See also People v. Peck,* 285 Ill. App. 3d 14, 220 Ill. Dec. 897, 674 N.E.2d 440 (1996) (Cook, J., specially concurring). The requirement that the child testify at the proceeding or be unavailable is satisfied regardless of whether the child's testimony at the proceeding conforms to the out-of-court statement. *People v. Rushing,* 192 Ill. App. 3d 444, 139 Ill. Dec. 403, 548 N.E.2d 788 (1989). The content of the child's out-of-court statement is admissible, including details pertaining to the act along with the identification of the alleged perpetrator. *People v. Priola,* 203 Ill. App. 3d 401, 148 Ill. Dec. 776, 561 N.E.2d 82 (1990); *People v. Coleman,* 205 Ill. App. 3d 567, 150 Ill. Dec. 883, 563 N.E.2d 1010 (1990); *People v. Smith,* 236 Ill. App. 3d 35, 177 Ill. Dec. 492, 603 N.E.2d 562 (1992). Sections 115-10(b)(1) and 8-2601(a)(1) encompass only the out-of-court statements of the child; a statement of another person made in response is double-level hearsay not admissible under the foregoing statutes. *People v. Petitt,* 245 Ill. App. 3d 132, 184 Ill. Dec. 766, 613 N.E.2d 1358 (1993). Similarly, statements other than by the child describing any complaint of such act or matter or detail pertaining to such an act of sexual abuse are not admissible. *Hannigan v. Hoffmeister,* 240 Ill. App. 3d 1065, 181 Ill. Dec. 323, 608 N.E. 2d 396 (1992). The foregoing principles apply as well with respect to hearsay statements of a physically abused child or a sexually or physically abused institutionalized severely or profoundly retarded person.

Section 5/115-10(d) and 5/8-2601(c) require that the proponent of the statement give the adverse party reasonable notice of the intention to offer the child's or institutionalized severely or profoundly mentally retarded person's statement and the particulars of the statement, a requirement that is satisfied only by notice of the specific content of the the hearsay statement of the child or institutionalized severely or profoundly mentally retarded person to be presented at trial. *People v. Carter*, 244 Ill. App. 3d 792, 185 Ill. Dec. 318, 614 N.E.2d 452 (1993). Section 5/115-10(b)(1) and 5/8-2601(a)(1) require that a hearing be conducted following the provision of notice of intention to offer a statement pursuant to the statute. *People v. Smith*, 221 Ill. App. 3d 605, 164 Ill. Dec. 109, 582 N.E.2d 317 (1991). The hearing must be conducted outside the presence of the jury to determine whether the statement possesses sufficient safeguards of reliability. The party intending to offer the statement, ordinarily the prosecution, has the responsibility of requesting the hearing. *People v. Kargol*, 219 Ill. App. 3d 66, 161 Ill. Dec. 710, 578 N.E.2d 1356 (1991). Thus in a jury trial, failure to conduct a hearing is error and possibly plain error when not requested by the defendant. *People v. Mitchell*, 155 Ill. 2d 344, 185 Ill. Dec. 528, 614 N.E.2d 1213 (1993). On the other hand, in a bench trial, it is not plain error for the trial court to fail to conduct the hearing required by both statutes. *People v. Roy*, 201 Ill. App. 3d 166, 146 Ill. Dec. 874, 558 N.E.2d 1208 (1990) (trial judge is presumed to have considered only admissible evidence). *Accord People v. Dugan*, 237 Ill. App. 3d 688, 178 Ill. Dec. 594, 604 N.E.2d 1117 (1992).

The text of 5/115-10 has been held to preclude the introduction of the *videotaped* statement of the victim to the extent that it constitutes a corroborative complaint and that admission of a *videotaped* statement denies the accused the right to confrontation. *People v. Mitchell*, 225 Ill. App. 3d 708, 168 Ill. Dec. 3, 588 N.E.2d 1247 (1992). It is suggested that the admissibility of a *videotaped* statement under 5/115-10 is not in fact prohibited by the text of the statute and that its admissibility is properly governed by the requirements of the statute itself and the confrontation clause as described herein and in §807.1 infra. In fact most *videotaped* statements should be excluded, but not for the reasons set forth in *Mitchell* supra. *Accord People v. Peck,* 285 Ill. App. 3d 14, 220 Ill. Dec. 897, 674 N.E.2d 440 (1996), *Mitchell* expressly not followed: properly authenticated audiotape of child included within concept of "testimony of an out-of-court statement," 725 ILSC 5/115-10 (a)(2); *People v. Bowen,* 289 Ill. App. 3d 378, 224 Ill. Dec. 892, 682 N.E. 2d 453 (1997), videotaped statement of child who testified at trial possessing sufficient safeguards of reliability, *see* infra, properly admitted. *See also People v. Peck,* 285 Ill. App. 3d 14, 220 Ill. Dec. 897, 674 N.E. 2d 440 (1996) (audiotape possessing sufficient safeguards of reliability is admissible).

Both statutes require that the statement possess sufficient safeguards of reliability, a requirement that is imposed regardless of whether the child declarant testifies at trial or is unavailable to testify. *People v. C.H.,* 255 Ill. App. 3d 315, 193 Ill. Dec. 326, 626 N.E.2d 359 (1993).

It is not necessary that an available child declarant testify at the hearing to determine whether the child's out-of-court statement possesses sufficient safeguards of reliability. *People v. Guajardo,* 262 Ill. App. 3d 747, 201 Ill. Dec. 431, 636 N.E.2d 863 (1994); *People v. Wilson,* 246 Ill. App. 3d 311, 186 Ill. Dec. 226, 615 N.E.2d 1283 (1993), the requirement of "sufficient safeguards of reliability is independent of confrontation clause considerations, a point apparently overlooked in *People v. Jahn,* 246 Ill. App. 3d 689, 186 Ill. Dec. 213, 615 N.E.2d 1270 (1993), where a variable standard was incorrectly suggested. Identical treatment is to be accorded institutionalized severely or profoundly mentally retarded persons.

The following factors are relevant to determining whether the time, content and circumstances of the statement provide sufficient safeguards of reliability with respect to the child's out-of-court statement describing a physical or sexual act perpetrated upon a child, 725 ILCS 5/115-10(b)(1) and 735 ILCS 5/8-2601(a)(1): (1) the child's partiality, that is, interest, bias, corruption, or coercion; (2) the presence or absence of time to fabricate; (3) the physical and mental condition of the child when the statement was made; (4) suggestiveness, brought on by the use of leading questions coupled with an evaluation of the child's relationship to the questioner, considered in light of surrounding circumstances; (5) the age of the child; (6) the nature and duration of the physical or sexual act; (7) the relationship of the child and the accused; and (8) whether the child has reaffirmed or recanted the statement. *See People v. West*, 158 Ill. 2d 155, 198 Ill. Dec. 393, 632 N.E.2d 1004 (1994) (important factors include the child's spontaneous and consistent repetition of the incident, the child's mental state, use of terminology unexpected of a child of similar age, and the lack of a motive to fabricate); *People v. Zwart*, 151 Ill. 2d 37, 175 Ill. Dec. 711, 600 N.E.2d 1169 (1992) (sufficient safeguards of reliability not present when *circumstances* indicated at least three prior interviews, possibly suggestive, respecting the alleged abuse, with the substance of these interviews not disclosed, with the *timing* of the statement being approximately five weeks following the alleged abuse; followed in *People v. Simpkins*, 297 Ill. App. 3d 668, 231 Ill. Dec. 748, 697 N.E.2d 302 (1998)); *People v. C.H.*, 237 Ill. App. 3d 462, 177 Ill. Dec. 906, 603 N.E.2d 1280 (1992) (no motive to lie shown; fact statement made in response to questions alone does not require inadmissibility); *People v. Back*, 239 Ill. App. 3d 44, 178 Ill. Dec. 895, 605 N.E.2d 689 (1992) (it is not necessary that the first person to whom the child victim reports abuse testify before subsequent receivers of the child's out-of-court statements can be permitted to testify); *People v. Anderson*, 255 Ill. App. 3d 636, 167 Ill. Dec. 435, 587 N.E.2d 1050 (1992) (fact alone made in response to a question does not require exclusion); *People v. Moss*, 260 Ill. App. 3d 272, 196 Ill. Dec. 685, 630 N.E.2d 850 (1993) (child's statement was spontaneous and consistently repeated); *People v. Peck*, 285 Ill. App. 3d 14, 220 Ill. Dec. 897, 674 N.E.2d 440 (1996) (trial court abused discretion in admitting audiotape by child in light of the frequent use of leading and suggestive questions by the sheriff's department).

In considering the "time" when the statement was made in

relationship to the event reported, the duration of time that lapsed must be evaluated in light of events occurring during such time period that might have affected the statement's reliability. *People v. Deavers*, 220 Ill. App. 3d 1057, 163 Ill. Dec. 26, 580 N.E.2d 1367 (1991). A delay in reporting alone does not require that the statement be found to lack sufficient safeguards of reliability. *People v. Land*, 241 Ill. App. 3d 1066, 182 Ill. Dec. 476, 609 N.E.2d 1010 (1993); *People v. D.R.R.*, 258 Ill. App. 3d 282, 197 Ill. Dec. 152, 630 N.E.2d 1276 (1994); *People v. Guajardo*, 262 Ill. App. 3d 747, 201 Ill. Dec. 431, 636 N.E.2d 863 (1994). *See also* §704.2 supra.

Matters of particular importance in determining the trustworthiness of a *young* child's hearsay statement of sexual abuse also include: (1) whether the child is likely, apart from the incident, to have sufficient knowledge of sexual matters to realize that the particular sexual act is both possible and sexually gratifying to some individuals; (2) whether the child's statement describes an embarrassing event that a child would normally not relate unless true; (3) whether the language is appropriate for the child's age; and (4) whether the child's statement is a cry for help. *See generally People v. Jahn*, 246 Ill. App. 3d 689, 186 Ill. Dec. 213, 615 N.E.2d 1270 (1993) (factors include the child's physical condition, the nature and duration of the sexual act, the relationship of the child and the accused, reaffirmance or recantation, whether the child is likely, apart from the incident, to have sufficient knowledge of sexual matters to realize the act is possible and sexually gratifying to some, whether the language is embarrassing and, therefore, only spoken if true, and whether it was a cry for help); *People v. Moss*, 275 Ill. App. 3d 748, 212 Ill. Dec. 40, 656 N.E.2d 193 (1995) (fact that 10-year-old in response to a question from a police officer to tell what happened in her own words used the word "intercourse" was not unusual and did not indicate unreliability).

In determining trustworthiness, 725 ILCS 5/115–10(e) provides that statements described in paragraphs (1) and (2) of Subsection (A) are not to be excluded on the basis that they were obtained as a result of interviews conducted pursuant to a protocol adopted by a Child Advocacy Advisory Board as set forth in subsections (C), (D), and (E) of section 3 of the Children's Advocacy Center Act or that in interviewer or witness to the interview was or is an employee, agent, or investigator of state's attorney's office. Similar factors are appropriately considered in determining the presence of sufficient safeguards of reliability with respect to the hearsay statements of a physically abused child or a sexually or physically abused institutionalized severely or profoundly mentally retarded person.

Videotaping of interviews with the child is helpful but not procedurally required. *People v. Wittenmyer,* 151 Ill. 2d 175, 176 Ill. Dec. 37, 601 N.E.2d 735 (1992); *People v. Coleman,* 205 Ill. App. 3d 567, 150 Ill. Dec. 883, 563 N.E.2d 1010 (1990). *See also Idaho v. Wright,* 497 U.S. 805 (1990). Corroborating evidence establishing the truth of the matter asserted by the declarant in the statement may *not* be considered under the confrontation clause. *Idaho v. Wright, id.* at 820 (we think the relevant circumstances include only those that "surround the making of the statement and that render the declarant particularly worthy of belief"; *excluded* evidence includes physical evidence of abuse, opportunity to commit the offense, and other crimes, wrongs, or acts evidence). *Accord People v. Barger,* 251 Ill. App. 3d 448, 191 Ill. Dec. 556, 642 N.E.2d 405 (1993). *See also People v. March,* 250 Ill. App. 3d 1062, 189 Ill. Dec. 456, 620 N.E.2d 424 (1993) (medical evidence may not be considered); *People v. Peck,* 285 Ill. App. 3d 14, 220 Ill. Dec. 897, 674 N.E.2d 440 (1996) (Section 115-10 incorporates the *Idaho v. Wright* criteria). The trial court may evaluate the credibility of the in-court witness testifying as to the child's or institutionalized severely or profoundly mentally retarded person's out-of-court statement in determining whether the time, content, and circumstances of the statement provide sufficient safeguards of reliability. However, the court may not make a determination of unreliability on the basis that the declarant's alleged out-of-court statement was not in fact made if an adequate foundation of making has been introduced. *People v. Ware,* 259 Ill. App. 3d

466, 197 Ill. Dec. 680, 631 N.E.2d 902 (1994). *See generally* §§104.1 and 104.2 supra. The difficulty in applying and weighing such a multitude of factors as developed in *Idaho v. Wright* and elsewhere is illustrated by *People v. C.H.,* 255 Ill. App. 3d 315, 193 Ill. Dec. 326, 626 N.E.2d 359 (1993), where the use of language unexpected of a child of similar age and the absence of a motive to fabricate were found adequately to support a finding of sufficient safeguards of reliability in spite of the fact that there was a delay in reporting accompanied by later inconsistent disclosures of abuse, and that the mental state of the child was nothing unusual.

With respect to the notion that children tend not to fabricate complaints of sexual abuse, *see People v. Nevitt,* 174 Ill. App. 3d 326, 123 Ill. Dec. 762, 528 N.E.2d 307 (1988); *People v. Fisher,* 169 Ill. App. 3d 785, 119 Ill. Dec. 760, 523 N.E.2d 368 (1988).

The court, following the hearing, need not set forth for the record the court's reasoning in support of its finding as to whether the statement possesses sufficient safeguards of reliability; 5/115-10(b)(1) does not require that the trial court state reasons for its finding and no need exists to create such a requirement, although a brief explanation, while not required, is appropriate. *People v. West,* 158 Ill. 2d 155, 198 Ill. Dec. 393, 632 N.E.2d 1004 (1994) (a highly questionable decision).

The trial court's determination will be reviewed on appeal applying the clear abuse of discretion standard. *People v. Zwart,* 151 Ill. 2d 37, 175 Ill. Dec. 711, 600 N.E.2d 1169 (1992); *People v. Land,* 241 Ill. App. 3d 1066, 182 Ill. Dec. 476, 609 N.E.2d 1010 (1993). The suggestion in *People v. Jahn,* 246 Ill. App. 3d 689, 186 Ill. Dec. 213, 615 N.E.2d 1270 (1993), that the improper admission of a statement under 5/115-10 is *always* harmless error when the child testifies in accord at trial is incorrect and should not be followed.

Unavailability as employed in both of the statutes discussed above includes each of the grounds provided in Federal Rule of Evidence 804(a), as well as incompetency. *People v. Rocha,* 191 Ill. App. 3d 529, 138 Ill. Dec. 714, 547 N.E.2d

1335 (1989). *See* §804.1 infra. Unavailability also includes those child victims who cannot or will not testify in court about their experiences. *Maryland v. Craig*, 497 U.S. 836 (1990); *People v. Coleman*, 205 Ill. App. 3d 567, 150 Ill. Dec. 883, 563 N.E.2d 1010 (1990). *Accord People v. Rocha* supra, unavailability includes children who are unable to testify because of fear, inability to communicate in the courtroom setting, or incompetence. Finally, unavailability includes a showing of a "substantial likelihood of severe emotional and mental harm" being suffered by the child if required to testify face to face in the presence of the defendant. *See Maryland v. Craig* supra. Notice that while *People v. Ely*, 248 Ill. App. 3d 772, 188 Ill. Dec. 651, 618 N.E.2d 1221 (1993), sanctions a finding of unavailability on the basis of a child's emotional reaction to testifying before the jury, *Maryland v. Craig*, supra, only sanctions a finding of unavailability based upon an emotional reaction to testifying in the presence of the defendant.

Section 5/115-10(b)(2)(B) and 5/8-2601(a)(2)(ii) require that if the child declarant is unavailable at trial that the child's out-of-court statement be corroborated. *People v. Wolfe*, 176 Ill. App. 3d 299, 126 Ill. Dec. 19, 531 N.E.2d 152 (1988). The determination of whether there is corroborative evidence of the act may await a determination that the child is in fact unavailable as a witness. *People v. Embry*, 249 Ill. App. 3d 750, 188 Ill. Dec. 882, 619 N.E.2d 246 (1993). The requirement of corroborative evidence refers to the existence of the physical or sexual act that is the subject of the statement; corroborative evidence that the physical or sexual act was committed by the accused is *not* required. Corroboration may consist, for example, of the testimony of an eyewitness, a statement by the accused, physical evidence at the scene, or the findings of a medical examination of the child victim. *People v. Embry*, 249 Ill. App. 3d 750, 188 Ill. Dec. 882, 619 N.E.2d 246 (1993); *People v. Ward*, 207 Ill. App. 3d 365, 153 Ill. Dec. 207, 565 N.E.2d 740 (1991). *See also In re C.C.*, 224 Ill. App. 3d 207, 166 Ill. Dec. 540, 586 N.E.2d 498 (1991) (interpreting 705 ILCS 405/2-18(4)(c); corroboration includes child's ability to describe semen and recreation of secret game using anatomically correct dolls). Neither evidence of prior acts of misconduct nor expert testimony relating to the credibility, character, or psychological state of being of either child or the accused, if admissible, should be considered as the type of corroborative evidence of the existence of the sexual act described in the hearsay statement required by 5/115-10(b)(2)(B) or 5/8-2601(a)(2)(ii). *Contra People v. Roy,* 201 Ill. App. 3d 166, 146 Ill. Dec. 874, 558 N.E.2d 1208 (1990)(post-traumatic stress syndrome). For a comprehensive discussion, *see* Graham, Indicia of Reliability and Face to Face Confrontation: Emerging Issues in Child Sexual Abuse Prosecutions, 40 U. Miami L. Rev. 19 (1985). *See also* Federal Rule of Evidence 807. Corroborative evidence of the act which is the subject of the statement is also required by 5/115-10(b)(2)(B) with respect to an unavailable institutionalized severely or profoundly mentally retarded person in prosecutions for sexual abuse and with respect to both an unavailable child and unavailable institutionalized severely or profoundly mentally retarded person in prosecutions for physical abuse.

Section 115-10 was upheld as complying with the confrontation clause in *People v. Rocha,* 191 Ill. App. 3d 529, 138 Ill. Dec. 714, 547 N.E.2d 1335 (1989), and *People v. Coleman,* 205 Ill. App. 3d 567, 150 Ill. Dec. 883, 563 N.E.2d 1010 (1990). Section 115-10 is not firmly rooted; particularized guarantees of trustworthiness must be shown. *People v. March,* 250 Ill. App. 3d 1062, 189 Ill. Dec. 456, 620 N.E.2d 424 (1993). As to the confrontation clause, *see* generally §807.1 infra. For a discussion of the relationship between corroboration and sufficient safeguards of reliability, *see Idaho v. Wright,* 497 U.S. 805 (1990), and *People v. Peck,* 285 Ill. App. 3d 14, 220 Ill. Dec. 897, 674 N.E.2d 440 (1996). (Section 115-10 incorporates the *Idaho v. Wright* criteria). As to the argument of *ex post facto* application, *see People v. Edwards,* 224 Ill. App. 3d 1017, 167 Ill. Dec. 54, 586 N.E.2d 1326 (1992).

If a statement is admitted pursuant to either 5/115-10 or

5/8-2601, the court must instruct the jury that it is for the jury to determine the weight and credibility to be given the statement and that, in making the determination, it shall consider the age and maturity of the child, or the intellectual capabilities of the institutionalized or severely or profoundly mentally retarded person, the nature of the statement, the circumstances under which the statement was made, and any other relevant factor. Failure to give the required instruction is plain error. *People v. Mitchell,* 155 Ill. 2d 344, 185 Ill. Dec. 528, 614 N.E.2d 1213 (1993); *People v. Scott,* 284 Ill. App. 3d 868, 219 Ill. Dec. 868, 672 N.E.2d 376 (1996); *People v. Guajardo,* 262 Ill. App. 3d 747, 201 Ill. Dec. 431, 636 N.E.2d 863 (1994). The statutory requirement of an instruction to the jury was upheld against an attack of being an unconstitutional exercise by the legislature of judicial power. *People v. Novak,* 163 Ill. 2d 93, 205 Ill. Dec. 471, 643 N.E.2d 762 (1994).

In addition, effective January 1, 1992, the legislature has provided that in a proceeding in the prosecution of an offense of criminal sexual assault, aggravated criminal sexual assault, criminal sexual abuse, or aggravated criminal sexual abuse, the testimony of a child victim under the age of 18 years may be taken outside the courtroom and shown in the courtroom by means of a closed-circuit television if the court determines that testimony by the child victim in the courtroom will result in the child suffering serious emotional distress such that the child will not be able to reasonably communicate or that the child will suffer severe emotional distress that is likely to cause the child to suffer severe adverse effects, 725 ILCS 5/106B-1:

(a)(1) In a proceeding in the prosecution of an offense of criminal sexual assault, aggravated criminal sexual assault, criminal sexual abuse or aggravated criminal sexual abuse, a court may order that the testimony of a child victim under the age of 18 years be taken outside the courtroom and shown in the courtroom by means of a closed circuit television if:

(i) The testimony is taken during the proceeding; and

(ii) The judge determines the testimony by the child victim in the courtroom will result in the child suffering serious emotional distress such that the child cannot reasonably communicate or that the child will suffer severe emotional distress that is likely to cause the child to suffer severe adverse effects.

(2) Only the prosecuting attorney, the attorney for the defendant, and the judge may question the child.

(3) The operators of the closed circuit television shall make every effort to be unobtrusive.

(b)(1) Only the following persons may be in the room with the child when the child testifies by closed circuit television:

(i) The prosecuting attorney;

(ii) The attorney for the defendant;

(iii) The judge;

(iv) The operators of the closed circuit television equipment; and

(v) Any person or persons whose presence, in the opinion of the court, contributes to the well-being of the child, including a person who has dealt with the child in a therapeutic setting concerning the abuse, a parent or guardian of the child, and court security personnel.

(2) During the child's testimony by closed circuit television, the defendant shall be in the courtroom and shall not communicate with the jury if the cause is being heard before a jury.

(3) The defendant shall be allowed to communicate with the persons in the room where the child is testifying by any appropriate electronic method.

(c) The provisions of this Section do not apply if the defendant represents himself pro se.

(d) This Section may not be interpreted to preclude, for purposes of identification of a defendant, the presence of both the victim and the defendant in the courtroom at the same time.

Section 106B-1 does not require on its face that the court's determination that testimony by the child victim in the courtroom will result in the child suffering serious emotional distress such that the child will not be able to reasonably communicate or that the child will suffer severe emotional distress that is likely to cause the child to suffer severe adverse

effects be made following a hearing, presumably one including the introduction of expert witness testimony but not necessarily (*People v. Scott,* 284 Ill. App. 3d 336, 219 Ill. Dec. 868, 672
N.E.2d 376 (1996), mother testified, child psychologist not
required). Nevertheless a hearing should be conducted. *See
People v. Weninger,* 243 Ill. App. 3d 719, 183 Ill. Dec. 224, 611
N.E.2d 77 (1993). *Cf. People v. Schmitt,* 204 Ill. App. 3d 820, 149
Ill. Dec. 913, 562 N.E.2d 377 (1990) (discussing the prior law,
§106A-3; a finding by the court based solely upon the representation of the prosecution does not violate the confrontation
clause). While not specified in the statute, the severe emotional distress the child will suffer must arise from the presence of the criminal defendant face-to-face in the courtroom
for the child to be declared unavailable under the confrontation clause. *Maryland v. Craig,* 497 U.S. 836 (1990).

725 ILCS 5/106B-1 was held by the Illinois Supreme Court
in *People v. Fitzpatrick,* 158 Ill. 2d 360, 198 Ill. Dec. 844, 633
N.E.2d 685 (1994), to be an unconstitutional denial of the
right to confront witnesses under the confrontation clause of
the Illinois Constitution, which, unlike the confrontation
clause of the United States Constitution, specifically provided the accused the right "to meet the witnesses face to
face." In November of 1994, the Illinois Constitution was
amended to delete the face-to-face provision substituting the
language of the confrontation clause of the sixth amendment of the United States Constitution, updated to be gender neutral, that is, "to be confronted with the witnesses
against him or her." For a description of the history of the
constitutional provision and a declaration that the amended
provision does not apply retroactively, *see People v. Dean,* 175
Ill. 2d 244, 222 Ill. Dec. 413, 677 N.E.2d 947 (1997). *See also
People v. Van Brocklin,* 293 Ill. App. 3d 156, 227 Ill. Dec. 637,
687 N.E.2d 1119 (1997) (statute as applied is constitutional).

In proceedings in the juvenile court, 705 ILCS 405/2-
18(4)(c) provides:

> Previous statements made by the minor relating to any alle-
> gations of abuse or neglect shall be admissible in evidence.

However, no such statement, if uncorroborated and not subject to cross-examination, shall be sufficient in itself to support a finding of abuse or neglect.

See generally In Interest of Marcus E., 183 Ill. App. 3d 693, 132 Ill. Dec. 34, 539 N.E.2d 344 (1989); *In Interest of B.W.*, 216 Ill. App. 3d 410, 159 Ill. Dec. 677, 576 N.E.2d 346 (1991); *In re N.S.*, 255 Ill. App. 3d 768, 194 Ill. Dec. 536, 627 N.E.2d 1178 (1994). In *In re A.P.*, 179 Ill. 2d 184, 227 Ill. Dec. 949, 688 N.E.2d 642 (1997), the Illinois Supreme Court stated that either cross-examination or corroboration is required and that corroboration refers to the fact that the abuse or neglect occurred; it is not necessary to corroborate the identity of the perpetrator.

The legislature added 735 ILCS 5/8-2701, effective July 23, 1998, which provides a hearsay exception for statements of an eligible adult as defined in the Elder Abuse and Neglect Act, 320 ILCS 20/1, describing any act of elder abuse, neglect or financial exploitation found to possess sufficient safeguards of reliability. 735 ILCS 5/8-2701 provides:

(a) An out of court statement made by an eligible adult, as defined in the Elder Abuse and Neglect Act, who has been diagnosed by a physician to suffer from (i) any form of dementia, developmental disability, or other form of mental incapacity or (ii) any physical infirmity which prevents the eligible adult's appearance in court, describing any act of elder abuse, neglect, or financial exploitation, or testimony by an eligible adult of an out of court statement made by the eligible adult that he or she complained of such acts to another, is admissible in any civil proceeding, if:

(1) the court conducts a hearing outside the presence of the jury and finds that the time, content, and circumstances of the statement provide sufficient safeguards of reliability; and

(2) the eligible adult either:

(A) testifies at the proceeding; or

(B) is unavailable as a witness and there is corroborative evidence of the act which is the subject of the statement.

(b) If a statement is admitted pursuant to this Section, the court shall instruct the jury that it is for the jury to determine the weight and credibility to be given to the statement and that, in making its determination, it shall consider the condition of the eligible adult, the nature of the statement, the circumstances under which the statement was made, and any other relevant factors.

(c) The proponent of the statement shall give the adverse party reasonable notice of an intention to offer the statement and the particulars of the statement.

Section 8-2701 contains the same requirements for admissibility provided for in 725 ILCS 5/115-10, discussed supra, which should be consulted as to matters of interpretation.

§804   Hearsay Exceptions: Declarant Unavailable

§804.1   An Overview

The several exceptions to the Hearsay Rule involving a requirement that the declarant be shown to be unavailable as a witness at the present trial are discussed in §§804.2 to 804.9 infra. *See* §803.1 supra with respect to the general requirements applicable to statements admitted pursuant to a hearsay exception.

Historically the determination in Illinois of what satisfies the requirement of unavailability has been derived in connection with each of these particular exceptions. Today this approach has little to commend it. McCormick, Evidence §253 (4th ed. 1992). Whether unavailability should be required is, of course, a question to be resolved in connection with each exception, but as uniform as possible a pattern of what constitutes unavailability is desirable and represents the current trend. McCormick supra.

The thrust of a uniform approach to unavailability is upon

the unavailability of the testimony of the witness, which in-cludes but is not limited to situations in which the witness is not physically present in court. *Naylor v. Gronkowski*, 9 Ill. App. 3d 302, 292 N.E.2d 227 (1972). The recognized grounds of unavailability, each alone sufficient, are delineated in Fed-eral Rule of Evidence 804(a), 65 F.R.D. 131, 158 (1977), as amended, as follows. Federal Rule of Evidence 804(a) was adopted implicitly if not explicitly in *People v. Johnson*, 118 Ill. 2d 501, 115 Ill. Dec. 384, 517 N.E.2d 1070 (1987).

"Unavailability as a witness" includes situations in which the declarant—

(1) is exempted by ruling of the court on the ground of privi-lege from testifying concerning the subject matter of the declarant's statement; or

(2) persists in refusing to testify concerning the subject matter of the declarant's statement despite an order of the court to do so; or

(3) testifies to a lack of memory of the subject matter of the declarant's statement; or

(4) is unable to be present or to testify at the hearing because of death or then existing physical or mental illness or infir-mity; or

(5) is absent from the hearing and the proponent of his state-ment has been unable to procure the declarant's atten-dance (or in the case of a hearsay exception [other than former testimony] the declarant's attendance or testimony) by process or other reasonable means.

A declarant is not unavailable as a witness if exemption, refusal, claim or lack of memory, inability, or absence is due to the procurement or wrongdoing of the proponent of a statement for the purpose of preventing the witness from attending or testifying.

Physical presence on the witness stand does not make a witness available if the witness exercises a privilege, simply refuses to answer, or lacks memory as to the subject matter of his prior statement. Conversely, mere reluctance of the witness to testify does not constitute unavailability. *People v. Johnson*, 118 Ill. 2d 501, 115 Ill. Dec. 384, 517 N.E.2d 1070 (1987). A child witness who is too frightened of the defendant or the courtroom to be able and willing to testify is obviously unavailable. *Maryland v. Craig*, 497 U.S. 836 (1990). *Accord People v. Coleman*, 205 Ill. App. 3d 567, 150 Ill. Dec. 883, 563 N.E.2d 1010 (1990); *People v. Rocha*, 191 Ill. App. 3d 529, 138 Ill. Dec. 714, 547 N.E.2d 1335 (1989), unavailability includes children who are unable to testify because of fear or inability to communicate in the courtroom setting. The same is true of a child found incompetent to testify. *People v. March*, 250 Ill. App. 3d 1062, 189 Ill. Dec. 456, 620 N.E.2d 424 (1993); *People v. Hart*, 214 Ill. App. 3d 512, 158 Ill. Dec. 103, 573 N.E.2d 1288 (1991), child witness unable to appreciate obligation to tell the truth. *See also Gregory v. State of North Carolina*, 900 F.2d 705 (4th Cir. 1990). The foregoing is equally applicable with respect to an institutionalized severely or profoundly mentally retarded person. A child whose testimony in the presence of the defendant creates a substantial likelihood of causing the child to suffer severe emotional distress is unavailable. *See Maryland v. Craig* supra. As to the use of closed-circuit television under similar circumstances, *see* §803.23 supra. The absence of an alternative right on the point in Federal Rule of Evidence 804(a) does not alter the result. The listed alternatives are illustrative, not all inclusive. In determining availability it is useful but not constitutionally required that the trial judge personally observe or question the prospective witness. *See Maryland v. Craig* supra.

A witness exempt from testifying on the grounds of privilege is unavailable. *People v. Rice*, 166 Ill. 2d 35, 209 Ill. Dec. 635, 651 N.E.2d 1083 (1995) (witness invoked fifth amendment). *See also People v. Taylor*, 264 Ill. App. 3d 197, 202 Ill. Dec. 217, 637 N.E.2d 756 (1994); *People v. Rice*, 247 Ill. App. 3d 415, 187 Ill. Dec. 152, 617 N.E.2d 360 (1993). Thus an actual claim of privilege must be made by the witness, other than a criminal defendant, and allowed by the court. *See* Federal Rule of Evidence 804(a)(1). One who persists in refusing to testify despite an order of the court that he do so is also unavailable. *See People v. Ramey,* 152 Ill. 2d 41, 178 Ill. Dec. 19, 604 N.E.2d 275 (1992). Silence resulting from misplaced reliance upon a privilege without making a claim, or in spite of a court denial of an asserted claim of privilege, constitutes unavailability under this subsection. *See* Federal Rule of Evidence 804(a)(2) supra. In addition, a witness who testifies to a lack of memory of the subject matter of his prior statement is unavailable. *See* Federal Rule of Evidence 804(a)(3). A witness may either truly lack recollection or, for a variety of reasons, including concern of a possible perjury prosecution, feign lack of recollection. In either event, the witness is unavailable to the extent that he asserts lack of recollection of the subject matter of the prior statement, even if the witness recalls other events. *People v. Ramey,* 152 Ill. 2d 41, 178 Ill. Dec. 19, 604 N.E.2d 275 (1992), a witness asserting lack of memory is unavailable, whether the assertion is genuine or feigned. For further discussion, *see* Graham, The Confrontation Clause, the Hearsay Rule and The Forgetful Witness, 56 Tex. L. Rev. 151 (1978).

Death and existing physical or mental illness or infirmity at the time of trial are grounds for finding of unavailability. *Curt Bullock Builders v. H.S.S. Development, Inc.,* 261 Ill. App. 3d 178, 199 Ill. Dec. 698, 634 N.E.2d 751 (1994) (quoting Handbook). *See* Federal Rule of Evidence 804(a)(4) supra. Death is the most obvious basis; mental illness or physical disability of a serious nature are equally compelling. *George v. Moorhead,* 399 Ill. 497, 78 N.E.2d 216 (1948). Similarly, Supreme Court Rule 212(b)(1) allows the introduction of an evidence deposition if the deponent is dead or unable to attend or testify because of age, sickness, infirmity, or imprisonment. If the reason for the prosecution witness's unavailability is only temporary, considerations of confrontation in criminal matters may require resort to a continuance pursuant to 725 ILCS 5/114-4. *See Dear v. Chicago Transit Auth.,* 72 Ill. App. 3d 729, 28 Ill. Dec. 920, 391 N.E.2d 119 (1979), temporary illness does not constitute unavailability. Continuances are also available in civil cases as provided in Supreme

Court Rule 231. *Accord Curt Bullock Builders* supra, if the witness would have been available following a reasonable continuance, the trial court should not have permitted the use of the transcript.

A declarant is generally found unavailable if her presence cannot be secured by process or other reasonable means. *See* Federal Rule of Evidence 804(a)(5) supra. In criminal cases, the Supreme Court of the United States in *Barber v. Page*, 390 U.S. 719 (1968), held that the confrontation clause imposes a requirement that the government make a good-faith effort to obtain the presence of the witness at trial, going beyond the mere showing of an inability to compel appearance by subpoena, before prior testimony may be introduced as a substitute for testimony. Where appropriate, this includes a showing of inability to procure the attendance of a witness pursuant to the Uniform Act to Secure Attendance of Witnesses from Within and Without a State in Criminal Proceedings, 725 ILCS 220/1 to 220/6, or, if the witness is in custody in another jurisdiction, inability to procure attendance through cooperation of authorities in charge. *See* §611.6 for discussion of ability to compel attendance of witnesses.

Whether the party has shown good faith in attempting to procure the witness's attendance by process or reasonable means is determined on a case-by-case basis after careful review of the particular facts and circumstances. *People v. Brown*, 47 Ill. App. 3d 616, 7 Ill. Dec. 730, 365 N.E.2d 15 (1977). The undertaking of reasonable means to procure attendance was not shown by the sending of two or three letters to the supposed address of the witness, *People v. Holman*, 313 Ill. 33, 144 N.E. 313 (1924); a failure to attempt to locate a witness in a town in Tennessee to which investigators had been told witness moved showed lack of a reasonably diligent effort, *People v. Brown* supra; failure to pursue various leads such as prior place of employment showed lack of undertaking of reasonable means, *People v. Payne*, 30 Ill. App. 3d 624, 332 N.E.2d 745 (1975); as did the mere making of telephone calls to the missing witness. *People v. Rogers*, 79 Ill. App.

3d 745, 35 Ill. Dec. 108, 398 N.E.2d 1058 (1979). On the other hand, good faith was established where government attempted on five occasions to subpoena witness who was traveling out of state over a year and whose location during that entire period was unknown to her parents, *Ohio v. Roberts,* 448 U.S. 56 (1980), and where the State's investigators tried to serve subpoenas on three occasions at two different addresses, had called the Public Aid Office, spoke with security at former apartment building, etc., and had no remaining investigative leads. *People v. Smith,* 275 Ill. App. 3d 207, 211 Ill. Dec. 746, 655 N.E.2d 1129 (1995).

In civil cases "reasonable means" are established by a showing of inability upon the exercise of reasonable diligence to serve a subpoena. *John v. Tribune Co.,* 28 Ill. App. 2d 300, 171 N.E.2d 432 (1961), *rev'd on other grounds,* 24 Ill. 2d 437, 181 N.E.2d 105 (1962). Supreme Court Rule 212(b)(3) permits introduction of an evidence deposition if the party offering the deposition has been unable to procure the attendance of the witness by subpoena. *Compare Burton v. Drake's Mayors Row Restaurant,* 53 Ill. App. 3d 348, 11 Ill. Dec. 20, 365 N.E.2d 771 (1979), due diligence was held not to be satisfied by reason of failure to check telephone directory or voting registration records or to locate witness through driving license records; *Dietrich v. Jones,* 172 Ill. App. 3d 201, 122 Ill. Dec. 191, 526 N.E.2d 450 (1988), due diligence not shown with respect to a witness residing in forum county at time of deposition by evidence that area telephone directory shows no listing, *with Buckley v. Cronkhite,* 74 Ill. App. 3d 487, 30 Ill. Dec. 405, 393 N.E.2d 60 (1979), due diligence shown where after witness, who had been served with subpoena and had also promised to appear, failed to appear and attempts were made to contact witness by visiting his residence and telephoning several times.

In addition, Federal Rule 804(a)(5) requires that it be shown that the deposition of the witness cannot be procured by process or other reasonable means before a hearsay statement may be admitted as a hearsay exception requiring unavailability other than former testimony. However, Illinois law also imposes the requirement of inability to obtain a deposition with respect to former trial testimony. *Brownlie v. Brownlie*, 351 Ill. 72, 183 N.E. 613 (1932), and *Stephens v. Hoffman*, 275 Ill. 497, 114 N.E. 142 (1916), absence from the state is not sufficient in civil cases to permit introduction of former trial testimony unless it further appears that the deposition of the witness could not, with the exercise of due diligence, have been taken. In view of the similarity between depositions and former testimony, the result is extremely questionable.

A witness is not "unavailable" if the circumstances that would otherwise constitute unavailability are due to the procurement or other wrongdoing of the proponent of the statement. *People v. Ramey*, 152 Ill. 2d 41, 178 Ill. Dec. 19, 604 N.E.2d 275 (1992). *See* Federal Rule 804(a) supra. *See also* Supreme Court Rule 212 (b)(2), qualifying the use of an evidence deposition at trial of a witness out of the county with the words "unless it appears that the absence was procured by the party offering the deposition."

Determination of unavailability is a matter for the court, §104.1 supra. The burden of showing unavailability is upon the party offering the statement. *Burton v. Drake's Mayors Row Restaurant, Inc.* supra.

§804.2 Former Testimony: An Overview

Testimony given as a witness at another hearing of the same or a different proceeding, or in an evidence deposition taken in civil cases, Illinois Supreme Court Rule 202, or in a criminal proceeding, Illinois Supreme Court Rule 414, is admissible as a hearsay exception if (1) the witness is unavailable, (2) the actions are the same or involve the same issues, and (3) the party against whom offered was a party to the prior proceeding or in civil cases in privity with a party to the prior proceeding. *See Laboy v. Industrial Commission*, 74 Ill. 2d 18, 23 Ill. Dec. 83, 383 N.E.2d 954 (1978); *Wilkerson v. Pittsburgh Corning Corp.*, 276 Ill. App. 3d 1023,

213 Ill. Dec. 633, 659 N.E.2d 979 (1995). It should be observed that Supreme Court Rules 202 and 414 supra also specify avenues of admissibility of depositions. In addition, regardless of availability, "[t]he evidence deposition of a physician or surgeon may be introduced in evidence at trial on the motion of either party regardless of the availability of the deponent, without prejudice to the right of either party to subpoena or otherwise call the physician or surgeon for attendance at trial." Illinois Supreme Court Rule 212(b). With respect to the use of closed-circuit television of the accused at a pre-trial or post-trial proceeding when the accused's personal appearance is not constitutionally required, *see* 725 ILCS 5/106D-1. With respect to the use of closed-circuit television of a child witness in a child sexual abuse prosecution, *see* §803.23 supra. *See generally* Graham, Indicia of Reliability and Face to Face Confrontation: Emerging Issues in Child Sexual Abuse Prosecutions, 40 U. Miami L. Rev. 19 (1985).

With respect to the use of closed circuit television of child witnesses in child sexual abuse prosecution, *see* §803.23 supra. Consideration should be given to creation of a statutory hearsay exception for a videotaped deposition of an "unavailable" child witness in child sexual abuse prosecutions. *See* Graham, Indicia of Reliability and Face to Face Confrontation: Emerging Issues in Child Sexual Abuse Prosecutions, 40 U. Miami L. Rev. 19 (1985).

The exception for former testimony involves the admission of testimony taken under oath and subject to cross-examination. Obviously, however, the demeanor of the witness has not been and will not be observed by the present trier of fact; thus the imposition of the requirement of unavailability represents a strong preference for the personal appearance of the witness as an aid in evaluating his testimony. The additional requirements relating to parties and issues are designed to ensure the presence of an adequate opportunity to develop the witness's testimony when it was given. Adequacy of the opportunity to develop testimony by direct, cross-examination, or redirect examination is unaffected by counsel's tactical decision not to inquire. Thus a decision not to cross-examine at a preliminary hearing assumes the risk that the witness will not be available at trial. Similarly, when the opponent takes an evidence deposition, counsel who refrains from laying bare the full story of his client or of a favorable witness assumes the risk that the deponent will be unavailable at trial so that his one-sided deposition becomes admissible. However, since the purpose of a suppression hearing with respect to a confession is to determine voluntariness and not truth or falsity, neither an adequate opportunity nor the same issue is present. *Lee v. Illinois*, 476 U.S. 530 (1986). *See* §806 infra with respect to attacking the credibility of the hearsay declarant.

In the discussion following, extremely strict requirements imposed by the early common law cases are compared with the modern trend. As was stated in connection with the general discussion of unavailability, the lack of recent authority viewed in light of general common law development makes ascertainment of the current Illinois position difficult.

With respect to adequacy of opportunity to cross-examine at a preliminary hearing, *see* §804.5 infra; as to proof as to the content of former testimony, *see* §1002.2 infra.

§804.3   *Former Testimony: Same Party or Privity*

The leading early Illinois common law case interpreting the requirement of identity of parties imposed the requirement of mutuality. *McInturff v. Insurance Co. of N. Am.*, 248 Ill. 92, 93 N.E. 369 (1910), testimony of witness for state in prosecution for burning building to defraud insurer excluded in action on insurance policy when offered by defendant because of a change in parties, although admission would have meant only that plaintiff in the second case was required to accept as adequate the cross-examination conducted by himself as accused in the first case. *Cf. George v. Moorhead*, 399 Ill. 497, 78 N.E.2d 216 (1948), former testimony admissible if parties are essentially the same. *McInturff* and the concept of mutuality were severely criticized and rejected in *Laboy v. Industrial Commission,* 74 Ill. 2d 18, 23 Ill. Dec. 83, 383 N.E.2d 954 (1978) (lack of identity of the parties in the two proceedings has no significance). Identity of counsel in both proceedings has never been a condition of admissibility. *People v. Jackson,* 41 Ill. 2d 102, 242 N.E.2d 160 (1968).

In civil cases privity serves to satisfy the requirement relating to parties. The common law requirement of privity in interest was stated to include privies in blood, in law, or in estate. *McInturff v. Insurance Co. of N. Am.* supra. Privity has been held to exist between owner and bailee, *Goodrich v. Hanson,* 33 Ill. 498 (1864), and between grantees and grantors, *Stephens v. Hoffman,* 263 Ill. 197, 104 N.E. 1090 (1914). However, in a litigation subsequently arising between parties who otherwise would be regarded as in privity, it has been held improper to require one party to accept former testimony in a case in which the other was a party. *London Guar. & Accident Co. v. American Cereal Co.,* 251 Ill. 123, 95 N.E. 1064 (1911).

While mutuality is no longer required, the party against whom the former testimony is now being offered must have been a party to the prior proceeding or in a civil case in privity with a party to the prior proceeding as otherwise a full and fair opportunity to develop the testimony by cross-examination or direct and redirect examination is lacking. *Laboy v. Industrial Commission,* supra; *Wilkerson v. Pittsburgh Corning Corp.,* 276 Ill. App. 3d 1023, 213 Ill. Dec. 633, 659 N.E.2d 979 (1995). *People v. Jackson* supra, introduction of former testimony proper where opportunity existed for cross-examination at prior trial of Officer Charles, now dead, upon same issue as in instant case by different counsel for same defendant. *Accord People v. Allen,* 56 Ill. 2d 536, 309 N.E.2d 544 (1974); Federal Rule of Evidence 804(b)(1), 65 F.R.D. 131, 158 (1975). In civil actions, Federal Rule 804 (b)(1) restricts the parties at the former proceeding to the same party or predecessor in interest, interpreted to mean community of interest. *See* Graham, Handbook of Federal Evidence §804.1 (4th ed. 1996).

§804.4 Former Testimony: Same Action or Same Issues

The leading case concerning the common law requirements of the same action or same issues indicates a slavish adherence to the requirement that issues be the same. *McInturff
v. Insurance Co. of N. Am.,* 248 Ill. 92, 93 N.E. 369 (1910),
testimony of witness for the state in prosecution for burning
building to defraud insurer properly excluded in later action
by accused on insurance policy, defended on ground of
fraudulent burning. More justifiable applications are found
in *Pittsburgh, Cincinnati, & St. L. Ry. v. McGrath,* 115 Ill. 172, 3
N.E. 439 (1885), issues in coroner's inquest (cause of death)
not same as in wrongful death action (negligence); *George v.
Moorhead,* 399 Ill. 497, 78 N.E.2d 216 (1948), issue in proof
of heirship (identity of heirs) not essentially same as in
will contest (capacity of testator to know natural objects of
bounty).

The modern trend is to require merely a similar motive to
develop the witness's testimony and the opportunity to do so;
identity of issues is relevant only to the extent of creating a
similar motive to develop the testimony of the witness by the
same party in the prior proceeding or in civil cases in privity
with a party to the prior proceeding. McCormick, Evidence
§304 (4th ed. 1992); Federal Rule of Evidence 804(b)(1), 65
F.R.D. 131, 158 (1975). *See generally People v. Rice,* 166 Ill. 2d
35, 209 Ill. Dec. 635, 651 N.E.2d 1083 (1995), the test is
whether the motive and focus of the cross-examination at the
time of the initial proceeding was the same or similar to that
which guides the cross-examination during the subsequent
proceeding. *See also People v. Taylor,* 287 Ill. App. 3d 800, 223
Ill. Dec. 138, 679 N.E.2d 82 (1997), motive to cross-examine
witness testifying on post-trial motion to establish the innocence of the defendant was the same motive the prosecution
would have at any subsequent retrial. For specific applications, *see* §804.5 infra.

For purposes of assessing adequacy of opportunity to develop testimony, Federal Rule 804(b)(1) specifically provides
that an opportunity to conduct direct and redirect examina-

tion is equivalent to cross-examination of an opponent's witness. In fact, in practice, direct and redirect of the witness on the former occasion is more likely to have been a superior method of developing the witness's testimony when compared with cross-examination.

§804.5　Former Testimony: Adequacy of Opportunity to Cross-Examine at Preliminary Hearing, Suppression Hearing, Grand Jury, and Post-Trial Motion for a New Trial

A difficulty arises in regard to the hearsay exception for former testimony when testimony of a witness given at a preliminary hearing is offered by the state against the same criminal defendant after the witness becomes unavailable. Analysis of the adequacy of opportunity to cross-examine is complicated by the nature of the preliminary hearing itself, as well as by Illinois Supreme Court Rule 411, which provides that the criminal discovery rules "shall not be operative prior to or in the course of any preliminary hearing."

A preliminary hearing is ordinarily a much less searching exploration of the merits of a case than a trial, simply because the function is the more limited one of determining whether probable cause exists to hold the accused for trial. *Barber v. Page,* 390 U.S. 719 (1968). Cross-examination at the preliminary hearing, unaided by adequate discovery, may not extend beyond the scope of direct examination and such further interrogation as is directed to show interest, bias, prejudice, or motive to the extent these factors are relevant to a determination of probable cause. *People v. Horton,* 65 Ill. 2d 413, 3 Ill. Dec. 436, 358 N.E.2d 1112 (1971). Moreover, the preliminary hearing is not intended to be a discovery proceeding. *Id.* Thus, in light of the limited nature of the proceedings and the frequent absence of meaningful discovery, the question whether adequate, sometimes referred to as ample, opportunity, *People v. Tennant* 65 Ill. 2d 401, 3 Ill. Dec. 431, 358 N.E.2d 1116 (1976), to cross-examine the witness existed at the preliminary hearing does not depend in its entirety upon what in fact transpired at the preliminary hearing. *People v. Horton* supra.

Resolution of the question whether adequate or ample opportunity to cross-examine existed does not lend itself to a per se determination but must be decided upon the circumstances of each case. Thus, adequate opportunity to cross-examine means an opportunity to cross-examine effectively; providing merely an opportunity to cross-examine at the preliminary hearing is not per se adequate opportunity. *People v. Horton* supra. Such an opportunity to be adequate must at least contain no undue restriction upon defendant's right to cross-examine, *People v. Allen*, 56 Ill. 2d 536, 309 N.E.2d 544 (1974); *People v. Bell*, 132 Ill. App. 3d 354, 87 Ill. Dec. 247, 476 N.E.2d 1239 (1985); defense counsel must be allowed to cross-examine the witness completely, vigorously, and comprehensively, *People v. Jackson*, 41 Ill. 2d 102, 242 N.E.2d 160 (1968). In addition, the length and extent of the actual cross-examination conducted, whether the same evidence would be covered by other witnesses, and whether discrepancies in the witness's testimony pertain to a material issue, are also properly considered. *People v. Sutton*, 260 Ill. App. 3d 949, 197 Ill. Dec. 867, 631 N.E.2d 1326 (1994); *People v. Kite*, 97 Ill. App. 3d 817, 53 Ill. Dec. 140, 423 N.E.2d 524 (1981). *See also People v. Smith*, 275 Ill. App. 3d 207, 211 Ill. Dec. 746, 655 N.E.2d 1129 (1995) (fact witness had recanted preliminary hearing testimony under oath at a bond hearing and in taped statement to defense attorney did not require that preliminary hearing testimony be excluded). A decision by counsel not to cross-examine or to do so only to a limited extent does not affect the adequacy of opportunity. *People v. Allen* supra; *People v. Behm*, 49 Ill. App. 3d 574, 7 Ill. Dec. 475, 364 N.E.2d 636 (1977); *People v. Kite*, 97 Ill. App. 3d 817, 53 Ill. Dec. 140, 423 N.E.2d 524 (1981) (fact that witness was evasive, nervous, and loquacious at the preliminary hearing does not prevent his testimony from being admitted at trial). *Compare* discussion, infra, dealing with grand jury testimony offered by the accused.

Where the opportunity to cross-examine on its face appears to conform to the foregoing standard, in the absence of a showing by the defendant how additional cross-examination would have benefited or in what manner lack of prior discovery affected the adequacy of the opportunity to cross-examine, the preliminary hearing testimony of the unavailable witness will be admitted. *People v. Horton* supra; *People v. Behm* supra; *People v. Griffin,* 47 App. 3d 1012, 8 Ill. Dec. 249, 365 N.E.2d 487 (1977). This position is in conformity with that of the Supreme Court of the United States. In *California v. Green,* 399 U.S. 149 (1970), the court pointed out that *Barber v. Page,* 390 U.S. 719 (1968), recognized that "there may be some justification for holding that the opportunity for cross-examination at a preliminary hearing satisfies the demands of the confrontation clause where the witness is shown to be actually unavailable," and further pointed out that counsel in the present case did not "appear to have been significantly limited in the scope or nature of his cross-examination," and hence admitting the testimony on a showing of unavailability would not have violated the confrontation clause. *Id.* at 166. *Accord Ohio v. Roberts,* 448 U.S. 56 (1980).

Since the purpose of a suppression hearing with respect to a confession is to determine voluntariness and not truth or falsity, neither an adequate opportunity nor the same issue is present. *Lee v. Illinois,* 476 U.S. 530 (1986). With respect to a suppression of evidence hearing, both an adequate opportunity for effective cross-examination and a similar motive to develop the witness's testimony must be present. *People v. Rice,* 166 Ill. 2d 35, 209 Ill. Dec. 635, 651 N.E.2d 1083 (1995). A similar motive is not present where the issue is not the same, id. at 41-42, 209 Ill. Dec. at 638, 651 N.E.2d at 1086:

> The focus of the cross-examination of codefendant at the suppression hearing therefore was the conduct of codefendant just prior to the search, his self-interest in testifying falsely at the suppression hearing, and the issues presented by the motion to suppress. At trial however, the State's focus would be on the guilt or innocence of defendant—a much different issue than

that presented at the suppression hearing—and any motive codefendant might have in making exculpatory statements on behalf of defendant. The issues at the suppression hearing and the purpose for which codefendant's testimony was later offered at defendant's trial are not so similar that we may say that the State had a meaningful opportunity to effectively cross-examine codefendant on the occasion his testimony was given.

Relying on *Rice, People v. Radovick,* 275 Ill. App. 3d 809, 212 Ill. Dec. 82, 656 N.E.2d 235 (1995) held that the *State* did not have a meaningful opportunity to effectively cross-examine a witness before the grand jury because the purpose for which the defendant offered the grand jury testimony at trial was not sufficiently similar — the State was not an opponent of the witness at the grand jury but was only developing facts to determine if an indictment was warranted and "locking in" the witness's testimony that someone else, James, had done the killing. Accordingly, if the State had not yet developed sufficient facts implicating the defendant at the time of the grand jury hearing, prosecutors would have had little motive to challenge the witness's version of events at the time. Obviously the tenor of the foregoing arguments would support inadmissibility of preliminary hearing testimony when offered against the defendant by the prosecution. *See* infra and supra. *Compare People v. Taylor,* 287 Ill. App. 3d 800, 223 Ill. Dec. 138, 679 N.E.2d 82 (1997), where it was held that the state's motive to cross-examine a witness testifying on post-trial motion to establish the innocence of the defendant was the same motive the state would have at any subsequent retrial.

§804.6   *Dying Declaration*

The hearsay exception for a dying declaration finds its guarantee of trustworthiness in the assumption that belief of impending death excludes the possibility of falsification by the declarant. *Starkey v. People,* 17 Ill. 17 (1855).

A statement under belief of impending death is a statement by the victim, concerning the cause and circumstances of what he believed to be his impending death, made under belief that death is impending and almost certain to follow immediately. *People v. Tilley,* 406 Ill. 398, 94 N.E.2d 328 (1950). While the victim must believe death is inevitable and at hand, *People v. Newell,* 135 Ill. App. 3d 417, 90 Ill. Dec. 327, 481 N.E.2d 1238 (1985), it need not be shown that the victim has given up every scintilla of a ray of hope. *People v. Davis,* 93 Ill. App. 3d 217, 48 Ill. Dec. 675, 416 N.E.2d 1197 (1981); *People v. Crayton,* 175 Ill. App. 3d 932, 125 Ill. Dec. 493, 530 N.E.2d 651 (1988). Belief in the imminence of his death may be shown by the declarant's own statements or from circumstantial evidence, such as the nature of his wounds, statements made in his presence, or opinions of his physicians. *Shepard v. United States,* 290 U.S. 96 (1933); *Mattox v. United States,* 146 U.S. 140 (1892); *People v. Odum,* 27 Ill. 2d 237, 188 N.E.2d 720 (1963); *People v. Lawson,* 232 Ill. App. 3d 284, 173 Ill. Dec. 356, 596 N.E.2d 1235 (1992); *People ex rel. Hatch v. Elrod,* 190 Ill. App. 3d 1004, 138 Ill. Dec. 643, 547 N.E.2d 1264 (1989); *People v. Crayton,* 175 Ill. App. 3d 932, 125 Ill. Dec. 493, 530 N.E.2d 651 (1988). The declarant must also have been sufficiently possessed of his mental faculties as to be able to perceive, record and recollect, and communicate the cause or circumstances surrounding his impending death. *People v. Rhoads,* 110 Ill. App. 3d 1107, 66 Ill. Dec. 747, 443 N.E.2d 673 (1982); *People v. Davis,* 93 Ill. App. 3d 217, 48 Ill. Dec. 675, 416 N.E.2d 1197 (1981). *See* §602.1 supra. Any adequate means of communication, including words or signs, will suffice, as long as the indication is positive and definite. *People v. Scott,* 52 Ill. 2d 432, 288 N.E.2d 478 (1972). *See People v. Cobb,* 186 Ill. App. 3d 898, 134 Ill. Dec. 664, 542 N.E.2d 1171 (1989) ("He" killed "me" was clear enough where defendant was the only one present). The court must determine that the declarant believed himself *in extremis* when the statements were made. *People v. Beier,* 29 Ill. 2d 511, 194 N.E.2d 280 (1963); *People v. Barnes,* 117 Ill. App. 3d 965, 73 Ill. Dec. 236, 453 N.E.2d 1371 (1983); *People v. Timmons,* 127 Ill. App. 3d 679, 83 Ill. Dec. 39, 469 N.E.2d 646 (1984); *People v. Newell,* 137 Ill. App.

3d 417, 90 Ill. Dec. 327, 481 N.E.2d 1238 (1985). The suggestion in *Beier* and *Lawson* following *Tilley* supra that the court must determine beyond a reasonable doubt rather than merely more probably true than not true that the declarant believed himself *in extremis* is highly unusual and excessively burdensome; it should not be followed. A declaration motivated by a desire for revenge has been held not admissible. *Tracy v. People,* 97 Ill. 101 (1880). For an extensive discussion of each of the requirements of the hearsay exception for a dying declaration, *see People v. Webb,* 125 Ill. App. 3d 924, 81 Ill. Dec. 134, 466 N.E.2d 936 (1984).

Admissibility of dying declarations is limited to criminal prosecutions for homicide and does not extend to civil cases. *Marshall v. Chicago & G.E. Ry.,* 48 Ill. 475 (1868). Dying declarations may be offered against or on behalf of the accused. *Mattox v. United States* supra; McCormick, Evidence §312 (4th ed. 1992). The declarant must be the victim of the homicide for which accused is being prosecuted. *People v. Cox,* 340 Ill. 111, 172 N.E. 64 (1930), error to admit dying declaration of another victim of same poisonous liquor.

Declarations phrased in terms of opinions are admissible. *See* §803.1 supra. A requirement of firsthand knowledge, §602.1 supra, is imposed.

§804.7 Declaration Against Interest

The assumption that people do not make false statements damaging to themselves furnishes the basis for the hearsay exception admitting declarations against interest. Such a statement will be that of a nonparty, for if the statement is that of a party, offered by her opponent, it comes in as an admission, *see* §802 supra; there is no occasion to inquire whether it is against interest, this not being a condition precedent to admissibility of an admission by an opponent. *People v. Ward,* 154 Ill. 2d 272, 181 Ill. Dec. 884, 609 N.E.2d 252 (1992) (quoting Handbook), statements of a party are not admissible as declarations against interest.

The common law requirements of this hearsay exception are (1) that the declarant be unavailable, *Levy v. American Automobile Ins. Co.*, 31 Ill. App. 2d 157, 175 N.E.2d 607 (1961), in action under uninsured motorist clause, error to admit statement of other motorists that they were uninsured in absence of showing of unavailability, (2) that the declaration have been against his pecuniary or proprietary interest when made, (3) that the declarant have had competent knowledge of the fact declared, and (4) that the declarant have had no probable motive to falsify. *See, e.g., German Ins. Co. v. Bartlett*, 188 Ill. 165, 58 N.E. 1075 (1900), declaration of husband, since deceased, that he was indebted to wife admissible on her behalf in suit to set aside his conveyance to her as fraudulent; *Haskell v. Siegmund*, 28 Ill. App. 2d 1, 170 N.E.2d 393 (1960), statement of insured, since deceased, that he owned car, as ownership raised presumption of agency of driver involved in accident; *Seward v. Griffin*, 116 Ill. App. 3d 749, 72 Ill. Dec. 305, 452 N.E.2d 558 (1983), statement of driver of car, since deceased, that he had purchased alcoholic beverage in defendant's bar prior to the accident; *Tucker v. County Mut. Ins. Co.*, 125 Ill. App. 3d 329, 80 Ill. Dec. 610, 465 N.E.2d 956 (1984), statement of insured, now deceased, that he had received notice of underinsurance coverage; *Carlson v. City Construction Co.*, 239 Ill. App. 3d 211, 179 Ill. Dec. 568, 606 N.E.2d 400 (1992), guilty plea to reckless homicide exposed driver to clear risk of civil damages. *Cf. People v. Ward*, 154 Ill. 2d 272, 181 Ill. Dec. 884, 609 N.E.2d 252 (1992), statement by declarant that he had stolen car but had not seen or harmed victim was substantially exculpatory in nature and thus inadmissible; *Jones v. DeWig*, 25 Ill. App. 3d 423, 323 N.E.2d 475 (1974), statement by assailant that he had gotten drunk in tavern not admissible as declaration against interest in action against tavern by victim of shooting, in light of probable motive of declarant to fabricate in support of his intoxication defense to the criminal charge; *People ex rel. Fahey v. One 1976 Monte Carlo, Etc.*, 81 Ill. App. 3d 735, 37 Ill. Dec. 506, 402 N.E.2d 396 (1980), statement of unavailable declarant that while he did not know what was in the bag in which drugs were found that he said belonged to another person, he did know that the other person did have small amount of cannabis, was inadmissible in light of probable motive to fabricate. A defendant who exercises his or her right not to testify is not unavailable for the purpose of offering his or her own out-of-court statements. *People v. Barnwell*, 285 Ill. App. 3d 981, 221 Ill. Dec. 241, 675 N.E.2d 148 (1996).

Direct acknowledgements of facts giving rise to liability are against pecuniary interest. *Karlin v. Inland Steel Co.*, 77 Ill. App. 3d 183, 32 Ill. Dec. 657, 395 N.E.2d 1038 (1979); *Naylor v. Gronkowski*, 9 Ill. App. 3d 302, 292 N.E.2d 227 (1972). Statements collateral to such pecuniary interest that are substantially connected with the same subject matter covered by the declaration against interest are also admissible. *Horace Mann Insurance Co. v. Brown*, 236 Ill. App. 3d 456, 177 Ill. Dec. 690, 603 N.E.2d 760 (1992). *See generally* McCormick, Evidence §319 (4th ed. 1992); 5 Wigmore, Evidence §1465 (Chadbourn rev. 1974). The trustworthiness of the declaration against interest imports credibility to the collateral statement. *Buckley v. Cronkhite*, 74 Ill. App. 3d 487, 30 Ill. Dec. 405, 393 N.E.2d 60 (1979), in Dramshop Act litigation, statement by driver of car that she was drinking together with collateral statement that she purchased liquor at defendant's tavern were properly admitted as declarations against pecuniary interest.

Since conventional doctrine required that the statement be contrary to the pecuniary or proprietary interest of the declarant, confessions of third persons were excluded in criminal cases. However, in *People v. Lettrich*, 413 Ill. 172, 108 N.E.2d 488 (1952), the court, while recognizing the conventional view, held that exclusion of the confession of a third person, shown to be unavailable, was error in view of the fact that the prosecution relied solely upon a repudiated confession that did not coincide with all the known facts. The principle of *Lettrich* was recognized as sound but found distinguishable on the facts in *People v. Craven*, 54 Ill. 2d 419, 299 N.E.2d 1 (1973), also containing a discussion of the admissibility of declarations against penal interest offered on behalf of the criminal defendant in light of *Chambers v. Mississippi,* 410 U.S. 52 (1973). In discussing *Chambers,* the Illinois Supreme Court emphasized that the reliance on objective indicia of trustworthiness is the key to determining the admissibility. The four indicia of reliability present in *Chambers* are: (1) the statement made to a close acquaintance occurred shortly after the crime; (2) the statement was corroborated by other evidence; (3) the statement was self-incriminating and a declaration against interest; and (4) there was an opportunity for cross-examination of the declarant. The fact that the statement was made as part of plea negotiations does not mean that the statement was not against the declarant's penal interest. *People v. Cruz,* 162 Ill. 2d 314, 205 Ill. Dec. 345, 643 N.E.2d 636 (1994). Evidence of other crimes, wrongs, or acts is admissible to corroborate the trustworthiness of the statement. Id. Unfortunately, these indicia present in *Chambers* were taken out of context and incorrectly interpreted as constituting the requirements for a hearsay exception for declarations against penal interest. *See, e.g., People v. Tate,* 87 Ill. 2d 134, 57 Ill. Dec. 572, 429 N.E.2d 470 (1981); *People v. Garza,* 92 Ill. App. 3d 723, 48 Ill. Dec. 44, 415 N.E.2d 1328 (1981); *People v. Nally,* 134 Ill. App. 3d 865, 89 Ill. Dec. 630, 480 N.E.2d 1373 (1985); *People v. Newell,* 135 Ill. App. 3d 417, 90 Ill. Dec. 327, 481 N.E.2d 1238 (1985). Notice that under *Chambers,* as thus incorporated into Illinois law, a declaration against penal interest was admissible *only* when the declarant is available.

In *People v. Bowel,* 111 Ill. 2d 58, 94 Ill. Dec. 748, 488 N.E.2d 995 (1986), the Illinois Supreme Court opined that the four factors enumerated in *Chambers* are to be regarded simply as indicia of trustworthiness and not as requirements of admissibility. *See also People v. Davis,* 254 Ill. App. 3d 651, 193 Ill. Dec. 636, 626 N.E.2d 1187 (1993). The supreme court went on to cite Federal Rule of Evidence 804(b)(3), noting with approval that the admissibility of a statement made against penal interest is determined simply by whether there are "corroborating circumstances [that] clearly indicate the trustworthiness of the statement"; "considerable assurance" of trustworthiness is required. *Accord People v. Cruz,* 162 Ill. 2d 314, 205 Ill. Dec. 345, 643 N.E.2d 636 (1994); *People v. House,* 141 Ill. 2d 323, 152 Ill. Dec. 572, 566 N.E.2d 259 (1990). *See also People v. Hoffstetter,* 203 Ill. App. 3d 755, 148 Ill. Dec. 651, 560 N.E.2d 1349 (1990). Accordingly under *Bowel,* a statement against penal interest accompanied by corroborating circumstances clearly indicating trustworthiness is admissible regardless of whether the declarant is available or unavailable, *People v. Anderson,* 291 Ill. App. 3d 843, 225 Ill. Dec. 854, 684 N.E.2d 845 (1997); *People v. Morris,* 148 Ill. App. 3d 471, 101 Ill. Dec. 907, 499 N.E.2d 495 (1986) (the availability of the declarant is not essential), and regardless of whether made to a close acquaintance shortly after the crime. *People v. Rice,* 247 Ill. App. 3d 415, 187 Ill. Dec. 152, 617 N.E.2d 360 (1993). For a thorough discussion of the four factors of *Chambers* as well as other factors indicative of trustworthiness, *see People v. Kokoraleis,* 149 Ill. App. 3d 1000, 103 Ill. Dec. 186, 501 N.E.2d 207 (1986); *People v. Scherzer,* 179 Ill. App. 3d 624, 128 Ill. Dec. 598, 534 N.E.2d 1043 (1989); *People v. Cathers,* 194 Ill. App. 3d 318, 140 Ill. Dec. 893, 550 N.E.2d 1018 (1989); *People v. Nally,* 216 Ill. App. 3d 742, 159 Ill. Dec. 281, 575 N.E.2d 1341 (1991); *People v. Villegas,* 222 Ill. App. 3d 546, 165 Ill. Dec. 69, 584 N.E.2d 248 (1991); *People v. Eyman,* 222 Ill. App. 3d 1097, 165 Ill. Dec. 364, 584 N.E.2d 543 (1991); *People v. Hampton,* 249 Ill. App. 3d 329, 188 Ill. Dec. 353, 618 N.E.2d 923 (1993); *People v. Rivera,* 260 Ill. App. 3d 984, 201 Ill. Dec. 321, 636 N.E.2d 753 (1994); *People v. Townsend,* 275 Ill. App. 3d 200 211 Ill. Dec. 599, 655 N.E.2d 982 (1995); *People v. Radovick,* 275 Ill. App. 3d 809, 212 Ill. Dec. 82, 656 N.E.2d 235 (1995); *People v. Swaggirt,* 282 Ill. App. 3d 692, 218 Ill. Dec. 150, 668 N.E.2d 634 (1996); *People v. Taylor,* 287 Ill. App. 3d 800, 223 Ill. Dec. 138, 679 N.E.2d 82 (1997). *See also People v. Green,* 179 Ill. App. 3d 1, 128 Ill. Dec. 902, 535 N.E.2d 413 (1988) (whether the statement was spontaneous is a factor to be considered). Statements admitted under the foregoing standard comply with the confrontation clause. *See Lee v. Illinois,* 476 U.S. 530 (1986); *Cruz v. New York,* 481 U.S. 186 (1987); *Williamson v. United States,* 512 U.S. 594, 114 S. Ct. 2431

(1994). Sometimes the factors of *Chambers,* in spite of *Bowel,* are treated incorrectly as requirements of admissibility. *See People v. Mack,* 238 Ill. App. 3d 97, 179 Ill. Dec. 333, 606 N.E.2d 165 (1992); *People v. Carson,* 238 Ill. App. 3d 457, 179 Ill. Dec. 531, 606 N.E.2d 363 (1992); *People v. Bradford,* 239 Ill. App. 3d 796, 180 Ill. Dec. 556, 607 N.E.2d 625 (1993); *People v. Jimenez,* 284 Ill. App. 3d 908, 220 Ill. Dec. 97, 672 N.E.2d 914 (1996). To the extent that *People v. Anderson,* 291 Ill. App. 3d 843, 225 Ill. Dec. 854, 684 N.E.2d 845 (1997), after acknowledging the correctness of the "totality of the circumstances approach" to determining the presence of "considerable assurance" of trust-worthiness, analyzes each of the four *Chambers* factors one at a time, it is unhelpful and should not be followed.

Statements collateral to the declarant's penal interest are admissible if they possess sufficient indicia of reliability. *See People v. White,* 209 Ill. App. 3d 844, 153 Ill. Dec. 910, 567 N.E.2d 1368 (1991). The United States Supreme Court in *Williamson v. United States,* 512 U.S. 594 (1994), a decision interpreting Rule 804(b)(3) of the Federal Rules of Evidence and thus not binding on state courts, held that collateral statements against penal interest are *not* admissible. After discussing *Williamson* and its concern that collateral inculpatory statements, especially arrest statements, may be motivated by a desire to implicate another and exonerate oneself, *see also Lee v. Illinois* supra, *People v. Wilson,* 271 Ill. App. 3d 943, 208 Ill. Dec. 716, 649 N.E.2d 1377 (1995) went on to find that the witness statements involved were properly admitted as state-ments against penal interest, highlighting that the statements did not directly implicate the defendant and were not arrest statements. *Wilson* is most interesting in that by distinguishing *Williamson* on the facts, the court may be implying that *Williamson* should be followed in Illinois, i.e., collateral inculpa-tory statements, at least arrest statements, should be found insufficiently trustworthy to be admissible. For further discus-sion *see* Graham, Handbook of Federal Evidence §804.3 (4th ed. 1996).

Admissibility of declarations on the grounds of being against penal interest raises the possibility of perjury by witnesses testifying as to confessions that never were made. Mc-Cormick, Evidence §318 (4th ed. 1992). Accordingly, in a criminal action a statement tending to expose the declarant to criminal liability and offered to exculpate the accused is not admissible unless corroborating circumstances clearly indicate the trustworthiness of the statement. *People v. Tate,* 87 Ill. 2d 134, 57 Ill. Dec. 572, 429 N.E.2d 470 (1981) (citing Handbook); *People v. Ireland,* 38 Ill. App. 3d 616, 348 N.E.2d 277 (1976); *People v. Pietrzyk,* 54 Ill. App. 3d 738, 12 Ill. Dec. 285, 369 N.E.2d 1299 (1977); *People v. Taylor,* 264 Ill. App. 3d 197, 202 Ill. Dec. 217, 637 N.E.2d 756 (1994). *See also People v. Hammers,* 48 Ill. App. 3d 1023, 6 Ill. Dec. 967, 363 N.E.2d 914 (1977) (Trapp, J., specially concurring). *Accord* Federal Rule of Evidence 804(b)(3), 65 F.R.D. 131, 159 (1975). The additional requirement, that the court find the presence of corroborative circumstances clearly indicating the trustworthiness of the statement against penal interest when offered to exculpate an accused, was imposed in response to an awareness of both the suspect nature of such statements and the impact such a statement would have upon a jury applying a standard of proof of guilt beyond a reasonable doubt. Once the declarant has been apprehended, circumstances surrounding plea negotiations, immunity, or the actuality of a conviction must be taken into consideration in determining whether the statement was, in fact, against penal interest when made. *Lee v. Illinois* supra; *United States v. Palumbo,* 639 F.2d 123 (3d Cir. 1981). While not required by Federal Rule of Evidence 804(b)(3), federal decisions have imposed the requirement that corroborating circumstances clearly indicate the trustworthiness of inculpating statements as well. *See United States v. Riley,* 657 F.2d 1377 (8th Cir. 1981).

While Federal Rule of Evidence 804(b)(3) does not elaborate as to the meaning of "corroborating circumstance," the requirement should be construed in such a manner so as to effectuate its purpose of circumventing fabrication. *See People v. Rice,* 166 Ill. 2d 35, 209 Ill. Dec. 635, 651 N.E.2d 1083 (1995). As to the meaning of "corroborating circumstances," *see generally* Graham, Handbook of Federal Evidence §804.3

(4th ed. 1996). *See also People v. Rice* supra (codefendant's statement made at a suppression hearing lacks sufficient trustworthiness since the codefendant stood to benefit by making the statement as the statement, if believed, would have resulted in evidence being suppressed); *People v. Rutherford,* 274 Ill. App. 3d 116, 210 Ill. Dec. 599, 653 N.E.2d 794 (1995) (other witnesses corroborated the blood in the bottle and bloody baseball bat, one of the declarants led the police to the burial ground, and neither statement attempted to exculpate the accused). As to the difficult issue of whether evidence undermining reliability may be considered in determining whether corroborating circumstances clearly indicate the trustworthiness of the statement *compare People v. Rice* supra (fact declarant had motive to falsify considered) with *People v. Swaggirt,* 282 Ill. App. 3d 692, 218 Ill. Dec. 150, 668 N.E.2d 634 (1996) (suspect credibility of defense witness presenting evidence corroborating the declarant's statement goes to weight and not admissibility as trustworthiness is determined on *objective* indicia). With respect to a similarly difficult issue of whether the credibility of the in court witness testifying as to the existence of the declarant's statement against penal interest may be considered, *see People v. Villegas,* 222 Ill. App. 3d 546, 165 Ill. Dec. 69, 584 N.E.2d 248 (1991) (fact witnesses establishing statement was made were related to defendant properly considered). *See generally* Graham Handbook of Federal Evidence §804.3 n.18 (4th ed. 1996).

The statement must be against interest when made. For a discussion of the balancing of self-serving aspects against disserving aspects of a declaration, *see* McCormick, Evidence §319 (4th ed. 1992).

For a discussion of paid bills or receipts, *see* §803.22 supra.

§804.8   Statement of Personal or Family History

A hearsay exception exists for statements concerning the declarant's own birth, adoption, marriage, divorce, legitimacy, relationship by blood, adoption, or marriage, ancestry, or other similar fact of personal or family history, even though declarant had no means of acquiring personal knowledge of the matter stated, *Champion v. McCarthy,* 228 Ill. 87, 81 N.E. 808 (1907); *Harland v. Eastman,* 107 Ill. 535 (1883), and for statements concerning any of the foregoing matters, as well as the death, of another person.

The common law exception as developed in Illinois apparently also requires that (1) the declarant be dead, *Harland v. Eastman* supra; (2) the declaration was made before the controversy arose, *Sugrue v. Crilley,* 329 Ill. 458, 160 N.E. 847 (1928); and (3) the declarant was related by blood or marriage to the family to which the declarations refer, *Welch v. Worsley,* 330 Ill. 172, 161 N.E. 493 (1928); *Jarchow v. Grosse,* 257 Ill. 36, 100 N.E. 290 (1912). *See Daniels v. Retirement Bd.,* 106 Ill. App. 3d 412, 62 Ill. Dec. 304, 435 N.E.2d 1276 (1982), restating the foregoing requirements. Moreover, the common law seems to require that when the subject of the statement is the relationship between two other persons, the declarant must qualify as to both. *Jarchow v. Grosse* supra. While ordinarily the required relationship of the declarant to the family must be established by proof other than his own declaration, a rule criticized in 5 Wigmore, Evidence §1491 (Chadbourn rev. 1974), the declarant's own statement is admissible to prove the relationship if it is sought to reach the estate of the declarant himself, rather than claiming the property of others through her. *Jarchow v. Grosse* supra.

Consideration should be given to bringing this hearsay exception into accord with modern practice. *See, e.g.,* McCormick, Evidence §322 (4th ed. 1992); Federal Rule of Evidence 804(b)(4), 65 F.R.D. 131, 159 (1975).

§804.9 Family Record

Statements of fact concerning personal or family history contained in family Bibles, genealogies, charts, engravings on rings, inscriptions on family portraits, engravings on urns,

crypts, or tombstones, or the like constitute a hearsay exception. *Gorden v. Gorden*, 283 Ill. 182, 119 N.E. 312 (1918). The
author of the statement need not be identified. The basis of
the exception is that the family would not allow an untruthful entry or inscription to be made or to remain without
protest. In addition, this hearsay exception apparently requires that the declarant be unavailable, that the statement
be made before the controversy or a motive to misrepresent
arose, and that the declarant be related by blood or marriage
to the family. *Sugrue v. Crilley*, 329 Ill. 458, 160 N.E. 847
(1928); *Jarchow v. Grosse*, 257 Ill. 36, 100 N.E. 290 (1912);
Champion v. McCarthy, 228 Ill. 87, 81 N.E. 808 (1907). *Cf.*
Federal Rule of Evidence 803(13), 65 F.R.D. 131, 156 (1975),
eliminating each of these requirements.

For statutory recognition in family Bibles, *see* 820 ILCS
205/11(2)(c) evidence of age of minor desiring employment certificate.

§804.10 *Witness Declarant Refusal to Testify*

725 ILCS 5/115-10.2 provides a hearsay exception in criminal proceedings for an out-of-court statement of a declarant
who as a witness persists in refusing to testify concerning the
subject matter of the declarant's out-of-court statement despite an order to do so, provided that the out-of-court statement is shown to possess equivalent circumstantial guarantees
of trustworthiness to statements admitted pursuant to recognized hearsay exceptions:

> (a) A statement not specifically covered by any other hearsay
> exception but having equivalent circumstantial guarantees of
> trustworthiness, is not excluded by the hearsay rule if the
> declarant is unavailable as defined in subsection (c) and if the
> court determines that:
>> (1) the statement is offered as evidence of a material fact;
>> and
>> (2) the statement is more probative on the point for

which it is offered than any other evidence which the proponent can procure through reasonable efforts; and

(3) the general purposes of this Section and the interests of justice will be best served by admission of the statement into evidence.

(b) A statement may not be admitted under this exception unless the proponent of it makes known to the adverse party sufficiently in advance of the trial or hearing to provide the adverse party with a fair opportunity to prepare to meet it, the proponent's intention to offer the statement, and the particulars of the statement, including the name and address of the declarant.

(c) Unavailability as a witness is limited to the situation in which the declarant persists in refusing to testify concerning the subject matter of the declarant's statement despite an order of the court to do so.

(d) A declarant is not unavailable as a witness if exemption, refusal, claim or lack of memory, inability or absence is due to the procurement or wrongdoing of the proponent of a statement for purpose of preventing the witness from attending or testifying.

(e) Nothing in this Section shall render a prior statement inadmissible for purposes of impeachment because the statement was not recorded or otherwise fails to meet the criteria set forth in this Section.

The purpose of the statute is to permit admissibility of certain prior statements of a witness who refuses to testify at trial despite a court order to do so, 5/115-10.2(c). In some cases, the witness will have been granted immunity, see §502.6 supra. In other cases the witness will simply not possess a privilege against self-incrimination because the subject matter of the prior statement does not tend to incriminate, see §502.1 supra, for example, when an occurrence witness to a crime describes her observations. In both of the foregoing situations, refusal of the witness to testify despite an order to do so may be the result of intimidation emanating from the accused.

The prior statement must be shown to possess "equivalent circumstantial guarantees of trustworthiness" to statements admitted pursuant to recognized hearsay exceptions, 5/115-10.2(a). The concept of "equivalent circumstantial guarantees of trustworthiness" is derived from the other reliable hearsay exceptions of Federal Rules of Evidence 803(24) and 804(b)(5), recently consolidated and retitled Federal Rule of Evidence 807. In determining the presence of "equivalent circumstantial guarantees of trustworthiness," the court will apply the same criteria employed in determining whether "sufficient safeguards of reliability" are present under 725 ILCS 5/115-10 relating to sexual or physical abuse of a child or institutionalized mentally retarded person discussed in §803.23 supra.

In addition, Section 115-10.2(a)(1)-(3) provides that the court determine that (1) the statement is offered as evidence of a material fact; (2) the statement is more probative on the point for which it is offered than any other evidence that the proponent can procure through reasonable efforts; and (3) the general purposes of the section and the interests of justice will best be served by admission of the statement into evidence. These requirements were similarly derived from Federal Rules of Evidence 804(24) and 804(b)(5). As understood in the context of current Federal Rule of Evidence 807, the requirement that the statement be offered as evidence of a material fact probably means that not only must the fact the statement is offered to prove be relevant, but that the fact to be proven must be of substantial importance in determining the outcome of the litigation. Section 115-10.2(a)(2) imposes a requirement of necessity; the hearsay statement must be necessary in the sense of being more probative on the point for which it is being offered than any other evidence that the proponent may reasonably procure. Whether a particular effort to obtain alternative proof of a matter may reasonably be demanded must, of course, depend on the fact at issue considered in light of its posture in the total litigation. Finally, the requirement that the general purposes of Section 115-10.2 and the interests of justice be best served by admission of the statement into evidence is of little practical importance in determining admissibility.

A statement may not be admitted under this exception unless the proponent of it makes known to the adverse party, sufficiently in advance of the trial or hearing in order to provide the adverse party with a fair opportunity to prepare to meet it, the proponent's intention to offer the statement and the particulars of the statement, including the name and address of the declarant, 5/115-10.2(b), a requirement also derived from Federal Rules of Evidence 803(24) and 804(b)(5).

Section 115-10.2(d) declares that a witness who refuses to testify despite an order by the court to do so, *see* Section 115-10.2(c), is not unavailable as a witness if exemption, refusal, claim or lack of memory, inability, or absence is due to the procurement or wrongdoing of the proponent of a statement for purpose of preventing the witness from attending or testifying, a requirement derived from Federal Rule of Evidence 804(a).

Finally, Section 115-10.2(d) states that nothing in Section 115-10.2 renders a prior statement inadmissible for purposes of impeachment because the statement was not recorded or otherwise fails to meet the criteria set forth in section 115-10.2. *See* §613.1 supra.

§805   Hearsay Within Hearsay

§805.1   *Commentary*

Hearsay within hearsay, often referred to as double-level or multiple hearsay, is admissible if each of two or more statements falls within an exception to the Hearsay Rule. *Horace Mann Insurance Co. v. Brown,* 236 Ill. App. 3d 456, 177 Ill. Dec. 690, 603 N.E.2d 760 (1992) (citing Handbook). *See also* McCormick, Evidence §293 (4th ed. 1992). An illustration is a business or public record coming within a hearsay exception, which includes within it information supplied by an informant not himself under a duty to provide such information. If the informant's statement itself qualifies as a hearsay exception — for example, an excited utterance, §803.3 supra — the record containing it is not barred from admissibility by virtue of the Hearsay Rule. *Bradley v. Booz, Allen & Hamilton, Inc.,* 67 Ill. App. 3d 156, 23 Ill. Dec. 839, 384 N.E.2d 746 (1978), results of survey admitted as first level of hearsay met then-existing state of mind exception while second level of hearsay met business record exception. Similarly, a hospital record admitted as past recollection recorded may contain a statement of a patient pertinent to medical diagnosis or treatment, *Minor v. City of Chicago,* 101 Ill. App. 3d 823, 57 Ill. Dec. 410, 428 NE.2d 1090 (1981). However, where the additional hearsay exception is lacking, the record may be admitted to prove that the statement was made but not to prove the truth of the statement. *People v. Chambers,* 179 Ill. App. 3d 565, 128 Ill. Dec. 372, 534 N.E.2d 554 (1989); *People v. Hawthorne,* 60 Ill. App. 3d 776, 18 Ill. Dec. 182, 377 N.E.2d 335 (1978). Double-level hearsay problems are sometimes overlooked. *See People v. Wilson,* 92 Ill. App. 3d 370, 48 Ill. Dec. 31, 415 N.E.2d 1315 (1981), testimony of state's attorney authenticating unsigned statement of questions asked and answers given orally by defendant. *See also* §803.10 supra. But not always. *See People v. Murphy,* 157 Ill. App. 3d 115, 109 Ill. Dec. 311, 509 N.E.2d 1323 (1987); *Kress Corp. v. Forbes,* 190 Ill. App. 3d 72, 137 Ill. Dec. 285, 545 N.E.2d 1046 (1989); *In re Estate of Holmgren,* 237 Ill. App. 3d 839, 178 Ill. Dec. 569, 604 N.E.2d 1092 (1992).

For a contention that not all double-level hearsay statements should be admissible when each statement falls within a hearsay exception, *see* Graham, Handbook of Federal Evidence §805.1 n.6 (4th ed. 1996).

§806   Attacking and Supporting Credibility of Declarant

§806.1   *Commentary*

The credibility of the declarant of a statement admitted under a hearsay exception may be attacked by any evidence that would be admissible for that purpose if the declarant had testified as a witness. Thus a witness's bias, interest, corruption, or coercion, his prior conviction of a crime, or his inconsistent statements may be shown. *People v. Smith,* 127 Ill. App. 3d 622, 83 Ill. Dec. 27, 469 N.E.2d 634 (1984). For example, if a dying declaration is admitted it is proper to introduce evidence that the declarant entertained feelings of malice and hostility toward the accused. *People v. Edgeston,* 157 Ill. 2d 201, 191 Ill. Dec. 84, 623 N.E.2d 329 (1993). Similarly, if the declarant's credibility has been attacked, it may be rehabilitated to the same extent as if he were a witness.

People v. Johnson, 271 Ill. App. 3d 962, 208 Ill. Dec. 730, 650 N.E.2d 1 (1995), takes the novel position that prior conviction impeachment of the nontestifying declarant of a hearsay statement admitted as an excited utterance, §803.3 supra, is not permissible since the basis of the hearsay exception is the stilling of capacity for reflection, thus making the veracity of the declarant not a fact of consequence. It is suggested that *Johnson* should not be followed. First, while an exciting event is treated in the law as stilling reflective thought enough to provide sufficient guarantees of trustworthiness to permit admissibility, that is not to say that in any given case such capacity for reflective thought did not in fact exist. In reality an exciting event reduces capacity for fabrication; it ordinarily will not eliminate such capacity. Secondly, it is simply better to have a unified approach to the impeachment of the nontestifying witness declarant of a hearsay statement admitted pursuant to a hearsay exception covering all avenues of impeachment and all hearsay exceptions. Incredibly little would be gained by adding the complexity that would be added by following *Johnson* in searching for underlying trustworthiness rationale for each exception. Moreover discretionary balancing mandated with respect to prior conviction impeachment, *see* §609.2 supra, would result in exclusion of the prior conviction to impeach if the trial court concluded that the prior conviction had little or no probative value on credibility.

A question arises as to whether evidence of an inconsistent

statement or conduct of the declarant is subject to any require-ment that a foundation be laid and the declarant afforded an opportunity to deny or explain. Where the inconsistent state-ment or conduct occurs subsequent to the hearsay statement admitted in court, the usually present impossibility of laying a foundation requires that it not be considered a prerequisite. 3 Wigmore, Evidence §1033 (Chadbourn rev. 1970); Mc-Cormick, Evidence §37 (4th ed. 1992). However, where the prior inconsistent statement or conduct occurs prior to tak-ing of a deposition offered in evidence at trial, the laying of a foundation and opportunity to deny or explain have been insisted upon. *See People ex rel. Korzen v. Chicago, Burlington & Quincy R. Co.*, 32 Ill. 2d 554, 209 N.E.2d 649 (1965); *Gilberto v. Nordtvedt*, 1 Ill. App. 3d 677, 274 N.E.2d 139 (1971). *Cf.* Fed-eral Rule of Evidence 806, 65 F.R.D. 131, 160 (1975), dispens-ing with the requirement of a foundation and opportunity to deny or explain under all circumstances when a hearsay state-ment is involved. *Compare also Kincaid v. Ames Dept. Stores, Inc.*, 283 Ill. App. 3d 555, 219 Ill. Dec. 215, 670 N.E.2d 1103 (1996), indicating that Illinois law is in accord with Federal Rule of Evidence 806.

§807   Hearsay: Confrontation and Due Process

§807.1   *Commentary*

The Constitution of Illinois at one time conferred on the accused in a criminal case the right "to meet the witnesses face to face. . . ." Art. II, §8. The Sixth Amendment to the United States Constitution provides that "in all criminal prosecutions, the accused shall enjoy the right . . . to be con-fronted with witnesses against him." In November of 1994, Art. II, §8, of the Illinois Constitution was amended to delete the face-to-face provision, substituting the language of the Confrontation Clause of the Sixth Amendment of the United

States Constitution updated to be gender neutral, that is, "to be confronted with the witnesses against him or her." With respect to the right to face-to-face confrontation under Art. II, §8, as amended, *see* §§803.23 and 804.1 supra.

Other Confrontation Clause cases fall into two broad categories: cases involving the admission of out-of-court statements and cases involving restrictions imposed by law or by the trial court on the scope of cross-examination. As to the scope of cross-examination, *see* §611.11 supra.

Under the Confrontation Clause as currently interpreted, substantive admissibility of prior inconsistent statements of an in-court witness testifying under oath subject to cross-examination is permissible even if the witness denies making or doesn't recall the prior statements. Prior consistent statements admitted under similar circumstances also do not run afoul of the Confrontation Clause, *See, e.g., United States v. Owens*, 484 U.S. 554 (1988); *Nelson v. O'Neil*, 402 U.S. 622 (1971); *California v. Green*, 399 U.S. 149 (1970).

With respect to a witness who does not testify at trial under oath subject to cross-examination, admissibility of the witness' hearsay statements is governed by *Ohio v. Roberts*, 448 U.S. 56, 66 (1980);

> The Court has applied this "indicia of reliability" requirement principally by concluding that certain hearsay exceptions rest upon such solid foundations that admission of virtually any evidence within them comports with the "substance of the constitutional protection." Mattox v. United States, 156 U.S. at 244. . . . This reflects the truism "hearsay rules and the Confrontation Clause are generally designed to protect similar values," California v. Green, 399 U.S. at 155 . . . and stem from the same roots," Dutton v. Evans, 400 U.S. 74, 86 . . . (1970). It also responds to the need for certainty in the workaday world of conducting criminal trials.
>
> In sum, when a hearsay declarant is not present for cross-examination at trial, the Confrontation Clause normally requires a showing that he is unavailable. Even then, his statement is admissible only if it bears adequate "indicia of reliability." Reliability can be inferred without more in a case where the

evidence falls within a firmly rooted hearsay exception. In other cases, the evidence must be excluded, at least absent a showing of particularized guarantees of trustworthiness.

In *Roberts,* although declining to "map out a theory of the Confrontation Clause that would determine the validity of all hearsay exceptions," id at 64-65, the Supreme Court stated without qualification that sufficient trustworthiness of hearsay statements of witnesses not called at trial, whether or not the declarant must be shown to be unavailable, can be "inferred without more" with respect to evidence falling squarely within a "firmly rooted hearsay exception." Most if not all of the traditional common law hearsay exemptions clearly fall within the description "firmly rooted." The Supreme Court also provided for the admission of statements not falling within a "firmly rooted" hearsay exception if such statement possesses "particularized guarantees of trustworthiness." Notably, the court's language exactly fits the requirements of the child sexual abuse hearsay exceptions discussed in §803.23 supra, and the witness refusal to testify exception discussed in §804.10 supra.

The quotation from *Roberts* presented above states that a hearsay statement falling within a hearsay exception may be admitted against the criminal defendant in the normal case only if the government produces the declarant so he can be subjected to cross-examination at trial, or, if not produced, the government has made a sufficient showing that the declarant is not availabe to testify. Presumably, production would include making the declarant available to be called by the prosecution for direct examination at the option of the accused and subjected to cross-examination concerning the hearsay statement. In addition, if the declarant is not available for cross-examination at trial, the hearsay statement may be admitted only if it bears adequate "indicia of reliability." However, indicia of reliability "can be inferred without more in a case where the evidence falls within a firmly rooted hearsay exception." Taken literally, almost all hearsay exceptions could require a showing of unavailability or the production of an available declarant when a hearsay statement is offered against the accused.

Several factors indicated that the United States Supreme Court had no radical change in practice in mind. First, the foregoing indication in *Roberts* was made in the context of a discussion of the former testimony hearsay exception, see §§804.2 to 804.5 supra, a hearsay exception that itself requires unavailability. Moreover, the casualness displayed in the making of the comment with respect to unavailability generally, in the context of a hearsay exception requiring unavailability, belied any intention to make a radical change in the law. As *Roberts* itself states, "competing interests . . . may warrant dispensing with confrontation at trial," *id.* at 64, and further relaxation of the Hearsay Rule may occur depending on " 'considerations of public policy and the necessities of the case.' " *Id.* at 64, quoting *Mattox v. United States,* 156 U.S. 237, 243 (1895). The opinion also indicated that a demonstration of unavailability or production of the declarant is not required when the utility of confrontation is remote. *Id.* at 65 n.7. In this context it is interesting to note that, generally speaking, neither the United States Court of Appeals, state courts, nor the leading commentators on the Federal Rules of Evidence construed *Roberts* as ushering in a radical change. *See, e.g., United States v. Hans,* 684 F.2d 343, 346 (6th Cir. 1982) ("The district court acknowledged that the checks were exceptions to the hearsay rule under Rule 803(6) and Rule 803(8), both of which could be utilized 'even though the declarant is available as a witness.' Clearly *Roberts* does not support exclusion of the instant checks.") Finally, any reading of *Roberts*'s "normally requires" language as mandating a requirement of unavailability or production with respect to almost every hearsay statement falling within a common law hearsay exception offered against the criminal defendant was completely out of character with other recent decisions of the United States Supreme Court, including *Dutton v. Evans,* 400 U.S. 74 (1970).

In *United States v. Inadi,* 475 U.S. 387 (1986), the United States Supreme Court addressed the question of whether the statement in *Roberts* that "the Confrontational Clause normally requires a showing that [the defendant] is unavailable" applies to co-conspirator hearsay statements. The Supreme Court held that considerations of reliability and necessity, benefit, and burden all support its conclusion that the confrontation clause does not mandate an initial showing of unavailability of the declarant before a statement of a co-conspirator may be received in evidence. In *White v. Illinois,* 502 U.S. 346 (1992), the Supreme Court in the context of the "spontaneous declaration," *see* §803.3 supra, and the "medical examination", *see* §803.8 supra, hearsay exceptions being employed in a child sexual assault prosecution, went even further declaring that *Inadi* held that "*Roberts* stands for the proposition that unavailability analysis is a necessary part of Confrontation Clause inquiry only when the challenged out-of-court statements were made in the course of a prior judicial proceeding." 502 U.S. at 352.

The second question raised by *Roberts* with respect to the admissibility of a statement of a co-conspirator under the Confrontation Clause — whether a statement of a co-conspirator admitted as a representative admission of a party-opponent falls within the notion of a "firmly rooted hearsay exception," or conversely whether such an admission of a party-opponent requires a "showing of particularized guarantees of trustworthiness," was answered by the Supreme Court in *Bourjaily v. United States,* 483 U.S. 171 (1987), in the affirmative: "We think the co-conspirator exception to the hearsay rule is firmly enough rooted in our jurisprudence that, under this Court's holding in *Roberts,* a court need not independently inquire into the reliability of such statements." 483 U.S. at 184. Interestingly, the majority opinion determines that the co-conspirator hearsay exception satisfies the second prong of *Roberts,* not on the basis of an assessment of reliability, but rather on the basis that the co-conspirator exception is of long-standing tradition. The fact that an agency and adversary system plus necessity rationale are commonly asserted to support the common law co-conspirator hearsay exception rather than an assessment of reliability was completely ignored. The fact that the adversary system rationale led the drafters of the Federal Rules of Evidence to provide that admissions of a party-opponent are not barred by application of the rule against hearsay through exemption by definition in Rule 801(d)(2) as "not hearsay" rather than inclusive as an exception in Rule 803 was completely overlooked. Thus in *Bourjaily*, the Court answered the second question posed by *Roberts* as to whether a statement of a nonappearing declarant admissible under the rules of evidence under an exemption or exception for a statement of a co-conspirator "bears adequate 'indicia of reliability' " without ever exploring the reliability of statements of a co-conspirator. In fact the Court in *Bourjaily* may fairly be said to have gone so far as to restate *Roberts'* second question so as to remove the concept of "firmly rooted" from being a means to infer "indicia of reliability" and reintroduce "firmly rooted" as an alternative method of satisfying *Roberts'* second question, i.e., any statement of a nonappearing declarant meeting the requirements of a "firmly rooted hearsay" exception does not run afoul of the confrontation clause. Under such a gloss, the Court will not examine a "firmly rooted" hearsay exception to determine whether it in fact possesses "adequate 'indicia of reliability' " — being of long-standing tradition is all that is required. Of course, the hearsay statement must in fact fall within a "firmly rooted" hearsay exception. *See People v. Smith,* 141 Ill. 2d 40, 152 Ill. Dec. 218, 565 N.E.2d 900 (1990), prison incident reports do not fit neatly into the public record exception and lack sufficient "indicia of reliability." Clearly, the hearsay exceptions in child sexual abuse cases, 725 ILCS 5/ 115-10 and 735 ILCS 5/8-2601, discussed in §803.23 supra, and the witness refusal to testify exception, discussed in §804.10 supra, are *not* firmly rooted; "particularized guarantees of trustworthiness" must be shown. *See, e.g., People v. March,* 250 Ill. App. 3d 1062, 189 Ill. Dec. 456, 620 N.E.2d 424 (1993) (725 ILCS 5/115-10 relating to child sexual abuse, §803.23 supra).

In short, *Inadi, White,* and *Bourjaily* support an interpretation of the confrontation clause that statements falling within *any* traditional common law hearsay exception are sufficiently reliable on their face to be admitted against the accused and that the imposition by the confrontation clause of a requirement of unavailability is required only when the challenged out-of-court statement was made in the course of a prior judicial proceeding. The Illinois Constitution is in accord. *People v. Smith,* 152 Ill. 2d 229, 178 Ill. Dec. 335, 604 N.E.2d 858 (1992). *See also People v. Moss,* 275 Ill. App. 3d 748, 212 Ill. Dec. 40, 656 N.E.2d 193 (1995).

The admissibility of confessions of a codefendant is governed by the United States Supreme Court decisions of *Bruton v. United States,* 391 U.S. 123 (1968); *Lee v. Illinois,* 476 U.S. 530 (1986); *Richardson v. Marsh,* 481 U.S. 200 (1987); and *Cruz v. New York,* 481 U.S. U.S. 186 (1987). Pursuant to *Cruz,* the fact that the codefendant's and the defendant's confessions interlock is not relevant (*Parker v. Randolph,* 442 U.S. 62 (1979), overruled). Pursuant to *Lee,* the codefendant's confession is only admissible against the defendant if an independent evidentiary basis, i.e., hearsay exception, exists. *People v. Moman,* 201 Ill. App. 3d 293, 146 Ill. Dec. 897, 558 N.E.2d 1231 (1990); *People v. Dixon,* 169 Ill. App. 3d 959, 120 Ill. Dec. 249, 523 N.E.2d 1160 (1988); *People v. Lincoln,* 157 Ill. App. 3d 700, 109 Ill. Dec. 958, 510 N.E.2d 1026 (1987). Sometimes the fact that an independent evidentiary basis is required for admissibility, and that possession of adequate indicia of reliability is not alone enough, is forgotten. *See People v. Sevier,* 230 Ill. App. 3d 1071, 174 Ill. Dec. 336, 598 N.E.2d 968 (1992).

ARTICLE IX

Authentication and Identification

§901   Requirement of Authentication or Identification

§901.1   An Overview

Authentication and identification represent a special aspect of relevancy, §401.1 supra. Thus, for example, a telephone conversation may not be shown to be relevant unless the person speaking is identified, nor may a purported letter of the defendant be relevant unless it is authenticated through the introduction of evidence sufficient to support a finding that the defendant actually wrote the letter. *Mann v. Russell*, 11 Ill. 586 (1850), advertisement purporting to bear defendant's name not admissible unless shown to have emanated from him; *St. Louis Loan & Inv. Co. v. Yantis*, 173 Ill. 321, 50 N.E. 807 (1898), printed statement of loan company inadmissible in absence of authentication; *McKaig v. Appleton*, 289 Ill. 301, 124 N.E. 596 (1919), letters purporting to have been dictated by blind man inadmissible in absence of evidence that he did in fact dictate them; *People v. Dinenza*, 356 Ill. 118, 900 N.E. 298 (1934), error to admit extortion letters without connecting defendant with preparation or mailing; *Summerville v. Rodgers*, 31 Ill. App. 2d 420, 176 N.E.2d 667 (1961), document purporting to authorize cancellation of policy on behalf of insured inadmissible without proof of authenticity; *Laughlin v. Chenoweth*, 92 Ill. App. 3d 430, 47 Ill. Dec. 180, 414 N.E.2d 1296 (1980), signature of person upon statement is insufficient authentication in absence of evidence that the witness read or understood the contents before signing. Similarly, a map or photograph of an intersection is not relevant unless evidence is introduced establishing that the map or photograph accurately depicts the intersection; nor is a gun relevant unless sufficiently connected to both the defendant and the crime.

Satisfaction of the requirements of authentication or identification is a matter of conditional relevancy to be approached as provided in §104.2 supra. Accordingly, once the court finds that evidence has been introduced sufficient to support a finding by a reasonable jury that it is more probably true than not true that the item in question is what its proponent claims, §104.2 supra; *Flynn v. Golden Grain Co.,* 269 Ill. App. 3d 871, 207 Ill. Dec. 202, 646 N.E.2d 1289 (1995) (citing Handbook), and the court finds that the item as claimed has any tendency to make a fact of consequence in the litigation more or less probable, §401.1 supra, the item, subject to objection on other grounds, should be admitted. Proof of authenticity or identification may be by direct or circumstantial evidence. The laying of the foundation must be conducted, to the extent practicable, so as to prevent inadmissible evidence from being suggested to the jury by any means. The trial court's determination as to the sufficiency of the foundation will be reviewed on appeal applying the clear abuse of discretion standard. *People v. Dixon,* 228 Ill. App. 3d 29, 170 Ill. Dec. 424, 592 N.E.2d 1104 (1992); *People v. Bell,* 273 Ill. App. 3d 439, 210 Ill. Dec. 164, 652 N.E.2d 1140 (1995).

After the proponent of the evidence completes laying the foundation, the court may permit opposing counsel to conduct a limited cross-examination, referred to as *voir dire,* on the foundation offered. *See Bazzell-Phillips & Assoc. v. Cole Hosp.,* 54 Ill. App. 3d 188, 54 Ill. Dec. 883, 369 N.E.2d 337 (1977). In reaching its determination as to admissibility, the court must view all the evidence introduced as to authentication or identification, including issues of credibility, most favorable to the proponent. If upon consideration of the evidence as a whole, the court determines that the evidence is sufficient to support a finding by a reasonable juror that it is more probably true than not true that the matter in question is what its proponent claims, the evidence will be admitted. *See Aguilera v. Mount Sinai Hospital Medical Center,* 293 Ill. App. 3d 967, 229 Ill. Dec. 65, 691 N.E.2d 1 (1998) (fact that date on CT scan films does not match date on other records including log showing that a CT scan was performed does not defeat admissibility). The party against whom the evidence has been received may during the trial offer contradictory evidence before the trier of fact or challenge the credibility of the supporting proof at the same time and in the same way that he disputes any other testimony. The ultimate decision as to whether a person, document, or item of real or demonstrative evidence admitted in evidence is as purported is for the trier of fact.

While ordinarily the authentication of a writing or record is satisfied by the introduction of evidence, in some instances a writing or record itself is treated as sufficient to support a finding of its authentication. *Pittsburgh, Ft. W. & C. Ry. v. Callaghan,* 157 Ill. 406, 41 N.E. 909 (1895), inscription on a vehicle is *prima facie* evidence of ownership or control; Uniform Commercial Code §1-202, 810 ILCS 5/1-202, third party documents authorized or required by a contract are *prima facie* evidence of their own authenticity. Self-authenticating writings or records are discussed in §902 infra. For discussion of *prima facie* evidence, *see* §302.8 supra.

Primarily in civil proceedings, the time and uncertainty incident to authenticating documents at trial may often be avoided by using available procedures before trial. An allegation in a pleading of the execution or assignment of a written instrument is admitted unless denied in a verified pleading, although verification may be excused by the court. 735 ILCS 5/2-605. In addition, authentication may be accomplished through an admission in open court or in a pleading, by requests to admit the genuineness of a document, by service of a copy of a public record pursuant to Supreme Court Rule 216(d), by stipulation, by deposition, by interrogatory, or as a result of agreement at the pretrial conference.

Following are ten illustrations of authentication or identification, each sufficient to support admissibility. The illustrations are not exclusive but serve only as examples. With respect to the illustrations, the terms *writing* or *record* are frequently employed. These terms should be interpreted to conform with the definition of *document* provided in Supreme Court Rule 201(b)(1); a document includes but is not limited to papers, photographs, films, recordings, memoranda, books, records, accounts, communications and all retrievable information in computer storage. Of course, compliance with the requirements of authentication or identification does not guarantee that the evidence is admissible, for the offered evidence may still be excluded because of some other bar to admission, such as hearsay or lack of relevancy.

§901.2   Testimony of Witness with Knowledge; Chain of Custody

An obvious method of identification or authentication is the testimony of a witness with personal knowledge, §602.1 supra, that a matter is what it is claimed to be. A witness may testify, for example, that the person who made a particular statement is the plaintiff, that the writing bears her signature, that she observed someone else writing the letter, or that the exhibit is a piece of the bottle found on the floor immediately after it exploded. *People v. Sansone*, 42 Ill. App. 3d 512, 1 Ill. Dec. 101, 356 N.E.2d 101 (1976), record albums; *People v. McKnight*, 55 Ill. App. 3d 1052, 13 Ill. Dec. 854, 371 N.E.2d 946 (1977), a watch and receipt; *People v. Starks*, 119 Ill. App. 3d 21, 74 Ill. Dec. 760, 456 N.E.2d 262 (1983), defendant was person appearing in a motion picture; *People v. Drake*, 131 Ill. App. 3d 466, 86 Ill. Dec. 639, 475 N.E.2d 1018 (1985), store manager, by use of label including store code number, could identify stolen merchandise; *People v. Knade*, 252 Ill. App. 3d 682, 192 Ill. Dec. 212, 625 N.E.2d 172 (1993), telephone book. In addition, if an object is involved, and if relevancy requires, evidence must be introduced sufficient to support a finding not only that the object offered is *the* object involved but also that the object is in substantially the same condition now as it was at the time relevant in the litigation. *Jones v. Greyhound Corp.*, 33 Ill. 2d 83, 210 N.E.2d 562 (1965), brake drum of vehicle must be shown to be in same condition when examined by expert witness as it was prior to the accident; *Cheek v. Avco Lycoming Div.*, 56 Ill. App. 3d 217, 13 Ill. Dec. 902, 371 N.E.2d 994

(1977), airplane engine parts not shown to be same parts in the same condition; *People v. Jarosiewicz,* 55 Ill. App. 3d 1057, 13 Ill. Dec. 857, 371 N.E.2d 949 (1977), piece of sheet metal; *People v. Houck,* 50 Ill. App. 3d 274, 8 Ill. Dec. 338, 365 N.E.2d 576 (1977), a torn jacket. *See also People v. Dixon,* 228 Ill. App. 3d 29, 170 Ill. Dec. 424, 592 N.E.2d 1104 (1992); *People v. Jackson,* 89 Ill. App. 3d 461, 44 Ill. Dec. 527, 411 N.E.2d 893 (1980), prosecution is not required to exclude all possibility that article was not altered prior to being taken into custody but rather to establish reasonable probability that article was not changed in any material respect. If the object possesses characteristics that are fairly unusual and readily identifiable and if the object is impervious to change, a sufficient foundation may be introduced by a single witness with personal knowledge identifying the object and establishing that the object is in substantially the same condition. *People v. Stewart,* 105 Ill. 2d 22, 85 Ill. Dec. 241, 473 N.E.2d 840 (1984); *People v. Hominick,* 177 Ill. App. 3d 18, 126 Ill. Dec. 422, 531 N.E.2d 1049 (1988); *People v. Winters,* 97 Ill. App. 3d 288, 52 Ill. Dec. 763, 422 N.E.2d 972 (1981).

Personal knowledge acquired from any of the five senses may form the basis for the testimony of the witness.

In order to assist identification of a particular object in court, it is common for the person, especially a police officer, to place identifying marks or labels on the object. *People v. Judkins,* 10 Ill. 2d 445, 140 N.E.2d 663 (1957); *People v. Ransom,* 65 Ill. 2d 339, 2 Ill. Dec. 721, 357 N.E.2d 1164 (1976), testimony concerning tag on body present at postmortem proper to show that it was same body delivered to funeral home; *People v. Rhodes,* 81 Ill. App. 3d 339, 36 Ill. Dec. 556, 401 N.E.2d 237 (1980), latent prints were placed on "lifter tape" on back of which police officer had written pertinent information concerning burglary and had placed his initials; *People v. Thibudeaux,* 98 Ill. App. 3d 1105, 54 Ill. Dec. 275, 424 N.E.2d 1178 (1981), labeling of fingerprints taken from various objects assisted officers in testifying as to uniqueness and unchanged conditions.

Where evidence that the object is in substantially the same

condition cannot be offered by one individual (i.e., the object is subject to alteration, substitutuion, or change of condition), such as where narcotics are involved, the object must be authenticated by means of a chain of custody. Either identification or chain of custody is sufficient; both are not required. *People v. Stewart,* 105 Ill. 2d 22, 85 Ill. Dec. 241, 473 N.E.2d 840 (1984). *See also People v. Arbo,* 213 Ill. App. 3d 828, 157 Ill. Dec. 348, 572 N.E.2d 417 (1991), chain-of-custody evidence is not required when an item is readily identifiable. Chain of custody requires testimony of continuous possession by each individual having possession, *People v. Maurice,* 31 Ill. 2d 456, 202 N.E.2d 480 (1964), together with testimony by each that the object remained in substantially the same condition during its presence in his possession. *People v. Irpino,* 127 Ill. App. 3d 767, 78 Ill. Dec. 165, 461 N.E.2d 999 (1984). *See People v. Brown,* 253 Ill. App. 3d 165, 192 Ill. Dec. 26, 624 N.E.2d 1378 (1993), chain of custody was not established where no evidence was introduced identifying the gas can offered in evidence as the gas can recovered at the crime scene. All possibility of alteration, substitution, or change of condition need not be eliminated. *People v. Stevenson,* 90 Ill. App. 3d 903, 46 Ill. Dec. 226, 413 N.E.2d 1339 (1980); *People v. Farmer,* 91 Ill. App. 3d 262, 46 Ill. Dec. 726, 414 N.E.2d 779 (1980); *People v. Creque,* 214 Ill. App. 3d 587, 158 Ill. Dec. 112, 573 N.E.2d 1297 (1991). For example, generally an object may be placed in a safe to which more than one person has access without each such person being produced. *People v. Anthony,* 28 Ill. 2d 65, 190 N.E.2d 837 (1963); *People v. Tribett,* 98 Ill. App. 3d 663, 53 Ill. Dec. 897, 424 N.E.2d 688 (1981); *People v. Bradney,* 170 Ill. App. 3d 839, 121 Ill. Dec. 306, 525 N.E.2d 112 (1988). To the extent that *People v. Gibson,* 287 Ill. App. 3d 878, 223 Ill. Dec. 234, 679 N.E.2d 419 (1997) is to the contrary, it is incorrect and should not be followed. The more authentication is genuinely in issue, the greater the need to negate the possibility of alteration, substitution, or change of condition. *People v. Judkins,* supra; *People v. Atchley,* 97 Ill. App. 3d 85, 52 Ill. Dec. 585, 422 N.E.2d 266 (1981); *People v. Shiflet,* 125 Ill. App. 3d 161, 80 Ill. Dec. 596, 465

N.E.2d 942 (1984); *People v. Dixon,* 228 Ill. App. 3d 29, 170 Ill. Dec. 424, 592 N.E.2d 1104 (1992). In the absence of any evidence of substitution, tampering, or other form of alteration, reasonable protection techniques are sufficient, i.e., the prosecution is required only to demonstrate a reasonable probability that the item has not been substituted, tampered with, or altered in any important aspect. *People v. Ryan,* 129 Ill. App. 3d 915, 85 Ill. Dec. 93, 473 N.E.2d 461 (1984); *People v. Hominick,* 177 Ill. App. 3d 18, 126 Ill. Dec. 422, 531 N.E.2d 1049 (1988); *People v. Carroll,* 227 Ill. App. 3d 144, 169 Ill. Dec. 91, 590 N.E.2d 1010 (1992); *People v. Bynum,* 257 Ill. App. 3d 502, 196 Ill. Dec. 179, 629 N.E.2d 724 (1994); *People v. Harper,* 279 Ill. App. 3d 801, 216 Ill. Dec. 414, 665 N.E.2d 474 (1996). Whether evidence of proper sealing of the exhibit has been introduced is an important factor in the court's decision. *People v. Noran,* 24 Ill. 2d 403, 182 N.E.2d 188 (1962), unsealed packet of narcotics inadmissible; *People v. Kabala,* 225 Ill. App. 3d 301, 167 Ill. Dec. 595, 587 N.E.2d 1210 (1992), exhibit neither tagged nor marked, placed in an unsealed envelope, variously identified, was improperly admitted; *People v. Irpino* supra, narcotics contained in sealed manila envelope at crime lab were admissible; *People v. Winters,* 97 Ill. App. 3d 288, 52 Ill. Dec. 763, 422 N.E.2d 972 (1981), unsealed vial of blood was inadmissible. Similarly, evidence of a discrepancy in a description such as variance in weight between the item seized and the item tested is also an important factor. *People v. Gibson,* 287 Ill. App. 3d 878, 223 Ill. Dec. 234, 679 N.E.2d 419 (1997), chain of custody foundation for crack cocaine inadequately established. The fact that items in addition to those introduced in evidence seized from the defendant are not accounted for does not affect admissibility. *People v. Holman,* 157 Ill. App. 3d 764, 110 Ill. Dec. 108, 510 N.E.2d 1139 (1987).

It is worth emphasizing that chain-of-custody showings are required only when the object or substance is not susceptible to identification on the basis of its distinctive appearance, e.g., a blood specimen or a powder claimed to be a controlled substance. *People v. Winters,* 97 Ill. App. 3d 288, 52 Ill.

Dec. 763, 422 N.E.2d 972 (1981), a chain-of-custody foundation is required when the offered evidence is not readily identifiable or is susceptible to alteration by tampering or substitution.

Requirements have sometimes been said to be rather strict in criminal cases. *See People v. Pittman,* 28 Ill. 2d 100, 190 N.E.2d 802 (1963) and cases cited supra. *See also People v. Kabala,* 225 Ill. App. 3d 301, 167 Ill. Dec. 595, 587 N.E.2d 1210 (1992) (citing Handbook). The prosecutor must show a chain of custody of sufficient completeness to render it improbable that the item has been altered by tampering or substitution. *People v. Slaughter,* 149 Ill. App. 3d 183, 102 Ill. Dec. 769, 500 N.E.2d 662 (1986); *People v. Terry,* 211 Ill. App. 3d 968, 156 Ill. Dec. 310, 570 N.E.2d 786 (1991); *People v. Gibson,* 287 Ill. App. 3d 878, 223 Ill. Dec. 234, 679 N.E.2d 419 (1997). On the other hand, the test has sometimes been stated less forcefully: unless the accused provides actual evidence of substitution, tampering, or altering, the State need only demonstrate a reasonable probability that the evidence has not been substituted, tampered with, or altered in any important aspect. *People v. Pavone,* 241 Ill. App. 3d 1001, 182 Ill. Dec. 372, 609 N.E.2d 906 (1993); *People v. Hermann,* 180 Ill. App. 3d 939, 129 Ill. Dec. 656, 536 N.E.2d 706 (1988); *People v. Schubert,* 136 Ill. App. 3d 348, 91 Ill. Dec. 254, 483 N.E.2d 600 (1985); *People v. Ryan,* 129 Ill. App. 3d 915, 85 Ill. Dec. 93, 473 N.E.2d 461 (1984). Unless the defendant shows actual evidence of tampering, substitution, or alteration, deficiencies in the chain of custody go to weight and not admissibility. *People v. Reed,* 243 Ill. App. 3d 598, 183 Ill. Dec. 695, 611 N.E.2d 1343 (1993). Accordingly, the absence of testimony as to the condition of the particular items during one or more links in the chain of custody does not alone mandate exclusion. *People v. Hominick,* 177 Ill. App. 3d 18, 126 Ill. Dec. 422, 531 N.E.2d 1049 (1988); *People v. Bynum,* 257 Ill. App. 3d 502, 196 Ill. Dec. 179, 629 N.E.2d 724 (1994). In civil cases, while every possibility of doubt need not be precluded, it was once nevertheless indicated that every person having knowledge of the object and the condition should testify.

Woolley v. Hafner's Wagon Wheel, Inc., 22 Ill. 2d 413, 176 N.E.2d 757 (1960). Arguably only if all persons testify would a discrepancy go to weight and not admissibility. *Woolley v. Hafner's Wagon Wheel, Inc., id.* It is likely that the less forceful test would be employed in civil cases.

In *People v. Pulliam,* 176 Ill. 2d 261, 223 Ill. Dec. 610, 680 N.E.2d 343 (1997), the Illinois Supreme Court stated that a book found in the defendant's apartment two days after a murder, entitled *The Force of Sex,* was improperly admitted in light of the absence of testimony that the defendant owned or had read the book and the fact that the apartment was unsecured for those two days. Obviously, *Pulliam* can't mean what it might seem to imply, for if it did, a gun found in the defendant's apartment three days after a murder would be inadmissible. The book in *Pulliam* should have been found inadmissible, if at all, solely on the basis of its probative value being substantially outweighed by the danger of unfair prejudice, misleading the jury, and confusion of the issues, *see* §403.1 infra.

Where a sample is offered, it is also necessary to establish that the sample is representative of the mass. *People v. Kaludis,* 146 Ill. App. 3d 888, 100 Ill. Dec. 382, 497 N.E.2d 360 (1986). Ordinarily, an opinion may be rendered with respect to the contents of a substance even though the opinion is based on testing of only random samples of the substance. However, where the weight of a substance is an element of the offense and the accused could be charged with a lesser offense, such as may occur with respect to possession of drugs, weight must be proven beyond a reasonable doubt. *People v. Robinson,* 167 Ill. 2d 397, 212 Ill. Dec. 675, 657 N.E.2d 1020 (1995). This requires that *each* of multiple packages be sampled even if discovered together; thus testing two of ten packages fails to establish the content of the remaining eight packages. *People v. Hill,* 169 Ill. App. 3d 901, 120 Ill. Dec. 574, 524 N.E.2d 604 (1988). *Accord People v. Miller,* 218 Ill. App. 3d 668, 161 Ill. Dec. 419, 578 N.E.2d 1065 (1991); *People v. Jones,* 260 Ill. App. 3d 807, 198 Ill. Dec. 756, 633 N.E.2d 218 (1994). It appears that if individual packages are combined, a sample taken from the combined substance is adequate. *People v. Little,* 140 Ill. App. 3d 682, 95 Ill. Dec. 101, 489 N.E.2d 322 (1986). Of course, if the weight of the package actually tested comprises more than the weight required for a particular offense, it is not necessary for all of the packages to be tested. *People v. Robinson,* supra.

With respect to authentication of photographs, *see* §401.8 supra.

With respect to the foundation for admissibility of the results of application of a particular scientific principle, technique, or test, *see* §702.4 supra.

§901.3   Nonexpert Opinion on Handwriting

A witness who is not an expert can give her opinion authenticating a writing or signature if she has sufficient familiarity with the handwriting of the putative writer, *People v. Williams,* 274 Ill. App. 3d 598, 210 Ill. Dec. 704, 653 N.E.2d 899 (1995), and remarkably little has been held to qualify the witness. *Woodford v. McClenahan,* 9 Ill. 85 (1847), seeing person write on one occasion held sufficient. The witness's familiarity may be acquired not only by seeing the person write but also by conducting a correspondence with him or, as in the case of a bank clerk or teller, by handling his checks or deposits. *Board of Trustees v. Misenheimer,* 78 Ill. 22 (1875); *Buckingham Corp. v. Ewing Liquors Co.,* 15 Ill. App. 3d 839, 305 N.E.2d 278 (1973). Whether the witness's familiarity, however acquired, is sufficient to allow her to give an opinion is a question of conditional relevancy, §104.2 supra; an assertion by the witness of familiarity coupled with a description of circumstances from which knowledge might reasonably be acquired will ordinarily be held sufficient. A showing of limited opportunity to become familiar with the handwriting generally goes to the weight given the witness's testimony by the trier of fact rather than to admissibility of the document. *Buckingham Corp. v. Ewing Liquors Co.* supra.

A nonexpert witness cannot rely upon familiarity acquired

for the purpose of litigation. *Board of Trustees v. Misenheimer* supra, familiarity acquired after controversy arose insufficient. Only an expert may testify to familiarity obtained for that purpose. *See* §901.4 infra.

A lay witness may be cross-examined with respect to the basis of his opinion, *Bevan v. Atlantic Natl. Bank,* 142 Ill. 302, 31 N.E. 679 (1892), and in spite of the holding in *Massey v. Farmers Natl. Bank,* 104 Ill. 327 (1882), the cross-examiner should be permitted to ask the witness to pick out a genuine writing from false copies prepared for such purposes. *Melvin v. Hodges,* 71 Ill. 422 (1874), such cross-examination permitted if specimen in file or in evidence for other purposes. While a nonexpert witness has been permitted to point out differences between the disputed specimen and a genuine handwriting sample, *Nagle v. Schnadt,* 239 Ill. 595, 88 N.E. 178 (1909), and presumably also similarities, such comparisons should be permitted to be made only by an expert witness and/or the trier of fact. *Yelm v. Masters,* 81 Ill. App. 2d 186, 225 N.E.2d 152 (1967), lay witnesses may not compare exemplar and disputed item before jury.

Since a lay person's ability to distinguish between an authentic specimen and a skilled forgery is minimal at best, where a genuine issue is raised as to authenticity, an expert witness should be employed. McCormick, Evidence §221 (4th ed. 1992).

§901.4   *Comparison by Trier or Expert Witness*

An expert witness may base her opinion as to authenticity upon a comparison between the questioned piece of evidence and an exemplar, the authenticity of which has been sufficiently established. *Rogers v. Tyley,* 144 Ill. 652, 32 N.E. 393 (1892). The process of authentication by comparison rests upon the notion that with respect to a particular item there are so many common identifying characteristics that it is possible by this means to establish that the item and the specimen have the same origin. Comparison is frequently used in connection with ballistics, handwriting, and typewriting. *Lyon v. Oliver,* 316 Ill. 292, 147 N.E. 251 (1925), identity of machine used to produce disputed typewriting proper subject of expert testimony. The same technique has also been used to authenticate tire tread marks, shoe prints, and other items where the presence of sufficient common characteristics is shown.

The common law originally did not permit the introduction of handwriting specimens to be used by the trier of fact to determine the genuineness of a disputed specimen by comparison. *Jumpertz v. People,* 21 Ill. 375 (1859). However, a writing in the files of the case or in evidence for other purposes, and admittedly genuine, could be compared with the disputed specimen by the trier. *Brobston v. Cahill,* 64 Ill. 356 (1872). *See also Stitzel v. Miller,* 250 Ill. 72, 95 N.E. 53 (1911). By statute enacted in 1915, comparison may be made by the jury or by an expert witness, provided, however, that the specimen is admitted to be genuine or proved to be genuine to the satisfaction of the court. *Cook v. Moecker,* 217 Ill. App. 479 (1920), court must first find on basis of evidence that specimen is genuine. Reasonable notice to the opposite party is required, plus reasonable opportunity to examine. For the latter purpose the court could order the specimens impounded with the clerk. 735 ILCS 5/8-1501 to 5/8-1503. Specimens introduced under the statute must be made prior to the origin of the controversy, *Shinn v. Settle,* 222 Ill. App. 463 (1921), and the comparison may be made by the jury only in open court. *People v. White,* 365 Ill. 499, 6 N.E.2d 1015 (1937); *People v. Clark,* 301 Ill. 428, 134 N.E. 95 (1922). *Cf. People v. Hoover,* 87 Ill. App. 3d 740, 43 Ill. Dec. 193, 410 N.E.2d 193 (1980), trier of fact may examine exemplars in jury room provided that in the first instance the comparison is made in open court. While the statute refers solely to the jury or an expert witness, in a case tried without a jury a comparison may be made by the trial judge. *1601 South Michigan Partners v. Measuron,* 271 Ill. App. 3d 415, 208 Ill. Dec. 86, 648 N.E.2d 1008 (1995).

Where comparison is of matters other than handwriting,

whether it is by comparison by the trier of fact alone, by expert testimony, or by the trier of fact aided by expert testimony, the genuineness of the specimen is treated as a matter of conditional relevancy, §104.2 supra, ultimately decided by the trier of fact. The court will admit a specimen into evidence for purposes of comparison if evidence sufficient to support a finding of its genuineness has been introduced. The specimen itself may be authenticated by any of the methods discussed in §§901 and 902, or by any of the methods available prior to trial discussed in §901.1 supra.

Cf. Federal Rule of Evidence 901(b)(3), 65 F.R.D. 131, 160 (1975), applying the concept of conditional relevancy to all comparisons, including handwriting.

Once the specimen has been sufficiently authenticated, the expert, whether, for example, testifying as to handwriting, typewriting, or ballistics, will commonly demonstrate the validity of his comparison by using blown-up photographic copies of both the specimen and the questioned item so as to be able to demonstrate graphically the similarities or differences leading to his opinion as to the origin of the questioned item.

The cross-examiner is afforded wide scope in examination of such expert witnesses. Where it is fair to do so, the cross-examiner should be permitted to require the expert witness to pick a genuine item from among false samples. *Contra Massey v. Farmers Natl. Bank,* 104 Ill. 327 (1882).

§901.5   *Distinctive Characteristics and the Like*

Appearance, contents, substance, internal patterns, or other distinctive characteristics may sufficiently authenticate an item of evidence when considered in conjunction with circumstances. *People v. Towns,* 157 Ill. 2d 90, 191 Ill. Dec. 24, 623 N.E.2d 269 (1993). Thus a letter may be authenticated by its contents with or without the aid of the physical characteristics just mentioned if the letter is shown to contain information that no one other than the purported sender is likely to possess. McCormick, Evidence §225 (4th ed. 1992). Authentication by distinctive characteristics and the like has also been found to be sufficient where evidence supported a finding that one of a small group of individuals including the defendant wrote the letter offered into evidence, *People v. Munoz,* 70 Ill. App. 3d 76, 26 Ill. Dec. 509, 388 N.E.2d 133 (1979), where a letter bearing the correct address of the Cook County jail and the defendant's home address referred to the incident for which the defendant was on trial, *People v. Buford,* 110 Ill. App. 3d 46, 65 Ill. Dec. 721, 441 N.E.2d 1235 (1982), and where letters bore defendant's return address, discussed many subjects that only the defendant knew about, and where the contents of the letters were discussed by the defendant with others. *People v. Faircloth,* 234 Ill. App. 3d 386, 175 Ill. Dec. 342, 599 N.E.2d 1356 (1992). A common aspect of this kind of authentication is the reply doctrine, which provides that once a letter is shown to have been written and mailed, a letter shown by its contents to be a reply to it is authenticated without more. *Consolidated Perfume Co. v. National Bank of the Republic,* 86 Ill. App. 642 (1899).

§901.6 *Voice Identification; Sound Recordings*

Voice recognition is sufficient identification if made by a witness having some familiarity with the speaker's voice. *People v. Nichols,* 378 Ill. 487, 38 N.E.2d 766 (1942). Familiarity may be gained either before or after hearing the voice to be identified. A voice heard firsthand may be authenticated by hearing it over the telephone and vice versa. *People v. Nichols* supra; *People v. Abrego,* 142 Ill. App. 3d 973, 97 Ill. Dec. 200, 492 N.E.2d 636 (1986).

Sound recording of voices is authenticated if a proper foundation is laid, including identification of the speakers. *Belfield v. Coop,* 8 Ill. 2d 293, 134 N.E.2d 249 (1956). The specific requirements for authentication in addition to voice identification of sound recordings of any kind vary depending upon the circumstances. Thus, for example, a person who overheard or participated in the entire conversation may lay a proper foundation by testifying that the sound recording fully, fairly, and accurately reflects the conversation. *People v. Lewis,* 84 Ill. App. 566, 40 Ill. Dec. 310, 406 N.E.2d 11 (1980); *People v. Williams,* 109 Ill. 2d 327, 93 Ill. Dec. 788, 487 N.E.2d 613 (1985); *People v. Gaurige,* 168 Ill. App. 3d 855, 119 Ill. Dec. 447, 522 N.E.2d 1306 (1988); *People v. Cochran,* 174 Ill. App. 3d 208, 123 Ill. Dec. 708, 528 N.E.2d 253 (1988). A sufficient foundation is laid through similar testimony by a person who heard the conversation by electronic transmission as it was taking place, provided the mechanical capability and proper operation of the transmitting device is also established. *People v. Melchor,* 136 Ill. App. 3d 708, 91 Ill. Dec. 485, 483 N.E.2d 971 (1985). In other instances a mechanical capability plus chain-of-custody foundation, including testimony as to (1) capability of the device for recording, (2) competency of the operator, (3) proper operation of the device, (4) preservation of the recording with no changes, additions, or deletions, as well as (5) identification of the speakers, may be necessary. *People v. Estrada,* 91 Ill. App. 3d 228, 46 Ill. Dec. 628, 414 N.E.2d 512 (1980) (quoting Handbook); *Estate of Jones v. Atwood State Bank,* 159 Ill. App. 3d 377, 111 Ill. Dec. 509, 512 N.E.2d 1050 (1987); *People v. City of Springfield,* 193 Ill. App. 3d 1022, 140 Ill. Dec. 846, 550 N.E.2d 731 (1990) (quoting Handbook). The recording, of course, to be admissible must not be barred by the eavesdropping statute discussed in §503.8 supra. The burden of showing a violation of the eavesdropping statute lies with the party *opposing* introduction of the recording. *Estate of Jones v. Atwood State Bank* supra. Sound recording in the court's discretion may be employed in the jury room. *People v. Manuel,* 294 Ill. App. 3d 113, 228 Ill. Dec. 472, 689 N.E.2d 344 (1997).

A transcript of the sound recording may be received in evidence if a sufficient foundation is presented establishing the accuracy of the transcript and the identity of the speakers. *People v. Melchor* supra; *People v. Rogers,* 187 Ill. App. 3d 126, 135 Ill. Dec. 65, 543 N.E.2d 300 (1989). The admission of a recording that is partially inaudible or that reproduces only part of a statement of conversation is a matter within the trial court's discretion. *People v. Manning,* 182 Ill. 2d 193, 230 Ill. Dec. 933, 695 N.E.2d 423 (1998). The jury should be instructed that the tapes and not the transcripts are the evidence they are to consider. *People v. Manuel,* 294 Ill. App. 3d 113, 228 Ill. Dec. 472, 689 N.E.2d 344 (1997).

In *United States v. Wade,* 388 U.S. 218 (1967), it was held that compelling a defendant to speak to provide voice identification does not violate his privilege against self-incrimination, even if he is asked to use words purportedly uttered by the person committing the crime of which he is suspected. *Accord People v. Davis,* 151 Ill. App. 3d 435, 104 Ill. Dec. 283, 502 N.E.2d 780 (1986).

§901.7   Telephone Conversations

Communications by telephone do not authenticate themselves. A mere assertion by the speaker as to his identity, being hearsay, cannot be taken as a sufficient showing of his identity. Testimony that the witness was familiar with and recognized the speaker's voice is obviously sufficient, §901.6 supra. *Bell v. McDonald,* 308 Ill. 329, 139 N.E. 613 (1923). The familiarity may be acquired prior to the conversation, *Bell v. McDonald, id.,* or afterward, *People v. Nichols,* 378 Ill. 487, 38 N.E.2d 766 (1942); *People v. Abrego,* 142 Ill. App. 3d 973, 97 Ill. Dec. 200, 492 N.E.2d 636 (1986). Authenticating evidence may also be circumstantial, such as contents of the statement or the reply technique. *People v. Poe,* 121 Ill. App. 3d 457, 76 Ill. Dec. 752, 459 N.E.2d 667 (1984) (citing Handbook). *See* §901.5 supra. *See also People v. Nichols* supra, subsequent statement indicating knowledge of contents of calls.

Regarding calls made by the witness, in distinction to calls received, an early decision recognized the sensible principle that calls to a place of business and relating to the business are admissible on the theory of assuming regularity and authority in the answering, and no further authentication is required. *Godair v. Ham Natl. Bank,* 225 Ill. 572, 80 N.E. 407

(1907). Later decisions unfortunately curtailed, though they did not overrule, the effect of this decision by holding its principle inapplicable when a particular person is asked for. *People v. Metcoff,* 392 Ill. 418, 64 N.E.2d 867 (1946); *Holland v. O'Shea,* 342 Ill. App. 127, 95 N.E.2d 515 (1950). *But cf. Smith v. Seiber,* 127 Ill. App. 3d 950, 82 Ill. Dec. 697, 469 N.E.2d 231 (1984), specifically approving *Godair* without mention of any restriction. *Cf.* Federal Rule of Evidence 901(b)(6), 65 F.R.D. 131, 161 (1975), which provides that a telephone conversation may be authenticated by evidence that a call was made to the number assigned at the time by the telephone company to a particular person or business, if (1) in the case of a person, circumstances, including self-identification, show the person answering to be the one called, or (2) in the case of a business, the call was made to a place of business and the conversation related to business reasonably transacted over the telephone. *Accord Tomaszewski v. Godbole,* 174 Ill. App. 3d 629, 124 Ill. Dec. 440, 529 N.E.2d 260 (1988).

§901.8   Public Records

The party may authenticate a writing or record in any form including a data compilation, §901.1 supra, by introducing evidence sufficient to support a finding that (1) the writing or record is a public record authorized by law to be recorded or filed, and (2) the public record is from the public office where such items are kept. *Bell v. Bankers Life & Cas. Co.,* 327 Ill. App. 321, 64 N.E.2d 204 (1945). Any writing or record authorized by law to be recorded or filed in a public office, such as tax returns, weather bureau reports, or documents affecting real property, are included, as are official records — for example, judicial records and data compilations prepared by the public office itself. *People ex rel. Wenzel v. Chicago & N.W. Ry.,* 28 Ill. 2d 205, 190 N.E.2d 780 (1963). A writing or record may be shown to be from the public office where such items are kept by the testimony of a person from the office or other person with knowledge. *People ex rel.*

Wenzel v. Chicago & N.W. Ry., id. Duplicates prepared in the ordinary course of business are treated as originals in civil matters under limited circumstances having to do with statements of account under the Dead Man's Act by 735 ILCS 5/8-401. General treatment of duplicates prepared in the ordinary course of business in criminal proceeding as originals is provided in 725 ILCS 5/115-5(b). *See* §§1003.1 and 1004.1 infra.

Production of the original public record, coupled with testimony as to its being a public record from the public office, is clearly not the only means of authenticating a public record or copy thereof. Certified copies of public records may be employed as specified in §902.2 infra. In addition, 735 ILCS 5/8-1206 provides for authentication of records of courts, municipalities, and private corporations by testimony of a person that she has compared a copy with the original and that it is correct. Finally, Supreme Court Rule 216(d) provides as follows:

> If any public records are to be used as evidence, the party intending to use them may prepare a copy of them insofar as they are to be used, and may seasonably present the copy to the adverse party by notice in writing, and the copy shall thereupon be admissible in evidence as admitted facts in the case if otherwise admissible, except insofar as its inaccuracy is pointed out under oath by the adverse party in an affidavit filed and served within 14 days after service of the notice.

With respect to the hearsay exception for public records, *see* §803.10 supra; as to transcripts of former testimony, *see* §1002.2 infra. The Original Writing Rule's applicability to public records is discussed in §1005.1 infra.

§901.9 Ancient Documents

A writing or recording affecting real property may be authenticated by evidence that the writing or recording (1) is in such condition as to create no suspicion concerning its authenticity, (2) was in a place where it, if authentic, would likely be, and (3) has been in existence 30 years or more at the time it is offered. *Cf. Lunger v. Sechrest,* 186 Ill. App. 521 (1914), marriage certificate admitted as ancient document. If a document has been recorded, the recording is evidence of age. *Reuter v. Stuckart,* 181 Ill. 529, 54 N.E. 1014 (1899). There is no requirement that possession of the real property be consistent with the document. Possession where it does occur is, however, a circumstance corroborating execution of the document. *Reuter v. Stuckart* supra. If an ancient deed is executed pursuant to a purported power of attorney, the existence of a valid power of attorney is presumed, *id.,* although this presumption has not been extended to include a "public" authority (i.e., administrator). *Fell v. Young,* 63 Ill. 106 (1872). The 30-year-old document only affects real property if it is in fact an official document, i.e., one commissioned under official authority or ratified as an official document by reason of having been recorded and relied on by the general public, for example, in the ascertaining of property lines. *People v. Village of Camp Point,* 286 Ill. App. 3d 247, 221 Ill. Dec. 641, 675 N.E.2d 1371 (1997).

Cf. Federal Rule of Evidence 901(b)(8), 65 F.R.D. 131, 161 (1975), applying the ancient document concept to documents in existence 20 years or more without regard to subject matter.

With respect to the hearsay exception for ancient documents, *see* §803.17 supra.

§901.10   *Process or System*

Evidence describing a process or system used to produce a result, showing that the process or system produces an accurate result when properly employed, and establishing that the process or system was properly employed in the case at hand, is sufficient to authenticate the result when offered at trial. Thus evidence describing, for example, the process of creating X-rays, photographs, tape recordings, computer printouts, or scientific surveys, when coupled with evidence showing that a particular process or system produces an accurate result when employed and that the process or system was in fact employed, constitutes sufficient evidence that the result is what it purports to be. *People v. Black,* 84 Ill. App. 3d 1050, 40 Ill. Dec. 322, 406 N.E.2d 23 (1980). Underlying documents and physical items need not be introduced but may have to be made available to the opposing party. *See* §1006 infra. The reliability of instruments used and of substances employed for comparison purposes need not be determined independently by the person performing the test. *People v. Schlig,* 120 Ill. App. 3d 561, 76 Ill. Dec. 144, 458 N.E.2d 544 (1983).

Computer-generated records may be introduced into evidence if a sufficient foundation is laid establishing that the electronic computing equipment is recognized as standard, the particular computer produces an accurate record when properly employed and operated, the particular computer was properly employed and operated in the matter at hand, and the entries were made in the regular course of business at or reasonably near the happening of the event recorded by or from someone within the business possessing personal knowledge, unless the court determines that the sources of information, method, or time of preparation indicate lack of trustworthiness. *Grand Liquor Co. v. Department of Revenue,* 67 Ill. 2d 195, 10 Ill. Dec. 472, 367 N.E.2d 1238 (1977); *Riley v. Jones Bros. Constr. Co.,* 198 Ill. App. 3d 822, 144 Ill. Dec. 924, 556 N.E.2d 602 (1990); *People v. Hendricks,* 145 Ill. App. 3d 71, 99 Ill. Dec. 20, 495 N.E.2d 85 (1986); *People v. Mormon,* 97 Ill. App. 3d 556, 52 Ill. Dec. 856, 422 N.E.2d 1065 (1981); *Department of Mental Health v. Beil,* 44 Ill. App. 3d 402, 2 Ill. Dec. 655, 357 N.E.2d 875 (1976). *Cf. Estate of Buddeke,* 49 Ill. App. 3d 431, 7 Ill. Dec. 285, 364 N.E.2d 446 (1977), declaring it reversible error to permit introduction of computer printout of hospital patient's account without supporting testimony of a witness as to the correctness of the figures and supporting documentation as to what was used to produce the figures. *See* §§803.10 and 803.11 supra; *see also* §901.6 supra, discussing sound recordings.

The authentication of "faxed" documents was addressed in *People v. Hagan,* 145 Ill. 2d 287, 164 Ill. Dec. 578, 583 N.E.2d 494 (1991), where the Supreme Court incorrectly looked for guidance to computer printouts, supra, which incorporate requirements for the introduction of business records. Faxed documents are properly authenticated by the introduction of evidence sufficient to support a finding either that the documents received accurately reflect the documents "faxed," or that the documents "faxed" were accurately received, which itself requires evidence that the machines employed to send and receive the fax are capable of producing an accurate reproduction when properly employed and that in the particular case the machines were properly employed. In addition it will be necessary to establish through the introduction of sufficient evidence that the faxed document originated with and was received by those asserted to have accomplished such tasks. *See generally* Graham, Handbook of Federal Evidence §901.9 (4th ed. 1996).

An e-mail message may be authenticated through various traditional common law methods such as the reply doctrine, distinctive characteristics, chain of custody, or process or system similar to the foundation presented above with respect to faxed documents. To further insure the accuracy of the message and the identity of the sender a digital signature, created and verified by cryptography, may be utilized. *See generally* Digital Signature Guideline: Legal Infrastructure for Certification Authorities and Secure Electronic Commerce, Information Security Committee, Section of Science and Technology, American Bar Association (1996).

With respect to proof of public records relating to a person's driving by fax or e-mail, *see* 625 ILCS 5/2-123(g) 6.

Evidence as to the process or system and its accuracy may sometimes come from an expert witness or be judicially noticed, §202.2 supra. In still other instances authentication is provided by statute, §901.11 infra. *People v. Black,* 84 Ill. App. 3d 1050, 40 Ill. Dec. 322, 406 N.E.2d 23 (1980), proper foundation for admission of breathalyzer examination includes evidence that the test was performed according to the Department of Public Health's uniform standard.

It is probably fair to say that in most instances evidence of the results of such a process or system is simply admitted without any objection being raised as to the capacity of the process or system, properly employed, to produce an accurate result. This is especially true, for example, where a physician testifies to the results of a test such as an electroencephalogram.

§901.11   Method Provided by Statute or Rule

Authentication or identification is sufficient if made in compliance with any statute or rule of the Illinois Supreme Court.

With respect to statutes, see, e.g., 625 ILCS 5/11-501.2, chemical tests of bodily substance for intoxication; 750 ILCS 45/1-45/26, blood tests for paternity; 765 ILCS 5/35, duly acknowledged title documents. See also §1002.2 infra for statutory provisions for authentication of certain former testimony. For statutory provisions making a fact presumptive or prima facie evidence of another fact, see §902.9 infra.

Certain Illinois Supreme Court rules also provide for authentication or identification. For instance, Supreme Court Rule 216(a) and (b) provide for requests to admit facts and the genuineness of documents; interrogatories, Rule 213; and depositions, Rules 202-212. The pretrial conference, Rule 218, may be employed for the same purpose. In addition, Supreme Court Rule 207(b)(1) provides that a record of a deposition properly certified requires no further proof of authenticity. Finally, Supreme Court Rule 191 provides that with respect to (1) motions for summary judgment, Code of Civil Procedure §2-1005, 735 ILCS 5/2-1005, (2) motions for involuntary dismissal, 735 ILCS 5/2-619, and (3) a special appearance to contest jurisdiction, 735 ILCS 5/2-301, affidavits shall have attached to them "sworn or certified copies of all papers upon which affiant relies." *See also* Supreme Court Rule 216(d), relating to authentication of public records, discussed in §901.8 supra.

§902   Self-Authentication

§902.1   *An Overview*

Certain kinds of evidence inherently possess sufficient indicia of authenticity on their face to support a finding that the item is what it purports to be. Thus evidence in each of the eight categories discussed in §902 is self-authenticating; no extrinsic evidence as to authentication or identification is required. The rationale in support of these instances of self-authentication is that the likelihood of fabrication or honest error is so slight in comparison with the time and expense involved in authentication or identification that extrinsic evidence is not required for a *prima facie* case of admissibility. Evidence of nonauthenticity is, however, not foreclosed. *See* §901.1 supra.

Out-of-court statements admitted as self-authenticating, i.e., sufficiently establishing that the writing offered into evidence is as purported to be, are received in evidence to establish the truth of the matter asserted. The concept of self-authentication thus operates as a hearsay exception on the limited question of authenticity. It does not, however, create a hearsay exception for matters asserted to be true in the self-authenticated writing itself. Although the writing may be self-authenticating, the writing must still meet other requirements with respect to its contents such as the Hearsay Rule, §801 supra, and the Original Writing Rule, §1002 infra, in order to be admitted.

With respect to each of the eight categories, which follow, the writing itself is self-authenticating when presented in court. A writing is not self-authenticating when a witness in court testifies that a given document observed out of court was, for example, a newspaper. The rationale of sufficient indicia of reliability requires actual production in court of the item claimed to be self-authenticating. To the extent *People v. Drake*, 131 Ill. App. 3d 466, 86 Ill. Dec. 639, 475 N.E.2d 1018 (1985) and *People v. Mikolajewski*, 272 Ill. App. 3d 311, 208 Ill. Dec. 443, 649 N.E.2d 499 (1995) are contrary they should not be followed. If the item is not produced, authentication should proceed through the production of evidence, §901.1 supra, rather than under the concept of self-authentication. Thus the requirement of actual production of the item as a prerequisite to self-authentication operates independently of the Original Writing Rule, §1002.1 infra.

§902.2 Certified Copies of Public and Corporate Records

Considerations of inconvenience and danger of loss or damage in removing a public record from its usual place of keeping led to the common law rule that a public record may be proved by a copy certified by the custodian under his official seal if he has one. *Stevison v. Earnest*, 80 Ill. 513 (1875); *People v. Brown*, 194 Ill. App. 3d 958, 143 Ill. Dec. 5, 553 N.E.2d 712 (1990); The certification is *prima facie* evidence of authenticity. See §301.4 supra; *People v. White*, 24 Ill. App. 2d 324, 164 N.E.2d 823 (1960); *People v. Smith* 113 Ill. App. 3d 101, 68 Ill. Dec. 669, 446 N.E.2d 575 (1983) (certified copy of record of Secretary of State is *prima facie* evidence that a driver's license has been revoked. 625 ILCS 5/2-108, 5/6-117). The copy must be a literal one, rather than a statement of its substance or effect. *Golder v. Bressler*, 105 Ill. 419 (1883), error to admit certificate of Secretary of State that his records showed appointment of named persons as trustees of State Bank of Illinois by governor, instead of actual copy of record. Matters provable by certified copy of public records include only matters that the officer is under a duty to record and that affirmatively appear of record. *Compare St. Louis Pressed Steel Co. v. Schorr*, 303 Ill. 476, 135 N.E. 766 (1922), certificate of secretary of Industrial Commission that files were lost inadmissible, *with People v. Love*, 310 Ill. 558, 142 N.E. 204 (1924), certificate of Secretary of State admissible to show failure to file documents under Securities Law (*semble* 815 ILCS 5/15). Where use of a chart, summary or calculation is appropriate, *see* §1006.1 infra, a certificate detailing such information and certifying that such information is contained in the records of the public office will be received. *Department of Pub. Aid v. Estate of Wall*, 81 Ill. App. 3d 394, 36 Ill. Dec. 798, 401 N.E.2d 639 (1980), certificate of director of Illinois Department of Public Aid presenting list compiled from records on file with the department indicating payments made was properly received in evidence. The concept of what is an official record has been applied liberally. *People v. Dolgin*, 415 Ill. 434, 114 N.E.2d 389 (1953), certified copy of letter from meter manufacturer in file of Revenue Department properly admitted in prosecution under Cigarette Tax Act (35 ILCS 130/10).

The common law rule has also been incorporated and expanded in numerous statutes. For example, proof of records of courts, municipalities, and private corporations in civil actions is treated in the Code of Civil Procedure, 735 ILCS 5/8-1202 to 5/8-1205:

> Section 8-1202.   The papers, entries and records of courts may be proved by a copy thereof certified under the signature of the clerk having the custody thereof, and the seal of the court, or by the judge of the court if there is no clerk.
>
> Section 8-1203.   The papers, entries, records and ordinances, or parts thereof, of any city, village, town or county, may be proved by a copy thereof, certified under the signature of the clerk or the keeper thereof, and the corporate seal, if there be any; if not, under his or her signature and private seal.
>
> Section 8-1204.   The papers, entries and records of any corporation or incorporated association may be proved by a copy thereof, certified under the signature of the secretary, clerk, cashier or other keeper of the same. If the corporation or incor-

porated association has a seal, the same shall be affixed to such certificate.

Section 8-1205.   The certificate of any such clerk of a court, city, village, county, or secretary, clerk, cashier, or other keeper of any such papers, entries, records or ordinances, shall contain a statement that such person is the keeper of the same, and if there is no seal, shall so state.

See also 305 ILCS 5/10-13.4:

Proof of Records. The books, papers, records and memoranda of the Illinois Department or of the administrative enforcement unit, or parts thereof, may be proved in any hearing, investigation, or legal proceeding by a photostatic or other copy thereof under the certificate of the Director of the Illinois Department. Such certified copy shall, without further proof, be admitted into evidence in the hearing before the Illinois Department or in any other legal proceeding.

A certification is sufficient compliance with such statutes, no opportunity to cross-examine the affiant being required. *Glos v. Garrett,* 219 Ill. 208, 76 N.E. 373 (1906). A facsimile signature of the proper person accompanying the certification is also adequate. *Estate of Zander v. Illinois Dept. of Public Aid,* 242 Ill. App. 3d 774, 183 Ill. Dec. 233, 611 N.E.2d 86 (1993).

Cases interpreting the foregoing statutes have sometimes applied the term *foreign* to sister states, a practice that should be abandoned. *Garden City Sand Co. v. Miller,* 157 Ill. 225, 41 N.E. 753 (1895), 8/1202 supra, applies to domestic and foreign judgments (Michigan); *People v. Funk,* 325 Ill. 57, 155 N.E. 838 (1927), 8/1202 supra, does not apply in criminal cases to foreign judgments (Missouri). Proof of a sister state judgment has to be made in accordance with 735 ILCS 5/12-650 to 5/12-657, a statute enacted pursuant to the full faith and credit clauses of the Constitution of the United States. *People v. Funk* supra.

With respect to transcripts of former testimony, *see* §1002.2 infra.

§902.3   *Foreign Public Documents*

Certification of public records of a foreign country is governed generally by the common law. *In re Ersch's Estate,* 29 Ill. 2d 572, 579-580, 195 N.E.2d 149, (1964), held that a document indicating the name of a Polish city had been changed was properly certified. The document provided:

> The Presidium of the National Council of the City of Bielsko-Biala certify hereby, that the locality LIPNIK, county Bielsko-Biala was in the year 1939 anected by the German occupations forces into the "Reich" and named "Kunsendorf." After the liberation in February 1945 the Polish Authorities have restored the formerly named LIPNIK. This was issue on the ground of general acts of law.

The document bore the seal of the National Council of the city and was signed by the chief of the division of Internal Affairs. The authenticity of the signature, seal, and the contents of the certificate were further certified to by the chief of the division of Internal Affairs of the Presidium of the National Council of the Province of Katowice, and the ministry of Foreign Affairs certified to the authenticity of the signature and the seal of the division chief. This was accompanied by legalization by the United States consul at Warsaw and the statement of the Polish consul in Chicago that the authentication was in accord with the laws of Poland.

Cf. the requirements for certification of foreign public documents provided in Federal Rule of Evidence 902(3), 65 F.R.D. 131, 162 (1975), as amended:

> A document purporting to be executed or attested in an official capacity by a person authorized by the laws of a foreign country to make the execution or attestation, and accompanied by a final certification as to the genuineness of the signature and official position (A) of the executing or attesting person, or (B) of any foreign official whose certificate of genuineness of signature and official position relates to the execution or attestation or is in a chain of certificates of genuiness of

signature and official position relating to the execution or attestation. A final certification may be made by a secretary or embassy or legation, consul general, consul, vice consul, or consular agent of the United States, or a diplomatic or consular official of the foreign country assigned or accredited to the United States. If reasonable opportunity has been given to all parties to investigate the authenticity and accuracy of official documents, the court may, for good cause shown, order that they be treated as presumptively authentic without final certification or permit them to be evidenced by an attested summary with or without final certification.

With respect to title documents, *see* §902.7 infra.

§902.4   *Official Publications*

Books, pamphlets, or other publications purporting to be issued by public authority are self-authenticating, *Illinois Cent. R. Co. v. Warriner,* 229 Ill. 91, 82 N.E. 246 (1907); 735 ILCS 5/8-1104(a), printed statute books of United States, the state, and the several states and territories purporting to be printed under authority shall be evidence; *id.,* 8/1106, books of reports of decisions of the courts of the United States, the state and the several states purporting to be published by authority admissible in evidence; 65 ILCS 5/1-2-6, municipal ordinance printed in book or pamphlet form is *prima facie* evidence of content. With respect to *prima facie* evidence, *see* §302.8 supra.

§902.5   *Newspapers and Periodicals*

Printed materials purporting to be newspapers or periodicals are self-authenticating. The realities of newspaper and periodical publications, including items such as telephone directories, make the risk of forgery extremely low. *Consolidated Perfume Co. v. National Bank of the Republic,* 86 Ill. App. 642 (1899), trade publication admitted to establish market value of corporate stock. *See* §803.18 supra for discussion of the hearsay exception for market reports and commercial publications. *See also Alimissis v. Nanos,* 171 Ill. App. 3d 1005, 121 Ill. Dec. 826, 525 N.E.2d 1133 (1988).

Notices and advertisements appearing in newspapers and periodicals should be considered self-authenticating with respect to the fact that they were inserted by authority of the person purporting to have inserted them. *Contra Mann v. Russell,* 11 Ill. 586 (1850), advertisement in newspaper purporting to bear defendant's name not admissible unless shown to have emanated from him.

§902.6   Trade Inscriptions and the Like

Inscriptions, signs, tags, or labels purporting to have been affixed in the course of business and indicating ownership, control, or origin, should be considered self-authenticating. The basis for self-authentication of these items is the day-to-day reliance by members of the public on their correctness and the unlikelihood of fabrication. *St. Louis Connecting Ry. v. Altgen,* 210 Ill. 213, 71 N.E. 377 (1904); *Pittsburgh, Ft. W. & C. Ry. v. Callaghan,* 157 Ill. 406, 41 N.E. 909 (1895). *See, e.g., People v. Mikolajewski,* 272 Ill. App. 3d 311, 208 Ill. Dec. 443, 649 N.E.2d 499 (1995) (price tag on merchandise quoting Handbook); *Robeson v. Greyhound Lines, Inc.,* 257 Ill. App. 278 (1930), inscriptions on train or bus *prima facie* evidence of ownership or control. Moreover, many cases will involve trademarks and brand names registered under federal and state laws prohibiting others from using them. *See also People v. Drake,* 131 Ill. App. 3d 466, 86 Ill. Dec. 639, 475 N.E.2d 1018 (1985) (store code number affixed to a label placed on merchandise was sufficient authentication). Similarly, a label required by law to be affixed to a product constitutes *prima facie* evidence of the contents of the product. *In Interest of T.D.,* 115 Ill. App. 3d 872, 71 Ill. Dec. 20, 450 N.E.2d 455 (1983), and a stated advertised price sufficiently establishes full retail value. 720 ILCS 5/16A-2.2.

§902.7 *Acknowledged Title Documents*

A certificate of acknowledgment of a title document acknowledged in accordance with 765 ILCS 5/24 is sufficient for the admission of the original in evidence without further proof of authenticity, *id.,* 5/35. *Matter of Estate of Shedrick,* 122 Ill. App. 3d 861, 78 Ill. Dec. 462, 462 N.E.2d 581 (1984). Upon a proper showing that the original of an acknowledged and recorded title document is not within the power of the party to produce, the record or a certified copy is admissible. *Id.,* 5/35.

The certificate of acknowledgment should provide in one form or another that the person executing the particular document in question has (1) come before a public official or a notary public authorized to take an acknowledgment, (2) that his identity was known to the said official or notary, and (3) that he stated to the notary that he executed the document of his own free will. *See also id.,* 5/20(4), providing for acknowledgment for person in armed forces. If a partnership, the person should indicate that he acknowledged the document on behalf of the partnership. If a corporation, the person should indicate that he executed the document or affixed the corporation seal, if so affixed, or both, by authorization of the corporation.

Notice that the mere execution of a jurat by the notary public does not establish the identity of a person being sworn.

No requirement is imposed that there be a further authentication, often referred to as a flag, of the notary's authority to take the acknowledgment or the genuineness of the notary's signature. *Id.,* 5/20. With respect to out-of-state or foreign acknowledgments, *see id.,* 5/20, 5/22.

§902.8 *Commercial Papers and Related Documents*

Commercial paper, signatures thereon, and documents relating thereto to the extent provided by the Uniform Commercial Code are self-authenticating. The following provisions of the Uniform Commercial Code are relevant: (1) 810 ILCS 5/1-202 makes certain documents required by an existing contract "*prima facie* evidence" of their own authenticity; (2) *id.*, 5/3-308 presumes the genuineness of the signatures on negotiable instruments; and (3) *id.*, 5/8-105(3) creates a presumption as to the genuineness of a signature on a negotiable instrument.

With respect to *prima facie* evidence, *see* §302.8 supra; as to the terms *presumption* and *presume, see* discussion of presumptions under the Uniform Commercial Code, §302.6 supra.

§902.9   Presumptions Under Acts of Congress and by Statute

Any signature, document, or other matter declared by Act of Congress or statute to be presumptively or *prima facie* genuine or authentic is self-authenticating. Statutory provisions may employ the terms *presumption* or *prima facie evidence* in reference to authentication. *See, e.g.,* 325 ILCS 325/33, order over seal of Department of Engineering *prima facie* proof that signature of Director is genuine; 65 ILCS 5/1-2-6, municipal ordinance presented in book is *prima facie* evidence of content; 735 ILCS 5/8-1201, printed copies of schedules, tariffs or rates, etc., of Interstate Commerce Commission *presumed* to be correct copies; 20 ILCS 2505/39c-(1)(b), signature on documents faxed to the Department of Revenue when authorized by rule, is *prima facie* evidence for all purposes that the document was actually signed by the person whose signature appears in the facsimile. For presumptions under the Uniform Commercial Code, *see* §902.8 supra.

With respect to presumptions generally, *see* §302.1; as to *prima facie* evidence, *see* §302.8. supra.

With respect to federal presumptions to be applied when federal law provides the rule of decision, *see* §302.11 supra. A partial listing of federal presumptions may be found in 4 Weinstein's Evidence ¶902(10)[01] (1983).

§903 Subscribing Witness's Testimony Unnecessary

§903.1 Commentary

An attesting or subscribing witness is a person who, at the request or with the consent of the maker, places her name on the document for the purpose of making thereby an implied or expressed statement that the document was then known by her to have been executed by the purporting maker. 4 Wigmore, Evidence §1292 (Chadbourn rev. 1972).

The ancient common law rule required in the case of all attested documents either the production of each attesting witness or a satisfactory accounting for his or her absence. This rule was abrogated generally by statute, 735 ILCS 5/8-1601; the testimony of a subscribing witness is not necessary to authenticate a writing unless the law governing the validity of the writing specifically requires attestation, such as wills. Moreover, 755 ILCS 5/6-4 now permits either the testimony or affidavit of attesting witness to a will to admit the will to probate, with an affidavit being admissible without first accounting for availability.

ARTICLE X
Original Writing Rule

§1007   Testimony or Written Admission of Party
        §1007.1   Commentary

§1008   Functions of Court and Jury
        §1008.1   Commentary

§1001   Definition

§1001.1   *The Original Writing (Best Evidence) Rule: Introduction*

Article X addresses what has misleadingly been named the Best Evidence Rule, a rule of preference for the production of the original of a writing, recording, or photograph when the contents of the item are sought to be proved. *Trustees of Soldiers' Orphans' Home v. Shaffer*, 53 Ill. 243 (1872). Better described as the Original Writing Rule, the rule applies only to writings, recordings, and photographs; there is no general rule of evidence that a party must produce the best evidence that the nature of the case permits. *People v. Tharpe-Williams*, 286 Ill. App. 3d 605, 221 Ill. Dec. 914, 676 N.E.2d 717 (1997). *See e.g., People v. Ristau*, 363 Ill. 583, 2 N.E.2d 833 (1936), condition of clothing may be described without producing the clothing itself; *Jones v. Greyhound Corp.*, 46 Ill. App. 2d 364, 197 N.E.2d 58 (1964), *rev'd on other grounds*, 33 Ill. 2d 83, 210 N.E.2d 562 (1965), if a sufficient foundation was laid establishing that brake drum examined by mechanic testifying to its condition was in the same condition prior to the accident, it need not be produced; *Sheldon Livestock Co. v. Western Engine Co.*, 13 Ill. App. 3d 993, 301 N.E.2d 485 (1973), witness may testify to lost profits, provided corporation's books produced for in-court inspection; *Jones v. Consolidation Coal Co.*, 174 Ill. App. 3d 38, 123 Ill. Dec. 649, 528 N.E.2d 33 (1988), the cost of repairs actually made may be proved without introduction of a paid repair bill. *See* §1006 infra.

The rule developed at common law to provide a guarantee against inaccuracy and fraud by insistence upon production at trial of original documents. While the great expansion of pretrial discovery has measurably reduced the need for the rule, it still has significant application in criminal cases, where a greater limitation on discovery exists, and in unanticipated situations. McCormick, Evidence §231 (4th ed. 1992).

The requirement of production of the original when the contents are in issue is addressed in §1002 infra; the admissibility of a duplicate under most circumstances is discussed in §1003.1 infra. Definitions of the terms *original* and *duplicate,* along with those of *writings, recordings,* and *photographs,* are suggested in §§1001.2 and 1003.1 infra. The circumstances under which the original is not required are stated in §1004 infra. To be admissible the writing or record must of course be relevant, §401.1 supra; be properly authenticated, §§901, 902 supra; and either not be hearsay or meet the requirements of a hearsay exception, §§801-805 supra.

With respect to the nature of an original, *see* §1001.2 to 1001.4 infra; as to when the contents of a writing, recording, or photograph are in issue, *see* §§1002.1 to 1002.3 infra.

With respect to public records, *see* §1005.1 infra.

§1001.2　Nature of an Original: An Overview

An "original" of a writing is the writing or recording itself or any counterpart intended to have the same effect by a person executing or issuing it. An "original" of a photograph undoubtedly includes the negative or any print therefrom. A "writing" and "recording" in today's society may reasonably be thought to consist of letters, words, or numbers, or their equivalent, set down by handwriting, typewriting, printing, photostating, photographing, magnetic impulse, mechanical or electronic recording, or other form of data compilation. *See generally* Federal Rule of Evidence 1001, 65 F.R.D. 131, 163 (1975). If data is stored in a computer or similar device, any printout or other output readable by sight, shown to reflect the data accurately, is properly classified as an original. *See People v. Sadaka,* 174 Ill. App. 3d 260, 123 Ill. Dec. 738, 528 N.E.2d 283 (1988). *Compare People v. Rushton,* 254 Ill. App. 3d 156, 193 Ill. Dec. 827, 626 N.E.2d 1378 (1993) (printout of computer record is "merely" a copy; incorrectly decided). Thus computer printouts are admissible in satisfaction of a statutory requirement that a "writing" be introduced. *People v. Menssen,* 263 Ill. App. 3d 946, 201 Ill. Dec. 669, 636 N.E.2d 1101 (1994); *People v. Rushton,* 254 Ill. App. 3d 156, 193 Ill. Dec. 827, 626 N.E.2d 1378 (1993); *People v. Ethridge,* 243 Ill. App. 3d 446, 183 Ill. Dec. 61, 610 N.E.2d 1305 (1993).

The question of whether a particular writing or record is an original must be answered in light of the purpose of the Original Writing Rule. The emphasis is upon assuring accuracy as to the terms of the writing, recording, or photograph by avoiding the uncertainties of recollection that are inherent in oral testimony and the chances of mistake that may be present in the handmade copy. *See Humphreys v. Collier,* 1 Ill. 297 (1829).

The original writing or recording is the writing or recording whose content is in issue, taking into account the particular situation. *Prussing v. Jackson,* 208 Ill. 85, 69 N.E. 771 (1904), in libel action arising from publication of a letter in a newspaper, the original held to be the letter itself and not what was printed, the action being against the writer and not against the newspaper publisher; *Fuchs & Lang Mfg. Co. v. Kittredge & Co.,* 242 Ill. 88, 89 N.E. 723 (1909), the blueprint from which the machine in controversy was assembled, rather than the drawing of which it was a copy, held to be the original for purposes of showing the operation of the machine.

The mere fact of identicalness does not make a copy into an original. *King v. Worthington,* 73 Ill. 161 (1874), regardless of accuracy, letterpress copy not an original. However, if the party executing or issuing intends that a writing, recording or photograph constituting a counterpart that otherwise would be considered only a copy have the same effect as the original, the counterpart then is an original. Thus, with respect to instruments executed in multiple copies, each is an original, *Hayes v. Wagner*, 220 Ill. 256, 77 N.E. 211 (1906), without regard to whether each party executed only one or all copies, for it is the intent of the parties that controls. Counterparts of writings, recordings, or photographs produced by the same impression as the original, or from the same matrix, or by means of photography or equivalent measures, if intended to be regarded by the party as originals, are also originals. *People v. Chicago, R.I. & P. Ry.*, 329 Ill. 467, 160 N.E. 841 (1928), printed election notices and ballots. Thus each photostatic or xerographic copy of a single original instrument constitutes an original if so intended by the parties.

Finally, a party by his conduct may confer the status of an original upon a writing, recording, or photograph originally produced as a copy. *People v. Munday*, 280 Ill. 32, 117 N.E. 286 (1917), retained carbons of letters in files of insolvent bank admissible as original "records" against a dominant officer in prosecution for conspiracy to defraud bank's customers; *People v. Stone*, 349 Ill. 52, 181 N.E. 648 (1932), duplicate sales slips mailed by a commission buyer to the seller held to be originals; *Illinois Tuberculosis Assn. v. Springfield Marine Bank*, 282 Ill. App. 14 (1935), carbon of a bank statement mailed to the depositor held to be an original. In the latter two cases it should be noted that the documents were offered against the party who gave them currency. *Cf. People v. Hauke*, 335 Ill. 217, 167 N.E. 1 (1929), a carbon of a typed confession held to be an original, but whether either copy was signed does not appear.

With respect to whether the contents of a writing, recording, or photograph are in issue, *see* §§1002.1 to 1002.3 infra; as to photographs, *see also* §1002.4 infra.

§1001.3   *Nature of an Original: Telegrams*

The original of a telegram is determined by analogy to contract rules governing risk of error in transmission. If the party sending the message selects the telegraph as the means of transmission, the original is the writing delivered to the addressee, but if the addressee makes the selection, then the original is the writing delivered to the telegraph company. *Anheuser-Busch Brewing Assn. v. Hutmacher,* 127 Ill. 652, 21 N.E. 626 (1889). If what would be the original if written is instead telephoned, the Original Writing Rule is inapplicable. *See* §1002.1 infra.

§1001.4   Nature of an Original: Business and Public Records

Retained copies, however produced, may qualify as the originals of business or public records. *Chicago & E.I.R. Co. v. Zapp,* 209 Ill. 339, 70 N.E. 623 (1904), letterpress copies of reports sent to Washington, retained by local weather bureau, held to be original public records; *People v. Munday,* 280 Ill. 32, 117 N.E. 286 (1917), retained carbons in files of insolvent bank held to be original records of bank. This principle is incorporated in the Code of Civil Procedure by its expansion to include "any other record or document" and the addition of the following:

> Where such book of original entries or any other record or document has been photographed, microphotographed, microfilmed, optical imaged, or otherwise reproduced either in the usual course of business, or pursuant to any statute of this State authorizing the reproduction of public records, papers or documents, and the reproduction, in either case, complies with the minimum standards of quality for permanent records approved by the State Records Commission, then such reproduction shall be deemed to be an original record, book or document for all purposes, including introduction in evidence in all courts or administrative agencies. [735 ILCS 5/8-401.]

Section 8-401 of the Code of Civil Procedure, *id.,* applies by its terms solely where the claim "[is] founded on a book, account or any other record or document. . . ." and only in connection with the exception to the Dead Man's Act, 735 ILCS 5/8-201, provided in subsection (c) thereof. *See* §606.6 supra. Where the action is not so founded, the stringent requirements for treating copies of business records as originals set forth in §8-401 are not applicable. Thus a carbon copy of ledger sheets was held admissible where complaint was for recovery of goods and material delivered and also upon an account stated. *Pope v. Kaleta,* 90 Ill. App. 2d 61, 234 N.E.2d 109 (1967); *Soft Water Serv. v. M. Suson Enter.,* 39 Ill. App. 3d 1035, 351 N.E.2d 264 (1976).

In criminal matters, 725 ILCS 5/115-5(b) provides as follows with respect to the admissibility of copies as originals:

If any business, institution, member of a profession or calling, or any department or agency of government, in the regular course of business or activity has kept or recorded any memorandum, writing, entry, print, representation or combination thereof, of any act, transaction, occurrence, or event, and in the regular course of business has caused any or all of the same to be recorded, copied, or reproduced by any photographic, photostatic, microfilm, micro-card, miniature photographic, or other process which accurately reproduces or forms a durable medium for so reproducing the original, the original may be destroyed in the regular course of business unless its preservation is required by law. Such reproduction, when satisfactorily identified, is as admissible in evidence as the original itself in any proceeding whether the original is in existence or not and an enlargement or facsimile of such reproduction is likewise admissible in evidence if the original reproduction is in existence and available for inspection under direction of court. The introduction of a reproduced record, enlargement, or facsimile does not preclude admission of the original. This Section shall not be construed to exclude from evidence any document or copy thereof which is otherwise admissible under the rules of evidence.

See People v. Mormon, 97 Ill. App. 3d 556, 52 Ill. Dec. 856, 422 N.E.2d 1065 (1981). With respect to the admissibility of hospital or medical records, *see* §803.11 supra; as to police investigative reports, *see* §803.13 supra.

Consistent with the purpose of the Original Writing Rule, the proper test for treating photostatic copies as originals focuses solely on the intent of the person while not imposing any requirement as to the quality of the copy. Since most retained copies, and copies of retained copies of business and public records, are intended by the person to have the same effect as the original, they should be treated as originals.

In *People v. Wells*, 380 Ill. 347, 44 N.E.2d 32 (1942), a prosecution for forgery, it was ruled that photographic Recordak copies of other allegedly forged checks to show the intent of the accused could not be regarded as originals. The decision, which predates 725 ILCS 5/115-5(b), is not necessarily inconsistent, for it may be distinguished on the ground that the appearance of the original is of particular importance on an issue of forgery and therefore a photographic copy is not an appropriate method of proof. *See* §1003.1 infra.

§1002   Requirement of Original

§1002.1   An Overview

To prove the content of a writing, recording, or photograph, the original writing, recording, or photograph is required, except as otherwise provided by decision, rule, or statute. *Larson v. Commonwealth Edison Co.*, 33 Ill. 2d 316, 211 N.E.2d 247 (1965). Thus, in order for the Original Writing Rule to apply, the contents of a writing, recording, or photograph must be sought to be proved. If the contents are not sought to be proved, then evidence other than the writing, recording, or photograph is admissible without reference to satisfaction of the Original Writing Rule.

When a happening or transaction itself assumes the form

of a writing, recording, or photograph, as with a deed or a written contract, proof of the happening or transaction necessarily involves the contents of the writing and calls for application of the Original Writing Rule. If, however, the event or happening does not take the form of a writing, recording, or photograph, it may ordinarily be proved by other evidence even though a writing, recording, or photograph was made. The proof is directed to the occurrence of the happening or transaction and not to the contents of the writing, recording, or photograph. The Original Writing Rule applies in this situation only when the happening or transaction is sought to be proved by the writing, recording, or photograph, not when it is sought to be proved by other evidence. *People v. Tharpe-Williams,* 286 Ill. App. 3d 605, 221 Ill. Dec. 914, 676 N.E.2d 717 (1997). To illustrate, consider an oral confession of an accused made to a police officer that is simultaneously tape recorded and taken down by a stenographer. Assume further that the stenographer types up her notes and that a copy of the confession is given to the defendant to sign. The police officer may testify to the oral confession without accounting for either the tape recording or the signed confession. If the police officer, however, attempts to testify as to the content of the tape recording or the content of the independently relevant signed confession, because the content of a writing, recording or photograph is being sought to be proved, the Original Writing Rule requires that such evidence be introduced by having the tape recording or signed confession authenticated and admitted into evidence prior to publication of its content to the jury. *See Jones v. Consolidation Coal Co.,* 174 Ill. App. 3d 38, 123 Ill. Dec. 649, 528 N.E.2d 33 (1988), the Original Writing Rule does not apply where a party seeks to prove a fact that has an existence independent of any writing by evidence other than a writing made to memorialize the fact; *People v. Spencer,* 264 Ill. 124, 106 N.E. 219 (1914), person hearing oral confession may testify thereto, though confession was taken in shorthand and transcribed; *Branch v. Lee,* 373 Ill. 333, 26 N.E.2d 88 (1940), payment may be proved by parol, though receipt was given; *People v. Mitchell,* 240 Ill. App. 281 (1926), number of bonds issued by corporation provable by parol, though appearing in records of corporation; *Sheldon Livestock Co. v. Western Engine Co.,* 13 Ill. App. 3d 993, 301 N.E.2d 485 (1973), witness may testify to lost profits provided corporation's books produced for in-court inspection; *Continental Ill. Natl. Bank & Trust Co. of Chicago v. Eastern Ill. W. Co.,* 31 Ill. App. 3d 148, 334 N.E.2d 96 (1975), letters setting forth plaintiff's expenses incurred as a result of defendant's mortgage default not barred by rule; *People ex rel. Person v. Miller,* 56 Ill. App. 3d 450, 13 Ill. Dec. 920, 371 N.E.2d 1012 (1977), plaintiff may testify to lack of payment for child support as such fact exists independent of any record of social services department; *In re Marriage of Collins,* 154 Ill. App. 3d 655, 107 Ill. Dec. 109, 506 N.E.2d 1000 (1987), attorney may testify to time and services expended as such facts exist independently of any writings; *People v. Boshears,* 228 Ill. App. 3d 677, 170 Ill. Dec. 507, 592 N.E.2d 1187 (1992) and *People v. Pelc,* 177 Ill. App. 3d 737, 126 Ill. Dec. 867, 532 N.E.2d 552 (1988), qualification to give a breathalyzer examination may be established by means other than by introduction of license; *People v. Tharpe-Williams,* 286 Ill. App. 3d 605, 221 Ill. Dec. 914, 676 N.E.2d 717 (1997), witness may testify to matter observed contemporaneously on a video monitor, even when a videotape recording was made of the event. *Dunn v. People,* 172 Ill. 582, 50 N.E. 137 (1898), in suggesting that a dying declaration reduced to writing and signed is within the rule, seems to miss the above distinction. Similarly, mere reference to a writing, recording, or photograph to prove its existence, execution or delivery but not its content does not call for application of the Original Writing Rule. Naturally there is often difficulty determining when the content is sought to be proved, and when the writing, recording, or photograph is being referred to for some other purpose. *See* 4 Wigmore, Evidence §1242 (Chadbourn rev. 1972). Nor does the Original Writing Rule apply when a witness testifies that books or records do *not* contain a particular entry. *Leischner v. Deere & Co.,* 127 Ill. App. 3d 175, 82 Ill. Dec. 120, 468 N.E.2d 182

(1984). *See also* Federal Advisory Committee's Note to Rule 1002, 56 F.R.D. 183, 342 (1973). However, where the witness's testimony constitutes a summary of the records, the original records must be made available to the opponent for inspection. *Kwai Paul Lam v. Northern Ill. Gas Co.,* 114 Ill. App. 3d 325, 70 Ill. Dec. 660, 449 N.E.2d 1007 (1983). *See also* 1006.1 infra.

With respect to statutory provisions relating to the rule, *see, e.g.,* 735 ILCS 5/8-401 and 725 ILCS 5/115-5(b), discussed in §1001.4 supra; as to Acts of Congress, *see* 5 Weinstein's Evidence ¶1002[04] (1983).

§1002.2   *Former Testimony; Depositions*

Testimony that was given on another occasion is a proper subject for the testimony of any witness who heard it, despite the fact that it was taken down in shorthand or otherwise contemporaneously recorded, thereby affording a means of proof far more accurate than the recollection of the witness. The Original Writing Rule does not apply, *Hutchings v. Corgan,* 59 Ill. 70 (1871), for it is the occurrence of the happening rather than the contents of the transcript that is sought to be proved.

In fact, even though the reporter's transcript was an official one, it has been asserted that the transcript is not in and of itself even acceptable evidence, except on appeal in the particular case. To prove testimony by use of the reporter's transcript, the reporter must be called to testify that the witness had been sworn, that certain questions were asked and answers given, that he had taken down the testimony in shorthand notes, and that the transcript was a correct and accurate reproduction of his notes. *People v. Berry,* 309 Ill. 511, 141 N.E. 132 (1923); *Vanderveen v. Yellow Cab Co.,* 89 Ill. App. 2d 91, 233 N.E.2d 68 (1968). In effect, the transcript was admitted under the recorded recollection exception to the Hearsay Rule. This attitude is clearly a carryover due to the nature of the old bill of exceptions, made from counsel's notes and designed only to present questions for review. *Roth v. Smith,* 54 Ill. 431 (1870). The advent of shorthand reporting removed the reasons for the bill of exceptions, but the old rule of exclusion apparently persists. *Illinois Cent. R. Co. v. Ashline,* 171 Ill. 313, 49 N.E. 521 (1898).

The strict foundation apparently once required for former testimony should no longer be followed. Several different avenues of proof of the prior testimony are potentially available: (1) by testimony of a firsthand observer of the former proceedings who can satisfy the court that he is able to remember the purport of all the witness said even if he cannot remember the exact words; (2) by the testimony of a firsthand observer who has refreshed his present recollection with a memorandum, such as the stenographer's notes or transcript; (3) by the official stenographer's notes or transcript which qualifies as a public record, §803.12 supra; or (4) by the notes of an observer at the trial if they meet the requirements of a memorandum of recorded recollection, §803.9 supra. In addition, of course, a certified copy of the transcript is self-authenticating, §902.2 supra.

Finally, a deposition certified and filed in accordance with the Supreme Court Rule 207(b)(1) is usable in evidence without further authentication.

Under the early procedure requiring the testimony at coroners' inquests to be written up and signed by the witness, the Original Writing Rule was held to be applicable, seemingly on the fallacious theory that the later signing converted what was originally said orally into a signed agreement. *Overtoom v. Chicago & E.I.R. Co., id.* The statute now provides alternatively for taking down the testimony in shorthand without signing by the witness, 55 ILCS 5/3-3031, which procedure, if followed, appears to eliminate application of the Original Writing Rule. The provision that the reporter shall certify the transcript as correct may well be construed as conferring an official status making it a permissible, though not required, method of proof. *See Carroll v. Krause,* 280 Ill. App. 52 (1935).

§1002.3   Cross-Examination on the Writing

Occasional statements are found that a witness who admits having signed a writing cannot then be cross-examined as to its contents, the writing being the best evidence thereof. *Momence Stone Co. v. Groves,* 197 Ill. 88, 64 N.E. 335 (1902); *Gerrard v. Porcheddu,* 243 Ill. App. 562 (1927). If the writing is desired as evidence of contradiction, it will, of course, be necessary to introduce or account for it in due course. However, the purpose of the questioning is not to establish the contents but to test the memory and veracity of the witness, which does not call for application of the Original Writing Rule at all. *Steele v. Bennett,* 50 Ill. App. 2d 70, 200 N.E.2d 10 (1964) (abstract only). Such a rule, to the extent it ever existed, is no longer followed. *See* §613.1 supra.

§1002.4   Photographs

Photographs, including still photographs, X-ray films, video tapes, and motion pictures, when their contents are in issue, should be subject to the Original Writing Rule. The original of a photograph should be defined to include the negative or any print therefrom. Federal Rule of Evidence 1001(3), 65 F.R.D. 131, 163 (1975).

The Original Writing Rule is said to apply to photographs only when the contents of the photograph possess independent probative value rather than being merely illustrative of a witness's testimony as to matters observed. *See* §401.8 supra. Photographic defamation, invasion of privacy, and charges of copyright infringement are instances where the contents of the photograph are sought to be proved. Use of an automatic photograph taken of a nighttime bank burglary requires that the contents of the photograph be proved, since there is presumably no one whose testimony the photograph may be said to illustrate. X-rays also fall into the latter category.

In a majority of instances the witness testifies that the photograph is a correct representation of events that she saw or of a scene with which she is familiar. Since the photograph itself is produced at trial and is in effect adopted by the witness as her testimony, no problem under the Original Writing Rule arises: the original is in fact in evidence. *See generally* Advisory Committee's Note to Federal Rule of Evidence 1002, 56 F.R.D. 183, 342 (1973).

As to the requirement of accuracy in photographic exhibits, *see* §401.8 supra.

§1003　Admissibility of Duplicates

§1003.1　Commentary

The common law authority does not specifically provide for the admissibility of duplicates in place of originals, although in practice it is very common for a duplicate to be introduced into evidence instead of an original so that the original may be maintained in its current location. For these purposes a duplicate is a counterpart produced by the same impression as the original, or from the same matrix; by means of photography, including enlargements and miniatures; by mechanical or electronic re-recording; by chemical reproduction; or by other equivalent technique that accurately reproduces the original. Federal Rule of Evidence 1001(4), 65 F.R.D. 131, 163 (1975). Thus a hand-produced copy cannot be a duplicate. A duplicate differs from a counterpart treated as an original in that a duplicate is neither intended by nor employed by a party as an original. *Schmidt v. Barr*, 333 Ill. 494, 165 N.E. 131 (1929), duplicate bank deposit slips, presumably carbons, not originals for purpose of proving deposits; *King v. Worthington*, 73 Ill. 161 (1874), letterpress copies not originals, regardless of accuracy.

Consideration should be given to making a duplicate admissible to the same extent as an original unless (1) a genuine question is raised as to the authenticity of the original or (2) in the circumstances it would be unfair to admit the duplicate in lieu of the original. *See* Federal Rule of Evidence 1003, 65 F.R.D. 131, 164 (1975). A duplicate, being a counterpart produced by a method providing assurance of accuracy and precision, provides a convenient substitute for an original under most circumstances. Thus under normal circumstances the convenience of placing into the record a photostatic or equivalent copy of an original should be provided for, since such a technical departure from the Original Writing Rule must almost inevitably be treated as harmless error. Where, however, there is some reason for the original itself to be required, such as where a genuine issue is raised as to its authenticity, the original would be required, and a duplicate could not be used since production of the original would facilitate resolution of the issue. *See People v. Wells,* 380 Ill. 347, 44 N.E.2d 32 (1942), discussed in §1001.5 supra; 4 Wigmore, Evidence §1179 (Chadbourn rev. 1972). A genuine question as to the accuracy of the duplicate as reflecting the original would also call for production of the original. *See People v. Bowman,* 95 Ill. App. 3d 1137, 51 Ill. Dec. 527, 420 N.E.2d 1085 (1981), stating that a duplicate "should be admissible in Illinois" as provided for in Federal Rules 1001(4) and 1003. *Accord Indian Valley Golf Club v. Long Grove,* 173 Ill. App. 3d 909, 123 Ill. Dec. 498, 527 N.E.2d 1273 (1988), Federal Rule of Evidence 1003 has been "implicitly" adopted in Illinois. Formal adoption of Federal Rule of Evidence 1003, 65 F.R.D. 131, 164 (1975), would eliminate many questions concerning admissibility of a facsimile or copy under 735 ILCS 5/8-401 and 725 ILCS 5/115-5(b), discussed infra. *See People v. Mormon,* 97 Ill. App. 3d 556, 52 Ill. Dec. 856, 422 N.E.2d 1065 (1981).

The admissibility of duplicates of business and public records prepared in the ordinary course of business is provided in civil cases by 735 ILCS 5/8-401, and in criminal matters by 725 ILCS 5/115-5(b). Both statutes are set forth in §1001.4 supra. The requirement that the duplicate be prepared in the ordinary course of business, thus making it an original for particular business purposes, obviously substantially curtails the usefulness of the statutory provisions. Moreover, 5/8-401 of the Code of Civil Procedure, *id.*, applies by its terms solely where the claim "[is] founded on a book account or any other record or document. . . ." and only in connection with the exception to the Dead Man's Act, 735 ILCS 5/8-201, provided in subsection (c) thereof. *See* §606.6 supra. On the other hand, Illinois Supreme Court Rule 216(d), applicable in civil proceedings, provides for the admissibility of a duplicate of a public record made in conjunction with litigation:

> If any public records are to be used as evidence, the party intending to use them may prepare a copy of them insofar as they are to be used, and may seasonably present the copy to the adverse party in notice by writing, and the copy shall thereupon be admissible in evidence as admitted facts in the case if otherwise admissible, except insofar as its inaccuracy is pointed out under oath by the adverse party in an affidavit filed and served within 14 days after service of the notice.

The admissibility of reproductions of documents by a corporate fiduciary in the regular course of business, whether the original is in existence or not, is provided for by 205 ILCS 620/2-12.

§1004   Admissibility of Other Evidence of Contents

§1004.1   *Competency of Witnesses: An Overview*

When the contents of a writing, recording, or photograph are sought to be proved, production of the original will be excused if the original is sufficiently established to have existed, *People ex rel. Yohe v. Hubble*, 378 Ill. 377, 38 N.E.2d 38 (1941); *Palmer v. Liquor Control Commn.*, 77 Ill. App. 3d 725, 33 Ill. Dec. 100, 396 N.E.2d 325 (1979), and if in addition the evidence establishes that the original (1) is lost or destroyed, *see* §1004.3 infra; (2) is not obtainable, *see* §1004.4 infra; (3) is in the possession of an opponent, *see* §1004.5 infra; or (4) relates to a collateral matter, *see* §1004.6 infra. Under any of these circumstances, other evidence, (referred to as secondary evidence) of the contents is admissible. *Rybak v. Provenzale*, 181 Ill. App. 3d 884, 130 Ill. Dec. 852, 537 N.E.2d 1321 (1989); *Pugh v. Bershad*, 133 Ill. App. 2d 174, 272 N.E.2d 745 (1971). *See* §1004.2 infra, with respect to degrees of secondary evidence. Whether an excuse for failure to produce the original has been shown is a preliminary matter for the court. *People v. Wells*, 380 Ill. 347, 44 N.E.2d 32 (1942); *Silberman v. Washington Natl. Ins. Co.*, 329 Ill. App. 448, 69 N.E.2d 519 (1946). The sufficiency of the evidence showing that it is not within the offering party's power to produce the original depends on the circumstances of each case. *People v. Baptist*, 76 Ill. 2d 19, 27 Ill. Dec. 792, 389 N.E.2d 1200 (1971); *Zurich Ins. Co. v. Northbrook Excess & Surplus Ins. Co.*, 145 Ill. App. 3d 175, 98 Ill. Dec. 512, 494 N.E.2d 634 (1986). Since the question is for the court, the rules of evidence, except with respect to privilege, do not apply. *See* §104.1 supra and §1008.1 infra.

The requirements generally applicable to the introduction of secondary evidence were stated in *Gillson v. Gulf, Mobile & Ohio R. Co.*, 42 Ill. 2d 193, 199, 246 N.E.2d 269 (1969), as follows:

> To introduce secondary evidence of a writing, a party must first prove prior existence of the original, its loss, destruction, or unavailability; authenticity of the substitute and his own diligence in attempting to procure the original . . . ; this requirement is no less applicable when the writing is offered as an admission.

When parties were at common law generally incompetent as witnesses, *see* §601.1 supra, they could nevertheless testify to loss or destruction of original writings as a preliminary to the introduction of secondary evidence. *Holbrook v. Trustees of*

Schools, 22 Ill. 539 (1859). Section 5/8-101 of the Code of Civil Procedure renders parties and interested persons generally competent to testify, but 735 ILCS 5/8-201 preserves the incompetency in Dead Man situations. Since the parties were already competent to testify to loss or destruction of original writings, 735 ILCS 5/8-201 as an exception to 5/8-101 would not render them incompetent. 735 ILCS 5/8-101, 5/8-201. This aspect of the Dead Man rule seems in practice to be overlooked, and no case deals with it. *See* §606 supra for a discussion of the Dead Man's Act.

With respect to public records, *see* §1005 infra.

§1004.2   Degrees of Secondary Evidence

Illinois common law recognizes degrees of secondary evidence. *Mariner v. Saunders,* 10 Ill. 113 (1848). If it appears that a copy was made, its nonproduction has to be accounted for before parol evidence of contents is admissible. *Illinois Land & Loan Co. v. Bonner,* 75 Ill. 315 (1874); *People v. Village of Camp Point,* 286 Ill. App. 3d 247, 221 Ill. Dec. 641, 675 N.E.2d 1371 (1997). If it does not otherwise appear that a copy was made, the party objecting to parol evidence of contents has the burden of proving the existence of better evidence and that it was known to the opposite party in time to be produced at the trial. *Wilson v. South Park Commrs.,* 70 Ill. 46 (1873). However, if the original is in the possession of the opposing party, §1004.5 infra, extension of the Original Writing Rule into degrees of secondary evidence has been said not to apply. *Mariner v. Saunders* supra.

With respect to the various degrees of secondary evidence, McCormick, Evidence §241 at 83 (4th ed. 1992) suggests the following order of reliability: (1) a mechanically produced copy, such as a photograph, a carbon, a letterpress copy, etc., (2) a firsthand copy by one who was looking at the original while he copied (immediate copy, sworn copy), (3) a copy, however made, that has been compared by a witness with the original and found correct (examined copy), (4) a secondhand or mediate copy, i.e., a copy of a firsthand copy, (5) oral testimony as to the terms of the writing, with memory aided by a previously made memorandum, and (6) oral testimony from unaided memory.

If parol evidence is given as to the contents, the witness must state the substance of the language, though not necessarily its exact terms, so that the effect of the writing may be determined from its language and not by the judgment of the witness. *See* §§602.3 and 704.5 supra.

Cf. Federal Rules of Evidence 1004, 65 F.R.D. 131, 164 (1975), recognizing no degrees of secondary evidence.

As to public records, *see* §1005 infra.

§1004.3 *Original Lost or Destroyed*

An original is not required, and other evidence of contents is admissible, if all originals are lost or have been destroyed, unless the proponent lost or destroyed them in bad faith. *People v. Baptist,* 76 Ill. 2d 19, 27 Ill. Dec. 792, 389 N.E.2d 1200 (1979), evidence of existence of letter and its destruction by fire sufficient to permit parol evidence of its content; *People v. Bowman,* 95 Ill. App. 3d 1137, 51 Ill. Dec. 527, 420 N.E.2d 1085 (1981), original confession and its loss sufficiently established to permit introduction of a photocopy. The circumstances of loss or destruction should be shown to establish that the original was not initially concealed, destroyed or disposed of for the purpose of introducing secondary evidence. *People v. Carter,* 39 Ill. 2d 31, 233 N.E.2d 393 (1968). *Accord Kwai Paul Lam v. Northern Ill. Gas Co.,* 114 Ill. App. 3d 325, 70 Ill. Dec. 660, 449 N.E.2d 1007 (1983), proponent of secondary evidence must rebut to the satisfaction of the court any inference of fraud. Proof of loss or destruction, a determination to be made by the court, §104.1 supra, will ordinarily consist of testimony in open court, *Becker v. Quigg,* 54 Ill. 390 (1870); *People v. Lopez,* 107 Ill. App. 3d 792, 63 Ill. Dec. 573, 438 N.E.2d 504 (1982); *People v. Klisnick,* 73 Ill. App. 3d 148, 28 Ill. Dec. 740, 390 N.E.2d 1130 (1979), but in appropriate cases, deposition testimony, *McDonald v. Erbes,* 231 Ill. 295, 83 N.E. 162 (1907), and proof by affidavit have been accepted. *Taylor v. McIrvin,* 94 Ill. 488 (1880). The Conveyances Act permits either testimony or affidavit to establish proof of loss or destruction. 765 ILCS 5/36 and 5/37. The rules of evidence, except those with respect to privilege, do not apply to the determination of the preliminary question, §104.1 supra. The foregoing principles also apply where it is impractical to bring the original into court. *People v. Black,* 84 Ill. App. 3d 1050, 40 Ill. Dec. 322, 406 N.E.2d 23 (1980), decal on breathalyzer machine.

As to writings, recordings, or photographs formerly in the possession of the party herself, it must be clearly shown that the original is lost or destroyed. *Hazen & Lundy v. Pierson & Co.,* 83 Ill. 241 (1876).

Destruction of the original in bad faith by the party or another person at his instigation precludes introduction of secondary evidence of the contents by the guilty party; voluntary destruction must be proved not to have been of fraudulent design. *Blake v. Fash,* 44 Ill. 302 (1867).

§1004.4 *Original in Possession of Third Person Not Obtainable*

Secondary evidence as to the contents of a writing, recording, or photograph may be introduced if no original can be obtained by any available judicial process or procedure or by the exercise of reasonable effort. When an original is traced to the possession of a third party, it must be shown that the third party cannot be subpoenaed to produce the original at trial or at a deposition, and that no other judicial procedure compelling production is available. *Electric Supply Corp. v. Osher,* 105 Ill. App. 3d 46, 60 Ill. Dec. 690, 433 N.E.2d 732 (1982); *Rybak v. Provenzale,* 181 Ill. App. 3d 884, 130 Ill. Dec. 852, 537 N.E.2d 1321 (1989) (quoting Handbook). Resort to the foregoing is compelled even where the original is located in another jurisdiction. *Dickinson v. Breeden,* 25 Ill. 167 (1861); *McDonald v. Erbes,* 231 Ill. 295, 83 N.E. 162 (1907). In addition, it must be shown that reasonable but unavailing efforts have also been made to secure the original from its possessor. *Prussing v. Jackson,* 208 Ill. 85, 69 N.E. 771 (1904), a search of papers must be proved unless shown to be impossible.

An original in the possession of an opponent is discussed in §1004.5 infra.

§1004.5   *Original in Possession of Opponent*

If, during the time an original of the writing is in the possession of the opponent, reasonable notice is given that the contents will be the subject of proof at a hearing and she fails to produce the original, secondary evidence of contents may be introduced. *Holbrook v. Trustees of Schools,* 22 Ill. 539 (1859). Notice may be contained in the pleading, or be given otherwise, including a notice to a party to produce a document at trial as provided in Supreme Court Rule 237(b). Reasonableness depends on circumstances and is considerably within the discretion of the trial judge. *Pittsburgh, C.C. & St. L. Ry. v. Gage,* 286 Ill. 213, 121 N.E. 582 (1919), two days' notice in open court during trial, client being a resident of the city where trial was held, was reasonable.

Notice is not necessary if from the nature of the case the opponent must know that the party will rely upon a writing in the opponent's possession, *Maxcy-Barton Organ Co. v. Glen Corp.,* 355 Ill. 228, 189 N.E. 326 (1934); *Continental Life Ins. Co. v. Rogers,* 119 Ill. 474, 10 N.E. 242 (1887), or if the opponent had already denied receipt of the original, making notice futile. *Soft Water Serv., Inc. v. M. Suson Enter.,* 39 Ill. App. 3d 1035, 351 N.E.2d 264 (1976). However, where the existence of a document is asserted for the first time at trial to be in the possession of the opponent, notice is required. *Electric Supply Corp. v. Osher,* 105 Ill. App. 3d 46, 60 Ill. Dec. 690, 433 N.E.2d 732 (1982).

§1004.6   Collateral Matters

Writings, recordings, or photographs may enter into a case only incidentally, with their significance being merely that an item of that general character exists or existed. Under these circumstances it is unlikely that the precise terms of the item can become a center of genuine controversy. Hence the original is not required when not closely related to a controlling issue. Illustrations of this necessarily indefinite concept are: testimony by witness that judgment rendering him incompetent had been taken against him, *Babcock v. Smith,* 31 Ill. 57 (1863); conveyance of property to a witness as supporting the purpose of defendant to avoid payment of note, *Massey v. Farmers Natl. Bank,* 113 Ill. 334 (1885); possession of transfer by injured plaintiff to show he was a passenger, *Chicago City Ry. v. Carroll,* 206 Ill. 318, 68 N.E. 1087 (1903); testimony that cards were in interstate commerce by witness who examined waybills, *Wagner v. Chicago, R.I. & P. Ry.,* 277 Ill. 114, 115 N.E. 201 (1917); testimony of clerk of court as to conviction of father where mother and new husband sought adoption of children without father's consent, *Smith v. Andrews,* 54 Ill. App. 2d 51, 203 N.E.2d 160 (1965); beneficiary permitted to identify parties to a trust since purpose was not to vary, alter, or contradict the terms of the instrument, *In re Village of Round Lake Park, Lake County,* 29 Ill. App. 3d 651, 331 N.E.2d 602 (1975).

§1005   Public Records

§1005.1   Commentary

The same policy that permits authentication of public records by certified copy, §902.2 supra, also exempts the certified copy from the requirements of the Original Writing Rule; there is no need to account for failure to produce the original. *Ramsay's Estate v. People,* 197 Ill. 572, 64 N.E. 549

(1902). *See also* 735 ILCS 5/8-1202, providing for the admissibility of judicial proceedings solely by means of an authenticated original or certified copy. *Schwartz v. Schwartz,* 38 Ill. App. 3d 959, 349 N.E.2d 567 (1976), original or certified copy of judicial record admissible pursuant to *id.,* §8-1202. *Cf.* Conveyances Act, 765 ILCS 5/35, 5/36; *Winter v. Dibble,* 251 Ill. 200, 95 N.E. 1093 (1911), requiring accounting for nonproduction of the original recorded instruments as a condition precedent to admission of either the record or a certified copy of the record.

Duplicates of court, municipal, and private corporate records are also admissible if sworn to be correct without accounting for the original. 735 ILCS 5/8-1206. In addition, Supreme Court Rule 216(d), set forth in §901.8 supra, provides for the admissibility of duplicate copies of public records. Other evidence of the contents of a public record may be introduced only if neither the original, a certified copy, nor a compared copy may be obtained by the exercise of reasonable diligence. *See Forsyth v. Vehmeyer,* 176 Ill. 359, 52 N.E. 55 (1898), in the event of loss or destruction of the public record, its contents may be established by secondary evidence upon proof that the record was in fact made. *Accord People v. Village of Camp Point,* 286 Ill. App. 3d 247, 221 Ill. Dec. 641, 675 N.E.2d 1371 (1997). *See also Indian Valley Golf Club v. Long Grove,* 173 Ill. App. 3d 909, 123 Ill. Dec. 498, 527 N.E.2d 1273 (1988), employing the concept of a duplicate as expressed in Federal Rule of Evidence 1003, §1003.1 supra, to admit a certified copy of a public record.

§1006   Summaries

§1006.1   *Commentary*

The results of examinations of masses of figures or of other voluminous writings, recordings, or photographs may be presented in the form of a chart, summary, or calculation as constituting the only method of intelligible presentation. *Joseph W. O'Brien v. Highland Const. Co.*, 17 Ill. App. 3d 237, 307 N.E.2d 761 (1974), summary of construction costs incurred because of defendant's breach; *People v. Crawford Dist. Co.*, 65 Ill. App. 790, 22 Ill. Dec. 525, 382 N.E.2d 1223 (1978), chart summarizing examination of 1,200 invoices relating to beer sales; *People v. Gerold*, 265 Ill. 448, 107 N.E. 165 (1914); *Smith v. Sanitary Dist. of Chicago*, 260 Ill. 453, 103 N.E. 254 (1913). A proper foundation must of course be laid establishing the correctness of the figures in the summary, *Grand Liquor Co. v. Department of Revenue*, 36 Ill. App. 3d 277, 343 N.E.2d 555 (1976), as well as the underlying records. *Veco Corp. v. Babcock*, 243 Ill. App. 3d 153, 183 Ill. Dec. 406, 611 N.E.2d 1054 (1993). The originals of the records thus summarized must be made available to the opposite party for examination or copying, or both, in advance of trial at a reasonable time and place. *LeRoy State Bank v. Keenan's Bank*, 337 Ill. 173, 169 N.E. 1 (1929); *In re Marriage of Westcott*, 163 Ill. App. 3d 168, 114 Ill. Dec. 411, 516 N.E.2d 566 (1987); *Landmark Structures v. F. E. Holmes & Sons*, 195 Ill. App. 3d 1036, 142 Ill. Dec. 595, 552 N.E.2d 1336 (1990); *People v. Wiesneske*, 234 Ill. App. 3d 29, 175 Ill. Dec. 252, 599 N.E.2d 1266 (1992); *Heller Financial, Inc. v. John-Byrne Co.*, 264 Ill. App. 3d 681, 202 Ill. Dec. 349, 637 N.E.2d 1085 (1994). However, the originals of the records need not be introduced into evidence, although the court may require that they be produced in court. *Sheldon Livestock Co. v. Western Engine Co.*, 13 Ill. App. 3d 993, 301 N.E.2d 485 (1973). The requirement that the original records be made available has been applied to computer printouts. *Estate of Buddeke*, 49 Ill. App. 3d 431, 7 Ill. Dec. 285, 364 N.E.2d 446 (1977). Employment of a chart, summary, or calculation may be used in conjunction with the public records hearsay exception, §803.12 supra, and presented in the form of a certified copy of a public record, §902.2 supra. *Department of Public Aid v. Estate of Wall*, 81 Ill. App. 3d 394, 36 Ill. Dec. 798, 401 N.E.2d 639 (1980), certificate of Director of Illinois Department of Public Aid presenting list compiled from records on file with the department indicating payments made was properly received in evidence; *People v. Wiesneske,* 234 Ill. App. 3d 29, 175 Ill. Dec. 252, 599 N.E.2d 1266 (1992), the public record but not the summary itself must have been kept in the ordinary course.

This technique may not be employed as a guise for placing before the jury a synopsis of oral testimony. *Morton Grove v. Gelchsheiner,* 16 Ill. 2d 453, 158 N.E.2d 70 (1959).

If adequate supporting data are presented, the coincidence of final computations with an ultimate issue is now of no moment. *People v. Albanese,* 102 Ill. 2d 54, 79 Ill. Dec. 608, 464 N.E.2d 206 (1984) (expert witness upon review of documentation could testify that person was in "critical financial condition"). *See* §704.1 supra. *Cf. Estate of Smythe v. Evans,* 209 Ill. 376, 70 N.E. 906 (1904), in claims for profits, improper for bookkeeper to testify to amount thereof, though his footings and calculations were otherwise admissible.

Testimonial evidence by a witness who has examined the mass of figures or voluminous records and is qualified to testify to the net result or content is admissible; a written summary, chart, or calculation is not required. *People ex rel. Wenzel v. Chicago & N.W. Ry.,* 28 Ill. 2d 205, 190 N.E.2d 780 (1963); *People v. Albanese* supra.

Charts, summaries, or calculations are not admissible if the original records on which they are based are inadmissible because they are hearsay or for some other reason, *Veco Corp. v. Babcock,* 243 Ill. App. 3d 153, 183 Ill. Dec. 406, 611 N.E.2d 1054 (1993), except to the extent that they have been reasonably relied upon by an expert, *see* §703.1 supra.

Charts, summaries, or calculations of testimony or documents actually admitted as evidence will also be received when such testimony or documents are too voluminous to be conveniently examined in court. *Department of Corrections v. Adams,* 278 Ill. App. 3d 803, 215 Ill. Dec. 631, 663 N.E.2d 1145 (1996); *Little v. Tuscola Stone Co.,* 234 Ill. App. 3d 726, 175 Ill. Dec. 812, 600 N.E.2d 1270 (1992); *People v. Wiesneske,* 234 Ill. App. 3d 29, 175 Ill. Dec. 252, 599 N.E.2d 1266 (1992).

§1007   Testimony or Written Admission of Party

§1007.1   Commentary

The English rule of *Slatterie v. Pooley*, 6 M. & W. 664 (Ex. 1840), that the contents of a document may be proved by evidence of an oral admission without accounting for the original, has never been followed in Illinois. *Bryan v. Smith*, 3 Ill. 47 (1839), in action for profits of land, oral admission by defendants that plaintiff was tenant in common not admissible without accounting for title documents. The risk of inaccuracy is substantial, and a contrary decision would be at odds with the purpose of the Original Writing Rule's preference for the original.

McCormick, Evidence §242 (4th ed. 1992), suggests that a desirable rule is to permit the contents of a writing, recording, or photograph to be proved, without accounting for the nonproduction of the original, by the testimony or deposition of the party against whom offered or by her written admission. *Accord* Federal Rule of Evidence 1007, 65 F.R.D. 131, 165 (1975). *Contra Prussing v. Jackson*, 208 Ill. 85, 69 N.E. 771 (1904), admission by party on witness stand inadmissible in absence of accounting for original, criticized in 4 Wigmore, Evidence §1256 (Chadbourn rev. 1972).

§1008   Functions of Court and Jury

§1008.1   Commentary

With respect to the Original Writing Rule, responsibility is allocated for determining preliminary questions of fact between judge and jury. The court decides, §104.1 supra, such issues as whether the contents of a writing, recording, or photograph are sought to be proved; whether nonproduction of the original has been satisfactorily accounted for, §§1004.1 to 1004.5 supra; and the priority of degrees of secondary evidence. These matters involving administration of a protective policy are solely for the court. Where, however, relevancy depends upon satisfaction of a condition of fact, the issue relating to the condition of fact is ultimately for the jury. The court determines only whether the evidence sufficient to support a finding as to the condition of fact has been introduced, §104.2 supra. Thus, when the issue is raised (a) whether the asserted writing ever existed, (b) whether another writing, recording, or photograph produced at the trial is the original, or (c) whether other evidence of contents correctly reflects the contents, the issue is for the trier of fact to determine, as in the case of other issues of fact.

To illustrate, assume the plaintiff desires to offer secondary evidence of an alleged contract's content after first introducing evidence that the one and only original is in the possession of the defendant. Assume further that the defendant counters with evidence that no such contract was ever executed. If the court were to decide that the contract was never executed and exclude the secondary evidence, the case would be at an end without ever going to the jury on the central issue. Accordingly, the court alone would decide whether plaintiff has introduced evidence sufficient to support a finding by a reasonable juror that a contract was executed, whether the plaintiff has established possession of the original by the opponent, §1004.5 supra, and its nonproduction at trial following proper notice thereby permitting the introduction of secondary evidence, and whether evidence has been introduced sufficient to support a finding by a reasonable juror that the secondary evidence accurately reflects the content of the original contract. Whether the contract was in fact ever executed and, if so, whether the secondary evidence correctly reflects the contents of the original would then be decided by the jury. In reaching its determination as to whether the proponent had established that it is more probably true than not true that the original is in the possession of the opponent, it is not necessary for the court to first decide whether the original ever existed, a decision reserved for the jury. The jury will be permitted to decide whether a contract was entered, provided evidence has been introduced sufficient to support a finding by a reasonable juror of its one-time existence. Once such evidence has been introduced, the court simply assumes the existence of the original in determining whether the proponent of secondary evidence has established possession by the opponent to be more probably true than not true.

Table of Illinois Cases

TABLE OF ILLINOIS CASES

Table of Federal Cases

TABLE OF FEDERAL CASES

TABLE OF FEDERAL CASES

Table of Cases from Other Jurisdictions

Table of Illinois Supreme Court Rules

Table of Illinois Statutes

TABLE OF ILLINOIS STATUTES

5/115-6	502.3, 706.1		5/115-12	611.16, 803.1
5/115-7(a)(1)	404.4		5/115-13	803.8
5/115-7(a)(2)	404.4		5/115-14	601.1, 601.3, 603.1, 604.1
5/115-7(b)	404.4			
5/115-7.1	601.2, 704.2		5/115-14(e)	601.2
			5/115-15	803.13
5/115-7.2	601.2, 704.2		5/115-16	503.3
			5/115-20	404.7
5/115-7.3	404.6		5/116-1	103.8
5/115-9(a)	401.4, 401.8		5/122-1 et seq.	103.10
5/115-10	611.15, 803.23, 804.10, 807.1		115/7.2	404.4
			125/6	502.4, 503.3, 506.3, 601.5, 601.7, 601.8, 607.7, 609.6
5/115-10(a)(2)	803.23			
5/115-10(b)(1)	803.23			
5/115-10(b)(2)(B)	803.23		125/7	611.6, 611.7
5/115-10(e)	803.23		125/8b(XIII)	403.2
5/115-10.1	611.16, 613.1, 801.9		140/1	604.1
			185/11	410.1
			200/1	404.4
5.115-10.1(b)	801.9		204/4	706.1
5/115-10.1(c)(1)	801.9		205/1.01 et seq.	502.3
5/115-10.1(c)(2)	801.9		205/1.01 to 205/12	404.1
5/115-10.1(c)(2)(A)	801.9		220/1	804.1
			220/1 to 220/6	611.6
5/115-10.1(c)(2)(C)	801.9		220/6	804.1
		730 ILCS	5/3-3-13	609.8
			5/5-2-5	702.2
5/115-10.2	615.1, 804.10		5/5-5-5	609.8
			5/5-6-3.1(f)	609.2
		735 ILCS	5/1-106	102.1
5/115-10.2(a)	804.10		5/2-301	611.8, 901.11
5/115-10.2(b)	804.10		5/2-605	901.1
5/115-10.2(d)	804.10		5/2-610(b)	202.4, 802.11

TABLE OF ILLINOIS STATUTES

Table of Federal Rules and Standards

Table of Statutes and Rules from Other Jurisdictions

[All references are to section numbers.]

California

Cal. Code Civ. Proc. §651 412.1
Cal. Evid. Code §801(b) 703.1
Cal. Evid. Code §802 705.1

District of Columbia

14 D.C. Code §305 609.2

Kansas

Kan. Code of Civ. Proc. 60-456
  705.1
Kan. Code of Civ. Proc. 60-457
  705.1

New Jersey

N.J. Evid. Rule 57 705.1
N.J. Evid. Rule 58 705.1

New York

N.Y. CPLR (McKinney 1963), Rule
  4515 705.1

Table of Illinois Pattern Jury Instructions

[All references are to section numbers.]

CIVIL		**CRIMINAL**	
Civil 1.01	203.2	Criminal 2.03	304.2
Civil 1.04	203.5	Criminal 2.04	506.3, 609.1
Civil 12.01	403.3		
Civil 21.01	301.6	Criminal 2.05	303.4
Civil 31.13	803.18	Criminal 3.14	404.5
Civil 34.04	803.18	Criminal 4.19	301.6
Civil 50.01	202.4	Criminal 13.34	304.1
Civil 50.02	202.4	Criminal 23.30	304.1
Civil 150.15	403.3		

Index

INDEX